The Papers of
HENRY CLAY

The Papers of
HENRY CLAY

James F. Hopkins, *Editor*

Mary W. M. Hargreaves, *Associate Editor*

VOLUME 3

PRESIDENTIAL CANDIDATE
1821-1824

UNIVERSITY OF KENTUCKY PRESS

Library of Congress Catalog Card No. 59-13605

Printed in the United States of America
at the University of Kentucky, Lexington, Kentucky

"My ambition is that we may enter a new and larger era of service to humanity."

Dedicated to the memory of
JOSIAH KIRBY LILLY
1861-1948
President of Eli Lilly and Company
Founder of Lilly Endowment, Inc.

Whose wisdom and foresight were
devoted to the service of
education, religion, and
public welfare

SYMBOLS

The following symbols are used to describe the nature of the originals of documents copied from manuscript sources.

AD	Autograph Document
ADI	Autograph Document Initialed
ADI draft	Autograph Document Initialed, draft
ADS	Autograph Document Signed
AE	Autograph Endorsement
AEI	Autograph Endorsement Initialed
AES	Autograph Endorsement Signed
AL	Autograph Letter
AL draft	Autograph Letter, draft
ALI	Autograph Letter Initialed
ALI copy	Autograph Letter Initialed, copied by writer
ALI draft	Autograph Letter Initialed, draft
ALS	Autograph Letter Signed
ALS copy	Autograph Letter Signed, copied by writer
ALS draft	Autograph Letter Signed, draft
AN	Autograph Note
AN draft	Autograph Note, draft
ANS	Autograph Note Signed
Copy	Copy not by writer (indicated "True" if so certified)
D	Document
DS	Document Signed
DS copy	Document Signed, copied
E	Endorsement
ES	Endorsement Signed
LS	Letter Signed

The following, from the *Symbols Used in the National Union Catalog of the Library of Congress* (8th ed., rev.; Washington, 1960), indicate the location of the original documents in institutional libraries of the United States.

CSmH	Henry E. Huntington Library, San Marino, California
CU	University of California, Berkeley
CtHi	Connecticut Historical Society, Hartford
CtSoP	Pequot Library Association, Southport, Connecticut
CtY	Yale University, New Haven, Connecticut

DLC	Library of Congress, Washington, D. C.
DLC-HC	Library of Congress, Henry Clay Collection
DLC-TJC	Library of Congress, Thomas J. Clay Collection
DNA	National Archives, Washington, D. C. Following the symbol for this depository, the letter M means Microcopy; R, Reel; and RG, Record Group.
ICHi	Chicago Historical Society
InU	Indiana University, Bloomington
KyHi	Kentucky Historical Society, Frankfort
KyLxT	Transylvania College, Lexington, Kentucky
KyU	University of Kentucky, Lexington
MH	Harvard University, Cambridge, Massachusetts
MHi	Massachusetts Historical Society, Boston
MWA	American Antiquarian Society, Worcester, Massachusetts
MiD-B	Detroit Public Library, Burton Historical Collection
MoKiT	Northeast Missouri State Teachers College, Kirksville
MoSHi	Missouri Historical Society, St. Louis
NBu	Buffalo and Erie County Public Library, Buffalo, New York
NBuHi	Buffalo Historical Society, Buffalo, New York
NHi	New York Historical Society, New York City
NN	New York Public Library, New York City
NNPM	Pierpont Morgan Library, New York City
NRHi	Rochester Historical Society, Rochester, New York
Nc-Ar	North Carolina State Department of Archives and History, Raleigh
NcD	Duke University, Durham, North Carolina
NcU	University of North Carolina, Chapel Hill
Nj	New Jersey State Library, Archives and History, Trenton
OCHP	Historical and Philosophical Society of Ohio, Cincinnati
PHC	Haverford College, Haverford, Pennsylvania
PHi	Historical Society of Pennsylvania, Philadelphia
PKsL	Longwood Library, Kennett Square, Pennsylvania
PPL-R	Library Company of Philadelphia, Ridgeway Branch, Philadelphia
PPPrHi	Presbyterian Historical Society, Philadelphia
PU	University of Pennsylvania, Philadelphia
RPB	Brown University, Providence, Rhode Island
ScHi	South Carolina Historical Society, Charleston
THi	Tennessee Historical Society, Nashville
TxU	University of Texas, Austin
ViU	University of Virginia, Charlottesville
WHi	State Historical Society of Wisconsin, Madison

The Papers of HENRY CLAY

From James De Wolf, Jr.

To the Honble Henry Clay New York 1st January 1821

Sir Having been informed that you have resumed the practise of Law, since retiring from Congress, I have to request your assistance in aiding me to eject from my lands, in Louisville Ky,[1] the persons composing the Corporation of the "Hope distillery Company" consisting of my Father James DWolf Senr of Bristol R. I., Mr. Ruggles Whiting (I beleive [*sic*] of Louisville); Mess Ebenezer & John Breed of Boston Mr: Tilley Whitcomb of Boston, the Heirs of Thomas Whiting deceased, formerly of New Orleans, always represented by R. Whiting; and Simon S. Goodwin[2] (as pr Charter—see Volume 5th of the Laws of Kentucky[3]) or whoever else may now compose said company[4]—They having entered my lands & erected there buildings &c without my consent, and having refused & neglected to purchase the lands from me which I was disposed to sell them at a fair price, I have determined to have recourse to the Laws to remove them; and I request you to bring an action in my behalf for that purpose. I notice by a Copy sent me of a Bill in Chancery filed by Mr. Ruggles Whiting against me & my Father, that he purposes to avail himself of some supposed advantage, in consequence of the inadvertence of the writer of my deeds of said Land in omitting to add the *Junior* to my name (or rather in omitting the Junior in my name)[5] to which bill I have replied, setting forth the facts which are;—that the whole of said land was purchased by me of Mr. Robert Todd,[6] for my sole use & benefit, and that my Father did not nor has he ever had any Interest in said purchase which he will verify on oath, it is a misfortune that the omission took place & that I had not discovered it at the time, but not being observed by me it remained untill about the 6th of Septem. 1819, when my Father executed to me a quit claim deed in order to rectify the error. Mr. Todd from whom I purchased the lands, & Mr. Pope, who wrote the deeds, I have no doubt will also testify the fact that they understood me to be the purchaser of the lands for my own benefit & use.—Mr. Worden Pope the register at Louisville, will furnish you with copies of my deeds if necessary. I desire you to bring the action in the Federal Court—Should reference be necessary I will correspond with Messrs Prather & Jacobs[7] of Louisville.—my Father will write you on this subject, as also an injunction to stay waste &c which I also request you to apply for immediately on bringing the action, as some of the Company may attempt to remove some of the fixtures &c to the injury of the rest of the Compy as well as myself—they have already made great waste in cutting down & destroying nearly all the Wood in a very unwarrantable manner & which I considered valuable to me.

I am Sir Very respectfully Your Obt. Servt.

JAMES D'WOLF, JR.

LS, "Duplicate." DLC-TJC (DNA, M212, R12).

1 In three transactions early in 1814 the younger De Wolf had purchased, for $10,720, a total of 107 acres of land in and adjoining the town of Louisville, on lower Main Street and along the road thence to Shippingport and Portland. Jefferson County Court, Deed Book 10, pp. 326-27, 328, 450.

2 As late as May, 1821, Whiting still claimed legal residence in Boston, Massachusetts. U. S. Circuit Court, Seventh Circuit, District of Kentucky, Order Book H, 20, 21. Simeon S. Goodwin resided in Louisville.

3 The title, but not the entire act approved January 27, 1817, was published in Littell (comp.), *Statute Law of Kentucky,* V, 458. The measure may be found in Ky. Gen. Assy., *Acts, 1816-1817,* pp. 54-55.

4 The act of incorporation also included the name of Martin Blake of Louisville. The Hope Distillery Company, capitalized at $100,000, erected buildings and installed equipment designed to make it the largest and most modern establishment of its kind in the United States. It proved unsuccessful, however, and soon closed operation. Its buildings were eventually destroyed by fire. McMurtrie, *Sketches of Louisville,* 127-30; Ben Casseday, *The History of Louisville, from Its Earliest Settlement till the Year 1852* (Louisville, 1852), 143.

At the May Term, 1821, of United States Circuit Court, at Frankfort, Kentucky, Clay and Robert Wickliffe, acting for James De Wolf of New York (James De Wolf, Jr.), instituted ejectment proceedings against Simeon S. Goodwin, who failed to appear. After various continuances of the case, a jury at the May Term, 1824, found "the defendant guilty of the trespass and ejectment." The Court thereupon ordered that the plaintiff recover 106 acres, with appurtenances, and one cent damages. U.S. Circuit Court, Seventh Circuit, District of Kentucky, Complete Records, U, 491-93.

5 The name of the purchaser appears as "James D'Wolf Junr" on only one of the deeds, for a one-half acre lot. The suit has not been found.

6 One tract, of a half-acre, was purchased from "Robert Todd (rs) and Barbara F. his wife"; the second, of 106 acres, from "Robert Todd (rs) and Fortunatus Cosby and Mary Ann his wife of Louisville in the state of Kentucky and William Lytle and Eliza N. his wife of Cincinnati in the state of Ohio"; and the third, of a half acre, from "Robert Todd (rs)." Todd, a justice of the peace in Jefferson County, Kentucky, was a nephew of William Lytle.

7 For many years one of the foremost mercantile firms in Louisville. Thomas Prather, born in Maryland in 1770, had established himself as a Louisville businessman at an early age. John I. Jacob, who became Prather's brother-in-law, had come to Kentucky in 1805, had begun working for the older man, and had been taken into partnership. Both were active in local civic, as well as business, affairs. Prather died in 1823. Jacob was for many years a member of the city council, and served successively as president of the Louisville Office of the Bank of the United States, the second Bank of Kentucky (established at Louisville in 1834), and the Louisville and Frankfort Railroad. He resigned from the last position in 1852, the year of his death.

From James De Wolf

Hon Henry Clay Bristol R.I. Jany 3rd 1821.

Sir—I had the pleasure of writing you a line on 25th May last on the subject of my action of ejectment against the Mess Johnsons for the lands mortgaged to me by James Prentice, and received your reply dated 15th. July[1] in which you was good enough to say you would assist me in said cause, which I presume you was able to attend to with Mr Wickliffe.[2] I have just been informed by that Gentleman that an other continuance has been granted them which I consider very unjust, as those Gentlemen can not have any hope of ultimate success. I desire you to be particular to have the proper merits of the case, on my side of it carried up to the Supreme Court in case I should unexpectedly lose it in the circuit court.—

I have also a very untoward business with Mr Ruggles Whiting at Louisville having been weak enough to be induced by him to advance a large sum of money for prossecuting [*sic*] a project of his for distillation of grain at that place in which I have been exceedingly ill treated by that Gentleman.[3] Mr Howe[4] (who may have informed you something of it) left the business in charge of Mess Denny & Thruston[5] of Louisville to whom I have lately wrote requesting them to move the master in chancery (before whom said Whiting has filed his bill of complaints) to remove the cause into the U. S. Court, and in case of success to call on you to manage it in my behalf. This man (Whiting) is catching at straws and endeavouring to evade payment of his notes, and defraud me of the moneys intrusted to his management for carring [*sic*] into effect said Distillery project.—one of his notes which last fell due I endorsed over & sold to Mr Hersey Bradford who I advised sending it to you for collection, two others of 3000 each have been sued in the State Court and I have also requested said Gentleman to carry the actions into the Federal Court.[6]—My Son James DWolf Jr who is the owner of the land on which the buildings for said Distillery have been erected, has determined to bring his action of ejectment, and I advised his writing to you on the subject, which I request you will assist him in doing. Mr Whiting supposes he can avail himself of some advantage in consequence of having discovered that the writer of my Sons deed omitted to put the Junior to his name—my own and Sons answer to Mr Whitings bill in chancery will develop the whole business.—In all these difficulties I am desirous of obtaining your assistance my principal object is to get the whole business properly submitted to the most respectable and independent men as arbitrators, or to get it into the Federal Courts, he has pretended to be willing to submit to Arbitrators but without sincerity, on which point Mr Howe fully tested him, if he could get creatures of his own for Arbitrators he would submit his present bent appears to be to forestall public opinion at Louisville, affect to be the injured man and is very grose [*sic*] in his abuse of me, Mr Wm Stackpole (who is another limping fellow citizen) has gone to your part of the

Country is the confidant of Mr Whiting and I am told is covering his property, he also makes use of Mr. S. S. Goodwin who from motives of humanity I employed as an Assistant to Mr Whiting, but now used as a witness against me, and as a pretended Agent for me, in the hands of Mr. Whiting.—Mr Wickliffe is aquainted [*sic*] with one transaction of his which is a sample of the whole.

I request you to undertake for me in earnest and employ such Assistance as you will need and to keep me informed of your opinion on the several subjects.

I expect to make a visit to the western country next summer, when I hope to have the pleasure to see you.

I am very Respectfully Sir, Your Obedient Servant

JAS. D'WOLF

LS. DLC-TJC (DNA, M212, R12). Endorsed by Clay: "Answered 29h. Jan. 21." Answer not found.

[1] Neither letter has been found. In 1815, in Bristol, Rhode Island, De Wolf had loaned James Prentiss $83,000, secured by a mortgage on Kentucky lands. Two years later the original agreement had been superseded by a new contract, for $62,000, signed in Kentucky. In March, 1818, Prentiss by deed of trust had conveyed his equity of redemption to William T. Barry, who on May 27, 1818, had sold the land at public auction to James and Richard M. Johnson "subject to the incumbrances of any previous mortgage or deed of trust." De Wolf in September of that year had filed a bill in the Federal District Court of Kentucky, asking foreclosure of the mortgage given him by Prentiss in 1817. Prentiss filed no answer; James Johnson set up the defense of usury in the original contract between De Wolf and Prentiss and denied notice of the mortgage, "except by vague report"; Barry also resorted to the defense of usury and, in addition, declared that he had held the public sale before the bill was filed; Richard M. Johnson denied knowledge of the mortgage and claimed that the assignment from Barry was the only security he had for a debt of nearly $500,000 which Prentiss owed him. De Wolf lost the case in the lower court but took an appeal to the United States Supreme Court, which reversed the decision and sent the cause "back to have a decree of foreclosure entered and carried into effect." 23 *U.S.* (10 Wheaton) 367-95 (1825); U.S. Circuit Court, Seventh Circuit, District of Kentucky, Complete Records, R, 1-100.

[2] Robert Wickliffe, who handled De Wolf's case in the Federal Circuit Court. Neither Clay nor Wickliffe argued the case before the Supreme Court.

[3] See above, James De Wolf, Jr., to Clay, January 1, 1821. [4] John Howe.

[5] James W. Denny and Charles M. Thruston. The former, a member of the Kentucky House of Representatives, 1819-1820, was State Senator from Jefferson County, 1823-1825, and Attorney General of Kentucky, 1825-1832. Thruston, son of a Jefferson County farmer, had studied law under Worden Pope and, while still a minor, had been licensed to practice. He became an outstanding lawyer and represented the city of Louisville in the State legislature, 1832-1833, 1844-1845.

[6] At the May Term, 1821, of the United States Circuit Court, at Frankfort, Kentucky, Whiting was made defendant in two suits, one instituted by De Wolf, the other by Bradford, of Bristol, Rhode Island (probably a kinsman of De Wolf's wife, who was a daughter of William Bradford, United States Senator from Rhode Island, 1793-1797). In each instance Whiting argued that the case was not properly a matter within the Court's jurisdiction, since neither De Wolf nor Whiting, himself, had held citizenship in Kentucky when the notes were executed, the plaintiff's writ was served, or the action begun. The cases were, nevertheless, continued. In June, 1823, Whiting withdrew his plea to the jurisdiction of the Court and asked for further continuance. On June 10, 1824, a jury, called in De Wolf's suit, found for the defendant, whereupon the plaintiff moved for a new trial, which was granted at the May Term, 1826. On May 8, 1827, on information that the defendant was dead, the suit was abated. Meanwhile, Bradford had discontinued his action on November 8, 1825, and the Court had ordered that the defendant recover costs. U.S. Circuit Court, Seventh Circuit, District of Kentucky, Order Book H, 20, 21, 79 (no. 2); I, 239, 252, 267-69, 302; K, 133, 439; L, 245, 405-406.

From James Taylor

Hon: H. Clay Columbus Ohio Jany 5th. 1821.
Dr Sir

You will receive herewith an Account setled [*sic*] between Jas. T. Eubank[1] D Q Master & Col Jas Morrison in which the balance is setled at $2222.06—.[2] John C Bartletts recpt for $10,000 paid by Jas. T Eubank to him as p recpt dated. 20h. May 1813 Also a Copy of sd Eubanks recpt given to James W. Biddle[3] asst. Depy QM by the hands of Majr A. Stoddard[4] &c. dated 15. of Apl 1813 for $10,000. Also the letter of Peter Hagner 3d Auditor of 6h. July 1818 inclosing the Copy refered to and also an account

the sum of	$2228.62
To which is added the sum of	10,000.—
	$12 228.62[5]

Mr Clay will discover that the money recevd by Jas T. Eubank of Biddle on the 15. of Apl 1813 is the same sum paid to J.C Bartlett on the 20h. of May 1813, and Genl Wm. H. Harrison declares it to be the same. Mr C. will discover Wm. Piatts[6] name is not named in the recipt [*sic*] & this Circumstance of Piatts having charged the recipt may have caused the Mistake, but Genl Harrison says the money came from him.

At any rate In Jas T. Eubanks account as setled with Col Jas Morrison he has credited the money Recd of Biddle & charged the money paid Bartlett, which closes the transaction and nothing remains but for Mr Eubank to settle for the $2228.62—I hope Mr Clay will endeavor to procure from Mr Crawford[7] or the proper department an order to Mr Bibb U States attorney to discontinue the Suit[8] and to allow me time to try & make up some funds from Mr. Eubanks estate which is very small. The greater part of the sum remaining in his hands, he having expended in endeavoring to restore his health which he distroyed [*sic*] by his exposures in the swams [*sic*] of the frontier, but in which he failed, having died on the 8h of December 1814, with a Consumption leaving a fine young wife who was delivered of a fine son in about eight days after his death and by which they were reduced to Poverty.

Mr. Eubank was an active young man, and I have no hesitation in saying that had he have lived to this time he would have now been in flourishing circumstances.

He was a young man of great industry & zeal and as a proof of this fact, Col Morrison late Qr Master Genl appointed him his first assistant and he continued as such till The Colo. appointment was done away by a new organization of it & Mr. Eubank declined continuing longer on account of his health. I assure you that he appeared to be blessed with one of the finest constitutions I ever knew & that his death was brought on by his exposures in the army.

If the claim which is due from his estate is now pressed one half of the demand cannot be made from it and his infant Son & late wife will be left destitute of their little support I have the honor to be with great respect Dr. Sir your Obed. St. JAMES TAYLOR

ALS. DNA. RG217, 3rd Auditor, Settlement File no. 8787.

1 Of Newport, Kentucky, a nephew of Taylor, who had reared the young man from early childhood. Cited for bravery during the siege of Fort Meigs in May, 1813, Eubank had been a deputy quartermaster on the staff of General William Henry Harrison.

2 Peter Hagner, in a letter to Taylor, June 20, 1816, had called attention to an error and stated that the balance should be $2,228.62.

3 Later a merchant at Mackinac.

4 Amos Stoddard, lawyer, soldier, author, and, briefly, civil and military commandant of Upper Louisiana after the purchase of that Territory by the United States. During the War of 1812 he had served on the staff of General William Henry Harrison until killed at the siege of Ft. Meigs.

5 The documents referred to herein, except Bartlett's receipt, may be found in Settlement File no. 8787.

6 Commissioned from New Jersey during the Revolutionary War, Piatt had long been in the Quartermaster Department of the Army and in June, 1813, had been made a colonel. After leaving military service at the close of the War of 1812, he had settled in Hamilton County, Ohio, down river from Cincinnati.

7 William H. Crawford.

8 George M. Bibb, who was again (by interim appointment, 1819; formally nominated and confirmed in January, 1820; and reappointed in January, 1824) United States Attorney for the District of Kentucky, had instituted the action March 10, 1820, in the Federal Circuit Court for the District of Kentucky, against Taylor, as Eubank's bondsman. The suit was continued and at the May Term, 1821, the Government was awarded a judgment to recover $2,228.62, interest on this sum at six per cent annually from October 4, 1819, until paid, and costs. U.S. Circuit Court, Seventh Circuit, District of Kentucky, Complete Records, P, 105-110.

Bond from Thomas S. Hinde

[January 6, 1821]

I have engaged H. Clay to appear before the Supreme Court for me in a Case adjourned there between Taylor and Myers in behalf of Myers;[1] and in the event of Taylor's success in the said Case I agree to pay said Clay five hundred dollars. Witness my hand and Seal this 6h. Jan. 1821.[2] The payment to be made by transfering the amt on W Lytle in case of success in the Circuit Ct U S—In Ohio[3] THS. HINDE. {L.S.}

DS, in Clay's hand (except as noted). DLC-TJC (DNA, M212, R15).

1 A case involving claims to land in the Virginia Military Grant in Ohio. The United States Supreme Court in February, 1822, ruled that the owner of a survey might abandon it after it had been recorded "but by doing so he will not cancel the rights of others." The cause had been argued in the previous term, but Clay was not listed among the attorneys participating in it. 20 *U.S.* (7 Wheaton) 23-27.

2 The remainder of the document is not in Clay's hand.

3 In January, 1822, Clay argued before the Federal Circuit Court at Columbus in support of Hinde's complaint against James Findlay, William Lytle, Charles Vattier, Robert Ritchie, and others, regarding title to lot no. 86 in the city of Cincinnati. Hinde won his suit in the Circuit Court, but on appeal by the defendants to the United States Supreme Court, in January, 1828, the decision was reversed and the

cause remanded for new proceedings. Clay was not active in the case at the latter date. Lexington *Kentucky Reporter,* January 28, 1822: 26 *U.S.* (1 Peter) 241-46.

Findlay, a Pennsylvania Scotch-Irishman who had early settled in Cincinnati, where he practiced law and was active in commercial concerns, had served in the Territorial legislative council, 1798, and the State legislature, 1803. He was receiver of public moneys of the Cincinnati Public Land office, 1800-1825; mayor of Cincinnati, 1805-1806 and 1810-1811; brigadier general of militia, commissioned for service in the War of 1812; and a Jacksonian member of the United States Congress, 1825-1833. Vattier and Ritchie, who currently held the disputed property, were also residents of Cincinnati.

To Gorham A. Worth and Thomas T. Crittenden

Gent. Columbus 6h. Jan: 1821.

Mr Richardson informs me that he has rendered some professional services for the Bank with which Mr. Worth is acquainted; and that he is desirous of having his account settled, paying up some part of the debt which he owes to the Bank & securing the residue at the office of Chillicothe. I of course know nothing personally of his account; but if you are satisfied of its justice, I do not hesitate to recommend the execution of the arrangement he proposes. If he be sued (as I understand he is) the legal costs should be comprehended in the settlement. With great respect I am Yr. ob. Servt. H. CLAY

Mess Worth & Crittenden &c &c &c

ALS. NNPM. Delivered to the recipients, "Agents of the B. U. States Cincinnati," by "S. Q. Richardson Esqr."

From Duncan McArthur

Dear Sir, Chillicothe Jany. 8th. 1821

Some years ago I conveyed to Philip Doddridge Esquire of Ohio County Va.[1] seven hundred acres of land on the waters of the Big Miami, west of what is called Ludlow's line & east of the line run in 1812 from the source of the little Miami to the source of the Scioto river by Charles Roberts in pursuance of instructions from James Kilbourn Samuel Herrick and William Ludlow Commissioners appointed on the part of the United States to establish the Westerly boundary of the Virginia military reservation.[2] For said seven hundred acres Mr. Doddridge is bound by agreement to prosecute his claim to said land to a final decision, and also to prosecute or defend all my claims to lands between the two said lines—A declairation [*sic*] in Ejectment was served upon Thomas Thompson tenant in possession and at the last term of the Circuit court, a case was maide [*sic*] between Mr. Doddridge and Mr. Jno. C. Wright, in which Thompson & Wright are made defendants and the facts admitted on both sides as they really exist. and the cause certified up to the supreme Court of the U.S. in such manner that I think, the merits of my claims West of Ludlow's line can be fairly tried.[3] Mr. Dodridge [*sic*] has spoken to Mr. Scott[4] to assist him in the prosecution of this suit, but as the latter does not expect much of a fee, he may be a little slack in the business—And as my interes [*sic*] is considerable between these lines, I have concluded to imploy you to assist in the prosecution of this suit (with the permission of Mr. Doddridge) and for your services, should you succeed in establishing the right of Mr. Dodridge [*sic*] to the said 700 acres of land, in opposition to the claims of those claiming the same, under purchases from the United States, I will convey to you in fee simple four hundred acres of land on the North line and in the North West corner of a survey No. 5092 on Millcreek in Union County Ohio, which survey was made in the name of Robert Means[5] and patented to me or I will convey to you in like manner two hundred acres in the N. W. corner of said survey for your servies [*sic*] in assisting to prosecute said claim in case the court shall decide against us. I am anxious to have you engaged in the prosecution of of [*sic*] this business, and I trust that the offer which I make you will compensate you for your trouble.

This land is situate on the North side of Millcreek near the mouth of Otter creek, there is 1333⅓ acres in the survey 600 acres of which, on the East side, I have sold to a Mr. Petty[6]—you may find persons at Columbus who can describe this land to you. It is heavy timbered with sugar tree beech, ash &c. and the soil is good. and is about 3 or 4 miles from Garwood's Mill.

I hope this cause will be tried at the insuing term of the supreme Court of U.S. If you and Messrs. Doddridge & Scott can be prepared to do the prosecution justice. I am Dear Sir, your Ob. Servt.

Henry Clay Esquir[e] DUNCAN MC.ARTHUR

ALS. DLC-TJC (DNA, M212, R12).

1 Born in Pennsylvania, Doddridge had begun to practice law in Wellsburg, Virginia (now West Virginia), in 1797. He served several terms in the Virginia legislature and was a member of the United States House of Representatives from 1829 until his death in 1832.

2 In 1802 Israel Ludlow, pioneer Ohio surveyor and settler, had been directed by the United States Surveyor General to run the western boundary of the Virginia military reservation northwest of the Ohio River, between the Little Miami and the Scioto rivers. Beginning at the source of the Little Miami, he had surveyed toward what he supposed to be the headwater of the Scioto when he had been stopped by Indians at the Greenville Treaty line and prevented from continuing. Congress in 1804 had designated Ludlow's line, extended to the Scioto, as the boundary of the reservation; but the act had been nullified when Virginia had refused to give her assent.

In 1810 Duncan McArthur and another speculator, contending that Ludlow had failed to find the source of either of the rivers and that all land lying "east, or north, of a line drawn from the headwaters of both rivers is subject to entry by Virginia military warrants," had located with such warrants a large area west of Ludlow's line. Their claims conflicted with those of purchasers of public lands within the same area.

By act approved June 26, 1812 (2 *U.S. Stat.*, 764-65), the President of the United States had been authorized to appoint three commissioners to serve with Virginians "to ascertain, survey and mark" the boundary in question. Meanwhile, Ludlow's line was to serve as temporary boundary. James Madison, on July 1, had appointed three prominent Ohioans, Kilbourn, Herrick, and William Ludlow, as the United States Commissioners; and later in the year this group, meeting with the Virginia Commissioners, had directed their surveyor, Charles Roberts, to run the line from the source of the Little Miami to the source of the Scioto. When a disagreement arose within the commission, the negotiation had been broken off, leaving the question of boundary still unsettled. See above, I, 653-54n; *American State Papers, Public Lands,* II, 123, 735; IV, 771; 2 *U.S. Stat.,* 274-75, 764-65; U.S. Sen., *Executive Journal,* II, 281. The rival claims to land between Ludlow's and Roberts' lines were for many years the subject of litigation and Congressional action.

3 See below, Clay to McArthur, January 26, 1821. 4 Probably Thomas Scott.

5 Of Richmond, Virginia, formerly McArthur's partner in land speculation in the Virginia Military District. Means had died in 1808.

6 Not identified.

From James Morrison

My dear Sir, Lexington, Jany 11th—1821—

I recover too slowly to justify the risk and fatigue incident to a Journey at this inclement season—must therefore commit my interest at Washn. City entirely to your supervision. I do this with confidence —knowing you have great capacity and influence—and I am satisfied you will use exertion to promote my views—

You will herewith receive the Petitions to Congress which you prepared for me.[1] I have had them copied—with a view to guard against miscarriage—the copies will be sent by a subsequent mail —The copies which you inspected, will be forwarded in such sized packets as will not subject you to postage. Should they miscarry, the originals are in Mr. Hagner's[2] office, from whom you can obtain them—

With the documents which I will forward, I will make such explanations as will enable you to understand the character of my demand—

I am Dear Sir Very sincerely Your friend JAMES MORRISON

The Honble Henry Clay

Copy. DLC-TJC (DNA, M212, R12).

1 See below, Morrison to Clay, January 16, 28, 1821; Motion on Report, February 21, 1821.

2 Peter Hagner.

From James Morrison

My Dear Sir Lexington, 16th. Jany 1821—

On yesterday I had the satisfaction of receiving your favor of the 6th. dated at Columbus—[1]

I have to offer you thanks for the trouble you had with Dr. Edmiston[2]—He is a strange man—this I may say of him at least with propriety—At Washington you will be more fortunate I trust.—

On the 11th. inst. I enclosed to you to the City in two packets the petitions to Congress, which you prepared with the duplicate of lost Abstracts and Copy of Bufords receipt[3]—With this you will receive sundry documents as listed at Bottom—

I have had something of a relapse, and am unable to sit more than a few minutes—So soon as I shall have recovered a little, will give you my views on the nature of my claims—With that respecting the loan to Buford, you are as well acquainted as I am.

Here we have nothing new, saving a deep snow which fell during the last night— I am &c. JAMES MORRISON

Papers forwarded—

Copy of Petition to Congress in Buford case & discts. pd. in Bank
Ditto do in case of lost Abstracts
Vouchers—A & B. for disct. pd. in Bank
3 Copies of Letters from Wm. Eustis Secy. of War dated 29th. October—6th. & 27th Nov. 1812—
Copies of Pindell & Scotts[4] depositions of 4th. Jany 1817.
Ditto . . . . . . do . . . . . . do 28 April 1820
Ditto . . J. Maccouns . . . . . . do . . . . . . 1 May. . . . . .
Copy of the 3rd. Auditors[5] opinion in Bufords case 17 June 1820
Ditto. . . . Comtrollers [*sic*] . . . . do. . . . . . do . . 21 . . . . Ditto
(Put up in 4 packets including this)

The Honble H. Clay. Congress—

Copy. DLC-TJC (DNA, M212, R12). 1 Not found.

2 Dr. John Edmiston, said to be the first physician to locate in Columbus, Ohio. A note which he owed Morrison was due in September, 1821. Fayette County, Will Book F, 234.

3 Thomas Buford. See below, Motion on Report, February 21, 1821.

4 Thomas Hart Pindell, who had served as Assistant Deputy Quartermaster General under Morrison during the War of 1812; possibly Robert Scott.

5 Peter Hagner.

To Simon Gratz and Brothers

Gent. Washn. 17 Jan. 1821.

I beg leave to introduce F. Preston Blair Esqr.[1] the bearer hereof to your acquaintance. He is a very worthy & intelligent Citizen of Kentucky, who is making his first visit to Philada., principally for the purpose of effecting some arrangements respecting the new bank just established in Kentucky.[2] In that object he may possibly require your friendly assistance, and I have ventured to say to him that it will be chearfully [*sic*] rendered, if wanted. The wife of Mr. Blair is the sister of the lady of Mr. B. Gratz—[3]

With much respect I am Gent. Yr. ob. Servt. H. CLAY

Mess. Gratz's

ALS. PHi.

1 Francis Preston Blair (1791-1876), son of James Blair, had been graduated from Transylvania University in 1811 and admitted to the bar in 1817 (although he never practiced law). Poor health had ended his brief participation in the War of 1812 and had led him to become a farmer. His strong interest in politics had involved him in the relief struggle in Kentucky, during which he was chosen Clerk of the new Court of Appeals. A close friend of Amos Kendall, Blair contributed frequently to the columns of the Frankfort *Argus of Western America*.

Although opposed to many of Clay's views, Blair supported his fellow Kentuckian politically until 1825. He then joined the forces of Andrew Jackson, who called him to Washington in 1830 to establish an Administration paper, the *Globe*, which Blair edited for fifteen years. He also became a member of Jackson's "Kitchen Cabinet." Later one of the founders of the Republican Party, he returned to the Democratic fold after the Civil War.

2 As a part of an extensive relief program (cf. above, II, 904n; below, Clay to Dougherty, December 7, 1821), the Kentucky legislature in November, 1820, had passed an act (approved November 29) creating the Bank of the Commonwealth, the entire stock of which was owned by the State. Capitalized at $2,000,000, the institution was authorized to issue $3,000,000 in notes for circulation. Twelve branches were established. Ky. Gen. Assy., *Acts, 1820*, pp. 55-65.

In accordance with one provision of the law the legislature on December 14 had chosen for the bank a president and a board of directors, of which Blair was a member. Lexington *Kentucky Reporter*, December 18, 1820.

3 Mrs. Blair was Eliza Violet, daughter of Nathaniel Gist; her sister, Maria Cecil, was the wife of Benjamin Gratz.

Address to American Colonization Society

[January 18, 1821]

Cited in Washington *Daily National Intelligencer*, January 25, 1821; American Colonization Society, *Fourth Annual Report* (Washington, 1821), 3. Called to the Chair at the annual meeting of the Society, Clay delivered an address (his remarks unrecorded), principally urging "persevering efforts in the prosecution of the original objects of the Society, and obviating the objections which have been made against its success, from the occurrences of the past year; and justly concluding, that, whilst there was much to animate the members to perseverance, there was nothing to create despondency or alarm."

The outcome of the first attempt of the Society to carry out its colonization scheme had been discouraging. By June 1, 1820, after the expedition had landed in Africa, death had struck down two agents of the United States Government, one agent of the Society, and twenty-four Negroes, almost one fourth of the number of prospective settlers in the expedition. Fox, *American Colonization Society*, 55, 66-67.

To Langdon Cheves

Sir Washington 22d. Jan. 1821.

I have received the letter which you wrote me on the 19h. inst.[1] transmitting a Memorial from the debtors of the Bank of the U.S. at Cincinnati, with a request, from the Commee. of the Board to which it was refered, to communicate any information or advice upon the subject of it which I may be able to give. My letter of the 16h. inst[2] could not have been received by you at the date of your's. Refering to that letter, in which there were one or two general statements with respect to those debtors, I will now add: That the memorial appears to ask for all the debtors of the Bank at the late office at Cincinnati, whose conditions must, from the nature of things, be as various as their number, a common measure of indulgence: It is a *joint* application for *separate* favors. If the memorialists proposed to consolodate the whole of the debts due from them respectively, and to make each liable for the whole, there would be some propriety in their request to extend to all the same period of forbearance; but that is not their intention, which is to unite themselves to obtain, by their combined exertions, a general rule of procratination [*sic*] for all, and then leave each to skuffle for himself in the application of it. The result of establishing such a general rule would be that the best debtors of the Bank would avail themselves of it, although they might be able to pay in a much shorter time, and the worst and the doubtful would not comply with it, and would probably come to the Bank for other & farther indulgence. I think, therefore, that it would be unwise to establish any general rule. Nor need there be any apprehension that those debtors will continue for any length of time to act in concert, there not being an essential element to such a lasting association, an equality in the actual condition of the parties. The causes which have led to their present embarrassments may be the same, but the degree in which those causes have affected them respectively is very different, and each will naturally seek to preserve his credit, and to extricate himself from debt according to his *own* means, without being regulated by those of his fellow debtor. Accordingly, as stated in my letter of last week, several have renewed their notes at Chillicothe, and more may be expected to do the same. The distance of Chillicothe is complained of, and I think on this point it would be just and reasonable that the Board there should be instructed to allow the debtors of the Cincinnati office to renew their notes, in terms of six months, instead of sixty days, taking proportionate precaution as to the safety of the security.

In regard to the duration of the period of indulgence, whilst that ought to be regulated by the capacity of the respective debtors, I do believe that the Bank will not be able in a less time than that suggested by you (2. 3. 4 & 5 years) to obtain reimbursement from any of their debtors, however solvent they may be, whose debts happen to be large. There is unexampled distress throughout the Western Country. The fall in all kinds of property, and in almost every description of produce, the diminution in the circulating medium, and the unsoundness of that which remains, have together contributed to produce a state of embarrassment unknown before in that quarter of the Country. The measure of each debtor's ability furnishing the rule which ought to be applied to his case, in the extension of indulgence to him, and it being impossible, if the parent board could command the time, that it could acquire all that minute information respecting the circumstances and situation of individuals which would be necessary to guide the judgment, the establishment of a local agency to apply the rule, and which would have a full knowledge of all the facts connected with the debtors' condition, is indispensible. Such an agency should be characterized by firmness, integrity, intelligence, and discrimination. It should be as little subject as possible to any local influence. With respect to the agents already there, Mr. Wilson's[3] knowledge, at least of Mr. Worth,[4] is better than mine, and as to him I will say nothing. Mr. Crittenden[5] may be altogether relied upon for integrity, and as being free from any local bias. He is a man of good sense and of good judgment. The want of industry is the only defect about which I should entertain any fears in him. He is firm and decided, and upon the whole I think may serve the Bank very faithfully. In regard to a third agent, to be associated with the other two, I should think it advisable to appoint one, especially if those large and liberal discretionary powers are vested in them which I think ought to be confided.

I concur entirely in the opinion that indorsers should, in no case, be released without getting a better security. A request for their discharge is prima facie evidence itself against the application. And the indorsers may indemnify themselves, if they choose, by taking the very security which their principals would substitute to them.

In the mean time before this Agency can commence its operations I submit whether it would not be advisable for the Board at Chillicothe to continue to allow the Cincinnati debtors to renew at that office and upon the longer term which has been suggested. I do not believe that as many will be disposed to arrange, either with the Agents, or with the Chillicothe office, as would be but for the question intended to be raised about the effect of the abolition of the Office at Cincinnati. That question I hope we may have decided at September.[6]

On the subject of the valuation of real estate, I am persuaded that public opinion will gradually come right and accommodate itself to the altered condition of things. But there ought not to be such reliance upon the effect of this change as to prevent the employment of every precaution to obtain just valuations.

The offer of Mr. Hammond was, without any condition, to use his best exertions, to return the sum of $95.000 or $98.000[7] I should not have acceded to it, if the money were to be returned on any condition which wd. have *even* implied a surrender of any right whatever appurtaining to the Corporation, under the Charter. A bill has been introduced, which I have not yet seen, in consequence of what occurred.[8]

I did think of visiting Philadelphia during the winter; but I am not sure that I shall be able to effect that intention If I should, it will be about the first of March.

I am writing in the Hall of the H. of R. during its Session, and should any thing further present itself to my mind I will take the liberty of communicating it.

With great respect I am Yr. obt. Servt. H. CLAY

L. Cheves Esq.

P.S. I return the memorial. H.C.

ALS. PU. Cf. above, II, 908-909.

1 Not found.

2 Not found.

3 Thomas Wilson.

4 Gorham A. Worth.

5 Thomas T. Crittenden.

6 Probably a reference to the pending court action. See below, Clay to Cheves, September 8, 1821.

7 During hearing of the case of the Bank of the United States against Ralph Osborn, John L. Harper, James McColister, John C. Wright, and Charles Hammond in an action of trespass *quare clausum fregit* (see above, II, 873-75), at the January Term of the United States Circuit Court for the District of Ohio, Clay had agreed "to withdraw a juror," thus necessitating a continuance, upon Hammond's promise to work for passage of a law by the Ohio legislature "for paying over to the bank, 90 or 95,000 dollars of the money, and retaining the balance as a tax." *Niles' Weekly Register,* XIX (January 20, 1821), 347, citing Columbus *Ohio Monitor,* January 6, 1821.

8 See below, Clay to Cheves, March 10, 1821.

To Greenberry W. Ridgely

My dear Sir Washington 23d. Jan. 1821.

I was gratified by the receipt of your letter of the 19h. inst.[1] from Philadelphia which gave me the first information concerning you, altho' I had frequently enquired after you, and which contains the agreeable assurance that your health is much improved. I have a letter from your father,[2] under date the 9h. inst, in which he expresses great solicitude about you, and says that the family is in the most painful state of suspense, in consequence of not hearing from you so long. I shall let him know where you are and that you have improved your health; but you had better write to him also. I have no packet of papers from your father for you, as you suppose. In his letter to me he mentions that he has directed some papers to be sent to me respecting business of the Estate of Mr. Edmunds;[3] but I have not yet received them.

My journey from Kentucky, via Columbus in Ohio, was attended with less discomfort than any journey I ever before performed in the winter. It was cold, but it was dry; and when I reached Wheeling the fine state of the roads allowed me to travel in a sleigh the principal part of the way to Fredericktown in Maryland.

I have reached this place time enough to give my vote upon every important question that has occurred or is likely to be agitated during the Session. Missouri will be taken up again in a day or two.[4] Strong fears exist however that it will not be admitted.

I shall be glad to hear from you & to see you,

G. W. Ridgely Esq. Your's faithfully H. CLAY

ALS. NcD.

1 Not found.

2 Dr. Frederick Ridgely. The letter, not found.

3 Possibly Elias Edmonds.

4 See below, Notice, January 24, 1821.

Remarks on Bill for Reduction of the Army

[January 23, 1821]

Cited in Washington *Daily National Intelligencer,* January 24, 1821; *Annals of Cong.,* 16 Cong., 2 Sess., XXXVII, 936. By the time Clay took his seat in Congress, January 16, 1821, the House had already for ten days devoted a large share of its attention to a bill proposing a reduction of the military peace establishment. On the last day of debate before House action on the measure Clay expressed his views (not recorded) on the reasons why he thought the interest of the country called for passage of the bill. Immediately afterward the bill was approved by the House and later, with some Senate amendment, was enacted into law. 3 *U. S. Stat.,* 615-16 (March 2, 1821).

Remarks and Motion on Relief of the Family of Oliver Hazard Perry

[January 23, 1821]

Mr. *Clay,* though decidedly in favor of the object of the bill, objected to that part of it proposing an allowance of 330 dollars per annum, during life, to the mother of the deceased; and, on his motion, that part was stricken out.[1]

Washington *Daily National Intelligencer,* January 24, 1821. Published also in *Annals of Cong.,* 16 Cong., 2 Sess., XXXVII, 938. The House in Committee of the Whole had taken up a bill, reported at the previous Session of Congress, for the relief of the family of the late Commodore Perry and for the education of his children at public expense. On motion of John Randolph the blanks in the measure were filled so as to provide annual stipends of $330 to Perry's mother, Sarah Wallace Alexander Perry; $400 to his widow (unless she remarried); and $150 to each of his four children, Christopher Grant, Oliver Hazard, Christopher Raymond, and Margaret, until they reached the age of twenty-one. Clay's motion was offered after the Committee had risen and reported the bill and after several proposed amendments had indicated strong disagreement on the measure.

1 Randolph tried unsuccessfully to add this sum to the allowance of $400 for the widow, making her annual stipend $730. The bill, as amended by Clay's motion, passed the House by a vote of 76 to 62 and was enacted in the same form on March 2, 1821. 6 *U. S. Stat.,* 260.

Notice of Motion on Missouri Statehood

[January 24, 1821]

Mr. *Clay* rose, and gave notice, that, if no other gentleman made any motion on the subject, he should on the day after to-morrow move to go into committee of the whole on the State of the Union, to take into consideration *the resolution from the Senate* on the subject of Missouri.

Washington *Daily National Intelligencer,* January 25, 1821. Published also in Lexington *Kentucky Gazette,* February 8, 1821; *Annals of Cong.,* 16 Cong., 2 Sess., XXXVII, 944. The compromise of 1820 (see above, II, 748n, 788) had not settled the Missouri question, for, although Maine had been admitted to the Union, Missouri had merely been authorized to draw up a constitution, to be submitted to Congress for approval. At the beginning of the Second Session of the Sixteenth Congress, in November, 1820, a copy of the constitution adopted by Missouri during the previous summer had been laid before Congress, and within a short time select committees in both houses had reported resolutions approving statehood. The Senate on December 12 had adopted, after amendment, the resolution submitted by its committee; but in the House of

Representatives on the following day this measure had been read and tabled. The House then had rejected the resolution reported by its own select committee, which had been the subject of a week's debate, and during the following weeks had shown no disposition further to examine the Senate proposal.

To Duncan McArthur

Dr. Genl. Washington 26h. Jan. 1821.

The letter which you did me the favor to write on the 8h. inst. and which you addressed to me at Columbus did not reach that place. until after my departure from it, and it has been slow in finding its way here. I have however received it; and having considered your request that I should appear in your behalf, in conjunction with Mr. Doddridge, at the ensuing term of the Supreme Court of the U. States, in the case from Ohio in the name of Mr. Doddridge, intended to try the validity of entries West of Ludlow's line, I have determined to appear accordingly.[1] I have not had an opportunity here of consulting with any on[e] as to the value of the land which you have offered me as a fee; but relying on your having made an offer to me of what is worthy of my acceptance, I am content to receive the compensation for my services which is proposed in your letter.

I will take an early opportunity of examining into the transcript of the record which has been sent up, and after having done so, I will write you what I think of the case— In the mean time I am, with great respect, Faithfy Yr ob Servant H. CLAY

Genl. McArthur

ALS. DLC-McArthur Papers (DNA, M212, R22).

[1] On appeal from an adverse ruling by the Circuit Court for the District of Ohio, Doddridge won a reversal when the case, with Clay representing the plaintiff, was argued before the Supreme Court in March, 1824. Chief Justice Marshall delivered the opinion that the land between Ludlow's and Roberts' lines had not been withdrawn from the territory to be surveyed for military warrants prior to passage of the act of June 26, 1812 (see above, Clay to McArthur, January 8, 1821, note).

To Smith Thompson

Sir Washington 26 Jan. 1821.

In the event of the U. States acquiring the Floridas, it is probable that the appointment of a Naval Storekeeper at the port of Pensacola may become necessary.[1] In that case, I take pleasure in recommending for that appointment John S. Williams, Esq. of Maryland,[2] whose integrity, capacity & other qualifications are such as will, I have no doubt, ensure a faithful discharge of the duties incident to that appointment, if he should obtain it. I have the honor to be with great respect Your obedient servant H. CLAY

The Honble. Mr. Thompson &c &c &c.

ALS. Nj. 1 No such appointment was made for Pensacola until 1830.

2 Probably the Brigade-Major and Inspector, 1st Columbian Brigade, District Militia, in the War of 1812, who later published a *History of the Invasion and Capture of Washington, and of the Events which Preceded and Followed* (New York, 1857).

From James Morrison

My Dear Sir Lexington Jan'y 28th. 1821—

Herewith you will receive the balance of the Documents which you examined previous to your departure—If they should be too voluminous will enclose a part to our friend Auditor Lee.[1] They are Documents of a public character, and ought to be exempt from Postage.

You will find a rough statement relative to my claims on Govet,—I cannot promise that a perusal will give you any Idea that may be important or Serviceable in pressing them on the Accounting Officers — My deficiencies will be abunantly [*sic*] supplied by your fertile Brain— and familiarity with claims and Accounts even on a single perusal of them. You will please direct Montgomery[2] to bring such papers as he may have in his possession, and which you may wish to examin [*sic*]— Where unsuccessful, please to return them to him— As you already have a pretty ample knowledge of my demands on Government, you will be able to Judge very soon by Conversing with Mr. Calhoun— and with our good friend Mr. Crawford,[3] if you can reach him—how far you ought to press decisions—I cannot ask that you should remain after Congress adjourns, attending to my business without Compensation or even during yr Session— If you succeed in having the allowance of 5* Cents for the issues at Forts Osage & Madison[4]—which will amount to about $3,800—you shall have $250— For lost Abstracts nothing more than an application to Congress & the passage of a Law to Justify the Accounting Officers to make payment, as Secretary Calhoun informed me was requisite —and that on reference to him, he would make such statement as would ensure the passage of the law— With this item you will have but little trouble— but you will have some, compensation $150— There are some circumstances not now necessary to communicate, which forbid the offer of a large sum for having the advance by Pindell to Buford passed to my Credit—but do for me all you can— if success full you shall have $300—

The original certificate of our friend Eustis—and Simmons's[5] Deposition, are either in the hands of Mr. Hagner—Mr. Cutts[6]—or in my Trunk in the possession of J. Montgomery—

My Health (altho' improving slowly) Coupled with the short time Congress will be in Session forbid leaving home— should I live you will find me where you left me—

I am My Dear Sir very sincerely, your friend JAMES MORRISON
The Honl. H. Clay
* On examination of my Books, the original charge was Osage 40. & Fort Madison 38. cents instead of 35. as mentioned in my statement— However I did agree to receive 40. & 35 Cents, and can claim no more
P. S. If you succeed in obtaining a decision that all issues made at Osage & Madison until a Contract was made— shall be 40. & 35. Cents —the sum will be more than I have stated say about $4269.89 John Abbett,[7] the old Gentleman who attends to the Contract business alone, will state the a/c fairly— He is an honest man—

You will receive by next mail a statement of the items—

ALS. DLC-TJC (DNA, M212, R12). See above, Morrison to Clay, January 11, 16, 1821; below, Motion on Report, February 21, 1821.

1 William Lee, of Massachusetts, Second Auditor, United States Treasury Department.

2 James Montgomery, of Pennsylvania, a clerk in the office of the Third Auditor and a relative of Mrs. Morrison.

3 John C. Calhoun; William H. Crawford.

4 Fort Osage, at the junction of the Kansas and Missouri rivers; Fort Madison, at the site of the present Iowa city of that name on the west bank of the Mississippi River.

5 William Eustis; William Simmons, a Pennsylvanian, an accountant in the War Department from 1795 to 1814.

6 Peter Hagner; Richard Cutts.

7 John Abbott, a native of New York, was a clerk in the office of the Third Auditor.

Motions and Speech on the Admission of Missouri

[January 29, 1821]

On motion of Mr. *Clay,* the House resolved itself into a committee of the whole on the State of the Union, Mr. *Smith,* of Md. being called to the chair; and the resolution from the Senate, for admitting Missouri into the Union, with a *caveat* against the provision, if there be any, which conflicts with the constitution of the U. States, was taken up.[1]

[John Randolph moved to strike out the *caveat,* "but waived his motion for the present, to accommodate Mr. Clay, who wished to address the Committee on the whole subject."]

Mr. *Clay* then delivered his sentiments at large on the present state of this question. He was in favor of the resolution from the Senate, and should vote for the resolution, even though more emphatically restricted against any supposed repugnance of one of its provisions to a provision of the constitution of the United States, the existence of which, however, he did not by any means admit.[2]

[At the conclusion of Clay's remarks Randolph renewed his motion, which, after some discussion, was defeated. Samuel A. Foot then moved to amend the resolution under consideration by adding a proviso under which Missouri would be admitted on condition that the offending clause be expunged from her constitution within two years. Henry Baldwin stated his intention of voting for Foot's proposal.]

Mr. *Clay* moved to amend the amendment by adding words to this effect: "so far as the same (the clause of the Missouri constitution) tends to deprive citizens of each state of the privileges and immunities of citizens of the several states." This motion, however, he subsequently withdrew.[3]

Washington *Daily National Intelligencer,* January 30, 1821. Published also in Lexington *Kentucky Reporter,* February 26, 1821; *Annals of Cong.,* 16 Cong., 2 Sess., XXXVII, 982, 984. See above, Notice, January 24, 1821.

1 Opposition to the admission of the new state centered around the provision of the Missouri constitution requiring the legislature, "as soon as may be," to enact laws "To prevent free negroes and mulattoes from coming to, and settling in, this state, under any pretext whatsoever. . . ." *House Docs.,* 16 Cong., 2 Sess., no. 2, p. 7. The Senate resolution included the following amendment, which had been proposed by John Henry Eaton, of Tennessee: "*Provided,* That nothing herein contained shall be so construed as to give the assent of congress to any provision in the constitution of Missouri, if any such there be, which contravenes that clause in the Constitution of the United States which declares that 'the citizens of each State shall be entitled to all privileges and immunities of citizens of the several States.' " *Annals of Cong.,* 16 Cong., 2 Sess., XXXVII, 43-45, 100, 102.

2 The speech is not more fully reported; but some indication of its content may be derived from the following allusions by Josiah Butler, of New Hampshire, on January 30:

"The gentleman from Kentucky, (Mr. Clay,) said, admitting the clause of the constitution of Missouri, respecting free negroes and mulattoes, to be incompatible with the constitution of the United States, it could not be an objection to her admission into the Union; because the legislators of Missouri would be bound by an oath to support the federal constitution, which would be paramount to the oath to support their state constitution, and of course would never make any enactment pursuant to that clause. Beside, he said, if they did enact any law in pursuance of that clause in their constitution, it would be declared void by the courts of the United States.

. . . .

"The gentleman from Kentucky, (Mr. Clay,) said, that a limitation or restriction upon the power of the legislature of Missouri might be imposed, by adding to the resolution under consideration a provision, that no law should be enacted under the clause in question, to affect the rights of citizens of other states.

. . . .

"Sir, I cannot doubt, that the clause in the constitution of Missouri, which requires the legislature to pass laws to prevent free negroes and mulattoes from going to, and settling in, that state, is wholly incompatible with the constitution of the United States, which gives the citizens of each state all the privileges and immunities of citizens of the several states, notwithstanding the construction given to that article by the gentleman from Kentucky, (Mr. Clay.) Had not that honorable gentleman represented this article in the constitution of the United States as equivocal and uncertain, I should have supposed it beyond the art of logic or subtlety of metaphysics to mislead any one who read it, or to pervert its very obvious signification." Washington *Daily National Intelligencer,* April 14, 1821.

The editor of the Georgetown, D. C., *Metropolitan,* referring to one of Clay's major speeches on the subject, either this one or that of February 13 (below), further reflected his comments:

"Mr. Clay, in his solicitude to cause the restrictionists to look well to the consequences of refusing Missouri, shewed too clearly the vast resources she had within herself—that she might open her land offices, and not retail it at two dollars an acre, as the general government did, but she would say to the hardy yeomanry inhabiting the states around and distant from her, '*here is our soil, come receive it, and defend us;*' the choice spirits which would then flock to her, would extend her possessions to the Pacific; and that if she receded from the general government, Kentucky, Tennessee, and Ohio must necessarily go with her. He alluded to the conflicting interests between the decisions of the state and supreme courts, the state banks and United

States' bank. He mentioned that the people in the west were goaded almost to desperation by pecuniary embarrassments, and that gentlemen were preparing further combustion, to which when the spark was applied the fire of inextinguishable discord would be lighted up. He thought the subject about the constitutionality of which they were debating, not sufficiently important to risque such disastrous consequences as might ensue. He took a view of ancient history, and cited, as examples, Greece and other countries, which from the slightest causes, had the proud pillars which sustained the fabric of their governments, dilapidated and torn down —turning to more modern dates, he instanced the bloody revolution of France, produced from the *slightest* causes, and which was only terminated by the valor, skill, and prudence of the immortal Bonaparte. . . ." Reprinted in Lexington *Kentucky Reporter*, March 5, 1821. The subsequent remarks, an encomium upon Bonaparte, were clearly the editor's elaboration, as were, probably, the laudatory words of the last line.

3 After further discussion the Committee rose, and the House adjourned.

Remarks and Motion on Missouri Question

[January 30, 1821]

Mr. *Clay* earnestly opposed this course, as going to close the door on the spirit of accommodation.

[Rhea's motion was defeated by a large majority.]

Mr. *Clay*, then, after an earnest appeal to all parts of the House to bring to the future discussion of this subject minds prepared to harmonize, and forever settle this distracting question to mutual satisfaction, and expressing his desire more fully to examine Mr. *Storrs'* proposition, to see whether he could bring his mind to assent to it, as he wished to do—moved, that the committee now rise, in order to have the several propositions for amendment printed.

[This motion being adopted, Clay gave notice that he would again call up the subject the next day. William Lowndes favored deferring the matter "until Friday next, to give more time."]

Mr. *Clay* said he would compromize with his friend for Thursday. He did not like the idea of taking up this question *on Friday*.

Washington *Daily National Intelligencer*, January 31, 1821. Published also in Lexington *Kentucky Reporter*, February 26, 1821; *Annals of Cong.*, 16 Cong., 2 Sess., XXXVII, 994-95. The House in Committee of the Whole had resumed consideration of Samuel A. Foot's proposed amendment to the Senate resolution for the admission of Missouri. After Josiah Butler (see above, Motions and Speech, January 29, 1821, note) and others had been heard. Henry R. Storrs moved to amend Foot's amendment so as to impose a "perpetual obligation" on Missouri, as a condition to statehood to be accepted by the legislature of that state acting as a convention, "that no law shall ever be enacted by the said state, impairing or contravening the rights, privileges, or immunities, secured to citizens of other states, by the constitution of the United States. . . ." Others joined the discussion, and finally John Rhea moved that "the committee should rise, with a view to demanding the previous question, which would preclude all debate and amendment, and present to the House a naked and direct question on the resolution from the Senate."

To Langdon Cheves

Sir Washn. 31 Jan. 1821.

I transmit for your perusal the inclosed letter which I have just received.[1] The amount which the bill mentioned by Mr. Hammond proposes to restore of the money belonging to the Bank is not as great as was promised.[2] I have not yet learnt its fate in the Senate.

You will observe that it is proposed still to continue to levy a tax, and the employment of the machinery of criminal jurisprudence is intended to be resorted to. The object of this is, doubtless, to oust the Federal Judiciary of jurisdiction of the subject matter. Should such a law pass, it will become very important for us to maintain the competency of the Court of Chancery to restrain by injunction the collection of the tax. I shall be, in due season, put in possession of information as to what the Legislature may do, and we will take the best care we can of the interests of the Bank—

L. Cheves Esqr. I am Your ob. Servant H. CLAY
&c &c &c

ALS. PU. [1] Not found.

[2] Cf. above, Clay to Cheves, January 22, 1821; below, Clay to Cheves, March 10 (1), 1821.

Remarks on Bill to Incorporate Columbian College

[January 31, 1821]

Cited in Washington *Daily National Intelligencer,* February 1, 1821; *Annals of Cong.,* 16 Cong., 2 Sess., XXXVII, 998. A Senate bill to incorporate Columbian College in the District of Columbia had progressed to its third reading in the House, when a lengthy debate arose on a motion to recommit the measure for revision. That motion having been negatived, Henry Baldwin offered an amendment providing that nothing in the act should be construed "to authorize said College to purchase or hold any real estate out of the District of Columbia, without the consent of the Legislature of the State within which such real estate shall be situated." When this proposal failed to obtain the unanimous consent required for amendment at this stage of the proceedings, John W. Campbell, of Ohio, moved to return the bill to committee with instructions to add this particular amendment. Further debate, in which Clay participated (his remarks not recorded), followed, the amendment being opposed by both friends and adversaries of the bill—"by its friends, as being unnecessary—by its enemies, on the ground that its insertion would leave an implication that, without its insertion, the College would have had the power proposed to be denied." Campbell's motion was then defeated, and the bill, for which Clay voted, was passed.

Columbian College ultimately became George Washington University.

Motion and Remarks on Missouri Resolution

[February 1, 1821]

On a motion by Clay, the House again resolved itself into Committee of the Whole on the Senate resolution. During the debate, not fully recorded, John Sergeant proposed that the admission of Missouri be deferred until the next Session of Congress. A correspondent to the editor of the Lexington *Kentucky Reporter,* in a letter from Washington dated February 4, cited Clay's "vehemence" in reply: "'Put off the question,' said he, 'to the next session—No! I would as soon sleep amidst the conflagration of a city, under the vain persuasion that in the morning, when I awoke, it would be time enough to endeavour to extinguish the flames.'" Lexington *Kentucky Reporter,* February 19, 1821. On the dating of this exchange see Everett Somerville Brown (ed.), *The Missouri Compromises and Presidential Politics, 1820-1825, from the Letters of William Plumer, Junior* (Missouri Historical Society, *Publications,* 1926), 30.

The day's business terminated with the defeat of Foot's amendment and the proposal of another amendment, by Louis McLane, of Delaware.

Motions on Missouri Resolution

[February 2, 1821]

Cited in H. of Reps., *Journal,* 16 Cong., 2 Sess., 194, 197; Lexington *Kentucky Reporter,* February 26, 1821; *Annals of Cong.,* 16 Cong., 2 Sess., XXXVII, 1026, 1027. The House, again in Committee of the Whole on the Senate resolution for the admission of Missouri, had agreed to the amendment offered by Louis McLane on the preceding day; but, after the Committee had risen and reported, the amendment was rejected. The Senate resolution was then again read. Henry R. Storrs moved to amend it by striking out most of the measure and substituting language providing for the admission of Missouri "on an equal footing with the original States, on the first day of the next session of Congress," under a condition similar to that which he had proposed on January 30 (above, Remarks and Motion), and providing that the Missouri legislature, as a convention, declare by public act its acceptance of this condition. On motion by Clay the amendment was changed "by striking out these words where they first occur, viz: on the first day of the next session of Congress." Storrs' amendment was, however, finally rejected, as was another, offered by Samuel Moore, of Pennsylvania. After protracted debate, Clay moved that the resolution be referred to a select committee. This proposal was agreed to, and Clay was named chairman of a committee of thirteen.

To John Q. Adams

2. Feb. 1821.

Mr. Clay has the pleasure to accept the invitation of Mr. and Mrs. Adams to dinner on thursday the 8h. inst.

AN. MHi-Adams Papers. Addressed: "The Honble J. Q. Adams. Present."

Motion on Missions to South America

[February 3, 1821]

Mr. *Clay* then rose to make a motion. It would be recollected, he said, by the House, that, by a majority very decisive, a resolution was adopted at the last session, declaring it expedient to make an appropriation, by law, for a mission to such of the governments of South America as had established their independence.[1] It remained for the house to carry that resolution into effect; and he thought that it was a solemn duty of this house to give complete effect to its own decision. He rose therefore to move that the resolution adopted at the last session be referred to the same committee of the whole house, to which was referred the bill making appropriations for the support of government, that it might come up for consideration, in a regular manner, and a clause be inserted in that bill to accomplish the object of the resolution. Mr. C. made this motion to prevent the imputation of taking the house by surprise. Conceiving it proper to act in the spirit of that resolution, he now proposed the preliminary step.[2]

Washington *Daily National Intelligencer,* February 5, 1821. Published also in Lexington *Kentucky Reporter,* February 26, 1821; *Annals of Cong.,* 16 Cong., 2 Sess.,

XXXVII, 1029-30. Upon completion of consideration of other matters by the House, Samuel Smith "moved to go into committee on the general appropriation bill, but temporarily withdrew his motion, at the request of Mr. *Clay*."

1 See above, II, 815n, 816n, 817-18.

2 "The motion was agreed to without a division, though not without dissenting voices."

From James De Wolf, Jr.

Hon: Henry Clay New York, 3d of Febry 1821

Sir

I addressed you, at Lexington, under date of the 1st of Jany—requesting you to commence an action against the Hope Distillery Company. (copy of which letter I now inclose you)

Subsequently, under date of 13th Jany, I wrote to you, duplicate of which I have since forwarded to Washington, in which I requested you to stay proceedings 'til you should hear further from me on the subject.[1]

I have now to request, that you will cause a suit to be commenced agst. the said company as mentioned in my said letter of the 1st Jany—and an injunction to be taken out to stay Waste of the property &c.

I am Sir, very respectfully Your Mo Obt Servt.

JAMES D'WOLF, JR.

LS. DLC-TJC (DNA, M212, R12). Endorsed by Clay: "Ansd. 7 Feb. 1821." Answer not found.

1 This letter not found.

Remarks Relating to Cumberland Road

[February 5, 1821]

Cited in Washington *Daily National Intelligencer*, February 6, 1821; *Annals of Cong.*, 16 Cong., 2 Sess., XXXVII, 1033. Christian Tarr having moved to amend the general appropriation bill so as to permit construction of a bridge over the Monongahela River at the crossing of the Cumberland road, by use of "the unexpended balance heretofore appropriated" for completing the road, Clay joined in the debate. His remarks were not recorded.

Motion and Speeches on Missions to South America

[February 6, 1821]

Mr. *Clay* moved the amendment, which he a few days ago intimated it to be his intention to propose to the bill,[1] and was as follows:

For an outfit and one year's salary to such Minister as the President, by and with the advice and consent of the Senate, may send to any government of South America, which has established and is maintaining its independency on Spain, a sum not exceeding 18,000 dollars.

Mr. *Clay* followed his motion with a speech of more than an hour's length, in its support.[2]

[William Lowndes stated "reasons why he conceived the adoption of the proposition at this time inexpedient, and the mode of obtaining the object improper." George Robertson, of Kentucky, also opposed the motion, while John Floyd, James Stevens, of Connecticut, David Trimble, and John Culpepper, of North Carolina, spoke in its favor.]

Mr. *Clay* again occupied the floor for some time in reply to Mr. *Lowndes,* and in a zealous support of the proposition.[3]

Washington *Daily National Intelligencer,* February 7, 1821. Published also in Lexington *Kentucky Reporter,* February 26, 1821; *Annals of Cong.,* 16 Cong., 2 Sess., XXXVII, 1042, 1055. The motion was offered immediately after the House had resolved itself into Committee of the Whole on the general appropriation bill.

1 See above, Motion, February 3, 1821. On February 5 the Committee of the Whole on the general appropriation bill had risen "and obtained leave to sit again, on motion of Mr. *Clay,* who was prepared to move an amendment, respecting a mission to South America, but thought the hour too late, and the house too thin." Washington *Daily National Intelligencer,* February 6, 1821; *Annals of Cong.,* 16 Cong., 2 Sess., XXXVII, 1034.

2 Not recorded.

3 His remarks were not recorded. John Rhea next spoke, in opposition to Clay, after which the amendment was defeated by a vote of 73 to 77.

Motion and Speech on Missions to South America

[February 9, 1821]

Cited in Washington *Daily National Intelligencer,* February 10, 1821; Lexington *Kentucky Reporter,* February 26, 1821; *Annals of Cong.,* 16 Cong., 2 Sess., XXXVII, 1071. The House had resumed consideration of the general appropriation bill, which had been tabled on February 7 "with the view of affording to Mr. *Clay* an opportunity of renewing, in the House, the motion unsuccessfully made by him in committee of the whole, on Tuesday [see above, Motion and Speeches, February 6, 1821]; that gentleman being now absent, on the committee appointed on the Missouri subject [see above, Motions, February 2, 1821]—which committee obtained leave yesterday to hold its sittings during the sessions of the House." Washington *Daily National Intelligencer,* February 8, 1821. Clay accordingly submitted his proposal to the House and "spoke at some length . . . on the grounds formerly and frequently taken in support of it." His speech was not recorded.

After several other speakers had been heard, the amendment was again rejected, by a vote of 79 to 86.

To Langdon Cheves

My dear Sir Washington 10h. Feb. 1821.

I have duly received your obliging letter of the 5th. instant[1] and thank you for your kind invitation to me to visit Philada. I am very anxious to see you, and if I can possibly go, without too great inconvenience, I shall take much pleasure in doing so. My being able however to gratify this wish depends principally upon the time

I shall be detained by the Supreme Court, after Congress adjourns.

I am very greatly obliged by the friendly manner in which you have alluded to the subject of my Law Agency &c. for the Bank. I had wished to write to you in relation to it, but the same considerations of delicacy which, it seems, have influenced you, produced some hesitation in refering to it, on my part. I had however, before the receipt of your letter, resolved to break it to you, and to throw myself on that friendship for me, on your part, which I so highly value, and of which, on several occasions, I have felt the most signal benefit.

I concur entirely in thinking that the best arrangement for both parties would be that of a fixed annual stipend. Indeed any other would be almost impracticable. When in the Western Country, I am almost daily applied to in person or by letter for some advice respecting the affairs of the Bank. During the sitting of the Federal Courts I am in constant attendance not knowing at what moment nor often in what particular cause I may be called on to render some assistance to the Solicitors, they being some times themselves unapprized of the character of the defence. This advice and assistance are often in matters not of very great moment, 'though it is some times otherwise. The small current business, as well as that of a more important description, will rather increase, at least for a time, than diminish. And the known fact that I am honored with the confidence of the Bank, and with your friendship multiplies applications to me for advice, owing to that common desire which men have to escape from, or to shift upon others responsibility. I of course answer all enquiries and reply to all letters, without regard to that responsibility, endeavoring to form the best judgment I can upon the case submitted, and then acting upon the rule of recommending for the Bank that to be done, which under analagous [*sic*] circumstances in my own situation I would do for myself. To make separate charges for all these various services, as they might be successively rendered, would be a tedious and endless affair. The Bank could have no certain or probable standard by which to test their accuracy; and even, as is not unlikely, if their aggregate amount at the end of a year should be greater than that of a fixed compensation I should prefer the latter.

As to the quantum of compensation I need not say that I am not a very disinterested judge. But there are some general facts which may assist in determining what would be a proper measure. Independent of that portion of the Capital of the Bank in the two Western States, which is not in suit, and of the occasions of taking counsel concerning transactions which may appurtain [*sic*] to it, there are I think (speaking from memory) not much less than four hundred suits on the dockets in the two States, involving an amount of about two millions of debt. Many of these, it is true, are plain causes; and many it is hoped may be compromised; but it may be pretty certainly assumed that in almost every instance of an attempt to recover the contents of a bill of exchange, or to charge indorsers, obstinate defence will be made. In Kentucky, owing to the want of a provision in the Charter of the Bank, or an equivalent provision in the laws of the State, placing discounted promissory notes upon the footing of foreign bills of exchange,[2] suits are necessarily multiplied, and the greatest caution is necessary in prosecuting the principal to charge the indorser. Complicated suits in Chancery must be brought, and one or two have already been commenced. Even after Judgment, questions will frequently arise about the execution of the final process, growing out of replevin,[3] property and other stay laws. And no doubt many cases may occur to unravel fraudulent conveyances to screen the debtors property. From this mass of business I really expect that the greater part of my time will be engrossed with the interests of the Bank. I have supposed, under these circumstances, that an allowance of $5000. per annum would be just and liberal. Such an allowance for any considerable length of time would be too large and more than the Bank would be justified in making. But I have thought that during the great pressure of its business, from the causes suggested, which may possibly last for two or three years, the magnitude of its interests at stake would warrant a compensation to that extent. However, such is my entire confidence in the Board, and at the same time my apprehension that I may be operated upon by a natural bias, that I shall be perfectly satisfied with whatever decision it may make. I should be glad, if it be convenient, that it would make some definite arrangement whilst I am here, and that you would have the goodness to communicate it to me.

With very great regard I am faithfully Your ob. Servt.

L. Cheves Esqr. H. CLAY

P.S. I thank you for the perusal of Judge Peters's[4] letter. I will write to him directly on the subject of it,[5] and not trouble you to be the organ of communication between us. H.C.

ALS. ScHi.
1 Not found.
2 See above, II, 723n.
3 See above, II, 904n.
4 Richard Peters.
5 No letter has been found.

Committee Report on Missouri Resolution

[February 10, 1821]

The Select Committee to whom was referred the resolution from the Senate declaring the admission of the state of Missouri into the Union, have, according to order, had the same under consideration, and beg leave to submit to the House the following REPORT:

That they have entered upon the discharge of the duty assigned them by the House with the most anxious desire to arrive at a conclusion which would give general satisfaction; that, in the prosecution of this purpose it seemed to them to be useful to ascertain, in the first place, by a full and frank comparison of opinions among themselves, whether any and what conditions ought to be prescribed to the admission of Missouri into the Union; that, on making this comparison the opinion appeared to be nearly unanimous in the committee, that no other conditions ought now to be required than those which were specified in the act of the last session of Congress, providing for the admission of Missouri into the Union; and that, considering all the circumstances attending that act, the settlement which it made of the question of restriction ought not to be disturbed;[1] that this opinion limited their subsequent inquiry to the consideration of the single question, whether the constitution which Missouri has formed for herself contained any thing in it which furnished a valid objection to her incorporation in the Union? And, on that question, they thought that there was no other provision in that constitution to which Congress could, of right, take exception, but that which makes it the duty of the legislature of Missouri to pass laws to prevent free negroes and mulattoes from going to and settling in the said state. In regard to that clause, the same diversity of opinion existed among the members of the committee which had been previously manifested in the House; one portion believing it liable to an interpretation repugnant to the constitution of the United States; and the other thinking it not exposed to that objection, or that if it were, the exceptionable interpretation was superseded by the paramount authority of the federal constitution.

With these conflicting opinions, the committee thought it best that, without either side abandoning its opinion, an endeavor should be made to frame an amendment to the Senate's resolution, which, compromitting neither, should contain an adequate security against any violation of the privileges and immunities of citizens of other states in Missouri; and, a majority of the committee thinking that such security could not be sufficiently afforded, without some previous act to be done by the legislature of Missouri, the amendment was finally agreed upon which they now beg leave to report.

According to this amendment Missouri is to be admitted into the Union, upon the fundamental condition, that she shall never pass any law preventing any description of persons from going to, and settling in, the said state, who now are, or hereafter may become, citizens of any of the states in this Union; and upon the legislature of the said state signifying its assent to that condition, by a solemn public act, which is to be communicated to the President of the United States, he is to proclaim the fact, and thereupon the admission of the said state into the Union is to be complete, without any further or other proceeding on the part of Congress. To prevent, however, this amendment from being considered as impairing any right which may appertain to Missouri, in common with other states, to exclude from her jurisdiction persons under peculiar circumstances (such as paupers, vagabonds, &c.) a further proviso is added, declaring that nothing in the said amendment is to be construed to take from Missouri, when admitted into the Union, the exercise of any right or power which the original states may constitutionally exert.

The modification which the committee thus respectfully recommend of the Senate's resolution, is the result of a spirit of concord, under the guidance of which they have anxiously sought, without the sacrifice of principle on either side, to reconcile the variant opinions among them. There cannot be a doubt but that Missouri, solicitous as she must be to participate in all the high advantages of our excellent union, will eagerly seize the opportunity of testifying her attachment to the federal constitution, by giving the solemn pledge which she is asked to make, to respect the privileges and immunities which it secures to citizens of other states—a pledge become necessary, in the opinion of a large and respectable portion of the House, by the terms which she has employed in a clause of her constitution. Nor will there be a doubt of the sincerity or efficacy of such a pledge. On the other hand, if, by postponing for a short period her admission into the Union, a circumstance every day less and less important, in consequence of the lapse of the time allotted to this session, those who thought her invested with a perfect right to be admitted, without delay, are not fully gratified, they will be consoled by the reflection, that the amendment requires only the performance of a precise and simple act, which cannot be mistaken by the highly responsible officer to whom the judgment of its execution is confided. And the whole House must be gratified with any proper disposition of the subject, which will henceforth free the public deliberations from the agitation and disturbance to which it is but too likely always to give rise. And your committee believe that all must ardently unite in wishing an amicable termination of a question, which, if it be longer kept open, cannot fail to produce, and possibly to perpetuate, prejudices and animosities among a people, to whom the conservation of their moral ties should be even dearer, if possible, than that of their political bond. Sharing as the committee do largely in this sentiment, they respectfully submit to the House the amendment which they propose, in the hope that it will be received and considered in the same spirit in which it has been devised.

Strike out all after the word "be" in the third line of the Senate's resolution, and insert

"Admitted into this Union on an equal footing with the original states, in all respects whatever, upon the fundamental condition, that the said state shall never pass any law preventing any description of persons from coming to and settling in the said state, who now are or hereafter may become citizens of any of the states of this Union: And provided, also, that the Legislature of the said State, by a solemn public act, shall declare the assent of the said state to the said fundamental condition, and shall transmit to the President of the United States, on or before the fourth Monday of November next, an authentic copy of the said act; upon the receipt whereof, the President, by proclamation, shall announce the fact; whereupon, and without any further proceeding on the part of Congress, the admission of the said State into this Union shall be considered as complete: And provided further, that nothing herein contained shall be construed to take from the said state of Missouri, when admitted into this Union, the exercise of any right or power which can now be constitutionally exercised by any of the original states."[2]

The report, *House Reports,* 16 Cong., 2 Sess., no. 60; the amendment, Washington *Daily National Intelligencer,* February 12, 1821. Published also in Lexington *Kentucky Reporter,* February 26, 1821; Lexington *Kentucky Gazette,* March 1, 1821; *American State Papers, Misc.,* II, 655-56; *Annals of Cong.,* 16 Cong., 2 Sess., XXXVII, 1078-80. See above, Motions, February 2, 1821.

1 See above, II, 788.

2 The resolution, with the report, was, on Clay's motion, tabled, he giving notice that he should call for its consideration the following Monday.

Resolution and Remarks on Missions to South America

[February 10, 1821]

Resolved that the House of Representatives participates with the people of the U. States in the deep interest which they feel for the success of the Spanish provinces of South America which are struggling to establish their Liberty and Independence; and that it will give its Constitutional support to the President of the U. States whenever he may deem it expedient to recognize the Sovereignty and Independency of any of the said provinces

In offering this resolution, Mr. C. said, he was influenced by the general solicitude which he felt on this subject, and by the conviction that there was a majority of the house in favor of an expression of a sentiment favorable to the cause of the people of the Spanish Provinces. The vote of yesterday,[1] to the contrary, was influenced, in a great degree, it was evident, by considerations of form. He had framed this resolution so as, he hoped, to be unexceptionable in that respect; and, though it did not go as far as he wished to go, it went to a certain extent in giving the countenance of this house to the exertions of the People of the South. Mr. C. said, as the subject was well understood, and he wished not to consume the time of the house, he should not debate the proposition, unless he should be obliged to do so by debate against it.

[Robert R. Reid, of Georgia, moved to table the resolution, not only because of the importance of the subject "and the propriety of acting on it with deliberation," but also because of the absence this day of William Lowndes, chairman of the Committee on Foreign Affairs.]

Mr. CLAY stated, that he had informed his friend at the head of the committee of Foreign Affairs, who was absent from a temporary indisposition, that he intended to submit such a proposition as this to-day; and received for answer that he did not care about being present at the discussion, and did not wish to be sent for.

[The motion to table was defeated, by a vote of 71 ayes to 72 noes. On the question of agreeing to the resolution a debate arose and continued throughout the day.]

Mr. CLAY then delivered a speech of half an hour's length in support of his motion. He opposed to one another the objections to the resolution, to shew that they would not stand together, and therefore denied their claim to respect taken separately. He quoted the precedent of the resolution of Congress to support the President in any consequences which might follow the dismission of the British Minister, Mr. Jackson, some years ago,[2] and alluded to other precedents of expressions of opinion by this House. He ridiculed and reasoned against the argument, that this resolution would hurt the feelings of the Executive, or encroach on his authority. It was on the contrary, he contended, assuming only a fair responsibility on the part of this House, and adding strength to the Executive. He referred to the vote of last session, and the counter vote of yesterday, which appeared to him imperiously to require the passage of this resolution. He protested against the argument of the gentleman from Georgia, drawn from the situation of Old Spain, as absolutely founded on the idea that the colonies ought to repass under the yoke of Spain.[3] The argument which denied the power of one Congress to bind its successors would, he contended, equally apply to the most important acts of legislation, such as declarations of war, &c. As to the sentiments of the people on this subject, Mr. C. said that was a matter of fact which each gentleman must determine for himself, and vote accordingly: for his own part, he had no doubt what were the sentiments of his constituents on this subject;

and, repeating a sentiment thrown out by Mr. Mercer, he said, if they did not entertain such sentiments, so help him God he would not represent them.[4] If the matter of fact was certain, he could see no reason against avowing it. With respect to the mode of recognition of foreign powers, Mr. Clay reviewed the various opinions which had been expressed at different times, as well as to-day, on this subject. He, concluded that both Congress and the Executive had this power, but that the most regular, ordinary, and usual course was by the Executive; and it was, therefore, proper to assure him of the support of this House, &c. There was a peculiar propriety, Mr. C. contended, in this House moving in this business, being the immediate representatives of the People, and the cause of South America being that of the People, as being the cause of human liberty, &c. Mr. Clay concluded by saying, if this proposition did not satisfy gentlemen, it was impossible for him to conceive in what shape a proposition on this subject could be placed, so as that they could vote for it.[5]

The resolution, AD, DNA, RG233, HR16A-B3; remarks, Washington *Daily National Intelligencer,* February 12, 1821. Published also in Lexington *Kentucky Reporter,* February 26, 1821; Lexington *Kentucky Gazette,* March 1, 1821; *Annals of Cong.,* 16 Cong., 2 Sess., XXXVII, 1081, 1088-89.

1 See above, Motion and Speech, February 9, 1821, note.

2 The resolution following the dismissal of Francis James Jackson had been approved January 12, 1810. 2 *U.S. Stat.,* 612.

3 Thomas W. Cobb had cited recent changes in Spain, where the people were "now regenerated and comparatively free," and "a probability . . . that old Spain would voluntarily do justice to the colonies" as reasons to delay action at this time.

4 This statement is not included in the reported version of Charles F. Mercer's remarks supporting Clay's resolution.

5 After further debate and the defeat of attempts to amend and table the measure, the resolution was approved. In preliminary voting the first clause was agreed to by a vote of 134 to 12; the second, by 87 to 68.

Motion and Remarks on Due Execution of Process

[February 12, 1821]

Resolved that the Committee on the Judiciary be instructed to enquire whether any & if any what provision by law is necessary to secure the due execution of process issuing from the Courts of the U. States—[1]

AD. DNA, RG233, HR16A-B3. Published also in Washington *Daily National Intelligencer,* February 13, 1821; *Annals of Cong.,* 16 Cong., 2 Sess., XXXVII, 1092-93. In presenting the resolution Clay made "a few explanatory remarks" (not recorded), citing the need for such an enquiry in view of the passage "by one of the States" of a law refusing the use of its jails to the United States. Cf. below, Clay to Cheves (1), March 10, 1821.

1 On February 21, John Sergeant, for the Judiciary Committee, presented a resolution providing that where any State or States had withdrawn, or should subsequently "withdraw, either in whole or in part, the use of their jails for prisoners committed under the authority of the United States," the Federal marshal, under direction of the judge of the district, should be authorized and required "to hire a convenient place to serve as a temporary jail, and to make the necessary provision. . . ." Washington *Daily National Intelligencer,* February 22, 1821.

The measure was promptly passed in both House and Senate and approved March 3. 3 *U.S. Stat.*, 646-47.

Motions and Remarks on Missouri Statehood Report

[February 12, 1821]

The House then, on motion of Mr. *Clay*, proceeded to consider the report of the committee appointed on the Missouri subject.[1] On motion of Mr. C. it was referred to the committee of the whole on the state of the Union. And, also on motion of Mr. *Clay*, the House forthwith resolved itself into a committee of the whole, to take the subject up.

[The amendment which formed the conclusion of the committee report was read from the Chair.]

Mr. *Clay* gave a detailed account of the proceedings in the committee, of the difficulty which interposed, and of the considerations which led to the recommendation of this amendment. This statement of course corresponded with that contained in the report of the committee. Mr. C. then went on to obviate some objections to the report which had been made by the friends of Missouri, as well as by those opposed to her admission into the Union. Although those in favor of her admission into the Union could not succeed entirely in their particular views, Mr. C. was of opinion that they had, as regarded the report of the committee, nothing to complain of. At the same time, the report was calculated to obviate the objections of those who had opposed the admission of Missouri on the ground of the objection to her Constitution which had been avowed. Thus consulting the opinions of both sides of the House, in that spirit of compromise which is occasionally necessary to the existence of all societies, he hoped it would receive the countenance of the House. Mr. C. concluded by earnestly invoking the spirit of harmony and kindred feeling to preside over the deliberations of the House on the subject.

[A protracted debate ensued, after which the Committee of the Whole voted in the negative, 73 to 64, on the amendment proposed by the select committee. This decision was reported to the House, which, after further consideration, refused by a margin of 83 to 86 to concur, and the amendment was consequently adopted. The question was then taken by roll call on ordering the Senate resolution, as amended, to a third reading. Before the Clerk could announce the result, two members who had not been in attendance when their names were called requested leave to have their votes counted. The Speaker[2] offered to receive their votes, contrary to the rule of the House, if unanimous consent were given for that purpose. An objection was made, however, and "It was evident, from the sensation which filled the house, that the vote was a close one, though its result had not been announced."]

Mr. *Clay,* finding that the objection to these gentlemen would not be withdrawn, moved to suspend the rule of the house which forbids a change of the rule without one day's notice, in order to suspend or repeal the rule which forbids these gentlemen from voting. After a while, however, he withdrew his motion, relying on the magnanimity of some member of the majority to move for a reconsideration of the question.[3]

Washington *Daily National Intelligencer,* February 13, 1821. Published also in Lexington *Kentucky Reporter,* February 26, 1821; Lexington *Kentucky Gazette,* March 1, 1821; *Annals of Cong.,* 16 Cong., 2 Sess., XXXVII, 1093-94, 1116.

1 See above, Committee Report, February 10, 1821.

2 John W. Taylor, Clay's successor in the post.

3 The result of the vote was then announced: "For the third reading 80, against it, 83." Arthur Livermore, though he had objected to the contested votes, thereupon "gave notice that he should, at 12 o'clock to-morrow, move for a reconsideration of this question, that every member might have an opportunity of voting on it. And then the House adjourned."

From James Morrison

My Dear Sir, Lexington 12th. Feby 1821

The last mail brought no letters from the eastward— I have received none from you since your departure from Columbus—nor can I look for more than one or two, from the short period you will remain in the City—

I mentioned in a former communication[1] the probability of the P. Master here being removed,[2] and your advice whether in such event I ought to ask for his birth [*sic*]— I think on reflection it would be improper for me to ask for it—and should the present incumbent be removed, which I trust will not be the case, don't think of or [*sic*] name as his successor—

I walked to your house[3] this morning, being the greatest exertion, save a tour to Frankfort, since your departure—Mrs. Clay and family are well—she thinks favorably of your overseer[4]—on the farm everything is said to be going on well—and as you intend raising Hemp, will this year make money from the farm—

A misunderstanding has taken place between Mr. Holly and the medical Students—The latter are I suspect, stimulated by those who are behind the curtain—I however hope the affair will be amicably adjusted in a day or two—[5]

My health and strength has improved but little since you left us —and the weather from having been extremely cold, has for two weeks and upwards been warm, or very moderate, and dul [*sic*] & rainy with the exception of a day or two—

Ere this you are I trust in possession of all my documents touching my claim on Government[6]—Do for me what you think proper— If the sums mentioned as compensation are deemed inadequate I will make them more ample— I am &c. JAMES MORRISON

Copy. DLC-TJC (DNA, M212, R12). [1] Not found.
[2] John Fowler was removed from office in 1822.
[3] Mrs. Clay had taken a town house, owned by Thomas P. Hart (see above, II, 313n), upon Clay's departure for Washington. See below, Memorandum and Receipt, June 29, 1821.
[4] Not identified—possibly Daniel Ford, later a property owner on the Georgetown road, in Fayette County.
[5] Incident not found. Cf. above, II, 583n, 613, 780-81; below, Morrison to Clay, February 18, 1821.
[6] See above, Morrison to Clay, January 16, 28, 1821.

To Joseph Anderson

Joseph Anderson Esqr. Washington City Feby 13th. 1821.
Sir,

We have the pleasure to be personally acquainted with Genl. W. E. Boswell & Colo Chs Smith,[1] surities [*sic*] of Paymaster Hayden:[2] They have desired us to solicit, for them, a further indulgence upon the judgment already recovered against them by the United States. It is a duty which we perform with great pleasure, and a sincere desire that it may prove availing. These unfortunate gentlemen are much esteemed, and have excited the sympathy of their numerous friends. We refer to previous communications, made by us, or some of us, on their behalf, for a more particular account of their situation. So far from the condition of the Western Country having become more favorable to their exertions, since the first indulgence, that it has been daily becoming worse; and their claim, to the kind indulgence of the government, is now stronger, than formerly. We are informed that they had hoped, among other means, to have sold some valuable out land, for their relief; which they had in vain tried to do, and, which, they still hoped, by further indulgence, to be enabled to do— We are the more earnest from a thorough knowledge, that if they are immediately pressed for the judgment, their respectable families must be driven, miserable and dependent, from valuable farms, supplied with negroes and stock, where they have long lived comfortably and independently—If this melancholy event must take place, it should be in the last resort—

Very respectfully your's &C.— WM BROWN
THOS. METCALFE
ISHAM TALBOT
H. CLAY
Joseph Anderson Esqr RH: M: JOHNSON

N.B. As Genl. Boswell resides near me, I should be glad that you would forward to me your determination, as soon as made— WB.

ALS by Brown, signed also by others. DNA, RG217, First Comptroller, Letters Received from Members of Congress. Anderson had been appointed Comptroller of the Treasury in 1815.

1 Probably Charles Smith, of Bourbon County, Kentucky; a justice of the peace; a member of the State legislature, 1792, 1795-1797, and of the State Constitutional Convention of 1799; a veteran of the Revolution; and an officer in the Kentucky militia.

2 William D. Hayden, of Montgomery County, Kentucky; a brother-in-law of Matthew H. Jouett. Hayden had served as a lieutenant and paymaster, possibly as successor to Jouett, in the 28th Infantry, United States Army, during the War of 1812. Indulgence against execution on a judgment for nearly $25,000 due on Hayden's account was granted until July, 1822, at which date orders were given that execution should issue without further delay. *House Docs.*, 17 Cong., 2 Sess., no. 32, p. 51.

Vindication of Action, as Speaker, on Missouri Bill

[February 13, 1821]

Mr. *Clay* seconded the motion, and took the occasion to make a few remarks explanatory of an incident which occurred at the last session, (on a question of re-considering the final vote of the House on the Missouri bill,) and to vindicate the then Speaker of the house from a presumed interference on that occasion, and to shew that the Clerk did no more than his duty required him to do, in carrying the bill to the Senate without waiting the motion for re-consideration.[1]

Washington *Daily National Intelligencer*, February 14, 1821. Published also in *Annals of Cong.*, 16 Cong., 2 Sess., XXXVII, 1117. As soon as the Journal of the preceding day had been read Arthur Livermore, "with the view of affording to members who were absent yesterday an opportunity of voting on the resolution from the Senate, rose to carry that purpose into effect; and, to obtain his object, moved to amend the journal of yesterday's proceedings, by striking therefrom the order 'that the clerk should acquaint the Senate with the decision of this house on yesterday'; that, by withholding that message, he might be enabled to move the re-consideration of the decision, when the time should arrive at which such a motion would be in order."

1 See above, II, 788n. Livermore's motion "was agreed to without a division," and the House turned to consideration of other business.

Appeal for Reconsideration of House Vote on Missouri Question

[February 13, 1821]

Mr. *Clay* replied, regretting the unfortunate situation in which he was placed, having to meet objections of an opposite nature, and from quarters of the house whence he had no right to expect them. Though gentlemen might not be in favor of the resolution as amended, they ought yet to vote for reconsideration, that the door might be kept open for a different amendment if a different one should be thought necessary. He threw himself on the frankness and courtesy of the house, to allow the members who were absent on yesterday an opportunity of recording their votes.[1]

Washington *Daily National Intelligencer,* February 14, 1821. Published also in Lexington *Kentucky Reporter,* March 5, 1821; *Annals of Cong.,* 16 Cong., 2 Sess., XXXVII, 1120. Soon after the adoption of his earlier motion of this date (above), Arthur Livermore "moved to re-consider the vote of yesterday, by which the resolution from the Senate, as amended, for the admission of Missouri, was rejected." In the discussion that followed Robert S. Garnett, of Virginia, who had voted for the third reading of the resolution, stated that he had come to the conclusion that no restriction could be placed on Missouri and, consequently, he opposed reconsideration. John Randolph, who had voted against the resolution, also protested against the proposed reconsideration as "under the circumstances, contrary to parliamentary usage, and as tending to prostrate the great constitutional barriers which surround the powers of this house."

1 Reconsideration was agreed to, by a vote of 101 to 66.

Speech on Admission of Missouri

[February 13, 1821]

Cited in Washington *Daily National Intelligencer,* February 14, 1821; Lexington *Kentucky Reporter,* March 5, 1821; *Annals of Cong.,* 16 Cong., 2 Sess., XXXVII, 1145. After reconsideration of the vote on the amended Senate resolution had been agreed to, debate again arose on the question of third reading of that measure. At one point "an explanation took place" (not more fully reported), between Clay and Thomas R. Ross, of Ohio, who had "reprobated the change of sentiment which some gentlemen had evinced, and intimated that, if honest in their first opinion, they had acted dishonestly, or under the influence of improper motives in voting differently now, &c." Clay concluded the main debate in a speech (not recorded) "of about an hour's length, in which he alternately reasoned, remonstrated, and entreated with the House to settle forever this agitating question, by passing the resolution before it." See above, Motions and Speech, January 29, 1821, note.

After Samuel A. Foot had spoken briefly in reply to Ross, the question was taken and third reading of the resolution was again rejected, 82 to 88.

Resolutions, Remarks, and Motions on Counting the Electoral Vote

[February 14, 1821]

Resolved, That the two Houses shall assemble in the Chamber of the House of Representatives, on Wednesday, the 14th of February, 1821, at 12 o'clock, and the President of the Senate shall be the presiding officer of the Senate, seated on the right of the Speaker of the House, who shall be the presiding officer of the House; that two persons be appointed tellers on the part of the House, to make a list of the votes as they shall be declared; that the result shall be delivered to the President of the Senate, who shall announce the state of the vote and the persons elected, to the two Houses assembled as aforesaid, which shall be deemed a declaration of the persons elected President and Vice President of the United States, and, together with a list of votes, be entered on the journals of the two Houses.

Resolved, That if any objection be made to the votes of Missouri, and the counting or omitting to count which shall not essentially change the result of the election, in that case they shall be reported by the President of the Senate, in the following manner: Were the votes of Missouri to be counted the result would be, for A B, for President of the United States votes. If not counted, for A.B. for President of the United States votes. But, in either event, A B is elected President of the United States. And in the same manner for Vice President.

Mr. *Clay* offered some remarks explanatory of the considerations which governed the committee in recommending the resolutions which had been reported. As convenience rendered it necessary for the Senate to meet this House here, in its own hall, it was due to that body, by courtesy and propriety, that the President should be invited to preside, he being the officer designated by the Constitution to perform a certain duty appertaining to the occasion which called the two Houses together.[1] As to the second resolution, the state of the votes for President and Vice President was well known, though unofficially, and, as the votes of Missouri could not affect the result, it was considered by the committee, to obviate the unpleasant difficulty which would otherwise arise in the joint meeting, better to provide for the case in the manner proposed. This course was deemed by the committee the most expedient, under all the circumstances, and he hoped the House would adopt it, the more especially as the Senate had already concurred in it.

[The first resolution was agreed to immediately, "though several noes were heard"; but John Randolph, David Trimble, and John Floyd expressed objections to the second.]

Mr. *Clay* said the constitution required of the two Houses to assemble and perform the highest duty that could devolve on a public body—to ascertain who had been elected by the people to administer their national concerns. In a case of votes coming forward which could not be counted, the constitution was silent; but, fortunately, the end in that case carried with it the means. The two Houses were called on to *enumerate* the votes for President and Vice President; of course they were called on to decide what *are* votes. It being obvious that a difficulty would arise in the joint meeting, concerning the votes of Missouri, some gentlemen thinking they ought to be counted and others dissenting from that opinion, the committee thought it best to prevent all difficulty by waiving the question in the manner proposed, knowing that it could not affect the result of the election. As to the condition of Missouri, he himself thought her a state, with a perfect moral right to be admitted into the Union, but kept out for the want of a ceremonious act which was deemed by others necessary to entitle her to admission. Though, in his opinion, a state in fact, yet not being so in form, her votes could not be counted according to form. He was aware that the question of her admission might come up and be decided in this very shape; for if Congress allowed her to vote for President and Vice President, and counted her votes, it would be a full admission of the state into the Union; but the committee thought, as there were other and more usual modes of admitting the state into the Union, it was better not to bring up the question in the discharge of this solemn and indispensable duty, but to allow that ceremony to proceed, if possible, without difficulty or embarrassment.

[Further opposition to the resolution was expressed by John Rhea, Trimble, Thomas Culbreth, of Maryland, and Albert T. Tracy, of New York.]

Mr. *Clay* said he would merely observe, that the difficulty is before us; that we must decide it when the two Houses meet, or avoid it by some previous arrangement. The committee being morally certain that the question would arise on the votes, in joint meeting, thought it best, as he had before stated, to give it the go-by in this way. Suppose this resolution not adopted; the President of the Senate will proceed to open and count the votes, and would the House allow that officer, singly and alone, thus, virtually, to decide the question of the legality of the votes? If not, how then were they to proceed? Was it to be settled by the decision of the two Houses conjointly, or of the two Houses separately? One House would say the votes ought to be counted—the other that they ought not; and then the votes would be lost altogether. Would the gentleman from New York prefer that it be decided in the joint meeting? In that case he would find himself in a much leaner majority than on the question yesterday.[2] In fact, Mr. C. said there was no mode pointed out in the constitution of settling litigated questions arising in the discharge of this duty—it was a casus omissus, and he thought it would be proper, either by some act of derivative legislation, or by an amendment of the constitution itself, to supply the defect.

[Following remarks by two other members, the second resolution was approved.]

On motion of Mr. *Clay,* it was then ordered, that a message be sent to the Senate, informing that body, that this House, on its part, concurs in the report of the joint committee, and is now prepared to proceed, with the Senate, in the performance of its constitutional duty.

. . . .

On motion of Mr. *Clay,* and by general consent, it was determined that the members of this House should receive the Senate, on their entrance into the House, standing and uncovered. In the same manner, it was determined that a sufficient number of the seats on the right hand of the chair, should be set apart for the Senators.

Mr. *Clay* moved that a committee of two members be appointed to receive the Senate, and conduct the President of the Senate to the chair, and the members to the seats assigned to them.

[Hugh Nelson stated that he saw no reason to change the usual procedure, whereby the Speaker of the House received the President of the Senate and invited "him to a seat beside him."]

Mr. *Clay* said it was true it never had been done before; but, having, whilst he had the honor to preside over this House, witnessed the embarassment occasioned by the want of such a regulation, he now thought it would be proper to adopt it.

[Clay's motion was approved. He and Mark L. Hill, of Massachusetts (of Maine after March 4, 1821), were appointed to the committee. Within a short time the Senate entered the hall of the House of Representatives, and the counting of the electoral votes began. When the votes from Missouri were announced, Arthur Livermore objected to receiving them on the ground that Missouri was not a State of the Union. The Senate thereupon retired from the chamber, and the House fell into debate on a resolution, offered by John Floyd, asserting that Missouri was a State of the Union and that her votes ought to be counted. After a time Clay was recognized but yielded to John Randolph, who spoke until Clay "claimed the floor, which he had yielded to the gentleman only for the purpose of making an explanation." Randolph then "took his seat, saying that he would give way to the honorable gentleman in every thing but one."]

Mr. CLAY said, he really saw no difficulty in this business; and, before he sat down, should make a motion, with a view to put an end to this discussion. The House and the Senate, have, by a conjoint act, this day agreed, that, in the event of an objection being made to the vote of Missouri, her vote should be counted hypothetically; that the whole number should be announced including the vote of Missouri, and that the number should also be stated as it would be, the vote of Missouri being excluded—and, the result not varying, that it should be declared that, in either case, the person having the largest number of votes was duly elected. The motive which operated on the joint committee, in recommending this course, and on the two houses in adopting it, was to avoid the very difficulty into which the House was about to precipitate itself. It was an effort to provide, by previous arrangement, for that very contingency which has arisen. The moment the objection was made, in that instant the rule adopted this morning took effect. Mr.

C. said it therefore appeared to him, with very great deference to the course of the presiding officer of the Senate, that he ought to have gone on, and, after the votes had been summed up, to have made the annunciation as proposed in the joint resolution adopted this morning.

The two houses ought not, in the opinion of Mr. C. to have separated until they had consummated what had been stipulated for. He was now not willing to take up any proposition on this subject or any other, however willing he might have been to meet it at any other time. He was opposed to do so, because to do so is a violation of good faith between the two houses, as pledged by the arrangement of this morning. He had not a doubt, he said, that Missouri might be admitted into the Union in a variety of ways, and very possibly, on proper examination, the mode now proposed might be one of them, by the two houses, jointly or separately, giving her the exercise of a right which, as a state, would belong to her. The house, however, as well as the Senate, had virtually determined to get round that question to-day, and to put an end to any controversy which might arise in respect to it, in the manner contemplated by the second resolution passed this morning. Mr. C. therefore moved that the subject now under consideration be laid on the table, in order to resume the business which had been interrupted by the retirement of the Senate.

[Henry R. Storrs next rose to point to a discrepancy between the House and Senate versions of the first joint resolution adopted this day, in regard to the presiding officer of the joint session. A discussion among Samuel Smith, Clay, Randolph, Nelson, Samuel A. Foot, and Thomas W. Cobb followed "as to the state in which matters would be, on the Senate's return. Some of the gentlemen contended that, on the Senate's return, matters would stand just as they did before, and the same difficulty as had already presented itself would again arise. Others contended, and the majority appeared to be with them, that, on the return of the Senate, the President would go on to declare the result, as directed in the second joint resolution of this morning." Eventually, Clay's motion to table Floyd's resolution was approved.]

On motion of Mr. *Clay,* it was ordered, that a message be sent to the Senate to inform that body that the House is now ready to receive the Senate in the Chamber of the House of Representatives, for the purpose of continuing the enumeration of the votes of the Electors for President and Vice President, according to the joint resolutions agreed upon between the two houses; and that the Clerk go with the said message.[3]

The resolutions, U.S. H. of Reps., *Journal,* 16 Cong., 2 Sess., 230-31; remarks and motions, Washington *Daily National Intelligencer,* February 15, 16, 1821. Published also in *Annals of Cong.*, 16 Cong., 2 Sess., XXXVII, 1147-53 *passim*, 1159, 1161-62, 1163; and, partially, in Lexington *Kentucky Reporter*, March 5, 1821. On February 8 the House had concurred in a resolution from the Senate providing "for the appointment of a joint committee to ascertain and report a mode of examining the votes for President and Vice President of the United States, and of notifying the persons elected of their election. . . ." Washington *Daily National Intelligencer*, February 9, 1821. Clay, John Sergeant, and Solomon Van Vechten Van Rensselaer, of New York, had been named to represent the House on this Committee. Clay brought the report before the House in the form of two resolutions.

1 The President of the Senate is the official directed to open the votes of the electors in the presence of the two houses of Congress.

2 Tracy had voted against the amended resolution for the admission of Missouri.

3 The Clerk delivered the message, the Senate returned, and the votes of Missouri were counted. With some difficulty, owing to an interruption by Floyd, Randolph, and Henry Brush, of Ohio, who were each ruled out of order, the President of the Senate announced the tally and declared James Monroe and Daniel D. Tompkins duly elected President and Vice President, respectively. After the Senate had retired from the hall, Randolph, amid confusion in the House, proposed resolutions declaring the election illegal. While he was putting his motion in writing, the boisterous session was terminated by approval of a motion to adjourn. On the following day the House decided against consideration of Randolph's resolutions.

To Langdon Cheves

Sir Washington 15h. Feb. 1821.

Inclosed I transmit to you a copy of a bill, pretty much in the shape in which I am told it has passed the Ohio Legislature.[1] The only provision, which it contains, which it appears to me necessary that Congress should now legislate to obviate is that which denies the use of its jails; and I have submitted a proposition on that subject to the Judiciary Commee.[2]

The bill for the restoration of the money passed the House without conditions, but conditions were put into it by the Senate of such a character as to render it impossible for the Bank, in my opinion, to accept the money; such as the withdrawal of the branches &c. &c.[3]

As the other side has thus failed to redeem its pledge; and as we have exhausted the cup of conciliation, nothing remains to us but to proceed firmly & temperately in our purpose. That shall be done, and in September next, if I live, we will have a Judgment or decree, or both for the money.[4] Yr. ob. Servant H. CLAY

Mr. Cheves.

ALS. PHi-Etting Collection.

1 The second act discussed below, Clay to Cheves (1), March 10, 1821.

2 See above, Motion and Remarks on Due Execution of Process, February 12, 1821.

3 The first act discussed below, Clay to Cheves (1), March 10, 1821.

4 See below, Clay to Cheves, September 8, 1821.

To Caesar A. Rodney

My dear Rodney. Washn. 16 Feb. 1821.

I recd. your obliging letter of the 6h. inst.[1] and am glad that you continue to take an interest in the affairs of Spanish America.

Going out of Congress as I am, I must commit them to your keeping in the future.

After two unsuccessful efforts, a third was attended with success, and I carried against the whole weight of influence, and a most determined opposition, my proposition about the acknowledgment &c.[2] I have since had the honor of presenting it to the President, who gave me a most gracious reception.

But my dear Sir this Missouri Storm is threatening to sweep every thing before it. Unhappy subject! Every attempt to settle it has yet failed. But I still cherish, perhaps vainly, hopes.

C. A. Rodney Esq   Your's faithfy H. CLAY

ALS. DLC-Rodney Family Papers (DNA, M212, R22). Addressed to Rodney at Wilmington, Delaware.

1 Not found.

2 See above, Resolution and Remarks, February 10, 1821.

To James Monroe

Sir,   Washington Feb 17th. 1821

Capt Adolphus F. Hubbard is desirous of filling a judicial station in Florida— we are acquainted with Capt Hubbard & recommend him as a person well qualifyed for the faithful discharge of judicial duties. He has been in the practice of the Law for five years. He has served in the Territorial & State Legislature of Illinois; he has been lately honored with the office of Elector of President & v. President of the U States— he is a gentleman of prudence, judgement, capacity experience & integrity and it would give us great pleasure to see him in some comfortable situation.

With great respect your ob svt RH: M: JOHNSON
FR: JOHNSON[1]
NINIAN EDWARDS[2]
THOS. VAN SWEARINGEN[3]
JESSE B THOMAS
H. CLAY
JONA. O MOSELEY.[4]

James Monroe Esqr.
President of the U States

ALS, by Richard M. Johnson, signed also by others. DNA, RG59, Applications and Recommendations for Office.

1 Francis Johnson, Bowling Green, Kentucky, lawyer, born in Virginia in 1776, had moved to Kentucky in 1796. He had been elected to the State legislature in 1812, 1813, and 1815, and was a member of Congress from 1820 to 1827. In 1829 he became a resident of Louisville, where he practiced law and served as Commonwealth's Attorney.

2 Now United States Senator from Illinois.

3 Of Shepherdstown, Virginia, a member of the State House of Delegates, 1814-1816, and of the United States House of Representatives, 1819-1822.

4 Jonathan O. Moseley, a Representative from Connecticut, 1805-1821, had been a legislator, justice of the peace, and State's attorney in Connecticut. He later moved to Michigan.

From James Morrison

My Good Sir Lexington 18th Feby 1821.

I had hoped that by tomorrows mail, I could have transmitted to you the record in the case of J. K Smith;[1] but the duplicate will not be ready for a day or two—you may however calculate on receiving it by the mail after this reaches you—No eastern mail—there are three or 4 now due—We are all solicitous to hear from you—read your speeches and be releived [*sic*] from suspense as to the admission of Missouri—

The misunderstanding between the medical students and Mr. [Holley] has been amicably and satisfactorily adjusted—and last evening [W. T. Bar]ry was appointed professor of law—so far, all goes on smoothly—[pub]lic sentiment began to be evidently with Mr. Holly—The Medical Students and that Gentleman will no doubt in future cultivate relations of [per]fect amity and respect for each other—[2]

Enclosed you have my check for Sixty dollars on the U States Branch in Baltimore—Speak to our friend Auditor Lee,[3] who thinks highly of you and will take pleasure in serving you and probably me also, to select two casks of Claret for us at the store of the Exporting and Importing Co. Georgetown—Genl Smith[4] is the Agent [a]nd have them forwarded if possible before leaving the City—if to [Pi]ttsburgh, to the care of Bean & Butler,[5] who are my particular friends—[It] is however likely that Colo. McKenney[6] Supert. Indn. Trade, Georgetown could have them forwarded at once—As it is the season when he is sending stores to Missouri &C—It would be advisable to have them, the Casks, *cased*—I beleive [*sic*] you tasted one of two bottles of Claret which Lee gave me when leaving Washington, which you pronounced good—the price then, and as times have not changed for the better, presume has not, become higher 30$ for 60 Gallons—If you succeed in procuring the wine and of the quality which Lee purchased, it will last us for years [an]d will be a cheap and wholesome beverage when deluted [*sic*] with [wa]ter—

As to my accounts,[7] I have nothing to add—resting satisfied you will endeavor to promote my interest—By next mail no doubt I will receive letters from you which will pro[bab]ly releive from suspense respecting the expediency of attempting a journey—which until roads and health become better I dare not attempt—

The Honble H. Clay I am Dr Sir &C— JAMES MORRISON

Copy. DLC-TJC (DNA, M212, R12). Some words obliterated by ragged margin.

1 The Kentucky Court of Appeals in December, 1820, had upheld a judgment of the Fayette Circuit Court awarding Morrison $45,774.90 due on merchandise supplied

the firm, Smith and Morrison. The suit had been instituted against John K. and Alexander Smith (the latter, a resident of Fayette County in 1810) as surviving partners of the firm, but action against Alexander Smith had been abated when he could not be located. 10 *Ky. Reports* (3 A. K. Marshall) 81-82; Fayette Circuit Court, File 430 (1819).

2 See above, Morrison to Clay, February 12, 1821. On May 3, in connection with another incident involving activities of students "derogatory to the Character of the Institution," Clay observed that "an intimation" of the matter "to the faculty was sufficient, that he hoped they would perform their duty without the interference of the Bd:, and it was determined that the immediate government of the College was the province of the faculty, and the subject was dropped." PPPrHi-Shane Collection, copies of fragmentary minutes of meetings of the Board of Trustees, Transylvania University, III, 67.

3 William Lee.

4 Brigadier General Walter Smith, who had commanded the District militia at the Battle of Bladensburg.

5 Isaac Bean and J. R. Butler, Pittsburgh merchants.

6 Thomas L. McKenney.

7 See above, Morrison to Clay, January 16, 28, 1821.

Report on President's Response to Spanish American Resolution

[February 19, 1821]

Mr. *Clay,* from the committee (himself and Mr. Allen,[1] of N.Y.) appointed to wait on the President of the United States with the resolution declaring the feelings of this house in regard to the Spanish provinces of South America, reported that the committee had, according to order, presented the resolution to the President; that the President assured the committee that, in common with the House of Representatives, he felt a great interest in the success of the provinces of Spanish America which are struggling to establish their freedom and independence; and that he would take the resolution into deliberate consideration, with the most perfect respect for the distinguished body from which it had emanated.

Washington *Daily National Intelligencer,* February 20, 1821. Published also in Lexington *Kentucky Reporter,* March 5, 1821; Lexington *Kentucky Gazette,* March 8, 1821; *Annals of Cong.,* 16 Cong., 2 Sess., XXXVII, 1179-80.

1 Nathaniel Allen.

Motion on Reimbursement to Planters' Bank of New Orleans

[February 19, 1821]

Resolved that the Comee. of Claims be instructed to enquire into the expediency of making provision by law for the reimbursement to the Planters Bank of New Orleans of certain advances made by it upon Pay Rolls of the Army.[1]

AD. DNA, RG233, HR16A-B3. Published in Washington *Daily National Intelligencer,* February 20, 1821; Lexington *Kentucky Gazette,* March 8, 1821; *Annals of Cong.,* 16 Cong., 2 Sess., XXXVII, 1180. In the fall of 1815 the Planters' Bank of New Orleans had responded to an appeal by a deputy paymaster of United States troops at New Orleans, the paymaster being without funds, and advanced money "to pay off several discharged soldiers." The Bank had possession of the pay and receipt rolls as documentation for the claim, which, however, had been rejected by the Treasury Department, partly because no muster-rolls or certificate of the commanding officer had been produced to show that the pay was due. *American State Papers, Claims,* 816.

1 Clay accompanied the resolution "with sundry documents in support of the claim," which together with the resolution were referred to the Committee of Claims, and no further action appears to have been taken at this time. In the next Congressional Session a Senate bill for reimbursement of the bank was enacted. 6 *U.S. Stat.,* 275 (May 7, 1822).

To John W. Hunt

Dr Sir Washn. 21 Feby. 1821

I received your letter[1] inclosing some drafts on the Treasury, which I left with the Secretary to be passed through the forms of office. As soon as that is done and the money is received I will remit it to the Cashr. of the Bank of the U.S. as directed.

I have also received your letter of the 7h.[2] inclosing one for Charleston, which shall be duly forwarded.

The Florida treaty is ratified by our Govt.[3]

John. W. Hunt Esqr. Yr's faithfully H. CLAY

ALS. KyU-Hunt-Morgan Papers. Endorsed: ". . . Recd. March 5th. 1821."

1 Not found. 2 Not found.

3 The treaty had been approved by the United States Senate on February 19; the ratifications were exchanged on February 22.

To John W. Hunt

Dr Sir H. of R. 21 Feb. [1821]

Since I wrote you I have been to the Treasury—There is some difficulty about your bills; one of them cannot be paid until the 3d. March; and the accounts, upon the foundation of which, the others were drawn, have not been forwarded, as they should have been. I will endeavor to get the difficulty obviated. In the mean time you had better write the drawers & tell them to forward their accounts for Contingent expences. Yrs H. CLAY

ALS. KyU-Hunt-Morgan Papers. Addressed to Hunt; endorsed: ". . . Recd. March 5th. 1821." See above, Clay to Hunt, same date.

Motion on Report of Secretary of the Treasury

On motion of Mr. Clay, [February 21, 1821]

Ordered, That the report of the Secretary of the Treasury, made on the 8th instant, in the case of James Morrison, concerning his advances to colonel Buford,[1] together with the additional documents presented by him on the 19th instant, be recommitted to the Secretary of the Treasury, with instructions to report thereon to the House of Representatives at the next session of Congress.[2]

U.S. H. of Reps., *Journal,* 16 Cong., 2 Sess., 255. Published also in *Annals of Cong.,* 16 Cong., 2 Sess., XXXVII, 1193. Clay, on January 30, 1821, had "presented a petition of James Morrison, a deputy quartermaster general of the army in the late war with Great Britain, praying to be allowed a credit for the sum of ten thousand dollars, advanced in his absence by an assistant deputy quartermaster general, out of public funds, committed to his, the petitioner's charge, which advance was for the purpose of being applied to the public service; and also, that he may be reimbursed the sum of 289 99/100 dollars, paid by him as interest on moneys borrowed on his private credit for the public use; which petition was referred to the Secretary of the Treasury, with instructions to report thereon to the House." A second Morrison petition, presented at the same time by Clay, had been referred to the Secretary of War. U. S. H. of Reps., *Journal,* 16 Cong., 2 Sess., 181-82.

On February 8 the Speaker had laid before the House a report from the Secretary of the Treasury on Morrison's petition. After a reading, the report had been tabled.

1 Thomas Buford.

2 Legislation for the relief of Morrison was enacted in 1823. 6 *U. S. Stat.,* 283, 288-89.

Motion on Bill to Reduce Salaries

[February 21, 1821]

Mr. *Clay,* with the expressed intention of putting the bill and amendment to sleep, as one which would be productive of nothing but a useless consumption of time, moved to lay the bill on the table. . . .[1]

Washington *Daily National Intelligencer,* February 22, 1821. Published also in *Annals of Cong.,* 16 Cong., 2 Sess., XXXVII, 1215. Members of the House, engaged in considering a bill to reduce salaries of officers of the Government, had not been able to agree on proposals to lower their own rate of pay. An amendment to an amendment to the bill had just been offered when Clay rose.

1 The motion was adopted.

Resolution and Motions on Missouri Statehood

[February 22, 1821]

Resolved that a Committee be appointed, on the part of this House, jointly with such Committee as may be appointed on the part of the Senate, to consider and report to the Senate and to the House respectively, whether it be expedient or not to make provision for the admission into the Union of Missouri,[1] on the same footing as the original States, and for the due execution of the laws of the U. States within Missouri; and if not, whether any other and what provision adapted to her actual condition ought to be made by law.

[After about an hour's debate, the resolution carried.]

On motion of Mr. *Clay,* with the expressed wish of the Speaker in favor of that course, it was ordered that the committee on the part of this house, consisting of twenty three members (corresponding with the number of states) should be appointed by ballot.

[This proposal having been adopted, John Randolph was defeated on offering a motion "that one member of the said committee be chosen from each state."]

Mr. Clay moved that the House do *now* proceed to the said election.[2]

Resolution, AD, DNA, RG233, HR16A-B2; intervening motion, Washington *Daily National Intelligencer,* February 23, 1821; last motion, U.S. H. of Reps., *Journal,* 16 Cong., 2 Sess., 262, 264. Published also in Lexington *Kentucky Gazette,* March 8, 1821; Lexington *Kentucky Reporter,* March 12, 1821; *Annals of Cong.,* 16 Cong., 2 Sess., XXXVII, 1219, 1220.

1 In the final version the last two words were deleted and inserted in strange hand after the word "admission."

2 Opposing proposals were offered to delay the election until "tomorrow at 12 o'clock," and until "Monday next" at that hour. Clay's motion was defeated and the election set for the following day.

On Clay's role in selection of this committee and in effecting compromise through its deliberations, see Glover Moore, *The Missouri Controversy, 1819-1821* ([Lexington, Ky.], [c. 1953]), 154-58; and below, Speech, February 6, 1850.

Speeches on Relief for Purchasers of Public Lands

[February 23, 1821]

Cited in Washington *Daily National Intelligencer,* February 24, 1821; Lexington *Kentucky Reporter,* March 12, 1821; *Annals of Cong.,* 16 Cong., 2 Sess., XXXVII, 1221, 1222. Clay, in Committee of the Whole on a "bill for the relief of purchasers of the public lands prior to the 1st of July, 1820," was among those who, in "a wide debate on the merits of the bill," supported the measure. He also participated in "a long debate" that arose later in the day on a proposed amendment to the bill. The speeches were not recorded in either instance.

Motion on Committee Appointments

[February 23, 1821]

Cited in Washington *Daily National Intelligencer,* February 24, 1821; Lexington *Kentucky Reporter,* March 12, 1821; *Annals of Cong.,* 16 Cong., 2 Sess., XXXVII, 1223. In the balloting for members of the committee on Missouri statehood (see above, Resolutions, February 22, 1821) votes had been cast for 157 members, of whom only 17, including Clay, had received a majority. Six committee members remained to be chosen when Clay moved that, "as the operation of balloting again to-morrow would be tedious and create delay, that the House agree, by general consent, to select the remaining six members from those having received the next highest number of votes."

Upon learning that the Speaker, if the choice of the six were left to him, would select the names next highest on the list, Clay withdrew his motion. Five additional members were then added to the committee, but the House adjourned before the Speaker had chosen between John Randolph and Henry Baldwin, who were next on the list with an equal number of votes. Two vacancies on the committee having developed by the following day, the Speaker was able to appoint both Randolph and Baldwin, as well as one other person.

From Langdon Cheves

Sir, Bank of the United States 23d feb.y 1821.

The Board have had under Consideration the Subject of Compensation for your highly useful & Valuable Services as the Counsel in the States of Ohio & Kentucky & have this day Confirmed a report of a Committee of the Board to Whom the Subject was referred. As this report will better communicate to you the views of the Board than any thing I can say I beg leave to send you a Copy of it[1] adding no more than that I hope it may be Acceptable to you.

I am Sir, With great respect, Your Obt. St L CHEVES Pres.

The Honorable Henry Clay, City of Washington.

ALS. DLC-HC (DNA, M212, R1). See above, Clay to Cheves, February 10, 1821.
1 Report not found; on compensation, see below, Clay to Cheves, June 23, 1822.

From Edmund W. Rootes

Dear Sir Richmond 23" Feby 1821—

Your favor of the 14" Instant,[1] (on the subject of George Penn's[2] Bond—) came duly to hand—You will find the Bond enclosed, dated "12" Decr 1812 on demand "for £633.17.4. Payable to Rob: & Allan Pollok & Co."[3] Receipt of which you will please to acknowledge—David Buchanan[4] is Surviving Partner of R & A Pollok & Co—of which circumstance I supposed you ought to be advised in bringing the Suit[5]—Colo Penn lives in PennsVille, Christian County, Ky—

On the point, on which you wish instruction, "as to the reception in payment of it—in notes of the Bank of Ky. which are at a depreciation of about 20 p Cent." I have only to say, you can advise me occasionally during the progress of the Suit, as to the probability of the debt being in that Species of paper—& if it should be—in that case I must do the best I can towards converting it into Eastern funds

I am truly yours E. W. ROOTES

H. Clay Esq

ALS. DLC-TJC (DNA, M212, R12). See below, Rootes to Clay, March 1, 1821.
1 Not found.
2 Formerly of Henry and Patrick counties, Virginia, where he had been a member of the Virginia legislature and a presidential elector at the turn of the century. He later moved to New Orleans.
3 Merchants of Petersburg and Richmond, Virginia. 4 Probably of Petersburg.
5 Suit was instituted in the United States Circuit Court for the District of Kentucky on April 19, 1821. At the November Term of that year judgment was rendered for the plaintiff in the amount of the bond, equal to $2,110.47½, with interest at six per cent annually from December 12, 1812, until paid, plus the costs of suit. U. S. Circuit Court, Seventh Circuit, District of Kentucky, Complete Records, Q, 347-48.

To John Quincy Adams

Washn. 24 Feb. 21

Mr. Clay's respectful compliments to Mr. Adams, and he will be obliged to him to forward the inclosed letter from a friend of Col. Todd,[1] with the first despatches.

AN. DNA, RG59, Misc. Letters. 1 Charles S. Todd.

Committee Report and Remarks on Missouri Statehood

[February 26, 1821]

Resolved, by the Senate and House of Representatives of the United States of America in Congress assembled, That Missouri shall be admitted into this Union on an equal footing with the original states, in all respects whatever, upon the fundamental condition, that the fourth clause of the twenty-sixth section of the third article of the constitution, submitted on the part of said state to Congress, shall never be construed to authorize the passage of any law, and that no law shall be passed in conformity thereto, by which any citizen of either of the states in this Union shall be excluded from the enjoyment of any of the privileges and immunities to which such citizen is entitled under the constitution of the United States: Provided, That the Legislature of the said state, by a solemn public act, shall declare the assent of the said state to the said fundamental condition, and shall transmit to the President of the United States, on or before the fourth Monday in November next, an authentic copy of the said act; upon the receipt whereof, the President, by proclamation, shall announce the fact: whereupon, and without any further proceeding on the part of Congress, the admission of said state into this Union shall be considered as complete.

[The resolution was read twice, then tabled in accordance with a motion by Clay, who announced his intention "of calling for its consideration in the course of this day." After some intervening business,[1] the House again took up the report.]

Mr. *Clay* briefly explained the views of the committee, and the considerations which induced them to report the resolution. He considered this resolution as being the same in effect as that which had been previously reported by the former committee of thirteen members; and stated that the committee on the part of the Senate was unanimous, and that on the part of this House nearly so, in favor of this resolution.[2]

The resolution, U.S. H. of Reps., *Journal,* 16 Cong., 2 Sess., 270-71; the remarks, Washington *Daily National Intelligencer,* February 27, 1821. Published also in Lexington *Kentucky Gazette,* March 15, 1821; Lexington *Kentucky Reporter,* March 19, 1821; *Annals of Cong.,* 16 Cong., 2 Sess., XXXVII, 1228, 1236. Clay presented the report for the joint committee appointed in consequence of his resolution of February 22.

1 See below, Remarks and Motion, this date.

2 William Henry Sparks later recalled Clay's remarks, on the day the compromise proposal was adopted, as follows: "I wish that my country should be prosperous, and her Government perpetual. I am in my soul assured that no other can ever afford the same protection to human liberty, and insure the same amount. Leave the North to her laws and her institutions. Extend the same conciliating charity to the South and West. Their people, as yours, know best their wants—know best their interests. Let them provide for their own—our system is one of compromises—and in the spirit of harmony come together, in the spirit of brothers compromise any and every jarring sentiment or interest which may arise in the progress of the country. There is security in this; there is peace, and fraternal union. Thus we may, we shall, go on

to cover this entire continent with prosperous States, and a contented, self-governed, and happy people. To the unrestrained energies of an intelligent and enterprising people, the mountains shall yield their mineral tribute, the valleys their cereals and fruits, and a million of millions of contented and prosperous people shall demonstrate to an admiring world the great problem that man is capable of self-government." W. H. Sparks, *The Memories of Fifty Years: Containing Brief Biographical Notices of Distinguished Americans, and Anecdotes of Remarkable Men . . .* (3d. edn.; Philadelphia, 1872), 232.

Despite opposition, the resolution was finally passed (87 to 81) and sent to the Senate, which concurred on February 28. The President signed the measure on March 2.

Remarks and Motion on Relief for Purchasers of Public Lands

[February 26, 1821]

This motion was opposed by Mr. *Clay,* as going to favor monied men only, who have no occasion for indulgence from the government. He concluded by moving that the bill and amendment lie on the table, with a view of taking up the Missouri resolution, which, he hoped, there was a general wish to see acted upon this day.

[The motion was approved, and action on the Missouri resolution was completed.[1]]

Mr. Clay moved that the House do now resume the consideration of the bill from the Senate, entitled "An act for the relief of the purchasers of public lands, prior to the 1st day of July, 1820. . . .[2]

The remarks, Washington *Daily National Intelligencer,* February 27, 1821; the motion, U.S. H. of Reps., *Journal,* 16 Cong., 2 Sess., 278. Published also in *Annals of Cong.,* 16 Cong., 2 Sess., XXXVII, 1235, 1236, 1240. During discussion of a bill for the relief of purchasers of public lands Clay spoke first (his remarks not recorded) in opposition to an amendment designed to strike out a reduction of 25 per cent on the amount due by purchasers, a change proposed in order that a discount for prompt payment might be substituted. The amendment was adopted and another was proposed to allow a deduction of 37½ per cent for prompt payment of sums still due by purchasers.

[1] See above, Committee Report and Remarks, this date.

[2] As soon as the question was stated, the House adjourned.

To Langdon Cheves

Sir Washington 27h. Feb. 1821

I have to acknowledge the receipt of your letter of the 23d. instant, inclosing a Copy of the Report of a Committee of the Board, to which was refered the subject of my compensation as the Counsel of the Bank in the States of Kentucky and Ohio. I am perfectly satisfied with the decision of the Bank. And I beg you to communicate to the Board my entire contentment with the arrangement which has been made; and also my assurance that I will dedicate, with the utmost zeal, my best services to the advancement of its interests. The liberality of the allowance which has been made to me is such as to admit of my time, almost exclusively, being applied to its service. In a few days more my public duties will have terminated, and I shall then be solely occupied with those of my profession.

There is one matter which I wish to suggest to you. The Bank has, in the two Western States, about two millions of debt in litigation. If no system is adopted for the regulation of payments, from time to time, as collections shall be made by the public officers, they will possibly pass through the hands of Solicitors &c. Money is a leaky thing. And I should think it hazardous, to say nothing of Commissions &c. which might be charged or expected, to allow such an amount of debt to pass through ordinary channels. These observations are not intended to imply any want of confidence, on my part, in any quarter, but arise out of some knowledge of human nature.

I would propose,

1st. That all payments of money collected on executions be made in Ohio, at the office of discount and deposit in Chillicothe; and in Kentucky at the offices respectively, out of which the business issues, or at a designated office; and that the Marshalls be instructed accordingly. and

2dly. That at the end of each term of the Federal Courts, a list of judgments obtained, be made out and furnished to the respective offices, and that they be instructed to inquire, from time to time, as to the progress made in collecting the amt. of those judgments.

Either some such system of checks as is above suggested ought to be adopted, or the local offices should be instructed to devise one, and provision be made for the case of the abolished office.[1]

I will thank you to have made out a Copy of the first order of the Board establishing the office at Chillicothe, and of the successive orders, afterwards made, appointing directors of that office down to the last appointment. This Copy I wish proven to be correct by a deposition, taken in the form prescribed by the Judicial act of the United States (see page 68 of 2 Vol. of Colvin's Ed.)[2] I want it to be used in the trespass action in Ohio, the title of which is The President Directors and Company of the Bank of the United States vs Ralph Osborn, John L. Harper, Thomas Orr, James McAlister,[3] Charles Hammond and John C. Wright. As the deposition must be sealed & addressed to the Court, I will thank you to send me a Copy of it, that I may be sure no mistake is committed. Both may be put under cover to me, and addressed to me either here or at Lexington.

I have the honor to be with great respect

L. Cheves Esq. &c &c &c Your obedient Servant H. CLAY

ALS. PHi-Etting Collection.

1 At Cincinnati. Cf. above, Clay to Cheves, January 22, 1821.

2 Section 30 of the act establishing "the Judicial Courts of the United States," approved September 24, 1789, provided that in civil cases in federal courts testimony of persons living more than one hundred miles from the place of trial might be taken *de bene esse* before certain magistrates. "And the depositions so taken shall be retained by such magistrate until he deliver the same with his own hand into the court for which they are taken, or shall, together with a certificate of the reasons as aforesaid of their being taken, and of the notice if any given to the adverse party, be by him the said magistrate sealed up and directed to such court, and remain under his seal until opened in court." 1 *U.S. Stat.*, 88-89. On Clay's citation, see above, II, 560n.

3 James McColister.

Remarks on Bill to Reduce the Military Peace Establishment

[February 27, 1821]

Cited in Washington *Daily National Intelligencer,* February 28, 1821; *Annals of Cong.,* 16 Cong., 2 Sess., XXXVII, 1242. During discussion of a bill from the Senate to reduce the military peace establishment, a motion was made to strike out a provision for "one Major General, with two Aids [*sic*] de Camp." Clay, and others, opposed the change "on the ground that as the Senate had made the amendment, they would probably adhere to it; that if disagreed to by this House, it might put the whole bill in jeopardy; that much would still have been done in the way of retrenchment even if this provision passed, and it would be better not to endanger the bill by rejecting this provision." When the question was called, the motion to strike out this provision was negatived.

Remarks on Relief for Purchasers of Public Lands

[February 27, 1821]

Cited in Washington *Daily National Intelligencer,* February 28, 1821; *Annals of Cong.,* 16 Cong., 2 Sess., XXXVII, 1243. The House resumed consideration of the bill for relief of purchasers of public lands, and Clay joined in the discussion on various amendments. His position on these questions is not recorded.

Remarks on Bill to Exempt French Ships from Certain Duties

[February 27, 1821]

Mr. *Clay* expressed the same sentiments. If a partial and rigorous construction had been given to the act of last session, the effects of it ought to be remedied. He was the more disposed to this course, since it was understood that an arrangement was in negociation between the two governments, which would produce a reciprocal revocation of the extra duties by both governments.[1] France, Mr. C. said, is our natural friend, and he should be glad that Congress would, by the passage of this bill, add another motive to a conclusion of the arrangement which is necessary to a good understanding between the two governments.[2]

Washington *Daily National Intelligencer,* February 28, 1821. Published also in *Annals of Cong.,* 16 Cong., 2 Sess., XXXVII, 1244-45. As explained by Thomas Newton, Jr., the proposed bill was designed to relieve certain French vessels which had not received sufficient notice of the extraordinary duties levied under the United States legislation of May 15, 1820 (see above, II, 846n.) Rollin C. Mallary, of Vermont, who had preceded Clay in the debate, had contended that "there was nothing whatever in this bill which went to defeat the legitimate effect of the act of last session, but rather to make that act what it was intended to be, an act with fair notice to the parties. Mr. M. further explained the cases to which the act applied, and expressed his hope that the bill would be passed."

1 The French, angered by Albert Gallatin's action in recommending the retaliatory legislation of 1820, had transferred negotiations to De Neuville in Washington in February, 1821. The discussions continued for more than a year before a "temporary convention of navigation and commerce," which included a separate article refunding the extra duties levied by both governments, was signed June 24, 1822. *American State Papers, Foreign Relations,* V, 149-213.

2 Following Clay's argument, the Committee rose and reported the bill, which was enacted. 3 *U.S. Stat.,* 641-42 (March 3, 1821).

Remarks on Bankruptcy Bill

[February 28, 1821]

Mr. *Clay* said, to commit the bill would place it at the foot of the docket, of business, and that course would be tantamount to a rejection of the bill. If gentlemen were sincere in a desire to examine it in committee, he would propose a compromise, and that was to agree by general consent to go into committee of the whole on the bill forthwith; and added some remarks on the imperious necessity which existed for taking up the subject, and deciding on it at the present session; as well as on the circumstances of the country which required its passage.

[Thomas W. Cobb, who "declared himself heartily sick of all compromises," and others joined the discussion. The motion was defeated; but a further motion to postpone the bill indefinitely prolonged debate, Clay advocating the bill "very earnestly, in a speech of some length." (His remarks were not recorded.) Three motions to adjourn and one to table the bill were then negatived.]

Mr. *Clay* made a few remarks in favor of deciding to-night the question of indefinite postponement, and then adjourning to discuss the subject in detail on the morrow.[1]

Washington *Daily National Intelligencer,* March 1, 1821. Published also in *Annals of Cong.,* 16 Cong., 2 Sess., XXXVII, 1259, 1260, 1261. Having taken up a "bill from the Senate to establish an uniform system of bankruptcy," the House was considering a motion by Weldon N. Edwards, of North Carolina, to commit the measure to Committee of the Whole.

1 Following additional discussion, motions to adjourn, and "some rather confused proceedings," the bill was ordered to a third reading and the House adjourned. On the following day the measure was laid on the table, and on March 3 the House refused to consider it further.

To John Quincy Adams

Sir 1 March 1821

I recommend Genl. Carroll[1] of Nashville to the consideration of the President as a suitable person to be Governor of Florida. His public services, in the battle of New Orleans, and in the South during the late War, and his personal merits in other respects are so well known, that it can only be necessary to mention his name, to ensure a just appreciation of them.[2] I have the honor to be with great respect Your obedient Servant H CLAY

The Honble Mr. Adams. &c &c &c.

ALS. DNA, RG59, Applications and Recommendations for Office.
[1] William Carroll. [2] Andrew Jackson received the appointment.

To [John Quincy Adams]

1 Mar. 1821.

Being long and well acquainted with the signatures both of John Adair Govr. & J. Cabell Breckinridge Secy. of the State of Kentucky, I certify that their signatures respectively to the Power of Atto from John Henry Orthgies[1] to William Chaloner[2] are genuine.

H. CLAY

ANS. DNA, RG59, Misc. Letters.
[1] Also written as Ortgees, Ortkies, Otkies—probably of Lincoln County, Kentucky.
[2] Not identified.

To [James Monroe]

Sir Washington 1st. March 182[1]

Whatever pecuniary misfortunes I have sustained (and they are not inconsiderable) are to be distinctly traced to my service in public life. I do not allude to those which proceeded from my abandonment of a lucrative practice in an honorable profession. They were voluntary. But I refer to those which have resulted from my absence from home, and the consequent withdrawal of my attention from my private affairs. This topic is touched not to ask the charity of Government, which I would not receive, but as furnishing a motive for the request which I make of its justice.

Upon my return from Europe, I thought I had a just claim to, at least, half an outfit for my public services in the negotiation at London, which terminated in the convention of 1815.[1] It appeared to me to be sanctioned by all former precedents, and particularly by that of Mr. Adams, in the instance of the allowance to him of half an outfit, for the negotiation which was intended to have been had, under the mediation of the Emperor of Russia, but which in fact never did take place.[2] This allowance to Mr. Adams received the legislative approbation.[3] When you acted as Secretary of State, you did me the honor to say, that you thought my demand well founded.

But as I experienced some difficulty about it, I waived it. I ought frankly to say, that it was my intention, then, even to abandon it but not from any sense of its being ill-founded. I should probably have never again adverted to it, if it were not for the misfortunes which I have mentioned. The service, however, such as it was, exists; and its existence is testified by the records and in the history of the Country. The compensation for it, as I think, has not been made; and I am unconscious of any forfeiture of my right to that compensation. If Mr. Gallatin did not bring forward such a claim, his forbearance cannot justly affect my right,[4] especially as Mr. Gallatin probably felt himself sufficiently remunerated, in the receipt of two entire outfits, in a short space of time, one for his mission to France, at or about the very time that he was negotiating with Mr. Adams and me in London.

I have taken the liberty to address you on this subject, in the hope that it may experience your favorable consideration; and that you may give your sanction to an act of justice, solicited by one who has had the honor of serving with you, in perilous times, in the councils of our common country, and who is about to retire, perhaps forever, from them. I have the honor to be with great respect

Your obedient Servant H. CLAY

The President

P.S. I will not trouble you to make a written reply. I will have the honor to call on you in person, on the subject of this letter, before I depart from the City.[5] H. CLAY

ALS. DNA, RG59, Misc. Letters.

1 See above, II, 57-59. 2 See above, I, 799n, 853n.

3 In September, 1815, Adams had noted the great expense of residence in London and had asked to be recalled the following spring, "if, upon the construction of the law, the Legislature should refuse an appropriation for the outfit." *American State Papers, Misc.*, II, 306. This statement was submitted to the House on April 15, 1816, in support of legislation to increase the compensation to American ministers abroad (cf. above, II, 190-91). Legislative action relating to Adams' specific request was apparently encompassed in the general appropriation bill.

4 Cf. above, II, 64, 101, 105-106.

5 Monroe, in view of the delicacy of Clay's request, owing to the personal opposition which had developed over the conduct of foreign policy during his Administration, referred the matter to Attorney-General William Wirt, rather than to Secretary of State Adams. Wirt presented a favorable report on Clay's claim before a meeting of Monroe's Cabinet on March 13; but, in consequence of Adams' protests, Monroe postponed final decision. Adams, *Memoirs,* 311, 323, 329-30. See below, Anderson to Clay, July 12, 1822.

From Edmund W. Rootes

Dear Sir Richmond 1″ March 1821

Yours of 25″ Feby[1] has just reached me—to which I hasten to reply —that David Buchanan is a Citizen of Virginia—that George Penn, was the Purchaser of Goods wares & mdze of R & A Pollok & Co. to the amot of £633. 17.4. & promised to give his Bond with Security, which Security was to be Green'sVille Penn,[2] who upon application being, made refused to sign the Bond—I inclose you a Letter from Colo. Penn of 1″ May 1819. wherein he promises to see me on the subject of his Bond in the course of that fall, or to name an Atto for the purpose of setling [*sic*] the same—since which I have neither seen Colo Penn, his atto, nor have I heard from him even

H. Clay Esqr I am Respectfully E. W. ROOTES

ALS. DLC-TJC (DNA, M212, R12). [1] Not found.
[2] Of Patrick County, Virginia; a younger brother of George.

To [Smith Thompson]

Sir Washn. 2 March 1821

I have the pleasure to recommend to you the bearer Mr. John Love Ball, as a Mid Shipman in the Navy. He is the orphan of the late Col. Ball of the American Army a gallant and distinguished officer.[1] Mr. Ball's connexions are otherwise highly respectable, and, should he succeed in his present application, I hope will sustain the high reputation of his father.[2]

I am, with great esteem Your obedient Servant H. CLAY.

ALS. CtHi.
[1] James V. Ball, a native of Virginia, had been an officer in the United States Army, 1794-1802, 1812-1815, and from 1816 until his death early in 1818. He had been brevetted lieutenant colonel in 1812 for gallant conduct in battle and had been promoted to the permanent rank of lieutenant colonel in 1817.
[2] Young Ball's appointment as midshipman was dated December 4, 1822.

Remarks on Road Bill

[March 2, 1821]

Cited in Washington *Daily National Intelligencer,* March 3, 1821; *Annals of Cong.,* 16 Cong., 2 Sess., XXXVII, 1272. Clay opposed a motion to reject a Senate bill marking out and making an additional appropriation for a road from Wheeling to the Mississippi River. On motion of Henry Brush, of Ohio, the bill was tabled.

Receipted Bill from Benjamin Binns

March 2d 1821

The Honble Henry Clay To Benjamin Binns Dr

To @ pair Mild blue cassimere pantaloons	$16 —
@ white mersales[1] vest	5.50
@ black cloth vest	7 —
	$ 28.50

Recd payment in full Benjamin Binns

ADS. DLC-TJC (DNA, M212, R15). Binns, not identified. [1] Marseilles.

Resolution of Thanks to Speaker

[March 3, 1821]

I rise to submit a motion, which, if it should conciliate the general concurrence of this House, I shall be extremely glad. The present session was commenced under very unpleasant auspices. In the appointment of a presiding officer of the House, the first manifestation was made of that unfortunate division of opinion which has been the peculiar characteristic of the session.[1] The storm has happily subsided; and we have the great satisfaction to behold the ship of our confederacy unimpaired by its rage; her hull, her rigging, and her patriotic crew completely fit for a long and glorious voyage, under the star-spangled banner which proudly floats aloft.

The moral of that agitating drama, of which, for more than two years past, our country has been the theatre, is that, whilst our Federal Union is admirably fitted to accomplish all the national purposes for which it was intended, there are delicate subjects, exclusively appertaining to the several States, which cannot be touched but by them, without the greatest hazard to the public tranquility. They resemble those secluded apartments in our respective domicils, which are dedicated to family privacy, into which our nearest and best neighbours should not enter. Let us terminate the session by making that officer the depository of our entire reconciliation, whose election first elicited our divisions, and whose situation has been extremely arduous and difficult. For my part, I have great pleasure in testifying to the assiduity, impartiality, ability, and promptitude, with which he has administered the duties of the Chair, since I was able to take my seat. I move the following resolution:

Resolved, That the thanks of this House be given to the honorable John W. Taylor, for the assiduity, promptitude, and ability, with which he has administered the duties of the chair.[2]

The remarks, Washington *Daily National Intelligencer,* March 5, 1821; resolution, U.S. H. of Reps., *Journal,* 16 Cong., 2 Sess., 320. Published also in Lexington *Kentucky Reporter,* March 19, 1821; *Annals of Cong.,* 16 Cong., 2 Sess., XXXVII, 1294-95.

1 Taylor had been elected Speaker only after twenty-two ballots over a period of three days.

2 When the question was taken, only "one negative voice" was heard.

From Langdon Cheves

My Dear Sir, (Private) Bank United States 3 March 1821.

I am much gratified by your favour of the 27th. ultimo[1] which I received yesterday afternoon. I beleive [*sic*] the Cashier was under the impression you did the business of *Solicitor* of the Office at Lexington. But the duties of such Office were not intended to be

Covered by the Compensation allowed and you will of Course be entitled to the Customary Compensation for these duties—These duties & Particularly the just compensation to be Allowed form One of the matters on which I Proposed to write to you or to converse with you about & in an Official letter with Which I trouble you this day[2] I will speak at length on the Subject.

You have abundant reason for the gratification you feel On the Subject of your Public duties since your last arrival at Washington and the Country owes you much for the important Services you have rendered, nor do I believe it will be Withheld from you in any Part of it—The Missouri question has done, irremediably, much evil, and the disease can never be Completely eradicated. But you have accomplished all that was Practicable & so much as leaves the Patient a whole Constitution—I Perceive while Writing that the metaphor is not Solemn enough for the Occasion & that to speak literally is best to express its importance & difficulty—The Constitution of the Union was in danger & has been Saved. It would have been a terrible spectacle to have seen Missouri independent & yet not a member of the Union, Without a Power in the latter to Coerce her, nor would the evil have been much diminished by the fact that it was Perhaps her duty not to do the act of Self humilitation which was required. The Whole Idea of restriction was a wicked conception which though it may be forgiven ought not to be forgotten.—I am My Dear Sir Very truly, With great respect & esteem Yr. Obt St

LANGDON CHEVES

The Honorable Henry Clay, City of Washington.

ALS. DLC-HC (DNA, M212, R1).

1 Possibly not the official letter of that date published above, but a personal letter not found.

2 Not found.

To Langdon Cheves

My Dr Sir Washington 5h. March 1821.

I hasten to reply to the two private letters, under date the 3d. inst. with which you have favored me.[1] I transmit a letter of introduction to Mr. Gallatin for Dr. Horner,[2] which I would have addressed to him directly at New York, but that I supposed it would pass more certainly through you.

No human being could have anticipated all the tremendous consequences of the exclusion from the Union of Missouri, for any length of time. My firm conviction is, founded upon a knowledge of several powerful local causes operating in the West, that one of them would have been an attempt at separation of some, and ultimately all, of the Western States from the confederacy. Wisdom and prudence may keep us united a long time, I hope for ever. But there are natural causes, tending towards disseverance, which ought to be counteracted by an enlightened policy. There may be occasions when it is necessary even to risk a rupture of the cord which binds us together. But they ought to be occasions worthy of such a risk. I perceive, however, that I am boring you with politics. I will desist.

The late law of Ohio has attracted, of course, my attention— It will do the Bank no harm— I will shortly answer your official letter on that and other subjects—[3] In the mean time

L. Cheves Esqr. I am faithfully & cordially Yours H. Clay

ALS. ScHi. [1] Only one of these letters has been found.

[2] Albert Gallatin; William Edmonds Horner. The latter, a Virginian, had been graduated in medicine from the University of Pennsylvania, had served as surgeon's mate in the War of 1812, and had practised for a brief time in Warrenton, Virginia. Late in 1815 he had removed to Philadelphia, where he had soon found employment in the Medical School of the University of Pennsylvania. Appointed adjunct professor of anatomy in this institution in 1819, he became professor in 1831, and for many years was dean. He was the author of numerous articles and books, chiefly on anatomy. No record of a visit by Horner to France at this time has been found.

[3] See below, Clay to Cheves (1), March 10, 1821.

To William Wirt

D Sir Washn. 9h. Mar. 1821

On the subject of my claim to half an outfit for negotiating, in conjunction with Mess. Adams and Gallatin, the Convention of London in 1815,[1] I rely upon the official usage for its support.

The case of Mr. Adams who was transfered from the Hague to Berlin,[2] and who I presume received a full outfit in both instances is apposite. The case of the same Gentleman, who in 1814, received half an outfit, if not more, with *the sanction of Congress* also applies. The case also of the same gentleman who was transfered from St. Petersburg to London in 1814-15 and, without returning to the U. States, received two entire outfits is also a precedent.

Mr. Monroe I believe, when he went to Spain, received likewise an outfit, having previously received one for his mission to France.[3]

Mr. Pinckney[4] recently on his Mission to Naples if he did not receive an outfit, received an equivalent in the payment of his expences, besides being allowed an outfit for his Russian Mission.

I am persuaded that the records of the State Department will prove that wherever the same individual has been on two Foreign Missions, outfit has followed as a matter of course, unless there was a special arrangement substituting a different rule. Such has been the case with Mr Gallatin in his two recent negotiations at London and at Brussells [*sic*].[5] His expences were allowed him, I think I have understood by a particular agreement.

My expences in London even have not been allowed me. It is said that outfit supposes establishments by the Minister to whom it is granted. The truth is I had two, one at Gottenburg & the other at Ghent, the first at my sole expence.

I have assumed the measure of half an outfit because that received the approbation of Congress, in Mr. Adams's instance.

Wm. Wirt Esq. With great respect I am faithfy Yrs H CLAY

ALS. DNA, RG59, Misc. Letters. 1 See above, Clay to Monroe, March 1, 1821.

2 After almost four years as United States Minister at the Hague, John Quincy Adams in 1797 had become Minister to the Court of Prussia.

3 Having been first sent to France to participate in the negotiations which resulted in the purchase of Louisiana, Monroe had thence proceeded to London, where he had held the post of Minister from 1803 to 1807. During the latter ministry, from January to May, 1805, he had joined Charles Pinckney in negotiations at Madrid (see above, I, 271n). Clay was correct as to the extent of Monroe's reimbursement but erred in detail: Monroe had received outfits for both the extraordinary mission to France and the regular mission to England but merely his expenses for the special assignment to Spain. Lucius Wilmerding, Jr., *James Monroe: Public Claimant* ([Trenton, N.J., c.1960]), 39-40, 45-46.

4 William Pinkney. See above, II, 256n, 505n.

5 In the summer of 1817 Gallatin had left his post as Minister at Paris to assist William Eustis in negotiations for a commercial treaty with the Government of the Netherlands. Initiated at Brussels, the conferences had been transferred to the Hague in the latter part of August. Unable to reach an agreement, Gallatin had returned to Paris in September.

The following year he had assisted Richard Rush in the negotiations at London which terminated in the Anglo-American convention of October 20, covering renewal of the commercial treaty of 1815, definition of the Newfoundland fishing privileges and the northwestern boundary of the United States, and provision for the joint occupation of Oregon.

To Langdon Cheves

Sir Washington 10h. March 1821

I duly received your letter of the 3d. inst.[1] transmitting copies of two acts of the Legislature of Ohio, in relation to the Bank of the U. States, and I proceed to comply with the request of the Board to communicate such views as present themselves to me respecting their legal operation. I will first notice that which provides for a restoration of $90.000, of the money of the Bank, forcibly seized, under the authority of the State.[2]

If the act had offered to return that sum unconditionally, according to the proposal made to me at Columbus in January last, and which produced a continuance of the action of Trespass,[3] I should have advised the reception of it, with an express reservation of the right of the Bank to prosecute any legal means for the recovery of the residue of the $100.000 seized, with interest and damages. But the offer is coupled with the conditions, that the Bank shall with draw the pending suits for the recovery of the $100.000, and submit, in future, to the payment of a tax equal to four per cent per annum upon the dividends arising from the business transacted at its Ohio office, or that it shall withdraw those suits, and also with draw its branches from that State, substituting to them an agency for the final closing of its business. If, therefore, the Bank were to accept the $90.000. upon the terms offered, it would, in effect, admit a right of taxation to exist on the part of the States, which has been solemnly decided by the Court in the last resort not to belong them [*sic*],[4] or that the States have a right, which most clearly does not appertain to them, to expel from their respective jurisdictions, any branches which the Bank may establish within them. To admit such a power in the Legislature of Ohio, is to admit it in every other State Legislature, and to acknowledge also that that of Pennsylvania may exert it in reference to the parent institution. To acknowledge its existence would be to allow that a Charter granted by the authority, and which must be sustained by the power, of all the States, may be impaired and destroyed by any one State. It would be a virtual surrender of the Charter. It is impossible, therefore, to hesitate in a peremptory rejection of the $90.000 upon the conditions which are proposed.

That section of the act, under consideration, which declares that any person who may resist or impede the collection of the tax which it imposes, shall be deemed guilty of a misdemeanor, by creating a criminal offence, was, doubtless, intended to place the party thus denounced under the jurisdiction of the State tribunals, and to exclude that of the Federal Courts. In this the authors of the act will find themselves deceived. By a recent decision of the Supreme Court, jurisdiction is affirmed in the Federal Judiciary in all cases, criminal as well as civil, in which it may be necessary to maintain the inviolability of the Laws of the U States, against the laws of any of the States.[5] Should, therefore, any prosecution take place under that section, the party may obtain the protection of the Supreme Court.

There is one admission, which the act clearly implies, and that is the enormity of the former tax,[6] of which a proper use will be made in the suits now existing. I believe the Injunction which we have obtained, to restrain the collection of the former tax,[7] covers the case of any new tax which the Legislature might subsequently impose. However, I will take care if it does not that a new injunction shall be procured.

The other act, which seems to have for its object to out law the Bank of the U. States,[8] is marked by a degree of intemperance which it is to be greatly regretted any deliberative body should allow itself to manifest. The first section denies to the Bank the use of the jails of Ohio, in cases in which it might be necessary to employ them. The effect of this section has been guarded against, by the adoption of a joint resolution of the Senate & H. of R. at the late Session of Congress, in consequence of an enquiry which I instituted, vesting powers in the District Judge of Ohio to supply the want of the State Jails.[9]

The second section of the act prohibits the State officers from receiving proof of deeds, or committing them to record, where the Bank is concerned. The right of the Bank to acquire real estate depends upon its Charter, and to the extent of the provisions and under the qualifications of the Charter, cannot be impaired by State legislation. By the laws of Ohio the proof of the execution of deeds, and their registry, are generally required. But, if in any particular case, those same laws forbid or dispense with the proof and the registry of conveyances, their validity will remain the same as if those ceremonies were actually performed. I would, however, advise that in all instances where deeds of trust, mortgages, or other conveyances are made to the Bank the effort should be made to get them proved and registered, just as if this act had not passed. If they are proved and registered, no question about their efficacy can afterwards be raised. If the officers charged with the duty of receiving proofs and registering them, will not do it, I would recommend an indorsement to be procured to be made upon the conveyances, by those officers respectively, stating the offer to prove or to register them (as the case may be) and the refusal in consequence of this act. If there should be several officers, designated by law for performing those duties, I would make the demand of each of them. The Bank will then have done all it can do, and no doubt, I think, can be entertained of the security of their rights, the refusal to take the evidence and to perpetuate the existence of which shall have been thus made.

The third section prohibits Notary publics, appointed under the authority of Ohio, from making protests of promissory notes and bills of exchange, belonging to the Bank of the U. States. It has been decided both in Kentucky and Ohio, by the State tribunals, not only that the protest of a promissory note is not necessary to charge any of the parties, but that the expence incident to the act of protest is not taxable against the defendants.[10] The same rule will be observed, I think, by the Circuit Courts. Taking that as the law, applicable to promissory notes, the section of the act I am examining, will produce no inconvenience to the Bank; and it will be better to seize the occasion which it affords for discontinuing an useless and expensive ceremony. In respect to bills of exchange I would recommend an application to the Notary or Notaries of the place, and after their refusal to make protest of them, which should be certified, I would have them protested in the mode known to commercial usage, where there is no notary to be had. I ought to have added that, altho the protest of promissory notes may be dispensed with, notice of their non payment must be given to the indorsers &c. with the same promptitude, as if they had been formally protested.

The remaining sections of this act having for their object the enforcement, by certain sanctions which are provided, of the three first sections, and to prevail upon the Bank to withdraw its branch, & to dismiss the suits brought for the recovery of the $100.000. need not be particularly observed upon.

I think it very probable that an act which is characterized by so little moderation, and which, whilst it evinces a disposition for annoyance, is in fact incapable of producing any, will not be enforced. The contrary supposition is, however, the prudent one to act upon. And, unless I shall hear from you in a way which shall restrain me, I shall give instructions, more in detail, in conformity to the opinions here expressed. As to the first act, nothing will be necessary to be done on the part of the Bank, unless an application should be made by the Governor or Auditor to know, if it will receive the money upon the specified conditions. And as to the other, the operation of it being postponed until the first day of September, there is ample intermediate time for further deliberation.

I have the honor to be with great respect Your obedient Servant
Langdon Cheves Esqr. &c &c &c H. CLAY

ALS. PU.

1 The "official letter," not found, mentioned above, Clay to Cheves, March 5, 1821.

2 Ohio General Assembly, *Acts Passed at the First Session of the Nineteenth . . ., 1820,* pp. 173-76 (February 2, 1821).

3 See above, Clay to Cheves, January 22, 1821, note. 4 See above, II, 673-74.

5 In the case, Cohens *vs.* Virginia (February, 1821), the Supreme Court had accepted jurisdiction even though the controversy lay between a State and one of its own citizens; and Chief Justice Marshall had declared that "the judicial power, as originally given, extends to all cases arising under the constitution or a law of the United States, whoever may be the parties." 19 *U.S.* (6 Wheaton) 392.

6 The statute provided that instead of the sum of $50,000 per annum, as originally assessed against the branches of the Bank of the United States, the State Auditor should issue his warrant for collection of $2,500, only, to be levied and collected as under the previous act; or, if the branch officers reported "the actual amount of the dividends arising from business transacted at such office of discount and deposit, for the preceding year," the Auditor should cause to be collected a sum equal to four per cent of the dividend thus reported.

7 See above, II, 723n.

8 Ohio Gen. Assy., *Acts, 1820,* pp. 108-10 (January 29, 1821).

9 See above, Motion and Remarks on Due Execution of Process, February 12, 1821.

10 See above, II, 327n; below, Clay to Cheves, October 26, 1821.

To Langdon Cheves

Sir Washington 10h. March 1821

Having limited my letter, bearing even date herewith, in answer to your's of the third instant, to an examination of the two acts of

Ohio, I will now reply to the other parts of your letter, which relate principally to the affair of solicitors.

Solicitors are at present appointed by the respective offices for the Bank. Being selected from the places where those offices are severally situated, perhaps the local boards constitute as good judges of their fitness and qualifications as any one else could be. I do not think, therefore, that any benefit is likely to arise to the Bank from a transfer of the appointing power from those boards to me, equivalent to the possible dissatisfaction which the offices might feel at the distrust which would be manifested of them, or supposed to be, by such transfer. Yet, if the Board take a different view of the subject, I would certainly conform to their wishes.

The compensation, allowed to Solicitors, is at present in the shape of a fee in the particular cause or causes which they may institute. This fee varies, according to circumstances, from ten dollars, the lowest, to twenty, the highest that is paid. And either the one or the other of these sums is paid or expected to be received in all cases, whatever may be their result. The Bank is reimbursed, if a recovery take place & the defendant is able to satisfy the execution, to the amount of the legal fee, which is, I believe, never more than ten dollars, some times five, and I think some times not more than $2:50. With respect to commissions I presume five per Cent would be charged in all cases where collection[s] are made, and that would be sanctioned by the usage of the Country, unless a specific agreement for a different sum were made.

Although I would not advise a change of the power of appointm[ent] of Solicitors, perhaps it would be best to submit the affair of their compensation to your Counsel, which might be done without any implication unfavorable to the local boards. I think it will be best to allow an average fee which may as often fall below as it will exceed the just standard, and which should be, in a considerable degree, regulated by the number of causes brought by the particular office. Between this mode, and that which the Bank has adopted in relation to its Atlantic offices the pecuniary difference is merely in form, and I think that the former, besides having the usage of the Country and of other local Banks (that I know of the Bank of Kentucky in particular) in its favor, has perhaps the recommendation of insuring greater zeal and fidelity. The duty of the Solicitor will not be without considerable importance. Besides the draft of the pleadings in ordinary cases, to him will be confided, in the first instance, the facts of the case, and the knowledge of the proofs of those facts. He will also assist in the argument. The truth is, and the Board will not conceal from itself the fact, that it has great interests which must be subjected to a course of litigation, in the Western States. And whilst it is called upon, in the execution of its high trust, to exercise a just œconomy, it ought not, one would think, to fail to command the best talents for the various services which it may require, if they can be procured with reasonable compensations.

In regard to collections from the public officers, they may be made by the Solicitors, or by the Offices directly. If by the former, and no specific agreement as to commission is made, five per Cent would probably be claimed & be recovered, if contested. But I persevere in thinking that the business of collection should be confided to the offices directly, as best, whether we consider œconomy or security. Both these considerations concur in recommending it, even if an additional Clerk were necessary to be appointed. A Clerk, either one now in office, or one to be appointed, if required by the state of the business, should be charged with keeping the accounts of cases put in suit; with watching their progress; with receiving and paying over to the Cashiers, from time to time, monies not paid in the offices directly as they may be received from Marshalls; with attending Sales advertized of debtors property taken in execution, and which, being required to produce a certain proportion of its assessed value it may be sometimes necessary to force, and to guard against collusions. In short, that such Clerk, under the immediate superintendance [*sic*] of the Cashiers or the Board, and advised by your Counsel, should take care of the prompt and faithful reception of all monies levied by execution. If however the Board shall think that the matter of collection had better be confided to the Solicitors, then some special agreement ought to be made, in regard to commissions, which should be regulated by the amount to be collected, and the solvency of debtors.

Even in the taking of depositions, and in riding through the Country for the purpose of attending Sales &c &c. the Clerk may in the general, if a judicious choice be made, be competent to the task. In taking of depositions in Chancery cases of great difficulty, the Solicitors may be occasionally required, and then some compensation must be allowed them.

I have received the letter which you did me the honor to write on the 6h. inst.[1] You are right in supposing that my intention was to ask for those orders only which relate to the establishment and organization of the office at Chillicothe down to and including the epoch of the trespass. Beyond that period they are not wanted.

I expect to leave here on monday evening next. Your future communications to me, therefore, had better be addressed to me at Lexington. With great respect I am Your ob. Servant. H. CLAY

Langdon Cheves Esqr. &c &c &c.

P.S. I have not had time even to copy this letter & that which accompanies it. May I ask the favor of you to have copies of them transmitted to me at Lexn. H.C.

ALS. PU. [1] Not found.

To Richard W. Meade

WASHINGTON, *March* 12, 1821.

SIR: I have attentively examined the papers illustrative of your demand upon the Government of the United States, founded upon your acknowledged claim on that of Spain, and arising out of the recent treaty concluded between them;[1] and although, from the variety and pressure of my engagements incident to my departure from this place, I have not time to prepare and present to you an argumentative opinion upon the whole case, I will take that to say that, in the instance of wrongs, including violence committed by one nation, or under its authority, upon the citizens of another, the latter has a right, in the preservation of its sovereignty and honor, to settle the grievance so as to conclude the rights of its citizens who have been aggrieved, even if the measure of redress falls short of the measure of injury; that such a settlement, however, ought not to be made but on weighty and urgent reasons; and that one nation ought never to avail itself of the claim to redress, for violent injuries committed by another upon its citizens, to acquire territorial or other advantages inuring to the benefit of the public at large.

In regard to contracts or commercial operations between the citizens of one country and a foreign Power which withholds from them justice, there is no absolute right of interposition on the part of that country, since those citizens have voluntarily put their trust in the foreign Power. The country may interpose at the instance of its citizens, but the extent of that interposition must depend upon the request of its citizens. The country then becomes a sort of agent, of a high and dignified character, to ask justice for its injured citizens. It must not abuse this agency which is submitted to the laws which regulate all delegated power. In your case, you asked the assistance of your country's minister to have your claims settled. You obtained it. You proceeded in their liquidation; and you completed the adjustment of them with Spain. After you had obtained the bond of Spain for the payment of the debt which it acknowledged to be due to you, your country acquits Spain of this bond by a provision in the recent treaty, to which you gave no express assent, nor, as I think, any implied assent. Now, if a country is not bound to go to war to support the rights of its citizens; if it is not even compelled to interpose its good offices in cases where those citizens have, with their eyes open, confided in a foreign State by contracting or voluntarily dealing with it, neither has it a right, especially in the latter case, to extinguish the just rights of its citizens arising out of such contract or voluntary trading. The treaty extinction of them is probably binding on them; but if it is, it appears to me that the rule of equity furnished by our Constitution, and which provides that private property shall not be taken for public purposes without just compensation, applies, and entitles the injured citizen to consider his own country as substituted to the foreign State.

As to you, the treaty must be considered as taking its date from the Spanish ratification or the last American ratification. Prior to the former event it was at an end. There had been a compact intended, but both parties, and each, were released from it. A new compact was proposed, the same in terms as the old one, by the act of the Spanish ratification. It was finally consummated by that of America. Taken in either view, the treaty came upon you whilst you were in the regular prosecution of your demand before the Spanish Government. It arrested your progress; it abated your suit, after you had got a verdict and judgment. Having taken from you the means of obtaining satisfaction by your execution, it seems to me that it is now incumbent upon your own country, which has thus thought proper, from public considerations, to check your career, to render you an equivalent, an entire satisfaction. H. CLAY.

R. W. MEADE, Esq.

American State Papers, Foreign Relations, VI, 786-87.

1 After his release from imprisonment (see above, II, 764n), Meade had succeeded in obtaining from Spain, in 1820, a certificate acknowledging an indebtedness of almost half a million dollars for claims which resulted from his furnishing funds and supplies to the Spanish Government during the Peninsular War. When the United States, under the terms of the Adams-De Onís treaty of 1819, assumed the claims of Americans against Spain, Meade returned to Philadelphia and, later, took up residence in Washington to promote his efforts to collect. He was never successful either in prosecuting his claim before the Claims Commission or in obtaining from Congress a bill authorizing payment.

From P[eter] H[agner]

Hon. Henry Clay Washington City 12th. March 1821

Sir, The voucher and explanatory statement deposited by you[1] relating to the account of the late James T. Eubank, Esq, as Quarter Master have been examined, and a statement of his account predicated thereon, which having been reported for decision to the 2d Compr. has been returned to this office resulting in a balance due the U.S. of $2228.62 which been [*sic*] accordingly reported to the first Comptroller who will furnish the Dist. Attorney with the necessary information on the subject—P,H,

Copy. DNA, RG217, Misc. Letters Sent, vol. 20, p. 179.

1 See above, Taylor to Clay, January 5, 1821.

Toast and Response at Washington Banquet

[March 14, 1821]

Our distinguished guest and friend, HENRY CLAY: and may the regrets and wishes of his country, coinciding with his private convenience, speedily restore him to the public councils, which his genius and experience should enlighten and sustain; and to the society of this city, which his manners have adorned.[1]

. . . . [Applause.]

Mr. *Clay* rose and, with visible emotion, acknowledged that though it had been his fortune, in the course of his life, to receive several similar marks of approbation from his fellow-citizens, he had never experienced, on any occasion of the kind, emotions so strong and so difficult to express; nor was this surprising, when he found himself thus honored by a company which he might view as a packed jury of his friends; from some of whom, it was true, he had differed, on important political questions, but who were, nevertheless, dear to him.[2] The verdict which they and all present had now rendered in his favor, he was proud of, and it would always be remembered with the fondest recollections.

Mr. C. adverted to his retirement from public life, and the causes of that determination. It was induced by the highest of all obligations—a man's duty to his family and to his own personal independence, which could only be maintained by such a competency as would secure him from the necessity of looking for support to official favor and emoluments. To remain longer in public life would be highly injurious to his private concerns, and to prevent them from running into disorder and derangement, he was obliged to retire. Personal independence of thought and action could in no other way be fortified and secured.[3] Mr. C. remarked upon our happy union, and the excellence of our political institutions, which, notwithstanding some defects might exist in them, and some occasional errors occur in their administration, were the best with which any nation was blessed, and ought to be religiously cherished by every patriot. Mr. C. next adverted to this city, its history and prospects. It had been visited by a great disaster, he said, by the sudden incursion of a barbaric enemy, whose course was marked with desolation.[4] But this calamity had no other effect than to enlist more strongly and deservedly the sympathies of the nation in favor of its infant metropolis; on the citizens of which he concluded by invoking every happiness, and on the metropolis itself a prosperity and splendor worthy of the immortal name which it bears.

Washington *Daily National Intelligencer,* March 17, 1821. Published also in Lexington *Kentucky Reporter,* April 2, 1821. On the morning of March 14, the *Intelligencer* had carried a notice of "a Public Dinner, to be given This Day, at Brown's Hotel," by citizens of Washington "to evince their respect for the distinguished public services of HENRY CLAY, especially during the last session of Congress, and also their sense of his steady friendship for this city." Those who wished to attend were requested "to leave their names at the bar of the Hotel by one o'clock." The hasty arrangements resulted from an understanding that Clay intended leaving the city "immediately." Dinner was to "be on the table precisely at 4 o' clock."

Jesse Brown's Indian Queen Hotel, on Pennsylvania Avenue, had formerly been known as Davis's Hotel.

1 Toast given by Walter Jones, who presided over the dinner.

2 Besides Jones, the listed guests included Judge Buckner Thruston; R. C. Weightman; Thomas Dougherty; Josiah and Return Jonathan Meigs; Henry Brush; Thomas Sidney Jesup; Baptis Irvine; William Elliot; John Payne Todd; Henry Johnson, Senator from Louisiana; James M. Varnum, a justice of the peace for the District of Columbia; Abraham Bradley, Jr., Assistant Postmaster General; John and Edmund Law; and William Davis Robinson. The Law brothers, residents of Washington, about this time received minor political appointments in the territorial government of Florida. Robinson, a citizen of the United States who had been imprisoned by the Mexican Royalists as a Patriot supporter at Vera Cruz in 1816, was author of several brochures urging closer relations with the new governments of Spanish America. His *Memoirs of the Mexican Revolution . . .*, a longer work published at Philadelphia in 1820, had roused widespread interest in the possibility of trans-isthmian commerce.

3 The speech as reported in the *Washington City Gazette* elaborated Clay's comments at this point as follows: "It fortified a man for independence of thinking and acting in public bodies; helped him to withstand the allurements of office, and to keep aloof from soliciting place or appointment; it undeniably contributed to keep a man erect before power, and promoted an independent discharge of duty." Reprinted in Lexington *Kentucky Reporter*, April 2, 1821.

4 See above, I, 989, 990n.

Receipted Bill from B. H. Blake

Mr. Clay Dr. March 14th. 1821
For board commencing 24th. Jan. & ending 13th. March
1821. which is 7 weeks at 13 dols per week . . . . $ 91 .. 00
Receiv'd payment in full B. H BLAKE

ADS. DLC-TJC (DNA, M212, R15). Mrs. Blake at this time was proprietress of a boarding house on Pennsylvania Avenue, Washington; later in the year she gave up the establishment and moved to a residence on Tenth Street.

From P[eter] H[agner]

Hon. Henry Clay Lexington Ky 14 March 1821

Sir, I have perused the memorandum from General Taylor to you,[1] wherein he requires copies of certain statements &C. relative to his accounts as late District Pay Master &C.

All the information necessary to establish the points General Taylor wishes, to enable him "to tell whether he is correctly charged or not" is contained in the statement of differences and notes on his accounts furnished him in my letter of the 4th of December last. These documents shew the difference both of debits and credits between his own account rendered and the official statement of his accounts; this besides is the only information usually furnished in like cases—

The disallowed vouchers so far as they are unconnected with those allowed are returned to you—

A like statement of his Quarter Master charges is also furnished to you. P, H.

Copy. DNA, RG217, Misc. Letters Sent, vol. 20, p. 188.

1 Not found. James Taylor's account at settlement on December 1, 1820, had shown the sum of $18,378.89 due to the Government. His case was reported for suit in May, 1821, but continued for one year at his request. *House Docs.*, 17 Cong., 2 Sess., no. 32, p. 106.

To John Quincy Adams

Dr Sir Brownsville[1] 18h. Mar. 21

I owe you an explanation, which I should have made to you in person, but that the intimation which I received and which renders it necessary was communicated just before I left the City. That intimation was that, in presenting my claim upon Governmt. I had passed you by. The truth is that, in our system, the practice I believe is not well settled as to the person to be addressed. Hence I some times address myself to the President and some times to his Secretaries. In this particular case, there was a special reason which induced me to make my application to Mr. Monroe,[2] and that was that I felt it necessary to advert to some circumstances within his memory. Nothing was further from my intention than to imply, in the mode of making that application, any neglect of you, or any distrust of your justice. And I should be extremely sorry if such an impression were made on the mind of one with whom, I shall always remember with satisfaction, that I have co-operated in some very important transactions of our common Country. I have the honor to be with great respect Your obt. Servant. H. CLAY

J. Q. Adams Esqr.

ALS. MHi-Adams Papers. 1 Maryland. 2 Above, March 1, 1821.

From Benjamin Smith

Sir Orton[1] 24h. March 1821—

Your favor dated Washington 16h. Feb:[2] but without any Post mark was unaccountably detained so that I could not write in time to that City for you to receive it previous to the adjournment of Congress; in which your "active & incessant engagement in pulic [*sic*] duties was certainly sufficient cause for your neglecting or rather postponing a reply to my letter or any other on private business. The best reward of a patriot, the warm & unadulterated praise of millions of free men must ever attend you & your memory for the indefatigable & noble exertions made in the Missouri business—Permit me Sir to assure you of my regret at your leaving the Councils of your Country & to express an hope that in due season you may return to them with double pleasure.

Whilst Mr. Langley[3] was here he informed me that the Court in which his Suit was to be tried would meet on the 3d. Monday of this month say the 19th.—As you only "expected to reach home about the 25th. of March", I am apprehensive you could not be at Lexington during the term & under this apprehension have not written quite as early as I might, but suppose you will have heard what was done in the case and will thank you to inform me as speedily as possible—For I shall wait to hear the result previous to my leaving home as that will have great influence in determining my departure for Kentucky—I propose to be prepared to leave this place immediately after hearing from you—& will thank you to inform me how long the Stage takes to go from Wheeling to Lexington—or say from Washington to Lexington—

The letter you were so good as to enclose from Col Morrison[4] of course was received—I [am] truly sorry he has been so seriously indisposed—In it he enclosed an account of the amount necessary to redeem my lands (as he mentions) the first of May—I could send it in No Carolina State Bank bills if that would do, but being uncertain in that respect & informed by your first letter that I can redeem at any time within two years, I shall delay remitting in hopes those who owe me in Kentucky will furnish the means—Respecting the draft of $200 in your favor I am much obliged by your delicacy in not forwarding it—Have written to Mr Langley to pay you immediately upwards of $150—And shall urge Capt. S. G. Hopkins by the next Mail to remit to you the balance which I will cheerfully pay to have your weight of Character & abilities enlisted in my favour—Should they fail I must remit from hence but as I have money due in Kentucky & think the Lands there ought to answer for themselves & it would also save the risk of remittance I would prefer that method & hope it will be no inconvenience to you—I remain Sir With great Respect, your very obedt. BENJA. SMITH

ALS. DLC-TJC (DNA, M212, R12). Addressed to Clay at Lexington. Postmarked at Wilmington, North Carolina, March 27. Smith was probably the veteran of the Revolution, donor of 20,000 acres in military land warrants for founding the University of North Carolina, Senator from Brunswick County throughout much of the period from 1783 to 1816, and Governor of North Carolina, 1810-1811, who died in great poverty in 1826.

1 Plantation near Wilmington, described as "the finest colonial residence now standing in North Carolina." R. D. W. Connor, *History of North Carolina . . .* (6 vols.; Chicago and New York, 1919), I, 150.

2 Not found. 3 Not identified; his suit, not found. 4 James Morrison.

From Nicholas Berthoud

Henry Clay Esqr. Shippingport April 1st. 1821

Dr Sir

In compliance with instructions received from Mr. John Clay of New Orleans—I have Shipped the Steam Engine[1]—Stored with me on your a/c—per the Steam Boat Columbus—Captn. John De Hart[2] & Consigned to Mr. Jno Clay—to be delivered Twenty four miles below New Orleans—as per Bill of Lading[3] enclosed—

Very Respectfully Yor. Mot. Obt. Svt N Berthoud

P

ALFRED CRAWFORD

LS. DLC-TJC (DNA, M212, R10). Crawford has not been further identified.

1 See above, II, 899.

2 Also a boatbuilder at New Albany, Indiana, in collaboration with Captain Robeson DeHart. The *Columbus,* however, had been built by others in 1819 at New Orleans.

3 Dated at Shippingport, Kentucky, March 29, 1821, and signed by DeHart, this document covers shipment "For account and Risk of Henry Clay Esqr. of Lexington Ky," of "Ten pieces fly wheel = Six fly wheel arms = One hundred & seven Grate Bars & Bearers = Six pieces Doors & frames = Six Boiler heads = One piston of air pump = Six Boxes sundry Irons = One flange fast Eighteen pieces pipe = Two Cranks = One Cylinder One piston = Three stay arms = One Valve Seat = One Valve cover = One Boiler cover = One mortar Three Boilers = Two upright shafts—and nine pieces Sundry Castings—weighing in all say Thirty thousand pounds——" DS, partially printed. DLC-TJC (DNA, M212, R10).

Rental Agreement with John Deverin

[April 4, 1821]

ADS by Clay. KyLxT. Deverin's copy; Clay's was probably covered by endorsement above, II, 350.

Receipt from William Allen

[April 6, 1821]

Attached to Promissory Note, July 15, 1820.

Receipt to William S. Dallam

[April 6, 1821]

[Clay acknowledges receipt from Dallam of two notes: one of Jacob Creath[1] for $200, dated April 18, 1817, payable on demand; the other of Daniel Bryan and Samuel Bryan[2] for $397.26, due February 20, 1819. From the proceeds of these notes, when collected, the sum of $503, with interest from the date of this receipt, is to be paid "to Edward Lloyd, of Md."[3] and the balance rendered to Dallam.]

ADS. DLC-TJC (DNA, M212, R15). Endorsed by Clay on verso: "Memo. on settlement with Majr Dallam up to 1st. Sept—1822—"

1 Prominent Baptist preacher in central Kentucky, subsequently a leader in the churches of the Disciples of Christ; commonly identified as elder Jacob Creath, Sr. On the note, see below, Assignment, June 15, 1821.

2 Of Fayette County, Kentucky; son of Daniel Bryan.

3 United States Senator, 1814-1826; formerly Congressman, 1806-1809, and Governor, 1809-1811.

Bill of Sale from Patterson Bain

[April 7, 1821]

[For the sum of $500, "in hand paid," Bain conveys to Clay "one negro man slave named Bristow, about thirty seven years of age," warranting him sound and warranting the title "against all persons whatsoever." Witnessed by Abner LeGrand.]

DS, in Clay's hand. DLC-TJC (DNA, M212, R15).

From George Talbot

Dr. Sir Millersburgh Ky. April 10th. 1821

In a suit now depending in the Court of Appeals between Olive Selden (plaintiff) & Anthony Sheriff Martin Baker & Co (Defendants) I wish you to attend to the side of Mrs. Selden, & look to me for remuneration.[1] I have long since paid the money to Mrs. Selden, as security for Sheriff, & finding that I had it in my power, or believing so, to recover a part back, I have had her to carry on the suit against Sheriff & Baker & Co—The History of the Case is a long one, & unnecessary to communicate as you can have full reference to the papers filed in the case. Executions were stayed by a writ of errors & supersedeas.—

I think you can have it before the present term of the Court, because you can make it clearly appear that it is an affair of aggravation, designed to postpone payment without any expectations of ultimately avoiding it—

As I have combatted with much perplexity expense & frustration in this matter, I do hope the more earnestly, that you will do your best for me; & the fees shall in full time be paid by your friend & humble servant GEO: TALBOT

Henry Clay Esq.

P.S. I will be glad to hear from you relative to this matter, as soon as convenient.

ALS. DLC-HC (DNA, M212, R1). Directed to Lexington, with the following endorsement on the cover: "If Mr. Clay is absent, this will be sent immediately after him, & the Post Master will confer a great favor on the writer &c." Talbot, who in his youth had been brought to Kentucky from Virginia, was a prosperous Bourbon County farmer.

1 The case, both in Bourbon Circuit Court and in the Kentucky Court of Appeals, was actually Sheriff and Baker *vs.* "Seldon." It had originated from an effort on the part of the plaintiffs "to set aside a replevin bond executed by them to the defendant, Seldon, under a distress warrant which she caused to issue from a justice of the peace, against sheriff [*sic*] and Talbot, for rent." The writ of error *coram vobis,* brought by the plaintiffs, had been quashed in the lower court, which judgment was affirmed by the Court of Appeals (Clay arguing for the defense) in December, 1821. 16 *Ky. Reports* (Littell, *Selected Cases*) 485-87.

To [Return Jonathan Meigs]

Dr Sir Lexington 14h. Apl. 1821.

I have taken the liberty of putting under cover to you, the Western Review,[1] a periodical work published here, for His Excellency Mr. Poletica,[2] the Russian Minister, who expressed to me a wish to possess it. May I ask the favor of you to have it sent to him, and to excuse the trouble which I thus give you?

I duly received the digest of the decisions of the Supreme Court which you had the goodness to send me.

With great regard I am faithfy Yr. ob. Servt. H. CLAY

P.S. As far as I can judge, I think the opinion of the public in this quarter entirely favorable to you, in regard to the late attack on you.[3]

H.C.

ALS. NcD. Recipient identified by NcD.

1 *The Western Review and Miscellaneous Magazine, a Monthly Publication, Devoted to Literature and Science,* published in Lexington, 1819-1821, by William Gibbes Hunt. Hunt, who had come to Kentucky from Boston, also published the *Western Monitor and Lexington Advertiser,* before removing to Nashville, Tennessee, where he died.

2 Pierre de Polética.

3 On February 28, 1821, a select committee appointed to investigate the affairs of the Post Office Department had submitted to the House of Representatives a report critical of the Department in respect to expenditures, reports, and the handling of public funds. A supplementary report had been made on March 3. *House Reports,* 16 Cong., 2 Sess., nos. 65, 69.

Speech at Laying of Cornerstone

[April 16, 1821]

Clay, as Grand Master of the Grand Lodge of Kentucky, delivered "an appropriate address" (not recorded) during Masonic ceremonies attending the laying of the cornerstone of St. John's Chapel, an "Independent Methodist Church" in Lexington. Lexington *Kentucky Gazette,* April 19, 1821.

Receipt from William Allen

[May 3, 1821]

Attached to Promissory Note, July 15, 1820.

Property Deed from William and Betsey Allen

[*ca.* May 4, 1821]

[On an unspecified date in 1821 William Allen and Betsey, his wife, of Shelby County, Kentucky, for the sum of $6,190, "in part paid[1] and the residue secured by note[2] the receipt whereof is hereby acknowledged," sell to Henry Clay a parcel of land on Water Street in Lexington bounded "beginning at the east corner of a lot late the property of James Kerns decd on a street called locust or lowest street thence feet to a continuance of water street beginning northeast thence with said street as continued or laid out by John Cocke[3] thence westerly binding on said street north westerly feet to a stake at the corner of the fence thence south westerly with said fence to Kerns line thence south easterly with said line to the beginning being five lots laid off by John Cocke and numbered one, two, three, four and five including the Tamany [*sic*] Mills being the property which was conveyed to the said Allen, by William West's Commissioner &c. by deed dated the 13th Oct 1820 together with the Steam Mill offices out-buildings dwelling houses the machinery engine mill stones and all other things belonging to said property. . . ."]

DS. DLC-TJC (DNA, M212, R15). Acknowledged by William Allen before James C. Rodes, Clerk of Fayette County Court, May 4, 1821, and by Betsey Allen before James S. Whitaker, Clerk of Shelby County Court, June 20, 1821. Recorded in Fayette County Court, Deed Book U, 413-14.

1 See above, II, 882. 2 Not found.

3 Lexington miller and baker, who had died in 1814.

To Langdon Cheves

Sir Lexington 5h May 1821.

I should have earlier acknowledged the receipt of your letter of the 16h. March,[1] which came duly to hand, with its inclosures, but that I supposed it was not material.

The deposition of Mr. Benson,[2] the Clerk of the Bank, contains all the substantial requisites, but it has not been certified (judging from the Copy which you sent to me) in the manner prescribed by the 30h. Sect. of the Judicial Act of the U. States, to which I refered in a former letter.[3] I take the liberty of transmitting inclosed the form of a Certificate which I should like to be observed.[4] The Caption and body of the deposition may be as it was formerly taken, and this Certificate then added at the end of it; and then the deposition inclosed & sealed by the Mayor & addressed as before.

I have addressed letters to the several offices and the Agency in Ohio and Kentucky in regard to the collection of money from Marshalls & other public officers, according to the request of your Board.[5] I have also prepared & transmitted to the office at Chillicothe a bill of injunction to restrain the collection of the tax imposed by the act of the last Session of the Legislature of Ohio. And I will give, in due season, instructions founded upon the other act of that Session.[6]

There is no very sensible change for the better yet in this quarter. Kentucky has more elasticity than Ohio and will sooner emerge from existing embarrassments. In the mean time our Currency is continuing, in Kentucky, to get worse. The depretiation of the paper of the Kentucky Bank has reached twenty seven per Cent. If that bank should determine to take indiscriminately the paper of the Bank of the Commonwealth, there is no doubt that the notes of both banks will continue to experience a depretiation, and that it will be progressive. The Bank of Kentucky is understood to be now deliberating upon the question whether it will receive or not the notes of the other institution. I have no doubt it will determine to do so, under some limitations, which will be, at least for the present, only nominal.[7]

We shall persevere in our course of taking the notes of neither of those Banks, as the general rule.

I am with great respect Your obedient Servant H. CLAY

Langdon Cheves Esq. &c &c &c.

ALS. PHi-Etting Collection. [1] Not found.

[2] Probably David P. Benson, who had served in the Philadelphia militia during the War of 1812 and later became an officer of the Erie, Pennsylvania, branch of the Bank of the United States.

[3] See above, Clay to Cheves, February 27, 1821, note. [4] Not found.

[5] The letters and the request have not been found.

[6] On these statutes see above, Clay to Cheves (1), March 10, 1821.

[7] The Bank of Kentucky received the paper of the Bank of the Commonwealth in payment of interest and call notes; and the depreciation of its notes, as well as those of the latter institution, confirmed Clay's fears. By early August the notes of the Bank of the Commonwealth had depreciated fifty per cent and during the next year and a half ranged at 170 to 205 relative to 100 in notes of the Bank of the United States. Washington *Daily National Intelligencer,* August 2, 1821; Lexington *Kentucky Reporter,* June 19, 1821; *Niles' Weekly Register,* XXI (December 29, 1821), 276; XXII (April 13, 1822), 97; XXIII (October 12, 1822), 96; XXIV (February 10, 1823), 16.

Deed of Release to Robert Grinstead

[May 7, 1821]

[Whereas Robert Grinstead has earlier conveyed to the executors of Thomas Hart, Jr., a certain lot, part of out lot no. 7 in the Lexington town plan, to secure payment of a debt of $650, and whereas the debt has been paid, Eleanor Hart, Henry Clay, John W. Hunt, and Abraham S. Barton, executrix and executors of Thomas Hart, Jr., release "and forever quit claim" the lot to Grinstead.]

Fayette County Court, Deed Book U, 339-40. See also above, I, 701n.

From William T. Barry and Others

SIR, LEXINGTON, 12th MAY, 1821.

In behalf of the citizens of the counties of Fayette, Woodford and

Jessamine, we invite you to partake of a public dinner, to be prepared for the occasion at Higbee's[1] Tavern, on the 19th of this month. Your constituents offer you this testimony of respect for the faithful and able manner in which you have discharged the important trust confided to you as their representative. It has been highly satisfactory to them to witness the series of enlightened efforts, that marked your course whilst a member of Congress, calculated to give elevation to our character as a nation and to promote in an eminent degree the happiness and prosperity of our common country. The sentiment of regret excited by your retiring from Congress, is most sensibly felt by your immediate constituents, who can at once appreciate your public worth and private virtues. The hope is fondly cherished that at no distant period it may be found compatible with your private duties for you to enter again on public life; & afford to the nation the advantages to be calculated on from an enlarged experience, and the aid of those talents that have already given to yourself and your country a distinguished standing.

With sentiments of unfeigned regard and friendship.

Your ob't. serv'ts.

W. T. BARRY,
J. MORRISON,
C. WILKINS,
T. BODLEY, } *of Fayette.*

JNO. M'KINNEY, JR.
WILLIS FIELD,
CHS. RAILEY, } *of Woodford.*

S. H. WOODSON,
ROBT. CROCKETT,
THO. B. SCOTT, } *of Jessamine.*

H. CLAY, Esq. *Committee of arrangement.*

Lexington *Kentucky Reporter,* May 21, 1821. Published also in Lexington *Kentucky Gazette,* May 24, 1821.

[1] John Higbee.

To William T. Barry and Others

GENTLEMEN— LEXINGTON, 14th MAY, 1821.

I have the honor to acknowledge the receipt of your note of the 12th inst. inviting me, in behalf of the citizens of the Congressional District which I lately represented, to a public dinner at Higbee's tavern on the 19th inst. I accept, with very great pleasure, the invitation. Ever anxious, in the course of my official duties, to deserve the public approbation, I have sought it by honestly supporting those measures which seemed to my best judgment most calculated to promote the real interests of the whole country. Acting upon this principle, I have sometimes risked the displeasure of the moment, in confidence that, on further & fuller consideration, any hasty or erroneous decision against me would be reversed; and

I have preferred to a policy, having for its object mere local or temporary benefit, that which had the most expanded or permanent operation. It gives me inexpressible satisfaction to find that, on a review of my whole public conduct, my constituents, in all parts of the District, are pleased to manifest their approbation of it in a manner at once decided and distinguished. Whatever may be my destiny hereafter; whether, as your partiality for me has induced you to hope, I may be again allowed to co-operate in the councils of our country, (a subject on which, depending as it does upon future time and circumstances, I have formed no resolution) I shall ever retain a fond and proud recollection of the many signal testimonies of their kindness and confidence which my constituents have given me. And to you, gentlemen, who are not only a part of them, but belong also to the number of my personal and particular friends, I beg leave to offer respectful assurances of my gratitude, and of the unabated esteem, with which I am cordially,

Your faithful and ob't. serv't. H. CLAY.

TO MESSRS.

W. T. Barry,	*Willis Field,*
James Morrison,	*Chas. Railey,*
Charles Wilkins,	*Saml. H. Woodson,*
Tho. Bodley,	*Robert Crockett,*
Jno. M'Kinney, Jr.	*Tho. B. Scott.*

Committee of arrangement.

Lexington *Kentucky Reporter,* May 21, 1821. Published also in Lexington *Kentucky Gazette,* May 24, 1821.

From Timothy Fuller

Dr Sir, Boston 15 May 1821—

Yrs of the 23 Apl, was recd. yesterday & the order of Mr Hart[1] has also been presented—The balance due to Mr. Hart & his wife[2] in her right on the Judgment on the Probate bond agt. the surety of Jas. Prentiss, deducting the expenses is Five hundred & forty six dollars & thirty cents. I shall take an early opportunity to have the a/c copied from the ledger & enclosed to yourself or Mr Hart agreeably to your request.

Since Maine has become a State the lands of nonresident proprietors have been taxed considerably higher than heretofore—The other proprietors of the land in which Mrs. Hart is interested have repeatedly called upon me to pay her proportion of the taxes, & I expected Mrs Hart would authorize me do [*sic*] so, or agree to a division of the land. Unless this is done the other proprietors, who have paid the taxes hitherto, will probably take the land in the name of the collector & proceed to sell by distress, or will attach it. Either of these would cause a considerable loss, & I have thought it best to retain the excess over five hundred dollars to be applied in payment of the taxes, provided I should be so request[ed]. If not I will pay the balance on the order into the bank.

The value of the land cannot be ascertained with exactness—it has been estimated at two thousand dollars, & if faithfully managed would probably considerably exceed that sum.—I cannot give much information of the number of acres which Mr. Prentiss gave bonds to convey upon certain conditions—none of the deeds I believe have been executed, but the agent has stated that several are ready to pay the consideration if they can have valid conveyances.

Your inquiries in relation to Nathl Gardner[3] will require the delay of a few days—I will ascertain the facts & inform you in a future letter.—

With great respect & consideration I am Sir,
Honble Mr Clay.— Your most ob Sert TIMOTHY FULLER

ALS. DLC-HC (DNA, M212, R1). [1] Thomas P. Hart.

[2] The former Mary Ann Lewis Gardner (Gardiner), ward of James Prentiss. Married in 1817, she died in 1822.

[3] Possibly the young man who had been clerk to General Henry Dearborn during the War of 1812.

Bill from [Benijah Bosworth]

Henry Clay	Dr	May 17th 1821
to 1 barrel of Shad—		\$ 18 —
to 3 barrels of whisky 104½ gallons		\$ 24 12½
to 3 barrels tare		3
		\$ 45 12½

D. DLC-TJC (DNA, M212, R15). See below, Account with Bosworth, *ca.* June 27, 1821.

Toast and Response at Public Dinner

[May 19, 1821]

2. HENRY CLAY.—His public services insure him the regard of his country, his private virtues the respect and confidence of his friends —Union his motto; conciliation his maxim; firmness and independence his principles of action.

. . . .

He [Clay] begged the President and his other fellow citizens there assembled, to allow him to make his profound acknowledgments for the sentiment just drank, incompetent as he felt his language must be to describe adequately the fullness of his gratitude, or the various emotions by which he was agitated. Considering the relation in which he had stood to them for so many years, the many and distinguished proofs of their confidence and regard which he had received, and that this relation had just terminated, some conception might be formed of the actual state of his feelings. It would have given him much satisfaction, if, prior to the close of his public career, some subjects in which his constituents had, with him, manifested a deep concern, could have had a completely successful issue. One of them was the recognition of the Independent Governments of South America. He was happy to be able to tell them, that the popular branch of the National Legislature, in accordance with the sentiments of the American people, had, at the last session of Congress, proclaimed to the world the wish of this country for that recognition, and the great interest which is felt here for the success of the Patriot cause.[1] And it might be reasonably hoped that the Executive branch of the government would not much longer delay to conform to the known sentiments of the whole union.[2] Among the motives which always appeared to him to recommend to this country to countenance, by all means short of actual war, that great cause, one, and not the least considerable, was that it would give additional tone, and hope, and confidence to the friends of Liberty throughout the world. It was evident, after the overthrow of Bonaparte, that the alliance by which that event was unexpectedly brought about, would push the principle of *legitimacy,* a softer and covered name for despotism, to the utmost extent. Accordingly the present generation had seen, with painful feelings, Congress after Congress assembling in Europe to decide, without ceremony, upon the destiny and affairs of Foreign Independent States. And if we, the greatest offender of all against the principle of legitimacy, had not been brought under their jurisdiction and subjected to their parental care, we owed the exemption to our distance from Europe, and to the known bravery of our countrymen. But who can say that has observed the giddiness and intoxication of power how long this exemption will continue? It had seemed to him desirable that a sort of counterpoise to the Holy Alliance should be formed in the two Americas, in favor of National Independence and Liberty, to operate by the force of example and by moral influence; that here a rallying point and an assylum [*sic*] should exist for freemen and for freedom. In the recent lawless attack upon the independence of unoffending Naples,[3] that alliance had thrown off the mask of religion, and peace and hypocrisy, and fully exposed the naked atrocity of its designs. A reform in the government of Naples had become necessary from the greatest abuses. The reform took place, peaceably, without bloodshed, and with the unanimous and enthusiastic concurrence of the whole nation, prince and people. This is the crime of Naples; and for this crime three individuals,[4] who if they have reached the height of human power, are displaying what is too often its attendant, the height of human presumption, are threatening to pour their countless hordes into her bosom and to devastate her land. The Holy Alliance professes to have no objection to Revolutions, but it denounces the severest punishment against all Revolters! If the people, as in the case of France, make the Revolution, why the peope are jacobins, disorganizers, the foes of order, and the revolution must be crushed! If the military aid the people in effecting the revolution, the example of military insubordination is most pernicious, and such a revolution must be put down! The Allies graciously allow Independent Nations to meliorate their institutions and the social condition, but these same Allies forbid the use of all the instruments to effect the object! They would indeed suffer monarchs to make the changes; that is, they would allow the mass of abuse and corruption and putrefaction, which may have been accumulating for ages, voluntarily to purify itself!

Mr. Clay also wished that some further encouragement to Domestic Manufactures could have been given. The truth was becoming more and more palpable, and diffusing every day a wider influence, that the old system of applying so large a portion of our labor to production for foreign markets, which have ceased to exist, would not do. We must cease to produce a surplus, which as things are, we can neither consume at home, nor sell abroad: and we must produce at home what we cannot buy abroad. And, although he never had thought that this desirable change was to be effected by legislation alone, he yet believed, that a judicious tariff, carefully devised, would powerfully aid the necessary sosial [*sic*] process. Owing to the extraordinary character of the times, he had also been anxious that a Bankrupt system should have been adopted, broad and comprehensive in its beneficence, at least of temporary duration, and to extend to the case of every man who was honestly and hopelessly indebted beyond his ability to pay, with modifications adapting it to the habits of the various classes in society.[5] With respect to that subject which no doubt suggested the expression of the leading sentiment of the toast, with which he had just been honored, he would say, that he had certainly felt most intensely the awful importance of an amicable settlement of the Missouri question; and he had devoted himself to it with his utmost zeal. Nor would he, under any affectation of humility, deny that his exertions may have somewhat contributed to putting it to rest.[6] But its adjustment ought to be mainly ascribed to those strong feelings of attachment to the Union which exist in all parts of it; to the deep conviction, that without it, our country would be exposed to the greatest calamities, rent into miserable petty states, and these convulsed by perpetual feuds and wars; and to those patriotic members of the House of Representatives, from the other section of the confederacy, who nobly risked their personal popularity for the good of the whole nation. The question, we may indulge the hope, is happily settled. And we should hasten to forget all the painful and disagreeable incidents by which the agitation of it was attended. For those few unprincipled men, if there were such, who sought to erect, upon the honest prejudices of the people, and upon the unhappy divisions of the nation, the foundation of the structure of their flagitious ambition, there ought to be no indulgence. But with respect to the great mass of the community, we should recollect that both sides were alike sincere and honest. If we believed that we stood upon the firm ground of the constitution, and were opposing principles fraught with the most direful ultimate consequences to us; they, on the other hand, were impelled by an honest zeal (misdirected as he verily thought) in behalf of that liberty, which we adore, and by an aversion from that slavery which we with them regret. Mutual forbearance and mutual toleration should restore, as he hoped they would, concord and harmony to our country.

He would not trespass further than to add, that feeling as he did, that if he had acquired any public consideration, he stood indebted for it to the repeated favors which his constituents had shewn him,—to their long continued and unshaken confidence in him, he should express again and again his thanks, and cherish a gratitude towards them as durable as his existence.

Toast, Lexington *Kentucky Reporter,* May 21, 1821; response, *ibid.,* May 28, 1821. Published also in Washington *Daily National Intelligencer,* June 6, 19, 1821; the toast and a brief report of the speech, in Lexington *Kentucky Gazette,* May 24, 1821. James Morrison presided over the affair, which was held at Higbee's Tavern and attended by "between two and three hundred, from different parts of the district, and a number of strangers from a distance." Among those who responded to toasts, and whose remarks were reported, was Thomas Hart Benton (Lexington *Kentucky Reporter,* June 4, 1821).

1 See above, Resolution and Remarks, February 10, 1821.

2 See below, Shaw to Clay, April 4, 1822.

3 See above, II, 863n. The Neapolitan revolt had been put down in March, 1821, by action of Austria under agreement of the Holy Alliance at the Congress of Laibach, held in January of that year.

4 Alexander I, of Russia; Francis I, of Austria; and Frederick William III, of Prussia.

5 See above, Remarks, February 28, 1821.

6 See above, Committee Report and Remarks on Missouri Statehood, February 26, 1821.

From J[ohn] C. C[alhoun]

Honble Henry Clay Lexington Ky.

Sir, Department of War 19th. May 1821.

I have received your letter of the 5th. inst;[1] and altho' Kentucky has recd. her full quota of the appointments of Cadets for this year, which have been already made, yet as there is likely to be a greater number of Vacancies in the Academy than was Originally calculated, I have conferred an appointment on your Son[2] notice of which is herewith enclosed. If he accepts it will be of material advantage to him to join as early as possible as he will before the Corps go into encampment have perfected himself in the drill and exercises so as to be able to march with it to Boston whither it will proceed in August next. Should he not accept, have the goodness to return the letter of appointment to me. J. C. C.

Copy. DNA, RG107, Military Books, vol. 11, p. 207. 1 Not found.
2 Thomas Hart Clay, who entered the United States Military Academy in July of this year but failed to qualify at the examinations the following September.

From Samuel Frothingham

Sir, Office Bank of the U S. Boston May 19. 1821.

Your letter of the 23d. ulto,[1] is received. I have collected on the order prefixed thereto Five hundred Dollars, and credited your account accordingly.—I am with much respect Sir, Your Obt st &c

Sam Frothingham, Cashr

The Honble. H. Clay, Lexington. (K)

ALS. DLC-TJC (DNA, M212, R12). Cf. above, Fuller to Clay, May 15, 1821.
1 Not found.

Receipt from Josh P. Gould, Jr.

[May 22, 1821]

Recd. New York May 22d. 1821 of the Hon. Henry Clay. the Sum of Eighty dollars, being in full for Books Sold him Recd. from J. J Astor & Sons.

$80,,00— S. Gould[1] for Josh P. Gould Jr.

[Endorsement][2]

Dear Sir, New York 22nd. May 1821

In the absence of my father I have had the honor to receive your letter of 4th. Inst.[3] addressed to him, enclosing a check for $1500 say Fifteen hundred dollars on the U S Bank at Philadelphia—80 dlls. of the amt. as you will observe by the above receipt have been paid to Mr. Gould & the balance will be applied to the payment of interest on your bond—The time you require as an extension in the payment of the interest will when requested be allowed you—My father who is now in Paris will return to this Country next summer or early in the fall when your suggestions relative to the rate of interest on your bond wi[ll] meet due attention—I am Sir, with great regard Your obdt. & humble Servt. WM. B ASTOR

To, The Honorable Henry Clay Lexington Kentucky.

ADS. DLC-TJC (DNA, M212, R12). Gould, not identified.
[1] Not identified. [2] AES. [3] Not found.

To Board of Navy Commissioners

Gent. Kentucky 29h. May 1821

Govr. Shelby,[1] his son Genl. James Shelby & their connexions Mess Nathl. and John Hart[2] intend to apply to your Board to contract for the supply of Pork and Beef for the use of the Navy at New Orleans and perhaps some other ports. Those gentlemen are all raisers of the articles respectively which they propose to furnish. And I have great pleasure in stating that they are among the most respectable & opulent of our Citizens; and that the most perfect reliance may be placed upon any contract which the above gentlemen or either of them may enter into. I have the honor to be with great respect Your obedient Servant H. CLAY

The Commissioners Of the Navy Board.

ALS. DNA, RG45, Navy Commissioners' Misc. Letters Received.
[1] Isaac Shelby. [2] John Hart, Senior.

Memorandum of Court Cases

Court of Appeals— [*ca.* June 1, 1821]

McConnell vs Brown &c. From Greenup—Appear with Mr. Haggin[1] for Appellant—Henry Daniel of Montgy is to pay me a fee of $200 if the Court reverse the Judgt. below on the point in whom the legal estate was vested on the death of Edmund Taylor[2]

John Alexr. vs John Leach[3]
Madison's Heirs vs Owens &c[4] } Appear H. Daniel to pay me

fees of $50 each for Appellants. H. CLAY

[Endorsement on verso][5]

Lampton vs Taylor &c From Clarke[6]—Spoken to by Mr. Payne[7]
Thomas ads Clarke[8]—Fee not paid

ADS. DLC-HC (DNA, M212, R6). [1] James Haggin.

[2] The case on appeal from Greenup Circuit Court related to an ejectment from certain lands patented in 1787 to the "legal representatives" of Edmund Taylor, a Virginia veteran of the Revolution, who had died in 1786. The Court of Appeals in December, 1821, reversed the decision of the lower court and remanded the case for new proceedings, based upon rulings that since Edmund Taylor had not held possession of the land at the date of his death, the provisions of his will were inapplicable; further that the "legal representatives" to whom the patent was granted were to be determined by the Virginia law of primogeniture, in effect at the date of

patent, and not by the will, which had devised Taylor's Kentucky lands to his ten children equally. 16 *Ky. Reports* (Littell, *Selected Cases*) 459-68. The parties of the suit are not fully named.

3 On appeal from Bath Circuit Court, an action on a charge of fraud in the sale of a mare. Clay represented Alexander, pioneer Kentuckian, who had been the plaintiff in the lower court. The Court of Appeals on June 9, 1821, reversed the earlier judgment, which had favored Leach (Leatch), and remanded the case for new proceedings. 10 *Ky. Reports* (3 A. K. Marshall) 503. The parties have not been further identified.

4 The suit, on appeal from Floyd Circuit Court, related to an action for ejectment brought by the heirs of the Reverend James Madison, to recover a tract claimed under a Virginia patent. The Court of Appeals in October, 1821, upheld the ruling of the lower court in favor of Owens and others (not fully named). On December 14, 1821, Clay delivered an extended plea for rehearing of the case (printed in the *Reports*), but his petition was rejected. 16 *Ky. Reports* (Littell, *Selected Cases*) 281-85.

5 AE.

6 Clay's client, James Lampton, deputy sheriff of Clark County, was appealing against a judgment in favor of Jonathan Taylor and others in an action for debt brought by Lampton in Clark Circuit Court. In October, 1821, the Court of Appeals reversed the judgment and remanded the case for new proceedings. 16 *Ky. Reports* (Littell, *Selected Cases*) 273.

7 Probably Daniel McCarty Payne.

8 Clay's client, Robert Thomas, formerly of Fayette County, had been a constable and was charged with recovery of money from Edmund Clark, also of Fayette County, under illegal replevin bonds. The Court of Appeals in June, 1822, setting aside the verdict of the Fayette Circuit Court at the March Term, 1817, ruled that no action should lie unless the bonds had been quashed. 11 *Ky. Reports* (1 Littell) 287-90; Fayette Circuit Court, File 371 (1817); Order Book Q, 194-95.

From Nicholas Berthoud

Dear Sir— Lexington June 2d. 1821—

Not having had the pleasure of Seing [*sic*] you during my Stay in this place I beg leave to hand you herewith My Account, the Balance of which I will thank you to remit me through the Kentucky Branch Bank,[1] or if more convenient You will please pay the Amount to Mr. John S. Snead for My Account—

I remain with Respect Your Most Obt. Servt. N. BERTHOUD

Henry Clay. Esqre.

[Enclosure][2]

[Debit entries on November 2,3,7,9,11, and 27, 1820, for "Carriage on Sundries from Lexington," amounting to $74.44; on March 29, 1821, for "Storage Drayage & Shipping 1 Engine,[3] $31.00; on May 3, 1821, for "Drayage Storage & forwarding 3 bbls & 3 Cases," $2.00; Postage, $1.00; "Commission on $39-16 advancd. to pay Carriage," $1.95—total debits, $158.64¼. Credit, November 6, 1820, "By Cash," $100.00. Balance due, $58.64¼.]

[Endorsement on verso][4]

Recd. the balance of the within a/c this 14h. July 1821

Jno. S. Snead
p JNO. KEATING[5]

ALS. DLC-TJC (DNA, M212, R12).
2 D. DLC-TJC (DNA, M212, R15).
4 ES, in Clay's hand.

1 Lexington Branch, Bank of Kentucky.
3 See above, II, 899.
5 A clerk, married in Cincinnati in 1826.

From Nathaniel Cox

Dear Sir, New Orleans 5. June 1821.

We have little news to detail from hence Yet that little is of quite a flattering nature for your unfortunate country. The Idea Even of a War in Europe[1] has created a demand & rise in Western cou[ntry] produce—flour was dull 2 Weeks since—2¼ to 2½$ and now in demand—3½$—This looks well—Pork is also improving a little—

The first installment of Breedlove & Cos. Debts is due and I am promised a dividend in a few days for the claim of our deceased friend Mr John Hart[2] when collected I will by some means transmit it.—For this Debt I gave Mr. Hart a draft on my brother at St Louis[3] 480$ he hearing of Breedlove & Cos failure before reachg. St. Louis had so much delicacy that the draft never was presented, it must therefore be amoing [*sic*] his papers—when found have the goodness to transmit to your Brother or myself—

Mr. John Clay showed me a late letter from you[4] relative to Mr Harts business, and some Enquiries have been made—but result in no profit I still think he must have had Goods of Some discription [*sic*] to the amount of 12 or 1500$ Either in St Louis or the Intended Scite [*sic*] for his Distillery[5]—I hope to get information on this head from my Brother now there. he has had a dreatfull [*sic*] sick family for 6 or 8 months which has heretofore prevented his attention to Even his own affairs—fearfull in this domestic calamity he may have neglected my former commns. on this subject I shall again write him particularly. I think I informed you at Washington that we had obtained an order of Court to compell your brothers Syndics to pay 10 P Cent[6]—I got the claims representing my house and I fear that is all that will Ever be got from there—Mr Livingston[7] representing what he calls a priviledged claim has got an injunction & stopping the Syndices [*sic*] from making any further payments—

Among the Creditors James Wier stands high—his claim is upwards of 6000$—when Harris[8] was here he spoke of purchasing it—This is of course with a view of pressing it in the United States Dist Court —and from the late decisions at Washington he will I think recover— In that case all others not barred by their own act in signing off will persue [*sic*] their claims I doubt not—Would it not be well to Endeavour to Soften down Mr Wier in Some way—or compromise with him on some terms or could not his own paper be purchased up at a great discount—

These are only hints not advice—and unknown to your Brother— should they prove of any use I shall be happy at having made them—& remain Very Sincerely D Sir Yr Most Ob S NATH: COX

ALS. DLC-TJC (DNA, M212, R12).

[1] See above, Toast and Response, May 19, 1821, note. The Piedmont uprising (see above, II, 863n), which had broken out in March, 1821, was promptly suppressed by action of the Austrians and Russians. Also in March, war with Russian backing had broken out against the Turks in Moldavia and the Morea, the prelude to a struggle for Greek independence which lasted until 1832.

[2] See above, II, 898.

[3] Caleb Cox, St. Louis merchant.

[4] Not found.

[5] Not located.

[6] John Clay had invoked the Louisiana bankrupt law in 1811. See below, John to Henry Clay, December 13, 1822.

[7] Edward Livingston.

[8] John Harris, Natchez and New Orleans merchant.

From Lafayette

My dear Sir Paris June 9h 1821

Permit me to Entreat Your kind Welcome and good Advice in Behalf of Mr *Pesse* and Mr. *Menardi*[1] the Later [*sic*] a [. . .][2] professor who are going to settle in the State of ohio. their partner M. La Barthe[3] is already fixed near New Athens, and there Enjoys the freedom which old Athens Now struggle [*sic*] to obtain.[4] Our Cause Has Been Unfortunate in italy.[5] But Cannot fail Ultimately to prevail. European liberty Chiefly depends on the interior politics of France. I Hope our American Newspapers take their paragraphs from the *Constitutionel,* the Courier, or at least the semi official *Moniteur* in what relates to the debates of the *Chambre of deputies*: all the other Journals make it a point to disfigure them scandalously. Where M. *Pesse* and M. *Menardi* will find You I do not know But am Sure You will Have the Goodness to give them the advices and recommendations in Your power. Most truly and Affectionately

Yours LAFAYETTE

ALS. DLC-HC (DNA, M212, R1). Addressed: "Hble Mr Clay Speaker of the House of Representatives Washington. favour'd by Messrs pesse and Menardi." Endorsed on envelope: "Cette recommandation de Mr. le Général la[Fayette] [mi]s et ne parvenue que le 10 février 1822 à Cittie de Bradford en Pensilvanie ou nous Sommes établis. Nous nous empressons de donner cours à la présente et d'y joindre la brochure que nous avons reçus et nous prions, Mr Speaker, d'agréer les Saluts respectueux Pesse et Menardi." The letter, without the endorsement, published in Colton (ed.), *Private Correspondence of Henry Clay,* 62.

[1] Neither has been identified. The manuscript at this point is defaced—the double "s" in Pesse crossed to make double "t" and the following five words deleted. Colton prints the name as "Pette"; but it appears as "Pesse" in the endorsement, and the letters are not crossed at other points in the document.

[2] Word illegible.

[3] Not identified.

[4] See above, Cox to Clay, June 5, 1821, note.

[5] Cf. above, II, 863; Cox to Clay, June 5, 1821, note.

From John Chambers

Sir Washington 10th. June 1821

When your letter of the 6th. inst.[1] reached this place I was attending the Fleming Court:[2] otherwise you would have had my Answer by the last mail.

Judgments were had at our late term in favour of M. T. Scott against Waters Sumrall, Murphy & Duke for the debts due the Farmers & Mechanics Bank[3]—Exons have not yet issued (ten days not having lapsed since the termination of the term) but will on Tuesday next I have ordered Fi: fa's and have been instructed by Mr. Scott not to make any indorsment [*sic*]. Waters has mortgaged to his securities some real estate and slaves which will probably sell for from 3 to 4000$ and I think it probable the equity of redemption will be released & the property given up to be sold the residue of the claim will have to be paid by the securities and I consider Sumrall & Murphy as perfectly safe for the whole sum, indeed the former alone is I presume good for 10000$—Our Sheriffs are safe and well disposed but not energetic.

I will with pleasure give you any further information you may wish on this subject, and regret that I could not have answered your letter "by the return Mail" as you requested.

With great respect Yours JOHN CHAMBERS.

ALS. DLC-TJC (DNA, M212, R12). Addressed to Clay at Lexington. Chambers, a Washington, Kentucky, lawyer, had been born in New Jersey and at the age of fourteen had been brought to Mason County. He had begun the practice of law in 1800, had sat in the State legislature, and during the War of 1812 had served on the staff of General William H. Harrison. He was elected to the United States House of Representatives in 1828, 1834, and 1836, was again a member of the Kentucky legislature (1830-31), and from 1841 to 1845 was Governor of the Territory of Iowa.

1 Not found. 2 Fleming County, Kentucky.

3 At the May Term, 1821, of Mason Circuit Court, Scott, Cashier of the Farmers and Mechanics' Bank of Lexington until its liquidation under act of February 10, 1820 (Ky. Gen. Assy., *Acts, 1819-1820,* pp. 908-10), had won two judgments against Richard L. Waters, Joseph K. Sumrall, Thomas M. Duke, and William Murphy, who "were solemnly called but came not." One judgment was for $3,626.19, the other for $3,570.25, with interest and costs in each case. Copies of the judgments are enclosed in the letter from Marshall Key to Clay, June 26, 1821. Sumrall, born in Scotland, had been brought to Pittsburgh as a child, had embarked on mercantile business at Philadelphia, and subsequently had transferred his operations to Maysville, Kentucky. Murphy, a veteran of the War of 1812, was postmaster at Washington, Kentucky, and, later, at Maysville. Waters, also, was a resident of Mason County; Duke has not been further identified.

To Langdon Cheves

Sir Lexington 11h. June 1821

I have just received your letter of the 28h. Uto.[1] [*sic*] covering the deposition for the Ohio case, which appears to be now taken in due form.[2]

We have just closed a most fatiguing term of the Federal Court of five weeks duration, in the course of which many causes of the Bank were tried, and many questions raised in them. I have the satisfaction to tell you that we did not lose a single contested point. And I have the pleasure further to add that our Court of Appeals (the Court of dernier resort in the State Judiciary) before which I argued last fall the appeal of the Bank from the decision of one of our inferior Courts, by which the right of the Bank to acquire promissory notes by assignment was denied, has within a few days past given in its opinion, reversing that decision, and affirming the right of the Bank, in the broadest terms, to purchase promissory notes.[3] I think the Bank may now confidently rely upon obtaining from the Superior Courts in this State the same justice that is measured out to other litigants.

I was embarrassed, during the term of the Federal Court, to know what disposition to make of the cases agt. Col. R. M. Johnson & his connexions,[4] as I have not received one line from Philadelphia of direct communication upon that subject. However as I had learnt, through indirect channels, that an arrangement had been made at Philadelphia with the Col., the execution of which was to take place in Kentucky; and as he informed me that he was ready to proceed upon its execution; I thought it best that the cases should be continued. Indeed the Court itself would, if appealed to, under the circumstances, have directed their continuance. I have apprehended that there has been some misunderstanding in regard to that subject. My opinion is that the sooner the arrangement is completed the better for the Bank.

I am, with great respect, Your obedient Servant H. CLAY

Langdon Cheeves [*sic*] Esqr. &c &c &c

ALS. PHi-Etting Collection. 1 Not found.

2 See above, Clay to Cheves, May 5, 1821. 3 See above, II, 901n.

4 James Johnson's financial difficulties growing out of the Yellowstone Expedition (see above, II, 599n) embroiled Richard M. Johnson and other family connections, his sureties (above, II, 605), in extensive litigation during the years 1820-1826.

On June 1, 1820, James and Richard M. Johnson and Uriel Sebree, partners in the Lexington mercantile firm of Sebree and Johnsons, with John T. Mason and John Fowler had signed a mortgage deed to the officers of the Bank of the United States, covering fourteen parcels of property in and around Lexington, as security for a debt of $50,000 at the Lexington office of discount and deposit. The instrument also pledged this property as a supplemental guarantee for a debt of Richard Johnson "and others Joined with him" amounting to $400,000 and interest from April 23, 1819, at the Philadelphia office of the Bank, and a further obligation of $164,469.13 at the Baltimore branch. On September 11, 1820, and again on September 22, 1821, the two Johnsons pledged two lots in Georgetown, Kentucky, and additional Lexington property as security for another $25,000. Surrender of the Georgetown property to the Bank was provided for in an arrangement during the fall of 1821 and relinquishment of the Lexington tracts was included as part of a general settlement of the Johnsons with the Bank in 1824. Fayette County, Deed Book T, 515-24; U, 520-23; Z, 225-27; Scott County, Deed Book E, 7-9, 58-60; below, Clay to Cheves, October 3, December 3, 1821; Clay to Biddle, December 31, 1823.

From William DuVal

Dear Sir, Virginia Buckingham June 14th. 1821.

Our old Friend Chancellor Wythe[1] & myself discovered in you when Young a Capacity that would make you an Ornament to your

Country—. I had your Grand Father Hudson & your Father[2] as my Friends, whose Virtues endeared them to me, & my Esteem & affection naturally extended to the Son of your Father.—

I observed that the supreme Federal Court decided in the Case of Green v Biddle that two laws of Kentucky were unconstitutional. 1st. the occupant Law.

2d the Law which allows the first Settler for lasting or permanent Improvements, when evicted by the Claimant. That on your motion the Court suspended the entrying of their Judgment untill next Term[3]—I have examined the Laws of Virg[inia] from 1619 to 1819—9 [*sic*] Volumns [*sic*]—We had so early as 1642 an Occupant Law Five Years quiet possession vested the Right in the possessor, which Law continued to be in Force un till [*sic*] 1705 when it was Repealed in 4th of Queen Anne, which extended the Claimants Right to 30 Years before he was bared [*sic*] by the Act of Limitation —see 1 Vol: page 260- & 443. 452 [*sic*]. 321 [*sic*]. Statutes at Large.[4]

Statute 1 Vol. Page 260. passed in 1642 allows for permanent improvements, to be valued by 12 Jurors; if the Plt does not choose to pay for the Improvements, The Deft is to keep the Land on paying the value, to be ascertained by a Jury, before the Settlement

do. 2 Vols Page 96 same continued with amendments[5]—It does not appear that the Remuneration Law, I call it, has ever been repealed untill about 3 Years ago. that all Laws of a public Nature which are not included in the last Revisal of the Laws of Virginia, were repealed—Mr William W. Henning who published the Statutes at Large, under the patronage of our Legislature, & myself, are of Opinion that the Law by mistake was pretermited. All our Laws were in Manuscrip [*sic*] untill about the Year 1733. Purvis[6] was the First Printer.

I think it equitable, that when a man settles [. . .] to which he supposes he has a Title, and make[s . . . improve]ments thereon, that the Claimant ought to be al[lowed . . .] permant [*sic*] Improvements. Why should a man imp [. . .] to the amount of 4,000 $ on a tract not worth [. . .] & the Claimant to have the entire benefit of [. . .] Labour, without Compensation to the Settler?

I am inclined to think your Occupant Law is [. . .] to the Compact between Virga. & Kentucky, [. . .] It appears to me that the other Law altho [. . .] was unrepealed at the time of the said Comp[act . . .] The Laws 7 Vol. Mr Harden[7] has; Mr Wirt[8] has them also. I have the Statutes at large from 1619 to 1763. Also the Revised code contains 2 Vol:

If you would call on me I should be happy to see you—I don't mean to tell any one the Contents of this Letter. You have rendered such faithful Services to your Country, at Ghent, in the Missouri Question & have showed such a laudible Zeal for Kentucky Rights that if any benefit or light can be given you, I wish the Credit to be yours—I am in my 73d Year. I emancipated my Slaves 20 Years ago —I work from 5 to 8 Hours a day, & have one among the neatest Farms in the County. Three Lads & a tradman [*sic*] of mine work it. I have paid including Interest & Cost more than Two hundred Thousand Dollars by Securityships and the failures of others, but I never was happier. I walk frequently Seven Miles to & from Meet[ing.] We make a plenty to eat & some thing to spare. To fear God & keep his Commandments, give that Peace which the World can not give, nor take away.

May the Lord who made heaven and Earth bless you & your Family, is the sincere prayer of your most Obedient Friend

WILLIAM DUVAL

ALS. DLC-HC (DNA, M212, R1). MS. torn; piece missing. DuVal (Duvall), the father of William Pope and Samuel P. DuVal, was a Richmond, Virginia, lawyer.

1 George Wythe.

2 George Hudson, of Hanover County, Virginia; John Clay, Sr.

3 The case of the heirs of John Green against Richard Biddle, tenant, for the recovery of certain lands in Kentucky, had been first argued before the United States Supreme Court in February, 1821. In its preliminary decision, rendered March 5, the Court had ruled that the Kentucky statutes—both the occupying claimant law of February 27, 1797 (Littell [comp.], *Statute Law of Kentucky,* I, 642), which, up to the date of institution of suit for adverse title, allowed an occupant compensation for improvements and exempted him from liability for waste committed or profits received on lands entered peaceably and occupied under "a plain and connected title, in law or equity, deduced from some record," and the amendment of January 31, 1812 (*ibid.,* IV, 346), which shifted the effective date to that of the notice of adverse judgment and provided that in no case might the holder of a superior title recover more than five years' payment for rent, waste, and damages against such an occupant —violated the Enabling Act, or Virginia Compact of 1789 (Hening [comp.], *Statutes of Virginia,* XIII, 17-21, December 18, 1789), governing the separation of Kentucky from Virginia. In particular, the laws were held to have controverted the clause which stated "that all private rights, and interests of lands" within Kentucky "derived from the laws of Virginia prior to such separation, shall remain valid and secure under the laws of the proposed State, and shall be determined by the laws now existing in this State [Virginia]." On March 12, Clay, in the role of *amicus curiae,* had moved for a rehearing on the grounds that Biddle's side of the cause had been unrepresented by counsel or argument and that the effect of the decision involved many Kentucky residents who had been allowed indemnities for improvements on lands which had been reclaimed by rightful owners. The Court had accordingly granted that final decision should be withheld pending argument at the next term. 21 *U.S.* (8 Wheaton) 1-18 (1823). See below, Clay and Bibb to Kentucky General Assembly, *ca.* May 13, 1822; Clay to Brooke, March 9, 1823.

4 Hening (comp.), *Statutes of Virginia,* I, 260, 443, 451, 331 (March, 1642-3; March, 1657-8· *ibid.;* October, 1646, resp.).

5 *Ibid.,* II, 96 (March, 1661-2).

6 John Purvis, a merchant-captain long in the Virginia-London trade, had carried the laws of Virginia to London for publication between 1684 and 1687, the work appearing without date, with the printer's identification as "T. J. for J. P." Hening (comp.), *Statutes of Virginia,* I, v.

7 Benjamin Hardin, who had acted as one of the attorneys for Green.

8 William Wirt.

Assignment from William S. Dallam

[June 15, 1821]

For value received I assign the within to Henry Clay this 15th June 1821 WILL S DALLAM

AES. Franklin Circuit Court, File 296. On verso of a promissory note for $200, dated April 18, 1817, from Jacob Creath to Dallam. Cf. above, Receipt, April 6, 1821. Endorsement indicates that a judgment on this note was confirmed in July, 1821.

Power of Attorney to Robert Snell

[June 16, 1821]

[Henry Clay and Isham Talbot, owners in joint right of a tract of 1500 acres in Scott County, patented to Henry Watkins,[1] which interferes with part of a survey held by Owen Owens,[2] hereby appoint Robert Snell, of Scott County, to settle the interfering claims by division in such portions as he may in his discretion deem proper. Signatures witnessed by one Coones[3] on the above date.]

Scott County Court, Deed Book F, 504. Recorded copy partially destroyed.

1 See above, I, 577-78n.

2 Who resided in Scott County.

3 Initial of first name not clear—probably F. or T. Both Frederick (a Revolutionary veteran) and Thomas Coons were residents of northern Fayette County.

Property Deed to Owen Owens

[June 17, 1821]

[Henry Clay and Isham Talbot, as joint owners of the following land claimed under patent of Henry Watkins in Scott County on the waters of Miller's Run,[1] within the patent calls also of Noel,[2] release unto Owen Owens for the sum of one dollar, paid and acknowledged, all claim to 18¾ acres, more or less, beginning at a stake on the Cynthiana road where Charles Whitaker's[3] old line, now Joseph Ewing's,[4] crosses the road, and extending in the direction of properties of Harroway Owens[5] and Eastin,[6] now Warren,[7] thence along the middle of the Cynthiana road to the beginning. Title guaranteed only against claimants under Clay or Talbot. Signed by Robert Snell for Clay and Talbot and recorded on the above date.]

Scott County Court, Deed Book F, 503-504. Recorded copy partially destroyed. See above, Power of Attorney, June 16, 1821.

1 Which rises near the village of Oxford, Scott County, and flows into Elkhorn Creek.

2 First name missing.

3 Pioneer settler and land locator in the Georgetown area of Scott County; removed to Shelby County by 1800.

4 Who resided in Scott County.

5 Of Scott County.

6 First name missing.

7 Probably William Warren.

Property Deed from Owen Owens

[June 19, 1821]

[For the sum of one dollar, paid and acknowledged, Owen Owens conveys to Henry Clay and Isham Talbot a tract of 14 acres, 2 roods, and 14 poles in Scott County on the waters of Miller's Run, being part that interferes with the patent calls of Henry Watkins, beginning at a stake on Noel and Watkins' old line, now Ewing's,[1] thence ultimately[2] to the Cynthiana road and along it to the intersection with Charles Whitaker's line. Title guaranteed only against claimants under Owens. Signature witnessed by Louden Snell, Garrett Snell, and Willis West;[3] deed recorded on the above date.]

Scott County Court, Deed Book F, 504-505. Recorded copy partially destroyed. See above, Power of Attorney, June 16, 1821.

1 Noel's first name missing; Henry Watkins; Joseph Ewing.

2 Boundary calls missing.

3 Louden Snell, of Scott County; Garrett Snell and West, not identified.

From Peyton Short

Dear Sir, Lexington June 20h. 1821

A short time after my last conference with you on the subject of Wilkenson's vexatious business, a motion was made by my Attorney for setting aside the answer of said Wilkenson—which motion was over-ruled by the Court.[1]

As I now foresee a long, vexatious & expensive litigation, I beg leave to avail myself of your kind & friendly offer of mediation between the opposite party & myself; provided the subject is entirely without the control of Genl. Wilkenson—With him I am disposed to hold no communication in any shape whatever—for to his *baleful touch,* in my early days, I owe nearly all the misfortunes of my subsequent life.

I observed, from your conversation on this subject, last evening, that you had made yourself acquainted with the history of this unfortunate business, that, in order to secure the payment of the balance of a much larger debt, you were apprized that a mortgage had been given me on certain lands lying on Slate & Licking rivers; and that these lands, after a lapse of many years, had been sold at twelve months credit, in order to foreclose the said mortgage. A small part of these lands were purchased by indifferent persons—the residue by Mr. James Hughes as Attorney in my behalf.—The whole of the transaction, from the execution of the mortgage to the sale of the lands by the Commissioners, had been confidently intrusted to the integrity & abilities of Mr. Hughes. I do not recollect ever to have seen the mortgage; and I am sure I never attended Court, a single term, whilst the Suit was before them. Trusting that they well knew their business, and that Wilkenson's title to the lands in question, had been fairly vested in me, I proceeded to sell a part of those, which had been purchased in my name.—After selling about 2000 Acres, discovering that there were some difficulties as to Wilkenson's title, I discontinued my sales, and have since, rather than be involved in an expensive law suit, refunded more than 2000$ (int: included) on a part of those lands, the titles to which were represented as the most questionable. This I did without the compulsion of Law—and am therefore unable to say whether Wilkenson or the adverse parties held the better tittle [*sic*].

Now the proposition, which, through you, I feel disposed to make, is this—If the gentlemen claiming these lands through Wilkenson, will refund to me the money, which I have paid back as aforesaid in specie or current money at the par of exchange & confirm the unrecorded Sales I have made, I will give a quit-claim deed to all the residue, amounting to about 10,000 Acres, independent of one fourth part of the lands purchased in my name, to which James Hughes was entitled for his services. As to the few purchases made by others on their own Acct. at the aforesaid Sales, feeling no other interest in their situation than every honest man ought to feel at the contemplation of injured justice, I have a right to say nothing on that head.—

Col: James Morrison & Genl: Fletcher[2] are said to have the management of this unpleasant affair. Should you be able to effect a compromize [*sic*] on the foregoing terms, *with those gentlemen,* or whoever else may have it in their hands, you would confer a lasting obligation on Dr Sir,— Your Obt. Sert, PEYTON SHORT.

Henry Clay Esquire

Since writing the within I have laid my hand upon an Acct. of Sales of the within mentioned lands as made by my Agent.—which I herein enclose.— *P.S* Should a Compromise be made on the terms suggested in this Communication I shall expect the adverse party to pay all Costs subsequent to the opening of the subject by them, including my two Lawyers fees.

ALS. DLC-TJC (DNA, M212, R12).

1 Short had been in partnership with James Wilkinson, 1789-1791, in a venture to sell tobacco on commission for Kentucky farmers shipping to New Orleans and to operate a store in Frankfort, Kentucky, as an outlet for goods brought upstream. When the project failed, settlement of their account had left Wilkinson in debt to Short for several thousand dollars. For this sum Wilkinson had executed a mortgage covering extensive acreage on the Licking River and its branches in Bath County, Kentucky. By decree of the District Court at Lexington in July, 1798, the land had been sold: but, at the rate accepted by the commissioners of the Court, a sum of over one thousand pounds yet remained due from Wilkinson to Short.

In a statement to the court, dated June 22, 1821, Short maintained that he had supposed the suit terminated at this time. Wilkinson, however, in 1805 had filed a bill of exceptions, arguing that he had received no notice of the earlier litigation and that the value of the pledged land was more than adequate to cover the debt. In 1811 Wilkinson's plea of *nil debet* on the basis of full payment, argued before the Federal Court for the District of Columbia, had been rejected under the Constitutional injunction that "full faith and credit" must be accorded to the judicial proceedings of the States. Meanwhile the case had been continued on the docket of the Fayette Circuit Court until 1817, when one of the purchasers under the sale of 1798 had petitioned for survey and conveyance of the property. In September, 1819, the deed for that tract had been approved and recorded, but in 1820 the Court had again appointed commissioners to appraise the mortgaged lands. James Hughes, Short's lawyer, having died in the interim, Short had apparently known nothing of the reopening of the case. His interest had been protected at the February Term, 1821, when James Haggin, who had taken over Hughes' business, petitioned for a continuance to permit him to consult Short. In March, 1822, upon Short's petition, the case was finally stricken from the docket. James Ripley Jacobs, *Tarnished Warrior* (New York, 1938), 99, 127-28, 147; 22 *Fed. Cas.* 15-16 (1811); Fayette Circuit Court, File 523 (1822); Fayette Circuit Court, Order Book Y (February 4-October 5, 1822), 22, 235, 303.

2 Thomas Fletcher, of Bath County, a militia officer in the early Indian campaigns and repeatedly a Representative in the Kentucky General Assembly.

Receipt from James W. Palmer

Lexington, June 22. 1821.

Received of H Clay Six dollars for one years Subscription to the Lexington Athenaeum ending May 1. 1821.

$6— JAS. W. PALMER, treasr.

ADS. DLC-TJC (DNA, M212, R15).

From John Chambers

Dear Sir Washington 25th. June 1821

Since the receipt of your letter of the 19th. inst.[1] I have not been able to see the Deputy Sheff in whose hands the fi:fa's in the name of Scott against Waters & others were placed[2] and am now just leaving home for Nicholas Court,[3] but will leave this to be forwarded with a schedule of the property taken in Exon as soon as it can be obtained together with the time at which the sale is to take place. I am inclined to believe that no other property will be sold than that Morgaged [*sic*] by Waters to the others and that the ballance [*sic*] of the debt will be replevied; I will see that the replevy bond includes all the defts.

Query as to the propriety of the sale of the Mortgaged property without a release of the Mortgage or of the equity of redemption: neither of which I am told has yet been given.

The idea which strikes me is that as the title of Waters is only an aquitable [*sic*] one and consequently not subject to Exon, and the legal estate of the Mortgagees subject to be defeated by a redemption, there may be a doubt at least whether the purchaser can acquire a title and consequently of the legality of the sale.

I shall leave instructions for Mr Boulton[4] the dy Sheff to extend his seizure of property if as I am told he has taken no other than the Mortgaged property— respectfully Yours JOHN CHAMBERS

Henry Clay Esqr.

ALS. DLC-TJC (DNA, M212, R12). 1 Not found.

2 See above, Chambers to Clay, June 10, 1821.

3 Nicholas County, Kentucky. 4 Possibly Rice Boulton.

Receipt from Barnaby Worland

Lexington June 25. 1821.

[Worland acknowledges receipt from Clay of $11.25, "the town tax Charged to the heirs of Thos. Hart Snr for the preasent [*sic*] year."]

ADS. DLC-TJC (DNA, M212, R15).

From Marshall Key

H. Clay Esq. Washington 26th June 1821

Sir

Yours of 18th. Instant[1] covering an assignment of two Judgments came to hand on Yesterday, the transfer is filed among the papers, on the preceeding [*sic*] page you have Copies of the Judgments with the amount of Costs,[2] Executions issued some time since (without endorsement) and have been levied as the sheriff informs me, on Waters' property and it will be sold on a credit of two years; the debts I Consider as perfectly secure— Accept my best wishes for your heath [*sic*] & happiness MARSHALL KEY.

ALS. DLC-TJC (DNA, M212, R12). Key, at this time Clerk of the Circuit Court of Mason County, Kentucky, later (1842-1847) served several terms in the Kentucky legislature.

1 Not found.

2 Copies by Key. See above, John Chambers to Clay, June 10, 1821, note. The assignment may have been made to John L. Martin, at this time proprietor of an Exchange Office in Lexington. Cf. below, Chambers to Clay, June 23, 1823.

Account with Nathan Burrowes

May 10th 1821 [*ca.* June 27, 1821]

	Nathen [*sic*] Burrowes to Henry Clay	Dr
	To 1 Bolting Reele	12.00
May 20	To 4 yars [*sic*] of old Bolting Cloth at 12/	8 00
	To 112 Feet of planke	2 24
		$ 22.24
June 27.	To 4 ½ yard [*sic*] of Bolting Cloth—	9 00
	JACOB MCCONATHY	$ 31 24

[Endorsement on verso][1]

Pay to Mr H. Clay or order in shoes & boots Nineteen dollars & 24 Cents in addition to the order heretofore given[2] for value received.

Thomas Gibbons[3] 28h. June 1821. N BURROWES

ADS. DLC-TJC (DNA, M212, R15). Burrowes was a Lexington inventor, manufacturer, and merchant.

1 Es, in Clay's hand. 2 Not found. 3 Of Fayette County.

Account with Benijah Bosworth

[*ca.* June 27, 1821]

[Entries on account of "Benijah Bosworth To Henry Clay Dr.," dated May, 1821, and May 17, include such items as "1 hoper Boy and Shafte," "1 Bolting Reele Shafte & head," "4 Bolting heads & 2 Shaftes," "1 allevater head," "old Fan," "Paten Ballen Scale," "1 Scriu to Rose mill Stone," plank, scantling, iron, boxes, butt hinges, and "pullies." The total charge is $220.08½, from which is deducted "for Whiskey & Shad" $45.12½,[1] leaving a balance due stated as $175.00.]

D. DLC-TJC (DNA, M212, R10). A second page contains a duplicate of Clay's account with Nathan Burrowes, above, *ca.* June 27, 1821. Endorsed by Clay: "Bosworth to H. Clay Amot. of his a/c. rendered by Mr. McConothy." Endorsed also: "The within a/c. settled by Careys note and Mr Bosworths own note for $84 which when paid is in full HC." Carey has not been identified.

1 Cf. above, Bill, May 17, 1821.

Order from Nathan Burrowes

[June 28, 1821]

Attached to Account, *ca.* June 27, 1821.

Memorandum and Receipt from Thomas P. Hart

29 June 1821.

I have this day settled with H. Clay the amount expended by him in repairs on the fences, steps &c. on the lots which he now occupies in Lexington rented of my mother[1] and me by him, and I find the said amount to be one hundred dollars which is to be taken out of the two first years rent in equal proportions.

[Endorsement][2] THOMAS P HART

Received of H. Clay one hundred & seventy five dollars being two quarters rent up to the 20h. July 1821 due on a/c. of the house & lots occupied by him now in Lexn. after deducting twenty five dollars on a/c. of repairs 29 June 1821 THOMAS P HART

DS, in Clay's hand. KyU-Wilson Collection.

1 Eleanor Grosh Hart. The property was probably that located above, II, 313n.

2 ES, in Clay's hand.

From William Murphy

H Clay Esqr Washington Ky July 3 1821

D Sir

Yours of the 23d Ulto.[1] was duly recd— Contents noted. The other Gentlemen concerned with me in the debt of *waters*[2] are much Oblige [*sic*] to you for your offer of further time— But Our Intention is to make the money for you as soon as possible— *Waters* has appeared to be Honest, so far in the transaction of this Affair. & I had until very lately anticipated that he would have had it in his power to have paid this debt without injuring his Securities But now I think the thing very doubtfull—he has given up to the executors abt. 96 acres of good land with excellent improvements thereon. (& would three years ago would [*sic*] have paid the debt itself) also seven negroes one man & one woman the Balance are five young negroes from the age of 15 down to 3 or 4 years Old— The sale is to be on the 16th Jul. and should be glad to see you here on that day; probably if you were present some arrange [*sic*] might be made with Waters' friends to pay you Sooner than the law would give it you—How we will succeed in makeing [*sic*] the payt. you have proposed, is a question I can not satisfactorally answer until after the sale—But you may rest assured its my wish & also that of my Co securities to have this debt paid as soon as possible—will you be so Oblidging as drop [*sic*] me a line informing me whether it will be in your power to attend on the day of sale, the sale is to be continued from day to day until all the property is sold—therefore perhaps if you could not be here on the 16th. you might on 17th.

I am D Sr Respectfully yours W. MURPHY

ALS. DLC-TJC (DNA, M212, R12). 1 Not found.
2 See above, John Chambers to Clay, June 10, 1821.

To J[osiah] Meigs

Dr. Sir Lexington 6h. July 1821

The inclosed survey, belonging to my neighbour and friend Mr. Clarke, is transmitted to you for the purpose of procuring a patent, which I will thank you to send to him or to me as soon as convenient.

I have to thank you for the Tables which you sent me. They are very useful, and I have deposited some of them in the University[1] where they will be ve[ry] serviceable.

You will hear, with satisfaction, that the Madrid Apricot which you gave me when I parted with you at Washington, is growing finely. I hope to treat you some day with fruit of its produce—

With great regard I am faithfy Yrs H. CLAY

J. Meigs Esq. &c &c &c

ALS. DNA, RG49, Letterbook, 1821, Misc. Letters Received, Series C. Addressed to Meigs, "Commr. of the L. Office Washington City." Endorsed: "H. Clay relative to Pat for G. Clarke [George Clark]."
1 Transylvania University.

To Langdon Cheves

Sir Lexington 8h. July 1821

I received your letter of the 22d. Ulto.[1] in due course of the mail. Prior to the reception of it I had addressed a letter[2] on the subject of it to the agents of the B. U.S. at Cincinnati in which I advised them 1st. to notify all persons whose debts had been transfered by the Miami Ex. Co. by way of security for the debt due to the B. U.S. of the fact of that transfer; and the consequent expectation of payment being made to the Agents &c. And as, if suit should be delayed, or credit should be given to those persons, by the B. U.S. the Miami Co. might assert a claim for the amount, if the debtors proved insolvent I advised 2dly. That an understanding should be had with that Co. on the subject of bringing suit &c.

On the point whether the debts which have been transfered can be extinguished, after notice of the transfer, by payment on the part of the debtors in the notes of the M. E. Co. acquired subsequently to such notice? nothing can be clearer than that it cannot be done on general principles. It could not be done, on those principles, even where the assignment vested only an equitable right to the contents of the paper assigned, and the assignee was bound to employ the name of the assignor to recover those contents. In intimating the opinion that it could be done, I presume the Agents were governed by an act of the State of Ohio, passed in 1820, regulating judicial proceedings in cases where Banks and Bankers are parties &c.[3] That act is not free from ambiguity on the point; but I think it admits of an interpretation compatible with the rights of the assignee and the justice which belongs to him. I am not yet advised what has been the construction given to it by the local tribunals; but I think they cannot have adopted that which it appears to me would be manifestly unjust, if not unconstitutional.

I have not yet received any communication from you respecting the arrangement which is understood to have been made at Philada. with Col. R. M. Johnson. I must repeat that I think any further delay in the execution of it will be prejudicial to the Bank. Judgments have been recovered against him & his connexions[4] and it is to be apprehended that liens may be acquired by other Creditors, on their property, which may obstruct their fulfillment of the agreement. I have the honor to be with great respect Your obedient Servant H. CLAY

L. Cheves Esqr. P. B. U.S.

P.S. I have again written to the Agents repeating the advice formerly given, and recommending further that they ascertain from the debtors, whose debts have been assigned whether they have any offsets, and to offer to receve [*sic*] any notes of the M. E. Co.[5] which they acquired before notice, and which they have ever since *retained*.

HC.

ALS. ScHi. [1] Not found. [2] Not found.

[3] The statute carried a proviso stating: "That in all suits or actions prosecuted by a bank or banker, or persons claiming as their assignees, or under them in any way for their use or benefit, the sheriff upon any execution in his hands, in favor of such bank or banker, their or his assignee as aforesaid, shall receive the note or notes of such bank or banker from the defendant, in discharge of the judgment"; and if the bank or banker, or assignee, "refuse to receive such note from the sheriff, the sheriff shall not be liable to any proceedings whatever, at the suit or upon the complaint of the bank or banker, their or his assignee as aforesaid." Ohio Gen. Assy., *Acts (General), 1819-1820,* p. 159 (February 18, 1820).

[4] See above, Clay to Cheves, June 11, 1821. [5] Miami Exporting Company.

Bond for James Morrison

[July 9, 1821]

[James Morrison, Richard Hawes, Jr., and Henry Clay sign a bond to the Commonwealth of Kentucky in the sum of $40,000 to assure "just and true" performance by Morrison as administrator of "goods, chattels and credits of Wilson Cary Nicholas deceased."[1] Should it hereafter appear that Nicholas left a will, and should Morrison in consequence be required to give up his letters of administration, this bond is to be void, "else to remain in full force and virtue." Signatures witnessed by J. C. Rodes, Clerk, Fayette County Court.]

DS. Fayette County Administrators' Bonds, no. 1 (1817-23), p. 132.

[1] Nicholas had died October 10, 1820.

From William Murphy

H Clay Esqr. Washington Ky July 10th 1821

D Sir

Yours of the 6th Jul.[1] is before me, and in answer to your enquiries will state to you that the sale is to take place at Minerva the seat of Mr Waters—[2] the negroes are all One family— Both land & negroes are unimcumbered except the Mortgage given to *Simeral* [*sic*], *Duke,* & *myself* for the purpose of secureing [*sic*] to us the property in Case he failed to meet the payt. of the notes due to M Scott &c.[3] Both land & negroes are given up Specially to pay those executions—

Will you be in Washington on Sunday evening next?

Yours very Respectfully W. MURPHY

ALS. DLC-TJC (DNA, M212, R12).

[1] Not found.

[2] Richard L. Waters. Minerva is located northwest of Maysville, in Mason County, Kentucky.

[3] See above, John Chambers to Clay, June 10, 25, 1821; Murphy to Clay, July 3, 1821.

From James Smith, Jr.

Esteemed Friend Philada. July 11h. 1821

Robert Ewing a partner of Saml Longsteth [*sic*][1] called on me a few days since, and says that, the ballance [*sic*] due from Woodson Wren can be had, if an allowance of £17.18/- which he claims as an Error in their Accot—will be made— It is now so long since the goods were sold that I cannot recollect such an error,[2] but nevertheless it will be best to allow it in order to get the ballance and have the account settled— He left word for me to write to you on the subject—and to say that Wodson [*sic*] Wren resides at Natchez— Will you be so good as to endeavour to get this ballance whatever it may be—

I received your favour of 2d. April[3] which should have been answered long since could I have made up my mind what to say to Mr Underwood—[4] I cannot see the necessity of a Power of Attorney— If he thinks the money can be recovered—he is my Attorney under you of course—& I wish him to get the money if possible— The fact is that his letter is written with such very bad Ink, that it is almost impossible to read it— I wish you to say to him, (if it is in your opinion likely the money can be had) to go on with the suit without delay—

I am very respectfully Yr Friend JAS SMITH JR

ALS. DLC-TJC (DNA, M212, R12). Addressed to Clay at Lexington; forwarded to Frankfort on July 25.

1 Ewing and Longstreth, merchants of Philadelphia.

2 See above, II, 228.

3 Not found.

4 Probably Joseph Rogers Underwood, born in Goochland County, Virginia, but as a child moved to Barren County, Kentucky. He had been graduated from Transylvania University in 1811, had studied law in Lexington, and, after being seriously wounded and captured at Dudley's Defeat in May, 1813, had completed his legal training the next autumn. He had then settled in Glasgow, Kentucky, and embarked upon a brilliant career as lawyer, jurist, and legislator. He represented Barren County in the State Assembly, 1816-1819; Warren County (after his removal to Bowling Green in 1823), 1825 and 1826, 1845, 1860-1863. He served as a judge of the Kentucky Court of Appeals, 1828-1835; member of the United States House of Representatives, 1835-1843; and member of the Senate, 1847-1853. He was an ardent Whig and a Clay supporter, serving as elector in the presidential campaigns of 1824 and 1844.

Receipted Bill from Hugh Foster

Henry Clay Esqr Dr to Hugh Foster July 14. 1821.

1821		
Aprile [*sic*] 21	To Making blue Coat son Theodore	6 50
	pad and stays	1 12½
	Sleave linnings [*sic*] and pockets	1 00
	Silk twist and thread	" 75
	one set of best gilt buttons	1 50

Making Coat son Thos	$ 6 - 50	
one set of fancy buttons	2 - 00	
pad and stays	1 - 12½	
Sleave linnings and pockets	1 - 00	
Silk twist and thread	0 - 75	
Cutting overalls son Thos	0 - 50	11 87½
		$ 22 75

Recvd payment HUGH FOSTER.

ADS. DLC-TJC (DNA, M212, R15).

To Langdon Cheves

My dear Sir Lexington 21 July 1821.

I duly received your favor of the 28h. Uto.[1] [*sic*] transmitting to me a Copy of your letter to Judge McLean.[2] With respect to the News paper paragraph, the occasion of your letter, I did not see it until some time after its publication, and then without any particular emotion.[3] I was quite sure that it was unauthorized by any thing you had said or written. Indeed it is just as probable that it may have originated from what fell from me, as I have had no hesitation in avowing, without reserve, the advice which I felt it my duty to give to the Bank. Altho' it was unnecessary for you to have taken the trouble which you have done to send me the Copy of your letter to Judge Mc. I thank you for the friendly sentiment which induced you to do it.

I have been placed in somewhat an embarrassing situation by the business of Col. R. M. Johnson with the Bank. I yielded, with some reluctance, my consent to superintend, on the part of the Bank, the execution of the arrangement which he had made with it. This reluctance proceeded from an apprehension that he might entertain the opinion of a favorable disposition towards him, on my part, which I could not indulge; and, on the other hand, from a fear that the Bank itself might suppose that such a disposition had been exercised, if its expectations should not be realized. Nevertheless, with a firm determination to discharge my duty, I gave that consent. I have not received one line of direct communication from you or from your board, altho' I have mentioned the subject in letters both to you and to Mr. Wilson.[4] In the mean time I have been urged by Col. Johnson to proceed in the execution of the arrangement upon the strength of letters addressed to him and to the office here. I said to him, some weeks ago, that I would proceed provisionally in the business, so far as to make selections of property, have it valued &c preparatory to the final adjustment. When I said so to him, I was in expectation of receiving by every subsequent mail a communication from you directly. No such communication having arrived, I believe

I shall decline doing any thing until I hear from you. For it appears to me to be entirely irregular that I should act upon letters addressed to others. In the mean time I fear his affairs are not improving, if they are not growing worse; and that, as I have already intimated to you, delay may be highly prejudicial to the Bank. I need not say, what I am sure you will be sensible of, that it will be very agreeable to me to be rid of the business.

I attended a sale of property yesterday under execution to prevent injury to the Bank which held a subsequent lien upon it.[5] The sale was so productive as to leave a residuum, free from any competing incumbrance, entirely sufficient to secure a debt of $3500 due to the office here. This was owing to the sale being dischargeable in Commonwealth Bank notes, their depretiation having produced the ordinary effect of an appretiation in the nominal value of property.

With great regard I am faithfully Your's H. CLAY

Langdon Cheves Esqr.

ALS. ScHi. 1 Not found.

2 John McLean, born in New Jersey but resident in Nicholasville and Maysville, Kentucky, prior to settlement of the family in Lebanon, Ohio, in 1793. He had studied law in Cincinnati, had been admitted to the bar in 1807, and had then embarked upon a political career as the founder of the Lebanon *Western Star*. He had served in the United States House of Representatives, 1812-1816, whence he had resigned to become Judge of the Superior Court of Ohio. He was appointed successively Commissioner of the General Land Office in 1822, Postmaster General, 1823-1829, and Associate Justice of the United States Supreme Court, 1829-1861.

3 On June 27, 1821, the Washington *Daily National Intelligencer* had reprinted a paragraph from the *Liberty Hall and Cincinnati Gazette* asserting "that the rash, impolitic, and barbarous step of indiscriminately suing all the debtors to the Branch Bank of Cincinnati, was brought about by this personage [Clay], or ordered by the mother board at his instance, contrary to the opinion of the cashier, Mr. Wilson. . . ." The writer suggested that "the injured parties, cut off as they are from other redress, would seem *justified, whenever in their power, to remunerate the author of this mischief with a coat of Tar and Feathers*!"

4 See above, Clay to Cheves, June 11, July 8, 1821; no letter from Clay to Thomas Wilson has been found.

5 Notice of the execution sale has not been found. James B. January, who had previously, in April, 1820, mortgaged a number of slaves and two lots on Wilkins Street, Lexington, to Thomas January, on May 3, 1821, had executed a mortgage deed for this property to the President and Directors of the Bank of the United States —subject to redemption if his debt of $3,515 and interest charges were paid by the following November 1. Thomas January in the mortgage deed had relinquished his right and title to the property. Fayette County Court, Deed Book T, 399; U, 325.

To John Quincy Adams

Sir Louisville (K) 2d. Aug. 1821.

I presume that the line between us and the possessions of Spain which lye [*sic*] on the South of us will be run in conformity to the late Treaty;[1] and that arrangements for that purpose will be shortly made. The Government will most probably avail itself of that occasion to ascertain the natural productions &c. of the Country. Should it think proper to adopt measures for that object, I have great pleasure in recommending John Audibun Esq.[2] of this place as a fit person to compose a part of the suite, Mr. Audibun is a French Gentleman of remarkable attainments, who has resided some fifteen or sixteen years in this State, and whose connexions by marriage and otherwise are highly respectable. He has an uncommon talent for drawing, and some of his sketches of birds &c which I have seen greatly excel those beautiful ones taken by the late Mr. Wilson.[3] There will, I am sure, be general gratification in witnessing the Department of State vying with that of the war in illustrating the Natural history of our Country.

I have the honor to be Your obedient Servant H. CLAY.

J. Q. Adams Esq. &c &c &c.

ALS. DNA. RG59, Misc. Letters. 1 The Adams-De Onís Treaty.

2 John James Audubon had been born on Santo Domingo, the son of a prosperous French merchant who had served with the French fleet at Yorktown. Educated in France, the young man had removed to "Mill Grove," his father's property near Philadelphia, Pennsylvania, in 1804. Three years later he had embarked upon a mercantile venture in Louisville, Kentucky, whence after successive failures there and at Henderson, Kentucky, terminating in a plea of bankruptcy in 1819, he had moved to Cincinnati and had undertaken seriously to study and draw the birds of the Ohio and Mississippi valleys. In 1821 he was tutoring in New Orleans and on a Louisiana plantation while observing the wild life of the Southwest. Publication of his *Birds of America* was begun serially at Edinburgh, Scotland, in 1827, and won him immediate international acclaim.

His wife was Lucy Bakewell, daughter of an Englishman who resided on an estate near the Audubon property outside Philadelphia. Benjamin Bakewell, her uncle, was a New York merchant.

3 Alexander Wilson, a Scotsman who had settled near Philadelphia in 1802, was at the date of Clay's letter recognized as the foremost American ornithologist, the first volume of his *American Ornithology* (8 vols.) having appeared in 1808. He had died in 1813. His drawings were more limited in scope and much less artistic in style than those of Audubon, but the earlier work was the more original and scientific.

To [Francis Walker] Gilmer

Dr Sir Lexington 4h. Aug. 1821.

I have duly received your letter of the 8h. Ulto.[1] I regret that I am not able to communicate to you more precise information than I possess respecting the payment of taxes &c. on the land of our late friend Mr. Burwell.[2] The laws of Illinois have undergone some alteration and I do not know their precise condition at present on this subject. The taxes are payable annually; and if not punctually paid, the land is sold or forfeited to the State, subject to a right of redemption, on the part of the owner, within two years, by the payment of the tax, cost of sale, and perhaps 100—per Cent per annum.[3] I own some lands in the neighbourhood of that of the Estate of Mr Burwell, on which I have paid taxes. Govr. Ninian Edwards (now a Senator in Congress) has been kind enough to attend to the payment of them for me. He would probably or Edward Coles, formerly Mr. Madison's private Secretary,[4] attend to the matter for Mr. Burwell's representatives. A local agency I think is indispensible to a faithful execution of the business. If I am not mistaken, Mr. B. informed me that he had made some provision in regard to the taxes. The land is good. I was upon it;[5] and furnished the location to Mr. B. It is richer than the finest Roanoake bottoms, and by the time young Burwell[6] arrives at age will be very valuable. It ought to be well taken care of. It is prairie, situated at the junction of an arm or branch of the Grand Prairie,[7] with the Grand Prairie & commands a prospect of the latter of boundless extent. On one side it is skirted by woodland, well timbered, which the owner of the Prairie will be able to command.

I share with you, my dear Sir, in the griefs which the lamented death of our friend has occasioned. He was indeed a most excellent and intelligent person. He was among my earliest & most highly esteemed friends; our acquaintance having commenced upwards of 25 years ago. Poor fellow! his habitual inclination to low spirits attended him to the last & perhaps contributed to his dissolution; for early in the disease, which deprived us of him, he expressed his consciousness that he would not recover. Too sanguine, perhaps, I did not think so, and a few hours only before his death I left him with a strong hope that he would be spared.

With great regard I am Dr Sir faithf'y Yr. ob Servant H. CLAY

Mr. Gilmer.

P.S. The residence of Edward Coles is Edwardsville Illinois. The land lies in Illinois near the Indiana line, about fourteen miles due West from Fort Harrison[8] on the Wabash. H.C

ALS. KyU (purchased for *The Papers of Henry Clay* by the University of Kentucky Library Associates). Recipient not positively identified. Gilmer, son of Dr. George Gilmer, a signer of the Declaration of Independence, was a Richmond lawyer, Reporter of the Virginia Court of Appeals (1820-1821), and an intimate friend of Thomas Jefferson and John Randolph. Gilmer accepted appointment to the first professorship of law at the University of Virginia but died in February, 1826, aged thirty-six, before entering upon these duties.

1 Not found. 2 William Armisted Burwell, who had died February 16, 1821.

3 See below, David Hart to Clay, November 2, 1821. Under "An Act For the relief of certain persons whose Lands, Bank Stock, &c. have been sold for Taxes," approved in February, 1821, the interest rate on unpaid taxes and costs was fixed at six per cent per annum, provided the sums due were paid before January, 1822. Lexington *Kentucky Gazette,* April 19, 1821.

4 Since March 5, 1819, Register of the Land Office at Edwardsville, Illinois.

5 In 1817, when he had also visited Indiana. See above, II, 354-55.

6 William MacCreary Burwell, later a Whig member of the Virginia House of Delegates for twenty years and founder and editor of the Lynchburg *Virginia Patriot and Southwestern Advocate* (1848-1860). After the Civil War he moved to New Orleans, where he was identified with the *Commercial Bulletin,* the *Republican, Price Current,* and *De Bow's Review,* serving the last journal as editor from 1868 until its demise.

7 Contemporaneously defined as extending "from about the base line near the third principal meridian, between the Kaskaskia and Wabash rivers, in a northeast direction; then veering to the north, between the head waters of Vermilion of the Wabash, Woman river of Tippecanoe, Iroquois and Ma-qua-pin-a-con of the Kankakee, on the north side, to near the junction of the Illinois and Kankakee rivers, leaving

on the southwest the Sangamo, Michilimacinac and Vermilion river of the Illinois; thence crossing the Kankakee, bordered with small skirts of timber, passing northeast to Chicago, leaving on the west the Illinois river, and on the east the Kalimick of Lake Michigan; thence continuing north between Lake Michigan and the River des Pleines, to the northern boundary of the state, and eastwardly between the waters of the Kankakee, to within nine miles of the Cowpen trading-house on St. Joseph's river [northern Indiana]." Lewis C. Beck, *A Gazetteer of the States of Illinois and Missouri . . .* (Albany, 1823), 116. Beck commented: "It is very questionable whether it will ever be thickly settled."

8 At Terre Haute, Indiana.

Mortgage Deed from Thomas Hall

[August 8, 1821]

[Whereas Thomas Hall of Fayette County on May 27, 1821, executed to Henry Clay two promissory notes,[1] each for $357.60, one payable on December 25, 1823, and the other on December 25, 1824, both bearing legal interest from the initial date, and on the same day Hall at Clay's instance gave his bond to Sarah Hall for the sum of $300, payable on demand, also bearing interest from date —in consideration of these obligations together with the payment of five shillings, hereby acknowledged, Thomas Hall conveys to Clay a tract, estimated at 84 acres, in Fayette County on the waters of Elkhorn, on which Hall now resides, purchased by Hall from Levi Bowyer and Harrison Blanton and bounded according to that deed:[2] now if Hall shall pay the aforesaid bonds to Clay and Sarah Hall according to the agreed terms, this indenture shall be void.[3] Thomas Hall's signature acknowledged before J. C. Rodes, Clerk of Fayette County, August 8, 1821.]

Fayette County Court, Deed Book U, 490. When Hall, who was a resident of the northern district of Fayette County, died in 1825, Sarah Hall became a major devisee, their exact relationship not specified.

1 Not found.

2 Bowyer (Boyer) had been an early resident of Fayette County; Blanton for many years resided in Frankfort, Kentucky, where he was one of the contractors for the Old State House. Their deed to Hall has not been found.

3 Payment of $444.75, principal and interest, on a note to Clay and two payments, amounting to $437.79¾ and $377.47½, on notes held by Sarah Hall were included in the settlement of Thomas Hall's estate. Fayette County Court, Will Book G, 405. One undivided half of the tract acquired by Hall from Bowyer and Harrison Blanton was purchased by Sarah Hall from Thomas' other heirs following his death. Fayette County Court, Deed Book 1, pp. 24-25 (October 10, 1825).

Receipt to William S. Dallam

[August 9, 1821]

Attached to Assignment, November 10, 1819.

To Caesar A. Rodney

My dear Rodney Lexn. 9h. Aug. 1821.

I recd. your favor of the 22d. Ulto.[1] I shall be extremely glad to learn that the issue which you confidently anticipate of the Court of Enquiry, in the case of Commodore Baron, shall take place.[2] I have ever thought him injured; and the reparation, 'though late, is better than never. Had it occurred earlier, the life of poor Decatur[3] might possibly have been preserved.

I concur with you entirely as to the character of the fourth of July speech[4] which you have drawn. So does every body in this quarter with whom I have conversed. What must we think of the state of the press and of the taste of that part of the Country, which have extolled it to the skyes! Of its author I will only repeat, what I have often said that it furnishes further proof of his total want of judgment and discretion. He ought never to have undertaken the task, and if he did he ought never to have published the composition.

We are in the West in a terrible condition with our currency of which there is but little prospect of its speedy melioration.[5] The effect from it which I most apprehend is collision with the Federal authority. Always I am Faithfully Yours H CLAY

C. A. Rodney Esq.

ALS. DLC-Rodney Family Papers (DNA, M212, R22). 1 Not found.

2 Commodore James Barron had been brought before a Court of Naval Enquiry in February, 1808, following the *Chesapeake-Leopard* incident (see above, I, 481, 482n) and had been convicted of "neglecting in the probability of an engagement to clear his ship for action." Suspended from the service for five years, he had returned to the Navy after the War of 1812 but had not been restored to active duty. A second Court of Enquiry, held at Norfolk in July, 1821, still failed to absolve him completely. It was rumored in August, 1821, and confirmed by the report of proceedings, not published until the following spring, that the Court criticized Barron's failure to return to duty more promptly. Clay had testified to the Court, in writing (not found), that while at Gothenburg in June, 1814, he had encouraged Barron's return to the service and had attempted to procure passage for him on the *John Adams*. Washington *Daily National Intelligencer*, August 6, 7, 16, 23, 1821; April 2, 1822. Barron remained on "waiting orders" till his death, in 1851.

3 Stephen Decatur, whose duel with Barron had been the outgrowth of the latter's resentment at his treatment in the Navy.

4 On July 4, 1821, John Quincy Adams had delivered in Washington an oration, strongly nationalistic and anti-British, which was criticized by his political opponents as an effort to raise popular support for himself.

5 See above, Clay to Cheves, May 5, 1821, note.

To Langdon Cheves

Sir Lexington 11h. Aug. 1821.

A bill of Exchange drawn by R. M. Johnson on the 6h. July 1819 for $3533 on Richard Smith Cashr. U.S.B. City of Washington payable to the order of W. S. Dallam ten days after sight at the U.S. Bank Philada was protested by C. Biddle[1] on the 5h. Aug. 1819 at Philada. for non payment. A suit has been brought for the B. U States in the Circuit Court of the U. States for the K. District against Mr. Dallam to recover the contents of the bill;[2] and in this suit it will be necessary to bring aforward [*sic*] the necessary proof of presentation, notice &c. It does not appear when the bill was presented to Mr. Smith. Will you have the goodness to cause depositions to be taken, conformably to the 30h. Section of the Judicial Act of the U States,[3] to prove 1st. the time of presentation of the bill; and 2dly. when notice of the protest was transmitted to this place, to whom addressed, and whether by the next mail or not after the protest. I mean conformably to that part of the act which provides for the case of witnesses residing more than 100 miles from the place of trial. If notice were transmitted of the Non-acceptance, let that also be proven. What is your practice, on the subject of giving notice, in the case of such inland bills as this of *non acceptance?* The depositions will be wanting by the first monday in November, and it will be necessary to be very particular in the Certificate of the Judge, before whom they may be taken, that it be agreeable to the above section.

With great respect I am Yr. ob. Servant H. CLAY

Langdon Cheves Esq. P. B. U. S.

ALS. DLC-George H. Stewart Collection (DNA, M212, R22).

1 Probably Charles, father of James Biddle. A veteran of the Revolution, Vice President of the Supreme Executive Council of Pennsylvania under its first constitution, and a successful merchant of Philadelphia, he had died in April, 1821.

2 The suit had been instituted April 9, 1821. At the May Term, 1823, a jury awarded the plaintiff $4,701.92. U.S. Circuit Court, Seventh Circuit, District of Kentucky, Complete Records, V, 81-83.

3 See above, Clay to Cheves, February 27, 1821, note.

Advertisement of Law Office

H. Clay & G. W. Ridgely. Lexington, August 18 [1821]

HAVE moved their Office from the Kentucky Hotel to the house lately occupied by Capt. Gaines;[1] where one or both of them may generally be found, unless when on professional business.

Lexington *Kentucky Reporter,* August 20, 1821. 1 Bernard Gaines.

Property Deed to John Keiser

[August 27, 1821]

[For the sum of $3,097.30, current money of Kentucky, paid and acknowledged, Henry and Lucretia Clay convey to John Keiser a tract of 42¾ acres and 11 poles, on the waters of Cane Run, beginning at a stake on the northeast side of Russell's Road and adjoining property lines of Dougherty,[1] Alexander Smith (now deceased), and Thomas January, according to survey by Richard Higgins—Keiser now being in occupancy of the deeded tract. General warranty of title. The indenture is witnessed by William S.[2] and F. Ridgely. Recorded on oath of the witnesses before J. C. Rodes, September 24, 1821.]

Fayette County Court, Deed Book V, 36-37.
1 First name not given. Probably Moses Dougherty, a resident of the northern district of Fayette County.
2 Younger son of Dr. Frederick Ridgely and, himself, later a physician in Cincinnati.

To George Gibson

Sir Lexington 28 August 1821.

Col. R. Taylor and John Todd Esqr. of Frankfort[1] are about to make some propósals for supplying with provisions the Posts of Baton Rouge and New Orleans and perhaps some others. I take great pleasure in communicating to you my perfect persuasion that, in the event of their making a contract, you may put entire confidence in their faithful execution of it. Both of the gentlemen have had some military experience, and that of Col. Taylor in particular have [*sic*] been very considerable. He was connected, during the late War, with the Quarter Master's Department and acquitted himself, I have always understood, in a manner that gave great satisfaction to Govr. Shelby and Genl. Harrison.[2]

I have the honor to be with great respect Yr. ob. Servant

Col. Gibson &c &c &c. H. CLAY

ALS. Owned by Thomas D. Clark, Lexington, Kentucky. Addressed to Gibson, "Commissary General &c &c &c Washington."
1 Richard Taylor; John H. Todd.
2 Isaac Shelby; William H. Harrison. Taylor had been Quartermaster General of Kentucky militia.

From James De Wolf

Hon Henry Clay Bristol R I Sept. 5th 1821.

Sir

I have not had the pleasure of a line from you since my return from Cuba last spring, that of 19th & 24th Jany while you was [*sic*] at Washington are the last I have received.[1] it was my intention to have made a journey to the western Country the past summer but found it was impossible to leave my business and Family.— I have put great dependence on your promise to assist me in my difficulties with Mr. R. Whiting (that man if he has any conscience must suffer much for his treatment to me) as I find on a reexamination that my account with the Hope Distillery Compy formerly sent Messrs Denny & Thruston[2] is incorrect as I had given credit for the Assessments on S. S. Goodwins share (after the expenditure of the $5000 pr share which I had agreed to advance him) which I ought not to have done as $45000 was all I agreed to advance pr original agreement— I have therfore [*sic*] stated my account anew and forwarded to those Gentlemen which I request you to take particular notice of as it shows that I am not a delinquent as Whiting pretends and have complied with the terms of said Agreement, and it can be fully vouched. The $3000. charged for ten acres of land to be paid my son,[3] was according to an understanding from the beginning that it should be so estimated and charged by me until my son should agree on appraisers to appraise the ten acres, according to agreement $300—pr acre being the price he always held his land at, but you will see that I am in advance independent of that charge—

I hope you will not suffer this man to get advantage of me by his complaint in the Chancery Court— I request you to petition the Judge of the Federal Court to have his suit removed into that court, or failing in that I request you to prevent my being injured for want of attention before the State Court should that court order commissioners appointed I hope you will see that none but proper men are appointed, men intirely [*sic*] independent who would examine into the truth of the business—I should prefer to have them of Frankfort than Louisville, as Whiting and Goodwin have made it a study to excite the sympathy of the people of that place in their favor and their prejudice against me I believe they have even lavished the money on them I had intrusted to their care, or with large sums in their hands have so misrepresented things as to effect their object— I do not understand how my being a delinquent with the Compy (was that the case) could be cause of complaint by Whiting when he has always been such, and in fact has never paid any thing, but has directed Goodwin to credit and debit his account with many things which makes a large bottom line, but when investigated it will be found he has paid nothing—

I suppose you have brought an action for my son to eject the Hope Distillery Compy off his land in which case I think it highly necessary and proper that a Commission be taken out to obtain my testimony to the fact that the land was not purchased for me as it seems Whiting and Goodwin are making pretentions that the Junior not having been added to my sons name makes the land belong to me, in which I never had any interest, and you will observe by the original agreement that all the Compy understood the land to belong to my son, the discovery was lately made of the "Junior" not being added, it is a straw they choose to catch at— I have thought proper to inclose a copy of my account corrected and have made Whiting and Goodwin the debtors as they were the actual receivers of the money, I believe I have formerly sent my account with the company to Goodwin, incorrectly crediting the Assessment on his share beyond the $5000—which was an error of mine. I had never obligated myself to advance any more on his one share, and I do not know how I came to credit the company with the Assessment on

Goodwins share it was an error and I pray leave to rectify it, as I have done by the within statement of account, the items of Debt in this account are the same as those in the said account stated with the compy and forwarded some time ago. Messrs Denny & Thruston have the papers and I presume understand the case, but I wish your counsel with them.

Am very Respectfully Sir Your Ob Sert JAS. D'WOLF

LS. DLC-TJC (DNA, M212, R12).
[1] Neither letter has been found.
[2] See above, De Wolf to Clay, January 3, 1821.
[3] James De Wolf, Jr.

From James De Wolf

Hon H. Clay Bristol R.I. Sepr 5th 1821.

Sir

I here hand you Mr B. Diman[1] Cashier order on Cash U.S. Branch Bank Louisville Ky for R Whitings Note of $3000.—and interest due 8th. next month which I caused to be negotiated at the Mount Hope Bank of which Corporation I am the presiding Officer, and wish you to cause a suit to be instituted against him, for the payment of said Note at the Federal Court of U.S. (in case it is not paid) in behalf of the Mount Hope Bank a corporation established here.— I am respectfully Sir your Obt Servt

JAS. D'WOLF Presdt. M. H. Bank

LS. DLC-TJC (DNA, M212, R12).
[1] Byron Diman, who as a youth had entered De Wolf's counting house and later engaged in whale-fishing and manufacturing. After serving many years in the Rhode Island legislature, he filled one term as Governor, 1846-1847.

To Langdon Cheves

Sir Columbus 8h. Septr. 1821.

The Circuit Court of Ohio commenced its Session on monday last, being holden by the District Judge[1] alone, in the absence of Judge Todd[2] from indisposition. During the week we have obtained a decree in the suit in Chy. respecting the seizure of the money of the Bank,[3] of which a Copy is inclosed. The terms of this decree were settled by an arrangement between the Counsel of the respective parties. According to that arrangement the decree was to be entered, and all the forms of law to be prosecuted to obtain a compulsory surrender of the sum now in the Treasury of Ohio, upon which the sum was to be restored, and thereupon the defendants were to appeal to the Supreme Court, giving bond and security, which was to suspend so much of the decree as relates to the $2000 not now in the Treasury and the interest and the Costs.

To this course of proceeding the Governor of the State and the Auditor[4] are understood to have yielded their assent; and I did not entertain a doubt that by this time we should have had in our possession the $9800 [*sic*]. I transmit you inclosed a Copy of the notes of an agreement signed by Mr. Hammond[5] and myself. By this agreement, I have undertaken to abstain from demanding interest upon that part of the sum seized which consisted of the notes of the Corporation, and to demand it only upon the Coin which was taken. I was induced to do this from several considerations. 1st. I thought it questionable whether we could recover interest upon our own notes. 2dly. The injunction, by which the defts were restrained from negotiating or parting with the amount seized, seemed also to be opposed to the recovery of interest. And thirdly supposing that the arrangement would be executed with good faith, I thought it desirable to have the business closed with as little cause for further irritation as possible. I have further agreed to dismiss the proceeding for contempt against Osborn & Harper, in disobeying the injunction,[6] at their Costs, and it is accordingly dismissed. This I was induced to do also from several considerations 1st. The prosecution for contempts, such at least as that was supposed to be, is always calculated to produce excitement in the public mind. 2dly. Osborn had prepared an answer to Interrogatories which so far purged him that I was satisfied the Court would not have ordered his imprisonment until the money seized was restored. 3dly. And, at all events, the most that we could possibly have gotten would have been to have had him & Harper imprisoned until the money was restored, and that we are equally entitled to under the decree which has been pronounced.

Contrary to all expectation, the Treasurer[7] now refuses to surrender the money, which he does for the want of an act, conformably to the constitution of Ohio, making an appropriation of the money, and the Auditors warrant in pursuance of such act. This unexpected course of the Treasurer (which I must believe is his own, contrary to the advice of his Counsel) left me but one alternative, which I instantly pursued. I moved the Court for an attachment against him for not performing the decree of the Court, which, after argument, was promptly granted by the Judge, and he is now in custody, and is to be imprisoned until the decree is executed. I have thought it not necessary, for the present, to ask of the Court to imprison the other defendants, all of whom it is believed are sincerely desirous that the money should be given up. I entertain no doubt that the Treasurer will either yet surrender the money before the meeting of the Legislature in December, or immediately after that event. The Marshall,[8] under the direction of the district Judge, is to hire a house for a Jail, according to the resolution of Congress at the last Session, where the Treasurer will be confined. New Lancaster, it is understood, is the place selected for that purpose.

Altho.' I have been disappointed in getting immediate possession of the money, I think the business is in a good train; and I shall be extremely glad if the Board shall be satisfied with the course I have taken. Our moderation has done us no harm; and the current of public sentiment, already turned & turning in our favor, is now impetuously directing itself against those, by whose Councils, the State is brought into its present predicament.

With respect to the sale of January s Estate, adverted to by me in a former letter,[9] and which is mentioned in your's of the 8h. of August,[10] which I duly received with its inclosure, the Bank by that sale has had the debt due to it rendered perfectly safe, payable in Specie and not in Commonwealth's paper as you appear to have supposed. I have the honor to be with great respect Your obedient Servant H. CLAY

Langdon Cheves Esqr.

N.B. Columbus 10h. Sept. 1821.

The defendant Sullivan has been committed for a contempt of the Court in disobeying the decree. Being thus in custody, I moved the Court this day for a Commission of Sequestration to seize his Estate real & personal and to take the *identical money* in the Treasury which was forcibly taken from the Bank. The Commission was granted, and, without opposition, the key of the office of the Treasury was taken from him by the Commissioners appointed to execute it, the office entered, and the $98.000, the only part of the $100.000. in the Treasury, were taken out and are now in the possession of Mr. Creighton,[11] the President of the Office at Chillicothe. As to the residue of the decree (the $2000 of principal, the interest & the Costs) the defendants have prayed an appeal to the Supreme Court & entered into bond with security to prosecute the appeal. There has been no tumult; no violence, and whatever of public excitement that exists is, I believe, favorable to us.

H. CLAY

ALS. PU.

1 Charles Willing Byrd, appointed March 3, 1803, remained on the bench until his death in 1828.

2 Thomas Todd.

3 See above, Clay to Cheves, January 22, February 15, 1821, note; below, Clay to Biddle, February 17, 1824, note.

4 Ethan Allen Brown; Ralph Osborn. In 1804 Brown, born in Connecticut and educated in law under Alexander Hamilton, had settled in Cincinnati and begun the practice of his profession. He had served as Associate Judge of the Supreme Court of Ohio, 1810-1818, prior to his election as Governor, and he resigned the latter post to fill a vacancy in the United States Senate in January, 1822. He remained in the last post until 1825, then served as Canal Commissioner of Ohio, 1825-1830; United States Chargé d'Affaires to Brazil, 1830-1834; Commissioner of the General Land Office,

1825-1836. Moving to Indiana in 1836, he was for one term, 1842, a member of the Indiana legislature.

5 Charles Hammond. The agreement, not found.

6 Complementing the chancery action, suit by the Bank of the United States against Ralph Osborn and John L. Harper "on criminal prosecution, for contempt of court" had been instituted at the January, 1821, Term of the United States Circuit Court at Columbus, Ohio. It also had been continued to the September Term. *Niles' Weekly Register,* XIX (January 20, 1821), 346, citing Columbus *Ohio Monitor,* January 6, 1821.

7 Samuel Sullivan, of Zanesville, who had been elected to the office in February, 1820.

8 John Hamm, formerly Surgeon of the 27th Regiment, United States Infantry, had held the post of Marshall in Ohio since December 30, 1813. On Congressional provision for the local jail, see above, Motion and Remarks on Due Execution of Process, February 12, 1821.

9 See above, Clay to Cheves, July 21, 1821.

10 Not found.

11 William Creighton, Jr.

Statement on Controversy between Ohio and Bank of the United States

[*ca.* September 12, 1821]

This controversy has, we understand, from an unquestionable source, come to a final issue in the Circuit Court of the United States for the District of Ohio. To give our readers a distinct comprehension of that issue, it is necessary to inform them, that a bill in chancery was filed against the collecting officers of the state to restrain the collection of the tax imposed by the state; on which an injunction was granted. Prior to the collection of the tax this injunction was served; but, as those officers supposed, and as they were advised by counsel, that it was illegally served, they proceeded notwithstanding to collect the tax, and levied $100,000, about $20,000 in specie, and the residue in the notes of the corporation. The counsel for the Bank, entertaining an opinion of the service of the injunction different from that of the opposite counsel, proceeded against the officers for an alleged contempt in disobeying the injunction, and the Court adjudged the injunction to have been legally served; but, at the instance of the counsel of the officers, continued the prosecution for the contempt until the late term of the Court.

The Bank also instituted an action of trespass, *quare clausum fregit,* against the officers and the sureties, in their office bond, for entering its office at Chillicothe, and forcibly seizing the $100,000; to which the defendants severally pled not guilty. After the seizure, the Bank amended its bill, and stated that fact, obtained an injunction to prevent the negotiation of the notes seized, and prayed a decree for the restoration of the specific money and notes which had been levied. Thus the Bank had in operation three remedies for the recovery of the sum taken: 1st, the bill in chancery; 2dly, the proceeding for the contempt; and, 3dly, the action of trespass—all of which were ready for trial at the late (September) term.

The Court pronounced a decree for the restoration of the identical

$100,000 which had been seized, with interest upon the specie part of it from the time of the seizure until payment; and granted a perpetual injunction against the collection of any tax in future under the act of Ohio. By an arrangement between the respective counsel, the attachment for contempt was dismissed at the costs of the defendants, and the action of trespass to be continued until the decision of the Supreme Court is also to be dismissed at the defendants' costs, in the event of the affirmation of the decree of the Circuit Court. The Treasurer refused to comply with that decree, and an attachment for a contempt was issued against him, and he was committed to prison. He still refused; whereupon the Court, upon the motion of the counsel of the Bank, awarded a writ of sequestration, by which the commissioners appointed in it were empowered to seize his whole estate, real and personal, and the identical $100,000 seized, wheresoever the same might be found, and to sequester the whole, subject to the future order of the Court. In virtue of this writ of sequestration, the commissioners named in it took the key of the Treasury from the Treasurer, entered the Treasury, and took thereout $98,000, the only part of the sum levied remaining, the other $2000 having been retained by the officer making the collection for his commission. The defendants appealed from the decree to the Supreme Court, which, by consent, was made to operate as a supersedeas upon the $2000, the interest, and the costs of the suit in chancery; and the Treasurer was thereupon discharged from custody.

No violence, no opposition, no forcible resistance, was offered to the execution of the writ of sequestration; and, if the original seizure of the money is to be regretted, it is highly consoling to have witnessed the silent but irresistible energy of the law, when that law was declared by the Constitutional organ. The execution of the process of the Court, without impediment or disturbance, is creditable to the people of Ohio, and to the population of Columbus in particular. Thus, the very circumstances which seemed at first to threaten the peace and quiet of the Union, and to weaken the authority of the government, terminates [*sic*] in evincing its strength, and in communicating to it new vigor.

Washington *Daily National Intelligencer,* September 21, 1821. On Clay's authorship, see below, Clay to Hammond, September 12, 1821. See also above, II, 721, 723n, 874-75; Clay to Cheves, January 22, September 8, 1821; below, Clay to Biddle, February 17, 1824.

To Charles Hammond

Dr Sir Chillicothe 12th. Septr. 1821.

On my arrival here, perceiving in one of the prints of this place a very imperfect and erroneous statement of the transactions at Columbus, respecting the restoration of the money of the Bank,[1] it appeared to me that it might be useful to present to the public a narrative of those transactions which should put it in possession of all the information which it might desire in regard to them. Such a narrative I hastily prepared, shewed to Mr. Dodderidge who is here and who approved it, and sent on to the Intelligencer by Mr. Graham,[2] who is proceeding immediately to the City. It will of course be published, without the parade or responsibility of any names; and I hope you will find it substantially accurate and unexceptionable, which it was my intention it should be— I subjoined to it a single reflection, called for by the occasion, which, far from throwing any censure, conveys I think a merited compliment to the people of Ohio for the good order with which the execution of the process of the Court was attended.[3]

I am faithfully & respectfully Yr. ob. Servant H. CLAY

Charles Hammond Esqr.

ALS. InU.

[1] A report from the Chillicothe *Supporter*, datelined September 12, reprinted in Washington *Daily National Intelligencer*, September 21, 1821.

[2] Philip Doddridge; probably George Graham, now president of the Washington Branch, Bank of the United States. See above, Statement, this date.

[3] See above, Clay to Cheves, September 8, 1821.

From Nathaniel Cox

Dear Sir New Orleans 12 Sept. 1821.

I have to acKnowledge your much Esteemed favr. of the 25 ult.[1] now before me—

The draft on my brother of $480 was the consideration given to Mr Hart for Breedlove & cos note of a like sum and who failed immediately after the transaction took place and which prevented him (Mr Hart) from presenting it.[2] The dft not being paid the note of Course for the benefit of his Estate; Some partial payments have been made on it and I gave Mr John Clay Two hundred dollars thereon to be passed to your credit— This will account to you Satisfacty. why I have made you no remittance. Breedlove & Co are hard handed men to get money from, but I still think the whole 480$— will ultimately be got out of them in time

I truly regret the want of instructions to have purchased the done [*sic*] Kelly[3] Plantation for you & Col Morrison[4] Such another opportunity may not again offer in our life time. It is a valuable spot, capable of producing 400 H hds of Sugar annually and with the Expences of 30 additional Negroes you might have at once stepped in [*sic*] a revenue of 35.000$— As regards another sale, I begin to think That we shall not be able to effect it Trudeau[5] Knows too well the Value of his bargain not to hold on at some additional Thousands— Our courts had all adjourned before the Sheriffs return, and no steps have yet been taken in the premises, but at their next Session steps will be taken to bring the question fairly before the Court— If the Plantation should be again put up for sale, and any Sum under 150.000$ obtain it, I should consider the purchasers fortune compleatly made—

I dont well Know what to say about hemp— At this moment yours cant be sold at 9 cents— Bale Rope is dull a [*sic*] 8—and heavy supplies in hand—but again our port is very thin of Shipping and no demand for Tar'd Cordage—The winter Season may bring round a considerable change in that article, and create a demand for Yarns—

Tobacco has done much better in Europe the present season than was Expected— Shipments from hence at 4 1/4 to 4 3/4 Cents, have paid the shippers very fair profits, so that I think we may safely calculate on about the same price for the growing crop which I presume pays the planter well for the cultivation of the Article—

I know of nothing else you can Send to Market— We are now at a Season when western produce is at the highest or nearly so for the state of our market I reffer [*sic*] you to the annexed quotation.[6]

And remain with great respect Yr most Obt. s[evt] NATH COX

ALS. DLC-TC (DNA, M212, R12). MS. water-stained. 1 Not found.
2 See above, Cox to Clay, June 5, 1821.
3 Possibly Don Juan Kely, former Spanish army officer.
4 James Morrison.
5 Probably Charles Leveaux Trudeau, Surveyor General of Louisiana under Spain and, after transfer of the province to the United States, for many years Recorder of New Orleans. He had also served as president of the City Council, acting mayor of New Orleans, and member of the Territorial General Assembly (1811).
6 The report lists flour, first grade, at $4 1/2 to $6; flour, "sour", 2 to 3; mess pork, 9 to 10; prime pork, 7 to 7 1/2; cargo pork, 6; lard, 5 to 6; bacon, 5 to 6; whisky 25; and "Kentucky Baging," 14 to 17.

Deed of Trust from Executors of Thomas Hart, Jr.

[September 13, 1821]

[Whereas by the will of Thomas Hart, Jr., deceased, it is provided that upon the marriage of any of his daughters, the portion of his estate allotted for that daughter shall be assigned to her and one half of such portion shall be conveyed to trustees to secure it to her and her heirs; and whereas Eleanor Murdock Hart, the eldest daughter, has lately married George Washington Anderson,[1] and her portion of the estate of her father has been assigned to her: now in further consideration of one dollar, paid and acknowledged, the executrix and executors of Thomas Hart, Jr., grant to Henry Clay, John W. Hunt, and Thomas Anderson, as trustees, 113¾ acres in Fayette County on the waters of South Elkhorn, beginning at William Todd's[2] corner and running with the lines of Parker[3] and Black,[4] being part of a tract of 455 acres belonging to Hart's estate, together with the appurtenances, also the following Negro slaves: Lewis, Milo, Edward, Edmond, Jack, Sophia, and Cornelia, with their increase—to be held by the grantees in trust that they will permit the profits of the land and slaves (which together constitute one moiety of the portion of Hart's estate allotted to Eleanor Murdock) to be applied to her support and maintenance and that of her children, and upon her death to be divided among her children or, if she have none, to be conveyed to her husband, if he survive her, or, if not, to her remaining heirs. The trustees pledge to conform to these terms. George W. Anderson gives his consent to such trust conveyance. Signatures are acknowledged before J. C. Rodes, September 30, 1822.]

Fayette County Court, Deed Book 3, pp. 120-21.

1 Formerly a student at Transylvania University and, like his elder brothers, Thomas and James, later a merchant in Louisville.

2 Either the cotton spinner, Tod, or William Todd, Jr., Lexington lawyer and former clerk of the town Board of Trustees.

3 John Parker, first name omitted in deed.

4 Alexander Black, first name omitted in deed.

From J[ames] L. E[dwards]

H. Clay, Esq. Lexington Kty.

Sir War Dept. Pension Office Sept. 13th. 1821.

Your's of the 25h. ulto.[1] enclosing an affidavit of Thos. Bodley, relative to the circumstances of Hiram Mitchell,[2] has been recd.— His claim will be submitted to the Secy. of War, for reconsideration, on his return to the seat of Government.— I am &c. J.L.E.

Copy. DNA, RG15, Letter Books: General, vol. 11, p. 245. 1 Not found.

2 A resident of Lexington since around 1796, Mitchell had served as a marine, sailing out of Philadelphia, during the Revolution. He had already received a pension dating from June 24, 1818. In March, 1819, he had been "struck with the dead palsy" and since January, 1820, had been deranged. Bodley asserted that he had recently found him in a deplorable situation, entirely helpless physically. Annie Walker Burns (comp.), Revolutionary War Pensions of Soldiers Who Settled in Fayette County, Kentucky (mimeog., Washington, 1936), 67. He was dropped from the pension rolls in February, 1822.

To David L. Ward

Sir Lexn. 17h. Septr. 1821.

Inclosed I transmit the note which I recd. at Louisville at the period of its date,[1] and which I have been unable to get discounted so as to apply the proceeds to your previous note,[2] as I have informed you. I was absent when Mr. Neil[3] called here & have not since heard from him. Your obedient Servant H. CLAY.

David L. Ward Esq.

ALS copy. DLC-TJC (DNA, M212, R10).

1 Promissory note, dated at Louisville, July 31, 1821, by which Ward engages 120 days after date to pay to "Frederic W S Grayson or order" the sum of $2043, "payable and negotiable at the Lexington Branch Bank." Endorsed by Grayson, Robert Breckinridge, and Joseph Cabell Breckinridge. Copy. *Ibid.*

2 See above, II, 888. 3 Not identified.

Deed of Trust from Wade Mosby

[September 29, 1821]

[Indenture by which for the sum of one dollar, paid and acknowledged, Wade Mosby and Susannah, his wife, of Virginia, convey to Henry Clay one undivided fourth part of a tract of 3,000 acres in Montgomery and Bath counties, Kentucky, entered December 14, 1782, in the name of John Mosby, assignee, and patented to Littleberry Mosby and by him transferred to Wade Mosby, on which tract John Jouitt resides—which one fourth part is the same as that sold by James Brown to Thomas D. Owings, respecting which a suit in chancery, brought by Owings against Brown and Wade Mosby, is now pending in Fayette Circuit Court[1]—together with the appurtenances, with title warranted only against claimants under Wade Mosby: In trust "upon this special confidence and purpose that the said Clay shall convey to the said James Brown or to the said Thomas D Owings in execution of the contract between the said Brown and Owings the said undivided fourth part of the aforesaid three thousand acres of land." Signed by Wade and Susan Mosby in the presence of J. Cabell Breckinridge, James Haggin, and Robert Wickliffe. Recorded by Achilles Sneed, on proof by the oaths of Wickliffe and Haggin.]

Ky. Court of Appeals, Deed Book V, 81-82. Mosby, a veteran of the Revolution, had attended Hampden Sidney Academy and lived almost his entire life in Powhatan County, Virginia. He was a brother of Littleberry Mosby. Mrs. Mosby's dower rights were relinquished before K. Miller and Littleberry Mosby, justices of the peace of Powhatan County, February 5, 1822, as recorded by Achilles Sneed, Clerk of the Kentucky Court of Appeals, October 26, 1822. *Ibid.*, 339.

1 In a chancery action against Wade Mosby, instituted on January 26, 1815, Owings had sought to obtain conveyance of the property, for which he had given bond to make payment to Brown. In separate answers filed by Clay as attorney for Mosby and Brown on September 29 and December 4, 1821, respectively (both DS, in Clay's hand), Mosby admits Brown's right to the property but denies that Owings has presented written authority from Brown directing its conveyance to Owings; while Brown admits that he has sold the tract to Owings and has given an order for the transfer. The case was continued until the April Special Term, 1823, when Owings' bill was dismissed and the costs assessed against him. Fayette Circuit Court, File 543.

From James De Wolf

Hon. Henry Clay Bristol R I. Oct 1821

Sir your favour of 29th ulto[1] is before me & its contents noted, I feel myself much injured by the delay of that Justice I had a right to expect in the Federal court had I been able to have made a Journey to Kentucky I should not have made any effort for a compromise with the Mess Johnsons;[2] it seems those Gentlemen plead usury and have some testimony to that point. If my first transactions with Mr J. Prentis[3] had been usurious they were contracts made in this State, and of course its Laws must be enforced against me by the Mess Johnsons which I am perfectly willing to defend—but that plea can not avail them in defending against my Mortgage our Laws being such.

2d. If the first contract had been usurious it was purged of it by the one made when I was in Lexington & deeded to him all the Property he had sold me in the first contract transaction taking from him the present Mortgage & notes in which nothing short of shear positive purgury [*sic*] can avail them. I never have recieved [*sic*] any benefit from Mr Prentise [*sic*] over Six pr ct. & that for only one years use of the $83,000 furnished him so many years ago— 3d. the Mess Johnsons title (I believe) recognise [*sic*] mine as a prior one & the Lawyers tell me it gives them the right of redeeming the Mortgage Property and nothing more.— I want all the truth of the cause on my side got into it & if I can get this done I care not how much of anything else is in it, to carry up to Washington for I am safe in this case if safty [*sic*] can be found in any case.— The Mess Johnsons must expect to respond for the rents they have enjoyed & the waste they have made which they most assuredly will do if they have the ability & the Government of the U.S. continue to exist. I beg you Sir to understand my determination to prosecute for my right & assist me to bring this business to a close as soon as possible for it is a Crying Sin, a shame & disgrace, to our Country that any man or set of men in it should have the ability (however meritorious) to stop Justice in the way the Mess Johnsons have stoped [*sic*] my course in a lawful & rightful way to come into posession of my own: My Confidence in Prentises ability to pay his debts was more confirmed by the conduct of those Gentlemen than any thing else, when I was at Lexington, I met them at his house and observing that such respectable & intelligent Gentlemen had full confidence in him giving him large credits & living in the same Neighbourhood & Community had a great tendency to suport [*sic*] my shaken confidence in him— I beg you Sir to inform me against whom the action of Ejectment is brought (for my Son) for the Louisville Property & if an injunction is taken out to prevent waste which is very importent [*sic*]—[4] if the action is not brought against all the Company I suppose it should be against Whiting & Goodwin as being in possession, but I have instructed my Agent Mr Hugh H. Hawes[5] to take forcible possession of those Buildings & property if practicable for me & to take care of the same to prevent pilfering and destruction which has been practiced by Goodwin & Whiting to a great extent and as I am fearful that the property is all I shall ever obtain to remunerate me for about $75000 I have paid in good money to carry on 4/12th of said works under the superintendence of Mess Whiting & Goodwin, & by what I can learn Whiting has put all his property out of his hands & never intends paying any thing for my advances on his 3/12. I advanced him the money in Philadelphia & Baltimore to carry it on & for which he gave me his notes, I hope Sir with such an able advocate as yourself I shall be safe in establishing my rights and God knows I have no desire for any thing more —usury seems to be the standing defence of all my adversarys in Kentuc[ky] I suppose with the hope of establishing a belief that I a[m] a very rich man and that it comes of course that all contracts with me are usurious on [*sic*] that trivial & light evidence will answer to establish the fact.— I hope the Novr term of the Circut [*sic*] Court will establish my title to the Mortgaged Lands, or on failure I desire you to take out an appeal to the Supreme Court— Am Sir very Respectfuly [*sic*], your most Obt Servent [*sic*] JAS. D'WOLF

LS. DLC-TJC (DNA, M212, R12). Forwarded from Lexington to Frankfort November 12, 1821.

1 Not found. 2 See above, De Wolf to Clay, January 3, 1821.

3 James Prentiss.

4 See above, James De Wolf, Jr., to Clay, January 1, February 3, 1821; James De Wolf to Clay, January 3, September 5, 1821.

5 Louisville attorney.

Receipt from Thomas Anderson

1st. Oct 1821

Recd of Henry Clay Thirteen dollars 33 cts as entrance for tuition in T U[1] for Thos Anderson T T U JAS ANDERSON

ADS. DLC-TJC (DNA, M212, R15). Thomas and James Anderson, brothers, were partners in a mercantile business in Lexington. Thomas, appointed treasurer of Transylvania University in 1821, relinquished the position the following year, and the brothers moved to Louisville around 1826.

1 Henry Clay, Jr., was at this time a student in the preparatory department. He remained at the University until graduation with the A.B. degree, in July, 1826.

To Langdon Cheves

Sir Lexington 3d. Oct. 1821

I agreed with Col. R. M. Johnson to select Col. James Morrison, formerly president of the office here, Richard Higgins, now one of its directors, and John Pope, whom you knew in the Senate of the U.S., to value the real estate proposed to be given to the Bank, in satisfaction of the debt due from Col. Johnson and his connexions. From the high standing, probity, and good judgments of these gentlemen, I supposed we might safely confide in a just valuation. We were engaged several days last week in Scott County on that object. I thought it best personally to attend to it. The property offered consisted, with the exception of 150 Acres of land, of first rate quality, in the neighbourhood of George Town, entirely of houses and lots in that place. It was not such as I should have prefered [*sic*] to take for the Bank, if there had been any scope for selection; but, from what I conceived to be the precarious condition of the debt intended to be discharged, I thought it advisable not to decline having submitted to valuation almost any property that might be offered. You will perceive in the sequel that my fears in regard to it are but too well founded.

No *standard* of valuation had been fixed in the arrangement made at Philada; and as Col. Johnson and I could not agree upon one, we concluded to leave that matter to the valuers, each party presenting to them, in the presence of the other any observations which he might think proper. It is not necessary to trouble you with a narrative of these observations. I employed every topic that presented itself to my mind to dissuade the valuers from adopting a standard derived from the paper currency of the Country, and they accordingly rejected any such standard. They aimed, I believe, to affix a sort of medium price between the two extremes of highest and lowest values.

There was another preliminary point which it appeared to me necessary to be settled. Anticipating that real estate would not be offered, sufficient to discharge the whole of the debts, which were allowed to be paid in that kind of property, the point was to *which* of the debts should it be applied, in the event of such deficiency? If property sufficient were offered, the question of course would not occur. If we were allowed to make the application, we should apply it to the worst secured debts; if Col. Johnson, he would direct its application probably to the extinction of the best debts. I proposed the alternative, in the event of a deficiency of property, that there should be a rateable application of the amount to each debt (proportionate to such debt) comprehended in the arrangement, or that we should proceed in the valuation and leave to the Bank at Philada. and Col. Johnson to settle the question. The property brought forward was principally that of John T. Johnson and Genl. John Payne,[1] and each of them said that he would not surrender his estate, without it was applied to the discharge of that particular debt or debts for which he was responsible. They prefered accepting the latter branch of the alternative.

We then proceeded to examine the several parcels of property exhibited, of which I transmit you inclosed a descriptive list or schedule taken by myself, at the time of examining each parcel, with the valuations affixed. These valuations amount, in the aggregate, to a little more than I had anticipated; but I do not think, upon the whole, that we ought to complain of them. If the property were brought into market, in the present depressed state of things, the Bank would not probably realize the amount. Should the times improve (and they can scarcely become worse) it is not unlikely, on the other hand, that the whole property will command something more than it has been estimated at. One piece of property (an unfinished house, apparently very well built, of William Sebree) is estimated in its incomplete state, and also if finished. I understand that the parties elect to finish it, as it was in fact in the progress of completion when we viewed it. Supposing the parties to be entitled to the five thousand dollars, at which that item of property was estimated in its completely finished condition, the total amount of property valued is $37.000 or a little more than one fourth part of the mass of debt which was intended to be liquidated. Mr. John T. Johnson offers me a tract of 300 Acres of land, principally prime Ohio bottom, at $7500, which, if further information that I mean to obtain, shall confirm what I have already received, I think I shall take, and which two of the valuers advise me to receive. If that be taken the total amount of real estate will then be $44.500 or a little more than one third of the debt to be paid.

Deeds have been already deposited with me for the greater part and, in the course of a few days, others will be for the residue of the property contained in the schedule. I have used every precaution in my power to ascertain the validity of the titles. These deeds have been deposited upon the condition that the parties and the Bank shall be able to agree & in fact shall agree upon the debts to which the property conveyed shall be applied. If they can make no such agreement, I am to return the deeds to be cancelled, and there is an end of the business. During the exhibition of the property and its valuation the conduct of the parties appeared to be candid & fair. In regard to John T. Johnson, in particular, I must observe that he deported himself with a manliness, frankness and decision which made a highly favorable impression on my mind. With the 300 Acres of land which he proposes to convey on the Ohio, he will have surrendered, I verily believe, all the property he has in the world, except about 2 or 3 thousand dollars worth belonging to his wife, and which could not be reached by any legal proceeding against him. Considering therefore that nothing further could be obtained from him by having recourse to law, I would, if the case were my own, agree to the application of his property to his discharge as far as it goes from his responsibility to the Bank. He is in no lucrative business. He belongs to the profession of the law, the profits of which, if he were steadily to pursue it, would barely support his family; but he is now a member of the H. of R. of the U.S. and that you and I both know is not a situation of profit.

After we had proceeded so far as to value the property contained in the schedule, I received from Col. R. M. Johnson the inclosed letter[2] which I have been requested to transmit to you. The contents of that letter speak sufficiently for themselves. They amount to a declaration of the inability of the parties to execute the arrangement made at Philada. I believe that inability exists. I always feared it. Col. R. M. Johnson is among the most sanguine of men. Acting under the illusions of his strong imagination he believed that he could command, among his friends and connexions, property to almost any amount, that high values would be placed upon this property, and that he would be enabled, if the Bank would receive it, to rid himself & friends of the load of debt which is upon them. The experiment has so far failed. I know not what to advise as to the acceptance of one or other of the two propositions contained in his letter. That the debt cannot be recovered from the parties by law, indeed that a small part of it only can be recovered, is perfectly clear. The debt for which Genl. Payne is bound I should think is safe. The debts for which John T. Johnson is bound are good to the amount of the property which he has given up & proposes to give, I should think; beyond these very little, if any thing further, can be recovered. Under the influence of these impressions, I believe, if it were my private affair, I would close with one of the two propositions offered.

If the Bank determine to retain the property contained in the schedule, it will be necessary to make some arrangements with respect to leasing it. Possession is to be delivered forthwith. Most of it is now rented out. A power of Atto. from the Bank will probably be necessary authorizing the execution of leases &c &c. The subject of the management of the real estate of the Corporation which, in spite of its just aversion to that sort of acquisition, it must necessarily become possessed of in the process of collecting its debts, ought to engage, & no doubt will, your early attention.

I have, since the receipt of the letter from Col. Johnson already noticed, received from him another letter[3] which I also herewith transmit relating to the Home Estates of himself & his brother

James. These estates give them an appearance of wealth which may deceive. For if the incumbrances exist which Col. Johnson mentions, and which I suppose do, though I know nothing personally of them, they will probably exhaust the whole of those Estates.

The other party desires as prompt a decision as can be conveniently made on the subject of the application of the property which I have noticed. The two brothers Richard and John T. will leave here about the middle of next month for Congress and would be glad to know that decision prior to their departure. I have the honor to be with great respect Your obedient Servant H. Clay

Langdon Cheves Esqr. &c &c &c.

ALS. PHi-Dreer Collection.

[1] On John T. Johnson's involvement, cf. above, II, 605. Payne was a brother-in-law, the husband of Betsy Johnson.

[2] Not found. [3] Not found.

From Robert P. Henry

Dear Sir. Hopkinsville 7th October 1821.

I am authorized by the Reverend George Flynn,[1] to engage you on his behalf in a suit which *has* or *will,* probably *be* brought to the Court of Appeals. It is an appeal or [*sic*] *writ of error* to reverse a judgment of the Livingston Circuit Court rendered in his favour, against Francis Prince, the plaintiff in the Court below.[2] If the record is complete, it will present the proceedings of two successive Terms;—at the first term a verdict for the plaintiff on a writ of enquiry, for $3000 in damages, a motion for a new trial on affidavit, new trial granted and Bill of Exceptions: and at the second Term, sundry Bills of Exceptions growing out of instructions and opinions of the Court, the verdict & Judgment.

The correctness of the Opinion of the Court in granting the new trial is the only point of importance in the case. If the decision of the Court of Appeals, be against Flynn, on this point, his situation is desperate. The verdict on the first trial will be fixed upon him, & he will be,—*but a ruined man.* In 1st Marshall, Haggin vs. Christian, will be found a very strong case of new-trial.[3] This case, I think clearly supports the opinion of the court in the case of Prince & Flynn. In one of the volumes of Bibb, (I don't exactly recollect which) you will find this principle decided; "that where the Court below in the exercise of the discretion lodged in it, has granted a new trial, the appellate Court will (not) [*sic*] upon Slight grounds reverse that opinion; especially where the subsequent trial on the merits eventuates in favour of the party to whom the new trial was granted."[4] This is substantially the principle decided by the Court, & Operates strongly in favour of Flynn.

The transcript of the evidence brought forward in the Bill of Exceptions, taken at the last trial, presents *only one ground;* "Whether Flynn could be guilty of the trespass, when he was two miles from the theatre of conflict, on the opposite side of the river, in a different state; was not even acquainted with the party who seized & bore away the boat; was not a confedarate [*sic*] in the enterprise & only went on board as the boat passed his own house two hours after the trespass was *Completed.*"

I am thus particular, because, I am anxious to save you some trouble in the management of the Case; and because, I am extremely desirous that Flynn should triumph, throughout. *He* has already enjoyed a species of Ovation, on his own count; and *I* have not been altogether, unnoticed, in the spectacle. I came into the cause at a most critical juncture; *after* the first verdict had passed; and had to manage it against three of the ablest Lawyers in this end of the State. The rapid growth of my practice since, demonstrates that I have gained no small share of credit by atchieving a victory so signal under circumstances so apalling [*sic*], &, apparently, so desperate.

You will be so good as to inform me, whether you will be on our side? Whether the record has yet been filed? And what fee you must have for your services?

If the Record has not yet arrived, please enquire from time to time, and let me know so soon as it comes to the office.

By request of Mr. Flynn, I enclose Twenty Dollars, which is intended as ernest [*sic*] of his future punctuality and is to be a part of such fee as you may determine to Charge. Very sincerely, Your friend & most obt. Most Humble Sert. ROBT. P. HENRY

ALS. DLC-HC (DNA, M212, R1). Addressed to Clay at Frankfort, for delivery through the "Politeness of Colo. Y. Ewing of the Senate or James C. Cravens Esq (of the H.R.)."

1 Proprietor of a ferry, Livingston County, Kentucky.

2 On an action of trespass growing out of seizure of a ferryboat owned by Prince, also a ferryman of Livingston County, the lower court had at first, in the absence of Flynn, ruled in favor of the plaintiff. Flynn appearing the next day, a new trial had been ordered, at which the judgment favoring Prince had been set aside. Prince's subsequent motion for a new trial had been overruled and the case appealed. The Court of Appeals in December, 1822, ruled that the lower court had correctly awarded the second trial but that the judgment of that trial should be reversed. Though Flynn had not initially taken the boat, he "must be considered as having come in aid of those by whom the boat was originally taken, and thereby so identified himself in their tortious acts as to become principal in the trespass. . . ." The lawyers participating in the case on appeal are not identified. 12 *Ky. Reports* (2 Littell) 240-44.

3 In the case of Samuel Haggin *vs.* Paul Christian, 8 *Ky. Reports* (1 A. K. Marshall) 579-81 (1819), on appeal from a decision of the Fayette Circuit Court, the Court of Appeals in a similar situation to that of Flynn had upheld the right to the second trial but, on the merits of the evidence, had also sustained the verdict.

4 No such statement relative to "new trials" previously held in the lower courts has been found in the *Kentucky Reports;* a similar conception of the caution to be exercised by the Court of Appeals in directing subsequent retrial was voiced in the case of Maxwell *vs.* M'Ilvoy, 5 *Ky. Reports* (2 Bibb) 215 (1810).

Promissory Note from Samuel R. Combs

[October 13, 1821]

On demand I promise to pay to H. Clay or order for value received Four hundred dollars Witness my hand & seal this 13th. Oct. 1821.

S R COMBS {L.S.}

DS, in Clay's hand. Clark Circuit Court, File 295. In June, 1825, Clay won judgment against Combs in Clark Circuit Court for collection of this debt.

Bill of Sale from Edwin Upshaw

[October 17, 1821]

Know all men by these presents that I Edwin Upshaw, of the County of King & Queen and State of Virginia, Acting as agent for all the legatees of Frank Waring Decd, late of Kentucky,[1] have this 17th. day of October, 1821. bargained and Sold unto Henry Clay of the State of Kentucky. the following Slaves. Coty for the sum of Three hundred & fifty Two dollars, and Jude for the Sum of One hundred & Seventeen dollars to me in hand paid. The receipt where of I do hereby acknowledge Which said Slaves. to Said Henry Clay. his heirs &c I bind myself as Agent for Said legatees. their heirs Exors. to warrant and defend against the Claim or Challenge of any person or persons whatever; in testimony where of I have hereunto set my hand & seal The day and Year above written

Benjn. S. Waller[2] EDWIN UPSHAW {SEAL}

[Endorsement on verso][3]

18th Octr 1821 I do hereby ratify the within bill of Sale so far as I am interested therein. SILAS M. NOEL.[4]

ADS. DLC-TJC (DNA, M212, R15).

1 Francis G. Waring, of Frankfort, Kentucky, had been killed in a duel with Jacob H. Holeman, editor of the Frankfort *Commentator,* in July, 1819, following a quarrel over Waring's having killed Holeman's dog. J. Winston Coleman, Jr., *Famous Kentucky Duels, The Story of the Code of Honor in the Bluegrass State* (Frankfort, Ky., 1953), 51-58.

2 Not identified. 3 AES.

4 A native of Essex County, Virginia, who had come to Kentucky in 1806, practiced law until 1811, then joined the Baptist Church and entered the ministry, holding a charge for a brief period at Big Spring in Woodford County. Interrupting his ministry, he had removed to Frankfort and resumed legal practice around 1815, and, on appointment from Governor Gabriel Slaughter, had become Judge of Franklin Circuit Court. Around 1824 he returned to the ministry at the Baptist Church in Frankfort and subsequently established a reputation as one of the leading clergymen of the State. He was a brother-in-law of Waring.

From Alexander Johnston, Jr.

Sir Bank of Pittsburgh 18 Oct 1821.

Neither Mr. Snyder[1] or myself have any memorandum by which we can ascertain the precise time at which the letter of the Notary containing the Notices to Morehead & Whitaker was recivd [*sic*] at Pittsburgh— Upon enquiry at the post office here as to the time of the arrival of the Baltimore & departure of the Western Mail it appears that the first arrived and the latter closed on the same afternoon so that if the Notices had been sent direct to Kentucky they would have remained only a few hours at this place— I think it was in the evening before the closing of the next Western Mail that I called at Cromwells[2] warehouse and not being able to obtain information of the place of residence of the parties I held them over for another[3] mail. If this delay will in your opinion defeat our claim against the endorsers it may perhaps be well not to go to the expence of a trial. On this subject however we submit intirely to you—

Neither of the young men who lived with Mr. Cromwell at the time I called are now in Pittsburgh so that their depositns cannot be taken. It is probable in deed, that if here, they would not be able to recollect a mere enquiry as to the residence of particular individuals, their customers, without communicating my reasons for the enquiry.

I enclose the Notarys letter on the subject of the Notices for non-acceptance by which you will perceive that his depositns would not increase our chance of a recovry—

I am with great respect Your Ob. St. ALEX: JOHNSTON JR Cr

HENRY CLAY Esqr.

ALS. DLC-TJC (DNA, M212, R12). Endorsed on verso by Clay: "I drew 18h. June 1823 on Mr. Johnson [*sic*] for the sum of $93:38 the amt. of my fee & Costs of the two Suits of Morehead & Whitaker in the Fed. Court." On December 26, 1820, Clay had filed suits for Johnston against Armistead Morehead, Russellville, Kentucky, merchant, and William W. Whitaker, also of Russellville, as Morehead's endorser, to recover the sum of $10,000, in damages, growing out of a protested bill of exchange for $4,500, dated July 18, 1819. The cases were continued until the May Term, 1823, when a decision was reached in the action against Morehead, awarding the plaintiff $5,930.50 in damages, plus the costs of suit; but the cause against Whitaker was nonsuited and the latter was discharged from his liability on the ground that notice of nonacceptance of the bill of exchange had not been given. Clay's motion to set aside the nonsuit was overruled, after which he filed a bill of exceptions. No further action in the cases has been found. U. S. Circuit Court, Seventh Circuit, District of Kentucky, Complete Records, U, 174-76, 204-207.

1 John Snyder, later Cashier of the Bank of Pittsburgh.

2 Thomas Cromwell, Pittsburgh commission merchant.

3 This word superimposed on "the next."

To Langdon Cheves

Sir Lexington 22d. Oct. 1821.

I have duly received your obliging favor of the 4h. inst.[1] communicating the entire satisfaction of the Board, with the result of the controversy in Ohio.[2] It has given me much pleasure to learn that my conduct in that particular has been approved by the Board.

Subsequent reflection has convinced me yet more fully that the conclusion of the cause has been happy. I was strongly urged by a Committee of Govr. Worthington, Mr. Morrow, Mr. Ross, Mr. Sloan, Col. Brush (all now or late members of Congress) [3] and Mr. Silliman[4] to defer taking the final cumpulsory [*sic*] step until after the intervention of the Legislature. I explained to them fully all the measures of lenity and forbearance which had characterized the conduct of the Bank, during the whole progress of the cause. I added that, if I had a certain assurance that the Legislature would unconditionally restore the money I would postpone taking that step. But even they could not concur in the opinion of that body ordering such restoration; and they left me thinking, I believe, that I would be justified in resorting to the final measure. Public opinion, as far as I could obtain knowledge of it, was either with us or not against us.

You mention the wish of the Bank that I should appear before the Supreme Court on the appeal. I will do so with great pleasure. And as I shall be taken there by other professional objects, the measure of compensation which is proposed is liberal and perfectly satisfactory. I think that the shape in which the suit was ultimately put is such that we may confidently now look for an affirmance of the decree. I entertained some doubts originally whether the Court of Chy could maintain jurisdiction of the subject, and would not leave the Bank to its redress at law, after the perpetration of the Trespass. But I think that the jurisdiction of that Court must now be supported under the aspect in which the Cause presents itself. To guard, however, against the possibility of mistake in this respect, the action of trespass has been continued.

You will have heard of the death of Mr. Salomon, the Cashr. of the Off. at New Orleans.[5] My correspondents there are very anxious that Mr. Nathl. Cox, whom I formerly recommended to the Board, should be appointed to succeed him. If the Board, should so far deviate from the policy, according to which it has generally heretofore deputed from Philada. Cashiers to the distant offices, as to make a local appointment, in New Orleans, I am persuaded it cannot entrust its important interests there to safer or more competent hands than those of Mr. Cox, whom I have long and intimately known.[6] I am with great respect Your obedient Servant H. Clay

P.S. I will thank you to place with the Cashier of the Bank the $2000, the residue of my fee for conducting the suit in Ohio, and that which the Bank has had the goodness to allow me for the Supreme Court; and I will draw for it as I may have occasion. H.C.

Langdon Cheves Esqr. &c. &c. &c.

ALS. PHi-Etting Collection. 1 Not found.

[2] See above, Clay to Cheves, September 8, 1821.

[3] Thomas Worthington; Jeremiah Morrow, United States Congressman, 1803-1813, 1840-1843, United States Senator, 1813-1819, and Governor of Ohio, 1822-1826; Thomas R. Ross; John Sloane, Congressman, 1819-1829, Secretary of State of Ohio, 1841-1844, Treasurer of the United States, 1850-1853; Henry Brush.

[4] Wyllys Silliman, born in Stratford, Connecticut, briefly resident in Marietta, Ohio, and after 1804 a prominent lawyer of Zanesville. He had been one of the founders of the Marietta *Ohio Gazette and the Territorial and Virginia Herald* (1801-1803); member of the Ohio legislature, 1803; presiding judge of the middle circuit, Court of Common Pleas, 1803-1804; and Register of the land office at Zanesville, 1805-1811. In 1825 he was a member of the State Senate and in 1828 and 1829, of the State House of Representatives. His wife was a sister of Lewis Cass.

[5] Ezekiel Salomon had died September 27.

[6] Charles S. West, Cashier of the office of the Bank of the United States at Fayetteville, North Carolina, was transferred to the New Orleans post in December, 1821. Clay's earlier recommendation of Cox has not been found.

Bond from William Pollock

[October 22, 1821]

I have sold & bind myself on demand to convey to H. Clay five acres three quarters & 20 poles of land,[1] being the same which Jno Pollock purchased of Jesse Bledsoe,[2] adjoining the land on which I live and also the tract lately purchased by the said Clay from the Bank of Kentucky,[3] in which deed I am to be bound to repay the consideration money of forty five dollars per acre with interest paid by said Clay if the title is defective but I am not to be bound to warrant against any claim of dower. Witness my hand & seal this 22d. Oct. 1821. Possession is hereby given by me to said Clay.

WM POLLOCK {SEAL}

DS, in Clay's hand. DLC-TJC (DNA, M212, R15).

[1] See below, Property Deed, July 4, 1825.

[2] Fayette County Court, Deed Book I, 234-35 (November 4, 1813). John Pollock resided in Fayette County.

[3] See below, Property Deed, December 26, 1821.

Property Deed from Daniel and Eliza P. Bradford

[October 23, 1821]

[Daniel Bradford and Eliza P., his wife, for the sum of one dollar, paid and acknowledged, sell to Clay two lots in the town of Lexington "bounded as followeth towit Beginning at a stake at the junction of the George town road and second street running thence with said street South East one hundred and nine feet to an Ally of fifteen feet wide, thence with the Ally South West ninety six feet and six inches to an Ally ten feet wide thence with said Ally North West to the George town road, thence with said road a Northwardly Course one hundred and six feet to the beginning, being two lots conveyed to Abner Le Grand by Coleman and Todd[1] and their wives on the 29h July 1818 and known in the said Coleman & Todds platt by their numbers fifteen and sixteen; and conveyed to the said Bradford by the said Le Grand by deed under date the 26h. day of March 1819 recorded in Book S. page 313, with the appurtenances." Signatures of the Bradfords acknowledged and dower relinquished before James C. Rodes, Clerk of Fayette County—that of Daniel Bradford on October 23, 1821, and that of his wife, December 24, 1821.]

DS, in Clay's hand. DLC-TJC (DNA, M212, R10).

1 James Coleman, of Fayette County, and Dr. John Todd (son of Levi Todd), formerly of Fayette County, at this time a resident of Madison County, Illinois Territory, later of Springfield, Illinois. Fayette County, Deed Book S, 158-59.

To Langdon Cheves

Sir Lexington 26h. Oct. 1821.

A question is about being stir ed [*sic*] in regard to damages upon protested bills of exchange, in which the Bank of the U.S. is materially concerned. Protested bills drawn upon places out of this State, have been long supposed here to entitle the holders to ten per Cent damages, without regard to the residence of the parties. Upon that supposition all the local banks have governed themselves, and it was the common understanding of the Country. The branches of your bank conformed to the general usage. But in a cause recently decided by our Court of Appeals (the tribunal of last resort) in which I happened myself to be a party, in a fiduciary character, that Court decided that the damages were not recoverable, unless the bill was drawn upon a *person out* of the State.[1] The case was this: I drew bills for a large amount upon the late Genl. Sam. Hopkins, payable in Balto. in favor of John Hart, both of them being Citizens and residents of Kentucky. The bills were accepted, but were returned protested for non-payment. After their return I took a deed of trust from the drawee to secure payment of the principal interest and *damages.* Hopkins filed a bill in chancery to be relieved against the payment of the damages, and the Court did relieve him. I transmit you a Copy of the section of our law, which is now repealed, on this subject,[2] to give you a clearer view of the question. Since this decision a debtor to the office in this place, has applied to the Board to be relieved or credited for the amount of damages which is comprehended in his note, and the Board has refered the question to me. When the bill was returned protested the amount of it, including damages was liquidated, and his note was given for it, which has been several times renewed. My opinion is that, if he files a bill in equity, he will be relieved upon the ground of a mutual mistake of the parties; that his title to relief will not be precluded by the subsequent renewals of his note, all of which will be considered as infected by the original error.[3]

If the question were limited to the particular case, it would possess less interest. But it is probable there is not less than twenty or thirty thousand dollars, at the two offices in this State, which may be affected by the decision of the particular case. If the credit be refused to the party, he will appeal to a Court of justice, and should that relieve him, as I apprehend, others will be tempted to follow his example. If without such appeal, the credit should be voluntarily allowed him, a knowledge of the fact may be diffused, and other applications founded upon it may be made. There is difficulty therefore in either alternative, perhaps less however in the latter. I think the Bank equitably entitled to the damages, because all the parties to the transactions supposed them the necessary consequence of protest, and because that supposition constituted, no doubt, a leading motive with the offices in negotiating the bills. Under this view of the matter had we not better so arrange with the particular case, if we can, as to present as little encouragement as possible to other persons similarly situated? If it be desirable to take the question to the Supreme Court, there will be no difficulty in making a preparation of it to that object. I shall defer reporting my opinion to the Board until I hear from you. There will be no impropriety in saying to the party that the matter is under consideration, or that it will be time enough to give him an answer, when he is ready, which he is not now, to pay the residue of the debt.

I have received your letter of the 8h. inst. relative to the debt of John J. Marshall.[4] All that has occured, since I wrote you in August, respecting the insecurity of that debt has tended to confirm the opinions which I then expressed. I shall see him in a day or two, and will lose no time in effecting the best arrangement I can.

I am, with great respect, Your obedient Servant H. CLAY

L. Cheves Esq. &c. &c &c

ALS. PU. 1 See above, II, 327n.

2 The statute as enacted February 6, 1798, had provided: "If any person or persons shall draw or endorse any bill or bills of exchange, upon any person or persons out of this state, on any other person or persons within any other of the United States of North America, and the same being returned back unpaid, with a legal protest, the drawer thereof, and all others concerned, shall pay the contents of the said bill or bills, together with legal interest from the time the said bill or bills were protested, the charges of protest, and ten pounds per. cent advance for the damage thereof, and so proportionable for greater or lesser sums. . . ." Littell (comp.), *Statute Law of Kentucky*, II, 103. This section of the law had been repealed relative to all future contracts by act of January 10, 1820. Ky. Gen. Assy., *Acts, 1819-1820*, p. 823.

3 The case involved a bill of exchange drawn at Lexington, October 12, 1818, by Robert Griffing, identified only as a Kentuckian, on James Daniel, of Clark County, Kentucky, for $10,000, payable 120 days after date at the New Orleans office of discount and deposit of the Bank of the United States. The bill, drawn in favor of Henry Daniel, Isaac Cunningham, and Samuel Hanson, the latter two also of Clark County and both, like Henry Daniel, repeatedly members of the Kentucky legislature,

had been accepted by James Daniel and endorsed by the drawees to the Bank of the United States. When the bill remained unpaid at its due date, it had been protested. In July, 1819, James Daniel had made a settlement of the debt which comprehended payment, partially in cash and partially in another negotiable note, covering the principal, interest charges, and damages for the protest. The following year, a further partial payment having been made, a third note had been negotiated by Griffing and the drawees for the balance. This last note becoming due and protested, a suit was ultimately instituted, asking an injunction against collection of so much of the debt as constituted protest damages on the original bill. The United States Circuit Court in November, 1827, granted the injunction till further order and, at a final hearing in November, 1836, perpetually enjoined execution on that sum.

The Supreme Court, at the January Term, 1838, reversed this decision and discharged the injunction. In reaching this decree the Court placed main emphasis upon its reluctance to extend relief against a mistake of law when the parties "with a full knowledge of the facts, and a presumed knowledge of the law," had paid or agreed to pay the damages. Furthermore, the Court held that the right to petition for relief had been forfeited under the act of limitations, the opportunity for disputing the charges having been neglected at the earlier dates of settlement in 1819 and 1820. Bank of the United States *vs.* James Daniel *et al.*, 37 *U.S.* (12 Peters) 32-57.

4 This letter and that next mentioned in the document have not been found. Marshall, son of Humphrey Marshall, was a native of Woodford County, Kentucky. He had been graduated from Princeton College, had represented Franklin County in the State legislature (1815-1817, 1833-1834), and was a member of the State Senate (1820-1824), reporter of the Kentucky Court of Appeals (1829-1832), and judge of Jefferson Circuit Court from 1836 until his death in 1846.

On March 28, 1821, the President, Directors, and Company of the Bank of the United States had instituted five suits in the Federal Circuit Court against Marshall and his cosigners, for liabilities amounting to a total of $33,498.95, contracted in notes given in 1819 and 1820 to the Louisville office of the Bank. At the Fall Term, 1821, judgments favorable to the plaintiff were rendered in each case. U.S. Circuit Court, Seventh Circuit, District of Kentucky, Complete Records, Q, 390-401, 407-410. On September 20, 1821, the Bank authorities had instituted three additional suits against Marshall, amounting to a liability of $6,940, on notes contracted in 1820 at the Lexington office of the Bank. Judgments for the plaintiff were awarded at the May Term, 1822. *Ibid.*, S, 168-70, 205-208, 214-17. At the Spring Term, 1827, four other suits brought for the Bank against Marshall were dismissed, with each party to pay his own costs, the controversies having been adjusted. *Ibid.*, Order Book L, 147-48; M, 4, 75.

To Peter B. Porter.

My dear Sir Frankfort 31st. Oct. 1821.

I have been requested to procure some information for an old soldier, formerly in the the service of New York, who supposes himself to be entitled to some land under the laws of that state; and I know no one more likely to obtain and communicate the information than yourself. The memo. which he has sent me is as follows: "Samuel Holly[1] a soldier who served four years in Clintons[2] Brigade, Courtlands[3] Regimt. Hamtrammock's[4] Company, has not got the land which he understands was drawn for him. He understood he drew lot No. 47 in Hector, now Tompkins County, and that the patent was delivered to William Campbell.[5] Mr. Holly has not been in the State of New York since the year 1784 and has given no assignment to any person for the land, nor does he know any thing about William Campbell. N.B. Mr. Holly enlisted in the State of New York with a promise of a section of land."

You will very much oblige the old man and me if you will have the goodness to satisfy his mind on the subject of this land. If he be entitled to it, I am persuaded that you will take pleasure in giving him any aid in your power to establish his right

Do me the favor to make my best respects to Mrs Porter[6] and believe me Truly & Faithfully Yours H. CLAY

P.S. I would thank you to drop a line communicating any information you may acquire respecting this land to George Pearry Shelbyville (K.). H C.

Genl. P. B. Porter.

ALS. NBuHi. Addressed to Porter at Black Rock, New York. Postmarked: "Travellers Rest P Os. office [*sic*] Ky 7th. November." Travellers' Rest was the home of Isaac Shelby, in Lincoln County.

1 At this time a resident of Shelby County, Kentucky, Holley had served during the Revolution as a private in the Second Regiment, New York Line.

2 George Clinton.

3 Philip Van Cortlandt, who had served as lieutenant colonel in command of the Second New York Regiment. Mustered out of service with the rank of brigadier general for gallantry at the siege of Yorktown, he had served in both houses of the State legislature, 1788-1793, and as member of Congress, 1793-1809.

4 John Francis Hamtramck, born in Canada, had served as captain of the 5th New York Regiment during the Revolution and as a lieutenant colonel in the Battle of Fallen Timbers.

5 Possibly Dr. William Campbell of Otsego County, New York, later State Surveyor General.

6 In 1818 Porter had married Letitia Breckinridge Grayson, widow of Alfred W. Grayson.

From David Hart

Dr. Sir Vincennes 2nd. November 1821.

I received yours of the 13th. Octr.[1] by the last mail; the new Certificates are not yet made out, when they are I will forward them to you— The following tracts of your Land lye in Illinois viz the W. half of *S. 18. T. 14 N. R. 10. W*— S. E. qr. *S. 12. T. 14. N. R. 11. W*— *S. W. qr. S. 8. T. 14. N. R. 10. W*— *S. E. qr. S. 6. T. 14. N. R. 10. W*—and S. 7. T. 14. N. R. 10. W—[2] The other Two quarters which you retain lye in Indiana,[3] and as you Know are not yet Subject to taxation, the five years from the date of the entry not having yet expired— By an act of the Legislature of Illinois, of 1819, all Lands in the State are divided into three Classes, the first Valued at four, the second at three, & the third at Two Dollars, per, Acre and an *ad Valorem* Tax levied, of one half per cent. all non residents' property is placed in the first Class & Taxed accordingly— If the tax be not paid at the time fixed by the act, the Land is offered for Sale & if not purchased by Individuals, Stricken off to the State— All lands heretofore Sold or Stricken off to the State may be redeemed by payment into the Treasury of the Sum due with interest & costs of Sale On or before the first day of January 1822—

The first payment for your Lands will become due on the First of March next
Yours &C D. HART.

ALS. DLC-TJC (DNA, M212, R12). Addressed to Clay at Lexington. Hart, nephew of Col. Thomas Hart, had settled in Princeton, Indiana, in 1815, after serving as a judge advocate with the Kentucky Volunteers in the War of 1812. A promising young lawyer, he had been appointed presiding judge of the circuit court in 1818, but had been suspended later in the year as the result of sending a duelling challenge. He had removed to Vincennes around 1820. W. Faux, *Memorable Days in America . . .* (London, 1823), in Reuben Gold Thwaites, *Early Western Travels, 1748-1846 . . .*, XI (Cleveland, 1905), 215 and note.
1 Not found. 2 In Edgar County. 3 Not located.

Agreements with Mary O. Russell

[November 3, 1821]

In consideration of the professional services heretofore rendered to me by Henry Clay, and those which he has undertaken to render me in the suit in Chancery now depending in Fayette Circuit Court brought by the Heirs or Representatives of John May against me for Land near Lexington,[1] I do hereby agree to pay the said Clay One thousand dollars, provided I succeed in defeating their claim to the said land, to be paid upon the decision of the said suit. It is however understood that the said Clay is to appear for me in the Court of Appeals, if the cause should be taken by appeal there; and that in the event of its being so taken to the Court of Appeals I am not to pay the said one thousand dollars, without I succeed in defeating the said claim in the Court of Appeals. Witness my hand & seal this 3rd. day of Novr. 1821. MARY O. RUSSELL {L.S.}

Teste
JAMES E. DAVIS

[Endorsement][2]

A suit having been brought in the Fed. Court by the sister of the late James Hughes Esq. to foreclose a mortgage given by him to her on a house & lot in Lexn. formerly owned by me[3] & now occupied by Leslie Combs, I do agree to give H Clay (whom I have employed to appear for me in the said suit) five hundred dollars, if I succeed in defeating the said mortgage; but if it should be established then I am not to pay him anything. Witness my hand & seal this 3rd. day of Novr. 1821. MARY O. RUSSELL {L.S.}

Teste
J. E. DAVIS

[Endorsement on verso][4]

Memo. I am willing to receive of Mrs. Russell a part of the land within refered to, at a fair valuation, in satisfaction of the within
6. Nov. 1821. H. CLAY

DS, in Clay's hand. DLC-TJC (DNA, M212, R15).

1 "John L. May, Daniel Epps and Polly his wife, heirs of John May, deceased," had begun action in chancery against "Mary O. Russell, Thomas Irwin and Jane his wife" to contest the validity of an assignment, made in 1780 to John Todd by George May as agent for John May, for a settlement of 400 acres and pre-emption of 1,000 acres lying northwest of the "Mansfield" tract, on Boone's road, in Fayette County, Kentucky. After the death of Todd, patents to the land had been issued to his daughter, Mary Owen Todd (later Russell), on December 20, 1784. In April, 1823, the suit was abated as to Daniel Epes (Epps, Eppes), who had died. At the September, 1823, Term of the Fayette Circuit Court the case was decided in favor of the defendants; and Clay won an affirmation of this decision at the Fall Term, 1824, of the Kentucky Court of Appeals. Charles R. Staples, "History in Circuit Court Records—Fayette County, Kentucky," Kentucky State Historical Society, *Register,* XXXIII (1935), [151]-59; 17 *Ky. Reports* (1 Monroe) 223-28. A notice of objection to reading of George May's deposition, filed September 20, 1822; an amendment to Mary O. Russell's answer to the bill of complaint, filed February 6, 1822; and a further amendment to her answer, filed October 12, 1822—all ADS by Clay, may be found in KyU.

2 ES, in Clay's hand.

3 Hughes, who had died at Blue Licks, Kentucky, in August, 1818, had sold the property, approximately one-fourth of out-lot no. 16, to George M. Bibb, who had transferred it to John Jordan, Jr., and the latter, in turn, to Mary Owen Russell, the deed dated December 29, 1806, reading from Hughes to Mrs. Russell. Fayette Circuit Court, Deed Book C, 290. Hughes' sister, Martha, having returned to Cardigan, South Wales and married John Edwards, suit was brought as Edwards and Wife *vs.* Hughes and Others, to obtain payment on a loan of £770, 2s, 4d, secured by mortgage on sundry lots in Lexington. The lower court dismissed the bill against all the defendants but Gabriel Tandy, Samuel Patterson, and Hughes' heirs and representatives, who were called upon to pay the debt or suffer foreclosure of the property. Clay argued their case on appeal to the Supreme Court in 1824, but the ruling of the lower court was affirmed, with costs. 22 *U. S.* (9 Wheaton) 489-501.

4 AES.

Rental Agreement with Dr. Charles Caldwell and Others

[November 5, 1821]

An agreement entered into this 5th day of Novr. 1821 Between Charles Caldwell, Samuel Brown, William H Richardson[1] and James Blythe, members of the Medical Faculty in Lexington in the State of Kentucky[2] of the one part and Henry Clay of the other part:

Whereas the said Clay has been at considerable trouble & expence in fitting up apartments in the town of Lexington for the said Faculty, in delivering their lectures and making their demonstrations during their annual Sessions.

The said Clay hereby covenants to lease to the said Caldwell, Brown, Richardson and Blythe for the use of themselves and their successors the two large rooms in the Kentucky Hotel, which have been fitted up for the above purpose, for the term of Five years, commencing on the first Monday in November 1821. And the said Clay hath also leased hereby to them for the same term, the room in the said Hotel in which their library at present is;[3] but he reserves the liberty, if it should become necessary in renting out the residue of the establishment, to take back the said library room, and to substitute in place of it another over the said lecturing rooms. And in case of his so taking it back, and substituting another room, twenty dollars are to be deducted from the rent hereafter mentioned.

In consideration whereof the said Caldwell, Brown, Richardson and Blythe covenant with the said Clay that they and their successors shall annually pay to him, during each and every year of this lease, the sum of four hundred and twenty dollars in advance, the first payment to be made on the first Monday in November 1821 and so on that day for every year thereafter during this lease.

They further covenant to cause to be put in all glass that may be broke & to repair other injuries that may be done to the property during that portion of the year when it shall be occupied for the above purposes; but they are not to be liable for natural decay & inevitable accidents.

During that portion of the year when the said apartments are not used by the aforesaid lessees for lecturing to the medical students, the said Clay is to be at liberty to use them (except the Library room.) for any purpose he may deem proper, and he is then to be responsible for necessary repairs.

The said Clay hereby reserves the priviledge of distress and also that of re-entry into the demised premises, in the event of default in the payment of the rent stipulated for or any part thereof.

Witness the seals of the parties the day and year first mentd.

Sealed & Delivered
In presence of

H. CLAY {L.S.}
CH: CALDWELL {L.S.}
SAM. BROWN {L.S.}
W. H. RICHARDSON {L.S.}
JAMES BLYTHE {L.S.}

[Endorsement][4]
Recd. Novr. 1821. the first years rent. H. CLAY
[Endorsement on wrapper][5]
$30 were agreed to be added for the other apartments in the house containing the Lecture rooms, for a Museum &c. making therefore the total rent $450. HC.

ADS, signed also by Caldwell and others. DLC-TJC (DNA, M212, R15).

1 Who had settled in Lexington in March, 1813, and held the professorship in obstetrics from September of that year until his death in 1845. His medical degree, conferred in 1819, had been received from the University of the State of New York. He had also been a trustee and president of the Kentucky Insurance Company during the latter years of that institution (its charter having expired in 1820).

2 That is, of the Medical Department of Transylvania University. Another of the professors, Dr. Benjamin W. Dudley, lectured in rooms back of his own office on Mill Street. In 1827 funds were raised and a building, the first "Medical Hall," was constructed for the use of this department. Peter, *History of the Medical Department of Transylvania University*, 29n, 43-46.

3 Originally rented by Dr. Caldwell. See above, II, 724, 882.

4 AES. Receipted below by Robert Scott as follows (all AES, with exception noted): November 10, 1825, received of "Doctr. Cross" $100 in Commonwealth's notes on account of rent due the 7th instant; November 11, 1825 (AE), received of Dr. Blythe

$100 more on the same account; November 12, 1825, received of Dr. Cross $220 "on Acct of said rent"; May 23, 1826, received of Dr. Cross $22.50, which with $7.50 paid earlier by Dr. Richardson made "together 30$ in full of balance of last years rent"; and November 20, 1826, received of "Mr. H. Graham" $450 "in full of One years rent."

Dr. James Conquest Cross, born in Lexington and graduated from Transylvania with the degree of M.D. in 1822, was Medical Librarian in 1824-1825. He subsequently held a professorship at the Medical College of Ohio, in Cincinnati, before returning to Transylvania as occupant of the chair in Institutes of Medicine from 1837 till his dismissal, as an outgrowth of controversy among the medical faculty, in 1844. He was Dean of that faculty in 1838.

Hosmer Graham, a resident of New York State, served as Medical Librarian at Transylvania from 1825 to 1827 and received the degree of M.D. there in March of the latter year.

5 AEI.

Bail Bond for Thomas A. Marshall

[November 5, 1821]

I, Henry Clay do hereby acknowledge myself Special Bail for the within named Thomas A. Marshall in the suit named in the within writ. Given under my hand this 5th. day of November 1821.

H. CLAY

U. S. Circuit Court, Seventh Circuit, District of Kentucky, Complete Records, S, 206. Endorsement on writ in case of The President, Directors, and Company of the Bank of the United States *vs.* Robert Brenham and John J. Marshall, under the firm of Brenham and Marshall, Thomas A. Marshall, Richard Taylor, and John Samuel, for a debt of $2,200, on a note contracted with the Lexington office of the Bank, one of the suits referred to above, Clay to Cheves, October 26, 1821, note.

Thomas A. Marshall, a brother of John J. and son of Humphrey, had been born in Woodford County, Kentucky, and graduated from Yale College (1815). Beginning the practice of law in Frankfort, he had settled in Paris, Kentucky, in 1819. He removed to Lexington in 1835, to Frankfort in 1857, and to Louisville in 1859. He was a member of the Kentucky legislature, 1827, 1828, 1863-1865, and of the United States Congress, 1831-1835, a judge of the Kentucky Court of Appeals, 1835-1856, 1866, and a professor of law at Transylvania University, 1836-1849.

Brenham and Samuel were residents of Frankfort.

Memorandum of Agreement with Mary O. Russell

[November 6, 1821]

Attached to Agreements, November 3, 1821.

Property Deed to Robert Snell

[*ca.* November 13, 1821]

[For the sum of one thousand[1] seventy two and 5/100 dollars lawful money of the United States of America Henry Clay and Isham Talbot sell to Robert Snell all their interest in 91½ acres, part of Josiah Watson's[2] survey, bounded with reference to points in the lines of Joseph Ewing, Charles Whitaker, John McKinney, Noel,[3] and the Cynthiana road. Title guaranteed only against claimants under Clay. Recorded by Willis A. Lee, Clerk of Franklin County, on the date above named, and on December 14, 1821, produced for record in Scott County Court.]

Scott County Court, Deed Book E, 85-86. Recorded copy partially destroyed. See above, I, 577-78n; Property Deed, June 17, 19, 1821. An indenture signed by Isham Talbot, dated November 16, 1821, apparently covering the same tract, was witnessed and proved by John McKinney and John Montgomery and admitted to record in Scott County Court on December 14, 1821. Scott County Court, Deed Book E, 82-83. Montgomery, probably one of the long hunters of 1771 and an early resident of Harrodsburg, Kentucky, now lived in Scott County. McKinney, brother-in-law of Montgomery and son of Alexander McKinney, was popularly known as "Wildcat" McKinney because of an encounter in which he had killed a wildcat in the schoolhouse outside the fort at Lexington in the spring of 1783. Having first come to Kentucky in 1779, he had lived near Lexington until 1785, then had moved to Bourbon County, which he had represented in the Kentucky Constitutional Convention of 1792. With the exception of a three-year residence in Missouri, 1808-1811, and four years in the Hickman Creek district of Fayette County, Kentucky, somewhat later, he spent the remainder of his life at Clintonville in the Green Creek area, south of Paris, in Bourbon County. He died in 1825.

1 Next word, or several words, missing.

2 Prominent merchant and banker of Alexandria, Virginia; one of the original patent holders in the Georgetown area, Scott County.

3 First name missing.

To Langdon Cheves

Sir Lexn. 21 Nov. 1821.

In collecting the debts of the B. of the U.S. in the Western States, it has necessarily acquired, and must acquire more, real estate, the present management and future disposition of which no doubt engage its serious consideration. Many of its debts are secured by mortgage, and payment of these may have to be enforced by sales of the estate pledged. It is desirable that the Bank should avoid, as much as possible, becoming a purchaser at those sales; but, with all its just indisposition to be encumbered with that description of property, it must some times buy to avoid loss. A discretion to this effect must be somewhere given. How can the authority be most safely confered? I know of no safer repository of it than that of the Agents at Cincinnati in regard to that office, and the Cashiers of the respective offices of Lexington, Louisville and Chillicothe, acting by the advice of those several boards, in respect to their different interests. They will be instructed, of course, to purchase in no instance where the security of the debt does not require it.

In respect to the property thus obtained or hereafter to be acquired three objects appear to me to demand attention:

1. To protect and preserve it from intrusion and waste.
2. To rent out such parts of it as are productive, and to collect the rents. and

3dly. To sell the estate, and to guard against improvident alienation.

The Bank will want the local taxes to be regularly paid; intruders kept off or put out; voluntary waste prevented; and, in some instances, necessary repairs made. It will wish, until sales can be effected, to rent it out, and the rents to be regularly collected. When sold, it will desire to replace that for which it was received, including interest and expences, and that it shall sell for at least as much as it will fairly command in the market. Considering the mass of real estate, which it is likely to acquire, these different objects will engross a large share of any one person's time, if he be engaged only in relation to the affairs of a particular office. The property is scattered scattered [*sic*] throughout the Western States, or at least two of them. The rural part of it, according to the custom of the Country, will be rented out annually; and the rents of that which is in towns, according to the same custom, are payable quarterly or half yearly. There will be much riding about, and a vigilant observation of the conduct of tenants and others should be exerted. In respect to sales, which it will be desirable to make whenever a fair price can be procured, provision should be made to guard against frauds and to secure responsibility.

When we thus clearly comprehend the nature of the service to be performed, we shall be better prepared to understand the character of the agency which should be employed. As to Cincinnati, I presume you will have to confide in the Agents whom you have placed there. It is not to be desired to multiply your agencies, as that would have the effect of weakening responsibility, and increasing your expences. As to the other three offices therefore, it would perhaps be best to place the business generally under the control of their respective Cashiers. I have heretofore recommended that a particular Clerk, at each of them, be charged with the duty of keeping the accounts of debtors who are sued, attending officers sales, taking care of the registry of deeds, mortgages &c.[1] The same Clerk, under the direction of the Cashier, might rent out estates, collect the rents, pay taxes, protect the property &c. As to sales, the Cashier might be empowered to effect them, subject to the ratification of the local board, whose information of their value will in the general essentially aid that officer; and at the same time a salutary check upon him will be secured.

In respect to Kentucky another plan has suggested itself to me. Let *one* person be engaged to attend to the Landed interests of both offices. Let him account to the offices respectively quarterly or half yearly & pay over the rents. Let him effect Sales subject to the ratification of that Board at which the Land was acquired; and let him receive a Commission upon the amount of rents and of Sales. It will in the general be best that payments be secured in Specie, and not the Current money of the Country. Whether the one or the other plan be adopted, a power of Attorney, under the Seal of the Corporation, will be requisite; and in that power should be inserted a restrictive clause, that the validity of all sales which the Agent may effect must depend upon their ratification by the local board. Without such a precaution too great opportunity would be given to collusion between the Agent and purchasers.

I have received your letter respecting the affairs of Col. Johnson, with its inclosures.[2] As soon as I can have the business completed, I mean to take possession of the property and cause it to be rented out. Mr. Marshall[3] moves slowly, and I begin to entertain fears that he will be unable to discharge his debt in the mode authorized.

I have the honor to be with great respect Your's faithfully

Langdon Cheves Esqr. &c &c &c. H. CLAY

P.S. I need not add that my advice is constantly given & shall continue to be given in respect to your Landed interests both as to matters of Fact and of Law. H.C.

ALS. PHi-Etting Collection.
1 Cf. above, Clay to Cheves, February 27, March 10 (2), 1821.
2 Not found. See above, Clay to Cheves, June 11, July 8, 21, October 3, 1821.
3 John J. Marshall. See above, Clay to Cheves, October 26, 1821.

Agreement with Joseph Lindsay

[November 21, 1821]

Whereas H. Clay and Isham Talbot have recovered a tract of land in Scott County and partly agreed to divide the same and ninety two acres part thereof has fallen to the share of the said Clay in part, according to a survey lately made by John Ewing,[1] of which ninety two acres Joseph Lindsey [*sic*] is in possession.

The said Clay doth hereby agree to let the said Lindsey remain on the said ninety two acres one year free from rent.

In consideration whereof the said Lindsey agrees to surrender quiet possession of the said ninety two acres of land on the first of March 1823. in good tenantable order; and in the meantime to commit no waste thereon. Witness the seals of the said Clay and Lindsey this 21 Nov. 1821. H. CLAY {L.S.}

JOSEPH LINDSAY {L.S.}

ADS, signed also by Lindsay, who lived on the Frankfort road, in northern Fayette County, probably adjacent to the tract mentioned. DLC-TJC (DNA, M212, R15). See above, I, 577-78n; Power of Attorney, June 16, 1821; Property Deed, June 17, 19, *ca.* November 13, 1821.

1 The bill, dated October 18, 1821, from Ewing, Deputy Surveyor of Scott County, Kentucky, amounted to $6.50, covering charges of $4.50 for surveying 210 acres and a connected plot, plus one dollar each for two chain carriers. ADS. DLC-TJC (DNA, M212, R15).

To Thomas Bodley

My dear Sir Frankfort 30h. Nov. 1821

I duly received your letter[1] upon the subject of the re-hearing which you wished to obtain of the principle that 20 years' possession constitutes a Bar to a bill in equity; and I this morning stated to the Court that there existed a wish with several members of the Bar, and myself among them, to obtain a rehearing; but as neither of us were counsel in the case decided,[2] and as the 15 days, within which, by the rules of the Court, rehearings must be applied for had expired, we could not make the application without an enlargement of the time. I urged that as other parties were interested in the principle, and as they did not know of the decision until some time after it was rendered, the period ought to be enlarged &c. The Court manifested I thought entire confidence in their opinion; stated that the question had been repeatedly argued, and had been long under consideration. So decided indeed was their manner that it appeared to me to be wholly useless to make the effort you wish. Such I am persuaded is the impression of all who were present. I regret it much; for it would have afforded me particular satisfaction to have been able to render you any service. I have supposed, bad as this news must be to you, that it may be well for you to know it whilst you are in Mason. Your's faithfly H. CLAY

Gen. Tho. Bodley.

ALS. KyHi. Addressed to Bodley at "Washington Mason Co. (K)."

1 Not found.

2 Joseph Mitchell and Others *vs.* Edward Owings, argued by Isham Talbot and Martin D. Hardin before the Kentucky Court of Appeals in April, 1821, on appeal from Bourbon Circuit Court, relative to an erroneous property division dating from 1789. The higher court had ruled that inasmuch as those who had a beneficial interest in the controversy had been infants and out of the country and since the error had been discovered in much less than twenty years before the commencement of the suit, "there can be no question that the lapse of time can not operate as a bar to relief." 10 *Ky. Reports* (3 A. K. Marshall) 316.

Receipt from William P. Roper

[*ca.* November 30, 1821]

Recd. of H. Clay a note of Basil Tout[1] for Two hundred and thirty five dollars due 17h. March 1821 given to Tho. Bodley and assigned to said Clay, for collection. W. P. ROPER

DS, in Clay's hand. DLC-TJC (DNA, M212, R15).

1 Of Fleming County, Kentucky.

To Caesar A. Rodney

My dear Sir Lexington 2d. Decr. 1821.

I received your obliging favor of the 8h. Ulto.[1] from Wilmington;

and assure you of my cordial & hearty participation with you in the pleasure which the recent glorious events in South America have produced.[2] That this Country ought long since to have given some signal proof of the interest which the people feel in the success of the great cause of the South I have fully testified; and it has been to me a source of great regret that others did not see the subject in the same light that I did. But I shall be prepared, whenever that proof is rendered, to hail it with inexpressible satisfaction. It is my intention to attend the Supreme Court, at the approaching Session, and should I be able to realize it, I will then have the gratification of conversing with you fully on that interesting topic, as well as on others. I have not perused Mr. Schmidts pamphlet,[3] though I have seen some valuable extracts from it.

We are all extremely anxious in this quarter to learn the condition of the public revenue; and are entertaining fearful apprehensions of a deficit. Will you persist in the ruinous policy of loans? tax us, or retrench?

I shall leave here in about three weeks for Ohio.

The Honble Mr. Rodney. Yours faithfully. H. CLAY

ALS. DLC-Rodney Family Papers (DNA, M212, R22). Addressed to Rodney at "H. of R. Washington City."

1 Not found.

2 On the recent success of the Patriots in Venezuela and Colombia see above, II, 505, n. 25.

3 Probably Conrad Georg Friedrich Elias von Schmidt-Phiseldek, *Europe and America: or, the Relative State of the Civilized World at a Future Period* (Tr. from the German by Joseph Owen; Copenhagen, 1820), a volume of 257 pages—published also in French, as well as the German, that same year.

To Langdon Cheves

Sir Frankfort 3d. Decr. 1821

I duly recd. your favor of the 7h. Ulto. relative to the question of damages.[1] That question has not yet got into Court. If it should arise there, I will take care and have the matters of fact stated in the manner the most likely to produce in the Supreme Court a decision favorable to the Bank. But one person has talked of making the question, who is a professional gentleman bound for a debt believed to be perfectly secure. I have requested Mr. Harper[2] to say to him, "that the Bank is advised by its Counsel that the damages are recoverable, that it will not relinquish them, and that, if necessary it means to carry the question up. But that as the debt comprehends much more than the damages, and as he is not prepared to pay up the residue, after deducting them, if he will continue to pay the discount upon the whole debt, his *claim* to an exemption from the damages shall not be prejudiced by any thing that may be done in future." My wish is to postpone for the present the agitation of the question. For I fear Mr. Sergeant[3] is mistaken. Our law clearly marks the distinction between Foreign, Inland and Domestic Bills, the former being those drawn upon persons out of the U.S. the second those drawn on persons within the U.S. and the third within the State.[4] Judge Washington's opinion (if indeed it could have any application to the affair of damages) must be understood to furnish a definition of a Foreign bill only where the local law does not.[5]

The Fed. Court here has now been in Session for four weeks and will continue two more. A question was stirred early in it, in a criminal case in which I was not concerned, involving the validity of the acts of the Marshall [*sic*] and his Deputies for the last four years. The Court in that case decided that they were invalid, in consequence of his failure to take the oath & give the bond required by law, under a new commission. Perceiving the confusion, and the prejudice to the Bank likely to result from that decision, I argued the question, on a motion made to discharge a person in custody at the suit of the Bank, and am happy to tell you that the Court changed its opinion, and has decided that all his acts are good, even if he is to be considered only as an officer de facto.[6]

Many judgments are obtained for the Bank, and now as at the last Court we have succeeded in every controverted case. The opinion of the Court on the Marshall's question, alone, I think entitles us to success in the False Imprisonment case in the State Court of Ohio. I shall send a Copy of it to Mr. Creighton.[7] It was my intention to have attended the State Court on the trial of that cause; but as the term of it commences the day after tomorrow, I am apprehensive that I cannot get off from this Court in time. I have communicated my instructions however fully heretofore to the Counsel there, and have requested them to prepare the case, in the manner which I have suggested, for the Supreme Court of the U.S., if we should lose it, which is not apprehended.[8]

Col. Johnsons agents (for he is absent) proceed slowly in completing the arrangement to which the Bank has assented, as communicated in your letter of the 27th. October.[9] I am assured that it shall be done before I leave Kentucky for Columbus.

I am Sir with great respect Your obedient Servant H. CLAY

Langdon Cheves Esqr. &c &c &c

P.S. I will transmit to Mr. Sergeant a Copy of our act at large and of the opinion of the Court of Appeals concerning Bills of Exchange.

H C

ALS. PHi-Etting Collection.

1 Not found. See above, Clay to Cheves, October 26, 1821. 2 James Harper.

3 John Sergeant, now an attorney for the Bank of the United States.

4 Littell (comp.), *Statute Law of Kentucky,* II, 101-102 (February 6, 1798).

5 In the second case of Lonsdale *vs.* Brown, decided in the Circuit Court, Eastern

District of Pennsylvania, at the October Term, 1821, Judge Bushrod Washington had considered at length the distinction to be made between "inland" and "foreign" bills and had concluded that, with respect to their municipal laws the states being foreign to each other, he was "at a loss to conceive how a bill of exchange drawn in one state, upon a person residing in another, can be considered as an inland bill." In this particular case, however, he had denied damages to the plaintiff, no evidence having been submitted to support such a claim. 15 *Fed. Cas.* 855-60. Judge Washington reiterated this distinction between inland and foreign bills in the case of William S. Buckner, of New York, *vs.* Thomas Findley (Finley) and John Van Lear, merchants of Maryland, before the United States Supreme Court at the January Term, 1829. 27 *U. S.* (2 Peter) 586-94.

6 The case involved John T. Mason, who had been appointed Federal Marshal for Kentucky in the summer of 1817, his commission to run until the next Session of Congress, after which time he had been recommissioned, in December, 1817, but had failed to repeat the official oath or to renew his bond. The court, which had initially denied the continuation of Mason's authority and ruled in favor of the defendants (charged with resisting one of Mason's deputies), later reversed its stand and overruled the motion to quash the marshal's return. Lexington *Kentucky Reporter*, November 19, 26, 1821.

7 William Creighton, Jr.

8 See above, II, 900, 901n.

9 Not found. Cf. above, Clay to Cheves, October 3, November 21, 1821.

To Thomas Dougherty

My dear Sir Frankfort 7h. Decr 1821

My note at the off. of Dt. & Dt. of which you have been so kind as to be the indorser becomes due some time in the last of this month. It is not my intention that it shall be renewed. To pay it, I left there a note, due at the same time and for the same amount, of Mr. Scott[1] of your house. Lest he should not pay it, I transmit to you enclosed a check for $1300 (which is rather more than my note) and which I wish put to my credit, and my note deducted from it if Mr. Scott fails to discharge his. Being very anxious that the amount of Mr. Scott's note should be received and applied to the discharge of mine, I have to pray you, my dear Sir, not to let him know that I have made an arrangement predicated on his default; and to request Mr. Smith[2] (the Cashr.) also not to apprize him of this fact. His note has been long due, or rather the debt, and it ought to be paid.

Our Legislature is still in Session. Relief is yet the order of the day.[3] I think however that the struggle is at its crisis and that evidences of reaction will be quickly seen. It is probable that I shall have the pleasure of seeing you at the City this winter during the sitting of the Fed. Ct. They speak of sending me as one of the two Commissioners to treat with Virginia and to appear before that Ct. about the Occupying Claimant law. The appointment by the Legislature will probably take place next week—[4]

The subject of the next Presidency begins to be discussed in the papers and in the circles. You may confidently believe in an entire union of the West in favor of some Western Candidate.

Thomas Dougherty Esq. Your's faithfully H. CLAY

ALS. ViU.

[1] John Scott. The two notes and the check mentioned here have not been found.

[2] Richard Smith.

[3] See above, II, 904n; Clay to Gratz and Brothers, January 17, 1821, note. Governor John Adair had been elected (above, II, 886) on a platform advocating relief legislation. In addition to the replevy and bank laws cited above, the program encompassed abolition of imprisonment for debt (Ky. Gen. Assy., *Acts, 1821,* pp. 340-43 [December 17, 1821]) and, lest the courts authorize imprisonment where debts had been previously contracted, extension of prison bounds for insolvent debtors to the limits of the Commonwealth (Ky. Gen. Assy., *Acts, 1822,* p. 12 [May 29, 1822]). Since its first legislative meeting Kentucky had had a bankruptcy law, releasing insolvent debtors, after twenty days' confinement, upon surrender of their property to sheriff's sale. Littell (comp.), *Statute Law of Kentucky,* I, 142-44 (December 20, 1792).

[4] See above, William DuVal to Clay, June 14, 1821; and below, Credential, December 22, 1821.

Account with Matthew Kennedy

[*ca.* December 18, 1821]

	Henry Clay esqr. To M. Kennedy	Dr
1819—		
Septr 1	To 13 ft white oak Joist @ 5 .... 65 —	
	To 2 lb Nails 12½	
	To Cartage & putting up frame Celler 1-37½	$ 2 — 15
1821		
October 28	To 2633 feet of inch popler @ 1½	39 — 50
	710 feet of 1½ inch @ 2½	17 — 75
	1087 feet of 1¼ inch @ 1¾	19 — 03
	1036 ft .... Do .... @ 2	20 — 72
	353 ft .... of .... 1¼ got @ yard @ 2¼	7 — 94
	367 ft .... of .... 1 inch Do .... Do @ 1¾	6 — 43
	To 12 Loads of Cartage @ 25	3 — —
	To 18 lb. Nails @ 20	3 — 60
	To 24 feet cedar Scantling @ 4	96
	To Cash paid for one Lock	1 — 25
	To Do. paid for Cleaning windows &c	2 ....
	To taking down partition—Shelves &c	4 — 50
	To fitting up two Lecture Rooms with Seats &c[1] & caseing one Door	$ 230 ....
		$ 358 — 83
Novr. 12	To Misners[2] bill for makeing Keys and Repareing Locks	5 — 75
	To Gibineys [*sic*][3] bill for plastering and white washing	9 — 37½
	To painting and Glazing pr bill	$ 23 — 25
		397 — 20
	Cr by Cash Rcd $150	
	by plank .... left .... 7 — 56 $157 — 56	
	Ballence Due $239 — 65	
	To Grinsteds[4] bill Brick work — 5	
	$244 — 65	

To my Services furnishing materials and haveing painting Glazing plastering Cleaning and Brick work done .... 15 ....
also getting 4 Stoves fixed &C ....

$259 – 65

18th Decr. 1821– Cr. by Cash
Rcd $150
by his Services as Att –10 $160 –
[Endorsement on verso][5]
Recd. the bal. in full of the within account. 21 Decr. 1821.

MATT KENNEDY

D. DLC-TJC (DNA, M212, R15).
1 See above, Rental Agreement, November 5, 1821.
2 Christopher Misner, Lexington whitesmith and blacksmith.
3 Alexander Gibney. 4 Robert Grinstead. 5 ES, in Clay's hand.

From Henry R. Warfield

My dear Sir– Washington 18h. December 1821.

When we parted last spring[1] I think I promised occasionally to write to you which I shall do with unreserved Confidence.

We have again had as you have perceived by the public prints some difficulty in Electing a speaker–[2] The Representation from new york is almost entirely Changed–[3] There is from that state a strong party of the Bucktails– I beleive [*sic*] about twenty– they are anti clintonians and in decided political Hostility to Taylor–[4] Their object in the onsett was to Elect Rodney but finding after several fruitless attemps [*sic*] that to be impracticable they wheeled round and Joined in the Election Barbour [*sic*]– This I fancy was the result of one nights caucusing–[5] Taylor appeared more mortified than I think any man under such circumstances ought to be–and worst of all he had not the address to conceal it– Some of the Eastern members were really vexed at the result and I am inclined to beleive it awakened much of the old Missouiri [*sic*] feeling– whether it will assume a more distinct shape and form on the question of forming a Government for the Floridas is yet to be assertained [*sic*]– I fear it will– I voted For Taylor as long as I thought there was a chance of Electing him–because I think him in Every point of View better qualified than Rodney, who from the little I have Seen of him has acquired quite as great a reputation for talents to say the least of it as he is entitled to– and I did not think the Election of a speaker a point of so much importance as to avoid as far as possible any act that might in the remotest Degree tend to revive feelings which the substancial [*sic*] Interests of Our County [*sic*] require to be buried in oblivion–

Almost one half of the House of Representatives is composed of new members— Of what stuff they are made we have as yet had no opportunity to asscertain— If in Electing them their Constituents have not been influenced by a View to better Interests, they certainly have as to appearance and deportment— For the greater part of the new members have the appearance and manners of Gentlemen and take us altogether we make a tollerably [*sic*] decent shew— as much so as perhaps cou'd be reasonably expected— It is thought the Session will continue till May—

There are already conversations as to Mr. Monroes Successor to the Presidency— To make professions of Esteem and Friendship is superfluous— Actions are the truest and least fallable test— I hear much that is said, I occasionally Join in conversation on the Subject, more with the design of assertaining the plans and Views of Others than to Express any opinion of my own— For a mans own opinion being once known on a Subject is frequently a barrier to his assertaining the ulterior Views others [*sic*]—and it is much Easier to defeat an Enemy after obtaining a full examination of his Encampment, than to assail him with an imperfect knowledge of it— on the Subject of great Elections discretion is all important, and Falstaffs Idea that prudence is the better part of Valour May Very properly apply— A man shou'd not only know how to talk but when to talk— For as old Governor Johnson[6] of our State used to say it requires on Such Occasions that man shou'd be *Foxy*— In a long conversation with Mr Gorum[7] of Boston a few Evenings since as to the Views of the Eastern States I spoke of your qualifications, without giving any opinion supposing that he was for Adams[8] and wishing to obtain all the information I cou d— Gorum is a man with whom I have the pleasure of being on intimate and Confidential terms and for whose character and principles I entertain the Highest respect— In this conversation he spoke of you in High terms of approbation and said that he had so frequently done so in Boston that Webster[9] and other friends had jestingly said they believed he wanted you as President— Upon the probable result of an Election of so much importance, in which there is to be as far as practicable a reconciliation of Various Conflicting Interests it is difficult to conjecture I am inclined to think that an Effort to Elect a President at the *next Election* Either from the South or West wou'd unite the North and the East to a man in opposition— altho' some have said Main [*sic*] is in [. . .][10]— In our Conversations Gorum whom I beleive to me [*sic*] a man of Honor and Sincerity suggested the following plan which I give to you— He says the thing has been spoken of but by a few who are assertained to be trustworthy and that it must not be hinted at to Others— He says the Eastern States may and can be secured to support at the next Election Rufus King as President and yourself as

Vice President under an Explicit understanding that at the expiration of the *first four years* Mr. King will retire and you supported [*sic*] by those States as his Successor— He told me he was confident from Conversations with Prominent men to the Eastward this arrangement on their part cou'd be made and said I migh[t] under the injunction of confidence use his name— They are not disposed to take Adams unless compelled so to do by an Effort to Elect a Southern man— This however my dear Sir is a Subject of delicacy and great moment— It requires Judgement prudence and great circumspection— I shall endeavour with caution to assertain the Views of men and assertain as far as practicable their plans of opperation— Great things may be atchieved by Judicious arrangements and the fairest prospects may be marr'd by Indiscretion— There is Sufficient time to look arround us before the next Election of President— If it cou'd be assertained beyond a doubt that Gorum is right in the opinion he has of the Eastern States on this question, I think it doubtful whether the Southern & Western States cou'd be brought in to Support Mr. King even for the four years— However this point involves a Variety of considerations, and time— I wish Quincy wou'd make one or two more fourth of July speeches—[11] one or two more such specimens wou'd effectually Silence his pretentions to the chair of State What I have or may say to you on this Subject must be received as it is Intended in perfect confidence and tho' I may not have as extensive means as others to Eleva[te] you to the Presidency yet of this you may be assured that you will find no one more firmly and immoveably your friend

If you shou'd see my uncle Dr. Walter Warfield will [*sic*] to remember me kindly to him, and tell him I shall soon write to him—

My best wishes to you & yours— HENRY R. WARFIELD

Since writing the above I dined with a party at which Mr Ware the new Senator from Georgia was present—[12] He appears to be a Gentleman and a man of talents— In the course of the Evening the Subject of the next Presidency was Introduced your name among others was mentioned— His opinion was that whole Contest wou'd be between Quincy the speech maker and Crawford,—[13] He was warm in his Eulogeising [*sic*] on Crawford and is his zealous friend— thinks the contest between Clark of Georgia and Crawford will not interfere with the Interests of the latter in that State—[14] Towards the close of the conversation, I remarkd that it was not improbable that some person might be brought into Vi[ew], who wou'd be taken in preference to Either of of [*sic*] them— He Asked me whether I had any particular person in View & whether there were any arrangements making to that Effect— I said no—that I merely spoke of the possibility of such an Event— The conversation changed— He seemed thoughtful and Sometime after that, making a little apology for what he termed his curiosity, he repeated his question To which I again replied that I spoke only of the possibility of such an occurrence— I have fixed myself this Session on the Capitol Hill at Miss Hay [. . .]—[15] We have in our Mess Mr. Sargeant & Mr. Milnor of Philadelphia— Mr. McSherry and Mr. Buchanan of Pennsylvania—[16] The latter is a gentleman from Lancaster— a Lawyer of Considerable Eminence & whom I have made Very much your Friend— I am pretty certain from what I hear that the Missouri question will be agitated in the Formation of a Government for the Floridas—we shall then feel in all its force your absence— H R. W

ALS. DLC-HC (DNA, M212, R1). Addressed to Clay at Lexington. The date "18" superimposed upon "13."

1 At the end of the Second Session of the Sixteenth Congress.

2 The matter had been settled on the twelfth ballot, on December 4, the second day of the Session. Cf. above, Motion and Remarks on Missouri Statehood, February 12, 1821, note.

3 Only six members of the New York delegation had sat in the preceding Congress.

4 The Bucktails were a faction of the Democratic Republican Party in New York opposed to DeWitt Clinton. John W. Taylor was a Clintonian.

5 Caesar A. Rodney had run second to Taylor on the first ballot, led on the second, tied with Taylor on the third, led on the fourth and fifth, and in subsequent voting dropped rapidly from serious contention. Philip P. Barbour, whose name had not appeared until the eighth ballot (the first on the second day of the Session), had tied with Taylor on the tenth, then moved ahead to win.

6 Thomas Johnson, lawyer, member of the Continental Congress, brigadier general of Maryland militia during the Revolutionary War, first Governor of the State of Maryland, one of the first Associate Justices of the United States Supreme Court.

7 Benjamin Gorham, Congressman from Massachusetts.

8 John Quincy Adams. 9 Daniel Webster. 10 Word illegible.

11 See above, Clay to Rodney, August 9, 1821, note.

12 Nicholas Ware, of Augusta, Georgia, appointed to fill a vacancy, had taken his seat as United States Senator on December 11.

13 William H. Crawford.

14 Crawford's bitter, longstanding rivalry with John Clark, of Wilkes County, Georgia, marked by personal encounter on the duelling field in 1806, was manifest politically in the gubernatorial contest between Clark and Crawford's friend, George M. Troup, in 1819 and 1821. Clark, a close friend of John C. Calhoun, won both elections, the latter by only two votes. He was succeeded by Troup as Governor, 1823-1827.

15 Not clearly legible.

16 All Pennsylvanian Congressmen: John Sergeant; William Milnor, a representative in the Tenth, Eleventh, and Fourteenth Congresses, and from March 4, 1821, until his resignation in the next year; James McSherry, member of the House, 1821-1823; James Buchanan, member of the House, 1821-1831, later President of the United States.

Acknowledgment to ———— Valentine

20. Decr. 1821.

On a settlement of the account of Valentine for articles furnished & payments made on account of the Garden rented by him, I acknowledge that he has paid up to this day sixty eight dollars & 44 Cents. H. CLAY.

ADS. NcD. Valentine, not identified. There were several persons of that name in Fayette County at this time.

To Joseph Cabell Breckinridge

My dear Sir Lexn. 21st. Decr. 1821.

I understand that I am appointed one of the Commissioners in regard to the Occupying Claimant law &c.[1] Intending in a few days to set out on my journey Eastward, I am desirous of carrying with me the proper evidence of my appointment. That I presume will consist either of a Commission, or of a Copy of the Legislative resolutions and proceedings which evince the fact; these to be certified & authenticated by the Certificate of the Govr. seal of State &c. Will you have the goodness to converse with my Colleague on this subject & send me by Theodore[2] such evidence of my appointment as will be satisfactory?

I am with great regard Your's H. CLAY

Mr. Breckenridge [*sic*]

ALS. DLC-Breckinridge Family Papers (DNA, M212, R20). Directed to Frankfort, where Breckinridge was now Secretary of State.

1 See above, DuVal to Clay, June 14, 1821. 2 Clay's son.

Credential as Commissioner

[December 22, 1821]

State of Kentucky Secretary's office

I John Adair Governor of the State of Kentucky do hereby Certify and make known, that Henry Clay & George M Bibb Esquires, were by a joint vote of the Senate and house of Representatives of said State, duly elected Commissioners persuant [*sic*] to resolutions adopted by the General Assembly at the October session 1821 "Concerning the occupying claimant Laws of this State and the decision of the Supreme Court of the United States thereon" Approved December 17th 1821.[1]

In Testimony whereof I have hereunto set my hand and caused the seal of the Said Commonwealth to be affixed at Frankfort this twenty second day of December, in the Year of our Lord one thousand eight hundred and twenty one & in the thirtieth Year of the Commonwealth. By the Governor JOHN ADAIR

{SEAL} J. CABELL BRECKINRIDGE Secretary

DS. InU. Possibly George M. Bibb's copy of the Credential. See below, Clay to Breckinridge, December 27, 1821.

1 Ky. Gen. Assy., *Acts, 1821*, p. 469; Ky. H. of Reps., *Journal, 1821*, p. 457.

Property Deed from Bank of Kentucky

[December 26, 1821]

[For the sum of $10,000, paid and acknowledged, the President,

Directors, and Company of the Bank of Kentucky sell to Henry Clay a tract in Fayette County on the waters of the Town Fork of Elkhorn, bounded beginning at a stake in the center of the road from Lexington to Frankfort, corner to the Steam Mill Company's[1] tract, thence with their line S 18¾° W 160 poles to a stake, corner to   Pollock,[2] with his line S 71½° E 40 poles to a stake, thence S 18¾° W 23 poles to a stake in William Pollock's line, thence S 70° E 68 poles to two locust trees, corner to land formerly owned by   Creath,[3] thence with his line S 89° E 104 poles to a stake in Samuel Trotter's line, thence with it N 16½° E 114 poles to a stake in the road, and along the road to the beginning, amounting to 200 acres, more or less—the tract having been conveyed to the President, Directors, and Company of the Bank of Kentucky by Charles Wilkins and Matthew T. Scott, as commissioners, under deed of July 12, 1821.[4] Title warranted only against claimants through the Bank. Signed by Farmer Dewees, attorney in fact for the grantors, as authorized by letter of attorney dated December 22, 1821. Recorded by J. C. Rodes, Clerk of Fayette County, December 27, 1821.]

Fayette County Court, Deed Book V, 172-73. 1 Tammany Steam Mills.
2 John Pollock, the first name omitted in the deed.
3 Jacob Creath, the first name omitted in the deed.
4 Executed following sheriff's sale of the holdings of Lewis Sanders. Fayette County Court, Deed Book V, 175-80.

Mortgage Deed to Bank of Kentucky

[December 26, 1821]

[Whereas the President, Directors, and Company of the Bank of Kentucky have this day conveyed to Henry Clay a tract of 200 acres, more or less, in Fayette County on the waters of the Town Fork of Elkhorn, in consideration of which Clay has executed to the grantors three promissory notes for $3,333.33⅓, each, dated December 26, 1821,[1] and payable on September 25, of 1822, 1823, and 1824, respectively, in notes of either the Bank of Kentucky or the Bank of the Commonwealth, at Clay's option; and whereas Clay is willing to secure payment of his notes: now in further consideration of one dollar, paid and acknowledged, Clay conveys to the President, Directors, and Company of the Bank of Kentucky his house and lot at the corner of Second and Mill streets, opposite the residence of John Bradford, in Lexington.[2] General warranty of title. If Clay shall pay his notes as due, this deed is to become void. Recorded by J. C. Rodes, Clerk of Fayette County, December 27, 1821.]

Fayette County Court, Deed Book V, 173-75.
1 Not found. 2 See above, II, 716-17.

To Joseph Cabell Breckinridge

My Dr Sir Lexington 27h. Decr. 1821.

I recd. the papers which you transmitted to me from Frankfort.[1] The printed Copy of the Report which you sent is not as it finally passed, but as it came from the Committee. I wish you would do me the favor to have one correctly made out, and the Governor's authenticated Certificate of my appointment attached to it, & inclose them to me under cover to Sam. H. Woodson Washn. City. I wish to be in possession of this evidence of my appointmt. to guard against any accident which may possibly attend Mr. Bibb or that which you have furnished him.[2]

I have no information respecting the proceedings of Marshall vs McConnels heirs.[3] My time has been, since my return from Frankfort, exclusively engrossed by preparations for my journey. Should the money ever come to my hands I will endeavor to arrange the subject of your fee satisfactorily.

Any lease you may make of the Fl—d Salt works[4] will be agreed to by [. . . .]

J. C. Breckenridge Esq.

AL, signature removed. DLC-Breckinridge Family Papers.

1 Not found. See above, Clay to Breckinridge, December 21, 1821.

2 George M. Bibb; possibly the Credential, above, December 22, 1821.

3 The Heirs of Henry Marshall *vs.* the Heirs of James McConnell, argued before the Kentucky Court of Appeals in June, 1821, a dispute over the valuation of land surrendered under a contract for indemnification against a faulty land title. 11 *Ky. Reports* (1 Littell) 419-24. The lawyers are not identified, but cf. above, I, 239, 477.

4 Floyd salt works. See above, I, 229n, 247-48, 481, 831-32.

Credential as Commissioner

[December 29, 1821]

Lexington *Kentucky Reporter,* February 18, 1822. This document is virtually the same as the Credential above, December 22, 1821. See Clay to Breckinridge, December 27, 1821.

Advertisement of Property

FOR SALE, AND TO LET. Lex. December 31, 1821

I OFFER FOR SALE, The House and Lot opposite to the residence of John Bradford, Esq. and fronting the University square;[1] payment for which, on reasonable time, will be received in notes of the Bank of the Commonwealth.

I would RENT the HOUSE and LOTS which I now occupy.[2] Also, the ROOMS which Abner Legrand Esq. lately used for auctions, on the public square—[3] the HOUSE and LOT lately occupied by Captain Bernard Gaines,[4] and the HOUSE and LOT which were occupied by Col. Whaley, on Market Street.[5] For terms apply, during my absence, to the Editor of this paper.[6] H. CLAY.

Lexington *Kentucky Reporter*, January 7, 1822.
[1] See above, II, 716-17; Mortgage Deed, December 26, 1821.
[2] See above, Morrison to Clay, February 12, 1821, note.
[3] See above, II, 362.
[4] See above, II, 362-63; Advertisement, August 18, 1821.
[5] See above, II, 890-91. [6] Thomas Smith.

To Jonathan Russell

My dear Sir Chillicothe 2 Jan. 1822.

The inclosed letter was handed to me at Lexington, by your friend and relation Mr. Corlis,[1] whose acquaintance, I regret extremely, circumstances prevented me from making until the day of my departure, though I had the pleasure of knowing some of the members of his family.[2] I transmit it to you because you will receive it earlier, and equally as safe, by the mail, as if I were to carry it.

I saw, with great satisfaction, that the Speaker had appointed you to a distinguished station (certainly the third, if not the second) in the construction of the House.[3] I hope you will aid the Executive department in getting us out of the difficulty which exists with France.[4]

I am here, in my vocation, travelling to one of my Courts, at Columbus. From that place I shall proceed, with all due diligence, to Richmond in Virginia, and hope to have the pleasure of seeing you in Washington by the middle of February. Until then, and offering you the compliments of the Season.

I remain truly & faithfully Yours. H. CLAY

The Honble Mr. Russell.

ALS. RPB. Addressed: "The Honble Jonathan Russell. Of the H. of Representatives. Washington City."

[1] John Corlis, Sr., born in Providence, Rhode Island, had been a merchant and importer of fine silks until, threatened with bankruptcy following the War of 1812, he moved to Bourbon County, Kentucky, around 1817. His first wife was Susanna Condie Russell, daughter of Joseph Russell, possibly the colonial jurist of Bristol, Rhode Island, Jonathan Russell's grandfather.

[2] Clay was probably acquainted with Mary Ann Corlis, who had married Charles Bradford in September, 1817, and with John Corlis, Jr., who was a student in the Medical Department of Transylvania University (later for many years a physician in Bracken County, Kentucky).

[3] On December 7, 1821, Russell had been appointed chairman of a select committee to which was referred "so much of the President's Message as relates to the foreign and diplomatic affairs of the United States, in their intercourse with all other nations."

[4] See above, I, 527, 878; II, 846n; Remarks on Bill to Exempt French Ships, February 27, 1821, note. The dual controversy over commercial regulations and over claims arising out of the spoliations of the Napoleonic wars had reached an impasse, discussed at some length by President Monroe in his annual message of December 5, 1821. Fol-

lowing a change of political power in France at this time, Albert Gallatin again presented the subject of American claims, in a series of notes during the spring of 1822, but met with the reply that no action could be taken pending the outcome of negotiations on the commercial treaty. *American State Papers, Foreign Relations,* V, 301-10.

Receipt from Thomas Anderson

LEXINGTON, KY. Jany 3rd 1822

Thomas Anderson, as Treasurer of Transylvania University, acknowledges payment by Clay of $13.31 for tuition. DS. DLC-TJC (DNA, M212, R15). See above, Receipt, October 1, 1821, note.

To Langdon Cheves

Sir Columbus 12h. Jan. 1822

The U. States Circuit Court began its Session on Monday last. The preparations which had been made for the trial of the Causes of the Bank were such as to authorize us confidently to count upon Judgments in most of them; the attendance of some of the witnesses, whose presence could not be procured at the last term, having been secured, and the depositions of the Notary having been legally taken, in the Cincinnati causes.[1] But unfortunately it was discovered that the appointment of the Marshall was limited, by the terms of his commission, to the 30h. of last month, and that the President had not sent on a new appointment or commission.[2] The Court thought that it could not, by any inherent power or statutory provision, designate any other person to perform the duties assigned by law to the Marshall, and that in cases requiring his co-operation there must be continuances: The effect has been to continue all causes where an issue has been made up requiring a Jury. Judgments by default have been taken in about forty or fifty causes, and the residue are continued.

There is one consolation.for this unexpected occurrence. That reaction, in favor of the Creditor, which was to be anticipated against the system of policy which has prevailed for some time past in behalf of the debtor, is beginning to manifest itself in the Legislature of this State, now in Session. There is the prospect of the passage of a bill, pending before it, by which the requirement that *personal* property shall command a certain proportion of its value or not be sold, is to be done away after the 4h. of July next;[3] and other manifestations are also given of a disposition to return to the antient state of the Law.

The Session of the Court will be terminated to day, by the incident to which I have refered. I shall proceed from here to Richmond and expect to be at Washington early in the approaching term of the Supreme Court. I have the honor to be with great respect Your obedient Servant H. CLAY

L. Cheves Esqr. &c &c &c

ALS. PHi-Etting Collection. [1] Cf. above, Clay to Cheves, July 8, 1821.

[2] John Hamm, whose last appointment as Federal Marshal had been confirmed on February 19, 1818, was replaced by William Dougherty, of Ohio, under an appointment confirmed on February 5, 1822.

[3] Such a measure was enacted February 1, 1822. Ohio Gen. Assy., *Acts of a General Nature, 1821-1822,* p. 80 (sec. 27).

From John W. Overton

My Dear Sir, Nashville Tenn. January 16th 1822.

The minds of the people in this Country begin to be agitated on the question who is to be our next President— My friendship to you, and the interest I feel in the welfare of my Country, has induced me to address you, on this all important Subject— I hope you will not consider it presumption, when you will evidently ascertain, that my motives for it, are of the best kind—

We have heard here, that you will probably be run for this elevated office, if it be so, it would be well for us to know it— I know very well, it is much desired in this Country, that you should suffer your name to be run—

I can assure you, as far as I know the public mind, you will get all the Votes in Tennessee in preference to any man whose name has been mentioned— And those mentioned are Dewitt Clinton, J. Q. Adams, & W H Crawford, Neither of those men, are the choice of the people in this state, I can assure you—

There has been some whispering conversation here, that Jackson would suffer himself to be run for that office, but I do not believe that he will— In fact, I am almost certain that he will not, and my information is derived, from good authority.

When I was at your house last fall, in Lexington, I never mentioned the subject to you, or heard it mentioned while there, or I would then have satisfied my mind on the Subject—

In this Country at this time, the Contention is between Crawford & Adams, and it is somewhat doubtfull who would beat—but Clinton is left entirely out of the question— If though it could be known, that you would offer, the minds of the people would be readily made up, in your behalf—

Your Coolness with Jackson, might in some measure Operate to your slight injury, but the great mass of the people, would warmly Support you— This is told you from one who knows some thing about your standing here, and collected from Others, who know much more than I do—

Of this though you can be well assured, that you would get *all* the votes in Tennessee in preference to those mentioned—and indeed, I know only of but one man, who is eligible, who Could beat you, and that is Jackson— Although probably he could beat you himself, in *propria persona,* yet he could not raise up any other man to do it— Although Jackson might be friendly to Adams or Calhoun, or any other man, yet I do not beleive [*sic*] *that* Circumstance would lead those people his way— Indeed I know it would be otherwise.

Inasmuch as I, and our family have always been friendly with Jackson, I should not like him to know of any interposition of mine on this Subject, I have therefore to beg of you to keep these matters to yourself—

I heard governor Carroll[1] Say a few days since, that you would get all the votes in this state in preference to those who are now before the people—

Accept my best wishes for your health and happiness and believe me to be your Your [*sic*] friend Jno. W. Overton

Hon. Henry Clay.

P.S. A letter from you would be highly acceptable to your friend—

(Confidential)

ALS. DLC-HC (DNA, M212, R1). Overton, a son of Waller Overton and a nephew of John Overton, had been born in Fayette County, Kentucky, but spent most of his life in Tennessee.

1 William Carroll, twice Governor of Tennessee, 1821-1827 and 1829-1835.

Receipt from Thomas P. Hart

Jany 21st. 1822.

Recd. of H Clay the rent of my house and lot for one year

Thomas P Hart

ADS. DLC-TJC (DNA, M212, R15). See above, Memorandum and Receipt, June 29, 1821.

To Langdon Cheves

My dear Sir Washington 23d. Jan. 1822.

I have the pleasure to introduce to you the bearer hereof Sam. Q. Richardson Esqr. of Cincinnati, a gentleman of our profession of highly respectable standing, and well informed in the interests and condition of that City. Mr. Richardson desires your acquaintance on several accounts, one of which is to hold a conversation with you in respect to the revival of the Off. of Dt. & Dt. at that place. I am perfectly persuaded that if it had entered into the policy of the Bank of the U. S. to have retained that office, the delinquency of the debtors there, in the payment particularly of accruing interest on their debts, would not have been as general & indiscriminate as it has been. The question of the reestablishment of the office is one depending upon so many considerations, of which I am not possessed, that I can not venture to offer at present any decisive opinion upon it. Of all these you will have a full view, and I have said to Mr. Richardson that you will converse with him on the subject with the utmost freedom & frankness.

With great regard I am faithfy Yours H. CLAY

ALS. ViU. Addressed on attached sheet to Cheves at Philadelphia.

To Thomas M. Randolph

RICHMOND, 31st January, 1822.

SIR—We have the honor to inform your excellency that we are appointed by the state of Kentucky, commissioners to invite the attention of the state of Virginia to certain provisions of the act of its legislature, "Concerning the erection of the District of Kentucky into an Independent State;" and that we have arrived here, in order to execute the public trust confided to us. An interpretation of those provisions has been intimated different from that which Kentucky supposes to be their genuine import; and believing that their true sense may be better ascertained, & the fidelity with which they have been fulfilled, be best known by a direct appeal to the candid judgment of Virginia, the original and principal party to them; we are charged with the duty of making and receiving those mutual explanations which are demanded by justice, and are due to the amicable relations which have ever happily subsisted between the two states. In the accomplishment of this object, being persuaded that we shall be favoured with the prompt and candid co-operation of your excellency, we have respectfully to request, that you will make such communication to the General Assembly, or indicate to us such other mode, as will enable us to execute the commission assigned to us. We have the honor to lay herewith before you the testimonial of our appointment.[1] With great respect, We have the honor to be, Your excellency's humble serv'ts,

H. CLAY,
His excellency Th: M. Randolph, &c. &c. GEO M. BIBB.

Lexington *Kentucky Reporter,* February 18, 1822. Randolph was now Governor of Virginia (1819-1822).

[1] See above, December 22, 29, 1821.

From Chapman Johnson and Richard Morris

Richmond February 2nd. 1822—

[Chapman Johnson and Richard Morris, chairmen, from the Senate and House of Delegates, respectively, of a joint committee of the

Virginia legislature, inform Clay and George M. Bibb that their communication to the Governor of Virginia[1] has been referred to the joint committee, which wishes to know "in what manner it will be most agreeable to you to make any further communication on the subject of your Mission–" The committee is scheduled to meet again on Monday morning.]

LS. InU. Directed to Clay and Bibb, "Commissioners from the State of Kentuckey–" Published in Lexington *Kentucky Reporter,* February 25, 1822. Johnson, born in Louisa County, Virginia, had studied law and commenced practice in Staunton, Augusta County, which district he represented in the Virginia legislature, 1810-1826. From 1819 to 1845 he was a member of the Board of Visitors of the University of Virginia and from 1836 to 1844 served as rector. Morris, a representative of Hanover County, was subsequently also a delegate to the State constitutional convention of 1830.

1 See above, Clay and Bibb to Randolph, January 31, 1822.

To Chapman Johnson and Richard Morris

Richmond, Feb. 2, 1822.

GENTLEMEN: We have the pleasure to acknowledge the receipt of the note which you this day did us the honor to address to us, informing us that our communication to His Excellency the Governor has been laid before the legislature, and referred to a joint committee of both Houses of the General Assembly.

We are sensible of the respect and high considerations which dictated the request to be informed in what manner it will be most agreeable to us to make any further communication on the subject which has brought us here. And, in the same frankness of spirit, which has dictated the request, we have to say, for answer, that we are desirous of addressing ourselves, at once, to that department of the government of Virginia which can act efficiently on that subject. Believing that to be the General Assembly, we should be pleased to have an opportunity of being heard directly by that body, if agreeable to them, at such time as may suit their convenience.

We have the honor to be, with great respect, your ob't servants,

CHAPMAN JOHNSON, Esq &c &c &c. HENRY CLAY,
RICHARD MORRIS, Esq. &c. &c. &c GEO. M. BIBB

Lexington *Kentucky Reporter,* February 25, 1822.

From Linn Banks

[February 5, 1822]

ALS. InU. Letter of transmittal for resolutions, approved by the Virginia House of Delegates on February 5, 1822, providing that Clay and George M. Bibb should "be received at the Bar of the House of Delegates, and heard in support, or explanation, of such communication or propositions," as they were "authorised to make, on the part of Kentucky, to this Commonwealth"; and that the Speaker of the House of Delegates be requested to inquire on what day the Kentucky commissioners desire to submit this communication. The resolutions, DS copy, by William Munford, Clerk, House of

Delegates, InU; published in Ky. H. of Reps. *Journal, Special Session, 1822,* p. 11. See above, Clay to Breckinridge, December 21, 1821; Credential, December 22, 29, 1821; Clay to Randolph, January 31, 1822. The reply of Clay and Bibb to Banks has not been found.

From Linn Banks

[February 6, 1822]

Not found, a letter of transmittal covering a resolution by the Virginia House of Delegates, on this date, which designated February 7, at 12 o'clock, as the time at which the Kentucky commissioners were to be heard in accordance with the resolutions transmitted by Banks on February 5. The resolution, DS copy, by William Munford, InU.

To the Virginia General Assembly

RICHMOND, 7th February 1822.

To the honorable the Senate, and the House of Delegates, of the General Assembly of Virginia.

THE undersigned, commissioners from the state of Kentucky, in conformity to the first resolution reported by the joint committee of the two houses of the general assembly, and adopted on the 5th current by the house of delegates,[1] have the honor to propose,

1st. That the general assembly of the commonwealth of Virginia do declare, by resolution or other act, that, according to their sense of the true intent and meaning of the act which they passed on the 18th day of December 1789, "concerning the erection of the district of Kentucky into an independent state," the legislature of Kentucky was not restricted from passing two acts, the one on the 27th of February 1797, entitled "an act concerning occupying claimants of land," and the other on the 31st day of January 1812, entitled "an act to amend an act entitled an act concerning occupying claimants of land."

OR,

2dly. That the general assembly of Virginia, in such mode as may be deemed proper, do concur, by a convention for that purpose to be entered into with the undersigned, in constituting a board of impartial commissioners, according to the provision contained in the 8th article of the conditions specified in the 4th section of the aforesaid act of Virginia, to decide upon the validity of the two acts above mentioned, of Kentucky; and also the act passed by its legislature on the 20th December 1820, entitled "an act to amend an act entitled an act to amend an act concerning occupying claimants of land."

The undersigned will not now bring forward all those facts and circumstances, nor urge those considerations which appear to them to authorise a confident expectation that, the general assembly of Virginia will adopt the one or the other of these two propositions; but will content themselves with referring to the explanation and discussion which they shall have the honor of submitting orally, under the supposition that this course is in consonance with the views of that body.

They lay before the general assembly authentic copies of the several acts of Kentucky above mentioned; and avail themselves of the occasion to tender to the general assembly the homage of their profound respect.

H. CLAY,
GEO. M. BIBB.

Ky. H. of Reps., *Journal, Special Session, 1822,* pp. 11-12. Published also in Lexington *Kentucky Reporter,* February 25, 1822; Lexington *Kentucky Gazette,* February 28, 1822.

1 See above, Banks to Clay and Bibb, February 5, 1822.

Speech to the Virginia General Assembly

[February 7, 1822]

Mr. Clay commenced by observing that the duty devolved upon him of opening the subject which, by the favor of the General Assembly, his colleague and himself had now to present to their consideration. He had never felt himself in a situation of more responsibility and embarrassment. The profound respect which he entertained for the General Assembly of Virginia; the honorable recollections, ancient and modern, associated with its distinguished name; the deep and vital interest which his state had in the objects of the commission; the general expectation, which he would not disguise, he saw had been excited, filled him with serious apprehensions as to the manner in which he should acquit himself. It was impossible, he said to contemplate this Assembly without recollecting that it was here that the indignant and eloquent tongue of Patrick Henry first depicted the enormity and fatal consequences of British pretension, and stimulated the patriotic spirit of resistance; that it was in this very Hall, in that very form (pointing to the Speaker's chair) that the bland, the graceful, the accomplished and the enlightened Pendleton[1] presided over one of the most august assemblies that the world ever saw; aided by that illustrious man[2] who, to the stern virtues of Cato united the justice of Aristides—to whom, he hoped he should be excused, for making this public acknowledgment of his gratitude for his generous patronage of him, extended when he was an orphan, bereft alike of paternal and pecuniary assistance, and to whose memory he begged permission to pay the poor tribute of his highest veneration; that at a later period, in 1799, it was from this body issued that memorable paper which, for the force and power of its reasoning, the good temper that pervaded it, and its admirable method, was unrivalled, and which, if it were the sole production of its eminent author, would secure immortality to his respected name.[3] He was but too well aware also of the activity of misrepresentation, and the prevalence of misconception in regard to the laws of Kentucky which were to be the subject of consideration. And feeling his own incompetency more than ever, he should be utterly unable to sustain himself, under the pressure of these united causes, if he had not the encouraging consciousness that he was addressing the General Assembly of a state, at once the parent of his own and the place of his nativity, in whose generosity and kindness he should find indulgence and countenance.

Mr. C. proceeded to call the attention of the House to the act of 1789, creating Kentucky into an independent state, which was the basis of the compact between the two states, on the terms of which he expatiated at large. He adverted to a violation on the part of Kentucky which he had heard insinuated here, in respect to the district of country south of Tennessee river, in forbidding the location of military warrants after the 1st of May 1792.[4] He contended that the compact itself had retained to Virginia the power of appropriating the lands, in that district up to that time; that this appropriation could only be effected by location of the warrants; that the issuing of warrants was no such appropriation; that the warrant was an *authority* to appropriate, but was of itself no appropriation: That the justness of this interpretation was manifest from the provision in the compact that Kentucky, after the 1st of May, was at liberty to dispose of the residue of the lands not appropriated which she could not do if there were an unlimited time, after that period, during which the holders of warrants were at liberty to locate them or not at their pleasure. Passing from this topic, he then proceeded to explain fully the several laws for securing the bona fide occupants of land compensation for the value of their improvements. If the first law were more favorable to the successful claimant out of possession, than the second, and the second than the third, it was because of the lapse of time, during which he forebore to come forward and assert his right, and the consequent supposition of a dereliction of his claim. —The two first of those laws had been drawn in question before the supreme court, and at the last term of it, in a case in which one of the parties had no interest, and on an ex parte argument, an opinion had been intimated that they were contrary to the compact.[5] It was far from his intention to add to the exasperation of the public against that august tribunal. He would allay, if he could, rather than add fury to the storm. He owed indeed to that court and particularly to the distinguished native of Virginia who presided in it,[6] the expression of his testimony to the deep concern, the anxious solicitude which they evinced to have the subject of those laws fully and fairly discussed, and he entertained the strongest conviction that on reconsideration the question would be seen in a different light. But he must, in great deference, say, that although the court had jurisdiction between the parties, in his judgment it was doubtful if it had over the subject; because by the compact a stipulation is expressly made for the case of any violation of it, by the appointment of a tribunal, and until there had been a refusal, by one of the parties to the compact to constitute that tribunal, the jurisdiction at the instance of at most a collateral party, did not appear to him to attach.

Mr. Clay undertook then to defend the justice and necessity of the several laws in question. He here entered into a copious explanation of the land laws of Va. of the multitude of claims; of the uncertainty of locations and entries which the parties were at liberty to direct, according to their own fancy and caprice; of the numerous interferences which were the inevitable consequence; the same identical tract was frequently shingled over by a dozen claims, the eagerness of adventurers being in proportion to the richness of the prize. Then the impossibility often of ascertaining even the existence of these claims; if known, of ascertaining the facts on which they depended; if the facts were known, the impossibility of anticipating the decisions upon them, which the courts might pronounce in the artificial rules of interpretation rendered necessary to be applied to a subject on which the ancient land marks of the law furnished not the remotest guide. Of all the evils which can afflict an unhappy country, scarcely any was so aggravated as that of having its soil, the source whence all our riches flow, and all our wants are supplied, the subject of endless litigation. Kentucky was in this sad predicament. The alternative was presented to her of suffering the country to remain unpeopled, or to provide for an evil so enormous. The laws in question are the best remedy which she could devise. Without the system which they compose, her rich virgin earth would have been unturned, her fields unploughed, the theatre of a yet doubtful and dreadful war waged between civilized and savage men: the silence of her luxuriant forest disturbed by no other sound than the horrible warwhoop, and the shrieks of innocent females and the cries of helpless children expiring under the agonies of the tomahawk and scalping knife. With this system, thousands of her sons have migrated as they would fly from pestilence and famine, to more favored states and territories where they could enjoy in peace and tranquility their beloved homes. Without this system, there could have been no Kentucky [t]o second, at the memorable epoch of 1798-9, your patriotic efforts to recall back, a mad administration of the general government, to the fundamental principles of Liberty and the constitution.[7] Her brave sons could not have fought on the fatal field of Raisin, or won on the more glorious fields of Thames and New Orleans, those laurels which adorn the American brow. The system supposes that innocent men have mixed their property together, the one, believing it to be his own, having improved it; and the other being ascertained by judicial investigation to have the best title. The principle is to give to each what is his. And since the subjects are inseparable, this equitable design is effected in the only practicable mode. It gives to the owner of the best title the land, and exacts only that he shall account for what he never bought, what he never paid for, what is not his. The justice of this arrangement may be proven by its own principles, by the principles of abstract justice, and by the practice of all other codes in like circumstances. The subject of the improvements, and the subject of the land on which they are made are capable of a distinct comprehension and of distinct rules. Land before it is improved may be compared to the raw material; with its improvements, to a fabricated article. A farm, with all its fields, houses, orchards, gardens, lawns and shrubberies no more resembles the same land in its native state before these various improvements are put on it, than a piece of Brussels lace does the flax out of which is [*sic*] wrought. And would it not be monstrous to say to the innocent possessor and manufacturer of a raw material that he should surrender the article uncompensated for his labor and expense? The receiver of a benefit owes the price of it. The possessor of my money, or my property who has acquired it through accident or mistake, must give it up. The rule is, that if ex æquo et bona it cannot be retained, it must be surrendered. If I labor for another, without special contract, he is bound to remuneration. Do not these principles apply, with undiminished force, to such a state of things as the Kentucky titles exhibit? Not to go into other codes, what is the provision made by the laws of our common ancestors, in the colony of Virginia when its condition bore a faint resemblance to that of Kentucky? Here Mr Clay quoted several laws of the colony of Virginia passed near two centuries ago providing that the owner should compensate the seater of land. He contended that they were more unfavorable than the laws of Kentucky to the true owner—because the first of them compensated even the *squatter,* none of them gave rents, and although all of them secured to the true owner, the election to take the land and improvements upon paying the value of seating to be assessed by a jury, or the value of the land without the improvements; the land was to be valued at *the time* of seating, not that of the assessment.[8] The same principles as being dictated by equity, was [*sic*] recognized by the highest judicial tribunal of Virginia, of which Edmund Pendleton was the president, as late as 1794,[9] and by a chancellor of Virginia still later.[10] This system was not made for Kentucky claimants litigating with Virginia claimants; but was made to operate between Virginia claimants themselves. It was a system on which Virginia might be emphatically called to bestow her approbation, since it corrects the injustice of which she was, by the mode of disposing of her waste lands, the unintentional author. It is said to be abused. He believed there was great exaggeration on that subject:—And that whatever abuses had occurred may be traced to the neglect of parties themselves. All that the legislator can do is, to incorporate in his enactments a just principle, and secure it by all reasonable precautions against abuse. These precautions are abundant in the system. In the first place, its benefits are denied to all but the person having an apparently good title. He is liable for waste and damage. Seven commissioners are to be appointed by the *court,* of whom five at least are to act. They are to go on the land, and view the improvements. They are to be sworn. They are to value only what combines the two qualities of permanency and intrinsic worth, excluding what is temporary, ornamental or without utility. Their assessment may be set aside by the court, on proper cause. If, notwithstanding all these securities, abuses still arise; he could only say such was the lot of every thing human. The system was not confined to contests between resident and non-resident proprietors; but its most general application was between residents. The difference was immense between the condition of resident and non-residents [*sic*]. The non-residents [*sic*] remains at home, in ease and comfort, surrounded by his household gods [*sic*], by his friends, his family, his connexions, in the midst of the tombs of his ancestors, enjoying all the benefits and blandishments of refined society. The early adventurer penetrated a wilderness, exposed himself to all the perils of savage war, experienced every species of suffering and privation, an exile from his country and home, and who is not ready to share in the sensibility and exclaim with the poet,

> Breathes there a man, with soul so dead
> Who to himself hath never said
> *This* is my own, my native land?

What are the emotions which are felt by the contemplation of the scenes of one's infancy and nativity, may be imagined. He has [*sic*] recently felt them. Describe them he could not. If all proprietors were non resident, what would be the value now even of the rich Elkhorn region?[11] Probably, instead of 15 or 20 dollars per acre, not more than the minimum price of congress lands. Whatever might be the opinion of this general assembly on the justice of those laws, Mr. Clay contended that they were not violatory of the compact between the two states. That there was no intention on the part of Kentucky to violate the compact, is clear from her having incorporated it in both her constitutions. What the third article meant is to be ascertained by the condition of the parties, and the language in which they have expressed themselves. Virginia was about to part with the sovereignty. She had come under various engagements to grant the soil, for money and for services. The claims to which he had before alluded, arose out of these engagements. They were in every possible state from the first incipient stage of the title to the consummation of it by grant. There were warrants yet afloat; and unlocated; locations not surveyed; surveys not recorded; others recorded though not registered; and others again registered but not patented. Virginia, faithful to her engagements, was desirous that the parties might be assured of their rights and interests, and that no injury was to accrue to them from the transfer of the sovereign power. Kentucky, without an express stipulation to the contrary, it was apprehended might suppose herself authorised to refuse to fulfill those engagements of Virginia. That there should be no misunderstanding on this subject; that individuals might know these interests had formed an object of particular consideration; the third article of the compact declares. That all private rights and interests of lands derived from Va. prior to the separation, shall remain valid and secure, under the laws of the new state, and shall be determined by the laws of Virginia then existing. The expressions "rights and interests" are used as alone sufficiently descriptive of the nature of the subject. "Rights" or "Titles," which mean what is perfect and complete, would not have comprehended those numerous cases where the title was inchoate and just begun, which are covered by the expression "interest." Be it title, right or interest, that and that alone was the object in view of the parties, and what was to be determined by the rule of the Virginia laws. They neither had in view, nor could have had, the subject of ameliorations not then existing. Virginia was bound to complete the grant; she was bound to decide conflicting titles by the rule existing when the claims originated. Beyond this she was not bound to individuals, she did not intend to bind the new state. She sold land, not houses. She desired that the purchasers should enjoy what they did buy and pay for, not what they did not buy nor pay for—If any doubt could remain, it would disappear from the next article of the compact which provides, that a neglect of cultivation or improvement of any lands within the proposed state, belonging to non-residents, shall not subject such non-residents to forfeiture or other penalty within the term of six years after the admission of the said state into the Union. This limitation upon the power of Kentucky, implies that but for it, Kentucky had a right immediately to impose forfeiture or *other* penalty for non-cultivation or non-improvement. For, if she had no such power, if the third article implied a prohibition upon the exercise of such a power, why insert the limitation? why limit what had no existence? Both parties then supposed that after the exportation [*sic*] of six years Kentucky might enforce improvement or cultivation even by forfeiture or any other penalty. Consider this system as having for its object the improvement and cultivation of the country; consider it even as denouncing forfeiture or other penalty, the most odious form in which it can be viewed, the compact implies an admission of the power of the new state to enact it. But it is not a system of forfeitures and penalties; it promulgates a rule of equity, adapted to the state of the titles of the country, and founded upon just equivalents. If the legislature of Kentucky has not gone to the utmost limit of its power, as Virginia herself, when a colony did; for by her laws, lands were liable to forfeiture if not cultivated within three years;[12] far from being condemned for what she has done, Kentucky ought to be admired for her moderation. If she might have done more, her authority to do less cannot be questioned. The third article, in the sense for which he contends, has received its full operation. Our courts constantly refer to the rule of the Virginia laws to decide the right and interest of every land claimant. The titles to the whole of the real estate in Kentucky would be shaken, if that rule were not applied. In confidence that the system was not forbidden by the compact, individuals the bona fide occupants of land for near 25 years past, have proceeded to improve their possessions. Can any injustice be more monstrous or intolerable than that would be, which would oust them of their possessions, without compensation for their improvements?

But, there was a most appalling latitude of interpretation according to which those laws was [*sic*] to be set aside. The instant you depart from the plain meaning of the words of the compact, there was no restriction. If because the compact secured the title, the new state was disabled from legislating in regard to the improvements subsequently made on the land, it could not legislate on any subject whatever in connexion with the land. The exact state of the Virginia laws, at the epoch of the separation, in regard to real estates [*sic*], must forever prevail, in all cases whatever. We could not subject lands to the payment of debts, after the law of descents [*sic*], provide for alienation and conveyances, change the law of dower, courtesy,

&c. Your laws, like those of the Medes and Persians, would be immutable. Even after you had abandoned them, at some future period, as then unfit and undapted [*sic*] to the progress of civilization and improvements in the science of legislation, they would bind us. If Kentucky had never been separated from you, could you not have passed such a system as she has adopted? Then Kentucky could, and your purpose must have been merely to enforce respect on her part to your engagements, leaving her free as a sovereign state in every other regard.

He contended that the compact neither has nor could strip either state of any essential attribute of sovereignty, common to other states, and this was such an attribute. It provided that the new state should be admitted into the Union. Congress did admit it. The moment it was received, it stood amidst its compeers, absolved from every condition which would restrain it from exercising any essential power of sovereignty which they could exert. The word "state," in its constitutional sense is technical, and means a sovereign body, endowed with every power not delegated to the general government. As in the creation of an estate in fee simple, every condition inconsistent with the nature of the estate disappears, so in the formation of a new state every impediment to the exercise of its just sovereign powers must be removed. You can neither abridge its federal rights nor those which appertain to it as a state.[13] This was our doctrine on the memorable Missouri Question. In vain did we invoke the humanity of our brethren in behalf of the objects for whom they professed to act. In vain did we invoke it for ourselves. But when we wrapped ourselves in the constitution of the land, we were covered with an impenetrable shield and we prevailed. You may call a body, stript of the power in question, a state, but it is no state. It is not even a corporation; for what corporation has not the power to stimulate or regulate improvements within the limits of its charter? It is the substance not the name which constitutes character. But it may be said that, according to this principle, Kentucky could not even have been bound to the observance of the engagements of Virginia in regard to land, and the application of her laws to the decision of titles. Not so. That was what Kentucky was bound in justice to do. And the express declaration of the rule was to guard against misunderstanding; and to give confidence to claimants. It was to substitute Kentucky to Virginia, in the completion and fulfilment of her contracts, which she, by parting with the sovereignty, was now no longer able to fulfil. It was to oblige the new sovereignty to act as the old one would have done within the limits of the proposed state, if there had been no separation, but to leave it free in all other respects. Of all the attributes of sovereignty, scarcely any can be deemed more essential than that of adopting a policy to redeem a wilderness and render it productive. It is not merely the right, but it is the duty of a state to advance its own prosperity by the enactment of wholesome & equitable laws, demanded by its peculiar condition.

Lastly he contended not only that the new state was not and could not only be restrained, but that Virginia *would* not have restrained her, from adopting the system in question. It would have been utterly inconsistent with her enlightened and parental views. You did not mean to erect a new state destitute of the powers to maintain a respectable existence. You did not intend to send forth, in the wide world, your first (and he hoped he might say) your favorite child, ricketty and crippled, devoid of the faculties necessary to preserve itself. No, no, no. It was your munificent purpose to advance her liberally; to place along side you a stout and hearty member of the Union, supporting and perpetuating your principles of liberty; and giving additional strength to the nation. Yes, it was your noble intention to plant a new star in the bright firmament of the American Confederacy which equally uniting in the congregated splendour should diffuse light and life and liberty around. Such, Mr. Speaker, are the views of Kentucky. But suppose she is wrong; suppose you think that we have violated the compact, then the compact itself has provided for the case. Either you think that we have, or we have not violated it. If the first, you will not hesitate to declare so, as is proposed in our first written proposition.[14] If the last, you will not hesitate to refer the question to the tribunal of the compact according to the second proposition. The first embraced only our two earlier laws, because they only were before the supreme court. The last proposition embraced the three laws, because, if you deem those two repugnant to the compact, you will of course think the third is. If you do differ with us, it is fitting that the family dispute should be settled by the family tribunal, and not by strangers. It had been insinuated to him that Virginia would do nothing; that she would condemn the decisions of the Supreme Court when they bore hard upon her state rights,[15] but that she should approve them whenever they benefitted any of her citizens, however they might trench on the rights of any other state. He had indignantly rejected the malicious insinuation; told these who had made it that they were utterly ignorant of the chivalry, and the unbending integrity of the Virginia character; and that faithful to her principles, she would be unaffected by all the allurements of self-interest.

Whatever, Mr. Speaker, may be the result of your deliberations, he was sure he expressed the feelings of his colleague, as he did his own, when he declared that they would carry back to their state a grateful remembrance of your respect, attention, and of all your numerous kindnesses, public and private, during their abode among you.

Lexington *Kentucky Reporter,* March 4, 1822 (from Richmond *Enquirer,* February 14, 1822). Summarized in Lexington *Kentucky Gazette,* February 28, 1822. See above, Banks to Clay and Bibb, February 5, 1822.

1 Edmund Pendleton had been president of the Virginia constitutional convention of 1776. Earlier he had practiced law, served as justice of the peace of Caroline County, sat in the House of Burgesses, and represented his colony in the First Continental Congress. In 1775 he had become president of the Committee of Public Safety which temporarily governed Virginia before the adoption of the State constitution. He later presided over the Virginia convention that ratified the Federal Constitution and was, from 1779 until his death in 1803, president of the Virginia Supreme Court of Appeals.

2 George Wythe had been a member of the Virginia Constitutional Convention but had left to perform other duties before its work was ended.

3 The committee report, written by James Madison, referred to above, II, 448, 464n.

4 Littell (comp.), *Statute Law of Kentucky,* II, 110 (February 12, 1798).

5 See above, DuVal to Clay, June 14, 1821.

6 John Marshall.

7 The Virginia-Kentucky resolutions of 1798, which had declared that the several states of the United States were joined by compact under which residual powers remained in the states, that the Alien and Sedition Acts violated the Constitution, and that the legislatures called upon their sister states for cooperative action to preserve their liberties, had been drafted by James Madison for presentation to the Virginia legislature and by Thomas Jefferson for similar action in Kentucky—the plan being that the two States should act concurrently. The measure had been adopted by the Kentucky legislature on November 13, 1798, and approved by the Governor three days later; the companion proposition of the Virginia legislature had been adopted on December 24.

8 See above, DuVal to Clay, June 14, 1821.

9 Southall *vs.* M'Keand, Mayo, &c., 1 *Va.* (1 Wash.) 339 (October Term, 1794).

10 Possibly a reference to the decree of the Supreme Court of Chancery for the Staunton District, April, 1803, in the case of Nelson *vs.* Matthews and Another, in which Nelson was to be recompensed for his land loss according to its value at the time of the original contract, not at a subsequent period. This decree had been reversed by the Virginia Court of Appeals, 12 *Va.* (2 Hen. & M.) 164-81 (1808).

11 In the Kentucky Bluegrass area.

12 Hening (comp.), *Statutes of Virginia,* III, 314 (October, 1705).

13 See above, II, 740-43 *passim,* 777n.

14 See above, this date.

15 Cf. above, II, 490n.

From James Morrison

My dear Sir Lex: 8th. Febr'y 1822—

On the 19th. Ulto, I had the satisfaction of answering your favor from Columbus—[1]

To guard against contingencies, you have herewith the Documents which were transmitted to you last year, relative to my claims on the Government,[2] and which you handed over to me, on your return to Lexn.

I beleive [*sic*] you had Genl. Wilkinsons[3] certificate, but am not certain, it is however now sent— I have retained a Copy. This document Certainly is Corroborative of Mr. Eustis's Certificate, and the affidavit of Mr Simmons[4]—and if my Judgment is not strangely perverted, makes my claim as to the price of the ration at Forts Osage & Madison most clearly established.

It is my intention to set out by the first Steam Boat for Wheeling, and reach Washington by the Stage: as I am very solicitous to have your aid in obtaining what I am fairly & equitably entitled to from the Government—

My health is rather better than when you left us—but as I am old, and may be prevented from causes not within my Control, I have earnestly to ask you to do whatever you may think necessary—in a word, act as if you did not expect me—'tho' it is my intention to go as stated above—

I transmit my documents under cover to our friend Mr. Woodson—[5]

As Mrs. Clay writes to you, I shall only say your family & friends are well, and leave your Good spouse to give you all local news—

I am Dear Sir very sincerely your friend JAMES MORRISON

The Honl. H. Clay

ALS. DLC-HC (DNA, M212, R1). [1] Neither letter has been found.
[2] See above, Morrison to Clay, January 11, 16, 28, 1821.
[3] James Wilkinson. [4] William Eustis; William Simmons.
[5] Samuel H. Woodson.

Toasts and Speech at Dinner

[February 9, 1822]

The State of Virginia—"the ancient dominion."

. . . .

Henry Clay and George M Bibb, native citizens of Virginia, we feel honoured that they should come among us.[1]

Lexington *Kentucky Reporter,* March 4, 1822. While in Richmond Clay and George M. Bibb resided at the Eagle Hotel, on Main Street, where they were honored with a dinner, given by members of the State legislature boarding there. Linn Banks presided. Clay offered the first of the toasts here published; Judge Spencer Roane, the second.
[1] In reply, Clay "on behalf of himself and colleague made an appropriate and feeling speech," not further reported.

From Caleb Cox

The Hon Henry Clay St Louis 14 Feby 1822

Sir

Inclos d you have Smith & Fergusons[1] Draft on the Cashier of the US Branch Bank at Louisville for one Hundred Dollars Should you have Drawn on me for that Sum[2] you'll please return the enclos d without presentation

Respectfully your Most Obt Servt. CALEB COX

ALS copy. DLC-TJC (DNA, M212, R12). [1] Not identified.
[2] The enclosure, a duplicate draft by Smith and Ferguson in favor of Caleb Cox, is dated from St. Louis, February 15, 1822. No draft by Clay on Cox has been found.

Account with Nicholas Berthoud

[*ca.* February 15, 1822]

[N. Berthoud bills Henry Clay for $18.94, shipping and commission charges on freight of "2 Barrels Sugar & 1 box," July 5, 1821, and 6 demijohns of wine, November 3, 1821. Postage charges are added on February 15, 1822.]

D. DLC-TJC (DNA, M212, R15). John Keating, for N. Berthoud, acknowledges receipt to Thomas Smith, February 22, 1822 (ES).

From José Maria del Réal

Sir Bordeaux February 23 1822

Both by honour of my Country and duty of friendship, I think myself obliged to make over to the posterity the image of Don Josef Ma. Garcia de Toledo[1] my particular friend and the first Defender of the rights of his country, and as I was favoured with the honour of your acquaintance in London, and convinced as I am of a great deal of interest, you lay hold of for the liberty and indenpendence [*sic*] as well as for all that belonging to the glorious revolution of South America, I take the liberty of send [*sic*] you six stamps of his portraits, which I intreat you to have the goodness of accepting as an acknowledment [*sic*] of my duty to you

After a few days I shall embark to Carthagena where, if it is in my way to render you any service, I should be very glad to be honoured with your command. I have the honour to be Sir Your most obedient & humble Servt. JOSE MA. DEL REAL

to Henry Clay Esq.

ALS. DLC-HC (DNA, M212, R1). Addressed to Clay at Lexington, "Favored by Mr. Bernabeu [Juan Bautista Bernabeu, Spanish Consul at Baltimore, later Consul General of Spain in the United States]"; postmarked at Baltimore, Maryland, May 18. Published in Colton (ed.), *Private Correspondence of Henry Clay*, 63. Del Réal, born in Cartagena, had early embraced the Patriot cause, spent the period from 1812 to 1819 seeking to win it support in London, and, upon his return to Colombia, served successively as judge of the court at Cartagena, intendant of Magdalena, and deputy to the convention of Ocaña and to the national legislative assembly.

1 A native of Cartagena, he had been elected alcalde of that city in 1810 and had subsequently taken an active part in the Colombian revolution against Spain. Captured by the Spanish, he had been executed in 1816.

From Robert Saunders

Sir, Williamsburg Va. Feby. 23d. 1822.

In reply to your letter of the 14th instant[1] from Richmond, I have to say, that, more than a dozen years ago, I received from the present Judge Francis Brooke a Bond given by the late Warner Lewis the younger of Gloster County to you, for the purpose of making title to a certain piece of Land in Kentucky, to put in suit—Suit was brought agt. him in the then District Court of this City, which was continued time after time for the execution of a Commission sent to Kentucky to take Testimony in the Case; and, after some time, on his death Suit was revived agt. his Exor— In this State it remained till the District Courts were abolished, and the present System of Circuit Courts substituted—Upon this Change, this suit with many others was transmitted to the Gloster Circuit; and, as I was unable, as well from infirmity as from other causes, to attend that Court, I put my docket and Papers for that Court in the hands of James W. Murdaugh[2] a young Man of talents and Character who attended that Court— This was in 1809— In 1811 a Judgment was obtained agt. the Exor quando &c. by reason that Warner Lewis had, in his life, conveyed his whole estate in Trust for the benefit of his Creditors and family—After this Mr. Murdaugh returned me my docket, saying he had written to Judge Brooke or yourself, which I don't recollect, informing him or you of the fate of the suit— When I gave him my docket for that Court, I apprized him of the Cases in which fees had not been paid, requesting he wd. apply to those who had not paid:—this was one— for, altho' Judge Brooke had said to me in his letter that he wd. be responsible for my fees, I had never demanded them—It was proper for me, therefore, to refer Mr. Murdaugh to him, or you, respecting them— In 1815 Mr. Murdaugh informed me that the Trust estate of Mr. Lewis was brought into the Chancery here; and, as he had receiv'd instructions from you or Judge Brooke, I do not now remember which, to endeavor to secure the Judgment he directed a suit in Chancery & filed his Bill for that purpose—Mr. Murdaugh having taken the direction of the affair, as he said, on your or Judge Brooke's authority, I declined to do any thing more respecting it—nor have I since known any thing respecting the suit 'till I received your letter— For six years past, I have withdrawn from the Bar on account of ill health; and, knew nothing of any affairs in the Court, all my business having passed into other hands.—This Suit, I now learn, was sent from the Chancery here to the Court at Richmond, by the late Judge Nelson,[3] because he had been the Counsel of the Exor & Trustee before his appointment to the bench—And I also learn that a decree has passed the Chancery at Richmond, and that Mr. Murdaugh has recd. from the Trustee the Amount, two or three years since— Mr. Murdaugh has been now confined in the Lunatic Hospital nearly a year; and his estate, under an act of Assembly, is committed to a Curator called a Committee, who is authorized & compelled to pay debts and receive his property & debts— His Committee, in this case, is John Dandridge Attorney at Law residing at Richmond;[4] who, as I am informed has, at command funds sufficient for Mr Murdaugh's debts.— I can have little doubt that Mr. Dandridge will, upon your representation and demand, make provision to pay what you may be entitled to receive of the Amount paid to him under the decree. Mr. Murdaugh's estate will be entitled to the fees in Gloster & for the Judgment at law, as I have not received any fee, and do not claim one.

very respectfully, I am, Sir, Your ob[n]t S[erv]t

RO: SAUND[ERS]

ALS. DLC-TJC (DNA, M212, R12). Addressed to Clay, "now at Washington City."

1 Not found. 2 Of Williamsburg, Virginia.

3 William Nelson, for many years a judge of the General Court of Virginia and professor of law at William and Mary College until his death in 1813.

4 Brother-in-law of Murdaugh, the two men having married Minge sisters.

From S[tephen] Pleasanton

Treasury Dept. 5th. Aud: Office, Feby. 26th. 1822.

S: Pleasonton presents his compliments to Mr Clay, and has the honor to inform him, in answer to his Note of the 25th instant,[1] that no instruction has been given to the Marshall of Virginia, relative to the proposition made through him, by Mr. Morris,[2] in consequence of the Marshall having Signified his intention of being absent from the Scene of his Official Duties; but, that it has been decided to accede to the proposition of selling the negroes, on a credit for the joint benefit of the United States and Mr. Morris, if they Shall Sell, as they probably will, for more than will discharge the lien of Mr. Morris. If they shall not sell for more, he will of course, be entitled to the esclusive [*sic*] benefit of the Sale, his lien being formed by a Special Deed of Trust from Mr Taylor,[3] anteriour to that of the United States. It is not So, however, with respect to the land embraced in the same Deed, as on that the lien of the United States commenced at the time Mr. Taylor as Collector, recieved [*sic*] the Tax lists from the assessor, Several years prior to the Deed to Mr. Morris.

S: Pleasonton requests Mr Clay to accept his best respects.

Copy. DNA, RG206, Letters on Debts and Suits, vol. 2, pp. 479-80. Pleasanton, of Delaware, had been appointed an auditor in the Treasury Department in 1817.

1 Not found. 2 Richard Morris.

3 In 1819 William D. Taylor, of Hanover, Virginia, Federal Collector of Revenue in that district, had conveyed his estate of five or six hundred acres, known as "Taylorsville," to trustees, one of whom was Richard Morris, for the benefit of Dr. James Maury Morris, of Louisa County.

To Richard Morris

Dr Sir Washn. 26 Feb. 1822.

I am requested by our friend Dr. Morris to communicate to you the result of an enquiry which he has requested me to make for him at the Department of the Treasury. Not having been able to call there I addressed a note to Mr. Pleasanton; and by the suspension of business today, in consequence of Mr. Pinckneys regretted death,[1] being allowed to call in person, I received from Mr. Pleasanton the inclosed note, which I hope will prove satisfactory to the Doctor.[2] I need not repeat the expression of my disposition further to serve him in this affair, if in my power.

I perceive that the House of Delegates has finally disposed on its part of the "Kentucky Mission."[3] I am glad that it abstained from the expression of any opinion on our laws, as it did not feel itself justified in acceding to either of our propositions. I think it would have been exposed to the imputation of some inconsistency, if it had declared an opinion and stopt there.

I pray you to communicate my best respects to Mrs. Cock and Mrs. Kempe[4] and to the gentlemen of your mess, and that you will believe that among the many sources of agreeable recollection connected with my recent visit to the "ancient dominion" is that of having made your acquaintance. Your's faithfully H. Clay

Richard Morris Esq.

ALS. ViU-Morris Family Papers. 1 William Pinkney had died the preceding day.
2 See above, this date. 3 See below, Resolutions, March 2, 1822.
4 Mrs. Hannah Kemp, operator of the Eagle Hotel in Richmond; Mrs. Cock (or Coch, the name not clearly legible), not identified.

Rental Agreement with Barry and Leavy

[March 1, 1822]

[Clay, by his agent, Thomas Smith, rents to Barry and Leavy for one year "the rooms of a building on Street, lately occupied by Benjn. Gratz,"[1] for the sum of one hundred dollars, to be paid in quarterly instalments.]

ADS by Smith (except for one emendation), signed also by Barry & Leavy. DLC-TJC (DNA, M212, R15). William T. Barry and Laurence Leavy, one of Barry's former students, a son of William Leavy, were partners in legal practice from September, 1819, until the fall of 1822. The younger Leavy then moved to Louisville, where he died the following year, at the age of twenty-five.

1 The building was on Main Street, opposite the court house. No lease to Gratz has been found.

Rental Agreement with John Deverin

[March 1, 1822]

[Henry Clay, by his agent, Thomas Smith, rents to John Deverin "two rooms on the first floor of the Hotel building, (which said rooms were lately occupied by Abner LeGrand for Auctions)[1] together with a brick building situated back of said rooms, now occupied by J. Deverin for a Coffee House," for the sum of two hundred dollars for the year, to be paid in quarterly instalments.]

ADS by Smith, signed also by Deverin. KyLxT.
[1] See above, Advertisement, December 31, 1821.

Rental Agreement with Frances Rawlins

[March 1, 1822]

[Henry Clay, by his agent, Thomas Smith, rents to Mrs. Frances Rawlins for one year "the House and Lot on Main Street, nearly opposite Keen's Inn[1] and lately occupied by Charles Cummens,"[2] for the sum of eighty dollars, to be paid in quarterly instalments.]

[Endorsement on verso][3]

Recd. an order of the County Court allowing Mrs. Rawlings [*sic*] forty dollars on a/c of the two first quarters rent.[4] 16 Aug. 1822

H. CLAY

ADS by Smith, signed also by Mrs. Rawlins. DLC-TJC (DNA, M212, R15).
[1] Operated by Sandford Keen.
[2] Lexington hairdresser and hat seller. No lease to Cummens has been found.
[3] AES.
[4] Not recorded.

Resolutions from Virginia General Assembly

[March 2, 1822]

[In regard to the first proposal submitted by Clay and Bibb,[1] the Virginia General Assembly declares that the rights of claimants whether under the Virginia compact or the Kentucky statutes are "fit subjects of judicial cognizance, and ought to be decided, and no doubt will be decided, without reference to the opinion of the general assembly." Further, that body is "not prepared to declare, that, according to the true interpretation of the compact between the two states, the legislature of Kentucky was not restrained from passing the acts in question." It therefore rejects this proposition.

[The second proposal is also unacceptable. The Virginia General Assembly considers, "so far as the occupying claimant acts alone are concerned," the judicial tribunals fully competent to protect the rights of the citizens of Virginia claiming lands in Kentucky." If a repeal of these acts were desired by Virginia, "the limited powers of the board proposed would constitute an insuperable objection to its formation. If it were organized, every subject of difference in relation to the Compact between the two states, ought to be submitted to it. . . ."]

DS copy, by William Munford, Clerk of the Virginia House of Delegates. DLC-HC (DNA, M212, R1). Published in Ky. H. of Reps., *Journal, Special Session, 1822*, pp. 12-15. The published version includes the following, not found in the MS. copy:

"*Resolved,* That a copy of these resolutions, and the preamble thereto, be communicated, by the speaker of the house of delegates, to each of the aforesaid commissioners, Henry Clay, Esq. and George M. Bibb, Esq."

On this same day the Virginia General Assembly adopted a report and resolutions stating that unsatisfied claims to land bounties by Virginia veterans of the Revolution entitled "the owners thereof" to land between the Tennessee and Mississippi rivers; that it was "incumbent on Kentucky to make provision by law for satisfaction" of these claims; that a commissioner should be appointed to present the case to Kentucky; and that, if Kentucky proved unwilling to enact such laws, the commissioner should request the Kentucky legislature "to co-operate with the general assembly of Virginia, in organizing a board of commissioners, under the eighth article of the compact between the two states, with authority to decide all matters in difference between them." Ky. H. of Reps., *Journal, Special Session, 1822,* pp. 17-47. Four days later, Benjamin Watkins Leigh was appointed commissioner to present these resolutions to the Kentucky legislature. *Ibid.,* 48-49.

1 See above, Clay and Bibb to the Virginia General Assembly, February 7, 1822.

To Benjamin Watkins Leigh

Dr Sir Washn. 8h. March 1822.

I recd. your favor of the 6h. inst.[1] and congratulate you on your appointment as Commr. to K.[2] We shall be very glad to see you there, and I pray you to be persuaded that it will give me very particular satisfaction to shew you every civility and to render you every facility in my power. Your best way, beyond all doubt, is to take the Stage by this place and Wheeling. It runs to Frankfort. 4½ days will take you from Richmond to Wheeling, and six more will set you down at Frankfort. We are to have an extra Session in the Spring; the time to be fixed by the Governor. Should I ascertain it, before my departure from this place, I will communicate it to you.

Nicholas[3] is at my elbow, desires to be presented to you, and asks the favor of you to take care of him in the Ct. of Appeals until wednesday, when he will be there. I offer my respectful Compliments to Madam and remain Faithfully Yours. H. CLAY

P. S. You will go through Lexn. Come to my house, sans ceremonie. otherwise I may not know of your being in town.

ALS. ViU. Addressed to Leigh at Richmond, Virginia.

1 Not found. 2 See above, Resolutions, March 2, 1822, note.

3 Probably Philip Norborne Nicholas, Richmond banker and lawyer, who in 1823 became Judge of the General Court of Virginia and held that post until his death in 1849. He was the youngest brother of George and Wilson Cary Nicholas.

Resolutions and Letter on Establishment of a General Grand Lodge of Masonry in the United States

[*ca.* March 9, 1822]

Resolved, That, in the opinion of this meeting, it is expedient, for the general interests of Freemasonry, to constitute a General Grand Lodge of the United States.

Resolved, That it be proposed to the several Grand Lodges in the United States to take the subject into their serious consideration, at their next annual communications, and that, if they approve of the formation of a General Grand Lodge, it be recommended to them to appoint one or more delegates, to assemble in the city of Washington, on the second Monday of February next, to agree on the organization of such Grand Lodge.[1]

Resolved, That if two-thirds of the Grand Lodges within the United States concur in the propriety of establishing a General Grand Lodge, it be recommended to them to instruct their representatives to proceed to the formation of a constitution of a General Grand Lodge, to be subsequently submitted to the several Grand Lodges in the Union, for their ratification, and which, being ratified by a majority of them, shall be considered as thenceforth binding on all the Grand Lodges assenting thereto.

Resolved, That the Most Worshipful *John Marshall,* of Virginia; *Henry Clay,* of Kentucky; *William H. Winder,* of Maryland;[2] *William S. Cardell,* of New York;[3] *Joel Abbot,* of Georgia; *John Holmes,* of Maine; *Henry Baldwin,* of Pennsylvania; *John H. Eaton,* of Tennessee; *William W. Seaton,* of Washington; *Christopher Rankin,* of Mississippi;[4] *Thomas R. Ross,* of Ohio; *H. G. Burton,* of N. Carolina;[5] and the Rev. *Thaddeus Mason Harris,* D. D. of Massachusetts;[6] be, and they hereby are, appointed a committee to open a correspondence with the respective Grand Lodges within the United States, and to take such measures therein as they may deem expedient to carry the aforesaid resolutions into effect.

The committee, in complying with the above resolutions, are aware that a meeting of individual Masons, however respectable in number and character, could delegate no regular authority in behalf of the Masonic body; and, if they could, it was unnecessary. This paper will, therefore, be understood as it is intended—a proceeding, originating in the necessity of the case, to adopt some mode by which the general views of Masons in the different states of the American Union may be ascertained.

The history of the Masonic Institution shows that, tho' established among various nations, it was, in each country, confined to a comparatively small number. The jurisdiction exercised by Grand Lodges, like almost every exertion of power or of moral influence, was concentrated in different capital cities. The subordinate Lodges were few in number, and their connection with the supreme head was very direct. Till within a recent period, it is believed, no great number of Lodges have been united under a single jurisdiction. The art of printing and other causes have produced great changes in the condition of the world, and these causes have operated in their full proportion on the society of Freemasons. The sphere of civilization is greatly enlarging its boundaries: intellectual attainments and the influence of moral operations are taking the place of brute force: known principles and laws are recognized, and the advantages of cultivated reason are shared by an increased proportion of mankind. Under these circumstances Masonry has been extended, and its Lodges so multiplied as to make their proper conduct a subject of much interest to the friends of the society.

There are two points which at once present themselves in connection with the idea of establishing a General Grand Lodge of the United States. The first is to acquire, in a correspondence with foreign nations, an elevated stand for the Masonry of this country; to unite with them in maintaining its general principles in their purity; and, secondly, to preserve, between our own states, that uniformity in work, and that active interchange of good offices, which would be difficult, if not impossible, by other means.

The committee do not presume to instruct their brethren in the nature of an institution in which they have a common interest. They are governed by a few plain considerations known to all who have attended to the subject.

The antiquity of the Masonic Society, extending so far beyond all other human associations, seizes the attention, and the mind is naturally impressed with feelings of interest for an institution transmitted to us through the long train of a hundred ages. Time, which destroys all perishable things, seems to have consolidated the pillars of this moral temple. We contemplate the long catalogue of excellent men who have been equally the supporters of Masonry and the ornaments of human nature; and, we say, almost unconsciously, that the present generation, with all its lights, must not tarnish the name of an institution, consecrated by so many circumstances calculated to endear it to the mind of a good man.

Without making invidious comparisons between the United States and other portions of the world, there are some great considerations of responsibility, which our intelligent citizens, accustomed to reflect on the affairs of nations, cannot overlook. The Masons of the United States, in character as such, have their full share of this moral responsibility. They will consider their institution as one of the great social causes to allay low-minded jealousies between nations at peace; and in war to mitigate the horrors which it cannot avert. While they offer their gratitude to a Beneficent Providence for their own blessings, they will not be regardless of their obligations to their brethren through the world.

These reflections, drawn from the external circumstances of Masonry, are strengthened by the consideration of its intrinsic nature. Its foundation is fixed in the social feelings and the best principles of the human mind. Its maxims are the lessons of virtue reduced to their practical application. It stands opposed to sordidness; to a jealous or revengeful temper; to all the selfish and malevolent passions; it coincides with the highest motives of patriotism; the most expanded philanthropy, and concentrates all its precepts in reverence to a Divine Creator, and good will to man.

The United States are supposed to contain near 80,000 Freemasons. They are generally in the vigor of manhood, and capable of much active usefulness. Notwithstanding the abuses in some places by the admission of unworthy members, they are, as a body, above mediocrity in character and talent. It becomes an interesting question how the energies of this body can be best combined to give effect to the benevolent design of their association.

From causes which need no explanation, the Masonic jurisdiction in this country has taken its form from the political divisions. The modification which it has undergone, from the spirit of our civil institutions, has its benefits and its defects. Each of our state jurisdictions is supreme within itself. Whatever collisions may exist; whatever abuses; whatever departures from the correct standard, in principle or in rites; whatever injury to the common cause; there is no mode assigned to obviate the wrongs which it is the interest of all to prevent. There is no provision for a systematic interchange of Masonic intelligence. In one or two instances there are already two or more Grand Lodges in the same state, each claiming superior jurisdiction, and with no acknowledged boundaries between them. Will not these evils increase as our population becomes more dense, unless means be seasonably used to guard against them? Is the difference now prevailing between different states an evil which calls for remedy? Every good Mason must wish chiefly for the harmony of the general institution: for the society is so formed that no particular part, however meritorious by itself, can continue to prosper, if the body at large is brought into disgrace. Is the Masonry of our country at present a great arch without a key stone? Is it not in danger of falling? Are not many of the books which are published in the name of the Masonic institution, derogatory to its character and interest?

It is not the design of the committee to enter into arguments on this subject; nor to lay down their own opinions as a guide for those better able to judge; but to proceed to the only duty required of them to perform.

According to the preceding resolutions the committee are to submit the question whether it be expedient that a Grand Lodge of the United States be formed; and secondly, to request those Grand Lodges which approve that object, to appoint delegates to meet at

Washington, on the second Monday of February next, to take such measures as may be deemed most proper for the organization of such General Grand Lodge.

It is requested that this letter may not be published in newspapers; but submitted to the several Grand Lodges, and distributed among Masons, as a subject concerning the affairs of their own body.

If the information furnished to the committee should render it expedient, perhaps another letter may be forwarded, giving a statement of such facts as may be interesting to be known, previous to a final decision on the course to be taken.

An answer is requested, with a free expression of opinion on the subject of this communication. Such answer may be directed to any member of the committee, or, in particular, to WILLIAM W. SEATON, Esq. Washington.

HENRY CLAY,
WILLIAM H. WINDER,
WILLIAM S. CARDELL,
JOEL ABBOT,
JOHN HOLMES,
HENRY BALDWIN,
JOHN H. EATON,
WILLIAM W. SEATON,
CHRISTOPHER RANKIN,
THOMAS R. ROSS,
H. G. BURTON,
THADDEUS MASON HARRIS.

Copy, printed. DLC-HC (DNA, M212, R1). Pursuant to a "Masonic Notice," dated March 9, 1822, and published in the Washington *Daily National Intelligencer,* March 9, inviting all Masons among members of Congress and visitors in Washington to a meeting in the Senate Chamber that evening, "a number of members of the Society of Freemasons" had assembled. Thomas R. Ross had been appointed chairman, and William Darlington, Congressman from Pennsylvania, secretary. Following discussion of the objectives of the meeting, Clay offered these resolutions, which were adopted unanimously and thereafter included in the accompanying letter, by Clay and others, circulated to the Masonic Grand Lodges of the United States.

1 The response to this proposal being unfavorable, no meeting appears to have been held. Other efforts to organize such a General Grand Lodge have since proved similarly unfruitful.

2 Baltimore lawyer, who, having risen rapidly from lieutenant colonel to brigadier general of militia during the War of 1812, had commanded at the disastrous Battle of Bladensburg. He was at this time Grand Master of the Masonic Order in Maryland.

3 Born in Bozrah, Connecticut, a scholar and teacher, author of an *Analytical Spelling Book . . . ,* published at New York in 1823, and of several grammars and a reader, published later in this decade.

4 Born in Pennsylvania, Congressman from Mississippi from 1819 until his death in 1826.

5 Member of the House of Representatives from 1819 to 1824, when he resigned to become Governor of North Carolina.

6 Clergyman, writer, editor, and librarian, long active in Freemasonry and an outspoken defender of the Order.

To John Quincy Adams

Washington 11h. Mar. 22.

Mr. Clay has the pleasure to accept the invitation of Mr. Adams and Mrs. Adams to dinner on saturday next.

AN. MHi-Adams Papers. Addressed: "The Honble J. Q. Adams. Secretary of State."

Rental Agreement with William North

[March 12, 1822]

[Henry Clay, by his agent, Thomas Smith, rents to William North for one year, for the sum of $130, payable in equal quarterly payments, "the Brick and wooden buildings near the E. Church, lately occupied by Col. Whaley."[1]]

ADS by Smith, signed also by North, a Lexington tailor. KyLxT.

1 See above, Advertisement, December 31, 1821; cf. below, Rental Agreement, *ca.* December 27, 1822. In April North advertised his intention to begin tailoring and habit making at a different location. Lexington *Kentucky Reporter,* April 15, 1822.

To John W. Taylor

Saturday [March 23, 1822].

Mr. Clay's Compliments to Mr. Taylor, and he will be obliged to him to transmit the inclosed letter to a mutual friend.[1]

AN. NHi. Addressed: "The Honble John W Taylor—H. of R." Endorsed, apparently by Taylor: "H. Clay March 23. 1822."

1 Letter not found. See below, Henry Shaw to Clay, April 4, 1822.

To Samuel H. Woodson

[*ca.* April 1, 1822]

On April 20, 1822, John Quincy Adams learned that Woodson had shown President Monroe "a letter from Clay at Philadelphia [not found]." Clay "had there seen [Manuel] Torres, who was, he says, exceedingly earnest that a Minister should immediately go to Colombia, and fears that otherwise all the good effect of the recognition will be lost. This letter Clay had requested Woodson to show to the President, which he did." According to Adams, Monroe "was staggered by this *a parte* negotiation between Clay and Torres." Adams, *Memoirs,* V, 494-95.

From Richard M. Johnson

Henry Clay Eqr. City of Washington 1 Apl. 1822

Dear Sir,

I have Seen the President, who has again assur[ed] me that he would get Mr Wirt[1] to reexamine your Claim[2]—& he will bring the thing to a close— I see that Ficklin has republished a piece from the Franklin Gazette in Favour of Mr Calhoun.[3] & some letters from our friends dislike his course. I do not know his motive in doing this. I have not written a word to him on the subject of the next President. I saw a letter of his to Fr. Johnson in which he says he is for you— It is very possible that some of your particular friends may think that as I am intimate with him I may have some influence in this respect—and knowing the disposition with some to place every thing to my account I hope you will not only believe me incapable of promoting any thing unfavourable to you but whenever a different sentiment is communicated or [hi]nted to you, my feelings may be explained. I intend in this business to keep a straigh [*sic*] forward Course, and while I consider it my duty to be on terms of personal friendship with others, if I find it reciprocated no person shall doubt my course when I can be of any service to you. With sincere respect & esteem your friend & ob st in haste Rh: M: JOHNSON

ALS. DLC-HC (DNA, M212, R1). Addressed to Clay at Wheeling, Virginia. Published in Colton (ed.), *Private Correspondence of Henry Clay*, 64.

1 William Wirt.

2 See above, Clay to Monroe, March 1, 1821; Clay to Wirt, March 9, 1821.

3 The Philadelphia *Franklin Gazette,* on March 14, 1822, had begun publication of a life of Calhoun, which ran for nine installments over a four-month period and constituted a strong endorsement of his candidacy. Johnson apparently erred, however, in attributing the Kentucky item to the *Franklin Gazette.* The Lexington *Kentucky Gazette,* also on March 14, had reprinted an endorsement of Calhoun from the Lancaster, Pennsylvania, *Intelligencer* and the following week had carried editorial reference to the article as "the commencement of an electioneering contest," during which the journal proposed to furnish its readers "with the names and history of all the candidates. . . ." The editor had then further commented: "It is probable, nay certain, that Kentucky will have a candidate at the approaching election; and although there is none of the feelings to influence us which appears among a people divided into tribes and clans, yet that candidate will no doubt unite the fourteen votes of the state, because he will deserve them." *Kentucky Gazette,* March 21, 1822.

Joseph Ficklin, publisher of the *Kentucky Gazette* from August, 1821, to February, 1824, had been brought from Virginia to Kentucky at an early age, had been postmaster at Russellville, Kentucky, 1802-1812, and United States Consul at St. Bartholomew's Island, 1816-1820. He became postmaster at Lexington in 1822 and, except for a brief interval, 1841-1843, held the post continuously until 1850.

To Thomas Dougherty

My dear Sir Philada. 3 Apl. 1822

I have been detained here by indisposition, which for the three last days has absolutely confined me to my room. I have written a letter to Genl. Stokes[1] requesting him to pay you for me $115 which he owes me for money lent &c. at the Russian Minister's—[2] I do not wish him however to pay it before the next session, if it be inconvenient to him. I could have wished to have heard what arrangement you made with Commodore Rogers [*sic*] about the Carriage,[3] before I left here; but as that is impracticable, will you drop me a line *by the return mail* addressed to me at Balto.? which may find me there.

Whatever information I have acquired, since my arrival here, tends to strengthen the convictions I expressed to you, on a certain subject, at your house. My best respects to Mrs. Dougherty.

With great regard I am faithfully Yours. H. CLAY

Tho. Dougherty Esqr.

ALS. CtSoP.

1 Probably Montfort Stokes, United States Senator from North Carolina, 1816-1823, who had served as major general of militia during the War of 1812. He was later (1830-1832) Governor of North Carolina.

2 Pierre de Polética.

3 See below, Rodgers to Clay, July 18, 1822.

From Henry Shaw

Dear Sir Lanesborough Berkshire Co Mass. Apl. 4. 22

I red. yours of the 22d. Ulto.[1] under cover from Taylor—[2] To know you were well and enjoying the good things of life has given me great pleasure,—to find I was not forgotten by you has added to my pleasure [. . .][3] *agreable* [*sic*] unction to my vanity— I reciprocate the congratulations in yous [*sic*], on the success of the South Americans,[4] and had I not long since ceased to marvel at the ductility of Politicians, I should on this occasion have exclaimed against that poverty and meaness [*sic*] of spirit, that could be cold in the cause of principle, while it stood upon a hazard, and weedle with flatteries, on the day of its Triumph— but I care nothing for the vote of Congress on the subject *now*. The day has long ago passed bye, in which our acknowledgement of Southern Independence could have shed a lustree [*sic*] on our name forever— There was a time when *recognition* would have looked like a noble and chivalrick defense of the principles of Freedom— It now flows from the calculations of sordid interest alone. There was a time when *recognition* would have stayed the desolations of War, lifted up the broken spirits of a brave & generous people, and bound together our Hemispheres, by the facination [*sic*] of a glowing & ardent simpathy— That moment it was your fortune to distinguish—but the *Evil Genius* of our Country forbade its improvement— But after all I should, nay, I do rejoice sincerely at this late & halting & reluctant step, so far as the South are concerned—but I regret it for the honor of our Name— we had far better have never recognized—negotiating with the *Holies* of Europe for a simultaneous recognition— Uniting our Character with theirs —fearing to advance in our own Course and moreover so managing as to have our conduct in regard to Spain wear the aspect of duplicity— for so it will appear in after time— we could do nothing 'till we got Florida—and then— well let it go— it is humiliating to see the fair form of our Empire daubed by — — —. And after all England, yes England will have the Glory of atchieving the Independence of the South— Cochrane D'Everough; & English;[5] men worthless at home, have circled the brow of England with imperishable Laurels— but I write to you as though you were a Stranger to the subject— forgive me— the feelings, like Truant schoolboys, will sometimes run wild—

I was highly pleased with your frankness on the subject of the next P.E.—[6] on that subject I most certainly do take an interest—& I hope it is such an one as will not be entirely without effect— you need not be told, by me, how much, or how little of personal attachment enter into the anxiety I feel for the results— laying these matters entirely aside. There is already before the Publick evidences [*sic*] enough of your devotion to Principle, of your enlarged and comprehensive views of the present and ulterior interests of your Country, of your frank & honorable mind, and of your services, to place you high on the list of candidates— but the prize, the most distinguished, in the Civilized world, is "not to be snatched"— preliminary measures are doubtless proper, to guide the People to a wise and judicious bestowment of it— In your Judgment on this head it was but fair your friends should implicitly rely— The movement should be concutanious [*sic*] to have effect— I can confess, that at the commencement of the Session of Crs.[7] when so much seemed to be doing for others, I felt that some cooling laxities, as the fever was running high, might have been salutary— but the Patients, in the restlessness of their own disease, have called in some Quacks, & it looks now, to me, very much like an undertaker Job— I rejoice that you have stood back—while little Cordelia has been scratching Crd.—,[8] and *Mars,*[9] with his Red bretheren [*sic*] & arrearages & Indian affairs, has fairly bolted the course— & what *Colt* would not bolt with such riders— as for the *Proffessor* [*sic*] he has too much *water in his Eyes* to see common things[10]—and I doubt much whether he gets his native State— The Old School Feds. regard him as an apostate & the Repns. can't. forget *the Family*— however, Granger thinks the *Old Domn.* will support him under the advice of Mr. J........—[11] you can guess better than him— One thing is most certain, that in the solution, the small matters of our Country will give way to the prevailing influence of some leading interests— doubtless much regard will be paid localities— without calling any Names, I had prepared a few nos. for the Publik [*sic*] Eye, while the fever *was* up, turning its attention rather westwardly. I dwelt upon the rising influence of the west—the Manufacturing Interests—the Internal Improvement of the Country—The necessity of removing local jeolesies—and above all, to take from the *Cabinet* the power, by an expression of publick sentiment, of perpetuating offices in itself—&c &c. but I fortunately kept them back— they may yet be usefull— it is True that no one of the Candidates are as yet a favorite in this District—and should we be left to choose among ourselves, as a District, I have no doubt of the success of - - - here— As it regards the State of N.Y—it is not to be counted on for any thing— altho the Clintonians appear now to be completely down—yet I concede it an equal chance That at the Nov. Eletion [*sic*], under the New Constition [*sic*] That a Maj. of the Senate, will be his friends[12]—& next winter may entirely change the state of things there— the Selection of Yates,[13] has soured a portion of the Bucks, and in Truth That Party has never had an acknowledged head and it is strange indeed it has so long held together—

C—n[14] may yet, *in him too,* be Lord of the ascendant in N.Y.— I mention these things, that you may derive from them any conclusions you please—but in my opinion, any connexion at present with any party in N.Y. would be attended with great hazard— My connexions in the State, together with a pretty general acquaintance enables me to speak of it with considerable confidence. The Comptroller, & Genl. Root,[15] both men of extensive influence, may be at all times counted upon— you know them both— Van Buren[16] has lost very conciderably [*sic*] the weight he for a time enjoyed— he is a cunning managing man— In Vermont a Corps of Young Men have sway— among the most influential are Mallary Buck, Haight & Bradley—[17] Van Ness,[18] is Chief Justice, but is a faithless Janus faced De-l— & is at present in Adams inflnce [*sic*]— much can be done in this State by a few preparatory steps. I should also have mentioned Skinner & Chase,[19] as worthy of all consideration— but if your hopes are well founded in the West, you need not fear much for the result— I have been tediously particular, but you know how to excuse it— to you it may be usefull to know The springs which may possibly move a State— But who do you think of for a Colleague— or do you hold this, where perhaps it ought to be held, *in nubibus.* It would give me pleasure however to have from you some *hints* on that point— And I submit to you, whether a confidential communication of your wishes, or such information of a local nature as may have a general bearing, from time to time, would not be of advantage— do you know what course Cheeves[20] will take—if he take any. In the prosecution of this great object I tender to you readily all that may be in my power to do in sparing neither Time, exertion or Expense.

It will give you pleasure to know that my "lines have fallen in pleasant places"—[21] My Family of 5 children are highly promising— my popularity is improving— and my fortune is ample.

entertaining for yourself an affectionate friendship, I pray God to speed you in the high & honorable course fortune has destined for you— with sincerity I am your friend HENRY SHAW

ALS. DLC-HC (DNA, M212, R1). Shaw had been a United States Congressman from Massachusetts, 1817-1821, and had been defeated for renomination.

1 Not found. 2 John W. Taylor. See above, Clay to Taylor, March 23, 1822.

3 One word not legible.

4 In response to a resolution from the House of Representatives President Monroe on March 8, 1822, had sent a message to Congress proposing recognition of "the provinces which have declared their independence, and are in the enjoyment of it" and suggesting that the necessary appropriations be provided for carrying such action into effect. Eleven days later Jonathan Russell, for the Committee on Foreign Relations, had submitted a favorable report, which had been agreed to on March 28. An appropriation for maintenance of "such Missions to the independent nations on the American continent, as the President of the United States may deem proper," was approved May 4, 1822. *Annals of Cong.,* 17 Cong., 1 Sess., XXXVIII, 825, 828, 1238-41; XXXIX, 1314-19, 1403; 3 *U. S. Stat.,* 678. Recognition was extended first to the Republic of Colombia, June 17, 1822.

5 Thomas Cochrane, tenth earl of Dundonald, British admiral, was from 1817 until November, 1822, commander of the Navy of the Republic of Chile. Thereafter he commanded the Brazilian Navy until 1825 and the Greek Navy from 1825 to 1828 and in 1832 was restored to rank in the British Navy. He was a nephew of Sir Alexander Cochrane.

"Don Juan" Devereaux (d'Evereux), son of an Irishman executed for activities in the rebellion of 1798, and one Colonel English were leaders of the foreign legion supporting Símon Bolívar in the struggle for Venezuelan independence (see above, II, 585n).

6 Presidential election. 7 Congress.

8 "Little Cordelia," not identified. Daniel Pope Cook had introduced two resolutions calling for investigation of Crawford's administration of the Treasury Department: the first, on January 3, had requested a report on the mode of inspecting land offices; the second, on January 8, had sought information on the arrangements for placing deposits of public money. Both resolutions represented efforts to check Crawford's use of these operations to generate support for his candidacy. The latter request was based upon charges that the Government deposits had been placed in banks known to be on the verge of bankruptcy, that engagements had been entered into which barred withdrawal of the deposits during fixed periods, without compensation for such loan arrangements, and that a depreciated currency of these local institutions had been accepted by the Treasury when not required under the terms of its agreements with the banks. *Annals of Cong.*, 17 Cong., 1 Sess., XXXVIII, 620-21, 663, 673-80; Adams, *Memoirs*, V, 482-84. Crawford had answered his critics with a letter of February 18 on the payments made for examination of the land offices and a report of March 28 on the money outstanding to the credit of the Treasury Department. *House Docs.*, 17 Cong., 1 Sess., nos. 71 and 100. The issues were revived the following year in the charges voiced by Ninian Edwards, Cook's father-in-law (see below, Clay to Porter, April 26, 1824, note).

9 The Secretary of War, John C. Calhoun, whose efforts to control abuses of the Indian trade through establishment of Government-operated trading houses and strict licensing of private traders had become the subject of severe attack, inspired by an alliance of disgruntled traders and political opponents, during the Congressional Session of 1821-1822. At the same time his vigorous program in administration of military affairs—extending the location of military posts deep into the Indian country, as evidenced in the Yellowstone Expedition (above, II, 599); constructing a large-scaled system of coastal fortifications; reorganizing the Army in such a way as to retain a cadre of trained officers; expanding the educational program at the United States Military Academy; and supplying the Army directly, rather than through contractors—together with Congressional enactment of the expanded pension program of 1818 (above, II, 681, 739, 844) and drastic reduction in the military allotments under legislation of 1820 and 1821 (above, II, 789-93) had occasioned arrearages in the departmental accounts which had compelled Calhoun to request deficiency appropriations in December, 1821.

10 John Quincy Adams suffered an "infirmity of a watery eye." Adams, *Memoirs*, VII, 462.

11 Gideon Granger and Thomas Jefferson. See Charles Henry Ambler, *Thomas Ritchie, a Study in Virginia Politics* (Richmond, Va., 1913), 89. Granger, who had resigned as Postmaster General after a disagreement with President Madison in 1814, had moved to Canandaigua, New York, and resumed practice of law. He had served in the New York State Senate, 1820-1821, but his death in December, 1822, cut short his activity in local politics of that State.

12 New Yorkers had adopted a completely revised State constitution in February, 1822, to become effective after the following December 21; elections in November, however, were to determine the personnel of the executive and legislative offices. The followers of DeWitt Clinton remained in almost complete eclipse at this period, winning only three seats among the State delegation to Congress, none in the State Senate, and a thin scattering in the State Assembly. Their strength did revive in the elections two years subsequently.

13 Joseph Christopher Yates, born in Schenectady and first mayor of that city, had served as State Senator, 1805, and judge of the State Supreme Court, 1808-1822; he was now to become the first governor, 1822-1824, under the new constitution. As a candidate he represented a fusion of support from both the Clintonians and the Bucktails. See Jabez D. Hammond, *The History of Political Parties in the State of New York from the Ratification of the Federal Constitution to December, 1840* (2 vols.; Albany, 1842), II, 97-100; *Niles' Weekly Register*, XXI (February 2, 1822), 354.

14 DeWitt Clinton.

15 John Savage, of Salem, in Washington County, graduated from Union College, Schenectady, and admitted to the bar, had been district attorney for the Fourth New

York District, 1806-1813, member of the State Assembly, 1814, member of Congress, 1815-1819, district attorney of Washington County, 1818-1820, and State Comptroller, 1821-1823. He later served as Chief Justice of the State Supreme Court, 1823-1836.

Erastus Root, a major general of militia, was now a member of the State legislature.

16 Martin Van Buren, at this time leader of the Bucktails and United States Senator from New York (1821-1828).

17 Rollin C. Mallary; Daniel Azro Ashley Buck, lawyer, veteran of the War of 1812, several times a member of the State Assembly, and United States Congressman (1823-1825, 1827-1829); possibly Jacob Haight, of Greene County, New York (not a Vermonter), a strong supporter of John Quincy Adams and, in 1839, State Treasurer; and William C. Bradley, United States Representative from Vermont (1813-1815, 1823-1827) and son of Stephen R. Bradley.

18 Cornelius P. Van Ness, a native of New York who in 1806 had moved to Vermont, where he had practiced law, served briefly as a judge of the United States District Court, held the post of Collector of Customs at Burlington, acted as a member of the boundary commission under the Treaty of Ghent, sat in the State legislature, 1818-1820, and was, in 1821-1822, Chief Justice of the State Supreme Court. He became Governor of Vermont, 1823-1825, and United States Minister to Spain, 1829-1837.

19 Richard Skinner, born in Litchfield, Connecticut, and educated at the Litchfield Law School, had begun practice of law at Manchester, Vermont, where he had become judge of probate for the Manchester district, 1806-1813; member of Congress, 1813-1815; assistant judge of the State Supreme Court, 1815-1816; member of the State legislature, 1815 and 1818; and Governor of Vermont, 1820-1823. He later served as Chief Justice of the State Supreme Court, 1823-1828.

Dudley Chase, born in New Hampshire, had been graduated from Dartmouth College and had embarked upon the practice of law at Randolph, Vermont, becoming a member of the State legislature, 1805-1812, and again in 1823 and 1824; United States Senator, 1813-1817 and 1825-1831; and Chief Justice of the State Supreme Court, 1817-1821.

20 Langdon Cheves, earlier considered an aspirant for the Presidency of the United States at the end of Monroe's administration, resigned from his post in the Bank of the United States, effective January, 1823, but foreswore personal involvement in politics. See below, Cheves to Clay, November 9, 1822.

21 "The lines are fallen unto me in pleasant *places;* yea, I have a goodly heritage." *Psalms,* 16:6.

To Richard M. Johnson

My dear Sir Wheeling 12th. April 1822.

In passing through Hagars [*sic*] town I met with Mr. Wirt, who enquired of me if the President had dec[ided] upon my demand.[1] I told him that he had not, and that I had und[erstoo]d he had given a second opinion contrary to the first. He said that that was not the fact; that his two opinions were coincident; and that the last had only entered further into detail. He added that he entertained no [doub]t of the perfect competency of the President to admit the claim; and he kindly asured me that he would endeavor to obtain a decision on his return.

The President told me that he thought the claim was equitable and just. Mr. Wirt says he has full power to allow it. Then why am I not permitted to receive it? I know of no claim that can make a stronger appeal than that which, having equity and justice in itself, is presented to a high functionary invested with power to admit it. My situation abroad was peculiar. The sole Commissioner at the point of Gottenburg, where the negotiation for peace was expected to have taken place, for several months I sustained an expence which would have been probably divided with my colleagues had they been present, by renting an establishment at the rate of $2400. per annum. I entertained my countr[*ymen*] &c &c. The Government paid one months rent[2] [. . . esta]blishment only, because, by the removal of the seat [of the negoti]ation to Ghent, I had to disburse that sum without [. . .]ing the premises. At this latter place, we took a [. . .] lived as expensively as the state of society at Ghent required, [entert]aining Company &c. At London I took furnished lodgings, kept a carriage, coachman, fo[otm]an and valet de chambre. If outfit is granted, in contemplation of establishments, then I had three, certainly two when abroad. If it be granted, in consideration of your visiting diff[eren]t Countries on public service, then I treated on two different and distant theatres, and participated in the ex[ecution] of two separate Commissions, by signing the Treaty of peace at Ghent, and the Commercial Convention at London. It is not the *form* but the *substance* of things [whic]h should govern the award of outfit. It is not that you are presented to two different monarchs, having credentials to each, that should alone entitle you to outfit; it is a much stronger claim to it *that you have transacted, in fact, highly important business in two several and separated Countries.*

I am highly sensible of the very great delicacy which influences the President; and I should regret extremely to appear to him to be importunate, or to give him any embarrassment. But I must think without intending to pass any opinion upon his own claims, that there are circumstances in the two cases which so essentially vary them that it is impossible that malignity itself should impute to him the unworthy motive of forming a precedent in mine to govern his.[3] With respect to submitting my claim to the Cabinet, the President must, I think, feel that, considering the relations in which the [gent]lemen composing it and I stand to each other, it would b[. . .] to them to pass a judgment upon my demand [. . .] President must at last decide; and, with great [. . .] I think he has, in effect, decided in my favor. [. . .] I implicitly confide in his justice and his judgment.

I should not so earnestly solicit a determination, if I were not most thoroughly convinced of the justness of my claim, nor then, if I had not found [my ju]dgment fortified and confirmed by that of some half a dozen others every one of whom concurred in thinking it a clear case. I might go with confidence to Congress, but I think the President ought to spare me the mortification of exhibiting myself as a petitioner for its justice in a sort of appeal from his decision. I shall rely, my dear Sir, upon your good office[s to] obtain the pleasure of the President upon my case, during the present Session, agreeably to his obliging assurance.

Can you do nothing for the Cumberland road? It is going to

decay with a much greater rapidity than it was erected? Suppose you were to suggest to the President the propriety of making its reparation the subject of a special message? It would have good effect in Congress and good effect upon him. He might take that occasion to make the promised exposition of his views on the question of Internal improvements.[4]

When will Congress rise?[5] Your's faithfully H. CLAY

The honb[le] [R.M.] Johnson.

ALS. DLC-James Monroe Papers (DNA, M212, R22). MS. defaced.

1 See above, Clay to Monroe, March 1, 1821; Clay to Wirt, March 9, 1821; Johnson to Clay, April 1, 1822.

2 Two or three words missing at each of the ensuing indicated omissions.

3 Monroe had longstanding claims against the Government, arising out of disputed accounts for his services abroad in 1794 to 1796 and 1803 to 1807. Among the issues involved were the interpretation to be followed in assignment of an outfit and what, if any, allowance might be rendered for the extraordinary expense of residence in London. Having deferred pressure for a settlement while he held public office, he expected an arrangement upon his retirement. In January, 1825, he finally presented the matter to Congress, which by act of May 22, 1826, awarded him $29,513 in full payment "of all demands whatever, against the United States." This sum, however, Monroe considered grossly inadequate; and, his claims having been continued, Congress on March 2, 1831, appropriated an additional $30,000 "in full of all demands" for his "public services, losses and sacrifices." As late as April, 1831, he protested that he would "rather lose the whole sum than give it [this settlement] any sanction," but payment was made to him the following month. Wilmerding, *James Monroe: Public Claimant,* 68-70; W. P. Cresson, *James Monroe* (Chapel Hill, N. C. [c. 1946]), 473-74; 6 *U. S. Stat.,* 354, 457-58; Monroe to James Madison, April 11, 1831, in Stanislaus Murray Hamilton (ed.), *The Writings of James Monroe . . .* (7 vols.; New York and London, 1898-1903), VII, 233; *Niles' Weekly Register,* XL (May 7, 1831), 168.

4 Johnson, for the Senate Committee on Roads and Canals, had already reported, on January 3, 1822, a bill providing for repairs to the Cumberland Road. Later in the month, on January 21, the House of Representatives had begun consideration of a measure, from its own Committee on Roads and Canals, for the preservation and repair of the road. After a delay of about three months the latter bill was agreed to by both houses and sent to the President, who vetoed it on constitutional grounds, May 4. In a long statement Monroe then explained in detail his views on internal improvements. *Annals of Cong.,* 17 Cong., 1 Sess., XXXVIII, 50, 52, 428, 439, 748; XXXIX, 1734, 1803-1805, 1809-63.

5 The First Session of the Seventeenth Congress adjourned on May 8, 1822.

To Peter B. Porter

My dear General. (Confidential) Ohio River 14h. April 1822.

I regretted much that I did not see you as you passed, on your return from Virginia, through Washington City. I was not aware of your being in the City until after you left it. I wished to have consulted with you on a subject of great interest to me personally, and respecting which I am persuaded you do not feel altogether indifferent. Two or three years ago I thought that if the State of New York could present to the Nation a suitable Citizen to succeed Mr. Monroe, her claims were very strong, and that it would promote good feeling and the general harmony to elect him. From the present state of things it is extremely unlikely that she will bring forward any one of her own Citizens. Nor is it likely that Pennsa., which also has strong claims, will ask the general suffrage in behalf of any of her sons. For myself, if I dared indulge the hope of attaining, at any time, the Chief Magistracy, I was content to wait the termination of the period of Mr. Monroes successor, if a Northern Candidate arose who was likely to unite, in any considerable degree, the general confidence. I think no such Northern Candidate will appear. In the mean time, in the South, there are springing up several candidates, my juniors in years and in the duration of the terms of our respective service. Under these circumstances my friends think that there are no public considerations which should restrain them from bringing forward my name; and I frankly confess that I do not feel myself required to discountenance or repress the exertion which they are disposed to make in my behalf. Their calculation, as to the chances of my success, is sanguine and plausible, if not solid. It is assumed that the Western States, from Ohio to the Gulph of Mexico, will be firmly and ardently united in my support. Of that I entertain no doubt. This, it is thought, will give me broader, firmer and more commanding ground than any other competitor can occupy. And, upon the supposition that there is no candidate in that portion of the union which extends from New York to North Carolina inclusive, we think that, guided by liberal & national considerations, it will, in the sequel, unite with the West. In respect to your State, we suppose that the grounds on which we may anticipate her co-operation with the West are very strong. A large part of it is Western. It is connected with the Western States by many ties. It is reasonable to imagine, if it cannot obtain, for one of its own Citizens, the Presidency at the next election, that it will desire to secure that office as soon after as practicable. By co-operating with the West, it silences a most formidable rival. It does more; it conciliates & secures the gratitude of that rival. Whereas, by lending its support, either to New England or to the South, it will not advance its own pretensions one inch. It will give to those who have always had the Presidency. And it will leave its Western Rival, for that office, to acquire additional strength and vigor, by the lapse of time and its rapid growth, so as to make a competition with it more powerful than ever. I have been desirous to prevent an obtrusion of my name upon the public notice; and, on that principle, I have repressed rather than stimulated the public expression of sentiment in my favor, particularly in Ohio and Kentucky. There is another point however not to be neglected; and that is that one's name should not be held back too long. Accordingly, if I am not greatly deceived, you will, in due season, see the most decided, if not enthusiastic, manifestations of the public sentiment in all the West.

This is the general subject on which I wished to have conversed fully and freely with you, as a friend. If, as I, perhaps presumptuously, hope you concur with my other friends, I meant to enquire of you, if some thing, in promotion of our wishes, could not be done in your quarter? If you could not find time to employ your own excellent pen in illustrating and enforcing those views of general and State policy which ought to determine the judgment of New York, and which we think obviously indicate the expediency of her looking Westwardly? The Secretaries have great advantages—their extensive patronage—and a considerable control over the press. A fair and free canvass, if one should apply such a term to such a subject; an open and manly discussion; an unprejudiced exercise of the public judgment, is all that I desire. If these circumstances should exist, I declare to you that I do not think the result even doubtful— I need scarcely say to you that I write all this in perfect confidence. I address you from a Steam boat on its descent of the river to Maysville.

Be pleased to present my respectful & affectionate compliments to Mrs. Porter, and believe me, my dear General,

Faithfully & cordially Your friend & servant H. CLAY

Genl. Peter B. Porter.

ALS. ViU.

From Adam Beatty

Dear Sir, Washington 17h. April 1822

Your letter of yesterday from the Blue lick[1] affords me the most sincere pleasure, and I should have been highly gratified, if it had been in your power to have called on me, on your return.

I most cordially approve of the effort your friends are making to place you in the chair, as the successor of Mr. Monroe; and it affords me pleasure to add, that I have anticipated your views, by writing ten or twelve since [*sic*], to both Colo. Rochester and William.[2] In those letters I have presented, pretty fully, most of the views, embraced in your letter, and some additional ones. The letter to Colo. Rochester, I enclosed to William unsealed, for his perusal, and which he will deliver on his return.[3] But as your letter contains one very strong view of the subject, not embraced in either of my letters, I have written Wm B Rochester again, of this date, in which I have presented that subject, almost in the language of your letter, from a conviction that it could not be strenghened [*sic*], by any changes or additions, which I could make. I did not keep copies of the letters I have heretofore written to Colo. Rochester and William, but enclose you a copy of that written to day, that you may have a full view of the subject before you; and may thus be enabled to Judge what additional steps should be taken.[4]

I have not learnt what are the views of either Colo. Rochester or William, in relation to the next Presidential election. But I shall probably be informed, by their answers to my letters; of which I will hasten to give you information.

You may rely upon my exercising, most cordially, and sincerely, every effort in my power, to promote your views, in relation to the Presidential canvass. And I hope you will not hesitate to communicate freely your wishes, as to any particular, in which you may suppose I can be of service to you.

In reply to the question "ought you to go into the next congress?" I will offer such reflections as occur to me. The election for electors will take place in October and November 1824. If you go into the next Congress you will be in the city during the winter 1823-4. Altho' a considerable impression will be made on the public mind before that time, yet it is probable that the members of congress returning from that session will still have great weights in such of the States as shall not have taken a very decided part on the subject. The influence of your personal presence under these circumstances, would doubtless have considerable weight. Even the knowledge of your being a member elect during the session 1822-3 would probably have a favourable effect, tho' not personally present. If there should be a caucus to nominate a candidate for the Presidency (tho' I hope there will not be) it will be still more import [*sic*] that you should be present. There is still another view, in which your being a member, would be very important. If no candidate get a maj[or]ity of the whole number votes, the ele[ction] is to be made by the H. of R. from [the] three highest. In this event your [being] a member will be very importan[t.]

There is one consideration only that w[ould] make me hesitate in advising you to [*go*.] Are your private affairs in such a stat[e] [as] would justify you in making the sacra[fice] which your taking a seat would require? This is a question which ought to be left to your own judgment. I know your liberality and disinterestedness are such as will make you sacrifice much, and I am willing to trust you will go the proper length. Cordially and Sincerely your friend A BEATTY

P.S. If N. Y. can be thrown into your scale, it will be decisive of the election. No pains should be spared to make the proper impression there. I recollect of no other person there to whom I could write advantageously, unless it be Mr Elmendorf, formerly a member of congress from that State, and one of the counsel of appointment. His name I think is Lucas. Is he still living, and where does he reside? If you think it would be useful, I will write him on the subject.[5] Pennsylvania, ought also to be attended to. A B.

ALS. DLC-HC (DNA, M212, R1). Addressed to Clay at Lexington; postmarked, by hand, at Washington, Kentucky. MS. torn.

1 Letter not found.

2 Nathaniel Rochester and his son, William B. Rochester. The former was Beatty's brother-in-law. William B. Rochester was a member of Congress, 1821-1823; a New York circuit judge, 1823-1826; secretary to the United States envoy to Colombia, 1826; and Chargé d'Affaires to Central America, 1827. He later removed to Buffalo, New York, where he became president of the local branch of the Bank of the United States, then to Florida, where he held the presidency of the Bank of Pensacola.

3 From Washington, D. C., upon the adjournment of Congress.

4 The letter, ALS copy, follows:

Dear Nephew, Washington, Ky, April 18th. 1822

I wrote you a letter 10 or 12 days since in which I stated some of my views in relation to the next Presidential election. It is now reduced to a certainty, that Mr. Clay will be run for that office, after the expiration of Mr. Monro's [*sic*] time. I have reflected much on this subject since I wrote you the hasty letter spoken of above. I am more than ever confirmed in the opinion, that New York and the west ought not to divide on this subject. I have already suggested some of the reflections, arising out of the grand Canal undertaking of New York. I am persuaded I cannot add any thing, which will have a tendency to increase the importance of this work, in your judgment, when considered merely as a work intended for the benefit of your own citizens, but when considered in a national and commercial point of view; and particularly when taken in connection with a canal, forming a direct communication between Lake Erie and the Ohio, its grandeur and importance exceed all calculation. The fertility of the western country generally, and its immensely rapid increase of population, must, in a very short period, lay the foundation of a commercial intercourse, between the western country and New York, which must forever Unite them in the bonds of commerce; of interest; and of brotherly affection. But this intercourse and friendly feeling can only be perfected by completing the chain of water communication between New York and the west. The election of Mr. Clay would certainly accomplish this great object. His defeat would throw a damp upon it, which would probably long postpone it, tho' I have no doubt, it would still be accomplished, but at a much later period.

My purpose, however, was not to enlarge on a subject, upon which I have already stated my views, in a previous letter, but to inform you that Mr. Clay will certainly be supported for the Presidency. I have no doubt he will receive the undivided support of all the western States. I am very sanguine in the opinion, founded on recent information, that Virginia, his parent State, will yield him her undivided strength. I also entertain strong hopes of Pennsylvania. There is perhaps no man (not a citizen of that State) more popular in all that section of this great State, which is now experiencing the benefit of the great national turnpike to Wheling [*sic*]. Altho' I have no particular information from Maryland, Delaware, and New Jersey, yet it seems to me (taking it for granted there will be no candidate from any of the Middle States, or any from those lying North and East of them, except Mr. Adams) that there are many considerations, which would naturally incline those States to prefer Mr. Clay to any of the Southern candidates. The South will probably produce three candidates. Mr. Crawford; Mr. Lowndes; and Mr. Calhoun. The former has long stood prominent as a candidate, in consequence of his having heretofore been supported for that office. Mr. Lowndes has the countenance of a Legislative recommendation of his own State [William Lowndes had been nominated by members of the South Carolina legislature in December, 1821]. And judging from your letter, some time since, Mr. Calhoun must have strong pretentions. Under these circumstances the South will probably be so much divided as greatly to weaken its efforts in favour of any of its candidates. Besides it seems to me that southern politics are not so well adapted to the interests of the middle States as those of the west, and particularly those of Mr. Clay.

It appears to me that there are particular besides general views of the subject, which New York must take, that ought to attach her to the west. Every thing considered, New York and the West are doubtless those quarters, which have the strongest claims. It is natural that New York should desire to obtain the Presidency. But as it has so happened that none of her distinguished citizens are, at this time, sufficiently in view to render the prospect of success tolerably certain, she acts wisely in not bringing forward her claims at this moment. But as she must desire to obtain the honor of that high office as soon as a favourable occasion shall offer, she cannot pursue a course better calculated to attain that object, than by giving her support, at the present, to the western candidate. If she give her weight to the North, or the South, she will leave her great western rival in the possession of all her present pretentions, with those strong additional ones, that will arise out of the lapse of time; and the rapid groth [*sic*] of its population, between the end of Mr. Monro's term and that of his successor. By supporting the west now, she will satisfy claims in this quarter, and may then step in as a matter of course. She will do more; she will not only get rid of a rival, but she will make a powerful friend. If she lend herself to the support of the New England Candidate, her own claims will, in no inconsiderable degree, be merged in those of New England. Moreover, between the west and New York there are many strong points of affinity. A large part of that State is Western. Many of her sons have migrated to the west, particularly to Ohio. By means of her great canal she is brought in direct contact with Ohio; and when the additional link shall be completed, from the Lakes to the Ohio river, she will be brought into contact with the very heart of the Western States. There are also numerous points of coincidence, in the opinions of the western people, and those of New York on subjects of National policity [*sic*], upon some of which I remarked in my last letter to you.

If you see my highly valued friend, your venerable father, on your return, present him these views, and I should like to have yours and his in return.

Yours &c. A:Beatty.

5 Lucas C. Elmendorf, United States Congressman from New York, 1797-1803, lived until 1843.

From Richard M. Johnson

My Dear Sir, City of Washington 20th. April 1822

I have rcd, your favour,[1] and I shall take the first moment to see the President on your Claim against the government— the just Claim, as I consider it; & you Shall know the result— I found that there was no prospect of passing a Bill for the relief of Col Morrison without taking it up in the Senate— I took the work upon my Self— reported a Bill giving him upwards of 10.000 $ refered the Bill to the Committee of Claims who reported, in its favour unanimously— But when called up as the devil would have it Col. Eaton & several others made the most inveterate opposition to it & we were upon the Point of victory, when Mr. Barton discovered a fact which induced the Senate to recommit the Bill. which report I have Sent to Col Morrison, with a letter of farther explanation as to the Course I have taken to avoid the defeat of the case—[2] I refer you to him. I knew that you could not doubt my friendship— My only object was to put it in your power to meet any fears that any friend of yours might ever Suggest to you if there be any Such, as some of my friends write to me, that I was blamed for a favourable publication towards Mr Calhoun which the Gazette contained.[3] the war has commenced in both house [*sic*] of Congress—but very little is Said or done in my opinion as to the next presidential election— I shall See you—very soon & therefore Shall not enter into detail [*sic*] matters & things In haste Sincerely & affectionately yours

Honbl Henry Clay RH: M: JOHNSON

ALS. DLC-HC (DNA, M212, R1). 1 See above, Clay to Johnson, April 12, 1822.

2 On James Morrison's claims, see above, Motion on Report, February 21, 1821. The Senate bill introduced by Johnson on March 21, 1822, had been reported five days later without amendment by the Committee of Claims. It was debated in Committee of the Whole on April 11 and 12 and, on motion by David Barton, was recommitted. Barton, for the Committee of Claims, reported on April 15, but no further action was taken during this Session of Congress. The brief report of debate does not mention John H. Eaton as a participant. *Annals of Cong.*, 17 Cong., 1 Sess., XXXVIII, 313, 316, 331, 379, 380, 382.

3 See above, Johnson to Clay, April 1, 1822.

From "Patrick Henry"

Dear Sir Private & Confidential Apl. 21— 1822

On a View of all the Circumstances attendant on the prospect before us as respects next Prest.—men, localities &c—

I have come to a Conclusion—that our passions &c must not move us to do wrong things— reason must operate— *I am your friend entirely so—and desire your elevation more than any other man*— but to do it—to effect it—*the right mode must be adopted,* You must not permit Crawford to be elected— from the immense time that Virginia has had the direct rule—if you do permit it—the Chance is—90 to 100—that you never will be Prest.— Crawfords term ended—it must then, or in 4 years—or 8 years travel North— beyond all doubt—as Confusion & parties will by that time be so much rent— as to insure it— but if you prevent his Success now he is a dead man—he has *no literature or weight of Character, to sustain him at all— & Adams can't be elected*— Penna will not— N York will not, go for him—nor Ohio nor Kentucky— he is *too Cold*—& has not the *popularity*—he is *hated*— his Father's memory is enough— you must make Clinton[1] Prest.— which with your force & talents *publick* & *private* you *can accomplish* he has pretentions *in every respect—a man of business* —is *bold & honorable* an *elegant Schollar—deeply read—liberal altogether, in his ideas*— he WD. RETURN THE FAVOR WITH FIDELLITY— he has no sneaking tricky Vices— *you would be the next Prest. from Character—pretentions—experience* & *Coming from the West—it wd. be expected* & *attended to by the nation*—you would *be Vice* Prest— or *Secty of State*— the former wd. keep you *out of tormoil* [*sic*] *& responsibility*— & perhaps be the Safest place—you wd. be happy in it—honored & Supported by everybody— to effect it, I wd. even solicit Calhoun to join or permit it—if it cd. not be done without—as he would Conspire agst. Crawford—who is his greatest enemy— the eastern people—would hail it, with pleasure—Adams wd. be Surrenderd— If Such a Phalanx as Clinton & Clay &c &c &c were to form a leauge [*sic*]— the party Opposed to Clinton in this State—wd. be broken down—as sure as frost Comes in winters— Clinton has done so much for the honor of this State—for the last 25 years that he will hold a Strong influence always here— he is now rising— it will be glorious—to join him— the Splendor of his Character is an earnest of that Splendid Admn. which wd ensue—

Adams—Crawford—& Calhoun—all are naturally now opposed to you— Calhoun & Crawford—both know— if you are in, they wd. be ruined—as it must then go North again—but put *Clinton in now* & *you will follow*—as *sure as the world is a world*— *Otherwise*—it will *be Crawford*—& then all is Chaos—& you then have no chance— any

Station with a Southern Man—in the Cabinet—wd. be of no Service to you— North it must Come after Crawford—& you wd. be left behind— You are young—4 or 8 years hence wd. answer all the Objects of a noble & reasonable ambition— the thing is as clear—as any problem in mathematics— let people say as they please—Clinton has more qualities & more merrit—than is allowed him by his adversaries—*any Combination—however extended*—to effect—*his election* —if you *only Come in the Cabinet* or *Vice Prest* will answer your Views—as you need not fear the rivalship of any of them—

—If Calhoun Comes in—very well it will Strengthen the party— he can't stand against you— for the future—& especially—if there is an honorable View of things— this road pointed out is *plain—honorable—reasonable—natural* & *feasable*—only *unite early—Confidentally* [*sic*]—& the *thing will go down*— Virga. is going for Crawford—but N York will be had—& Ohio Pennsyla. Kentucky & so west— the East will come in—in preference to Crawford—Adams being Out of the question— *Calhoun will join a Northern man, I know* to *prevent Crawfords Success*—as he cannot Succeed himself—& the Sooner, you join Clinton the better— his principles & notions every way—are as yours—S America—internal improvements &c &—are all, as yours— & Altho Jackson is up—& is Cool to you—That Can all be got clear of— by an arrangement *& an* adjustment— —I know Crawfords friends —*here* are working hard—& promise to support Clinton— the moment they can't Succeed themselves—it may be so— but there is no affinity between them— they may come together—as Crawfords hopes are desperate or it is his last throw—& he feels desperation.— But Clinton & Clay—would make an admn.—Splendid in history—as well as Most potent—& honorable in their own time— look at it & act So Says your devoted friend—tho' under an anonymous Signature— I have a peep behind & know how things are moving—both *at Washington* —& in N York—and I speak the words of Candor & truth—& they are all that a noble man requires & are not the less true for being unknown from whom they are derived— It is yet 2 years—Sufficient time—If you began to work in Season—& continue to the end—

As to Adams & Crawford—you have no fellowship with them—they both prevented your nomination to the South—from jealousy—tho Opposed to each other— they both supposed you would obtain a niche that wd. place you above them in the temple of fame—— When Mexico & Colombia were both Spoken of as proper unitedly for you to Visit—they were rank agst. it— & Munro was glad of it—as an excuse also—[2] Who is as weak as he is rotten— I dont Consider it any great evil, yr. non appointment—but just mention it as indicative of the air at head Quarters— *but unite* & *resolve*—& *success is Certain*—or *divided* you *fall*— the batterys will soon be let loose agst.

Crawfords Treasury futile reports & his reports on Currency which will shew his disqualification to fill [the] place—[3] & as a Writer or Civilian or a Diplomatist he has no pretentions— indeed what talents has he ever displayed—to warrant it much less to merrit it— Clinton —has name—fame talents & useful & lasting honors to Sustain him for any or in any Station he may fill— It would be worthy of Clay & Kentucky to Join N York & Clinton in so Glorious a Cause in Serving the Union— PATRICK HENRY

ALS. DLC-HC (DNA, M212, R1). Extract published in Colton (ed.), *Private Correspondence of Henry Clay,* 67. The writer, apparently a resident of New York, has not been identified. A series of letters signed "Patrick Henry," discussing the issues of the presidential election in terms supporting the candidacy of DeWitt Clinton, was published in the New York *Statesman,* reprinted in the Lexington *Kentucky Reporter,* November 4, 11, 1822.

1 DeWitt Clinton.

2 According to Adams, Monroe had commented that "from the letter which Mr. Clay had written to Woodson, to be shown to him [above, *ca.* April 1, 1822], he had conjectured that Clay himself was disposed to accept one of these new missions." Monroe had then remarked that he was disinclined to make such an appointment because of Clay's "uniform hostility to this Administration." Adams had replied that in a conversation with Clay the preceding year, when asked if he would accept "a vacancy in any of the missions abroad" should such occur, the Kentuckian had declined because of "the state of his private affairs." But Adams, also, now concluded that Clay "wished for the offer of one of these missions, and that he would accept that of Mexico, and perhaps that of Colombia, but not either of the others." Adams would have been content to send Clay to Buenos Aires or Chile, where it was believed "he could do no harm"; but the Secretary of State "distrusted so much Mr. Clay's views in relation to South American affairs, and was so apprehensive of their tendency to entangle us," that he doubted the propriety of either of the acceptable appointments. Adams, *Memoirs,* V, 495-96.

3 See above, Shaw to Clay, April 4, 1822, note.

Marriage Bond for Susan Hart Clay

[April 22, 1822]

Know all men by these presents, that we Martin Durald, and Henry Clay are held and firmly bound, unto the Commonwealth of Kentucky, in the Just sum of £50. current money of said Comth. to the payment of which, well and truly to be made, we bind our selves our heirs &C. Jointly and Severly [*sic*], firmly by these presents Sealed and dated this 22nd. day of April 1822.

The Condition of the above obligation is such that whereas there is a marriage shortly intended to be solemnized,[1] between the above bound Martin Durald, and Susan Clay of the County of Fayette. Now if it should always hereafter appear, that there is no legal obstruction to said Marriage, then and in that case the above obligation to be void, else to remain in full force and virtue, of Law.

M. DURALDE JUR. {SEAL}
H. CLAY {SEAL}

DS. Fayette County Marriage Bonds.

1 The same day.

To Walter Dun

Dear Sir Lexington 23d. April 1822

I have duly received your favor of the 25h. March,[1] inclosing three several obligations executed by Thomas Mountjoy Jr.[2] of Miss State to James Taylor junr.[3] exor of James Herron[4] deceased, one payable on the 29h of August 1819 for $1575; another payable nine months after the date, of the 24h April 1819, for $788; and the third payable twenty one months after the same date for $787. And I have ordered suits on these bonds, according to your directions, in the Federal Court.[5] Your instructions shall be complied with not to receive the paper Money of Miss State.

With great respect I am your ob. Servant, H. CLAY

Walter Dun Esq.

Copy, from original in Ross County Historical Society, Chillicothe, Ohio. Dun, a native of Scotland, resided at Chillicothe, where he conducted an extensive business in land speculation. Three or four years after the date of this letter he removed to Fayette County, Kentucky. Thereafter, until his death in 1838, he devoted considerable attention to importing and breeding blooded cattle.

1 Not found.

2 Formerly of Mason County, Kentucky, whence he had served as an officer in the United States Army during the War of 1812.

3 Of Norfolk, Virginia.

4 James Heron, of Richmond, Virginia, a merchant and banker.

5 Suits on each of these bonds were instituted in the Federal Circuit Court for the District of Kentucky on April 26, 1822. At the May Term, 1823, the defendant acknowledged plaintiff's demands and judgments were entered for recovery of the amount of the notes, interest at six per cent annually from their respective maturity dates until paid, and costs of suit. U.S. Circuit Court, Seventh Circuit, District of Kentucky, Complete Records, U, 177-85.

From ———

My dear Sir— N. O. Apl. 26. 22

I should have answered your last friendly letter[1] sooner—but my professional duties hang so heavy on me as almost to forbid attention to anything else. My mind has been so long bent down by pecuniary slavery— (for what is debt but slavery) that I rarely lift it up from the toilsome path which promises redemption. Yet to be candid there is no subject nor pursuit which yields half the satisfaction of those coupled with the political career & character of our Country.

I was so warm an advocate for Mr. Monroes election and have been so disappointed in his Administration (having so completely destroyed the republican party as to leave us without guide without concert and almost without National purpose) that little is left but mere speculations as to future events—

National purposes seem to have give [*sic*] place to individual objects, and the promotion of *this* or *that* member of the administration Constitute [*sic*] its prominent measures. In their zeal for elevation they remind me of untained [*sic*] Attendants at a Banquet, jostling each other out of place—

Poor Adams will have to make his exit without time or opportunity to thank his friends (if he has any) for past favours.

What with his 4th. July garlands flowers of etiquette,[2] taunts of triumph over Senators wives[3] and last tho' not least the glory of advocating the Surrender of the navigation of two thirds of the union to the British, he has secured himself early, if not dignified, *retirement.*

I have yet to learn Crawfords claims to the Presidency—He has given stronger evidence of ability in a Congressional Caucus than upon any other theatre he has occupied—[4]

Lownds [*sic*] is destined to be President should he live until his virtues and talents are known—[5] He cannot I think succeed at the ensuing election— He may however materially mar your prospects,— What will Virginia do? Will she not take up Lownds? There are many of the old republican party who will stil [*sic*] look to & venerate the counsel of Jefferson & Madison— I have recently understood them to be cautious upon this subject—tho' warmly attached to you, and perhaps desirous for your success.

I formed an opinion of Calhoun[6] while public servants dug. the war— He was then the most presuming man in Congress— He is now the most presuming man in the *Nation*—

With fewer claims to the chair of state than any other individual named, he is making bolder efforts to attain it—

If he can secure the federalists (& he can alone do so by apostacy) and with them Cheves and the Bank,[7] he will secure a vote by individual effort, which the nations voluntary voice would not accord.

Will not the slave question, so called, divide us? If it should, Clintons[8] prospects are better than they seem to be.

Duane[9] & his party (& the feebleness of the present administration has given Duane & his friends strength) will support Clinton—New York will I presume support him: should success promise reward they will be more than vigilent [*sic*] in his support. Ohio, Indiana, Illinois are not sufficiently enlightened to free themselves from this pretended Crusade for African emancipation— They hate us, not because we have slaves, but because they have none. If the *West* are true to themselves—and some partial support can be had from the middle states your election might be calculated on with confidence.

You have I know warm friends in Pensylvania [*sic*] & New York and unless some sectional feeling or the slave question should interpose I presume you would find some support in these states.

In Louisiana, Our bales of Cotton & hogsheads of sugar absord [*sic*] all other considerations— The dependants on the present administration and the expectants for office, are devoted to Mr. Adams— You are the only Candidate for the P. known here, and the only one having warm personal friends— The aggricultural [*sic*] part of our Community whether creole or american is sound & you may I think rely on their support The press is the leveer [*sic*] which must be used here— The

AL, part of MS. missing. DLC-HC (DNA, M212, R1). Erroneously attributed to James Brown and published in Padgett (ed.), "Letters of James Brown to Henry Clay," *Louisiana Historical Quarterly*, XXIV (October, 1941), 934-36. Possibly from Eligius Fromentin, a native of France, who had settled in New Orleans, become a lawyer, and served as United States Senator from Louisiana, 1813-1819. In May, 1821, he had been appointed "Judge of the United States for West Florida, and for that part of East Florida which lies westward of the cape" and, later in the year, had become involved in a bitter quarrel with Andrew Jackson, Governor of Florida. Although paid to June 1, 1822, Fromentin had given up his post and returned to New Orleans several weeks before the date of the present letter. He died later in the year.

1 Not found.

2 See above, Clay to Rodney, August 9, 1821.

3 In January, 1822, Adams had released for publication a private letter which he had written to the Vice President of the United States, December 29, 1819, in which as Secretary of State he had rebuffed the suggestion by "some of the members of the Senate, entertaining the opinion that a formal visit in person or by card is due from each of the Executive Departments, at the commencement of every session of Congress, to every Senator upon his arrival at the seat of government. . . ." Adams explained that, while he was a Senator, he and his wife had themselves paid first calls upon "the Heads of Departments," "not from any opinion that it was an obligation of duty, but because we understood and believed it to be usual, and because we did not think it improper." Upon his return to the capital in 1817, he had supposed the usages to be as heretofore, that while as a member of the Administration he had no claim to a first call, any interchange was optional. In issuing the letter at the later date, he commented that it replied to an allusion by a correspondent of the Richmond *Enquirer*. Washington *Daily National Intelligencer*, January 15, 1822.

4 The election of Philip Pendleton Barbour as Speaker of the House of Representatives (above, Warfield to Clay, December 18, 1821) had constituted a victory for the Crawford supporters. Charles M. Wiltse, *John C. Calhoun, Nationalist, 1782-1828* (Indianapolis and New York, [c. 1944]), 237. Toward the end of December and into early January rumors had been widely circulated that efforts were underway to get up a Congressional caucus for nomination of a presidential candidate. By mid-January, however, the project had been abandoned. Washington *Daily National Intelligencer*, January 7, 19, 1822; Frankfort *Argus of Western America*, January 31, February 14, 1822; Adams to Henry A. S. Dearborn, January 8, 1822, and Adams to Joel Lewis, February 20, 1822, in Worthington Chauncey Ford (ed.), *Writings of John Quincy Adams* (7 vols.; New York, 1913-1917), VII, 196, 208.

5 Suffering from tuberculosis, William Lowndes resigned his Congressional seat the following May and died at sea in October, while on a voyage to Europe in an effort to recover his health.

6 John C. Calhoun.

7 Langdon Cheves; Bank of the United States.

8 DeWitt Clinton.

9 William Duane.

Receipt from Thomas Anderson

LEXINGTON, KY. April 26th. 1822.

Thomas Anderson, as Treasurer of Transylvania University, acknowledges payment by H. Clay of $13.35 for tuition. DS. DLC-TJC (DNA, M212, R15). See above, Receipt, October 1, 1821, note.

From Thomas Hart Benton

Senate Chamber, April 26th. [1822]—

D. Sir, All the information from Pennsylvania goes to confirm what we have understood, that there is nothing substantial in the shew that is made there in behalf of Mr. Calhoun.[1] One of Mr. Crawford's friends has just lamented to me the existence of a deep feeling in Penn— against him. Some of the best of the Virginians here say that this state will go for you if it does not go for Mr. Crawford. —John Q.[2] seems to be going off. —Mr. Russell gave me a letter stating your decisive conduct at Ghent. A copy has gone to Ohio and will be published there.[3] —The Senate will again reject the army nominations.[4] yours truly. T. H. BENTON.

ALS. DLC-HC (DNA, M212, R6).

1 See above, Johnson to Clay, April 1, 1822; below, Toland to Clay, August 8, 1822.

2 Adams.

3 Not found. See below, Benton to Clay, May 2, 1822.

4 During the preceding month the Senate had refused to approve nominations of James Gadsden, of South Carolina, as Adjutant General and Nathan Towson, of Maryland, as a colonel in the 2d Regiment of Artillery. On April 12 President Monroe had renominated these two officers and had sent to the Senate a letter explaining his interpretation of the Army Act of 1821 (see above, Remarks, January 23, 1821). The Senate, on April 29, again refused to approve the appointments.

From John Horne

Hon. Henry Clay Bristol April 30th. 1822

Dear Sir,

I lately sent you some documents[1] to be used in the Case of DeWolf vs Johnson if required, & now take the liberty to give you my view of that Case, with a few references which I hope may not be useless.[2]

. . . .

I am Sir with great respect your Obt. Servt. JOHN HORNE

P.S. If you should go out to South-America for a short period, as most of our Eastern Politicians anticipate,[3] I should be proud to accompany you as a Secretary, & will write again, if this hurried scrawl seems to denote that I should be a very bad one, for the sake of trying to remove such an impression— J. Horne

ALS. DLC-TJC (DNA, M212, R12). Directed to Frankfort, Kentucky. Horne has not been further identified.

1 Not found.

2 On the case, see above, De Wolf to Clay, January 3, October, 1821. Three pages of argument on the issues involved are here omitted by the editors.

3 See above, "Patrick Henry" to Clay, April 21, 1822, note.

From John Speed Smith

Dear Sir, Washington City April 30. 1822

You recollect when you arrived at this place from Richmond I expressed to you my opinion, that of the secretaries, who were candidates for the Presidency, I thought Mr. Calhoun was in the ascendant. That opinion I still believe was correct. During the previous part of the session, the enemies of Mr. Crawford had affected his standing by calls made upon his department, which, whether founded upon truth or not, had created suspicion, in the public mind and he was injured. Mr. Crawford's friends have turned the tables upon the friends of the Secretary of war and most adroitly too, at the close of the session, when members from every part of the Union will depart with impressions unfriendly to Mr. Calhoun's pretensions.[1] This warfare between the partizans of the two gentlemen, will eventuate in their ultimate prostration I have very little doubt. Your friends here have, I think so far, managed remarkably well, in not pressing you before the public. The course that is pursued and which I have indicated will be pursued by those gentlemen's friends, will turn the public eye from them and fix it upon yourself. My fixed opinion is that the nation will not select a president out of the number of Secretaries. Were I the President and my cabinet was as divided as his is, I should not hesitate to dismiss all of them. I have within the last few days conversed with several members, who declare their dissatisfaction at the conduct of the partizans of Crawford & Calhoun—and express their hope that you may be run. If your friends here are not over-anxious upon the subject, it seems to me most probable that N. York will take you up—for King & Thompson & Tompkins[2] are out of the question. The only fear to be entertained is that the idea will be started that Kentucky & N. York have combined—but this impression will be [less] if N. York gives the lead.

When I see you I will explain every thing in this letter that is [unclear.][3] With real respect Yr friend J. SPEED SMITH

ALS. DLC-HC (DNA, M212, R1). Addressed to Clay at Lexington. MS. faded.

1 On the counter-actions of the Crawford and Calhoun forces during the Congressional Session of 1821-1822, see above, Shaw to Clay, April 4, 1822, notes.

2 Rufus King: Smith Thompson; Daniel D. Tompkins.

3 Bracketed words illegible.

Receipted Bill from William Gilliam

[*ca.* May 1, 1822]

1822 Henry Clay Esqr. To Town Tax Dr

To Tax on $28,400 – at 20 cts. pr hundred $ 56.80.

Recvd Payment W: GILLIAM C, T, T

DS. DLC-TJC (DNA, M212, R15). Gilliam, who had served as a constable and who was at this time also acting as Clerk of the Upper Market House, had been selected Collector of the Town Tax at the meeting of the Lexington Board of Trustees, January 17, 1822. His collector's book had been certified to him according to the assessors' report and rate approved by the Trustees on April 4. Lexington Board of Trustees, Minute Book, III, 193, 200, 202.

From Thomas Hart Benton

D. Sir, Senate chamber, May, 2nd. [1822]

Mr. Russell will inform you of a pleasant interview with Mr. Adams, which ended in "a long farewell." He has read me his letter, but the President declines sending it in. It must and will come out some way.[1] The one he gave me goes to Cincinnatti [*sic*], and will appear there.[2]

We are all unanimous here in the opinion here *that affairs go on well.* I think your friends here have been judicious. They have made no enemies, and have conciliated good will and good feelings from all sides. The friends of all the others will support you in preference to any of their old opponents.

Yours truly. BENTON.

ALS. DLC-HC (DNA, M212, R6).

[1] The famous "duplicate letter" controversy between Jonathan Russell and John Quincy Adams, for which Adams considered Clay responsible, had begun in January, 1822, when John Floyd introduced in the United States House of Representatives a resolution calling upon the President to lay before the House "all the correspondence which led to the Treaty of Ghent, which has not yet been made public, and which, in his opinion, it may not be improper to disclose." Changed to include also a call for the Protocol, the resolution had been adopted.

Among the documents submitted, late in February, in response to this call had been a letter from Russell to Secretary of State Monroe, dated December 25, 1814, in which Russell had declared his intention of explaining in a subsequent communication his reasons for differing with a majority of the American Commissioners, who had favored "offering to the British plenipotentiaries, an article confirming the British right to the navigation of the Mississippi, and ours to the liberty as to the fisheries. . . ." In April the House had adopted another Floyd resolution, calling for the second letter from Russell to Monroe. Learning that the State Department files disclosed no such letter, Russell on April 22 had "delivered there 'a paper purporting to be the duplicate of a letter written by him from Paris, on the 11th of February, 1815, to the then Secretary of State, to be communicated to the House, as the letter called for by the resolution.'" Meanwhile, Monroe had found among his personal papers the letter in question, marked "private." Having discovered that the document was of a controversial nature, having learned that Russell's "duplicate" was not an exact copy of the original, and having been requested by Adams to transmit with it to the House "a communication respecting it," the President was reluctant to release the documents and delayed taking any action. U.S. H. of Reps., *Journal,* 17 Cong., 1 Sess., 152, 157-58, 292, 468, 471, 554; below, Russell to Clay, June 6, 1822.

On April 29 Russell had called upon Adams, regarding another matter, and a dramatic scene had occurred. Adams charged him with "extraordinary" conduct in connection with the "duplicate" letter. Russell, attempting to explain and defend his actions, declared that "there was no alteration of *facts.*" Adams "told him he was mistaken." After further exchanges, Adams closed the interview by observing that "of private and individual intercourse, the less there is between us from this time forward the more agreeable it will be to me." Adams, *Memoirs,* V, 504-507.

[2] See above, Benton to Clay, April 26, 1822.

From William Creighton, Jr.

Dear Sir. Chillicothe May 2. 1822

I am much gratified with the prospects communicated in yours of the 12 ultimo.[1] By the same mail yours reached me I received a letter from our friend Francis Johnston of your State from Washington, authorising me to publish an extract from his letter exposing the Intrigue carrying on in Pennsylvania for promoting the views of the Secretary of War.[2]

From all the letters I have received from Washington I think with you that the movement in Penna. is artificial and will be short lived, from that consideration and others I deemed it inexpedient to have it published.

As far as my correspondence and information extends I think there is no doubt but Ohio will come out decidedly for you. As neither of the three great States New York, Pennsylvania and Virginia have a candidate of their own the calculation is a correct one that they will go with the West if we shew them we are united on a Western Man. As Ohio takes rank with the large States her pride as well as her interest will be excited to lead of[f] and have the credit of giving a President to the Union.

The views communicated as to the time and mode of operation meets [*sic*] my approbation and will be acted on by your friends in this State. During the Winter a number of your friends here were anxious to come out at once for you, among this number was McArthur[3] who is a very warm friend of yours. I thought then it was too soon. Much can be done through the ensuing Summer and the pulse of the Legislature can be gently felt at their Session at Columbus on the third Monday of this Month.

From every consideration I have been able to give the question you proposed Whether you ought to go into the next Congress, My opinion is that you ought not. There may be views and bearings that I have not considered. In my Judgement your present situation gives you a decided preference in the Nation and that you left Congress at a most auspicious moment. Your reputation by your exertions the last Session you served was greatly increased and you carried with you the affections and good wishes of all parties. The Members of the Cabinet with the left handed aid of the Radicals[4] are doing their business most effectually. The Country has already become disgusted with the intrigues of the Cabinet Candidates, and will turn from them to seek a private Citizen unconnected with the administration or Congress.— The scene that has been acted in Congress during the last Winter will be repeated at every Session until the Presidential election. Should you return you would have to take a leading part in all the prominent Measures and in others which some of your zealous but imprudent friends might think important. As many of your friends in Congress were carrying the War into the Cabinet you would frequently be placed in a most embarrassing situation. You are sufficently [*sic*] before the public. The continuance of your practice in this State will be of great service.

And your attendance at the Session of the Supreme Court at Washington will give you all the opportunities and advantages without the embarrassing inconveniences that would result from being in Congress.— You see I have given you my opinion with the frankness of a friend. but as before observed there may be views and considerations that I have overlooked, your better Judgement will decide the question.

I propose visiting Kentucky with my family in the month of June when I shall have the pleasure of seeing you

Your friend W. CREIGHTON JUN.

H. Clay Esqe.

ALS. DLC-HC (DNA, M212, R1). 1 Not found.

2 Shortly after Congress met for the Session of 1821-1822, rumors had been circulated that the Pennsylvania delegation had caucused and endorsed John C. Calhoun for the Presidency. The Philadelphia *Democratic Press* thereafter reported that two members of the delegation, one a Senator and the other a Representative (probably William Findlay and Thomas James Rogers), had been sent as emissaries to the Pennsylvania legislature on a "mission . . . said to be political and important." Lexington *Kentucky Reporter,* February 25, 1822, reprinting report from *Democratic Press;* William H. Crawford to Charles Tait, June 3, 1822, in Shipp, *Giant Days,* 232 (Appendix). The first story had been promptly repudiated by "*One of the Pennsylvania Delegation,*" writing in Washington *Daily National Intelligencer,* January 17, 1822: and the same journal, on February 7, 1822, had denied the report that emissaries had been sent to Harrisburg. It seems probable that Calhoun's friends were at least considering a formal nomination by caucus of members of the Pennsylvania legislature. Adams subsequently asserted that the movement had for a time embraced the possibility of a Congressional caucus. Adams, *Memoirs,* VI, 42-43.

William Findlay, born in Mercersburg, Pennsylvania, had commenced practice as a lawyer at Franklinton and served as a member of the Pennsylvania legislature (1797, 1804-1807), State Treasurer (1807-1817), Governor (1817-1820), United States Senator (1821-1827), and Director of the United States Mint (1827-1841). Thomas James Rogers, a manufacturer of Easton, Pennsylvania, had been editor of the *Northampton Farmer* (1805-1814), author of *A New American Biographical Directory* . . . (Easton, 1813), brigadier general of State militia, and Congressman (1818-1824).

3 Duncan McArthur.

4 William H. Crawford's supporters, so identified because of their adherence to States' rights and strict construction of the Constitution, who had led the attack in Congress upon the program of Calhoun. See above, Shaw to Clay, April 4, 1822, note.

From Agustín de Itúrbide

Mexico 6th of may 1822.

My dear Sir: through the means of the captain of the navy Don Eugenio Cortes, I have been informed of the great Services by which you have furthered the Success of his commission and contributed to the prosperous advantages that resulted from it;[1] this generous course the fruit of this enlightened age, excites my gratitude and obliges me to give you my most Sincere thanks and offer you my friendship; for this philanthropic conduct that emanates from a liberal education, and whose end is the civilisation of nations, though it relates to the whole Mexican Empire, if its success should be in proportion to its efforts, I offer you the gratitude which is due to you by all, and my most particular thanks for the present of the books and for the value you Set on my portrait. In exchange of it I am waiting for yours which is announced by our common friend Cortes; and without Seing [*sic*] it, it gives me a satisfaction from that common effect which can not be explained, in which men reciprocally love without Knowing each other, in which the mind forms favorable prepossessions, and gives to the person (for so it delights in) as many virtues as it pleases, takes for true what it conjectures and goes so far as to give to the portrait expression and gestures; but our case is different from this; your works are distinguished, my correspondence is a debt of justice to their merit, an[d] I promise myself the continuance of duties so praise worthy and protest to render you the same in like circumstances, accept all the considerations and respect of your most affectionna[te] [*sic*] friend. Q. B. S. M.[2]

AGUSTIN DE YTURBIDE

Translation. DLC-HC (DNA, M212, R1). Published in Colton (ed.), *Private Correspondence of Henry Clay,* 64-65. Itúrbide (Ytúrbide), born and educated at Valladolid, Mexico, a royalist military leader during the first decade of the revolutionary movement, had joined with Mexican conservatives in rebellion against the Spanish Government when in 1820 Ferdinand VII again acknowledged the liberal constitution of 1812 (above, II, 789n). During the spring of 1821 the revolutionary forces were victorious, and in August the King's representative signed the treaty of Córdoba, recognizing Mexican independence. Though the Spanish Cortes refused to ratify this treaty, Itúrbide headed a provisional government; and in May, 1822, the Mexican Congress proclaimed him Emperor of Mexico.

1 In January, 1822, Eugenio Cortés had been appointed agent of the Mexican government in the United States, his principal object being to purchase vessels for the formation of a navy. In October of this year he was named Minister to the United States in the event that the regular appointee should fail to arrive, and for several months he served as the medium of liaison between the governments. His relations with Clay have not been traced.

2 Que Besa Su Mano.

To the Kentucky General Assembly

[*ca.* May 13, 1822]

To the General Assembly of the Commonwealth of Kentucky.

IN pursuance of the powers and authorities to us confided, on the subjects embraced by the resolutions of the general assembly, adopted at the last session, "concerning the occupying claimant laws, and the decision of the supreme court of the United States thereon,"[1] we deemed it expedient, in the first instance, to open a communication with the government of Virginia. For this purpose, we repaired to the City of Richmond; and having presented ourselves to the governor, he promptly laid before the general assembly of that state, the object of our visit to that metropolis, and our wish to be heard in the manner most agreeable to the general assembly.[2] On the 5th February last, we received from the honorable Linn Banks, speaker of the house of delegates of Virginia, the accompanying resolutions, designated by the letter A. On the 7th we addressed to each branch of the general assembly, a letter, enclosing two written propositions in the alternative, of which copies are hereto annexed, designated B. On the 7th and 8th of that month,[3] we were heard in support of those propositions, by both houses of the general assembly, convened for that purpose. We afterwards received their resolutions and decision, also annexed hereto, as document C.[4]

Whilst we regret that the general assembly has taken that view of the subject, we have particular satisfaction in testifying to the very prompt and respectful attention which was given by the government of Virginia, to the communications from the state of Kentucky. We had reason to believe, that if our powers had been more comprehensive, Virginia might have been disposed to co-operate with Kentucky, in constituting a tribunal, according to the act of separation, for adjudicating on all matters of difference, which either party should submit to its decision.

After this issue of the business at Richmond, we appeared before the supreme court of the United States, as friends of the court, and were heard upon the various questions involved in the case of Greene against Biddle. The court was composed of five of the judges only, and after the close of the argument, took time, until the next term, to consider and decide the cause.[5] One of us was informally assured, that the court did not feel itself compromitted, and would not be at all biassed by the opinion formerly intimated on an *ex parte* argument. What its ultimate decision, however, may be, we cannot venture to say. If we might anticipate it, from a strong persuasion of the wisdom, policy and justice of the acts of 1797 and 1812; from their long continued operation; from the uninterrupted sanction given to them by all the judges who have held judicial stations in our state, in the courts of original and appellate jurisdiction; from the solemn decision of the court of appeals; and from the very clear convictions, strengthened by the recent discussions, which we entertain, that there was full authority to enact them, we could not doubt that the ultimate decision of the court, on a review of the whole subject, will be consonant to the wishes of the general assembly of Kentucky.

We have the honor to be, with great respect, Your obedient servants,

H. CLAY,
GEO. M. BIBB.

Ky. H. of Reps., *Journal, Special Session, 1822,* pp. 10-11. Published also in Lexington *Kentucky Gazette,* May 23, 1822.

1 See above, Credential, December 22, 1821.

2 See above, Clay and Bibb to Randolph, January 31, 1822; Johnson and Morris to Clay and Bibb, February 2, 1822.

3 See above, Speech, February 7, 1822. Bibb spoke the following day.

4 See above, Resolutions, March 2, 1822.

5 See above, DuVal to Clay, June 14, 1821. Bibb began the argument in response

to Green's attorneys on March 8; Clay continued it during the next two sittings of the court. His remarks are reported at length in 21 *U.S.* (8 Wheaton) 38-58. On the decision, see below, Clay to Brooke, March 9, 1823.

From Alexander Macomb

Engineer Department Washington 13th May 1822

Henry Clay Esq Lexington Ky.

Sir By the request of the Secy of War,[1] I made a private communication to Major Thayer the Superintendent of the Military Academy at West Point,[2] respecting the different Accounts raised by your son Thomas H Clay at that place.

The Answer of Major Thayer has just been received, of which Copy is herewith transmitted together with the Account of Saml Wilton[3] which accompanied it.

I have the honor to be &c Alex Macomb Mr. Gl[4]

Copy. DNA, RG77, Misc. Letters Sent, vol. 1, p. 281. Macomb, in 1821, had been appointed head of the Corps of Engineers, United States Army, and inspector of the Military Academy.

1 John C. Calhoun.

2 Sylvanus Thayer, a graduate of the Military Academy, had served in the War of 1812 and, in 1815, had been sent to Europe to study army organization, fortifications and education in military schools. He was Superintendent of the Academy from 1817 to 1833; engineer in charge of fortifications at the entrance to Boston Harbor, 1833-1863; and, following his retirement from military duty, founder of Thayer School of Engineering at Dartmouth College, 1867.

3 Tailor, of West Point, whose account amounted to $119.50. For Thayer's letter and the account, see DNA, RG94, Letters from Supt. of Military Academy—no. 287.

4 Major General (by brevet).

Toast and Response at Public Dinner

[May 20, 1822]

11. *H. Clay and Geo. M. Bibb*—Late Commissioners to Virginia, Kentucky thanks them for their able vindication of her rights.

Mr. Clay in a short but impressive address returned for himself and his colleague, thanks for the favourable sentiment expressed approbatory of their conduct.

Frankfort *Argus of Western America,* May 23, 1822. Published also in Lexington *Kentucky Reporter,* June 3, 1822. On May 18, Benjamin Watkins Leigh had received and accepted an invitation to "a Public Dinner at the Mansion House, on Monday next, at three o'clock." The affair was "very numerously attended by the members of the Legislature, as well as private citizens; the table was sumptuous and well provided; and the day passed in harmony and conviviality." The Mansion House, in Frankfort, built about 1805 by John J. Marshall, who still owned it, was operated by Richard Taylor.

From Mordecai Gist

Dear Sir, Middleburg 30th May 1822. M.d.

I had the pleasure some few days ago to have a good deal of

conversation with my intimate friend Henry R. Warfield our representative in Congress from this district of Maryland. Who to my surprise only that you differ in political sentiments is very warmly your friend— Mr. Warfield confidentially communicated a discovery in the Cabinet at Washington just before the rise of Congress relative to the Mississippi part of the Treaty at Ghent[1] that has opened the eyes of the people who I have conversed with I candidly believe you are now their choice for the next presidency should you be a candidate Inasmuch as I have known you so long and have taken the Liberty to say some thing in your favour— I should be pleased to correspond with you—

Sincerely MORDECAI GIST

ALS. DLC-HC (DNA, M212, R1). Addressed to Clay, "Near Lexington Ky." Postmarked at Middleburg, Maryland. Gist, son of Joshua and grandson of Thomas Gist, had been born in Frederick County, Maryland, had married a niece of Clay's friend, James Clark (a granddaughter of Robert Clark, the magistrate of Clark County, Kentucky), had inherited a large tract in Fleming County, Kentucky, and had lived at least a decade in Clark and Fayette counties of Kentucky.

1 See above, Benton to Clay, May 2, 1822; below, Russell to Clay, June 6, 1822.

From Henry R. Warfield

My dear Sir— Frederick County 30th. May 1822

I received your letter[1] a few days before the adjournment of Congress, but such is the hurry and bustle on those occasions that proper attention cannot be bestowed Either on public [or] private business— Soon after your return from Richmond to Washington I left that place for Frederick and on my return to Washington I found you had set out for Lexington—those occurrances prevented my seeing you as often as I wished and Intended—

In the Early part of the Session I was with a mess on Capitol Hill with Sargeant Milnor Buchanan &c.[2] It was a Very pleasant one— Sargeant after some acquaintance with him put aside his usual reserve we got on Very friendly terms and passed some social Evenings in Each others rooms— But haveing [*sic*] more acquaintances in Georgetown— upon my return from Frederick I joined the old mess at Bradeys [*sic*] (Crawfords) [3] It consisted of Messrs. King Van Beuren [*sic*] & Mills of the Senate—McLane Mercer Genl. Stephen Van Rensselear [*sic*] Gorham & myself—[4] In our general conversations respecting the successor of Mr Monroe, your name was mentioned together with Crawfords Calhouns & Adams's— There were Various conjectures as to the result but no opinion or preference of a decided character given— With Genl. Van Rensselaer I had repeated confidential conversation, respecting your Election— on the Evening before he left George Town he invited me into his room—

The Conversation was renewed— He said he did not hesitate to avow his decided preference for you but was fearful you were not strong enough to succeed— we had some Conversation on that point— as I knew him to be a man of strict Honor & haveing assertain [*sic*] he was your firm Friend—I told him I cou'd furnish him with more information on that point than he was aware of, and under the strictest injunctions of confidence I wou'd shew him a letter I received from you—[5] He read it with great pleasure and expressed Very high gratification at the prospect— He enquired whether I intended writing to you Soon— I told him I shou'd— He went on to speak of the situation of parties in New York— He said that amidst the Various contrarient Views and contending interests in that state he thought he had a good foot hold (which I suppose is the case as I understand he holds a county and a half thickly inhabited) —[6] He spoke of several distinguished men of the Democratic party, amoung [*sic*] others of DeWit clinton [*sic*] as personally attached to him and a family connection[7] (and who I know from good authority is under considerable obligations to him) that he wou'd retire from Public Station, but with a powerful party in that state attached to him— That there was a Strong party of Federals in the State—with whom he had an intimate connection— The Federals he says have not on questions of a General Character taken any part but their cooperation with such force as Clinton can bring into action takeing the chance of *scatterers* can decide the fate of New York— now sir as to Van Beuren with whom I was on the most scocial [*sic*] terms, and who is a pleasant good tempered facetious little fellow, is at the same time a deep observer, looks quite through the Deeds of men— Subtle and intrigueing,—I was afraid to trust him— He is searching ambitious Indefatigable—no particular attachment to Either of the candidates—Trying to find out whose chance is the best— If he cou'd be secured & I have no doubt he might you wou'd unquestionably take New York— He is now inclined for Crawford because he thinks his chance the best— I have frequently told him in our General pleasant conversations, that altho it was a matter of little or no consideration with me who might be the president yet I had no more doubt of your Election than that we were then Engaged in conversation— That if the unbiased Votes of the people of this country cou'd be taken you wou'd out number Either of the other candidates fifty to one & this he wou'd find to be the fact whenever the question shou'd be fairly brought before the people— I pointed out a number of objections to Crawford, the Deplorable condition of our fiscal concerns &c. &c. difficulties it was impossible for him to surmount— That Calhouns know [*sic*] prodigallity [*sic*] in Expenditure of the Substance of the people together with his known preference to Military Establishments his inexperience, Impetuosity of feeling &c &c. prevented even a remote chance of his Election some twenty years hence— That as to John Adams 'twas only necessary to say that his head Glistened too much like a Sun Dial— He had neither the manners nor appearance of a Gentleman— He cou'd not make a bow, and had not learned to Dance when he was young &c. Van Beuren after several general conversations in a pleasant way Either was or pretended to be favourable to you he told me he intended to forward you some dispatches— I do not believe he is fixed, nor has he any decided personal partiallity [*sic*]—

When General Van Renselaer [*sic*] & myself were about to part on the Evening I have been speaking of he said, when you next write to Mr. Clay assure him from me that I will use every Exertion to secure his Election in New York—

With McLane of Delware [*sic*] I consider it my good Fortune to be on terms of the most unreserved confidence & the sincerest friendship— He is not only a man of fine talents but of intrinsic Excellence of Character— We passed much of our time in Each others society— You were frequently the subject of our conversation He always spoke of you with feelings of regard, but I thought from the general tenor of his remarks he inclined to Crawford for he woud frequently conclude the conversation by saying—well Warfield Either Crawford or Clay— Poor fellow, he is in bad health, he intends travelling this summer for the benefit of his health and has promised me a Visit— He had prepared to decline a reelection— I had the good fortune to prevail on him not to Do it— In our last conversation when I pressed him on the subject, he said why Warfield to be candid with you, the reason why I incline to Crawford is amoung other things that I understand Rodney[8] has been paying great court to Clay— He has been my uniform Enemy— I put every thing at hazzard [*sic*] on the Missouiri [*sic*] Question— Rodney if he had it in his power woud forever press me down in a political point of View— He Expressed not only a high opinion of your qualifications, but great personal regard— Well then said I, McLane, the first time I write to Clay I will on terms of the strictest Confidence and Honor, If you have no objection mention this Conversation to him— He replied none in the World you may on those terms mention it to Mr. Clay— now I shou'd regret that those impressions on McLanes mind knowing his personal regard shou'd deprive you of his political Friendship—

Gorham remains warmly and zealously your friend— He says there is no Doubt the New England States wou'd prefer a *man of their own*— But he did not think it possible to unite them in support of Adams, and there was no other person they cou'd bring forward— He thinks the question will turn between Crawford and yourself, on such an Event he said there was not the least question or Doubt, but that the New England States wou'd be decidedly with you— after his return to Boston he said he wou'd make some enquiry into their Views and movements & write to me fully on the Subject— When Webster[9] was in Washington last Winter Calhoun Was most particularly attentive to him—

I dined frequently with Hemphill[10] during the winter— You have not a more decided and zealous friend in the United States— He says much will depend on the Election of the next Governor in Pennsylvania as to the vote she may give on the Presidential Election He says he will Visit different parts of the State— He told me he intended to send you some despatches I believe the report of the Committee on Roads & Canals—[11] He says he will make Every Effort to secure your Election— Hemphill is an Honest Worthy fellow & most Esteemed by those who know him best—

A few days before Congress rose I had a conversation with Doctor Kent—[12] Lloy'd[13] he told me was decidedly for Crawford, and in our general remarks said he thought *he* shou'd be for him— Why Dr. there is our old Friend Clay— I am said he Clays personal friend but I do not think he is strong enough to be Elected— I did not let him know that I had heard from you— But made some general observations on the strength I thought you had, which I considered a Very fair calculation, and that in my Judgment your chance of being Elected was much greater than any person spoken of— I have no doubt the Doc. will be with you if he thinks there is a chance of your Election, and this my Dear Sir is the feeling of nine tenths of the persons I have heard speak on the Subject of the Presidential Election— I Verily believe that you have a hundred to one of the people generally, and depend upon it the moment they see a *probable prospect* of your Election they will arise in numbers greater than you suppose— you know in all political contests there are a number of persons of a certain description who *always* go with what is considered the strong side—

I cannot say at this time what will be the probable result in this State, I shall be the week after next at Annapolis when the Supreme Court will be in Session at which place Gentlemen of of [*sic*] information will be convened from different parts of the State— It is divided into Districts, each Electing one or more Electors according to its size and population— A part of the District which I represent is attached to Nelsons,[14] This Elects two Electors— Nelson is with you of course you get two Votes in this District— The residue is Joined to Dr Kents— This I think you can safely count on—and I can assure you no Effort will be wanting to secure you the whole State— you know Elections with us are carried by what is called Harangueing [*sic*] the people—and at a *Stump* speech I feel myself so perfectly at Home, that there is *no man I have Ever seen* I shou'd fear to meet in such a rencounter—

A few days before the close of Congress a Pamphlet was was [*sic*] laid on the Desk of Each member Signed a native of Virginia— I see by the late papers Mr. Jefferson has written to the Editors of the Richmond Enquirer a long letter in answer to some charges made in it against him—[15] If you have not seen the work let me advise you to get it— Read it and I think you will concur with me, that a general Circulation of it to the west and Indeed throughout the United States wou'd be attended, with the best Effects— Mr. Jefferson has Explained—those who cannot or will not, mus[t] bear the force of the charges— I must close this long and I fear tiresome letter— If you write Direct to Middleburg Fredk County maryland—

With Every kind wish yrs. c. HENRY R. WARFIELD

[Marginal note]

I have agreed during the Summer to correspond with Genl. Van Rensselaer Mc.Lane & Gorham and may perhaps have something worth communicating to you—

ALS. DLC-HC (DNA, M212, R1). [1] Not found.

[2] See above, Warfield to Clay, December 18, 1821.

[3] The Union Tavern, on Bridge Street, Georgetown, of which Joseph Crawford had been proprietor about twenty years, had recently been taken over by Peter Brady.

[4] Rufus King; Martin Van Buren; Elijah Hunt Mills; Louis McLane; Charles Fenton Mercer; Benjamin Gorham. Van Rensselaer, a major general of volunteers in the War of 1812, had been elected to the Seventeenth Congress to fill the vacancy caused by the resignation of his distant kinsman, Solomon Van Rensselaer. Stephen was the founder, in 1824, of Rensselaer Polytechnic Institute, Troy, New York.

[5] Not found. [6] Albany and Rensselaer counties.

[7] By marriage, probably through Clinton's second wife, Catherine Jones, of New York City.

[8] Caesar A. Rodney. [9] Daniel Webster. [10] Joseph Hemphill.

[11] "Report on Internal Improvements," *House Reports*, 17 Cong., 1 Sess., no. 98 (April 26, 1822).

[12] Joseph Kent, who had begun the practice of medicine in 1799, had been a Congressman from Maryland from 1811 to 1815, had been elected again in 1819, and served until elected Governor of his State in 1826. He was a member of the United States Senate from 1833 until his death in 1837.

[13] Probably Edward Lloyd.

[14] John Nelson, Congressman from Maryland (1821-1823), later Chargé d'Affaires to the Two Sicilies (1831-1832) and United States Attorney General (1843-1845).

[15] In two letters, dated May 13 and June 10, addressed to Ritchie and Gooch, Jefferson undertook to refute, so far as related to himself, "the arraignment of the Presidents of the United States generally, as peculators or accessories to peculation," which had been published over the signature, "Native Virginian" (not identified). Noting that he had seen the same charges against himself published in the Baltimore *Federal Republican* of August 28, which had been sent to him by a friend, together with the real name of the author, Jefferson explained that he had dismissed the matter as "the ferment of a warmly-contested election." He now explained the error in settlement of his accounts after his return from the mission to France, in the spring of 1790, which had occasioned repayment to him of $1148 by the Treasury upon his retirement from office in 1809. Andrew A. Lipscomb and Ellery Bergh (ed.), *The Writings of Thomas Jefferson* . . . (Monticello Edition, issued under the auspices of the Thomas Jefferson Memorial Association; 20 vols.; Washington, 1904-1905), XV, 365-70, 374-82.

Claiborne W. Gooch had joined Thomas Ritchie in partnership as publishers of the Richmond *Enquirer* with the issue of March 3, 1820.

Credential as Commissioner for Kentucky

[June 1, 1822]

[Governor John Adair certifies that Henry Clay has been appointed by the Kentucky legislature "to consort with Benjamin Watkins Leigh Esquire Commissioner from Virginia the necessary arrangements and stipulations preparatory to the organisation of the tribunal Contemplated by the 8th Article of the compact between the States of Virginia and Kentucky, agreeably to Resolutions of the General assembly of the Commonwealth of Kentucky . . . Approved May 29th 1822."[1] Signed by Adair and Secretary of State J. Cabell Breckinridge.]

DS. DLC-HC (DNA, M212, R1).

1 See above, Resolutions, March 2, 1822, note. On May 8 Leigh had informed Governor Adair that he, having been appointed by the Virginia General Assembly as "Commissioner to the legislature of Kentucky," had come to Frankfort "to fulfill the duties committed to me." Ky. H. of Rep., *Journal, Special Session, 1822,* pp. 50-51. The resolutions of the Kentucky legislature on May 29 acceded to the proposal that a board of commissioners be set up, "under the eighth article of the compact to determine all matters of controversy between the two states" and had provided that a commissioner be appointed by Kentucky "with authority to enter into the necessary arrangements and stipulations with the Virginia commissioner preparatory to the organization of the tribunal under the compact, and report the same to the legislature of Kentucky at their next session, to enable them to appoint commissioners on the part of Kentucky. . . ." Ky. Gen. Assy., *Acts, 1822,* pp. 15-17. Clay was the sole nominee in both the House and the Senate to fill the post under the second resolution.

Convention between Kentucky and Virginia

[Lexington, June 5, 1822]

[Certain differences having arisen between Kentucky and Virginia, "concerning the construction, effect and execution of the compact between the two states, contained in the act of the Legislature of Virginia, passed on the 18th day of December 1789, entitled 'an act concerning the erection of the District of Kentucky into an independent state,' " and the two States having appointed commissioners to organize a board of commissioners under the eighth article of the compact, "with authority to decide all matters in difference, between the two states," it is now agreed between Benjamin Watkins Leigh, as commissioner on the part of Virginia, and Henry Clay, for Kentucky as follows:[1]

[I. The proposed board shall be organized conformably to the eighth article of the compact, in such manner that none of the commissioners shall be citizens of either Virginia or Kentucky;

[II. The four commissioners so to be chosen shall meet in Washington on the fourth Monday in January, 1823, "or as soon thereafter as may be," whereupon they shall appoint two additional commissioners; the board so constituted shall meet "according to its own adjournments" and shall present its award in writing to the agents of the parties on or before the first day of April, 1823; otherwise the board shall be dissolved;

[III. The commissioners shall be allowed eight dollars for every day in attendance at Washington on the business of the commission and also eight dollars for every twenty miles in going and returning from Washington to their respective places of residence, the charges to be common to Kentucky and Virginia;]

IV. The matters of difference between the two states, to be submitted to the judgment and decision of the said board of commissioners, on the part of the state of Kentucky, are the following acts of the Legislature thereof, that is to say: "an act concerning occupying claimants of land," passed on the 27th February 1797; "an act to amend an act, entitled an act concerning occupying claimants of land," passed on the 31st of January 1812; "an act to amend an act, entitled an act to amend an act concerning occupying claimants of land," passed on the 20th of December 1820; "an act to compel the speedy adjustment of land claims," passed on the 9th of February 1809; and "an act to amend an act, entitled an act to amend and reduce into one, the several acts or parts of acts concerning limitations of actions, and for other purposes," passed the 22nd of January 1814: all which acts, the state of Kentucky insists, are valid, and no way repugnant to the said compact between the two states; on the contrary, the state of Virginia insists, that they are repugnant to the said compact and invalid. The board of commissioners is, therefore, to determine, whether the said acts, or either of them, or any part of either of them, be consistent with the said compact and valid, or not?

The points of complaint and difference to be submitted to the said board, on the part of the state of Virginia, are all the matters of complain[t] and dispute, set forth in a certain report of a select committee of the house of Delegates of Virginia, touching the claims of the officers and soldiers of the revolution for bounties in lands, which was agreed to by both houses of the General Assembly of Virginia at its last session, and was communicated to the General Assembly of Kentucky at its last session:[2] as to all which matters of complaint and dispute alledged by the state of Virginia, that state insists, that the state of Kentucky hath failed to observe and fullfil the compact between the two states, according to its true intent and meaning; on the contrary the state of Kentucky insists, that she has faithfully observed kept and fullfilled [*sic*] the said compact on her part, in respect to all the said matters of complaint and difference. The board of commissioners is, therefore, to determine, whether in respect to the said matters of complaint and dispute alledged by Virginia, or either or any part thereof, the state of Kentucky has observed kept and fullfilled the provisions of the said compact touching the same, or not?

[V. If these articles be ratified, the States are to choose their commissioners and exchange ratification through their Executives.][3]

ADS by Leigh, signed also by Clay. DLC-HC (DNA, M212, R1). Published in Ky. H. of Reps., *Journal, 1822,* pp. 37-40; Ky. Sen., *Journal, 1822,* pp. 33-36; Washington *Daily National Intelligencer,* December 16, 1822; Lexington *Kentucky Reporter,* November 11, 1822; Lexington *Kentucky Gazette,* November 14, 1822.

1 See above, Credential, June 1, 1822, note.

2 See above, Resolutions, March 2, 1822, note.

3 In Kentucky a resolution, which originated in the House of Representatives, approving and ratifying the Convention and the Contingent Provisions of the Convention (see below, this date) was approved by the Governor on November 16. Ky. Gen. Assy., *Acts, 1822,* pp. 248-49. Ratification failed, however, in the Virginia General Assembly. See below, Leigh to Clay, March 1, 1823, note.

Contingent Provisions of Convention between Kentucky and Virginia

[June 5, 1822]

The States of Kentucky and Virginia, having by their respective Commissioners, Henry Clay and Benjamin Watkins Leigh, this day entered into a Convention making certain arrangements and stipulations for organizing a Board of Commissioners to determine all matters of complaint or dispute between them, arising under the act of the 18h day of December 1789, entitled "An act concerning the erection of the District of Kentucky into an Independent State," passed by the General Assembly of Virginia; and the said Commissioners, deeming it proper that certain contingent provisions should be made, dependent upon the decision of the said Board, have entered into these separate articles, proposed on the part of Kentucky, that is to say:

I. That if the decision of the Board of Commissioners, to be organized as aforesaid, shall be in favor of Kentucky, on the claim asserted to have permission now to locate, below the Tennessee river, all unlocated land warrants granted by Virginia to her State line, the State of Virginia shall and doth hereby guarrantee to Kentucky that the proprietors of all such unlocated warrants shall submit to and abide by the said decision; and also shall and doth hereby agree to indemnify Kentucky against any claim which they or any of them may subsequently assert against Kentucky, or against persons deriving titles to land from Kentucky, on account of the said unlocated warrants, if the said proprietors or any of them should refuse to submit to and abide by the said decision.

II. That in no event is the decision of the said Board of Commissioners to affect the sales of land brought into market by the act of the General Assembly of Kentucky entitled "An act providing for the sale of the vacant lands West of the Tennessee river," passed on the 21st. December 1821; but, on the contrary, the said land is to be considered as altogether reserved by Kentucky, and to be exempt from all and every claim brought forward by Virginia.

III. That it is understood and agreed by the contracting parties that the amount of unlocated warrants, granted by Virginia to her State line, prior to the first of May 1792, does not exceed 109.449. Acres; that the amount of those granted subsequent to that day to the said line, does not exceed 37.409⅓ acres; and that the amount of those, granted prior and subsequent to that day, respecting which the line, whether Continental or State, has not been designated, does not exceed 186.520 Acres. And it being unknown what part of this latter quantity has been located, it is further agreed between the contracting parties that, if the decision of the said Board of Commissioners shall be in favor of the claim now to locate unlocated warrants, it shall nevertheless be competent to Kentucky to require the production of satisfactory proof of the facts both of the line to which any of the said warrants were granted, and that they have not been previously located.

IV. That, if the said Board shall decide in favor of the claim now brought forward to make locations below the Tennessee river, Kentucky retains to herself the power to regulate the making of such locations, in some convenient and equitable mode, allowing the claimants the full substantial benefit of the original appropriation for their bounties; and also the power to prescribe a reasonable time within which, if the proprietors of any warants, who may be adjudged now to have such right of location, do not make their locations in conformity with the mode so prescribed, their rights shall be forfeited.

V. These articles are to be binding on the parties when ratified by them respectively, and are to have the same effect as if inserted in and made a part of the Convention which has been this day agreed upon.

In faith whereof we the Commissioners aforesaid have respectively signed this agreement and have hereunto affixed our seals.

Done, in duplicate, at Lexington the fifth day of June one thousand eight hundred and twenty two. H. CLAY
B:W:LEIGH

ADS by Clay, signed also by Leigh. DLC-HC (DNA, M212, R1). Published in Ky. H. of Reps., *Journal, 1822,* pp. 40-42; Ky. Sen., *Journal, 1822,* pp. 36-37; Washington *Daily National Intelligencer,* December 16, 1822; Lexington *Kentucky Reporter,* November 11, 1822; Lexington *Kentucky Gazette,* November 14, 1822.

Toasts and Speech at Public Dinner

[June 6, 1822]

14. *Our guest* HENRY CLAY—Our friend and fellow citizen.

{MR. CLAY rose, and assured the company, that he felt proud of being thus named, and that he reciprocated most sincerely their friendly sentiments. He had in the course of his life received so many proofs of the kindness of his fellow citizens, that he felt utterly at a loss for words to express his gratitude; but he hoped on this occasion, they would accept all he had to offer,—his humble thanks.}

. . . .

VOLUNTEERS.

. . . .

By Mr. Clay—*The improved Hemp Breaker*—[1] May it prove a new *tie* to the different parts of the Union; and a new source of wealth to our country.

Lexington *Kentucky Reporter,* June 10, 1822. The "Volunteer" by Clay was published also in *Niles' Weekly Register,* XXII (July 6, 1822), 289. The dinner, given at Keen's Inn, Lexington, honored Benjamin Watkins Leigh.

1 Probably "Dey's Flax and Hemp Machine," advertised by Anthony Dey, of New York, in Lexington *Kentucky Reporter,* April 1, 1822.

From Jonathan Russell

My Dear Sir Mendon 6 June 1822

You will have seen, before this reaches you, the communication to Congress of what Mr Adams calls my original & duplice [*sic*] of a letter written at Paris 11 feby 1815 & his remarks on these papers—[1] I have really a great contempt for his part of the performance & I might remain silent but for the desire expressed, by some friends whose opinions I respect, that I should present to the public at least an explanation on some points— I shall do so accordingly &, as it will be necessary to appeal to you for confirmation of some of the views & facts which I shall present particularly those in which you are exclusely [*sic*] or jointly interested, it is important that our memories should perfectly accord with each other—

Mr Adams pretends to remember that a dispatch received on the 24th Novr 1814 released us, by permitting the Status ante bellum as the basis of negotiation,[2] from the obligation of observing the instruction of the 15 April 1813 (see paper annexed) which forbid us to renew the article of the treaty of 1794 "allowing the Northwest company and British traders to carry on trade with the indian tribes within our limits, a privilege the pernicious effects of which have been most sensibly felt in the present war"— & commanded us to "*avoid* any stipulation which might restrain the United States from increasing their naval force to any extent they may think proper on the lakes held in common, or excluding the British traders from the lakes & rivers exclusively within our jurisdiction"—[3] He also insinuates if he may not be said to assert that being thus released by the dispatch received on the 24th November, the proposition relating to the navigation of the Mississippi & the fishing privilege had been discussed at the meetings of the mission on the 28h & 29 of November & that in consequence of these discussions that proposition was made to the British Plenipotentiaries on the 1st of december following—[4] Now I remember distinctly that the meetings of the mission at which that proposition was seriously discussed were commenced as early at least as the 3d of November & probably the first & the sense of the American Ministers thereon when you & I were in the minority was taken before the 10th of that month— The following facts may serve to refresh your memory— On the 24h of October we addressed a note to the British Ministers & repeated our request that they would communicate all the other specific propositions (the preliminary article proposed by the British government having been accepted by us) offering a simultaneous exchange of projects [*sic*] by both parties— The British Ministers by their note of the 31st of that month declined acceding to this proposal saying they had already by their note of the 21st of that month communicated to us all the points upon which they were instructed to insist— After the receipt of this note, I beleive [*sic*] we met together every day to decide first if we should present a complete project on our part & then, having decided to do so, to digest this project, until the 10 of November when it was presented— During this period the proposition, in question, after having been repeatedly discussed was carried in the affirmative notwithstanding your & my opposition to it.— I am very certain that one among our objections was its incompatibility with our instructions of the 15h April 1813, above mentioned— When I had the pleasure of seeing you at Washington a few months ago you then intimated a recollection that this proposition was against our instructions— I examined in consequence all our instructions, & finding none other so much in point—a prohibition to bring [*sic*] our right to the fisheries into discussion not being equally so—I was satisfied from your intimation & from my own recollection that the instruction which you referred to was that of the 15 Apl 1813—[5] It was from this circumstance that I was induced to add this objection to those which I had stated at Paris—[6]

After the majority had decided on making the proposition, above mentioned, as a part of the project—our continued opposition, particularly yours, for it was then that you declared that you would sign no treaty of which such an article should make a part, induced the majority particularly Mr Bayard to relax—& to consent to present the project to the British Ministers without such an article,[7] declaring however, in our note which accompanied that project, that "in answer to the declaration made by the British Plenipotentiaries respecting the fisheries the undersigned, referring to what passed in the conference of the 9h of August can only State that they are not authorized to bring into discussion any of the rights or liberties which the United States have heretofore enjoyed in relation thereto. From their nature & from the peculiar charact[er][8] of the treaty of 1783, by which they were recognized no further stipulation has been deemed necessary by the government of the United States to entitle them to the full enjoyment of all of them"— This paragraph was drawn up by you, as Mr Adams himself admits—[9] & your sole object in drawing it up was to get rid of the offer of the navigation of the Mississippi as *an equivalent* for the fishing liberty— To induce the majority to go with you on this point you adopted the doctrine of the peculiarity of the treaty of 1783—

On the 27 of Novr the British Ministers returned our project with marginal alterations & suggestions & with an explanatory note dated the 26h the preceding day— The meetings of the American Mission on the 28 & 29 were to deliberate on this communication from the British Ministers in which not a word was said concerning either the navigation of the Mississippi—or the fishing privilege.[10] If this subject was mentioned by us at those meetings & possibly it might be, still it is certain that the proposition in relation to it which had been first carried & then waived by the majority previous to the 10h of that month was not decided on again, as Mr Adams more than insinuates I distinctly remember & I doubt not your recollection will perfectly accord with mine, that a majority of the mission were surprised when that proposition was offered at the conference on the 1st of december, as such an offer was then *entirely unexpected by them*.[11] Mr Bayard, in returning with you & me to our Hotel expressed his disapprobation in very strong terms that such an offer should have been made so long after the affirmative decision had been taken on it *without again consulting him*— To show you that my memory has been correct on this point I will give you an extract from a letter which I addresed to you at Stokholm [*sic*] on the 15 of October 1815—& which I hope you still have in your possession—[12] In that letter, speaking of Mr Gallatin, I say "who after having explicitly avowed that the contested liberty of the fisheries was *no equivalent* for the free navigation of the Mississippi not only insisted that the latter should be offered in consideration of the former but actually himself made this offer to the British Ministers in a manner unexpected & *unauthorised* by at least a majority of his colleagues."

To show you also that I remember correctly concerning the time when the proposition was really discussed & decided & the majority relaxed in relation to it, I will give you here extracts from two letters which I wrote to Mr Crawford[13] at the time—

In a letter to him, dated at Ghent the 4h Novr 1814 is the following— "The question which perplexes us the most is that concerning the fisheries & we have not yet decided on the mode of proceeding in relation to it. They have told us that the liberty of taking, drying & curing fish within the exclusive jurisdiction of Great Britain will not be continued to us without an equivalent. We cannot relinquish this liberty & we cannot offer territory as an equivalent. Shall we then offer the free navigation of the Mississippi which they apparently suggested with this view— I think this will be carried in the affirmative although I have very serious objections to the measure"—

In another letter to him of the 24 Novr 1814 I say "without having been deceived relative to the disposition of the majority on the subject of the free navigation of the Mississippi I am happy to inform you that this disposition was *not inflexible* & we finally transmitted our project without the article that had at first been carried— This article was as follows—"

"The right & liberty of the people and inhabitants of the United States to take, dry & cure fish in places within the exclusive jurisdiction of Great Britain as recognized (and secured) by the former treaty of peace and the privilege of the navigation of the Mississippi within the exclusive jurisdiction of the United States (as secured to the subjects of Great Britain by the same treaty) are hereby recognised & confirmed."

"Besides the objections to such an article which had occurred to you[14] and which had not escaped us—the blending the two points together & making them mutually dependant on each other, which was not done in the treaty of 1783, made this article the more objectionable"—

I think we must remember alike concerning the transactions above referred to & I leave you to draw inferences— There are other points in which we ought & I believe, shall agree— Mr. Adams in his remarks you will perceive has made us *assent* to his principle & even to the proposition, in question, 1st—because you presented the paragraph above mentioned of our note of the 10 of Novr admitting the *peculiar* character of the treaty of 1783 & because the mission unanimously accepted it—

He says that I &, of course you, *assented* to the proposition because it "was made by the *whole* of the *American mission* as may be seen by the protocol of the conference of the 1 december 1814 & by the letter from the American to the British plenipotentiaries of the 14h decmer [*sic*] 1814 which says "to such an article *which they viewed as merely declaratory* the undersigned had no objection & have offered to accede" & Mr Adams says that to that letter the name of Mr Russell is subscribed—[15] He might have added also your name— Now I consider all this as quibbling & shall so treat it—& I trust I shall be supported by your opinion— With regard to the adoption of the principle of Mr Adams with respect to the peculiar character of the treaty of 1783 &c in the paragraph which you furnished for the note of the 10h of Novr., it was assented to by us on that occasion as the only means of obtaining the consent of the majority to the only expedient which was left to get rid of the proposal, already decided on by that majority, of giving the free navigation of the Mississippi for the fishing privilege— That principle was admitted by us for that object & on that occasion only. We considered it as a mere pretext that thus used might do good but could so far do no harm— Whatever influence it might have on the British ministers it had a salutary one on our Colleagues by inducing them to waive their proposal— Whenever that principle (or pretext, or any other was advanced to sanction the British claim to the free navigation of the Mississippi we uniformly held it to be unsound & resisted it accordingly—

With regard to the protocol of the first December it was like all other protocols a mere record of facts—& the fact that that proposition was made to the British Mininisters [*sic*] in no way implied the *unanimous* consent of the American Ministers to such proposition—

Our signing the letter of the 14h of December 1814—after the proposition *had been made* acknowledging that fact cannot be evidence of your consent or mine to its being made or of our approbation of it— On the contrary, our assent to view it as merely *declaratory* was to diminish the evil which it might produce as it stood when offered & preventing it, as far as possible from being considered as containing mutual equivalents & thus permitting the British claim to the navigation of the Mississippi to stand on other or better ground than that on which it would have stood under the mere revival of the treaty of 1783— If we had not been able to prevent its being offered still we were willing to circumscribe its meaning as much as possible.

I showed to you, at the time the letter which I wrote at Paris & you coincided with me in the grounds there taken for our opposition— I shall state this fact & hope should occasion require you will confirm it—

Mr Adams throughout his remarks asserts or insinuates that I took no part in the debate on this subject—or said less on it than any other member of the mission or gave perhaps a silent vote &c—[16] now although I do not pretend to have said as much as you against this proposition yet I did say more against it & with more earnestness than on any other subject where there was a diversity of opinion—

In the publication which I intend first making & which will appear before I can hear from you[17] I shall controul my feelings as much as possible & act on the defensive only— There will be time enough afterwards to take a different course—

I have hastily written to you, my good friend, this long letter to freshen your memory & to throw myself on your justice & friendship to do all you can, with truth & propriety, to rescue me from the virulence & falshood [*sic*] of my malignant & mean calumniator—

It consoles me not a little that Mr Adams by avowing in his rage, that the free navigation of the Mississippi is of no more importance than the right to us of navigating the Bridgewater Canal or the Danube[18] has settled his fate in your quarter & will gain him nothing here—

A line from you, under existing circumstances would be particularly satisfactory— faithfully & cordially yours JONA RUSSELL

I cannot close this letter without taking notice of the conduct of Mr Adams in getting his remarks before the public— After the first strange message of the President Mr Adams seeing that no call in consequence of it was made went on the 6th May to the House of Representatives in person, & applied to Eustis[19] to make the call but he declined— Mr Adams then procured little Mr Fuller to perform this task— Fuller made the call the same day—the papers were communicated on the 7th & the house adjourned on the 8th— I had left Washington on the 5h. Was it fair towards me was it respectful towards the House thus to time the obtrusion of such a scurrilous pa[per on the][20] house to abuse an absent member—I hope some member may be found properly to notice this next Session—

ALS draft. RPB. Published in Washington *United States Telegraph,* October 23, 24, 1828.

1 President Monroe had resolved his dilemma in regard to the "duplicate letter" (see above, Benton to Clay, May 2, 1822) by informing the House of Representatives, May 4, that he had decided to withhold the document unless the House, with a knowledge of the circumstances connected with it, "should desire it; in which case the document called for shall be communicated, accompanied by a report from the Secretary of State. . . ." The original letter had then been deposited in the State Department, where anyone interested could obtain a copy.

Two days after Monroe's communication had been read in the House, Representative Timothy Fuller of Massachusetts had submitted a resolution calling for the Russell letter. On May 7, the resolution had been adopted, and the President had immediately complied by sending a report from the Secretary of State which included Russell's original and "duplicate" letters and "Remarks" by Adams. In his comment the Secretary had harshly criticized Russell for discrepancies between the two versions of the letter and attacked the "duplicate" as "a tissue of misrepresentations—of the subject, of the conduct and sentiments of his colleagues, and of his own conduct in opposition to them."

The report had been published in the Washington *Daily National Intelligencer,* May 21, 22, 23, 1822, and soon afterward in other papers over the country. See also U.S. H. of Reps., *Journal,* 17 Cong., 1 Sess., 554-55, 576, 585, 599; *House Docs.,* 17 Cong., 1 Sess., no. 131.

Later in the year Adams published at Washington the pertinent documents (the "private" and "duplicate" letters arranged side by side, with notation of 172 discrepancies), his own comments, and other material in a volume entitled *The Duplicate Letters, the Fisheries and the Mississippi, Documents Relating to Transactions at the Negotiation of Ghent.*

2 See above, I, 991.

[3] Donnan (ed.), *Papers of James A. Bayard,* 205. This part of the instructions is included in one of the confidential paragraphs omitted when Monroe's letter was published in *American State Papers, Foreign Relations,* III, 695-700.

[4] In his "Remarks," Adams had written: "The proposition relating to the navigation of the Mississippi, and the fishery, was made to the British Plenipotentiaries on the 1st of December, 1814. It had been discussed at the meetings of the American Mission, on the preceding 28th and 29th of November. On the 24th of that month, the American Plenipotentiaries had received a letter of instructions from the Secretary of State, dated 19th October, 1814 . . . ." *House Docs.,* 17 Cong., 1 Sess., no. 131, p. 34.

The proposal made in a conference with the British commissioners on December 1 had been discussed on the dates mentioned by Adams. Adams, *Memoirs,* III, 71-76.

[5] According to Adams' diary, discussion of these points had begun on October 30, at which time Albert Gallatin had proposed a renewal of the two articles of the Treaty of Peace of 1783 relating to the fisheries and the navigation of the Mississippi. Clay had objected and had appealed "to our instructions forbidding us to permit our right to the fisheries to be brought into discussion." On November 1 Clay had again stated his objections, declaring the navigation of the Mississippi "a privilege much too important to be conceded for the mere liberty of drying fish upon a desert." Four days later, after additional debate, a ballot had been taken on the proposal, and Clay and Russell had voted as a minority against it. Adams, *Memoirs,* III, 60-64.

[6] Unfortunately for Russell, he had in his "duplicate," with specific reference to the instructions of April 15, 1813, enlarged to a considerable extent on what he had written in the original letter from Paris. Adams, in his "Remarks," had taken full advantage of the opportunity thus offered for a devastating attack on Russell. See *House Docs.,* 17 Cong., 1 Sess., no. 131, pp. 33-36.

[7] On October 5, after the majority of the American commission had approved Gallatin's proposal (above, note 5), "Mr. Clay said that he should not sign the communication by which the proposal would be made." Two days later Clay offered a substitute article. After some discussion "Mr. Bayard said that rather than differ among ourselves he would agree to substitute Mr. Clay's paragraph instead of the proposed article; and this was ultimately assented to by us all." Adams, *Memoirs,* III, 64-65.

[8] MS. torn.

[9] See above, I, 999-1000; *House Docs.,* 17 Cong., 1 Sess., no. 131, pp. 43-44.

[10] Russell's statement is not correct. The communication of November 26, 1814, from the British Commissioners had included a provision concerning navigation of the Mississippi; and when the subject was taken up by the American Commissioners on November 28, "Mr. Clay lost his temper, as he generally does whenever this right of the British to navigate the Mississippi is discussed." Adams, *Memoirs,* III, 71.

[11] Again, Russell's statement is incorrect. At the conclusion of the discussion of November 28, "It became necessary to determine by a vote whether Mr. Gallatin's proposal to offer an article making the navigation an equivalent for the fisheries should be adopted, and it was determined that it should." The discussion of Gallatin's draft, on the following day, "was now on all sides good-humored." *Ibid.,* 75.

On December 1, before joining the British for a conference arranged for that day, the Americans met and agreed upon a mode of procedure. To this meeting Gallatin brought "a minute of the alterations and amendments which we wish to obtain to the British projet, and an article for restoring the British rights to navigate the Mississippi, and our right to the fisheries within the British jurisdiction." During the conference with the British negotiators, Adams presented the American argument concerning fisheries and navigation of the Mississippi. *Ibid.,* 75, 79, 84-85.

[12] Above, II, 72-80.

[13] William H. Crawford.

[14] On November 29 Russell had produced a letter from Crawford urging "in very strong terms objections against granting the navigation of the Mississippi as an equivalent for the fisheries, and had used the same arguments against it as those he had adduced." *Ibid.,* 76.

[15] *House Docs.,* 17 Cong., 1 Sess., no. 131, pp. 35-36.

[16] *Ibid.,* 40.

[17] "Mr. Russell's Reply to Mr. Adams," published in the Boston *American Statesman,* June 27, 1822, reprinted in Washington *Daily National Intelligencer,* July 3, 1822, and in Adams, *Duplicate Letters,* 119-37.

[18] Adams' actual statement had been that, under a mutual surrender of the fisheries and the navigation of the Mississippi, "we should have surrendered, in direct violation of our instructions, a real, existing, practical liberty . . . ; while the British would have surrendered absolutely nothing—a right which, by inference from their own principle, was abrogated by the war; a right which, under the treaty of 1783, they had enjoyed for thirty years, without ever using it, and which, in all human probability,

never would have been of more beneficial use to the British nation, than would be to the people of the United States the right of navigating the Bridgewater Canal, or the Danube." *House Docs.*, 17 Cong., 1 Sess., no.131, p. 51.

19 William Eustis. 20 MS. torn.

To Stephen F. Austin

SIR Lexington 7 June 1822.

I beg leave to introduce to you Mr. Elijah Noble who is attracted to Texas by the advantages which its fine soil, climate and cheap hands [*sic*] are supposed to offer. Mr. Noble is associated with other Citizens of this State who contemplate a removal thither, if the results of his present visit shall seem to favor their enterprize.[1] I have no doubt that they would prove a valuable addition to the population of the province; and I shall be obliged by your rendering to Mr. Noble every facility towards the accomplishment of his object which may be in your power

I have the honor to be Your ob. Servant H. CLAY.

Stephen F. Austin Esqr.

Eugene C. Barker (ed.), *The Austin Papers,* Part I (American Historical Association, *Annual Report . . . for the Year 1919,* II [Washington, 1924]), 526.

1 Noble resided in Lexington in the 1830's.

To Return Jonathan Meigs

Dr Sir (Confidential) Frankfort 8h. June 1822.

I seize an hours leisure from my professional engagements here to acknowledge the receipt of your obliging favor of the 20h. Ulto.[1] for the contents of which I offer you my sincere thanks. I concur with you in thinking that the name of any individual ought not to be prematurely thrust on the public notice, for the high office to which you refer. It is offensive and indiscreet in every possible aspect of the subject. And I think that any recommendation, by a public body, now or heretofore, of a suitable character for that office would be liable to that objection. On the other hand, one's friends ought not to delay bringing his pretensions into public view so long as to expose them to the danger of being forgotten or obscured. Some of mine think that the next winter will be a proper time to announce me by Legislative nominations; and that Ohio, if she is favorable to the object (as she is believed to be) had better begin those recommendations. What think you of that? In this State, there is great ardor and almost perfect unanimity. You will be surprized when you hear of some names, amongst us, who are forward in my support. My information from other parts of the West is also highly favorable and encouraging. My effort will be, as it has been, to repress any premature expression of public sentiment here, through the Legislative organ, and particularly to prevent this State being the first to declare itself in my favor.

An effort has been making to produce a diversion in the West favorable to Mr. Calhoun, but it has been unattended with any success; and I am greatly deceived if there is not ultimately a zealous and animated unanimity for me in this quarter.

I have been finally prevailed upon to consent to offer for Congress in the District in which I reside, and my name is now before the public. I am not aware of any opposition, actual or intended. It so happened, in the recent arrangement of the Districts, that no one of the present members was left in that in which I live.[2]

I shall be glad to hear from you occasionally, when your leisure will permit you to write.

Mr Meigs With great regard I am faithfy Yours H. CLAY

ALS. NcD. 1 Not found.

2 Under the Congressional reapportionment following the Fourth Census, 1820, Kentucky had acquired two additional representatives. Clay's candidacy had been announced in the Lexington *Kentucky Reporter,* June 3, 1822. See below, Clay to Porter, August 10, 1822.

To John White

Sir Frankfort 8 June 1822

I received a letter from you[1] when I was last at the City of Washington, respecting the protested bill of T [*sic*] W Hawkins on Sproul,[2] which I would have answered from that place, but that I was not in possession of the requisite information to enable me satisfactorily to reply to you. The bill, before the Law concerns of the Bank were committed to me, was placed in the hands of another professional gentleman, who brought suits upon it against the parties, but was subsequently compelled to suffer nonsuits. During my attendance on the Courts here, I have endeavored to acquire all the information I could about the bill and the parties, and I have this day possessed myself of the bill itself.

It is alleged by Mr Harvie[3] (the only responsible name on the bill) that a previous bill having been drawn on Finley and Vanlear,[4] this was sent on to them to be sold and the proceeds applied to the payment of that, on its maturity; that Finley and Vanlear could not negotiate it, and that the first bill was therefore protested, returned and taken up. Thus Finley and V. had no property in this bill but were the mere agents of the drawer. Still, if they had passed it off, on their own account, in a regular negotiation, there is no doubt that the parties to the bill would be now responsible to the innocent holder. But Mr Harvie alleges that it never was negotiated by F. & V.

but that it was only lodged at the office in Baltimore to be sent on to that at N. Orleans for collection on a/c of F and V.; and Mr. Harvie has shewn me several of their letters which tend to prove that statement.

If the Bank recd. the bill only for collection, it must be considered as standing in the character of an agent for F. and V.; and it would not be competent for the Bank afterwards to change, on its own separate will, that relation, and convert itself into a proprietor of the bill. Now, assuming the above statements of Mr Harvie to be correct, it is very clear that F and V. could not recover on the bill. And it follows that their agent could not. Upon their failure, the Bank might justifiably retain the bill as a collateral security, but it could not, in that state of things, vary the nature of the obligation of the parties to F. and V.

If the Bank has given credit to the Bill, in whole or in part, by negotiating it, or advancing money in faith of it, a recovery may be had of the parties, supposing (as I presume to be the fact) that notice of the protest &c has been regularly given.

I have thought it best to make this communication to you before suit is brought, that you may give such further directions as may be thought best. There is time enough for me to hear from you and have the suit ready for trial at the November term, the earliest at which it would be ready, if it were ordered without my communicating with you.

The indorsements on the bill are said to prove that, according to Bank usage, it never was negotiated by the Bank of the U. S.– The indorsement of F. and V. being in blank, and the bill transmitted in *that* state, without being filled up, to the office at N Orleans Of any such usage you will be the most competent judge.

I am Your ob. Servt. H. CLAY

John White Esqr. Cashr &c &c &c

ALS. DLC-HC (DNA, M212, R1). White was cashier of the Baltimore branch of the Bank of the United States.

[1] Not found.

[2] James W. Hawkins, postmaster of Frankfort, Kentucky; Charles Sproule, also of Franklin County. See below, Clay to White, June 3, 1823.

[3] John Harvie, who had come to Kentucky from Virginia in 1813 and had settled in Frankfort three years later, had been made president of the Bank of Kentucky in December, 1820. He held this post for nearly a decade and later served briefly in the State legislature. He died in 1838, having long been a warm friend of Clay.

[4] Thomas Findley and John Van Lear.

To Langdon Cheves

Sir Lexington 16h. June 1822.

I duly received your letter of the 30h Ulto.[1] transmitting to me a Copy of the mortgage of John H. Piatt to the Bank of the U. States, and a letter from his administrators[2] making certain propositions to the Bank; and requesting my opinion upon those propositions, and also upon several points and questions suggested in your letter.

Having considered the several subjects refered to me, I will first state what I understand to be the Law, applicable to the case of Mr. Piatt, on the various points which you have suggested for my consideration, and in the order in which you have stated them. The law of Ohio is not, in relation to the office of Administrator, essentially variant from that of England. In both Countries, either the Heir or Administrator may redeem mortgaged estate, by paying the debt which it was pledged to secure. In neither can the Administrator *release* the equity of redemption, which passes, upon the death of the mortgagor, to his heir, unless it be devised by his will. I do not, indeed, understand the admors of Mr. Piatt to assume a power in themselves to release the equity of redemption; they speak of having consulted "with the widow and heirs, who have consented, by their advice" &c, and no doubt intended, if the proposition submitted should be acceded to, that it should be effectuated by suitable conveyances from the proper parties. I do not know the family of the late Mr. Piatt. I have understood generally that he left no children, but that he has brothers and perhaps sisters who survived him. These brothers and sisters, and the issue of such of them as are dead, if there be any dead, will be his heirs at law. Should the Heirs comply with the proposition of the Administrators, and release to the Bank the equity of redemption in the mortgaged property, I think the other Creditors of Mr. Piatt could, within reasonable time hereafter, come in and redeem it Upon the release of the equity of redemption, effected by proper conveyances, executed by proper parties, to the Bank, it will become vested with the absolute Estate; and if it were subsequently to sell and convey it to a purchaser, I do not think that the Creditors would be able to pursue the Estate in the hands of such purchaser. But still they might compel the Bank to account for the real value of the Estate, and, if that exceeded the amount of the mortgage debts, with interest &c; [*sic*] to pay the excess. Mrs. Piatt having relinquished her right of dower in the Estate mortgaged, can have no legal claim to one third of the rents and profits of it either during her life, or the term of five years proposed by the Administrators. I do not understand them as advancing any such claim, as a legal claim. Their proposition to that effect seems to be founded upon the notion that you will have to encounter certain unavoidable delays, in foreclosing the mortgage; and that, in the mean time, the representatives of Mr. Piatt will have the right to receive and appropriate to themselves the rents and profits. To what extent this notion is correct will be seen hereafter.

If after having completed the proposed arrangement with the Admors and Heirs, and allowed the widow to receive, during the term of five years, one third of the rents and profits, should the creditors come in and claim to redeem the Estate, will the Bank be chargeable with the amount which had been so received by the widow? It would be very clear that what she had thus received, if the Estate be incompetent to pay all its debts, ought to have been applied to the satisfaction of the Creditors. But I incline to think that the Bank would not be liable to them, but that the widow herself would be, for what she had received.

What are the rights of the Bank as to the rents and income of mortgaged property? Upon filing a bill to foreclose the Equity of redemption, and suggesting in it the incompetency of the Estate to pay the debt for which it is pledged, I think the Chancellor would appoint a receiver to receive the rents and profits, pending the suit, or enjoin the tenants from paying them over to the Representatives of the mortgagor. The mortgagee has a right, at the same time, to file a bill of foreclosure, and to bring an action of ejectment against the tenant in possession. Upon recovery in this action, the tenant would I think be liable for the mesne profits, by a prosecution of the usual remedy, from the time of the ouster laid in the declaration. Thus, I think, the Bank is invested with a double remedy to prevent the perception and appropriation to their own use of the rents and profits, by the representatives of Mr. Piatt and the tenants in possession. Either remedy accomplishing its object would, of course, preclude the final enforcement of the other. The rents and profits which are received *prior* to the commencement commencement [*sic*] of suit or prior to notice from the Bank to the tenants in possession not to pay them, I do not think the Bank will have any specific lien upon. They may be liable, in the hands of the persons receiving them, to the creditors of Mr. Piatt generally, including the Bank.

There are two modes practised in Ohio to foreclose mortgages; one is provided for in the Statutes of that State, by Scire facias, and the other is the common proceeding by bill in Chancery. The delay to which each is incident is about the same. A judgment or decree of foreclosure, I should think, may be obtained in one year, that is to say if the proceeding be commenced, for example, to the approaching September term, by the September term twelve-month, the decree may be procured. The Bank may immediately proceed to foreclose for what is now due, without waiting 'till the maturity of the other instalments; and the Chancellor will, as they successively become due, make such decretal orders as may be necessary to the purposes of justice. I do not think the expence of foreclosure, if the remedy by bill in equity alone be adopted, will exceed $100; and if the Bank bring both ejectments and a bill in Chancery, the whole cost will not probably amount to five hundred.dollars. Should the Bank be inclined to agree to the proposal made to it, under all circumstances I would recommend, as the safest course, that a bill be filed to foreclose the equity of redemption; and to sell the mortgaged property. The very trifling expence, which would attend this proceeding, is not to be weighed against the security which would be derived from it against the future claims of all persons, creditors and others.

Having thus treated of the Law applicable to the case, I will now express my opinion of the proposition itself. My information, in regard to the condition of the Estate of Mr. Piatt, is not as full as that, no doubt, is which Mr. Jones[3] possesses and has communicated to the Bank. From what I have understood of it, I should think it would be as well for the Bank to receive the mortgaged property in full discharge of the debt, provided immediate possession of the whole property is given, and the accruing rents and profits are allowed to come to the Bank. A suit in Chy., such as I have suggested, could then be instituted to perfect and quiet the title. But this is not what has been proposed. The proposition is, a surrender of the whole Estate, coupled with the condition that the widow shall receive, during the term of five years, one third of the rents and profits of it. So far as this condition is founded upon any right in the widow to dower, it has been seen that it cannot be sustained. So far as it has been proposed upon the supposition, either that the Bank has no right to sue until the *whole* instalments are due, or that certain delays would attend the prosecution of a suit, during which the representatives of Mr. Piatt might receive the rents and profits upon the entire estate, it has been also seen that there is no support for it. If the condition is placed upon the claim which the widow of an enterprizing and unfortunate man, suddenly cut off in the prime of his life, has upon the generous consideration of the Bank, I have nothing to say against it. The Bank is the most competent and fitting measurer of its own charities.

Finally, if all compromise be unattainable, I would advise 1st. That notice, in writing, be so given to the several tenants in possession of the mortgaged premises as to be susceptible of proof hereafter, forbidding them to make payment of any rent *now* due or which shall become due, to the representatives of Mr. Piatt; and requiring them to pay all such rent to the Bank.

2dly. That a bill in equity be forthwith filed to foreclose the equity of redemption, and to have a sale decreed of the mortgaged premises. And that at the next term of the Court an injunction be applied for to restrain payment of the rents to any but the Bank, and to appoint a receiver &c. And

3dly. That Ejectments be also brought, returnable to the next

Court, against all tenants who refuse to pay the rent to the Bank and who will not now attorn to the Bank.

I presume Mr. Jones is invested already, by power of Attorney duly executed under the Seal of the Corporation, with authority to enter upon Lands to which the Bank is entitled, to take possession thereof, and to lease them out &c. If he is not possessed of such authority, he ought to be furnished with it— I will observe, by the way, that a similar authority is necessary in respect to the offices in this State.

In respect to the lien and effect of Judgments in the State of Ohio, the Legislature at its last Session passed a law which commenced its operation on the first day of this month.[4] The Law of that State at present is this, Lands are bound by the Judgment from the first day of the term at which it was rendered, that is all the lands lying within the County where such judgment is recovered; and all lands in other Counties and goods and chattels from the time they are seized in execution. If the Judgment creditor neglect for one year, next after the first day of the term at which such judgment was rendered, to sue out execution thereon and cause it to be levied, the judgment loses its lien upon the debtors Estate, so far as other bona fide judgment creditors are concerned. No other circumstance, short of actual satisfaction of the debt, will affect or destroy the lien incident to judgments.

Real estate, when taken in execution, must be appraised by five freeholders, resident within the County where it is situated, who are required on oath to make an estimate of the actual value in money of the Estate, and it is not to be sold unless it will command two thirds of such estimated value. When real estate has been so appraised, and two ineffectual attempts have been made to sell it, the Court is bound on motion to set aside the appraisement, at the cost of the plaintiff, who is authorized to proceed to have a second appraisement. The lien remains unimpaired. The Law of valuation is permanent in regard to Lands. It does not apply to mortgages or deeds of trust. It has not been decided whether Judgments in the Federal Court only bind lands within the County, where that Court happens to hold its Sessions. The reason of the limitation, in regard to State tribunals, arises out of the limitation of jurisdiction to the respective Counties. No such reason being applicable to the Federal Court my opinion is that the Judgments of that Court will bind co extensively with its jurisdiction.

I have again, as I have done frequently heretofore, pressed the Agents of the Bank at Cincinnati to prepare for the trial of its Causes at the next term of the Federal Court; and I have every reason to hope that your wishes, on that subject, will be fulfilled.

I have also received your letters of the 25h. and 31st. of May respecting the business of Mr. Marshall.[5] You will perceive, by a letter which must have reached you about this time, that the debt of McClanahan and Bogart[6] had engaged my attention. I have found Mr. Marshall inflexible in his resolution not to except that debt from the general arrangement which he proposed; and, in his last conversation with me, he said, that if all arrangement were defeated, and the Bank should press McC. and B. he would place the means of their indemnity in their hands out of the funds which he designed for the Bank. I shall not close the arrangement with Mr. Marshall until I hear from you in reply to my last communication. I believe better terms than I have there mentioned cannot be procured; and I believe it for the interest of the Bank to accept them rather than depend upon the precarious fruits of coercive measures. Still the property offered is of such a description, and objectionable in character as it is, falls so far short of the aggregate amount of debt proposed to be extinguished, that I have some reluctance in making the compromise. This reluctance is somewhat increased by the office at Louisville persisting in the belief that the Marshalls are good for their responsibilities at that place. I believe my own information, as to their actual condition, is superior to that which is possessed at that office, and it obliges me to adopt a widely different conclusion. Feeling myself in the predicament which I have described, I shall be glad to learn from you as soon as possible, if the views of the Board have undergone any change since the receipt at Philadelphia of my last communications on this subject.[7] I have the honor to be with great respect Your obedient Servant H. Clay

Langdon Cheves Esqr. &c &c &c.

P.S. I have according to your request sent to Mr. Jones at Cincinnati a Copy of this letter. And I have also sent to him a form of the notice to the tenants of the Mortgaged property, which I have advised him to cause to be served upon them immediately. It will do no prejudice, if you complete the compromise. H.C.

ALS. PHi-Dreer Collection. 1 Not found.

2 The letter not found. In February, 1822, Piatt had died at a boarding house in Washington, where he had gone to press for payment by the Government on his claims as an Army contractor during the War of 1812. His brother, Benjamin M., and Nicholas Longworth, both Cincinnati lawyers, served as administrators of the estate. Benjamin M., with Abraham S. Piatt, probably another brother; Hannah C. Grandin, a sister; Philip Grandin, a brother-in-law and prominent Cincinnati businessman; and Mrs. Frances Dunn, probably another sister, a resident of Lawrenceburg, Indiana, constituted the heirs at law. The mortgage to the Bank of the United States covered the property on Broadway known as the Cincinnati Hotel, erected by Piatt and at this time the town's leading hostelry, which subsequently became the object of litigation in the suit, Robert Piatt *vs.* Charles Vattier and Others and the Bank of the United States, 34 *U.S.* (9 Peters) 405-16 (1835).

This case, which was not initiated until December, 1827, indicates that the President and Directors of the Bank of the United States acquired possession of the property through a mortgage which had been executed in 1820. It was foreclosed, with conveyance of a quitclaim deed in 1823, under proceedings (not found) to which Clay here refers. As an accompaniment of the transaction the Bank paid the widow $11,000 for release of her dower rights. On the temporary arrangement relating to interim handling of this property, see below, Clay to Cheves, September 13, 1822.

3 Earlier in the year George W. Jones, later president of the Cincinnati Savings Institution, had been named agent of the Bank of the United States in Cincinnati.

4 Ohio Gen. Assy., *Acts, General, 1821-1822,* pp. 62-65 (February 2, 1822).

5 John J. Marshall. Letters not found. See above, Clay to Cheves, October 26, 1821.

6 Firm not found—probably Thomas McClanahan and James L. Bogert, Louisville commission merchants.

7 Not found.

From [Samuel B.] G[oddar]d

Hon. Henry Clay Lexington Kentucky 17th June 1822

Sir

I have the honor to acknowledge the receipt of your letter of the 19th ultimo[1] upon the subject of late Pay Master Charles Carr's account[2] and by the same mail I also received his vouchers to which your letter alludes, they have been examined & the result communicated to him at Frankfort. An authenticated Transcript of the present statement of his account which embraces the vouchers above mentioned has been furnished the Agent of the Treasury— GD.

Copy. DNA, RG217, Records of the 3rd Auditor, Misc. Letters Sent, vol. 26, p. 90. Goddard was a clerk in the office of the Third Auditor in the United States Treasury Department.

1 Not found.

2 According to the records of the Treasury Department, Carr, who had been paymaster to William Dudley's regiment of Kentucky militia in the War of 1812, had been, in 1820, still indebted to the United States for $39,884.37. His accounts were then under examination and he claimed already to have refunded the balance, which by June, 1821, had been reduced to $5,321.50. A suit instituted against him in Federal Court early in 1822 had been continued to the Fall Term, when the plaintiff was awarded the sum of $914.04 yet due, plus interest at six per cent per annum until paid, and the costs of litigation. *House Docs.,* 16 Cong., 2 Sess., no. 32, p. 29; U.S. District Court, Kentucky, Order Book H, 242. See below, Clay to Hagner, October 4, 1823.

To Langdon Cheves

Sir Lexington 19h. June 1822

The Territorial Government of Arkansas, thinking it just and expedient to spread the very heavy expence incident to the commencement of its operations over several years, and to divide it between the present inhabitants, and emigrants who may arrive there here after, instead of making an immediate provision for the whole of it, by imposing a tax upon the present inhabitants exclusively, to be collected within one year, has authorized, by an act passed in October last, a loan to be effected by the Governor of Ten thousand dollars. Robert Crittenden Esqr.[1] the Secretary of the Territory, now in this State, is authorized to contract for this loan,

and, at his request, I take great pleasure in recommending the application which he intends making, for that purpose, to the Bank of the U.S., to your favorable consideration. Mr. Crittenden is a gentleman of strict honor, in whom you may put entire confidence; and I should be extremely glad, should the Bank be not absolutely discouraged by its experience of Western Loans, if it would accommodate the Territory of Arkansas, whose rich staple production will, doubtless, enable it, without the least inconvenience, to reimburse the Loan, in strict conformity to the terms which Mr. Crittenden may stipulate. I am, with great respect, Your obedient Servant
Langdon Cheves Esq. President of the B. U. S. H. CLAY

ALS. PHC-Charles Roberts Autograph Collection.
[1] Brother of John J. and Thomas T. Crittenden. Robert, a young Kentucky lawyer, had been appointed Territorial Secretary March 3, 1819, and served in that capacity and as acting Governor of the Territory until 1829. He remained a resident of Arkansas, head of a powerful, anti-Jacksonian political organization, until his death in 1834.

From Eugenio Cortés

The honorable Henry Clay: Philadelphia 19th of June 1822

I have the honor to deliver to you the inclosed letter from the Supreme Chief of the Mexican Empire,[1] who directed me to present it to you personally, as a testimony of the gratitude, esteem, and distinction which the Supreme Chief of the Mexican nation entertains for the virtues, talents and Services displayed by you in favor of the just cause Sustained by all the States of South America to gain their independence.

This occasion affords me the opportunity of offering to you my respects and of assuring you that I am your most faithful and obedient Servant. Q. B. S. M. EUGENIO CORTES

Copy. DLC-HC (DNA, M212, R1). Published in Colton (ed.), *Private Correspondence of Henry Clay,* 65.
[1] See above, Itúrbide to Clay, May 6, 1822.

Rental Agreement with James Minter

[June 20, 1822]

[Under an agreement entered into June 20, 1822, Henry Clay leases to James Minter the property in Lexington known as the Tammany Mills, including the mill house and other buildings on the lots as they are now enclosed, for the term of seven years commencing on January 1, 1823. Clay is to give Minter immediate possession of the property, except that "Mr. Loney"[1] may occupy the house in which he is now dwelling, for the period of two months, "to enable him to look out and provide himself with another residence." Minter is at liberty to take down the house formerly used as an engine house and, in lieu thereof, to erect a shed, "or covering for a horse power," provided that he does no damage to the principal building, heretofore used as a mill house. The expense attendant to these alterations and all other repairs to the property during the term aforesaid is to be borne by Minter, unless a new roof should be needed, as provided under the following arrangement: if during the term of this agreement a new roof should be deemed necessary in the opinion of two persons, one to be chosen by each of the parties, and their umpire, Clay is to bear the cost. It is further agreed that if Minter, for his own accommodation, should erect any wooden buildings on the property, except the above-mentioned shed "for the Horse Power," he is at liberty to remove them at the end of the rental period, provided that no injury is thereby done to Clay. Clay reserves the right to remove the stones and other articles belonging to the mills now on the premises. Minter further covenants, at the end of the term, to surrender the premises to Clay in good tenantable order, natural decay and inevitable accidents excepted, with the lots enclosed "by a good substantial board fence." In consideration of the above premises Minter agrees that during each and every year of the term commencing January 1, 1823, the sum of $300, lawful money of the United States is to be paid, one half on the first day of July and the other half on the first day of January of each year. He is not to sell or assign this lease to any other person, without Clay's assent; and Clay reserves the right to distrain, re-enter, and take possession of the premises in case of default in Minter's payments. Minter's signature acknowledged June 20 and Clay's on June 22, 1822, before J. C. Rodes, Clerk of Fayette County.]

Fayette County Court, Deed Book V, 453-54. Minter was proprietor of the short-lived Hamilton Cotton Factory, located at his residence, five miles east of Lexington on the Boonesborough road. While he conducted some operations at the Tammany Mills site as late as 1825, the bulk of his equipment remained at the Hamilton factory when financial difficulties engulfed him at the latter date.

1 Thomas Loney.

From Amos Kendall

Dear Sir Frankfort June 20th 1822

Herewith you will receive the sheets[1] which I was preparing while you were here. You will find it somewhat enlarged and I think greatly improved. But do not hesitate to make any alteration you or your friends may think proper. I have no pride of authorship in it—all I wish is, that it may effectually answer the purpose. Alter or suppress it as with your views.

I have just heard read a letter from Richmond Va. to Robt Triplett.[2] I know not the writer; but he avows himself your friend in the next election. According to his representations Mr. Russells letters and Mr. Adams' strictures[3] have produced unutterable disgust towards [the] former and a favorable sentiment towards the latter. Many, he says, who were before opposed to Mr. Adams now declare for him; and there is some suspicion in some minds, that you had a hand in bringing forth these documents, which is calculated to injure you. He thinks it would be useful to you to disavow any agency in the business, or cause it to be done by your friends. Ritchie,[4] he says, is for Crawford, and he thinks the same of Judge Roane,[5] but of the latter he does not speak positively. From a conversation with Jefferson, he thinks, he is for Lowndes;[6] but is not certain. Virginia, he says, would be satisfied with yourself, Crawford or Adams; but he thinks the election will be decided in Congress.

I state these things merely for your information, without giving an opinion. If you wish to state any facts to the public, command my pen or my paper.

You have something to apprehend at home. The *Relief party* are very jealous of you.[7] It is important that this jealousy should not break out into public expression and criticism. I am considered rather the advocate of the *power* under which they act, than of the *policy* of many of their measures. Many of them have been jealous of me, because I have not gone the *whole;* but there is no danger of their discarding me. In this situation I can do much to suppress their jealousy of you, by shewing that in case of a break with you, they would be divided. But this cannot be done in public.

You are the centre of information relative to your distant prospects. If you think proper, I should like a free communication with you on the subject, that I may shape my course in such a manner as best to accomplish the great end. Give my compliments to Mrs. Clay and my regards to your family. If I can assist you now, it will be some compensation to your estimable lady for the kindness she exhibited towards me when I was moneyless, friendless and powerless.[8] Your friend &c. AMOS K[ENDALL]

P.S. I forgot to observe that if the [. . .][9] production be published at Chillicothe or C[incinna]ti it would be important to have it copied as m[y] handwriting is known to many persons in those places and to some of the printers. It may be divided into numbers to suit the convenience of the printer.

ALS. DLC-HC (DNA, M212, R1). Document is badly faded.

1 Not found. They were comprised of a series of four letters, addressed "To the People of Ohio," which appeared over the signature "Wayne" during the fall of 1822 in the *Liberty Hall and Cincinnati Gazette,* then edited by Isaac G. Burnet (founder of the Dayton *Ohio Centinel* in 1810 and in 1826 mayor of Cincinnati). Extensively revised and reprinted by Kendall in the Frankfort *Argus of Western America,* October 31, November 7, 14, 21, 1822, they stressed the interest of Ohio in support

by the Federal government for internal improvements such as the National Road and the proposed Ohio Canal, cited the opposition to such works previously demonstrated by Presidents Madison and Monroe, and analyzed the stand of the prospective presidential candidates on this and other issues deemed important to the West. John Quincy Adams was particularly censured for his stand during the Ghent negotiations relative to the British right of navigation on the Mississippi and for his abandonment of the United States' claim to Texas in the Florida Treaty. Only Clay among contenders for the Presidency was deemed representative of Ohio's peculiar interests. Yet his appeal was not found limited to Ohio: a universal feeling of friendship toward him required only the impulse of Ohio endorsement to set rolling his wave of support. Ohio must speak quickly, or the voice of popular approval would be lost amidst the clamor set up by "some triumphant chief" of a partisan corps.

2 Of Frankfort, Kentucky, where he served as attorney for numerous Virginians holding property claims in Kentucky. From 1825 to 1827 he held appointment as agent for the State of Virginia to superintend settlement of the grants of military bounty lands southwest of the Tennessee River, in Kentucky.

3 See above, Russell to Clay, June 6, 1822.

4 Thomas Ritchie.

5 Spencer Roane.

6 Thomas Jefferson; William Lowndes.

7 Those Kentuckians who advocated the relief legislation of 1819-1822. See above, II, 904n; Clay to Dougherty, December 7, 1821, note.

8 See above, II, 54n.

9 Possibly two words torn out.

To Langdon Cheves

Sir Lexn. 23 June 1822.

Will you have the goodness to direct to be placed to my credit, with the Cashier of your Bank, fifteen hundred dollars, the half year's compensation which it allows me, payable on the first of the next month?[1] When I had the pleasure of seeing you at Philada.[2] I understood from you that it would be ágreeable to the Bank to pay it semi annually. Under the expectation that this would be done, I have checked for a part, and shall shortly for the residue. I have the honor to be with great respect Your obedient Servant H. CLAY

Langdon Cheves Esqr. President &c &c. &c.

ALS. PHi-Etting Collection.

1 Endorsement by Assistant Cashier indicates the sum was credited July 8, 1822.

2 In late March or early April. See above, Clay to Dougherty, April 3, 1822.

To Martin D. Hardin

Dr Sir Ashland 23d. June 1823 [*i.e.,* 1822].

I have sent my son[1] to Hawkins twice with Mr. Lewis's assignment to us.[2] He did not see him the first time, but he saw him yesterday, and he promised to come to the Clerk's office tomorrow and pay the amount of the assignment, upon satisfying himself of the affirmation of the judgment.

I thank you for your friendly communication, under date the 20h. instant,[3] founded upon the letter received by Mr Triplett from Virginia.[4] With respect to Mr. Russell's letter, I had nothing upon earth to do with its composition, nor any concern whatever, direct or indirect, in the recent call which has been made upon the Executive for it. I did not know that such a letter was in existence; and I will add, that, if I had known it, I would not have called for it, nor, if I had been the President, would I have communicated such a private document to Congress. With respect to the suspicions that I have had an agency in the production of that letter, they are unworthy of me; nor can I condescend myself, or permit any friend for me, to make a public disavowal of any participation in it. Such suspicions if persisted in could only, I think, originate from a predisposition to assail me. I am persuaded that if they have been seriously entertained, by any one at Richmond or elsewhere, that they must have been hastily and inconsiderately suggested, and that, upon further reflection, their injustice will be apparent. I think it would display too great a sensitiveness on my part to take any sort of notice of them at present. I certainly felt very grateful to Mr. Russell for his concurrence with me in opposing, at Ghent, the proposition respecting the navigation of the Mississippi; and his whole conduct, during the continuance of the mission, and since I have known him has inspired me with esteem for him. I must acknowledge, however, that I have seen with great surprize and regret the discrepancy between his original letter and the duplicate. He owes it to his own character to make a satisfactory explanation of that fact. After all, that is an affair exclusively personal to himself.

The family of Capt. Smith, as you may suppose, are highly gratified with the favorable result of their cause.[5]

With great regard I am faithfly Yours H. CLAY

Genl. M. D. Hardin.

ALS. ICHi.

[1] Probably Theodore W. Clay.

[2] Case not found.

[3] Not found.

[4] See above, Kendall to Clay, June 20, 1822.

[5] Weathers (Withers) Smith, a Virginia veteran of the Revolution, had entered over 3,000 acres on Licking River and Stoner's Fork in Kentucky and subsequently had settled near Paris. Involved in extensive litigation by rival land claimants, he had been represented by Hardin, who had won a decision in the Kentucky Court of Appeals on June 12, 1822, rejecting an earlier judgment of the Bourbon Circuit Court relative to compensation for improvements after an order for eviction rendered against Smith in 1804. Weathers Smith *vs.* Daniel Hornback, 11 *Ky. Reports* (1 Littell) 272-73. Smith, who had died in December, 1813, was survived by his wife, Jane, four sons, and three daughters. Hornback was also a resident of Bourbon County.

To Amos Kendall

LEXINGTON, 23 June, 1822.

Dear Sir: I received your obliging favor of the 20th inst. and thank you most sincerely for the friendly sentiments towards me which it contains. Mr. T. Crittenden has retained the production which accompanied it, and which he has undertaken to divide, and to dispose of in his place of residence[1] according to our wishes.

I am also greatly obliged by your kind communication of the contents of the letter from Virginia. The effect produced at Richmond by the letters of Mr. Russell and the strictures of Mr. Adams, was the first impression. That it should have been unfavorable to the former, is quite natural. For undoubtedly Mr. R. owes it to his own character to explain, most satisfactorily, how the discrepancy has arisen between his original letter and the duplicate; and if he fail to vindicate himself, the prejudice to him must be permanent. With respect to the alleged suspicions that I have had some agency in bringing forth those letters, they are so unworthy of me, and are so unfounded themselves, that I do not think that I ought myself, or any friend for me, to take any public notice of them whatever. The truth is, that I did not know that such a letter was in existence; I would not have called for it, if I had known it; I would not have communicated to Congress such a private document, if I had been the President. I had myself not the slightest concern, direct or indirect, in the call for the letter. There is one reflection which must suggest itself to any person upon reading it, that it is calculated to make the impression that Mr. Russell, and not me, was the prominent person in opposing the Mississippi proposition. My name, or my opposition, is not, I believe, hinted at in the whole letter. Is it likely, therefore, that I should have been anxious to bring out a letter which thus keeps out of view my own strenuous opposition, and puts forward that of another? The sensation at Richmond must have been the result of indignant feeling excited by the disagreement between Mr. Russell's letters. However that may injure him, if he do not explain it, there ought to be no benefit nor prejudice to others arising from the circumstance.

Should these suspicions, so unjust towards me, assume a shape of more consequence hereafter, it will be time enough then to repel them. For your kind offer of your pen and your paper, I am infinitely obliged; and no doubt I shall have occasion for the friendly employment of both. I am aware of the jealousy, from a certain quarter, to which you refer. I am inclined to think with you, that it will not burst out upon me; but if it should not, I know that I shall be indebted for its restraint to yourself and other friends.

I will, without reserve, communicate freely to you any information that may be useful, in regard to the object on which my friends place so much solicitude. That which I am constantly receiving, is most encouraging. With great regard, I am faithfully yours, H. CLAY

A. KENDALL, Esq.

Frankfort *Argus of Western America,* July 9, 1828. Published also in Washington *United States Telegraph-Extra,* I (July 26, 1828), 318.

1 Cincinnati.

From Benjamin Owen Tyler

Dear Sir Washington June 24th 1822

Your polite letter of the 29th ult.[1] was duly recd. enclosing the prize ticket. the other ticket is yet in the wheel— The $100,000, 25000. 10.000 5000. 32 1000 &c are yet to be drawn—[2] only five more drawings and I sincerely wish you the $100,000—as it would do you more good than it would me. After one more drawing the lottery will be postponed six weeks to give time to sell the tickets before the 100,000 comes out. Draws the 26th.

As our friend Mr Dougherty[3] will hand you this letter I shall write more freely than I should were I writing by Mail. I assure you Sir without deigning to attempt to to [*sic*] flatter, that your prospects are every day brightening in this section, both North & East. A few days since I recd. a letter from *your sincere friend* Wm S. Cardell N.Y, [*who*][4] says "no man in this country ever gained popularity [fast]er than Mr Clay has of late. He has many very influential friends in this city. they think it best policy not to come out at present openly in the public papers but to pursue a still course until some of the other candidates have exhausted their ammunition—then open a battery upon them and take them by Storm. He further states that he believes that it would be worth to the U.S. $20,000,000 were you now President for the last 3 years of Mr Monroes administration in regard to South America. I am confident that no man can so strongly unite the interests of the East and West as yourself. I shall set out in about ten days on a tour with Mrs Tyler thro all the eastern States and the western part of the state of N.Y. and shall improve every opportunity to do all the good I can, and obtain all the information possible. I never put my hand to the plough and look back[.] As Mrs T. will accompany me I can best serve the cause by a prudent course, but at the same time with entire *confidence* of *success*. I have traveled thro' the country so much selling my Declaration of Independence[5] that I presume no man of my age in the U.S. has a more extensive acquaintance than myself and however small the real weight of my opinions, Yet I am confident that among the common class of people coming *from Washington* they will have more weight than they deserve. I presume you are well aware that the common and uninformed class of people at a distance, have a much more exalted opinion of their public officers and those who reside at Washington than they deserve, or Jimmy Monroe would never have been President— I recd. a letter a short time since from Mr Irvine, who is writing his book on S. America in Phia.[6] he says that he believes that Pa. will be almost unanimous in your favor

☞ Capt. Thomson[7] has this moment arrived here from Mexico—

you I presume will recollect he recd. an appointment as a Capt. in the Emperors life Guard. about the time you left here was one of Minas[8] men, he returns again in about six weeks. He was there when the Congress elected him (Iturbide) Emperor, he says all is tranquil, is much pleased with him, and says that it was the almost unanimous wish of the Congress that he should take the title of Emperor; not his own—ambition, He says when your name is mentioned it is like an electric fire. Capt Thomson says if you were now President of the U S you could obtain any thing you would ask for— Genl. Wilkinson is there—and expects he will yet be an important Personage there.[9] Capt. Thomson sends his best wishes to you for your utmost *success* and happiness, and will write you when he returns to Mexico. I expect Col. Bradburn[10] & Col. Cortez[11] here to be introduced to me every moment— Should I see them before I close this letter I will give you all the information I can obtain. Mr Dougherty starts in a few minutes therefore I hope you will excuse this blundering scrawl—as I am obliged to write in great haste. Thompson is highly pleased with Mexico and says that the Americans are very much respected there and Dams. the President for not sending out Ministers to Mexico & S America. While I think of it I will cut out two articles from the N.Y. Statesman on the last mentioned subject and enclose you. Why in Gods name the President does not send out Ministers none can tell. unless he is afraid of his own Damd. shadow. it is a subject of general conversation here and to the east. I shall be absent about 10 weeks. as soon as I return I write you all the *news*.

Very Respectfully your ever devoted friend B. O. TYLER

P.S. If you cannot translate this letter please apply to the professor of *Dead* Languages in Transylvania University or send it back to me. B O. Tyler

ALS. DLC-HC (DNA, M212, R1). Addressed to Clay at Lexington. Tyler, of Washington, D. C., a confectioner and liquor dealer, proprietor of a lottery office, and publisher, had recently issued "An elegant likeness of HENRY CLAY. . . ." Lexington *Kentucky Reporter*, June 3, 1822, advertisement reprinted from New York *Daily Advertiser*.

1 Not found.

2 See Tyler's advertisement of the Grand National Lottery, in Washington *Daily National Intelligencer*, June 20, 1822.

3 Thomas Dougherty, whose home was in Flemingsburg, Kentucky, died in Lexington, August 9, 1822.

4 MS. faded.

5 In April, 1818, Tyler had published an engraving of the Declaration of Independence, priced at five dollars on paper, seven dollars on parchment. Washington *Daily National Intelligencer*, April 2, 1818.

6 Baptis Irvine, *On the Commerce of South America, A Canal at Darien* (Philadelphia, 1822).

7 Probably William Thompson.

8 Francisco Xavier Mina.

9 In March, 1822, James Wilkinson had gone to Mexico, where he died December 28, 1825.

10 John Davis Bradburn, a Kentuckian who had served in Mina's forces and subsequently remained in the Mexican Army. His harsh measures in 1832, as commander

of the garrison at Anahuac, on Galveston Bay, precipitated conflict with the Texas colonists which culminated in their revolt from Mexico.

11 Eugenio Cortés.

From Andrew Hynes

Dear Sir, Nashl. June 30. 1822.

I had the pleasure of of [*sic*] receiving your letter of the 23d. instant[1] by the last mail, and have to state that Gov. Carroll has recd. the letter addressed to him by you with much satisfaction, and that he has sent a reply by this days mail.[2] He regretted that you should have felt any solicitude on account of postage.

You will have the opinions of the Gov. in regard to the Politics of this state, in which I Coincide. We have not yet made any public movement in your favour, but we have not been idle with the general mass of the people: and when their opinions are formed, it will not be easy for any others to supercede you in their esteem; and I have no doubt, but public sentiment will Carry the whole of the electors in your favour.

The Gov. from his popularity and being so immediately associated & Connected with the members of our Legislature, will have a great opportunity of making favorable impressions with them. He can Confirm the wavering—Soften opposition, and win over those who may be indifferent about an opinion. The election being so distant, that no zeal or anxiety ought to be manifested, and [*sic*] I think that silent perseverance the best Course.

The Gov. has intimated to you the possibility of Genl. Jackson being a Candidate. In that event, it will alter the affairs of this state in a material manner. When I addressed you last winter, we had no idea that he would have any pretensions, or that his name would be thought of for President It is now necessary to apprize you, that our situation in regard to him is so delicate, *that we would not willingly be opposed to him under any Circumstances.*

I think that Mr. Adams and others will be very glad to have more than *one* gentleman held up to public attention in the West as Candidates, as a division among ourselves would weaken, if not destroy the chance of either succeeding: and it may be, that Genl. J. has had overtures, not so much with a view of promoting his elevation, as to subserve an Eastern or Northern interest: which by Creating a division in the west, would be the most effectual means of destroying our influence.

Should Genl. Jackson's name be run, *our state pride,* will most probably induce us to support our own citizen in preference to any other, provided he had a probable chance of success; and it will be a great matter, in an election of such Consequence, for the people to believe their Candidate will be successful, (toward getting their votes), as none of them will be willing to vote for a man whom they thought ha[d] no prospect of succeeding. I believe it very natural for the weak to Combine with the strong, and if there should be a caucus nomination among th[e] members of congress, there will be much bartering of interests among the small states with the great. Colo. Cannon[3] has said to Gov. Carroll since his return[4] that you are the strongest man before Congress. When you are elected to Congress, you can consider if it be for your interest to be re-elected Speaker— will it not be gratifying to Virginia to retain that honor?

I will be happy at all times to hear from you and am most respectfully Your friend ANDW. HYNES

ALS. DLC-HC (DNA, M212, R1). Addressed to Clay at Lexington; postmarked at Nashville, Tennessee. Hynes was an early Nashville merchant and manufacturer of copper and tinware, elected in 1820 as president of the Farmers and Mechanics' Bank of Nashville. He had been associated with Andrew Jackson during the latter's military expeditions of 1813 and 1814 and had encouraged the General's presidential aspirations in the fall of 1815. See Hynes to Jackson, October 24, 1815, in Bassett (ed.), *Correspondence of Andrew Jackson*, II, 219.

1 Not found.

2 Neither Clay's letter to William Carroll nor the reply has been found.

3 Newton Cannon.

4 From Congress.

Property Deed to John Brand

[July 1, 1822]

[For the sum of $220, current money of Kentucky, paid and acknowledged, Henry Clay and Arthur Patterson, the latter a resident of Shelby County, Kentucky, convey to John Brand three quarters of an undivided tract of thirteen and a half acres on the waters of Cane Run, bounded beginning at Richardson Allen's corner, thence N 20° E 177 poles to an ash and red oak, thence S 70° W 24 poles to a hackberry, thence S 10° 32′ W 80 poles to the beginning, with the appurtenances. General warranty of title. Signed by Clay and Patterson, with an endorsement: "The within deed is made by my Consent 21st. August 1822," signed by Patrick Vance[1] and attested by Waller Rodes.[2] Patterson's signature attested by James S. Whitaker, Clerk of Shelby County, August 31, 1822; Clay's, by J. C. Rodes, Clerk of Fayette County, September 4, 1822.]

Fayette County Court, Deed Book W, 20-21.

1 A resident of the northern district of Fayette County.

2 Brother of James C. Rodes. Among the Fayette County offices filled by Waller Rodes were those of Deputy County Clerk, Deputy Circuit Clerk, and Sheriff.

From Charles Hammond

Dear Sir St Clairsville July 1 1822

I think I heard you mention in court at the last January term, that

Col Watt[1] was in Georgia endeavouring to find testimony to prove the transfer from ONeal to Scott of the entry which he claims adjoining Chilicothoe [*sic*],[2] and the impression made on my mind was that he encountered some difficulty in effecting it— A few days since I fell in with a gentleman resident of Ross County who informed me that in the early settlement of the Country he made up his mind to purchase ONeals Entry, and for that purpose travelled to ONeals residence in Georgia; that upon making application to purchase ONeal informed him that he had sold to Scott that he afterwards applied to Scott by letter and received information in reply by letter that Scott had sold to Watt. This gentlemans testimony would I presume compleatly make out your case I have given the information to Doddridge,[3] but least [*sic*] he should neglect it, I now communicate it to you— I have taken measures to ascertain the name of this gentleman which if his testimony is necessary for you, you can be informed of—

I see you are again a candidate for Congress, and I am glad of it. Our state is so districted as to throw Mr. Wright[4] and myself into different districts and we shall both be candidates, We hope therefore that we may meet you at Phillipi[5]

I received a note from you dated at Wheeling on your way home from the City—[6] I am engaged in preparing a written argument at length upon all the points I shall raise in our bank case—[7] This will be entirely too volumnious [*sic*] to furnish you with a copy. I shall not probably complete it before fall— When it is done I will supply you with a brief of the points made such as I shall prepare for the Court— I cannot well go further—

We have been visited by a very severe droughth [*sic*] which has greatly injured the flax oats & meadows, and will ruin the corn if it continues much longer— Crops of rye are generally good, wheat tolerable— All the Northern and Eastern section of the country seems to have been in the same situation— Flux dysenteries and billious fevers have begun to appear among us: a sickly season is anticipated—

I see you have been putting forth some more high handed doctrines in behalf of the Bank of the United States.[8] Do you really think that it is competent for Congress to give to suitors in the federal courts remedies unknown or contrary to the State Laws upon the same subjects?— God-a-mercy upon us if the federal courts once decide that this may be done— We shall see the Bank petitioning for summary process Judgement and Execution and immediate sale of property for what it will bring. Such proceeding as has been lately provided for in case of public debtors— Certainly this would be a most convenient mean of preserving that institution and therefore might be considered necessary and proper—on this subject permit me to say one thing to you in candour and sincerity. It is my earnest wish to see a western man at the head of our government but I scarcely know how to reconcile to myself the propriety of placing in that station, the advocate of doctrines so hetrodox [*sic*] as those maintained and repeatedly and in different forms advanced by the champions of the United States Bank appear to me— Nor is this all— There are, I am well persuaded, many who will feel it their duty to make opinions upon this subject something like a *sine qua non*— Respectfully yours Cs: HAMMOND

Mr. Henry Clay—

ALS. DLC-HC (DNA, M212, R1). [1] John Watts.

[2] In 1821 the United States Supreme Court had considered the case of Kerr and Others *vs.* Watts, which had grown out of Watts' effort to enforce his earlier judgment against Nathaniel Massie (above, I, 456n). While the Court at the second hearing had confirmed the original decision so far as the current occupants of the land claimed title through Massie, its opinion had reversed the lower court ruling against Kerr and several others who based their claims on entries independent of Massie's. The case had been remanded for new proceedings in which Watts must again prove his chain of title through Captain Ferdinand O'Neal, formerly of Williamsburg, a veteran of the Virginia Continental Line, and "the Scots" (not identified). 19 *U.S.* (6 Wheaton) 550-65.

[3] Philip Doddridge.

[4] John C. Wright. Under the Congressional reapportionment following the Census of 1820, Ohio's delegation in the House of Representatives had been increased from six to fourteen. Redistricting of the State had been the principal business of a special session of the State legislature held May 20-23.

[5] See below, Wright to Clay, November 2, 1822. [6] Not found.

[7] See above, II, 723, n. 4; Clay to Cheves, September 8, 1821.

[8] See below, Clay to Hammond, July 14, 1822.

From Hezekiah Niles

Dr Sir, Balt. July 1, 1822

I sincerely thank you for your favor of the 15th ult. and its enclosures.[1] I am sure that they will be of use to my son,[2] & the kindness with which they were granted shall not easily be forgotten. My dear boy has started on his journey, & I *now* feel a delightful confidence that if he succeeds he will not dishonor those who have interested themselves for him. Still, I much regret the course of conduct that was seemingly *forced* upon me

It was with much pleasure I heard that you had consented to serve again in congress, though I know that the place is incompatible with private comfort. In times like these *national* men must not all quit the field. The liberality & broadness of your views (I do not mean to flatter) are inestimably valuable just now. The legislation or direction of the public affairs seems to regard a quintal of codfish, a hhd. of tobacco *or* a bale of cotton, instead of keeping an eye to the whole.

I shall really regret the loss of our friend Col Trimble—but from his letter to me, he apprehends a defeat.[3]

With my best wishes for your health & happiness, I am sincerely your obliged friend H NILES

Our friend Col. C S. Todd left here this morning for Norfolk to embark on the John Adams.[4] He was quite well.

ALS. DLC-HC (DNA, M212, R1). Addressed to Clay at Lexington. Niles, a Pennsylvanian, had settled in Baltimore in 1805 and had become editor of the Baltimore *Evening Post.* In 1811 he had founded his *Weekly Register,* which he published until 1836.

1 Not found.

2 Samuel Niles, aged twenty-two, who died of yellow fever at the Barrancas, near Pensacola, the following October.

3 David Trimble was re-elected to a seat in Congress.

4 Bound for Colombia. Because of ill health, Todd had been permitted to return to the United States in 1821.

From Nathaniel Beasley

Dear Sir Decatur 4th July 1822

on yesterday I saw John W Campbell of west union whom you informed me at Columbus last Winter, you had authorised to sell Thomas Harts Part of the above Survey, Mr Campbell informs me that he is not authorised by you to sell, tho you had spoken to him that you would do so, for your information how the land lies I have above laid down a Platt of the whole Survey. the Divition line between the Part I Purchased & Harts as Divided by Commissioners appointed by Court agreeable the Statute of Ohio, I have Sold out the Part I had, and as the land lies in my neighbour [*sic*] I will buy Harts half if you will sell it at what I think a fair Price, for the Purpose of makiang [*sic*] a Sheep farm as I Sugestd. [*sic*] to you last winter at Columbus, the land is So very Broken as you my [*sic*] See by the Creek & Branches that Pass through it, that it is unfit for Cultivation in any other way than Pasture, and the Creek Spreads out So wide in byous that it destroys much Part of what little bottom their is on it. I will give one Dollar & fifty Cents Pr acre, which will be five hundred Dollars for your half & Pay one half Down the other half in twelve months, and give you good Surety for the Payment if you Required it, if you think Proper to let me have it, Please to let me know by letter Directed to Decatur Brown County Ohio, or I will give you two dollars Pr acre Payable in horses at Valuation in the Same time as above Stated, which was what I gave for the other half, only I made the Payments in three instalments yearly at a time two when land Sold much hier than it now does in this State, as the best of Congress land Can be had for $125[1]

you will Please let me hear from you as early as Convenient, So if we dont trade, I may turn my attention to Some other Place, I Presume you have but a Slight acquaintance with me, as I only had the Pleasure of being introduced to you while at Columbus, and my acquaintance is but limited in Lexington, but I will Refer you to Col Alexander Parker of Lexington with whom I am acquainted for information Relative to my Character, or to all most any gentleman of Maysville Paticular [*sic*] to Either of the Langhorns Sumralls & Chaimbers,[2] I have given you a Correct account of the Situation of your land, that it is hilly Very much so and Badley timberd what good oak timber & hickory was on it the Catta Pillers destroyed Some few years ago a Part of the land is tollorable rich Say one half the other but middling Second rate Soil. with due respect I am Sir your Very Humble Servt N BEASLEY

Henry Clay Esquire

ALS. DLC-TJC (DNA, M212, R12). Attached to "Platt of Daniel Balls Survey for 666⅔ acres No 746 & Patented to Thomas Hart & Cuthbert Banks, on the 18th day of April 1800 Assinee [*sic*] of Daniel Ball & Banks half Conveyed to Nathaniel Beasley." Beasley, a native of Virginia, had settled in Ohio in 1789. Cf. above, Orr to Clay, February 15, 1820; Clay to Meigs, February 28, 1820.

[1] The Land Act of 1820 had established $1.25 per acre as the minimum price for public lands. 3 *U.S. Stat.*, 566-67.

[2] Maurice, Jack H., and John T. Langhorne; James, John, and Joseph K. Sumrall (Simrall); John and James Chambers (the last, a Maysville tavern-keeper).

To Langdon Cheves

My dear Sir Lexington 5 July 1822.

My brother John Clay of New Orleans is desirous of being appointed a director of the office at that City, and has requested me to suggest his name to you. He was once unfortunate in business in that place, but I hope and believe maintained his character for honor and probity. For several years past he has been engaged as a broker in the purchase and sale of the rich staples of Louisiana and Mississippi, and as an inspector of tobacco from the upper Country. The profits of his business, which he pursues with unremitted industry, have enabled him to repair his misfortunes, and have placed him in a very eligible and comfortable condition. I am quite sure that he does not wish the situation from any pecuniary accommodation which may be incident to it. Since however he attaches importance to it, on other accounts, I should be glad, if the Bank cannot be better served, that he might be gratified.[1]

I am faithfly & cordially Your's H. CLAY

P.S. If my brother has not already, he will have, the Stock in the B. necessary to his qualification. H.C.

Langdon Cheves Esq.

ALS. ScHi. [1] See below, Cheves to Clay, July 27, 1822.

From Thomas B. Robertson

My dear Sir Baton Rouge 5 July 1822

Your friendly letter of this 1st April[1] would have been answered at an earlier date—but I asked Hawkins[2] who was writing to say to you that there was a most perfect coincidence between us in the opinions which he entertained on its principal subject

You have done well to allow yourself to be considered as a Candidate for the Presidency. Your pretentions are fair and your chance of success equal to that of any other person. You may count on the votes here, you have the advantage of being known personally —and of having some warm friends— Lowndes is very universally admired—and Crawford much respected but the first is not considered as a candidate and the second will not be dangerous—

You say I was spoken of at Washington as minister to one of the late acknowledged american govts— I do not believe the part I have taken in their behalf will be of any service to me nor indeed do I care for I am in all respects well and happily situated and content to remain at least for the present in that employment[3]

I am much pleased to see that you are about to return to Congress your being there cannot fail to promote the interest of both yourself and the Nation— we shall have now in that body three members among them Edward Livingston than whom no man in the United States possesses truer talents[4]

Remember me kindly to Mrs. Clay Durald[5] & Lady and if they are with you to Mr & Mrs Brown[6]

sincerely & respectfully Yours TH B ROBERTSON

Mr Clay

ALS. DLC-HC (DNA, M212, R1). 1 Not found.

2 Joseph H. Hawkins. His letter to Clay has not been found.

3 Robertson, a Louisiana Congressman from 1812 to 1818, was Governor of that State from 1820 until November 15, 1824, when he resigned to accept appointment as Judge of the United States District Court of Louisiana. He held that post until a year before his death in 1828.

4 Louisiana's Representatives in the Eighteenth Congress were Livingston, William L. Brent, and Henry H. Gurley.

5 Martin Duralde, Jr. 6 James Brown.

To Felix Grundy

Dr Sir (Confidential) Lexington 7h. July 1822

You are no doubt apprized of the controversy which exists between the States of Virginia and Kentucky, respecting the interpretation and execution of the compact entered into between them, on the occasion of their separation. The Legislature of this State, at its last session, having appointed me to concert with Mr. Leigh, the Virginia Commissioner, the necessary arrangements for determining all the matters of difference between the two States, I have accordingly agreed with him to submit them to a Board of Commissioners, in pursuance of one of the articles of the compact.[1] By our agreement, this board is to consist of six Commissioners, two to be appointed by each State, and these four to appoint the remaining two. They are to assemble at Washington City on the fourth monday in January next, are to decide the matters refered to them on or before the first of April next, and are to receive the same compensation, and travelling allowance, as members of Congress. The questions submitted to them are our several laws in favor of occupying claimants of land and the acts of our Legislature for limiting real actions, and the claim lately set up by Virginia to have the unsatisfied warrants of her officers and soldiers located beyond the Tennessee. We have also agreed that neither of the Commissioners shall be taken from Virginia or Kentucky.

We shall naturally turn our attention to the adjoining States States [*sic*] of Tennessee and Ohio in selecting the two Commissioners on our part; and some of us have thought and spoken of you. We have apprehended however that, either in your character of judge, legislator or Citizen in this State, you may have been so far committed on the questions, as not to feel at liberty to act in our behalf. And the object of this letter is to ascertain from you if you have any objections on that or any other account to serve? Your knowledge of the condition of this State and of the necessity of such provisions as are contained in those laws, provided we were not restrained from passing them would be of essential service to us in the Board.

Mr. Leigh's agreement and mine is subject to the ratification of our respective States. If ratified, which is probable, the G. Assembly of K. will appoint the two Commissioners on our part.[2] I do not belong to that body, but it is likely that many of the members will consult with me about the gentlemen to be chosen; and I was desirous of using your name or not, according to circumstances. With these views, and without any authority from the Legislature itself to open this communication, I shall be greatly obliged to you for the information sought for as soon as may be convenient. With high regard I am faithfully Yours H. CLAY

Felix Grundy Esq.

ALS. DLC-Felix Grundy Papers (DNA, M212, R21).

1 See above, Credential, June 1, 1822; Convention, June 5, 1822.

2 See below, Clay to Leigh, November 18, 1822.

From William B. Astor

Dear Sir, New York 8th. July 1822.

I have had the honor to receive your letter of the 23d ulto[1] enclosing a check on the U S Bank for $1400—Fourteen hundred dollars at your credit.—My father arrived here in April last & in good health,[2] he is at present at Boston whence we expect him here in about ten days. I am with great regard your most obedient Servant

Wm. B Astor.

To The Honorable Henry Clay Lexington Kenty.

ALS. DLC-TJC (DNA, M212, R12). 1 Not found. 2 See above, II, 863n.

From Peter B. Porter

Dear Sir, Black Rock July 8th. 1822

Your favour of the 14th. of April, and the envelope of your friend Mr Johnston,[1] reached Black Rock during my absence on the business of the Boundary Commission,[2] which will account for the tardiness of my reply. I appreciate the frank & open manner in which you have thought proper to address me on the important & delicate subject of your letter; and hardly need assure you that the confidence which it reposes will, under no circumstances, be violated.

It has been the misfortune of this State, that, for a number of years past, its political concerns have been managed, or rather distracted, by a few ambitious men whose views have extended only to their own personal aggrandisement, and on almost every great national question, our strength has been scattered & wasted by premature & unadvised commitments made by these headlong & selfish politicians. As regards the interesting question which is the subject of your letter, a new & more circumspect course of proceeding has been adopted. A mutual understanding now exists amongst the principal republicans of the State that it is yet too early to act on this question, and that, whatever may be the private sentiments & predilections of individuals, it would be imprudent at present to promulgate them. Whenever the proper time shall arrive (& perhaps the next winter's session of our Legislature may be selected as such) a full & friendly consultation & interchange of sentiments will take place; and we are not without hopes of producing, by this course, a unanimity that will ensure to this State (what it has never possessed) an influence proportioned to its population & wealth. Whoever may be the candidate fairly designated by the majority, I shall consider myself bound, as a republican, to give him my support— I have indeed been one of the advisers of this cautious & circumspect policy, because I have deemed it the wisest that this State, under present circumstances, could pursue. If we had a favourite Candidate in one of our own citizens it would afford a fair apology for our taking the field early: But we have none, and you are aware of the jealousy that exists, particularly in the South, against the growing power of the *Great State of New York,* and if we were to manifest our solicitude by making an early selection, that very circumstance might weaken the chance of our candidate & perhaps throw him into a minority.

Having thus answered your letter by an array of the cold & calculating policy adopted by us on this occasion, I can now assure you with all the sincerity of my heart, that there is not a man in the U. States whom I should be more gratified to see in the presidential chair than yourself; and that, so far as my best wishes & efforts (in conformity with the principles we have assumed) can aid in producing this desirable result, they will be faithfully executed.

The Republicans of this State have been so often & shamefully deceived & abused by the professed friendship as well as open hostility of the opposite party, that the first requisite in their candidate will be, that he be a *Republican of the old school,* and I know of no one who, in addition to so many other splendid qualifications, can better sustain the integrity of this character, than my friend from Kentucky.

In approving the cautious policy of *this State* I mean not to condemn a different course by other States. On the contrary, my decided opinion is that an early manifestation of the wishes of Kentucky in your favour, and, after her, of the other western States, who will be considered as thereby advocating their own particular & local interests, will be highly favourable to your success— By bringing a formidable force, whose fidelity may be relied on, early into the field, you will probably secure the cooperation of many, whose course might otherwise be doubtfull.

I expect to see a number of my political friends at my house during the summer, & amongst them Mr Van Buren[3] of the Senate. The subject of the next presidency will of course be canvassed, & I will, in a future letter, give you my impressions in regard to the prevailing views of the republicans of this State.

Mrs P. is in excellent health & desires her best respects to you. I remain, Dr Sir, with great respect & regard.

Honbl. H. Clay. your Obt Sert. PETER B. PORTER

ALS. DLC-HC (DNA, M212, R1). Published in Colton (ed.), *Private Correspondence of Henry Clay*, 65-66.

1 Probably Francis Johnson. 2 See above, II, 162n. 3 Martin Van Buren.

To Jonathan Russell

My dear Sir. Lexington 9th July 1822

Your letter of the 6th Ulto. arrived here whilst I was absent from home, at one of the watering places,[1] and hence the delay of my answer. I had read the communication of the President to Congress of your letters and Mr. Adams remarks. And I must frankly say to you, that the variance between your two letters has given in the public judgment, a great advantage to Mr. Adams, at least for the moment, and that, unless satisfactorily explained, it will do you a lasting prejudice. I saw it with very deep regret, and shall anxiously look for such an explanation.

On many of the circumstances stated in your letter my memory accords with yours; on one or two only it does not. I recollect distinctly that the paragraph offered by me and inserted in our dispatch to the B. Comms of the 10th Novr. terminated, at that time, the discussions respecting the navigation of the Mississipi [*sic*], and the privilege concerning the Fisheries within the British jurisdiction. It was prior to the adoption of that paragraph that it had been proposed, I think, by Mr. Gallatin to grant the one for the other; that the discussion which was long, earnest, animated, often renewed, had taken place; that a majority consisting of Mess. Gallatin, Adams, and Bayard appeared to be in favor of it; and that I had declared that I would sign no treaty in which such a stipulation should be included. After this declaration, Mr. Bayard came over to us and made us the majority. It was then necessary that we should, as we were about to send in to the B. Comms. the projet of a treaty of peace, give some written answer to their notification of the 8th of August, concerning the Fisheries.[2] We were forbidden, by our instructions,[3] to suffer our right to the Fisheries to be brought into discussion. The majority had now determined, not to offer for the renewal of our right the navigation of the Mississipi. We had, in short, no equivalent to offer. We had therefore no other ground to take than that which the above paragraph assumes. Whether solid or not it was the best we could occupy, and had the advantage of being in conformity to our instructions.

After the B. Comms. returned our projet, with an alteration proposing the renewal to them of the right to navigate the Mississipi; I think the same question, though in a form somewhat different, came up in our Commission. We received their note with their proposed alterations and suggestions on the 27th Novr.. We had a conference with them on the first of Decr. I think it must have been between those two days that the question was again considered. You and I (such at least is my recollection) proposed to strike out that part of the British alteration of the 8th article which had for object the renewal of their right to navigate the Mississipi; but the same majority that was at first in favor of making the offer of the navigation of that river, was now willing to accept the British proposal upon the condition of their renewing to us the Fishing liberties within their jurisdiction. The article, proposed at the conference on the first of Decr. expressed the sense of the majority.

My determination on this subject, had been deliberately formed, and communicated frankly to my colleagues. I did not probably repeat the communication of my resolution, because it would have worn the appearance of menace. I have some recollection of Mr. Bayard, on our return from the conference of the 1st. of Decr. having expressed his dissatisfaction at something which Mr. Gallatin said or did at the conference, but what it was I do not recollect. I cannot think it possible that we should have gone into that conference without being prepared to say something to the B. C. on the subject of the Navigation of the Mississipi, and my recollection is very strong that the above majority was in favor of accepting their proposal, with the condition which I have mentioned. I regret I cannot put my hands upon your letter from Stockholm mentioned in your last.

Nothing can be more unfounded than Mr. Adams' inference (if he intended to draw an inference) of our assent to the doctrine of the imperishable character, in all respects, of the treaty of 1783, & to the proposal, in regard to the navigation of the Mississipi, from the fact of our signature to the communication, respecting those subjects, to the British Comms, and that of our being present at the conference of the 1st Decr.

1st As to the durable character of the treaty; I think all of us (except Mr. Adams) concurred in believing that the provisions respecting the Fishing Grants, *within the British exclusive* jurisdiction, and the navigation of the Mississipi, expired on the breaking out of the war. Why he calls it the American doctrine[4] I do not know. If it be true, it is the doctrine of the public law. If he means to say, that it is American, because we were most interested in maintaining it, he is mistaken. If the superiority of interest should determine the national character of the doctrine, it ought to be called British. Then why did we take the ground which we did, in our note of the 10th Novr.? For the reason already assigned, It was the best we could occupy. It was plausible, and might serve, as it probably did subsequently serve, to enable us to make some satisfactory arrangement with Great Britain in regard to the Fisheries. We were bound to say something, or acknowledge by our silence the principle asserted by the British Comms on the 8th of August. By taking the ground which we did, if it were not absolutely tenable, we were better off than to have stood mute.

2. As to the navigation of the Mississipi; that the offer of it was the work of a majority, in which we did not participate, can not be denied. What puts this matter conclusively at rest is the despatch signed by all the American Comms to the Secretary of State, under date the 25th of Decr., accompanying the treaty, in which it is stated;

"To place both points {i.e. The navigation, & the Fisheries} beyond all future controversy, a *majority* of us determined to offer to admit an article confirming both rights."[5] You will no doubt recollect that I suggested, when we went to sign that despatch, the insertion of the words, "a majority"; and my purpose for doing it was not mistaken.[6] Why did we sign the communication to the B.C. of the 14h of Dec; and why were we present at the conference of the first, without objecting to that article? If we had failed to subscribe that [*sic*] communication, or if we had objected to the article at the conference, it would have, in effect, notified to the British Comms a serious division amongst us, than which nothing could have been more unfortunate. Our signatures, nor our presence no more proved our assent to the article than the signature of an arbitrator to an award proves his asent to it, when it was carried by the majority against his opinion, or the assent by a member of an aggregate body to all the transactions of that body, which happened during his presence.[7] All that it was material to the B. C to know was, that the offer was the act of the American Commissioners, which it would equally have been whether carried unanimously, by a majority of four, or a majority of three. How it was carried, (that is, by wha[t] majority) it was not necessary for them to know, but might to us have been highly injurious. But it was material that our own government, to which we were responsible, should know how we did act; and accordingly when we came to address it, we informed it that it was the affair of the majority &c.

It was the less necessary for us to disclose the fatal secret of our divisions to the enemy, because the proposition might be rejected, might be modified during the negotiation so as ultimately to be acceptable or less objectionable to us, or finally might be withdrawn. It was withdrawn; and thereby that was ultimately done which we at first proposed, and a clear demonstration was given of the indiscretion which would have characterised a gratuitous disclosure of the divisions among the A. Commissioners.

When I spoke to you at Washington of our instructions being opposed to the article in question, I alluded more particularly to that part of them which related to the Fisheries, our right to which we were forbidden to discuss &c.

The authority to treat on the basis of the status ante bellum which we did not recieve [*sic*] until two or three weeks after the discussion in our board, which, as before mentioned, was closed by the paragraph in our despatch of the 10th of Novr. did not authorise us to propose the article which we did, concerning the navigation of the Mississipi, if as I think that article would in effect have amounted to a grant of the navigation, in the whole extent of the river from the source to the Balize. For what was the status ante bellum of that subject? The subjects of G. B. had no right, either by the treaty of 1783 or by that of 1794 to navigate that river within the Spanish jurisdiction and the sovereign rights of Spain, over that river, were not vested in us until the conclusion of the treaty of Louisiana in 1803. It has been said that, during thirty years, no use was made by British subjects of the navigation of that river.[8] During a grea[t] part of the same thirty years (until the year 1795) no use for purposes of commerce, was made of it by the citizens of the U.S. and for the same reason, in both instances that is, that Spain held both sides of it from the mouth to the 31st degree of North latitude; and the West side up to its source.

Nothing would be more painful to me than to be drawn even remotely, into the unhappy controversy between Mr. Adams and yourself, a controversy in which the party most successful will be a loser in the public estimation. I certainly thought that the public ought to have been put into possession of the whole of the official transactions of the Mission of Ghent, not knowing myself of any sufficient reason for withholding any part of them. But I do not think that any *private* letters ought to have been communicated by the President. Far from stimulating as I think he did, perhaps unintentionally, a call upon him for your letter along with Mr. Adams' remarks, he ought in my opinion to have refused such a call, however unequivocally made. Your letter, which I believe you shewed me at Paris, I supposed was written to explain the grounds on which you had proceeded; and to be used defensively, upon the possible contingency of a misrepresentation, or misconception of your course. No such contingency had occurred.

What would aggravate the pain which I should feel, even at the necessity of testifying to any of the transactions at Ghent, in a controversy between two of my colleagues, is a consideration of the ralation [*sic*], in regard to the subject, in which I stood to Mr. Adams; the relation in which I now stand to him; and in which we both appear to the public; and the friendly relation which I have ever borne to you. I should hope that a necessity may not arise for me to appear in any form before the public. Would it not be most advisable for you to state what really occured, without appealing to any person to confirm your statement? Would not such an appeal be a departure from self-respect and self dignity, as implying a consciousness that it was necessary? Already, I understand, it has been said, at the metropolis of a great state, that *I* have prompted the call for *your letter,*[9] than which nothing can be more incorrect. I mention the incident not that I care for it, but to shew you the distrustful state of the public mind. This letter is not written for the public eye, but for your own. I am most anxious to see the publication, which you intimate was shortly to appear after the date of your letter. So far as the subject and the argument are concerned you cannot fail to achieve a signal triumph over your antagonist. And I repeat, in conclusion, the hope that so far as as [*sic*] there is any thing personal, you will be able fully to vindicate yourself in respect to the variance between your two letters.

Be pleased to present my best respects to Mrs Russell; and believe me Sincerely & cordially yours H. CLAY

The Honble. Mr. Russell

P. S. In the Session of Congress of 1815-16 in a debate on the state of the Union, I addressed the H of R in vindication of the war, the terms of the peace &c. In the course of my speech I stated that a *majority* of the A. C. had made the offer of the Navigation of the Mississipi for the Fishing liberties.[10] My speech was published in the Intelligencer & other prints of the day. H. C.

Copy. DLC-HC (DNA, M212, R1). Endorsed by Clay: "Rough Copy. . . ." Published in Washington *United States Telegraph,* October 24, 1828.

1 Not identified—probably either the Olympian Springs, to which eighteen new cottages had been added the preceding year and which under the new management of George and John Landsdowne, sub-lessees of Thomas Deye Owings, were being regularly advertised in Lexington papers at this period, or the Greenville Springs, near Harrodsburg, Kentucky, which, opened as a resort as early as 1808, had also undergone extensive improvements in the early twenties. Lexington *Kentucky Reporter,* July 9, 1821; June 10, 1822; J. Winston Coleman, Jr., *The Springs of Kentucky, an Account of the Famed Watering-Places of the Bluegrass State, 1800-1935* (Lexington, Ky., 1955), 17-22.

2 See above, I, 953, 958.

3 Of April 15, 1813. See above, I, 857.

4 In his "Remarks," Adams terms as "the American principle" the argument that the right to the fisheries had not been forfeited by the war. *House Docs.* 17 Cong., 1 Sess., no. 131, pp. 42-43.

5 *American State Papers, Foreign Relations,* III, 733.

6 Adams merely notes that his "draft of a dispatch to the Secretary of State had passed through the hands of all my colleagues, and had been altered and amended by them all." He had agreed to all the amendments except one, by Clay, relating to the interpretation of the Treaty of 1783 as a permanent contract. Adams, *Memoirs,* III, 127-28.

7 For Clay's proposal of a substitute for the note sent on December 14, 1814, see above, I, 1003-1005.

8 See above, Russell to Clay, June 6, 1822, n. 18.

9 See above, Kendall to Clay, June 20, 1822.

10 See above, II, 144.

To Richard M. Johnson

My dear Sir Ashland 12h. July. 1822.

I am greatly obliged by the perusal which you have allowed me of the letter of the President, respecting my demand on the Government, as well as for the very friendly exertions which you have made in support of it. I always entertained the highest confidence in the judgment and the justice of the president; and never doubted that, if the more weighty concerns of the public would allow *him* to exercise the one, I should have the other administered to me.

Should you have occasion to write to the President, I will thank you to convey to him an expression of my lively gratitude, for the favorable decision which he has been pleased to make in my case.[1]

I recd. also your note[2] covering the proposition of Mess. Sebree &c.[3] I will take the promptest steps in my power to have an estimate made of the value of the land offered.

With high regard I remain faithfy Yours H. CLAY

Col. R. M. Johnson.

ALS. DLC-James Monroe Papers (DNA, M212, R22).

1 See above, Clay to Johnson, April 12, 1822; Johnson to Clay, April 20, 1822. Monroe's opinion, dated June 22, 1822, is found in DNA, RG59, Misc. Letters (M179, R54).

2 Not found.

3 Uriel Sebree and James and Richard M. Johnson. Cf. above, Clay to Cheves, June 11, 1821, note. At the May Term, 1822, of the United States Circuit Court, Sebree and the Johnsons had been found liable for $1,902.07 to the Bank of the United States on an assigned note. U. S. Circuit Court, Seventh Circuit, District of Kentucky, Complete Records, S, 144-47.

From J[oseph] A[nderson]

Treasury Department Comptroller's Office 12th July 1822

Honble. Henry Clay, Arkland [*sic*], near Lexington Kentucky.

Sir,

I enclose you the result of the settlement of your account at the Treasury, relative to your claim to half an outfit for your services in the formation of a Commercial Treaty with Great Britain, jointly with Mr. Adams & Mr. Gallatin in the year 1815.[1]

You will perceive from the enclosed Statement, that the President of the U. States has allowed you $4,500 for your services in the capacity above mentioned; from which has been deducted the sum of $220, heretofore allowed you for your travelling expenses from Ghent to London.—

The balance of $4,280 will be paid to your Order on application at the Treasury.— With, &ca J. A.

Copy. DNA, RG217, Records of the 1st Comptroller, Misc. Letters Sent, vol. 21, p. 37.

1 See above, Clay to Johnson, July 12, 1822.

From Joseph Vance

Honble H, Clay Urbana. July the 12th. 1822

Sir since my return, I have been through the State in diferent [*sic*] directions and feel gratified to find that your Suport [*sic*] for the Next Presidency will be almost universal—and—without division—, I yesterday returned from Chillicothe and—found—our mutual friend Genl. McArthur[1] Hearty in the cause—, all the sst. [*sic*][2] men of the north western part of the State—that I have conversed with and I have been through most of the counties and attended several courts, are not only Friends but—warm ones; *Judge* McLeans pieces *in* favour of J. C. C. notwithstanding[3] yours with respect JOS. VANCE

ALS. DLC-HC (DNA, M212, R1). Vance, born in Pennsylvania, had been brought as a child to Vanceburg, Kentucky, where he had lived until removing to Urbana, Ohio, in 1805. He had risen to the rank of major general of Ohio militia during the War of 1812, had been a member of the State House of Representatives for several terms, and in 1820 had been elected to Congress, where he served from March 4, 1821, to March 3, 1835. He was Governor of Ohio, 1836-1838, a member of the State Senate, 1840-1841, again a Congressman, 1843-1847, and a delegate to the Whig National Convention in 1848.

1 Duncan McArthur. 2 Probably meant to read "1st."

3 John McLean had written a series of eight letters signed "Benjamin Franklin," published in the *Liberty Hall and Cincinnati Gazette* between February 23 and April 13, praising John C. Calhoun and criticizing his opponents. Harry R. Stevens, *The Early Jackson Party in Ohio* (Durham, N. C., 1957), 40.

To Charles Hammond

Dr Sir Lexington 14h. July 1822.

I duly recd. your favor of the first instant and thank you for the information which it communicates for the benefit of Col. Watts. He has taken, we hope, sufficient testimony to establish the several transfers from O'Neal down, but as it may be useful to procure corroborative proofs I will thank you for the name of the person, when you have ascertained it, who can prove the acknowledgment of O'Neal of the sale to Scott &c.

I am almost ashamed to admit of my being again a Candidate for Congress, as it was my intention, on retiring from that body, to have dedicated to my private affairs more time than I find I shall now be able to bestow on them; but you know how customary it is to have "those numerous friends" who bring out, in spite of him, the reluctant and unwilling candidate. I have, to be serious, given much weight to the opinions and wishes of many friends, both in and out of the State, who think that I ought to return. I am glad to hear that you and Mr. Wright are candidates. If I should be elected, which is probable, as I am not aware of any opposition,[1] it will give me much satisfaction to co-operate with both of you in promoting the welfare of our common Country.

Although I should have liked to have seen your entire argument in the Bank case, which I anticipate will be characterized by much ingenuity and ability, I must be content with and shall be greatly obliged to you for the points on which you mean to rely as promised in your letter. I really do not know to what "high handed doctrines" you allude as having been recently put forth by me, in behalf of the Bank of the U.S. Do you refer to the motion for a Ca Sa, of which I believe the prints took some notice?[2] If you do, I think if you have turned your attention particularly to the subject of the Execution

Laws of the U.S. and of the States, you will have observed it involved in great confusion & uncertainty. It was to attain some thing like precision that I made the motion, a favorable decision of which in the Circuit Court I was indifferent about, as the question was one which would, sooner or later, go to and ought to be decided by, the Supreme Court. I made up no positive opinion on the question; for I need not say to you that it would be most unfair always to infer the private opinions of an individual from his professional movements, as Counsel. I understand that, perhaps, in every Circuit in the U. States, other than the seventh, in the execution of the judgments and decrees of the Federal Courts no regard is paid to the State laws, as from time to time they vary, in regard to executions. Thus, I have been distinctly informed, in Pennsylvania, Sales are made upon executions, emanating from the Federal Courts, of real estate, without regard to the appraisement laws of that State. Now, there ought to be uniformity; the rule, practised upon in the seventh Circuit ought to be observed either in all the Circuits or in none.

In candor, I ought to say to you that, without having had occasion to make any very particular examination of the point, I have supposed it quite clear that, in respect to those subjects relative to which jurisdiction is confered on the Federal Judiciary by the Constitution of the U.S. it is competent to Congress to pass an Execution system of its own, different from that which may prevail in any of the States. Whether it will be expedient at any time, and to what extent, to act on that power is another question. I have no prejudices whatever in favor of the Bank of the U.S. As its Counsel I wish to discharge honorably my duty, which I shall certainly fearlessly, on all occasions, attempt to do; but, as its Counsel, I do not wish, in any case, that law or justice should be meted out to it in other quantities or qualities than what is extended to every other suitor in like cases having occasion to appeal to the same tribunals. Will you allow me, my dear Sir, whilst you kindly intimate to me cautions on this topic, in my turn, to ask you if there be not danger, from the part which your public duty has, according to your sense of it, required you to act, of your feelings transporting you too far and disturbing the calm exercise of your good judgment?

Whilst you are complaining of an afflicting drought, we have been, I may say, for the last three or four months, literally drowned. At this time we have the verdure of May, and our streams run with a Winter's fullness. The season has been so extremely wet that we have every reason to apprehend its usual incident o[f] dysentery, if not other maladies.

With high regard I am faithfly. Yours H. CLAY

Charles Hammond Esqr.

ALS. InU. [1] See above, Clay to Meigs, June 8, 1822.

[2] At the May Term of the Federal Circuit Court for the District of Kentucky, meeting in Frankfort, Clay had moved that the Clerk be instructed to issue writs of *capias ad satisfaciendum* (writs commanding the sheriff to hold offending persons for appearance in court to satisfy judgment), notwithstanding enactment of the State law abolishing imprisonment for debt (above, Clay to Dougherty, December 7, 1821, note). Clay argued that under the Constitution the Congress of the United States was empowered to regulate the process of Federal courts and that it had done so. The opposing argument maintained that personal liberty as affected by contract was matter for State regulation exclusively and that Congress had regulated process of the Federal courts only to provide that it should follow that used in the State courts. The Circuit Court had agreed that court precedent followed the latter argument and had overruled Clay's motion. Lexington *Kentucky Reporter,* June 10, 1822; U.S. Circuit Court, Seventh Circuit, District of Kentucky, Order Book H, 92, 254-55. This opinion was not upheld by the Supreme Court, which in 1825 in the case of William Wayman and John Clark, merchants of New York City, *vs.* Daniel R. Southard and Daniel Starr, merchants of Elizabethtown, Kentucky, on appeal from the Federal Circuit Court for the District of Kentucky, ruled that a State law on executions enacted subsequent to passage of the Federal Judiciary Act "is not applicable to executions issuing on judgments rendered by the courts of the United States, unless expressly adopted by the regulations and rules of those courts." In a second decision rendered by the Supreme Court at the same term, in the case of the Bank of the United States *vs.* January, reference being made to the process of a *capias,* the Court ruled that the judiciary acts of 1789 and 1792 having specifically mentioned this process, Congress must be understood to have adopted it "as one that was to issue permanently from the courts of the United States, whenever it was in use, at the epoch contemplated by those acts, as a state process." 23 *U.S.* (10 Wheaton) 48, 65n.

From William Duane

Henry Clay, Esqr Phila. July 15, 1822

Sir,

Frendship [*sic*] and confidence have enjoined in me a task painful but honorable— your earnest admirer and sincere friend Manuel Torres, is no more. He expired this day at 2 o'clock, after a lingering tho' not painful waste of life. The buoyancy of his spirit would not admit of any premonitions as to his life for some time past, but I considered as due to a long and close friendship rather to forfeit his present good will than prove untrue to a long established esteem— and I yesterday invited him to a consideration of his public duty and his reputation, so that he became sensible of the propriety of my suggestions, and gave such information upon four specific heads of his affairs, as enabled me to frame a will in something like the ordinary form, which being accomplished, Mr Meade[1] fortunately arrived soon after, and the will being read to poor Torres in Mr Meades presence, he subscribed his name to it. He afterwards directed me to write for some letters of introduction in favor of Mr Ravenga,[2] who is appointed the Political Agent of Colombia at London, to obtain from the Secretary of State and Gen. John Mason, letters of introduction to Mr Rush[3] in favor of Ravenga. He afterwards spoke of his friends here and elsewhere, among the few most esteemed yourself— he regretted that he would not see you for a few hours—but playfully observed—if I should go as you seem to think, you must not neglect to express my respects and best wishes to Mr Henry Clay; and he added some very warm sentiments in relation to you

It is in conformity with this occurrence that I now write you

He has placed his public papers in the hands of Mr Meade and myself. His private papers to me with an instruction how to dispose of them, and requested me to apprize his government if anything should happen

No one knows better than you do the heavy loss which the great common cause of America—and particularly Colombia, sustains by the death of this uncommonly wise and sagacious and profoundly learned man. He if he had lived would have been a link of union & a repository of sedate and matured counsel for the South and the North—such as I do not believe can be supplied or suited and prepared with Stores of every kind of intelligence and an intuition which sometimes assumed the appearance of a prophetic spirit.

Apprehensive of this unfortunate event I two two [*sic*] months ago, warned his government, by letter to Don Pedro Wale[4] of the apprehensions I entertained over the necessity of sending a successor here, were it only to acquire counsel should not the issue I feared arise. Poor Torres also entrusted me to write to President Bolivar in the like case—and to the Secretary of State and the President—which I do by the same mail that carries this.

Having no other object than that which I have fulfilled tho' unsatisfactorily, perhaps owing to my feelings for my friend—I can add only That I am, Sir with the greatest Respect Your obed Sert

WM DUANE

ALS. DLC-HC (DNA, M212, R1). [1] Richard W. Meade.

[2] Joseph Rafael Revenga, native of Caracas, who in 1811 had represented the Venezuelan revolutionary forces in the United States and in 1821 held the position of Minister of State and Foreign Relations for the combined states of New Granada and Colombia, was en route to London to negotiate a readjustment of the tangled fiscal arrangements of his government. He returned home in 1825 with an additional loan to develop Colombian agriculture.

[3] Richard Rush.

[4] Pedro Gual, like Revenga, a native of Caracas and also for a time during the early years of the Venezuelan revolution a refugee to the United States, in 1822 held the post of Secretary of State and Foreign Relations of Colombia.

Receipt from Daniel B. Price

[July 16, 1822]

Recd. 16 July 1822 of H. Clay the Sum of Four hundred dollars in various notes of the Farmers Bank of Jessamine which are filed by the said Clay as exhibits in a suit in Chy commenced by him in the Circuit Court of Jessamine against Hord and others Commissioners of the said Bank[1]

Danl B Price Clk
by J M HENDERSON D C

DS, in Clay's hand. DLC-TJC (DNA, M212, R15). Price, a native of Virginia, had been brought to Kentucky at an early age and, as a boy, had been appointed Deputy Clerk of Jessamine County. Succeeding to the post of Clerk in 1816, he held it for thirty-five years until 1851.

1 The bank, located in Nicholasville, Jessamine County, was one of the "Independent Banks" (see above, II, 442n), the charters of which had been repealed by act of February 10, 1820. Ky. Gen. Assy., *Acts, 1819-1820,* pp. 908-11. George J. Brown, Francis P. Hord, and Thomas E. West were the commissioners in liquidation of the Jessamine bank. See below, Agreement, November 6, 1824.

From John Rodgers

Dear Sir Washington July 18th. 1822

I have received your letter Enclosing a draft on the Honble James Barbour, Senator, for ($) which I have deposited in the United States Branch Bank at this place for collection—Mr. Smith[1] the Cashire [*sic*] has written to Mr. Barbour on the subject of the draft, which no doubt will be duly honored— The Ballance [*sic*] of the $500 for which I sold you Mrs. Pinkneys[2] carriage I will thank you to remit to Mr. Charles Goldsborough of this place[3] when convenient, as I am about to leave here, & shall not probably be back again before the 6th. of October. With great respect I have the honor to be yr Ob St JNO RODGERS

The Honble Henry Clay &c.&c &c

ALS. DLC-TJC (DNA, M212, R12). Endorsed by Clay:

Bill on Barbour	$180
Check on B. U. S.	100
	280
Check on B. U. S. in favor of Comm. Rogers [*sic*] sent to Mr. Goldsborough the 22d. Aug. 1822 for	220
	$500

1 Richard Smith.

2 Ann Marie Rodgers Pinkney, widow of William Pinkney and sister of John Rodgers. On the purchase of the carriage, see above, Clay to Dougherty, April 3, 1822.

3 Charles W. Goldsborough, Chief Clerk of the Navy Department, cousin of Charles Goldsborough.

To Joseph Anderson

Dr Sir Ashland 24h. July 1822.

Having learnt through a letter from the President[1] that "On full consideration of Mr. Clay's claim to half an outfit for services in the formation of a Commercial treaty with G. Britain in 1815 he had decided in its favor, and communicated that decision to the first Comptroller," I addressed a letter[2] to the Secretary of the Treasury[3] requesting that he would oblige me by depositing the sum to which I am thus entitled to my credit with the Bank of the U. S. at Philadelphia. I was not aware at the time of writing that letter that Mr. Crawford was gone to the South— Owing to that circumstance, I take the liberty of applying directly to you to enable me to obtain what the justice of the President has awarded to me. For this purpose I hereby vest in you all powers to sign any instrument of writing and to do any other act in my behalf necessary to entitle me to draw the sum refered to; and when drawn I will thank you to have it put to my credit as above mentd. with the Bank of the U.S. With high regard I am Your obt. Servant H. CLAY

Jos. Anderson Esq. &c. &c. &c.

P.S. Will you do me the favor to write me by the return mail? H. C.

ALS. DNA, RG217, Records of the 5th Auditor, Settlement File, no. 1139.
1 To Richard M. Johnson. See above, Clay to Johnson, July 12, 1822.
2 Not found. 3 William H. Crawford.

From Langdon Cheves

My Dear Sir, Philada. 27 July 1822

Your favour of the 5h Instant was duly received— I have put your Brother in nomination & his & your wish will be duly & respectfully considered—[1] The appointments for the Orleans office will be made on the 27th. november next at which time I will be merely nominally an Officer of the Bank as I have determined to leave it a few weeks after.[2] I perceive you are again a candidate for Congress in which I suppose you are right— The *great question* seems to be but little agitated yet— You will perceive from the "Sentinel" of this City,[3] which is one of the Oracles of the Democratic party in this part of the State—the Franklin Gazette is the Other[4]—that there is a Schism Schism [*sic*] among the active men— The Sentinel appears to incline to Crawford— New York appears to be completely undecided & apparently asking for an offer, But I really know nothing about it & hear little—

I am My Dear Sir With great respect & esteem Very truly Yrs

L CHEVES

The Hon'ble Henry Clay, Lexington Ky

ALS. DLC-HC (DNA, M212, R1). Published in Colton (ed.), *Private Correspondence of Henry Clay*, 66-67.
1 Appointment not found.
2 On July 1 Cheves had addressed a letter to the stockholders of the Bank of the United States, announcing his intention to retire as President of the Bank at the end of the year. Washington *Daily National Intelligencer*, July 4, 1822.
3 The Philadelphia *American Sentinel and Mercantile Advertiser*.
4 The Philadelphia *Franklin Gazette* (see above, Johnson to Clay, April 1, 1822, note).

From Andrew Hynes

Dear Sir, Nashville [July] 31. 1822.

I Did not reply to your letter of the 8 instant[1] at the time of receiving it, but beg leave now to state that the enclosure was delivered to Governor Carroll[2] immediately on its arrival.

Our Legislature commenced its session on the 22d. [*sic*] instant, and among its proceedings since that time, will be found a resolution recommending Genl. Jackson for the next President.[3] It was a kind of resolution that hardly any member would vote against, who was anxious for the *Political importance* of his own state. This measure, perhaps, was brought forward thus early, in order to have an influence on the election of United States senator, in the room of Colo. John Williams,[4] whose term of service expires before the next regular session of our Legislature, and I presume some calculations are made, that as the opponent of Colo. Williams will be a great friend of Genl. Jacksons, and Colo. Williams himself being some what unfriendly to him, that the Legislature having Committed themselves in favor of the Genl., that they must needs have a particular friend of his as senator.—[5] This is a kind of secret rumor that is afloat in the air, but has no tangible form.

I am afraid the Yankees will out manoeuver the western people Which, by the division among ourselves, will add greatly to the strength of their own Candidate. At present I have no more to add but presume Gov. Carroll will write you after the close of the present Session who will be enabled to give more correct & particular information in regard to the sentiments of the people of the state.

I am your friend ANDW. HYNES

ALS. DLC-HC (DNA, M212, R1). Addressed to Clay at Lexington; postmarked July 31.

1 Not found.
2 William Carroll.
3 On July 20 the lower house of the Tennessee legislature had adjourned for a few minutes while the members adopted a resolution expressing their opinion that Jackson's name "be submitted to the consideration of the people of the United States, at the approaching election for the chief magistracy." The measure was approved by the members of the State Senate on August 3.
4 United States Senator from Tennessee, 1815-1823, brother of Lewis Williams.
5 Jackson was himself chosen United States Senator in this election.

Testimonial on Lexington Female Academy

[*ca.* August 1, 1822]

Absence and indispensable engagements prevented us from being present at the public examination above noticed;[1] but from the many other opportunities which we have had of judging of Col. Dunham's school, we take great pleasure in expressing our belief, that it merits all the praise which is given it, and that no similar institution any where is more deserving of the public confidence and the public patronage.

H. CLAY,
JAS. HAGGIN,
JOHN BRADFORD.

Lexington *Kentucky Reporter,* August 19, 1822, reprinted from the Lexington *Western Monitor.* Appended to a report of the school's Board of Visitors, of which Clay was a member. The Lexington Female Academy, later named the Lafayette

Female Academy, had been established in the preceding year by Josiah Dunham, a native of Connecticut, formerly an officer in the United States Army, and, prior to his Lexington venture, head of a similar school at Windsor, Vermont.

1 Among the activities of the affair, held on July 31, was the reading of compositions, one of which had been presented by Clay's daughter, Lucretia.

From Thomas B. Reed

Dear Sir Natchez, August 2nd. 1822.

At the late session, in July, of the District Court of the United States, for the District of Mississippi, a judgment was recovered, on behalf of the U. States, against Parke Walton Esqr., a highly respected and valuable citizen of this State, for upwards of forty thousand dollars.

Mr. Walton had been, for many years, Reciver [*sic*] of Public monies, for the District west of Pearl river, in this state,[1] and had discharged the duties most satisfactorily to the people and, as was supposed, untill lately, to the Government. He acknowledges that, about twenty thousand dollars are still due from him to the Treasury, and, that sum he is willing to pay. I give full credit to the statements of Mr. Walton, in this regard. And believe the Government has done him, among a great number of other public accountants, very great injustice in this affair. Experience has shewn and you are, no doubt, well apprised, how extremely incorrect the public accounts have, in many instances, been kept and how much injustice has been done to many meritorious public Officers, from this Cause.

As the counsel of Mr. Walton, I have advised him to prosecute a writ of error, returnable to the February Term of the Supreme Court of the United States. Having emigrated from Kentucky[2] and holding your character in high consideration, he has requested me to enquire of you, if you will attend the Supreme Court at the February Term! And, if so, he wishes to retain you, as his counsel, upon this writ of error.[3] You are, in that event, authorized, at any time after the first of January, to draw upon me at thirty days sight, for any fee you may deem reasonable and just. An answer, to this letter, is requested by Mr. Walton at an early day. It being a matter of great moment to him, in case of your retainer, I will enclose you a Copy of the bill of Exceptions, taken on the trial, which will shew the points upon which we rely for a reversal of the Judgment.

I rejoice to hear that, you are again a Candidate for a seat in Congress. The contest here is a very warm one between Mr. Rankin, the present incumbent, and Mr. Poindexter, an ex member of Congress, whom you formerly knew. I have strong hopes and so have most good men that, the former will succeed.[4] The latter, at the time I am writing, is traversing the country and addressing the people, in his own behalf, and, as though he were the *pensioned* Orator, not like Anacharsis Clootz "of the human race"[5] but of John Q. Adams. He has also been pursuing his old vocation of writing books,[6] full of the grossest calumnies against his rival and his friends—not sparing Mr. Crawford, by the way, whom he cudgels as soundly, as he eulogizes his friend Mr. John Q. Adams. I have just room to remark to you that, this man, of whom I am speaking, from some mysterious cause, is using every endeavor to beat up a sentiment, in this state, favorable to his northern friend, as well as hostile to every other citizen, who may have pretentions to the first Executive office in the Union. I need not say to you, there are persons here, of no mean consideration, who have their eyes open to those projects and will advocate the true interests of this Country, by considering them as indissolubly connected with interests of the *West*. I think, I can say, the public sentiment here, is already or will becom[e . . .]d[7] on this subject. And, that we will prefer a Western to a Northern man, for our next President. If you will excuse the remark I would say that, your own inclinations on this matter, are not known with sufficient clearness or precision in this quarter. Your friends, however, have taken the liberty to advance pretensions on your behalf and to urge the reasons which would justify them.

Yours ever and truly THO: B: REED

Henry Clay Esqr. Lexington (Ky)

ALS. DLC-HC (DNA, M212, R1). Reed, born near Lexington, Kentucky, in 1787, had begun the practice of law there in 1808, one year before removing to Natchez, Mississippi. He was Attorney General of his adopted State, 1821-1826, and was twice a United States Senator (from January 28, 1826, to March 3, 1827, and from March 4, 1829, until his death on November 26, 1829).

1 He had been appointed to that position in 1810. Prior to that time he had been private secretary to the Governor of Mississippi Territory and, beginning in 1808, Clerk of the Supreme Court and Auditor of Public Accounts of the Territory.

2 Area not located.

3 See below, Reed to Clay, *ca.* September 1, 1822.

4 Christopher Rankin defeated George Poindexter in the election, held later this month.

5 Baron Jean-Baptiste, called "Anacharsis," Clootz, a Prussian Utopian whose ideas of universal emancipation and world brotherhood appeared to have reached fruition in the French Revolution, when he addressed the National Assembly "au nom du genre humain." Robespierre's enmity, which subsequently forced him from leadership of the Jacobins, led to his arraignment as an enemy of the Republic. He was guillotined in 1794, protesting against the iniquity of the judgment "au genre humain."

6 In 1815 Poindexter had published a pamphlet addressed *To the Public,* defending himself against charges of cowardice during the Battle of New Orleans and violation of the code duello during an encounter in which he had killed Abijah Hunt. No copy of the pamphlet is known now to exist, but excerpts may be found in the Natchez *Mississippi Republican,* July 26, 1815. Mack Buckley Swearingen, *The Early Life of George Poindexter, a Story of the First Southwest* . . . (Chicago, 1934), 135. No publication by Poindexter in 1822 has been found.

7 MS. torn, several letters missing.

From Anthony Butler

My dear Sir, Hazlewood[1] 3. August 1822

I have but this moment returned to my plantation from a tedious and fatiguing journey, and find your two letters of the 15h. & 25. July[2] on my table. I shall most certainly be in Lexington by the 20th. of this month agreable to the desire you express, where I hope to meet with you: there are many things about which we might converse that cannot so well be reduced to shape for a letter, and there are moreover some facts, that I should not chuse to hazard by the uncertain conveyance of a Mail.

Genl. Jackson's *nomination* for the Presidency has by resolution passed the House of Representatives in Tenn. *unanimously*— it seems to hang in the Senate, for several days had elapsed, by my last accounts from thence and no notice is taken of it by that body:[3] I shall probably hear from Gov. Carroll[4] before I leave this for Lexington.

What do the movements in New York & Pennsylvania indicate—can you tell? I have written a long letter to Mr. Cheves[5] on the subject, for the purpose of ascertaining not only his own opinions, but his views in regard to what N. York & pennsylvania will do. —

Don't leave home before I see you, as it is probably the only opportunity that will present itself previous to my leaving this for the State of Mississipp[i] and I should like to confer with you before my return to that State. I am very much of opinion that you have as much to fear from Alabama & Mississippi as from Louisiana—but we will talk of this when we meet.

most sincerely yours, A. BUTLER

ALS. DLC-HC (DNA, M212, R1). Addressed to Clay at Lexington; postmarked at Russellville, Kentucky, August 6.

1 Apparently the name of Butler's plantation. 2 Neither letter has been found.

3 See above, Hynes to Clay, July 31, 1822, note.

4 William Carroll. 5 Langdon Cheves.

From J[oseph] A[nderson]

Treasury Department Comptroller's Office 6th Augt. 1822

Honble. Henry Clay, Arkland [*sic*], near Lexington, Kentucky.—

Sir,

By this day's mail I received your letter, dated the 24th ulto. in which you request that the money due to you on account of half an outfit, recently authorised by the President, might be placed to your credit in the Bank of the U. States at Philada.—

In consideration of the powers vested in me by your letter, I have appointed Richard Smith, Esq. (Cashier of the Office of Discount & Deposit in this City) your Agent; in whose favor as such, the warrant has issued for $4280, being the balance found due to you, as advised by my letter of the 12th July last; which, however, does not appear to have been received on the 24th ulto. the date of your letter to me.—

Mr. Smith has undertaken to place the money to your credit in the U.S. Bank at Philada. which I expect will be done in a day or two; of which you shall be immediately thereafter advised.—

With, &ca. J. A.

Copy. DNA, RG217, Records of the 1st Comptroller, Misc. Letters Sent, vol. 21, pp. 56-57.

From Jonathan Russell

My dear Sir— Mendon 7 Aug 1822

I received by the last mail your letter of the 9 Ulto— All the abuse of Mr Adams & of his satelites has not given me so much pain as the mild intimation of your disapprobation— What is done cannot be undone— My greatest error, however, has been in placing any confidence in the candour of Mr. Adams— It was my intention to have acquainted him with the variations and to have left him, with this knowledge, free to act as he might think proper— It was for this purpose I called at the department with the exact copy in my pocket, but before I saw him, he & *the President* had found the original & the mischief was done— The coarse & violent manner in which he introduced the subject made it impossible for me to deprecate his hostility by declaring the intention with which I had called on him— Such a declaration, indeed, under such circumstances was not only repugnant to my feelings but would have been worse than useless & merely exposed me to an additional affront—[1] I now make this declaration to you because you are my friend but on the rack I would not make it to my enemies— After this explosion with Mr Adams I called on Mr Monroe & stated to him what had been my intentions & my willingness that either paper should be communicated or neither & he emphatically assured me that neither should be communicated—as he would not become the organ of personal hostility— Yet two [*sic*] days afterwards he sent his strange message of the 4th of May, which took from him all controul over the proceedings—[2] Thus I have been made the victim of the ferocity of the one & of the perfidy of the other— There is a circumstance in the conduct of Mr Adams relative to the fishing question with which perhaps you are not acquainted— He wrote to his *father* at the time an account of the transaction & the part which he had taken & the doctrine which he had asserted— His father sent this letter to James Lloyd, now a Senator in Congress, with a request to furnish his views on the subject— Mr Lloyd on the 8h of March 1815 addressed a letter of several sheets to the ex President in which he gave a most exaggerated account of the importance of the fishing privilege & a very jesuitical comment on our imperishable right to it— He says "it is a gem which should never be surrendered, nor can it ever be abandonned *by any statesmen alive to the interests of their country.* Compared in its consequences with a free right of navigating the Mississippi it is even a much more unequal stake than would be six French rapiers imponed against six Barbary horses" In another place he says— "She" (Great Britain) "has therefore notwithstanding *the opinion of two of the American Commissioners* and her own probable pretensions of fairness given up *nothing* in point of value compared with the fisheries, which upon the same ground she is undoubtedly desirious [*sic*] of fortifying herself in withholding"— This sapient treatise of Mr Lloyd was sent by the Father to Washington & is there carefully preserved in the department of State— I have reason to believe that it has even been sent to the legation at London to have an influence there— Thus it is that notwithstanding Mr. Adams' rage against *private* letters that we have been denounced in secret— All this in confidence for I do not wish it to be known at this time that I possess a copy of this letter— It may possibly be used with some advantage hereafter— You will perceive that I appealed to your recollection in my explanations on one point only & as on that your memory does not, it appears, accord precisely with mine it is of the less importance as you can decline answering, as undoubted [*sic*] you will do without affecting me— All I meant to say in my explanation on this point was that the instructions received on the 24h of november had no influence on the decisions of the board in relation to the Mississippi & that the majority & minority continued the same as before & that there was then no serious discussion or regular division on the subject. I am clear in my recollection that the dissatisfaction of Mr Bayard related to the offer made on the 1 Decr. & although he was still with the majority yet the offer was made at a time & in a manner unexpected by him— Now, my good friend, you may rest assured that I shall do nothing that can injure you Although Adams has hurt the feelings of my friends & perhaps injured me, he has gained nothing for himself by indulging in a tone unbecoming a candidate for the highest & greatest dignitity [*sic*] in this republic— All this in confidence—

For the present I shall take no further public notice of Mr Adams or his rapsodies [*sic*]— He smothers the merits of the case in a cloud of vituperation. His rejoinder is a mere *duplicate* of his remarks—[3] He avoids all argument & deals only in abuse. Any further explanation on my part would be followed by another repetition of the same scurrility on his, & tend only to keep up, I am sorry to say, the unfavourable excitement of the public— However pure & patriotic might have been my views—however just to myself or friendly towards you, still my indiscretion in confiding to any thing like magnanimity or liberality in Mr Adams, has unfortunately given him such an accidental advatage [*sic*] which he is disposed to abuse even to excess against me, that I cannot hope at present to obtain a triumph over the prejudices which he has sought to enlist against me— He has too many *printers* & *clerks* under his patronage to furnish essays & evidence to leave me a chance of encountering him with advantage— Some of the assertions in his rejoinder are totally unfounded & the declarations of Brent & Bailey, particularly the latter, contain many things worse than mistakes[4] Besides these objections to the continuance of a personal & Newspaper controversy with Mr Adams on the *present ground* I have on my hands a libel which more seriously affects my good fame & which will leave me no time & scarcely inclination to attend to lesser slanders— You will have seen in the public papers the infamous libel to which I allude—[5] With you I trust I need no defence against such a charge. I will however enclose you a copy of a letter which I have just received from Mr Frederick Mullett, a partner in the house designated by Hunt;[6] Mr Mullett is the very best witness the case admits & you will perceive that he is disposed to do me ample justice—

I will frankly confess that all these things weigh upon my heart & make me feel the want of, at least, the charity of my friends to lighten it Mrs Russell who has since her return home presented me with another daughter, gratefully acknowledges your kind remembrance of her— Remember me, in return I pray you respectfully to Mrs Clay— With great respect & regard Devotedly & faithfully Your friend JONA RUSSELL

ALS draft. RPB-Russell Papers. Published in Washington *United States Telegraph*, October 24, 1828; Washington *United States Telegraph-Extra*, I (November 8, 1828), 550-52.

1 See above, Benton to Clay, May 2, 1822, note.

2 See above, Russell to Clay, June 6, 1822, note.

3 For "Mr. Adams' Rejoinder to Mr. Russell," see Washington *Daily National Intelligencer*, July 17, 1822; Adams, *Duplicate Letters*, 138-54.

4 Adams had printed, as something of an appendix to his rejoinder, separate statements by Daniel Brent and John Bailey relating the circumstances under which Russell's letter had been delivered to the State Department, designated as a "Duplicate," and dated. Each also reported certain details of conversations with Russell. Washington *Daily National Intelligencer*, July 17, 1822; Adams, *Duplicate Letters*, 155-58.

5 A letter, signed "Ariel," had appeared in a New York newspaper charging that Russell, during the negotiations at Ghent, had sent to a London commercial firm information of a confidential nature and that he was to have profited from the resulting speculations. Upon demanding the name of the author, Russell had received from Seth Hunt, who designated himself a resident of Bennington, Vermont, an acknowledgment of authorship of the "Ariel" letter. Russell thereupon instituted in the State of New York a libel suit against his accuser. After having been several times postponed, owing in part to the desire of both parties to obtain evidence from France and England, the case was heard in 1828 and resulted in Hunt's conviction. *Niles' Weekly Register*, XXII (July 27, August 3, 24, 1822), 340, 353, 401; XXVII (October 2, 1824), 68; XXIX (December 10, 1825), 226; XXXI (November 11, 1826), 163; XXXV (October 18, 1828), 117.

6 In a published letter to Russell, July 27, 1822, Hunt had named Thomas Mullett,

I. I. Evans, and Company as the London house to which Russell allegedly had conveyed information. Evans had died before American entry into the War of 1812, and, according to Hunt, Thomas Mullett, Russell's friend, had died in December, 1814, leaving the business to his son and junior partner. *Ibid.,* XXII (August 10, 1822), 378.

Agreement with John Sheley and Matthew Barkley

[August 8, 1822]

[Henry Clay agrees to sell to John Sheley and Matthew Barkley, both of Scott County, a tract of land in that county containing 90 or 100 acres, the balance of Clay's share of a tract "recovered by the said Clay of John McKinney,"[1] from which is deducted about 26 acres which "old Mr. Montgomery"[2] lives on and "may hereafter purchase." Clay promises to deliver possession of the land, "at present in the occupation of Geo. Murray," early in the following year, "as soon as the permission expires which he gave to Joseph Lindsey to live on the same."[3] In the division of the tract "Barkley is to have about eighteen or twenty acres adjoining his land, and the said Shely [*sic*] is to have the residue."

[Sheley and Barkley agree to pay, in notes of the Bank of the Commonwealth, $20 per acre, of which "Shely has now paid . . . two hundred dollars." The remainder is to be paid by September 20, 1822.]

ADS, signed also by Sheley and Barkley. DLC-TJC (DNA, M212, R15). Endorsed on verso by Clay: "$200 at the date of the contract as within. $1274 on 20 Septr. 1822. $226 on 15 Oct. 1824 $69.20 paid 25 June 1825 122 paid 2 July 1825."

1 See above, I, 577-78n. 2 John Montgomery.

3 See above, Agreement, November 21, 1821.

Receipts from Joshua Humphreys

[August 8, 1822]

[Joshua Humphreys, Treasurer of Transylvania University,[1] acknowledges receipt for tuition in the University, of $15 from "Thomas Hart by H Clay," a like sum from "Henry C Hart[2] by H Clay," and $14 from "Henry Clay."[3]]

Each DS, printed form. DLC-TJC (DNA, M212, R15).

1 Appointed July 17, 1822, he died the following year.

2 Thomas and Henry Clay Hart were sons of Nathaniel G. S. Hart.

3 For Henry Clay, Jr.

From Henry Toland

Lexington, Ky. Philada. Augt 8h 1822

Henry Clay Esqr.

Dear Sir

I have recd. your esteemed favor of the 10th July[1] enclosing James Brown's dft. on Price & Morgan[2] at 10 days sight for five Hundred

Seventy five dollars, and requesting me to purchase five Shares of Stock of the Bank United States, and have them transfer'd to John Clay of New Orleans.[3]

I have now the pleasure to hand you enclosed the Certificate for the five Shares of Stock, with the bill of their Cost, amtg. to $516 29/100, and a check drawn by the asst. Cashier of the Bank of the United States, on their Office at Lexington, for fifty eight 71/100 dollars, in your favor, being the residue of the bill, after purchasing the Stock.

I have the pleasure to inform you that Mrs. Toland, had a fine son on the 2nd. inst, and that she, as well as the rest of my family are in good health.

Mr. and Mrs. Meade and family are in good health, and I believe their is no one to whom they all appear more attached, than to yourself. Mr. Meade has an appointment from the *new Emperor* of Mexico,[4] It is one of a mercantile nature, which will no doubt make him a good deal of money, of which their are few more deserving.

The time I suppose has not yet arrived for the demonstration in your favor relative to the ensuing election, be assured that no individual in the U States, more ardently desires your success than myself, and all my humble efforts will be used to promote what I Consider a public good– It is very Certain that Mr Calhoun never had any ground in Penna., and with the exception of Mr. Norvell[5] and a few others I have never heard an individual say that they Considered him as having just pretensions to the Presidency.

I wrote you on the 12th Ulto. on the subject of the debt due me by the Bank of Kentucky, and I soon expect to hear from you in reply thereto.[6]

In case myself or friends have any law business in Kentucky, Would it be agreeable for you to attend to it? and if not have you any friend you would wish me to employ or reccommend [*sic*]?

Please make my very sincere respects to Mrs Clay and your family and believe me Very truly your friend HENRY TOLAND

ALS. DLC-HC (DNA, M212, R1). 1 Not found.

2 Mercantile firm, composed of Chandler Price, of Philadelphia, and Benjamin Morgan, of New Orleans. Price was also a director of the second Bank of the United States. Morgan, who had moved to Louisiana from Philadelphia early in the century, had been a member of the first Territorial legislative council and subsequently of the legislature, a director of the New Orleans branch of the first Bank of the United States, and president of the Bank of New Orleans.

3 See above, Clay to Cheves, July 5, 1822; Cheves to Clay, July 27, 1822.

4 No appointment of Richard W. Meade by the Emperor Itúrbide has been found.

5 John Norvell. 6 Letter not found.

To Peter B. Porter

My dear Sir (Confidential) Ashland 10h. Aug. 1822.

I duly received your obliging favor of the 8h. Ulto. which reached this place, during my absence from home. at one of the Watering places of this Country.[1] I thank you, most sincerely, for the interesting communication contained in your letter and for the very friendly sentiments towards me which it expresses, and which were such as I anticipated, reciprocating them most fully as I do on my part.

The resolution to which many of the distinguished republicans in New York have come, as noticed by you, appears to me to be extremely judicious. If adhered to, it will doubtless give to that State, what it has not heretofore had, a weight in the National Councils proportionate to its numbers, its patriotism, and its talents. We think, in this quarter, (you are however much better judges) that all the considerations connected with that object as well as those which appertain to the Nation at large, and which you will of course not neglect, must urge you ultimately to turn your attention to the West for supplying a Successor to Mr. Monroe.

Since I last addressed you, I was induced some what reluctantly to present myself as a Candidate for the next Congress. My election has just terminated, without any opposition.

You will also have noticed another event, the recommendation of Genl. Jackson, by the Legislature of Tennessee, as the next President.[2] It has excited some surprize with us, because it is believed to have been only recently thought of even in that quarter. It is uncertain whether it has been stimulated to produce division in the West, or was intended as a mere compliment to the Genl. from his own State, without an expectation that it would be seconded by any other. I think it may be asserted very confidently that no other Western State will lend its support to him. My friends in Tennessee continue to assure me that, if the General be out of the way, I shall receive its undivided support; and they think that it will not persist in bringing him forward, with out probability of a considerable support in other States. All the information which is received from other Western States, and particularly Ohio, continues to be encouraging in the highest degree.

Mrs. Clay unites her respects with mine to Mrs. Porter; and I pray you to believe me, as ever, Faithfy & Cordially Your friend

Genl. P. B. Porter. H. CLAY

ALS. NBuHi.

1 See above, Clay to Russell, July 9, 1822, note.

2 See above, Hynes to Clay, July 31, 1822.

From William Meredith

Honble. Henry Clay Lexington Ky Philad. August 12th. 1822

Sir

My Brother, Mr David Meredith,—his health not being such as to admit of his paying attention to his concerns,—has handed to me a correspondence which he has had with James Brown Esqr & yourself in relation to a claim upon the House of Brown & Bell.[1] In your letter of 21st. April 1818.,—the last he has had the honour to receive from you,—you express a belief that Brown & Bells account had, two or three years before, been sent to the Circuit where Brown resides for collection—but promise on your return to Kentucky to look into the affair—

I shall feel myself exceedingly obliged if you will inform me what has been the result of this examination and am

Very respectfully Your Most Obt. Servt. W. Meredith

ALS. DLC-TJC (DNA, M212, R12). Forwarded to Columbus, Ohio. Meredith was a lawyer, banker, and, for a time, City Solicitor of Philadelphia.

1 Correspondence not found. John Brown and David Bell had been partners in a mercantile venture at Washington, Kentucky, before the turn of the century. Brown remained a resident of Mason County until his death in 1833; Bell had moved to Danville, where he continued in business as a merchant.

From George C. Thompson

Dear Sir, Shawanee Springs[1] 12th Augt. 1822

Col. McClung[2] from the neighborhood of Knoxville, a particular friend of mine & highly respectable old gentleman, was here two days since, and in conversation about the strange Caper of the H. of Representatives of Tennessee in nominating Genl. Jackson for the Presidency; he explained the the [*sic*] thing to me in this way.[3] The term of Mr. Williams one of their Senators in Congress is about to expire, and at this extra session an election is to take place. Williams is again a Candidate, and at the meeting of the Legislature appearances were altogether favourable to his re-election. But Pleasant Miller,[4] a Representative from Knox County, being exceedingly hostile to Williams, and knowing that Williams was not a friend to Jackson, has played off this manouvre to bring Jacksons name to bear, & make a point in the Election of Senator. Whether Genl. Jackson had been consulted or not Col. McClung does not know; but his impression is strong that so soon as the Election of Senator is over, we shall hear no more of a Tennessee Candidate for the Office of President. He thinks too that Williams will still be elected easily who it seems belongs to Carrols[5] party. The Col. says that Genl. Jackson would by no means be generally supported in his own State, and he believes will not ultimately be a candidate. If Col. McClungs idea be correct, there is perhaps no danger yet of the desertion of Tennessee from the Western Forces.

Retired as I am from the bustle of politics I still feel considerable solicitude on this subject not only as a personal friend of our Kentucky Candidate, but as a Citizen of the West; I have therefore taken the liberty of communicating to you this suggestion of my friend McClung; Altho' I ought to presume that you will not be without much more ample information of the real intention of the Tennesseans. I am Dr. Sir very respectfully yr. friend & mo Obt.

GEO. C. THOMPSON

ALS. DLC-HC (DNA, M212, R1). Addressed to Clay at Lexington; postmarked at Harrodsburg, Kentucky.

1 Thompson's estate, "Pleasant Fields," was located on Shawnee Creek, a few hundred yards from the Shawnee Spring, site of an early Indian attack, and about four miles north of Harrodsburg, Kentucky. It became a popular retreat for those visiting at the Greenville Springs resort.

2 Charles McClung, a native of Lancaster, Pennsylvania, who had laid out and surveyed the townsite of Knoxville, Tennessee. A merchant and a lawyer, he served as Clerk of the Knox County Court, 1792-1834, member of the State constitutional convention, 1796, and presidential elector, 1796 and 1800.

3 Cf. above, Hynes to Clay, July 31, 1822.

4 Miller, a former member of Congress, 1809-1811, and a veteran of the War of 1812, was a prominent Knoxville lawyer. Around 1824 he moved to western Tennesee and served as Chancellor of that judicial division in 1836 and 1837.

5 William Carroll.

To Charles Hammond

Dr Sir Lexington 14h. Aug. 1822.

I have duly received your obliging letter of the 6h. instant,[1] and I should now proceed to notice the several interesting topics of which it treats, but that I expect to have the pleasure of seeing you at Columbus in about a fortnight, when we can converse, at large, and much more satisfactorily upon them. I do not think that we can differ, after a full comparison of our respective sentiments, about the power of the General Government to provide *remedies,* in regard to those subjects of cognizance, which are confided to the Federal judiciary.[2] There is, doubtless, great difficulty in an accurate discrimination between right and remedy; between the rule, and the mode of enforcing it. But when they are both clearly defined, we have made a considerable advance in the ascertainment of the powers which appertain to the Federal & State Sovereignties.

Our elections have just terminated both for Congress and the State Legislature. For the latter body, they have been warmly contested; and, although the Relief party has so far prevailed as to have the majority, a powerful re-action was demonstrated, to an extent which leaves but little doubt that in another year a reform in our Laws will be effected.[3] My own election was without opposition.

I remain faithfly & Cordially Your ob. Servt. H. CLAY

C. Hammond Esqr.

ALS. InU. 1 Not found.

2 See above, Clay to Hammond, July 14, 1822.

3 On the repeal of the replevy laws, see above, II, 904n. The Lexington *Kentucky Reporter,* August 12, 1822, discussing the very close contest in which the relief candidates of Fayette County had been elected observed: "They [the antirelief forces]

may with confidence look forward to a period of *Relief* from the unjust oppression and unexampled usurpation of a violent party."

Receipt to Frances Rawlins

[August 16, 1822]

Attached to Rental Agreement with Mrs. Rawlins, March 1, 1822.

To John S. Skinner

Dear Sir, ASHLAND, 19th August, 1822.

Your letter under date the 11th ultimo,[1] reached Lexington, whilst I was absent from home, on a visit to one of our watering places,[2] and on that account there has arisen some delay in my answer. I received the portraits by mail, shortly after I addressed you on the subject of them.[3]

You request some account of my imported English Cattle, which I give with great pleasure. In 1816, I wrote to my friend, Peter Irving at Liverpool, the brother of our distinguished countryman, Washington Irving, and requested him to purchase for me two pair of English Cattle, one of the beef and the other of the milk breed.[4] I gave him a carte blanche, both as to price and races. He took great pains to satisfy himself of the best breeds in the kingdom, by a resort to all the means of information at his command; and he became convinced that the Hereford reds was the best, as combining in themselves the three great qualities, beef, milk and draught, which it is desirable that cattle should possess.— Accordingly he caused to be selected and purchased for me, in January 1817, two pair of that breed of cattle. Two of them were two year-olds, and the other two yearlings; the sum of their cost was £105 sterling. They were shipped at Liverpool, in March 1817, on board the same ship, which imported the English Cattle, for some gentlemen in this neighbourhood, an account of which you have already published,[5] but that was altogether accidental, there having been no concert whatever between those gentlemen and me, in making our respective importations. They were received by Messrs. McDonald and Ridgely, in April or May 1817, and I immediately upon hearing of their landing in the United States, despatched a messenger for them. He brought them about one hundred and fifty miles from Baltimore into the State of Virginia, and owing to the great heat of the season and the wearing away of their hoofs, he was obliged to leave them there to rest, until the weather became cooler; so that it was late in August before they reached Kentucky. One of the bulls died on his way from Baltimore to Virginia, from over feeding on red clover. Estimating the first cost of the cattle, and all incidental charges from the time they were purchased in England, until I received them in Kentucky, and charging the three survivors with what was lost by the death of their companion, those three have come to me at five hundred dollars each. My cattle are very beautiful, fine form, symmetry and color.— They are all without exception, a deep red, white faces, white under the belly, at the tip end of the tail and on one or more of the feet. As I have generally parted with the young, I am not able yet to pronounce, with certainty, whether they will realize the high expectations, which were entertained of them by my friend, Mr. Irving; but I believe he has not been deceived as to their qualities.

We have been for some years breeding in this State, very extensively, from some English Cattle, imported forty or forty-five years ago, by, I believe, Mr. Gough, of Maryland, and Mr. Miller Virginia [*sic*].[6] This race of cattle attains a larger size, than any of those of the late importations which we have made. The latter do not, however, want size, and the circumstance of their being smaller than the descendants of the old importation is abundantly compensated by their having less bone, being greatly superior in symmetry, and distributing their flesh on the carcase much better, so as to produce more meat on the good parts. Animals which are ill made, are difficult to keep in good order, because they cannot struggle for subsistence as well as those which are well built. I may, at some future period, inform you how my cattle turn out.

With great respect, I am your obedient servant, H. CLAY.

J. S. Skinner, Esq.

The American Farmer, IV (October 4, 1822), 223. 1 Not found.

2 See above, Clay to Russell, July 9, 1822, note.

3 Clay's letter has not been found.

4 Letter not found. For Irving's reply, see above, II, 252-53.

5 *The American Farmer,* II (December 29, 1820), 313-14.

6 Harry Dorsey Gough, wealthy planter and Baltimore merchant, elected in 1786 as the first president of the Society for the Encouragement and Improvement of Agriculture in Maryland, was long interested in improving livestock by importations from abroad. Descendants of cattle imported shortly after the Revolutionary War by Gough and Miller, the latter of Augusta County, Virginia (possibly Henry Miller, son of the pioneer Pennsylvania-German settler in the Shenandoah Valley), had been brought to Kentucky about 1785 by sons and a son-in-law of Matthew Patton. Patton himself settled in Clark County, Kentucky, in 1790, bringing additional animals of the Gough and Miller strain. Edith Rossiter Bevan, "Perry Hall: County Seat of the Gough and Carroll Families," *Maryland Historical Magazine,* XLV (March, 1950), 33-34, 40-41; Rice, "Importations of Cattle into Kentucky, 1785-1860," *Kentucky Historical Society Register,* XLIX (January, 1951), 36-37.

Credential as United States Congressman

[August 20, 1822]

ADS, by John Watkins, deputy for Henry Watkins, Sheriff of Woodford County; signed also by John C. Richardson, Jr., Sheriff of Fayette, and John B. Ryon, deputy for Thomas Wornall, Sheriff of Clark County. DNA, RG233, HR18A-H1. Similar to Credentials, above, I, 484. Wornall had been a member of the Kentucky House of Representatives, 1809-1810; and Ryon later, 1833-1835, served in the same body.

Toast and Response at Public Dinner

[August 28, 1822]

Our guest, Mr. Clay—His public services are cherished in the gratitude and recollections of the people: we hail with gratitude and confidence his return to the councils of the nation.

Mr. Clay said that, in rising to make his respectful acknowledgments for the sentiments just drank, and for the flattering marks of kind attention which, on the occasion of a former as well as his present visit, he had experienced in this city, he trusted he should violate no usage nor offend against any sense of propriety which prevailed here. He should be sorry indeed if there existed any restraint to the expression, however inadequate it might be, of the grateful emotions which he felt. He had been long desirous to see Cincinnati. He had been prevented from having that gratification until about two years ago, when he was brought here principally by a professional duty, painful to himself, and which, had its citizens been less liberal, less magnanimous, might have induced them to have given him a cold and cheerless reception. They then received him with a warm and hearty cordiality which he should never forget.* He was anxious to see this city for many reasons. It held indisputably the first rank among our western towns. All had a rapid and unexampled rise. Whilst towns in other countries rose gradually and so imperceptibly that their origin was obscured in their antiquity, this city had sprung up, on the banks of the most beautiful river in the world, as it were but yesterday, by a sort of enchantment. If causes, common to the whole of the western towns, for a moment seemed to cloud its prospects, he had no doubt that it would emerge, by its native energies, by the industry and by the enterprise of its citizens, and exhibit a renewed activity and an increased splendor and expansion.

He was extremely gratified to find that the gentlemen here assembled approved of his return to the national councils. He had left them with regret, and for imperious private motives which it would be impertinent here to relate. In going back again he should endeavour to carry with him those broad and comprehensive principles, by which he had ever sought to guide his public conduct, and by which every part and every interest of this great confederacy ought to be fostered and encouraged and protected.— And it would be to him a source of proud and agreeable recollection if he should be enabled hereafter to deserve the distinguished favor which, on this occasion, had been shewn him.

* Mr C. was understood here to allude more particularly to the offer then made him of the compliment of a public dinner, which he was obliged to decline.[1]

Lexington *Kentucky Reporter,* September 9, 1822. Published also in Lexington *Kentucky Gazette,* September 12, 1822; *Niles' Weekly Register,* XXIII (September 21, 1822), 48. The dinner, honoring Clay and Thomas Sidney Jesup, was held in Cincinnati.

[1] Cf. above, II, 888. No invitation and reply have been found.

From Thomas Jefferson

Dear Sir Monticello Aug. 28. 22.

In the general sufferings by the misfortunes of the late Colo. Wilson Carey Nicholas, my grandson Thos. Jefferson Randolph[1] & myself are in danger of a heavy participation. we were bound to the bank of the US. in Richmd. jointly and severally for him in the sum of twenty thousand Dollars, and my grandson was under some additional obligations. a plank however seems to float within our reach, which, if we can secure it, will save us from the wreck. this happens to be in the state of Kentucky, and we are anxious to engage your professional services in our behalf. Thomas Deye Owings of that state was indebted by bond to W.C. Nicholas in the sum of 10,000 pounds Kentucky money, the principal payable July 1, 1805. There is reason to presume that no payments, either of principal or interest have been made on this bond; and our request to you is to have suit brought on it immediately in the Federal district court of Kentucky. Colo. Morrison[2] of that state acted during mr Nicholas's life as his Attorney in fact, as to all his property and interests in Kentucky; and in order to enable him to transact the business with effect, that property was conveyed to him absolutely, but expressly in trust: and Owings' bond was specifically included in the conveyance. but, at the same time, the bond itself was retained by mr Nicholas in his own possession; and at his death it has come to the hands of his executors, in whom the legal property, as well as possession, of course is, and in whose name alone can a suit on it be maintained. they do not know whether Colo. Morrison sets up any claim of personal right in this bond. if he does we shall ask your assistance against him also. uncertain whether a letter might find you in Kentucky, and indeed whether it might be agreeable to you to undertake the cause, I inclose all the necessary papers to my friend and relation Dabney Terril,[3] who will be so kind as to form a point of communication between us, and those who may be interested or concerned in the case. these papers are so full and particular that I need go into no further details here. a copy only of the bond is sent, which may serve to commence the action on, and we reserve the original to go by a safer conveyance than the public mail. altho' I can have nothing to do in the action on this subject, in my own name, I am really interested as deeply as the parties themselves. because if the exrs can pay the debt out of this property of Colo. Nicholas, it will shield me from being called on for it.[4] my grandson, as exr, will attend to the duty of a proper compensation for your trouble, and he writes to mr Terril on that subject. should your law, like ours, require a plaintiff, not a resident of the state, to give security for costs of suit in case of failure, my antient friend John Brown of Lexington will I trust give me the benefit of his responsibility for the costs, as perhaps will mr Terril himself, on my assuming, as I do assume, to idemnify them against all loss on that account. in hope we shall not fail in the advantage we promise ourselves of your kind aid to help us out of the difficulties in which this unfortunate engagement has involved us, I pray you to accept the assurance of my very sincere esteem for you, and of my high respect. TH: JEFFERSON

the honble Henry Clay esquire.

ALS. ViU.

1 Jefferson's favorite grandson, a son of Thomas M. and Martha Jefferson Randolph. He had several years earlier been entrusted with management of Jefferson's financial affairs, and, upon Jefferson's death in 1826, he became chief executor of the estate. He was for many years a member of the Board of Visitors of the University of Virginia and served several terms in the State House of Delegates. Randolph's wife, to whom he was married in 1815, was Jane, daughter of Wilson Cary Nicholas.

2 James Morrison.

3 Dabney Carr Terrell, of Louisville, who died in 1827 at an early age. Jefferson was his great-uncle.

4 A suit, brought in Fayette Circuit Court, February 24, 1824, in the name of W. C. Nicholas' Administrator *vs.* Thomas Deye Owings, was decided in favor of the plaintiff at the September Term of that year. An execution was issued for £20,000, to be discharged by payment of £10,000, plus interest from July 1, 1805, and costs. The sheriff's return, however, was marked, "no property." D. DLC-TJC (DNA, M212, R16); Fayette Circuit Court, File 583. At the same time, Clay, as Nicholas' administrator brought two other actions to collect debts due on earlier judgments issued in Fayette Circuit Court against Owings, one for $5,338.46 and the other for $8,711.30, both with interest at six per cent annually from November 18, 1819, and court costs. These judgments were accordingly revived at the March Term, 1824. *Ibid.,* File 571.

Settlement with William S. Dallam

[September 1, 1822]

Attached to Assignment, November 10, 1819.

From Charles W. Goldsborough

Sir Washington 3 Septr 1822.

Your letter of the 22nd ins [*sic*][1] with a check on the Bank of the U S at Philadelphia for 220$ payable to the order of commre.

Rodgers, has just been received, & transmitted to Him at Boston. I have the honor to be respy, Sir, Yr mo ob st.

CHS: W: GOLDSBOROUGH

To the Honorable Henry Clay Lexington Ky.

ALS. DLC-TJC (DNA, M212, R12). Endorsed by Clay: "Commodore Rogers [*sic*] Rect. for $220. on a/ct. of Carriage—This was the bal. in full 180$ having been remitted him in a bill of R. Wickliff [*sic*] on James Barbour and $100 in a check on the bank of the U.S." Cf. above, Rodgers to Clay, July 18, 1822, and note.

1 Not found.

From Return Jonathan Meigs

Dr Sir, Marietta Sepr. 3d 1822

Yours of Augt. 21t.[1] was recd but yesterday—so late that I fear this will not find you at Columbus—

I cannot think that the legislative nomination of Gen Jackson will be adopted in other States;—but it may serve as a precedent for nominations of others in other States, & I do not think that an unfavourable Event—

Gen J will decline eventually— The public esteem him *only* for his military Energy— He is too much of a Soldier to be a civilian that is

"Impiger—iracundus—inexorabilis, acer,

"Jura sibi—negat—nati se"[2]

There is more of the Dictator—than of the Consul in his Character.

This Nation is to be governed by moral, not physical Force—I am decidedly favourable to a legislative nomination in Ohio—at the next Session & shall in conjunction with Colo Barber[3] & others endeavour to have it effected.— The measure will be more readilily [*sic*] adopted —as Tennessee has already set the Example—

I shall next week attend the Commencement of the Ohio University at Athens—with Mr Barber, where I expect to meet with many Gentlemen Trustees of the College[4]—& shall be able to learn their Sentiments— In the East—they are silent in general— I expect to return to Washington in 30 days With Esteem & Regard Yrs.

H Clay Esqr. R J MEIGS

ALS. DLC-HC (DNA, M212, R1). Addressed to Clay at Columbus, Ohio.

1 Not found. 2 Horace, *Ars Poetica,* lines 121-22.

3 Levi Barber, who had represented Washington County in the Ohio House of Representatives, 1806-1807.

4 Earlier in the year both Meigs and Barber had been appointed trustees of this institution, founded by the Ohio legislature in 1804.

To Jonathan Russell

My dear Sir Columbus 4h. September 1822

Being at this place attending the Federal Court of Ohio, your letter under date the 7h Ulto addressed to me at Lexington, has been forwarded to me here. I assure you, most sincerely, that it gave me as much pain to make, as it could possibly you to receive, "the mild intimation of my disapprobation" in regard to the unfortunate error which, I think, you committed in the variance between your two letters. I thought it due to our mutual friendship that I should speak, in its genuine spirit, without disguise. But I will not dwell on that unpleasant subject. "What is done cannot be undone," and I would rather soothe your feelings than add, in the smallest degree, to your afflictions. I have no doubt that you were dealt with, by the persons to whom you refer, with great duplicity, and that one of them even sought to produce the very state of things which exists. So far as the controversy is a personal one, I do not see that a continuance of it in the news papers is likely to be profitable to you. So far as it respects the public grounds of difference between Mr Adams and you—the respective values of the Fishing liberty and the navigation of the Mississippi, and the continued operation of the provisions of the former treaty of peace—much more might be said, and advantageously said. These are, in truth, the only grounds in which the public at large has a deep and extensive interest, and it has so happened heretofore that they have occupied the least prominent position in your controversy. As Mr Adams has avowed his intention of appealing to the public, in another form, in relation to those grounds, you may have an opportunity, if you think proper to embrace it, to resume the subject under better auspices.

I think I have seen the letter of Mr Lloyd to which you refer. I recollect it rather from his strange figure of the French rapiers and the Barbary horses, than from its argument. I feel so perfectly confident in the propriety of the opinions which we held at Ghent, in regard to the navigation of the Mississippi and the Fishing liberty, that I should not be provoked, by the eccentricities of Mr Lloyd to engage in any public vindication of them. A great part of the nation is now surprized, and all of it will before long wonder, that any person could ever think of exchanging the one for the other.

I had seen the production of Ariel, and have read the correspondence which subsequently passed between its author and you, as I have also observed the proceedings which you have instituted against him. I never could doubt the baseness of his calumny, and rejoice to find, from the copy of the letter which you transmitted to me, that you will have it in your power to expose its atrocity and to manifest to the world that the opinion which it has entertained of your probity rests upon a solid foundation. In this controversy I am persuaded that you have all the sympathies of the public on your side. And I trust that your complete vindication, which I anticipate as certain, will go far to efface any unfavorable impression which has been made by your affair with Mr Adams.

Our elections to Congress have just terminated in Kentucky. I was returned without opposition, 'though with some reluctance on my part.

With great regard I am faithfully & cordially Your friend

Jonathan Russell Esq H. CLAY

ALS. RPB. Published in Washington *United States Telegraph*, October 24, 1828.

From Thomas B. Reed

Dear Sir Natchez, Sept. 5th, 1822.

I have received your letter of the 17th. Ult.[1] I am much pleased to learn that, you will attend the next Session of the Supreme Court of the U. States and that, you Will appear for Mr. Walton, upon the Writ of error, which he has sued out against the United States. The recovery, against him, is for much more, than is due in justice. And his Case presents one of the strongest instances of injustice which has appeared upon the books of the Treasury Department. Inclosed, I send you, a Copy of the bill of Exceptions, taken upon the trial, in the Court below. It presents the only points of defectiveness, in the Record, upon which, it is sought, to reverse the Judgment. I had myself, upon the trial below, most confidence in the third ground, assumed in the Exceptions. The principle decided Case, upon this point, on which I relied, is to be found in Second Wash. rep. 172 Overton & Wife vs. Hudson.[2] You will pardon the liberty I take in refering you to it.

I feel much gratified, in knowing more explicitly, your sentiments, On an Other Subject, to which you have been so kind as to advert, in answer to my former letter. I had myself supposed there Would be the Concert you mention, among the States West of the mountains and as far South as the Gulf of Mexico, in favor of some person. And I saw no One, upon whom public favor, in this regard, was so likely to fix itself, as upon you. An effort, indeed, was made, as I mentioned to you in my former letter, to beat up a sentiment in favor of Mr. Adams; but, I think, but little progress has been made in his behalf. Mr. Crawford is not, for some reason Or Other, in good Odour, with the people here; and Mr. Calhoun is but little known and has, as yet, excited no industry Or interest in his behalf. You will pardon the frankness I use, in saying that, nothing opposes itself to your interests, in this State, but the part you took, upon the question growing Out of the Seminole War.[3] Genl. Jackson was thought and, in truth, had rendered important services to the Country and more especially to this part of it. And some artful persons have essayed to connect your admirable Speech, delivered

On that Occasion, into [an] attack upon him; instead of considering it [as] it really was, an enlightened and indep[endent] discussion of the high political concer[ns of the] Country. In other respects, I think, no [one is] fairer, for political promotion, than you[;] and, I think, that this illusion will eas[ily] yield to the strong Claims to admira[tion,] gratitude and confidence, which you [hold] upon Our Common Country.

I am pleased to Commun[icate to] you that, I was Wrong in my assert[ion] that the Contest Would be Warm [between] Mr. Rankin and Mr. Poindexter. The [former] is elected by nearly two to One.

I hope at some future day [to have] the pleasure of seeing you at Wa[shington,] but as the fervor of youth has ab[ated] also has diminished passion for [public] life. And, tho I think I could be se[nt] to the Senate, yet my more substant[ial in]terests will forbid it.

I embrace you With Cordiality & affect[ion] THO: B: REE[D]

The honble. Henry Clay Esqr.

ALS. DLC-HC (DNA, M212, R1). Right margin ragged. Cf. above, Reed to Clay, August 2, 1822.

[1] Not found.

[2] Overton *et ux*, Administrator and Administratrix of Josiah Hunley, *vs.* Charles Hudson, Executor of Christopher Hudson, 1 *Va.* (2 Wash.) 172-80 (April Term, 1796).

[3] See above, II, 636-62.

To Return Jonathan Meigs

My dear Sir Columbus 11 Sept. 1822.

I received your obliging favor addressed to me at this place,[1] and I am very thankful for the opinion which it communicates respecting the subject of a Legislative nomination. My friends here who have conversed with me on that topic entirely coincide with you; and think that the public sentiment is so fixed, that there will be a general disposition on the part of the Legislature to manifest, in the form of such a nomination, the public wish. It undoubtedly belongs exclusively to Ohio to adopt what opinion it may think proper on that point, and to declare it or not, in any mode that may be deemed expedient. But the effect of a declaration in my favor I believe throughout the Union would be very great, and tend more to decide the question than almost any other single circumstance that can be mentioned. Nor do I think that the time spoken of will be unseasonable. On the contrary it is my firm belief that it is the fittest that can occur, and that all the good effect to be anticipated from it would be lost, if it were longer deferred.[2]

There is some sickness in this place. My own health continues as good as I expected. That you may continue to enjoy your's is the sincere wish of Your faithful friend H. CLAY

The Honble Mr. Meigs

ALS. NcD. [1] Above, September 3, 1822.

[2] See below, Sloane to Clay, December 19, 1822, note; Clay to Brooke, January 8, 1823, note.

To Langdon Cheves

Sir Columbus 13h. Septr. 1822.

In coming to this place to attend the Federal Court I determined to take Cincinnati in my route that I might stimulate the Agent and Solicitor,[1] if it were necessary, in their exertions to prepare the causes of the Bank for trial. I found them sufficiently zealous in their endeavors to make full preparation. Mr. Jones came up to the Court and brought with him, in his own carriage, the principal witness, and the two other witnesses were also punctual in their attendance. I have therefore the satisfaction to inform you, that we have obtained two hundred and eleven judgments, in cases issuing from the Cincinnati office alone, and that there were only about twenty causes continued. These were continued owing to some peculiar circumstances affecting them, either at our instance or at that of the defendants; such as, that arrangements were pending for an amicable adjustment the absence of witnesses, alleged necessary for the defence, &c &c.

Our success both as to matters of fact and of law, controverted in the course of the trials, has been remarkably great. We lost but three or four cases, on account of notice to the indorsers, one where it was given too soon, another of them where it was too late, a third where it was left at an improper place. We suffered a non suit in the case of one indorser, respecting whom we thought the evidence insufficient, and that we could hereafter strengthen it. The developements, during the progress of the trials, evinced a degree of attention, on the part of the late office at Cincinnati, to the delivery of notices, which agreeably surprized me.

We did not receive the communications from the Bank, in regard to the case of John H. Piatt,[2] time enough to institute suits returnable to the present term. Nevertheless, before they came to hand, I prepared a bill to foreclose the equity of redemption of the representatives of the mortgagor, and had the parties notified that I should move the Court to restrain them, by injunction, from proceeding to collect the accruing rents and profits and for the appointment of a Receiver. They came forward, and have entered into an agreement with Mr. Jones, under my advice, which is to last until the end of the January term. According to this agreement the Bank is to be let in immediately to the receipt of two thirds of the rents, and the Admors are to be responsible to the Bank for the retained third, if the Court shall be of opinion hereafter that the

Bank has a right to the rents. The cause is to be docketed at the next court, the answers then filed, and we are not to be prejudiced by forbearing at this time to exhibit the bill & to make the motion which I contemplated. On the part of the Admors the motive avowed, for this temporary arrangement, was to afford them the opportunity of the intermediate time, to endeavor to effect at Philadelphia an amicable arrangement. On our part I was influenced by the considerations 1st. that we were immediately to receive two thirds of the rents. 2dly. that the suit could not be made *returnable* to the present term. But 3dly. & principally because I had some fears on the question of jurisdiction, some of the *heirs residing out of this district,* and if they answer the bill, as agreed upon, I hope to obviate that difficulty. I really think that Mrs. Piatt has a strong claim upon the generous consideration of her case, on the part of the Bank. I believe that no other creditor of Piatt will fare as well as the Bank. And I should be glad, if the Board shall feel itself justified to do something for her. In considering of the case, the circumstance of obviating, by an arrangement, all difficulties in regard to possession, ought to have some weight. If such an arrangement be effected, there will be no point of contest remaining, and nothing left to be done but the prosecution of a formal suit to bar the equity of redemption.

Mr. Jones will doubtless put you in possession of all the information which he can collect respecting the condition of Piatt's Estate; and I shall request him to forward you a copy of the agreement recently entered into as above mentioned

Mr. Worthington, our Solicitor, executes his intention of leaving the State, and consequently the service of the Bank. A successor to him will be necessary. Who shall he be? You ought to hear Mr. Jones on that point. I think Mr. Crittenden[3] has claims upon you for the appointment which, if there be no one in whose favor there exist stronger considerations, I should be glad he might receive.

Your communication respecting the business of Piatt and Mr. Marshall,[4] addressed to me at Lexington, has found me here. It shall be attended to. I have the honor to be with great respect Your obedient Servant. H. CLAY

Langdon Cheves Esqr. &c &c &c

ALS. PHi-Dreer Collection.

1 George W. Jones, and probably William M. Worthington, Cincinnati lawyer.

2 See above, Clay to Cheves, June 16, 1822, note.

3 Thomas T. Crittenden does not appear to have received the appointment. The solicitorship went to David K. Este, born in New Jersey and educated at the College of New Jersey, who had studied law and, in 1809, settled in Cincinnati. He removed briefly to Hamilton, Ohio, but in 1814 returned to permanent residence in Cincinnati, where in 1835 he was elected President Judge of the Ninth Circuit of the Ohio Courts of Common Pleas and in 1838 the first judge of the newly established Superior Court of Cincinnati.

4 John J. Marshall. The letter has not been found.

From Jacob Burnet

Dear Sir Cincinnati Sepr 18 1822

On my return from the circuit I found your very friendly confidential letter, of Aug 27—[1] I have since turned my attention, seriously, to the subject—I mean the propriety, or expediency of my undertaking to discharge the important trust referred to in your letter, should the Legislature be inclined, by your friendly interference, to honor me with the appointment.

While on the circuit last Summer, Mr Cotton[2] put into my hand the communication of Govr. Adair, on the subject of the claim set up by Virginia, which I read hastily.[3] The impression made on my mind was, that the holders of the warrants had acquired an equitable claim by the different laws passed on the subject, prior to the separation. This however, was the impression of the moment without much reflection, and ex parte.

On reading the opinion of the Supreme Court, relative to your occupying claimant law,[4] which was also a hasty perusal not accompanied with much deliberation, my impressions were unfavorable to the decision, but those impressions might have been produced, as much, perhaps more, by a conviction of the injury that would result from the decision, and the impropriety of the existence of such a restraint, as it imposed on your Legislature, than by an opinion, formed on the import of the compact. It is probable that I have expressed myself, when speaking of that decision, as would be natural for a person to do, in a transient conversation, with impressions on his mind, similar to those I have stated.

But in addition to the ground of objection, I feel a conviction which candor requires me to communicate, that the State of Kentucky, ought to seek for a person, more acquainted with the subject in controversy, and better able to discern and secure the rights, than myself. I feel so sensibly, my inability to execute the trust, with safety to the parties, or satisfaction to myself, that I must beg you not to mention my name and let me assure you, that this is not the result of an affected modes[ty,] but the real conviction of my judgment.[5]

I am fully sensible of the compliment which your proposition contains, and the honor that such an appointment, from the Commonwealth of Kentucky, must necessarily confer and I should anticipate it with much feeling if I elieved [*sic*] myself equal to its duties.

I duly appreciate the favorable impressions that have been made on your mind, in regard to myself, and can only add, my wishes that I were better entitled to them

I am Very respectfully Your friend J BURNET

Hon Henry Clay

ALS. DLC-HC (DNA, M212, R1). Burnet, a judge of the Ohio Supreme Court (1821-1828), had moved to Cincinnati from New Jersey in 1796. He had been a member of the legislative council of the territorial government, a member of the State legislature (1812-1816), and president of the Cincinnati branch of the second Bank of the United States. In 1828 he became United States Senator from Ohio, filling the vacancy caused by the resignation of William H. Harrison. A conservative in politics (calling himself a Federalist), he was active in business, education, and civic affairs in Cincinnati. He was a half brother of Isaac G. Burnet.

1 Not found.

2 Possibly John Cotton, of Washington County, Ohio, member of the Ohio House of Representatives, 1824-1825.

3 Probably Governor Adair's communication to the Kentucky legislature in Special Session, May 14, 1822, presenting the report and resolutions of the Virginia Senate and House of Delegates outlining the latter State's position in the controversy with Kentucky on the military grants between the Green and Tennessee rivers. Ky. H. of Reps., *Journal, Special Session, 1822,* pp. 16-47; Ky. Sen., *Journal, Special Session, 1822,* pp. 15-45.

4 See above, DuVal to Clay, June 14, 1821.

5 See below, Clay to Leigh, November 18, 1822.

To Joseph Gales, Jr.

Dr Sir Lexington 21st. Sept. 1822.

Your letter of the 28h. Ulto.[1] reached here a few days prior to my return from the Federal Court in Ohio, and on that account some delay has arisen in my acknowledgment of the receipt of it.

I am greatly concerned and mortified by the delinquency of poor Dougherty, and the bad state of his affairs.[2] He was the last man of whom I could have expected any irregularity in his public account. There must be some unexplained cause of it. It cannot be attributed, I think, to any extravagance in his living.

I have communicated the contents of your letter to his son in law Mr. Tilford,[3] a deserving good man, who had however previously received similar information from the City. G. W. Botts Esqr. the brother in law of Mr. Dougherty,[4] and who has administered here upon his Estate, will reach the City about the time you may receive this letter; and he goes there for the purpose of arranging the affairs of the deceased. He is a man of respectable standing and I understand of good property. He will be able to inform you fully of the condition of his means in this Country. I recommend him to your good offices.

My respects to Mr. Seaton[5] I am Your ob. Servt. H. CLAY

Jo. Gales Jr. Esqr.

ALS. NNPM. 1 Not found.

2 Thomas Dougherty had died in Lexington, August 9, 1822. A suit against his administrators for a balance of $1,338.15, due on his contingent account as Clerk of the House of Representatives, resulted in an interlocutory decree in May, 1831, binding the assets of his estate. Suit was renewed against his administrators and another instituted against his sureties, but the balance (reduced to $1,298.15 in 1835) was reported through 1839 as unpaid. *House Docs.,* 19 Cong., 2 Sess., no. 137, p. 3; 24 Cong., 1 Sess., no. 16, p. 5; 25 Cong., 2 Sess., no. 186, p. 6.

3 Robert Tilford, who had married Mary Ann Dougherty, in Flemingsburg, Kentucky, in 1819.

[4] Nancy Scott Dougherty, widow of Thomas, was the sister of Ann Scott Botts (Mrs. George W. Botts).
[5] William W. Seaton.

From Peter B. Porter

Dear Sir, Black Rock Sept. 30. 1822

I received, some time ago, your friendly letter of the 10th. of August, and am much gratified to learn that you have been returned to the next Congress— It is an event calculated to produce the most favourable results. You have undoubtedly observed that the *National Advocate* of N. York, commenced the Campaign, several months ago, in favour of Mr Crawford. Noah[1] was undoubtdly put up to this by some of our active & ambitious politicians; but you would judge wrongly if you considered this as any thing like a decisive indication of the course which this state will eventually pursue. I have seen many of our politicians during the summer, and amongst the rest, our senator, Van Buren. He *professed* not even to have ascertained his own choice amongst the candidates. I have no doubt however that he is under some pledge to support Mr. Crawford, *if found practicable,* and that it is he who has put Noah forward to feel the pulse of the state. The course, however, has been an unwise one on his part, & has produced a good deal of dissatisfaction amongst the Republicans—being in direct violation of a stipulation into which they had entered by common consent. If he finds he cannot succeed, he will have no difficulty in retracing his steps.

The new Paper at Washington[2] will I think produce some effects—unfavourable to the two Secretaries whom it attacks & supports, but favourable to the other candidates. It is certainly edited with ability and will injure Mr Crawford in this part of the country, where it has an extensive circulation. On the other hand, it will produce severe recriminations, by his freinds [*sic*], on Mr Calhoun. For the latter Gentleman I have a very sincere respect & esteem, and confess myself much more his admirer than Mr. Crawford's; But I have no belief in his success in the present contest— Indeed I feel convinced that he will ultimately withdraw & throw his influence into the scale of Mr. Crawford's most prominent competitor. In such an occurance [*sic*] (or perhaps without it), I should presume (although you are a much better judge of this than myself) that Pennsylvania would give its support to you. *This state* Pa. I think would be influenced in no little degree, by the course of Ohio; and again, the united influence of these two great states, would produce a serious, if not *decisive* impression on New York— and thus "The *trio*" adopt Mr Noah's plan, but not his candidate. I shall spend some weeks in Albany during the session of our Legislature which will commence in January. The question in this state will most probably be between yourself & Mr Crawford; and my greatest fear at present is that the course which Van Buren is pursuing, will have the effect to bring out the *Clintonians* in your favour, which would be a most unpropitious circumstance. It would be a great point gained if Kentucky & Ohio & perhaps some other of the *North* western States, would give some decided expression in your favour[.] Excuse me for the intimation that (as there [are][3] so many candidates in the field) it would [*be*] policy in your friends to look for success by a generous & manly *support* of you, rather than by *attacks* on your competitors & their friends.

Mrs P. joins me in expressions of the sincerest respect & esteem for yourself and Mrs Clay. P. B. PORTER

ALS. InU.

1 Mordecai M. Noah, born in Philadelphia and reared in Charleston, South Carolina, had served as clerk in the United States Treasury Department, reporter of the sessions of the Pennsylvania legislature, and United States consul to Tunis and Algiers prior to becoming editor of the New York *National Advocate* in 1817. He later founded and edited the New York *Enquirer,* the New York *Evening Star,* and the New York *Union* and was briefly an associate judge of the New York Court of Sessions.

2 On August 7, Thomas L. McKenney, Superintendent of Indian Trade until that office had been abolished by act of May 6, 1822 (3 *U.S. Stat.,* 679-80; cf. above, Shaw to Clay, April 4, 1822, note), had established a semiweekly Washington paper called *Republican and Congressional Examiner,* which supported Calhoun's candidacy. In May, 1823, McKenney relinquished the editorship; and in March, 1824, he became head of the newly established Bureau of Indian Affairs in the War Department.

3 MS. defaced.

Tax Receipt from Elijah C. Berry

STATE OF ILLINOIS, AUDITOR'S OFFICE, VANDALIA,
$ 27.20 3d. October 1822.

Received into this office of Henry Clay, by D. Rockwell[1] *the Treasurer's receipt for* Twenty Seven *dollars and* twenty *cents, being the amount of* his *land tax for the year* 1822 on SE 6. Section 7–SW 8– & W. half of 18, in township 14 N–R10W & SE12–14N–11W.

Signed Duplicates. E C BERRY Aud

DS, partially printed. DLC-TJC (DNA, M212, R15). In 1816 Berry had moved from Kentucky to Illinois, where he became Auditor of Public Accounts, first of the Territory and in 1818 of the State. Until 1820 he had also been a partner in the publication of a Kaskaskia newspaper, the *Western* (after 1818, the *Illinois) Intelligencer.*

1 Not identified–he was acting for Clay's agent, Ninian Edwards. The document is endorsed on verso (AES): "Received of Govr. Edwards, three dollars in full for my commission for the payment of the within taxes. Dennis Rockwell." Cf. above, Clay to Gilmer, August 4, 1821.

To Langdon Cheves

My dear Cheves (Confidential) Ashland 5h. Oct. 1822.

So you have executed your intention, intimated to me in Apl. last, of announcing publicly your fixed determination to resign the Presidency of the Bank.[1] What next? You do not mean to deliver yourself up to inglorious inactivity; in other words, to surrender yourself to ennui? Have you resolved upon your future course of life? I need not say to you that the deep interest I feel in your fortunes, fame and happiness makes me desirous of information on all these matters.

As for me, you see, I return to Congress, I may say, in spite of myself; for I would have prefered remaining a year or two longer in private life. But my friends, every where, concurred in thinking my presence there might be material in relation to another object, and one must, though he should do it rarely, yield his own opinion to theirs. With respect to that object, do you still pursue your determination to maintain a perfect neutrality on the question? I think that determination proceeded from an unwillingness to interfere between friends. But Lowndes[2] is no longer pressed—pressed he never was—on the public notice. And it must be now quite apparent that Calhoun is not likely to obtain much support. That is to happen, which I think I mentioned to you, the contest will be between the Secretary of the Treasury[3] and me. Here are my prospects in this quarter: You may be perfectly assured that the Western States to Louisiana inclusive will co-operate in the support of my election. In Ohio, from which I am but just returned, public sentiment is strong, ardent, and almost unanimous. My friends there think that it will manifest itself in the form of a Legislative recommendation of me.[4] The recent event in Tennessee[5] will not disturb the harmony of the Western effort. Genl. Jackson's name will be withdrawn, when it is perceived that the nomination of him is not seconded elsewhere. When withdrawn, I am assured by Govr. Carroll,[6] in a letter of the 1st. of Septr. after his return to Nashville from the Legislature at Murfreesborough, that no doubt will remain of my obtaining the unanimous support of Tennessee.

What prospects I have, on the other side of the Mountains, your own observation will best supply you with information. I think the recent progress of public sentiment there appears favorable to Mr. Crawford. But if Pennsylvania should determine to give me her support, I think that State, backed as she will be by all to the West, will yet decide the contest. The union of Penn: and the West will present a stronger mass of solid interest than any other competitor can claim. In my conscience I believe the people of Penns: generally prefer me to any other, and greatly to Mr. Crawford. But there is wanting, in the Press, fit organs to express and to enlighten public sentiment there. These would in my opinion be decisively furnished, if the National & Franklin Gazettes[7] were to espouse my interests. How is our friend Walsh now? Is he still allured by the literary acquirements of the Secretary of State? For Mr. Crawford, I would suppose, after all that he has said and written, it would be impossible that he should exert himself.

Will you favor me with your opinion of the *present state* of public sentiment in Pennsylvania? And also whether you think it would be judicious for the Legislature of Kentucky, at its ensuing Session, which begins on the third monday in this month, to express the public wish here?[8]

I began to write about your interests, and after dedicating a few lines to them, have employed the residue of a tedious letter about my own. A most equal division! Whatever inference may be drawn from that circumstance, allow me to say, in great truth, that I am Faithfully & Cordially Your friend H. CLAY

Langdon Cheves Esqr.

ALS. ScHi. 1 See above, Cheves to Clay, July 27, 1822.
2 William Lowndes. 3 William H. Crawford.
4 See below, Sloane to Clay, December 19, 1822, note; Clay to Brooke, January 8, 1823, note.
5 See above, Hynes to Clay, July 31, 1822.
6 William Carroll. The letter has not been found.
7 See above, Johnson to Clay, April 1, 1822, note. The Philadelphia *National Gazette and Literary Register*, published by Robert Walsh, Jr., had been serving as the organ of John Quincy Adams in the "duplicate letters" controversy (above, Benton to Clay, May 2, 1822, note; Russell to Clay, June 6, 1822, note) and, while not yet definitely committed, was friendly to his presidential aspirations. See Adams to Walsh, November 27, 1822, in Ford (ed.), *Writings of John Quincy Adams*, VII, 330-31.
8 See below, Clay to Porter, October 22, 1822.

From William C. Cowan

Dear Sir Near Danville Oct. 11th 1822

I am not a little surprised at the information recd. by your son,[1] as the note[2] assignd. by those Gentlemen to you was to be paid in the Currency of the Country—which was well understood both at the time of contracting & since as McConathy[3] did about the time when the Note became due tell me that he would receive Commonwealths paper as long as any body would receive it—at which time I askd. indulgen[ce] for 6 or 8 months the reply was that they would wait And that he would be glad to get it as fast as I could pay—even one or Two Hundred Dolls at a time—

The Money I have endeavoured to get as fast as possible and have now the greater part in Deposit for the special purpose of paying that debt—The Circumstances which caused delay—of payment was made known to the gentlemen though now not necessary—

I will come over to se [*sic*] you in 10 or 12 Days and know the whole of the matter. I would come at this time if in my power to

leave home— Your friend And Servent [*sic*] WM. C COWAN
H Clay

ALS. DLC-TJC (DNA, M212, R12). Cowan, a resident of Danville, had been a private in the War of 1812 and was prominent in civic affairs.
1 Probably Theodore W. Clay. 2 Not found. 3 Possibly Jacob McConathy.

From John Sloane

Dr. Sir Wooster Oct 16th. 1822

It has long been my intention to write you on the subject of the Presidential election, and I was only prevented from writing in the early part of Summer by a desire more fully to ascertain the public mind. and the expectation that I should have the pleasure of seeing you at Columbus in September. The indisposition of my family prevented me from visiting Columbus; and having delayed writing so long I concluded to defer it until after the elections which has [*sic*] eventuated in the choice of a number of my particular friends to serve in the next Legislature. Your recent visit to our seat of Government[1] where you would see a number of your friends from the western & middle parts of the State must have made you better acquainted with public opinion in that quarter in regard to the Presidential election than I can be. I shall therefore in Speaking on the Subject confine my observations principally to that part of our State lying east of the Scioto. I have not been much from home during the summer but have seen gentlemen from all parts of the Eastern section, and am happy to hear from them that you continue to stand high in public estimation as a candidate, & were it not the recollection of the Missouri question,[2] there would scarcely be a dissenting voice. Indeed my hopes that you may be nominated at the ensuing Session of our assembly, are stronger than when I conversed with you at Washington. I think Ohio has not elected one member to the next Congress who will be unfriendly to your election. I have heard from but a few districts. Mr. Wright[3] of Steubenville is elected. I have had no opposition to a reelection What do the people of Tennessee mean by nominating of Genl. Jackson?[4] They surely do not intend to throw away their votes on him who will get none other, I hope they will abandon him. Appearances in Pennsylvania I think indicate a disposition to drop Mr Calhoun should that be the case I flatter myself she will throw her interest in your favour, as I feel pretty confident she will never vote for Mr. Crawford. and as for Mr Mr [*sic*] Adams Pennsylvanians will be content to let him have the credit of flogging Mr Russell[5] and receive the gratitude of the fishermen— I think things are going well at the City Mr Crawford, & Mr Calhoun, by means of the Gazette &

Republican[6] are drubbing each other thoroughly. The people will say "if one tenth part of what these folks say be true it is time we make choice of a man unconnected with the administration." This is what I wish to see pressed on the public attention Some persons I have conversed with are of opinion that the Subject ought to be discussed more at large in the Ohio papers. I have myself entertained a different opinion If a nomination can be effected this winter it had better be done without much newspaper discussion. The truth is neither are necessary in order to ensure the electorial [*sic*] votes of Ohio. But a nomination would give confidence to our friends in other States. I shall be happy in hearing from you before I leave home which will be the 18th. of Nov.—

I am Sir very respectfully your Obt. Sert J. SLOANE

The Honbl. Henry Clay

ALS. DLC-HC (DNA, M212, R1). Endorsed on verso by Clay: "Mr Sloane—Answd." Answer not found.

1 See above, Clay to Meigs, September 11, 1822.

2 A reference to Clay's pro-Southern sympathies expressed during the controversy over the admission of Missouri to Statehood. See, e.g., above, II, 670n, 740-48 *passim*.

3 John C. Wright.

4 See above, Hynes to Clay, July 31, 1822.

5 See above, Clay to Russell, July 9, 1822.

6 See above, Porter to Clay, September 30, 1822, note. The daily *City of Washington Gazette,* established by Jonathan Elliot in 1817 as a continuation of his *Washington City Weekly Gazette,* had received large printing contracts from Secretary of the Treasury William H. Crawford and supported the latter's presidential candidacy.

Receipted Bill from William S. Dallam

Oct. 17 1822

The bill, D; the receipt, AES. DLC-TJC (DNA, M212, R15). The bill, "Mrs. Harts house Dr. to Repairs," amounts to $146.52, including $49.65 for 13,500 shingles, $11.00 for two locks, glass, and glazing, $10.00 for laying kitchen hearth and two back chimneys, $12.25 for rails, $56.12 for "McCrackens bill," and $7.50 "overpaid Theodore 1 Sepr. 1821." The work was done on the home of Mrs. Susannah Hart. "McCracken" was probably John McCracken. The overpayment to Theodore Clay covered rent due as above, II, 719, 724, 865, 882. The dated receipt, to Clay as executor of Col. Thomas Hart, is endorsed on verso.

To John Quincy Adams

Sir Lexington 18h. October 1822.

There being a general expectation that missions will be sent, early in the approaching Session of Congress, to the Independent Governments of Spanish America, in that event, I beg leave to recommend to the President William Blair Esqr.[1] of this place as a suitable person to be Secretary of Legation to one of them. Judge Blair is a gentleman of good education, obtained at Transylvania University, and possesses a highly cultivated mind. He was among the most respectable members of the Bar of this place, and has lately filled the

Judicial station, in our Circuit Courts, with great credit and ability, displaying in it uncommon firmness and independence. I will add that Judge Blairs connexions, both by blood and marriage,[2] are highly respectable. I have the honor to be with great respect Your obedient Servant H. CLAY

The Honble John Q. Adams &c. &c. &c.

ALS. DNA, RG59, Applications and Recommendations for Office (MR1).

1 William W. Blair, who did not receive the appointment. The following year, however, Blair was appointed Land Commissioner in Florida, and in 1824, Judge of the Middle District of Florida. He died July 29, 1824.

2 Blair had been married, in 1818, to Anna H. Warfield, daughter of Dr. Walter Warfield.

Agreement with William S. Dallam

[October 18, 1822]

An agreement entered into this 18h. day of October 1822 between Henry Clay of the one part and William S. Dallam of the other part.

The said Clay hereby agrees to sell to the said Dallam the tract of land lying in the County of Fayette, below the town of Lexington, which the said Clay purchased of the Bank of Kentucky, and the small piece adjoining which he purchased of William Pollock,[1] amounting together to two hundred and six acres, possession of which said land the said Clay will deliver to the said Dallam on the Second day of January next.

The said Dallam hereby agrees to pay to the said Clay fifty dollars per acre for each and every acre in the said tracts of land, amounting to ten thousand three hundred dollars, with interest thereon, after the rate of six per Cent. per annum from the 2d. of January 1823.

The said Dallam, in order to make payment of the said principal and interest, has this day assigned to the said Clay the notes of Daniel Bryan and William Romane,[2] of Daniel Bryan and Samuel Bryan and of Thomas January (of which a list is hereto annexed) amounting together to the sum of sixteen thousand five hundred and sixty four dollars and fifty four Cents, all payable to the said Dallam, in lawful currency of the United States.[3]

The said Clay is to proceed with reasonable diligence to collect the said several notes, and out of the amount collected he is to retain the aforesaid sum of ten thousand three hundred dollars, with legal interest thereon from the 2d. January 1823, and the residue he is to pay over to the said Dallam or his order.

But it is agreed between the parties that the said Clay shall retain the legal title of the land hereby sold, as a security for the above mentioned consideration money; and that, if he is not able, out of the notes assigned to him as aforesaid, to collect the said sum of Ten thousand three hundred dollars, with interest as aforesaid, in lawful money of the United States, he is to have a lien upon the said land for the said consideration money or for whatever part he shall fail to collect short of the said sum of ten thousand three hundred dollars, with interest as aforesaid.

The said Clay agrees to make the legal title of the said land to the said Dallam upon receipt of the consideration money as aforesaid; and in the mean time the said Dallam is to pay the public taxes accruing thereon.

A survey shall be made, if either party desire it, of the said land, and if the quantity shall not be two hundred and six acres, there is to be a deduction or addition, as the case may be, from or to the aforesaid consideration money.

It is understood that the said Clay is to omit no legal step, incumbent upon him as the assignee of the said notes, to recover the amount thereof.

Signed & Sealed in duplicate the day and year first above written.

H. CLAY {L.S.}
WILL S. DALLAM {L.S.}

[Endorsement][4]
Memorandum after the Draft of the Agreement the two Notes of the Messrs. Bryans were added to the List making the aggregate $17359.6., instead of $16 664.54. mentioned above[5]

H. CLAY {L.S.}
WILL. S. DALLAM {L.S.}

[Endorsements on verso][6]

We have this day settled all accounts and transactions whatever growing out of the within agreement and the several debts within mentioned, with the collection of which H. Clay was charged. On which settlement a balance was found due to W.S. Dallam of ninety six dollars and fifty six Cents, which balance the said Clay has paid to the said Dallam—

There is a balance uncollected by the said Clay of the debt due from Thomas January, which balance belongs to the said Dallam. Witness the hands and seals of the parties this day of November 1831.

H. CLAY {L.S.}
WILL S. DALLAM {L.S.}

Memo. There are two notes for Comths paper given by Maj Dallam amounting to $2000 not included in the above. And he is entitled to some real property sold as Thomas Januarys a year or two ago by the Shf of Fayette under a decree.

H. CLAY
WILL S. DALLAM

It is this 29h. day of October 1832 agreed between William S.

Dallam & H. Clay as follows: The said Dallam hereby agrees to sell to the said Clay the tract of land containing Two hundred and six acres in the within agreement mentioned, for which the said Clay has paid him in hand the sum of four thousand six hundred and six dollars in Commonwealths paper, and given his note for thirteen hundred and ninety four dollars payable in specie two years after date, without interest; which said two sums amounting together to six thousand dollars, the said Dallam acknowledges to be the consideration for the said land. The said Clay is entitled to and is to be deemed in possession of the land from this day. Witness the hands and seals of the parties. WILL S. DALLAM {L.S.}

Teste H. CLAY {L.S.}

P. T. Johnson[7] WILL S. DALLAM

ADS, signed also by Dallam. DLC-TJC (DNA, M212, R17).

1 See above, Bond, October 22, 1821; Property Deed, December 26, 1821; Property Deed, July 4, 1825.

2 William Roman, who a few years later resided five miles from Lexington, on the Nicholasville Road.

3 The list, in Clay's hand and signed by both Clay and Dallam, includes "Daniel Bryan and William Romane's note dated 7h. Novr. 1816, due eight years and one month after date for $6621."; three notes of Daniel Bryan and Samuel Bryan, for $397.26, each, due February 20, 1822, February 20, 1823, and February 20, 1824; an additional note of the Bryans, for $231.76, due February 20, 1825; "Thomas January's note dated 2 January, 1815 payable 1 January 1825 for 6000:"; and seven additional notes of January, for $360, each, dated January 2, 1815, and falling due on the first of January annually from 1819 through 1825. To these entries were subsequently added two notes of Daniel and Samuel Bryan, for $397.26, each, one due February 20, 1820, and the other on the same date the following year, bringing the total face value of the notes listed to $17,359.06.

4 AES by Dallam, signed also by Clay.

5 See above, this document, n. 3.

6 All AES, signed also by Dallam.

7 Of Lexington, a medical student at Transylvania University (1835-1836, 1838-1839), graduated in 1839.

Assignment of Notes from William S. Dallam

18th. Octo. 1822.

Pay to H Clay WILL S. DALLAM

ES, on verso of a note from Thomas January to Dallam, for $360, due January 1, 1819, "the same being the legal interest for the year 1818 of a note . . . for $6000 payable the 1 January 1825. . . ." Fayette Circuit Court, File 536. Four additional assignments of similar text, as endorsements on notes from January to Dallam for $360 due January 1 of the years 1820-1823, are also located in this file. See above, Agreement, this date.

To Peter Mason

To Mr. Peter Mason— 18h. Oct. 1822.

Having sold to Majr. Dallam the Land which you have rented of me[1] and by the contract of sale being bound to deliver possession of it to him on the second of January next, you will be pleased to deliver him possession accordingly; and in the mean time allow him any privileges which he may desire H. CLAY

ANS. NcD. Mason had earlier been a justice of the peace in Fayette County, Kentucky (appointed in 1796).
1 See above, Agreement, this date. No rental agreement with Mason has been found.

Receipt from Richard Hawes, Jr.

21st. October 1822.

Received of H. Clay the following notes: Four given by Daniel Bryan and Samuel Bryan to William S. Dallam, all bearing date the 7h. November 1816 and each given for the sum of three hundred and ninety seven dollars and 26 Cents, and due and payable on the 20h. February of the successive years of 1820. 1821. 1822 and 1823. Also five notes given by Thomas January to the said Dallam, all bearing date the 2d. January 1815 and each of them given for the sum of three hundred and sixty dollars, and due and payable on the first of January of the successive years of 1819. 1820. 1821. 1822 and 1823— All of which notes above mentioned are assigned to the said Clay, and which I have received for the purpose of prosecuting suits thereon and executions upon the Judgments so as to entitle the said Clay to recourse against the assignor, if the makers shall prove insolvent.

[Endorsement][1]

The first mentioned note of Bryan's was not recd.

RICHD. HAWES JR

[Endorsement on verso][2]

Recd. 8h. Novr 1823 of H. Clay a note of Danl. Bryan and Saml. Bryan for $397 26/100 due 20h. Feby next; and a note of Thomas January for $360 due 1st. Jany next both given to W. S. Dallam and assigned by him to the said Clay— Recd. them for the purpose of suit and collection as within. R. HAWES JR

DS, in Clay's hand (except as noted). DLC-TJC (DNA, M212, R15). See above, Agreement, October 18, 1822.
1 AES. 2 ES, in Clay's hand.

To Joseph C. Breckinridge

Dr Sir Tuesday evening. [*ca.* October 22, 1822]

I will look over the papers on O Mealy's suit[1] in the morning, and for that purpose will go to the office immediately after breakfast, if the weather is not very bad. Your's faithfy H. CLAY.

ALS. DLC-Breckinridge Family Papers (DNA, M212, R20). Addressed: "J. C. Breckinridge Esqr Present—"

1 A chancery case, brought in 1816 by Michael Omealy, of Baltimore, and others against the heirs of John Breckinridge, to cancel a deed for land in Oldham County, Kentucky, which had been granted for services which Breckinridge had failed to perform prior to his death. In November, 1822, a decree was entered in favor of the complainants; and on May 25, 1826, Breckinridge's heirs finally conveyed title to the property. See 32 *U.S.* (7 Peters) 180, 190-91, 202-203 *et passim* (1833).

To Peter B. Porter

My dear Sir (Confidential) Ashland 22d. Oct. 1822–

I have just received your obliging favor of the 1st. instant,[1] for which be pleased to accept my thanks. I had conjectured that the hand which you name had touched the string of the N. Advocate. That gentleman reconnoitred about me last winter, and although I treated him with respect and attention, I held out no inducements to him to avow himself my friend. I declined doing this because it is my fixed determination to enter into no arrangements, to make no bargains, but, if I should be elected to the great office in question, to hold myself free & unshackled, to pursue the public good according to my best judgment. In the course of conversations which he himself broached with me, on that subject, he gave to two of the Secretaries (Mess. Adams and Calhoun) their congé, without much ceremony, speaking of their prospects as being altogether hopeless. Whilst he very positively asserted who would *not* be elected, and thereby limited very much the field of competition, he abstained from mentioning (and I gave him no encouragement to say) who would be elected. Is it possible that he has met with more favor elsewhere? Is it possible that the Republicans of New York are to be put in motion by a single individual, without consulting their wishes? I need not I trust say to you that I never have nor can intrigue with any person or party on this subject. If my cause should be espoused by that interest which you suppose will prove injurious to it, in New York, it will be without any prompting from or concert with me.

The hopes and expectations of my friends, in the West will be, *you may rely abs outely* [*sic*] *upon it,* completely realized in this quarter. In Tennessee, Govr. Carroll of that State assures me, that I shall receive its unanimous support, if Jackson be out of the way.[2] This letter was written after his late attendance on the Legislature, which he says will *unanimously* recommend me if Jackson be withdrawn; and both he and others of my friends in that State believe he will not be pressed by Tennessee, when it perceives that the nomination of him is not well received in other States.

I returned from attending the Federal Court in Ohio about a month ago; and I declare to you most sincerely that I believe the zeal of that State in my behalf is not surpassed by that which prevails here. My friends there believe that the Legislature will at its session, beginning on the first monday in Decr. speak out its wishes in the most unequivocal manner.[3] Here in Kentucky, my effort hitherto has been directed to the suppression of what I considered would be a premature annunciation of the public wish, on the part of the Legislature. But it began its autumnal Session yesterday, and from what I hear, I doubt if it will be possible to restrain any longer the expression of its opinion.[4]

In short, my dear Sir, without travelling over the whole ground, I think I may take upon myself to assert, with the greatest confidence, that all the Western States to the gulph of Mexico, Alabama inclusive, will be cordially united in my support.

Assuming that ground is it possible that you, politicians, in New York can fail to see distinctly the course of policy, which it seems to us, it is your interest to pursue? Whether you look at what concerns your separate advantage, or the National welfare? This is a topic however on which it is not perhaps fitting that I should dwell even confidentially to a friend.

I shall be obliged to you to write to me from Albany— I shall be at Washn. attending the Supreme Court when you are there. In the mean time, I may possibly address you again—

I have just recovered from a severe fever, with which I was attacked, in consequence of my trip to Ohio—[5] My best respects to Mrs. Porter— Your faithful friend H. CLAY

P.S. I am assured that every person recently elected from Ohio to Congress is friendly to me H.C.

Genl. P. B. Porter

ALS. NBuHi. 1 That is, of September 30, 1822.

2 See above, Clay to Cheves, October 5, 1822.

3 See below, Sloane to Clay, December 19, 1822, note; Clay to Brooke, January 8, 1823, note.

4 Members of the legislature met in the House Chamber on November 18 and unanimously nominated Clay for the Presidency.

5 Clay's illness, "of the bilious fever," around October 1, had led to a report, circulated in Louisville, that he was dead. Washington *Daily National Intelligencer*, October 16, 19, 23, 30, 1822.

Report to Kentucky General Assembly

HON. RICHARD C. ANDERSON, October 22, 1822.

SIR: *Speaker of the House of Representatives.*

THE General Assembly having, at its last spring session, done me the honor to appoint me commissioner, on the part of Kentucky, to treat with Benjamin W. Leigh, Esq. commissioner on the part of Virginia, "on the necessary arrangements and stipulations, preparatory to the organization of a board of commissioners, according to the compact existing between the two states," to determine all matters in controversy between them, which have arisen under it; and having directed a report to be made of the result of the negotiation,[1] I have now, respectfully to submit to the general assembly the following report:

Shortly after the close of the session of the legislature, I had several interviews with Mr. Leigh, in the course of which we mutually made a free and full exposition of the objects of our respective appointments; and finally, for the accomplishment of those objects, concluded and signed two conventions, which I herewith transmit to the general assembly. By the first, which is designated by the letter A,[2] provision is made for the organization of a board of commissioners, in conformity with the eighth article of the compact; the time and place of its meeting are appointed; a day is limited [*sic*][3] on which the convention is to cease, and the board is to be dissolved, if, in the mean time, it shall not have made out and delivered its award to the agents of the respective parties; the compensation of the commissioners constituting the board is fixed, and its mode of payment; the several questions to be submitted to the final decision of the board, are stated, and issues made up on them; and lastly, it is stipulated that each state, ratifying the convention, shall forthwith proceed to choose commissioners on its part, and communicate to the other, the fact of such ratification, and the names of the commissioners so appointed.

It will be observed, that the validity, as well of the acts which relate to occupying claimants of land, as of those which prescribe a limitation of actions, founded upon the land law of Virginia, is submitted to the board of commissioners. All of these acts are drawn in question, upon the allegation, that they are repugnant to the compact between the two states, and causes involving them all, are understood to be pending before the federal judiciary. I supposed it, therefore, to be consonant with the views of the legislature, to subject them all to the test, for which the compact itself, said to be violated, has made provision.

The particular time and place, stated in the convention, for the meeting of the board, were adopted from two considerations: First, to afford an opportunity to have the award made and published, prior to the decision, by the supreme court of the United States, of the cause argued at its last term, embracing the validity of the occupying claimant laws; so that the award might have the effect and influence which justly belong to the opinion and judgment of the special tribunal of the parties. And, secondly, it was thought that, from the annual assemblage, at the City of Washington, of eminent men, drawn there from all parts of the Union, by public business, or by curiosity, there would be less delay and difficulty, on the part of the four commissioners, appointed by the two states, in selecting the remaining two, necessary to the completion of the board, than would occur at any other place that could be agreed upon.

By the second convention, which is designated by the letter B,[4] it is agreed between the two states, first, that if the decision of the board of commissioners, on the claim asserted by Virginia, shall be in favor of Kentucky, Virginia guarantees that the proprietors of all unlocated warrants shall submit to, and abide by the decision; and indemnifies Kentucky against any claim which they may subsequently assert. Secondly, that in no event is the decision of the board to affect the sales of land authorised to be brought into market by the act of the legislature of Kentucky, entitled "an act providing for the sale of the vacant lands west of the Tennessee;" but that land, on the contrary, is to be considered as specially reserved from the operation of such decision. Thirdly, that the quantity of the several descriptions of land warrants, remaining to be satisfied, does not exceed that which is specified in the convention; and that, if the award be against Kentucky, it shall be lawful for this state, in regard to that class of warrants in which the line, whether continental or state, has not been designated, to require the production of satisfactory proof of the line to which they were severally granted, and that they have not been previously located. And lastly, that the state of Kentucky, if the award be against it, retains the power to regulate the making of locations upon the warrants, in some convenient and equitable mode; and that of prescribing a reasonable time within which, if the proprietors of warrants do not make their locations, agreeably to the mode so required, their rights shall be forfeited.

The state of Virginia, in preferring the claim which she has done,[5] has proceeded without any authority expressly delegated to her by the proprietors of unlocated warrants. After settling with her the question as to the right of those proprietors now to locate their warrants, it might happen, that, disavowing her acts they would institute fresh measures to be let in to the satisfaction of their warrants. To guard against any such attempt, Virginia has stipulated that they shall abide by the determination of the board of commissioners; and that she will indemnify Kentucky against any claim which they may subsequently exhibit.

I was desirous that we should have agreed upon a precise limitation of the definite quantity of land comprehended in the Virginia claim. But as it could not be ascertained what part of those warrants which had issued, without a designation of the line, belonged to the state corps, or what portion of them had been located, it was found impracticable. The best substitute, for such a limitation, that occurred to me, has been adopted, in the provisions which specify the aggregates of the three classes of warrants, of which the satisfaction is now sought; and which throw upon the holder of the ambiguous warrant, the *onus probandi* of the facts, both of the line, on account of which it issued, and that it has not been previously located.

The utility of the other stipulations, contained in the instrument B, is sufficiently obvious. However just our confidence may be, in a favorable result of the appeal which is proposed to the tribunal of the compact, it was deemed advisable to guard against all contingencies. Perhaps most of the stipulations, inserted in that instrument, were not called for by the occasion, since they merely express what would have been necessarily implied from the nature of the whole transaction. But it seemed to me that, in laying the foundations of an amicable settlement of all past differences between the two states, it was better, even at the hazard of superfluous precaution, to make ample provision against future misunderstanding. That the ultimate issue of what has been done, may tend to the conservation of the harmony, which ought ever to be cherished between our parent state and us, I take pleasure in stating, appeared to be the sincere and anxious desire of the gentleman with whom I had the satisfaction to be associated, as it is that of Your obedient humble servant.

H. CLAY.

Ky. H. of Reps., *Journal, 1822,* pp. 34-37; Ky. Sen. *Journal, 1822,* pp. 30-33. Published also in Lexington *Kentucky Reporter,* November 11, 1822. ALI draft in DLC-HC (DNA, M212, R1).

1 See above, Credential, June 1, 1822, note.

2 See above, Convention, June 5, 1822.

3 The word "prescribed" was used in Clay's draft.

4 See above, Contingent Provisions, June 5, 1822.

5 This phrase written in Clay's draft as: "in asserting the claim which she has brought forward."

To Benjamin W. Leigh

Dr Sir Lexington 29h. Oct. 1822.

I am sorry to have to say that I have not found you, in all respects, a man of your word. You promised to write me how you got home, but I have never received your letter. I had the pleasure to learn, through other channels, that you arrived at Richmond in health and safety.

I transmit to you inclosed a Copy of my report to the Legislature of the two agreements which we entered into for our two States,[1] which I suppose you would like to have. There is every reason to believe that they will be ratified, and the arbitration consummated, as far as it can be done by Kentucky.

Our Assembly has met, under better auspices, in regard to our currency and relief laws, than when you saw it. Altho' the Relief party was successful generally at the late elections, many of them were so warmly and equally contested, that the leaders of that party begin to discover that its predominance will be only momentary, and they are, therefore, disposed to take shelter in time, and to provide for the currency and for the restoration of our antient laws. The Governor has transmitted, at the opening of the Session, quite an Anti-relief Message[2]—In short, we begin to see day break. I should not be surprized nevertheless if nothing very material was done during this Session; but by the next, I think public sentiment will have been so far corrected that the impulse which it will give cannot be resisted. But little has been said and nothing will be done, I understand, during the present Session, on the affair of the attack made at the last upon Judge Clarke.[3] Tell Ritchie[4] that after having done so much, by the able and ingenious publications in his paper, against the Judiciary, to kindle the spirit which has existed in this quarter, it is a little unkind, on his part, to treat his deluded followers so roughly as he has recently done.

You see I write to you, on Kentucky subjects, as if you were a Kentuckian. The interest which you seemed to take in them when here must be my apology. With great regard I am faithfly & Cordially Your ob. Servt H. CLAY

B. W. Leigh Esq

ALS. ViU.

1 See above, Report, October 22, 1822; Convention, June 5, 1822; Contingent Provisions, June 5, 1822.

2 In his message of October 22 Governor John Adair had said "that the great and complicated concerns of finance, can receive but little advancement from the frequency of legislation. The constancy and patience of virtuous economy, the victorious energies of well directed industry, and the demands of foreign commerce, regulate the wants and acquisitions of every people." He believed that the legislation previously enacted, sanctioning "means not heretofore usually employed," had been effective and "that the hour is near at hand, when we may change, without the fear of injury our precautionary attitude. . . ." He suggested passage of an act calling for "the Bank of Kentucky to pay, in a short period of time, into the Bank of the Commonwealth, in the notes of the latter, the whole amount of capital stock owned by the state in the former." This measure, he said, would lead to appreciation of the paper of the Bank of the Commonwealth, and he hoped that the Bank of Kentucky would within the coming year resume specie payments. Ky. H. of Reps., *Journal, 1822*, pp. 12-14.

3 During the special session of the Kentucky legislature, May 13-29, 1822, a determined but unsuccessful effort had been made to unseat Judge James Clark, who in the case of Williams *vs.* Blair, Bourbon Circuit Court, earlier in the month had held "that the law which gave to the defendant a stay of execution for two years, . . . unless the plaintiff consented to receive bank paper in payment of the debt, was unconstitutional and void." See above, Clay to Cheves, November 20, 1820, note. The resolution that Clark "ought to be removed from office" had been approved by a vote of 59 to 35, which fell short of the two thirds requirement for impeachment. Ky. H. of Reps., *Journal, Special Session, 1822,* pp. 64, 67-73, 96-97, 105-16.

4 Thomas Ritchie.

From "Albion"

Near Washington City, 30th Oct. 1822.

TO THE HON. HENRY CLAY.

SIR—I have just seen in the American Farmer, your letter of the

19th August, addressed to J. S. Skinner, Esq. respecting your English Cattle, and as I, some years since, was a breeder and feeder of the kind of stock you allude to, I take the liberty to offer a few remarks on your letter.

The description you give of your Cattle and their offspring, is quite sufficient to satisfy any person acquainted with this breed, that your's are of the thorough Herefordshire blood, but unless I saw them, or knew the names of their breeders, I would not undertake to say, they are of the best blood of that country, and indeed from the price your's cost in England, I have my doubts on this head—as I never knew the most celebrated breeders inclined to take so little money for their choice stock; but times are much altered since I left England, and perhaps this may account for the depreciation in price.

Nearly all the cattle of Herefordshire are of the color you mention; namely, the feet, belly, end of the tail, and face, white, and the rest of the animal a dark mahogany red—but some of the breeders, I may say, have private marks, such as a small piece of white on the top of the shoulders, others a red rim round the eyes.—It is wonderful to observe how they can obtain such peculiarities as they do in this respect, and they show what may be effected in breeding stock, by the man who is possessed of a steady perservering [*sic*] judgment. Indeed, it is this peculiarity in the character of the English yeomanry, and perhaps I may say nation, that renders their endeavours in almost every undertaking, ultimately successful, and their farming stock of almost every description unrivalled.

In order that you may have an opportunity of comparing your English stock with my view of what I consider the best blood of Herefordshire, I will just give you a description of the cattle I was in the habit of breeding and feeding in England; which originally, I personally selected from the stock of the most celebrated breeders in that county, at a cost of sixty and one hundred and fifty guineas for two Bulls, and from thirty to forty guineas each, for heifers and cows.

I consider the most choice blood of the Herefordshire Cattle to be of the color described above, including the white on the top of the shoulder—Hide, thick, soft, and feels between the fingers like rich fat, covered with fine soft thick-set hair, which occasions the skin to feel like a piece of fine thick rich velvet. Lips thin—nostrils, wide and full—eyes, bold and dark colored—eye sockets, prominent and wide apart—ears and face rather short—(which is the reverse of the Durham and other short horned cattle)—the tongue roots rather full—no loose dulap—bosom, not very prominent but wide—belly or paunch, very small and much drawn upwards—horns, yellow white, turning upwards, rather long, very smooth, bright, free from wrinkles, and fine, not resting *on,* but growing *out* of the head—Neck thin and fine—chine, thin when lean, well joined to the loin; when fat, very broad, and particularly full at the sides, the shoulders fitting it equally nice as in the blood horse, without any projection of the elbow—ribs, not hanging from, but rising out of the back, very wide —and when the animal is fat, I have seen the flesh on them three inches higher than the back bone, which was ascertained by laying a stick in various places across the back, and running a three inch rule along the centre of the back, from behind the hips to the centre of the chine, without touching the stick—short ribs, at the side of the loin, very projecting, and thick at the ends with fat—hips, projecting, remarkably large and fat, and when the hand is placed on them, feel like the back of a man's head, and a very fat head too—rump, remarkably long and full of fine flesh; indeed it is here and in the loin and chine that the Herefords principally excel, which occasions those parts to sell in London, to the Beef-steak houses at full double the price of those from many other kinds of cattle—Twist, or where the hind legs unite, very low and full, the outside of the thigh, flat, and free from flesh, which occasions the round to be nearly free from coarse, and full of fine meat—flank, full and driving forward when the animal is walking.

The peculiarities of the Herefordshire cattle are, the color, horns turning upwards, long and smooth—lightness of offal, length of rump, size and fatness of the hips; every part where gentlemen usually eat, remarkably full of fine fat beef, while those parts usually eaten by plebians are very scanty, which occasions these cattle to be much sought after by butchers, who supply gentlemen's families with beef.

With respect to size, these animals are so disposed to fatten, that by good management they attain a weight equal to any cattle in England, not excepting the Holderness and Durham, but when low in flesh, they appear small, from their bones being so remarkably light, and the paunch so very small and drawing upward.

As milkers, they are, perhaps, equal to any of the distinguished feeders—but here a distinction must be made, as none of the famed beef cattle are good for milk; indeed we ought not to expect it, it is too much like blowing hot and blowing cold with the same breath.

For working, they perhaps surpass any other breed in England, unless the North Devonshire cattle can be considered as equal to them—but every good property being taken into consideration, I prefer the Herefordshire cattle to any other breed in England; these, and the North Devons, always sell at a higher price, according to their weight in London, than any other cattle, unless the Fifeshire and Kyloe Scotch Cattle can dispute the palm with them; indeed these four breeds nearly supply with beef all the first families in the kingdom, and may be considered amongst cattle, what the Barb and the Arabian are amongst horses.

There are to be found of course in Herefordshire, cattle of various qualities, according to the judgment of those persons who undertake to breed them, but generally speaking, they are good workers, good feeders, make excellent beef, and are first rate *handlers;* but the latter good property appears to be of little value in the United States, although the English Grazier, in selecting cattle or sheep, depends more on his fingers than his eyes. Should these observations furnish you or any of the readers of the American Farmer, with information that may in any manner assist the cause of agriculture, I shall be well pleased: and, that you may rise pre-eminent as a farmer and grazier, as you so justly have done as a Senator [*sic*], is the wish of ALBION.

The American Farmer, IV (November 8, 1822), 262. Published also in Lexington *Kentucky Gazette,* November 28, 1822.

From John C. Wright

Dear Sir, Steubenville O. 2d Nov 1822

Since I saw you at Columbus I have been constantly engaged on the Circuit. Our Court here has just adjourned. This must be my apology for not having before written you as I engaged.

Recently much alarmed at the account of your dangerous illness[1] we are now very much gratified to learn through the medium of the newspapers that you are again restored to health, your family & Country.

In relation to election, my engagements have been such as to preclude any settled arrangement, with your friends in this quarter as to what measures shall be pursued to secure the interest of the west, but I have had opportunity to converse with many, and think our cause is gaining daily. A repugnance is felt by some to a nomination by the members of the Assembly. Our people generally feel hostile to caucusses, and that hostile feeling will be more or less arranged [*sic*] in opposition to bringing you or any other person forward in that way. I do not, however, despair. of such a nomination if proper measures are resorted to. Daily we hear in conversation that it is time for the western world to be *felt* at the *seat of the national government,* & yet all is unsettled as to what mode we shall resort to to effect the object. Every thing is crude & undigested. Col. Sloane[2] & myself, shall make it a business to write our acquaintances in the assembly on the subject & hope to do something.[3]

Could a well *"argued"* circular letter signed by some of your most distinguished citizens be addressed to our members of Congress Elect, some of the principeler [*sic*] men thro' the State, & particularly to the members of Assembly, urging the claims of the *west*, your attachment to *domestick manufactures* & *internal improvement*—your *exertions* for the *Land relief Bill*, your intimate acquaintance with our concerns, wants, &c, & mollifying, if possible your *Missouri vote* & *slave residence* it would I think, have an excellent effect.[4] I regret however the measure had not been resorted to in season to have addressed the members before they leave home—that is now impracticable. If Worthington, Williams of Cincinnati, Hallock of this County, Richardson from Columbiana Harper & Sloane from the Reserve, Trimble, Morrow & McArthur[5] be enlisted, I think all would be safe. Some of the Newspapers might be *touched* by letter, properly worded, reminding them of the importance of their influence, &c. Mr Wilson,[6] our editor, is inclining to you—he was for Adams, but is cured— He *talks* of removing to take charge of the Aurora & if he does, it would be the more important that he be secured. His establishment here is offered for sale. No suitable person has yet offered to buy.[7] It would be an object for some young man of intelligence, with a little money— A letter to Wilson, *inquiring barely* how the publick pulse [bea]t hereabouts, from some of your friends could be [all] that is *necessary* for him now, as he is in a good [. . . .][8]

You must excuse my crude ideas— I have not time to be careful or particular. And please remember that I write *in confidence*. I should be glad to hear from you. So far as I can learn east, you are gaining. but the newspapers seem to be declaring for Crawford.

The result of my election you will have seen in the papers, majority 636. Whittlesey is elected—[9] Hammond was run down.[10] Both I think are with you I am, Sir, with great respect your friend & humble Servt J. C. WRIGHT

Hon. H. Clay

ALS. DLC-HC (DNA, M212, R1).

1 See above, Clay to Porter, October 22, 1822.

2 John Sloane, who had been a colonel of militia in the War of 1812.

3 See below, Sloane to Clay, December 19, 1822.

4 A committee of correspondence, comprised of members of the Kentucky legislature, on November 20, 1822, directed a letter to the members of the Ohio legislature, inviting them to follow Kentucky's lead in nominating Clay.

5 Thomas Worthington, now a State representative from Ross County; Micajah T. Williams, representative from Hamilton County; Jeremiah H. Hallock, representative from Jefferson County; Joseph Richardson, representative from Columbiana County; Robert Harper, representative from Ashtabula County; and, probably, Jonathan Sloane, of Portage County, a representative in the previous legislature but not now a member (both Ashtabula and Portage counties are in the Western Reserve, located in the northeastern corner of the State); Allen Trimble, State Senator from Highland County and acting Governor (later, 1826 and 1828, elected Governor); Jeremiah Morrow, incoming Governor; and Duncan McArthur, now State Senator from Ross County.

6 James Wilson, born in northern Ireland, had been employed by William Duane as editor of the Philadelphia *Aurora* during the War of 1812. In April, 1815, Wilson had purchased the Steubenville, Ohio, *Western Herald*, which in 1817 had become the *Western Herald and Steubenville Gazette*. He was several times a member of the

Ohio legislature and in 1832 was elected a judge in Jefferson County. He was a grandfather of President Woodrow Wilson.

7 Wilson's plan to return to Philadelphia was not carried out. Having already purchased the *Aurora,* he was unable to sell his Ohio establishment and early in November resold the Philadelphia journal, to John Sanderson, of Philadelphia, a teacher of the classics and one of the publishers, in 1820, of the first two volumes of the projected multivolumed *Biography of the Signers of the Declaration of Independence.*

8 MS. torn—one or two words missing. Elsewhere in this sentence, MS. faded.

9 Elisha Whittlesey, a native of Connecticut, had moved to Ohio in 1806 to practice law. He had been secretary to General William Henry Harrison during the War of 1812 and had represented Trumbull County in the Ohio legislature, 1820-1822. He was a member of Congress from 1823 until his resignation in 1838, Sixth Auditor of the Treasury, 1841-1843, and First Comptroller of the Treasury, 1849-1857 and from 1861 until his death in 1863.

10 Shortly after his unsuccessful campaign for election to Congress, Charles Hammond moved to Cincinnati and became associated with the *Liberty Hall and Cincinnati Gazette* (see below, Godman to Clay, July 1, 1823, note).

From William Warren

Dear Sir Geortown Novr. 4th. 1822

Capt Buckner[1] waits on you with the negroes mortgaged to me as his security to the U. S. Bank— I wish it was in my power to accompany him but I am so afflicted at this time with rheumatizm [*sic*], that I can't ride except in great pain— I have transfer'd all my interest to you, and if any thing else is necessary to invest you with my title, I will do it with pleasure

The Capt will relinquish his right of redemption— Please write to me by the Capt.[2] with great respect Your Ob. Sert.

W. WARREN

ALS. DLC-TJC (DNA, M212, R12). Addressed to Clay at Lexington. See below, Bill of Sale, this date.

1 John C. Buckner, of Georgetown, Kentucky. Buckner had been one of the first trustees of Covington, Kentucky, in 1815, and was later, until his death in 1825, a resident of Lexington.

2 No letter has been found.

Bill of Sale from William Warren

[November 4, 1822]

For and in consideration of the Sum of one thousand one hundred dollars, money of the United States of America, paid by H. Clay to the President and directors of the U. S. Bank at Lexington to be applied to the credit of John C. Buckner on his note payable in said bank and indorsed by W. Warren, and W. Sebree,[1] I W. Warren do hereby release, relinquish and transfer to the said H. Clay all my right title and interest to four negroe slaves, towit Precilla a woman and her three children John, Joe and Caroline: In testimony whereof I have this 4th. day of Novr. 1822 set my hand and seal.

Witness W. WARREN {SEAL}

U B Chambers[2]

[Endorsement on verso][3]

For and in consideration of the sum of Eleven hundred dollars paid me by H. Clay, I have bargained sold & delivered and by these presents do bargain sell & deliver to the said Clay four Negro slaves being the same four within mentioned, that is to say Priscilla and her three children, John, Joe, and Caroline. And I do hereby release to the said Clay all equity of redemption which I have in the said slaves in consequence of any mortgage by me heretofore executed.

Witness my hand & seal this 4h. day of Novr. 1822,

Teste JNO C BUCKNER {L.S.}
Cha. Wilkins

ADS. DLC-TJC (DNA, M212, R15). See above, Warren to Clay, this date.
1 William Sebree. 2 Uriel B. Chambers, of Scott County.
3 ES, in Clay's hand.

From Lafayette

My dear Sir,— Paris Novembre 5h. 1822

I am ever Happy in an opportunity to keep up our friendly acquaintance, and Would be still Happier to Converse with you on the business of freedom as it relates to both Sides of the Atlantic. You Have Had the pleasure, in which I was long ago ready to Sympathise, of the Acknowledgement of Colombian independence by the United States.[1] May every part of that Continent be also free, independent, and universally Acknowledged! it is to Be expected the NonSense of an American Emperor[2] cannot last long. But While I rejoice in the Emancipation of what was Called the Spanish dominion, while I lament the Hesitation of the Cortes in the Acknowledgment Which policy and Necessity point out to them, I would Be very Sorry to Hear of a Serious quarel [*sic*] Between Spain and the United States. The Embers of European freedom are Now to Be Cherished in the peninsula. Old governments, England particularly, Employ a great deal of Cunning in fomenting divisions Among the Nations, and in Every Nation Among the parties, nay the Individuals who Enlist in the Cause of Mankind. Their friendship is almost as bad as their Enmity. The British papers, Whig and tories, Seem to vie in recommending an intervention, Under the form of protection, in the Affair of that very Greece Against whom Great Britain and Austria Have Acted so Cruel and disHonorable a part.[3] How Happy Should I Be to See an American Squadron in those Seas! The American flag Would be the Natural disinterested protector for the Grecian Confederacy. Should the ottoman Navy prove impertinent, it Might Be Crushed at once. a Grecian Citisen who has left Corinth with orders from the federal Government tells me that two Millions of dollars, two Ships of the line or three or four large frigates, Could they obtain that sum and naval Means from Mercantile Enterprise would Suffice to insure the liberties of that Classic Country. it is to be feared the Assistance will Be either With Held or lent With interested Views, if not Under degrading Conditions. the decisions of the Verona Congress[4] are every day Expected. While a Common Antipathy to the Rights of men and Nations link them together, the old Systems and present Views of Each Cabinet interfere with the General plan of the Holy Alliance. The Situation of France, under its Counter revolutionary Government is better understood by a Series of intelligences, lately Collected from the papers of Both parties than I Could express it in a letter. An actual invasion of Spain by foreign troops May be postponed from the fear of Uniting the Whole people in the defense of the Country; but Every Countenance and protection shall more and more Be Afforded to the Ennemies [*sic*] of the Constitution, and if the patriots are driven to Excesses, in Consequence of their provoked irritation, it Will Be Made a pretence Against them, Against the liberals of Every Country, and the Cause itself. much depends on the Spirited resistance of Spain in the present Crisis.

I Have Been Requested By My former Aid de Camp in the National Guards and Constant friend M. de la Rue[5] to Mention to you a Claim of His Lady, Beaumarchais's daughter, now Under the Examination of Congress.[6] Their Wish is that the Affair may be Referred to a Judicial, I Suppose the Supreme Court. it does not Belong me [*sic*] to decide on the propriety of the Measure, nor the Circumstances of the Claim, further than to Say I Have Been a Witness to very Active Exertions of Beaumarchais in the first period of our American Contest. But I owe it to those remembrances, and to My Affection for M. de la Rue to Make to you the desired Mention of this Affair Very important to Him and family. it Appears that American Claims Upon france, are on the point of Being Examined in this Country.[7] I much Wish Justice may be Rendered on all Sides.

I Have often the pleasure to talk of you with two amiable friends of ours Misses Wright[8] Who are Now in france and most of the time in our family Colony of La Grange.

Receive, My dear Sir, the expression of my most Sincere friendship

LAFAYETTE

ALS. DLC-HC (DNA, M212, R1). Addressed: "Henry Clay Esq. Washington." Published in Colton (ed.), *Private Correspondence of Henry Clay*, 67-69.

1 See above, Shaw to Clay, April 4, 1822, note.

2 See above, Itúrbide to Clay, May 6, 1822, note.

3 Metternich and Castlereagh had both reminded Emperor Alexander in October, 1821, that his own principle of "universal union" in preservation of the existing state of Europe barred his intervention in aid of the Greek rebellion against Turkey. By the fall of 1822, however, Greek successes had convinced the British Ministry that

sooner or later the belligerent rights of *de facto* government must be accorded to the Morea. While the British were not prepared to intervene, they were ready to extend "good offices" in any proposed intervention.

4 The Holy Alliance had met at Verona in October, 1822, to consider questions arising from the resurgence of liberalism in Spain (above, II, 789n). With the British abstaining, it was determined to request certain changes in the Spanish Constitution on threat of intervention; and when the Spanish Government rejected these demands, French forces under Louis-Antoine de Bourbon, Duke of Angoulême, invaded Spain, in April, 1823.

5 Not further identified.

6 The accounts of Pierre Augustin Caron de Beaumarchais for arms, military stores, and other supplies provided to the United States at the beginning of the American Revolution had been closed by the Treasury Department in 1805, with payment of all but one million livres plus interest on that sum, which the United States Government believed had been previously paid by France. The following year, Beaumarchais' only daughter and heiress, Amélie Eugénie Beaumarchais de la Rue, appealed to Congress from the Treasury decision. Both James Madison and James Monroe, during their presidencies, had recommended Congressional action on the claim, and a select committee of the House of Representatives in February, 1818, had recommended a bill for relief of Beaumarchais' heirs. A similar report was filed by a House select committee in January, 1823, and by other House committees in subsequent Sessions. In the fall of 1822, however, the topic had been incorporated in the discussions on United States claims against France for spoliations during the Napoleonic wars, and the matter was not settled until included as an offset in the final settlement of the latter controversy in 1835. *House Repts.*, 20 Cong., 1 Sess., no. 220, pp. 1-3, 111, 112, 125; Richard Aubrey McLemore, *Franco-American Diplomatic Relations, 1816-1836* (University, La., 1941), 29-30, 87.

7 In August, 1822, following completion of the Franco-American commercial treaty (see above, Remarks on Bill to Exempt French Ships, February 27, 1821, note), Gallatin had pressed for resumption of the discussions on conflicting Franco-American claims. Several notes were exchanged in November before negotiations were again discontinued until Gallatin might receive new instructions relating to a disputed interpretation of the commercial clause in the treaty for cession of Louisiana.

8 Camilla and Frances Wright, Scottish by birth, orphaned at an early age and reared in England, had travelled in the United States in 1818-1820 and the following year had visited Paris to meet Lafayette. They remained in residence at "La Grange" until 1824, when they again returned to America for an extended stay. Frances became noted, both in this country and abroad, as a lecturer and editor in advocacy of political liberty, social reform, and free thought. In 1821 she had published *Views of Society and Manners in America,* an enthusiastic panegyric, which contrasted with the general tone of British travel accounts.

The sisters had been in Washington during the tariff debate of 1820. Commenting upon Clay's oratorical and conversational skill, with which they had then become acquainted, Frances described his voice as "without exception the most masterly . . . that I ever remembered to have heard." She concluded: "From the perusal of his speeches, you may have formed some idea of the ardour of feeling and expression which characterize this statesman; but you must have heard one delivered to understand their effect in the national senate." Wright, *Views of Society and Manners in America* . . . (New York, 1821), 374-75.

From Langdon Cheves

My Dear Sir, (Confidential) Philada. 9th Novemr 1822.

I ought long ago to have replied to your Confidential letter of the 5th. Ultimo—: But I was encumbered with much business and much intercourse which left me no leisure for reflection or writing and to say the truth I should have written earlier if I had known distinctly what to write in answer to your request that I would give you my opinion of the present State of Public Sentiment in Pennsylvania. To proceed, without further preface to give that Opinion. I incline to think public Opinion in this State is not yet *settled* and that causes may occur to give it a final determination different from its present leaning. The Activity at Washington last winter of a few of the representatives from the State in Congress, particularly General Rogers, almost made the State itself as well as the exterior public believe that Pennsylvania would Support Calhoun.[1] The Franklin Gazette (and News papers & Seats in the Cabinet seem to be the pivots on which this question turns) was at once decided, The Sentinel[2] rather Chimed in with the Other & they are, in this part of the State the principal Organs of the great Majority of the Democratic Party. It soon began to be doubted, however, Whether there was not some mistake on this point.— Lowrie[3] & other persons of Some influence—Lacock[4] for example—were known to be favourable to Crawford— Those who are always looking which way the wind blows, began to be apprehensive they had mistaken the propitious point of the Compass— The Sentinel became an apologist for Crawford & is finally rather an Advocate. As to yourself it does not appear to me that you have any party in the State, but that, their favourites aside, you probably Stand well with both divisions of the democrats. The general impression is that Calhoun will not be supported by Pennsylvania finally because he will not have much Support elsewhere; and that Crawford will be Supported because it is believed he will be Strongly Supported elswhere [*sic*]: It is believed that Virginia will support him & even New York, among the large States, while it is not doubted buthat [*sic*] he will have No. Carolina & Georgia— with the exception of New England of which we will Speak hereafter there seems to be a general disposition on the part of the Newspapers & the active politicians to ascertain who (Calhoun Crawford or Yourself) will be most likely to succeed and as soon as the favourite is pretty well ascertained to give *him* their Support. it is said Crawford will have some Western & some Eastern Support. In relation to him I recollect a remark which I think material— I said to Lowndes[5] last winter at Washington that I did not think Crawford would Stand any Chance, & Such was my impression at the time, but he replied "you are Mistaken his Chance is the best"— It was at Brown's Ball[6] & there was no room for a discussion which would elicit his reasons. A friend of his, however, recently told me he had often declared to him the the [*sic*] same Opinion & had given as his reason for it the fact, that he was the only Candidate who had an *Organised Party*— The fact I believe is pretty well founded & it is one of great weight. I incline then to think his Chance is the best *at this time* in Pennsylvania, as well as several other points, particularly Virginia & New York, and, if Supported by them, Smaller States will follow. The National Advocate[7] & Van Buren (for I understand that Gentleman has become his partizan) having come out for him are I believe the principal Circumstances which lead the public to believe New York is for him. I understand it is pretty well ascertained that Virginia is for him. Mr. Gaillard,[8] who is said by some to be friendly to him, tho' it does not accord with his language to me, told me he had a Conversation with a busy politician of this place of the name of *Randall*[9] (one of *Binns'*[10] friends, who by the by is said to be for Crawford) who said he had been travelling thro' the western part of Pennsylvania & he thought the people of that part of the State were for Crawford & that he (Randall) had written to *Ritchie*[11] who had answered Cautiously that he had not made up his Mind yet, but that if called upon to decide immediately he should be in favour of Crawford.

I think, on the whole, present prospects afford Calhoun little Chance—Lowndes none— I have no Idea that Genl. Jackson would be Supported in the Atlantic States & I Suppose you will think out of Tennessee he would have little Chance in the west, while the newspapers have recently said he declines all offices & will retire— It is supposed by some here that it was not Contemplated by the Legislature of Tennessee Seriously to Support him, but that it was done to injure you. I believe then the Contest will be be [*sic*] between Yourself, Crawford & Adams. of Crawford we have said enough— Of Adams & new England. I have always thought New England generally would finally support Adams: tho' until recently even Massachusetts appeared not to be in his favour. Now you perceive she is Supporting him with zeal & I think Connecticut & the Other new England States will go with him, tho' I believe he will have many opponents. On the part of Connecticut there will be a strong disposition nevertheless to receive the bids of the most promissing [*sic*] Candidates— Whittlesey[12] of Louisville, who has recently been in Connecticut said Casually to me that he thought that State was in a good measure for Sale & this is probable tho' I think she must go with the rest of new England. Her new politicks, however, are neither Manly nor Moral & no calculation I think Can be made upon her. His Contest with Russell has elevated Adams immiensely [*sic*], both as an honest Man & as a Man of talents: But I see no evidences of Support from New York for him; nor do I think, except in thevent [*sic*] of Occurrences which I can not Conceive, he is likely to be supported South of New York & I presume he will not have any support in the west, tho' I believe some think he has friends in Ohio—but there you are at home & can better judge for yourself than others can for you.

Now as to yourself. It is Supposed you will be Supported, of Course, by Kentucky but it is doubted whether you will have the

Support of the western States generally and this prevents you from being so much in the view of the Calculators as you would be if there were a general & especially an Unanimous *western demonstration.*— A demonstration of power & the time of making it are I think Vastly material if they shall not be decisive of the question The time appears to me to have arrived & I think it will pass away before the close of the next meeting of Congress. Crawford, for example is rising by that demonstration & is becoming fixed in the public eye & thoughts—

The Gazettes— the Franklin hangs on with all the tenaciousness of a first love & the irritation of disappointed ambition to our friend Calhoun— the Sentinel is Cautious but obviously devoted to Crawford: But both promise, as the whole tribe do, to follow the indications of public Sentiment as it may be expressed by a regular republican nomination— You perceive the Washington City Gazette is decidedly in favour of Crawford—at least so I learn from other papers for I do not see it,—while McKinneys paper,[13] which is regularly sent to me as I believe it is to many others who like me are not Subscribers, supports Calhoun with great zeal & attacks Crawford with violence & virulence— The Intelligencer[14] fights shy though I think there is no doubt it is in favour of Crawford. Walsh[15] is, I have no doubt, decidedly in favour of Adams tho' he has made no declaration. next to Adams I think he would support Calhoun & yourself in preference to Crawford. The *Aurora* has been recently Changing hands—[16] It has lately had several Chapters in Opposition to Cabinet Candidates— But after all I know nothing about the Subject of which I have been Speaking. You are really, I have no doubt, better able where you are to judge even of Pennsylvania than I am. I incline to think the inhabitants of our Atlantic Cities are not the proper persons to form Correct Opinions of the public sentiment of the nation—They are like a proud Vain man whose thoughts always turn in upon himself & as he wishes so he presumes the world thinks. I forgot to Say that I think Should Calhoun discover his case to be hopeless, which I do not think he will suppose to be the fact before there is some general public declaration by a Caucus of Congress or the like, he will give any influence he may have to Adams; and some therefore even Calculate that Adams may receive the Support of Pennsylvania.—

Finally. I think nothing is yet *decided* in Pennsylvania, tho' it is verging to a decision. That all the other *neutral* states, in which I would include those who offer no prominent Candidates except the small New England States who will probably unite in favour of Adams, are yet open to the influence of Circumstances which may occur altho' some of those are verging to a decision. Among these circumstances I think the first & most important is the demonstration of Power or Support by States & Sections of Country—Editorial Support—Union & Concert with leading Partizans, organization of friends at Washington, Cabinet influence & Caucus Nomination &c &c &c— If you shall be generally & zealously Supported by the west I then think the west will not yield to the Caucus Nomination. If New England shall generally & zealously support Mr. Adams then I think New England will not yield to that Nomination, and if these sections do not yield, the question will remain open for new Combinations & infinite intrigue. If these If these [*sic*] new Combinations shall Unite one or two large States with either the East or the west, there may be an Election in the usual manner.— But if not then neither Candidate will have a majority & the Election will take place in the Hall of Congress, which I think is on the whole the most probable event— In that event I presume your being in Congress will be favourable to you on the whole, as it will probably be in a Congressional Caucus. You have asked me for facts & I have given a long disquition [*sic*] on probabilities & Chances which you Can Calculate with much greater accuracy than I Can. Enough then on this Subject.

Of myself. I leave the Bank in January & then, probably (Entre nous as all I have said is) will begin at 46 the practice of the Law again, in New York or Philadelphia.[17] I find I can't do otherwise— My family is so large & so expensive that I must either labour or go into retirement in some inexpensive place & the habits of my family are too much formed to make the Change an easy one, besides my wife's mother[18] is now old & a good deal infirm & I should do an act of great violence to the feelings of both if I were to Separate them far from each other. If I begin the law again I shall be obliged to give the rest of my life to it—at least ten Years—I am therefore done with Politicks & public life in all likelihood.— On the Subject of the Presidential Candidates, of Course, for the reasons I gave you, I must be neutral: But it is of no importance to any friend, for I have not the influence of a feather situated as I am. The Contest is I think between you Crawford & Adams & without doing doing [*sic*] the invidious act of declaring between you & *other* friends, who probably, will not stand in your way, of the *trio* I heartily wish you success— Very truly & sincerely Yours LANGDON CHEVES

The Honble Henry Clay Lexington Kentucky.

ALS. DLC-HC (DNA, M212, R1).

1 See above, Creighton to Clay, May 2, 1822, note.

2 The Philadelphia *American Sentinel and Mercantile Advertiser*.

3 Walter Lowrie, United States Senator from Pennsylvania, 1819-1825, Secretary of the United States Senate, 1825-1836, Secretary of the Board of Foreign Missions of the Presbyterian Church from 1836 until his death in 1868.

4 Abner Lacock, Congressman from Pennsylvania, 1811-1813, United States Senator, 1813-1819.
5 William Lowndes.
6 Probably the Washington's Birthday Ball at Jesse Brown's Indian Queen Hotel.
7 New York *National Advocate.*
8 John Gaillard, United States Senator from South Carolina, 1804-1826.
9 Josiah Randall, a Philadelphia representative in the Pennsylvania legislature.
10 John Binns, an Irishman who upon release from political imprisonment in England had come to America in 1801 and in the following year had begun publication of the Northumberland, Pennsylvania, *Republican Argus.* He had moved to Philadelphia in 1807 and established the *Democratic Press,* which he published until 1829.
11 Thomas Ritchie.
12 Probably Chauncey Whittlesey, Louisville, Kentucky, lawyer.
13 Thomas L. McKenney; Washington *Republican and Congressional Examiner.*
14 Washington *National Intelligencer.* 15 Robert Walsh, Jr.
16 See above, Wright to Clay, November 2, 1822, note.
17 After his resignation Cheves remained in Philadelphia. In February, 1823, he was appointed commissioner for the United States under a convention with Great Britain to determine "the true construction of Article I of the Treaty of Ghent," and in 1827 he was appointed one of the commissioners under a convention, concluded in the preceding year, by which Great Britain agreed to pay a lump sum in settlement of claims arising under this article of the Ghent Treaty. He also practiced law in Philadelphia and Lancaster, Pennsylvania, before returning to South Carolina in 1829.
18 Sophia Heatly Dulles, widow of Joseph Dulles, a Charleston, South Carolina, merchant who had died in 1818. Their daughter, Mary Elizabeth, had married Cheves in 1806.

From Benjamin Watkins Leigh

My dear Sir Richmond, Nov. 9. 1822.

I had the happiness to receive your letter of the 29th October, this morning; and I am heartily thankful to you for it. It was the more welcome, as it served to assure me of the re-establishment of your health. The newspapers represented you, some weeks ago, as very dangerously ill; and one of them killed you outright[1]—which your distant friends regard as a very unpardonable abuse of the freedom of the press.

It was considerate and kind in you, to send me your report of our arrangements, to the legislature of Kentucky—the more so since I must plead guilty to the charge of having broken my promise to write to you, on my return home. The truth is, that when I got home, I had to write so many letters which I was obliged to write, that I soon came to a conclusion to write none but such as were absolutely indispensible. I trust to your own experience in like cases, to estimate the worth of this apology.

You are right in supposing that I take the deepest interest in Kentucky affairs. I not only wish, but I hope the best for you. Property is the ballast of the vessel of state; and Kentucky has so much of it, that I have no doubt she will soon be righted; tho' (of a truth) she carries more sail than is prudent, and is too venturesome for troublesome and stormy times. To drop the metaphor, you have so many and such substantial and solid grounds to expect public prosperity, that I should not despair of you, in much more serious agitations that [*sic*] any you have experienced. If your legislature pause at the present Session; if the excitement in that body, and in the public mind, abate; if you come to that condition, in which you can look back upon the past with coolness, and forward to the future with a patient reliance on the natural energy of your resources: this were as much as can be reasonably expected for the present; perhaps, as much as should be wished. In all sudden and violent changes of policy, (in popular governments especially) passion is apt to get the mastery, and proceed to demolish, where wisdom would reform and correct.

As to yourself in particular, I shall take this occasion to say, that there was no part of your conduct in regard to the peculiar state of your local politics (and I was very observant of it all), which impressed me with such high respect, and excited so warm a sentiment of approbation, as the constant effort I saw you making, to impress it upon all parties, that there was no desperation, either in the distemper of the state or in the remedies that had been applied, and that it behoved all men, to treat *them both,* with patience, temper and moderation, as well as frankness and steadiness.

In Virginia, all things are in a state of profound calm and quiet; not to say indifference; nor has any change occurred interesting to our sister states or even to ourselves, since you were here last winter, except the death of Mr Roane.[2] The leader of his party on every occasion when state rights were involved, or were supposed to be involved, and especially in every opposition to the supreme court of the U. States, his loss will doubtless be felt here, if not elsewhere, as an important political event. On all such subjects, The Enquirer[3] had no opinions but such as he dictated; and you will see, that its tone will be changed, tho' (I dare say) unintentionally; for, while his feelings remain the same, he[4] will be now without a guide, as he has always been without knowledge, concerning the topics of controversy.

I do not remember, that Ritchie himself has been peculiarly harsh in his censure of your anti-judiciary proceedings: I remember he admitted a communication into his paper sometime ago, that was foolishly ill-natured towards Kentucky, in respect not only to that, but many other subjects. I endeavoured, but in vain, to find out who was the author. I am under an impression, (tho' I forget how it was produced) that it came from the other side of the Alleghany [*sic*].

What the Editor said about the proceedings in Judge Clarke's case (at least, all that struck my attention) was drawn from him by a curious mistake. There was a paper published in the National Intelligencer, signed A. B. vindicating the right of the judges to decide on the constitutionality of acts of the legislature;[5] which Gales[6] recommended to Ritchies particular attention. It was neat in its style, and sensible enough; but I saw in it no original thoughts, nor any very forcible combination of old ones. Ritchie, some how or other, took it into his head, that it was written by Mr Madison;[7] and broke forth into the warmest admiration and assentation, accordingly. It was in fact written by George Hay: *I* thought his hand was visible in every sentence; but the National Intelligencer said the same mistake had been often made. Now—knowing Hay, as you and I do—is it possible to conceive a more exquisite gratification of human vanity, than this mistake must have given him? I could not help being really pleased at the thought of his pleasure.

Meaning to leave enough of this sheet for an envelope, I shall stop here. Tell my friends in Kentucky, that I remember them as I ought. Have the goodness to present my best respects to Mrs Clay.— And believe me, always, with sincerest respect & regard, Yr: ob: serv:

B:W:LEIGH

Henry Clay Esq

P.S. I had almost forgot to tell you, that I hope to bring your suit in the federal court[8] to an end at the approaching term.

ALS. DLC-HC (DNA, M212, R1). Published in Colton (ed.), *Private Correspondence of Henry Clay*, 69-70.

1 See above, Clay to Porter, October 22, 1822, note.

2 Spencer Roane had died September 4, 1822.

3 The Richmond *Enquirer*.

4 Thomas Ritchie.

5 Washington *Daily National Intelligencer*, September 11, 1822.

6 Joseph Gales, Jr.

7 James Madison. See excerpt from Richmond *Enquirer* reprinted in Washington *Daily National Intelligencer*, September 23, 1822.

8 For the recovery of "Euphraim."

From Richard Rush

Dear Sir. London November 9. 1822.

I received a fortnight ago your letter of the 8th of September, since which I have made inquiries respecting John Tench,[1] but can hear nothing whatever of such a person. My inquiries have been among the native Americans living in London, including some of an ancient day, amongst others Mr Murdoch,[2] but none of them can afford me any information on the subject. If you can refer me to any other source whence I may be likely to trace any of the family, I will, on hearing of the proper individual, make the proper use of your letter. My inquiries shall be continued as occasion my [*sic*] offer, though with little hope of hearing any thing for you, unless you can supply me with other lights. I remain, with great respect, your most faithful & obt. Sert.

RICHARD RUSH.

The Honorable Henry Clay.

ALS. DLC-HC (DNA, M212, R1).

1 Not identified; letter not found.

2 Partner in an English mercantile firm.

From John Norvell

Dear Sir, Philadelphia, Nov. 14, 1822.

I had the pleasure duly to receive your interesting letter, dated "Ashland, October 5."[1] Severe illness at the time of its reception, and an engagement since which I could not permit even my indisposition to prevent me from fulfilling, have delayed a reply: Indeed, as every thing on the important subject to which your letter relates is more or less a matter of conjecture and speculation, I fear that it will be impossible to make you a satisfactory answer: My impression is still very decided, that Mr. Calhoun is the favorite of Pennsylvania;[2] that Mr. Adams has some friends scattered over the state; that Mr. Crawford is very unpopular, and could not, at this time, without the aid of a congressional nomination, command two thousand votes in this great republican commonwealth; and that you are gaining ground, at least in this city and district, and in western Pennsylvania. If your friends should act discreetly, and should pursue a conciliatory policy towards Mr. Calhoun, Mr. Adams and General Jackson, it is, in my judgement, more than probable that you will become the candidate in opposition to Mr. Crawford, and be elected. The liberal and honest republicans in this quarter, and throughout the Atlantic states, are very much opposed to the radical system of politics,[3] upon which Mr. Crawford seems to rely for his success: and eventually their votes will be concentrated in favor of *one* candidate against him. In that event, he stands no chance, and the candidate of the republicans in opposition to the radicals will inevitably succeed. Your friends are very anxious that you should act with a view to this state of things. Your return to congress, and election to the chair of Speaker, will put it in your power to shew yourself to every advantage.

Mr. Calhoun's friends do still hold him up, and you may rely upon it, that unless a very great revolution take place in public sentiment, he will be pushed by Pennsylvania as far as patriotism and a due regard to the unity of the republican party will permit. If she find that he cannot be carried, she will probably agree to unite for any other republican candidate in preference to Mr. Crawford. How important is it, then, to your personal and political friends, here and elsewhere, that you should be her next choice? And this, I am still persuaded, may be effected by shewing yourself to be, what you always have been, a liberal republican, an enemy equally to radical meanness and to federal extravagance, and a friend to that administration of which the republican party approve, and which was elected by them.

I am sincerely rejoiced at your bright western prospects, and trust that they may be more than realized. I do firmly believe that you have your own destinies in your own hands: and though, from local causes, I cannot afford you direct aid at present, you may rely upon it that we have never lost sight of you. At the same time, candor [req]uires the declaration that we can see [no] earthly objection to Mr. Calhoun. His talents and patriotism amply qualify him for the station. With equal talents, if not superior, longer service, and stronger party attachments, you have the personal preference of many of us: and we wish to see you honorably placed where your splendid abilities could be exerted with most effect for the honor and welfare of your country. I have the honor to be, Very respectfully, Your most obt. servt. JNO: NORVELL

Mr. Dallas and Mr. Bache[4] warmly reciprocate your friendly regards.

ALS. DLC-HC (DNA, M212, R1). Addressed to Clay at Lexington.
1 Not found.
2 Cf. above, Johnson to Clay, April 1, 1822, note; Cheves to Clay, November 9, 1822.
3 See above, Creighton to Clay, May 2, 1822.
4 George M. Dallas; Richard Bache. The latter was the husband of Dallas' sister, Sophia.

To [Joseph Gales, Jr., and William W. Seaton]

LEXINGTON, 15th Nov. 1822.

Gentlemen: I have witnessed, with very great regret, the unhappy controversy which has arisen between two of my late colleagues at Ghent. In the course of the several publications, of which it has been the occasion, and particularly in the appendix to a pamphlet which has been recently published by the Honorable John Q. Adams,[1] I think there are some errors, (no doubt unintentional,) both as to matters of fact and matters of opinion, in regard to the transactions at Ghent, relating to the navigation of the Mississippi, and certain liberties claimed by the United States in the Fisheries, and to the part which I bore in those transactions. These important interests are now well secured; and, as it respects that of the navigation of the Mississippi, left, as it ought to be, on the same firm footing with the navigation of all the other rivers of the Confederacy, the hope may be confidently cherished, that it will never hereafter be deemed even a fit subject of negotiation with any foreign power. An account, therefore, of what occurred in the negotiations at Ghent, on these two subjects, is not, perhaps, necessary to the present or future security of any of the rights of the nation, and is only interesting as appertaining to its past history. With these impressions, and being extremely unwilling to present myself, at any time, before the public, I had almost resolved to remain silent, and thus expose myself to the inference of an acquiescence in the correctness of all the statements made by both my colleagues; but I have, on more reflection, thought that it may be expected of me, and be considered as a duty on my part, to contribute all in my power towards a full and faithful understanding of the transactions referred to. Under this conviction, I will, at some future period more propitious than the present to calm and dispassionate consideration, and when there can be no misinterpretation of motives, lay before the public a narrative of those transactions as I understood them. I will not, at this time, be even provoked (it would, at any time, be inexpressibly painful to me to find it necessary) to enter the field of disputation, with either of my late colleagues.[2]

As to that part of the official correspondence at Ghent, which had not been communicated to the public, by the President of the United States, prior to the last session of Congress, I certainly knew of no public considerations requiring it to be withheld from general inspection. But I had no knowledge of the intention of the honorable Mr. Floyd to call for it, nor of the call itself, through the House of Representatives, until I saw it announced in the public prints. Nor had I any knowledge of the subsequent call which was made for the letter of the honorable Mr. Russell, or the intention to make it, until I derived it through the same channel.

I will thank you to publish this note in the National Intelligencer, and to accept assurances of the high respect of Your obedient servant, H. CLAY.

Washington *Daily National Intelligencer,* December 17, 1822. Published also in *Niles' Weekly Register,* XXIII (December 21, 1822), 246; Lexington *Kentucky Reporter,* January 6, 1823; Lexington *Kentucky Gazette,* January 16, 1823; Adams, *Memoirs,* VI, 116-17.

1 See above, Russell to Clay, June 6, 1822, note.

2 This letter drew from Adams the following communication to the Editors of the *National Intelligencer,* published December 19, 1822:

Gentlemen: In your paper of yesterday I have observed a note from Mr. Henry Clay, which requires some notice from me.

After expressing the regret of the writer at the unhappy controversy which has arisen between two of his late colleagues at Ghent, it proceeds to say, that, in the course of the several publications of which it has been the occasion, and *particularly* in the appendix to the pamphlet recently published by me, "he thinks there are some errors (no doubt unintentional) both as to matters of fact and matters of opinion, in regard to the transactions at Ghent, relating to the navigation of the Mississippi, and certain liberties *claimed* by the United States in the fisheries, and to the part which he bore in those transactions."

Concurring with Mr. Clay in the regret that the controversy should ever have arisen, I have only to find consolation in the reflection, that, from the seed time of 1814 to the harvest of 1822, the contest was never of my seeking, and that, since I have been drawn into it, whatever I have said, written, or done in it, has been in the face of day, and under the responsibility of my name.

Had Mr. Clay thought it advisable now to specify any error of fact or of imputed opinion which he thinks contained in the appendix to my pamphlet, or in any other part of my share in the publication, it would have given me great pleasure to rectify, by candid acknowledgment, any such error, of which, by the light that he would have shed on the subject, I should have been convinced. At whatever period hereafter he shall deem the accepted time has come to publish his promised narrative, I shall, if yet living, be ready, with equal cheerfulness, to acknowledge indicated error, and to vindicate contested truth.

But as, by the adjournment of that publication to a period "more propitious than the present to calm and dispassionate consideration, and *when there can be no misinterpretation of motives,"* it may chance to be postponed until both of us shall have been summoned to account for all our errors before a higher tribunal than that of our country, I feel myself now called upon to say, that, let the appropriate dispositions, when and how they will, expose the open day and secret night of the transactions at Ghent, the statements, both of fact and opinion, in the papers which I have written and published, in relation to this controversy, will, in every particular, essential or important to the interest of the nation, or to the character of Mr. Clay, be found to abide unshaken the test of human scrutiny, of talents, and of time.

Washington, 18th Dec. 1822. JOHN QUINCY ADAMS.

Promissory Note to Bank of the Commonwealth

[November 16, 1822]

$960 *No.* 1869 *Due* 16. March

One hundred and twenty days after date, we, Henry Clay Abm S Barton & Jno Tilford jointly and severally, promise to pay the President and Directors of the *Bank of the Commonwealth of Kentucky,* or order, Nine hundred & Sixty Dollars Cents; negotiable and payable at their Branch Bank at Lexington, for value received this 16th day Novr. 1822

H. CLAY
JNO TILFORD
ABM. S. BARTON

[Marginal note][1]

59.20/100 paid

[Endorsement on verso][2]

Recd payment of the within note amount Nine hundred & Sixty Dollars. by the hand of J Humphreys Treasurer of Trana University Jany 15h 1822 [*sic*][3] JOHN H. MORTON Cashr.

ADS by Barton, signed also by Clay and Tilford, partially printed. KyLxT. By means of this personal note, three members of the Board of Trustees of Transylvania University obtained funds for the use of that institution. The step may have been taken in anticipation of payments provided in an act of December 18, 1821, by which one half the profits of the Lexington Branch of the Bank of the Commonwealth were to be set aside to discharge debts of the University to a maximum of $20,000. Ky. Gen. Assy., *Acts, 1821,* pp. 353-54. Several months earlier a similar private loan had been negotiated for this purpose, the University itself being unable to borrow because of a provision in the charter of the bank which forbade loans to a corporation. James Morrison, Chairman of the Board of Trustees, to Richard C. Anderson, Speaker of the House of Representatives, October 26, 1822, in Ky. H. of Reps., *Journal, 1822,* pp. 54-55.

1 AE by Barton. 2 ES.

3 Joshua Humphreys had been appointed to this post in July, 1822, and continued in that capacity until his death, November 23, 1823, when he was succeeded by John H. Morton.

From Charles Miner

Henry Clay, Esqr west Chester Penn, Nov. 16—1822

Sir,

Your frank and honourable character emboldens me to write you this letter; the interesting matter treated of must be my apology. You are looked to by a large and liberal portion of citizens in Pennsylvania as a candidate for President. The grounds of their preference are wholly national. We know that the general denomination of your politics is the same with those of Mr. Crawford, Mr. Calhoun and Mr. Adams. But you are prefered

1 Because it is thought to be wise, at times, particularly at this time, to select a man who is not one of the Presidential Secretaries

2 Because your opinions in favour of moderate, but the sure protection, of Domestic Manufactures, are known.

3 Because you favour a liberal system of National Internal Improvemt in Roads and Canals

4 Because the part you have taken in favour of acknowledging the Independence of the New Southern nations would give you their confidence and enable you to make such preliminary arrangements with them (guarded by a wise caution, yet partaking of a spirit frank, liberal and generous) as should be useful to both and lay the foundation of future good will {For myself I look with earnest and affectionate solicitude to their growth in freedom and power, that the liberal nations of the new world may be a counterpoise for the despotic nations of the old.}

I cannot speak of your high personal qualifications without seeming to flatter you, and shall therefore, pass them over without remark

But it is understood here that the western presses and your western friends, under your advice, are comparatively silent on the subject of your claims thinking the Presidential question prematurely agitated

So zealous and active are the friends of the other candidates that it has become necessary that your western friends should every where speak out distinctly. It is thought the nomination of Henry Clay should appear as a western nomination. Every moment of delay cannot now but be injurious. I *think* in Pennsylvania, if the friends of Mr. Calhoun find there will be no chance of his election, they will unite in an electoral ticket for Mr. Clay; and, on the other hand, if there should appear no reasonable prospect of carrying Mr. Clay his friend [*sic*] (with a few exceptions) would unite in an electoral ticket for Mr. Calhoun

The Presidency is an object worthy the noblest ambition and to which the purest patriotism may aspire. The mountain did not go to Mahomet— It is a law of God and nature that great heights are only to be attained by great labour. Zeal must be met with zeal; ardour with ardour. With the motto on our shields of "*God–Liberty* and our Country" if we go forth with spirit I am sure we may return with "Clay and Victory" on our banners. I am very respectfully yours

CHARLES MINER

Henry Clay, Esqr

P. S. I take no copy of this letter.— I wish no reply. But as a token that it has come to hand please send me a Lexington paper with the word "Received" on the margin

ALS. DLC-HC (DNA, M212, R1). Postmarked November 22; addressed to Clay at Lexington, but forwarded to Frankfort. When a young man, Miner had moved from Connecticut to Pennsylvania, where in 1802 he had joined the staff of the Wilkes-Barre *Luzerne Federalist and Susquehanna Intelligencer,* of which he became owner and publisher two years later. He subsequently edited another paper in Wilkes-Barre and, briefly, a daily journal in Philadelphia. In 1817 he had removed to West Chester and had begun publication of the *Village Record,* in its day a widely known weekly newspaper. He had served two terms in the Pennsylvania legislature and in 1824 and 1826 was elected to the United States House of Representatives. He retired from politics because of deafness and in 1832 gave up his newspaper work. From 1834 until his death in 1865 he lived in Wilkes-Barre.

To Benjamin Watkins Leigh

Dr Leigh Frankfort 18h. Nov. 1822

I have the satisfaction to inform you that the General Assembly has unconditionally ratified the Conventions.[1] Mr. Rowan[2] proposed a condition imposing upon the two States the reciprocal obligation that claimants of Lands, within this State, should abide by the decision of the Board of Commrs on the Laws of limitation and Occupancy. Without sufficient deliberation and a clear comprehension of the effect of the proposed condition a majority in the H. of R. voted for it. But an immediate reconsideration took place, and the condition was rejected 66 to 20 in the House,[3] and the ratification carried in the Senate unconditionally with one dissentient.[4] The Legislature will probably appoint Jacob Burnett Esqr. of Cincinnati and Hugh L. White of Tennessee, Commr. under the Florida Treaty,[5] Commrs on the part of this State. Mr. Rowan will probably be associated with me as Counsel to appear before the Board.[6] Mr. Bibb[7] declines offering. There will be, on our part, as I have no doubt there will be on yours', a faithful compliance with the engagements which we contracted between our respective States.

With great regard I am faithfully Your's H. CLAY

B. W. Leigh Esq

ALS. ViU. [1] See above, Convention, June 5, 1822. [2] John Rowan.

[3] Ky. H. of Reps., *Journal, 1822,* pp. 91-92, 96, 125. The *Journal* does not name the author of the condition.

[4] Ky. Sen., *Journal, 1822,* pp. 95-96.

[5] White, who had held office in Tennessee as a judge of the Superior Court (1801-1807), State Senator, United States Attorney, and presiding judge of the State Supreme Court of Errors and Appeals (1809-1815), had been appointed in 1821 a member of the claims commission set up under the terms of the Adams-De Onís Treaty.

[6] The election of commissioners and counsel, with results as here foreseen, was held by both houses of the legislature on November 19. Ky. H. of Reps., *Journal, 1822,* pp. 148-49; Ky. Sen., *Journal, 1822,* pp. 108-109.

[7] George M. Bibb.

To Benjamin Watkins Leigh

Dr Sir Ashland 21 Nov. 1822

As I anticipated in my last letter to you[1] the General Assembly has appointed Mess. Burnett and White Commrs on the part of this State, and Mr. Rowan and myself Agents. We have no information whether the Commrs will act or not. To guard against their Non-acceptance, or nonattendance, a contingent power will be vested in some persons (probably the Agents) at Washington to supply their place.[2] The above gentlemen were the only persons nominated as Commissioners. With great regard I am truly Yours. H. CLAY

B. W. Leigh Esqr.

ALS. ViU. [1] See above, November 18, 1822.

[2] This power was granted in a resolution adopted by the House on November 20, concurred in by the Senate on November 21, and approved by the Governor on the latter date. Ky. H. of Reps., *Journal, 1822,* p. 153; Ky. Sen., *Journal, 1822,* p. 118; Ky. Gen. Assy., *Acts, 1822,* p. 249.

From José Manuel Herrera

Mexico 23 de Noviembre de 1822.

Ha recibido con sumo aprecio S.M. el Emperador la atenta y afectuosa carta q. con fha. 25 de Marzo último se sirvió V. dirijirle; y lleno de los mas vivos sentimientos de reconocimiento y estimacion, me manda contarle á V. manifestandole las buenas disposiciones q. lo animan en favor de los habitantes de ese pais á quienes recibirá como amigos y tratará siempre con las consideraciones q. se deben las naciones vecinas destinadas á vivir en la mas perfecta é inalterable armonia.

El Sor. Poinsett[1] ha correspondido completamte. a la ventajosa idea q. V. dá oi [*sic*] en México, y en el ha encontrado el Ymperio un hombre adornado delas mas recomendables prendas.

Espero se sirva V. recibir la manifestacion de mis sentimientos q. tengo la honra de dirijirle con el feliz motivo de estar encargado por S.M. para darte esta contestacion en la q. me sirve de la mayor complacencia aseguararte q. soy

Su muy adicto y Seguro Servidor J. M. HERRERA

A Mr. H. Clay

ALS. DLC-HC (DNA, M212, R1). Endorsed by Clay on verso: "Mr. Herrera Iturbide's Minister of Foreign affairs." See above, Itúrbide to Clay, May 6, 1822.

[1] Joel R. Poinsett.

To Smith Thompson

Sir Lexington 25h. Nov. 1822

I beg leave to recommend for Midshipman's warrants William Farrar, and James Farrar, sons of Doctor B. G. Farrar of St. Louis.[1] I have the pleasure of personally knowing Dr. Farrar, and can speak of him, with great truth, as a man of honor and a gentleman of the

highest respectability. Although I do not know his sons, the account which I have received of them and upon which I can entirely confide, is that they are uncommonly promising and manly youths. I have the honor to be with great respect Your ob. Servant H. CLAY
The Honble Mr. Thompson &c &c &c

ALS. CtHi.
[1] Dr. Farrar, brought to Fayette County, Kentucky, in his infancy, had been educated at Transylvania and the University of Pennsylvania and had moved to St. Louis in 1807. He had been a surgeon in the United States Army during the War of 1812, after which he had returned to private practice. The two sons here mentioned, children of his first wife, died unmarried. They did not receive appointments.

Report to Board of Trustees, Transylvania University

[November 25, 1822]

The Committee appointed to consider and report upon the subject of the Salaries of the Officers of the University have, according to order, taken the same into consideration, and now beg leave to report,

That the state of the actual currency of the Commonwealth has induced the Board to assign the present duty to the Committee: That the losses which arise to individuals, in consequence of its depreciation, and particularly to Salary Officers, are greatly to be regretted: In considering the subject, however, two inquiries must be made 1st What is the actual loss arising from the depretiation of the Currency and? 2dly. Has the University the ability to make an adequate indemnity for it?

1st. The salaries allowed were when granted understood doubtless to be payable in the curent [*sic*] money of the U States, that is in Specie. They are now paid, and have for some time past been paid, in the paper currency of the State. The nominal loss therefore to the Officers of the University is the difference between specie and that paper currency, which difference has been as great as two dollars of paper for one of specie, and it is now nearly that. But if we compare (as we ought) the value of Specie, at the time when those salaries were granted, with its present value, we shall find that the actual loss will be much less than the nominal loss to the officers. All domestic commodities are believed to have fallen, on an average, nearly of fifty per Cent. Those of foreign industry have not fallen in the same proportion, but have fallen considerably. If all articles of consumption, house rent, servant hire &c had fallen fifty per Cent, the Salaries, although paid in a medium worth only fifty per cent. in specie, would have sustained no actual diminution And the mitigation of the evil of a depretiated currency, to the officers of the Institution, is in the proportion, therefore, of the fall in the price of all the objects of their Expenditure. Viewing the subject in this light, we shall perceive that their loss is much less considerable than it might appear at first to be. Even that reduced loss the Trustees ought to prevent if the University has the means to prevent it. And this leads us to the second inquiry.

All will agree that, since the University must mainly depend upon its receipts from tuition, the expences ought to be graduated by the fund which is to be bear them; that these expences ought not to exceed the revenue; and that it would be unwise to place any considerable reliance upon the contingent aid derivable from charitable Contributions, flowing either from the public or from individuals. The present income of the University, it is notorious, is scarcely sufficient to meet its current disbursements. To augment therefore materially the Salaries of the officers would be, in effect, to make promises without any certain ability to comply with them. If the revenue can be increased (and that must depend upon the exertions chiefly of the Professors and tutors) the trustees would certainly take great pleasure in an equitable appropriation of it. For in the performance of the public duty assigned to them, they can have no wish but so to execute it as to produce the greatest sum of public good, and at the same time to promote the comfort & happiness of the Officers of the University.

If it be impracticable to make at this time to the Professors & tutors any indemnity for the loss sustained by them in receiving payment of their Salaries in the paper money of the State, they are nevertheless not without many strong motives to animate and encourage them. The depretiation, it is to be hoped, will be temporary. The general expectation, excited by the measures of the Legislature at Frankfort, is that the currency will progressively improve.[1] We may, therefore, console ourselves with believing that we have passed through the most difficult period. The Country and the University are so identified in interest that they cannot be separated from each other. None are wholly exempt from the evils of a depretiated currency. All may reasonably hope to gain something by its amelioration, of which there is now an encouraging prospect. It would be injudicious, both as to the University and its officers, to predicate a permanent arrangement of their Salaries upon a depretiation, which is temporary. It could only be justifiably done by resorting to a less fluctuating standard, than that of the paper currency. And if that were done a considerable reduction of their specie amount must be made, which in the end might be more injurious to the officers themselves than the temporary mischiefs of which they complain.

In a solitary instance a specie salary or its equivalent has been engaged. The peculiar considerations which led to that measure are within the recollection of the Board[2] If the currency shall be greatly improved in its value, as is generally anticipated, the condition of the officer who receives that Salary, in comparison with that of his Colleagues, may not then be quite as enviable as it now appears to be.

Under all the circumstances of the times and of the subject your Comee. recommend the adoption of the following resolution:

Resolved that it is inexpedient at this time to make any alteration in the Salaries of the Officers of Transylvania University.

JOHN W. HUNT C.C

DS, in Clay's hand. KyLxT. John D. Shane, in his notes from the records of Transylvania University, stated that the Committee on Salaries reported to the Board of Trustees on November 25, 1822, but that the report was "not entered." PPPrHi-Shane Collection (microfilm at KyU); cf. above, II, 583n.

On February 7, 1820, and again on December 13, 1821, Clay had been re-elected for successive terms as a trustee of the University. Ky. H. of Reps., *Journal, 1819-1820,* p. 362: *1821,* p. 405. He thereafter served continuously in this capacity until 1828. He was again re-elected on May 14, 1829, but resigned from the post early in the following year. See below, Clay to Bradford, January 5, 1830.

1 In response to that portion of Governor Adair's message of October 22, 1822, concerning banks, each house of the legislature had begun considering means to reduce the amount of paper currency in circulation. On November 23 the Senate had approved and sent to the House of Representatives "an act to reduce the quantity of paper currency," and, earlier on the same day, had begun consideration of a bill to repeal the charter of the Bank of Kentucky. These measures were eventually combined in an act, approved December 5, which revoked the charter of the Bank of Kentucky and provided for cancellation, by burning, of certain notes, both of that institution and of the Bank of the Commonwealth. The notes of the latter were to be reduced by periodic burnings, according to a schedule, throughout the following year. The first of the burnings was held January 8, 1823. Ky. H. of Reps., *Journal, 1822,* pp. 12-14, 17, 43, 94-95; Ky. Sen., *Journal, 1822,* pp. 55, 128, 132; Ky. Gen. Assy., *Acts, 1822,* pp. 119-24; Lexington *Kentucky Reporter,* January 13, 1823.

2 In July, 1822, the Board of Trustees had established a committee to employ a principal of the grammar school at an annual salary of $500 "in lawful money of the U.S." Later in the month the Board had decided, as an added inducement to prospective applicants, that the principal of the grammar school might enroll his sons at the University without charge; and on August 1, the proffered salary was raised to $600. Two days afterward Mann Butler, then a teacher in Frankfort, Kentucky, was elected to the position. Butler was later the author of *A History of the Commonwealth of Kentucky* (Louisville, 1834).

Debit Account with the Estate of Samuel Hopkins

[*ca.* December 3, 1822]

AD by Clay. DLC-TJC (DNA, M212, R15). This statement differs from that above, II, 916-18, only in that the minor error in the column of figures has been corrected, the interest has been calculated to December 3, 1822, making the total amount due $10,841.57, and no credits are shown.

From John C. Wright

H. Clay Esq Steubenville, 4th Dec 1822

Dr Sir

From conversation with members of the Legislature & information from others I am well assured that but one obstacle remains to your nomination at Columbus about or before the first of January and that is the idea that Clinton will be a candidate— I have solicited information from Washington to be sent to Columbus on that subject, but lest it should fail altogether or be received [*sic*] in season, I write this hasty line while the mail is closing, supposing your friends might already have obtained certain information on that subject or could perhaps obtain & communicate sooner than it could be gotten elsewhere. No time should be lost in conveying information on that point to Columbus if favorable I have just been writing to several members assuring them of my confident belief that Clinton will not be out, & pressing a nomination in this month, to give time your [*sic*] state & the other western states— As popular as Clinton is we may calculate, if our legislature nominate another, the state will act accordingly. Reports from Pennsylvania are becoming more favorable.

Some resent [*sic*] attempt to advance your interest in the Cincinnati papers has drawn down upon your head some abuse—and it has been tho't that as the time is so short as not to allow a rejoinder in case an attack in reply upon you is provoked—We have concluded in this quarter to let the newspapers alone.

I have rec'd no acknowledgement of my former letter,[1] and must apologise for again writing you in the pressing necessity of the case. I shall be happy to serve you in any way in my power

In great haste yours respectfully J. C. WRIGHT

ALS. DLC-HC (DNA, M212, R1). [1] See above, November 2, 1822.

To John Quincy Adams

Frankfort 5h. Decr. 1822—

Mr. Clay's respectful compliments to Mr. Adams and he will be obliged to him by his forwarding the inclosed letter to Mr. Rush[1] with the first despatches from Government.

AN. DNA, RG59, Misc. Letters. [1] Richard Rush. The letter, not found.

From Thomas Wilson

Sir, Bank United States Decem. 6th 1822

I have the honor to transmit the annexed report of a Committee, on the case of J. J Marshall Esq, a debtor to this Bank at the Offices of Lexington & Louisville, adopted by the Board this day.[1] I am, very respectfully Sir. Yr Ob: Servt. THO WILSON Cash

Honble. Henry Clay Lexington, Ky

ALS. DLC-HC (DNA, M212, R1).

1 The enclosure is an extract from the minutes of a meeting of the President and Directors of the Bank of the United States, at which the committee "to whom was referred the letter of Mr. Clay dated 7th. Ultimo submitting a new proposition from Mr. J. J. Marshall" reported adversely on the proposal. Clay's letter, here mentioned, has not been found. See above, Clay to Cheves, October 26, 1821.

To [James Monroe]

Sir Ashland 8h. Decr. 1822.

Presuming that, in the course of the present Session of Congress, missions will be sent to Spanish America, in conformity with your recommendation made at the last,[1] I beg leave to recommend, for the appointment of Secretary to one of them, Robert J. Breckenridge Esq.,[2] Son of the late John Breckenridge Esq. Atto. General of the U. States. Mr. Breckenridge has received the best education which the institutions of our Country could confer; and has availed himself of the fine opportunities which he has possessed to improve and cultivate his mind. Young, ardent and emulous, we consider him among those promising young men, of whom the State has a right to entertain high expectations and sanguine hopes. Should he be favored by being selected for the service which he solicits, I have no doubt that whilst he would discharge its duties faithfully, he would embrace every occasion to qualify himself to perform hereafter still higher duties.[3] I have the honor to be with great respect Your obedient Servant H. CLAY

The President Of the U. States.

ALS. DNA, RG59, Applications and Recommendations for Office (MR1).

1 See above, Shaw to Clay, April 4, 1822, note.

2 Robert Jefferson Breckinridge (1800-1871), after attending Princeton and Yale, had been graduated from Union College, Schenectady, New York, in 1819 and had returned to Lexington. In 1824 he began practice of law and in the next year was elected to the first of several terms in the State legislature. He became a Presbyterian minister in 1832, attended the Theological Seminary at Princeton for a short time, succeeded his brother, John, as pastor in Baltimore, and became nationally influential in the Church. After two years as president of Jefferson College, Cannonsburg, Pennsylvania, he returned to Kentucky in 1847 to become pastor of the First Presbyterian Church in Lexington. In the same year he received an appointment as State Superintendent of Public Instruction, a post which he held with distinction until 1853, when he became professor in the Theological Seminary at Danville, Kentucky. Loyal to the Union during the Civil War, he was temporary chairman of the convention of the National Union Party, composed of the Republicans and Unionist Democrats, which met at Baltimore in 1864. Strong minded and disputatious, he was a popular lecturer and a prolific writer. He founded and published journals in both Baltimore and Danville and was a successful Kentucky farmer.

3 He was not nominated.

To Robert J. Breckinridge

8h. Decr. 1822

Mr. Clay's compliments to Mr. Breckenridge and he has the pleasure to inclose him herein a recommendatory letter[1] as requested by Mr B.

AN. DLC-Breckinridge Family Papers (DNA, M212, R20). Addressed: "Robert J. Breckenridge Esq. Cabells Dale."

1 Above, this date.

From John Breathitt

Mr. Clay, Frankfort, Decr. 8, 1822,

Will much oblidge the undersigned, If, when, He goes on to Washington, He will use his endeavour to have Wm. Y. C. Ewing a resident of Lillard County Missouri appointed to be Receiver; or Register at a Land Office expected to be established in the N. Western part of said state;— He is a man of unexceptionable character—and of the strictest integrity, & would make a good officer.[1]

Your friend &c, JOHN BREATHITT

ALS. DLC-TJC (DNA, M212, R12). Breathitt, a lawyer and former member of the Kentucky legislature, had been brought, when a child, from Virginia to Logan County. He became Lieutenant Governor of Kentucky in 1828, and in 1832 was elected Governor. He died in 1834, before the end of his term of office.

1 Ewing, who had been a member of the First Regiment, Kentucky Mounted Militia, in the War of 1812, apparently did not obtain an appointment (although a "Young Ewing, of Missouri," was appointed "Receiver of Public Moneys for the Western District of Missouri" in the spring of 1826 and resigned before the end of the year).

From Francis Johnson

Dear Sir (Confidential) Washington City 10 Decr. 1822

Your favors of the 21 & 22 Ulto were recd. today—[1] The Subject matters thereof have been duly attended to.

From the intimations I have had I look every day to hear that Ohio has taken up the Subject of the next president.— I had thought it most prudent for Ky to have forborne her expression, and permitted some other State to have started your nomination—but I begin to think the measure a salutary & a very timely one[2]—for I have my doubts, which perhaps a few days may Confirm or dissipate —that the exertions made here last winter by Certain individuals to inculcate the idea, that Ky would not unanimously support you, had been pushed to the extent, that many who felt strongly inclined to support you, were either silenced, become lukewarm or felt disposed to look to some other as the prominent man—and the act settles the question—supports your friends in their declarations—and puts the feret [*sic*] and grovling [*sic*] or open & avowed, if they please, enemies to the blush. or ought to do it— tis not forgotten, that I was enquired of by several gentlemen here last Session, how it came that a Certain person was opposed to you— I answered that I expected they were mistaken— they said not, I then replied it made no difference, the Current in Ky was so strong for you that person would have to go along with it, and they would see it—and it has happened— Genl Smyth[3] of Virginia has published a Circular to his Constituents in which he tells them it is possible if he should be re elected that he may have to vote for President, he does not say who he will vote for but he says he will tell them now that he will not vote for J Q Adams and assigns his reasons— It is published in the Richmond enquirer of the 7 & Washington Gazette of the 9th. you probably get one or the other before this reaches you— It is beleived [*sic*] it will have considerable effect against Mr A. I can entertain no doubt but it was intended more for Mr Adams, than his Constituents— in a conversation today with a leading member from New Hampshire—he expressed himself for Mr Adams and said it would be gratifying to the North to have the next President— I observed we should be pleased if we could consistently gratify the north in any of its pretentions, [but upon some real principles, some rational grounds]—he said you were a m[an] of broad & liberal principles—and after some further conversation, I put the question to him—if the contest should turn between Mr. Clay & Mr Crawford, did he not beleive that you would beat him— expressed himself that he thought you would and that easily— I find some of Mr. Adams friends are very willing to make you Vice President— In a conversation to day with a Senator from New Jersey, somewhat to my surprize he was in favor of Mr Smith Thompson as next President—that he preferr d him to any other man— he said Moreover that in his opinion it was well settled that his State would not support Mr Adams—and hereon hangs the indecision of the North— they want the next President— they cant unite on Mr A. and they are sounding to see if any other will do—and if Ohio Comes out for you—the impression on Pensylvania [*sic*], in my Opinion will be manifested early—and Virginia & other states will not long suspend their indications— the West once united, the Current will flow easily and without obstructions of a serious Cast— no section of the Union owes you illwill or dislike that I have heard of— Virginia Certainly in my opinion leans more to you than she did a twelve month ago—

The Vice President[4] has made his appearance here with his family —much reformed in health &c. I have thought some hopes still hovered over his immagination [*sic*]—but perhaps not— Cambreleng[5] in a conversation the other day suggested to me some things which were calculated to induce a beleif, that some of the prominent men in N York who favor d Mr Cds. pretensions were on the decline in influence and seemed I thought to rank himself rather in opposition to them—but the whole of his Conclusion amounted to this, that the only understood settled point was that Mr A. was not to get NY.— It is possible that State may entertain some hopes of Mr. Thompson— tho' not one from the State, has as I have heard ever named him—or the fact as relates to that State is as I suggested to you long since—

Yancy of Barren came with me here and the President has given him an appointment—[6] he is & I have no doubt will continue to be your Warm friend—

You will not surprized [*sic*] I hope, when I tell you Mr H. Nelson is to go Mexico [*sic*]— Mr. C A Rodney to Buenayres]*sic*[and Mr R C Anderson to Columbia [*sic*], as Ministers Plen:[7] (but this to yourself only) — Unless something should change the dye that is the throw now—

Be assured of my best wishes Yr friend FR: JOHNSON

I think there are symptoms of a surrender on the part of Mr. Calhoun and his friends—some [. . .][8] think—he will unite his interests with Mr. A— but I do not beleive it— One thing pretty Certain—he cant carry all his friends with him— the Election for a Senator in So. Carolina is just over— Hayne, the Calhoon [*sic*] Candidate got 71. and Judge Smith the present Senator the Crawford Candidate got 73—[9] upon this point it is said the Election turned— So that Mr Cn. is not so strong in his own State, as was wont to be represented— after the nomination of Mr Lowndes[10] and this Election I think Mr. Cns. friends will say nothing more about the unanimity of So Carolina—

The last accts from Mr Lowndes were unfavorable to his ever reaching alive his native shore— FR: JOHNSON

ALS. DLC-HC (DNA, M212, R1). MS. faded. 1 Neither letter has been found.
2 See above, Clay to Porter, October 22, 1822, note.
3 Alexander Smyth. 4 Daniel D. Tompkins.
5 Churchill C. Cambreleng, born in North Carolina, had in 1802 moved to New York, where he became a merchant. He was a member of the United States House of Representatives, 1821-1839, and Minister to Russia, 1840-1841.
6 Joel Yancey, of Barren County, Kentucky, had been nominated on December 9 as Collector at Key West, Territory of Florida, and his appointment was confirmed three days later. He had been a member of the Kentucky House of Representatives, 1809-1811, and of the State Senate, 1816-1820. He again sat in the Senate, 1824-1827, and was a member of the United States House of Representatives, 1827-1831.
7 The nominations as here indicated, except that Hugh Nelson was named to succeed John Forsyth at Madrid, were sent to the Senate on January 13, 1823, and approved a few days later. No minister was sent to Mexico by the United States until 1825.
8 Word or two illegible.
9 Actually, the election was won by Robert Y. Hayne, Charleston lawyer, who had been a member of the South Carolina legislature (including one year as Speaker of the House) and State Attorney General. He was United States Senator from 1823 until he resigned in 1832 to become Governor of South Carolina.
William Smith had served in the United States House of Representatives, 1797-1799, and in the Senate, 1816-1823. He had also held several local offices.
10 See above, Fromentin to Clay, April 26, 1822, note.

From Henry R. Warfield

My dear Sir— Washington 10th. Dec[ember] 1822

I shou'd have written to you after the receipt of your letter last Summer[1] but being most of my time at Home I had nothing as I thought worth your attention— we had also accounts of your illness—[2]

I need not assure you of my cordial congratulations on your restoration to health— I am now at Pecks (Crawfords old stand) [3] in a Mess composed of Mr. King of New York, Mercer Gorham Edwards of Pena. Van Beuren Genl VanRenselear McLane of Delaware[4] & myself, Tho we think it po[ssible] we shall have our mess much enlarged in a few [days], Mills of the Senate Stevenson of Richmond[5] & several others are inclined to Join us— I shall at present write you only a few lines— Congress as you may suppose has done nothing as yet— The Presidential Election is the daily theme— It is generally understood and believed here that Calhoun will withdraw from the contest— His friends speak of it in that way, and I have no doubt of [its truth]— I understand from a correct sourse [*sic*] that he [is late]ly spoken of in [*very*] high terms as an able statesman, which it was [understood] was *not altogether* the case last winter— With regard to Mr. Adams from conversations with Eastern Gentlemen, I consider it an unquestionable fact that he cannot unite the Eastern States,— Some of the best informed Gentlemen from that quarter speak of this as certain—and without unanimity and a zealous Cordial cooperation in that Section his most Sanguine friends must perceive, there is not the remotest prospect of his Election— Depend upon it the question will rest between Crawford and yourself unless some one not yet spoken of, (and I know of no such person in any part of the union) shou d be brought into view— Shou'd this not be the case you have Pennsylvania. I know— a highly respectable Member from that State who was 'till half past Eleven P. M. at Myers,[6] which is the Pennsylvania boarding House a few Evenings past assured me of this— New York 'tiz thought here by some is favourable to Crawford— *I doubt it for strong reasons*— If She is at this time I think there will be a radical change before the Election* Genl. Van [Rensselaer] who has been with me in my room for [some] Hours this Evening is your fast friend— I read to [him] the part of your letter to me in which you speak in such friendly terms of him— Every Service he can render you will be [*gladly render*]ed— But there are other Springs to be [*tapped* in that] State— More however on this point at some [other] period—

That Crawford will get some of the New England States as they are called I think Extremely probable— Holmes of Main[7] [*sic*] report says is with him— That you will get some of them also is most certain— I am not at this time in possession of materials to make Even a probable calculation— In the course of the Winter I shall be able to count with considerable accuracy— As to Virginia & the Southern States I do not undertake to give an opinion; but from the result of the Election of Senator in the place of Judge Smith which has lately taken place[8] (Calhoun out of the question) I shou'd consider South Carolina for you, for the Election turned as it is understood here upon the question of Calhoun or Crawford— In Maryland we vote by Districts I consider two thirds of the votes for you certain—perhaps the whole State— Crawford friends some of whom are sagatious and Influential are busily Engaged— From some of the states there are men of talents and information who are not *positively determined*— The reason why 'tis Easy to conjecture— one plan adopted, and attempted to be put in opperation [*sic*] by Crawfords friends is to impress a belief that he is so strong that all opposition wou'd be useless— 'tis frequently said in speaking of the Election [". . .][9] I like Clay very well I wou'd as soon see [him Preside]nt as any of them but I do not think him [strong eno]ugh—" This impression must & will be done away—we [recei]ved in our mess room this Evening a paper contain[ing] your nomination by the Kentucky Legislature—[10] Its Effect will be great— It will tend to fix the opinions of many of those "*not positively determined Gentlemen*"— I cou'd give you the names of a number of *prominent men* both for & opposed to you, but I do not like to trust to paper— I give you these few outlines for the present— but as your Engagements are numerous & Extensive I know not that this letter will find you at Lexington— at what time will you probably be here, Let me have a few lines to know where to direct for I remember last year you did not receive a letter of mine for some six or Eight weeks after it was written—[11] There are but three persons in the District who know that I correspond with you & they are your fast friends— Hemphil[12] [*sic*] is your open *avowed* & zealous friend— Others whom I will hereafter name are loocking [*sic*] out to see how the wind blows— Tis now almost 12 & I have to meet the [Naval] Committee Early in the morning— Tis contempl[ated] Immediately to put in action a sufficient force to Exterminate the Pirates. Come.[13] [Porter of]fered his resignation as Commissioner on Condition [of receiv]ing the Command—[14]

I shall Communicate to you more fully hereafter as this is hastily written— I am no Prophet—but in the approaching Contest I shall nail my colours on the mast head— all we ask of you is to stand firm on the quarter deck—and I predict you will command the ship Constitution for the next Eight years; and whether the Voyage is to be performed on a calm unruffled sea, or agitated by contending billows—of one thing you may be certain that you will not find in the whole crew a more firm and Stefast [*sic*] friend than

[Marginal note] HENRY R. WARFIELD

* This I think I can demonstrate to you—

ALS. DLC-HC (DNA, M212, R1). MS. foxed, partially illegible.

1 Not found. 2 See above, Clay to Porter, October 22, 1822, note.

3 Hiel Peck, formerly proprietor of Rossburg Tavern, had taken over Joseph Crawford's Union Tavern in the spring of 1822.

4 Rufus King; Charles Fenton Mercer; Benjamin Gorham; Samuel Edwards, lawyer of Chester, Pennsylvania, United States Congressman, 1819-1827; Martin Van Buren; Stephen Van Rensselaer; and Louis McLane.

5 Elijah Hunt Mills; Andrew Stevenson, lawyer, member of the Virginia General Assembly (1809-1816, 1818-1821), United States Congressman (1821-1834), Speaker of the House (1827-1834), Minister to Great Britain (1836-1841).

6 Mrs. Myer's boarding house, Seventh Street, one door south of Pennsylvania Avenue, opposite the center market house.

7 John Holmes. 8 See above, Johnson to Clay, this date, note.

9 Possibly two or three words missing.

10 See above, Clay to Porter, October 22, 1822, note.

11 Possibly above December 18, 1821. 12 Joseph Hemphill. 13 Commodore.

14 On December 9 President Monroe had sent a special message to Congress, noting the "multiplied outrages and depredations which have been committed on our seamen and commerce, by the pirates, in the West Indies and Gulf of Mexico," and asking that a force of vessels of light draft suitable for campaigning in shallow waters be provided. On December 15 the House approved a bill for this purpose, which was accepted by the Senate the following day and approved by the President on December 20. *Annals of Cong.*, 17 Cong., 2 Sess., XL, 32-35, 371-84; 3 *U.S. Stat.*, 720. Commodore David Porter, who had been appointed a Commissioner of the Navy Board in 1815, resigned this post and was assigned to purchase the vessels and direct the action.

From John Clay

My dear Brother New Orleans, 13th Dec. 1822.

Mr Duralde Susan & Ann[1] arrived in this City a few days ago in good health. they have done us the pleasure to stay with us till suitable arrangements are established in a house which Mr D. has rented & which is situated in the Same Street & contiguous to mine. Mrs. Clay seems to be proud of our Neice [*sic*] Ann. We shall both duly appreciate the trust. & we will do all we can to contribute to her amusement & happiness. We regret most Sincerely the death of our venerable father Mr. M Duralde Sen.[2] of which event you have been already apprised.) & that this circumstance should also deprive us from accompanying to the different amusements offer'd at this season in our City. I received your letter per Duralde of the 9th oct inclosing me Certificates of five Shares in the U S Bank Stock[3] I thank you for attention to this business. You will have received some time ago a Bill of Exchange to refund you the am't you paid for them. The Suit Smith vs. myself which has been for a long time hanging over my head was decided on Yesterday to my great mortification & disappointment. In the U States Dt. Court of this City. the Conduct of Judge Dick[4] was marked with hostility against me. in the whole pleadings & particularly the charge he gave to the Jury he evinced partiality. I have appealed to the S. Court at Washington It is possible it may be called for feby term.[5] If so, I wish you to attend to it & get some eminent Lawyer to join you. if it should be for Jany term 1824. I have engaged Mr Livingston[6] to assist you his acquaintance with the Laws & Languages of this Country joined with his eminent talents would benefit my case. I will allow you 500 dollars for your attention to this business & in the event of Success $2000. I could not pay you immediately. but you may rest assured so soon as I can conveniently; for the other attorney you will endeavor to procure one on reasonable terms.

Should this suit go against me. I am parralized [*sic*] for the rest of my life. I already begin to feel the loss of credit here. by getting a successfull [*sic*] issue I am confident in a few years to be enabled to pay all my just debts. & I could do it in that way.not to be felt & at the same time preserve my Credit. There is So much justice on my side & as it would be So unjust on the other hand to decide agt. me. that I still have hope of a favorable decision. Mr. H. Johnson & J S Johnson[7] delegates from this Country to whom I have communicated freely will furnish considerable information on my case. I will however in a few days make you a Statement of the circumstances attending my Bankruptcy & forward it to you at Washington.

I regret not being able to loan you 5000 dollars I have not got over the embarrassment, occasioned by my Building my last Season was not so productive as formerly. I have also met with some losses, add to these the most distressing times. Short Crops & decline in prices, a heavy pressure for funds pervades our Country

Julie joins me in our best wishes for yourself Mrs C. & family

Yr Affectionate Brother JOHN CLAY

ALS. DLC-TJC (DNA, M212, R10). Addressed to Clay at Lexington. Published in Smith and Clay, *The Clay Family*, 123-24.

1 Mr. and Mrs. Martin Duralde, Jr., and Anne Brown Clay.

2 Martin Duralde, Sr., had died earlier in the month.

3 Letter not found. See above, Clay to Cheves, July 5, 1822; Cheves to Clay, July 27, 1822; Toland to Clay, July 27, 1822.

4 John Dick, formerly United States Attorney for the district of Louisiana, was District Judge from 1821 until his resignation in 1824.

5 Abraham Smith, of Kentucky (possibly of Shelbyville), had brought suit against John Clay for the recovery of a debt incurred in 1808. Clay, who had failed in business, sought refuge in the Louisiana bankrupt law, under which Smith, as one of several creditors had already received ten percent of the amount due him. The case, on appeal, was argued before the United States Supreme Court at the January Term, 1828, and was held under advisement until the January Term, 1830. In its decision the Supreme Court held that Smith, by voluntarily participating in the proceedings under the bankrupt law of Louisiana, had "abandoned his extra-territorial immunity" from that act and was bound by it. The decision of the lower court was, therefore, reversed. 28 *U. S.* (3 Peters) 411-12.

6 Edward Livingston, who argued the case before the Supreme Court in 1828.

7 Henry Johnson; Josiah Stoddard Johnston. The latter, born in Connecticut, had been brought as a child to Washington, Kentucky, where his parents settled. After graduation from Transylvania University, he had studied law and in 1805 had begun practice at Alexandria, Louisiana. He had been a member of the Louisiana Territorial legislature from 1805 until the State was admitted to the Union in 1812, member of the State legislature in 1812, and State district judge, 1812-1821. He served as Congressman from Louisiana, 1821-1823, and United States Senator from 1823 until his death in 1833.

Credential as Counsel

[December 17, 1822]

[John Adair, Governor of Kentucky, certifies that Henry Clay has been duly elected one of the counsel for the State pursuant to the "Resolutions providing for the appointment of a board of Commissioners under the eighth article of the compact with Virginia, and ratifying the Convention of the Commissioners appointed to make the necessary arrangements for constituting said board," approved November 16, 1822.[1] Countersigned by J. Cabell Breckinridge, Secretary of State.]

DS, by Breckinridge. DLC-HC (DNA, M212, R1).
[1] See above, Clay to Leigh, November 18, 1822.

From Edward Shippen

Dear Sir Office Bank U. States Louisville Dec. 19. 1822

I enclose you an affidavit for the purpose of obtaining further time to file the record in an appeal in the case of Harrison vs Luckett & Maupin &c.—[1] You will please attend to this immediately, as the adverse party are about applying to the Court of Appeals for a dismissal; Should the Court refuse time to file the Record, I wish to apply for a writ of Error with Supers., and therefore will thank you to inform me by return of the bearer of that fact.

I am very respectfully Your obt. Servt. EDWD. SHIPPEN Cashr.

ALS. DLC-Breckinridge Family Papers (DNA, M212, R20). Addressed: "Henry Clay Esq. or in his absence, Cabel Breckinridge Frankfort." Endorsed, in strange hand: "attended to & answered —21 Decr." Shippen, a native of Philadelphia, had been appointed Cashier of the Louisville office, Bank of the United States, in October, 1821, and held that office until his death in December, 1832.

[1] The principals in the case, not found, were probably Benjamin I. Harrison, Craven P. Luckett, and Richard A. Maupin, all of Louisville, Kentucky, who, a short time earlier, had been involved in settlement of a suit in Federal court which had been won by the Bank of the United States over Maupin, Luckett, and others. U.S. Circuit Court, Seventh Circuit, District of Kentucky, Complete Records, R, 487-503.

From John Sloane

Dear Sir Washington Decr. 19th. 1822

The last advice I have received from Columbus was a letter from my brother, who is a member of the Senate;[1] it was dated the 9th. Knowing the zeal he felt I hope he is mistaken in the apprehensions he entertained of the result of the meeting which was to have been held on the 10th.[2] I am sorry they met to nominate so soon because it was important that letters which were writen [*sic*] from here, should have been received before the meeting took place— Those letters I think would have removed all difficulty from the minds of those friendly to Mr. Clinton, Appearances here remain equal to my expectation, Mr. Adams still remains confined to a part of New England— If Ohio does her duty the contest will be mainly, between Mr. Crawford and yourself—

Some of the politicians of the Richmond school[3] seem very uneasy and indicate a disposition to enter warmly into the election, One of them a few days since proposed to bet that you could not get 500 votes in Virginia, he was offered a bet that in case the State was districted you would get one third at least. On the subject of the negociations at Ghent I will take the liberty of making a few observations. I perceive by the Intelligencer of this morning that Mr. Adams has replyed to your note of Nov last in a Style that many here suppose will draw you forth into a full discussion.[4] Contrasting my experience in public life with yours it might well be considered an act of suppererogation [*sic*] in me to express my opinion as to what course you ought to pursue in this business, nor will I presume so to do. Nevertheless I feel constrained by the desire I have for your success to state briefly how the matter presents itself to my mind

In the controversy between Messrs Adams, and Russell, the public attention has been entirely diverted from all consideration of the merits of the point in dispute, and become wholly directed to the disputants. It has settled into a mere personal contest, and the interest felt by the public is little more than a desire to see which of the parties can say things the most cuting [*sic*] and sarcastic. Considering it in this light it does appear to me that circumstances are such, as to render any defence of your conduct wholly unnecessary; and that there are many reasons why a discussion on your part had better be avoided. It is that kind of discussion in which even victory will be no gain, but a certain loss. A discussion the motives of which will not fail to be misrepresented by the numerous writers who will present themselves before the public on the occasion— Confident that these observations will be considered in the spirit in which they are writen [*sic*] I remain with great respect & esteem your

Obt. Sert J. SLOANE

Hon Henry Clay

ALS. DLC-HC (DNA, M212, R1).

1 David Sloane, State Senator from Harrison-Jefferson counties, Ohio.

2 Members of the Ohio legislature, assembled in caucus on December 10, had opposed by a margin of three votes the nomination of any candidate for the Presidency. Report of this action was carried in the Washington *Daily National Intelligencer* on December 23.

3 The so-called "Richmond Junto," led by Thomas Ritchie, John Floyd, John Tyler, and James and Philip Pendleton Barbour—States rights advocates, strict constructionists in interpretation of the Federal Constitution, and supporters of William H. Crawford.

4 See above, Clay to Gales and Seaton, November 16, 1822, note.

Mortgage Deed to James Harper

[December 24, 1822]

[For the purpose of securing the debt herein mentioned and in consideration of five shillings, paid, Henry Clay conveys to James Harper the house and lot on Mill Street in Lexington, presently occupied by Mrs. Susannah Hart, opposite the house of John Bradford and Transylvania University, it being the same house and lot formerly owned by John Hart, purchased by Clay from the Bank of Kentucky[1]—in trust that the property may be sold to satisfy and pay a note given by Clay to the President, Directors, and Company of the Bank of the United States for the sum of $1666, bearing date of October 1, 1822,[2] and due two years after date, in payment for the purchase of two Negroes, sold as the property of Samuel Ayres, and for four others bought from John C. Buckner.[3] In the event of nonpayment of this note, the property is to be sold under a decree of court of equity. General warranty of title. If the note is paid, this deed shall be void. In the meantime, Clay is to retain possession of the property and to receive its rents and profits. Clay's signature acknowledged before J. C. Rodes, December 24, 1822.]

Fayette County Court, Deed Book W, 131-32.
1 See above, Property Deed, December 26, 1821.
2 Not found.
3 See above, Bill of Sale, November 4, 1822.

Power of Attorney from Richard Biddle

[December 24, 1822]

Know all men by these presents that I Richard Biddle of Bourbon County in the State of Kentucky have nominated and appointed and do hereby nominate and appoint Henry Clay and John Rowan to appear for me as my Counsel jointly & severally or any other Counsellor practising before the Supreme Court of the U. States, and to prosecute defend or dismiss (as to my said Counsel so appearing for me may seem best) an action or suit depending before the said Court between the Heirs of Jno. Green deceased and me from Kentucky—[1]

Hereby ratifying and confirming whatever my Counsel may do for me in the premises.

Witness my hand and seal this 24th day of December 1822.

RICHD BIDDLE {L.S.}

DS, in Clay's hand. DLC-TJC (DNA, M212, R15). Subscribed and acknowledged before Robert Trimble, Judge, United States Court, Kentucky District, on the same date.

1 See above, DuVal to Clay, June 14, 1821; Clay and Bibb to the Kentucky General Assembly, *ca.* May 13, 1822.

From Thomas B. Reed

Dear Sir, Natchez Decr. 24, 1822

Inclosed you will find the *duplicate* of a Check, drawn by the Cashier of the "Bank of the State of Mississippi," on the "Farmers and Mechanics Bank of Philadelphia," in favor of Park Walton, Esqr. and, by him, endorsed, for two hundred and fifty dollars,[1] in part of your fee in the Case of Mr. Walton v.s. the U.S. in the Supreme Court.[2] Thinking it probable that, you will have departed for Washington, before this reaches you, I have inclosed, in a letter bearing date on this day,[3] the *Original* Check and addressed it to you at Washington; but, have thought it prudent, to inclose you this duplicate, least Something may have detained you in Kentucky. In my letter, addressed to you at Washington, I have said several things, which Mr. Walton had given me in Charge, relative to his business; and to this, permit me to refer you.

There is a young gentleman, in this City, by the name of Jessee [*sic*] Perkins, who is extremely anxious to be appointed Mid-shipman in the Navy. He has applied to me, for my interposition in his behalf, and I have written to Several of the Senators, on the Subject. He is a young Man, of great Modesty and Merit, and is fired with the Ambition of signalising himself in the Naval Service. The Signal Zeal which he displays, added to the amenity of his Character, has excited in me a deep interest in his behalf. I know, full well, that your feelings will be inlisted in favor of so Much Merit, and I have assured Mr. Perkins that, you would not permit an opportunity to escape of serving him, where you can do it with propriety[4]

Yours ever and truly THO: B: REED

ALS. DLC-TJC (DNA, M212, R12).

1 The enclosure, DS by Pat Tichener, Cashier of the Bank of the State of Mississippi, was drawn at Natchez, December 23, and endorsed (AES): "pay to Henry Clay Esqr. Parke Walton."

2 See above, Reed to Clay, August 2, September 5, 1822.

3 Not found.

4 The young man did not receive an executive appointment.

From Richard Biddle

Sir Decr 25th 1822

I should have been happy to have put the papers[1] in your hands myself but am somewhat unwell to day & have therefore sent them on by a borrowed hand you'll see the alterations & additions occasiond [*sic*] by my not finding the $400. Receipt[2] the first search but you must Excuse me as I did for the best, & if you should want any thing more of me at any time hereafter in the process of the suit you are only to send me word by mail or otherwise & I shall take pleasure in doing any thing I lawfully may do for my fellow citizens who are or may be Injured by taking away the benifits [*sic*] of the Occupying Claimants law from us & wishing you Great Success in your philathropic [*sic*] Endeavours I subscribe myself as in duty bound your Obt. Hble. sevt. RICHD. BIDDLE

ALS. DLC-TJC (DNA, M212, R12). Addressed to Clay, "Fayette County Kentucky."

1 See above, Power of Attorney, December 24, 1822. Biddle also enclosed an affidavit (with supporting documents), dated December 24, 1822, sworn to before Robert Trimble, outlining the facts in the case of Green *vs.* Biddle. Several years earlier Biddle and others had been sued in Federal court, Kentucky District, by John Green for a large amount of land in Bourbon County, of which Biddle claimed only 99 acres. After having recovered judgment, Green had died, "about four years ago." Afterward Biddle had bought from one of the heirs of John Green the 99 acres he had originally claimed, at fifteen dollars per acre, with the assurance that the other heirs would ratify the purchase. Following this step, Biddle "no longer supposed himself engaged in any dispute with the said Green's heirs about the land itself its improvements or its profits; and he was surprized when he saw in the public prints his name as a litigant adversely to the said Green's heirs before the Supreme Court of the United States." Had he known "any question interesting to him, on account of his improvements made on the said ninety nine acres of land, or the rents thereof, had been depending before the Supreme Court of the U. States, he should have employed Counsel to defend and protect his interests; but that not being aware of any such question pending, in which he was at all concerned, he has employed no counsel heretofore." DS, in Clay's hand (except for three lines of correction, noted below, and notation of appendage of the assent of John Green "the Younger"). DLC-TJC (DNA, M212, R15).

2 The statement, in the original wording of the affidavit, that a receipt was enclosed, was crossed out; the following was added: "but the receipt for four Hundred dollars of the purchase money is at present mislaid: altho Some where in his possession."

Power of Attorney to Matthew T. Scott

[December 26, 1822]

Whereas the Bank of the State of Kentucky is indebted to me in the sum of Ten thousand one hundred and twenty six dollars and ninety six Cents, by notes which the said Bank has regularly issued and which have come to my hands and become my property, in the course of my dealings and transactions: And where as I have deposited the notes aforesaid, according to law and to usage, with the Branch of the said Bank established in the town of Lexington, which Branch hath acknowledged in a book kept by itself, the aforesaid balance of $10.126: and 96 Cents to be due to me for notes deposited with it, on the 24h. day of this month: I do hereby, therefore, nominate and appoint my friend M. T. Scott Esqr my attorney for me and in my name to demand of the President Directors & Company of the said Bank of Kentucky, in lawful money, the aforesaid sum of $10.126:96; and the same being paid I do hereby authorize and empower my said Attorney to receipt therefor or to grant acquittances for the payment thereof, by drawing a check for the amount afd., in behalf of the said President Directors and Company of the Bank of Kentucky upon the Branch Bank afd., or in any other manner more agreeable to the said President Directors & Co. of the Bank of Kentucky: Hereby ratifying and confirming whatever my said Attorney may do for me in the premises.

In testimony whereof, having written with my proper hand the whole of this power of attorney, I do hereunto set my hand & affix my seal this 26h. Decr. 1822. H. CLAY {L.S.}

[Endorsement on verso][1]

Memo I wish Mr. Scott to demand of the Cashier of the Bank of K. in the Banking house and in Banking hours the within sum of $10126:96 in specie or lawful currency of the U. States (which is the same thing.) I wish on the same day and at the same place a similar demand made of the President; but if he be not in the bank, the demand of him may be made wherever Mr. Scott finds him.

I then request that Mr. Scott would make a memo. in my bank book of the circumstances of the demand, similar to that which Mr. LeGrand[2] has signed. H. CLAY

26h. Decr. 1822.

ADS. DLC-TJC (DNA, M212, R15). 1 AES. 2 Abner LeGrand.

Memorandum of Assets

Memo. made 26 Decr. 1822.

The Bank of K. owes me $10126:96 which is shewn by the Books of the Branch Bank of the said institution at Lexington.[1]

Majr. W. S. Dallam owes me $10.000 for the Bledsoe farm below Lexington (see his agreement with me in bundle including letter D. among my private papers) That debt carries interest from the 1st. Jan. 1823. He has assigned me, in security for it, a parcel of notes, some of which are in Mr. Hawes's hands, and the residue with the afd. agreement.[2] I am bound to pursue the makers of the notes with due diligence.

There is due me in Mason County about $5000 on replevy bonds (enquire of Lawyer Chambers[3] & see the Circuit Court Clerks office) — a debt assigned me by the Farmers & Mechanics Bank of Lexington—[4] The bonds are due in July next—

The Bank of the U S. owes me four or five thousand dollars for doing the business of its Solicitor in the Lexn. off. of Dt. & Dt. the amt. to be ascertained by the number of suits to be obtained from the off. of the Fed. Ct. in Kentucky which I have brought for it. The rate of allowance is fixed by what was given to Mr. Wickliffe[5] before I became their Solicitor {☞ See Mr. Cheves's letter among the papers of the B. of the U. S. in my office shewing that I was to be paid as Solicitor beyond and independent of what I was allowed as their Counseller}.[6]

I have also transfered to the Bank U. S. a debt of $2000 due me by D. L. Ward for which judgt. has been obtained in the Fed. Court[7] & a replevy bond given to the Bank, which is to be credited agt. the debt I owe.

I have sued the Bank of Jessamine in Jessamine Ct Ct. for $400 suit pending.[8]

I hold the note of Robert Crockett for $2000–[9]

R. Breckenridge [*sic*], J. C. Breckenridge &c for about } 500–[10]

Besides sundry other notes {see the bundles in my private papers}

I have in Missouri 2500 acres or thereabouts of Military Land paid for[11] {deeds among my papers; enquire of Col Benton[12]}

About 16 or 1700 Acres of Land (excellent in quality) in Indiana & Illinois bought of the public, not all yet paid for {See titles &c & enquire of David Hart Vincennes.}[13]

I own a lott unimproved on Limestone Street, conveyed to me by Adam Rankin,[14] near Weirs[15] Rope Walk–

Two or three lots on Geo Town road near Charles Carr's conveyed by D. Bradford–[16]

I have R. Hickman's bond[17] given to me & R. Wickliffe for One hundred acres of land–

Mr. Talbot & I are suing for some land in Scott Court conveyed to me by H Watkins–[18]

All the above, besides my property well known to my family & evidences of debt & contracts among my papers in my private desk–

H. CLAY

There is a debt due to me of 4 or 500 hundred [*sic*] dollars for which judgt is obtained in Clarke (Mr. Hanson's[19] hands) I have sent the Execution to Ch. H Allen in Henry.[20]

ADS. DLC-TJC (DNA, M212, R10). 1 See above, Power of Attorney, this date.
2 See above, Agreement, October 18, 1822; Receipt, October 21, 1822.
3 John Chambers. 4 See above, Chambers to Clay, June 10, 1821.
5 Robert Wickliffe. 6 See above, Cheves to Clay, March 3, 1821.
7 At the November Term, 1823. U. S. Circuit Court, Seventh Circuit, District of Kentucky, Complete Records, P, 278-80. See above, II, 888; Clay to Ward, September 17, 1821.
8 See above, Receipt, July 16, 1822; below, Agreement, November 6, 1824.
9 Not found.
10 Note not found. See above, II, 888. 11 See above, II, 578-79.
12 Thomas Hart Benton. The deeds have not been found.
13 See above, Clay to Gilmer, August 4, 1821; Hart to Clay, November 2, 1821.
14 See above, I, 793. 15 James Weir.
16 See above, Property Deed, October 23, 1821. 17 Not found.
18 Cf. above, I, 577-78. 19 Samuel Hanson. 20 Henry County, Kentucky.

Agreement with Robert Wickliffe

[December 26, 1822]

I am entitled to one-half of whatever Land may be saved in the appeal on the Case of Jno Stephens agst Radford MCCargo & others now depending in the Supreme Court & Mr. Clay has undertaken to appear for Stephens in the Supreme Court[1] In consequence of which I agree to Let Mr. Clay have one equal moiety of my half or of whatever I may recived [*sic*] In consequence of my contract with Stephens. In witness whereof I have hereunto Set my hand &c this 26h day of Decr 1822. R WICKLIFFE {Seal}

ADS. DLC-TJC (DNA, M212, R15).

1 Stephens, a Virginia veteran of the Revolution, had appealed from the decision of the United States Circuit Court for the District of Kentucky, which had directed him to convey to McCargo, of Clark County, Kentucky, and others certain lands on Four Mile Creek, in Clark County, claimed by Stephens under Virginia military grant. The appeal was unsuccessful, and on March 16, 1824, the decree of the lower court was "affirmed, with costs." 22 *U.S.* (9 Wheaton) 502-15.

To [Nicholas Biddle]

Sir Lexington 27h. Decr. 1822

According to the directions[1] of Mr. Cheves, I have had causes, in the name of the Bank of the U. States and of others prepared for the Supreme Court, by adjournment, from the Circuit Court, upon a division pro forma of the judges to have certain questions settled, arising under the execution Laws of Ohio and Kentucky, in which the Bank has a material interest. I shall take my departure from this place tomorrow to attend the Federal Court in Ohio and to proceed from thence to the Supreme Court, and I shall carry with me transcripts of the records in some of the above causes, others of them being already at the City of Washington. These causes will present to the Supreme Court for their decision, among other points, the following:

1. Are the State replevin laws, by which the debtor is allowed upon giving bond and security to defer, for a specified time, payment of his debt compatible with the constitution of the U. States?

2 Are the Execution laws of the States; as modified from time to time, by the authority of their respective Legislatures, to be considered as binding upon the Federal judicial tribunals in the enforcement of judgments rendered by them?

And in particular

3dly. Are the State laws binding on those tribunals which forbid a sale of the debtors property unless it produce a prescribed proportion of its value? And

4thly. Is the Law of Kentucky which interdicts the use of the Casa in the recovery of the debts of individuals to be regarded by the Federal Courts?[2]

My own opinion is that it is not for the interest of the Bank to agitate the first question. For I believe the existence of the Replevin laws has enabled the Bank to secure, in Kentucky, debts which were in considerable jeopardy; the debtor being able to procure security on long time whose property, if sold on prompt payment, would not be competent to discharge his debts. And the local Courts have decided that whatever may be the true character of those laws, the *debtor* cannot be permitted to avail himself of their invalidity so as to avoid his Replevy bond.

The third point stated is that which involves the greatest impediment to the Bank in the coercive recovery of its debts, particularly in the State of Ohio. And it is also matterially [*sic*] concerned in the last.

I have thought proper to make this communication that the Board may, in due time, engage the requisite Counsel to appear for the Bank before the Supreme Court. From the practice of that Court I apprehend there will be no difficulty in getting the Court to take up the questions refered to it at the approaching term. Although for several reasons, some of which I communicated to Mr. Cheves, it will not be in my power to argue for the Bank the above questions before the Supreme Court, I shall be chearfully disposed by conference with its Counsel to put him in possession of all the information which I can give. I expect one or two other causes of the Bank will be taken up from Ohio and Kentucky to which (if it has made no other arrangement) I shall attend, as well as to that with the State of Ohio. During the late term of the Circuit Court in this State, as well as during all preceding terms, we have experienced the most unexampled success in all the various questions which arose, in causes of the Bank.

I have to mention my regret that there is not a prospect of doing much business at the January term of the Court in Ohio, owing to the non-attendance of Judge Todd[3] from indisposition. I shall endeavor to have the question, about the immediate perception of the rents of the property mortgaged by the late John H. Piatt, settled at that term, unless I shall hear of an arrangement having been made at Philadelphia with his representatives.[4]

I have received the letter of Mr. Wilson announcing the decision of the Board in the case of John J. Marshall.[5] I have the honor to be with great respect Your obedient Servant H. CLAY

The President of the Bank of the United States.

ALS. PHi-Etting Collection. Endorsed: "recd. 13 Jany." Biddle, son of Charles and brother of James Biddle, had been born in Philadelphia, educated at the University of Pennsylvania and the College of New Jersey, and admitted to the bar (1809). He had held minor diplomatic posts abroad, as secretary to the American Minister to France (1804-1806) and Secretary of Legation in London (1806-1807), and had served in the Pennsylvania legislature. In 1819 he had been appointed one of the directors of the Bank of the United States and, following announcement of Langdon Cheves' decision to retire, was in November, 1822, nominated to the presidency of that institution by delegates of the stockholders. His formal election occurred January 7, 1823.

1 Not found.

2 See above, Clay to Hammond, July 14, 1822, note. The constitutionality of the Kentucky replevin laws had also been among the questions certified to the Supreme Court in the case of Wayman and Another *vs.* Southard and Another. As defined by the Court in its ruling on that case: "The question really adjourned is, whether the laws of Kentucky respecting executions passed subsequent to the process act, are applicable to executions which issue on judgments rendered by the federal courts?" 23 *U.S.* (10 Wheaton) 47-48.

3 Thomas Todd. 4 See above, Clay to Cheves, June 16, September 13, 1822.

5 See above, December 6, 1822.

Settlement with Francis Hawkins

27h. Decr. 1822.

We have this day settled all accounts up to the first January 1823 and H. Clay has paid me the sum of Two hundred & six dollars in full

H. CLAY—

his
Teste Sarah Hall FRANCIS X HAWKINS
mark.

ADS, signed also by Clay for Hawkins, his overseer, for many years previously a resident of Woodford County, later of Mercer County. DLC-TJC (DNA, M212, R15).

Rental Agreement with Benjamin Whaley

[*ca.* December 27, 1822]

An agreement between H. Clay and Benjamin Whaley.

The said Clay hereby leases to the said Whaley the Brick house on market street in the town of Lexington, at present in the said Whaley's occupation, and the small frame house adjoining for the term of one year commencing on the 12h. day of March 1823

In consideration whereof the said Whaley agrees hereby to pay to the said Clay the sum of one hundred and thirty dollars payable quarterly; and to surrender the demised premises at the end of the term in as good order as he receives them, natural decay and inevitable accidents excepted.

The said Clay reserves the right of distress for any of the rent in arrear.

Witness the hands & seals of the parties.

H. CLAY {L.S.}

[Endorsements on verso][1] BENJN. WHALEY {L.S.}

Warrant of distress issued for rent to 11h. March 1824—& replevied—

R SCOTT

Colo. Whaley left the house 11 May 24.

ADS, signed also by Whaley. KyLxT. Dated in accordance with Clay's activities preparatory to an extended absence from Lexington.

1 AES; AE by Scott.

From John Adair

Frankfort Executive Department Jany. 7h. 1823.

John Rowan & H Clay Esqrs.

Gentlemen,

I avail myself of the earliest opportunity after hearing from the gentlemen elected Commissioners on the part of this State, under the late convention between her & Virginia, to inform you that Mr. Burnet has accepted, & Mr. White has declined accepting the appointment. The task of selecting a fit person to fill the place of the latter gentleman of course devolves on you.[1]

I have the honour to be, very respectfully, Yr. Ob: Hb: Servt.

JOHN ADAIR

LS. DLC-HC (DNA, M212, R1). Directed to "Washington City."
1 See above, Clay to Leigh, November 21, 1822.

To Francis T. Brooke

My dear Sir Columbus 8h. Jan. 1823.

You will have seen a note which I addressed to the Editors of the Intellr. on the subject of the business at Ghent.[1] I wish to say one word to you on it. To those who have attentively read the controversial papers between Mess Russell & Adams, and particularly the appendix to the book of the latter,[2] it must be apparent that the Honble Secretary has labored to draw me into the controversy, by the manner in which he has alluded to my name, and the inconsistency which, on one occasion, he imputes to me. I had but one alternative, either to acquiesce, by my silence, in all misrepresentations, or, by a sort of protest, to reserve to myself the right of correcting errors on some future fit occasion. I might indeed have rushed into the controversy between those two gentlemen, or commenced a new one; but I hope my friends will believe me incapable of committing such an indiscretion as I conceive that would be of doing at this time the one or the other. I chose the latter branch of the alternative stated, and I hope you will approve of the step which I have taken. My purpose is answered; my ground is taken, and those who know me will not want to be assured that I [sha]ll adhere to both. I shall write no more until I think the period has arrived which I have indicated. The Honble Secretary seems to deplore its possible distance. I shall remain unmoved by any regrets which he may feel on account of the want of fresh aliment for new strife.

The news papers will communicate to you the events which have occurred here.[3] As they chose to have a second Caucus, I was glad it took place before I reached Columbus. Considering the great efforts made from without to prevent any Legislative expression of public opinion, the proof which is afforded by the vote here is extremely strong. My friends believe that from 80 to 90 out of the 103 members who compose the General Assembly are in my favor. And there is among the former the greatest zeal, animation and confidence.

I am anxious to learn the names of your Commissioners.[4] Expecting to reach Washington by the 22d. instant I shall be glad to have the pleasure of hearing from you on my arrival there.

I am faithf y & cordially Your friend H CLAY

The Honble Francis Brooke.

ALS. KyU. Published in Colton (ed.), *Private Correspondence of Henry Clay,* 70-71.

1 See above, November 15, 1822.

2 See above, Russell to Clay, June 6, 1822.

3 After the failure of the first effort to procure a nomination of Clay by members of the Ohio legislature (see above, Sloane to Clay, December 19, 1822), his friends had undertaken a second caucus. On January 3, 1823, in a meeting from which most of the opposition had withdrawn, he was nominated by a vote of 50 to 7, with Clinton receiving five votes and Calhoun and Adams one each. Washington *Daily National Intelligencer,* January 17, 1823; Stevens, *Early Jackson Party in Ohio,* 54-55.

4 See below, Leigh to Clay, February 12, March 1, 1823, note.

To Horace Holley

Dr Sir Columbus 9h. Jan. 1823.

I have made a promise which you will oblige me by redeeming, which is to send a Copy of the By-Laws of Transylvania to a gentleman in this State. I will thank you to inclose by mail a copy of them to Capt. Joel Collins Oxford, Butler County Ohio.[1]

I will be further obliged by your saying to Majr. Barry that his Report upon Education is much read and admired here,[2] where they are engaged in a similar project; and that if he has so many spare Copies he would render an acceptable service by sending half a dozen of them to Caleb Atwater of Circleville, who is one of the persons appointed by Ohio to collect and digest materials for a system.[3] With great respect I am faithfy yours H. CLAY

The Revd. Mr. Holley

ALS. Owned by John P. Crosby, Lexington, Kentucky.

1 Member of the State House of Representatives, later a State Senator. He had been an infantry captain in the United States Army during the War of 1812.

2 The Kentucky legislature, under the act of December 18, 1821, which had established a "Literary Fund" from one half the profits of the Bank of the Commonwealth (cf. above, Promissory Note, November 16, 1822), had appointed a group, of which William T. Barry became the head, to gather information "to enable them to digest a plan of schools of common education" for the State. At the next session of the legislature, a year later, the committee had submitted two reports, one including its own recommendations and the other composed of replies to letters of inquiry that had been sent to distinguished persons outside the Commonwealth. The Senate had ordered 1,000 copies of both reports printed; the House had ordered 500 copies. Ky. Gen. Assy., *Acts, 1821,* pp. 351-55; Ky. Sen., *Journal, 1822,* pp. 163-86, 189-219; Ky. H. of Reps., *Journal, 1822,* pp. 225-48, 253-83.

3 Atwater, a graduate of Williams College, had conducted a school for girls in New

York City, had studied theology and become a Presbyterian minister, then, having given up the ministry for reasons of health, had studied law, had been admitted to the bar, and in 1815 had settled in Circleville, Ohio. In 1821 he had been elected to the State House of Representatives, where he became an advocate of internal improvements and public schools. His work as chairman of a board appointed to devise a plan for public education has led to his being called the founder of the school system in Ohio. He was the author of several books, including the first history of that State.

From Joseph Cabell Breckinridge

Dr Sir Frankfort January 11—1823.

Your letter from Cincinnati of the 1. instant[1] was not received untill yesterday. The convention of the states of Kentucky and Virginia, entered into by Mr. Leigh and yourself,[2] has never been of record in my office; and the originals, in the hand writing of the commissioners, are now in the hands of Mr. Burnet.[3]

By this mail I send you two copies of the Journals of the last session,[4] which contain all that you desire on this subject. Very respectfully your obedient servant J. CABELL BRECKENRIDGE [*sic*]

ALS. DLC-HC (DNA, M212, R1).

1 Not found.

2 See above, Convention, June 5, 1822.

3 Jacob Burnet.

4 Of the Kentucky legislature.

From Daniel Call

Dear Sir, Richmond January 18th. 1823

Your letter of the 29th of October last[1] came to hand; but owing to the antiquity of the transactions; the difficulty of investigating matters with which I had no previous acquaintance; sickness; and the necessary attendance on courts, I have not been able to prepare my answer to Banks's suit[2] until to day. It is now inclosed; and, if, upon perusing it, you find any thing wanting, please inform me of it, that it may be attended to. I am, dear sir, with great respect your very sincere well-wisher DANIEL CALL

Henry Clay Esquire near Lexington

ALS copy. CSmH. Call, an eminent Virginia lawyer, was compiler of *Reports of Cases Argued and Adjudged in the Court of Appeals of Virginia* (6 vols.). He, Chief Justice John Marshall, and Edward Carrington had married sisters.

1 Not found.

2 Case not found.

From Martin Duralde

Dr. Sir, New orleans 22d. January 1823

Inclosed you have the duplicate of the check I sent you in my letter of the 18th. Instant.[1] I have nothing interesting to tell you. Our Legislature has yet done nothing important.— A motion made in the Senate, last monday, by Mr. Moreau, to expel some of the

Senators from Florida takes up all its time.[2] I did not speak of Mr. Hawkins[3] in my last letter because he told me he would write to you by the same mail.[4] Mr. & Mrs. Worsley,[5] on their way to the Eastward, arrived here a few days ago. I have received by the Steam Boat Colombus [*sic*] the Horse you were good enough to send me. I shall leave here for Attakapas, about the 6th. of next month & will be absent two or three weeks. We continue to enjoy good health.

I am Dr. Sir Your obedient Servt. M. DURALDE

Henry Clay Esqr. Washington City

ALS. Owned by J. Winston Coleman, Jr., Lexington, Kentucky. Duralde has been previously cited as Martin Duralde, Jr. On his father's death, see above, John Clay to Henry Clay, December 13, 1822.

1 The letter and checks have not been found.

2 Louis Casimir Elisabeth Moreau-Lislet, who had emigrated from Santo Domingo to New Orleans around 1800, was an eminent jurist and compiler of several legal works (some in collaboration with other Louisiana lawyers). He was a leader of the French faction in Louisiana politics, which in January, 1823, undertook to expel from the State Senate the members from parishes east of the Mississippi River on the ground that this area, part of what was once West Florida, was not a part of Louisiana. The attempt was unsuccessful. *Niles' Weekly Register,* XXIII (March 1, 1823), 402.

3 Joseph H. Hawkins.

4 No letter found.

5 In March, 1819, William W. Worsley had retired as editor of the Lexington *Kentucky Reporter* (the *Reporter* until the issue of October 3, 1817), leaving Thomas Smith as sole editor.

From Nicholas Biddle

Sir, Bank of the U.S. Jany. 25. 1823

Your letter of the 27th ulto from Lexington was duly received, & would have been sooner acknowledged had not the intention which you announced of going immediately to Ohio & thence to Washington rendered it uncertain how to address to you an answer. I have this day had the pleasure of receiving your letter from Columbus of the 12th inst.[1] To both these communications particular attention has been given. The causes which you will not have it in your power to argue before the Supreme Court have been committed to the care of Mr Sergeant & Mr Cheves[2] with whom the Board are desirous you should confer, as you have the goodness to propose, & communicate your information & your views. The other causes will be left as heretofore to your own management. The powers which you advised for the Agent at Cincinnati & the Cashiers of Lexington & Louisville have been forwarded to them and the Solicitor of the agency of Cincinnati will soon be named.[3] We had hoped much from the late sitting of the Court in Ohio, but the disappointment was unavoidable, & the regret is lessened by your previous successes, of which I learnt with great pleasure tho without surprize. The original measure of procuring your general superintendence over the interests of the Bank in the Western country was adopted during my past connection with the institution—and my observation then as well as every step of the enquiries which occupy me now, realize all the benefits which I had anticipated from it. If there be anything which you deem of sufficient interest to the Bank to repay you for the trouble of writing, it will give me great pleasure to hear from you. I should be still more gratified if any purpose of business or relaxation should tempt you to visit Phila. & enable me to renew an acquaintance which personal as well as official motives would conspire to render very agreeab[le] to yrs very respectfully N BIDDLE

Henry Clay Esq Washington Cola.

ALS draft. DLC-Nicholas Biddle Papers (DNA, M212, R20).

1 Not found. 2 John Sergeant; Langdon Cheves.

3 See above, Clay to Cheves, September 13, 1822.

From James Smith, Jr.

Esteemed Friend/ Philada. Jany. 27h. 1823.

I wrote you some time in last year[1] that Woodson Wren desired a Gentleman of this place to tell me he was willing to pay the ballance [*sic*] against him, provided I would consent to deduct an Over charge (as he called it) in the account of £1.7..18— In my letter to you, I desired you to allow it and close the business since which I have not heard from you—this ballance must be upwards of One hundred Dollars— In your letter of December 26' 1819,[2] you say, "One of the Notes left with me by Wren (on a G Walker) was put into the hands of a Mr. Haggin—[3] Walker is dead,[4] and the sum as Haggin told me, not yet collected"— and in yours of the 18 Jany 1820—you say—"I will transmit you the insolvent Note you desire upon my return, since which I have not heard from you—

Walkers Note, I believe was dated 27' August 1809 for 194.49 & D M Sharps note 27 July 1808 for $192— Quere—Is not W. Wren liable for both these Notes, if they have not been paid?— I have no doubt you are tired of this business, and as for myself—I am extremely anxious to have it closed, and do let me ask the favour of you to turn your attention to settling it, if not already done, and excuse the Urgency of this application— I am very respectfully Yr Friend

pray, have you any Accot from Sharp? JAS SMITH JR.

ALS. DLC-TJC (DNA, M212, R12). Addressed to Clay at Washington. Endorsed by Clay, "Answd." Answer not found.

1 No letter in 1822 found, but see above, Smith to Clay, July 11, 1821.

2 Not found. 3 James Haggin. 4 George Walker had died in 1819.

To Nicholas Biddle

Sir Washington 28th. Jan. 1823.

I have received your favor of the 25h. inst. and avail myself of the occasion to offer you my congratulations upon your recent appointment as President of the Bank. The event, I assure you, gives me great satisfaction in all the relations in which I have to regard it. I am very glad that you have committed to so good hands, as those of Mr. Sergeant and Mr. Cheves, the adjourned causes which particular circumstances will not allow me to take a part in. I have already said to the former gentleman that I shall take much pleasure in communicating to him and his coadjutor any local information or views which I may happen to possess.

I am at this moment engaged in preparations for the cause of the Bank with the State of Ohio.[1] It will be recollected by you that it is a suit in Chy. involving not only the same point, respecting the power of the States to tax the institution, which was decided in McCullok [*sic*] and Maryland, but also the question whether the Court of equity can entertain jurisdiction of such a cause. I do not apprehend the slightest difficulty upon the first point; and I think the last is with us. If I should however be mistaken, and the bill should be dismissed for want of jurisdiction, it is not unlikely that an attempt would be made to obtain a restitution of the $98.000 which we have received, leaving the Bank at liberty, as it then would be, to prosecute the action of trespass which is yet pending. Such a result would be very unpleasant, and would put the ultimate recovery a good deal at hazard. I do not think that it is probable that such a result will occur. But I submit to you whether the Bank, under all the circumstances of the case, would not feel itself more secure if its interests were in the hands of two Counsel instead of one. Whether I stand alone or am associated with another, the Board, I trust, need not be assured of my utmost zeal and my best exertions. Indeed I feel animated in the cause by considerations higher than any which can arise out of professional obligations. I understood, at one time, from Mr. Hammond[2] that he expected to be aided by Mr. Ross,[3] 'though I now doubt whether this gentleman will attend, and do not certainly know whether Mr. Hammond will have any or what assistance.

It is my intention to visit Philadelphia in March; and, in the hope that nothing will occur to prevent the execution of it, I will defer, until that occasion, several interesting communications which I wish to make to you. It will give me great pleasure to seize that opportunity of cultivating your acquaintance as it now does to assure you that, with great respect, I am Your faithful and obedient Servant

Nicholas Biddle Esqr. &c. &c. &c. H. CLAY

ALS. PHi. Endorsed: "recd Feby.1.1823."

1 See above, II, 723n; below, Clay to Biddle, February 17, 1824, note.

2 Charles Hammond.

3 Probably Thomas R. Ross, who practiced at Lebanon, Ohio.

From Peter B. Porter

Dear Sir, Albany Jany 29th. 1822 [*i.e.*, 1823]

I arrived two days ago, at this place, where not only the members of our Legislature, but most of the active political talent & mischief of the state are now congregated. I have not, during this period, been inattentive to the great question that at present engages the speculations of the politicians throughout the Union— And I think I do not deceive you when I say that your prospects here are highly flattering. You are probably aware that some 6 or 8 months ago there was a partial understanding & commitment amongst some of our most active politicians in favour of Mr C-d,[1] & It is to this class that my conversations & views have been principally directed. Many of them are now ready to change their ground, and even the most zealous are willing to lie still at present, and eventually to be governed by future & clearer indications of public sentiment on this subject.

You will see Mr Van Buren[2] in Washington, and I beg you to pay him some attention. I am decidedly of opinion that he will yet be for you. His best & strongest friends here are so, and I know that his own views have been essentially changed since last spring. He will not I presume awow [*sic*] his preference of any Candidate during the present session of Congress, and perhaps it is desirable that he should not. Be civil also to Rochester[3] of our state who is a very clever young man & strongly your friend. A rumor is in circulation here that you & D. Clinton are playing in concert, & that you & he will run on the same ticket. I need not tell you that such a rumour, once believed, would prostrate all your hopes here. The recent, & all but unanimous, rejection of the Clintonian Judges, by our Senate, shows the temper of the state in regard to that class of politicians.[4] Can you with propriety say something in a letter to me on the subject of this supposed coalition which I may shew confidentially to two or three persons?[5] It might be attended with good consequences. Noah, the Advocate man,[6] is now here. I have had several conversations with him, & altho' his predilections are still for Mr C-d, his zeal & confidence have greatly abated. He finds that the state is not disposed to go with him, and expresses a willingness to be quiet, untill the sentiments of the old republican party shall be more fully developed.

I send you by this mail a pamphlet on the subject of the western termination of our Second Canal.[7] I can hardly suppose that you will have leasure or curiosity to read it— But whether you do or not, you will oblige me by taking it to Kentucky & giving it to Cabell Breckenridge or one of his brothers.[8] I shall remain a month at this place, where I should be pleased to hear from you, & I will write again should any thing of moment transpire. With the greatest respect & regard, I am &c P. B. PORTER

Mr King is *said* to be for Mr A-s, but you will understand that his sons here (as well as the one in Ohio) [9] are warmly for you & will give most of his influence as well as their own for you.

ALS. DLC-HC (DNA, M212, R1). Published in Colton (ed.), *Private Correspondence of Henry Clay*, 62-63. Endorsed on verso by Clay: ". . . answd." Answer not found.

1 William H. Crawford. 2 Martin Van Buren. 3 William B. Rochester.

4 One of the judges nominated in New York for membership to the State Supreme Court was rejected by a vote of 29 to 2, another by 28 to 3, the third by "a bare majority." *Niles' Weekly Register*, XXIII (February 8, 1823), 355.

5 See below, Clay to Porter, February 3, 1823. 6 Mordecai M. Noah.

7 Besides the Erie Canal, the New York canal system encompassed a northern branch, the Champlain Canal, begun in October, 1816, navigable by November, 1819, and completed in 1823.

Porter was working to have the outlet of the Erie Canal fixed at Black Rock rather than at Buffalo. The pamphlet, not found, was probably a part of his campaign, which was ultimately unsuccessful.

8 Three brothers of Joseph Cabell Breckinridge lived to manhood. Besides Robert J., they included John and William L. Breckinridge. The Reverend John Breckinridge had been graduated from the College of New Jersey (Princeton) in 1818 and had attended the Theological Seminary at Princeton. He was Chaplain of the United States House of Representatives, 1822 and 1823; pastor of Presbyterian churches in Lexington, Kentucky, and Baltimore, Maryland; head of the Presbyterian Board of Education; and professor in the Princeton Theological Seminary. In 1840, the year before his death, he was elected president of Oglethorpe University.

The Reverend William L. Breckinridge (1803-1876), pastor of a church at Maysville, Kentucky, and, for nearly a quarter of a century, of the First Presbyterian Church at Louisville, subsequently became professor of ancient languages at Centre College, Danville, Kentucky, later president of Oakland College in Mississippi, and, from 1863 to 1868, president of Centre College.

9 Rufus King became Adams' appointee to the Court of St. James in 1825. His sons living in New York in 1823 were Charles, an editor of the New York *American*, which he had founded with a group of friends in 1819, and John Alsop, member of the State Assembly, 1819-1821, and of the State Senate, 1823-1825. Contrary to Porter's observation, John Alsop King, a leader of the "Bucktails," endorsed Adams; and the New York *American* also took this position. Edward Hale Brush, *Rufus King and His Times* (New York, 1926), 108; below, Shaw to Clay, February 11, 1823; Porter to Clay, May 26, 1823; Rochester to Clay, June 28, December 20, 1823. Edward King, who had married a daughter of Thomas Worthington, was a lawyer in Ross County, Ohio, removing shortly hereafter to Cincinnati, where he became one of the founders and first professors of the Cincinnati Law School, established around 1834. Edward was an active Clay supporter.

To Francis T. Brooke

My dear Sir Washington 31st. Jan. 1823.

I have recd. your obliging favor of the 29h. instant.[1] The considerations were so many and so powerful, calling upon your State to ratify the convention with Kentucky,[2] that I confess to you frankly I did not anticipate the event which you say will probably happen.[3] In that event, I shall deeply regret that Virginia ever again opened the negotiation, after rejecting the propositions which Mr. Bibb and I submitted to your Legislature last winter.[4] Why did Virginia ask a reference of the claim of her State line?[5] Could she suppose that Kentucky would refer it, and leave herself exposed, after the decision of the referees, to the claim as if it had never been submitted to arbitration? Could she think that the mockery of creating a tribunal was to be presented to *decide* a controversy, respecting which the parties were to be as free and unbound after the decision as before the reference? If she had no power to refer; if she had no authority to bind her constituents, then she ought not to have moved in the business; and the first error was committed at Richmond and not at Lexington. For my part, I believe the State line *bound* by the decision; and that the guarranty [*sic*] is a mere expression of a fair implication from the whole transaction without it. And it was only to render the convention more explicit, and to preclude the necessity of resorting to any interpretations, about which disputes might arise, that it appeared to me to be expedient to insert the clause of guarranty. Upon the whole I must say that if you reject the Convention, I think the impartial world will look upon you as being clearly in the wrong.

I am extremely sorry to find that any of my friends believe that I was not called upon to address the note which was recently published in the Intellr. respecting certain questions arising at Ghent.[6] Had Mr. Adams either before or after his several publications deigned to consult me about the use which he has freely made in them of my name; had he said to me, "Mr. Clay I have imputed to you such & such opinions, and made statements about the part you acted at Ghent; if I am inaccurate in any of them, I will take pleasure in correcting the error," I should have felt myself required to address Mr. Adams personally and not the public. But he never communicated to me any one of his publications, and I never had an opportunity of even seeing his book until since my arrival here. Having chosen, without my knowledge or consent, to usher my name into the public journals; having imputed to me, as he does in his Appendix, inconsistencies, and by an inuendo insinuated that I was the author of an editorial article in Kentucky, and which I never saw until I read it in the paper in which it was printed,[7] I felt myself absolved from all obligation to make any direct appeal to Mr. Adams himself. In addressing the note which I did to the public, it was my intention merely to enter a caveat against the correctness of all his statements, and to exhibit a public reservation of a right on my part to rectify mistakes, when the proper occasion should arrive. Considering the relation in which both of us now stand to the public, I thought the present an unsuitable moment to even hazard any controversy with him; and if I could prostrate him in the dust, I would not write at this time.

I thank you for your kind information respecting the state of the public mind in Virginia on the presidential question. Here, my friends are animated by the greatest zeal & confidence; and do not entertain a doubt that the nine western and south western States will be heartily united in my support. A great change has been undoubtedly wrought at this place, in regard to opinions on the subject, within the last two months. Those who then thought I stood no chance now believe that my prospects are equal (many think them superior) to those of either of the two other Candidates.[8] Very little doubt is entertained that Pennsylvania will finally give me her support; and it is believed that in New York my prospects at this time are not surpassed by those of Mr Crawford, whilst all admit that my friends are gaining ground & his are declining in that State. Still, my dear Sir, I look on upon this struggle with all the philosophy which I ought to do. On one resolution, my friends may rest assured, I will firmly rely, and that is to participate in no intrigues, to enter into no arrangements, to make no promises or pledges; but that, whether I am elected or not, I will have nothing to reproach myself with. If elected, I will go into the office, with a pure conscience, to promote with my utmost exertions, the common good of our Country. & *free* to select the most able and faithful public servants. If not elected, acquiescing most chearfully in the better selection which will then have been made, I will at least have the satisfaction of preserving my hands unsullied and my heart uncorrupted.

I shall remain here during the greater part of the term of the Supreme Court, in which I have some professional business particularly the cause between the Bank and the State of Ohio.[9]

I shall be glad that your leisure may allow you to give me the pleasure of again hearing from you. With great regard I am faithfully Your friend H. CLAY

The Honble Francis Brooke.

P.S. What course does Virginia mean to take after rejecting the guarranty? Does she mean again to open the negotiation? To propose that the Board of Commrs. shall *now* proceed, without the clause of guarrantee [*sic*]? Or to make a rupture of all negotiation & fly to arms—I mean *forensic* arms? H.C.

ALS. KyU. Published in Colton (ed.), *Private Correspondence of Henry Clay,* 71-73.

1 Not found.

2 See above, Convention, June 5, 1822.

3 See below, Leigh to Clay, March 1, 1823.

4 See above, Clay and Bibb to the Virginia General Assembly, February 7, 1822; Resolutions, March 2, 1822; Credential, June 1, 1822.

5 See above, Contingent Provisions, June 5, 1822.

6 See above, Clay to Gales and Seaton, November 15, 1822.

7 The article, entitled "The Ghent Mission," from the Frankfort *Argus of Western America,* July 18, 1822, is found in Adams, *Duplicate Letters,* 233-34; Adams' remarks on it follow, 234-43.

8 Adams and William H. Crawford.

9 See above, Clay to Biddle, January 28, 1823, and cf. below, Clay to Biddle, February 27, 1823. On February 6, Clay reported to the Court the Virginia-Kentucky Convention (above, June 5, 1822). See also, below, Clay to Brooke, March 9, 1823,

note. He argued for the appellants in the cases of Stephens and Others *vs.* McCargo on February 8 and 11 and Kirk and Others *vs.* Penn's Lessee on March 10. See above, Agreement with Wickliffe, December 26, 1822; below, Agreement with Kirk and Rutter, March 14, 1823; Washington *Daily National Intelligencer,* February 7, 10, 11, March 12, 1823.

To Philip Ricard Fendall

Tuesday— [February, 1823]

Mr. Clay's compliments to Mr. Fendall and he regrets that upon coming home he found that Mrs. Brown[1] had lent out to one of her acquaintances the Voice from St. Helena.[2]

AN. Owned by J. Winston Coleman, Jr., Lexington, Kentucky. Endorsed on cover sheet: "H. Clay Feby 1823." Fendall, an Alexandria, Virginia, lawyer, had been graduated from the College of New Jersey (Princeton) in 1815. In January, 1825, President Monroe appointed him Judge of the Orphans' Court for the County of Alexandria, District of Columbia. He was a clerk in the State Department during the Administration of President John Quincy Adams, and he later served as District Attorney in the District of Columbia. He had a reputation as an able lawyer and writer and projected a history of the Adams' Administration, which he never completed.

1 Probably Mrs. James Brown.

2 Barry E. O'Meara, *Napoleon in Exile: or, a Voice from St. Helena: the Opinions and Reflections of Napoleon on the Most Important Events of His Life and Government, in His Own Words* (2 vols.; London, 1822). Among the numerous subsequent editions of this work was one published by Thomas Smith, Lexington, Kentucky, in 1823 (2 vols. in 1).

Receipted Bill from Gales and Seaton

[February 1, 1823]

Hon. Henry Clay To Gales & Seaton. Dr.

1823.		
Feb. 1.	To printing 30 copies Brief, Bank of the United States vs. Osborn &c in the supreme Court Composition 9000 ins.—	6.75
	Paper & press work	1.25
		$ 8.00

Recd payment, for Gales & Seaton THOS. DONOHO.

ADS by Thomas Donoho, long a clerk for the Washington *National Intelligencer.* DLC-TJC (DNA, M212, R15). Endorsed on verso by Clay: "To be charged to the Bank of the U S." See above, Clay to Biddle, January 28, 1823.

From William Carroll

My dear Sir, Nashville February 1st. 1823

Previous to the receipt of your letter of the 13th. of January[1] I had been informed of the nomination which had taken place at Columbus.[2] The decided stand that Ohio has taken in your favor has had a very good effect in this and some of the adjoining States, as it was confidently asserted by many, that the support of that State would be given to an other Gentleman.

As I stated to you in a short note[3] a few days ago, you may rely with the utmost confidence on the support of Tennessee, if General Jackson should cease to be a competition. It is true that there are some gentlemen at Washington from this State who believe, and no doubt say so, that Mr. Crawford will receive a majority of the votes of Tennessee. This opinion has been formed, not from a knowledge of the wishes of the great body of the people, but because it is supported by a few individuals who *have* been considered as capable of wielding the political sentiments of this country. You are supported by the people, and the young, prudent polititions [*sic*], who are growing in Strength every day. In a conversation with Mr. Grunday[4] a few days ago, he assured me, that if the prospects of General Jackson became hopeless, he would be for you, and that he would endeavour to have you nominated at the next meeting of our Legislature. But it is said, that he is so cautious in the expression of his sentiments that he can render very little service to those whom he may wish to befriend; this may be true when his interest bids him be silent. But it is equally true, that he has more influence than any other person in our Legislature; and when he brings forward any measure in that body, he supports it fearlessly, and most generally succeeds. Perhaps it would not be amiss to write to him— You know him however better than I do, and can determine what would be proper.

The Legislature of Alabama adjourned a few days ago without an effort to make a nomination. I had supposed that, that State would have given some expression of its approbation of General Jackson. As it has not, I believe that you may calculate on its support. I am warranted in this belief by many circumstances, and particularly by a letter from an intelligent gentleman written from Cahaba when the Legislature was in Session, in which it is stated "the contest for the presidency will be between Mr. Crawford and Mr. Clay, the latter of whom is the strongest." This gentleman is the decided friend of Mr. Crawford.

As I have before stated, much depends on the support you may receive from Virginia. Pennsylvania and New York Should either of those states be unanimous in your favor, the issue cannot be doubted. I have written by this days mail to a friend in Harrisburgh, giving him correct information, so far as my knowledge extends, of the views intertained [*sic*] in relation to the presidency, by many of the Western and Southern States. By to morrows mail I shall make a simelar [*sic*] communication to a friend in Pittsburgh.

Colo. Hynes,[5] who has Just returned from New Orleans informs me, that Louisiana will favor your pretensions.

If your leisure permits I shall be happy to hear from you. With sentiments of the most sincere regard, I am sir,

Respectfully Yr. friend WM. CARROLL

The Honble. Henry Clay.

ALS. DLC-HC (DNA, M212, R1).
1 Not found.
2 See above, Clay to Brooke, January 8, 1823.
3 Not found.
4 Felix Grundy.
5 Andrew Hynes.

To Peter B. Porter

My dear General (Confidential) Washington 2d. Feb. 1823.

I learnt on my arrival here, with much regret, that you were detained at Black Rock by indisposition; but I heard yesterday that you had arrived at Albany; and I hope therefore you have entirely recovered. We are looking with great solicitude towards that important point, not merely on account of the momentous transactions which are taking place there in relation to your internal concerns, but in respect to movements and indications on the Presidential question. New York is now placed, on this latter subject, in the interesting attitude, in which I think in a former letter I stated to you she would be put—she unquestionably has the power, *if she decides for the Western Candidate,* of settling the question who shall be President. Such a decision would draw after it Pennsylvania New Jersey and Maryland, and those four states united to the vote of the Western and South western states secures the election. It woud [*sic*] do more; it would draw after it the vote of Virginia and perhaps the three Southern States, leaving Mr. Adams supported by New England alone. An intelligent friend of Mr. Crawford said to me the other night that if New York did not declare for him he might strike his flag.

The demonstrations which have been recently made in the West have produced at this place the greatest change in opinion. Those who, two months ago, affected to believe that I had no chance of being elected now acknowledge that my prospects are equal (many of them own they are superior) to those of either Mr. Adams or Mr. Crawford. Those demonstrations afford evidence only of what I stated to you would be the fact, that is a zealous and hearty cooperation among the Western States. And I now assure you, upon information which cannot deceive me, that the nine Western and South Western States, will be firmly united in my support. There may be some difference in point of time, and even of zeal, as to the exhibition of their preference, but depend upon it they will finally co-operate. Pennsylvania is already favorably disposed, and Mr. Calhoun out of the way, that State will bestow its suffrage on me. Assuming these facts, let us look at the position in which we find New York now placed. If, instead of following in the wake of Virginia as heretofore, she choose to speak out her sentiments & declare in my favor, Pennsylvania will undoubtedly be confirmed in her present predilections for me, and Maryland & New Jersey will go along, and these four States acting in concert with the Nine States already mentioned determines the election. Would Virginia in that state of things separate herself and exhaust her weight uselessly upon Mr Crawford, to the prejudice of all her future views of influence in the National Councils? Would she not, on the contrary, feel herself urged and obliged to *follow* instead of *leading* New York? I verily believe that if your State declare in my favor, the election will be decided by two thirds or three fourths of the Union.

Let us now suppose that New York, blind to the advantages of her present commanding position shall lend herself either first to Mr. Adams or secondly to Mr. Crawford.

In the first supposition, she will probably be sustained by New England; but that, in all likelihood, Mr. Adams can not come south of New York. Should Pennsylvania declare for me & Virginia should, perceiving that the contest is between Mr. Adams and me, take part with me (as in that event she undoubtedly would) the question would be settled, and New York would be left in the minority.

In the second supposition, if New York should unite with Virginia in the endeavor to elevate Mr. Crawford; and Pennsylvania should, on observing the contest to be between Mr. Crawford and me take part on my side (as most undoubtedly she will in that contingency) my election would be again secure, provided New England & South Carolina should (as is very probable) prefer me to Mr. Crawford.

Again, even if both Pennsa. & New York should concur in supporting Mr. Adams, my election is yet safe, provided all the South including Maryland should unite with the West. In Maryland I have every reason to believe that I shall, in all contingencies, obtain some votes.

From these views the following results may be deduced:

1st That New York has now the power of settling the question, if she decides in my behalf.

2. That if she decides in favor of either of the two other most prominent Candidates, his election may not be secure, even if Virginia or Pennsa. should unite with New York.

And 3. That my election may be safe with *either* of the three great States in my favor; whilst the election of neither of my competitors would be certainly secured, even with the concurrence of *two* of those States in his support.

I have thought your friendship would excuse the suggestion of these views. There is one point, on which I am extremely solicitous that my friends should uniformly be as explicit as I am firmly resolved, and that is, that I shall participate in no intrigues, enter into no arrangements, have no understandings with others formal or informal, make no pledges or promises. I am determined, if elected, to enter the office unmanacled, free to promote the interest of our Common country with the utmost of my exertions, and at liberty to command the best & most faithful public servants. If not elected, chearfully acquiescing in the better choice which, in that event, will have been made, I will have the satisfaction of preserving my hands unsullied, my heart uncorrupted & my conscience perfectly pure.

Let me hear soon from you and believe me as ever Faithf y & cordially Your friend H. CLAY

Genl. P. B. Porter.

ALS. NBuHi.

To Peter B. Porter

My dear General Washington 3d. Feb. 1823.

After I had committed to the Mail on yesterday my letter to you bearing that date, I received last night your obliging favor of the 29th. Ulto. which confirmed the intelligence which I had previously received of your arrival at Albany.

I have been greatly mortified and chagrined at a report which I am told has circulated in some parts of your State, that an arrangement existed between Mr. Clinton and myself for mutual support. Such a report must have originated and been propagated by some not very scrupulous friends of the other gentlemen, who are held up for the Presidency, or some of Mr. Clintons. I trust that you know me well enough not to require, for its refutation, my solemn declaration that it is a base calumny, for which there is not the slightest foundation. I have never had any correspondence with Mr. Clinton, direct or indirect, in my life, except possibly to give and receive occasionally, whilst he was Governor, a letter of introduction. The course of conduct imputed to Mr Clinton, during the most gloomy and discouraging period of the late War, and respecting which I have never seen any satisfactory vindication of him, entirely lost him my confidence; for you know he was here during the Session at which it was declared and avowed himself unequivocally in its favor, reproaching Judge Stow and others of the New York delegation for their opposition to it.[1] In the state of Ohio I have been vilely traduced by some of his friends, who in conjunction with the friends of the gentlemen of the Cabinet made the most strenuous exertions to distract and divide that State and to thwart my nomination. And you will be surprized to learn, what is nevertheless the fact, that, in order to accomplish that object, they represented in Ohio that Mr. Clinton and the Republicans had become reconciled; that they were going to take him up for the Presidency; and the names even of Mr. Vanburen, Judge Van Ness[2] &c &c. were given as among those who were about to lend him their zealous support. Ohio was earnestly entreated not to commit herself but to reserve her strength for co-operation in the elevation of Mr. Clinton. No! my dear Sir Mr. Clinton would not dare to propose to me any such arrangement as has been insinuated; because he knows that I would repel it with scorn and indignation. I am mortified at the prevalence of such a rumor because it at once assails both my integrity and my judgment —my integrity, in supposing me capable of countenancing or concurring in such an understanding—my judgment, in supposing that I could lend myself to such an injurious, foolish & ridiculous scheme. This story is one of the common tricks of electioneering, and I should imagine ought to deceive no body. In other quarters it has been just as falsely represented that an understanding existed between Mr. Crawford and me.

My friends may confide in my faithful observance of a resolution which I have deliberately and solemnly made, to enter into no "entangling alliances", to make no arrangements with any one, to come into no understandings, formal or informal, with any body, to make no pledges, no promises; but if I enter the office, to enter it pure and without a single compromitment or ground of self-reproach. And, in the event of the election of another, most chearfully acquiescing in the better selection which the Country will then have made, I will at least retain the very great satisfaction of an unstained conscience.

There is one point which I omitted in my last. You want in New York a Congressional caucus. The Republicans of the West do not I think generally desire it. What do you want it for? Not surely to increase your power or influence over the subject. For now, New York most indisputably, by concurring in the Western nomination, has it completely in her power conclusively to settle the question. No one here I believe doubts this. If you enter a Caucus at this place, you may find yourselves controlled, instead of giving the Law. For my part, altho' I neither wish a Congressional caucus, nor a Congressional election, I have no apprehensions from either, provided the members who compose it speak the sentiments of those

whom they represent— My life upon it, that if New York now decide with the West, there is an election by two thirds of the Nation at least, without the agency of the H. of Representatives. I remain faithf ly & Cordially Your friend H. CLAY
Genl. P. B. Porter.

ALS. NBuHi.

1 Silas Stow had voted against the declaration of war. However, Clinton, while believing the United States wronged by Great Britain, had also thought the country unprepared for war and had recommended that the Madison Administration seek to avoid it. In the ensuing presidential election of 1812 he had been supported in opposition to Madison by a large segment of the Federalists, as well as by "preparedness" Republicans. Despite his efforts to obtain a military command, Clinton had been held on the sidelines by political foes who dubbed him "pacifist." Dorothy Bobbé, *De Witt Clinton* (New York, 1933), 181-88; Hammond, *History of Political Parties in the State of New York,* I, 317.

2 Martin Van Buren; William P. Van Ness. The latter, a brother of Cornelius P. Van Ness, had been born in New York, had been graduated from Columbia College, and had studied law under Edward Livingston. He had been an ardent follower of Aaron Burr and had been Burr's second in the duel with Alexander Hamilton. He published *Laws of the State of New York* (1813) and other works and from 1812 till his death in 1826 was Federal Judge for the Southern District of New York. As the author of a virulent political pamphlet defending Burr and attacking Clinton in 1803, he had generated a longstanding political enmity.

From Peter B. Porter

Dr Sir, Albany Feby 3. 1822 [*i.e.,* 1823]

In my letter of last week[1] I told you, I believe, that *Noah,* altho' decidedly in favour of Mr C—d, had expressed to me a willingness be [*sic*] silent for the present, & wait the further development of public sentiment. I soon discovered, however, by his movements here, as well as by the unaltered complexion of his paper, that I had been decieved [*sic*]. Some ten days ago, one of the two Editors of the "Argus," and who are the *State Printers,* died.[2] Noah, at once, concieved [*sic*] the idea of getting that appointment, which is made by the concurrent or joint vote of the two branches of the Legislature. This obtained, he would come out with a flaming paper in fav. of Mr C. & give his own appointment as a conclusive indication of the sentiments of the members in favour of his candidate— He being the only editor in the state who has openly espoused his cause. N. has refused an offer made by Mr Lake,[3] the survivor of the state printers, to take him into partnership; and the contest for the office will now be between these two men. A *caucus* of the Rep. members will be held tomorrow eveing [*sic*] to designate the candidate for this, as well as those for several other legislative appointments.[4] Lake is a very clever man, and altho it has heretofore been conjectured that he was inclining to Mr C-d I *now know* that he is decidedly your friend. Much exertion is, & has been for a week past, made for N. & the friends of his opponent have not been idle; and I feel great confidence in a highly favourable result. I can only add that your prospects in this state are daily improving. You observe the course of the *American*,[5] and I presume *understand* it. Many of its influential patrons are now here & are *right*. I hope you will not engage in *writing Books* with Mr. A.[6]

Yours respectfully & truly P. B. PORTER

ALS. InU. [1] See above, January 29, 1823.

[2] Moses I. Cantine, lawyer and former New York State Senator, brother-in-law of Martin Van Buren. Cantine had joined with Isaac Q. Leake in 1820 to take over the anti-Clintonian *Albany Argus*.

[3] *I.e.*, Leake.

[4] See below, Porter to Clay, February 8, 1823.

[5] See above, Porter to Clay, January 29, 1823, note.

[6] See above, Russell to Clay, August 7, 1822, note.

To Peter B. Porter

Dr Sir Washington 4 Feb. 1823.

There is one subject on which I wished to offer you a few explanations, and that is the letter which I had occasion to address to the public respecting transactions at Ghent.[1]

So far as the personal controversy existed between Mess. Adams and Russell,[2] I have no hesitation in pronouncing that the latter was, in my opinion, clearly in the wrong, and that, if his letter from Paris ought ever to have been written, he has altogether failed to make out any justification for his alterations in it. But I do not think Mr. Adams had any right, without my knowledge or consent, to make the free and frequent use which he has done of my name; to impute to me (as he does in his Appendix) inconsistent opinions, and changes of opinion; and to insinuate pretty distinctly that I was the author of an editorial article in a Kentucky print, shrinking from the responsibility of affixing to it my name.[3] If he had deigned to consult me, before or after his several publications, as to the accuracy of his statements concerning me, I should have felt myself impelled to reciprocate his politeness, by pointing out to him personally any mistakes which I thought he had made. But this he never did; he never transmitted to me any of his controversial papers; and I never, until my arrival here on the 21st. Ulto., possessed even an opportunity of perusing his book. Under these circumstances I certainly felt myself absolved from all obligation, on the score of delicacy, to address myself to Mr. Adams directly.

Thus dragged by the Secretary of State before the public, I had to choose one of four courses which were presented to my consideration. Either to remain silent altogether; or to remain so until Mr. Adams and myself were both withdrawn from before the community; or to undertake, at this time, the correction of his errors; or finally to enter the caveat and make the public reservation, which I have done, at the bar of the same tribunal to which he had unceremoniously brought me.

In the first case, Mr. Adams's statements would have found their way into history, and affected my reputation, which is just as dear to me as his can be to him; for it would have been said that Mr. Clay was a contemporary, and an agent in those transactions, and died without contradicting the statements of the Secretary of State. In regard to Mr. Russell the historian would have concluded that he had, in some measure, discredited himself; and moreover he does not testify at all on several of the points material to the public character of Mr. Clay.

If I had remained silent for an indefinite term of years, during which Mr. Adams or I might happen to be in public stations or so before the public as to render it unfit to exhibit ourselves as public disputants on an important National transaction, when I did come forward I should have found it extremely difficult to have obtained a patient and impartial hearing. It would have been said, that this man has laid by, acquiescing in the statements of Mr. Adams for so many years, and now asks us to believe him. And my testimony would, by that circumstance, have been greatly impaired, if not rejected.

Of all the indicated courses the third was most abhorrent to my feelings, that of entering the lists at this time with Mr. Adams. It would have been impossible for me (every body who knows him will believe it) if I had now offered to the public my memoir to have escaped a personal controversy. And can any honorable high minded man think that it would be fitting and proper, considering the relations in which both of us now stand to the American people, that we should publickly exhibit ourselves as two literary or, if you please, diplomatic gladiators? Would not the public have said these men are not writing for the cause of truth, or in their own vindication, but to place themselves respectively in a certain high office? No! if I could achieve over Mr. Adams the most signal triumph that was ever won; if I could prostrate him in the dust, I would not, at this time, engage in a News paper controversy with him.

The last appeared to me, and I yet think it was, the most respectful course towards the public and the one that most became me. By the note which I have published, and which is I hope perfectly decorous towards all parties, I have simply announced the existence of errors, which I imagine to be unintentional, and declare my purpose to be to correct them at a suitable moment. This reservation entitles me to be impartially heard, when the condition of the parties concerned shall make it proper to address the public.

It may be said that by failing to specify the errors refered to I leave a large scope for the exercise of the imagination, and thereby do Mr. Adams an injury. But he has done me a positive injury; mine towards him, to say the most, is only imaginary: and at last there can be no great injury done to one to whom an *unintentional* error is imputed, unless that person should happen to be the Pope.

I will freely own to you that I had another object in view. I had understood that it had been industriously circulated in New England, and I know it had been said even at Richmond, that I had instigated the calls for the Ghent papers. Now, as in truth, that was a most unjust surmise against me, the occasion which my note to the public furnished allowed me to deny that groundless charge.

Such, my dear Sir, are the explanations which I have to offer to you; and I shall be abundantly compensated for the trouble of writing this letter, if you, in that which I give you in perusing it shall find sufficient grounds to approve of my motives. I am always Your faithful friend H. CLAY

Genl. P. B. Porter.

ALS. NBuHi.
1 See above, Clay to Gales and Seaton, November 16, 1822.
2 See above, Benton to Clay, May 2, 1822, note; Russell to Clay, June 6, 1822, note.
3 See above, Clay to Brooke, January 31, 1823.

Receipted Bill from Isaac Clarke

Henry Clay Esq. February 5th. 1823

To Isaac Clarke .... Dr.

To 1 large size Trunk .... $ 3.75

Recd. payment. ISAAC CLARKE

ADS. DLC-TJC (DNA, M212, R15). Clarke was probably a resident of Washington, D.C.

From [Richard W. Meade]

My Dear Sir Phila. february 8. 1823.

I wrote you some days since,[1] to which I have no answer, I suppose you to be much engaged, as I understand that the Kentucky & Virginia business was likely to proceed.[2]

My business before the Commissioners can be so arranged with those Gentlemen,[3] thro: Doctor Watkins,[4] as to wait your perfect leisure, & to be called up whenever you please. It is merely necessary to advise Dr Watkins whenever you are at leisure, & he will arrange matters so as to have the day fixed, which you may appoint for calling it up.

The present will be delivered to you by Mr George Dallas, who drew up the several Statements relative to my Citizenship, & the last memorial under the inspection & approbation of Mr. Binney—[5]

You some time ago, in the early stage of the business suggested the propriety of my shewing that I had acquired, or possessed property to an amount equivalent to such a large sum—

The certificates presented shew that my Contracts as far back as 1810. 11. & 1812. amounted to many millions of dollars, & that in September 1812 the then Government of Spain owed me above eight hundred thousand dollars. Fortunately, or unfortunately, I was then compelled to publish my complaints against the Regency & Treasurer General, & from hence all my subsequent troubles may be dated— The publication which contains my account[6] I send to you by Mr. Dallas, as it will at once shew the nature of my Contracts— One of my friends sent one of these books to Mr. Tazewell,[7] at least he so assured me, but I send you several copies, that you may give him one if you please, as the publication was made in 1812— No one can doubt its authenticity when presented to my Enemies who never attempted to doubt it. Indeed it was the cause of removing the Regents and Minister—their removal & subsequent employment when Ferdinand[8] came was the cause of all my persecution, as stated in my memorial to Congress, when I appealed to that body in 1817—[9]

At the end of the book, or near to it, you will find a note of the principal articles imported by [me] into the port of Cadiz during the siege, the value of which exceeded seven millions of Dollars—three fourths of the whole, on my own account, having at one time more than fifty American vessells [*sic*] in the port to my consignment—

I went to Cadiz in 1803, and established the only American house at that time in that City and such was my success & credit that in 1810 I had acquired a property of seven or eight hundred thousand dollars, My Credit was so extensive that one house alone in London gave me a credit to the extent of One hundred thousand pounds Sterling *per month,* if required this House Mess. Bainbridges & Brown[10] will testify to the fact— My credit in the U. States was unlimited, & I was ruined & lost the whole by the unwarrantable conduct of the Spanish Governments towards me—

These facts were notorious in Spain, and it is equally so, that I alone supported the government when the French laid siege to Cadiz & during that siege never had cause to complain— It was not till after the siege was raised in July 1811, that I was no longer wanted that I began to experience the ingratitude of those encharged with the finances of that Country

I have thought it proper to mention these facts, in consequence of your suggestions to me, & because they are on record—& can easily be proved if required—

The Cortes, who always behaved well to me, publickly requested me to become a Spanish Citizen, which I declined, & which fact is sworn to by one of our Citizens, who was there in Cadiz & is among the [. . . .]

AL. DLC-HC (DNA, M212, R1). The latter part of the MS. is missing.

1 Letter not found. 2 See above, Credential, December 17, 1822.

3 See above, Clay to Meade, March 12, 1821, note.

4 In December, 1821, Tobias Watkins, a native of Maryland, had been appointed secretary to the Commission created under the eleventh article of the Adams-De Onís Treaty. Having been graduated from the Philadelphia Medical College in 1802, Watkins had begun practice at Havre de Grace, Maryland, and had afterwards moved to Baltimore. He had been an army surgeon during the War of 1812 and Assistant Surgeon General of the United States from 1818 to 1821. From 1824 to 1829 he was Fourth Auditor of the United States Treasury. He was at various times an editor, a contributor to periodicals, and a translator. In 1821 he had published at Baltimore a translation of Luis de Onís, *Memoir upon the Negotiations between Spain and the United States of America, which Led to the Treaty of 1819. . . .*

5 Horace Binney, for many years a leading Pennsylvania lawyer, had been born in Philadelphia, had been graduated from Harvard, and had returned to Philadelphia to practice his profession. Elected to the State legislature in 1806, a director of the first Bank of the United States, several times a member of the governing body of the city of Philadelphia, and a member of Congress from 1833 to 1835, he was the author of numerous works, including *Reports of Cases Adjudged in the Supreme Court of Pennsylvania . . .* (6 vols.; Philadelphia, 1799-1814). In 1822 Meade had published *Documents in Relation to the Claim of Richard W. Meade, on the Government of Spain* (Washington, 1822), to which Binney had supplied a lengthy opinion.

6 Richard Worsam Meade, *Contestacion . . . á las exposiciones impresas y publicades por el ex-ministro de hacienda D. José Vasquez Figueroa, y el tesorero general en exercicio D. Victor Soret* (Cadiz, 1812).

7 Littleton W. Tazewell, of Virginia, was a member of the commission appointed in December, 1821, under article eleven of the Adams-De Onís Treaty. A graduate of the College of William and Mary, he had studied law and in 1796 had been licensed to practice. He had been a member of the General Assembly (1798-1800) and of Congress (1800-1801) before moving to Norfolk, where he rapidly achieved professional prominence. He was again elected to the General Assembly, 1804-1806, 1818-1817, and in 1823 was sent to the United States Senate. Re-elected to the latter post, he served until 1832, when he resigned. He was elected Governor of Virginia in 1834 but resigned two years later.

8 Ferdinand VII. 9 See above, II, 764n.

10 Merchants, engaged in trade with the United States.

From Peter B. Porter

Dear Sir, Albany Feby 8. 1822 [*i.e.*, 1823]

I received, this morning, your two favours of the 2d. & 3d. and am much gratified with the frank & explicit manner in which you repel the charges of coalition &c. It will be attended with great effects.

I believe I stated to you, in my last, that a Legislative caucus would be held on tuesday evening of this week at which a state printer would be nominated.[1] The meeting took place, but as there were several other nominations to be made which created a good deal of discussion & consumed much time, this & some others were not acted upon, but will probably be decided at an adjourned meeting to be held next tuesday night. The candidates for the office are, Noah on one side, & on the other, Leake (one of the former state printers) and a very clever young man from one of the interior counties with whom he is associated.[2] This appointment will have a strong squinting toward the presidential candidate, & Noah puts it upon that ground amongst the partizans of Mr C-d.[3] In case of the success of Leake & partner, of which I scarcely have a doubt, they will soon take the proper stand on the presidential question.

The attention of our members is at this time & will be for some days or weeks to come, principally engrossed by our state concerns—particularly the appointment of officers, of which, under the new order of things,[4] an immense number must now be appointed in every part of the state. When the interest & anxiety, occasioned by this circumstance, is passed, they will begin to look abroad. I shall leave Albany in the morning to visit my father who lives about 60 miles distant.[5] On my return, which will be six or seven days hence, I will again write you. In the meantime I can assure you that as far as my observations extend, your prospects are daily improving.

very respectfully & truly yours P. B. PORTER

ALS. DLC-HC (DNA, M212, R1). Addressed to Clay at Washington.

1 See above, Porter to Clay, February 3, 1823.

2 After the death of Moses I. Cantine, Isaac Q. Leake was joined in the editorship of the *Albany Argus* by Edwin Croswell, a journalist from Catskill, New York.

3 William H. Crawford.

4 See above, Shaw to Clay, April 4, 1822, note.

5 Joshua Porter, a native of Lebanon, Connecticut, who had been graduated from Yale, had studied medicine, and had practiced that profession in Salisbury, Connecticut, for about forty years. He had been a colonel of militia during the Revolutionary War, had held several local public offices, and had served in the State Assembly.

From Henry Shaw

Dear Sir Feby. 11. 1823

You was sick, I mourned over it—you died I wept for you[1]—you regained your health, I rejoiced & thanked my God for your deliverance— The Papers gave us the above facts, & my heart bore the above Testimonies— you have reached Washington— I have looked for some intimation from you that I still was regarded as a friend— in your last[2] you, say "when I reach W. I will tell you all that is going" —a plain & very proper intimation that 'till then I had better hold my peace. I have done so— believe me my dear Sir if you have a friend it is him who now writes you— you have nothing to give, nor ever will have, except your Esteem, that I shall ask for— The compact between us is the homage which an honest heart pays to the noble & disinterested virtues of another— but let all this pass— The most I could do at our last Eletion [*sic*] for Congress, was to obtain the solemn pledge of *both* the Candidates, for your support, in consideration of my forbearance to oppose either. This I have got—& in the end if Dwight[3] does not play true, this I will give to the Publick—this District is a Maj. in your favor, & if the Election of Electors is left to the People, your friend[4] will be the Man— so much for this Circle— you had better look graciously on Dwight— you must have perceived his weak side— he told me of your complaint at the last Session, he will bear a heavy dose—and he is withal a generous, good feeling fellow— he has strong partialities for Calhoun—but thinks him too young &c— The Federalists have got our *Asses* in the Legislature to nominate Adams—[5] But if he gets the vote of Mass, it must be by Federalists— They dare not nominate him—but may vote him. It looks a little quer [*sic*], to see Adams a Candidate for P. & Otis for Govr.—[6] but so the game goes—no Party at Washington, but Party enough at home. In this State however things will go at that Election as Webster[7] says—he is the Man of this State, that can speak with certainty— I believe if the vote of Masstts. could make the P. Calhoun would be the Man. The Party have more confidence in him than in Adams— There is a sort of Undefined attachment toward a native—but you know how far this goes with Politicians—would not a Union with Calhoun, be rather natural—Pensa. [*sic*] sems [*sic*] to look towards Cn.— Inclosed you will find a Calculation of Genl. Smith of Md.[8] which he sent me some weeks since— you know how to weigh it— you should have everything & take your steps accordingly— New York sems to be playing a deep game at W.—[9] Van B.[10] is a cunning Man—but there is many things to be taken into viw [*sic*] in regard to this State. I have many friends & all my connexions are there & their politicks are much more interesting to me than those of my own State— I spend considerable time at Albany paticulaly [*sic*] in the Winter—have just returned from there & shall be out again in about 10 days— I'll attempt a brief outline of there present condition. The late Convention[11] was got up by the Buck Tail Party, its success gave to that Party a vast ascendancy— The Govr. & all the offices [*sic*] of the State together with both branches of the Legislature are Bucks— The 1. Jany. the new Govt. was organised— The Party was without a head—it was too strong to admit of one— The first step was one of dissension— There is now an opposition formed in the Senate to the Govr.— at the head nominally is Genl. Root[12] —if you know him, you need not be told how long, or how ably he can conduct a Party—vain arrogant & factious, he has acquired the popularity of Demagoge [*sic*], without making a single friend— under him, but really controlling him are a number of enterprising & really able Men—Van Buren— Skinner Young[13]—Suydam Cramer Tallmage Tallcot[14] & others— The war is as yet under the rose, but will soon be open. The Govr. nominated the Old Sup. Court— It was highly honorable to his feelings as a Man— It was expected of him—and the rejection of them by the Senate was equally expected—[15] all this was well enough, & neither the Gov. or S. lost by the step each took— but then the Senate sought to dictate a Court— Root told the Gov.— "You must send us Sir Van Buren Talcot [*sic*] & Duer[16] or you will bring a Storm upon your head"— "I shall send you Sir my friends & your friends, & reject them if you dare"— Savage Sutherland & Betts,[17] were sent— The S. dare not reject the first, for altho not a great Lawyer, yet a very popular Man— the 2d. hard [*sic*] got a Maj pledged— the last was rejected— The Senate have been obliged to intimate to the Gov. that they would confirm Woodworth, one of the old Court, & the least obnoxious, if he would again send his name— he did so, & the Judge is app'td.—[18] I have been thus particular for the purpose of showing you the origin of Two parties that will probably before long, divide this State— The Gov will probably hold a large part of the old Republicns [*sic*]— Root & Co, take the rest, & the ballance will be held by the Federalists— Root & I Judge Van B. are the friends of Crawford at present— The Gov. has not as yet, as I can learn, expressed a preference some of his immediate friends are in favor of Adams but more of them in favor of yourself— Noah[19] who is the immediate organ of Van B. is for Cd. The "American"[20] gave us the strongest assurances, but in the end has come out for Adams— these Two papers are the leading ones in the State— but will be opposed—[21] But after all the People of the State have not as yet expressed any opinion— & with proper Management can be made to act right— I found a number of good Old Substantial Repub. decidedly your friends—& there is depend upon it throughout the State a feeling of a kindly nature towards you Those who are friendly to Crawford, can give but a poor account of themselves— They do not [a]cc[ount] for their friendship in any of those ways, that Men, who are devoted to anothers interest are accustomed to do— I have rather endeavored, in my intercourse with them, to neutralize, then [*sic*] proselite [*sic*]— Parties are not sufficiently formed as yet— and to disseminate among substantial country Gentlemen favorible [*sic*] impressions, withot [*sic*] appearing a partizan of any one, appeared to me the most judicious— The little band of Clinton[22] in Congress, Taylor Tracy[23] &c are at bottom your friends, but an avowal of it would at present do you hurt— There is this [*sic*] State certain local Influences, that are powerfull within their circle. & by the bye, let me tell you, that New York, will never again be under the controul of any Man— The new Constitution has so subdivided the patronge [*sic*] of the State, that no one through that medium can ever govern, as heretofore— after the appointmt this Winter, anything of a great nature, will be effected by addressing local influens [*sic*]— there will not be the same Party connexion as heretofore & depend upon it there is no Man at W. that can pledge N Y to the Support of any one—

Taylor & Tracy can both of them secure the Repns. of their Counties— but the most important local influenc [*sic*] in the State is a certain Virginia Party in the West— at its head stands Rob. S. Rose,[24] a Member Elect into the next Congress— here is a shrewd Managing Man— This influence, is composed of the Familis [*sic*] of Nicholas of Ontario—[25] [. . . .][26] Carroll & Fitchugh [*sic*] of Livingstone Counties—[27] They always act in concert & commonly effect their purposes— S. [*sic*] B. Rochester, at present a Member is of the Corps.— he will probably be appointed a District Judge[28] & will thereby have his influenc augmented— It is of the utmost importance that N.Y. should be secured, for independent of the vote she gives, She is the first State in the Union that will choose Electors, or rather she will have a Legislature that will have the earliest opportunity of expressing officially a preference for a Candidate— Rose says Van B. meas [*sic*] to Try Thompson—[29] I doubt it— V. is a Man—ah—you know him by this time better than I do—

Genl. Smith, calculation

"from present sentiments I would say

Mr. Adams will have ..		Mr. Crawford ..		Calhoun	
N.Hampshire	8	N. York	36	Pen	28
Massachusetts	15	Jersey	8	S. Carolina	11
Connecticut ..	8	Delware [*sic*] ..	3		39
Rhod [*sic*] Island..	4	Maryland	5		
Vermont	7	Virginia ..	24	Clay	
Maryland	6	N. Carolina	15	Kentuc.	14
	48	Georgia	9	Missouri	3
		Tennessee	5	Illinois	3
Jackson		Maine	9	Indiania [*sic*] ...	5
Louisanna [*sic*] ...	5		114	Ohio	16
Miss	3				41
Alla [*sic*]	5				
Tenssee [*sic*]	6				
	19				

whole number 261 ..

Majority .... 132 .. If Calhoun declins [*sic*] it will be to be made Secty. State under Adams, & S. Carolina will go to him, making his 59, & if Jackson declins he may get Alabama 5— making him 64— it is possible he may get Pen.—but not very probable—yet his friends [. . . .][30] That is all he can get in any event— If Jackson declins— Crawford will get 6 more from Tennssee [*sic*] & maybe 3 from Missippie [*sic*], making him—123 In that case Clay will get Louisiana 5, which will give him 46—if Clay is satisfied he can get no more he may concnt [*sic*] to be V P. in which case Crawford will get the West— indeed in any case Mr Noble[31] says he will get

Indiana"—so much for the General— This was not confidential, but yet, but—you [. . . .][32] not instruct, it may am[. . . .]—[33]

If you can get through this letter thank your stars— I should be pleased to hear from you I salute you with sincerity H: SHAW

The Envoy to Chili[34] = ! ! oh Lord. oh Lord —

I wrote you a letter in Oct.,[35] but before I sent it I heard of your illness— it contains some thigs [*sic*] that may amuse you, I thefore [*sic*] stick it in— but burn it, as a part of it is confidential—

ALS. DLC-HC (DNA, M212, R1). Several lines faded, as indicated.

1 See above, Clay to Porter, October 22, 1822, note. 2 Not found.

3 Henry W. Dwight, of Stockbridge, Massachusetts, recently elected to the second of his five successive terms in Congress. A graduate of Williams College, he had studied law and had been admitted to the bar in 1809. He had been a member of the State legislature in 1818 and was again elected to that body in 1834.

4 That is, Shaw, himself.

5 A resolution favoring Adams for President had been adopted unanimously "at a meeting of the republican members of both branches of the legislature of the commonwealth of Massachusetts, and of republican delegates from various towns of the commonwealth not represented in the legislature, held at the old court house, in the city of Boston, on Thursday evening, Jan. 23, 1823. . . ." *Niles' Weekly Register,* XXIII (February 1, 1823), 342-43.

6 Harrison G. Otis was defeated by William Eustis in the contest for Governor of Massachusetts in 1823.

7 Daniel Webster. 8 Samuel Smith.

9 Washington. 10 Martin Van Buren.

11 See above, Shaw to Clay, April 4, 1822.

12 Erastus Root, who had been elected lieutenant governor in 1822 but was defeated for re-election later in 1823.

13 Roger Skinner; Samuel Young. The former had been a member of the New York Council of Appointment, had for a time held simultaneously the offices of State Senator and United States Judge for the Northern District of New York, and remained in the judicial post until his death in 1825.

Young, of Saratoga, had been Speaker of the New York State Assembly, a State Senator, one of the first canal commissioners, and a member of the constitutional convention of 1821.

14 John Suydam, a lawyer, of Kingston, Ulster County, and a member of the State Senate; John Cramer, Senator from Saratoga County (1823-1825), formerly a member of the State House of Representatives, a delegate to the constitutional convention of 1821, and, from 1833 to 1837, a United States Congressman; James Tallmadge, now a State Senator; Samuel A. Talcott, of Oneida County, State Attorney General, 1821-1829.

15 See above, Porter to Clay, January 29, 1823.

16 William A. Duer, of Dutchess County, member of the State Assembly (1814-1820), Circuit Judge (1823-1829), President of Columbia College (1829-1842), author of numerous articles, pamphlets, and books. Van Buren had recommended him earlier in January, 1823, for an appointment to the State Supreme Court, but the Governor had refused to nominate him. He was appointed to the circuit judgeship in April. Denis T. Lynch, *An Epoch and a Man: Martin Van Buren and His Times* (New York, 1929), 242-43.

17 John Savage; Jacob Sutherland, earlier an Albany lawyer, Federal District Attorney, and Schoharie County farmer, who had been elected to the State Senate in 1822 but had refused to serve in anticipation of the judicial appointment, and who in 1835 resigned from the State Supreme Court to become Clerk of that body (Hammond, *History of Political Parties in the State of New York,* II, 102, 106, 111-12, 455); Samuel R. Betts, Orange County lawyer and United States Congressman (1815-1817). Later in the year Betts was appointed a State circuit judge and, from 1826 to 1867, was Judge of the United States District Court for the Southern District of New York.

18 John Woodworth, Albany lawyer, had been a State Senator, Attorney General, and, from 1819 until the new constitution went into effect, a judge of the New York Supreme Court. Following his reappointment, he served in the last post until 1828.

19 Mordecai M. Noah. 20 The New York *American.*

21 A movement to establish a Clay paper at Albany failed early in 1824. Thurlow

Weed, *Autobiography of Thurlow Weed* (ed. by Harriet A. Weed; Boston, 1883), 108-109.

22 DeWitt Clinton.

23 John W. Taylor; Albert H. Tracy.

24 Born in Amherst County, Virginia, in 1774, removed to Seneca County, New York, in 1803, a farmer and a member of the State Assembly (1811, 1820, 1821), the constitutional convention of 1821, and the United States House of Representatives (1823-1827, 1829-1831).

25 John Nicholas, brother of George, Wilson Cary, and Philip Norborne Nicholas, had practiced law in his native Virginia and had served four terms in Congress (1793-1801) before removing to Geneva, Ontario County, New York, in 1803. He was a State Senator, 1806-1809, and Judge of the Court of Common Pleas from 1806 to his death in 1819. His son, Robert C. Nicholas, was later elected to the New York legislature and became identified with the Anti-Masonic Party.

26 One line of text faded.

27 Charles Carroll and William Fitzhugh, both of Maryland and veterans of the Revolutionary War, had been associated with Nathaniel Rochester in the purchase of lands in western New York in 1803. Both had moved to Livingston County, New York, shortly after the War of 1812. Carroll's son, Charles H., became a county judge in 1823, later sat in the legislature, and was elected to two terms in Congress (1843-1847). One of Fitzhugh's sons, Henry, became a prominent merchant; another, William, a medical doctor.

28 William B. Rochester's appointment, as Judge of the Eighth Circuit of New York, was made in April of this year.

29 A few days earlier Smith Thompson had solicited Van Buren's support for the presidential nomination. Van Buren made no reply until March 4, the day after Congress adjourned, when he gave a discouraging appraisal of Thompson's chances as a candidate. Lynch, *An Epoch and a Man,* 244-46; Martin Van Buren, *Autobiography* . . . (ed. by John C. Fitzpatrick; American Historical Association, *Annual Report, 1918,* II [Washington, 1920]), 141n.

30 Three-fourths of line faded.

31 James Noble, a native of Virginia who had lived in Campbell County, Kentucky, before moving to Brookville, Indiana, in 1811. He had been a member of the Indiana constitutional convention, 1816, had served briefly in the State House of Representatives in the same year, and was a United States Senator from 1816 until his death in 1831.

32 Two-thirds of line faded.

33 One-half line faded.

34 On January 27 the Senate had confirmed the appointment of Heman Allen, of Vermont, as Minister Plenipotentiary to Chile. Allen, a lawyer, had held local offices and had been elected to Congress, but had resigned in 1818, before the end of his term, in order to accept an appointment as United States Marshal for the District of Vermont. He was Minister to Chile until 1827 and was later (1830-1836) president of the Burlington, Vermont, branch of the Bank of the United States.

35 Not found.

From Benjamin Watkins Leigh

My dear sir, Richmond, Feb. 12. 1823.

I have received your truly kind friendly letter.[1] Far from being surprised at the indignation, which the conduct of the Virginia Legislature, in respect to the convention agreed on between us last summer,[2] has excited in your breast, I unite in the sentiment; but my indignation is aggravated by the sense of personal mortification at such a defeat of my best efforts for the public service, and of burning shame for the ridicule and dishonor which Virginia has brought on herself. If *you* be thus indignant, what must be the feelings of your colleague mr Rowan?[3] I fancy I can see his resentment, disdain and contempt. Yet, my dear sir, this deed must not be imputed to us the people of Virginia, nor even to the body of her representatives—it must lie at the door of a bare majority of the Senate. I am not sure, that Kentucky is bound to take the distinction; but I hope you will. I beli[eve] that the sentiment of the people of Virginia towards Kentucky, is the same with my own individually; and that, I am sure, is what it ought to be.

It is impossible to say what our assem[bly] m[e]ans to do in this business. Some answer must be given to Kentucky.[4] What it will be, or how it can be agreed on, considering the difference of opinion between the two houses, I am wholly at a loss to conjecture. The majority in the Senate for the present, so far as I can learn, are perfectly careless about it. But it is impossible, I hope, that they can continue so regardless of self respect, so unconcerned about the comity due to a sister State, as to leave matters in their present condition. Mr Johnson[5] desired me, a day or two ago, to tell you, that he did not think it absolutely hopeless, that the Senate will yet consent to the ratification of the Convention.

Your suit in the federal court, was not tried at the last term[6]—and the only reason of it was, that there was such a mass of business, and the whole bar was so jaded and worn out, that we all came to a conclusion to adjourn all unfinished business to the next term.

I remain, ever, my dear sir, faithfully and cordially yours

Henry Clay Esq B:W:LEIGH

ALS. DLC-HC (DNA, M212, R1). Published in part in Colton (ed.), *Private Correspondence of Henry Clay*, 73-74.

1 Not found.

2 The Contingent Provisions of the Convention (above, June 5, 1822) had been rejected by the Virginia Senate on January 3; on January 13 the House of Delegates had insisted upon its original bill providing for acceptance of this guarantee; a committee of conference between the two houses had failed to reach agreement; and on January 31 and February 8, respectively, the Senate and House had reiterated their former positions.

3 John Rowan.

4 See below, Leigh to Clay, March 1, 1823.

5 Chapman Johnson.

6 For the recovery of "Euphraim." Cf. above, Leigh to Clay, November 9, 1822.

From Peter B. Porter

Dear Sir, Albany Feby 12. 1823

I have received your favour of the 4th. and have to regret that the sportive allusion I made to your letter respecting the transactions at Ghent,[1] should have subjected you to the trouble of a serious exposition of its object & propriety. My own impression was that there was nothing in Mr Adams' writings which rendered it necessary that you should appear before the public to sustain your character; and such controversies are rarely attended with advantage to either of the parties.

I informed you, in my last, that I was about making an excursion, for a few days, to the East,[2] but have delayed it untill this time, waiting the arrival of my stepson, Grayson, from west point.[3] He came in last night, and we shall leave Albany in the course of half an hour. A Legislative Caucus was held last night and the general indication of its proceedings was favourable, but they did not touch the question of State Printer, which has a much more direct bearing on the presidential question than any other. This, in point of grade, is one of the lowest of the legislative appointments, and they did not progress so far; and Noah[4] and his friends, who have lately been joined by *Mathew L. Davis*[5] (a character of whom I presume you have heard) took care to manage the other subjects in such a manner as to prevent the discussion of this. The Caucus is adjourned to the 1st. Monday in march, in order to give those Members who are "Supervisors of Towns" (and, who, as such, have the appointment of Justices of the peace in their respective counties) an opportunity to go home to attend to this duty. I shall return again in about 5. days. I beg you to excuse the manner & matter of this letter which is in great haste & on the eve of my departure.

with great respect & regard P. B. PORTER

Cannot Van Buren be brought right—

ALS. DLC-HC (DNA, M212, R1).

1 Cf. above, Porter to Clay, February 3, 1823. Clay could not, however, have received this letter prior to his explanation of February 4.

2 See above, Porter to Clay, February 8, 1823.

3 John Breckinridge Grayson, son of Alfred W. Grayson, had been appointed to the United States Military Academy in 1821. He was commissioned in 1826, attained the brevet rank of lieutenant colonel in 1847 for meritorious conduct in the Mexican War, continued in service until July 1, 1861, when he resigned to become a brigadier in the Confederate Army, and died a few months afterward.

4 Mordecai M. Noah.

5 New York newspaperman and politician, close friend and political adherent of Aaron Burr, for whom he worked in the campaign of 1800 in New York and served as companion at the duel with Alexander Hamilton. Davis was long a leader of the Tammany Society and, later in life, was Washington correspondent for newspapers in London and New York. After Burr's death, Davis had charge of his private papers and published *Memoirs of Aaron Burr, with Miscellaneous Selections from His Correspondence* (2 vols.; New York, 1836-1837) and *The Private Journal of Aaron Burr, during His Residence of Four Years in Europe; With Selections from His Correspondence,* (2 vols.; New York, 1838).

From Thomas J. Randolph

Dear Sir, Feby. 14. 1823

The only paper of importance which I find I have retained relating to the transactions between T. D. Owings and Colo. W. C Nicholas is the bond of Owings which I enclose to you. The mortgage and other papers were forwarded to Mr. Terrell,[1]

with great respect Your obt. Servt. TH J. RANDOLPH.

Copy. DLC-TJC (DNA, M212, R12). Followed by the following comment, in the same handwriting: "Note place of date not legible." Endorsed by Clay: "Copy of Th. J. Randolph's letter referred to in Clay's Amended ansr." Cf. above, Jefferson to Clay, August 28, 1822.

1 Dabney Terrell.

From Richard W. Meade

My Dear Sir Phila. february 15. 1823.

I am in receipt this day of your esteemed letter of the 13th.—[1]

Do me the favor to procure from Mr Cheeves[2] an opinion in writing. It will be extremely satisfactory to me to have an opinion from him—

My business, as well as my health prevent me from going down,— besides what utility can I be? With such friends as yourself & Mr Cheeves, what cause can be better defended? It is only the prejudices of Mr. Tazewell[3] that you have to combat. I am certain that if he has not imbibed some very erroneous impressions against me, that he cannot resist the justice of my claim.

I am most desirous to convince Mr Tazewell & anyone else who may wish to examine the case of the fairness & correctness of my conduct. If it was only possible to get him to sit down & look over the evidence brought forward with calmness & dispassionately I feel an inward conviction, that my claim would not be rejected— The Spanish Govt. declare positively that it is the *only* value received by them for the Floridas—

I am perfectly satisfied with the mode proposed by you of bringing forward the claim— I wish this done as early as your Convenience will permit— It must be done at all events whilst you & Mr Cheeves are on the spot, because I shall then know exactly on what I have to depend, and if you should be so fortunate as to have it admitted at once without further difficulty—It will be rendering me the most essential service.—

It is now 11 years since my troubles commenced in Spain, and since May 1816, the date of my last imprisonment, my whole time has been exclusively taken up, in this unfortunate business, so that I have spent a very considerable portion of my life, in endeavouring to save a portion of my property— The motives which induced me to embark my fortune in the revolution of Spain I know will not be appreciated by the Commissioners; & by the world It may be termed weakness, if not folly— Yet If I had the same thing to do over again, I might perhaps be inclined to act as I then did— I had acquired my fortune in that Country, I had become personally attached to many of its most respectable inhabitants— I saw them oppressed by a Tyrant & struggling for their liberty & independence— I was appealed to, to aid & assist them— No one in the Nation wuld [*sic*], from his foreign connections in the Commercial world do it so well as myself, & name it folly, rashness, or what you please. I could not resist the call— I embarked my all— the result is too well known for me to repeat it— If Spain had been unable to pay me, I should not say one word, but to know that she was able, & has provided liberally for my demand, & to know & feel that my own Government is instrumental in preventing me from recovering my demand is what annoys me, I should have preferr'd much taking my chance in Spain, I would soon yet prefer it, as I know the ground I stand on *there;* & the language I can hold out to the Nation, where I have thousands & thousands of Eye witnesses to testify to the services I rendered— Where-as here, those very services are imputed as crimes. The Commissioners cannot feel & see the claim in the same manner as I do, & as it is viewed in Spain, but they have laid it down as a general rule, that every person claiming under the treaty must substantiate his demand on the Spanish Government, that is he must make out a case to prove that he has a fair claim on Spain, & for which she was bound to make compensation— On this principle, what claims can be compared to mine?— It is not only a case made out against Spain, but admitted, & ratified by all the most solemn forms known to the Tribunal and highest Executive Authority, being sanctioned by the king himself, called for by my own Country, & ratified by both, in as formal & solemn a manner, as the treaty of Cession for Florida itself—

But I am trespassing on your valuable time, & I must conclude— To you & your friend Mr Cheeves I leave the matter & pray you to let me have every particular relative to it, so soon after it has been taken up, as possible. With Sincere regard & respect I remain

Yrs. Sincerely R W MEADE

Henry Clay, Esqr. Washington—

ALS. DLC-HC (DNA, M212, R1). See above, Meade to Clay, February 8, 1822.
[1] Not found. [2] Langdon Cheves. [3] Littleton W. Tazewell.

To Amos Kendall

WASHINGTON, 16th Feb. 1823.

Dear Sir: I have just received your favor of the 2d inst.[1] I wrote a few days ago to our friend Crittenden,[2] and must refer you to that letter for some topics not touched in this. With respect to the question whether, after the conclusion of the treaty of Louisiana, the right did not accrue to the British, under that of 1783, to navigate the Mississippi in its whole extent, I hope you will not commit yourself until I see you. My opinion is very strong that it did not; and although your suggestions are ingenious, I do not think them conclusive. I have not time here to discuss the question. But I would ask if more can be granted than the grantor has? What had the United States to grant in 1783? What was the consideration which the British paid? Although in name it was a grant of the right of navigation, in the whole extent of the river, the grant must be interpreted, not by its *words,* but by the power to grant. The equivalent given, was measured by what was received. The case of a grant of a right of way by a private individual will not illustrate the argument, because the grantee might have been deceived. Here England was not deceived, because she knew how far we had power to grant. We procured from Spain a right of deposit by the treaty of 1795.[3] Did that also inure to England? If, when we got a *part* of the subject, she could not claim to be let in under the treaty of 1783, how can she assert the claim when we got the whole? If England had tendered to us a part of the fifteen millions which we paid for Louisiana proportionate to the right claimed by her to navigate the river, within the former limits of Spain, she might then have made out a case, not of right, but strongly addressing itself to our equity.

The treaty of Louisiana furnishes another strong illustration. France by it was to be put on the footing of the most favored nation.[4] After the convention of London in 1815,[5] France claimed to be put, in regard to the tonnage of the respective countries, upon the same footing with England. But our government, through Mr. Adams, said, no, we have received pay from England for that privilege, and when you pay us the same (that is, adopt the principles of reciprocity) you shall be admitted as the vessels of England are admitted.[6]

Do you put it on the ground that the inhabitants of the head of a stream have a right to follow it to the ocean, although its debouchement belongs to another power? England at least could not take that ground, because she refuses to allow the application of the principle to the case of the St. Lawrence.[7]

When I shall have the pleasure of seeing you, we will further discuss this matter.

Mr. Talbot[8] promised to-day to send you one of Mr. Adams' books which I never saw until I came here. I will see that it is done.

Judging from present appearances, the contest will be between Mr. Adams and me. Mr. Crawford's prospects have greatly and evidently declined within the last three months. Still there may be other phases exhibited before the question is settled. I think, therefore, that the policy of my friends should be that of maintaining at least respectful relations with the other gentlemen and their friends. That is the best course under all circumstances. You may rely upon it, that New-York is perfectly uncommitted; that Mr. Crawford does not stand better there than I do, if so well now; that my cause is gaining whilst his is losing ground in that state; and that in Pennsylvania my prospect is far better than either his or Mr. Adams'. In two of the three great states, with which the decision of the question now mainly rests, I stand better than Mr. Crawford, and in two better that [*sic*] Mr. Adams. Mr. Calhoun is generally thought to be entirely out of the question.

Our Virginia business has taken a most unexpected turn.[9] Whilst I certainly should regret that the seeds should have been sown of a permanent alienation between the two states, I do think that we have been so right and they so wrong, that some notice ought to be taken in our papers, in pretty strong terms, of the rejection of the guarranty. I am not sure, that it might not have good effect on the very question, respecting which your solicitude exists for the preservation of the harmony between the two states.

In your notices of Mr. Adams, I need scarcely repeat the idea of the great advantage which will attend a perfectly decorous course. I do not know that I can add any suggestions that will be useful. As I hope to be at home early in the spring it will be then time enough to make any that may occur.

The prospect of war between France and Spain seems to have diminished.[10]

The rumor of a cession of Cuba to England I do not believe is well founded.[11]

With great regard, I am faithfully yours, H. CLAY

AMOS KENDALL, Esq.

Frankfort *Argus of Western America,* July 16, 1828. Published also in Washington *United States Telegraph-Extra,* I (August 2, 1828), 324-25.

1 Not found. 2 John J. Crittenden. Letter not found. 3 Pinckney's Treaty.

4 France was to have for twelve years preferential treatment in New Orleans and all other legal ports of entry in the Louisiana Territory, and "In future and for ever after the expiration of the twelve years, the Ships of France shall be treated upon the footing of the most favoured nations in the ports above mentioned." Miller (ed.), *Treaties,* I, 503-504.

5 See above, II, 57-59.

6 For the French protest (December 15, 1817), Secretary of State Adams' reply (December 23, 1817), and subsequent correspondence during the Monroe Administration, see *American State Papers, Foreign Relations,* V, 640-74. The issue had constituted a major bar to agreement on the commercial treaty with France (above, Remarks on Bill to Exempt French Ships, February 27, 1821, note) and remained a complication in negotiations on the United States spoliation claims (above, Lafayette to Clay, November 5, 1822, note).

7 Great Britain did not permit free navigation of the St. Lawrence by American citizens until the reciprocity treaty of 1854, under which the privilege was granted in exchange for concessions.

8 Isham Talbot. 9 See above, Leigh to Clay, February 12, 1823.

10 See above, Lafayette to Clay, November 5, 1822, note.

11 Since the preceding summer, members of Monroe's Cabinet had been alarmed by the fear that Great Britain might obtain Cuba as the price of her support for the policies of the Holy Alliance (cf. above, Lafayette to Clay, November 5, 1822, note). This apprehension continued at least until the end of April. See Adams, *Memoirs,* VI, 112, 139; Ford (ed.), *Writings of John Quincy Adams,* VII, 376-481.

Bill from B. Wells and Company

Hon. Henry Clay To B. Wells & Co Dr Steubenville Feby 17. 1823

To 3½ yds. Black Cloth @ 10 . . . . $ 35.00

" 6 " Blue " " 60"—

" 1	Pair Merino Sheep of W. R. Dickinson	50 –
		$ 145 –
Cr		
	By Cash remitted W. R. Dickinson	50 –
	To Balance	$ 95 –

[Endorsement][1]

Recd. 29 Apl. 1823 the above bal. of $95 in a check on the Off. of Dt. & Dt. Washington City– B. Wells & Co

pr D. B. BAYLESS[2]

D. DLC-TJC (DNA, M212, R15). Bezaleel Wells, one of the founders of Steubenville, Ohio, member of the Ohio Constitutional Convention and State Senator (1803-1804), had been a leader in the economic development of his community. During the War of 1812 he had formed a partnership with William R. Dickinson (Dickenson) for the manufacture of wool, and their cloth acquired a widespread reputation for excellence. Dickinson was a Virginian who had settled in Steubenville in 1807 and, around 1812, had begun bringing in Merino sheep. By the mid-1820's he owned a flock of 2,500, while Wells, who had embarked upon a similar enterprise around 1815, owned 3,500. W. H. Hunter (comp.), "The Pathfinders of Jefferson County," Ohio Archaeological and Historical Society, *Publications,* VI (1898), 210, 234-38.

1 ES, in Clay's hand. 2 Presumably a clerk.

From Francis T. Brooke

My Dear Sir Richmd Feb 19h 1823

I wrote you some days ago[1] and expected that I should again have the pleasure to hear from you before I left Richmd our Court will adjourn tomorrow to the 10h of March–and if your time will admit of it Shall expect a letter directed to Fredericksg Since my last I have had the opportunity to make more minute inquiry into the grounds of the revived opinion that Mr Crawford is the preferred Candidate in Virginia, and find what I conjectured that it is a very vague and undefined only [*sic*] in conversation with Genl Tucker[2] who is entitled in some degree to give the tone to public feeling, I perceived that he himself had no well defined preference– from the Western gentlemen, I understand that in their quarter you have been more in the public eye than any other– from Colol Cambpell [*sic*] of the Senate and Genl F Preston[3] who is here as well as others I get this information, so that it is at least doubtful when the legislature meets the next year who will be first in the opinion of a majority for that I think will decide who will have the vote of Virginia, Mr Adams Seems to be out of the question, I regret that you Should feel any disappointment in the course persued here in relation to the Kentuckey convention,[4] I have not examined the Subject very maturely, but still entertain the opinion that Virga was not called on to make any additional compact with Kentuckey[5] She was will [*sic*] to carry the one under which the difference arose into full effect, and to leave her citizens to the courts in the event that the commissrs decided against her, I think there was no change in the circumstances existing when the compact was made with Kentuckey requiring her to Superadd the guarranty—whether the decision of the co[mmiss]rs would have been conclusive in the courts I think is very uncertain—indeed the State ought not to pledge itself for any opinion of the Federal Courts, after what has occurred, but if *conclusive* there the guarranty was Superfluous which of itself is an objection to it, there is now a pretty Strong impression here that the whole course on that Subject has been wrong— Virginia as I thought then, ought to have Simpathised with Kentuckey last year, and to have proposed a reference of all the matters, finally agreed to be referred, without the guarranty which would probably then have not been thought of, I have Stated this much to you because I was told yesterday by Mr Herring[6] that I was quoted in the Senate by Genl. Tucker and that my opinions had some weight in that body— Mr Johnston[7] he informed me proposed to refer the question whether the warrant holders to get into the Federal Courts to the Judges of the court of appea[ls] which was not acceded to— for[. . .][8] reasons I think might have [. . . .] Yours very Sincerely F BROOKE

ALS. DLC-HC (DNA, M212, R1). Addressed to Clay at Washington.
1 Letter not found.
2 Henry St. George Tucker, now (1819-1823) a member of the Virginia Senate.
3 David Campbell; Francis Preston. The former, a veteran of the War of 1812, had been Clerk of the Washington County, Virginia, Court until elected to the State Senate in 1820. He was again Clerk of Washington County, 1824-1836, and in 1836 was elected Governor of Virginia.
4 See above, Clay to Brooke, January 31, 1823.
5 See above, Contingent Provisions, June 5, 1822.
6 Probably John S. Herring, agent for the State of Virginia in behalf of persons entitled to military lands in Kentucky.
7 Chapman Johnson.
8 MS. torn and illegible; two or three words missing here and at end of sentence.

From William Carroll

My Dear Sir, Nashville February 19th. 1823

I have this moment been informed that General Jackson will not accept the appointment of Ambassador to Mexico.[1] Should that be the fact, I know of no selection to fill that office, that would be more acceptable to the people of Tennessee, than that of Colo. Henry Crabb United States district Attorney.[2] He is certainly a young man of the most distinguished abilities, both as a lawyer and a politician; in proof of which, I refer you to Judge White. Judge Todd[3] and to our Senators and representatives in Congress, should they still be in the city.

As the mail is about closing, I have only time to request the favor of you to present the subject to the President, to whom be pleased to communicate, that the most satisfactory testimony can be given of the capacity of Colo. Crabb to discharge the duties of the situation.

If the recommendation of the most eminent men in our State, would have any weight in his behalf it can be procured and forwarded. With a tender of the most sincere friendship. I am respectfully Yr. Obt. Servt. WM. CARROLL

ALS. DNA, RG59, Applications and Recommendations for Office (MR1). Addressed to Clay at Washington.

[1] The nomination, and Senate confirmation, of Jackson as "Envoy Extraordinary and Minister Plenipotentiary of the United States, at Mexico" had occurred during the preceding month. See Jackson to John Coffee, March 10, 1823, in Bassett (ed.), *Correspondence of Andrew Jackson*, III, 192.

[2] Crabb had been appointed United States Attorney for the district of West Tennessee in 1818 and 1822 and was reappointed in 1826.

[3] Hugh L. White; Thomas Todd.

To Nicholas Biddle

Sir Washington 21st. Feb. 1823

I have received your letter under date the 18h. instant[1] with the Report of the Committee on the offices in the case of J. J. Marshall Esqr. The report is quite intelligible, and there will be no difficulty in the execution of its terms, if Mr. Marshall create none, and I have no reason to apprehend, from his past conduct, that he will create any. In one point only, perhaps, it might have been a little more explicit, and that is in the fixation of a period within which the property shall be conveyed, and the assignment made of his claim to arrears of rent &c. as specified in the two first clauses of the resolution. Would it not be well enough to intimate to him, if he be yet in the City, or by letter, if he has left it an expectation of the Board that the whole arrangement must be consummated by a day to be indicated by the Board?

I have no hesitation in expressing my firm conviction that the best interests of the Corporation have been consulted in this arrangement; and that, although the property &c. will not realize any thing like the aggregate amount of the debts which are to be cancelled, more will be thus obtained than could have been probably coerced out of the parties. The substitution of the cash engagement for the Sandy lands is a great improvement of the terms formerly proposed.

We have not yet reached the case with the State of Ohio in the Supreme Court,[2] although I have been anxiously expecting to arrive at it for some days past. Mr. Cheves,[3] whose zeal for the interests of the Bank, appears to be undiminished by his recent separation from it, has been preparing to volunteer his assistance of [*sic*] me. I have the honor to be with great respect Your ob. Servant H. CLAY

Nicholas Biddle Esqr. &c. &c. &c.

ALS. DLC-HC (DNA, M212, R1).

[1] Not found.

[2] See above, Clay to Biddle, January 28, 1823.

[3] Langdon Cheves.

Bill from Surveyor of Scott County

February 25th. 1823

[Henry Clay and Isham Talbot are debtors to the surveyor of Scott County for $2.50, charges on one plat at $1.00 and three copies at 50 cents each. Signed by John Ewing, Deputy Surveyor.]

ADS. DLC-TJC (DNA, M212, R15).

To Francis T. Brooke

My dear Sir Washn 26. Feb. 23.

I duly recd. your friendly letter of the 19h. inst. as I did the preceding one to which it refers. The course which the business between our respective states has taken fills me with so much regret and concern that I will not dwell upon it, especially as it has probably terminated finally, and had therefore better be forgotten as soon as it can be. What is done cannot be changed and it is not conformably to my temper or habit to indulge in unavailing regrets. I prefer always looking to the future.

I observe what you state with respect to the condition of the public feeling in Virginia, in regard to the next Presidency I ever thought that the line of conduct which the Virginia gentlemen had marked out for that State, that is to take no forward part in the ensuing election, but rather to leave the decision of it to the residue of the Union, was wise and discreet. It would have been thought that Virginia was dictatorial, if after ceasing to furnish a Chief Magistrate, she should have displayed any early and anxious solicitude about the successor of Mr. Monroe. But has Virginia acted in consonance with this avowed purpose? Has not that print, which heretofore has invariably indicated her pleasure, distinctly taken its ground?[1] Has it not been confidently proclaimed and been believed, every where out of Virginia, that her choice was fixed? May not the effect of all this be to jeopardize not only that preference, if it be actually made, but also the election of him who would be her secondary choice?[2]

Virginia may possibly decide the election by bestowing her suffrage on the gentleman refered [*sic*] to, 'though I doubt it extremely. But she certainly *can* decide it by lending her support to him who is said to be her second choice. She will of course, as she ought to determine as she pleases, in such contingencies.

Late information which I have received from Louisiana leaves me *no doubt* that I shall receive the votes of that state whether Genl. Jackson be with drawn or not; and the tendency of all that I have obtained here from the West & South West is to confirm what I have heretofore said to you, that there will be, in the end, no division there. That which I get from New York assures me of the rapid growth of my cause there. And I feel quite confident that I occupy, in one respect, more advantageous ground than either Mr. Crawford or Mr. Adams, that is, that a decision for me by either of three States, from its direct and collateral consequences (if the decision be not defered too long) insures my election, which cannot be affirmed as to either of those gentlemen.

In saying that it is my firm conviction that Mr. Adams is at present the most formidable of those two gentlemen, I pray you to believe that I do not mean (far from it) to indicate any preference for him, nor am I moved, at Mr. Crawfords expence, by the desire of advancing my own interests.

Unless your objections to me are insuperable, or your preference for Mr. Crawford is so strong as to induce you in Virginia to hazard all consequences, it is to me wonderful that you should hesitate or fail to seize the commanding position, in the affairs of this Nation, which evidently presents itself. Connect yourselves to the fortunes of Mr. Crawford and lose his election (which I verily believe is to be the result) and where are you? Connect yourselves with the West, and are you not, whether the election is won or lost, on the 'vantage ground? You see, my dear Sir, that I write you with all the freedom of our antient friendship, which could alone excuse the presentation to you of views which I dare say have often been taken by you.

There is but little news here of any sort. I believe it true that our Government has received from the British Minister some contradiction of the rumored cession of Cuba to England.[3] Congress is much occupied with the business of the Session, now near its close. I shall be yet detained here ten or twelve days by the Supreme Court. I pray you to give my best respects to your associate Judge Green,[4] whose acquaintance I had the pleasure of making last winter, and for whose character I have a high regard.

I am faithf ly & cordially Your friend H. CLAY

The Honble Francis Brooke.

ALS. KyU. Published in part in Colton (ed.), *Private Correspondence of Henry Clay*, 74-75.

1 Thomas Ritchie's Richmond *Enquirer* had moved close to avowed support of Crawford. See above, Kendall to Clay, June 20, 1822; Ambler, *Thomas Ritchie*, 86-91.

2 Clay, himself.

3 See above, Clay to Kendall, February 16, 1823.

4 John W. Green, appointed to the Virginia Court of Appeals to succeed Spencer Roane, remained on the bench until his death in 1834.

To Nicholas Biddle

Sir Washington 27h. Feb. 1823.

I recd. this morning your two letters bearing date the 24h.

instant.[1] I immediately caused an enquiry to be made for Mr. Hunt[2] and regret to have to communicate that he had taken his departure four or five days ago. He had been here it seems several weeks. If fortunately I had received the transcripts a week ago his arrest here might have been effected.

From what you state as having been the understanding with Mr. Marshall,[3] I hope and presume no difficulty will occur in the completion of the arrangement which has been made with him. I expect to reach home early in April. I find that I shall be yet kept here by the Supreme Court eight or ten days. The cause with the State of Ohio[4] has not been yet reached. I have just received a long letter from the Lexington office, respecting the mode of proceeding upon Replevy bonds, which shews how desirable it would have been to have ascertained the opinion of the Supreme Court upon our local laws regulating executions.[5] That, at the present term, not having been found practicable, I shall transmit the best advice I can give in the actual state of things. I retain my purpose of a short visit to Philadelphia. With great respect I have the honor to be Your obedient Servant H. CLAY

Nicholas Biddle Esq. &c &c &c

ALS. ViU. 1 Not found.

2 Probably Jesse Hunt, against whom the Bank of the United States about this time obtained a judgment for collection of a large sum. Hunt, a merchant in Cincinnati since before the turn of the century and one of the founders of the Miami Exporting Company, as district paymaster of the army under General William Henry Harrison during the War of 1812 yet owed the Federal government over $20,000. See below, Benham to Clay, January 30, 1826.

3 John J. Marshall. 4 See above, Clay to Biddle, January 28, 1823.

5 See above, Clay to Hammond, July 14, 1822, note; Clay to Biddle, December 27, 1822.

Receipt from Jacob Burnet

[February 27, 1823]

Allowance for travelling to, and from the city of Washington, 1120 miles—	$448,00
Thirty-seven days attendance at the city of Washington,	$296,00
	$744,00.

WASHINGTON CITY, February 27, 1823. Received of Henry Clay Esq. seven hundred and forty-four dollars, in full of the above account, it being the compensation allowed by the Commonwealth of Kentucky to the commissioners under the convention with Virginia.

J. BURNET.

Ky. H. of Reps., *Journal, 1823-1824*, p. 57. See above, Adair to Clay and Rowan, January 7, 1823.

From Hezekiah Niles

Dr. Sir, Baltimore, Feb 27. 1823.

I have the pleasure to introduce to you my much respected friend, Mr. William S. Cross—he is a very worthy gentleman. He has some little business in Kentucky, about which he desires your advice, which to him will be grateful either in your professional capacity, if it comes within the range of your practice, or as a private gentleman. With great respect Your much obliged & sincere frd H NILES

ALS. DLC-TJC (DNA, M212, R10). Addressed to Clay at Washington. Endorsed on cover by Clay: "Mr. Crowes note to Mr. Cross." Crowe and Cross have not been identified.

From Benjamin Watkins Leigh

My dear sir, Richmond, March 1. 1823.

I enclose you a copy of the resolution, to which our Legislature came at last, on the subject of our convention.[1] It was handed me, for the purpose of being sent to you, by my friend mr Johnson—[2] who desired me to say to you, that if the legislature of Kentucky should think proper to extend the time for the meeting of the board of commissioners, at its next Session, it is possible, and and [*sic*] not improbable, that our Legislature may ratify the convention as it stands, next winter; so that it would be well, that the supreme court should forbear to give judgment on the occupying claimant law question till the term of 1824.[3]

I remain always with sincerest regard, Your friend & obt. Servt.
Henry Clay Esq. B:W:LEIGH

ALS. DLC-TJC (DNA, M212, R10).

1 The resolution outlined the action taken by the two houses of the Virginia legislature on the bill for ratification of the conventions agreed upon by Clay and Leigh (see above, Leigh to Clay, February 12, 1823, note), noting that the Senate had amended the measure "on account of its disapprobation of the contingent provisions," and, accordingly, instructed the Governor of Virginia to inform the Executive of Kentucky of the failure to ratify the documents.

2 Chapman Johnson.

3 Cf. below, Clay to Brooke, March 9, 1823.

From Henry St. George Tucker

My dear Sir Winchester March 1. 1823.

I beg leave to enclose to your attention a letter for our common friend R. C. Anderson,[1] as I am not informed in what manner it should be directed in order to reach him with certainty. Its object is to request his friendly enquiries as to the fate of a young man long since supposed to be no more, who went off to the Patriot army several years ago, and of whom nothing has been heard by his afflicted father until within a few weeks, when his hopes of his son's existence have been revived by the intelligence given by a stranger who passed thro his vicinity.

I have just returned from Richmond after an absence of three months and have the happiness of finding all my family well. My winter has been laboriously, and somewhat anxiously spent. I fear you will think it worse than unprofitably employed during a part of my time. On that subject I have only the consolations afforded by the reflection that I have conscientiously discharged my duty, & have the support of the opinions of many of our wisest and most distinguished men. I have often thought of you during our discussions, and the regrets I have felt at the necessity of rejecting the Convention[2] have arisen only from the conflict of such a measure with your wishes. They were much lessened in the course of the debate, by percieving [*sic*] that your reputation grew in proportion to the disapprobation of the measures of the last session, and the aversion to the arrangements made between yourself and Mr. Leigh: Not that the latter were considered as evincive of any want of ability in our commissioner, to whom we cannot be too thankful for the able exposition of our rights and a Cauti[ous] reservation of a power of rejection, but that the negotiation had at last resulted in the reference of the dispute of Green & Biddle[3] which at first had appeared so hopeless a measure and which your address is supposed to have affected. We were indeed, twelve months ago, most clumsy diplomatists: for we sent to Kentuckey to solicit the passage of laws, which (if passed) would exclude her from a reference & *if not passed,* would give what she desired. This was our great error. We are now placed *"in statu quo"* and I hope that means may yet be found to adjust the warrant claims in a manner satisfactory to the holders, and calculated to relieve the fine country which Kentuckey is desirous of selling, from [. . .][4] dormant claim, the existence of which must embarrass the sale and produce a sacrifice of that valuable part of her national treasure.

I know not whether I ought to have touched upon a subject so interesting to us both, and on which our opinions are so opposite, but I have had the pleasure of knowing you too long to fear that such differences can influence your feelings. I hope to have the gratification of meeting you in Washington next winter, as I shall probably make a flying visit there, being [. . .][5] in any public station. I should however be yet more pleased to see you here on your way to the western Country and wish you would make Winchester a Stage & my house your home. Mrs. T.[6] will be very happy to meet with you

I am my dear Sir with great regard Your friend H:S:G:TUCKER

ALS. DLC-HC (DNA, M212, R1). 1 Richard C. Anderson, Jr.
2 See above, Leigh to Clay, February 12, 1823, note. Tucker had been the foremost speaker in opposition to the Contingent Provisions of the Convention.
3 See above, DuVal to Clay, June 14, 1821, note.
4 One word obscured.
5 MS. torn—one or two words missing.
6 Tucker and Anne Evelina Hunter had been married in 1806.

To Francis T. Brooke

My dear Sir Washington 9h. March 1823.

You will have seen that the Supreme Court has decided against the validity of our occupying claimant laws.[1] The dissatisfaction which will be felt by the people of Kentucky with the decision will be aggravated, in no little degree, by the fact, that the decision is that of three judges to one, a minority therefore of the whole Court, and this aggravation will be further increased by considerations which belong to each of those three judges.[2]

At the moment of some vexation about this unhappy result of a cause, the effects and possible consequences of which fill me with extreme concern, I wrote you my last letter;[3] and I fear that I have expressed myself in it, on some points, in a manner which I ought not to have done even to one whom I have ever regarded as among my best friends. I must pray you therefore to commit it to the flames, and its contents to oblivion.

Since that letter & within a few days past I have received a letter from Genl. Peter B. Porter, under date at Albany,[4] where he has been attending the Legislature of New York during the greater part of its present Session. He says that there will be probably no expression of public opinion by the Legislature, during the present Session; but he adds that "there is scarcely a doubt if there were a vote at the present Session, you would get a majority of the whole." All accounts from that State concur in representing a great and obvious progress in the public sentiment in my favor—

I have recently received information also from Louisiana that there is the greatest unanimity there, among the French and American population, in their determination to support me.

I shall leave this place in a few days for Kentucky by the way of Philadelphia, and I shall be glad to have the pleasure of hearing from you when I reach home. I am faith ly & cordially Your friend

The Honble Francis Brooke. H. CLAY

ALS. KyU. Published in part in Colton (ed.), *Private Correspondence of Henry Clay*, 75.

1 Rendering its decision upon the arguments in the case of Green *vs.* Biddle as presented during the preceding term (see above, Clay and Bibb to the Kentucky General Assembly, *ca.* May 13, 1822, note), the Court on February 27 had again held the Kentucky acts of 1797 and 1812 unconstitutional. 21 *U.S.* (8 Wheaton) 107-108. A petition for a reconsideration of the case, drawn by John Rowan and Clay

immediately after the Court ruling, was denied. For the petition see Ky. H. of Reps., *Journal, 1823-1824*, pp. 60-83; *House Docs.*, 18 Cong., 1 Sess., no. 69, pp. 3, 29-49.

2 The three judges supporting the decision were: Bushrod Washington, who wrote the opinion; Joseph Story; and Gabriel Duval. John Marshall and Thomas Todd abstained. Brockholst Livingston was ill and absent. William Johnson opposed the ruling. On March 17, before leaving Washington, Clay called on John Quincy Adams, who recorded that his visitor "Wants a special Supreme Court U.S. to try the Kentucky cause over again; thinks all the present Judges but one superannuated. Salvo for the Chief Justice." *Memoirs,* VI, 138.

Kentucky's dissatisfaction at the limited participation in the decision on this case was expressed in the State legislature's adoption of a series of resolutions condemning the Green-Biddle decision and calling for remedial action in Congress "either by passing a law requiring, when any question shall come before that tribunal, involving the validity of a law of any of the states, that a concurrence of at least *two-thirds* of all the judges, shall be necessary to its vacation; or increasing the number of the judges, and thereby multiplying the chances of the states, to escape the like calamities, and of this state to escape from its present thraldom, by exacting the exercise of more deliberation, and an increased volume of intellect, upon all such questions." Ky. Gen. Assy., *Acts, 1823-1824,* pp. 488-516, 520-27 (quotation, p. 527).

3 No letter since the philosophical statement of February 26 has been found.

4 Not found.

To Thomas Wilson

Sir Washington 11h. March 1823.

I inclose a check drawn by R. W. Meade Esq. in my favor for Two hundred and fifty dollars, which you will be pleased to pass to my credit.[1] I am Your ob. Servt. H. CLAY

Thomas Wilson Esq.

ALS. PPL-R. Endorsed: "$250 Cr. March 14, 23."

1 At the Philadelphia office, Bank of the United States.

From Hugh Mercer

My dear Sir, Fredericksbg March 11th. 1823

In my last[1] I informed you, that a letter which I expected from Mr Walker at Philada. would decide whether I would be willing to go into the friendly Suit in Chancery for Peart's[2] estate— That letter is just received—it is inclosed, that you may see the Ground he takes, to which we cannot object; & of course we will expect you to bring the Suit immey, & have it decided if possible, at the May term of the Fed—Court— Your fee of 100$ will be paid you, but for this I must beg you to wait, as my funds are exhausted very much, by my having to pay all the expences heretofore in this Suit, & by the disappointment I have met with from Genl Taylor,[3] in my private Business with him— Before I make further advances, I must collect what is now due, & your fee of 100$ will not be forgotten— I hope it will be attended with no inconvenience to you to wind up the Business for us as proposed, your fees in the former Trial,[4] of 600$ having been paid— Mr Walker has made Judge Marshall[5] Say, what he has never said—for he has communicated with no one but myself; & in his letters to me, was very guarded & concise, in his reasons for declining to arbitrate the Business for us— I allude to where Mr. W— says as you will see—"adding," meaning the chief Justice, "that the Will was doubtful also, whether the property should go to the Children or Grandchildren"[6]— Judge Marshall never gave any such opinion or made such a declaration—directly or indirectly—& I will let Mr W— know immey in my ansr— to his letter, which I inclose, that he is mistaken on this point—

It is of little or no Moment however, except that such an opinion, if it had been really expressed by him, & were known, *might have* some influence in the Decision of the friendly Suit now proposed— The Court will of course give I suppose, the same opinion *judicially* in the friendly Suit in Chany, which they gave *extrajudicially,* in the trial before the Jury on the action of Ejectment— viz— that the Children of C. & J.T. Griffin, to the exclusion of the Grandchildren, were entitled to the property— This is the Question we want settled, & one equally important *to me,* how the expences of the Suit are to be paid in what proportions by the parties—the property being bound by the Decision of the Court, for the payment of those expences— In this way, & this only, shall I ever receive a Dollar from Walker, as he is a Bankrupt— The Children of Cyrus Griffin are John Griffin, Mary Griffin wife of Thomas Griffin[7] her Cousin, Louisa Mercer—my wife & Saml S. Griffin[8]— Those of John T. Griffin, are Maria Walker & Thomas Lightfoot Griffin, her brother, lately deceased— Walker's children, I know not how many, but 6 or 8 I believe, were all born in England— the Names of the grandchildren of C. Griffin, I could ascertain if absolutely necessary—but I shall trust they will not be wanted, as it would give much trouble &c to get them

Walker, while he & his friend Mr Wickliffe,[9] of whom I know nothing, not even from report as to his character, will contend for the rights of the grandchildren, does not seem to be aware that his Children's rights would escheat to the commonwealth of Keny[10]—tho' he calculates, I know, that in such an event, the Legislature of Keny would listen to a Memorial or petition from him, to give up the State's right in favor of his Children—all this Mr Wick— may have induced him to believe, would necessarily follow— Walker & Wick— have had long correspondencies [*sic*] on this Subjt, & the latter knowing the former's poverty, & his high expectations from this estate, has given Walker reasons to think, that he is entitled to more than the Court will sustain him in, I am sure— Walker's conduct thro' out has been extremely obstinate, shewing no disposition to do right—except *now* as to the friendly Suit, & the signing the inclosed agreements, when we supposed Judge Marshall would have no difficulty in arbitrating the Business for us— I had difficulty in geting him to sign those agreements, particularly that relating to the expences—but he found that my course with him was immoveably determined, & he at length complied— He denied for some time his liability to pay any part of the expences of the Suit, which secured to us this property, upon the most ridiculous & flimsy pretexts, whilst at the same time he & Mr Wick— were laying their Heads together, to grasp as much of the property as possible— His course shewed such a want of principle, that I was completely disgusted with him, & had determined at one time to have nothing more to do with him, & told him so in my letters—but he knows he can do nothing without my co-operation, & has been urging me in the most pressing terms, to go on in aiding him to bring the business to a close— My interest now requires that I should do so—

As Walker's letter speaks freely of Mr Haggin,[11] you will please consider it, as entirely confidential as this of mine to you will be— Haggin's course has certainly been, & is, inexplicable— after receiving 600$ from me in our Suit, he turns about & brings another Suit, in Scott Co, for one parson Elliott[12]— professionally, this is no derogation from his Character but taking all the circumstances into view, there is something which looks very much, as tho' there was some—Collusion between him & the parson— Knowing as you do all the parties in Keny, I need say nothing more to put you on your guard— You will have to contend with Mr Wickliffe I presume, as the Counsel of Walker— I shall write him (Wal) — immey & let him know that you are employed for us, that he may proceed in any way he pleases— If the receivg your fee of 100$ should be necessary, when the Suit is brought, will you endeavour to *squeeze* it out of Jas Taylor, & if you receive it from him, you can apprise me— You know, I suppose, that Haggin purchased out long since the interests of those in Keny to 1/4 of the estate, & that he resides on it, &c— He is writing me, proposing to buy, & offering in part beef Cattle & horses— I am reserved with him, as I know his character, from those well acquainted with him— Wishing you a safe return to your family & friends, I am yrs, Dear Sir, very truly, H. MERCER

P.S. Majr. Wm. Taylor of Floyd's fork, Shelby County, Keny, will manage for us any Agency which may be necessary in this business— He is a most worthy, correct Man, & every confidence may be placed in his steady & faithful attention to any business committed to him— I never saw him, but his Character is fully shewn, from the many letters I have received from him, on business in Keny, which he has there to manage for me, as Executor of my brother—[13] H. M.

The Letter of Walker—inclosed I have supposed would be important & useful to you, which you can *read* to Mr. Wickliffe, if he is employed by Walker, & it is in any wise necessary— This & the other papers inclosed you will please carefully preserve, in the event of there being necessary or useful hereafter—but this is not probable, as the friendly Suit in Chany will I trust settle the whole business, fully & clearly, forever—as I am almost worn out, & broken down with it— H. M.

ALS. DLC-TJC (DNA, M212, R12). Addressed to Clay at Washington. Mercer, of Fredericksburg, Virginia, was the youngest son of the Virginia Revolutionary War general, Hugh Mercer, for whom Mercer County, Kentucky, was named.

1 Not found.

2 Francis Peart, of Woodford County, Kentucky, who had died in 1815, without issue. In March, 1826, Chief Justice John Marshall delivered the opinion of the United States Supreme Court, on appeal from error in the Circuit Court for the District of Kentucky, in the case of Martin Walker and Wife *vs.* Cyrus Griffin's Heirs, a friendly suit for division of the property among Peart's heirs. The decision of the lower court was reversed in so far as it directed distribution among the children of Cyrus and John T. Griffin *per capita* and not *per stirpes.* The Supreme Court also provided for apportioning costs of the case in like proportion—the heirs of Cyrus Griffin to be chargeable with one half of the expenses and Walker and his wife, Maria, as the heirs of John T. Griffin, chargeable with the other half. 24 *U. S.* (11 Wheaton) 375-80.

Cyrus Griffin, born in Virginia and educated in the law in Great Britain, had been several times a member of the State legislature, member of the Continental Congress (1778-1781, 1787, 1788), president of the Congress in 1788, judge of the "Court of Appeals in Cases of Capture" (1780-1787), and judge of the United States Court for the District of Virginia from 1789 to his death in 1810. John Tayloe Griffin was his brother.

3 James Taylor. See below, Mercer to Clay, April 1, 1823.

4 The earlier suit had been instituted on October 6, 1817, on a declaration of trespass and ejectment brought by a tenant of Francis Peart's devisees against Thomas Guthrie and others, residents of Woodford County, Kentucky. At the November Term, 1821, of the Federal Circuit Court, a jury had found the defendants guilty and awarded the plaintiff the remainder of his term of lease. U. S. Circuit Court, Seventh Circuit, District of Kentucky, Complete Records, Q, 276-81.

5 John Marshall.

6 Peart had provided that, as a contingent grant, one fourth of his property was to be given to various devisees; "the balance to be given to the families of Cyrus and John T. Griffins children, in equal proportion."

7 Yorktown, Virginia, lawyer and judge. He was a member of the State legislature (1793-1800, 1819-1823, 1827-1830) and of the United States Congress (1803-1805) and had been an officer in the War of 1812.

8 A physician of Yorktown.

9 Robert Wickliffe.

10 Cf. above, I, 213n. The Kentucky Court of Appeals had ruled, in Hunt and Others *vs.* Warnicke's Heirs (1806), that aliens could not inherit lands in the State. 3 *Ky. Reports* (Hardin) 66-67.

11 James Haggin, who had acted with Clay in presenting the plaintiff's amended declaration in the suit, Doe Dem: Peart's Devisees *vs.* Guthrie and Others, above n.4.

12 Suit not found, apparently involving the Reverend James Elliott, of Woodford County, Kentucky, the second husband of Sarah Griffin Peart, sister of Francis Peart. Cf. the suits Doe Dem: Peirsol and Others *vs.* Elliotts and Others, instituted in the Federal Circuit Court, May 31, 1823, and James Elliott, the Younger, and Others *vs.* The Lessee of William Peirsol and Others, decided in the United States Supreme Court in 1828, relating to the claims of the heirs of Mrs. Elliott to a tract of 1200 acres overlapping Woodford, Scott, and Franklin counties. U.S. Circuit Court, Seventh Circuit, District of Kentucky, Complete Records, Z, 18-24; 26 *U. S.* (1 Peters) 328-42.

13 In addition to other bequests, General Hugh Mercer (who had died in 1777) had left to his son, John, 3,000 acres of land about seventeen miles above the Falls of the Ohio, in Jefferson County, Kentucky. John, in turn, by a will recorded in Spotsylvania County, Virginia, in 1817, had devised this tract to his brother, Hugh, and also made him executor of the estate. Katharine G. Healy (comp.), "Calendar of Early Jefferson County, Kentucky, Wills. . . ," *Filson Club History Quarterly,* VI (1932), 172.

William Taylor, the Kentucky merchant, brother of Edmund and Francis, and an uncle of Hubbard and James (of Newport), had himself held a location of 500 acres adjoining Hugh Mercer.

Agreement with Caleb Kirk and Samuel Rutter

Caleb Kirk et alia Plantiffs [*sic*] in Error [March 14, 1823]
Vs
Richard Smith lessee of John Penn Defendants[1]

I have agreed (as Counsel for the Plantiffs in Error) to prosecute the above suit to its final Issue in the Supreme Court of the United States; and to render my best services in the case, on the following Conditions (to wit) the sum of one hundred and twenty five dollars to be paid to me before the commencement; and the further sum of one hundred and twenty five dollars to be paid to me immediately after the argument is over: And in case the Judgment of the Circuit Court shall be reversed by the Supreme Court in such manner as that the Plantiffs in Error shall hold the lands in controversy, then and in that case, they are to pay me the further sum of two hundred and fifty dollars, within ninety days after such decision of the Supreme Court.

February 1823 the first above mentioned sum of one hundred and twenty five dollars was paid to Henry Clay Esqr. and in March 1823 the second above mentioned sum of one hundred and twenty five dollars was paid to Henry Clay Esqr. and the third above mentioned sum of two hundred and fifty remains to be paid to him according to the tenour [*sic*] of the above agreement. Witness our hands this 14th day of march 1823 CALEB KIRK

SAMUEL RUTTER

DS. DLC-TJC (DNA, M212, R15). Kirk and Rutter were probably residents of York County, Pennsylvania.

1 This case, on appeal to the United States Supreme Court from a decision of the Circuit Court of Pennsylvania, involved land in York County, Pennsylvania. The claim of Kirk and others stemmed from a survey made in 1747, for which title and possession had passed to the claimants. No grant had ever issued for the land, however, and there was no proof of payment of the full purchase price. The matter was further complicated by the Pennsylvania Statute of Limitations of 1705 and by legislation, enacted during the Revolutionary War, which vested estates of the proprietaries in the Commonwealth. An ejectment had been brought in 1819, and the Circuit Court, holding that these legislative acts were not applicable, had found for the plaintiff. The defendants in the lower court had thereupon appealed. On February 15, 1824, Chief Justice Marshall delivered an opinion affirming the judgment of the Circuit Court. 22 *U.S.* (9 Wheaton) 241-325.

John Penn (1760-1834), a grandson of William Penn, had succeeded to a share of the proprietorship of Pennsylvania, "with hereditary governorship," in 1775. Following the close of the Revolution he had lived for several years in the United States while looking after his property.

To Charles Jules de Menou

Washington ce 17 [*sic*][1] mars 1823

Légation de France aux Etats Unis

M. Clay présente ses compliments à M. le Comte de Menou. Il a reçu les certificats, envoyés par M. le Comte le 15, qui prouvent l'authenticité de l'appel du Cape. Edon interjetté à la Cour Suprème dans l'affaire de l'Apollon.[2] Muni de ces pièces M. Clay a obtenu l'ordre, samedi dernier, de faire enrégistrer l'appel du Cape. Edon. Il est enrégistré de manière à être Jugé en tems convenable. M. Clay regrette que les désirs que M. le Comte de Menou a si souvent et si vivement exprimés, d'obtenir le Jugement de l'appel dans le cours de la session qui vient d'expirer, n'aient pas pu se réaliser—

Copy (translation). DLC-Charles Jules, Comte de Menou Papers. The Count de Menou, Secretary of Legation of France in the United States, 1822-1830, had assumed the duties of Chargé d'Affaires upon De Neuville's departure from the country in the summer of 1822 as a protest to recognition of Colombian independence by the United States (see above, Shaw to Clay, April 4, 1822, note).

1 Possibly an error for 16. See below, De Menou to Clay, March 17, 1823.

2 The *Apollon*, a French merchant vessel bound for Charleston, South Carolina, in the spring of 1820, had avoided that port after the enactment of retaliatory legislation against France (see above, II, 846n) and had gone instead to Amelia Island. After paying Spanish duties and selling a part of his cargo, Captain Edon, the master of the vessel, early in September had removed his craft up Belle River to St. Joseph's, where the Spanish authorities were planning to establish a new port of entry near the United States boundary. Later in the month Archibald Clark, the Collector of Saint Mary's, an official of the United States, had seized the vessel and its cargo on the ground that their presence at that spot was for the purpose of evading American law and carrying on an illicit trade across the border.

An admiralty case, brought by the United States Attorney in the District Court of Georgia, to subject the cargo to forfeiture and the ship to payment of tonnage duty, had resulted, however, in a defeat for the Government, with an order for restitution of the ship and cargo. An appeal was initiated by the United States but was abandoned.

Meanwhile, a libel for damages against Clark, instituted in the District Court, had resulted in a decree for the plaintiff. The Circuit Court, on appeal, had confirmed this decree and added 33⅓ per cent to the demurrage allowed by the lower court. Not yet satisfied, the master of the vessel had then appealed to the United States Supreme Court and employed Clay as one of the lawyers to present the case. The cause was argued in March, 1824, whereupon the Court decreed a reversal in part of the decision of the Circuit Court (deducting $602.31 for two items which had been allowed the appellants) and ordered that the remainder ($8,093.06), plus interest at six per cent per annum on this sum from the date of the decree in the Circuit Court, be paid the appellant. 22 *U.S.* (9 Wheaton) 362-80.

To [Josephus B.] Stuart

Dr Sir Washington 17h. March 1823.

I received this day your obliging favor, under date the 7h. instant at James Ville;[1] and I am greatly indebted to you for the very interesting and important information which it communicates, and which is corroborated by that which I have received through the unsolicited favor of other friends. My intelligence from many other quarters is highly flattering; from none is it at all discouraging.

After you left the Judge[2] and myself, he became extremely ill, and suffered most excrutiating pain. He was confined several weeks on his first arrival at this place; and took his departure for Cincinnati near three weeks ago. The object of his journey here was entirely defeated by the refusal of Virginia to ratify the convention which her commissioner had negotiated with Kentucky.[3]

War it seems is again lighted up in Europe. France applies the torch to Spain;[4] and if Spain does not at once succumb (and her priests and her dissentions make me tremble for her) there is I think but little doubt that the flames will spread in every direction. With great regard I am Your ob. Servt. H. CLAY

Dr. Stuart.

ALS. NcD. Stuart, a physician of Albany, New York, had served as a surgeon in the War of 1812.

1 Onondaga County, New York. The letter has not been found.

2 Jacob Burnet. 3 See above, Leigh to Clay, February 12, March 1, 1823.

4 See above, Lafayette to Clay, November 5, 1822, note.

From Charles Jules de Menou

March 17th. 1823—

Mr. de Menou has the honor of presenting his respects to Mr Clay & while acknowledging his polite note of yesterday[1] begs leave to thank him for his attention to the affair of Apollon which he regrets was not tried this term: he hopes mr. Clay will have the goodness to give it his Continued Support next year.

Should Mr Clay have no further use at present for the different papers relating to this business & think fit to Send them to Mr de M. he would Keep them in readiness to be returned to Mr Clay on his return to Washington.

AN. DLC-HC (DNA, M212, R1). Published in Colton (ed.), *Private Correspondence of Henry Clay*, 75-76. Addressed: "The Honble. H. Clay, at Mrs. Clarkes F. Street," where Mrs. Eliza Clark kept a Washington, D. C., boarding house.

1 See above, Clay to de Menou, March 17, 1823.

From Hugh Mercer

Dear Sir, Fredericksbg March 17th. 1823

Your favor of the 14th.[1] is just received— I am satisfied that Walker is very much in earnest in co-operating in the friendly Suit, & will doubtless instruct his counsel, Mr Wickliffe, accordingly—

You will see by the agreements sent you, which have been regularly executed, the importance I attach to the expences— It having been fully understood & agreed upon by us, that Judge Marshall should decide how & in what proportions the expences should be paid by the parties who take the property; & the Judge having declined to act, the same principle will be fully embraced, we wish, by the Court—*making the property* at *the same Time liable for these expences*— Walker being worth nothing, it is in this way only, that I shall ever get a Dollar from him— We must have the Judgment of the Court in this Way, & I must beg you to have this particularly attended to— I am not willing to depend upon what

Mr Walker might be disposed to do privately, if he had the power or discretion to act as he pleased; & it will be best for us all, that we should be equally *bound* by the decree of the Court, to render to each other strict Justice— This decree I shall confidently rely, will be in accordance with the extrajudicial opinion given by the Ct formerly—viz—"that the property should go to the Children of C. & J. T. G., to the exclusion of the Grandchildren—" & in this expectation I feel as a friend of Mrs Walker, who I wish to see fully participating in the property, agreeably to Her just rights— I have, I believe, nearly as many Children as Walker— but it seems to me, that if the decree should give the property in this Way, that Mr W— would have difficulties & new perplexities to encounter, of which he seems not to be apprised— He will no doubt write Mr Wickliffe immey,[2] as I will apprise him of your being engaged to bring the friendly Suit, about which he has been of late so solicitous—

I am Dr Sir, Yr friend & Ob St, HUGH MERCER

To shew you that I am acting in a disinterested way— I have 5 Children— Walker I know not how many, but I believe 6 or 7— Majr. Griffin[3] 2, Dr Griffin[4] 3, & Judge Griffin[5] at Detroit none, as he is a Bachelor— H. M.

NB—With respect to the expences, those incured [*sic*] already, as well as such as *may hereafter be incured,* you will please have embraced in the Decree— In much haste— H. M.

ALS. DLC-TJC (DNA, M212, R12). Addressed to Clay at Washington, with a note directing that it be forwarded if Clay had left that city. Cf. above, Mercer to Clay, March 11, 1823.

1 Not found. 2 Immediately. 3 Thomas Griffin. 4 Samuel S. Griffin. 5 John Griffin.

To Charles Jules de Menou

18 mars [1823]

M. Clay a reçu la note que M. le Comte de Menou lui a fait l'honneur de lui adresser hier.[1] Conformément à sa demande, M. Clay renvoie à M. le Comte les papiers qu'il avait reçus de lui relativemen[t] à l'affaire de l'Apollon. Les deux copies destinées à être remises à la Cour ont été rendue du greffier. M. Clay espère que rien ne se présentera qui puisse l'empêcher de consacrer tous ses soins à terminer entièrement ce procès dans la prochaine session de la Cour Suprème—Il sent vivement l'outrage fait au pavillon Français (quoique ce soit sans la participation du gouvernement) et les dommages causés à la propriété de l'armateur de l'Apollon—

Copy (translation). DLC-Charles Jules, Comte de Menou Papers.

1 See above, Clay to De Menou, March 17, 1823.

To Peter B. Porter

My dear General Washington 18 March 1823.

I ought before to have acknowledged the receipt of your kind favor of the 24th. Ulto.[1] which I have taken the liberty to shew to a few friends with the view of animating and encouraging them, I hope without your disapprobation. I shall leave this place, where I have been detained by the Supreme Court, for Philadelphia in a few days. I shall not remain there more than a week; possibly I may go to New York upon an affair of business.[2] I shall be greatly obliged by a letter from you, addressed to me in Kentucky, giving such information as you may think it interesting to me to know, written at your perfect leisure, and after a full view of the whole ground. I shall return with a full persuasion that, unless my friends are greatly deceived, my prospects are superior to those of any of the other gentlemen. Information from all quarters justifies this encouraging conclusion. By the bye, Mr. Van Buren is understood to have left here with a pretty explicit commitment to the Secretary of the Treasury.[3] Has he any object of personal ambition to gratify at present? Does he wish to supplant or to succeed Mr. Tompkins?[4] I have heard such an intimation. Hear what you may, rely upon it that the nine Western & South Western States will unanimously, in the end, render me their support; and I am much deceived if unequivocal demonstrations to that effect are not given in the course of the year.

Judge Livingston[5] expired to day. He has been ill ill [*sic*] some time. Speculation is already actively engaged in the designation of his successor. The Secretary of the Navy[6] is spoken of.

Be pleased to offer my best respects to Mrs. Porter and believe me

Faithf ly Your friend H. CLAY

Genl. P. B. Porter.

P.S. I shall inclose this letter to the P.M. at Albany,[7] to be forwarded to you, if you shall have left that City. H C.

ALS. NBuHi. 1 Not found.
2 Cf. below, Astor to Clay, March 26, 1823. 3 William H. Crawford.
4 The Vice President, Daniel D. Tompkins.
5 Brockholst Livingston. Cf. above, Clay to Brooke, March 9, 1823, note.
6 Smith Thompson, who was appointed, during the recess of the Senate, as Livingston's successor. His nomination was approved December 9, 1823.
7 Solomon Van Rensselaer, Postmaster, 1822-1839 and 1841-1843.

To Solomon Van Rensselaer

Dear General, Washington March 18, 1823.

I take the liberty of inclosing to your care a letter for Gen. Porter,[1] not knowing whether he may not have left Albany, in which case I pray you to have the goodness to give it the proper destination to reach him.

I seize the occasion to assure you of my continued esteem and regard for you, and to say that I have derived great pleasure from learning that your friendly sentiments towards me, inspired during our mutual service in the H. of R. remain unabated.

Be pleased to say to the Patroon[2] that I hope he found on his arrival at home, every thing as he would have it.

I am faithfy & Cordially yr. ob. Servt. H. CLAY.

Gen. Solomon Van Rensselaer P. M. Albany, New York.

Catharina V. R. Bonney (comp.), *A Legacy of Historical Gleanings* (2 vols.; Albany, N. Y., 1875), I, 405.

[1] See above, this date.

[2] Stephen Van Rensselaer.

Account with Bank of the United States

[March 25, 1823]

Dr. Henry Clay in a/ct. with Bank U. States Cr.

Dr.					Cr.			
1822					1822			
Jany	4	1	Check	$ 1.300.	Jany	1	Balance brot. forwd.	$ 2.000.
Mch	5	1	"	645.				
April	19	1	"	54 40	July	8	Cash by B.U.S.	1.500.
July	9	1	"	1.400.	Augt.	9	"	4.280.
Septr.	24	2	"	1.000.	1823			
	28	2	"	320.	Jany	10	" "	1.500.
Octr.	8	1	"	500.	Feby	8	by Note	500.
	12	1	"	500.		14[1]	"	250.
	14	1	"	700.				
	30	1	"	400.				
Decr.	2	1	"	460.				
1823								
Jany	10	1	"	1.500.				
Mch	25		Balance	1 250 60				10.030.
				10.030.	Mch 1823	25	By Balance	1.250 60

D. DLC-TJC (DNA, M212, R15).

[1] Should be March 14. Cf. above, Clay to Wilson, March 11, 1823.

From John Jacob Astor

My Dear Sir New Yorke [*sic*] 26 March 1823

I have this moment your letter of 25 It[1] In which I am glad to See that your prospect is So good. what I wish to Say to you Was Chiefly about mr Gallatin[2] who you think can Do nothing in this State he has Some Influancs—& if he coms out to the U S. he will not use it to your Intrest. better if he remain in frances [*sic*] of this Mr Adams must also be Sensible— I Should be very hapey [*sic*] to See you here[3] & if you could com & Remain Some Weeks it might be usefull that You Should com but for a few Days only my opinion is that you had better not com because it will be Sayd. that you came for Some other purpose—in which you can Do no good unless you can Spend Some time— I hope you will excuse my giving you opinion unaskd for it pourd from nothing but good wishes—on which you can rely— about the Buissness between us that can be arrangd without your coming here however if you can I hope it will be soon & that you will let me know as soon as you can & the Day on which you will be here—& tell me if you wish to See any person particularly that I may Invite them to meet you at my house— I am Dear Sir very Resptfuly [*sic*] Your Obed Servt.

Honle Henry Clay J.J.ASTOR

P S. Letters from Spain Recd here to a [. . .][4] Discouraging of the Spanish cause[5]

ALS. DLC-HC (DNA, M212, R1). 1 Not found. 2 Albert Gallatin.
3 See above, Clay to Porter, March 18, 1823.
4 MS. faded—two words missing.
5 See above, Lafayette to Clay, November 5, 1822, note.

Toasts and Speech at Public Dinner

[March 29, 1823]

12. Our Distinguished Guest, HENRY CLAY. {Twelve cheers}

Mr. CLAY rose to return thanks to the meeting. He should feel, he said, that he was perfectly inexcusable to the state of which he was an humble and unworthy citizen, if he did not, even at the hazard of trespassing on their own precious usages, publicly make his most respectful acknowledgments for the distinguished notice which they had taken of it, in one of the toasts recently drank,[1] and in his own person. As for himself, if he were made of stone, he could not be insensible to the very flattering circumstances in which he found himself; to the unexpected and unmerited but highly distinguished honor which they had been pleased to confer upon him. For them all, he could offer only his sincerest thanks, and the assurance of a lasting and grateful recollection. Whilst I am up, continued Mr. CLAY, with your permission, I will take the liberty of proposing a sentiment, on which I am quite sure all American hearts will be cordially united. It will be an allusion to a subject on which you have just expressed the most lively and enthusiastic interest.[2] I might indeed, without going beyond the Atlantic, derive a fit topic, to present to your consideration, from the established and notorious patriotism of the State of Pennsylvania; from this city, its well known science, its flourishing literary institutions, its munificent patronage of the arts, its rich commerce, its rising and interesting manufactures. But, in the selection of that which I mean to submit to you, I feel perfectly persuaded that I shall find a full justification in your magnanimous sympathies and your generous philanthropy. More than ten years past have the people of the United States felt and manifested the deepest interest in the success of the struggles of Spanish America, throughout all its fortunes and vicissitudes. These honorable feelings were excited by their abhorrence of a foreign domination, by their love of liberty, and by their high and just estimate of the inestimable privilege of self-government. The encouraging progress of that great cause is such as to lead irresistibly to the speedy consummation of the independence of all of the Spanish provinces. It is a most remarkable dispensation of Providence that Spain herself is now called upon to maintain, on her own fair fields, the very principles which she combatted on the crimsoned plains of Venezuela; and to sustain in her own behalf, against a presumptuous foreign dictation, that right of self-government which she would have denied to her provinces.[3] The same principles which interested our wishes and hopes, on the side of the colonies, must now urge us to cherish a solicitude for the success of the parent country. And how has the Spanish government brought down upon the devoted peninsula the vengeance of France? Has it menaced France with invasion? Has it sought to propagate in the bosom of France free principles, to disturb there the quiet rule of the Bourbons? Has it set up new and alarming principles in the international law? Has it aimed to aggrandize Spain at the expence of her neighbors? No! No! No! What, then, is the offence of Spain? Her institutions wanted reformation; a shocking mass of abuses had been accumulated, during the lapse of ages; she was swimming in corruption. Sensible of the disadvantages of her political condition, she has sought to correct them; to purify her government and adapt it to the great object of social happiness.— Her revolution has been characterised by no excesses, sullied by no atrocities, stained by no blood, except that which has been shed at the instigation or with the countenance of foreign powers. She has moved on slow and measured and dignified, with a mildness like that of the bright sun of her delightful climate. And France comes to check her in her noble and patriotic career. And for what purposes, and with what principles? She breaks the unthreatened peace, that she may not have war! She would have peace! She appeals to arms that she may restore the absolute sway of the monarch, and, I suppose, all the blessings of the inquisition! The Bourbons of France, the modern

Stuarts, enter Spain, sword in hand, with the principles of the divine right of kings, and of the non-resistance and passive obedience of the people, as their motto; principles which our British ancestors, a century and a half ago, successfully combatted, and which lost to one of the Stuarts his head, and to the whole race the three kingdoms. With what little benefit does history hold up to these Bourbons its instructive examples? One pleasing effect upon the people of this country with regard to this war will be, that, unlike the late wars of Europe, it will create no divisions of opinion among us. In spite of all our partiality to France; in spite of all the grateful recollections with which her name is associated; in spite of our sincere desire to maintain with her, especially, the most amicable relations, there will be here but one feeling and one hope as to the issue of this wanton and unprovoked contest. We shall, in regard to it, be "all federalists—all republicans;" all Spanish—none, no, not one, French. We may be disappointed in our ardent wishes. Spain, torn by her unhappy dissentions, may be overwhelmed. The scene at Naples may be re-exhibited in the Peninsula.[4] And I confess, when I contemplate the appalling power which is about to be exerted to subdue her, that I tremble for the event. We may be destined to behold the afflicting spectacle of the extinction of the light of liberty in the land of Homer and Leonidas,[5] and in the adopted country of Columbus; and all Europe may be encircled in the thick and dark mantle of inexorable despotism. Whatever may be the issue, we shall, at least, have the consolation of cherishing our own principles, and of giving all that is consistent with our posture and our institutions to communicate—our fervent prayers and our best wishes for every people, wherever situated, whether in the old or new world, who are struggling to establish and preserve their liberties. And, in all the changes of human affairs, let us cling, with a closer and fonder embrace, to our own excellent governments, and be thankful to the kindness of Providence for having removed us far from the power and influence of a confederacy of kings, united to fasten forever the chains of the people, and for having given us the blessing of a confederacy of free states, united to secure the liberty and to promote the welfare and happiness of millions of freemen. But I have already detained you too long from the sentiment which I would propose, and which, though already drank, will bear repeating again and again. It is—

"Success to the cause of the Country under whose auspices the New World was discovered."

Washington *Daily National Intelligencer,* April 8, 1823. Published also in *Niles' Weekly Register,* XXIV (April 12, 1823), 94-95; Lexington *Kentucky Reporter,* April 21, 1823. The dinner was held at the Western Hotel, Philadelphia, Pennsylvania, with from 80 to 90 guests in attendance.

1 "4. The state of Kentucky. [Three cheers.]"
2 "9. The illustrious Patriots of Greece and Spain—Engaged in a glorious struggle for the imprescriptible rights of human nature, may Heaven crown their efforts with success. [Nine cheers.]"
3 See above, Lafayette to Clay, November 5, 1822, note.
4 See above, Toast and Response, May 19, 1821, note.
5 See above, Cox to Clay, June 5, 1821, note; Lafayette to Clay, November 5, 1822.

To Caesar A. Rodney

My dear Sir Philada. Sunday 30 Mar. 1823.

I was extremely mortified, when I had, at length, found out your abode in this City and called there to day to see you, to learn that you had left it yesterday, and regretted more that you left it indisposed. I spent at least an hour and a half the day before yesterday in quest of you, but could not find the house at which you stopt, owing to your imperfect direction, or my ignorance of the locale of the place. I wished much to have seen you; but as I have not had that gratification, I beg you to allow me to assure you, on paper, as I do most sincerely, that you have my best wishes for your success in your mission[1] and for your prosperity in all respects.

The Honble C. A. Rodney. I am faithfy Your's H. CLAY

P.S. I do not know whether the hand writing of yourself or Bonaparte is most illegible. I understood the direction in your note for example, to be Mrs. Chamberlane South street, and away I went there without success. Whereas it seems you meant South 4 corner of Arch. H.C.

ALS. DLC-Rodney Family Papers (DNA, M212, R22). Directed to Wilmington, Delaware.
1 See above, Johnson to Clay, December 10, 1822.

Receipt from Joshua Humphreys

LEXINGTON, Ky. Apl. 1st 1823—

Joshua Humphreys, as Treasurer of Transylvania University acknowledges payment by Henry Clay of $15.00 for tuition (of Henry Clay, Jr.). DS. DLC-TJC (DNA, M212, R15).

From Hugh Mercer

My dear Sir, Fredericksbg April 1st—1823—

A Day or two ago I received a long letter from Genl Taylor,[1] dated the 3d. Ulto. in reply to mine of the 18th. Novr. last—

The Genl apologizes for his long silence, & says it has been owing to much & necessary absence from Home— "You ask me," he says, "how the suit progresses for the land you sold me— The Compts.

have not had a Survey executed as yet, but if they do not proceed I shall endeavour to have one executed, so as to progress with the Business so as to have it ready if possible by the July term, as Mr Clay informs me he would attend & argue it— There is considerable trouble in giving notices as the Heirs of Kennedy & Beale[2] are much scattered, but you may be assured I shall do all in my power to defeat them— To make out the report & lay down the different claims will take much time & expence, as they are numerous— I got Mr Clay to converse with one of our Counsel (meaning Route[3] I suppose) as to the management of the cause, & I requested him to govern himself entirely by Mr Clay's advice— I want Mr Route to be present when the Survey is made as he is a practical Surveyor, & I mean to attend myself"—

Thus it would seem, that Genl T— is very much in earnest about supporting our rights to this land, & with your aid, every thing I will trust, will terminate favorably for us—

A late letter from Mr Walker of Philada. on our interests in Peart's estate,[4] says "&c, & I have accordingly written to Mr Wickliffe urging him by all means to cooperate with Mr Clay that our Business may be finally settled—& have particularly stated, that it is our wish to act upon the principle already extra judicially expressed by the court in the former Suit— & I have also requested that he would use his endeavours to persuade Mr Haggin, to join in the Business that a final Division may be effected—proposing that we either *give* or *take* a proper proportion of Land as an equivalent for the Mansion house the whole with the Value of the life interest of Mrs Peart (now Haggin's) to be adjusted by the Court— now my dear Sir, if you are in correspondence with Mr Haggin, do beg of him to meet us in the business— I am most truly glad that we have at length come to a proper arrangement, assuring you that no obstacle will be obtruded on our part"— So much Mr Walker—to save postage I do not inclose his letter— his letters to Mr Wick— of which he speaks, will tally no doubt with what I have transcribed of his to me— I am not in correspondence with Mr Haggin, & shall not write him— you & Mr Wickliffe will have more influence with him than I could— I have lately heard from him, proposing to buy our interest &c, I answered in a few lines, refering him to *our* agent in this business; to my friend Majr. Wm. Taylor, of Shelby—whose steady & correct attention to other business of mine in Keny, as Exor. of my late brother, & from the many letters I have received from him, have given me a very high opinion of him, as a worthy & strictly honest & correct Man—

Genl T— says he will cheerfully pay any Money for me in Keny— I shall write him by this mail, & ask him to pay you one hundred [do]llars—your fee in the friendly Suit in Chany— for your Services in our joint business in Campbell,[5] he will doubtless be prompt in paying your fees— I remain Dr Sir, Sincerely yr friend, & ob St,

HUGH MERCER—

ALS. DLC-HC (DNA, M212, R1). Addressed to Clay at Lexington.

1 James Taylor.

2 Not identified; the suit not found.

3 William Rout, who practiced in the courts at Frankfort, Kentucky; probably the son of William Rout of Bourbon County.

4 See above, Mercer to Clay, March 11, 1823.

5 County, Kentucky.

Receipt from Robb and Winebrener

[April 1, 1823]

Recvd Aprile 1. 1823 of Mr H Clay Seventeen Dollars 75 in full Robb & Winebrener $17:75

ADS. DLC-TJC (DNA, M212, R15). Robb and Winebrener were tailors, of Philadelphia, Pennsylvania.

To Langdon Cheves

Dr Sir Philada. 7h. Apl. 1823.

I believe you are already acquainted with Majr. Smith.[1] Allow me to express a wish that you will afford him an opportunity of cultivating more particularly your acquaintance. I have known him for many years, and feel a particular interest in his welfare.

Langdon Cheves Esqr. Your's with great regard H. CLAY

ALS. ScHi. Addressed: "Present."

1 Probably John Speed Smith.

From Edward Shippen

Henry Clay Esq Office Bank U. States Louisville April 12th. 1823

Sir

Your letter dated Phila. 26 Mar:[1] was received this day and I have obtained payment of A Phillips[2] check therein enclosed viz:

Amount of check—	$400.
Int: from Protest to this day—	26.33
Cost of Protest &c—	2.25
	428.58

which amount ($428 58/100) is to your credit in this Office.— You will observe that the Interest is calculated from the date of the Protest, which Mr. Phillips is advised is all that could be recovered from him, as the check would have been paid had it been presented within a reasonable time after its date.— If however you insist on the Interest from the date of the check it will be paid rather than have any difficulty about it. Yours respectfully EDWD. SHIPPEN Cashr.

ALS. KyLxT. Directed to Lexington.

1 Not found.

2 Probably Asher Phillips, of Louisville.

To Simon Gratz and Brother

Gent. Washington 14h. April 1823.

By the request of Col. James Morrison I transmit to you inclosed a draft of the Treasurer of the U.S. on the Cashier of the Bank of the U. States for the sum of Eight thousand four hundred and thirty nine dollars and three Cents in his favor and by him indorsed to you, the receipt of which you will be pleased to acknowledge by letter addressed to him. I am Your ob. Servt. H. Clay

P.S. Col. Morrison is a little better to day. Mrs. M. not yet arrived.

Mess. Simon Gratz and Brother. H. C.

ALS. PHi.

To Jonathan Russell

Dr Sir Washington 19h. April 1823.

Detained here by the dangerous illness of a highly esteemed friend (Col. Morrison) [1] whose case it is to be feared will terminate fatally in a few days, I am enabled to transmit you the Kentucky Argus containing the third of a well written series of essays on the subject of the Fisheries and the Mississippi.[2] They are I believe entirely from the pen of Mr. Kendall the editor of that paper. I suppose that such productions never find their way into the papers of New England. If they did they could not fail to present the matters of which they treat in new and different lights from those in which they have been heretofore viewed in that quarter.

I congratulate you on the Massachusetts verdict and judgment recently rendered against the Hartford Convention.[3] Your's truly

Jonathan Russell Esqr. H. Clay

ALS. RPB-Russell Papers. 1 James Morrison.

2 The series, begun in the issue of March 19 and continued through ten letters published at intervals until August 13, was subsequently released as *Letters to John Quincy Adams, Relative to the Fisheries and the Mississippi, First Published in the Argus of Western America* (Rev. and enl.; Lexington, 1823). They constituted a campaign document defending Clay against the charges of sectionalism in his stand at Ghent, as expounded in Adams' *Duplicate Letters.*

3 One of the issues in the campaign between William Eustis and Harrison Gray Otis for the Governorship of Massachusetts (see above, Shaw to Clay, February 11, 1823, and note) had been the participation of Otis in the Hartford Convention.

From George Graham

[April 23, 1823]

Wednesday Morning, 6 o'clock.

Dear Sir—I hasten to advise you of the event anticipated when you left us yesterday morning, but which has taken place earlier than we then expected. Our friend[1] expired this morning about one o'clock, without a struggle, retaining his senses to the last moment and exhibiting one of the most remarkable instances that ever was witnessed of the sleep of death. You will readily conceive the effect, which this melancholy event has produced on Mrs Morrison, but I beg you to be assured that every service, which it is in my power to render her, will be offered as well while she remains here as in facilitating her return to Kentucky by whatever route she may designate. Yours very respectfully, GEO: GRAHAM

H CLAY, ESQ.

Horace Holley, *Discourse Occasioned by the Death of Col: James Morrison, Delivered in the Episcopal Church, May 19, 1823* (Lexington, 1823), 35.

1 James Morrison.

From George Graham

Dear Sir Washington April 26th. 1823

I advised you on the 23d Inst of the death of Coll. Morrison, and wrote in duplicate one Copy of which was inclosed to Mr. Skinner[1] the Post Master at Baltimore, with a request that he would forward it to Pittsburgh if you had left Baltimore, and the other was forwarded direct to Lexington, endorsed "to be opened by Mr. R. Scott should you be absent"—

The body was enter'd [*sic*] on Thursday forenoon, in that part of the burial ground at the Navy Yard allotted to Public Characters, at the request of the President, who has been particularly kind & attentive— In compliance with his own request the body was opened but no formation of pus could be discovered, the strong pulsation which you frequently felt, appeared to have been occasioned by an enlargement or prolongation of the internal part of the spine, which obstructed the passage of the blood in the large Artery that passes over it this pulsation became more perceptible as the entestines [*sic*] became more completely emptied— This affection of the spine will account for that deep seated complaint which the Coll. has for so many years complained of, and also for these palpitations of the Heart to which he was subject—but it did not appear to me to be a sufficient cause for the fatal termination of his last illness— The lungs were sound so far as they were examined— one lobe of the Liver was materially affected— I have requested the Physicians to draw up and sign a particular statement of the appearances on dissection, which shall be forwarded to you, as soon as they can furnish it—

Mrs. Morrison findind [*sic*] herself unable to undertake the Journey to Wheeling immediately, and her Brother Mr. John Montgomery,[2] who arrived here the day you left us, being very solicitous that she should go with him to Baltimore, she determined to take that route, and left this with him this Morning— I furnished

Mrs. Morrison with five hundred dollars as she obtained but few articles of Mourning here, and may probably wish to procure some other things in Baltimore; I have requested her should she want any further supply to let me know and I would furnish it to her— All the papers have been put in a small Trunk which is well secured, and I have given John[3] Instructions to be particularly careful of it, I enclose you the key by Genl. Rector[4] who takes charge of the Trunk containing Coll. Morrisons Clothing. Mrs. Morrison had not decided how long she would remain in Baltimore I requested Mr. Montgomerie to ascertain where Mr. & Mrs. Harper[5] were, & when they proposed to go out— She proposes to take the route by Wheeling— The Check for the five hundred dollars which Coll. Morrison owed you & for which he had given you a memorandum,[6] was not made out as he had directed me to do the Morning you left us— It was our Bank day and I was detained untill late, on getting to his lodgings I found him so weak that I did not like to disturb him—

Coll. Morrisons Bank Book with this office[7] I have kept—the balance in his favor on the 19th Inst. was $4644:72—and two notes for collection amounting to $700— Exclusive of the money advanced Mrs. Morrison, the other expences will be about $250, exclusive of the Physicians bills, and any donation it may be deemed proper to make to the Clergymen—

You will please remember me to Mrs. Clay—

H. Clay Esqr. Yours very respectfuly [*sic*] GEO: GRAHAM

ALS. DLC-TJC (DNA, M212, R10). 1 John S. Skinner.

2 A native of Carlisle, Pennsylvania, who had begun the practice of law in Harford County, Maryland, in 1791. He had been a member of the State legislature, 1793-1798, and of Congress, 1807-1811. After moving to Baltimore in 1811, he had been State Attorney General, 1811-1818, captain of militia in the War of 1812, a member of the State legislature in 1819, and Mayor of the city, 1820-1822. He was again Mayor, 1824-1826.

3 Possibly a slave, left to Mrs. Morrison by her husband's will and emancipated at her death. Fayette County, Will Book F, 61; P, 281.

4 William Rector, by whom this letter was conveyed, was in Washington probably in connection with a Congressional inquiry into his contracts as Surveyor General of the Public Lands in Illinois, Missouri, and the Territory of Arkansas. See *American State Papers, Public Lands,* III, 618-20. A native of Virginia, he had removed to the Illinois country in 1806, had been commissioned a brigadier general of militia, Illinois Territory, in 1811, and, after long service as a surveyor of public lands, had been appointed in 1816 as Surveyor General for the Territories of Illinois and Missouri. After 1816 he made his home in St. Louis.

5 James Harper. 6 Not found.

7 Washington, D. C., branch, Bank of the United States.

From Albert H. Tracy

Hon. Henry Clay Buffalo, New York 27 April 1823—

My dear Sir

Owing to unexpected delays on the road I did not reach home until last week where I found your esteemed favour of the 28th ult[1]

In reply I can only say that the sentiment of this state upon the ensuing Presidential election has not yet been sufficiently indicated to authorise a prediction of the result— Our violent local politicks have so completely engrossed the public mind that but little attention has been given to national concerns Some efforts are making principally by Mr. Crawfords friends to awaken popular feeling on this subject but so far as I can judge the effect as yet has been inconsiderable— The nature as well as the result of our state controversies have been to repress that political intrepidity and generous enthusiasm which are so honorable to our natures and to resolve all our measures into questions of selfish security and cautious expediency— In a condition of things like this, when every body appears more anxious to be on the *strong* side than the *right* side you will readily perceive how impossible it is to foresee the result— So far however as I can penetrate this "palpable obscure [*sic*]" I think I discover that Mr Crawford has exceeded his competitors in satisfying our leading politicians that he will succeed though he probably will find it more difficult than some of them to persuade the people that he ought— the only advantage he now has over his rivals arises from his having friends among the dominant party of this state who are willing to incur the responsibility of openly taking ground,[2] which the friends of the other candidates appear afraid to do— This circumstance produces the worst possible effect for them by inducing the belief that their friends have no confidence of their success. The impression can only be countervailed by open and decided conduct, by those who are legitimate members of this party— by others it would be worse than useless—

When at Philadelphia I first ascertained from Mr Van Beuren that he had determined to enter the lists as a decided champion of the Secy of the Treasy. Afterwards at Albany I found that he was pursuing openly and unequivocally the course he had indicated— What the influence of his example will be I cannot say— It cannot fail however of being considerable— For independently of his direct personal influence, his reputation for astuteness and his known reluctance to be on the losing side joined with the superior opportunity he is supposed to possess of judging correctly on this point will give to his opinion the weight of authority with many politicians whose sole purpose is to be with the successful—

By the hasty view I have afforded you will discover that nothing certain can be told of of [*sic*] the course which this state will take except that her votes will not be given for a losing candidate if it is possible for her politicians to guard against such a result— It only remains for any one of the competitors to produce the conviction that he will succeed in order to do so— With much respect and esteem I am Sincerely Yours ALBERT H TRACY

ALS. DLC-HC (DNA, M212, R1). [1] Not found.
[2] See above, Clay to Porter, March 18, 1823.

Receipt from B. Wells and Company

April 29, 1823

Attached to Bill, February 17, 1823.

To Langdon Cheves

Dr Sir Lexington 8h. May 1823.

Allow me to introduce to your acquaintance Mr. J. J. Mercier, a young gentleman of Louisiana, who has been some time at Transylvania University, where he has graduated.[1] I have known him intimately and participate, with numerous other friends, in the interest which has been excited by his promising talents, his amiable disposition and his correct deportment. In performing a tour which he is about to make in the Eastern States, he desires to make the acquaintance of distinguished gentlemen who reside in them; and it is for that reason that I have to solicit your kind reception of him. I am with great regard Faithfully Yours. H. CLAY

Langdon Cheves Esqr.

ALS. ScHi. Addressed to Cheves, "Counseller [*sic*] at Law Philadelphia."

[1] John James Mercier, who had just received a degree in law, became a New Orleans attorney and a leader in civic affairs.

From Charles S. Todd

My dear Sir, Bogota. May 8th. 1823.

I had the pleasure of addressing you a short note from Merida in December last[1] and avail myself, now, of the return of the Swedish Consul General[2] to Phila. to transmit a Correspondence with the Authorities here, produced by the presentation of some of Tyler's engravings of you,[3] 3 Copies of which I had procured for the purpose; the receipt of that presented to General Soublette,[4] Intendant General at Caracas, has not been acknowledged.—The Correspondence was originally in Spanish and you will see in the translation that I have made some progress in a Language, which, besides its preeminent beauties, may become emphatically that of America—

I hope you know me sufficiently to be aware that I have not received with indifference, the account of the indications in Kentucky Ohio and Missouri[5] and in the prints of other States, favorable to your pretensions to the next Presidency.— Death and some Siberian Missions may lessen the number of your Competitors[6] and whatever may be the feeling of the U States singly on the subject, there can be no doubt but that the United Voice of Continental America would elevate you to a station full of unexampled responsibility and of unrequited Solicitude— I am persuaded, however, that you are yourself too National in your feelings, to give all the point which the people and Governments in the new States of Spanish America would wish to convey by their unqualified approbation of your Conduct in relation to their supposed interests; since it has been made the occasion and the pretext for indulging in cold and unworthy feelings towards our Government and extending, in a much greater degree than we Could wish, even to our people and institutions.—

I might refer you to Col Duane for detailed information with respect to the State of Affairs here; and his opinions would be entitled to great consideration, having devoted many years to the acquisition of an extensive knowledge of the Country and in Support of the Cause which the people supposed they were maintaining—[7] Being myself in the *diplomatic* service and, moreover, under the immediate eye of a Statesman, who is Characteristically known, never to express more than he means to say,[8] I may be excused from giving an opinion on the Condition of things—but Col Duane, if he were to meet with you, would undeceive you with respect to many matters about which, he says, he has been heretofore under misapprehensions.— He would tell you that though the Country is separated from Spanish dominion and Misrule, yet that Spanish duplicity in the Governors and Spanish superstition in the people are but too painfully prevalent; whilst the hopes of the public Councils are directed to Europe and especially G. Britain in the vain delusion, that it is by those powers alone, their interests [can] be promoted—

If the arrangement made conditionally with the Bank of the U States at Phila. in June last, has been carried into effect, I shall be grateful for whatever influence you may have exercised in the effectuation of a result, so auspicious to my future hopes.—[9] With respect to the Secretaryship, I shall continue until the arrival of Mr. Anderson,[10] in the condition of our learned judges when they say. "Curia advisare vult."— What is the present tone of our Judge breakers?[11] Did their ill humor evaporate in the burning of the Bank Notes?[12] I need not say, Dr. Sir, that any Communication you may find it convenient to make me, will be peculiarly acceptable,

Yours faithfully, C. S. TODD

H. Clay Esq.

ALS. DLC-HC (DNA, M212, R1). Published in Colton (ed.), *Private Correspondence of Henry Clay*, 77-78.

1 Not found.

2 The Chevalier Severin Lorich, Consul General from Sweden to the United States, had arrived at Bogotá in February, 1823, after a journey across the plains from Caracas. He had been authorized by his Government to negotiate exclusive commercial privileges and to observe conditions as a preliminary to recognition of Colombian independence.

3 See above, Tyler to Clay, June 24, 1822, note.

4 General Carlos Soublette, later Venezuelan Minister to Spain and Vice President and acting President of Venezuela.

5 See above, Clay to Porter, October 22, 1822, note; Clay to Brooke, January 8, 1823. Missouri, by action of members of its legislature November 7, 1822, had been the first State to nominate Clay for the Presidency.

6 On the death of William Lowndes, see above, ——— to Clay, April 26, 1822, note; on Andrew Jackson's appointment as Minister to Mexico, see above, Carroll to Clay, February 19, 1823.

7 William Duane, who had been traveling in South America, returned to Philadelphia early in July.

8 John Quincy Adams.

9 In December, 1821, Todd had concluded a written agreement with Clay on behalf of the Bank of the United States, which cancelled Todd's debt to the Cincinnati office of the Bank by transfer of some property in Louisville. At the same time he was liable, with George M. Bibb and Peter G. Voorhies, the latter of whom was insolvent, for a judgment on a note at the Louisville office of the Bank amounting to $5590, interest at six per cent annually from February 23, 1820, until paid, and costs. At the May Term of the Federal Circuit Court in 1823 judgments were also issued against Todd for two notes payable at the Lexington office of the Bank, the first, for $3800, signed with Bibb, John T. Pendleton, and Francis P. Blair; the second, for $7500, chargeable to these parties together with John H. Todd and Achilles Sneed. Todd had not been successful "in the general proposition made to the Mother Board at Philadelphia in Novr. [1821] to pay the whole debt in real property at valuation." No further record of an intervening arrangement has been found; but at the May Term, 1827, of the Federal Circuit Court, the Bank of the United States discontinued two additional suits against Charles S. and John H. Todd. Todd to Isaac Shelby, December 20, 1821 (DLC-Shelby Papers, microfilm in KyU); U.S. Circuit Court, Seventh Circuit, District of Kentucky, Complete Records, Q, 430-32, 434; V, 106-108, 111-13; Order Book, L, 404.

10 Richard C. Anderson, Jr.

11 See above, Clay to Leigh, October 29, 1822, note.

12 See above, Report, November 25, 1822, note.

To Jabez D. Hammond

Dr Sir Ashland 12h. May 1823.

I perceive with great pleasure, by your letter of the 23d. Ulto.[1] which I have just received, that you retain a recollection, which I assure you is not forgotten on my part, of our having served together in the H. of R. several years ago. I received along with your obliging letter the prize poem of Mrs. Land[2] which I have perused with very great satisfaction. It is highly creditable to her taste and talents. Should circumstances carry me to Indiana (which is not improbable) I shall seek an opportunity to cultivate the acquaintance of the fair authoress, and to make one complaint to her that is, that she has not permitted her Muse to bestow one look, or describe one object on the Southern shore of the Ohio river.

I thank you for the information communicated in the postscript to your letter. Your State, by such a decision as you suggest it to be probable she will make, would conclusively settle the question to which you refer; and assume, what she has never yet had, a primary rank in the affairs of this Union, to which she is entitled by all the circumstances of position, population, wealth & talents.

The Honble J. D. Hammond. [. . . .]

AL (signature removed). NHi. Hammond, born in Massachusetts and reared in Vermont, had studied medicine and practiced as a physician before turning to the study of law. Admitted to the bar, he had begun practice in Cherry Valley, New York, in 1805. He had sat in the United States House of Representatives, 1815-1817, and, immediately afterward, in the New York State Senate for four years. He then practiced law in Albany for several years before returning to Cherry Valley, where he resided the rest of his life and was for almost a decade a judge of Otsego County. He is the author of the notable historical work cited above, Shaw to Clay, April 4, 1822, note.

1 Not found. 2 Not identified.

From George Graham

Dear Sir Washington May 17th. 1823

I received a Letter yesterday from Mr. Montgomery[1] informing me that Mrs. Morrison and Miss Sidney[2] had left Baltimore on the 10th Inst. for Lexington in company with Mr. & Mrs. Harper[3] he says that Mrs. Morrison was very weak, but he hopes that by making short stages she will be able to accomplish the Journey—

Mrs. Morrison has not required any further advance of Money from me, and for that collected in Baltimore by Mr. Montgomery she takes out a Post Note— I send you a Statement[4] of the accounts paid by me on account of the Estate of Coll. Morrison. I have paid them by giving checks on the accounts, and have had them charged up in Coll. Morrisons Bank Book— Dr. Cutbush[5] has not yet presented his account, his charge will I presume be greater than that made by Doctor Sim,[6] as he was longer in attendance— The amount paid to Mr. Jas. Montgomery was on account of money loaned by him to Coll. Morrison— It is usual to give the attending ministers of the Gospel, something, but as they could make out no account I have left that for you to settle—[7]

I now enclose the Report of Drs. Cutbush & Sim,[8] which I mentioned in my last Letter—

Whenever the Exrs. of Coll. Morrison may deem it proper to shew the amount standing to his credit on the Books of this office, it will be necessary to accompany their draft by a certificate of Administration— With great respect Yr. obt. Sert. GEO: GRAHAM

H. Clay Esqr.

ALS. DLC-TJC (DNA, M212, R10). 1 John Montgomery.

2 Mrs. James Morrison; Sidney S. Edmiston, Mrs. Morrison's niece, who had become a member of the Morrison household and who continued to reside in Lexington until her death in 1874.

3 James Harper. 4 D. DLC-TJC (DNA, M212, R10).

5 Edward Cutbush, a graduate of the medical school of the University of Pennsylvania, surgeon in the United States Navy from 1799 to 1829 (stationed in Washington

much of the time). After resigning from the Navy, he retired to Geneva, New York, where he became professor and dean of the medical faculty of Hobart College.

6 Thomas Sim, one of the founders of the Medical Society of the District of Columbia.

7 See below, Graham to Clay, July 15, 1823.

8 ADS. DLC-TJC (DNA, M212, R10).

To [Charles S. West]

Sir Frankfort 20h. January [*i.e.*, May][1] 1823.

In your letter of the 30th. November last[2] you promised that my request respecting depositions in the case of McKinney's bill for $2000 should be attended to in a few days. As the depositions have not been received, I fear that, if taken, they have miscarried, or that some thing has occurred to prevent their being taken. The consequence has been that I have been obliged to continue the suit of the Bank of the U.S. against N. B. Cooke & Co., in which they were desired, from the present Session of the Court until the next term in November.[3]

The bill is under date Versailles October 27. 1819, in favor of N. B. Cooke & Co. or order, upon Mess. McNeill, Fisk and Rutherford New Orleans, payable at your office, one hundred days after date. The deposition of Mr. Pedesclaux,[4] the Notary public, is wanted, to prove that a demand was made at the office of discount and deposit as well as at the House of the payers. If the fact were that both the drawers and payers had no funds in the Bank on the day of the protest, that is the 7h. Feb. 1820, I wish it also proven; or if one of those parties only had no funds, I wish that proven. I wish the proof which can be made either by the Notary or by your office also to be furnished as to the transmission of notice to the parties to be affected, that is that it was by the next mail after the protest. The depositions should be taken, under the act of Congress and to be read as evidence in the action now depending in the Circuit Court of the U. States of the Bank of the U. States against N. B. Cooke & Co. I will thank you to have them taken and forwarded as soon as convenient, under cover addressed to the Cashier of the Lexington office.

I learnt with regret that you were obliged to suffer a Nonsuit in the case agt. McClanahan & Bogart for the want of the letter of credit which they gave to Mr. Marshall.[5] He informed me that it was on file in some other suit depending at New Orleans to charge the same persons upon another bill, growing out of the same transaction. Has it been found? With great respect I am Your ob. Servt.

The Cashier of the Off. of Dt. & Dt New Orleans. H. CLAY

ALS. PHC-Charles Roberts Autograph Collection. Addressed on attached sheet: "The Cashier of the Off. of Discount & Deposit of the Bank U. S. New Orleans."

1 Postmarked at Frankfort on May 23. Clay was not in Kentucky on January 20.

2 Not found.

3 On April 29, 1822, the President, Directors, and Company of the Bank of the United States had brought suit against John McKinney, Jr., for collection of the bill described below. At the May Term, 1822, McKinney acknowledged the demand and the court ordered payment of $2,507—the amount of the bill, ten per cent damages, interest on the bill and the damages, and costs of suit. On May 19, 1823, the Bank's suit against Norborne B. Cooke and Company, that is, the partnership of Cooke and Nathaniel Hart, merchants of Kentucky, had been docketted for jury trial but was never called up. U. S. Circuit Court, Seventh Circuit, District of Kentucky, Complete Records, S, 162-63; Order Book I, 154.

4 Peter Pedesclaux, French by birth, who had been for a time public auctioneer, Notary, Recorder of Mortgages, and Clerk of the Cabildo in Louisiana under Spanish rule. After the United States obtained possession of the province, he was made Notary Public and Keeper of Mortgages, although removed from the latter office in 1808.

5 Cf. above, Clay to Cheves, June 16, 1822.

From Richard M. Johnson

Dear Sir. Great Crossings 22d. May 1823

In conversing with Mr. Scott[1] I find that he has effected every object of your memorandum[2] to effect. the titles to the property conveyed[3]

Two things he says remains to be done the delivery of the house of Sebree which was not finished— Sebree disappointed me in not having the house finished altho he has had much of the woork [*sic*] done. I am willing to finish it fourthwith [*sic*], or I would as leave let Mr Scott come up & get men to value the work to be done & I will give a note with approved security for the amount & I think the Bank had better take immediately possession at all events, as the house is the Bank's in any event, whether they finish or I finish it; the other unfinished business is the conveyance of the house & lot in Burlington[4] which better answers the discription [*sic*] given in by me. I have had great difficulty in making this arrangement & had offered 2000$ in property to effect it & thought it was done—but it has not been. I understand from Robt J. Ward[5] that Capt Benj. Johnson[6] will be up in ten days & will accept my prposition [*sic*] & make the deed to the Large house. I have done every thing in my power to effect & consummate the arrangement according to the understanding. of the parties & over this last difficulty I have had no controul— Sincerely yours RH: M: JOHNSON

ALS. DLC-R. M. Johnson Papers (DNA, M212, R21). Published in James A. Padgett (ed.), "The Letters of Colonel Richard M. Johnson of Kentucky," Kentucky State Historical Society, *Register*, XXXIX (1941), 186. Addressed to Clay at Frankfort.

1 Probably Matthew T. Scott. 2 Not found.

3 See above, Clay to Cheves, October 3, 1821.

4 County seat of Boone County, Kentucky.

5 Son of William Ward and nephew of Richard M. Johnson. Young Ward, several times a member of the Kentucky legislature and during the session of 1824-1825 Speaker of the House of Representatives, was a Georgetown lawyer. Later he removed to Louisville, where he acquired wealth, first as a commission merchant and subsequently as head of two successive firms, based in New Orleans, dealing in cotton.

6 Richard M. Johnson's brother, an officer during the War of 1812, now serving the first of several four-year terms as Judge of the Territory of Arkansas, later a Judge of the Supreme Court of the State of Arkansas.

From David Woods

State of New York Town & County of Madison
Sir 22d. May 1823.—

Though a stranger, I take the liberty of addressing you, on a subject in which I, in common with the citizens of the United States in general, feel a deep solicitude; I mean the subject of the approaching Presidential Election. I might naturally be asked my reasons for addressing you on this subject—I will give them. In the first place, I disapprove of the interference of a president, in disignating to the people who his successor should be, more especially when the selection is confined to some favorite of his own Cabinate. I think that the publick aught to be left free, so that a spontanious expression of the publick will, untrammeled with Presidential influence, shaught disignate the man whom the people would wish to preside over their Government.

And in the second place, it is not to be disguised, but that Jealousies do exist to a very general extent, throughout the United States, that abuses have crept in to the administration of the Government, and no small share of those abuses are charged on the present heads of the different departments of government. Whether those Jealousies are well or ill founded, I have not the means of Judging correctly, but as long as they do exist, sound policy would seem to dictate to the people, the propriety of selecting some Gentleman, who is wholly unconnected with that Cabinate. If those Jealousies are ill founded, no evil could result to the people from adopting this course, And if well founded, much good might be the consequence. I am free to acknowlidge that Mr. Clinton of this state, would be my favorite Candidate; but from the state of publick feeling here, misguided as it is, I fear that his prospects, to say the least, are inauspicious.

Although I venerate Gen. Jackson as a military commander, yet I cannot believe that he will be seriously thought of, by any considerable portion of the people of the United States for the office of president. The proceedings lately had in the County of Cumberland, in the State of Pennsylvania, I can view in no other light, than as a manoeuvre to defeat Mr. Calhoun's nomination,[1] or perhaps with a view to some ultirior object.

I therefore believe, that your prospects are more flattering than those of any of the other gentlemen taulked of, who are unconnected with the Cabinate at Washington.

Our Senate Consists of thirty two members, nine of whom, together with the whole of our assembly, will be Elected next October, when they will choose the presidential Electors by joint ballot— What the political complexion of our next legislature will be, is impossible to predict, but from the confusion that at present prevails, among the men in power here, I do not believe that Mr. Van Beuren will be able to manage so, as to procure a majority in favor of his favorite Candidate, Mr. Crawford. I do not think he will be able to effect much, as his popularity is evidently on the decline.

Mr. Van Beuren, at our last Election, effected considerable in relation to the Election of Members of Congress, a considerable number of them, when they were Elected, were no doubt willing to be subservient to his views, as respected the presidential question, but I think the mutation of the human mind would be exemplified in many of those members, should interest, or popularity open to their view. Mr. Crawford has nothing to expect from Mr. Van Beuren, further than his own views are subserved, for, to use a vulgar phrase, he is as slippery as an Eel. As to the meeting held in April last by the members of our Legislature,[2] there was but little meaning attached to it, It was understood that Mr. Van Beuren got it up with a view to feel their pulse, in relation to the presidential question, and that he furnished his friends, among the members, with two sets of resolutions, one set embraceing the nomination of Mr. Crawford, if the members could be brought up to the sticking point, and if that could not be effected then to adopt the other set, which recommended a Congressional nomination, the last set were adopted. In that meeting, I have no doubt but that you had more friends than any other Candidate. I fully believe from present appearances, that the Electors of this State, are more likely to be your friends, than the friend of any other Candidate— I should be happy in communicating to you from time to time, any information in my power, which might be useful to you. It is unnessary [*sic*] for me, to state to you that this is confidential I do not know but that I have misjudged in writing thus to you, if I have, I can only say it was well intended. I am Sir your obedt. Servant DAVID WOODS

Hon. Henry Clay

ALS. DLC-HC (DNA, M212, R1).

1 At a meeting in Carlisle, Pennsylvania, scheduled for the nomination of Calhoun, a motion withdrawing his name and substituting that of Jackson had carried by a large majority. Lexington *Kentucky Reporter,* May 5, 1823.

2 At a caucus in Albany on April 22, 1823, the legislators had adopted a resolution favoring a Congressional caucus as a means of nominating a candidate for President.

To John Quincy Adams

Sir

Lexington 23d. May 1823.

Being informed that Mr. Charles Savage is desirous of obtaining a Foreign Consulate, I take pleasure in saying that I have known him for several years past, as a highly respectable and intelligent mer-

chant, in this place and Louisville, and that I am persuaded he would honorably & creditably discharge the duties of the station which he solicits, if it should be confered on him.[1] I have the honor to be with great respect Your obedient Servant H. CLAY
The Honble J. Q. Adams &c. &c. &c

ALS. DNA, RG59, Applications and Recommendations for Office (MR1). Endorsed: "Recd. 26 June."
[1] Savage, who was also recommended by Richard M. Johnson, was appointed Consul at Guatemala in April, 1824, and remained in this post until his resignation in 1838.

From Peter B. Porter

Dear Sir, Black Rock May 26. 1823.

I have neglected to write to you for some time past, because I had nothing new to communicate on the subject to which our late correspondence has related. I left Albany on the 29th. of March & a few days before Van Buren returned from Washington. At that time—and my impressions are still the same—I considered the public sentiment in this State to be much divided, and in the manner I have before represented to you, that is to say. A certain portion of the Republicans, perhaps a fourth or third, are the honest friends of Mr. Adams, and will give him their support as long as they can perceive any reasonable prospect of his success; but in case of dispair [*sic*] will unite on you. As regards the *balance* (as we Kentuckians say) of the Republicans, my opinion is that the spontaneous sentiment of a decided majority of them is with you. But Mr Crawford possesses the advantage (and it is no inconsiderable one) of having most of the *active* & *managing* politicians on his side—such as V. B. & others who are looking for place & preferment, and the host of Treasury dependants [*sic*] who have already got places. It was the intention of V.B. & his friends to have procured a legislative expression in favour of their candidate, and I protracted my stay at Albany for some days waiting his arrival from New York where he spent some time, in labouring to bring the Republicans of that city in to the measure.

On reaching Albany, however, he found the attempt fruitless, and was obliged to be satisfied with the farce (which, as it effected nothing, all concurred in) of approbating Congressional caucusses.[1]

I think I informed you last winter, that the Patrons of the "American" in New York, & eventually the paper itself, would come out in your favour.[2] My authority for beleiving [*sic*] & saying this was John King (son of Rufus) who is a member of our Senate, and one of what Noah[3] calls the "high minded men" who established the paper. *He* is, or professes to be, still your friend, but I knew that the clans were divided between you & Mr. Adams, and I think they will all yet support you the moment they find Mr A's success, in this State, doubtfull.

It is utterly impossible to say at this moment what will be the course of this State. One circumstance however decidedly in *your* favour is, that should the friends either of Mr Adams or Mr. Crawford find it necessary or expedient to abandon their man, they will, in either event, be much more likely to support you than the opposing candidate. Our public Journals are, as yet, extremely coy —not one in ten having selected its candidate. We have a fair prospect of bringing out, in the course of a few weeks, some 6 or 8 papers in this section of the State, simultaneously, or nearly so, in your favour. Should we succeed, & I think we shall, it will produce considerable effect in the eastern & southern parts of the State.

The Vice President arrived at Albany a few days before I left. I made some attempt to sound him, but he is an old politician, and, *situated as he is at this moment,*[4] he will avoid taking any active part, altho.' his opinions should he express them, would have an important, if not controuling, influence in this State. He expressed, &, as I know, feels great personal regard for you. He intimated to me, very pleasantly but not without meaning, that you *neglected* him while at Washington. He told me that, *if he could raise a little money,* he would visit Niagara in the course of the Summer & spend a week with me. P. R. Livingston, our late Speaker,[5] will also be here. Can you not make it convenient to visit us in July, August or September—look at the Fall & take a trip on the Canal as far as Sarat[oga.] If you can, please advise me as early [as possible o]f the time when we may expect you.

I have the satisfaction to in[form you] that I have a *Daughter* between five & six weeks old, and although she is very small, she is still, *in the opinion of her parents,* very handsome & very clever.

Mrs Porter, who is in good health, joins me in the expression of our respect & regard for Mrs Clay & yourself. P. B. PORTER

ALS. DLC-HC (DNA, M212, R1). Addressed to Clay at Lexington.

1 See above, Woods to Clay, May 22, 1823.

2 Cf. above, Porter to Clay, February 3, 1823.

3 Mordecai M. Noah.

4 Probably an allusion to the political eclipse into which Daniel D. Tompkins had fallen, when he was unable to account for large sums of money which he had handled, much of it borrowed on his personal credit, in support of the public military effort during his service as Governor of New York and Commandant of the Third United States Military District in the War of 1812. A bill to settle his accounts with the State of New York had been enacted, after political controversy, in 1820 but had contributed to his subsequent defeat in the gubernatorial race of that year (see above, II, 820n). His accounts with the Federal government were in process of adjustment. See below, Remarks, December 11, 1823.

5 Philip R. Livingston, of Dutchess County, New York, distant kinsman and brother-in-law of Robert R. and Edward Livingston, had been elected Speaker of the New York House of Representatives in January, 1823.

From Gabriel J. Johnston

Hon. H. Clay. New Castle 27 May 1823.—

Sir.

Your Speech upon the "Seminole War"[1] being frequently the subject of public Conversation and Comment—and much handled by your political enemies, with a view to your injury, as a Candidate for the first Office in the gift of the people—and never having had an opportunity of perusing that production, as your political friend, I am desirous to have a Copy of it, and of any other of your speeches which you may have, or Can conveniently procure. The "Missouri Question," "Domestic Manufactures"[2] &c.

To you I am *personally* an entire stranger, and will probably ever remain so—but of your character as a Statesman and Orator I should be ashamed to say I am ignorant— it is identified with the History of my Country, and is as imperishable as Patriotism, and Feeling, and Taste.

I contemplate a removal to the seat of Governmt. in Indiana the ensuing Fall— with the Legislature, or at least some of its' members, I may be able to render you some service—

Believing that the interest and honor of the Union and especially of the West, will be subserved & promoted by your elevation to the Presidential Chair I most heartily wish for your success—

Most respectfully I am Sir Yrs &c GABRIEL J JOHNSTON

ALS. DLC-HC (DNA, M212, R1). Johnston, son of Gabriel J. Johnston of Louisville, Kentucky (who had died in 1815), had attended Transylvania University. He appears to have returned to Louisville in later years.

1 See above, II, 636-62.

2 See above, Speech, January 29, 1821; II, 826-47.

From William Murphy

H. Clay Esqr. Washington Ky May 28h. 1823

D Sr

Your's of the 19th Int.[1] is recd. and I Omitted writing you; Owing to the absence of Mr. Waters[2] (on a trip to New Orleans) who has now returned—& says he will be able to pay *$1000.* by the first day of July next. If this payt. is made, Mr Waters wishes to Know what indulgence Could be given for the Balance of Col Picketts[3] debt which was for the House & lott where Waters lives— enclosed I send you a Copy of the Bonds &c.— Respectfully yours &c W. MURPHY

Col. Jno Picketts Bond is for $2885 with Dt. from 16h July 1821
Capt. James Byres[4] do. 1900 ditto—
W Murphy do 615 $700 paid by Col Pickett
this is from recollection & I think Correct

ALS. DLC-TJC (DNA, M212, R12). [1] Not found. [2] Richard L. Waters.
[3] John Pickett, of Mason County, Kentucky, a native of Virginia; member of the Kentucky House of Representatives, 1795, and of the Senate, 1819-1822; commissioned Lieutenant Colonel, Commandant, 15th Regiment, Kentucky Militia, in 1806.
[4] James Byers, also of Mason County, a captain of militia and later a member of the Kentucky legislature. See below, Byers to Clay, June 22, 1823.

To Horace Holley

Sir Ashland June 1823[1]

Agreeably to the wish which you expressed to me, I proceed to state some circumstances attending the last illness of our late highly respected friend and townsman Col. James Morrison.

Upon my reaching Washington, late in January last, I learnt that he was sick and had been indisposed for some weeks. I immediately went to see him, and found him, though much reduced, still capable of transacting business and occasionally going out. I saw him every day, from that time until the day of his death, except about two weeks during which I was absent from the City.[2] His loss of strength and decline were gradual, but quite perceptible. Shortly after I first saw him I formed the opinion that he never would leave the City. He entertained however hopes himself until within a few days of his death, and was very attentive, in the execution of the prescriptions of his physicians, and to every particular which he supposed might conduce to the restoration of his health. All the soothing attentions and acts of unaffected kindness, which occurred to any of his numerous friends and acquaintances, were promptly and sedulously performed. The President took the most lively concern in his recovery, daily sending to enquire about his condition, transmitting from his table choice articles of food, and frequently calling in person to see and cheer him.

Shortly after my arrival at the City, I communicated to him my apprehensions about him, and advised him to make all necessary preparations for the most awful event. He kept by him the New testament, which he continued to read as long as his strength permitted him. He was often visited, towards the latter period of his illness daily, by one or the other of two highly respectable Clergymen (Mess Holley and McCormick)[3] and joined them in religious exercises. On the occasion of one of those visits, I was present when the Clergyman asked him if he should read a chapter in the bible and continue their accustomed devotions. He answered yes, and I retired, supposing he would prefer to be alone. Upon his remarking, on my return, that I had not united with them in prayer, I took the opportunity of expressing to him my hope that he felt himself contented and at ease in his religious relations. He promptly replied that he had not now to form his opinions on that subject; that they had been long settled; that these gentlemen (alluding to the Clergymen) were pious good men, and had good intentions; and that he thought it right that they should perform the duties incident to their station. What was the precise nature of his opinions I did not inquire, nor do I certainly know. It was enough for me that *he* was satisfied with them.

No man ever bore with more fortitude protracted illness than he did. A groan, a complaint never escaped him. No man could contemplate, with more perfect calmness and composure, his dissolution than he did. He requested his kind and attentive friend George Graham Esqr. and me, a few days before his death, to have his body opened. The morning I left him he stated to me that he could not survive, enquired when the ensuing County Court of Fayette would be, and observed, upon my informing him, that his executors might then qualify and "go to work." The pressure of duties at home, from which I had been detained much longer than I anticipated when I left it, obliged me most reluctantly to separate myself from him on the 22d. April. It was then expected that he might linger some days, if not weeks. But he expired the next morning, about eighteen hours after my departure, and exhibited (to quote the language of Mr. Graham) "one of the most remarkable instances of the sleep of death ever witnessed."

With great respect I am faithfully Your's H. CLAY

The Revd. H. Holley.

ALS. KyLxT. Published in Holley, *Discourse Occasioned by the Death of Col: James Morrison*, 33-35.

1 Month and year not in Clay's hand.

2 See above, Toasts and Speech, March 29, 1823; Clay to Cheves, April 7, 1823.

3 William Hawley; A. T. McCormick—both Episcopal. The former, originally of Virginia, was for many years rector of St. John's Church in Washington. McCormick was rector at Christ Church, in Georgetown.

From Benjamin Warfield

Dr. Sir, Cyna.[1] June 1. 1823

I recd. yours of the 15h. On friday last and am highly gratified to here of the favourable prospects for you [*sic*] election to the Presidential Station, I desire to say one thing, after making the enquiries in my letter to you about it[2] I was sensible that I might have asked too much & intended before I sent the letter to have added that if my enquires [*sic*] were imprudent that you must not answer them, as they were perhaps too particular; as I would not that you should let one word escape you to your best friends that could if known to the world would in the slightest degree injure your prospects with a reasonable man in the nation

Anxiety prompted me to the enquiries & I know you have viewed them in the proper light enough of this at present—

Colo. Morrison is dead. There are suits in this quarter for his benefit in which I am engaged for him— Who are his Executors in whose name revivors Can be had. I am told you are one[3] Our Court Sits on 2d Monday in June & until we know this Cannot proceed?

I have red[4] of Samuel $698. in Com.[5] Notes to be exchanged for Specie, & is in the hands of Elisha Warfield, (Lexington) for you on the bond. See him & get the money & receipt for it at what it will bring in Specie— Since Which he has Sued out a writ of Error & got a supersedeas, You will notice it on file in the Court of appeals. —When you examin [*sic*] the Errors will you write me as I Cannot think any thing but delay is intended.[6] Yr friend BEN. WARFIELD

[Endorsement][7]

Recd. 9h. June 1823—the within sum of $698 which (exchange being at ninety five) I receipted for at $358 in specie.[8] H C

ALS. DLC-TJC (DNA, M212, R12). Addressed to Clay at Lexington. Postmarked: "Ruddells Mills June 2." Endorsed by Clay: "B. Warfield Priestman's debt" (possibly a reference to William Priestman).

1 Cynthiana, Kentucky.

2 Neither of these letters has been found.

3 James Morrison had named his wife executrix and Clay, Robert Wickliffe, Farmer Dewees, and Richard Hawes (Jr.), executors; but Clay served alone in this capacity. Fayette County, Will Book F, 68, 122. At the June Term, Fayette County Court, Clay "took the oath required by Law; no security being required of said Clay by said will, none was therefore required by the Court." Fayette County Court, Order Book no. 5, pp. 275-76.

4 Received; Samuel, not identified.

5 Bank of the Commonwealth.

6 Case not found.

7 AEI.

8 Receipt not found.

To John White

Sir Frankfort 3d. June 1823.

It will be necessary for me to have by the next term of the Federal Court the depositions and proofs upon which your office intends to rely to recover of John Harvie the amount of the bill for $4200 drawn by James W. Hawkins on Charles Sproule at New Orleans and indorsed to the Bank by Finley and Vanlear. The next Court will commence on the first monday in November— Notice of the nonpayment and protest of the bill must be proven to have been given to the parties in due time. I shall write to the Cashier of the office at New Orleans to have the deposition of the Notary public there taken and forwarded to me with such other proofs as that office can furnish.[1] The point of most difficulty in the case (if notice shall be proven) I apprehend will be that the bill was lodged with the Bank for collection merely. The depositions should be taken under the act of Congress in such cases made & provided.[2] The title of the suit is the President Directors and Company of the Bank of the

U. States against John Harvie.[3] The title of the Court is the Circuit Court of the U. States for the Kentucky District. Be pleased, after having the depositions certified & sealed as the act of Congress directs, to inclose them directed to the Cashr. of the Lexington office. I am respectfully Your ob. Servt. H. CLAY

Mr. White Cashr. &c. &c &c

ALS. DLC-HC (DNA, M212, R1). Cf. above, Clay to White, June 8, 1822.

1 No letter found.

2 See above, Clay to Cheves, February 27, 1821.

3 In May, 1827, Harvie filed answer to the suit, denying that he had assumed the obligation as charged and calling for trial. A year later, the plaintiff having failed to appear in court, the case was nonsuited, with costs chargeable to the plaintiff. U. S. Circuit Court, Seventh Circuit, District of Kentucky, Order Book L, 467; M, 273.

From John McKinley

Dear Sir Florence[1] June 3rd 1823

Yours of the 20th ult.[2] has just been recd & I am on the eve of setting out for Cahawba[3] to attend the Supreme court of this State, & regret that I have not more time to devote to the subject of your letter. Every little community has its own views of matters however important & however incompetent they may be to judge of them. Such is the case here in relation to the Presidential election. Tennessee has by its Legislature declared for Gen Jackson[4] & "to make assurance doubly sure" the people in some parts of the State are confirming that act. The contagion is even spreading to this country through the influence of Gen Coffee (who is connected by marriage with Gen. Jackson) James Jackson & many others from the neighbourhood of Nashville who now reside in this county.[5] In my absence on Saturday last a meeting was goten [*sic*] up in this town & a vote given for the Gen. Though many as I am informed, were dissatisfied with it & now it seems some of his friends think his election certain Your friends here have at present a difficult part to play Believing as we do that Gen Jackson will not finally be a candidate we have deemed it bad policy to give the Slightest offence to his friends in general as it will be very easy to turn the large majority of the people in your favour when he is out of view. He & his warm partizans are however as perhaps you know inimical both to you & Mr Crawford & will prefer Mr Adams next to him. Whenever we can get them to urge the claims of Mr Adams their influence is gone here for Mr Adams will never under existing circumstances be supported by the people of the South & Mr Crawford from peculiar circumstances is very unpopular in the Northern & middle Section of this State[6] From this data you may infer what your prospects are. At the last Session of the Legislature of this State there was a strong disposition on the part of some of the members to bring Gen Jackson forward as a candidate but finding that an attempt of that kind might result in a majority in your favour it was abandoned. The present proceeding before the people is designed as the basis of Leslative [*sic*] nomination but it is certain to fail I think. The union of the West upon this subject is very important as you justly remark & therefore the better the public mind is prepared for that result the better To effect that object & produce that union in your favour the violence & bitterness of Some of the Generals friends ought to be met with temperance, but firmness by you & your friends as I concieve [*sic*] From these considerations I hinted to Doctor Pindall[7] last winter the propriety of a conciliatory course in Kentucky towards General Jackson. As far as my little influence will go it will be exerted in your favour & you know I am not *lukewarm* on subjects of this kind. On my return if any thing seems worthy of con[sider]ation I will advise you of it. By the [way t]he present Governor of this State[8] is for Mr Adams. Doctor Chambers[9] his opponent at the ensuing election is for you & we have great hopes of the Doctors election.

Your friend J. McKINLEY.

ALS. DLC-HC (DNA, M212, R1). Addressed to Clay at Lexington.

1 Alabama.
2 Not found.

3 Cahaba, established at the confluence of the Cahaba and Alabama rivers as the first capital of the State of Alabama.

4 See above, Hynes to Clay, July 31, 1822.

5 John Coffee, husband of a niece of Mrs. Andrew Jackson, had been an early business partner and a trusted military subordinate of General Jackson during the War of 1812 and the subsequent Indian campaign. James Jackson, a wealthy Nashville merchant, was not related to the General. Coffee and James Jackson headed one of the companies formed for land speculation in the vicinity of the Muscle Shoals, following the opening of that area after its cession by the Chickasaws. The town of Florence had been founded in 1818 in connection with this speculative venture.

6 Early Alabama politics had been dominated by settlers from Georgia, who looked to William H. Crawford for leadership. The Georgia faction, opposed by immigrants from North Carolina and elsewhere, and injured by its connection with an unpopular bank at Huntsville, had been defeated in the gubernatorial election of 1821. Albert B. Moore, *History of Alabama* (University, Alabama, [c. 1934]), 114-16.

7 Richard Pindell.

8 Israel Pickens, a native of North Carolina, was Governor of Alabama for two terms, 1821 to 1825. He had practiced law in North Carolina, had been a member of the legislature of that State (1809), and had served three terms in Congress (1811-1817) before removing to Alabama, where he practiced law, was register of the land office, and became president of a bank. He was briefly (February 17-November 27, 1826) a United States Senator.

9 Henry Chambers, originally a Virginian, a graduate of the College of William and Mary and of the University of Pennsylvania Medical Department (1811), had moved to Alabama in 1812 to practice his profession. He had served as a surgeon under Andrew Jackson during the War of 1812, as a member of the State Constitutional Convention in 1819, and as a State legislator in 1820. He had been defeated in the gubernatorial election in 1821 and was again beaten in 1823. He held a seat as United States Senator from March 4, 1825, until his death early in 1826.

Promissory Note from John Todd

[June 5, 1823]

I promise to pay H. Clay on demand fifty dollars; and if Todds heirs succeed in the cause now depending in the Court of Appeals with the Bates's and which is expected to be argued at the present term of that Court I promise to pay to said Clay the further sum of one hundred and fifty dollars.[1] Witness my hand & seal this 5th. day of June 1823. JOHN TODD {L.S.}

[Endorsement on verso][2]

Memo. This is to be void if I do not argue the Cause. H CLAY

DS, in Clay's hand. DLC-TJC (DNA, M212, R15). Todd, son of Robert Todd and brother of Levi L. Todd, later practiced medicine in Danville, Kentucky.

1 The case, Bates, &c. *vs.* Todd's Heirs, &c. stemmed from an agreement by which Robert Todd in 1784 had bound himself to make conveyance of 6,000 acres. Under successive assignments, one third part of this obligation in 1807 had come into the hands of John and James S. Bates (Bate), of Jefferson County, Kentucky, the former subsequently becoming identified with the United States Saline in Illinois (above, II, 166n). When the Bateses demanded of Robert Todd a conveyance, an additional agreement had been concluded; when this later obligation had also not been satisfied, a suit had been instituted against Todd but had been dismissed upon his execution of two bonds, calling for payments in money and land. These bonds had then been assigned to another party, suits had been brought upon them, and judgments recovered. After the death of Robert Todd, his heirs had won a suit in chancery, in Fayette Circuit Court, enjoining the judgments at law and cancelling the two agreements between Todd and the Bateses. The defendants had thereupon appealed. When the case was argued by Clay and others at the Fall Term, 1823, of the Court of Appeals, the latter court ruled that the Todd heirs were not "entitled to any relief against the contracts made by Todd with the Bates," but that the heirs of the parties holding the other two thirds of the original agreement had no "just cause to assert their claim under the agreement of 1784" against the Todds. 14 *Ky. Reports* (4 Littell) 177-86.

2 AES.

Memorandum of Receipt to Benjamin Warfield

[June 9, 1823]

Attached to Warfield to Clay, June 1, 1823.

To Nicholas Biddle

Sir Frankfort 11h. June 1823.

I have been attending the Circuit Court of the U. States at this place almost ever since my return from the Eastward, and the term is now about drawing to a close. I have the satisfaction of communicating to you that in many causes of the Bank, which have been tried during the term, our usual good fortune has attended us, and that we have not lost one cause of any importance. The Court has finally settled two principles of great moment, as they affect the interests of the Bank, both in Ohio and Kentucky. The first is, that sales of real estate, mortgaged or conveyed in trust to the Bank, are to be made for lawful money of the U. States, without regard to the valuation and other stay laws; and consequently for whatever it will produce. And the second is that, in cases of mortgages and trusts, where the Estate is insufficient to pay the debt intended to be secured, and the debtor is insolvent or doubtful in his circumstances, the Court will appoint a Receiver of the rents and profits of the

Estate, and order immediate possession of it to be taken, without waiting for the decision of the bill to foreclose or other suit. The rents and profits to be applied to the extinction of the debt. This decision is in conformity with the opinion I formerly gave to the Bank in Piatt's mortgage.[1]

The arrangement with Mr. Marshall[2] is not finally completed but the execution of it is in progress. He has conveyed the Mansion House and other real estate in this town (excepting a small part of the Stable lot, a conveyance of which will be made) and delivered to the Agent of the Bank possession of the whole. Most of the property has been since rented out, 'though on very low rents. He has also assigned $2500 in Kentucky currency on Taylor[3] the tenant, for arrears of rent. I fear however that but little if any of these arrears will ever be realized. Mr. Marshall has yet to secure payment of the $4000 and he has experienced considerable difficulty in obtaining such notes as I am willing to accept.

I have directed a Survey to be made of the Mansion House with a view to the Bank's effecting an insurance upon it, and I now transmit the survey herewith. The property has, during the last two or three months, been twice in imminent danger of being consumed by fire, and I beg leave to urge strongly the propriety of taking out a policy on such part of it as can be insured.

Mr. Jones,[4] the agent at Cincinnati, requested my attendance there to argue before a State Court a motion which Lytle[5] was about to make to quash the Judgment obtained against him at the instance of the Bank. The motion, it was expected, would be made on the 7h. instant. Although it was not exactly within the scope of my engagement to the Bank to appear there before a State Court, I should have gone, with great pleasure, but for two reasons, one was that my presence was necessary here to attend to the various concerns of the Bank before this Court; and the other was that one of my children is extremely ill, and I could not think of separating myself from her so far as Cincinnati.[6] I was happy to learn from Mr. Jones that he did not apprehend any danger from the motion; and I hope therefore that the interests of the Bank, in that motion, have been well taken care of by its Solicitor[7] and other local Counsel. Indeed it appears to me to be impossible that the Court should set aside that Judgment, unless there is a total disregard of all the law applicable to the case. I have the honor to be with great respect
Your obedient Servant H. CLAY

Nicholas Biddle Esqr. &c. &c. &c

P.S. The survey does not include the dwelling house and its offices adjoining the Mansion House, which were also conveyed by Mr. Marshall. I will have a survey made of them, if it be desired.

H.C.

ALS. PHi. Endorsed: "recd June 24."

1 See above, Clay to Cheves, June 16, 1822. As examples of the rulings of the Circuit Court for the District of Kentucky, at its May Term, cf. the case of The President, Directors, and Company of the Bank of the United States *vs.* Henry Johnson and Hugh Offutt, of Scott County, Kentucky, and that of the same plaintiff *vs.* John T. Johnson and Offutt, in both of which the defendants having failed to make payment on the first of a series of notes falling due in consecutive years, the court had appointed commissioners to take over the property pledged as security and, if payment had not been rendered by the following October, to sell the mortgaged tracts for "lawful Currency of the United States." U. S. Circuit Court, Seventh Circuit, District of Kentucky, Complete Records, W, 182-92.

2 John J. Marshall. See above, Clay to Cheves, October 26, 1821; Clay to Biddle, February 21, 1823.

3 Richard Taylor. 4 George W. Jones. 5 William Lytle.

6 Lucretia Hart Clay died one week later, June 18, 1823. 7 David K. Este.

To Martin D. Hardin

Dr Sir Ashland 14h. June 1823.

Mr Beall[1] has requested me to furnish you with a Certificate that the Judgt. Ormsby agt. Owings & Co. was for a Company debt. I prosecuted two writs of Error for the Co. about 15 or 20 years ago on that Judgt. & if you will examine the record perhaps it will shew the fact wanted.[2]

In 13 Johnson's Reports (page 127) you will find the whole doctrine treated on the subject of the mode of suing Corporations.[3] It appears that a summons should issue in the first instance. If the arrangement is acceded to for delaying the bringing the suit, as intimated, there ought to be a provision, as suggested by you, to guard against the death of the witnesses, and that I should have all the advantage which would flow from suing out process at this time. I mean this latter provision to cover the subject of interest, if the demands do not entitle me, as I think they do, to it. I am with great respect Your's H. CLAY

Genl. Hardin.

ALS. ICHi.

1 Probably Norborne B. Beall, executor of the estate of Walter Beall, who had died in 1810.

2 When control of the iron works property in Bath County passed to John C. and Thomas D. Owings in 1803 (see above, I, 135n), they had executed a mortgage to their former partner, Walter Beall. After Beall's death, his heirs had been forced to pay certain demands, owed by John C. Owings at the date of the mortgage, including two judgments (one in Federal court, the other in Nelson Circuit Court) to Peter B. Ormsby. 13 *Ky. Reports* (3 Littell) 104-105. The suits mentioned have not been found.

3 Lynch *vs.* Mechanics' Bank, 13 *Johns. R.* 127 (N. Y. Sup. Ct., 1816).

To Peter B. Porter

My dear Sir (Confidential) Lexington 15th. June 1823

Prior to the receipt of your very welcome letter of the 26th. Ulto. I had heard of the birth of your daughter and had shared with your

other friends in Kentucky the gratification which so pleasing an event was likely to produce. I offer to you and Mrs. Porter my hearty congratulations on the occasion, and particularly for her safe recovery from a condition at once the most interesting and perilous to which her sex is exposed.

I thank you for the very satisfactory information which your letter contains on the state of public sentiment in New York in regard to the Presidential election. Mr. Crawford possesses over his competitors the advantage, which you notice, in your State, that of having to espouse his cause some of the *most* bustling and active politicians, and Mr. Van Buren among them. I do not recollect whether I ever related to you an anecdote concerning this gentleman. The winter before the last he opened with me, on two several occasions, without the smallest invitation or encouragement on my part, a conversation on the Presidential election. In the first, he considered the prospects of Mr. Calhoun, of whom he said that he had not known an instance, so signal, of a gentleman of acknowledged talents, who was so evidently allowing himself to be made a dupe and victim, by a few noisy clamorous members of Congress, without influence at home; and he pronounced that he did not stand the slightest chance of being elected. In the second, he treated of the pretensions of Mr. Adams, who he said never could be President of the U.States; that his name was odious; that he had apostatized from his party; and that he was quite sure that in no event would New York render him her support. Well, this circumscribed the list of Candidates very much, reducing it perhaps to Mr Crawford and myself. I could not but feel (perhaps unjustly) that Mr. Van Buren's motive was to sound me, and that if I had, at that moment, said any thing very explicitly encouraging to him, his zeal would have been given a different direction from that which it has since taken. I need not, of course, say to you that, adhering to the resolution which I have deliberately formed, to make no promises, to hold out no individual inducements to any one, I forebore to excite his interest or stimulate his ardor in my behalf. Shortly before the close of the last Session I said jocosely to him "you said last winter who would not be elected, but did not tell me who whould [*sic*] be; it is time for you to fill up the blank." he replied that there was much more difficulty in pronouncing an affirmative judgment than a negative one. Have hopes of personal advancement been raised in his mind from another quarter? I am very unwilling to believe that Mr. Crawford would present any. But without any such intention on his part, may they not have been cherished by the other side?

It appears to me that the apparent advantage which the Secretary of the Treasury possesses, from the circumstance already mentioned, might be turned against him. If the public could believe that Mr. V.

Buren is actuated by the desire of personal aggrandizement it would certainly neutralize all his efforts. And if the public of New York were made to feel, as it might be, the controlling influence which that State could exert, on the Presidential question, the aims of the friends of the Secretary of the Treasury would I think be frustrated. If the alleged preference of Virginia for that gentleman really exists, on what ground does it rest? Is it not because he is supposed to possess views of certain great National interests more congenial with her own than mine are? Is it not, in short, for causes which ought to induce New York rather to oppose than support him? Is not the attempt of Virginia, if she means to bestow her suffrage on him, to continue her dynasty, after she is no longer able to present from among her own Citizens to the American people a suitable candidate, in the person of a Citizen of Georgia? And will New York, entitled as she is to perform a leading part in the affairs of this Union, ingloriously content herself with following in the wake of Virginia, and that at the hazard of defeating those great principles which she wishes transfused into the general administration? And after having thus lent herself to the Virginia notions, in opposition to her own views of the welfare of the Nation; after having acted the part of an humble sattellite [*sic*] is she even sure of winning this secondary honor? I do believe the election of Mr. Crawford very doubtful even if the weight of New York, ponderous as it is, should be cast into his scale. In a contest between him and Mr. Adams (should the election take that turn) I verily believe that the Secretary of the Treasury would lose every State West of the Mountains, except *perhaps* Kentucky, of which, in that contingency, he would by no means be certain. Majr. Hamilton,[1] the best informed, most active and most influential member of Congress from So. Carolina, assured me last winter that Mr. Calhoun, out of the way, that State would support me; and if I were out of the way also, he believed it would support Mr. Adams. And when we take into view the border war that has been so long carried on between the States of Georgia and So. Carolina,[2] we shall be prepared to admit the probability of his conclusion. Give Mr. Adams, then, New England, the West, with the exception mentioned, Pennsylvania (which he would I think certainly obtain in opposition to *Mr. Crawford*) South Carolina, and a share of votes in Maryland & New Jersey, and his election would be certain.

If New York were to declare for Mr. Adams, there would I think be more probability of his election than there would be of that of the Secretary of the Treasury, if she were to support him. And she would then at least have the merit of acting a primary part. She would not then move in subordination to Virginia. And she would seem to be obeying the law of the vicinage, and pursuing a course

more correspondent with her natural position. In the event of such a declaration for Mr. Adams, the issue of the contest would be between him and me, and it would depend upon the Southern States, including Maryland, and I am quite confident, whatever you may hear or see to the contrary, that those States would take part with me.

The result then is that New York would not be sure of her man, in the support either of Mr. Crawford or Mr. Adams. The truth, I verily believe, is (you will say possibly that I exhibit my vanity or selfishness in stating it) that she would only be certain of effecting an election, by the influence of her own weight, in taking me up. I have before communicated to you this opinion,[3] and I will now only say that, if during her next Legislature, New York comes out in my favor, my election is absolutely secure by the vote of two thirds of the Union. The immediate and inevitable consequence of such an annunciation of her will would be the relinquishment of Mr. Crawford by his Southern friends; the confinement of the contest to Mr. Adams and me; and I should obtain the support, probably without exception, of all South & West of New York.

In laying the preceding views before you, I pray you not to understand me as intimating any preference between the honorable Secretaries. I merely meant to open the chapter of probabilities.

I concur with you entirely as to the weakness & inefficiency of the measure adopted at Albany of recommending a Congressional Caucus. It ought to be considered only as a proclamation of the serious divisions, from which it no doubt emanated, among the members of your Legislature. Instead of heaving the difficulty of deciding the question from themselves & throwing it into a Caucus at Washington, it would have been much more becoming (if I dare speak my sentiments) the gentlemen at Albany to have reconciled their own differences, and told us their mind. Such a course would have greatly contributed to prevent popular agitation & might have secured to New York the preponderance which belongs to the first State in the Union.

Will there be a Caucus at Washn.? I doubt it. The difficulty first of ascertaining and then of combining the elements of such an assemblage, so as to produce a practical result, will be almost insuperable. Are federalists to be admitted or excluded? In either contingency many republicans will stay away. Are members from States which have committed themselves capable of binding their respective States, to the decision of a Caucus, if in opposition to the declared preference of those States? Do those States which are uncommitted & those which are committed, in other respects, stand on equal ground? Will not the friends of the respective Candidates be influenced in attending it by the probability of the success of their favorite? As no one may possibly have a majority, in the first in-

stance, of the whole, will it be possible to anticipate what the secondary combinations will be? Will not these secondary combinations lead to infinite intrigue? When the friends of each may fear the result, will not a majority or a great part absent themselves?

Would the decision of a caucus at Washn. have the effect which attended the resolution of former Caucus's there? I doubt it. As this subject will by the next winter or Spring reach every hamlet and every bosom, may not the promulgation of a vote in Caucus rather exasperate than allay previous differences?

I thank you for your kind invitation to visit you this summer. It would give me infinite pleasure to have that gratification; and if I live I intend some day or other to enjoy it. But I am such a slave to my professional & other business at this time that it will not be possible for me now to allow myself such an indulgence. I regret it the more because, besides the pleasure of meeting Mrs. Porter & you, there would be a probability of my meeting P. R. Livingston (whom I am very desirous to see) and the Vice President, for whom in all the vicissitudes of his fortunes I have cherished the greatest respect. If he supposed me capable of any intentional neglect of him last winter, he does me great injustice. The Country owes him a debt of gratitude on many accounts but particularly for his patriotic zealous & efficient support of the late War, which it can never cancel. He knows, I presume, through Mr Secretary Thompson[4] the high wishes which I sincerely entertained for him.

I have extended this letter to a most unreasonable length. I pray you to believe that it is not my habit to be thus unreasonable with my friends.

With my best compliments to Mrs. Porter & best wishes for the young lady, I remain Faithfully Your friend H. CLAY

P.S. Be pleased to inform me if the Editorial movement should be made which you have mentd. as being probable. H.C.

Genl. P. B. Porter.

ALS. NBuHi.

[1] James Hamilton, Jr., a Charleston, South Carolina, lawyer, had been elected to Congress in 1822 to fill the vacancy caused by the resignation of William Lowndes. Hamilton had risen to the rank of major in the United States Army during the War of 1812, had been Mayor of Charleston, and had served in the State legislature. He remained in Congress till 1829 and was Governor of South Carolina from 1830 to 1832. He later moved to Texas.

[2] Cf. above, Warfield to Clay, December 18, 1821, note; Smith to Clay, April 30, 1822; Porter to Clay, September 30, 1822.

[3] See above, Clay to Porter, February 2, 3, 1823. [4] Smith Thompson.

From Charles Miner

Sir

west Chester, June 19. 1823

My friend Wm H. Dillingham[1] has just returned from an Eastern tour. On Saturday the 31st May, on the Steam boat from Phila to

New York he fell in company with Maj. Haughton, the new editor of the Washington Republican,[2] a man, evidently of more zeal than discretion, from whom he learned:

1 That a great effort is to be made to elect Mr. Calhoon President.

2 That President Munroe is taking an active part in his favour.

3 That to advance their plan, Mr. Meigs and one of the Mr. Bradleys were to be removed from the offices of Post Master, & assistant P. M. Gen. (The first part of this prediction was verified in a week after it was announced, which gives much weight to all he said.) [3]

4 That Mr. McLean, of Ohio, in Mr. Calhoons interest was to be appointed P. M. G.[4]

5 That Smith Thompson, a partizan of Mr. Calhoon, was to be appointed a Judge of the Supreme Court in the place of Judge Livingston, deceased.[5]

6 That Mr. Southard of N. Jersey was to be appointed Secy of the Navy,[6] being a friend to Mr. Calhoon.

7 That the new paper "The Patriot" lately set up in N. York was to come out for Mr Calhoon[7]

8 That the "Virginia Times" was also to come out for Mr. Calhoon[8]

9. That there would be a Caucus of members of Congress; Mr. Crawford would go down; Mr. Calhoon would be nominated, and be elected as the Southern candidate.

Maj. Haughton was on a political mission; he intended to have gone to Albany, but finding that Mr. Van Beuren & Mr. Savage[9] of N. York had gone on a journey to Boston to promote Mr. Crawfords views, he went on after them.

From Mr. Dillingham I learned further, that Mr. Tallcott[10] Attorney General of N.Y. is the advocate of Mr. Crawford, but if he cannot be run with a prospect of success, his next choice would be Mr. Clay. Mr. Daggett—Mayor of New Haven[11] would prefer Mr. Calhoon, his, & his friends'—second choice, would be Mr. Clay. Mr Clay has, in Pennsylvania more friends than any other candidate, and would be the second choice of two thirds of those who are for the other candidates. The numerous meetings in favour of Gen. Jackson[12] are deceptive. Under certain circumstances the Gen might have a powerful vote here, but will not. A majority of those who attend those meetings I am confident are for Mr. Clay. Mr. Adams has some respectable friends, but not numerous. He could not, under any circumstances now conceivable, unless as the opponent of Mr. Crawford, obtain the electoral vote of Penna.

But, perhaps I am wearying you with uninteresting details. I would give you a particular account of Pennsy parties & politics but it might not be acceptable. Our contest for Gov. will be a severe one, your friends much divided. Neither the sentiments of Mr. Gregg nor Mr. Shulze[13] known, but the latter supposed to be a Calhoon man.

As I write without your knowledge, an apology is certainly due I thought the contents of Maj. Haughtons budget of consequence enough to warrant a letter.

May God preserve you long to your Country, is the wish of your most obed. Servt CHARLES MINER

Henry Clay Esqr

P.S. I ought to have mentioned that Mr. Meigs was suspected to be *your friend.*

ALS. DLC-HC (DNA, M212, R1). [1] West Chester, Pennsylvania, lawyer.

[2] Richard Haughton and Company had succeeded Thomas L. McKenney in proprietorship of this newspaper.

[3] Return Jonathan Meigs had resigned earlier in the month. Abraham Bradley, Jr., remained as Assistant Postmaster General some years longer.

[4] John McLean was named to the post under an interim appointment on July 1, 1823; he was formally nominated for the office on December 8, and his appointment was approved the following day.

[5] See above, Clay to Porter, March 18, 1823, note.

[6] Samuel L. Southard, Senator from New Jersey, was appointed to the post in September, 1823, and the nomination was confirmed December 9. Southard had held several local offices in New Jersey, had been an associate judge of the State Supreme Court (1815-1820), and had been elected to the United States Senate in 1820. After leaving the cabinet in 1829, he became Attorney General of New Jersey, was elected Governor in 1832, and in 1833 returned to the United States Senate, where he served until his death in 1842.

[7] Established by friends of John C. Calhoun, this journal was launched on May 28, 1823, and discontinued in December, 1824. Its editor, Charles K. Gardner, had been an officer in the United States Army, 1808-1818, and, from 1820 to 1822, editor of the New York *Literary and Scientific Repository, and Critical Review.* He was later Assistant Postmaster General, an auditor of the Treasury Department, Postmaster of Washington, D. C., Surveyor General of Oregon, and a clerk in the Treasury Department. He published, in 1819 and 1820, two works relating to infantry training and, in 1853, *A Dictionary of All Officers . . . in the Army of the United States . . . 1789-1853.*

[8] Published at Richmond, Virginia, this journal had been established in Calhoun's interest by Samuel Saunders in February, 1823. William Ramsay, former editor of the Richmond *Daily Mercantile Advertiser,* succeeded Saunders as editor later in July of this year, and the paper ceased publication toward the end of August.

[9] John Savage. [10] Samuel A. Talcott.

[11] David Daggett, New Haven, Connecticut, lawyer, who had served several terms in both branches of the State legislature and had been a United States Senator, 1813-1819. In 1822 he had been appointed an associate justice of the Superior Court of Connecticut and the same year had become Kent Professor of Law at Yale University, a position he filled for over two decades. He was again Mayor of New Haven, 1828-1830, and for about two years from 1832 was Chief Justice of the Supreme Court of Errors.

[12] Friends of Jackson had met at Greensburg, in Westmoreland County, Pennsylvania, on December 28, 1822, and agreed to establish a committee of correspondence to organize a campaign in that State for his nomination. A second meeting of his supporters had been held at Harrisburg toward the end of January, 1823. On the Cumberland County meeting in April, see above, Woods to Clay, May 22, 1823.

[13] Andrew Gregg; John A. Shulze. The former, after having been a member of the United States House of Representatives (1791-1807), had been elected to one term in the Senate (1807-1813). He had become a banker in Bellefonte, Pennsylvania, in 1814 and was now (1820-1823) Secretary of State of Pennsylvania. He had been nominated for the Governorship by the independent Republican faction in Pennsylvania. His opponent, Shulze, nominee of the Republicans, had been educated as a clergyman

but had retired from the ministry in 1802. He had become a successful businessman, had served for eight years as an official of Lebanon County, Pennsylvania, and had been elected to several terms in the State legislature. Shulze won the gubernatorial election by a large majority and was overwhelmingly approved for a second term.

Receipt from John Wirt

[June 20, 1823]

DS. DLC-TJC (DNA, M212, R15). John Wirt, Collector of the Lexington town tax, acknowledges receipt of eight dollars for the tax of the current year, paid by Clay as executor of the estate of Thomas Hart, Sr. Wirt was also a silversmith and engraver.

To Martin D. Hardin

Dr Sir Ashland 21st. June 1823.

I recd. your favor of the 18h. inst.[1] and thank you for the kind communication respecting Col. Arnold.[2]

You will be pleased to order the suit against the Bank, having on my part exhausted all measures in my power to avoid the necessity of instituting it at this time.[3] I wrote you a few days ago refering you to 13h. Johnson's reports page 127 in which the doctrine is fully considered and established as to the mode of suing Corporations aggregate by summons.[4] Your's with great regard, H. CLAY

Genl. Hardin

ALS. ICHi. 1 Not found.

2 Possibly John Arnold, formerly a Franklin County, Kentucky, militia officer, member of the State legislature, 1813-1814.

3 See above, Power of Attorney, December 26, 1822. On June 9, 1823, the President of the Bank of Kentucky had reported to the Board of Directors that Clay had stated orally his willingness to postpone suit until the next year, provided the Board would be ready for trial at that time. The Board, however, had declined to commit itself. Bank of Kentucky, Frankfort, Record Book D (July 19, 1821-October 22, 1828), 157.

4 See above, Clay to Hardin, June 14, 1823.

From Nicholas C. Horsley

Henry Clay Esqr Henderson, June 21st. 1823

Dear Sir,

Becoming one of the heirs of Genl. Hopkins's Est by marriage, I feel authorised to communicate with you, without ceremony, on the debt due you by the Estate[1]—and particularly, on finding the Deed Trust covers all the negroes I recd from the Est and particially [*sic*] only, the negroes of the other heirs, except Miss Hopkins's,[2] who is rendered very uneasy by your letter to Judge Towles[3] of your intention to close the Trust by immediate sale—the heirs are generally, I believe, much attached, from family association, to their negroes, & would dislike very much to having them forced out of the family if there be a remidy [*sic*]

Saml. G. Hopkins is the administrator of the Est, and most ample funds had been provided by his farther [*sic*] before his death to pay off all the debts he owed, but unfortunately for the rest of the heirs (at present) he has very improperly applied those provisions of his Farther to his private purposes; but immediately on seeing your letter, I have called him to a settlement of his administratorship, and am determined to coerce that settlement as soon as practicable—

You would certainly be extending to the rest of the heirs an act of great Kindness, to suspend a coercion of this debt until they can make the administrator disgorge—which will be done immediately by law, if no other alternative will effectuate this most desired wish.— Please communicate with us if any arrangement for our relief may be expected.

I am shure, I could pledge myself, that the rest of the heirs would not Keep you out of the money a moment longer than can be made out of the administrator

I have the honour to be, Very Resply Yr ob St N. C. HORSLEY

ALS. DLC-HC (DNA, M212, R1). Horsley, a resident of Henderson County, had married Sarah P., daughter of Samuel Hopkins.

1 See above, II, 916-18; Account, December 3, 1822.

2 Probably Mary B., another daughter of Samuel Hopkins.

3 Thomas Towles. Letter not found.

From James Byers

Dr. Sir Mason County June 22 1823

When I purchased the negroes at the sale of R. L. Waters[1] I intended them for my plantation on Red River Louisiana, but yielded to the tears and entreaties of Mrs. Waters and did not remove them. She had raised them all, & very naturally felt for them a warm & unconquerable attachment, a seperation would have been cruel so long as there remained even a hope that Mr Waters would redeem them, I was assured most solemnly by Mr. W. (& had the utmost reliance upon the man) that he would pay the money before my note fell due, the negroes were left with him, & I went on to Virginia & purchased others in their stead, —altho I have some fears that Waters will not pay the money, I still think it probable he will do so for he assured me a few days Since that he would pay the money. but to guard against events & to be prepared for any possible contingency I have thought proper to ask of you a stay of execution or delay of payment, if Waters should disappoint me (thro my frend John Chambers), until I can have time to Sell the negroes, —I ask no more that [*sic*] what I am to pay, but should I not be able to get it here I shall be compelled either to take them below, or send them to a frend of mine Judge Johnston[2] on Red River who will cash them for me, seperately they will bring $2,500 however I do not wish to seperate them if they can be sold together, one has been added, to the number—the other children have increased in value beyond all reasonable calculation, —the woman is likely & about 32. her eldest a girl uncommonly likely about 15 or 16. the next a boy, about 13 or 14— a girl about 10 or 11 & the balance boys.— I feel perfectly satisfied they will Sell for more than I am to give, but if a Sale is forced at this time they will Sale [*sic*] for little or nothing—

I do not *beg* this as a favour, nor do I ask it as a right. but to be candid with you, to force out of me at this time $2,000 would ruin me— I am a farmer, & poor, yet able to pay the debt & intend to do so but you must indulge me if you *possibly* can,— I should like to hear from you in a few days. Yours respectfully JAMES BYERS

ALS. DLC-TJC (DNA, M212, R12). Addressed to Clay at Lexington.
1 See above, Murphy to Clay, July 3, 1821; May 28, 1823.
2 Josiah Stoddard Johnston.

From Samuel G. Hopkins

Dear Sir Spring Garden[1] Henderson County 22d June 1823

I was yesterday favored with a perusal of your letter to Mr. Towles on the subject of closing your trust upon the estate of my deceased father[2]

After the conversation which passed last winter in Frankfort, I determined to wait on you in Lexington before I returned home: and make arrangements for its final payment; but was arrested, in this intention, by the severest spell of sickness with which I was ever visited, and was compelled, (after being confined in Frankfort until subsequent to your departure for Washington) to avail myself of a Steam Boat to get home. Since that period, your absence from the State has precluded the opportunity of seeing you with this view; and now (our circuit court commencing tomorrow) renders it impossible for either Mr. Towles or myself to come up within the time limitted [*sic*] in your letter— As soon thereafter as possible one, or both of us, will wait upon you. The Severe pressure of pecuniary distress, which seems, indiscriminately to afflict every portion of our State, will make it necessary for us to encounter great sacrifices in raising the money for you— Should you persist in your determination, to close the trust immediately but little will remain of the estate, to support an aged widow and several indigent orphan grand children, who had hoped to derive subsistence from it. At present we have a growing crop upon the land; and depend exclusively upon [the] negroes conveyed in the deed, for its cultivation— To divest us of these before it is har[vested][3] would bring additional injury which would result in nothing short of ruin— I therefore appeal to your liberality; and hope when it is considered, that only a portion of the original debt is now due; and even that portion effectually secured that you will grant us additional time– Of this, I must beg you to inform me as early as your convenience will permit

I am with great respect your obedient servant S. G. HOPKINS

Honble Mr. Clay

ALS. DLC-TJC (DNA, M212, R12). 1 Residence of Samuel Hopkins.
2 See above, Horsley to Clay, June 21, 1823. 3 MS. torn.

To Simon Gratz and Brother

Mess Simon Gratz and Brother Lexington 23d. June 1823.

I will thank you to transmit to me, as soon as convenient, the state of the account of the late Col. James Morrison with your house.

By the will of the deceased[1] he has bequeathed sundry pecuniary legacies to a large amount.. It is my wish and my duty to pay the legatees as soon as may be practicable; and I desire particularly to discharge a rateable proportion of them in October next. In drawing upon you for the balance in your hands, I would like to consult your convenience as far as I can consistently with my duty. May I therefore now enquire of you, if it would comport with your convenience to pay the balance in your hands in the above month? With great respect I am Your obedient Servant H. CLAY

only acting Exor of James Morrison deced

ALS. PHi. Endorsed: "Ansd 9 July." Answer not found.
1 Fayette County, Kentucky, Will Book F, 61-70.

Advertisement of Estate Management

June 23, 1823.

[Clay, *"only acting Executor"* of the estate of James Morrison, requests those indebted to the estate "to make immediate arrangement for the discharge of their respective debts," and "those who have demands against the estate . . . to exhibit them, that prompt provision may be made for payment of such as are not contested."]

Lexington *Kentucky Reporter,* June 23, 1823.

From John Chambers

Dear Sir Washington[1] 23d June 1823.

Captn. Byers who purchased the negroes sold under Martin's[2] Exon against Waters requests me to state his situation to you and to request that if you can conveniently do so, you will extend the

time of payment on his bond. Byers purchased the negroes for his own use but from the extreme anxiety of Waters and his wife to retain them & his positive assurances that he could raise the money by the time it would become due, Byers permited [*sic*] him to keep possession of the negroes and purchased others for his own use, he now entertains doubts of Waters ability to raise the money & in the event of his failure will not be prepared himself to make the payment without selling the negroes which I have no doubt he will do as soon as possible and the growth of the young negroes and the increase of one in number will notwithstanding the depreciation in value of that kind of property enable him to get the money for them— Byers and his securities are each good for a much large [*sic*] sum than his bond is for and if you can conveniently indulge him I assure it will seldom be in your power to extend a favour to a more honorable or Amiable man. I have adised [*sic*] him to write to you on the subject. Accept the renewed Assurance of the very high estimation in which you are held by Your Mo: Obt: Servt. JOHN CHAMBERS
Honble Henry Clay

ALS. DLC-TJC (DNA, M212, R12). See above, Byers to Clay, June 22, 1823.
1 Kentucky. 2 Possibly John L. Martin.

Agreement with Jacob Payton

[June 24, 1823]

I have this day received of H. Clay Two hundred & 54 lb pounds weight of Merino wool which I promise and bind myself to manufacture for him in the following proportions that is to say Fifty yards of flannel, and four fifths of the residue in Casimere and one fifth in Casinette, the said Clay to pay for the Cotton warp & to furnish Madder and Indigo. I am to manufacture the above articles of the best kind which the quality of the wool will admit of, the color of the Casimere and Casinette to be a dark blue mixture; and I am to deliver the several species of Cloth above mentioned on or before the first day of November—next; the Casimere & Casinette when fulled to be not less than three quarters wide. As a full compensation for my services in manufacturing the above wool I am to receive one half of the Cloth which it makes. I am to call on said Clay when I want the Indigo and Madder—

Witness my hand this 24h. June 1823. JACOB PAYTON

[Endorsement][1]

the Wool deliverd [*sic*] to Jacob payton two Hundred & Seventy pounds Tare Sixteen pounds

270
Tare 16
254

Witness Present Emd. Kenna.[2]

[Endorsement on verso][3]

We have settled the within agreemt. and H. Clay has paid Twenty two dollars & fifty Cents in full 17 June 1824 H CLAY

DS, in Clay's hand (except for the weight "54 lb," in Payton's hand). DLC-TJC (DNA, M212, R15). Payton was a Lexington, Kentucky, weaver.

1 ES, in Payton's hand. 2 Not identified. 3 AES.

Agreement with John Bruce and Benjamin Gratz

[June 26, 1823]

[Whereas James Morrison, John Bruce, and Benjamin Gratz on July 1, 1822, entered into copartnership as the firm of Morrison, Bruce, and Gratz for the manufacture of "spun Yarns, Cordage, Bale rope, twine and other articles usually made in a rope walk and also Cotton bagging"; whereas Morrison has died and although the articles of copartnership made provision for continuance in such eventuality, it is nevertheless deemed best to dissolve the firm so far as Morrison was therein concerned—the remaining partners have agreed with H. Clay, only acting Executor of Morrison, that the dissolution shall be accomplished under the following terms: 1st, Bruce and Gratz shall pay all debts, receive all profits, and bear all losses of the company; 2nd, Clay, as Executor, shall be paid the amount of all advances made by Morrison to the concern, with legal interest from the time such advances were made, such payments to be rendered in the kind of money in which they were originally rendered, the specie advances amounting to $9452.71, with interest of $664.38 for the period to the next October 23, for which sums Bruce and Gratz have executed promissory notes payable on the latter date, with the understanding that they shall have an additional four years, with interest payable semiannually at the rate of six per cent per annum—and the advances in notes of the Bank of the Commonwealth, totaling $4950.31, inclusive of charges up to next April 1, for which Bruce and Gratz have issued promissory notes payable on that terminal interest date; 3rd, Bruce and Gratz agree to give Clay a mortgage upon all the real estate and slaves of the firm to secure payment of the above-mentioned notes; 4th, Bruce and Gratz are to retain all the real estate of the firm, but they are to pay the Executor $6,000 on January, 1828, with accrued interest, which they had agreed to pay Morrison for houses and lots sold the partnership; and 5th, the present agreement does not "comprehend any settlement of the affairs of the late Concern of Morrison and Bruce,[1] which is to be effectuated" between Clay and Bruce. Signed by Clay, "only acting Exor. of James Morrison deceased," and by John Bruce and Benjamin Gratz; witnessed by Robert Scott. Recorded by J. C. Rodes, Clerk of Fayette County Court, November 1, 1823.]

Fayette County Court, Deed Book X, 112-14.
[1] James Morrison and John Bruce had initiated the ropemaking business under a partnership announced on January 12, 1822. Lexington *Kentucky Reporter,* January 21, 1822.

Mortgage Deed from John Bruce and Benjamin Gratz

[June 26, 1823]

[John Bruce and Benjamin Gratz, in order to secure payment of the several sums hereafter mentioned and for the further consideration of one dollar, paid and acknowledged, convey to Henry Clay, as executor of James Morrison, deceased, a lot of ground and the buildings thereon, in Lexington, two acres and 104½ poles on Short Street, between the property owned by T. W. Hawkins and that held by the representatives of Thomas Hart, Jr., deceased—which lot and buildings were transferred by James Morrison on July 1, 1822, to the firm of Morrison, Bruce, and Gratz, as recorded in Fayette County Court, Deed Book V, 499; also 38 slaves, now in the possession of Bruce and Gratz, together with the increase of the females: on condition that whereas Bruce and Gratz have this day executed to Clay, as Morrison's executor, three promissory notes, one for $9,452.71, payable October 23 next, another for $664.38, also payable on that date, both payable in specie, and the third for $4,950.31, payable on April 1 next, in notes of the Bank of the Commonwealth or its branches, now if Bruce and Gratz, or either of them, pay the several notes as due, this indenture is to be void. Witnessed by W. Rodes, Deputy Clerk; the signatures of Bruce and Gratz acknowledged before James C. Rodes, Clerk of Fayette County, June 27, 1823.]

Fayette County Court, Deed Book W, 352-54. See above, Agreement, this date.

Receipt from David Grisham

26 June 1823.

I have this day settled with H Clay all my blacksmith's accounts and I have this day received of him the sum of sixty four dollars being the balance in full of all accounts. DAVID GRISHAM

DS, in Clay's hand. DLC-TJC (DNA, M212, R15). Grisham (Gresham) was a resident of Fayette County.

From William B. Rochester

Dr Sir Bath, Steuben County, N.Y. 28. June 1823

I owe you an apology for not having replied sooner to your letter of the 15h. March,[1] tho' it did not in fact get into my hands until about the 7h. May, the day on which I got home

I found the politicians at Albany much more at odds on subjects of a national concern than I anticipated— The Federal Corps are almost nemine contradicente for Mr. A.[2] but they do not really compose a third of our population and they constitute all *his* strength, so that his chance is perfectly hopeless in this State— I think I Speak truly on this hunch tho' the American of N. Y. holds a different language—[3] altho in this Section of Country the western candidate is indubitably the most popular, some of our leading Repubs. in the Eastern part of the State are decided and open for Mr. Crawford so much so, that, inasmuch as the legislature here resolved to abide by a nomination at Washngtn[4] they will spare no pains to give such bias to our members in the next Congress— Among the most influential of those are the Lieut Gov:[5] Mr. Van Buren of Albany and Mr. Bowne of N. Y.—[6] with our Legislature, these three Gentlemen are a host in themselves—

The Govr.[7] is rather shy— I think he inclines to Mr. Calhoun I judce [*sic*] from the late course of some of his ardent friends in N. Y. City our old Repubs. are very much opposed to Mr. A. and they generally identify Mr. Calhoun with him— extraordinary exertions are making for Mr. Crawford, and a regard for truth compels me to express my belief that he will be the N. Y. Candidate— our mode of choosing (as you know) will make them all alike—

I have in my feeble way remonstrated with V. Buren, Root & Bowne, but to no purpose— It is not to be disguised that Mr. V. Buren is a great favorite with the democratic party in this state on account of the persecutions he has undergone for our opponents and very many who are indifferent in these piping times of peace are willing to do as he does because they have his interests and advancement very much at heart.—I am glad that not one of them dared to find fault with the merits of my candidate and indeed they frequently acknowledged the force of my reasoning as a matter of policy, but they talk about principle, the age of Mr. Crawford, his former pretensions & support from this State—

I pray you not to understand that I am alone—far from it—but we have a Sort of tripartite contest, so conducted that your friends should not be too confident of N.Y.— as far as my feble [*sic*] example & advice & exertions may avail you shall have friends in the next Congress from our State—

The political fates have decreed that I shall not be at Washington next winter[8]—indeed my residence there had nearly killed me—

I trust that my Dist: will find a better man & one who thinks as I do, on all political matters— I have the honour to be Dr Sir Very truly Yr. friend W B ROCHESTER

Hon: Henry Clay Lexington Ken:

ALS. DLC-HC (DNA, M212, R1). [1] Not found. [2] John Quincy Adams.
[3] See above, Shaw to Clay, February 11, 1823; Porter to Clay, May 26, 1823.
[4] See above, Woods to Clay, May 22, 1823, note; Porter to Clay, May 26, 1823.
[5] Erastus Root.
[6] Walter Bowne, wealthy hardware dealer of New York City, who had turned to politics, had been a member of the State Senate and the Council of Appointment, and had been in 1820 Grand Sachem of the Tammany Society. He became Mayor of New York for five years, beginning in 1827.
[7] Joseph C. Yates. [8] See above, Shaw to Clay, February 11, 1823, and note.

From Adam Beatty

[Dear] Sir Washington, June 30th. 1823

It would have afforded me much pleasure to have seen you on your return from the Eastward, but was prevented, in consequence of my absence at the Bracken[1] court. I have, within a few months recd. two letters from my [wor]thy frie[nd Nathaniel Roches]ter. He is cordually [*sic*] your [. . . .][2] first letter, febr. 11th tho' he enter[tai]ned strong hopes of your succeeding in the State of New York, he was not without apprehensions that the Yankee interest, governed by their prejudices in favour of an Eastern man, would give Mr. Adams a majority. In his last letter (May 24th.) he is deci[dedly] of opinion, that the interest of Mr. Adams is [decl]ining. He says, "The Republicans, (he speaks of the west) since they find the [Feder]al papers, in every part of the Union, advocating [his e]lection, suspect his Republicanism; at any rate [they] think it will not be best to have a President [who] will be indebted to the Federalists for his elli[*vati*]on to office, and they are now divided be[tween] Clay and Crawford." He speaks of the resolution [en]tered into by the republican members of the Legislature of New York, last winter, relative to a congressional caucus[3] but says nothing about the vote said to have been taken, in which you are represented as having stood highest on the list. Mr. Craw[ford] second, Mr. Adams third &c. The following is an [extract] from his letter of the 24th. May. "The republi[can mem]bers of our Legislature (being 9/10 of that body) [in session] at Albany, last winter, entered into a reso[lution] condemning State nominations, and recommending a nomination in the old way, by the Republica[n] members of Congress. It is thought, that if the[y] had nominated, *last winter,* Crawford would [have] had a majority, in [. . .][4] but [. . .][5] is declining [. . .][6] in this State." As I had understood Colo. Ro[chester] was a member of the Legislature (but perhaps it w[as] of the one preceding)[7] I was surprised at his maki[ng] no mention relative to the vote spoken of above. You however must have correct information on this subject. I thought it proper h[ere] to give you a statement of Colo. Roch[ester's] views. He is decidedly of opinion, that your [*election*] will best promote the great and leading [*objects*] of New York; and entertains strong hopes [*that*] it will be ultimately found to be in you[r favour.] Their election, he says, will take place in N[ovember] for the State Legislature, which will cho[ose] electors, and he expresses an opinion "that t[hey] will support the men, whose opinions may coincide with theirs, as to who shall be President. I regret to find that William Rochester will n[ot] be in the next Congress. Since the election [of] [me]mbers of Congress, he has been appointed a judge [of] the Western District, under a late law arrang[ing] the State into Districts, and has accepted the [a]ppointment. I hope however he will be able to do something for you, within his circuit.

I suppose you have seen the Account of the Woodbe [*sic*] family.[8] I think it places you on very favourable [g]round. I was pleased to find, that it originated in [New] Y[ork *and hope that it* wi]ll be of some service to [*you*] there, [*as*] w[*ell as i*]n other States.

If you are not too much pressed with business, I should like to hear your views respecting your prospects to the Eastward, and in [t]he middle States. I remain cordually and sincerely Your friend

A BEATTY

ALS. DLC-HC (DNA, M212, R1). Addressed to Clay at Lexington. MS. torn.
1 County, Kentucky. 2 Four to six words missing.
3 See above, Woods to Clay, May 22, 1823, note.
4 Two or three words missing. 5 One word missing.
6 Half a line missing.
7 Nathaniel Rochester had been a member of the legislature in 1821-1822.
8 Late in May, 1823, a Cincinnati correspondent to the Lexington *Kentucky Reporter* noted receipt of the pamphlet, "A Sketch of Several Distinguished Members of the Woodbee Family in a Letter from a Gentleman to His Friend," which he supposed to be the production of a former resident of that city. Originally published in New York and reprinted in the Lexington *Kentucky Reporter,* June 9, 1823, the work was sharply ironical in description of William H. Woodbee's (Crawford's) pretensions to the Presidency, balanced in its appraisal of John Q. (Adams), and very generous in its conclusions relative to Henry Woodbee (Clay). The author has not been identified.

From John D. Godman

Dear Sir, Philadelphia, the 1st of July, 1823.

Since your departure many exertions have been made by our friends, to induce a generally favorable sentiment, relative to the subject of our last conversation. Much more could have been done, but that the editors have been very unwilling to be impartial, to say nothing of being active, for our cause. They will not publish unless the article be *mild* even to insipidity, and so free from sectional feeling as to be of no service to any one.

We have been considerably dispirited to find the Western papers so obstinately silent; because our opponents consider it an evidence of the despondency of the most sanguine.

Dr. Drake[1] has excellent talents for composition of the kind which would be most serviceable for the present occasion. He is very friendly to you, and would be rejoiced at your success. In writing to him I have stated the necessity of his becoming active in promoting our wishes; this I have done without speaking of any understanding with you or your friends. Should you think proper to let him know anything on this subject, I feel sure that he will do his best.

Mr. T. T. C.[2] of Cincinnati is one of your warmest friends, and if he would occupy the columns of the Cini. Gazette,[3] it would be to our advantage. You can best judge of the propriety or utility of inviting him to cooperate with your friends in this city. As our opponents will certainly endeavour to profit by the remissness of the Western papers, we shall be very happy, that this source of gratulation should be closed to them.

Before this, you have doubtless felt fatigued by the intrusion of so much of my inexperience, on your notice. The blame, however, rests with you, who have bestowed your complaisant attention where it could be as little merited as expected, although your regard will ever be ardently wished for by Sir, Your friend & Servant.

H. Clay, Esqr. Lexington Ky. JOHN D. GODMAN.

ALS. DLC-HC (DNA, M212, R1). Sent, "Politeness of Mr. R. Best"—Robert Best, who this year came to Transylvania University as adjunct professor of chemistry, received the M. D. degree from this institution in 1826, and died in Lexington in 1830. Endorsed by Clay: "Answd." Answer not found. Godman, who had served in the United States Navy during the War of 1812 before beginning the study of medicine, had been graduated from the University of Maryland in 1818, had begun practicing his profession in Lancaster County, Pennsylvania, and, after brief residences in Maryland and Philadelphia, in 1821 had become professor of surgery in the Medical College of Ohio, located at Cincinnati. He had resigned that position after one term, though he had remained in Cincinnati a few months longer as editor of a medical journal. He had returned to Philadelphia late in 1822 and, in the next year, became head of the Philadelphia School of Anatomy. In 1826 he moved to New York to fill the chair of anatomy at Rutgers Medical College but was soon forced by ill health to resign. He was the author of several works on medicine and natural history.

1 Daniel Drake, noted physician and author, had at an early age been brought from New Jersey to Mays Lick, Kentucky. He had studied medicine with a physician in Cincinnati and at the Medical College of the University of Pennsylvania, where he had received the M. D. degree in 1815. After practicing briefly at Mays Lick and Cincinnati, he had taught in the Medical Department of Transylvania University, 1817-1818, and had founded the *Western Medical and Physical Journal*. In 1819 he had established the Medical College of Ohio (later the University of Cincinnati College of Medicine), which was soon torn by dissension to the extent that he had been forced to leave. In 1823 he returned to the Transylvania University Medical School, where he was dean for several years. Subsequently he went back several times for brief periods to the Ohio Medical College; taught at the Jefferson Medical College, Philadelphia, and the Louisville, Kentucky, Medical Institute; and founded the Medical School of Miami University of Ohio and the Medical Department of Cincinnati College. Outstanding among his publications is *A Systematic Treatise, Historical Etiological and Practical, on the Principal Diseases of the Interior Valley of North America* . . . (2 vols.; 1850, 1854).

2 Thomas T. Crittenden.

3 Two Cincinnati newspapers, *Liberty Hall* (founded in 1804 as *Liberty Hall and Cincinnati Mercury*) and the *Cincinnati Gazette* established in July, 1815), had been consolidated in December, 1815, as *Liberty Hall & Cincinnati Gazette*.

To Walter Dun

Dr Sir Ashland 2d. July 1823.

I duly received your favor, under date the 12th Ulto.[1] which I defered answering until I received the inclosed copy of Banks's bill from Frankfort, which I got yesterday. You will perceive from it that I obtained a Judgment against him at the late term of the Federal Court, and that he has procured an injunction. He had of course to give security which may render the debt safe, 'though I did not much like the person received, but he qualified according to law, and the Court was therefore obliged to take him.[2] The sooner your answer is prepared and sent to me the sooner we shall be able to dissolve his injunction, for which I take it for granted he has no just grounds.

I did not receive the papers to which you refer in the case of Mr. Call Exor of Means agt. Carneals heirs & the action is consequently not brought. If you will forward other Copies in the course of a few weeks I will institute the suit to the next Court and it will be as forward as it could have been, if I had before received them.[3]

I inclose herein a statement of the Costs in the three suits agt. Mountjoy, brought in the name of Taylor Exor &c[4] and in that against Mr. Banks amounting together (excluse [*sic*] of my fees) to $54:67, which I have paid. If it be perfectly convenient to you, I would be obliged if you would deposit to my credit with the off. of discount and deposit at Chillicothe the amount and also my fees according to a statement below and transmit me a Certificate of the deposit. With great regard I am faithfully Your ob. Servant

Walter Dunn Esq. H. CLAY

Amt. of Clerk & Marshalls fees in Taylor exor of Heron against Mountjoy in three actions at common law	$45:81
To my fees in those three actions $25 in each	75:
Amt. of Clerk & Marshalls fees in Dunn agt. Banks	8:86.
To my fee in do.	25:
	$154:67

H. CLAY

ALS. Ross County Historical Society, Chillicothe, Ohio. 1 Not found.

2 At the May Term, 1823, Dun, an executor of the estate of his uncle, John Graham, a merchant of Richmond, Virginia, who had died in September, 1820, had been awarded a judgment against Henry Banks for $691.14, claimed on an overdue note, together with interest at six per cent from the due date, July 11, 1818, until paid, and costs. Clay had served as Dun's attorney in the action, instituted in December, 1820.

In June, 1823, Banks had opened a countersuit in chancery, claiming that he had already provided Dun with funds sufficient to offset Graham's demand but that his accounts were sent to Graham and fell into Dun's hands, also that Dun had failed to credit other payments. With Stanley P. Gower, Frankfort, Kentucky, jailer, as security, Banks had been awarded a temporary injunction barring enforcement of Dun's decree, pending action on the countersuit. At the May Term, 1824, the injunction was dissolved and Dun was awarded benefit of his earlier judgment plus ten per cent damages. A year later, however, Banks in chancery proceedings was awarded an injunction to stay the earlier judgment on the basis of three separate credits, totaling $783.27, the latest dated March 4, 1823. U. S. Circuit Court, Seventh Circuit, District of Kentucky, Complete Records, U, 111-13; W, 222-34; Order Book I, 330-32.

Banks, in 1823 a resident of Frankfort, had been, during and immediately after the Revolution, a prominent Virginia lawyer, merchant, and land speculator, with interests ranging from Philadelphia and Richmond west to the Kanawha (which district he had represented in the Virginia House of Delegates in 1792) and into central Kentucky and Ohio. Around the turn of the century he had been declared insolvent under the laws of Pennsylvania, at which time he was already in debt to John Graham, among others. Cuthbert Banks represented Banks' interests in Kentucky but was not apparently a member of his immediate family.

3 The suit, Daniel Call, executor of Robert Means, deceased, against Thomas D. Carneal, in chancery, was brought up on October 15, 1824, and a decree *nisi* awarded to the plaintiff for collection of $2,580 and interest at six per cent from September 23, 1801, plus costs. Carneal thereupon called for filing of exhibits. The case was continued until May, 1830, when on motion of the plaintiff it was discontinued at his costs. U. S. Circuit Court, Seventh Circuit, District of Kentucky, Order Book K, 156, 283; N, 7, 179, 186.

4 See above, Clay to Dun, April 23, 1822.

To Martin D. Hardin

Dr Sir Lexn. 3d. July 1823.

I came into town this morning with the inclosed letter for you, and found in the office your's addressed to me.[1] It appears that, without knowing it, we were both engaged on the same object—

I send you the draft which I prepared[2] & you can compare it with your's & avail yourself of any suggestions which it may contain. Mine has a count upon *an account stated* which I think had better be in. Do you think the demand of lawful currency is sufficiently avered [*sic*] at this place & in Frankfort in your sketch?

Anxious that the writ shd. be issued to the next Court & supposing it shd. be executed 10 days before the Court, I return it in haste confiding altogether in your better judgment.

If the cause can be tried at the next term be pleased to inform

Your's faithfully H. CLAY

ALS. ICHi. Addressed to Hardin at Frankfort.

1 Neither letter has been found. 2 Not found.

Account with Lexington Post Office

1823 H Clay Esqr [July 3, 1823]

Apl	1	due to this day	12.17
		Nat Intel[1] to July	57
		Nat Gazette	57
		Cincinnati	19
		Indianapolis	19
		Commentator	13
		Argus	13
		Box to July	30
			14.25
8. & 9		– Letter postage	20
12 . 13		– do	50
14 . 17		– do	1-10
19 . 20		– do	1 43½

22	— do	....	.16
May			
1 & 3	— do	....	-55
4 & 6	— do	....	52
7 & 11	— do	..	1.06½
12 . 13	— do.	.. ....	62½
14 . 15	— do	....	1.27
16 18	— do		1 40
		Carried over	23.08
	Amt brot over		$23- 8
May			
20 & 21—	letters	....	1.62
23 25—	do	....	87
27 28	— do		68½
29 30	— do	....	59
June 1	— do	....	35
4 5	— do	....	37
7. 9	— do	..	75
11. 12	— do		72
13- 15	....		56
17 19	....	....	48½
21 24	....		45
27 —	....		65½
July 1	....	....	18½
2 & 3	....		1.17½
			32„55

Amt of Postage from 1 Jany 1823 to 3 July

[Endorsement][2]

Recevd paymt JOSEPH FICKLIN

AD. DLC-TJC (DNA, M212, R15). Endorsed on verso by Ficklin: "Post office Acct to 3 July 1823."

1 Newspapers received by Clay were: Washington, D. C., *National Intelligencer;* Philadelphia *National Gazette;* Cincinnati *Liberty Hall and Cincinnati Gazette;* probably Indianapolis *Gazette,* established in 1822; Frankfort, Kentucky, *Commentator,* founded in 1817; Frankfort *Argus of Western America.*

2 AES.

From Hersey Bradford

Honble. Henry Clay Bristol R. I. July 3d 1823

Sir I have to acknowledge your letter of 10th. ulto.[1] with endorcd [*sic*] order of Court for a letter from R. Whiteing [*sic*] to James DWolf on the subject of interest on the note I sent you for Collection.[2] I have called on Mr. DWol [*sic*] for Said letter which he informs me he deliverd [*sic*] the original to you at Washington last winter with sundry other papers which I hope you will find accordingly, and in a few days I will send you the depositions of Mr. DWolf & others, he informs me that the contract with Whiting for the loan was made & executed in this place and the usury laws of this state have never been more severe then [*sic*] the forfeit of one third the principal & the intrest [*sic*], I will write you more particularly in a few days, and Am Respectfully sir your Ob. Servt.

N HERSEY BRADFORD

Please refer to Mr DWolfs letter[3] for further information.—

ALS. DLC-TJC (DNA, M212, R12). [1] Not found.
[2] See above, De Wolf to Clay, January 3, 1821.
[3] See below, De Wolf to Clay, July 5, 1823.

Rental Agreement with John Deverin

[July 5, 1823]

[Henry Clay agrees to lease to John Deverin, for four years from June 1, 1823, "that part of the Kentucky Hotel . . . now in his possession, that is to say, the large house (with the exception of the two large rooms above, one occupied by the Athaneum [*sic*], and the other by the Medical Faculty for their Library[1]) and the small house adjoining the Hotel and Tibbatts[2] house, and the back buildings to the fence which separates the Stables and the lot attached to them from the residue of the said property, including also the Ice house."

[Deverin agrees to pay in quarterly payments, $430 per year "for the demised premises." Clay reserves the right to distrain for the rent and to take possession of the property in case of default in payment of rent "and also access through the passage to the room of the Atheneum [*sic*]—"]

ADS, signed also by Deverin. DLC-TJC (DNA, M212, R16).
[1] See above, Rental Agreement, November 5, 1821. [2] Thomas Tibbatts.

To Smith Thompson

Sir Ashland 5h. July 1823.

Mr. D. Mallory[1] informs me that there is some vacancy expected shortly to occur in the Administrative branches of your department, which he is desirous to procure. I have known him for several years and take great pleasure in recommending him to your consideration as a gentleman of capacity & who may I think be entirely relied upon to discharge the duties of any such place that you may please to bestow on him. I will add that I should be highly gratified to see him in a place in which he could at the same time be serviceable to government & benefically [*sic*] employed as it regards himself. I have the honor to be with great respect Your obedient Servant

Honble S. Thompson Secretary of the Navy. H. CLAY

ALS. DNA, RG45, Misc. Letters Received, 1823, vol. 4, p. 83.
[1] Daniel Mallory, of New York City, author, publisher, and minor politician. His two-volume work, *The Life and Speeches of the Hon. Henry Clay,* first published in

1843, appeared in several editions. He also published *Short Stories and Reminiscences of the Last Fifty Years, By an Old Traveller* (2 vols.; New York and Philadelphia, 1842). He apparently did not receive employment in the Navy Department.

From James De Wolf

Honble H. Clay Bristol R I 5th July 1823—

Sir

Mr Hersey Bradford has shown me your letter of the 11th ulto[1] by which I observe Whitings plea of usury, the truth is that all the contract I ever made with Whiting was made in this place, the circumstance of the note being made in Boston was that Whiting neglected and refused to consumate [*sic*] his contract (for associating to erect the Distillery at Louisville) by giving his notes (after he had taken and converted to his own use about $50,000 of my money & the prospect of the Distilling project was on the wane in his estimation) I was obliged to go to Boston, where I had learned this Gentleman was, and by complying with some new requisitions I obtained such notes as he was pleased to give, the last of which I now enclose to you dated 20th Feby 1817— for 3000 Dollars with six years interest, and due 20th Feby last. The original note written to me by R. Whiting saying he would allow ten p cent for those funds I handed to you at Washington last winter, with a number of other papers, the said letter, or note, was numbered 7. & I expect & believe was dated in this place, as was the original contract, but as the place is not named in said original contract, it may be necessary to send a commission for taking evidence. The two witnesses to the said Agreement Robert Davis & Stephen S. Falls were my clerks, the former is dead, and the latter is residing in Cuba, near Matanzes General George DWolf[2] of this place, the witness to the notes given by Whiting has some knowledge of the fact, if you think it advisable to take the depositions of Mr Falls & Gen G. DWolf I wish the captions of the Commissions so made as they can be used in all the courts, particularly the Chancery Court where Whiting has filed his bill of complaints against me— (you do not mention the fate of my Sons action of ejectment.)

Mr H. W. Hawes & Messr. Denny & Thruston of Louisville have many papers concerning my affairs about that Distilley [*sic*] project &c & touching said Whitings bill in Chancery. & request you to communicate with said Gentlemen and direct them in said business—

I find that by the usury laws of this State in 1815. (when my unfortunate business with those people commenced) the interest only is forfeited, as will be seen by refering to the Statutes of this State on the subject copies of which I will send to you soon— You will judge whether it will be promoting my interest to commence another suit for the recovery of the within note, or bring it into the account in defending against his bill in Chancery The latter I suppose you will advise—

I wish you to include the names of Sanford Horton of Providence in this State, & Nathaniel Church of this town in the commission [*sic*] should you think it advisable to send them—one must be for Matanzes in the Island of Cuba Mess John I. Latting, Thomas Adams & Stewarts are respectable merchants there, who would be suitable persons to be commissioned: there are many other respectable Americans residing there, Zacheus Atkins, Joseph Oliver Wilson— my object is to prove that the original contract was made & consumated in this place, Whiting & S. S. Goodwin ought to be prevented if possible from being evidences for each other, as they are both delinquents, and both stand nearly in the same situation toward me & towards the Distilling Comy— I enclose the acts on usury from the Statute Book of this State— I find I stand no chance in Kentucky, it needs but to charge that contracts with me are usurious & it is confirmed as a matter of course.—

Should you think it necessary to take my testimony on the subject, you will please order a Commission for that purpose—please direct whatever is necessary to be done—

In the hope of the pleasure of seeing you in Washington next Decr I am very respectfully Sir Your Obt Servant JAS. D'WOLF

LS. DLC-TJC (DNA, M212, R12). See above, De Wolf to Clay, January 3, 1821.
1 Cf. above, Bradford to Clay, July 3, 1823.
2 Brigadier general of Rhode Island militia, 1818-1821; major general, 1822-1825.

From William B. Astor

Dear Sir, New York 7th July 1823

In the absence of my father who sailed for Havre on the 1st. ulto. I have received your letter of the 23d. June[1] inclosing a check on the Bank of the United States for $1400 say Fourteen Hundred dollars— Should you be desirous to make payments on your bond either next winter or in the Spring I will receive the same for my father as his attorney— Your letter of 13 May[2] to him was received a few days before he sailed & I believe remains unreplied to— I am with great regard your most Obedient Servant WM. B ASTOR

To, The Honorable Henry Clay Lexington Kentucky.

ALS. DLC-TJC (DNA, M212, R12). 1 Not found. 2 Not found.

From James Byers, Arthur Fox, and James W. Coburn

Mason County July 7th. 1823

If you extend the time of payment on a bond given by James Byers principal Arthur Fox & James W. Coburn Security for the Slaves purchased at the Sale of R. L. Waters to the first day of October next you may rest satisfied that the money will be *punctually* paid on or before that day.

JAMES BYERS
AR FOX
JAS W COBURN—

Honble. Henry Clay.

ADS by Byers, signed also by Fox (son of Arthur Fox) and Coburn. DLC-TJC (DNA, M212, R15). See above, Byers to Clay, June 22, 1823; Chambers to Clay, June 23, 1823.

Power of Attorney to John C. Sullivan

[July 8, 1823]

[Henry Clay, only acting executor of the estate of James Morrison, deceased, constitutes Colonel John C. Sullivan, near St. Louis, Missouri, his lawful attorney to sell Julia, a slave, now in the possession of Charles S. Hempstead,[1] of St. Louis, she being the property of the Morrison estate. Clay's signature acknowledged before James C. Rodes, July 8, 1823.]

Fayette County Court, Deed Book W, 354. Sullivan, a resident of St. Ferdinand, fifteen miles from St. Louis, was a surveyor who had held numerous contracts covering work on the public lands.

1 A lawyer, formerly of Ste. Genevieve, Missouri, where he had served at least two terms as public attorney for the Southern Circuit, Missouri Territory.

From James Byers

Dr. Sir

Mason County July 8th. 1823

I have recieved [*sic*] your letter of the 26th June[1] in which you say, that you would be willing to wait with myself & Securities until the first of October next, if you were perfectly certain of recieving the amount of the debt at that time, & request me to get my Securities to join me in the assurance that the money will certainly be paid on that day.—

I enclose you the Statement of Messrs. Fox & Coburn—[2]

I have this moment returned from Minerva Mr. Waters tells me that he has part of the money, & will obtain the balance this week, but I still do not believe he will get it all, whatever he does raise shall be paid over to your Atty.[3] & the balance of the debt paid before the first day of October next, should Waters disappoint me & [*sic*] shall proceed immediately to sell the negroes for whatever they will bring— I wish to save the commission & would be glad you [*sic*] would let me hear from you immediately, or write to your Atty. by the return mail Yours respectfully

JAMES BYERS

I do not wish Mr. Waters to know any thing of the delay, or he might not use proper industry.

ALS. DLC-TJC (DNA, M212, R12). Addressed to Clay at Lexington.
1 Not found. 2 See above, Byers, Fox, and Coburn to Clay, July 7, 1823.
3 John Chambers.

Land Patent from James Monroe

[July 11, 1823]

JAMES MONROE, President of the United States of America,

TO ALL TO WHOM THESE PRESENTS SHALL COME, GREETING:

KNOW YE, That Henry Clay of Lexington Kentucky ________ having deposited in the General Land Office a Certificate of the Register of the Land Office at Vincennes whereby it appears that full payment has been made for the North East quarter of Section Seven, in township Fourteen North, of Range Ten West, containing one hundred, and Sixty Acres ________ of the Lands directed to be sold at Vincennes by the Act of Congress, entitled "An Act providing for the sale of the Lands of the United States, in the Territory north west of the Ohio, and above the mouth of Kentucky River," and of the Acts amendatory of the same, There is granted, by the United States, unto the said Henry Clay, the Quarter lot or section of Land above described: To have and to hold the said quarter lot or section of Land, with the appurtenances, unto the said Henry Clay ________ his heirs and assigns for ever. ________________

[Seal] In Testimoney Whereof, *I have caused these letters to be made PATENT, and the seal of the* GENERAL LAND OFFICE *to be hereunto affixed.*

GIVEN under my hand at the city of Washington, the Eleventh *day of* July *in the year of our Lord one thousand eight hundred and* twenty three *and of the Independence of the United States of America the forty*-eighth

By the President. JAMES MONROE

[. . . V]olume 3 Page 425 GEO: GRAHAM *Commissioner of the General Land Office.*

DS, partially printed. DLC-TJC (DNA, M212, R10).

From Joseph R. Underwood

Dr Sir Glasgow 11th July 1823.

I have received ninety one Dollars in Commonwealths paper[1] from Edmd Hall late D Sheriff of this county[2] paid me for James Smith on account of money collected by him from James Burnett.[3] Hall agreed to pay as much more in Comths. paper as would be equivalent to $91 specie in case you would not receive this paper at par but requests that he may be dealt with favourably as he once before paid the whole amt recd to S P Sharp or your brother P Clay & has lost the vouchers at least this is his statement. I have stipulated for the additional payment in my recpt to him. John C Hall[4] late D Sheriff has collected for Mr Smith $162.38 from Burnett & has paid no part of it to me He says he has lost his vouchers but avers it was paid over long since. Before payment can be coerced it will be necessary that Mr Smith should forward me written authority to demand payment. Write to him to do so & to acknowledge his power to me before a notary. I have seen & taken copies of three receipts given by your brother P Clay for money paid him collected of Burnett for Smith The first is to Leander J Sharp[5] for three hundred Dollars dated 4th July 1811. The second to Solomon P Sharp for sixty Dollars dated 8th August 1811 and the third to Edmd Hall for two hundred & seventy Dollars dated 9th August 1811 making the whole sum recd by him $630.

I thought it best to take the $91 as offered by E Hall stipulating to return it should specie be required. Write me soon & say what course I shall take. I sent you such information as I could procure relative to the line between the lands belonging to the state & continental troops of Virginia under cover directed to F. Johnson Esqr according to your request.[6] Mr Johnson informs me my letter never reached Washington City. with esteem Your Obt Sert

J, R, UNDERWOOD

ALS. DLC-TJC (DNA, M212, R12). Addressed to Clay at Lexington.

1 Notes of the Bank of the Commonwealth.

2 Barren County, Kentucky. Hall, a lieutenant in the United States Army during the War of 1812, was one of four sons of a pioneer family in the county.

3 See above, II, 228, 567. About 1811 Burnett had probably been proprietor of a Barren County paper mill, which he had shortly sold.

4 Probably a brother of Edmund Hall.

5 A physician, who had represented Warren County in the Kentucky legislature, 1813-1814, 1822, then moved to Frankfort to practice his profession. He was a younger brother of Solomon P. Sharp.

6 Not found.

Account with Nicholas Berthoud

Shippingport [*ca.* July 14] 1823.

Henry Clay Esqr. To N: Berthoud Dr.

1822			Specie Currency
Sept.	6	To draye. of 10 Bags Salt to WH.[1]	" 37½
	7	" Freight on ditto 1775 @ ¼ p................	22 18¾
		" Commn. on advance of do 5 pct.	1 10¼
Jany.	3	" Storage on 4 Bags Salt & forwd do	1 25
	10	" do........ on 6 " ....".... "	1 87½
			26 79

Apl.	21	"	Carriage of 2 Boxes Bacon	....	21 "
		"	Coopering do & Nails		2 "
	23	"	Storage on 2 Boxes Bacon 140[1]	1 18	
		"	draye. to Boat & Shipping	1 25	
May	28	"	draye. of Brl & boxes to WHouse	" 25	
		"	Freight of do p Rob Roy[2]	2 16	
June	12	"	1 Brl sugar 1 Box Storage & forwdg.	" 50	
	27	"	Storage on 1 Box forwd	" 25	
July	8	"	Freight Keg rum 62½¢ draye. 12½¢	" 75	
	14	"	Storage & forwdg. Keg rum	" 25	
		"	Postages	" 20	
		"	Commn on advance Carriage $21.—5 pct.	" —	1 05
			do do Freight p R. Roy	— 15	....
				$ 33 73	$ 24 05

D. DLC-TJC (DNA, M212, R15). 1 Warehouse.
2 Steamboat, 240 tons, built at Cincinnati and put into service earlier this year.

From George Graham

Dear Sir Washington July 15th. 1823.

Your favor of the 20th of June[1] has been received—and I now forward a statement of the Money paid by me on account of the estate of Coll. Morrison,[2] and also of the balance on the books of the Office of Discount & Deposite subject to your draft— It will not be necessary for you to draw in my favor for the amount paid by me, as Checks signed by me "for the Exor. of Jas. Morrison" were in all cases shewn in the back of the accounts, which were enter'd in Coll. Morrisons own Check book— they will be given up to you on your arrival here with the Check book, and will constitute your vouchers— The balance to the credit of Coll. Morrison in Bank on the 23d. of April was $5144:72—
the amount of Checks paid by me is 1144.52
leaving a balance of $4000:20
subject to your draft as Executor—

Mr. Abbots[3] Note for $400, the only one deposited for collection, was protested & remains unpaid— I gave a check to Mr. Laurie[4] & Mr. Hawley[5] for $30 each— I was disposed to have made this a larger sum, but understanding that the Exrs. of Judge Livingston[6] had given to Mr. Hawley, $25 for similar services, with which he was satisfied, I thought it prudent to take that as a precedent— I believe that every claim of every description in this place against the estate has been paid, except, one made by a Barber, of five dollars for shaving Coll. Morrison after death, which I refused to pay—.[7]

You will be so good as to make my best respects to Mrs. Morrison

& Miss Edmiston[8]— I most sincerely sympathise with Mrs. Clay & yourself for your late affliction[9] With great respect Yr. obt. Sert
H. Clay Esqr— GEO: GRAHAM

ALS. DLC-TJC (DNA, M212, R12).
1 Not found.
2 James Morrison.
3 Possibly John Abbott.
4 James Laurie, minister of the Associate Reformed Church. Educated at the University of Edinburgh, he had emigrated from Scotland to the United States about 1802 and the following year had become pastor of a congregation in Washington, D. C., where he remained until his death in 1853. In addition to his pastoral duties, he was for years an employee of the United States Treasury.
5 William Hawley.
6 Brockholst Livingston.
7 Clay's account in settlement of Morrison's estate shows that on December 20, 1823, M. Brockenborough was paid $5.50 for this service. Fayette County, Will Book F, 372.
8 Sidney S. Edmiston.
9 See above, Clay to Biddle, June 11, 1823, note.

To Amos Kendall

Dr Sir Olympian Springs 21st. July 1823.

Your favor of the 16h. instant[1] has found me at this place. The Earl of Selkirk[2] when at Washington City in 1817 or 1818 (I forget which, the same winter however that he passed through this State) called on me and stated what he represented to be the object of his visit to that City. He said he was desirous of obtaining permission to introduce into his settlement from the Western States, particularly Illinois and Indiana which lie most convenient to it, breeding cattle & stock of all kinds, as he could obtain them through that route much easier than from Canada or England. Perhaps (though I am not sure he said so) he desired a permanent priviledge of trading with those States. I did not understand him as desiring that of introducing British goods, nor do I think he mentioned it to me. If he had, it would have made an impression on my mind. I asked him if he had not better make his application through the British Minister? He replied in a way which satisfied me that he had more reliance on his own diplomatic skill. What communications passed between him and the Department of State I do not know. I believe he did not succeed in the object of his mission.

With high regard I am faithfy Yours H. CLAY

Amos Kendall Esqr.

ALS. NcD.
1 Not found.
2 Thomas Douglas, 5th Earl of Selkirk, who had founded a colony on Prince Edward Island in 1803, had, even earlier, become interested in such an establishment on the Red River in Hudson Bay Company territory. After having acquired a controlling interest in the Hudson Bay Company, Selkirk in 1811 had sent out a group of settlers. Friction, to the extent of armed conflict, had ensued between his group and employees of the Northwest Fur Company, which also claimed the area. At the end of the Napoleonic wars he had employed ex-soldiers to accompany him to the Red River Valley, where his activities in 1816 and 1817 had incurred legal action. To stand trial at York, Canada, he had traveled by way of the United States during the fall of 1817 —through "Mendota, now in Minnesota, down the Mississippi to Prairie du Chien and

St. Louis and across Illinois and Indiana to Ohio; from there to Lexington (Kentucky), Washington, Philadelphia, New York, and Albany." Apart from his wish to avoid the embarrassment of arrest by an agent of the Northwest Company stationed at Fort William, Selkirk had been motivated in his routing by plans to purchase cattle and sheep in the Ohio and Missouri country for his colony and by a desire to reach agreement with United States officials relative to conflicting land claims. John Perry Pritchett, *The Red River Valley, 1811-1849, A Regional Study* (Carnegie Endowment for International Peace, Division of Economics and History, *The Relations of Canada and the United States;* New Haven, Toronto, and London, 1942), 206. Heavily fined as a result of the Canadian litigation and broken in health, Selkirk had returned to England late in 1818 and died in April, 1820.

From Thomas Hart Benton

Dear Sir, Nashville, July 23d. 1823.

I have been in this state two months, and in this town two weeks. I have been entirely through the state from one end to the other, and know it as well as any one that lives in it. The names for the Presidency now stand thus with the people: Jackson, Clay, Adams, Crawford. Jackson out of the way the state will go for you, and there is hardly any one who thinks he has any chance, and many see in his offering nothing but a diversion in favor of Adams. The friends of Crawford admit to me that he is now behind, but that single handed against Adams they could carry him, and that I think probable. Your friends here do not push you in opposition to Jackson. They would consider it bad policy, but go for you next after him. I have seen almost all the candidates for congress, and have a good guess who will be elected. Of the new ones they will be chiefly young men with the best dispositions in your favor. Col. Williams[1] will be very hard pressed for the Senate, and cannot possibly be elected unless he *gives in* for Jackson. Cocke[2] will be re-elected without opposition. He stands thus—Crawford, Clay, and would as lief go for the devil as any of the others.

The most active and influential paper in this state is edited by Darby.[3] He is for Jackson, Clay; with very little prospect for the former. He will be in Kentucky in a few weeks, and will call on you. Will also be at Washington this winter.

Shall be in this state two or three weeks longer, and then return to Virginia.[4] Yours truly. THOMAS.H.BENTON.

ALS. DLC-HC (DNA, M212, R1). Addressed to Clay at Lexington. Endorsed by Clay on cover: "Answered." Answer not found.

1 John Williams. See above, Hynes to Clay, July 31, 1822. 2 John Cocke.

3 Patrick Henry Darby, admitted to the bar in Franklin County, Kentucky, in 1822, had recently become editor of the Nashville *Clarion*. By the fall of 1824 he had returned to the practice of law in Frankfort, Kentucky, where in September, 1825, he acquired the *Harbinger*, renamed it the *Constitutional Advocate*, and established the journal as a powerful conservative, political organ. Darby's virulent attacks upon Solomon P. Sharp brought the editor under suspicion when Sharp was murdered two months later. Though exonerated, Darby merged the *Advocate* with the Frankfort *Commentator* in June, 1826, and retired to Brandenburg, in Meade County, Kentucky, where he died in 1829.

4 Where he had presumably been visiting relatives of his wife, the former Elizabeth McDougal, in Rockbridge County.

From George McClure

Bath Steuben County N. York—23d, July 1823—

Honrl, Henry Clay.

Dear Sir

As I have not the pleasure of a personal acquaintance with you, I have taken the liberty of introducing myself through the medium of a letter. Our mutual friend Judge Rochester[1] assured me that a corraspondance [*sic*] would be verry [*sic*] agreeable to you, and I can assure you Sir, that notwithstanding I am an entire stranger to you, personally, I can write to you as to an old friend and acquaintance, with that freedom which results from a consciousness of a perfect simularity [*sic*] of views as to men and measures, policy and politicks, which certainly exist between us— It had been my intention some time since not to have taken an active part in the approaching Election for President—but it seems almost impossible to preserve my neutrality— There is an impulse of public duty on my mind which urges me to enter into the contest, and I have at length given way to it, for the subject appears to me inseperable [*sic*] from the protection of National industry— And I now find myself enlisted and irresistably drawn to my favourite subject, and cannot keep silent when matters of deep concern are agitating the Country,— I have often noticed with great satisfaction your remarks on the subject of our manufactures when in Congress— In the sentiments You have often expressed, you are secure in the concurrence of all those who have bestowed any considerable attention on the subject, and although certain flippant and shallow opinions of an opposite character seem yet to prevail, and are asserted with an audacity which nothing but ignorance or prejudice is capable of, Yet it will be rendering the public a great service to bring up the subject in the next Congress—for while events are illustrating the doctrines you have always maintained, in relation to the protection and promotion of our agriculture manufactures, and internal improvements, it is desireable [*sic*] they should be held up to the view of the People—

You will readily perceive Sir that I have given you the preference over all the other candidates for President— and you may rest assured that I will use every exertion within my power to promote your Election— You must not be discouraged in consequence of the result of our Legislative caucus at the close of their Session—[2] The resolutions passed by that caucus was [*sic*] verry far from being the expression of the sentiments and views of the majority— It was a mere trick of a certain U. *States Senator*[3] and two or three others who had previously laid their plans, in order to promote Crawford's Election, and to injure you, by disapproving of State nominations, the trick was not discovered until too late— I was a member of the

House at the time but being out of Town knew nothing of the caucus until it was over— This fact I am verry confident of, that a majority of both Houses were in your favour, and I am clearly of the opinion that a majority of the People of this state (though much divided in opinion) are with you— Much depends on our next Legislature, they choose the Electors—

I am one of six candidates in this District to fill Mr. Rochesters place in Congress; if I succeed in geting [*sic*] the nomination by this District convention (which will shortly take place) I will be Elected, but should I fail in geting the nomination, I shall in all probability be a member of our next Legislature,[4] in either case I flatter myself that I can be of some service to you—

In relation to the other Candidates for President, it is the prevailing opinion in this Country that there is not one of the three Cabinet candidates on whom the friends of National industry could rely for any support, if they or any of them have exibited [*sic*] different opinions I think it may be fairly attributed to Electioneering views— it is at all events certain that neither of them have given any pledge or public assurance, They neither have or will array themselves against the ruinous and mistaken policy of the south, and therefore I am decidedly of opinion that they ought not to have our support, Southern policy is unbending and inveterate, there is between them and us no community of interest & feeling— their products are protected by duties and have market [*sic*] in Europe, their only concerns [*sic*] for the Middle and Western States is for their votes— they may flatter us, but they flatter because they fear us, —I find (with a few exceptions) that southern men are embodied firmly against every attack on their narrow selfish policy, the only impression to be made on them is by taking from them their influence in the public councels [*sic*], we have the votes and must not put them into their hands, and unless we avail ourselves of this oppertunity [*sic*] it may be our last— It is however but Justice to Messrs Adams Crawford & Calhoun to say that they are all men of talents which qualify them for the highest Office— that their acquirements are extensive are all familiar with the history and policy of the Country if the internal policy of the Government in relation to the great interests of the Country were fixed and setled [*sic*]— if there were no measures of National importance on the adoption or regection [*sic*] of which the prosperity of the Nation depended, I could say that either would make a good President, and that it would be unwise to agitate the Country by a contest for the choice— the laws would be Executed at home and and [*sic*] our rights be respected abroad— But it seems to me that the situation of the Country calls on us to look to higher considerations, There is a question depending which is of infinitely more importance to the People than the Execution of the laws, or our foreign relations, the protection of our manufactures and agriculture— before this question all others seem small, and with sentiments on this subject like such as prevails in the Middle and Western States, we are bound to make a test for every candidate— The People are sattisfied [*sic*] that there is at least two of the Cabinet candidates who cannot stand this test— It is presumed that Mr. Adams [is a]t heart favourably disposed but will not offend the Eastern merchants or southern planters, and publickly he expresses no Opinion on the subject of manufactures—

You are doubtless led to believe from the complexion of some of the public newspapers in this state that Mr. Crawford will get the votes of this State, depend upon it that will have but little influence with the People, and much less with the Legislature Those printers are bought over by the friends of Crawford & the People know it— they will think and act for themselves— You have many warm friends throughout the State and after our next falls Election they will be found at their post— For my own part I took my stand last winter, I am identified with you, and I do not dispair [*sic*] of success —Thus Sir have I given you my sentiments freely and without reserve—and if my advice was asked, I should say persevere to the end— I shall be happy to hear from you,—in the meantime accept assurances of the highest consideration & regard of your friend & servt.— GEO, MC,CLURE—

P.S. It has not been for want of high respect for Genl. Jackson that I have omited [*sic*] to mention his name as a Candidate, but that it is on acct of a certainty that He will not have any support in this state hower Just his claim may be—

ALS. DLC-HC (DNA, M212, R1). McClure, a native of Ireland, had emigrated first to Baltimore and, around 1793, had settled at Bath, Steuben County, New York, where he became a merchant. A brigadier general of New York militia during the War of 1812, he was renowned for directing the destruction of the Canadian town of Newark, for which the British had retaliated in the burning of Buffalo and Black Rock (cf. above, II, 270-71, 563-64). He had held office as Sheriff of Steuben County in 1815 and was three times elected to the State legislature. In 1834 he removed to Elgin, Illinois, where he died.

1 William B. Rochester.

2 See above, Woods to Clay, May 22, 1823, note; Porter to Clay, May 26, 1823; Clay to Porter, June 15, 1823; Beatty to Clay, June 30, 1823.

3 Martin Van Buren.

4 The special election to fill the vacancy caused by Rochester's resignation was won by McClure's fellow townsman, William Woods, a lawyer.

To Duncan Cameron

Sir Ashland 26h. July 1823.

W. H. Caperton Esqr. of Richmond in this State having desired me to communicate to you his standing at the Bar, I take great pleasure in saying that it is highly respectable, and that he has the reputation of assiduity punctuality & integrity. I have no doubt that

he will faithfully discharge any professional engagements which he may come under to you. I am with great respect Your ob. Servt.
Duncan Cameron Esq. H. CLAY

ALS. NcU-Southern Historical Collection. Cameron, born in Mecklenburg County, Virginia, had read law in Charlotte County, Virginia, before moving to Martinsville, Guilford County, North Carolina, in 1798. He had shortly thereafter removed to Hillsboro, North Carolina, where he rapidly rose to prominence, as representative in the State House of Commons (1802, 1806, 1807, 1812, 1813), State Senator (1819, 1822, 1823), judge of the Superior Court, and, for twenty years from 1829, president of the State Bank of North Carolina. He had been a leader of the Federalists in North Carolina.

From Jacob Payton

H. Clay Esqr. 1 Augt. 1823—
Sir,

I have been in town for the purpose of Seeing you to get the indigo necessary to dye your wool—[1] It will require $4\frac{1}{2}$ lb which will cost 6$ per lb— & $5\frac{1}{2}$ lb Madder 75c. per lb— I would come to town tomorrow but have to go to Cyntha. Will be in town on Monday Morning. Respectfully J. PAYTON

[Endorsement on verso][2]
5 Augt 1823 recd of H Clay Thirty one dollars to purchase the dye Stuffs within Mentioned JACOB PAYTON
Test
Robt. Scott

ALS. DLC-TJC (DNA, M212, R1). [1] See above, Agreement, June 24, 1823.
[2] AES, signed also by Scott.

To John D. Godman

ASHLAND, *9th August,* 1823.

I need not contradict to you, a report of a coalition between Mr Crawford and me. I have come to no understandings, entered into no arrangements, made no promises, entangled myself with no engagements of any sort, with any candidate, nor with the friends of any candidate—and so help me God, I will not. I neither can, nor have, nor will, seek to influence or control the choice of my friends, in regard to the other candidates. I believe them incapable of being influenced by me, or I am sure I should not consider them worthy of being my friends. Faithfully your friend, H. CLAY.

JOHN D. GODMAN, M.D.

Washington *Daily National Intelligencer,* December 3, 1827, reprinted from Philadelphia *United States Gazette,* December 1, 1827. Published also in Lexington *Kentucky Reporter,* December 19, 1827.

From Cornelius Comegys

Sir, Philadelphia 9 August 1823

It has been a long time since I had this honor, & longer since I had the pleasure of a line from you— I am now more than anxious on accot of my age, with a large Family dependent on me, to bring all my Concerns to a Close, and this letter is predicated on some information I have recently received respecting Wm Bradford, the same I presume against whom you have a Suit pending for the late firm of C & J Comegys,[1] and as the Surviving partner State what I have heard, and if true I trust you will be able to recover that debt which is of considerable importance to me, and if Mr Bradford is an honest Man disposed to redeem his Character as such, I have no doubt of your Success if the affair is revived with vigor—

"Major William Bradford lives in Crawford County
"Arkansas Territory and reported to be worth Thirty
"thousand dollars"—[2]

The gentleman from whom I have derived this information advises me to send the Claim to William Trimble Esqe. Attorney at Law Little Rock Arkansas—[3] No doubt you have some knowledge of this gentleman, as well as most other Lawyers in that direction, and will thank you to make enquiry into the Correctness of this information and if such are the facts, I beg you will endeavor to have the amot of the debt against Wm & Ira Bradford Collected— the last information reced from them was to advise the payment to you of $300 and that the whole would be ultimately paid, and is certainly worthy of pursuit. I have suffered so much by debtors in the Western Country, and more considerably in Kentucky than any other State that I am in a fair way to loose [*sic*] all my labours in the mercantile way for thirty years past by bad debts, depreciation of their Currency and the fall of real property, on which I hold liens, and produce— The great change in times appears to have changed the disposition of the People and made them indifferent about paying their debts as if they were under no obligation to fulfill their Contracts— The time was when I preferred the Trade of Kentucky to any other and could always calculate on them with some degree of Certainty, and I hope the time is not far distant when they will return to their former soundness— Excuse these remarks persuaded you will duly appreciate my motive for stating them to you, and beg you will not suppose that I intend them to apply generally— for yourself and many other Citizens of Kentucky I have the highest regard and Consideration— Will you be so obliging as to favor me with a few lines on the subject at your leisure— By & bye I hope you will receive the highest reward which our Country can bestow for the Services you have rendered in your day & generation. I have the honor to be very respectfully, your obt Servant CORNS. COMEGYS

To the Honble Henry Clay Lexington Ky

ALS. DLC-HC (DNA, M212, R1). [1] See above, I, 572-73; II, 195-96, 319.

[2] Bradford, who had remained in the Army after the War of 1812, had been commandant at Ft. Smith, Arkansas Territory, from 1817 to 1822. Rather than accept reassignment elsewhere, he decided to give up his commission. His resignation became effective in 1824, whereupon he became brigadier general of Territorial militia. He was an unsuccessful candidate for delegate to Congress in 1821 and 1823 (while still an Army officer) and for the Territorial legislature in 1825. He died in 1826. Lonnie J. White, "The Arkansas Territorial Election of 1823," *Arkansas Historical Quarterly*, XVIII (Winter, 1959), 325, 327-28.

[3] Trimble, who had moved to Arkansas after receiving his legal education in Kentucky, was one of the holders of the original pre-emption entry for the site of Little Rock. He had been a circuit judge of the First Judicial Circuit (1819-1820), had served as a member and Speaker of the Territorial House of Representatives, and, in September, 1823, was appointed a magistrate of Hempstead County, from which post he resigned to accept appointment (1824-1830) as Judge of the Superior Court of the Territory. He was a brother of David Trimble.

From Richard Wistar, Jr.

Henry Clay Esqr. Phila 11th. August 1823

Dear Sir

Your highly esteemed favor of 10h. Ulto[1] was recd. in Course Covering your chk as acting Exr to the estate of Mr Morrison[2] deceasd. for Seven hundred and ninety one dollars which was duly honoured and is in full of my Claim vs Geo. B. Thompson[3] given to you for Collection.— Please accept my best thanks for your attention in Collecting and your punctuality in remitting me With much respect I remain Your assured Friend RICHD WISTAR JR.

ALS. DLC-TJC (DNA, M212, R12). Wistar (Wister) was a Philadelphia merchant, descended from a German emigrant to Pennsylvania, who had established prosperous shipping and manufacturing enterprises.

[1] Not found. [2] James Morrison.

[3] Of Mercer County, Kentucky, a nephew of George Thompson, and a cousin of George C. Thompson.

From Thomas I. Wharton

My dear Sir Philad. 13 August 1823

If I have not performed my promise of writing to you at an earlier period it [is] not that I have been thoughtless of you or unwatchful of your interests or indifferent to the gratification of communicating with you. The truth is that I have had nothing very agreeable or encouraging to communicate— I had no disposition to trouble you with my crude speculations upon political prospects. Not that I despair by any means of your final success in Pennsylvania but the unfortunate nomination of Gen. Jackson has so possessed the public mind & the disorder has broken out in so many fresh places[1] that your friends here have been unable to make much headway. I am confident that if this unfortunate nomination had not been made you would have carried the state by an overpowering majority & the great misfortune is that Jackson is supported by exactly that school of politicians who would otherwise have been decidedly & unanimously for you. I have no doubt however that in the end his friends finding that he will receive no support out of Tennessee & Penna. will transfer their support to you & that they will reject with scorn the project which is said to be in contemplation by Jackson of ceding them to Mr Adams. It has indeed been already suggested to me by one of Mr Calhouns principal ci-devant advocates, (for his hopes are quite extinct) that it would be advisable to frame an electoral ticket pledged to vote for either yourself or Jackson as circumstances may render expedient in opposition to the Adams party. If this or a similar arrangement is not made I should not be surprised if the friends of Adams should carry their electoral ticket as the federalists are still a strong party here. I speak of things you will observe from present prospects. There may & probably will be many circumstances to change the course of the existing Currents. A nomination by the Caucus at Washington would I think ensure your success in this state. I doubt whether even that could gain Mr Crawford the vote of Penna. As matters stand his adherents are a miserably diminutive band.

What operates very much against your prospects is the want of a newspaper here & in New York devoted to your interests. There is no *democratic* paper earnest on your side. In every quarter they are setting up presses for Crawford & Adams while it is with difficulty that we can find admittance for articles in your favour. Dr. Godman[2] & myself especially have not been wanting in exertions to shed ink on the subject but the difficulty is to find a proper vehicle. I find in many Editors a fear of committing themselves as yet. This is the case with Niles[3] of the Baltimore Weekly Register whom I have urged to publish some articles I wrote for him but he hangs back for the present. The Statesman of New York[4] has published some things for me but I fear its circulation & influence are small. Our papers in this state are at the present moment given up almost entirely to state politics. The question is whether Mr Shulze or Mr Gregg[5] shall be Governor. The presidential question has nothing to [do] with the subject.

In the discussions which have taken place here on your qualifications &c. one fact has been stated which has evidently made a favorable impression on the public mind. It is said that at the outset of your political career you advocated the gradual emancipation of slaves in Kentucky. This fact has been doubted & denied by some paragraphists & it is proper that your friends should be able to make some proof of the correctness of the statement. Is there any printed evidence of this either in the newspapers of the time or in the proceedings of the Convention? This in fact is my object in now writing to you. If you can furnish me with the evidence it can be used to advantage.[6]

At all events it will give me great pleasure to hear from you.

I am my dear Sir very truly & respectfully Yr. friend.

H. Clay Esquire T. I. WHARTON

ALS. DLC-HC (DNA, M212, R1). MS. torn. Wharton, a native of Philadelphia, was an eminent lawyer and writer. He had been graduated from the University of Pennsylvania and had studied law, served as an officer of volunteers during the War of 1812, contributed to the *Port Folio,* and edited the *Analectic Magazine* before devoting his attention almost exclusively to law. As compiler and as author he published several legal works and was one of a group of three appointed in 1830 to codify the civil statute law of Pennsylvania. He was a founder of the Historical Society of Pennsylvania, a member of other learned societies, and, from 1837 until his death in 1856, a trustee of the University of Pennsylvania.

[1] See above, Hynes to Clay, July 31, 1822; Woods to Clay, May 22, 1823; Miner to Clay, June 19, 1823.

[2] John D. Godman. [3] Hezekiah Niles.

[4] In January, 1822, the Albany *New York Statesman* and the New York *Evening Journal* had been combined as the New York *Statesman,* under the editorship of Nathaniel H. Carter and George W. Prentiss. Items from this journal sympathetic to Clay's candidacy were reprinted in the Lexington *Kentucky Reporter,* February 10, August 4, 18, 1823; but the New York editors, commenting on such a piece, a letter by *"One from the West,"* which appeared in the fall of that year, observed that they published it with some hesitation as they found it "objectionable in several points of view." Reprinted in *ibid.,* October 13, 1823.

[5] John A. Shulze; Andrew Gregg.

[6] See above, I, 5-6, 12-14. Clay's reply to this request has not been found.

From Francis T. Brooke

My Dear Sir August 14h 1823

I have to apologise to you for not writing you sooner as intended when I wrote you last,[1] I delayed it, with the hope that Something might occur, more favorable to your prospects, the truth is that great apathy Still exists in Virginia on the Subject of the Presidential Election, it is impossible to excite the zeal of the people in behalf of any one individual in the absence of any pledge that their great interests are to be much promoted by his Election, the negative business of obviating objections instead of advancing pretensions has no kindling influence to warm them— it is an up hill work as is deeply felt by Some of our Editors to Stimulate the people by the mere finding and proving without the ability to put their fingers upon any tangible measures that place one competitor greatly above the others— you have many warm friends in Virginia and your patriotism and Talents have I am perfectly persuaded placed you in the highest rank in public opinion— if an opportunity was afforded you of giving some pledge that you would take care of the great interests of the South and the west, there is nothing so Settled that great change might not be expected— whatever may be said to the contrary the mass of the people of the South and the west, must feel the progress of their impoverishment by the extraction of the profits of their labour by the northern and eastern capitalists, under the operation of the protecting System, they must feel also that they pay the enormous pension lists, and that they, in fact Support a large portion of the paupers of the north and the east under the imposing pretext that they are remunerating the old revolutionary Soldier for his blood & his Toils— they do feel if their acts can demonstrate anything that the assumed power of extending the given duties of the Federal courts is fast undermining the State governments and must Sooner or later demolish the System for which their ancestors fought and bled— you See I express myself with the frankness of a Sincere friend, I know we differ as to some, of what I pronounce encroachments on State powers, but the broad doctrine now inculcated, that Congress have the right to extend, not to regulate only, the jurisdiction of the federal courts is one which I presume none can differ on who will read the constitution and reflect on its objects, without Some Sinister intention, it would have afforded me great pleasure at this time to have held a more extensive and free communication with you than is attainable by Letter, I shall however be very happy to hear from you— I promised to pay a visit to Colo Taylor[2] on the first of next month he I am told is very lukewarm and by no means decided as to the course he will persue [*sic*], or that he will persue any, he has certainly not put pen to paper on the Subject of the Presidential election, if I know him however, I think he will take a part, and will have great weight, this between our selves—

with Sincere Esteem FRANCIS BROOKE—

N B I wish some of your friends would publish your Speech on the war— it is in Niles Register I think 16 vo—[3] I ought to apologise for this desultory and illy written Letter, in the country without time & good materials it must be so—

ALS. DLC-HC (DNA, M212, R1). Addressed to Clay at Lexington.

1 Last letter found, above, March 9, 1823. 2 John Taylor of Caroline.

3 Volume XVI of *Niles' Weekly Register* contains no major speech by Henry Clay. His speech on the Seminole War (above, II, 636-62) was published in this journal, XV, Supplement, 124-35.

Receipted Bill from George Trotter and Son

Lexington 14th Aug. 1823.

[George Trotter and Son bill Henry Clay for purchase, during July and August, 1823, of 6-penny and unspecified size "wrought nails" at 50¢ per pound and 6-, 8-, and 10-penny cut nails at 20¢ per pound. One entry, on August 3, cites "4d. Cutt nails" at 25¢ a pound. The bill, amounting to $10.75, is noted as paid in full.]

DS. DLC-TJC (DNA, M212, R10). Margin of MS. torn. George Trotter, Sr., had taken his son Franklin into partnership in 1817 or 1818 to establish the firm, George Trotter and Son, Lexington merchants.

Account with Wilkins, McIlvaine, and Company

[*ca.* August 16, 1823]

Dr Henry Clay Esq on acct with Wilkins Mc I & Co—
1823

May — 21 — To Cash paid for Mendg pump	....	$ 10 —
Aug — 16 — " Do ...... paid him ...... "		115
		$ 125
6h. By rent of house[1] for ½ year ending June 1— 1823		$ 125

WILKINS MCILVAINE & Co

DS. DLC-TJC (DNA, M212, R15). [1] Cf. above, II, 786-87, 882.

To James Gambier

My Lord Kentucky Lexington Agst 20th 1823

I beg leave to introduce to your Lordship the Reverend Philander Chase Bishop of the Protestant Episcopal church in the State of Ohio,[1] who visits England on some object connected with the prosperity of the church— Mr Chase is a learned, pious and highly esteemed clergyman, deserving of all kindness and civility, I hope it may be convenient to allow him the honor of the acquaintance of your Lordship. for whose character he has a high regard—

It has been some time since I had the pleasure of hearing directly from your Lordship, the last time I think was through my friend poor Lowndes,[2] who has since paid the debt which we have all to discharge— I pray you, nevertheless, to believe, that I still cherish those strong sentiments of esteem and respect for your Lordship which were excited during our acquaintance in Europe; and that I have the honor to be Faithfully Your Lordships Obedient servant

Lord Gambier &C. &C H. CLAY

Copy. DLC-Decatur House Papers. Published in Philander Chase, *The Reminiscences of Bishop Chase, (Now Bishop of Illinois)* (2 vols.; New York, 1844), I, 251-52.

[1] Chase, born in New Hampshire, had been elevated to this post in 1819. He had determined to establish a theological seminary in his diocese and was now on his way to England seeking funds. His success in this venture led him to name the college for George Kenyon, second Baron Kenyon, and its site for Gambier. Chase was later Bishop of Illinois, and presiding bishop of the Church.

[2] William Lowndes, who had traveled in Europe during the summer of 1819.

To Alexander Baring

D,Sir, Kentucky 20th Agst 1823

I have the honor to introduce to your acquaintance the Reverend Philander chase, Bishop of the Protestant Episcopal church in the State of ohio, who will deliver you this letter— Intending to visit England, he is desirous of availing himself of that opportunity to cultivate an acquaintance with some of its most distinguished inhabitants, and, amongst others you, Knowing that your kindness is always shown to my country men I present Mr Chase to you without hesitation being persuaded that his piety learning and amiable disposition would secure him your favourable reception whatever country he might represent— I have the honor to be with great regard Your Ob Servt H, CLAY.

Alexr Baring Eqr &C &C

Copy. DLC-Decatur House Papers.

To Charles Hammond

Dear Sir Ashland 21st. Aug. 1823.

I was so anxious to visit Columbus, at the approaching term of the Fed. Court, that I have not, until the very last moment, and then most reluctantly, relinquished the intention. The state of my health has compelled me to adopt this resolution; my physicians assuring me that all the good effects which are anticipated from a course of medicine & regimen that I am pursuing will be greatly hazarded, if not lost, by the journey, for which also my strength is not competent.

I inclose two letters for Bishop Chase,[1] according to the request contained in your favor of the 14h. inst.,[2] which I hope may be of some service to him. I have no acquaintance with Mr. Brougham.[3] I could have transmitted other letters to Sir James Macintosh, Goulburn[4] &c. but I presumed he would hardly want them.

I hope that you and the rest of the Gentlemen of the Bar will take care of me in Court and not allow any of my little business to suffer.

Your letter contained the first information which I received of "the New York pamphlet."[5] I have seen no such production. In the papers in that City I observe a pamphlet noticed on the question of the appointment of Electors, that is whether it should be popular or legislative,[6] but I suppose that not to be the one to which you refer; but that has not reached us here—

I think it probable that the Executive patronage will be distributed so as to promote the views of one or other of the two Cabinet Candidates whom you have named. In the recent appointment of the Post Master General two birds were killed with one stone, provision was at once made for a favorite of the Secretary of War, and a favorite of the President (Mr. Graham.) [7] I think it likely that Southard will be appointed to succeed Mr. Thompson, who is put in the place that Chancellor Kent[8] should have filled. After all, much cannot now be done by any exertion of partonage [*sic*]. I think it will rather injure the cause which it is intended to subserve.

My information from N. York is good; highly encouraging.

You may reply I think upon these results:

If N. York promulgate her preference, by some unambiguous act, so long before the election as that it will influence other States, if that preference be for Mr. Crawford, there is an end to Mr. Adams, and the contest will be between Mr. Crawford & me; and New England will probably have to decide it.

If it be for Mr. Adams there is an end to Mr. Crawford, and the contest will be between Mr. Adams & me.

If it be for me, my election will take place by at least two thirds of the Union.

Should N. York make no annunciation of her choice, and it remain a matter of contestation to the last which way she will vote, there will be no popular election, unless produced by a Congressional Caucus.

I think there will be no such Caucus.

If there should be one, it will either not decide at all or its decision, being by a small majority, will not be respected.

I have heard nothing from Ohio very particularly lately. What you state about one or two individuals does not surprize me. What you mention about the Miami Country generally. [*sic*] I always supposed Mr. Adams had some interest throughout Ohio, as indeed he has in most of the Western States; but I imagined it not to be an available interest.

Our elections have terminated more favorably in K. to a sounder currency & sounder legislation than they have done for some year or two; but it is not certain that there is a majority obtained in the *H. of R.*. The Senate has improved more than the other branch. Doubtless a sudden & violent return to a more wholesome regimen is to be avoided. The work must be accomplished cautiously & gradually.

Be pleased to make my best respects to Wright[9] &c.

Your's faithfully H. CLAY

Charles Hammond Esqr.

ALS. InU. Addressed to Hammond, "Counseller at Law Columbus [Ohio]."

1 See above, Clay to Gambier and Clay to Baring, both August 20, 1823.

2 Not found.

3 Henry Peter Brougham, born and educated in Edinburgh, was a lawyer, a versatile and prolific writer, an antislavery agitator, and a highly vocal member of Parliament. Later, in 1831, he was raised to the peerage as first Baron Brougham and Vaux and was commissioned Lord Chancellor of England.

4 Sir James Mackintosh; Henry Goulburn.

5 Possibly the anonymous *Sketches of the Public Services of Adams, Clay and Crawford . . . By a New-York Republican* (New York, 1823).

6 Pamphlet not found. The New York *Patriot* during the summer of 1823 had campaigned strongly for popular election of the presidential electors. Hammond, *History of Political Parties in the State of New York,* II, 131.

7 Upon the resignation of John McLean as Commissioner of the General Land Office, to become Postmaster General (see above, Miner to Clay, June 19, 1823, note), George Graham had received an interim appointment as his successor. Graham's nomination was approved by the Senate December 15, 1823.

8 Samuel L. Southard; Smith Thompson; James Kent. Kent, whose long service as a jurist had begun with his appointment to the New York Supreme Court in 1798, had been Chancellor of the New York Court of Chancery from 1814 until forced, under a mandatory provision of the State constitution, to retire from the bench in July, 1823, at the age of sixty. Thereafter he taught briefly at Columbia College, then published his *Commentaries on American Law* (4 vols., 1826-1830), which appeared in six editions before his death in 1847.

9 John C. Wright.

From Charles Wilkins

Henry Clay Esqr Lexington 25th. Augt. 1823

Sir

I was present at several intervies [*sic*] between Mr Morrison & Mr. McIlvaine[1] previous to the latter seting off for the Illinnois— in all of which Mr Morrison urged him to proceed promising ample compensation, but did not absolutely fix upon any Sum saying that if he succeeded he should have a commission upon the amount obtained. Mr McIlvaine refused positively to go unless he was to be compensated for his trouble whether he succeeded in obtaining his claim, or not & demanded five pr. pt. [*sic*] upon the full amount claimed or half if he did not succed & his expences— Mr. Morrison preferd a fixed Sum & Said that he believed that Mr Cowan[2] would go for $300 & his expences— I had nothing to do with the appointment of Mr. Mc.Ilvaine, being opposed to employing any person, & urged a communication to the governor by mail, which would Save the expence, Mr Morrison thought differently & employ'd Mr McIlvaine & made his own bargain with him I am of opinion that Mr Morrisons executors ought to pay the claim of Mr McIlvaine & deduct it from the amt. when recoved from the Genl. Goverment.

I am Sir, very respectfully Yr Obt. St. CHA. WILKINS

ALS. DLC-TJC (DNA, M212, R12). Endorsed by Clay: ". . . Bussiness [*sic*] of the Saline—. . . ." See above, II, 165-66.

1 James Morrison; B. Reed McIlvaine. 2 Probably James Cowan.

From John Chambers

Dear Sir Washington 26th. August 1823

Captn. Byers[1] has put three hundred and ten dollars in silver into my hands for you in consequence of the refusal of the Branch Bank[2] here to take it in deposite, and not having been able to convert it into Specie paying paper so as to transmit it by Mail I must hold it subject your Order.

Some intelligent men from Indianna have recently been in this neighbourhood who inform me that the Kenty papers are not generally taken there and suggested the propriety of geting the Editors of the Reporter and Indianna Statesman (printed at Connersvill [*sic*][3] to exchange papers, the latter they say is *well disposed.*

With great respect Your Mo. Obt. JOHN CHAMBERS

ALS. DLC-TJC (DNA, M212, R12). Addressed to Clay at Lexington. Sent by "Mr. Herndon," probably Edward H. Herndon, a resident of Lexington, later (1837) one of the incorporators of Mays Lick, in Mason County, Kentucky.

1 James Byers.

2 Bank of Kentucky. On the liquidation of this institution, see above, Todd to Clay, May 8, 1823, note.

3 Thomas Smith of the Lexington *Kentucky Reporter;* Abram Van Vleet, of the short-lived *Indiana Statesman,* established earlier in the year. Van Vleet had previously been editor and publisher of the Lebanon, Ohio, *Western Star.*

From Lucas Alamán

PRIMERA SECRETARIA DE ESTADO. *Seccion de Estado.*

Mexico 27 de Agosto de 1823

Al Honorable Señor Henrrique Clay

El Supremo Gobierno Provisional de la Nacion Mexicana lleno de gratitud por el interes que V con tanta energia ha manifestado por este Pais, se ve en la grata obligacion se manifestarte cordialmente aquella, tanto en su nombre como en el de todos los habitantes de México.

El Soberano Congreso de la Nacion reinstalado por los heroicos esfuerzos de los Patriotas, ocupado infatigablemente en trazar la lineas del grandioso edificio de nuestra futura prosperidad, identificada con la de nuestros hermanos de esos Estados, al paso q. ofrece testimonios del reconocimiento mas sincero á los q. han peleado pr. la Yndependencia Mexicana sabe ser agradecido á los buenos deseos y oficios de quantos los han prestado en ese Pais para hacer valer sus Derechos y contribuir á su bien estar futuro.

Entre todos ocupa V un lugar muy distingui- [*sic*] y asi es tambien el aprecio q. el Supremo Poder Executivo en consonancia con aquellos sentimientos tributa á sus singulares talentos y sublimes virtudes Patrioticas, Congratulandose al considerar q. quando todo nos anuncia aqui el establecimiento firme y duradero de un sistema de Gobierno análogo á las circunstancias de nuestro Pais, destruido el q. se habia instalado y q. sobre haber sido obra de la violencia habia degenerado en despótico con demasiada velocidad, hallará en

V un firme Amigo q. contribuirá generosamente á consolidar nuestra apetecida felicidad.

Hecha como está hace tiempo la Convocatoria para el nuevo congreso constituyente q. debe reunirse á lo mas tarde el dia ultimo de Octubre de este año, y q. toda la Nacion aguarda con la mayor ansia, y las mas felices disposiciones, deben esperarse de tan augusta asamblea toda clare de bienes y quantas ventajas son imaginables para este naciente Estado,[1] q. tiene el mor. anelo [*sic*] por estrechar mas y mas los vinculos de amistad y fraternidad con los Norte Americanos y reproducir á V. los sentimientos mas puros de benebolencia [*sic*]

Con ellos y los de la mayor consideracion me protexto [*sic*] su mas obediente Servidor.

LUCAS ALAMAN

Secretario de Estado y del Despacho de Relaciones esteriores [*sic*] e interiores

LS. DLC-HC (DNA, M212, R1). Alamán, Mexican statesman and historian, was a minister in the provisional government established after the fall of Itúrbide (March 19, 1823). Though he retired to private life two years later to devote attention to his extensive mining interests, he again held the post of chief minister from 1829 to 1832 and in 1853. He was organizer of the Archivo General, founder of the National Museum, and author, among other writings, of two multivolume works on Mexican history.

1 The Congress assembled on November 7, 1823, adopted a constitution (the Constitution of 1824) based on that of the United States, and made of Mexico a federal republic.

From David Woods

Sir Madison[1] 27th. Aug. 1823.—

Yours of the 14th. of June last,[2] I recd. on the 5th. July, at the at the [*sic*] moment I was seting out on a journey for the Eastern and Southern part of the State. I have been absent the greater part of the time since, that, and the dearth of information must be my appoligy for not writing to you sooner. In travelling through the State, I found a very great discordance in the views and feelings of those Members of Congress, who at, and after our last Election, were expected to act in concert on the Presidential question. It was then expect[ed], that out of our 34 Members, and 2 Senators, 5/6 of them would act with Mr. Van Beuren, and further his views, but recently an astonishing change has taken place in the mind of this community. When I was in N. York, in the latter part of July, I found that the prejudice against that Gentleman, had burst out in to a flame—the ferment had become general. I think I speak within bounds, when I say that ¾ of the Electors of that City are arrayed in hostility to him. I should now consider it as a misfortune for any of the presidential candidates, to have him act publickly as their advocate in this State. It may naturally be asked What has caused such a change? I answer that a very general belief has gone abroad (whether true or false is not for me to say) that he has offered to barter this State, for the purpose of furthering his own views. This belief has been produced, by his recent journey through the Eastern or New England States, to Philadelphia, and lastly, from the circumstance of his present location at the Saratoga Springs.[3]

My opinion now is, that Mr. Crawford has no prospect of obtaining the sufferages of this State. I think the state is nearly balanced between your friends, and those of Mr. Adams, I think your friends have the preponderance. Mr. Cahoun [*sic*] has not yet been much taulked of and a general impression prevails that Gen. Jackson can not be Elected. Indeed there has not been a very general expression by the people who their favorite candidate would be; the opposition to Mr. Crawford seems to absorb every other consideration.

Our people have become Clamourous for a reform in the mode of choosing the Electors of President & Vice-President they ask for the repeal of the law which is now in force authorizing the members of our legislature to choose those Electors & to transfer the right of choosing them immediately to the people I think our next legislature will not be able to resist the force of publick feeling on this subject and that the members will be elected with a view to that object.[4] Should the right be given to the people it will probably be by general ticket: in that event I think you have much to expect from this State thoug [*sic*] important changes may take place in the minds of the people before Novr. 1824. when the Electors will be chosen Yet I think our Election in Novr. next will give such an indication on the subject as will afford a ground of rational probability as to the character of the presidential electors.

I shall now proceed to give you my views of our Members of Congress according to the best light I have. The medium through which I view this subject is an uncertain one and may be so changed by circumstances as to render the appearances of objects entirely different. Messrs. Wood, Craig Strong, Van Rensselaer, Cady, Taylor, Marvin, Haydon & Tracy[5] I think will act in concert and I hope for you. Mr. Wilson has the certificate but Mr. Adams is the member elected by a majority of the votes and I think will be admitted to his seat[6]—he will act with the above named persons. In the vacancy occasioned by the resignation of Mr. Rochester I have no doubt but that a gentleman will be elected who will be friendly to you.[7] Messrs. Foot, Storrs, Herkimer, Rose, Sharp & Cambreleng[8] I hope will be in your favor. The other members Messrs. Tyson, Morgan, Frost, Van Wyck, Jenkins, Hogeboom, Eaton Williams,

Martindale Richards, Teneyck, Collins, Dwinnell, Clark, Litchfield, Day and Lawrence[9] are wholly uncertain. Martindale is for Adams. Storrs will endeavor to assume high ground Rose is a Verginian [*sic*] and an honorable man. Litchfield Dwinel [*sic*] Day Hogeboom and Lawrence in common with many others are men of weak intellect Van Buren will endeavor to flater them and others with a view to his own interest. Richards is a stuborn Welchman and very Jealous should he imbibe an idea that any person was attempting to exercise an influence over him he wold [*sic*] certainly go against him. My view however of those members is not to be relied on I have given you the best information I could. Many things may appear in this note invidious and might injur [*sic*] feeling which I would wish to preserve. I should feel highly gratified by a [co]mmunication from you I am Sir your obedt. Servt. DAVID WOODS

Hon. H. Clay.

ALS. DLC-HC (DNA, M212, R1). 1 New York. 2 Not found.

3 Van Buren had visited John Adams at Quincy during a journey to Boston earlier that summer. Reference to his situation at Saratoga Springs has not been found.

4 Cf. above, Clay to Hammond, August 21, 1823. Although the matter was debated in regular session, and a special session was called in August, 1824, to consider the passage of a new law, the legislature failed to change the method of choosing electors.

5 Silas Wood; Hector Craig; James Strong; Stephen Van Rensselaer; John W. Cady; John W. Taylor; Dudley Marvin; Moses Hayden; Albert H. Tracy.

6 Isaac Wilson served until January 7, 1824, when he was replaced by Parmenio Adams, who had successfully contested Wilson's election.

7 See above, McClure to Clay, July 23, 1823, note.

8 Charles A. Foote; Henry R. Storrs; John Herkimer; Robert S. Rose; Peter Sharpe; Churchill C. Cambreleng.

9 Jacob Tyson; John J. Morgan; Joel Frost; William W. Van Wyck; Lemuel Jenkins; James L. Hogeboom; Lewis Eaton; Isaac Williams, Jr.; Henry C. Martindale; John Richards; Egbert Ten Eyck; Ela Collins; Justin Dwinell; Lot Clark; Elisha Litchfield; Rowland Day; Samuel Lawrence.

To Francis T. Brooke

Lexington 28h. August 1823.

I received, my dear Sir, your very obliging letter of the 14h instant, and I pray you to believe that I do not place less value on your friendship because you have nothing to communicate "more favorable to my prospects." On the subject to which you allude I assure you, most sincerely, I look with great calmness, and with a most perfect determination to acquiesce chearfully in whatever choice the Nation may make. It would be a poor compliment to our institutions to say that their solidity, or the public happiness, materially depended upon any selection that shall take place. I really think however that Virginia cannot justify herself to the Union for the apathy which you say prevails there on the question. Judging as I have done, at this distance, from the Enquirer[1] and other Virginia prints I had supposed that great interest was felt and generally taken in its decision; and that there was even danger of her oversteping the line of cautious circumspection which her leading politicians were understood to have marked out for her.

This indifference, you say, arises from the absence of any pledge that the great interests of the people of Virginia will be taken care of by any of the competitors for the Chief Magistracy. If indeed no such pledge is to be found in the principles, integrity & character, as heretofore developed, of either of the Candidates, it is, I should think, quite too late in the day now for any pledge to be given or received. But, my dear Sir, what interests have Virginia and the South separate from the Union? You have mentioned a single subject only, that of the encroachments of the Federal Judiciary on State rights; and, as connected with this, the "broad doctrine now inculcated that Congress has the right to extend not to regulate only the jurisdiction of the Federal Courts." On that subject I am entirely at a loss to conceive any peculiar interest in the State of Virginia and the Southern States. All are equally concerned in the preservation of the State Sovereignties. All would be equally affected by Fœderal usurpation. But I must confess that it is the first time that I ever heard asserted such a doctrine as you say is now inculcated. The limit of the Federal Judiciary is to be found in the Constitution; and Congress can vest in it no power which is not there found. If such a doctrine as you state is really attempted to be inculcated you will find Kentucky now, as in the epoch of 1799,[2] in spite of all your unkindness towards her,[3] ready to co operate with you in opposing it. And no man in the Union will be more prompt than I shall be to second the opposition. I cannot suppose you to refer to the power which is claimed for the General Government to give effect to its laws through its own judiciary. For without that power; without Federal means to effectuate the constitutional resolves of the Federal will, there is an end to the General Government; there is inevitable if not instantaneous anarchy.

But, my dear Sir, on this subject of the Federal Judiciary and State rights I mean to say a few words to you, in the spirit of Virginia Independence, and in the frankness of sincere friendship. Has not Virginia exposed herself to the imputation of selfishness by the course of her conduct, or of that of many of her politicians? When, in the case of Cohens and Virginia,[4] her authority was alone concerned, she made the most strenuous efforts against the exercise of power by the Supreme Court. But when the thunders of that Court were directed against poor Kentucky, in vain did she invoke Virginian aid. The Supreme Court it was imagined would decide on the side of supposed interests of Virginia. It has so decided;[5] and, in effect, cripples the Sovereign power of the State of Kentucky noore [*sic*] than any other measure ever affected the Independence of any state in this Union, and not a Virginia voice is heard against the decision. The Supreme Court is viewed with complacency, and as a very different sort of tribunal, from that Supreme Court which decided Cohens s case. Again. Of all the irregular bodies none can be more so than a Congressional Caucus at Washington. None have a more consolodating tendency. Indeed it is espoused upon the principle of preventing the exercise of State or Federal rights through the medium of the H. of R. Yet the Virginia politicians (at least if we are to judge from the papers) warmly advocate the constitution of such a Caucus. Will it not be said that they are influenced by the consideration, not of preserving unimpaired State rights, but of giving to the State power of *Virginia* the utmost effect of which it is susceptible? Or that of securing the election of the alleged favorite of Virginia who, without the instrumentality of such an assemblage, is in danger of losing the election?[6] It is in vain to speak of the inconveniencies of a warmly contested election. They are incident to our system; and are happily provided for by it. And the transitions from a Congressional Caucus, to a Prætorian Cohort or Hereditary Monarchy, to escape from those vexations, are not so great as we might at first imagine.

I am aware that on two subjects I have the misfortune to differ with many of my Virginia friends—Internal Improvements and Home Manufactures. My opinion has been formed after much deliberation, and my best judgment yet tells me that I am right. I have not time nor would it be fitting as regards your comfort now to discuss the policy or the power of fostering those interests. I believe Virginia & the Southern States as much interested, directly or indirectly, as any other parts of the Union, in their encouragement. When this Government was first adopted, we had no interior. Our population was inclosed between the Sea and the Mountains which run parallel to it. Since then the West part of your State, the Western parts of N. York & Pennsa. & all the Western States have been settled. The Wars of Europe & the emigrants to the West consumed all the surplus produced on both sides of the Mountains. Those Wars have terminated; and emigration has ceased. We find ourselves annually in the possession of an immense surplus. There is no market for it abroad; there is none at home. If there were a foreign market, before we, in the interior, could reach it, the intervening population would have supplied it. There can be no Foreign market adequate to the consumption of the vast & growing surplus of the produce of our Agriculture. We must then have a Home market. Some of us must cultivate; some fabricate. And we must have reasonable protection against the machinations of Foreign powers. On the Sea board you want a navy, fortifications, protection, foreign commerce. In the Interior we want Internal Improvements, Home Manufactures. You have what you want, and object to our getting what we want. Should not the interests of both parties be provided for?

It has appeared to me, in the administration of the General Government, to be a just principle, to enquire what great interests belong to each section of our Country, and to promote those interests as far as practicable consistently with the Constitution, having always an eye to the welfare of the whole. Assuming this principle, does any one doubt that if N. York, N. Jersey, Pennsa. Delaware Maryland & the Western States constituted an Independent Nation, it would immediately protect the two important interests in question? And is it not to be feared that, if protection is not to be found to vital interests, from the existing system, in great parts of the Confederacy, those parts will ultimately seek to establish a system that will afford the requisite protection? I would not, in the application of the principle indicated, give to the peculiar interests of great sections *all* the protection which they would probably receive if those sections constituted separate & independent States. I would however extend some protection & measure it by balancing the countervailing interests, if there be such, in other quarters of the Union.

I concur entirely with you in thinking that the North & East, but particularly New England, have laid in a great measure, the other parts of the Union under contribution. And of all the ill advised measures; of all the wasteful expenditures of public money, the Revolutionary pension list preeminently takes the lead. Never was there more public money spent with less practical benefit. But who proposed it? Your own Monroe.[7] I thought of it then as I think of it now; but opposition would have been silly & vain.[8]

You will oppose my election I suppose in Virginia. I have no right to complain. Silence & Submission are my duty. You will oppose me because I think that the interests of all parts of the Union should be taken care of; in other words, that the interests of the Interior, on the two subjects mentioned, as well as those of the Maritime coast ought to be provided for. You will give your suffrages to Mr. Crawford or to Mr. Adams; and if Mr. Crawford or Mr. Adams be elected I venture to predict that we shall find either in his inaugural speech, or in his first message or speech (perhaps the latter mode of communication may be revived) to Congress, a recommendation of efficient encouragement to Domestic Manufactures & Internal improvements.

I am afraid that you will think me in a very bad humor. Far from it. I repeat, that I never enjoyed more perfect composure. My health, it is true, is extremely bad; and I am now confined at home by the endeavor to re establish it. But it neither affects my tranquillity nor gives me the spleen. In regard to the election, as to which I will make no professions of apathy or indifference, which I do not feel, my friends continue to be very confident; and my own opinion is that my prospects are not surpassed by those of either of the other gentlemen. Still I am not unaware that all things are uncertain. And I therefore continue resolved to preserve my philosophy, my principles & my conscience, be the event what it may.

Has not our friend Southard[9] been rapidly advanced? He certainly has merit; and his friend the Secretary of War[10] has discernment.

It would have given me great pleasure to see you. as it will to meet you any where again. Can you not run up to Washn. next winter? To a close observer there will be a scene then exhibited worth surveying. Wherever you are I pray you to be persuaded that the best wishes attend you of Your faithful friend H. CLAY

P.S. I send you my effusions as they are poured out through a mercurial course, on which the Doctors have put me. I keep no copy; and wish no copy for others— I write for yourself alone— H C.

The Honble Francis Brooke—

ALS. KyU. Published in Colton (ed.), *Private Correspondence of Henry Clay*, 78-83.

1 Richmond *Enquirer*.

2 See above, II, 448; Speech to the Virginia General Assembly, February 7, 1822.

3 See above, Convention, June 5, 1822, note.

4 See above, Clay to Cheves (1), March 10, 1821.

5 See above, Clay to Brooke, March 9, 1823.

6 William H. Crawford.

7 The pension law of March 18, 1818 (see above, II, 681n), had been enacted after President Monroe, in his annual message, December 2, 1817, had called attention to needy Revolutionary veterans who were not eligible for pensions under existing legislation. "These men," he said, "have a claim on the gratitude of their country, and it will do honor to their country, to provide for them." *Annals of Cong.*, 15 Cong., 1 Sess., XXXI, 19.

8 Cf. above, II, 739, 844.

9 Samuel L. Southard.

10 John C. Calhoun.

From Richard Alsop

Henry Clay Esqre. Lima September 1st 1823.

Sir

Presuming upon the reputation, which you have so ably sustained, of an enlightened statesman and independent republican, feelingly alive to whatever may affect the welfare of his country, or impede the glorious march of Freedom; as well as the peculiar interest you have always manifested to the cause of suffering humanity, in South America, I consider it my sacred duty, as an American citizen, to call your attention to a subject, which not only involves our national character, and jeopardises our commercial relations; but is completely subversive of the righteous principles we are taught to venerate, and painfully degrading to our Naval establishment.

The subject, to which I allude, is the conduct of some of our naval commanders on this coast; but more especially to that of the commander of the present squadron, who has, apparently, manifested a malignant hostility to the cause of Patriotism on the shores of the Pacific:[1] Without recapitulating any of the well attested facts, which are in every one's mouths, or dwelling upon the unhappy and, to me, altogether unlooked for, prejudice and ill will entertained by the people of these countries towards us; continually drawing disparaging comparisons between the policy of our country {the parent and advocate of colonial independence and liberty} and that of England {the mere Pander of her own monopolists and manufacturers}: comparisons which are, as it were, tangible, and which are constantly presenting themselves to their observation and animadversion, namely, in the different line of conduct pursued by the commanders of the national vessels of the two countries, for they cannot seperate [*sic*], but, judging from the extrinsic evidence of things, confound these commanders with their respective Governments;[2] and it would be surprizing were it otherwise: Without detailing the various circumstances, which have fallen under my own observation, since March last, while conducting considerable commercial concerns in these seas, and from which the most unfavourable inferences might be drawn: or without entering into any investigation of the causes which may have produced unfriendly feelings in the mind of Captain Stewart, and have influence[d] both his public and private conduct, I beg leave to lay before you the accompanying copy of a document which has been furnished to John B Prevost Esq the private agent of the Government of the United States, to be submitted by him to the Department of State, containing a general history of the proceeding[s] of the United States Ship Franklin, while on this coast drawn up by Platt H Crosby Esqre., a gentleman of much observation and favourably Known in the United States as the author of Passos [*sic*] The story of South America,[3] an[d] who has been sometime in this country, and has had every opportunity of acquiring correct information, of the subject upon which he writes.

It is with Mr Crosby's permission, and at his instance, that I have taken this copy of a history of truth abjured, good faith violated, honour and justice trampled to the earth: a history, of facts, to rouse the indignant spirit of every honest man, and mantle his cheeks with burning blushes of shame at his country's dishonour: of facts, the most material of which can be proven by the officers of the two vessels, Franklin & Dolphin; and which Mr Crosby pledges himself to substantiate, if ever called upon so to do.

Mr Provost [*sic*], I understand, has been, for the last four years, continually representing to the Department of State, the injurious effects of the system pursued by the commanders, of our Ships of War, on this coast, without any apparent attention having been paid to his representations: and, I am further informed, that for more than two years he has not received any letters, or instructions whatever, from our Government.[4]

I mention these facts, respecting Mr. Provost, which have come accidentally to my knowledge, as indicating, at least, a great degree of negligence somewhere and submit, to your superior intelligence, the proper mode to be adopted to elicite [*sic*] the truth, to wipe out this foul blot from our heretofore unsullied escutcheon and to strangle, in its infancy, a monster, inordinate lust of gain, which would profane the fair Temple of our holy Liberty, convert our national Ships into huxters' shops, and our high minded chivalric officers into Jew Brokers.

As I have not the honour of being personally known to you: it appears to me proper that you should have some warrant for paying the attention it merits to the matters I have communicated. I, therefore, refer you to Messrs. Eyre & Massey,[5] merchant[s] of Philadelphia, who are concerned with me in the Ship Kensington of that port now on this coast and remain, with m[y] respectful consideration, Sir Your humble fellow citizen RICHARD ALSOP.

ALS, "Duplicate." DLC-HC (DNA, M212, R1). Alsop, a native of Connecticut, was a member of the mercantile firm, Alsop and Company, operating in Lima, Peru, and Valparaiso, Chili. He later became a director of the Bank of the United States in New York, an association formed under New York law to resume banking operations in the city after termination of the charter of the second Bank of the United States.

1 Captain Charles Stewart, born in Philadelphia, had been commissioned a lieutenant in the United States Navy in 1798 and had served with distinction in the undeclared war with France, the Tripolitan War, and the War of 1812. From 1821 to 1824 he was commander of a squadron, which included the *Franklin* and the schooner *Dolphin*, stationed in the Pacific. In performance of this duty his refusal to honor the ineffective blockade established by the Patriot naval forces before Royalist ports of the Spanish colonies incurred charges against him which led to court-martial proceedings in 1825. Among the specifications of complaint were allegations that a merchant of the United States, trading with the Royalists, had been transported with his goods and samples in the Navy schooner *Dolphin;* that several schooners, supposed to be under Stewart's command in the service of the United States, had been employed "in traffic and carrying merchandise on private account"; that sails had been made by seamen of the *Franklin* out of Government materials for the use of a privately owned vessel; and that Navy vessels were used to transport bullion for private traders. The Court not only cleared Stewart but took occasion to praise his conduct. *American State Papers, Naval Affairs,* II, 487-610.

2 The distinction properly belonged at the governmental level, for the United States had persistently maintained a narrow definition of blockade, while Great Britain had upheld the loose and broad interpretation consonant to belligerent sea power. Though discharged from the British Navy, Thomas Cochrane in his activities (see above, Shaw to Clay, April 4, 1822, note) served to promote, and was popularly identified with, the British as opposed to the American stand.

3 Crosby, a New York lawyer, who in January, 1820, had taken up residence in Buenos Aires, was the translator of Pazos' book (see above, II, 685n). In a comment to Clay officially as Secretary of State, May 26, 1825 (omitted from the letter as presented below), Crosby explained that he had only recently learned that Prevost had forwarded the paper to the State Department, that it had not been intended for such use,

and that Prevost himself had made additions and alterations which, while not changing its factual content, had rendered it "rather a second edition, revised and enlarged by him." Crosby regretted that the submission of the document might have been interpreted as "the part of a thankless volunteer in a business in which it may perhaps be thought I had no proper concern."

4 As early as 1820 Secretary of State Adams had concluded that Prevost, a favorite of the President, though possessed of "more ability than any other of the informal Agents who have been employed in South America, has not escaped the common error of making himself a blind partisan, not only to their struggle for independence, but to their internal feuds; and . . . he has been, to say the least, very remiss in supporting the rights and interests of his countrymen." Adams had further complained: "No satisfaction has been obtained from them [the South American states] upon any complaint, and they have been constantly endeavoring to entangle us with them and their cause. Prevost has been one of their dupes, if not worse, and by his correspondence has contributed all in his power to make us dupes also." Adams, *Memoirs,* V, 157, 164-65.

In January, 1823, President Monroe had nominated Prevost as Chargé d'Affaires of the United States in Peru; but, after the Senate had postponed action on the matter, the nomination had been recalled. U. S. Sen., *Executive Journal,* III, 320, 327, 340. Early in 1825 Prevost was given permission to return to the United States and notified that "it was deemed advisable that there should be an investigation of his conduct." Adams, *Memoirs,* VI, 462. He died in March of that year.

5 Manuel Eyre; Charles Massey.

From John T. Hawkins

[September 1, 1823]

I am to give H Clay an order for One hundred dollars[1] on James Barbour Esqr. of Va. the price of a gig & harness bought of him 1 Septr. 1823. JOHN T. HAWKINS

DS, in Clay's hand. DLC-TJC (DNA, M212, R15).

1 Not found.

Property Deed from William W. Whitney

[September 1, 1823]

[William W. Whitney, of Fayette County, for the sum of $500, current money of Kentucky, sells to Henry Clay, acting executor of James Morrison, five acres, more or less, comprising the major portion of lot no. 44 "in the general plan of the Town of Lexington."]

Fayette County Court, Deed Book X, 27-29. Recorded September 1, 1823. Whitney was a Lexington physician.

From Henry Whiting

Sir/ Chicago 2d. September 1823

I have the honor to acknowledge the recpt. of yours of the 15th. May,[1] & beg leave to request of you the favor to transmit the Accnt. that may be due on Mr. Phillips draft.[2] to Messrs. Ben. De Forest & Co. Merchants New York

I am Sir With great respect Your Mo. Obt— HENRY WHITING

Hon. Henry Clay &c. &c

ALS. KyLxT. Postmarked at Fort Wayne, Indiana, September 13. Endorsed by Clay: ". . . Sent a check according to the within for $400. drawn by the Lexn. Office on the B.U.S. 27 Septr. 1823. HC." Whiting, a career officer in the United States Army—a captain at this time, chief quartermaster to Zachary Taylor in the Mexican War, brevetted brigadier general for gallantry in the Battle of Buena Vista, February, 1847—and author of several published poems and prose works.

1 Not found. 2 See above, Shippen to Clay, April 12, 1823.

To Nicholas Biddle

Dr Sir Ashland 4h. Septr. 1823.

Col. Richard M. Johnson is on his way to Philadelphia and desires me to say to you that the arrangement which he made some time ago with the Bank for the discharge of certain debts with property, the execution of which was confided to me on the part of the Bank,[1] is completed except in two particulars, the finishing of a house in Geo. Town, and the conveyance of a house and lot in Burlington, one having been conveyed instead of another through mistake.

Col. Johnson informs me that he is about to make some proposition to the Bank, and wishes me to express to you my opinion about the ability of himself, his brother Col. James Johnson, and John T. Mason. I have no hesitation in declaring my full conviction that all of those gentlemen are utterly unable to discharge their debts; and that any attempt to coerce the payment, by legal means, will be totally unavailing.

The state of my health obliged me most reluctantly to decline going to Columbus.[2] I have taken all the precautions in my power to prevent prejudice to the interests of the Bank from my absence, and I believe they will not sustain any. I have the honor to be with great respect Your ob. Servant H. CLAY

Nicholas Biddle Esqr. &c. &c. &.c

ALS. CSmH.

1 See above, Clay to Cheves, October 3, 1821; Johnson to Clay, May 22, 1823.

2 To attend Federal court.

From Peter B. Porter

Dear Sir, (Confidential) Black Rock Sept. 6th. 1823.

Altho' I am a very negligent correspondent, I beg you not to suppose that I have been equally inattentive to the political interests & movements that have constituted the subject matter of our late letters. Your favour of the 15th. of June did not reach this place untill late in July, & two days after I had left home for Albany. It is only a few weeks since the presidential question began to develope itself to any considerable extent in the interior of this State; and I have delayed writing to you from day to day, in the hope of improving my information on this subject. I will however wait [n]o longer, but will write you again in the course of two or three weeks.

From the imperfect lights I now possess, the [follow]ing are the speculations I should make on the present state of public sentiment. Mr Crawford, I think, stands lower with the people of this State, and particularly with those of the western part of it, than any other candidate, with the exception perhaps of Genl. Jackson. His strength is entirely factitious & is limited to the personal influence of a few active political partizans. He has no chance of the vote of this state unless he should obtain a caucus nomination in which case Mr Van Buren & his friends may perhaps attempt to push him— But I much doubt whether, *even then,* [the r]epublicans of the state could be induced to vote for him. Mr Calhoun's strength is confined principally to the city of New York, with a few scattering friends in other parts of the State.

The republicans in the city who are opposed to Mr Crawford (and they constitute a very decided majority) are again divided between Mr. Calhoun & yourself. A majority of them are favourable to Mr Calhoun, if the new political paper, *The Patriot,* is to be considerd [*sic*] as the index of their sentiments. This is not surprising when we consider the personal popularity of Mr. C. and the government, & especially the *army,* influence & patronage which he is able to weild [*sic*]. There is however no asperity, but, on the contrary, a state of very good feeling, existing between Mr C's & your friends; and it is well understood that the former will readily unite with the latter whenever it shall be discovered, as I think it soon will be, that he has no chance of carrying the vote of the State. Such I have understood to be the state of things in the City for two or three months past, & it was confirmed by Judge Ogden Edwards of N.Y., the Classmate & friend of Mr Calhoun,[1] who spent two days with me this week, & who I beleive [*sic*] has become pretty well satisfied on his journey through the country that Mr. Calhoun's prospects are extremely slender. Indeed, I consider that the approaching contest will ultimately settle down between Mr Adams and yourself, and I am glad it is taking that turn because it will in that case inevitably resolve it self into the old party question of federalist & democrat. Independently of Mr. Adams' equivocal character as a politican, the zeal & interest already manifested by many of our federal & Clintonian presses are calculated to give that direction to the contest.

My opinion is that at the next meeting of our Legislature the *Republican* [mem]bers will have an amicable meeting, and indicate their candidate (whom I assure you I have strong reasons to believe will be yourself) and instruct our members of Congress to support him in Caucus, if a Caucus shall be held. In case their instructions shall be disobeyed, the proceedings of the Caucus will of course be disregarded.

Within the last 15 or 20 days, four or five newspapers in this part of the State have, for the first time, declared in your favour; and we expect as many more to come out in the course of the ensuing fortnight. If I can lay my hands on any of them before the mail closes I will send them to you. My brother[2] was, last week, at Utica where he saw Judge Skinner,[3] whom you may recognise as the political coadjutor of Van Buren. He acknowledged his doubts of the practicability of sustaining Mr. Crawford in this state; and expressed his willingness in such case to join in supporting you. I, yesterday, received a letter from a friend of mine in Oswego County, who is also your friend and one of the most influential members of our State Senate.[4] He has recently b[een] informed by a Gentleman from N.York that you are shortly to be in this part of the country—appears to be much gratified with the intelligence, and begs me to inform him, if in my power, at what time you may be expected. Can you not make it convenient to pass through this State on your way to Congress? Whatever remarks might be made on it by your enemies, I am satisfied that such a journey would not only be gratifying to you personally, but would be politically auspicious. Come to Columbus where you will probably have professional business. From that place it is only 110 miles to Sandusky, where you will take the Steam Boat & arrive at Buffalo & Black Rock in 36. hou[rs.] From this you will go to the falls (only 20 miles) & then proceed on the Canal to Albany. Mrs P. joins me in the expression of our great respect & regard. P. B. PORTER

Hon. H. Clay.

ALS. DLC-HC (DNA, M212, R1). Holes in MS.

1 At Yale. Edwards, a native of New Haven, had removed to New York City, which he represented in the State legislature, 1817-1818, and the State constitutional convention of 1821. He was appointed Judge of the First Circuit, New York, in April, 1823, and served in that post until he reached the age of mandatory retirement in 1841.

2 Augustus Porter, pioneer surveyor and settler in western New York and, in partnership with his younger brother, Peter B. Porter, highly successful as developer of the area adjacent to Niagara Falls. Augustus had been elected to the State legislature in 1802, had been appointed Judge of Niagara County in 1808, had served in the Commissary Department during the War of 1812, and was for years Postmaster of Niagara.

3 Roger Skinner.

4 Alvin Bronson, a merchant, who retired from the State Senate in 1824.

To John J. Crittenden

Dr. Crittenden. Ashland 13h. Septr. 1823.

I recd. your letter[1] by Mr. Davis.[2] I participate most cordially with you in the just solicitude which the dispute between Mess.

Breckenridge and Wickliffe[3] awakens. When it was first mentioned to me, considering its peculiar circumstances, and the character of one of the parties, I feared that all private interference would be unavailing; and that the best course would be an appeal to the civil authority with its chances of delay, cooling of the passions & possible ultimate accommodation. Supposing the intervention of the civil power would not Mr. W. be relieved from the necessity of having the interview and Mr. B. be stript of any ground to carry into effect the other alternative which it is said he menaced?

There is no incompatibility, however, between the two courses which may be tried in succession or simultaneously, according to circumstances. I have therefore prepared and on my part signed a letter, addressed to the parties,[4] and which may be signed by both or either of you and the Governor— If the relation of your brother to one of them[5] should induce you to with hold your signature that of the Govr. may be affixed without your's. I would advise a copy of this letter to be also delivered to each of the Seconds of the parties. And considering that it is uncertain where they may meet, I would suggest that one of the Judges of the Court of Appeals or Circuit Courts be applied to for a warrant to bind the parties. The public rumor of their intention to meet will form a sufficient ground for his acting.

One of the motives which took me to Woodford was to see you. The melancholy event which occurred there of private affliction to you[6] (on which I offer you my sincere condolence) deprived me of that pleasure. My health is not re established, but is improving, and I begin to feel that I see land, or rather that I may not get under it. I am faithfully Your friend H. CLAY

J. J. Crittenden Esq.

ALS. DLC-John J. Crittenden Papers (DNA, M212, R20). Published in Coleman (ed.), *The Life of John J. Crittenden,* I, 59. Addressed to Crittenden in Frankfort.

1 Not found.

2 Probably James E. Davis, who in 1819 had opened a law office in Lexington.

3 Further reference to the pending duel has not been found.

4 Not found.

5 In 1813 Thomas T. Crittenden had married Mary W. Parker, daughter of Alexander and Mary Howard Parker of Lexington. Her mother was a sister of Margaret Howard (Mrs. Robert) Wickliffe and a first cousin of John and Alexander Breckinridge, fathers of Robert J. and James D. Breckinridge, respectively, either of whom might have quarreled with a Wickliffe at this time.

6 Possibly the death of Crittenden's mother, Judith Harris Crittenden.

Advertisement of Morrison Property

Ashland, 15th Sept. 1823

[Clay, acting executor of the estate of James Morrison, advertises a public auction, to be held October 21 on the Morrison farm,[1] adjoining Clay's residence, of "about TWENTY SLAVES, and all the moveable property on the farm," including livestock, tools, and the portion of the crop still on hand. "The slaves, most of whom are young and likely, composed principally of women and their children, will be sold in families; but the bid of no person will be received whose intention is known to be to carry them out of this state." The sale is to begin at eleven o'clock in the morning; payment must be in specie; one year's credit may be allowed for sums above $100; and Morrison's legatees may purchase on credit to the extent of their respective legacies. If necessary the sale will be continued a second day; if the weather be bad, the sale will be postponed to October 28. Immediately before the sale the farm will be rented to the highest bidder.]

Lexington *Kentucky Reporter,* September 22, 1823.

1 "Carlisle Farm."

Receipt from T. H. Clarke

[September 15, 1823]

Received Terre-Haute September 15th. 1823, from Henry Clay by the hand of Col. T. H. Blake,[1] eight dollars and thirty two cents, in full of the State, County, and Road Taxes on the following described tracts of land lying in the County of Vigo for the year 1823, to wit:

S. E. qr. S. 6. T. 13. N. of R. 9. W. —	State $1.60 —	Cy. $1.06 —	Road $1.50
NE. " " 7. " 13. " " " 9. "	" 1.60 —	" 1.06 —	" 1.50
	$ 3.20	$ 2.12	$ 3.00
Second Rate Land—	2 12		
	3.00		
	$ 8.32		

T. H. Clarke Collector
By HENRY ALLEN[2]

ADS, by Henry Allen. DLC-TJC (DNA, M212, R15).

1 Thomas Holdsworth Blake, a native of Calvert County, Maryland, who had studied law in Washington, D. C., served in the militia during the War of 1812, then moved to Kentucky and from there to Terre Haute, Indiana, where he had begun the practice of law. After brief service as a judge of circuit court, he abandoned legal practice and went into business, at a later date becoming president of the Erie & Wabash Canal Company. He was a member of the State legislature at the approaching session, from 1827 to 1829 a Congressman, and from 1842 to 1845 Commissioner of the General Land Office.

2 Not identified.

From Caleb Cox

The Hon H. Clay St Louis 19 Sept. 1823

Sir

Inclos'd you have a/c. sales & a/c. current of goods benonging [*sic*] to J. Harts Estate[1] [in w]hich you will find a balance of

	$67.02	67.02
Due by Bright[2] (faild)	61.50	
Post Since the a/c. was made—	״.25	
Cash I now Inclose you	5 ״	66.75
balance		״.27 Cts

Respectfully your most obt St CALEB COX

ALS. DLC-TJC (DNA, M212, R12). [1] AD. DLC-TJC (DNA, M212, R12).
[2] Probably Jonathan Brown Bright, a native of Massachusetts, who had settled in Missouri and engaged in commission business to the southward. In 1823 he removed to New York and became a cotton broker.

To Walter Dun

Dr Sir Lexington 26h. Sept. 1823

Inclosed I transmit to you receipts for the amount of Costs which you have paid in the cases of Taylor exor &c against Montjoy and that in your own name against Banks, which I hope you will receive in due time.

Mr. Call requested me to draw on you for a fee in the suit ordered in his name as executor of Mr. Means against Thomas D. Carneal; and he wished me to do so whilst he was in Chillicothe. The suit is in Chancery and will be I apprehend a pretty troublesome one, from what I learn of our antagonist and what I know of his character. You will be pleased therefore to remit me $100 in the same way that you made the former remittance, if perfectly convenient.

I heard with much concern of your indisposition, from which I hope you have entirely recovered. I lament exceedingly the very great sickness which prevails in Ohio; and tremble to hear from my friends at Columbus & in Chillicothe.

With great regard I am Yours faithfully H. CLAY

Walter Dunn Esq.

P.S. I have had notice delivered to Montjoy of a motion to dissolve his injunction at the next Court. H.C.

ALS. Ross County Historical Society, Chillicothe, Ohio. Endorsed: ". . . Answered Nov. 20.1823." Answer not found. See above, Clay to Dun, July 2, 1823.

From John McKinley

Dear Sir Florence Septr 29 1823

In June last I gave you a hasty & desultory answer to your letter & promised to advise you further after the election[1] Contrary to my aticipation [*sic*] Pickens is reelected Governor & so far as his influence extends it will be exerted against you & in favour of Mr Adams Candour requires that I should state to you that at present General Jackson would get a large majority of the people of this state & although many & perhaps a majority of the most inteligent [*sic*] are strongly your friends yet such is the influence of public opinion many of them conceal or abstain from an expression of their preference The personal friends of Genl Jackson (as I before informed you) are your bitterest enemies & will use every exertion to transfer his friends & interest to Mr Adams if they find he can not succeed But they consider his prospects brightening daily & will probably in a short time become jealous of Mr Adams also & operate against him as they now do against others The expression of public opinion throughout the nation as far as it can be collected from the public papers leaves the main question as doubtful as it was six or even 12 months ago & indeed there seems to be a suspension of open & public effort but I apprehend there is at this time more Secret intrigue going forward than at any former period As a confidential correspondence has commenced I must beg a continuance of it that I may be the better able to *act* & *counteract* in the darkness which is likely to pervade future operations. That you be upon your guard at Washington next winter I will give you information upon which you may rely with safety in relation to the representation of this State Mr King[2] you know perhaps better than I do & knowing him can appreciate his professions He is for Adams Mr Kelley[3] is like St Paul "All things to all men" Mr Owen[4] is a vain young man pretends sometimes to be for Genl Jackson but is in reality for Adams Col McK[5] is an honest blunt independent man & is no doubt for Mr Crawford at present Mr Moore[6] is a man in whom little confidence can be placed He declared himself for Mr Calhoun first, then for Mr Adams, but finding neither suited his constituents he pretends now to be for Jackson Write to me freely you risque nothing by doing so except the transportation by mail Your friend J McKINLEY

ALS. DLC-HC (DNA, M212, R1). Addressed to Clay at Lexington.

1 See above, McKinley to Clay, June 3, 1823. 2 William Rufus de Vane King.

3 William Kelly, Huntsville lawyer, who had been elected United States Senator to fill a vacancy and served from December 12, 1822, to March 3, 1825. He subsequently moved to New Orleans, where he died in 1832.

4 George W. Owen, a native of Virginia, had lived for a time in Tennessee, had been graduated from the University of Nashville before studying law, and, having been admitted to the bar in 1816, had begun practice in Claiborne, Alabama. He had been a member of the Alabama House of Representatives, 1819-1821, Speaker in 1821. After having sat in Congress from 1823 to 1829, he became Collector of the Port of Mobile until 1836, when he was elected Mayor of Mobile. He died the following year.

5 John McKee, a pioneer settler in Tuscaloosa County, Alabama, had been educated in his native Virginia and had become identified with the Mississippi-Alabama area through his services on several occasions as Agent to the Indians. He was a member of Congress from 1823 to 1829.

6 Gabriel Moore, a graduate of the University of North Carolina, had been admitted to the bar in 1810 and had settled in Huntsville, Alabama. After having been a member of the Territorial legislature, delegate to the State constitutional convention in 1819, and State Senator, he was elected to Congress, where he sat from 1821 to 1829. In the last year he became Governor of Alabama and, upon expiration of his term in this office, was chosen United States Senator, 1831-1837. He was defeated in the Congressional election of 1836, moved to Texas in 1843, and died there two years later.

Receipt from John C. Richardson

[*ca.* October, 1823]

Recd. payment from H Clay J. C. RICHARDSON

ES, in Clay's hand. DLC-TJC (DNA, M212, R15). Endorsement on verso of a statement, attested by Thomas Bodley, Clerk of Fayette Circuit Court, that Richardson had served as commissioner in the chancery suit of William S. Dallam against Thomas January. A decree rendered at April Special Term, 1823, of Fayette Circuit Court, had required sale of January's property to cover payment of principal and interest on his overdue notes to Dallam (cf. above, Agreement and Assignment, October 18, 1822). The sale, at public auction, had been held in Lexington, June 24, 1823. Lexington *Kentucky Reporter,* June 16, 1823. Richardson's claim to twenty dollars for his services in this transaction had been authorized under order of the court at September Term, 1823.

From William Carroll

My dear Sir, Murfreesboro Oct. 1st. 1823

The political movements here, since the meeting of our Legislature have been so strange and uncertain, that I have declined writing you at an earlier day, and even now I have only time before the mail closes, to inform you of an important event that has Just taken place.

A determination had been manifested for the last twelve months to defeat the election of Colo. John Williams to the Senate.[1] At the commencement of the Session Pleasant M Miller, appeared as the opposing candidate, but it was soon discovered that he could not be elected. Mr. Rhea[2] and others were spoken of but it was ascertained that no successful stand could be made; and as a last resort General Jackson was mentioned who consented that his name should be used. The contest is Just over and it has terminated in the election of the General. Jackson, thirty five and Williams twenty five votes— Thus you see a man known to be unfriendly to the Genl. has obtained a very honorable vote. I forbear to comment on the subject; for I cannot tell how it will operate

I have not time to add any thing further,—at present Yr. friend

WM. CARROLL

ALS. DLC-HC (DNA, M212, R1). The address has been torn from the document.
[1] See above, Hynes to Clay, July 31, 1822. [2] John Rhea.

Receipt from Joshua Humphreys

Lexington, Ky. Octr 1st. 1823

Joshua Humphreys, Treasurer of Transylvania University, acknowledges receipt of $20 from Henry Clay for tuition (of Henry Clay, Jr.). DS (partially printed). DLC-TJC (DNA, M212, R15).

To Peter Hagner

D Sir Ashland 4h. Oct. 1823

An act passed at the last Session of Congress (Chapter 103) for the relief of my neighbour and friend Charles Carr.[1] The vouchers and papers on which that act passed are on file with one of the Clerks of the two houses of Congress. Mr. Carr has, to my knowledge, paid to the U. States Atto. all of the Judgment recovered against him which he thinks is justly due. I was his Counsel in the suit and take pleasure in saying that he used no evasions, sought no improper delay, but went manly into the trial. He believes that the papers on which Congress acted will be deemed by you sufficient to enable you to carry into effect the act. And the object of this letter is to request of you, as a personal favor to me, to obtain those papers and if practicable to liquidate his account upon them. If they should be defective, and you think it probable that the defect can be supplied, be pleased to indicate it, and if possible it will be supplied. And I will thank you for an answer as soon as your convenience will admit of transmitting one. With great regard I am Your ob. Servt.

P. Hagner Esqr. &c &c &c H. CLAY

ALS. DLC-Henry Clay Papers (unbound) (DNA, M Supplement).

1 The act directed the Treasury Department to allow Carr "such credits as he may prove that he is entitled to by the best evidence which the nature of the case will admit of, and which it may be in his power to produce." Meanwhile, further prosecution of the judgment against Carr (see above, Goddard to Clay, June 17, 1822) was to be suspended for a year. No credits in excess of the claim against him were to be allowed, and the Treasury Department was to require of him "good and sufficient surety" for payment of whatever sum might be found due upon settlement of his accounts under this act. 6 *U.S. Stat.*, 289.

To Peter B. Porter

Dr. General Ashland 4h. Oct. 1823.

Before you receive this letter, the distressing tidings will have reached you of the death of J. C. Breckenridge Esqr—an event which has filled us all with the deepest regret and concern. I have rarely witnessed the death of any person which has been so generally & sincerely lamented. South Frankfort, in which he resided, has been visited during the two past months by fever of a most extraordinary mortality, to which he fell a victim. The health of other parts of our State has been bad. Mr. Breckenridge had intended to retire to his mothers[1] previous to his attack, but was detained at home by the illness of Genl. John Preston from Virginia,[2] lying sick there. Be pleased to offer to his sister[3] my sincere condolence for the very great loss which she and her family have sustained. I have myself sustained in his death the loss of one of my best friends

I duly recd. your very obliging letter of the 6h. Ulto. The information which you have had the goodness to communicate to me, respecting the state of public sentiment in N. York on the Presidential election, corresponds with that which I derive through other channels. One gentleman indeed tells me in his letter that there is a general burst of indignation against Mr. Van Buren, to whom the most injurious motives are imputed.[4] Mr. Crawford, I assure you, stands quite as low in the West as in N. York. He is the most unpopular here of all the candidates. I do believe that if the contest were limited to him & Mr. Adams, he would lose every State West of the Mountains except Missouri & Kentucky, and even of the latter there is much doubt. I do not mean of course to indicate in the smallest degree my own wishes, adhering as I have done and mean to do to a system of perfect neutrality in regard to the other Candidates.

I retain the opinion that there will be no Congressional Caucus. In this quarter it is strongly opposed. Grundy has introduced into the Legislature of Tennessee, now in Session, resolutions denouncing such a Caucus, and instructing the representatives and Senators of that State no [*sic*] to attend it, if one be held. These resolutions will most probably pass.[5] The question of a Caucus ought to be decided on principle. But it is to be apprehended that it will be according to interest. Assuming that basis, it will be opposed by the friends of each of the Candidates who suppose that the recommendation will not be favorable to their choice. It is not likely that any one Candidate will be able to anticipate, with probable certainty, the result, from the difficulty of ascertaining what the secondary combinations may be. And I should not therefore be much surprized if the friends of all the Candidates oppose a Caucus. Certainly those of Mr. Crawford, who have been most favorable to it, will find a state of his interest in the next Congress very different from that which prevailed in the last. In N. York, Virginia and Pennsa. a caucus is most popular. Can the representations from those three States form one, if it be refused to be attended by those from most of the other States? I think not. It would be too invidious. Moreover, they differ so essentially about the fittest person, that there is no likelihood of a concert between them, acting in Caucus separately from the other States.

I do not know of any intention in other Western States to follow up Mr. Grundy's example; but I should not be surprized if there be other similar expressions of public sentiment.

How is your member Tracey?[6] He has spoken to me, of his own accord, in the most friendly way.[7] Is he sincere?

I had intended to have asked your opinion about the expediency of my serving again as Speaker, if the place should be offered to me;

but I fear I have omitted it too long, unless you could address me at Washn. I shall go there with a determination to avoid any doubtful contest about the Chair; but at the same time if a disposition generally exists to replace me there not to oppose it. Such a disposition I have reason to believe will prevail.

I regreted extremely that the state of my health would not allow me to visit you, if other circumstances had favored the gratification of my wishes. I was prevented from attending the Court at Columbus, from which place I had thought seriously of making an excursion by the route suggested by you. My health is not yet reestablished, but I think it is in a condition of progressive improvement.

How do you dispose of yourself this winter? Will you be at Albany, Washn. or remain at Black rock?[8] Wherever you may be, I shall be glad to hear from you when your leisure will allow you to write— With great rega[rd] I am faithfully Your friend

Genl. P. B. Porter. H. CLAY

ALS. NBuHi. [1] Mary Hopkins Cabell Breckinridge, widow of John Breckinridge.

[2] Brother of Francis Preston and first cousin of Joseph Cabell Breckinridge's father. A general of the Virginia militia, John Preston had been a member of the Virginia House of Delegates (1783, 1791, and 1803), a State Senator (1792-1799), and Treasurer of Virginia (1808-1819).

[3] Mrs. Porter. [4] See above, Woods to Clay, August 27, 1823.

[5] The first of the resolutions offered by Felix Grundy, and adopted early in October, 1823, provided "That the Senators in Congress from this State be instructed, and our Representatives be requested to use their exertions to prevent a nomination being made during the next session of Congress by the members thereof in Caucus. . . ." Lexington *Kentucky Reporter,* October 6, 1823.

[6] Albert H. Tracy. [7] See above, Tracy to Clay, April 27, 1823.

[8] Cf. below, Porter to Clay, November 17, 1823.

From Newton Cannon

Dear Sir Nashville Tennessee Octr. 4th. 1823

The bearier [*sic*] hereof. Mr. James Erwin.[1] has intimated to me a wish that I would give him a Letter to you in relation to his Standing and character in this country, which request it gives me great pleasure to grant I have been personally acquainted with him Several years and during the whole time I have consider d him a young man of the first Ta*len*ts and respec*ta*bility. I know of none that are his Superiour in either respect and I believe So far as I have ever heard him Spoken of, that is his character both here and elsewhere. I have known his father[2] from my boyhood and in every Situation of Life in which he has been placd. he has uniformly Supported the character of an honest and honourable man.

I am glad to hear you are recovering your health, present my respects to Mrs. Clay and accept yourself my good wishes for your health and prosperity with great respect Your obt. Servt.

The Honble Henry Clay N. CANNON

ALS. Owned by M. W. Anderson, Lexington, Kentucky.

1 A partner in the Savannah, Georgia, mercantile firm of Erwin and Company and associated in the farflung commercial and land operations of his father. He was at this time, briefly, a resident of Cahaba, Alabama.

2 Andrew Erwin, formerly an innkeeper and merchant at Wilkesboro, North Carolina, member of that State's House of Commons from Wilkes County (1800 and 1801), and Asheville's first postmaster, in 1814 had removed to Augusta, Georgia, where he had established a mercantile business with connections in Savannah, Charleston, Nashville, and New Orleans. He was also engaged in developing extensive land holdings in Tennessee and Alabama. By 1819 he had suffered serious financial reverses and at this time had shifted his residence to Bedford County, Tennessee, where he had sought political office as Marshall for the Western District and, in the early 'twenties, as a member of Congress. Representing forces allied with William H. Crawford and in opposition to Andrew Jackson, Erwin had been defeated.

Report to Trustees of Transylvania University

October 5, 1823.

Mr. Clay reported from the Comee. apptd: for that purpose, that an excellent likeness of Col: James Morrison[1] had been painted by M. H. Jouitt, and that a frame had been made by James McIntosh,[2] & was ready for delivery—that Mr. Jouitt's charge was $120.—and Mr. McIntosh's $30.—in specie.

Copy. PPPrHi-Shane Collection, TU62-T68N, III, 107.

1 At his death Morrison had bequeathed to the Trustees of Transylvania University the sum of $20,000 "to vest the capital in some permanent productive fund; and out of the anual [*sic*] interest, or dividends accruing thereon to pay the sallery [*sic*] of a professorship . . . to be denominated the 'Morrison Professorship'; or to apply the said twenty thousand Dollars to the purchase of a Library, to be denominated the 'Morrison Library'; as the said Trustees may think, will best promote the interest of learning and science." The residuum of his estate, after very numerous bequests, was also given to the University "to be applied to the erection of another edifice for its purposes, to be denominated 'Morrison College,' in the Town of Lexington." Fayette County, Will Book F, 63, 67.

It was contemporaneously reported that Clay's influence had led to the latter bequest after Morrison had first proposed to leave the residual estate to Clay's youngest son, John Morrison Clay, born February 21, 1821. Lexington *Kentucky Reporter*, September 22, 1827.

2 "Carver and Gilder," located on Upper Street at the Public Square, Lexington.

Account with Lexington Post Office

[*ca.* October 10, 1823]

The account with the Lexington Post Office, similar to that above, July 3, 1823, covers Clay's postal charges for the period from July 3 through October 8, 1823. Included in the total sum of $26.38 are postage for two quarters (to January, 1824) on the Washington *National Intelligencer, City of Washington Gazette,* Cincinnati *Liberty Hall and Cincinnati Gazette,* Frankfort *Argus of Western America,* and Frankfort *Commentator;* nineteen cents postage, October to January, for "N. H. paper" (the Keene *New Hampshire Sentinel,* established in 1799 by John Prentiss, brother of George W. Prentiss, and continued under this editorship for nearly fifty years); box rent, from April 1 to December 31, ninety cents; and letter postage, $22.11. D. DLC-TJC (DNA, M212, R15). Endorsed on verso by Clay: "Paid by a check on the Off of Dt & D 10 Oct 1823 [query—I am charged improperly with postage on news papers to 1st. Jan.]" Clay's check has not been found.

Speech to Synod of Kentucky

[October 11, 1823]

He considered the subject in two points of view: 1st, Is it *desirable* to colonize the free blacks of America; 2d, Is it *practicable* to do so. On both these subjects he expressed his thorough conviction of their importance, and the entire possibility of carrying them into effect. In the course of his remarks he adverted to some of the leading objections that had been raised, and the obstacles thrown in the way of this scheme; and demonstrated their erroneous foundation, and mistaken tendency. One of them we have heard often repeated, which is, that the people of colour would refuse to go to Africa, and that it would be criminal to take them to a place where the sickly climate would prove their immediate destruction. This has turned out to be untrue. Mr Clay observed that the society had found more willing to go than they had the means of accommodating; and that the climate, when they become a little seasoned and accustomed to it, was congenial to their health. All colonists in settling a new country experience the same effects in almost any clime or country.

Lexington *Kentucky Reporter,* October 27, 1823, from Lexington *Western Monitor.* Clay's "short address . . . delivered before the Synod of Kentucky, composed of all the Presbyterian Clergy in the state," was on the subject of the American Colonization Society. He "appeared before them on a short notice, and without any written document, but spoke from memory, and gave a very interesting view of the progress of the Society since its first institution."

Statement to James Byers

[*ca.* October 13, 1823]

Statement of Capt. Byers' debt—

Amount of his bond	$ 1900 —
Int thereon from the 16 July 1821 to the 26 August 1823 . .	240:66
	2140:66
By Cash paid Mr. Chambers (supposed to have been paid)[1] 26 Aug. 1823	310:
	1830:66
Int. thereon from the 26 August 1823 to 1 Oct. 1823	10:67
Amount to have been paid by Capt. Byers on the 1 Oct. 1823 exclusive of the above paid to Mr. Chambers	1841:33
Amt. passed by Theodore to the care of Capt Langhorne[2]	310:—
Amt. to be brought home by Theodore . .	$ 2151:33

Memo. If Capt. Byers did not make paymt on the 1st. Oct. interest is to be calculated up to the time when he makes it.—

H.C.

[Endorsement][3]

Theodore W. Clay is authorized to receive the above for 13 Oct. 1823.

H. CLAY.

ADI. DLC-TJC (DNA, M212, R15).
1 See above, Chambers to Clay, August 26, 1823.
2 Maurice Langhorne. 3 AES.

Legal Opinion to Bank of United States

13h. Octr. 1823

In eleven manuscript pages Clay examines the desirability of the Bank's acceptance of a contract by Nicholas Longworth for transfer of an "undivided moiety of three hundred lots of ground in Cincinnati," the tract being 52¼ acres on the western perimeter of the city, in settlement of Longworth's debt to the Bank. The decision hinges upon the status of Longworth's title, the consideration of which well illustrates Clay's services to the Bank. ADS. NHi.

From Lafayette

My dear Sir La Grange October 15h 1823

I Have Been applied to By the Amiable Mde de la Rue for a letter of introduction to My friend Mr Clay; She is daughter to the Celebrated Beaumarchais Whose Name Has Been Connected With the five years of our American Contest; She is the Wife of one of my faithful and zealous Aids de Camp in the National guard; two motives Which Make it a Very agreable duty for me to present Her to You.

Mde de la Rue Has a claim upon the public Treasury, long debated in Congress, the documents of which Have Been laid before You. it does Not Belong to me to Anticipate your opinion in a matter Upon which you Have more data than I could offer; But I find a pleasure in Contributing to gratify Mde de la Rue's wishes to be introduced to your personal Acquaintance.

Most truly and affectionately Yours LAFAYETTE

You will find in the News papers a Sad account of the Spanish Counter revolution;[1] the effects of ignorance and superstition Might Be foreseen; not So for the influence of corruption. this Momentary triumph of Aristocracy and despotism Has Been directed against the french People still more than Against the peninsula itself. Whatever may Have Been the defeats and defections, the tranquillity of those Countries is far from Been secured.

ALS. DLC-HC (DNA, M212, R1). Published, without postscript, in Colton (ed.), *Private Correspondence of Henry Clay*, 83. Addressed: "Mr Clay M. C. Washington favour'd by Mde de la Rüe." See above, Lafayette to Clay, November 5, 1822.
1 The Spanish constitutional regime had collapsed at the end of September.

From R[obert] R[ead]

Hon. Henry Clay Lexington, Kentucky 18th October 1823

Sir, Your letter of the 4th Inst.[1] came to hand this morning– Foreseeing the necessity of acting on Mr Carr's case, within the time limited by the law referred to by you, I addressed a letter on the 1st May last, to the Clerk of the House of Representatives,[2] requesting him to transmit to this office, the Petition and papers upon which the Act was passed by Congress. To that letter I have received no reply. I have however, addressed another letter to the Clerk, this morning, and requested him, should the papers in question, not be on [*sic*] the files of his office, to refer the letter, to the Secretary of the Senate,[3] and request him to have them transmitted to this office without delay–

As soon as I am put in possession of the papers they shall be examined, and the requisite information communicated to you–

R,R,

Copy. DNA, RG217, Records of the Third Auditor, Misc. Letters Sent, vol. 31, p. 135. Read (Reed) was a clerk in the office of the Third Auditor.

1 See above, Clay to Hagner, October 4, 1823.

2 On December 3, 1822, the House of Representatives had elected Matthew St. Clair Clarke to fill the vacancy occasioned by the death of Thomas Dougherty. Clarke, a resident of Pennsylvania, had studied law in Washington, D. C.

3 Charles Cutts, of New Hampshire, filled this post from 1814 to 1825.

Receipt from Robert Scott

[October 18, 1823]

[Robert Scott acknowledges receipt from Clay, only acting Executor of the estate of James Morrison, deceased, of a letter[1] requesting Nathaniel Cox to pay Samuel Scott, brother of Robert, any monies Cox might hold for the estate, in return for which Robert Scott binds himself to be accountable for the funds received by Samuel, provided that Robert is to be allowed a discount equal to the premium for checks on Lexington, Kentucky, payable in New Orleans at the period the money is received, minus interest from then until it shall begin to accrue on his legacy[2] due from the estate.]

ADS. DLC-TJC (DNA, M212, R15). 1 Not found.

2 See below, Receipt, October 31, 1823.

To Benjamin W. Leigh

My dear Sir Ashland 20th. Oct. 1823.

I duly received your obliging letter under date the 29h. Ulto.[1] Inclosed is a deposition[2] to prove the facts you directed to be established in relation to my deceased brother Geo. Henry W. Watkins of Powhatan, near the Coal pitts of Mr. Heth,[3] formerly and perhaps now a representative from that County, and Henry Perrin or Saml. Perrin of Hanover, near the Merry oaks, can testify to the same facts. The first (Mr. Watkins) is the most intelligent man, and if it be deemed necessary by you I will thank you to have him summoned. Our antagonist will fail in making out that the Legatees of my father received the proceeds of the illegal sale of the land, otherwise at least than such a fact may be inferred from the following statement: My father was much embarrassed at his death: A Mr. Chapman of Hanover and Col N. Wilkinson of Henrico were his exors: Upon the marriage of my mother with her present husband, Henry Watkins, he administered upon the estate, in her right, who I believe was also an executrix: There has been no settlement of the general administration either of the exors or of Mr. Watkins, at least if there be I am not aware of it: There may have been possibly some partial settlements: There has been no settlement with either of the legatees: All that they have received of the Estate has been two slaves specifically bequeathed to each,[4] and one other slave a piece which my mother surrendered of her dower slaves, since her removal to this State: It is possible, but of that I am not informed, that the proceeds of the sale of the land were applied in a course of administration. If that be the fact, it must be made out by the other party; for not knowing it, it will not be admitted

It appears to me as it does to you that the defense cannot be available at law. In equity the most that could happen would be, if it appeared that we received the benefits of the amount of sale, to hold us responsible for that amount, which I presume would be more than counter-balanced by the rents and profits, unless you should set up in Virginia the occupying claimant law, which she has been so anxious to put down in Kentucky.[5]

Will the death of Col. Morrison have any effect upon the Ejectment?

I am greatly obliged by your very kind enquiries upon the subject of my health. The state of it has improved since I saw Dr. Adams,[6] by a course of medicine and regimen which I commenced immediately after I saw him. It is however not re established entirely, but I have strong hopes, inspired by its better condition and the great confidence of my physicians, that I shall regain it.

Some person sent me a Copy of the Boston pamphlet,[7] which I have perused. It exhibits as much egotism vanity & folly as one ever met with in the same compass. To you and me, however, it sheds no new light upon the character of the father or son.[8] It furnishes evidence indeed which a large portion of the public might not have before possessed, I see, it is said, that Pickering is about to write (who by the bye 'though a political bigot is the honester man of them) and we shall thus have the whole truth.[9] After all, I think we may begin to content ourselves with the son as our next President. The probabilities appear to me to be greatly in his favor. The irreconcilable divisions between the South and the West must tend strongly to his success. They will succeed in N. York in having a popular election of electors,[10] and in that event the chances are very much with him. In the West, if local partialities are dismissed, I do believe he will obtain a decided plurality of votes. Upon such a supposition there is no State West of the mountains that can be counted against him but Missouri certainly and Kentucky probably.

You will have seen that Genl. Jackson is elected to the Senate.[11] The event has produced much excitement in Tennessee, as may be infered from the state of the vote. I understand that the General has altered essentially his course of personal conduct; and has become extremely gentle, affable & conciliatory. It is said that he has extinguished some of his most antient and bitter enmities; and is on all occasions seeking to reconcile himself with his enemies. What would *you* think of receiving from him a sincere and cordial shake of the hand?

Mrs. Clay joins me in best respects to you, and in hearty wishes for your welfare. I pray you also to communicate mine to Mrs. Leigh and to Mrs. Wickham;[12] and believe me Faithfully Your friend

H. CLAY

B. W. Leigh Esqr.

P.S. Will you do me the favor to inform me, by a letter addressed to me at Washn., of the event of the suit? H C.

ALS. ViU. See above, II, 726-27, 735-36, 821.

1 Not found. 2 Not found.

3 John Heth, an officer of Virginia Volunteers during the War of 1812, lived in the Midlothian area of Chesterfield County, Virginia, where his family's land holdings included extensive coal fields.

4 Cf. above, I, 2n.

5 See above, Convention, June 5, 1822; Leigh to Clay, February 12, 1823.

6 John Adams, a prominent physician of Richmond, had been a member of the Virginia House of Delegates (1803, 1804) and became Mayor of Richmond (1824).

7 In response to a request, in 1803, from William Cunningham, of Fitchburg, Massachusetts, former President John Adams over a period of several years had written letters critical of Thomas Jefferson and the Republican administrations. Although Adams had stipulated that the correspondence should not be published during his lifetime, after Cunningham took his own life in May, 1823, his son, Ephraim May Cunningham, in the following September had published *Correspondence between the Hon. John Adams . . . and the Late Wm. Cunningham, Esq., Beginning in 1803, and Ending in 1812* (Boston, 1803). According to John Q. Adams, "The malignity of the publication consists in its being now made for the purpose of injuring me, by exciting personal enmities against me among leading men of both parties and their families and friends." Adams, *Memoirs*, VI, 176; Henry S. Randall, *The Life of Thomas Jefferson* (3 vols.; New York, 1858), III, 493.

8 John and John Q. Adams.

9 In 1824 Timothy Pickering published *A Review of the Correspondence between the Hon. John Adams, Late President of the United States, and the Late Wm. Cunningham, Esq., Beginning in 1803, and Ending in 1812.* A second edition appeared in the same year, both published at Salem, Massachusetts.

10 See above, Woods to Clay, August 27, 1823, note.

11 See above, Carroll to Clay, October 1, 1823.

12 Julia Wickham Leigh, third wife of Benjamin W. Leigh, and, probably, her mother, Elizabeth Selden McClurg Wickham, the second wife of John Wickham, eminent Richmond lawyer. Mrs. Wickham was a daughter of Dr. James McClurg.

To James C. Rodes

[October 21, 1823]

To Mr. James C. Rhodes, Clerk of the County Court of Fayette

Having given my consent to the marriage of my daughter Anne B. Clay with Mr. James Erwin, I authorize you to issue a license for that purpose. Witness my hand & seal this 21st. Oct. 1823.

Teste H. CLAY {L.S.}

T H Clay

Theo. W Clay

ADS. Fayette County Marriage Bonds.

From R[obert] R[ead]

Hon. Henry Clay Lexington, Ky 25th October 1823

Sir, Since writing to you on the 18th Instant I have been put in possession of the papers of Charles Carr Esq referred to in your letter of the 4th Instant—

On examining the petition and accompanying documents in connection with Mr Carr's accounts in this office several difficulties to an immediate decision on Mr Carr's case under the Act for his relief present themselves, which I will endeavor to point out in this communication—

It appears that on the last settlement of Mr Carr's accounts in June 1822 a balance of $1165.15 was reported against him, whilst it appears by his petition, that the judgment was for only $914, There is nothing among the papers with the petition, to shew what portion of the items deducted from Mr Carr's Accounts by the Accounting officers, was allowed by the Court and Jury, whilst it is obvious that allowances must have been made by the latter to the amount of $251.15, the judgment being so much less than the balance claimed of him— It becomes necessary therefore before the Accounting officers, can Act understandingly upon the law of last session, that they should be apprized of the particular items that were allowed by the Court and jury—

There is another difficulty to making a final settlement of Mr Carr's Accounts at this time, of which it is proper you should be apprized— It appears that the District Attorney, has as yet, furnished no evidence to the Agent of the Treasury of his having deposited in Bank to the Credit of the Treasurer the $750 which it appears was paid to him on the 11th December last, on Account of the judgment obtained against Mr Carr— According to my instructions that sum cannot be carried to Mr Carr's credit on the Books of this office, until evidence shall be furnished of the same being placed to the credit of the Treasurer—As the payment, however, to the District Attorney, releases Mr Carr for that part of the judgment, it would perhaps be advisable for him to forward to the agent of the Treasury, or to this office, the Original receipt of the District Attorney—It is only necessary to add, that as soon as I am furnished with a statement of the items that were allowed by the Court and jury Mr Carr's Account will be taken up, and such allowances made as the law for his relief will warrant— R,R,

Copy. DNA, RG217, Records of the Third Auditor, Misc. Letters Sent, vol. 31, pp. 161-62.

Promissory Note from William S. George and Others

[October 28, 1823]

[William S. George, Francis G. Hawkins, and John R. Hawkins bind themselves to pay to Henry Clay, only acting executor of James Morrison, $101.25 in gold or silver coin by October 21, 1824. Witnessed by Robert Scott.]

DS (printed form). Woodford Circuit Court, File 1491. George and the Hawkinses were probably all residents of Woodford County. A suit filed in 1824 in Woodford Circuit Court for collection of this note was decided the following year by a verdict for the plaintiff and one cent damages. *Ibid.*

Account with Samuel Redd

[*ca.* October 29, 1823]

The document, three manuscript pages, covers charges over a period beginning July 27, 1822 (the date heading the account), and ending October 29, 1823, for repairs and new parts for Clay's Dearborn, the family carriage, a coachee, and harness. To the sum of these charges, $90.75, was added on the latter date $520 for "One Light Carrige [*sic*] & Harness—Baize Cover & foot curtain," bringing the total to $610.75. Clay was credited on October 29, 1823, for a cash payment of $300 "in part for the carriage," for $50, "My Due Bill for Cabinet work," and for $1, allowed for "a Small quantity of Stufing [*sic*] hay." AD. DLC-TJC (DNA, M212, R15). An endorsement (AE) supplies credit entries, dated July 3, 1824, for a cash payment of $220 and for "20 Cords of Wood," $50, erroneously computed as leaving a balance of "11-75." On July 4, 1825, Redd acknowledges receipt (AES) of "the above in full."

To [David K.] Este

Dr Sir Ashland 29h. Oct. 1823.

I recd. from Mr. Evans[1] the Clerk of the Federal Court the declaration and record against Lytle,[2] sent at your request, to prepare an amendment. The reason that I did not put in the Costs originally was that the transcript shewed *no Judgment* for Costs. It shewed a taxation of Costs, without a Judgment for them. And as that was a mere clerical act; the omission or performance of which could not increase or diminish the actual judgment, it did not appear to me that I could declare for the Costs as a part of the Judgment. Such I think ought to have been the view which the Court should have taken of the matter. It seems that it took another, and you got leave to amend the declaration, and I understood from Judge Todd[3] the writ also. If you obtained leave to amend both, I suppose your design was to include the Costs, and in that case the draft which I have prepared and which is inclosed will answer for the amended declaration. If your design were merely to amend the declaration, without comprehending in it the Costs, then the amendment which you have already made to the original declaration will serve. There is another difficulty I perceive about the interest. I declared upon the Judgment according to its legal effect, claiming interest from its date. The Clerk I observe says the Judgt. is to carry interest from the 15 Sept 1820. How is this? The draft I now send corresponds with that date; but if there be nothing of record to abridge our right to interest, it would follow the Judgt. from its date— There is safety however in declaring from the 15h. Septr., since if we are entitled to it from the 28h. Aug. we are of course entitled to it from the subsequent day—

Be pleased to transmit the declaration, to correspond with the fact as to your leave to amend, to the Clerk of the Court. I hope Judgt will be got at the next term—

I should be glad to have from you a general statement of the business of the Bank for the next term.

Mr. Este— With great regard I am faithfy Yrs H. CLAY

ALS. DLC-David K. Este Papers (DNA, M212, R21).

1 Harvey D. Evans, who had removed from Chillicothe to Columbus with the transfer of the Federal court in 1821.

2 See above, Clay to Biddle, June 11, 1823.

3 Thomas Todd.

To Charles Hammond

Dr Hammond Ashland 29h. Oct. 1823.

I received your obliging letter under date the 15h. inst.[1] for which I am greatly indebted to you. I have heard of you frequently during the summer, and learnt with pleasure that your prospects at Cincinnati are good. You have only to be discreet to realize all your expectations from the exchange of the hills of Indian Wheeling[2] for the flourishing and populous streets of the Western Metropolis. Society is somewhat unsettled there at present, but it must 'ere long right itself, and I think Cincinnati possesses natural advantages which must make it a great City, which it is indeed now.

I concur with you entirely in thinking it highly important, on the Presidential question, thoroughly to impress the friends of Mr. Crawford with the truth in regard to the sentiments of the Western States. If the contest be reduced to him and to Mr. Adams I scarcely entertain a doubt that Mr. Adams would obtain the support of every State West of the Mountains but Missouri certainly and Kentucky probably. Many here even think that he would get Kentucky. He will strongly contest Mississippi with Genl. Jackson or me. In Tennessee the candidates may be arranged, as it regards their popular estimation, in this order: Jackson, Clay, Adams, Calhoun, Crawford. Have you any correspondents at Richmond? Letters from you, communicating the condition of public sentiment in this quarter, would have the best effect there from two considerations: first that you are there well known; and secondly from your being disposed to support Mr. Crawford as your second choice. The Chief Justice[3] would be a good person to address. He thinks highly of you I know, and you could employ as an occasion to write him that of transmitting a Copy of your argument in the Bank case.[4] There is not a doubt that Virginia prefers me next to Mr. Crawford.

Depend upon it that the Secy of the Treasury stands no earthly chance of being elected. He has most rapidly declined for the last twelve months every where but in Virginia & I suppose Georgia. I have concurrent testimonies, communicated from all parts of New York, without concert, representing his prospects there as utterly hopeless. Genl. Porter says in a late letter that he is the most unpopular of all the Candidates, except Genl. Jackson; and that he does not believe that he would get the suffrages of that State, even if recommended by a Congressional Caucus.[5] I think they will succeed in New York in getting a popular electoral ticket,[6] and in that event Mr. Crawford will be absolutely out of the question. You recollect a singular man at Columbus last winter, Dr. Stuart.[7] He seemed to know every body, every thing; to have been every where, in Europe and America, and to recollect whatever he had seen, heard, thought or dreamt. He travelled with Judge Burnett[8] and myself to Wheeling, and amused and instructed us much. He has ever since volunteered a correspondence with me in which, on my part, I have treated him with politeness, without considering him one in whom I ought to implicitly confide. I transmit you a letter which I have just received from him[9] for your perusal, and to be transmitted to me at Washington, when you have read it. Shew it to the Judge also, who thought very highly of him. If the statements which he makes depended upon his sole testimony I should receive them with caution, but they are fully corroborated by numerous other sources of information.

I think my friends in Ohio have sustained my interests there with much prudence and judgment. Nothing could have been more injudicious than to have urged me obtrusively upon the people or to have treated me, as I think Calhoun's friends have him, by the application to my name and character of ridiculous superlatives. To compare him to Washington; to pronounce him a prodigy of genius! What nonsense. Whatever was necessary to be done for me within the State I believe has been done—[10] There is only one point on which it might perhaps be desirable to do more and that is to afford further manifestation of your wishes to the exterior American public. That perhaps can be accomplished next winter at Columbus, on the occasion of forming an electoral ticket, which I imagine will then be done—[11]

The election in Pennsa. is now over; and I presume Shulze is elected.[12] We shall now begin to see some unequivocal evidence of its disposition on the Presidential election. Mr. Crawford has no chance there; nor ever had. Calhoun will make a great push at that State, and, as his friends have constantly done, they will probably overshoot the mark.

I have seen the Boston pamphlet to which you refer.[13] My friend who sent it to me says it is the production of a Mr. Fuller[14] of the H. of R. and that it has been a complete abortion. It is about on the level of his capacity. I have seen a still more recent Boston pamphlet (published in Rhode Island) on the same subject, written with more discretion, but not likely I think to advance the pretensions of its Hero.[15] I have also read the Boston correspondence to which you refer of the elder Mr. Adams.[16] Such a composition of bloated egotism, extravagant vanity and folly I never before perused. You Federalists have more to complain of about it than we republicans. He treats poor Hamilton[17] and Pickering without mercy. He does not even allow Hamilton talents! and represents him the most profligate and licentious of men.

I do not know that it will be in my power to visit Steubenville. If I can, I will with pleasure call there. I shall leave home about the 10h. and the debility which I yet feel will compel me to make short stages, and I may not have it in my power to deviate from the direct route.

I think no direct overtures will be made to me to negotiate with the other Candidates. I hope my character will protect me from the affront which such overtures would comprehend. I should repel them with scorn and promptitude. It is not a subject for negotiation. That portion of the public which has shewn its confidence in me will act for itself as, in its judgment, the public welfare will require. It will act without any effort on my part to control it. If I should be elected, I am resolved to enter upon the office perfectly free and untrammeled, without compromitment bargain, or understandings of any sort with any person. If I am not elected, I will at least lay up no reproaches for myself but preserve my conscience pure and uncontaminated.

Let me hear from you occasionally as your leisure will permit and believe me Faithfully Your friend H. CLAY

Charles Hammond Esqr.

ALS. InU. 1 Not found.

2 A small stream in Ohio, which rises in Harrison County, flows across southeastern Belmont County, and empties into the Ohio River opposite Wheeling.

3 John Marshall. 4 See below, Clay to Biddle, February 17, 1824.

5 See above, Porter to Clay, September 6, 1823.

6 See above, Woods to Clay, August 27, 1823, note.

7 Josephus B. Stuart. 8 Jacob Burnet. 9 Not found.

10 See above, Clay to Brooke, January 8, 1823, notc

11 See below, Clay to Porter, April 26, 1824.

12 See above, Miner to Clay, June 19, 1823, note.

13 *The Election of President of the United States, Considered, Addressed to the People, By a Citizen* (Boston, 1823).

14 Timothy Fuller.

15 Probably Principles and *Men Considered in Reference to the Election of President, By a Citizen of Rhode Island* (Providence, 1823), advocating the election of Andrew Jackson.

16 See above, Clay to Leigh, October 20, 1823. 17 Alexander Hamilton.

Agreement with Mrs. James Morrison

[October 30, 1823]

[Whereas by the will, and a codicil, of James Morrison his widow, Esther Morrison, is empowered to make testamentary disposition of $15,000 worth of land, valued in accordance with a schedule annexed to Morrison's will, Clay, "acting Executor of James Morrison deceased," agrees to convey to the widow in fee simple "the Carlisle Farm and the 26 Acres formerly owned by James Hughes and by J Dougherty,"[1] with title warranted against claimants under Morrison, "subject however, to the condition that the same are to be in lieu of and full satisfaction for the Fifteen thousand dollars worth of land which the said Esther hath the power as aforesaid to dispose of by her will."

[Esther Morrison agrees to accept and abide by the provisions of the will and codicil "in full satisfaction of her dower and legal claims" upon the estate. All her rights, except her power to devise the $15,000 worth of land, "are to remain valid and in full force."

[Since the "Carlisle Farm" has been rented until March 1, 1825, it is understood that possession is not to be delivered until that date; meanwhile, Mrs. Morrison is to receive the rent in lieu of possession and "is to enjoy an unrestricted liberty of taking firewood from the said farm." Clay authorizes her to take immediate possession of the 26-acre tract. Signed by Clay and Esther Morrison; witnessed by Thomas H. Pindell.]

Copy, in Robert Scott's hand. KyLxT. 1 James Dougherty.

Receipt from Robert Scott

[October 31, 1823]

[Robert Scott acknowledges receipt from Clay, "acting Executor of James Morrison decd.," of $2,361.75 "in Negroes &c.," purchased by Scott at the sale of Morrison's property at the "Carlisle Farm," and of $1,500 in cash, making a total of $3,861.75 "on account of the legacy of Fifteen thousand dollars left me by the Will of the deceased[1]—"]

ADS, "Duplicate." DLC-TJC (DNA, M212, R15).
1 In addition to the monetary bequest, Morrison left to Scott "lands to the value of thirty thousand dollars, . . . to be estimated according to the valuation contained" in a list annexed to the will.

Settlement with Francis Hawkins

1st. Novr. 1823.

Dr Francis Hawkins		
Jno. McNair for 3 bush. of Hemp seed	$ 3.	
Spencer[1] for hide & Calf Skin	5:25	
Recd. from Mrs. Clay to pay Hall[2] hireling during harvest	2:25	
Sandford Keen for stack of rye	21:25	
Logan for hemp seed	1:50	
Webster ½ bushel	" 75	
A. Campbell[3] for hemp seed	7:50	
Mr. Montmillen [*sic*][4]	6:75	
Bal. of Cash given to get my horse	1:87½	
From David Bell[5] for wheat	21:	
Cow	21:	
	$ 92:12½	[$ 92:12½]

. . . . Creditor	
Wheelbarrow to Howe[6]	$ 6
20 bush. of Oats of Steel	7.
1 dog skin (Smith)	1:
Mitchell for Curing horse	8.

Howe for Axle tree &c	1:75	
Geo Hall during harvest	5:	
Tanner for repairing horse mill	2:—	
Bryan[7] for two Collars	5:—	
Grisham[8] for	1:50	
Curry Combs	:75	
Mill rounds	3:—	
Joseph George[9]	17:50	
	$ 58:50	$ 58:50
		33:62½
By Cash		120:
		153:62½
Cash		86:37½
		240

Upon a settlement of all accounts this day made with H. Clay there appears to have been paid by him to me on account of my present years wages Two hundred and forty dollars and there remains to be paid me at Xmas next sixty dollars in full of my wages.

Teste Theo W. Clay

his
FRANCIS X HAWKINS
mark

DS, in Clay's hand (including Hawkins' signature). DLC-TJC (DNA, M212, R15).

1 Not identified—there were several men of that name in Lexington and its environs at this date. The same circumstance occasions inability to identify other names below in this account: Logan, Webster, Steel, Smith, Mitchell, and Tanner.

2 George Hall, a resident of the southern district of Fayette County.

3 Archibald Campbell.

4 Probably Frederick Montmollin, Lexington wholesale grocer and commission merchant.

5 Formerly of Virginia, whence he had come to Kentucky in 1806 and had begun farming three miles north of Lexington. He was a stock raiser on an extensive scale and proprietor of a large distillery on the Tate's Creek road.

6 Edward Howe, wagon maker, Third Street, Lexington.

7 John Bryan. 8 Probably David Grisham. 9 Of Woodford County.

Receipt from Samuel Redd

1 Novr. 1823.

Recd. of H. Clay Three hundred dollars on a/c of a new Carriage which he has this day purchased of me the bal. of Two hundred and twenty dollars for the Carriage, cover & front curtain he is to pay me on his return from the Eastward. SAML REDD

[Endorsement][1]

To be paid in currency. SAML REDD

DS, in Clay's hand. DLC-TJC (DNA, M212, R15). Cf. above, Account, *ca.* October 29, 1823, note.

1 ES, in Clay's hand.

From William B. Rochester

Dr Sir Albany 1. Novber 1823

In conformity with the wish indicated in yr. letter of the 12th. Aug:[1] I Sit down to submit to you some of my unripe speculations upon the probable course which our State will take on the Presidentl. question

We are now just on the eve of a genl. election— the friends of the respective Gentl. Spoken of for the Chief Magistracy of the Union are drawn up in array determined apparently to go all lengths in pursuit of that object regardless of local questions In one thing all agree— The Electors will be chosen by the people by a general ticket—[2] No member of the legislature will have the hardihood to advocate an adherence to our present mode— altho' this burst of the public feeling has been mainly brot. about by the friends of Mr. Adams,[3] yet as all the others fall in with the proposition & will compete for the honor of consummating this mode of choosing Electors, he (Mr. A) will at last gain little or nothing by it— You may indeed take it for a moral certainty— N. Y. will not, cannot go for Mr. Adams

Those politicians who either do or affect to, stand aloof, say that Mr. Crawford will be the choice of N. Y, tho' they admit that the question will be violently & *ferociously* contested to the last & that it will not be without much suppressed feeling on the part of a vast many reps. & much expressed by the Feds. I took occasion on this day to ascertain how the 8 Circuit Judges of whom I am one, stood— and found it as follows viz:

for Mr. Crawford	3.	for Mr. Calhoun . .	2
for Mr. Clay	2	for Mr. Adams	1

Mr. Crawfd. out of the question—2 of his friends wd. join yours & the other Mr. Calhoun's—

Mr. Clay out of the question—his friends would divide on Mr. Crawfd. & Mr. Calhoun

Mr. Calhoun out of the question—his friends would divide between Mr. Clay and Mr. Adams

Mr. Adams out of the question—his friend would transfer to Mr Calhoun

I have been thus particular in making this Statement, because I verily believe that it presents in miniature the aspect & bearing of the question throughout the State, both positively and contingently in the event of any withdrawal

You will then readily observe that I have been led (I need not say how reluctantly) to think that Mr. Crawfords prospects are at present the best Govr. Yates, Lieut: Govr. Root, Mr. V. Buren,[4] & indeed every effective advocate of Mr. Crawford's pretensions—prefer you next to him— indeed you two are considered the only *democratic* candidates—for as for Genl. J. he is considered as being (unconsciously on his part) a mere make-weight for the Secretary of War—

It was no longer ago than yesterday that Mr. V. Buren told me frankly, that he "would not give a Straw to choose between you & Mr. Crawford; but that he thot. Mr. Crawford could be run with the greater chance of success ags. A. & Calhoun"

This was his language to an avowed friend of yours— he meant, I conceive however more than civility— it is a concession which, I am apt to think, he would not make in all companies, but he Spoke his honest feelings— Mr. V. B. & I have so long been fellow labourers in the same political Vinyard [*sic*] & his course has been such as to attach me to him I shall be exceedingly gratified to learn that, when you meet, he may have no occasion to suppose that he is looked upon as an implacable enemy I shall go to the City of New York on the 3d. inst. whence I I [*sic*] shall write you again after the close of the polls there

I know not who will be elected as my successor— if *Cruger*[5] my Sworn personal enemy—he is avowedly for Adams really for Mr. Calhoun— if Wm Woods, —he is my particular friend and I admire him the more because he professes to think as I do on the great question

the defeat of Col: John Williams of Tenessee [*sic*] has damped Some of Mr. Crawford's friends here very much

I understand that there is a project to run Govr. Yates for the Vice Presidency— & in that event to hold out to Col: Samuel Young the chair of our State— if so—& Col: Young be captivated by the temptation and declare for Crawford—then & in that case the assurance of this State for Mr. Crawfd. will be "doubly sure"— Col: Young is a most powerful man— he and Mr. V. B. have not been very cordial of late, but a union of their interests in this State cannot be resisted— The Col:'s opinion is not yet kno[wn] each claims him for all want him— I have had a conversation with Mr. Storrs[6] this evening, who says that you must be in the next administration— I take it for granted that *his* wish is to see you at the head of it— Storrs will be able to acquaint your friends fully as to the State of the matter here—

In answer to that part of yr. letter which inquires as to the dispositions of the N. York members— I set down for Messrs. A. & Calhoun pretty certainly, Silas Wood, Sharpe, Strong, Cady, Taylor, Martindale, Rose—& Cruger if he be elected & perhaps 3. or 4. more —say in all about 12— I set down for you Storrs, V. Rensellaer, Tracy, Adams, if he obtain his seat and Wm. Woods if he be elected instead of Cruger—also most probably Marvin and Genl. Herkimer—perhaps Van Wyck & possibly Hayden and Litchfield[7]—say, in the first instance about one fourth of the Delegation— & for Mr. Crawford the residue—vibrating from 12—to 16—or 17. the maximum. My venerable and revered Father[8] made me promise to mention him to you in the most friendly terms— We both cordially unite in sincere wishes for your continued health, and in the anxious hope that our common Country may place you in the Situation where of all others you may be most eminently useful and tributary to its glory, its honor and its independence WILLIAM B. ROCHESTER

pardon my haste & carelessness I write in the midst of noise

ALS. DLC-HC (DNA, M212, R1). Addressed to Clay at Washington, D.C.; postmarked at New York, November 7.

1 Not found. 2 See above, Woods to Clay, August 27, 1823, note.

3 The Clintonians, who very largely transferred their support to Adams as DeWitt Clinton's candidacy faded, had not introduced but had seized upon the suggestion of popular choice of electors. Cf. above, Miner to Clay, June 19, 1823; Hammond to Clay, August 21, 1823; Wiltse, *John C. Calhoun, Nationalist, 1782-1828,* p. 274.

4 Joseph C. Yates; Erastus Root; Martin Van Buren.

5 Daniel Cruger, a Pennsylvanian who had settled in New York, had for a brief period edited newspapers, first in Union, then in Owego, before embarking on a career as a lawyer, in Bath, in 1805. He had been a militia officer in the War of 1812; a member of the State Assembly, 1814-1816 (Speaker in the last year) and 1826; United States Congressman, 1817-1819; District Attorney for the Seventh District of New York, 1815-1818, and for Steuben County, 1818-1821. He subsequently removed to Wheeling, Virginia (now West Virginia), where he died in 1843.

6 Henry R. Storrs. 7 Cf. above, Woods to Clay, August 27, 1823.

8 Nathaniel Rochester.

To Walter Dun

Dr Sir Frankfort 3d. Nov. 1823

As I anticipated Montjoy has obtained a continuance until May next of the motion to dissolve his injunction against Mr. Taylor.[1] His plea was sickness, which he says prevented him from obtaining some depositions which he wants.

Your answer to Banks's bill has not been recd.

Walter Dunn Esqr. Yr's with great respect H. CLAY

ALS. Ross County Historical Society, Chillicothe, Ohio. See above, Clay to Dun, April 23, 1822; July 2, 1823.

1 At the May Term, 1823, of the Federal Circuit Court, Mountjoy had obtained an injunction restraining execution of the judgments obtained at that time by James Taylor, Jr., pending equity proceedings. The injunction was dissolved November 19, 1825, but the equity action dragged on until November, 1828, when Mountjoy was given leave to withdraw his bond posted at institution of the latter suit. U.S. Circuit Court, Seventh Circuit, District of Kentucky, Order Book, I, 134; K, 484; M, 97, 226, 441.

To the Kentucky General Assembly

Frankfort Nov. 4, 1823.

REPORT.

THE undersigned, appointed by the General Assembly, counsel to represent the state before the board of commissioners, which was expected to be organized at the City of Washington in January last, in conformity to the convention which was concluded and signed by the respective commissioners of the states of Virginia and Kentucky on the 5th day of June, 1822, have the honor now respectfully to report:

That, on considering the duties incident to their appointment, it appeared to them, that if they remained in Kentucky until the decision of Virginia, on the convention, was communicated to the Governor of Kentucky, if that decision were in favor of its ratification, there might not be time for them to reach Washington, so as to afford the requisite co-operation, in the constitution of the proposed board, by the day prescribed in the convention: and not doubting that Virginia would ratify the solemn act of her own commissioner, to which the general assembly of Kentucky had promptly yielded its assent, the undersigned determined, shortly after the close of the last session of the legislature, to proceed, without delay, to the City of Washington: That accordingly, they arrived there some days before that which was assigned for the assembling of the board, thus manifesting a ready disposition to execute, in good faith, on the part of Kentucky, a convention which had been concluded and ratified by it, in good faith. That greatly to their surprise, they there learnt that difficulties existed at Richmond about the ratification of the convention; and that, although the House of Delegates of Virginia, by a large majority, had resolved to approve and execute it, on the part of that state, its fate in the Senate, the other branch of the General Assembly of Virginia, was extremely doubtful: That the deliberations of this body were long protracted; the senate, disagreeing in opinion with the house of delegates, an unavailing attempt was made to reconcile the two branches; and it was not until the 18th of February last, several weeks after the board should have been organized, that the final decision of Virginia was made, to reject the convention: That this decision was communicated to the undersigned some days after, and may be seen in the paper which is hereto annexed, marked A:[1] That, during the continuance of those deliberations, they thought it their duty to remain at their post, and thus to exhibit to the world a further proof, that if what had been conceived and agreed upon in a spirit of concord and concession, were not carried into complete effect, in a similar spirit, the fault was not on the side of Kentucky:

That the honorable Jacob Burnet, having accepted the appointment of commissioner, conferred upon him by Kentucky, proceeded[2] to Washington and arrived some days before the one fixed for the assembling of the board,[3] and continued there until the decision at Richmond was known: That they would suppress their feelings, if they did not make this public acknowledgment, to that gentleman, for the promptitude with which he repaired to that city, under circumstances, at that inclement season of the year, of great personal suffering and inconvenience, and for the patience with which he remained until the pleasure of Virginia was known: That the honorable Hugh L. White, for reasons which the general assembly will deem satisfactory, declined accepting the appointment of the other commissioner; but the undersigned were always ready, in execution of the power with which they had been invested to supply, without loss of time,[4] the vacancy which they regretted had been thus created:

That, after the fate of the convention at Richmond was known at Washington, the supreme court of the United States delivered its opinion and judgment, on the occupying claimant laws, the validity of which was involved in the cause of Green and Biddle;[5] That they were delivered by associate justice Washington, in a court composed of four judges, the chief justice, and associate justice Todd not having sat in the cause, and associate justice Livingston being confined by extreme indisposition;[6] That, upon observing that a division in opinion existed among the justices who constituted the court, an enquiry was made by the undersigned, whether Mr. Justice Livingston had formed and expressed an opinion in the case, to which Mr. Justice Washington answered that he did not know what his opinion was, if he had made up one, and Mr. Justice Johnson added that the decision was that of three to one:

That, when the determination of the court was thus announced, believing it to be erroneous, the undersigned resolved to make another effort to sustain those laws, of the validity of which they could not yet doubt, after the most respectful and deliberate consideration of the argument of the majority of the actual court: That they accordingly prepared, with great labor and as much care as the limited time would admit, a respectful petition to the court, praying a re-hearing of the cause. When they presented this petition, the court manifested a decided repugnance even to receive and read it; Mr. Justice Story stating, that he could not conceive it possible, that his mind could be further informed on the subject. A majority of the Justices, however, decided to take the petition and read it, at their chambers. It was returned the next morning, with an intimation from the court, that it had produced no change in its opinion.

That the Treasurer paid to the undersigned the sum of $6000 in specie, in pursuance of provisions made by the General Assembly for that purpose. Of that sum, they have expended in payment to Judge Burnet, for his travelling allowance and compensation for his attendance at Washington, the sum of seven hundred and forty-four dollars, as will appear by the receipt annexed and designated {B.}[7] That five thousand two hundred and fifty six dollars, the residue of the sum advanced, remain in their hands, subject to the order of the General Assembly; they have returned no part of it to the Treasurer, because no law or order indicated that to be their duty.

All which is respectfully submitted. HENRY CLAY.
JOHN ROWAN.

Ky. H. of Reps., *Journal, 1823-1824,* pp. 53-56. ADI draft in DLC-HC (DNA, M212, R1). Except as noted, the differences between the draft and the printed version are minor.

1 "*Preamble and resolutions for announcing to the Executive of Kentucky, the refusal of this state, to ratify the convention concluded between the commissioners of the two states,*" February 18, 1823. Ky. H. of Reps., *Journal, 1823-1824,* pp. 56-57.
2 The words, "with one of the Undersigned," are in the draft.
3 The preceding thirteen words not in draft.
4 The preceding four words not in draft.
5 See above, Clay to Brooke, March 9, 1823.
6 Clay had written in the draft: "and Justice Livingston having shortly before died."
7 See above, Receipt, February 27, 1823.

Account with William North

[*ca.* November 5, 1823]

1823		Mr. H Clay To W North	
June	30	Theodore[1] fashionable blue dress coat making & trims. Gilt butts. & trims.	14. –
July.	1	Negro coat Cutting	1. –
	28	Thos Clay blue coat pressed &c	37½
Sepr.	11	young Clay[2] Roun about [*sic*] cutting	62½
	14	H Clay set of buttons set on &c	1.50
Octr.	–	do black coat md	– 50
Novr.	5	2¾ of twist cloth at 11 $ pr. yd.	30.25
		Spencer making & trims.	8.00
		pair of pantaloons making & trims	3.50
			$ 59.75

[Endorsement][3]
Recd. with thanks the above amt. WILLIAM NORTH Novr. 12th. 1823

AD. DLC-TJC (DNA, M212, R15).
1 Theodore W. Clay.
2 Probably Henry Clay, Jr.
3 AES.

Property Assignments to Heirs of James Morrison

[November 8, 1823]

[In five separate indentures, all dated November 8, 1823, Henry Clay, only acting executor of James Morrison, and Esther Morrison, Robert Wickliffe, Farmer Dewees, and Richard Hawes, Jr., "nominated but who have not qualified or acted as Executrix and Executors," make the following assignments of land to devisees under the terms of Morrison's will, the land to be valued according to a schedule annexed to the will: to Robert Scott, six parcels, including the Sanders Garden tract of 84¾ acres on the Georgetown Road,[1] four adjoining plots, and the major portion of lot no. 44 in the Lexington town plan,[2] in satisfaction of $12,671 of the $30,000 worth of land devised to him; to Mary Ann Dewees,[3] in full satisfaction of her devise of $10,000 worth of land, two adjoining lots, containing together over four acres, bordering on Main and Back streets in Lexington; to Sidney Edmiston, in full satisfaction of her devise of $1,000 worth of land, a house and lot on Main Street in Lexington (part of lot no. 31 on the town plan), a house and lot "near the first Presbyterian Church" in Lexington, and one quarter section, 160 acres, of military bounty land in Missouri; to Morrison Boswell,[4] in full satisfaction of his devise of $1,000 worth of land, an undivided moiety of two lots on Upper Street in Lexington, an adjoining lot "immediately back" of the other, and three 100-acre tracts in Logan County, Kentucky; and to Mary Pindell,[5] in full satisfaction of her devise of $2,000 worth of land, a lot fronting 28½ feet on Short Street in Lexington, 160 acres in Missouri, and 400 additional acres in Missouri (a moiety of five quarter sections held in partnership with J. C. Sullivan).]

Fayette County Court, Deed Book X, 148-60, 176-78. All recorded November 25, 1823.

1 Part of the property formerly held by Lewis Sanders. Cf. above, Property Deed, December 26, 1821, note.

2 See above, Property Deed, September 1, 1823.

3 Morrison's niece, Mary Ann Holmes, who had married Farmer Dewees in 1815.

4 James Morrison Boswell, son of Dr. Joseph Boswell.

5 Mary Edmiston Pindell, Mrs. Morrison's niece, wife of Thomas Hart Pindell.

Property Deed to Joshua Collins and William Jones

[November 8, 1823]

[Henry Clay, only acting executor of James Morrison, and the executrix and executors nominated but not qualified, in consideration of one dollar, in hand paid, convey to Joshua Collins and William Jones a lot in Lexington, fronting 60 feet on Short Street and extending back to Cross Street.]

Fayette County Court, Deed Book X, 160-61. Recorded December 11, 1823. Collins, formerly of Philadelphia, was a resident of Versailles, Kentucky; Jones lived in Lexington.

Receipt from Susannah Hart

[November 8, 1823]

Recd. 8h. Novr. 1823 of H. Clay one hundred dollars for the

Board of Thomas & H. C. Hart children of Capt. Hart[1] deceased, up to the first instant. SUSANNNA HART

DS, in Clay's hand. DLC-TJC (DNA, M212, R15). 1 Nathaniel G. S. Hart.

Receipt from William S. George

[November 9, 1823]

Recd. of H Clay 9h. Novr. 1823 a sorrel horse, which has a blemish in one eye, and which horse I am well acquainted with, being the balance in full of all accounts. WILLIAM S GEORGE
Teste T H Clay

DS, in Clay's hand. DLC-TJC (DNA, M212, R15).

To William Hendricks

My dear Sir (Confidential) Lexington 10h. Novr. 1823

Confiding in our amicable relations, I take the liberty of addressing you on the subject of the approaching Presidential election. Information, coming to me from many sources in New York, fully authorizes me to believe that there the only real contest is between Mr Adams and me; that my friends are zealous and sanguine of success; that Mr. Crawford has no chance whatever of obtaining the vote of that State; that he is the most unpopular of all the Candidates except Genl. Jackson; that he would not probably obtain its support, even if nominated by a Caucus at Washington; and finally that there is every reason to believe that a popular election of Electors, instead of one by the Legislature will be decided on.[1] If Mr. Crawford should fail to be supported by N. York, there must be an end of his prospects, and in that event there is no doubt but that Virginia will bestow her suffrage on me. From all quarters of Ohio I have been informed that I shall be unanimously supported in that State. Pennsylvania has been so agitated by her recent Governor's election[2] that nothing positively can be affirmed of her determination. Unless my friends are however greatly deceived, there is much reason to anticipate her favorable decision. I will say nothing more at present of other States, supposing you may be well informed of them.

There is no event that I know of that can now happen in the West that would so much tend to promote my election, as a recommendation of me by your State, which next to Ohio, Kentucky and Tennessee, is the most important Western State. Whatever may be said of the Caucus's of State Legislatures, there is no doubt that they are the most influential expressions of public sentiment which have been yet employed, and that their effect is very great. There is reason to believe that other States, and among them Virginia; will announce their preference, in the course of the ensuing Winter. It is far from my intention to interfere in this concern in Indiana so as to indicate any measure which your own judgments do not approve. I mean merely to communicate my conviction that a public declaration of your choice will have powerful effect, let it be for whom it may. I need not say or attempt to disguise that I should feel very greatly the value and honor of such a declaration, if it be your pleasure to make it for me.

I shall set out to day for the City, and shall be greatly obliged by a letter from you addressed to me at that place—

I need not say that I write for your own view only.

With great regard I am faithfully Your's H CLAY

His Excellency W. Hendricks.

ALS. MoKiT. Hendricks, Governor of Indiana, 1822-1825, had been born and educated in Pennsylvania; had lived for a short time in Cincinnati, where he taught school and studied law; and in 1813 had settled in Madison, Indiana, where he practiced law and joined in publication of the *Western Eagle*. He had been a member, and Speaker, of the Territorial legislature, secretary of the Indiana constitutional convention, and United States Congressman from 1816 until his resignation to become Governor. In 1825 he resigned the governorship to enter the United States Senate, where he remained until 1837. He died in 1850.

1 Cf. above, Woods to Clay, August 27, 1823, note.

2 See above, Miner to Clay, June 19, 1823; Wharton to Clay, August 13, 1823.

Promissory Note to Esther Morrison

[November 10, 1823]

I promise to pay to Esther Morrison or order the sum of One thousand dollars one year after date, with interest thereon from the date to be paid half yearly

Witness my hand & seal this 10h. Novr. 1823. H. CLAY {L.S.}

[Endorsements on verso][1]

Paid the interest up to the 10h. Novr. 1824 by a check on the B Bank of the U. S.

Paid the interest up to 10 November 1825 by a check on the Office of the Bank of the U S. 7 August 1826. H. CLAY

Do. Do. 13 July 1827 up to 10 Novr 1826. H.C.

Do. Do. 5 Septr. 1829 up to the 10h. Novr. 1828 in a check on the B. B. of the U. S. at Lexington. H.C.

Do. Do. 17h. Nov. 1829 up to 10 Nov. 1829 in a check on the B. B. of the U. S. at Lexington H C.

Int. paid 22 Novr. 1831 in a check on the Off. B U. S. H. C.

Int. paid in a check 17h. Nov. 1831. H.C.

do. do. 24 Nov 1832. H.C.

ADS. DLC-TJC (DNA, M212, R15). Signiture crossed out on MS.

1 All by Clay; the first, AE; the second, AES; each of the remainder, AEI.

Agreement with Bank of Kentucky

[November 10, 1823]

An agreement between the President Directors & Co. of the Bank of Kentucky of the one part and Henry Clay of the other. The said party of the first part being indebted to the said Clay in the sum of $10,126 96/100 with interest thereon from the 3d. day of January 1823 and costs of suit in order to pay the said debt interest and costs hereby agrees to assign and has assigned to the said Clay the following notes.

John Tilford	with	G Trotter & son secy	due	17 Nov:	1150.
W. Warfield	"	Alex: Parker	"	8 Decr:	1320.
Ed C. Payne[1]	"	D. M. Payne	"	" "	1350.
James Wier	"	H. Wier & G Robinson[2]	"	5 Jany:	1350.
Alex: Parker	"	W. Warfield	"	22 Decr:	2400
Sam. Trotter	"	James Trotter	"	17 Nov:	1800.
Thomas Wallace	to	D. Castleman	"	22 Decr:	1600.
				Dolls	10,970.

The said Clay agrees to receive the said notes without recourse to the said Bank on account of the insolvency of the parties or any of them if they should prove insolvent If the full amount of the said notes or any of them shall not be recovered on any other account or if offsets shall be established against them the party of the first part agrees to pay in gold or silver coin the amount which shall not be recovered or the amount of such offsets as soon as it is ascertained in either case by suit against the makers. payment to be made to the said Clay or his assigns.

Witness the seal of the said corporation and of the said Clay this 10. Nov 1823.— {L.S.}

Test F Dewees H Clay {seal}

Copy. DLC-TJC (DNA, M212, R15). Endorsed: "The foregoing is a correct from [*sic*] the original. S.I.M. Major CBDBK" (Samuel I. M. Major, Clerk of the Board of Directors of the Bank of Kentucky and a farmer and mill owner in Frankfort). The Agreement with a transposition of the names of the two notes dated December 8, thus making that of the Paynes read as "1320," while that of Warfield and Parker amounts to "1350," also appears in Bank of Kentucky, Record Book D (July 19, 1821-October 22, 1828), 178-79. Cf. below, Assignment, November 18, 1823. Clay to Paynes and Statement, both November 20, 1823.

See also above, Power of Attorney, December 26, 1822; Clay to Hardin, June 21, 1823. The Agreement was offered by Clay in response to action taken on November 7 by the Board of Directors, who, wishing to avoid the suit already begun by Clay against the Bank for the collection of his demand for $10,126 with interest, had "Resolved that the President and Cashier of the Lexington Branch Bank be instructed to compromise with said Clay for the amount of said demand Provided he will agree to receive *without recourse* the sum in the Bills receivable of the Lexington Br: Bank and that they attempt to effectuate the compromise by the transfer of such debts as have been longest under accommodation or protest excepting however such as are secured by a pledge of stock." Bank of Kentucky, Record Book D, 175-77.

1 Brother and law partner of Daniel McCarty Payne.

2 Henry Weir, Lexington merchant, nephew of James Weir; George Robinson, also a Lexington merchant.

Administrator's Bond

[November 10, 1823]

[Henry Clay and Richard Hawes, Jr., are bound for $30,000, current money of Kentucky, that Clay, as administrator of the estate of Wilson Cary Nicholas shall "make a true and perfect inventory of . . . the goods, chattels, and credits" of Nicholas and exhibit this record to the Fayette County Court when required.]

DS, partially printed, signed also by Hawes and the signatures witnessed by J. C. Rodes, Clerk. Fayette County, Administrators' Bonds, no. 2, p. 27.

Memorandum to Robert Scott

H Clays Memo. for Robert Scott Esq. 10h. Nov. 1823.

I leave you S. Cooper & Cos.[1] bond payable at Christmas next for the hire of Jonathan, which may be received in currency	$ 100. *pd*
" Winns[2] do. for Shadrach's hire do. *pd. 27* do *Decr 23*	100
Mr. Deverin's[3] lease, upon which a a quarters rent will be due on the 1st. day of Decr. next, on account of which he has paid me $33 leaving then due . . . . *pd 4 Decr 23*	74:50
$107„50 pd. 2 March 1824	
Benj. Whaley's lease on which there is now due ½ years rent which became payable on the 12h. Sept. last	65:
" On the 12h. Decr. another quarter will be due . .	32:50
" On the 12h. March next another quarter	32:50
Mess Wilkins, Mc Ilvaine & Co. on which on the first January next a quarter's rent will be due of *pd*	62:50
Mrs. Rawlings s[4] lease on which I promised her if she would pay this sum I would give up the lease	40:
	$ 507

Altho' I am entitled to demand specie, you may take Currency for any part of the above. If Col. Whaley does not pay he must be distrained upon before or at the end of the year. Get Mr. Hawes.[5] to attend to the distress.

Be pleased to pay over to Mrs. Clay any part of the above as you receive it.

I must trouble you to hire out Jonathan and Shadrach for me at the end of the year. Shadrach has been taught to weave, and if Mr Winn gets him I was promised that his hire should be increased another year. I ought to receive for him $150 in currency, but do the best you can H. CLAY

ADS. DLC-HC (DNA, M212, R1). Italics, supplied by editors, delineate subsequent annotations by Scott.

1 Spencer Cooper and Joseph and George Boswell, all of Lexington, manufacturers of gunpowder.

2 J. Winn, possibly Jacob Winn, who in 1828 advertised the establishment of a new cotton factory in Lexington.

3 John Deverin.

4 Frances Rawlins. Cf. above, Rental Agreement, March 1, 1822.

5 Richard Hawes, Jr.

Receipt from William North

[November 12, 1823]

Attached to Account, *ca.* November 5, 1823.

From William Woodbridge

Sir, [*ca.* November 15, 1823]

This letter will be presented to you by our Delegate elect, the Hon. Gabriel Richard.[1] This gentleman, tho' a native of France, has been for more than twenty years past the principal catholic pastor of this people—He is a man of fine native parts—and of an understanding, most highly cultivated— As a Theologian his equal it is presumed can scarcely be found— while at the same time as a belles lettres scholar, he is deservedly celebrated. —If there be any topick in the wide range of human learning, of which he is ignoran[t,] it is that of politics, with which he has not I know been conversant— He did not seek the employment upon which he is sent—but being elected he feels desirous to do all the good he can:—and as one important mean by which to render himself useful, he is most desirous Sir to [. . .][2] aid, which your coun[sel, advice] & favour cannot fail to give him. And with a feeling of certainty that it will secure to him that favour, I take pleasure in testifying in his behalf, that he is zealously attached to this nation— I know of but one instance in which he ever occupied himself with the political concerns of the Country— It was when the enemy were in possession—it was when destruction stared this people in the face—when the Tomhawk [*sic*] was over every man's head—it was when every persuasive was at the same time used to alienate the affections of this people from the nation—it was then that Mons Richard came forward zealously—boldly & with devotedness to the cause—using that powerful influence which he had acquired over the minds of his people & kept them fast in their faith—not one within his influence ceased for a moment to remain true & faithful to the United States— His efforts terminated in his being cast into prison by Proctor & in his chivalric rescue by a far more noble spirited man Tecumseh![3]

Such is the man Sir, I ask leave to present to you; and such an one for whom I respectfully ask your counsel and indulgent aid [. . .][4]

you for any thing crude or slovenly y[ou] see in this letter—for which I may justly apologyze—as the messenger of Mr Richard is waiting in great impatience for it—and allow me only to superadd that with very Great respect I remain Sir Yr obedt servt WM WOODBRIDGE
Hon. Henry Clay Esquire

ALS. MiD-B. Woodbridge, born in Connecticut, in 1780, had removed to Marietta, Ohio, around 1800. Admitted to the bar in 1806, he had held office as county prosecuting attorney, State Representative, and State Senator before receiving an appointment, in 1814, as Secretary of Michigan Territory and Collector of Customs at Detroit. From 1819 until his resignation the following year he had been the first delegate to Congress from the Territory. He was afterwards judge of the Territorial Supreme Court (1828-1832), delegate to the State Constitutional Convention (1835), State Senator (1838-1839), Governor (1840-1841), and United States Senator (1841-1847).

1 Born, educated, and ordained to the priesthood in France, Richard had fled to America during the French Revolution and had been assigned to missionary work, first in the Illinois country, then, in 1798, at Detroit, where he had become pastor of St. Anne's Church. He had also become a leader in education and had established an active press. He had been elected Territorial Delegate to the United States Congress in 1822.

2 MS. torn—four or five words missing.

3 In the spring of 1813 Henry A. Procter had imprisoned Richard for refusing to take an oath of allegiance to the British Crown. After about three weeks he had been released, according to the traditional account, through the intervention of Tecumseh in his behalf. Frank B. Woodford and Albert Hyma, *Gabriel Richard, Frontier Ambassador* (Detroit, 1958), 75-76.

4 Four or five words missing.

Receipt from George F. Strother

RECEIVER'S OFFICE, at St. Louis, Novr. 15th, 1823

[George F. Strother, Receiver of Public Moneys at St. Louis, acknowledges receipt from Clay, as executor of the estate of James Morrison, of the sum of $200, payment "in full for W½ of NW qr. of 28 & E½ NE qr. of section No. 29. township No. 47N. range No. 7 East. containing one hundred & Sixty acres, at the rate of $1.25 per acre."]

DS, partially printed. DNA, RG49, Land Entry Papers, Cash Entry no. 683, St. Louis, Missouri.

Accompanying this document, and bearing the same date, is a certificate, signed by William Christy, Register of the Land Office at St. Louis, entitling Clay to receive a patent for the land involved. DS, partially printed. *Ibid.* An endorsement on verso of the certificate reveals that a patent, dated January 13, 1824, was issued. According to a later endorsement, written across the face of the document, the transaction was cancelled in 1855 owing to "conflicts with New Madrid location as per survey No. 2495," and the "Purchase money refunded."

The "New Madrid location" was a claim, antedating purchase of the tract for the Morrison estate, under an act approved February 17, 1815, which had authorized owners of land in the county of New Madrid, Missouri Territory, whose holdings had "been materially injured by earthquakes" to give up their land to the United States and "to locate the like quantity of land on any of the public lands of the said territory, the sale of which is authorized by law." 3 *U. S. Stat.*, 211-12.

From Peter B. Porter

Dear Sir, Black Rock Novr 17th 1823.

I received your favour of the of September[1] some days ago.

The singular results in our late Elections, with the speculations on them in our news papers, will show you the uncertainty of the ultimate vote of this state on the Presidential question. The zeal & pertinacity with which Van Buren & his friends have pushed Mr Crawford (who has no substantial popularity here) without any other argument in his favour than the necessity of *party discipline,* have disgusted the Republicans of this state, & produced great dissatisfaction & division in our ranks.—and the consequence has been that an unexpected number of Federalists & Clintonians have been returned to our next Legislature. I consider it settled that our mode of appointing Electors will be changed; and that they will hereafter be chosen by the *people,* by a *general* ticket—most of the members of our next Legislature having already pledged themselves to advocate that course.[2] And I consider it equally certain that Mr Crawford can, in no event, obtain the vote of the State. Who will eventually be the fortunate Candidate it is impossible, at present, to tell. I have no hesitation however in saying that your chance has been improved by the issue of the late election—inasmuch as the friends of Mr Crawford, who seemed almost desperate in his favour, will now perceive the absolute necessity of giving him up. Mr Adams is, at present, unquestionably the strongest Candidate in the State, and there is scarcely a doubt that, if the [elec]tion were to be put to the people, tomorrow, he would have the greatest number of votes—although I doubt whether it will ever be possible for him to obtain a majority of the whole votes of the State. Adams, Crawford & Calhoun have all strong Supporters in the city of New York— The two latter have few, & the first many, friends scattered over every part of the state. The partizans of these three candidates have become so violently & vindictively arrayed against each other that it will be next to impossible that they should unite on either of them —while your friends who are composed of the more temperate & reflecting part of the community (principally the Yeomanry of the West) have done nothing to render them obnoxious to either of the other sects. There will doubtless be two tickets—one for Adams, and the other I have reason to hope will be supported by your friends & united with the friends of Crawford, Calhoun & even some of the present friends of Adams who have been drawn to him by their dislike of Crawford, & be in your favour. When I say that one ticket will be for Adams, it is upon the presumption that D-Clinton will not be a candidate—for you will understand that in consequence of the number of Federalists & Clintonians in our Legislature, an attempt will be made to bring him forward; but this can be effected only by drawing off a considerable part of Mr Adams strength to his support which I think he will not be able to accomplish.

Our Board of Commission[3] will meet in January at Albany, where I shall spend several weeks & be happy to hear from you.

In answer to your enquiries about T-y,[4] I can only say that I consider him as low, intriguing & heartless a man as any country can produce. He has not, as yet, declared for either of the Candidates—waiting I presume to ascertain who will be the *successfull* one, & when he can make the best bargain for himself. His predilections would be first for Clinton, & next for Adams—*but for anybody else* if he could make a better bargain. His vote might be of use to you, but beware of his friendship.

The cleverest fellow in our delegation is Dudley Marvin, a new member from Ontario, to whom I have given a letter of introduction to you. He was from New England & educated a federalist, but is a Republican in principle & practice, & has for some time been in the confidence of our party. He possesses a heart as well as head, of the first order. I hope you [w]ill notice him in *public* as well as in private, [an]d I am confident your attentions will be ampl[y] repaid in the pleasure you will derive from his acquaintance. Col. Herkimer,[5] our member from Montgomery County, called at my home a few weeks ago, on his way to Cincinnati, where he intended to proceed direct to Washington. He was formerly a member of Congress & is I believe known to you. He is a worthy & honest man & your firm friend on the presidential question. I fully concur with you in opinion that you ought neither to court nor decline *the chair,* which I hope & trust you will obtain.

I conclude that you will have no Congressional Caucus, & I hope you may not. Situated as you are, *delicacy* would probably forbid your taking a very active or open part on the question of caucus, or no caucus. Excuse me for suggesting that, in my opinion, policy, as regards both the friends of Mr Crawford & Mr Calhoun in this state, requires that you should not become a champion on either side of the question. Excuse this letter which is written in great haste.

Hon. H. Clay Yours very respectfully P. B. PORTER

ALS. DLC-HC (DNA, M212, R1). Published in part in Colton (ed.), *Private Correspondence of Henry Clay*, 83-84.

1 *I.e.*, October 4, 1823.

2 See above, Woods to Clay, August 27, 1823, note.

3 The Boundary Commission. See above, II, 162n.

4 Albert H. Tracy.

5 John Herkimer.

Assignment of Note from Bank of Kentucky

[November 18, 1823]

The President Directors & Co. of the Bank of Ky assign the within note to H. Clay without recourse as to the sufficiency of the parties.

Witness their Common seal hereby authenticated by the signature of the Prest. thereof this 18 Nov 1823.— J HARVIE. Prest. Bk Ky.

ES, on verso of note for $1350 dated October 6, 1823, and due December 8, from Edward C. Payne, with Daniel McCarty Payne as security, to the Bank of Kentucky. Fayette Circuit Court, File 581. Clay also received on this date similar assignments of notes from Samuel Trotter, with James Trotter as security, to the Bank of Kentucky, dated September 15, 1823, due 60 days thereafter, amounting to $1800 (ES, *ibid.*); from James Weir, with Henry Weir and George Robinson as securities, dated November 3, 1823, due January 5, 1824, for $1350 (ES, *ibid.*); from Thomas Wallace to David Castleman, endorsed to the Bank of Kentucky, dated October 20, 1823, due December 22, amounting to $1600 (ES; Fayette Circuit Court, File 585). Assignments of notes from the remaining parties mentioned in the Agreement, November 10, 1823, have not been found.

Statement of Account with Bank of Kentucky

[November 20, 1823]

[Henry Clay's deposit in the Lexington Branch Bank is stated at $10,126.96, which with interest for one year from January 3, 1823, amounts to a debt due him of $10,734.58. This sum is balanced by payments due on the notes which Clay holds on James Tilford, for $1150, due November 17, 1823; Walter Warfield, $1320, due December 8, 1823; Edward C. Payne, $1350, due December 8, 1823; James Weir, $1350, due January 5, 1824; Alexander Parker, $2400, due December 22, 1823; Samuel Trotter, $1800, due November 17, 1823; and Thomas Wallace, $1600, due December 22, 1823—which with interest in each case computed to January 3, 1824, amount to $11,012.38. Clay's balance owed to the Bank, in paper of the Bank of the Commonwealth is $277.80, from which sum is subtracted entries for error and costs, leaving a total of $271.15. On November 20, 1823, the Bank draws on Clay in favor of James M. Pike[1] at five days sight for $131.65, which at an advance of 106 per cent for bank paper, amounts to $271.19.]

[Endorsement on verso][2]

Recd the within balance of Two hundred Seventy one 15/100 Dollars in Comths paper from Mr J Harper.[3] Nov 21 1823

F DEWEES Cas

D. DLC-TJC (DNA, M212, R15). See above, Agreement, November 10, 1823; Assignment, November 18, 1823.

1 Lexington hairdresser, who soon thereafter moved to Nashville, Tennessee, where he died in 1832.

2 AES.

3 Clay's attorney.

To Edward C. and Daniel McCarty Payne

LEXINGTON NOVEMBER 20th, 1823.

Messrs. EDWARD C. PAYNE & DANIEL McC. PAYNE,

Gentlemen—Please to take notice, that the President, Directors and Company of the Bank of Kentucky, have assigned to me your note made payable to them for thirteen hundred and fifty dollars, due the 8th day of December next, and you will be held accountable to me for the payment of the same. Respectfully yours,

Henry Clay,

By his Attorney, J. HARPER.

☞The above mentioned note is left at the Lexington Branch Bank for collection.

Printed copy, accompanying Daniel McCarty Payne to the "Gentlemen of the Senate and House of Representatives" (broadside). DLC-TJC (DNA, M212, R15). See above, Agreement, November 10, 1823; Assignment, November 18, 1823. The Agreement under which Clay had obtained possession of the Payne note, among others, occasioned great controversy during the following year. Daniel McCarty Payne phrased the protest in a petition to the Kentucky General Assembly:

"The Bank of Kentucky at Frankfort has ordered the Bank at Lexington, to permit Mr. H. Clay to select out of her *Bill Box* notes to the amount of ten thousand dollars, and to assign the notes thus *selected* to him. This has been done, and the individuals whose notes have thus been assigned, have been required, and are now required to pay them in *Gold* or *Silver;* and although several of the individuals, both before and when their notes became due, have tendered their amount in notes on the Bank of Kentucky, yet they have been refused in payments, and I understand Mr. Clay has offered to transfer those notes to the United States Branch Bank at Lexington, with a view of bringing suit in the Federal Court, and thereby avoiding the 'Relief Laws of Kentucky [see above, II, 904n],' and being more certain of recovering *Gold* or *Silver;* and among other notes, one of my brother's, on which I am bound as security, has been transferred.

"While I am candid to declare that I did not expect Mr. Clay would receive from the Bank an offer of this kind, which would involve him in a suit with his private and political friends and neighbours, and while I did not expect the members who formed the Board at Frankfort could feel any wish to oppress or ruin any portion of their debtors, yet the act in its consequences is oppressive and unjust,

"1st. Because it gave Mr. Clay as a creditor of the Bank a *preference* above other creditors, and this is a species of *favoritism,* which ought not to exist in a public institution: and I know of none, nor have I heard of any good reason assigned why Mr. Clay should have had a preference.

"2d. This act of the Bank operates *unequally* upon the debtors of the institution, for it compels those, whose notes are assigned to pay them in gold or silver, while other debtors can discharge their notes in Bank paper of one half the value of Gold or Silver, thereby compelling some debtors to pay *double* the amount of others.

"3d. It is a violation of all banking rules to permit an individual (not an officer of the Bank, and of course not bound by its rules) to examine and pry into their Bill Box, and thereby discover the condition, number, and circumstances of its debtors.

"4th. This act of the Bank operates against the implied agreement of the persons who borrow its money, in this way. When a person borrows money from a Bank, it is always understood that he is to conform to the rules and usages of the Bank, in giving such notes, at such dates, and with such securities as the Bank shall require to make payments at the Bank offices, and in the hours required for banking business, in their own paper and such other as the Bank may be willing to receive, but since those notes have been assigned, the poor debtors will have to consult the *will and pleasure* of Mr. Clay, and not the Bank rules and usages, and to his mercy (and I fear there is none) they will have to appeal for indulgence.

"5th. By this act of the Bank those debtors will be brought before the Federal Court, and it is well known, that the Inquisition of Spain was never more alarming to the citizens of Spain, than the Federal Court is to the citizens of Kentucky. . . . I have no wish to injure Mr. Clay in his Presidential Election, nor to involve myself with the officers of the Bank. All I ask is only to be relieved from this act of *oppression.*

DANIEL MC. PAYNE.

"P. S. It will appear by the annexed documents, that notes of the Bank of Kentucky have been tendered in payment of the above note before it fell due, on which I am bound as security, and refused."

The Lexington *Kentucky Gazette* on November 27 and December 11, 1823, carried letters to the editor, commenting upon the assignment of the notes and critical of the role of "the few men, who have hoarded the Bills of the old Kentucky Banks," but without naming Clay. Similarly a report of a joint committee of the Senate and House of the Kentucky General Assembly, appointed "for the purpose of enquiring into the situation of the Bank of Kentucky," again without denominating Clay, felt "constrained to notice a practice which has recently been adopted by the bank, of transferring the notes of individuals, under discount and accommodation to persons holding claims against the institution, in payment of those claims." Such transfers "are, as far as your committee are informed, unusual in the operations of banking institutions, and highly injurious to those who may be the unfortunate subjects of such traffic. Your committee cannot, however, in justice to the bank, refrain from stating that in their opinion, nothing but the most imperious necessity, has induced the adoption of this course on the part of the bank; that it has been reluctantly resorted to, in only one or two instances; and they entertain the fullest confidence, will never be pursued, when it can be avoided without great loss to the institution." Ky. Sen., *Journal, 1823-1824*, pp. 268-69; Ky. H. of Reps., *Journal, 1823-1824*, p. 359.

From Nicholas Berthoud

Henry Clay Esqre. Lexington Shippingport Novr. 23d 1823.
Dear Sir

Enclosed you will please find Bill of Lading for the Two Cows sent by you, and Shipped to Mr. Durald per the Steam Boat Rob Roy agreably to your request—[1] Annexed is an account which I have against Mr. Durald to which I have added the charges for the Shipment of the Cows Amounting together to \$24.73½/100 in Specie and \$34.50/100 in Currency, Which if convenient you will Oblige m[e . . .][2] by remitting— I remain Respectfully Your Obt Servt.

N. BERTHOUD

ALS. DLC-TJC (DNA, M212, R15). Forwarded from Lexington, November 27, to Clay at Washington.

1 Request not found. The bill of lading, dated at Shippingport, November 22, 1823, and signed by George F. Bartlett, a clerk, covers shipment of "Two Cows with their provender consisting of 700 lbs Hay 16 Bushels corn & 19 Bushels of Brann" aboard the *Rob Roy*, J. Pierce, master, to Martin Duralde, New Orleans, *"or to* his *assigns, he or they paying freight* at Fifty dollars for the whole." DS, partially printed. DLC-TJC (DNA, M212, R15).

2 MS. torn—possibly one word missing.

From Robert Scott

Dr. Sir, Lexington 23rd. Novr. 1823

Your favor dated Chila. [*sic*] 15 inst.[1] has been recd— The executorial Accounts to which you allude, are in the packet I made up in the office and by request handed to Theodore Clay in the carriage— examine and you will find them there— I will forward the land Account in a few days.— I have not seen Mr Payne since I received your letter, but will present your order by first oppy.[2]— The convention Bill I understand has recd. its death in the Senate[3]— I have been once at the farm since you left us and saw Mr. Hawkins[4] yesterday—your domestic affairs are I beleive [*sic*] all doing well— In the packet I gave you, is a letter from Mr. Creighton Esqr.[5] of

Chila. giving a partial statement of money collected on Acct. of Harris & Donaldson and which is to their credit in Acct. with Colo. Morrison; but the House and Lot in New Ark which has been devised to E. Harris has not been credited because no statement has been recd. from Colo Creighton of that transaction[6]— In the papers is H & Ds. Acct.— I do not know that you can do any thing with it but if you intend to, it will be necessary to have the statement from Colo. C— I have heretofore written to him for it, but without effect— Perhaps if you drop him a line it will have the desired effect— That will be necessary only in case you contemplate a close of H & Ds. Acct.—

You have been very fortunate as to weather on your journey— I trust you have been equally so in an improvement of your health— We are all well— very respectfully Yr. obt. Servt. ROBT. SCOTT.

ALS. DLC-TJC (DNA, M212, R12). Addressed to Clay at Washington.
1 From Chillicothe, not found. 2 Cf. above, Clay to Paynes, November 20, 1823.
3 In an effort to obviate the difficulties placed in the way of relief legislation by a conservative judiciary (see above, Clay to Leigh, October 29, 1822, note), the advocates of the program had led a campaign to call a State constitutional convention which should provide for popular election of judges and for fixed terms of judicial office. The proposal for a convention had passed the House of Representatives on November 14, 1823, by 59 to 36, but was defeated in the Senate on November 21 by a tie vote, 18 to 18, which failed to satisfy the requirement for a majority. Ky. H. of Reps., *Journal, 1823-1824*, pp. 130-31; Ky. Sen., *Journal, 1823-1824*, pp. 98-99.
4 Francis Hawkins. 5 William Creighton, Jr. Letter not found.
6 Under a codicil to his will, James Morrison had bequeathed a house and lot in Newark, Ohio, to "Hester" (Esther) Morrison Harris, daughter of Mrs. Morrison's sister Sarah, and of Colonel David Harris, Baltimore merchant. For the firm of Harris and Donaldson, see below, Harris to Clay, April 24, 1824.

Acceptance of Speakership

[December 1, 1823]

Gentlemen: I pray you to accept my most respectful thanks for the honor you have just conferred on me. The station of Speaker of this House has been always justly considered as one of great respectability and dignity, as well as of high responsibility. But at the present period, when we are assembled under a new census, with our number considerably enlarged, and the highest interests of a greatly augmented population committed to our charge, it has acquired much additional importance, which requires from the favored object of your selection his most grateful acknowledgments, and the expression of the profoundest sensibility. The principles which should regulate the execution of the duties of the incumbent of the chair are not difficult to comprehend, although their application to particular instances is often extremely delicate and perplexing.— They enjoin promptitude and impartiality in deciding the various questions of order, as they arise, firmness and dignity in his deportment towards the House, patience, good temper, and courtesy, towards the individual members, and the best arrangement and distribution of the talent of the House, in its numerous subdivisions, for the despatch of the public business, and the fair exhibition of every subject presented for consideration. They especially require of him, in those moments of agitation, from which no deliberative assembly is always entirely exempt, to remain cool and unshaken, amidst all the storms of debate, carefully guarding the preservation of the permanent laws and rules of the House, from being sacrificed to temporary passions, prejudices, or interests. It is on such occasions as these, too, that the Chair stands most in need of your support, of your candor, of your liberality, of your unbiassed judgment. I am not so presumptuous, gentlemen, as to promise you that I shall perform the arduous duties, of which I have presented an imperfect sketch. All I dare say, is, that I will exert an anxious, faithful, and unremitting endeavor to fulfil the expectations by which I have been so much honored. And may we not indulge the hope, that, with the blessing of Divine Providence, all our deliberations and all our proceedings may tend to sustain the dignity of the House, to maintain the honor and character of the country, and to advance the public welfare and happiness.

Washington *Daily National Intelligencer,* December 2, 1823. Published also in Lexington *Kentucky Reporter,* December 22, 1823; *Annals of Cong.,* 18 Cong., 1 Sess., XLI, 795. On the first day of the Session, the Clerk having called the roll and found a quorum present, John W. Taylor had arisen to declare that he was not a candidate for the Speaker's Chair. The House then elected Clay, by a vote of 139 to 42 over Philip P. Barbour. Upon being conducted to the Chair, Clay "made acknowledgments to the House" in this brief address.

From Charles Wilkins

Dear Sir Lexington 3d. Decr. 1823

I enclose to you under several covers all the papers I am in possession of in relation to the Claim of the late Lessees of the United States Saline. I must beg you will endeavour to Settle this affair for us.[1] The claim against Mr. Leonard White[2] stands in an unpleasant Situation. Mr. Taylor & Mr. White were conserned [*sic*] in Some transaction, by which, I suppose, the former became indebted to the latter, or for the purpose of releasing White from the claim of the goverment [*sic*], Mr. Taylor gave a rect. in the name of Wilkins, Taylor & Co for the amt. which White was indebted to the Govt. This rect. Still Stands against us although entirely unauthorised by the other parties concerned in this transaction— Taylor now contends that he never recd. one cent from White, that White did not comply with the conditions Stipulated for between them besides the rect. was given long after the copartnership of Wilkins, Taylor & Co expired. Be these facts as they may, I doubt very much whether we shall not be obliged to recognize them, but I would prefer making application for the whole amt., unless you should be of opinion, that it might operate against us, but do in this business as you may think best— I would now be satisfied to receive $12.061 99½/100 being the Amt. of the Valuation of the metal & leave us at liberty to demand from White the amt. due from him— I cannot pretend to give you instructions upon this subject, I only suggest this mode as one with which I would be satisfied myself. You are the representative of the late Mr Morrison & I am willing to submit the whole, to your management. If an arrangment [*sic*] cannot be made with the Secy. of the Treasury, it might be well to petition Congress in our names.

Very respectfully Yr. Obt St CHA: WILKINS

The hble. H. Clay—

ALS. DLC-TJC (DNA, M212, R12). 1 See above, II, 165-66.

2 An early settler at the United States Saline, where for a time he had been Postmaster and United States Agent. He had also been an officer in the Illinois territorial militia and a judge in Gallatin County. He was a member of the State Senate, from White County, 1822-1824.

To Walter Dun

Dr Sir

Washington 4h. Decr. 1823

I duly received your obliging letter of the 20h. Ulto. with the Check inclosed[1] for the amount of my fee in the suit in Chy of Mr. Call as exor of Means against Carneal, and send you a receipt inclosed.[2]

I expected to have had the pleasure of seeing you at Chillicothe,[3] but arrived late in the evening very much fatigued, and left it too early in the morning to call on you, otherwise I should have had that satisfaction.

When your answer is prepared to Banks's bill be pleased to send it to me here or a copy of it—

Montjoy means to take some depositions, and I told him to notify you of the time and place— Be pleased to prepare your deposition and forward it to me or to Frankfort.

Walter Dun Esqr. With great regard I am faithfy Yrs. H. CLAY

ALS. Ross County Historical Society, Chillicothe, Ohio. See above, Clay to Dun, July 2, 1823.

1 Neither letter nor check has been found.

2 Not found. 3 En route to Washington.

From Philip P. Barbour

Dear Sir,

Wash. Dec. 4th. 1823.

In answer to your note[1] of this evening, I beg leave to say, that I should regret exceedingly as far as I am personally concerned to give you the slightest difficulty in the arrangement of committees. My own individual wish would be decidedly to be on no committee; but as that might *possibly* give rise to some misconstruction, I now so far modify my wish, as to desire to be put upon none whose labor is very great, and further not to be chairman of whatsoever committee I may be placed on. Above all, the Committee of Ways and means, I should most object to. Wheresoever your general arrangement may make it convenient to place me, I assure you in sincerity I shall be perfectly satisfied.[2] Resp'ly your's &c P. P. BARBOUR

ALS. DLC-HC (DNA, M212, R1). Published in Colton (ed.), *Private Correspondence of Henry Clay,* 84. Addressed: "Honble Henry Clay Speaker H. R. Davis's," a new stand of John Davis, near Pennsylvania Avenue, on Ninth Street.

1 Not found.

2 The Washington *Daily National Intelligencer,* December 6, 1823, reports the Speaker's appointment of Standing Committees, with Barbour as a member, only, of the Judiciary Committee, as an action of December 5. The dating of this action as December 3 in U. S. H. of Reps., *Journal,* 18 Cong., 1 Sess., p. 24; and *Annals of Cong.,* 18 Cong., 1 Sess., XLI, 798, appears to be erroneous.

From Robert Scott

The Honble H Clay Lexington 4th Decr 1823

Dr. Sir

I have recd. a letter from Colo. Sullivan[1] of Missouri, in which came the enclosed receipt,[2] and in which he says—"Since I last wrote you, I have succeeded in defeating Mr. Coopers Second Sale, and in order to secure the improvems. I thought it advisable to hold a qr. Section by preemption, and for the purpose of covering the improvement and the most valuable of the land I took the ½ of 2 qr. Sections touching the improvement and herewith send the Receivers receipt for the money 200$, which you can forward to the City and get the Patent on—I have lately heard that Tanner, the person from whom the land was purchased) has been among those who were minors when they conveyed and probably he may get them to confirm the former sale, which he promised me he would do—Should he not do so and Evans's claim under those minors be good, a compromise can be made on good terms as the improvements and best of the land are secured by the preemption"—[3]

By the mail which conveys this I send you the Schedule of debts due the estate of Colo. Morrison, supposing it probable that you might wish to look over it and give me some instructions about the debtors—By advice of Mr. Hawes I will file a copy at the Cy. Court on monday—[4] The Clerk mentioned to me that it should be filed and on consulting Mr H. he is opinion [*sic*] it may be done without your presence Two or three days since I sent you the land Acct.[5] My impression is, that Mr. Nourse may have some U States Stock,[6] but am not certain of it—Perhaps it would be well to enquire—He did owe a small Acct. as per balance list unless he paid it to Colo. Morrison last winter—

Mr. Wilkins informs me he will send on the papers relating to the claim of C Wilkins & Co.—or Old Saline Co. agt. the goverment [*sic*]—[7]

We are all well— Wishing you good health and a sucessful [*sic*] campaign toward the P y—

I am Dr Sir most respectfully Yr. obt. Servt. ROBT. SCOTT

P.S. The Estate own 5 Shares U S Bank Stock—had it not better be sold?[8] If you think so will send you the Evidence of the Shares— If you wish the Ky. B. Stock sold send me or Mr. Deweis[9] Power of Atty giving authority— R S.

ALS. DLC-TJC (DNA, M212, R12). [1] John C. Sullivan.

[2] See above, Receipt, November 15, 1823.

[3] Transaction not found—possibly involving Samuel Cooper, for years a justice of the peace in New Madrid County, Missouri, and Edward Tanner, also a justice of the peace in the same county, a militia officer, and a businessman. Evans, not identified.

[4] Richard Hawes, Jr. See Fayette County, Will Book F, 231-33.

[5] See Fayette County, Will Book F, 71-73.

[6] See below, Nourse to Clay, January 12, 1824.

[7] See above, Wilkins to Clay, December 3, 1823.

[8] See below, Clay to S. Gratz and Brother, February 1, 1824.

[9] Farmer Dewees.

To Nicholas Biddle

Sir Washington 6th. Decr. 1823.

I am indebted to the Bank at the Lexington office a sum of considerable amount,[1] which I diminished a little before I left home, and I have been struggling to obtain the means to liquidate the whole debt, which was principally thrown upon me as an indorser. A considerable part of those means consisted of about $10.000 which the Bank of K. owed me and for which I sued it. The day before I left home that Bank sent up an Agent[2] to me to offer in paymt. of its debt my choice of notes out of its bill box in Lexington. I acceded to the proposal and received the notes.[3] These notes I left with Mr. Harper to be offered to your Board at Lexington as a *collateral security* only. Mr. Harper writes me that the measure adopted by the Bank of K. has produced considerable excitement with the makers of the notes,[4] and he anticipates a refusal on the part of the Board at Lexington to receive them. The truth is that two of the notes are made by two of the directors of that Board, Mess Trotter and Tilford. I foresaw, duly weighed, and care not for this excitement. There is no just cause for it; and I have long since made up my mind to disregard all clamor, whether on public or private account, for which there is no reasonable foundation. In wishing to transfer the notes to you my motive is to have suits brought in the Federal Court, which cannot be otherwise done, and to have the inforcement of the Judgments and the collection of the debts with the Marshall instead of the Sheriff of a County.[5] On your part, I should think the motive of having your debt from me further secured, without any additional expence to you, would determine you to accept the notes as Collateral security. And the object of this letter is to ask the favor of you to lay the matter before your Board in the hope that it will make the requisite order to receive the notes. Supposing that to be done, what will be the amount of the transaction? One debtor (the B. of K) pays his debt to his creditor, with the notes of his debtors, by contract and by the law payable in specie, which the assignee again transfers in payment of his debt to his creditor, the B. of the U. S. Now what will the parties be able to make of an arrangement so simple so compendious, so equitable?

If there be any prejudice created by it, it will fall on me, and I am quite willing to bear it. I trust the order will be made and that you will have the goodness to favor me with an early answer.

I transmit a list of the notes which I wish to assign to the B. U. S.[6] I have the honor to be with great respect Your ob. Servant

Nicholas Biddle Esqr. &c. &c. &c. H. CLAY

ALS. ViU. Endorsed: "recd. Dec 8th. 1823. . . ."

1 See above, II, 877.

2 Charles Miles, Frankfort merchant, for many years a director of the Bank of Kentucky.

3 See above, Agreement, November 10, 1823.

4 Letter not found. Cf. above, Clay to Paynes, November 20, 1823, note.

5 Cf. below, Clay to Harper, December 22, 1823, note.

6 Not found.

Receipt from John Jacob Astor

[December 8, 1823]

Received New York 8 December 1823 from the Honorable Henry Clay Five Thousand Dollars being on account of principal on his Bond for Twenty Thousand Dollars to me dated the 18th [*sic*] Day of April 1819[1] which said Five thousand Dollars as payment on that bond have been thereon endorsed.[2]— for John Jacob Astor

(Duplicate Receipt) WM. B ASTOR

[Endorsement][3]

Dear Sir, (Duplicate) New York 8 Decr. 1823

I have received your favor of the 4th inst,[4] covering a check for payment of $5.000 on your bond to my father a receipt for which you have above I remain with great regard Your Obedient Servant.

WM. B ASTOR

To the Honorable Henry Clay &c &c &c Washington (DC)

ADS by William B. Astor, "Duplicate." DLC-TJC (DNA, M212, R15).

1 See above, II, 686.

2 AES, by William B. Astor for J. J. Astor, on wrapper of the bond.

3 AES, "Duplicate."

4 Not found.

From R[obert] R[ead]

9th. December 1823.

Hon. Henry Clay Speaker of the House of Representatives

Sir, I have had the honor of receiving your note of the 5th Inst.[1] with its accompaniments in relation to the Accounts of Charles Carr, late Pay Master Kentucky Militia—and having also received from the Agent of the Treasury, a communication appraising me that he has been furnished with evidence of the District Attorney having deposited in the office of the Bank of the U States at Lexington to the credit of the Treasurer, the $750 paid to him by Mr Carr on the 11th December 1822, another statement of Mr. Carr's Accounts has been made, and the following items passed to his credit, by the Accounting officers—

Items rejected by the Accounting officers but allowed by the Jury—	$251.11
On a/c of money lost— (admitted under the late Act of Congress)	160.
Payment to the District Attorney	750
Making an Aggregate of	$1161.11

The balance reported against Mr Carr on the last settlement of his accounts in June 1822, was $1165.15

Besides this balance, he has been charged in the present settlement with the sum of $70.54 on account of Interest that accrued upon the Judgment against him up to this time—A statement of which is enclosed The foregoing debits being added together, makes the sum of $1235.69—deducting from which the foregoing credits, there remains a balance of $74.58 still due from Mr Carr—arising principally from the Interest that has accrued on the Judgment—

I observe by Mr Carr's letter to you that he speaks of a claim, he has for transportation which he wished applied to the payment of the Interest that would be due from him—Before any decision can be made on this transportation claim, it will be necessary for Mr Carr to state the number of miles for which he claims this allowance—make out an a/c & depose to its accuracy & that no public transportation was furnished to him— R,R,

Copy. DNA, RG217, Records of the Third Auditor, Misc. Letters Sent, vol. 31, p. 338. See above, Read to Clay, October 25, 1823.

1 Not found.

To Peter B. Porter

My dear Sir Washn. 11h Novr. [*i.e.*, December][1] 1823.

I duly received your obliging favor of the 17th. Ulto.[2] The result of the Election of Speaker was most gratifying to my friends and myself.[3] If I had possessed the power of controlling events the circumstances which preceded & accompanied the issue could not have been more favorable. It will have a beneficial influence on another election. There is an effort making, I understand, to get up a Caucus, but it does not promise to be successful. Indeed I think the zeal of Mr. Crawfords friends for one has much abated, seeing that it is not likely to advance their wishes. It is now more wanted for their sakes than for his. I shall take no particular part in regard to it. My opinions have been fortunately promulged at a time when I could not be supposed to be biased by any personal wishes; and to these opinions my friends appeal when necessary.

Is there a real design to bring out Mr. Clinton? or is it a mere rues [*sic*] de guerre? Seeing that the election is likely to come to the H. of R. may he not be influenced by the hope that he can command a sufficient number of votes to make him one of the three from whom the selection is to be made? But, if he can even obtain the vote of his own state, where will he be able to procure the residue? You may rely upon it that Ohio is stedfast [*sic*] in its declared preference.[4] If he is brought out, Rochester seems to think that he may probably succeed in N. York.[5] Judge Thompson[6] is of a different opinion.

I have made the acquaintance of most of your delegation. I am pleased with many of them and particularly Mr. Marvin. I understand that the gloomy prospects of Mr. Crawford have dispirited Mr. Van Buren and those associated with him very much. Mr. Van and myself are very civil, but we have had no conversation in regard to the Presidential election.

Genl. Jackson has buried the hatchet and we are again on good terms.[7] The Tennessee delegation has been remarkably attentive to me, and I understand are nearly unanimous for me, if Jackson be out of the way.

We have not yet fairly commenced our Legislative labors. The Committees are preparing business. I have no doubt of our passing a Tariff bill & I hope a good one—

My best respects to Mrs. Porter. Your's faithfully H. CLAY

Genl. P. B. Porter.

ALS. NBuHi.

1 The incorrect month was crossed out and "Dec." substituted for it by Porter.

2 November.

3 See above, Acceptance, December 1, 1823.

4 See above, Clay to Brooke, January 8, 1823.

5 Cf. below, Rochester to Clay, December 20, 1823.

6 Smith Thompson.

7 On the circumstances of this reconciliation, see below, Clay to Johnson, October 6, 1827.

Remarks on Bill for Relief of Daniel D. Tompkins

[December 11, 1823]

Mr. CLAY (the Speaker) then rose, and said, that, to him, it appeared that the considerations urged by the gentleman from Tennessee would have been in their proper place, if urged at the last Session—but were certainly out of place at this time, when we are called upon, not to investigate a new claim, but to redeem the pledged faith of the Public. On such a question, it was entirely unnecessary for the friends of the Vice President to refer to the public services, eminent as they had been, of the distinguished gentleman in question. This was not a fit occasion to introduce them. If the claimant were the meanest and the most obscure individual in society, the House were equally bound to pass that bill. For, what was it? The accounts to which it refers, had long been pressing on the public for liquidation; they had at length been brought before this House; and, after deliberate consideration, an act is passed for their final settlement. The accounts were quietly examined and liquidated by the accounting officer. But, mark the precaution by which that act is characterized! Not only were those accounts to be submitted to the severe scrutiny of the most rigid officer of this Government; an officer whose scrupulous accuracy, in the admission of accounts against the Government, is as deservedly approved as it is universally known;[1] but, after they had gone through the crucible—after they had been subjected to all the jealous scrutiny of this vigilant officer, they are to be submitted to the President for revisal. The President revises them, and then he sends to this House a message, in which he declares, not only that he is satisfied that this balance is justly due, but that much more is due to him. Under such circumstances, all that is now asked is, that we shall pay so much as has been thus ascertained to be due. It is, in fact, to do nothing more than supply the defect of the act of the last Congress, in which, by some omission, no appropriation had been made to meet the balance, if, according to the provisions of that act, a balance should have been ascertained to be due to Mr. Tompkins. Now, what does the gentleman from Tennessee tell us? He wishes to know *the ground* of the settlement? He wants, in short, to settle this account himself—to see the basis on which the officers of the Treasury proceeded, in coming to the decision which they have laid before the President. This, Mr. C. said, might have been proper when the subject was under consideration at the last session; but Congress had committed the liquidation of these accounts to another tribunal. It had committed it to the accounting officers of the Government—gentlemen whose characters were unimpeached, and on whose accuracy, in this settlement, no reflections had been cast. The gentleman from Tennessee, whose vigilance over the Treasury was the admiration of the country and of the House, should have reserved the remarks with which he had favored the House, until the time when a final settlement of the demands of the Vice President on this government is called up in this House—but now, when the sum reported is incontestable, when all the guards of the Treasury unite in declaring it justly due, when all that is asked is to supply a deficiency in the law of the last session, those remarks, however eloquent, would, he trusted, have no weight.[2]

Washington *Daily National Intelligencer,* December 12, 1823. Published also in *Annals of Cong.,* 18 Cong., 1 Sess., XLI, 821-22. See above, Porter to Clay, May 26, 1823, note. By an act approved February 21, 1823, Congress had authorized "the proper accounting officers of the Treasury . . . to adjust and settle the accounts and claims of Daniel D. Tompkins . . . on principles of equity and justice, subject to the revision and final decision of the President of the United States" (6 *U. S. Stat.,* 280). On December 8 Congress had been informed by special message that the accounting officers of the Treasury had reported a balance of $35,190 in favor of Tompkins and that, after considering the report and a claim from Tompkins for an additional sum, the President had concluded that a larger allowance should have been made. In view of the fact that no appropriation had been included in the act of February 21 and upon being informed by Tompkins "that the sum reported would afford him an essential accommodation at this time," Monroe had submitted the matter to Congress. The message had been referred to the Committee on Ways and Means, which had reported a bill, on December 10, "appropriating $35,190 for the relief of Daniel D. Tompkins." In Committee of the Whole on the measure, the following day, John Cocke had moved to strike out the enacting clause. He wished to know upon what vouchers the report in favor of Tompkins had been made, he was suspicious of a claim which had "lain dormant for a number of years" and "was brought forward after all the circumstances of it are forgotten," and he was apprehensive because he expected another demand for a much larger sum in the same case. Others joined in the debate, in which Clay participated after Cocke had spoken a second time.

1 Peter Hagner.

2 Several other speakers were heard, after which Cocke's proposal was defeated, as was an amendment, also offered by him, which would have declared "that the amount now appropriated should be *in full* of the claim of Mr. Tompkins." The bill was passed by both houses and was signed on December 22, 1823. 6 *U. S. Stat.,* 290.

To Nathaniel Rochester

My dear Sir Washn. 13h. Decr. 1823.

I duly recd. your obliging favor of the 3d. inst.[1] with its inclosure, for which be pleased to accept my best thanks. The interest which you and your family so kindly take in my success is most gratifying to me. The prospect of my success daily brightens. The flattering manner of my election to the Speaker's Chair cannot fail to promote that object. I have just recd. a letter from Govr. Carroll[2] of Tennessee, in which he says that the unanimity there in my favor, as their second choice is as great as it is for Genl. Jackson, as their first. If N. York decides for me, and promulgates her purpose to do so by some incontestible evidence within four or five months, I do believe I should be elected by two thirds of the Union. The inclination for a Caucus here has abated. Still there is an effort making to get up one. I doubt its success; unless they determine to hold one, with a small minority of the Republicans. It is quite evident that Mr. Van Buren and the other friends of Mr. Crawford begin to despair of this gentleman's success. They want a Caucus rather for themselves than for him.

My health is greatly improved and nearly re-established. Mrs. Clay did not accompany me. I left her and my family well. We have two daughters married, and I have one grand child.[3] Dr. Pindell[4] and his children were all well. By the generosity of the widow of the late Col. Morrison, the situation of Thomas H. Pindells family is likely to be much bettered.[5] Mr. Brown, you will have seen, is appointed Minister to France.[6]

I shall be glad to be favored with a line occasionally from you; and I pray you to believe me Faithfly & Cordially Your friend

Col. N. Rochester. H. CLAY

ALS. NRHi. 1 Not found. 2 William Carroll.

3 Mrs. Martin Duralde (Jr.); Mrs. James Erwin; Martin Duralde (III), born earlier this year.

4 Richard Pindell.

5 No immediate benevolence from Mrs. Morrison to the Pindells has been found. Under her will, dated November 22, 1836, the "Carlisle Farm," conveyed to her under the Agreement, above, October 30, 1823, was granted to her grandnephews, Richard and James Morrison Pindell, and the 26 acres of land, also conveyed under the above Agreement, was bequeathed for the education of a third grandnephew, Henry Clay Pindell. Fayette County, Will Book P, 280-81.

6 As successor to Albert Gallatin, who had resigned. James Brown's appointment had been approved on December 9, and he had resigned from the United States Senate the next day.

From Thomas Cromwell

My Dear Sir, Baltimore December 13th 1823.

Your very many.acts of Friendship in soothing the unhappiness and distress of our fellows.Justifies me asking this favour., [*sic*] A young man by.the name of Daniel Campbell and who is now in this City and whose relatives and friends.are of the most respectable Character was left a Fatherless Boy. and from the want of Paternal Care has.been to much indulged. his friends aided him in acquiring an excellant understanding.added to which is a heart warm to every feeling and Sensibility but being thus thrown on the world, as is often unfortunately the case.got into the habits of Intemperance, the only evil I may Say.he possesses

every means that could be devised has been made use of to ward him from the fate.attendant thereto.and all so far of no avail, We have thought of one other and perhaps.the only remedy.which offers a prospect of restoring him to his friends and Society. That is by some means to get him on board of some of our National Ships likely to make a long Voyage. Information has been given me that Commodore Hull[1] is fitting up a Vessell & will Shortly Sail from Norfolk.for the Pacific Ocean.— May I beg the favour of your Interposition with the proper Authority at Washington City for.permission for this young man to be taken on board this vessell, *in any Capasity whatever.* he I may Say is well anured to Hardships, having recently Served a five year tour in the American Army & from which he has received an honourable discharge

Should your.Business and good disposition afford you time to make the necessary enquirey respecting these my wishes, I shall always feel obliged and as.Commodore Hull is now fitting out for this Voyage I Should be glad how Soon I hear the result.So that means may be taken to place the young man under the Commodores. direction as Soon as possible

In addition to what I have said respecting the Character of Mr Campbell, permit me to refer you to Genl. Duncan McArthur now at Washington City who is well acquainted with his Brother Mr Francis Campbell of the hous [*sic*] of Barr & Campbell Merchants of Chilicothee [*sic*] Ohio. Pardon the trouble I give you. & if I can remunerate you in any way. It will afford me much pleasure.

very Respectfully your Ob [Svt] THOMAS CROMWELL

Henry Clay Esqr. formerly of Pittsburgh Pa.

PS will you Just Enquire.whether.Harry D Hunter[2] is now on Service & where, or on furlough, he is attached to the Navy. T.C

ALS. DNA, RG45, Misc. Letters Received, 1823, vol. 7. 1 Isaac Hull.

2 A native of Pennsylvania and a midshipman in the United States Navy since November 30, 1814, Hunter had been on furlough during a part of the year 1823 and afterward sailed on the vessel commanded by Hull. His name does not appear in the "Naval Register" after 1824.

To David K. Este

Dr Sir Washington 15h. Decr. 1823.

I received your favor of the 6h. Ulto.[1] in respect to the business of the Bank in the Federal Court at Columbus, and thank you for the communications which it contains. I presume you will have no difficulty now in obtaining Judgment against Lytle on the amended declaration.[2] Judge Todd spoke of the case to me and appeared to be perfectly clear that the Judgment of Hamilton was to be treated and considered as a Judgment—a point so absolutely free from all difficulty that I did not expect Counsel would be got seriously to urge the opposite doctrine. I will thank you to see that Mr Evans takes the necessary steps to place the Chancery suit against Lytle for trial at the Septr. term, which is as early as it can be done under the rules of the Supreme Court. I have seen Lytle's answer, to refute which we want no evidence, unless it should be rendered necessary by that which he may take. Should he have taken any be pleased to direct a copy of it to be sent to me.

I will write to Mess Creighton and Bond[3] to request them to represent me in the cases of the Bank agt. Stone, Mack, Bates[4] & ad. Be pleased to say to them that I shall be thankful for them to appear for me.

The question of Costs in causes under $500 is perplexing The truth is that the Court in K. has intimated pretty distinctly that it thinks we are not entitled to them.[5] I wish to bring the question before the Supreme Court, which you know can only be done by a division of the Court, real or formal. And on the other hand I did not desire to bring up the question until the jurisdiction of the Federal tribunals, in cases in which the Bank is a party, was well settled in the Supreme Court. Considering that at its last term it took jurisdiction, without question being however made, in a case from Louisiana,[6] I think we may venture to bring up the question of Costs, if you can prevail on the Judges to certify a division. We may prosecute it or not afterwards as may seem expedient.

It is probable that at the approaching term of the Supreme Court the Kentucky execution laws will be decided on;[7] and as they involve the valuation principle, the doctrines which the Court must necessarily settle will enable us to see whether that of Ohio will stand the test.

Should any of the Mortgages cases come on, the point has been fully argued & firmly settled in Kentucky by Judge Todd and Judge Trimble that the mortgage Estate must sell for what it will bring, without reference to the valuation laws.

I shall be glad to hear from you, from time to time, and if at any time I can give any aid in the conduct of the business of the Bank it will afford me much pleasure to render it.

With great regard I am Yours faithfy H. CLAY

D. K. Este Esqr.

ALS. DLC-David K. Este Papers (DNA, M212, R21). [1] Not found.

[2] See above, Clay to Biddle, June 11, 1823; Clay to Este, October 29, 1823.

[3] William Creighton, Jr., and William Key Bond. The latter, a native of Maryland, had studied law at Litchfield, Connecticut, before settling in Chillicothe, Ohio, where he had begun practice in 1813. He became a member of Congress, as a Whig proponent, 1835-1841, then, declining renomination, removed to Cincinnati and resumed legal practice.

[4] Probably Ethan Stone, lawyer and former president of the Bank of Cincinnati. Mack and Bates not identified; suits not found. Cf. below, Clay to Biddle, August 7, 1824.

[5] See below, Clay to Biddle, May 11, 1824.

[6] William Fleckner *vs.* The President, Directors, and Company of the Bank of the United States, in which Justice Joseph Story on February 28, 1823, had expressed the opinion of the Court that the Bank of the United States was not barred from discounting promissory notes. 21 *U. S.* (8 Wheaton) 338-65.

[7] See above, Clay to Hammond, July 14, 1822, note; Clay to Biddle, December 27, 1822, note.

To Samuel L. Southard

Dr Sir 15h. Decr. [1823]

Will you be good enough to inform me if either of the objects of the writer of the inclosed letter be attainable, which I send you just as I have recd. it?[1] I have the honor to be Yr's with high respect

H. CLAY

P.S. Be pleased to return the letter with your reply.[2]

ALS. DNA, RG45, Misc. Letters Received, 1823, vol. 7. Addressed: "The Honble Mr. Southard Secty of the Navy."

1 See above, Cromwell to Clay, December 13, 1823.

2 Apparently this request was not granted.

From Robert Scott

H. Clay Esqr. Lexington, 15 Decr. 1823.

Dr. Sir

We have the agreeable intelligence of your election to the chair in the house of Reprs. this we anticipated but the vast majority in your favor is quite gratifying to us— It's ominous I hope of the result which will be realized for even a more elevated situation— We have the Presidents Message too—[1] It is generally believed to be the best that has emanated from the same source—

In looking over your professional account I observe a fee charged in the case of Morrison vs Beach in the U S Court—[2] If I am not very much mistaken this was as Navy Agent— Could you not in that case obtain a credit to the estate from the Government 25$ is the fee—[3]

Enclosed is a letter from the old man Himpy Ball who lives on the Carthage land—[4] I am unable to give the power he requires— therefore the papers are enclosed to you— I dislike troubling you but feel a strong desire that the old man should be relieved— As I understand the matter it is about this— Originally he leased from those men the Tuckers[5] and without giving possession or removing off the land, leased from Colo. Morrison— The Tuckers therefore are pursuing him for the rents—

I have unpleasant news from Natchez— none of our rope has been sold owing to the fever which prevailed there this last summer &c. Cox[6] has remitted one 1000$ on acct. of Morrison & Bruce—

I was at the C Farm[7] to day— did not see Mr. H.[8] as he was at Ashland— Your domestic affairs are I beleive doing well—

Mr. Harvey[9] requested me to inform you of what I knew respecting a certain John Baker who has petetioned [*sic*] Congress for a pension— Altho' I did not beleive it would do any good I promised and now do it— In the Winter 1813 & 14 I transacted the business of the Qr. Mr. Dept. in this place and knew said Baker well— he was then a soldier in the regular service and remained here during that Winter or the greater part of it— He was remarkable for his sober and orderly conduct and was one of those entrusted with the hospital— he left here with the troops in the spring 1814 I am pretty certain and beleive did not return until after the peace— he has almost constantly resided in this place ever since— He stil [*sic*] continues to be a sober and orderly man; but has been so much afflicted with complaints in his head and neck &c that he is unable to do much; but what little he can he does—[10]

We are all well— Wishing you good health and Success in your views— Respectfully Yr. obt. Servt ROBT. SCOTT

ALS. DLC-HC (DNA, M212, R1).

1 The annual message, delivered December 2, 1823, which included the basic pronouncement of the Monroe Doctrine.

2 There had been two suits for breach of contract, instituted in May, 1810, by James Morrison against John Beach, a shipper, possibly of Natchez. Both cases had been dismissed after out-of-court agreements—the first, at the November Term, 1814, a personal suit brought by Morrison and John W. Hunt, related to a cargo of yarns; the second, at the May Term, 1817, with Morrison acting as Navy Agent, concerned a shipment of powder. U. S. Circuit Court, Seventh Circuit, District of Kentucky, Order Book B, 306, 387; C, 49; D, 9; E, 87.

3 No reference found.

4 Morrison had owned 300 acres, part of a military survey, on the Ohio River, including the town of Carthage, in Campbell County, Kentucky. Ball has not been identified.

5 Not identified.

6 Nathaniel Cox.

7 Clay had placed some of his livestock on Morrison's "Carlisle Farm," adjoining "Ashland."

8 Francis Hawkins.

9 Possibly Joseph H. Hervey.

10 In 1813 Baker had enlisted from Madison County, Kentucky, as a private in the 17th United States Infantry. As a result of exposure and injuries suffered during military service, he had a neck paralysis and had lost the use of his right arm. He was placed on the pension rolls in 1830.

From Samuel L. Southard

Sir Navy Depmt 16th Decr 1823

I have had the honor to receive your note of yesterdays date, enclosing a letter from Thomas Cromwell Esqr—

I take pleasure in informing you that the young gentleman alluded to in that communication, can go out in the frigate U States, Capt Hull,[1] now bound on a cruise to the Pacific— He will be regularly shipped as a boy, or ordinary Seaman, but instructions will be given to Capt Hull, to give to him such duty as is within the range of his capacity, and will at the same time, associate him with the young Gentlemen on board, should his conduct render such course justifiable—

The necessary instructions are herewith sent, and he can take them with him to Norfolk, and report to Capt Hull—[2]

with great respect I am Sir your ob sv— SAML L. SOUTHARD

Honbl Henry Clay Speaker of the H R

LS. DNA, RG45, Misc. Letters Received, 1823, vol. 7.

1 Isaac Hull.

2 Southard to Campbell, December 16, 1823 (LS. DNA, RG45, Misc. Letters Received, 1823, vol. 7). The young man was not a willing participant in this arrangement. In a

letter of protest to Commodore Hull, dated December 26, 1823, Campbell stated that he had handed the letter to Hull with the understanding that it was merely a message to be delivered from Cromwell, whereupon he had been detained by force—the latter step also having been prearranged by Cromwell, in accordance with a note to Hull dated December 24. Campbell concluded: "Mr. Clay never could have done this if he knew I was not acquainted with his undertaking Mr. Southard the Gentleman who it appears has interested himself through Mr. Clay for Mr. Cromwell I had no knowledge of; neither were either of the Gentleman [*sic*] aware that this transaction was Sacrafiseing [*sic*] my happiness." *Ibid.*

To Amos Kendall

Washington, 17th Dec. [1823]

Dear Sir: Several inquiries have been made about your pamphlet on the Fisheries,[1] by members of Congress, and I have promised to request a copy to be sent to Mr. David Sloane, of the Ohio Senate, at Columbus; another to the Hon. Henry R. Storrs, and another to the Hon. John Sloane, here. Will you be good enough to have them forwarded?

There is an effort making to get up a Caucus. I doubt its success. Mr. Adams is weaker to the North than I supposed him to be; if one is to judge from what he hears at this place. My prospects are very good. Yours with great esteem, H. CLAY.

Frankfort *Argus of Western America,* July 9, 1828. Published also in Washington *United States Telegraph-Extra,* I (July 26, 1828), 318.

1 See above, Clay to Russell, April 19, 1823, note.

From S[amuel] L. S[outhard]

Hon. Henry Clay, In Congress. Navy Dep'mt. 17. Dec. 1823.

Sir,

In reply to your letter of this date,[1] I inform you that no appointments of Midshipmen can be given at present. The claims of Mr. Loofborough[2] shall be duly regarded when further appointments are necessary. I am, respectfully, &c. S.L.S.

Copy. DNA, RG45, Letters to Members of Congress, 1820-1826, p. 88.

1 Not found.

2 Probably Preston S. Loughborough, of Frankfort, Kentucky, who by the 1840's became a prominent lawyer, serving as United States Attorney for Kentucky and publishing *A Digest of the Statute Laws of Kentucky . . . Passed since 1834* (Frankfort, 1842).

Legislative Act Providing Payment for Services

[December 18, 1823]

WHEREAS Henry Clay and John Rowan, Esq's. were, at the last session of this General Assembly, appointed counsel to represent this state before the board of commissioners which was expected to be organized at the City of Washington in January last, in conformity to the convention, which was concluded and signed between the state of Virginia and the state of Kentucky on the fifth day of June, one thousand eight hundred and twenty-two; and the said counsel having attended at Washington City in discharge of said duty, and having also appeared before the Supreme Court of the United States, in defence of our occupying claimant laws;

Be it therefore enacted by the General Assembly of the Commonwealth of Kentucky, That the said Clay and Rowan shall respectively retain out of the monies in their hands advanced to them by the state,[1] the sum of one thousand dollars, in full for their services. The balance in their hands, after deducting seven hundred and forty-four dollars, paid Jacob Burnett,[2] is to be paid by them to the Treasurer; for which they are to take the said Treasurer's receipt, and lodge the same with the Auditor of public accounts.

Ky. Gen. Assy., *Acts, 1823-1824,* pp. 344-45. See above, Convention, June 5, 1822; Clay to Leigh, November 18, 1822; Report, November 4, 1823.

[1] By an act approved December 7, 1822, the Kentucky General Assembly had directed the State Treasurer to pay over to Clay and Rowan the sum of $6,000 "in specie or United States paper," from which they were to compensate the Commissioners representing Kentucky under the Convention with Virginia and to cover "such contingent expenses as may be found necessary, in conducting said mission." Ky. Gen. Assy., *Acts, 1822,* pp. 152-53.

[2] See above, Receipt, February 27, 1823.

To Thomas Cromwell

Dr Sir 19h. Decr. 23

I transmit to you inclosed the result of my application to the Secy of the Navy in behalf of your friend.[1] I should be glad if the situation which he has the power of accepting would produce the wished for reformation. Yr ob Servt. H. CLAY—

ALS. DNA, RG45, Misc. Letters Received, 1823, vol. 7. Addressed: "Thomas Cromwell Esqr. late of Pittsburg. Baltimore."

[1] See above, Southard to Clay, December 16, 1823.

To Josephus B. Stuart

Dr Sir Washington 19h. Decr. 1823.

I received your favor of the 8h. instant from Albany as I did that to which it refers,[1] which came to hand just as I was about taking my departure from home for this City. I am greatly indebted to you for both communications. On the subject to which they relate I have the satisfaction to say to you that Caucus or no Caucus, my friends believe, as I do myself, that my prospect of success is better than that of either of the other Candidates. There is a considerable effort making to get up a Caucus here, but it is thought that it will not succeed, unless a small minority of the Republicans should determine to hold one, which is not very likely. If there be one, my friends would carry into it as great a positive weight, if not greater than that of either of the other gentlemen. And there is a much stronger disposition on the part of the friends of all of the other candidates to come to me than to go to either of them. If the election devolve on the House not a doubt is entertained that the probabilities there are strongly with me. On the first ballot it is likely that I should receive the vote of not less than eleven States.

New York continues to be uncertain as to its preference. If that State thought proper to declare for me there would be a popular election of me by not less than two thirds of the Union; and it cannot be said of any other Candidate for whom she might declare that his election would be even certain by a bare majority. Considering the similarity of interests, the coincidence in views of national policy, and the amicable dispositions which reciprocally exist between the West and New York, I cannot but think that this great state will yet see it conformable to her soundest policy to unite in a choice with the West. On the recent election of Speaker I was honored by almost an undivided vote of the delegation.

We are told here that Mr Clinton has under consideration the propriety of his coming out. Is it possible that he can exhibit such a want of knowledge of the character of the people of this Country as would be implied by his countenancing an exertion made at this late period for him? Had New York been united in his behalf two years ago, there would have been much probability of his election, but her decision now for him would have no such effect. He is most egregiously deceived if he counts upon Ohio. That State is as much determined to support me as Kentucky is. And the little exertions making for him at Steubenville & at Cincinnati serve only to expose his cause there to ridicule.[2] They no more manifest a determination on the part of Ohio to support him than a similar demonstration, at Louisville, last spring, for Genl Jackson,[3] would indicate that Kentucky will support the Genl. Tennessee, by the bye, is just as decided to bestow its suffrage, in the second instance, on me as it is in the first on Genl. Jackson— The delegation here, I understand, is unanimous, at least with but one exception, in that purpose.

I adhere to my purpose of spending no money on printers for two reasons, one of which is that I think it wrong, and the other is that I have none to spare to such an object—

I write you in confidence and remain Respectfully Your's

Dr. Stuart. H. CLAY

ALS. NcD. [1] Neither letter has been found.

[2] A meeting in Steubenville on December 2 had adopted resolutions recommending DeWitt Clinton for President and Andrew Jackson for Vice President. The same resolutions had been adopted two weeks later by a large crowd assembled at the Baptist Church in Cincinnati. Stevens, *Early Jackson Party in Ohio*, 74-76.

[3] At a meeting, called by friends of Andrew Jackson, at Louisville in April, 1823, a resolution had been offered favoring Jackson for the Presidency. James D. Breckenridge had thereupon proposed a substitute resolution expressing the opinion that it was inexpedient at that time to nominate Jackson or anyone else "as a fit person for the next President of the United States." Breckenridge's motion had been defeated by a small margin (170 to 164), and the meeting had adjourned. Lexington *Kentucky Reporter*, May 5, 1823.

To Francis T. Brooke

Washington Dec. 20, 1823

My Dear Sir: A friend informs me that, at Richmond, my arrangement of the committees of the house of representatives has been the subject of some animadversion, in consequence of Mr. Barbour, late speaker, not being at the head of any committee. The truth is, that it was my intention to have appointed him chairman of one of the most prominent committees of the house; but he entreated me not to put him at the head of any committee, nor on any committee, which might require much of his time, as he wished to employ it exclusively in study.[1] I should certainly not offer, even to a friend, any explanation of my official conduct, in such a matter, if it were not to prevent misconception of my motives in respect to a gentleman between whom & myself unfortunately some competition existed. I am sure if he were apprized (he is now absent from Washington) of the erroneous impression existing at Richmond, he would himself hasten to correct it. I have a full share of human frailties; but a want of consideration for a competitor, in relation to any object, does not, if I know myself, happen to be one of them.

Did you get a *lengthy* letter that I wrote you in august or September last?[2] With great regard I am faithfully Yours, H. CLAY:

The Honble F. Brooke &c &c &c
(Richmond Va.)

Copy. DLC-TJC (DNA, M212, R12). Published in Colton (ed.), *Private Correspondence of Henry Clay*, 84-85.

[1] See above, Barbour to Clay, December 4, 1823.

[2] See above, August 28, 1823.

From William B. Rochester

Hon. H. Clay Bath Steuben County N. Y. Dec 20 1823

My Dear Sir

Your election as Speaker, considering the Majr[1] and that you were opposed by a professed friend of Mr. Crawford,[2] has had the effect of making the few friends of the last named Gentl whom I have since conversed with, admit that he is not so strong a man throughout the Union as they had previously supposed— you were right in taking it, had you declined, you would have been charged with chaffering, indeed Rufus King's paper in N. York City has already in substance charged you with having graduated some of the first of your official acts (ex. gr. appts of Committees) with a view to serve private views— That Editor (Verplanck)[3] is a sad fellow, for it is only about a twelve month since he avowed to me his preference of you and ever since he has been, tôtis viribus, for Adams!

The hollow apology which he made to me, was your publication disavowing any co-operation with Mr. Russell in his affair with Mr. Adams.[4]

In answer to the inquiry in your favor of the 6h. inst.,[5] whether I correspond with Mr. V. Buren I reply affirmatively, tho' I have not as yet heard directly from him since his arrival at Washington

I have just finished a hasty letter to him, which lies before me & shall be forwarded by the same mail which takes this

In it I submit to him a variety of propositions in hæc verba, viz:
"1st. That the choice of electors in N. Y. will be given to the people"
"2d. That Mr. Clinton will be a candidate"
"3d That, that whether he be or not, Mr. Crawford cannot (owing to his location) get the vote of this State by a popular ticket"
"4th. That by such ticket Mr. Clinton will probably succeed in this State"
"5. That in such event, the choice must devolve upon the H. of Rep."
"6. That Clinton calculates on such event"
"7. That in such event, Mr Clay's chance will be the best"
"8. That Mr. Clay or Mr Adams might be brought out in this State against Mr. Clinton with a better prospect of success than either Mr. Cr. Genl. J. or Mr. Calhoun—but that the chance of the first named Gentl. is by far the best"

"The result of this Speculation, is"

"That N.Y. by supporting Mr. Clay *may* make a democratic President without risquing the question in the H. of Rep. but by taking up Mr Crawford, she jeoperdizes [*sic*] all her influence"—

to this I add in conclusion

"I am aware that you appreciate the talents & principles of Mr. C. very highly or I should not have ventured once more to press his pretensions upon your notice"

I repeat to you that Mr. V. B's preference will be of vast importance to his favourite, in this State, let the choice be made as it may— I have been thus particular in copying what I have written him to enable you to judge from his subsequent carriage how far he allows such views of the question to arrest his attention— he has no reason to beleive that you & I correspond— I am told your health has been poor, and as your duties are doubtless arduous, let me once more beg of you to beleive that I do not write with a view of extracting answers I need hardly say that my letters to you are written for the indulgent eye of friendship only I have not time to transcribe & to correct, but shall occasionally drop you a hasty scroll as the tide moves on— I am Dr Sir Yours Sincerely WILLM. B. ROCHESTER—

(Confidential!)

I have recently recd. from a distinguished and highly gifted individual, *one of our State Senators* (Mr. Sudam,)[6] a reported friend of Mr. Crawford a long letter in which among other things, he says "if the electoral vote is given to the people it will produce one of the most contested elections ever known in this State; Ought not the SENATE to resist their infatuation for the moment &c &c"? requesting an answer and I shall take care to give the proper response— in fact it is little less than treason for any man in this quarter to object to such mode of election— An adherence by the majr. to the present mode will destroy the Rep: party in this State for 10 years to come— You must know that a vast majr. of our lower House are pledged to give to the people the choice of electors—the Senate is of course not so immediately responsible for their acts.

WBR

[Marginal note beside postscript]

Sudam writes me as your friend without indicating his own preference—but I am apt to think that he is in the field for Mr. Crawford

ALS. DLC-HC (DNA, M212, R1). Published in part in Colton (ed.), *Private Correspondence of Henry Clay,* 85-86.

1 Majority.

2 See above, ——— to Clay, April 26, 1822; Acceptance, December 1, 1823, note.

3 Among the young men associated with Charles King in founding and editing the New York *American* was Johnston Verplanck, who had "assumed the direction" of the paper in 1820 but had retired from the editorship in May, 1823. J. Verplanck to Rufus King, February 27, 1820, in Charles R. King (ed.), *The Life and Correspondence of Rufus King . . .* (6 vols.; New York, 1894-1900), VI, 283; Dixon R. Fox, *The Decline of Aristocracy in the Politics of New York* (Columbia University, *Studies in History, Economics and Public Law,* LXXXVI; New York, 1919), 286n.

4 See above, Clay to Gales and Seaton, November 15, 1822.

5 Not found.

6 John Suydam.

To Nicholas Biddle

Sir

Washington 22d. Decr. 1823

I received your favor under date the 14h. inst.[1] in answer to mine of the 6h. I am sorry that the Board thinks it is its duty to decline the additional security which I have offered it for the debt I owe. That debt is large and has been principally cast upon me as an indorser. Throughout all our bad times I have continued to pay the discount at the end of every sixty days and I have even paid several thousand dollars of the principal. I have never before asked any accommodation whatever in respect to it. Had the Bank accepted the notes as a collateral security I should have asked it to incur no costs in the suits which might have been brought upon them, but such as would have been reimbursed. However I acquiesce in its decision.

Mr. Hammond has sent me his argument in the case of the Bank and the State of Ohio. It makes a book of nearly 100 pages.[2] Would the Board or yourself like to peruse it?

I have the honor to be Your obedient Servant H CLAY

Nicholas Biddle Esqr. &c. &c. &c

ALS. KyU. Endorsed: ". . . recd Decr. 26. 1823." [1] Not found.

[2] *State of the Case and Argument for the Appellants, in the Case of the Bank of the United States, versus the Auditor and Treasurer of the State of Ohio, and Others, in the Supreme Court of the United States* (Cincinnati, 1823). See below, Clay to Biddle, February 17, 1824.

To [Samuel] Breck

22d. Decr. 1823.

Mr Clay's respectful Compliments to Mr. Breck, and he regrets extremely that a prior engagement will not allow him the pleasure of accepting Mr Bs. polite invitation to dinner on Xmas day.

AN. PPL-R. Addressed: "The Honble Mr. Breck. Of the H. of R." Samuel Breck, born in Boston, had removed to Philadelphia, where he became prominent as a writer, churchman, opponent of slavery, and politician. He had been a member of the Pennsylvania Senate (1817-1821) and was now (1823-1825) serving his only term in Congress.

To James Harper

Dr Sir Washn. 22d Decr. 1823

If Majr. Tilford and Geo. Trotter Esqr. will give their bond with such security as you approve to pay the amt. of the note assigned me by the B. of K. in three years, the accruing interest to be paid annually, I will give that indulgence. I require security because the time is long and they are both in business which is always more or less precarious. I fix upon a shorter time than in the case of Majr. Parker and Dr. Warfield because the sum is less.

The rest of the notes received from the B. of K, except those of Majr. Parker & Dr Warfield I will thank you to hand to Mr Hawes, and theirs also, if they decline the above proposition, to be sued upon.[1] If the above described bond is given be pleased to take it for me—

Mr Biddle[2] was here for a day or two but I did not see him.

James Harper Esqr. Yr's with high regard H. CLAY

ALS. DLC-HC (DNA, M212, R1). Cf. above, Agreement, November 10, 1823; Assignment, November 18, 1823, note.

[1] In an endorsement on verso, dated January 6, 1824, Richard Hawes, Jr., acknowledges receipt of specified notes, the list corresponding to that above, Agreement, November 10, 1823, except that the notes of Alexander Parker and Walter Warfield are not included.

Suits were brought upon all but the Parker and Warfield notes, in Fayette Circuit Court, under bills of complaint filed January 8, 1824. Those against John Tilford and George Trotter and Son were "Dismissed agreed" in June; that against Thomas Wallace was also dismissed, under an agreement in September, 1824. Fayette Circuit Court, Files 574, 575, 585. The other cases were tried at the September Term, 1824. In Clay *vs.* James Weir and George Robinson the Court ruled in favor of the defendants, they having tendered $1350 in notes of the Bank of Kentucky and its branches in open court and this sum being "deposited in the Branch Bank of the United States at Lexington: subject to the order of the Court or of the Plaintiff. . . ." Fayette Circuit Court, Order Book no. 2, p. 484; *ibid.*, File 581. The suits against Samuel and James Trotter and against Edward C. and Daniel McCarty Payne went to trial by jury, which decided in Clay's favor on the issue of payment, which the defendants claimed to have satisfied in offering the requisite sum in notes of the Bank of Kentucky on the date it was due. Fayette Circuit Court, Order Book no. 2, pp. 484-86; *ibid.*, File 581. The defendants appealed these last decisions, but no further action was reported. The improvement in the exchange rate of the bank bills as a consequence of the burning of the inflated currency (see above, Todd to Clay, May 8, 1823, note) may have resolved the controversy.

[2] Nicholas Biddle.

To Benjamin W. Leigh

My Dear Sir Washington 22d. Decr. 1823.

I thank you for your obliging letter of the 19th. inst.[1] communicating the disposition made, at the late term of your Fed. Court, of the Ejectments for the Henrico land.[2] I do not think that our antagonist can make any thing out of a Chy. suit, should we recover at law. I hope at the next term you will be able to obtain Judgments on the special verdicts.

I am glad to find that you, who know something of us in K. take an interest in our affairs and sympathize with us. The Governor was ill advised in his message.[3] It was the occasion of some warm conversation between us. My late information continues to assure me that nothing extravagant will be done in regard to the General Government. They may possibly send us a memorial here with some intemperate paragraphs;[4] but you know all that is mere expression. The mouth and the pen are happy conductors to let off bad humors. Not that I do not really think that we have much justly to complain of in respect to the fate of our Occupying claimant laws. But then I do not think that we ought to make any Civil war about them.

Ten judges to the Supreme Court are perhaps too many. For myself, I should prefer a system by which the Judges of that Court should be detached from the Circuits; but there is much diversity of opinion on that point. And as mankind is more inclined to adhere to an existing institution than to create a new one, from habit and from indolence, I think it most probable that the present system will be simply extended to the new States.[5] None can deny to them the right, when claimed, at [*sic*] it now is, to be placed on an equal footing with the old states, be that what it may, in respect to the Judiciary

Reciprocating, with great cordiality, the compliments of the Season I remain Faithfully Your's H. CLAY

B. W. Leigh Esqr.

ALS. Nc-Ar, Misc. Papers, Series One, vol. 2 (1789-1830), p. 103.

1 Not found.

2 "Euphraim." Cf. above, Leigh to Clay, February 12, 1823.

3 In his annual message to the legislature, November 4, 1823, Governor John Adair had protested strongly against the decision of the United States Supreme Court in the case, Green *vs.* Biddle (see above, Clay to Brooke, March 9, 1823, note). "I need not be told," said he, "that the General Government is authorised to use physical force to put down insurrection, and enforce the execution of its laws. I know it; but I know too, with equal certainty, that the day when the Government shall be compelled to resort to the bayonet, to compel a state to submit to its law, will not long precede an event of all others most to be deprecated." He hoped that the legislature, on this as on every subject to come before it, would "act with that cool, dispassionate, manly deliberation which will always be found the surest, as well as the shortest road to a correct decision." Ky. H. of Reps., *Journal, 1823-1824,* pp. 13-16.

4 See above, Clay to Brooke, March 9, 1823, note; below, Remarks, May 3, 14, 1824, notes.

5 Proposals to expand the Federal circuit system and to abolish circuit duties for members of the Supreme Court had been under consideration since 1816. On December 10, 1823, Richard M. Johnson in the United States Senate and, on December 24, Francis Johnson in the House of Representatives offered resolutions looking to the establishment of additional judicial districts for the Western Country. On February 23, 1824, "sundry counsellors and attorneys at law, admitted as practitioners in the Court of the United States, for the Seventh Circuit, and Kentucky District," also sought legislation to reorganize and extend the judicial system. These efforts, while coinciding with Kentucky's dissatisfaction with the existing procedure of the Supreme Court (cf. above, Clay to Brooke, March 9, 1823, note), were specifically related to the problem of expanding the Federal judicial system to serve the growing nation. On February 28, Daniel Webster, for the House Committee on Judiciary, offered a bill for general revision and extension of the judicial organization, subdividing the Seventh Circuit and establishing four additional circuits. This measure and a separate bill, reported by Webster for the Judiciary Committee on April 16, dividing Kentucky into two judicial districts, both died in Committee of the Whole. Similar proposals, urged again during succeeding Sessions of Congress, were repeatedly dismissed, largely because of political considerations relating to the increase of presidential appointments. The circuit system was not further extended until 1837, and provision for separation of the circuit duties from those of the Supreme Court was not adopted until 1869. *Annals of Cong.,* 18 Cong., 1 Sess., XLII, 1701-1702; U.S.H. of Reps., *Journal,* 18 Cong., 1 Sess., pp. 92, 254; Warren, *Supreme Court in United States History,* I, 672-84; II, 39-40, 501.

From [William Hendricks]

Dear Sir (Confidential) Corydon 22 Dec. 1823.

I acknowledge the reception of yours of the 10 ultimo & with much pleasure reply agreeably to your wishes & this reply would have been made some time ago but for the pendency of a proposition in the Senate on the subject of congressional caucuses

Your warmest friends would not venture on the proposition of a caucus nomination in your favor. The danger was too great that the result would be unfavorable and do you injury. But a Senator friendly to the prospects of Mr. Adams introduced a resolution against congressional caucuses for the nomination of Presidential candidates concluding with instructions to our Delegation at the city on that subject. This for some time laid on the table during which time the project of amending it [so] as to instruct the Delegation that if they could not prevent a caucus to attend & endeavor to effect your nomination This was attempted & succeeded & but for an additional amendment which no one liked it would so have been reported to the H. Reps. The resolution however with the amendments was withdrawn by the mover. The same resolution was moved the next day & the Senate as if by common consent voted for and against it without amendment. The Senate was equally divided & the Lt. Gov. presiding gave the affirmative casting vote.[1] It was sent to the other House & there laid on the table where it will in all probability continue to lie.[2] It is easy to see that if the proposition as amended had been sent to the H. Reps. & there concurred in that the expression would have been altogether certain in its character & the proposition could not have been charged upon your friends

The result however shewed your strength in the Senate. That body consists of 17. members 11. of whom are friendly to you & there is a division among the other 7. [*sic*] One at least is for Jackson. In the H. Rs. there are 46 members. About 27 or 28 of whom are believed from the safest calculation to be friendly to your election to the Presidency & the rest are divided It is however very certain that if you be not a prominent candidate with such prospects of success as will encourage your friends to take a firm stand for you that Mr. Adams will get the votes of this state. but it is equally certain and so at this time admitted on all sides that if you are a candidate with good or reasonable prospects of success that you will get the votes of Indiana As evidence of this opinion your friends in the Legislature last year wished the state districted afraid that you could not succeed on general ticket Last session the bill on that subject fell and now the electors bill for general ticket has already passed one branch and there is no doubt of its success in the other.[3]

You will perhaps think it strange after this exhibit of your strength in the Legislature that a nomination could not be effected. This however is the case. So strong is the popular sentiment here on the subject of caucuses & against them

I regret not having had it in my power at an earlier day to have given you this line. Sooner I could only have given you opinions much less satisfactory to myself & to you. Your friends in other parts of the Union Should they succeed in making you one of the two prominent candidates (for it is probable there will not be more) may I think repose with much confidence on the aid of Indiana Should any thing further present itself on this subject important for you to know, I will make it the subject of another letter. & in the mean time and whenever convenient should be happy in hearing from you— With the greatest respect your obdt Servt—

AL draft, on verso of letter to which it replies. MoKiT.

1 John H. Thompson, State Senator from Clark and Floyd counties, had introduced his first resolution on December 6, had withdrawn it on December 12, and on December 13 had substituted a statement calling upon the State's Senators and Representatives in Congress to oppose any caucus nomination on the ground "That it is the legitimate and exclusive right of the people of the United States to elect a President and Vice-President without the aid or influence of caucus nominations, and that any attempt to assume or exercise this invaluable privilege, either by Congress or State Legislatures, is travelling beyond the sphere of Legislative authority, and ought to be regarded by a free and enlightened people as anti-republican. . . ." The vote was 8 to 8 before the Lieutenant Governor, Ratcliff Boon, cast the deciding vote. Ind. Sen., *Journal, 1823-1824*, pp. 40, 56, 58-59.

2 Introduced in the Indiana House of Representatives on December 13, the Thompson resolution was scheduled for debate on the following Monday, but no further action was reported. On January 7, however, Ezra Childs, of Washington County, and Thomas Holdsworth Blake each presented similar resolutions. The first was tabled and never acted upon; the second was taken up but on motion of Reuben W. Nelson, of Clark County, was indefinitely postponed by a roll call vote of 36 to 8. Ind. H. of Reps., *Journal, 1823-1824*, pp. 80, 182-83, 186-87.

3 The bill, introduced by William Graham, State Senator for Jackson, Scott, and Bartholomew counties, had passed the Senate after heavy amendment during the session of 1822-1823 but had then been postponed until the next year in the House. During the session of 1823-1824 Senator Graham on December 11 had been defeated in an effort to win approval of a compromise proposal that the State be divided into districts, that the electors be chosen "by general ticket throughout the state; but in such manner, that the person in each district having the highest number of votes, shall be considered an elector. . . ." In the House, John Law, of Knox County, on December 31 proposed that the bill be sent to a select committee with instructions for amendment to provide for district choice of electors. This motion was adopted by a vote of 23 to 22, but the subsequent amendment was then rejected. With minor alteration, to which the Senate agreed, the bill to provide for election under a general ticket was approved and signed by Governor Hendricks on January 10. Ind. Sen., *Journal, 1822-1823*, pp. 56, 101; *1823-1824*, pp. 51, 89, 124; Ind. H. of Reps., *Journal, 1822-1823*, pp. 175-76; *1823-1824*, pp. 172, 224; Lexington *Kentucky Reporter*, February 16, 1824.

To Peter B. Porter

My dear General Washington 24h. D[ecember, 1823]

I duly recd. your favor of the 11h. instant.[1] Should the subject of the compensation to the Boundary Commissioners be brought up I will not fail to give it particular attention.[2] Undoubtedly there should be no difference in respect to it between the British and our Commissioners.

There was a strenuous effort to get up a Caucus made at the commencement of the Session.[3] It is suspended for the present with an intention, it is understood, of renewing it about the middle of January. If a Caucus were generally attended I think if any one obtained a majority I should ultimately, because the friends of *all* the Candidates would sooner unite on me than on any other. No one would get a majority until after repeated ballottings, if at all. In the first instance Mr. Crawford and I would have the greatest and about an equal vote. But a Caucus will not be generally attended. The delegations from Tennessee and Maryland, both of which I should finally get, will not attend. If the election devolve upon the House, as is now most probable, I should receive on the *first* ballot the votes of 11 or 12 states should the three highest be Crawford Adams and myself.

Will Mr. Clinton be brought out? It is affirmed and denied believed and disbelieved here.

I have seen but little of Van Buren. I have met him always civilly when I have seen him. He boards in Geo. Town and I near the Avenue.[4] I shall be glad to hear from you frequently when you are at Albany. I think they are paving the way to refuse in the Senate of your State a popular election of electors.[5]

With the compliments of the season to Mrs. Porter and yourself I remain faithfully Your friend H. CLAY

Genl. P. B. Porter

ALS. NBuHi. Dated erroneously in endorsement by Porter on verso: "Decr. 24. 1824."
1 Not found. 2 No reference found.
3 See above, Clay to Porter, December 11, 1823.
4 See above, Barbour to Clay, December 4, 1823.
5 Cf. above, Woods to Clay, August 27, 1823, note.

To Samuel L. Southard

Washn. 24h. Decr. [1823]

Geo. Norton, a Constituent of mine, is desirous to contract with the Navy department for the supply for its use of manufactured tobacco. Will you have the goodness to inform me if it wants that article and in what way it would contract for it?

With great respect Yr. ob. Servant H. CLAY

Honble Mr. Southard

ANS. DNA, RG45, Misc. Letters Received, 1823, vol. 7, p. 98. Endorsed on verso: "24 Dec: 1823. . . ." A few years earlier Norton had become a tobacconist in Lexington.

From S[amuel] L. S[outhard]

Hon. Henry Clay, In Congress. Navy Dep'mt. 26. Dec. 1823.

Sir, In reply to your note of the 24th. inst. I have the honor to enclose herewith a letter from the Commissioners of the Navy, upon the subject.[1] I am, respectfully, &c. S.L.S.

Copy. DNA, RG45, Letters to Members of Congress, 1820-1826, p. 95.

1 John Rodgers to Southard, December 24, 1823 (Copy, DNA, RG45, Navy Comrs., Letters to Secretary of the Navy, 1822-1826, p. 80), in which the Commissioners of the Navy cite their "particularly unfortunate" experience in previous contracts "with Mr. Norton and other Gentlemen residing in the Western States," because of the rapid deterioration of tobacco during shipment in warm climates, unless it had previously undergone a process called "Sweating." Norton had been awarded a contract the previous spring. Rodgers to Norton, April 23, 1823 (Copy, DNA, RG45, Navy Comrs., Misc. Letters Sent, III, 151).

From G[eorge] G[raham]

Hon Henry Clay Spr. of the H. of Reps 30th December 1823

Sir A. Patent shall issue for the Receiver Receipt dat [*sic*]: St. Louis 15th ulto received in your note of yesterday as soon as the returns from that office exhibiting the Transactions for the last month are received, which will be about the middle of the ensuing month Your &C G. G.

Copy. DNA, RG49, Letter Books, 1822-1824, Misc. Letters Sent, vol. 12, p. 388. See above, Scott to Clay, December 4, 1823.

From Robert Scott

Dr. Sir, Lexington, 30th. Decr 1823.

Last mail brought to hand your favor of 17th Currt.[1] I rejoice at the prospect of your regaining good health— Be careful of your self and you will probably succeed— Agreeable to your request I called on Mrs. Clay, and mentioned what you requested— She seems to think she will not require any aid except such as your own funds from collections &c. will afford her—I have collected for you the following sums—say of Deverin 74$50— Payne 50$— & of Winn 100$ and have recd. of Gratz & Bruce 1022$50—[2] of these I have pd. Mrs. Clay 230$—and discharged your check to the estate[3] of 1000$— I have hired Shadrach to Winn for 150$ Curry Jonathan is not yet hired—

Thro' Mr. Pindell,[4] I learn that Mr Bibb[5] would be glad to have the original check given Buford[6] for 4000$. on L. B. Bank[7] on 4 Novr. 1812, being the advance made him on his draft on the Receiver of public monies Chilicothe [*sic*]— That check as well as the one on Bank of Ky. for 10,000$[8] Uncle Morrison had with him— Please mention this to Mr Hagner—[9]

Enclosed is a receipt given by a Mr. Nesbit of Maryland for some papers relating to a claim against a certain L. Owings— From the length of time which has intervened since its date I suppose nothing will be obtained—but if you find it convenient you will ascertain—[10]

Our Legislature are doing all the evil they can— A Bill has passed the lower house repealing all execution laws except such as the

Judges have determined unconstitutional!!!— It is said some Bill in relation to the Judges has passed the lower House also I do not know enough of it to say what it is—but of the same character as the other— Our only hope of safety is in the Senate and that is but slight—[11] Should they give way, which is much feared, the Commth will be thrown into confusion and ruin—

Your family and domestic affairs are all doing well I beleive [*sic*]— The family here are also well, Respectfully Yr. Obt. Servt.

The Honble H. Clay— ROBT. SCOTT

ALS. DLC-TJC (DNA, M212, R12). [1] Not found.

[2] Cf. above, Agreement with Gratz and Bruce, June 26, 1823; Memorandum, November 10, 1823; Clay to Paynes, November 20, 1823.

[3] Of James Morrison. The check has not been found.

[4] Thomas H. Pindell. [5] George M. Bibb. [6] Thomas Buford.

[7] Lexington Branch, Bank of Kentucky.

[8] See above, Motion on Report, February 21, 1821, note.

[9] Peter Hagner. [10] Cf. above, I, 650, 654. No suit found.

[11] An act to repeal all laws which authorized issuance of executions in any way contrary to the act to abolish imprisonment for debt, approved December 17, 1821, or that "to amend an act to regulate endorsements on executions," approved December 7, 1822, had been passed by the Kentucky House of Representatives on December 27, 1823, and by the Senate on December 30. Ky. H. of Reps., *Journal, 1823-1824,* p. 351; Ky. Sen., *Journal, 1823-1824,* pp. 245, 256-57; Ky. Gen. Assy., *Acts, 1823-1824,* pp. 390-91. The amendatory act relating to endorsements embodied the replevy principle (see above, II, 904n), which had been declared unconstitutional, as a violation of contract, by the Kentucky Court of Appeals in the cases of Blair and Others *vs.* Williams (cf. above, Clay to Leigh, October 29, 1822, note), decided October 8, 1823, and Lapsley *vs.* Brashears and Barr *e Converso,* October 11, 1823. 14 *Ky. Reports* (4 Littell) 34-116.

The dissatisfaction of Kentucky legislators with the role of the judiciary exemplified in the above decisions, as well as in the Green-Biddle decision of the United States Supreme Court (above, Clay to Brooke, March 9, 1823, note; Clay to Leigh, December 22, 1823, note), was expressed in several proposals before the General Assembly at this Session, notably in a lengthy preamble and resolutions, adopted by both houses and already approved on December 29, which denounced the above-mentioned decisions of both the Court of Appeals and the Supreme Court and called for preparation of a remonstrance presenting its views to Congress; in the subsequent remonstrance directed specifically against the Supreme Court decision; and in a measure passed by the State House of Representatives, but already defeated in the Senate, which would have provided for a convention to revise the State constitution so as to limit the terms of State judges. The Washington *Daily National Intelligencer,* January 19, 1824, reported that a law had "passed, or is about to pass," reducing the compensation of judges of the Court of Appeals to 25 cents a year. This proposal had not been formally introduced in the House, and on January 28 the *Intelligencer* described the scheme as "probably, from the beginning, a piece of badinage merely."

Receipt from Robert Scott

[December 30, 1823]

Recd. the 30 Decr. 1823 of Henry Clay Executor of James Morrison decd. by my brother through Nathaniel Cox of New Orleans, the sum of Four thousand four hundred and twenty three dollars and ninety five Cents on account of the legacy of Fifteen thousand dollars bequeathed to me by the Will of the said James Morrison Duplicate

$4423„95 ROBT. SCOTT

ADS, "Duplicate." DLC-TJC (DNA, M212, R15). Cf. above, Receipt, October 18, 1823.

From Nicholas Biddle

Sir, Bank of the United States. Decr. 31. 1823

During the recent visit of Col. Johnson to Phila,[1] he made certain propositions with regard to the debts of himself & his connexions which have led to a [par]ticular examination of the origin history & present state of his & their transactions with the Bank. The general impression is I think favorable, but before coming to any final determination it will be necessary to institute certain enquiries the result of which must decide the course to be pursued by the Board. In the meantime however there is one branch of the subject on which they are prepared to decide immediately. Our impression is, that the arrangement for the transfer of property made under your superintendence, with whatever loss it may be attended, was on the whole the best which under existing circumstances, could have been made and we are therefore willing to close the transaction rather than suffer it to remain indefinitely open. With this view we have acquiesced in the proposal of Col. Johnson for time to make up the difference in value between the house conveyed & that intended to be conveyed, & in order to set the seal on what has been already done without leaving it open until this comparatively small matter shall be adjusted, it was determined to take Col Johnson's agreement to make up this difference hereafter, & then close the whole arrangement. Col Johnson also represented that the house in Georgetown had been finished, a fact wh[ich] if not within your own knowledge, you could it was pr[es]umed readily ascertain. With these impressions the Bo[ard] have adopted the following resolution.

"Resolved That if Mr Clay is satisfied that the hous[e in] Georgetown which was to be finished is actually finish[ed] according to the understanding of the agreement; and if R[.] M. Johnson will give his obligation that within twelve mon[ths] from this date, he will convey to the Bank real estate equ[al] in value to the difference between the house in Burling[ton] intended to be conveyed & that actually conveyed—which difference is to be ascertained by valuation in such man[ner] as Mr Clay may direct, then Mr Clay is hereby authorized [to] close definitively the arrangement made by him with R. M. Johnson, for the discharge of a certain amount of his debt with property by virtue of the resolution of this [*sic*] passed Octr. 26. 1821."[2]

The agency assigned to yourself by this resolution you will have the goodness to execute whenever Col. Johnson is prepared. On the general & more important concerns of that gentleman & his connexions I propose to take an early opportunity of writing [to] you. In the mean time, I remain Very respy yrs N BIDDLE Pres

Honble Henry Clay Washington

ALS. DLC-HC (DNA, M212, R1). Margin ragged.
1 See above, Clay to Biddle, September 4, 1823.
2 Cf. above, Clay to Cheves, October 3, December 3, 1821.

To Nicholas Biddle

Sir Washington 3d. Jan. 1823 [*i.e.*, 1824].

I have duly received your letter of the 31st. Decr. in relation to the business of Col. R. M. Johnson, or rather that part of it the arrangement of which was specially confided to my care. The Board will be pleased to bear in mind that, after we had made some progress in the valuation of property tendered by Col. Johnson, in execution of his original proposition, he alleged his inability to comply with it, and proposed to the Bank to mortgage or to transfer, in full satisfaction of the debts intended to be arranged, certain pieces of property which he particularized, and on which he set his *own* values. The Bank accepted the latter alternative; and doubtless the loss which it will sustain on this property will be very great. With respect to that part of it which was valued by the late Col. Morrison, Mr. Pope and Mr. Higgins,[1] I attended in person and viewed every piece of property, combating the arguments of Col. Johnson which had for their object a high valuation, and urging those which occurred to me as tending to shew the propriety of applying a lower standard. The valuation, upon the whole was, at the time, I thought fair. Property has since fallen, and it would not now command the estimated value; but I do not think the Bank will sustain on this part of the property received as much loss as the office at Lexington supposes. Mr. Scott,[2] the Land agent of the Bank, is a very faithful and intelligent servant of the institution, but in his estimates of real estate he is always disposed to apply the lowest standard. And you will readily conceive how men perfectly honest, and intelligent may, by a different process of reasoning, arrive at very variant results on a subject which admits of so little precision as that of the value of real estate, at a period of general stagnation.

Notwithstanding the losses which the Bank will experience in the property thus received from Col. Johnson I have ever believed that it will finally realize more than it would have done, if, rejecting all compromise, it had depended exclusively on coercion. On this point also I differ in opinion with the office at Lexington. They think that more might probably have been forced out of the persons jointly responsible with Col. Johnson. On the contrary I conceive that nothing would have been obtained in all probability from any of the parties except Mr. Warren and Genl. Payne.[3] Some of the others have some property but they were embarrassed and are yet so. Had they been pushed they would have prefered other Creditors or made such disposition, in other respects, of their property that it could not be reached.

With regard to Col. Johnson and his brothers[4] I have believed for several years that they are hopelessly insolvent. It is well known that they have nothing which can be reached by execution. They retain possession of considerable property yet but it is by the favor of creditors who have incumbrances upon it, and who being friendly disposed towards them allow them a temporary occupation and use of it. There are large judgments against them, and heavy suits yet pending; among others one from the Balto. office of the Bank, which I hope to try in May, for upwards of $100.000. With respect to the nature of this demand I am not yet fully instructed by that office.[5] But even if the Mess. Johnsons should as I understand they expect, defeat the recovery of a Judgment against them, there are other heavy demands on the part of your bank and others, which are indisputable, against them to an amount which I do not see how it is possible they can ever discharge.

Entertaining these views, I concur with you entirely in thinking that the arrangement, little as it is likely to be productive, the execution of which was refered to me, upon the whole, was eligible. In respect to the two points to which your letter specially relates I have to say 1st. As to the unfinished house in Geo. Town. I understood before I left home that Mr. Scott took exception to the quality of the Locks, the quality & color of some of the painting, and some other small particulars, the aggregate amount of all of which was not considerable. I advised, as there was danger of injury to the house by its being left unoccupied, that possession of it should be taken and that it should be rented out, making a bill of what was necessary to be done to complete it according to Col. Johnson's contract. That I believe has been done. 2dly. As to the two houses in Burlington, I also directed Mr. Scott to personally examine and ascertain the difference in their values, which he had done before my departure. I do not recollect the difference in value, but I believe it was about $1200.

Col. Johnson proposes to give me his bond, without security, to make up the deficiences [*sic*] in the Geo Town house, and to secure the difference in value between the two houses in Burlington. I do not understand from the resolution, of which you have transmitted me a copy, that I am to take security from him. He has left with me a bond to that effect, but I shall not receive it without your instructions. If the bond should be received, after what I have said, it is scarcely worth observing that the reliance for its fulfillment must be upon the honor of Col. Johnson, and not upon our ability to enforce it by law. If the Board be desirous of immediately closing this affair, and will be content with the bond (of which he has sent you a Copy) and such a reliance as I have suggested, you will have the goodness to give me orders accordingly. If you prefer a more precise statement of the expence of finishing the Geo. Town house, according to contract, and of the difference in the values of the two Burlington houses, I expect I shall be able in about a month to furnish it from home. Or if you would rather that this business should abide my return home, that course can be taken.

There will still remain another small matter to give the finishing hand to the above arrangement. There are ten or a dozen suits on the docket of the Fed. Court at Frankfort for the debts comprehended in this arrangement against the parties bound. These suits have been continued from term to term, waiting its execution. Their costs may amount to some where about $250 or $300. The arrangement does not expressly provide who is to pay these costs. I have heretofore told Col. Johnson that I should expect him to do it. He rather resented the demand, and thought that the suits should be dismissed, each party paying his own Costs. I should be glad if you would signify the pleasure of the Board on this point.

I have the honor to be Yr. ob. Servant H. CLAY

N. Biddle Esqr &c &c &c

ALS. PHi-Etting Collection. Endorsed: "recd Jany. 7. 1824."

1 See above, Clay to Cheves, October 3, 1821.

2 Matthew T. Scott.

3 Probably William Warren; John Payne.

4 Cf. above II, 605; Clay to Cheves, June 11, 1821, note. Benjamin Johnson, another brother, was also under suit on a claim of the Bank of the United States. U. S. Circuit Court, Seventh Circuit, District of Kentucky, Order Book K, 216.

5 No suit found.

To Charles Hammond

Dr Sir Washn. 3d. Jan. 1824.

I recd. the letter which you did me the favor to write me by Mr. Senator Brown,[1] and I have also recd. your printed argument in the case of the Bank and Osborne &c.[2] for which be pleased to accept my thanks.

The business of Congress moves on but slowly, according to usage. It is in a course of preparation in the Committees. We shall have on monday next a report probably from that on manufactures.[3] What engrosses most of the conversation in the circles is the Presidential Election. The Cause of a Caucus is on the decline, and I do not think there will be one, unless in a state of despair the friends of Mr. Crawford determine to hold one of a minority of the republicans. I believe I should have nothing to fear from a Caucus composed of all Congress or of all the republican members, to the exclusion of Federalists. A different result might happen if the Caucus should be attended by *all* Mr. Crawford's friends, with but a partial attendance of the friends of other Candidates. If there be no Caucus, or being one, if its recommendation shall not be respected, the election will go into the H. of R. and there it is generally conceded mine is the best prospect of success. In that view of the subject the great aim of my friends will be to secure my being one of the three highest. I do not think there is much doubt of that, although it is *possible* it may so turn out that I shall not be one of them. If Ohio allow herself to be distracted by rumors of Mr. Clinton becoming a Candidate; if she bestow her suffrages on him, it might happen that neither Mr. Clinton nor me would be brought into the House. For even, if at this late day, his friends should be so deluded as to bring him out (which is not yet decided) it is far from certain, it is not probable, that he will get the vote of his own state. Ohio, by taking a firm decided and unequivocal stand, may command a weight in the Union which would be felt for a long time. All the great States are much divided, so much so as to have but little collateral influence. If therefore your's should be united and pursue steadily & distinctly its object may it not acquire an influence, from that circumstance superior, to any of them?

All my information recd. at this place tends to assure me in regard to N. York 1st. that there will be a popular electoral ticket. 2dly. that, in that event, Mr. Crawford cannot obtain the suffrage of that State; and that in all probability I shall: & 3dly. that, if the Legislature retain the power of choosing Electors, it is quite uncertain that the Secretary of the Treasury will obtain their vote.

The Legislature of Va. meets on monday next in Caucus to recommend Mr. Crawford and an electoral ticket favorable to him.[4] Will not your's also recommend a ticket?[5]

With the Compliments of the Season I remain Faithfully Your's

H. CLAY

Charles Hammond Esqr.

ALS. InU. [1] Ethan A. Brown. The letter has not been found.

[2] See above, Clay to Biddle, December 22, 1823.

[3] The report was made on Friday, January 9, when John Tod, of Pennsylvania, Chairman of the Committee, reported a bill to amend the tariff legislation.

[4] Crawford was not nominated in Virginia on Monday, January 5. Presented as an issue of the expediency of adoption of such a resolution by the House of Delegates in its legislative capacity, the proposal was defeated by a vote of 77 to 76. That evening a large proportion of the Republican members of the Assembly met and adopted resolutions urging that a nomination be made by a caucus of the Republican members of Congress and that the State's Republican congressional members endeavor

to procure such a nomination. Washington *Daily National Intelligencer*, January 6, 9, 1824. Finally, on February 21, a caucus comprising 163 of the 234 members of the Virginia legislature met and voted on a nominee: for Crawford, 139; Adams, 7; Jackson, 6; Clay 5; Nathaniel Macon, 4. Albert Gallatin was nominated for the Vice-Presidency. In a second caucus, on February 25, an electoral ticket pledged to support of Crawford and Gallatin was named. *Niles' Weekly Register*, XXV (February 28, 1824), 408: XXVI (March 6, 1824), 5.

5 See below, Clay to Porter, April 26, 1824.

To Joel R. Poinsett

Monday morning [*ca.* January 5, 1824]

Mr. Clay's Compliments to Mr. Poinsett, and he returns to him his Manuscripts, for the opportunity of perusing which he is much obliged. Mr. C. hopes that Mr. P. intends publishing these M.S. which, besides most of the information contained in Walton's book,[1] much better detailed and in a smaller compass, comprehends other interesting topics not noticed by the Author of that work.[2]

AN. NN-Ford Collection. Addressed: "Mr. Poinsett at Mrs. Wilsons." Mrs. Wilson has not been identified.

1 Probably William Walton, *An Exposé on the Dissentions of Spanish America . . . Intended as a Means to Induce the Mediatory Interference of Great Britain, in Order to Put an End to a Destructive Civil War and to Establish Permanent Quiet and Prosperity, on a Basis Consistent with the Dignity of Spain, and the Interests of the World . . .* (London, 1814), which had devoted special attention to Mexico.

2 Poinsett's work was published anonymously at Philadelphia, around midyear in 1824, as *Notes on Mexico, Made in the Autumn of 1822, Accompanied by a Historical Sketch of the Revolution, and Translations of Official Reports on the Present State of that Country . . . By a Citizen of the United States.*

Receipt from John H. Morton

Transylvania University, January 5th 1824.

John H. Morton, Treasurer of Transylvania University, acknowledges receipt of $20.25 from Henry Clay "for Tuition in C P. [College Preparatory] also 25 cents fine." DS (partially printed). DLC-TJC (DNA, M212, R16). Payment was probably for Henry Clay, Jr. Morton had succeeded Joshua Humphreys as Treasurer of Transylvania University late in 1823.

From Robert Scott

The Honble H. Clay,
Dr. Sir, Lexington 5 Jany. 1824.

The last of your favors recd. is that of 17th. Ulto.[1] the rect. of which I acknowledged on the 30th. I have received a copy of the check I requested, as certified by the Clerk of the Bank. I am not certain, but believe Colo. Morrison had with him the original check and Acct. with the Bank of Ky.—Neither were amongst his papers brought back last summer—Probably James Montgomery may know some thing of them—Have the goodness to make the enquiry—

Herewith are your Accounts with Colo. Morrisons estate from 8th. Novr. down to 31st. December Ulto. inclusive[2]

Doctr. Pindell[3] enquired if I had credited the Amt of their Medicinal Acct on his note due the estate to which I replied in the negative as is the fact—Something was said about this debt and Acct. last fall, but do not recollect precisely what—If you wish the credit entered, direct it and it will be done immediately—tho' I know it was not Colo. Ms intention to receive any other than specie for this debt as in such it was advanced more than 4 Ys since and saved to the Doctr. property worth much more—However your instructions are quite sufficient for me and are so considered—I have hired out Shadrach for 150$ and Jonathan for 100$ Curry.—Of Colo. Whaley I have been unable to get any thing and have issued a distress Warrant against him—The amt due by Wilkins McIlvain & Co & S. Cooper, I will get in a day or two and hand it to Mrs. Clay—

From our News Papers you will see the destructive course our Legislature are pursuing—From the obstructions thrown by them in the collection of debts I really begin to fear the estate will fall far short of what it provided on paper—

The Season with us has been uncommonly mild and wet—Very little freezing and none severe—

Mrs Morrison requested me to mention to you, that if you hear of a good plain Cook for sale, of 30 to 40 Yrs. of age—of good character, constitution and health, she would thank you to buy her—as old Rachel, her present one is very desirous to be sold to her husband—The cook desired must have no children with her—nor likely ever to have any—

Your family and domestic affairs are I beleive [*sic*] all well—Mrs. Morrison & family are well—

Very respectfully Yr. Obt. Servt. ROBT. SCOTT

ALS. DLC-TJC (DNA, M212, R12). 1 Not found.
2 Private account not found. For the executor's accounts, see below, *ca.* June 8, 1824.
3 Richard Pindell, whose note to the Morrison estate, dated May 26, 1819, amounted to $500.

To Margaret White

Washington 6h. Jan. 1824

I this day received your letter of the 3d. instant[1] inclosing your petition to Congress with an accompanying document inclosed. I shall take great pleasure in presenting it to the House of Representatives on monday next, now the earliest day that it can be offered.[2] It certainly makes a very strong appeal to the liberality; if not to the justice of Government; and I shall be extremely glad if the hopes which you indulge about it should be realized.

I am, with great respect, Your obedient Servant H. CLAY

Margaret White.

ALS. Owned by William Parlin Lillard, New York, New York. Margaret Ellis White was the widow of Anthony Walton White, a native of New Brunswick, New Jersey, a colonel of cavalry during the Revolutionary War, brigadier general of cavalry in the expedition against the Whisky Rebels in 1794, and brigadier general of the United States Army from 1798 to his retirement from military service two years later. On July 4, 1780, White, having been placed in command of cavalry in the South, had raised on private loan $150,000, with which to procure necessary supplies for his regiment. Although he had begun petitioning Congress for reimbursement as early as 1788, this sum remained unpaid, as did an earlier loan of $7,000 for which certificates had been issued to him by the loan office in South Carolina. After his death, in 1803, White's widow had continued to seek redress. Her efforts were finally rewarded in 1838, when Congress directed that "the representatives of Anthony White" be paid $3,750, "being the specie value, at the rate of forty for one, of one hundred and fifty thousand dollars, continental currency, advanced by Colonel White . . . for the use of his regiment." *House Reports*, 24 Cong., 1 Sess., no. 145; 25 Cong., 2 Sess., no. 315; 6 *U. S. Stat.*, 729 (July 7, 1838).

1 Not found.

2 The petition, presented by Clay on Monday, January 12, was referred to the Committee on Pensions and Revolutionary Claims, which reported it unfavorably, February 18.

From Simon Gratz and Brother

Dear Sir Philadelphia January 8. 1824

We enclose you two Certificates of United States stock in the name of our late friend Colo Morrison[1]— some years ago finding them in the Loan Office, on one of his visits to the City we mentioned it to him & he received & left them with us, the Interest has been transferred to the books of the Treasury.

The policy of Insurance against fire on his late dwelling will expire on the 16' Inst. we will pay premium & continue it for another year Very Respectfully Your Obed Sevts

Honle. Henry Clay Washington City SIMON GRATZ & BROTHER

ALS. DLC-TJC (DNA, M212, R12).

1 James Morrison. See below, Nourse to Clay, January 12, 1824.

Remarks on Relief of Sarah Perry

[January 9, 1824]

Mr. CLAY (the Speaker) said, he regretted extremely that the views which he entertained of this subject were such as would not allow him to accord with the gentlemen who supported the bill. If it were a question merely of feeling, he should probably accompany his assent to it with those eulogiums so eloquently bestowed upon the Victor of Lake Erie, and so justly merited. If the amount of money which the bill proposed to disburse was the only objection to it, he should not have offered any opposition; but it was the *principle* of the bill against which he protested, and he conjured gentlemen, before they gave their assent to this bill, to pause, lest, under the influence of the bursts of eloquence which had been heard to-day, they should be instrumental in establishing a principle which he believed to be pregnant with infinite mischief. The principle of the present system of pensions is, that, for the support of him who is disabled by wounds, or the family of him who falls in battle, provision shall be made from the Treasury. Commodore Perry neither fell, nor was he wounded, in battle. In the case of his wife and children, then, there had been already a departure from the principle of our pension list, and now a still further departure from it was proposed, in order to provide for another relative of the same officer. Mr. Clay called upon gentlemen not to suffer themselves to be led away from the true view of this question, by the seductive illusions of military or naval glory. Was there no service but the military or naval? Was there no instance, in *civil* service, of meritorious individuals dying whilst in the public employ, and leaving families, pining in want and overwhelmed in distress? Mr. C. here alluded to the case of a distinguished individual, (Mr. GERRY, it is supposed) who, not many years ago, holding a high civil office, died literally in the discharge of his public duty, far advanced in years, and leaving a destitute family. That case, said he, is well remembered; and do we not all know that every species of relief or compensation was refused to his afflicted family?[1] Mr. C. asked gentlemen to regard all services with an equal eye, and not make unjust discriminations. And, on the score of gratitude, he asked, is there to be no limit to the operation of that feeling on the public counsels? What, he asked further, is the basis of our present pension list? Gratitude. What is the basis upon which, in other countries, aristocracies are erected, and titles and honors showered on individuals, to be transmitted down to their remotest posterity, but the same principle? Mr. C. said he should not, however, have risen, but for some general observations on this subject, which had fallen from the gentleman from South Carolina, on national glory. If you wish to make your country illustrious, said Mr. C. you must *diffuse* your glory. It is not your heroes—God knows we have had enough of them within the last twenty years—every man now is a hero—it is not your heroes, but the body of the people, the men who fight your battles, to whom you are indebted for your safety and your eminence as a nation. But the gentleman from South Carolina, talking of the soldiers, says they fight for pay only, whilst their commanders fight for glory.[2] Is this the case? Look, sir, at the battle of New Orleans, rendered more familiar to our memory by the very recent celebration of its anniversary: the militia who poured down the Mississippi upon the enemy, and met him step by step as he advanced, were *they* actuated by a mercenary principle? No, sir; far otherwise. Mr. C. went on to say, that he had ever been disposed, as far as possible, consistently with the public interest, to reward our successful commanders and illustrate their services; but the body of the People it is on whose virtue and valor we must depend for the preservation of our liberties. If, in awarding pensions, Congress went one step beyond the principles already recognized, where would they stop? They must go on without limit, examining in detail the circumstances which constitute each particular claim preferred upon the public bounty, and measure it out accordingly. Under the present system, which allows pensions for death or disability incurred in the public service, we have a general rule which does not depend on circumstances, and may be safely applied. It is one which depends upon facts, and not upon eloquent appeals to the feelings, by yielding to which, principle might be disregarded. This was the danger to be apprehended from the precedent, should the present bill pass. What has become of him, said Mr. C. who was second to Com. Perry in his memorable conflict? He too has fallen, and his family, it is within the knowledge of some of us, is suffering from the want of the necessary means of aid.[3] Turning to the State from which he came, where, Mr. C. asked, is the widow of Col. WHITE, born to splendid fortune, the whole of which was expended in the revolutionary war? She is old, and in need of aid. I have, said he, a petition to present to this House from this venerable lady, making the most feeling appeal to Congress in her behalf; yet, in answering her letter, assuring her of the pleasure I should have in presenting her memorial to the House, I did not venture to hold out to her the most distant hope of success in her application.[4] Look abroad, said Mr. C., in all the walks of life, and see how many indigent families there are of individuals who have rendered most distinguished services to their country. Shall we select the families of those who wore epaulettes on their shoulders and swords by their sides, for peculiar favor, whilst we leave to pine in penury the families of those who have spent their lives in civil service? Not, Mr. C. said, that he would extend the principle of pensions to civil life; but he would restrict it to its present limit, within which it is safe. There was nothing more insinuating than applications of this description. But, he said, look to what they had led in other countries. Look to the pension list of England, swelled to an amount enormously great. Nay, look to our own pension list, already amounting to nearly two millions of dollars annually. Let us not, said Mr. Clay, surrender ourselves to the captivating eloquence which we have heard on this occasion, on all sides of the House; let us rather be influenced by reason, principle, and precedent. Let us put some limit to this principle of gratitude, however justly it has been extolled. When the honorable gentleman from S. Carolina, now no more, first introduced a bill containing this provision, as well as the one which passed for the relief of the widow and children of Com. Perry, I told the gentleman (said Mr. C.) that we were going too far.[5] When I appealed to his better judgment, and pointed out the fatal consequences of this precedent, he consented to strike out the provision for the mother. I hope we too shall, on this occasion, availing ourselves of his enlightened wisdom, pursue the course which it dictated to him, and refuse to pass this bill.

[John Randolph asked Clay "how, upon his own principles, he reconciled his support of the bill making provision for the widow and children of Commodore Perry with his opposition to this bill? Whether the bill first mentioned was not the very departure from principle against which the gentleman has warned the House this morning?"]

Mr. CLAY said, it was a departure from the general rule. But, having already departed from it, shall we make another and much wider departure? With regard to that bill, however, Mr. C. said, he had rendered it no special support, and he did not know whether or not he had voted upon it. It was a departure, but it was a *safe* departure when compared with that which was now proposed.[6]

Washington *Daily National Intelligencer*, January 12, 1824. Published also in *Annals of Cong.*, 18 Cong., 1 Sess., XLI, 980-82. Cf. above, Remarks and Motion on Relief, January 23, 1821. After the House had resolved itself into Committee of the Whole on a bill proposing a pension of $300 for the relief of Sarah Perry, Timothy Fuller had explained that a similar measure at the preceding Session, "from the pressure of business or some other cause," had not been acted on. He hoped that the bill would meet no opposition, but a debate had ensued. Several speakers had been heard before Clay took part.

1 Elbridge Gerry, signer of the Declaration of Independence, delegate to the Constitutional Convention of 1787, United States Congressman, member of the unsuccessful mission to France in 1797, Governor of Massachusetts, and Vice President of the United States from 1813 until his death at the age of seventy, in the next year. He had once been a man of considerable wealth but had been deeply in debt at the end of his life. The Senate late in 1814 had adopted a bill authorizing payment to his widow of the salary he would have earned had he lived to complete his term of office. The House of Representatives had postponed the measure indefinitely. *Annals of Cong.*, 13 Cong., 3 Sess., XXVIII, 132, 1173.

2 George McDuffie, of South Carolina, had maintained that "there is a broad distinction between the case of a high-spirited and distinguished officer and that of a common soldier. The latter . . . enters the service for his daily bread. Not so the officer. He chooses the profession for its own sake, and is tempted to the choice by the love of fame." *Ibid.*, 18 Cong., 1 Sess., XLI, 976.

3 The reference apparently is not to Jesse D. Elliott, ranking officer under Perry at the Battle of Lake Erie, but to Lt. John J. Yarnall, who had been second to Perry in command of the flagship, the *Lawrence,* during this battle. Yarnall, a native of Pennsylvania, had been on board the *Épervier* when that vessel, returning from Europe in 1815, had disappeared at sea.

4 See above, Clay to Margaret White, January 6, 1824.

5 The subject of relief for the Perry family had been introduced in Congress by William Lowndes, who on February 22, 1820, had offered a resolution calling on the Committee on Naval Affairs "to enquire into the expediency of extending to the widow and children of Captain O. H. Perry, the provision which is now made by law for the widows and children of naval officers who died from wounds received in action." Immediately after this resolution had been adopted, John Randolph had moved "That provision be made, by law, for the support of" Perry's family and the education of his children. This proposal also had been adopted, and a committee had been appointed to formulate a bill, which Randolph had presented on February 28. Though sent to Committee of the Whole for action the following day, the measure had not been returned during the Session. Randolph's effort to revive consideration of it in April had been negatived. U. S. H. of Reps., *Journal,* 16 Cong., 1 Sess., 236, 253, 366.

6 When discussion had ended, the Committee voted to strike out the enacting clause and thus reject the measure. The House, however, upon receiving the report, agreed by a small majority to recommit the bill. No further action was reported.

Remarks on Bill for Surveys for Roads and Canals

[January 12, 1824]

Mr. CLAY, (the Speaker,) took occasion to observe, that the discussion ought to be left free upon the broad principle of the bill, before going into a discussion of its details. Two questions of principle, he conceived, were involved in this bill: first, whether Congress possessed the constitutional power to legislate on the subject of internal improvement; and, secondly, whether it was expedient for Congress to exercise that power. Until it should be settled what was the opinion of the House on both these points, it was useless to go into a discussion of dollars and cents, in regard to the amount of appropriation to be included in the bill.

[Charles F. Mercer did not think this measure would test the opinion of the House on the two points mentioned by Clay, and he hoped that a bill involving the constitutional question would be placed "fairly before the House" during this Session of Congress.]

Mr. CLAY said he knew it was possible, according to one interpretation of the Constitution, to pass this bill without involving, in the discussion, the general principle of the power of the government in regard to internal improvement. But he thought, for his part, that the House could not fairly give its approbation to this bill, unless it also gave its assent to the general power. For what, he asked, does the bill propose? The making of certain surveys, with a view to opening channels for the distribution of the means of the government, and, through the Post Office, the communication of intelligence from one part of the country to the other. If the government has no right to open these communications, it has no right to make the surveys which are preparatory to them. He adverted to the fact that when, some sixteen years ago, a proposition had been made in the Senate for authorizing a survey for a canal around the Falls of the Ohio, a member, now high in office, was of opinion that, so absolutely was the government divested of the power over internal improvement, it could not authorize a survey looking to such an object.[1] Mr. C. said, that he was one of those who do believe the power of making roads and canals to belong to the government.— There were some who differed from him, and deduced the power to give money for such objects from the power to appropriate public money; whilst *he* considered the power to make the improvements as drawing after it the power to make the appropriations for them. According to the view which he took of the subject, the power of the government in regard to internal improvements was a necessary and indispensable topic of discussion which this bill involved. It would be better, then, he thought, to bring on the general discussion first, and, after the House should be satisfied of its power, to take into consideration the sum of money which it might be necessary to appropriate to these national purposes.[2]

Washington *Daily National Intelligencer,* January 13, 1824. Published also in *Annals of Cong.,* 18 Cong., 1 Sess., XLI, 999-1000. At the insistence of Joseph Hemphill, who on December 9, 1823, had offered a resolution "That the subject of roads and canals be referred to a select committee," the House had gone into Committee of the Whole on a bill, introduced December 15 by Hemphill, as chairman of the select committee, "to procure the necessary surveys and estimates on the subject of roads and canals." Following a speech by Hemphill, Philip P. Barbour moved to strike out the enacting clause of the measure in order "that the sense of the House might first be obtained on the general principles involved in the bill, before any thing should be determined as to its details"; and, wishing more time in which to express his views, "he moved that the Committee should rise, and ask leave to sit again." During the subsequent discussion, in which Clay was the first participant, Barbour withdrew both motions.

1 John Q. Adams had opposed passage of the bill to which Clay refers (above, I, 286-87) and had requested that a roll-call vote be taken, but his remarks were not recorded. Adams, *Memoirs,* I, 463; *Annals of Cong.,* 9 Cong., 2 Sess., XVI, 96.

2 Barbour renewing his two motions, the Committee rose "and obtained leave to sit again."

From Joseph Nourse

Dr Sir. City of Washington 12 Jan 1824

I had the honor of your Letter of this morning[1] and beg leave to inform you that I had formerly an Agency from the late Col James Morrison in the receipt of some Dividends of Interest, but which have been closed as P his Receipt in my Ledger page 375 on the 15 April 1820 at which time I paid him a balance of $95.13/100. A few days previous to his serious Illness I paid him a small sum of about $6. wch. he had paid at my request in Kentucky, so that all transactions were then closed. I have in relation to his small amount of public Stocks to state That on the Books of the B U S. Philadelphia, he has

$249. 18. 6 PC. Stock. Int. paid to 1 Jany 1823 to Col. Morrison himself.
124. 58. deferrd [*sic*] do. do
186. 89 3 PC. do. do
123. 37 6 million Loan. Int paid as above

These appear the whole of the Stocks

I have the honor to be Sir, with the greatest respect Your very obedt hum Sert JOSEPH NOURSE

Honorable Henry Clay.

[Endorsement on Margin][2]

In a few days, I shall do myself the honor of transmitting the forms of transfer, & Power to receive Dividends.

ALS. DLC-TJC (DNA, M212, R12).
1 Not found. 2 AE.

To S[olomon] Van Rensselaer

Dr Sir 13 Jan. 1824

I am glad of the occasion of acknowledging the receipt of your letter of the 6h. inst.[1] transmitting me the message of Govr. Yates,[2] since it allows me an opportunity of renewing to you assurances of my sincere regard.

I think you or I would have been a little more explicit, one way or the other, than his Excellency is in his recommendation respecting the choice of Electors.[3] Yr's faithfully H. CLAY

ALS. CSmH. Addressed: "Genl. S. Van Rensselaer Albany New York—"
1 Not found. 2 Joseph C. Yates.
3 The Governor's message, favoring a constitutional amendment to establish throughout the United States a uniform method of choosing presidential electors and submitting to the "wisdom and discretion" of the General Assembly whether the existing method should at that time be changed, has been termed "palpably an attempt to evade a direct expression of an opinion by the executive against giving to the people the power of choosing electors at the then next presidential election." Hammond, *History of Political Parties in the State of New York,* II, 140-42.

From William Hendricks

Dear Sir Corydon Jan. 13. 1824

In obedience to the enclosed I herewith forward you a preamble and joint resolutions of the General Assembly of this state in relation to the National road from Wheeling to the Mississippi[1] and have the pleasure to state that this copy is desired to be forwarded to you as the peculiar friend of the great interests of the West as well as on account of your being the presiding officer of the House of Representatives

Some time ago I took the liberty of addressing you a line[2] My opinions in all respects are now the same that they were at the time of that letter With much respect your obedt Servt.

The Honble Henry Clay. WILLIAM HENDRICKS

ALS. DNA, RG233, HR 18A-F20.3.

1 In these resolutions, approved January 7, 1824, the Indiana General Assembly proclaimed "the completion of the National Road from Wheeling to the Mississippi river . . . a work of great and general importance to the Union and to the Western States," and called upon its Representatives and Senators in Congress to use their exertions "to effect the completion of said Road by obtaining from Congress a donation of Land or appropriation of money for that purpose. . . ."

2 See above, December 22, 1823.

To Robert R. Henry

Sir Washington 14h. Jan. 1824

I duly received your letter under date of the 6h. instant[1] in relation to certain alleged malpractices of officers of Government. Most undoubtedly if they exist in the degree and extent which you suppose they ought to be seriously investigated and the proper remedy applied. Situated as I am, it is however impossible for me to take the iniative [*sic*] in the affair. I can only present to the House over which I have the honor to preside any petition which shall be respectfully couched, and transmitted to me for presentation.[2] With high respect I am Yr. ob. Servant. H. CLAY

ALS. ViU. Addressed on attached sheet: "Robert R. Henry Esqr. Albany New York." Endorsements indicate that Henry, a New York merchant trading in the South, received the letter on January 20 and replied four days later (letter not found), enclosing a memorial and petition with his answer.

1 Not found.

2 On February 2 Clay presented to the House "a memorial and petition of Robert R. Henry, of St. Mary's, in the state of Georgia, charging Archibald Clarke [*sic*] Collector of the Customs for the port of St. Mary's, with malpractices in office," and requesting an investigation. The petition was referred to the Committee on Commerce, which held it nearly four months without a report. Meanwhile, Stephen Van Rensselaer on April 12 presented another petition from Henry, "reiterating the charges of improper official conduct on the part of the Secretary of the Treasury and the Collector of the Customs for the port and district of St. Mary's." The latter document was tabled. Finally, on May 26, one day before the end of the Session, the Committee on Commerce reported on the earlier memorial and was discharged from further consideration of the matter. U. S. H. of Reps., *Journal*, 18 Cong., 1 Sess., 193, 388, 583.

To Josephus B. Stuart

Dr Sir Washn. 14 Jan 24

I duly recd. your letter of the 9h. inst.[1] transmitting the Govr. Message,[2] and the report of your Commee. of the Senate[3] for which

I thank you. I also recd. that enclosing the letter of Mr. Henry, to whom I have written.[4]

We have nothing new here. No caucus, and none likely to be.

Dr. Stuart. Yr's respectfly H. CLAY

ALS. NcD. [1] Not found.

[2] See above, Clay to Van Rensselaer, January 13, 1824.

[3] A select committee of the New York State Senate, having considered the resolutions of the General Assembly of Tennessee relative to nomination of candidates for the Presidency and Vice-Presidency by caucus of the members of Congress (see above, Clay to Porter, October 4, 1823), had concluded to oppose the resolutions: "Upon the whole . . . the committee are unable to discover any well founded objection, either in the constitution, or in public policy, to the mode of nominating candidates . . . which has heretofore obtained; and they are also decidedly of opinion, that its adoption at the present juncture, is both politic and expedient, and the only practicable mode of preserving the harmony of the Union, and securing the attainment of the will of the majority." At the same time, they held that since such nominating caucuses were not an "official act" of the members of Congress, "it would be improper for the Senate and the Assembly of this State, to instruct their Senators, or to request their representatives in Congress, to promote" or "to prevent a nomination from being made." Washington *Daily National Intelligencer,* January 16, 1824.

[4] Above, this date. The letter of transmittal has not been found.

Speech on Internal Improvements

[January 14, 1824]

Mr. CLAY, (Speaker) in rising, said, that he could not enter on the discussion of the subject before him, without first asking leave to express his thanks for the kindness of the Committee, in so far accommodating him as to agree unanimously to adjourn its sitting to the present time, in order to afford him the opportunity of exhibiting his views; which, however, he feared he should do very unacceptably. As a requital for this kindness, he would endeavor, as far as was practicable, to abbreviate what he had to present to their consideration. Yet, on a question of this extent and moment, there were so many topics which demanded a deliberate examination, that, from the nature of the case, it would be impossible, he was afraid, to reduce the argument to any thing that the committee would consider a reasonable compass.

It was known to all who heard him, that there had now existed for several years a difference of opinion between the Executive and Legislative branches of this government, as to the nature and extent of certain powers conferred upon it by the Constitution. Two successive Presidents had returned to Congress bills which had previously passed both Houses of that body, with a communication of the opinion that Congress, under the Constitution, possessed no power to enact such laws. High respect, personal and official, must be felt by all, as it was due, to those distinguished officers, and to their opinions thus solemnly announced; and the most profound consideration belonged to our present Chief Magistrate, who had favored that House with a written argument, of great length and labor, consisting of not less than sixty or seventy pages, in support of his exposition of the Constitution.[1] From the magnitude of the interests involved in the question, all would readily concur, that, if the power is granted and does really exist, it ought to be vindicated, upheld, maintained, that the country might derive the great benefits which may flow from its prudent exercise. If it has not been communicated to Congress, then all claim to it should be, at once, surrendered. It was a circumstance of peculiar regret to him, that one more competent than himself had not risen to support the course which the legislative department had heretofore felt itself bound to pursue on this great question. Of all the trusts which are created by human agency, that is the highest, most solemn, and most responsible, which involves the exercise of political power. Exerted when it has not been entrusted, the public functionary is guilty of usurpation. And his infidelity to the public good is not, perhaps, less culpable when he neglects or refuses to exercise a power which has been fairly conveyed, to promote the public prosperity. If the power which he thus forbears to exercise, can only be exerted by him—if no other public functionary can employ it, and the public good requires its exercise, his treachery is greatly aggravated. It is only in those cases where the object of the investment of power is the personal ease or aggrandisement of the public agent, that his forbearance to use it is praiseworthy, gracious, or magnanimous.

He was extremely happy to find, that, on many of the points of the argument of the honorable gentleman from Virginia, (Mr. BARBOUR) there was entire concurrence between them, widely as they differed in their ultimate conclusions. On this occasion (as on all others on which that gentleman obliged the House with an expression of his opinions) he displayed great ability and ingenuity; and, as well from the matter as from the respectful manner of his argument, it was deserving of the most thorough consideration. He was compelled to differ from that gentleman at the very threshold. He had commenced by laying down as a general principle, that, in the distribution of powers among our Federal and State governments, those which were of a municipal character were to be considered as appertaining to the State governments, and those which related to external affairs, to the General Government. If he might be allowed to throw the argument of the gentleman into the form of a syllogism, (a shape which he presumed would be quite agreeable to him) it amounted to this: Municipal powers belong exclusively to the State Governments; but the power to make internal improvements is municipal; therefore it belongs to the State Governments alone. He (Mr. C.) denied both the premises and the conclusion. If the gentleman had affirmed that certain municipal powers, and the great mass of them, belong to the State Governments, his proposition would have been incontrovertible. But if he had so qualified it, it would not have assisted the gentleman at all in his conclusion. But surely the power of taxation—the power to regulate the value of coin—the power to establish an uniform standard of weights and measures—to establish post offices and post roads—to regulate commerce among the several states—that in relation to the judiciary—besides many other powers indisputably belonging to the Federal Government, are strictly municipal. If, as he understood the gentleman in the course of the subsequent part of his argument to admit, some municipal powers belong to the one system, and some to the other, we shall derive very little aid from the gentleman's principle, in making the discrimination between the two. The question must ever remain open—whether any given power, and of course that in question, is or is not delegated to this Government or retained by the States.

The conclusion of the gentleman is, that all internal improvements belong to the state governments; that they are of a limited and local character, and are not comprehended within the scope of the federal powers, which relate to external or general objects. That many, perhaps most internal improvements, partake of the character described by the gentleman, he (Mr. C.) should not deny. But it was no less true that there were others, emphatically national, which neither the policy, nor the power, nor the interest, of any state would induce it to accomplish, and which could only be effected by the application of the resources of the nation. The improvement of the navigation of the Mississippi would furnish a striking example. This was undeniably a great and important object. The report of a highly scientific and intelligent officer of the Engineer Corps, (which Mr. C. hoped would be soon taken up and acted upon) had shewn that the cost of any practicable improvement in the navigation of that river, in the present state of the inhabitants of its banks, was a mere trifle in comparison to the great benefits which would accrue from it.[2] He (Mr. Clay) believed that about double the amount of the loss of a single steamboat and cargo, (the Tennessee[3]) would effect the whole improvement in the navigation of that river, which ought to be at this time attempted. In this great object twelve states and two territories were, in different degrees, interested. The power to effect the improvement of that river was surely not municipal, in the sense in which the gentleman used the term. If it were, to which of the twelve states and two territories concerned did it belong? It was a great object, which could only be effected by a confederacy. And here is existing that confederacy, and no other can lawfully exist: for the constitution prohibits the states, immediately interested, from entering into any treaty or compact with each other. Other examples might be given to shew, that, if even the power existed, the inclination to exert it would not be felt, to effectuate certain improvements eminently calculated to promote the prosperity of the Union. Neither of the three states, nor all of them united, through which the Cumberland road passes, would ever have erected that road. Two of them would have thrown in every impediment to its completion in their power.[4] Federative in its character, it could only have been executed so far by the application of federative means. Again: the contemplated canal through New Jersey; that to connect the waters of the Chesapeake and Delaware; that to unite the Ohio and the Potomac,[5] were all objects of a general and federative nature, in which the states, through which they might severally pass, could not be expected to feel any such special interest as would lead to their execution. Tending, as undoubtedly they would do, to promote the good of the whole, the power and the treasure of the whole must be applied to their execution, if they are ever consummated.

Mr. Clay did not think, then, that we should be at all assisted in expounding the constitution of the United States, by the principle which the gentleman from Virginia had suggested in respect to municipal powers. The powers of both governments were undoubtedly municipal, often operating upon the same subject. He thought a better rule than that which the gentleman furnished for interpreting the constitution might be deduced from an attentive consideration of the peculiar character of the articles of confederation, as contrasted with that of the present constitution. By those articles, the powers of the thirteen United States were exerted collaterally. They operated through an intermediary. They were addressed to the several states, and their execution depended upon the pleasure and the co-operation of the states individually. The states seldom fulfilled the expectations of the general government in regard to its requisitions, and often wholly disappointed them. Languor and debility, in the movement of the old Confederation, were the inevitable consequence of that arrangement of power. By the existing Constitution, the powers of the General Government act directly on the persons and things within its scope, without the intervention or impediments incident to any intermediacy. In executing the great trust which the Constitution of the United

States creates, we must, therefore, reject that interpretation of its provisions which would make the General Government dependant [*sic*] upon those of the States for the execution of any of its powers; and may safely conclude that the only genuine construction would be that which should enable this government to execute the great purposes of its institution, without the cooperation, and, if indispensably necessary, even against the will of any particular State. This is the characteristic difference between the two systems of government, of which we should never lose sight. Interpreted in the one way, we shall relapse into the feebleness and debility of the old confederacy. In the other, we shall escape from its evils, and fulfil the great purposes which the enlightened framers of the existing constitution intended to effectuate. The importance of this essential difference in the two forms of government, would be shown in the future progress of the argument.

Before he proceeded to comment upon those parts of the constitution which appeared to him to convey the power in question, he hoped he should be allowed to disclaim, for his part, several sources whence others had deduced the authority. The gentleman from Virginia seemed to think it remarkable that the friends of the power should disagree so much among themselves; and to draw a conclusion against its existence from the fact of this discrepancy. But he (Mr. C.) could see nothing extraordinary in this diversity of views. What was more common than for different men to contemplate the same subject under various aspects? Such was the nature of the human mind, that enlightened men, perfectly upright in their intentions, differed in their opinions on almost every topic that could be mentioned. It was rather a presumption, in favor of the cause which he was humbly maintaining, that the same result should be attained by so many various modes of reasoning. But, if contrariety of views might be pleaded with any effect against the advocates of the disputed power, it equally availed against their opponents. There was, for example, not a very exact coincidence in opinion between the President of the United States and the gentleman from Virginia. The President says, (page 25 of his book,) "The use of the existing road by the stage, mail carrier, or post boy, in passing over it, as others do, is all that would be thought of; the jurisdiction and soil remaining to the State, with a right in the State, or *those authorized by its legislature,* to *change* the road at *pleasure.*"[6] Again, page 27, the President asks, "If the United States possessed the power contended for under this grant, might they not, in adopting the roads of the individual states, for the carriage of the mail, as has been done, assume jurisdiction over them, and preclude a right to interfere with or *alter* them?"

They both agree that the General Government does not possess the power. The gentleman from Virginia admits, if he (Mr. C.) understood him correctly, that the designation of a state road as a post road, so far withdrew it from the jurisdiction of the state, that it could not be afterwards put down or closed by the state; and in this he claims for the General Government more power than the President concedes to it. The President, on the contrary, pronounces that "the absurdity of such a pretension" (that is, preventing, by the designation of a post road, the power of the state from altering or changing it) "must be apparent to all who examine it!"[7] The gentleman thinks that the designation of a post road withdraws it entirely, so far as it is used for that purpose, from the power of the whole state; whilst the President thinks it absurd to assert that a mere county court may not defeat the execution of a law of the United States! The President thinks that, under the power of appropriating the money of the United States, Congress may apply it to any object of internal improvement, provided it does not assume any territorial jurisdiction;[8] and, in this respect, he claims for the general government more power than the gentleman from Virginia assigns to it. And he (Mr. C.) must own that he so far coincided with the gentleman from Virginia. If the power can be traced to no more legitimate source than to that of appropriating the public treasure, he yielded the question.

The truth is, that there is no specific grant, in the constitution, of the power of appropriation; nor was any such requisite. It is a resulting power. The constitution vests in Congress the power of taxation, with but few limitations, to raise a public revenue. It then enumerates the powers of Congress. And it follows, of necessity, that Congress has the right to apply the money so raised to the execution of the powers so granted. The clause which concludes the enumeration of the granted powers, by authorizing the passage of all laws "necessary and proper" to effectuate them, comprehends the power of appropriation. And the framers of the constitution recognize it by the restriction that no money shall be drawn from the Treasury but in virtue of a previous appropriation by law. It was to him wonderful how the President should have brought his mind to the conclusion, that, under the power of appropriation, thus incidentally existing, a right could be set up, in its nature almost without limitation, to employ the public money. He combats with great success and much ability, any deduction of power from the clause relating to the general welfare. He shews that the effect of it would be to overturn, or render useless and nugatory, the careful enumeration of our powers; and that it would convert a cautiously limited government into one without limitation. The same process of reasoning by which his mind was brought to this just conclusion, one would have thought, should have warned him against his claiming, under the power of appropriation, such a vast latitude of authority. He reasons strongly against the power, as claimed by us, harmless and beneficent and limited, as it must be admitted to be, and yet he sets up a power boundless in its extent, unrestrained to the object of internal improvements, and comprehending the whole scope of human affairs. For, if the power exists, as he asserts it, what human restraint is there upon it? He does, indeed, say, that it cannot be exerted so as to interfere with the territorial jurisdiction of the states. But this is a restriction altogether gratuitous, flowing from the bounty of the President, and not found in the prescriptions of the Constitution. If we have a right, indefinitely, to apply the money of the Government to internal improvements, or to any other object, what is to prevent the application of it to the purchase of the sovereignty itself, of a state, if a state were mean enough to sell its sovereignty—to the purchase of kingdoms, empires, the globe itself? With an almost unlimited power of taxation; and, after the revenue is raised, with a right to apply it under no other limitations than those which the President's caution has suggested, he could not see what other human power was needed. It had been said, by Caesar or Bonaparte, no doubt thought by both, that, with soldiers enough, they could get money enough; and, with money enough, they could command soldiers enough. According to the President's interpretation of the Constitution, one of these great levers of public force and power is possessed by this government. The President seems to contemplate, as fraught with much danger, the power, humbly as it is claimed, to effect the internal improvement of the country. And, in his attempt to overthrow it, sets up one of infinitely greater magnitude. The quantum of power which we claim over the subject of internal improvement is, it is true, of greater amount and force than that which results from the President's view of the Constitution; but then it is *limited* to the object of internal improvements: whilst the power set up by the President has no such limitation, and, in effect, as Mr. C. conceived, has no limitation whatever, but that of the ability of the people to bear taxation.

With the most profound respect for the President, and after the most deliberate consideration of his argument, Mr. C. could not agree with him. He could not think that any political power accrued to this government, from the mere authority which it possessed to appropriate the public revenue. The power to make internal improvements drew after it, most certainly, the right to appropriate money to consummate the object. But he could not conceive that this right of appropriation drew after it the power of internal improvements. The appropriation of money was consequence, not cause. It follows: it does not precede. According to the order of nature, we first determine upon the object to be accomplished, and then appropriate the money necessary to its consummation. According to the order of the Constitution, the power is defined, and the application, that is, the appropriation of the money requisite to its effectuation, follows, as a necessary and proper means. The practice of Congressional legislation was conformable to both. We first inquire what we may do, and provide by law for its being done; and we then appropriate, by another act of legislation, the money necessary to accomplish the specified object. The error of the argument lies in its beginning too soon. It supposes the money to be in the Treasury, and then seeks to disburse it. But how came it there? Congress cannot impose taxes without an object. Their imposition must be in reference to the whole mass of our powers, to the general purposes of government, or with the view to the fulfilment of some one of those powers, or to the attainment of some one of those purposes. In either case, we consult the Constitution, and ascertain the extent of the authority which is confided to us. We cannot, constitutionally, lay the taxes without regard to the extent of our powers; and then, having acquired the money of the public, appropriate it, because we have got it, to any object indefinitely.

Nor did he claim the power in question, from the consent or grant of any particular state or states, through which an object of internal improvement might pass. It might, indeed, be prudent to consult a state through which such an improvement might happen to be carried, from considerations of deference and respect to its sovereign power; and from a disposition to maintain those relations of perfect amity which are ever desirable, between the general and state governments. But the power to establish the improvement, must be found in the Constitution, or it does not exist. And what is granted by all, it cannot be necessary to obtain the consent of some, to perform.

The gentleman from Virginia, in speaking of incidental powers, had used a species of argument which he intreated him candidly to reconsider. He had said, that the chain of cause and effect was without end; that if we argued from a power expressly granted to all others, which might be convenient or necessary to its exertion, there were no bounds to the power of this government; that, for example, under the power "to provide and maintain a navy," the right might be assumed to the timber necessary to its construction, and the soil on which it grew. The gentleman might have added, the acorns from which it sprung. What, upon the gentleman's own hypothesis, ought to have been his conclusion? That Congress possessed no power to provide and maintain a navy. Such a conclusion would have been quite as logical as, that Congress has no power over internal improvements, from the *possible* lengths to which this power may be pushed. No one ever had, or could, controvert the existence of incidental powers. We may apply different rules for their extraction, but all must concur in the necessity of their actual existence. They result from the imperfections of our nature, and from the utter impossibility of foreseeing all the turns and vicissitudes in human affairs. They cannot be defined. Much is attained when the power, the end, is specified and guarded. Keeping that constantly in view, the means necessary to its attainment must be left to the sound and responsible discretion of the public functionary. Intrench him as you please, employ what language you may, in the constitutional instrument, "necessary and proper," "indispensably necessary," or any other, and the question is still left open, does the proposed measure fall within the scope of the incidental power, circumscribed as it may be? Your safety against abuse must rest in his interest, his integrity, his responsibility to the exercise of the elective franchise; finally, in the ultimate right, when all other redress fails, of an appeal to the remedy, to be used only in extreme cases, of forcible resistance against intolerable oppression.

Doubtless, by an extravagant and abusive enlargement of incidental powers, the State governments may be reduced within too narrow limits. Take any power, however incontestibly granted to the general government, and employ that kind of process of reasoning in which the gentleman from Virginia is so skilful [*sic*], by tracing it to its remotest effects, you may make it absorb the powers of the state governments. Pursue the opposite course; take any incontestible power belonging to the governments, and follow it out into all its possible ramifications, and you may make it thwart and defeat the great operations of the government of the whole. This is the consequence of our systems. Their harmony is to be preserved only by forbearance, liberality, practical good sense, and mutual concession. Bring these dispositions into the administrations of our various institutions, and all the dreaded conflicts of authorities will be found to be perfectly imaginary.

He said, that he disclaimed, for himself, several sources to which others had ascended to arrive at the power in question. In making this disclaimer, he meant to cast no imputation on them. He was glad to meet them by whatever road they travelled, at the point of a constitutional conclusion. Nor did their positions weaken his;

on the contrary, if correctly taken, and his, also, were justified by fair interpretation, they added strength to his. But he felt it his duty, frankly and sincerely, to state his own views of the constitution. In coming to the ground on which (said Mr. C.) I make my stand to maintain the power, and where I am ready to meet its antagonists, I am happy, in the outset, to state my hearty concurrence with the gentleman from Virginia, in the old, 1798, republican principles, (now become federal, also,) by which the constitution is to be interpreted.[9] I agree with him, that this is a limited government; that it has no powers but the granted powers; and that the granted powers are those which are expressly enumerated, or such as, being implied, are necessary and proper to effectuate the enumerated powers. And, if I do not shew the power over federative, national, internal improvements to be fairly deducible, after the strictest application of these principles, I entreat the Committee unanimously to reject the bill. The gentleman from Virginia has rightly anticipated that, in regard to roads, I claim the power, under the grant, *to establish* post offices and post roads. The whole question, on this part of the subject, turns upon the true meaning of this clause, and that again upon the genuine signification of the word *"establish."* According to my understanding of it, the meaning of it is, to fix, to make firm, to build. According to that of the gentleman from Virginia, it is to designate, to adopt. Grammatical criticism was, to me, always unpleasant, and I do not profess to be any [*sic*] proficient in it. But I will confidently appeal, in support of my definition, to any vocabulary whatever of respectable authority, and to the common use of the word. That it could not mean only adoption was to me evident; for *adoption* pre-supposes establishment, which is precedent in its very nature. That which does not exist, which is not established, cannot be adopted. There was, then, an essential difference between the gentleman from Virginia and me. I consider the power as original and creative; he as derivative, adoptive. But I will shew, out of the mouth of the President himself, who agrees with the gentleman from Virginia, as to the sense of this word, that what I contend for, is its genuine meaning. The President, in almost the first lines of his message to this House, of the 4th of May, 1822, returning the Cumberland bill with his veto, says, "a power to *establish* turnpikes, with gates and tolls, &c. implies a power to adopt and execute a complete system of internal improvement."[10] What is the sense in which the word "establish" is here used? Is it not creative? Did the President mean to adopt or designate some pre-existing turnpikes, with gates, &c. or, for the first time, to set them up, under the authority of Congress? Again, the President says, "if it exist as to one road, {that is, the power to lay duties of transit, and to take the land on a valuation,} it exists as to any other, and to as many roads as Congress may think proper to *"establish."*[11] In what sense does he here employ the word? The truth is, that the President could employ no better than the constitutional word, and he is obliged to use it in the precise sense for which I contend. But I go to a higher authority than that of the Chief Magistrate—to that of the Constitution itself. In expounding that instrument, we must look at all its parts; and if we find a word the meaning of which it is desirable to obtain, we may safely rest upon the use which has been made of the same word in other parts of the instrument. The word "establish" is one of frequent recurrence in the constitution; and I venture to say that it will be found uniformly to express the same idea. In the clause enumerating our powers, Congress has power "to *establish* an uniform rule of naturalization," &c. In the preamble, "We, the people of the United States, in order to form a more perfect union, *establish* justice, &c. do ordain and *establish* this constitution," &c. What pre-existing code of justice was adopted? Did not the people of the United States, in this high, sovereign act, contemplate the construction of a code adapted to their federal condition? The sense of the word, as contended for, was self-evident when applied to the constitution.

But let us look at the nature, object, and purposes of the power. The trust confided to Congress was one of the most beneficial character. It was the diffusion of information among all the parts of this Republic. It was the transmission and circulation of intelligence; it was to communicate knowledge of the laws and acts of government; and to promote the great business of society in all its relations. This was a great trust, capable of being executed in a highly salutary manner. It could be executed only by Congress, and it should be as well performed as it could be, considering the wants and exigencies of government. And here I beg leave to advert to the principle which I some time ago laid down, that the powers granted to this government are to be carried into execution by its own inherent force and energy, without necessary dependence upon the state governments. If my construction secures this object; and if that of my opponents places the execution of this trust at the pleasure and mercy of the state governments, we must reject theirs and assume mine. But the construction of the President does make it so dependent. He contends that we can only use as post roads those which the states shall have previously established; that they are at liberty to alter, to change, and of course to shut them up at pleasure. It results from this view of the President that any of the great mail routes now existing, that, for example, from

South to North, may be closed at pleasure or by caprice, by any one of the states or its authorities through which it passes, by that of Delaware or any other. Is it possible that the construction of the constitution can be correct, which allows a law of the United States, enacted for the good of the whole, to be obstructed or defeated in its operation by any one of twenty-four Sovereignties? The gentleman from Va. it is true, denies the right of a state to close a road which has been designated as a post road. But suppose the state, no longer having occasion to use it for its own separate and peculiar purposes, withdraws all care and attention from its preservation. Can the state be compelled to repair it? No! the gentleman from Virginia must say and I will say. May not the general government repair this road which is abandoned by the state power? May it not repair it in the most efficacious manner? And may it not protect and defend that which it has thus repaired, and which there is no longer an interest or inclination in the state to protect and defend? Or does the gentleman mean to contend that a road may exist in the statute book, which a state will not, and the general government cannot, repair and improve? And what sort of an account should we render to the people of the United States of the execution of the high trust confided, for their benefit, to us, if we were to tell them that we had failed to execute it, because a state would not make a road for us?

The roads, and other internal improvements of states, are made in reference to their individual interests. It is the eye only of the whole, and the power of the whole that can look to the interests of all. In the infancy of the government, and in the actual state of the public Treasury, it may be the only alternative left us to use those roads, which are made for state purposes, to promote the national object, ill as they may be adapted to it. It may never be necessary to make more than a few great national arteries of communication, leaving to the states the lateral and minor ramifications. Even these should only be executed, without pressure upon the resources of the country, and according to the convenience and ability of government. But, surely, in the performance of a great national duty imposed upon this government, which has for its object the distribution of intelligence, civil, commercial, literary, and social, we ought to perform the substance of the trust, and not content ourselves with a mere paper inefficient execution of it. If I am right in these views, the power to establish post roads being in its nature original and creative, and the government having adopted the roads made by state means only from its inability to exert the whole extent of its authority, the controverted power is *expressly* granted to Congress, and there is an end of the question.

It ought to be borne in mind that this power over roads was not contained in the articles of confederation, which limited Congress to the establishment of post offices; and that the general character of the present constitution, as contrasted with those articles, is that of an enlargement of power. But, if the construction of the opposite side be correct, we are left precisely where the articles of confederation left us, notwithstanding the additional words contained in the present constitution. What, too, will the gentlemen do with the first member of the clause to establish post *offices*? Must Congress adopt, designate, some pre-existing office, established by state authority? But there is none such. May it not then fix, build, create, *establish* offices of its own?

The gentleman from Virginia sought to alarm us by the awful emphasis with which he set before us the total extent of post roads in the Union. Eighty thousand miles of post roads! exclaimed the gentleman; and will you assert for the general government jurisdiction, and erect turnpikes on such an immense distance? Not today, nor to-morrow; but this government is to last, I trust, forever; we may at least hope it will endure until the wave of population, cultivation, and intelligence, shall have washed the Rocky mountains and mingled with the Pacific. And may we not also hope that the day will arrive when the improvements and the comforts of social life shall spread over the wide surface of this vast continent? All this is not to be suddenly done. Society must not be burthened or oppressed. Things must be gradual and progressive. The same species of formidable array which the gentleman makes, might be exhibited in reference to the construction of a navy, or any other of the great purposes of government. We might be told of the fleets and vessels of great maritime powers which whiten the ocean; and triumphantly asked if we should vainly attempt to cope with or rival that tremendous power? And we should shrink from the effort, if we were to listen to his counsels, in hopeless despair. Yes, sir, it is a subject of peculiar delight to me to look forward to the proud and happy period, distant as it may be, when circulation and association between the Atlantic and the Pacific and the Mexican Gulf, shall be as free and perfect as they are at this moment in England, or in any other the most highly improved country on the globe. In the mean time, without bearing heavily upon any of our important interests, let us apply ourselves to the accomplishment of what is most practicable and immediately necessary.

But what most staggers my honorable friend, is the jurisdiction over the sites of roads and other internal improvements which he supposes Congress might assume; and he considers the exercise of such a jurisdiction as furnishing the just occasion for serious alarm. Let us analyse the subject. Prior to the erection of a road under the authority of the General Government, there existed, in the State through which it passes, no actual exercise of jurisdiction over the ground which it traverses *as a road*. There was only the possibility of the exercise of such a jurisdiction when the state should, if ever, erect such a road. But the road is made by the authority of Congress, and out of the *fact* of its erection arises a necessity for its preservation and protection. The road is some thirty or fifty or sixty feet in width, and with that narrow limit passes through a part of the territory of the State. The capital expended in the making of the road incorporates itself with and becomes a part of the permanent and immovable property of the State. The jurisdiction which is claimed for the General Government, is that only which relates to the necessary defence, protection, and preservation, of the road. It is of a character altogether conservative. Whatever does not relate to the existence and protection of the road remains with the State. Murders, trespasses, contracts, all the occurrences and transactions of society upon the road, not affecting its actual existence, will fall within the jurisdiction of the civil or criminal tribunals of the State, as if the road had never been brought into existence. How much remains to the State! How little is claimed for the General Government! Is it possible that a jurisdiction so limited, so harmless, so unambitious, can be regarded, as seriously alarming to the sovereignty of the States! Congress now asserts and exercises, without contestation, a power to protect the mail in its transit by the sanction of all suitable penalties. The man who violates it is punished with death or otherwise, according to the circumstances of the case. This power is exerted as incident to that of establishing post offices and post roads. Is the protection of the thing in transitu a power more clearly deducible from the grant, than that of facilitating, by means of a practicable road, its actual transportation? Mails certainly imply roads, roads imply their own preservation, their preservation implies the power to preserve them, and the Constitution tells us, in express terms, that we shall establish the one and the other.

In respect to cutting canals, I admit the question is not quite so clear as in regard to roads. With respect to these, as I have endeavored to shew, the power is expressly granted. In regard to canals, it appears to me to be fairly comprehended in, or deducible from, certain granted powers. Congress has power to regulate commerce with foreign nations and among the several states. Precisely the same measure of power which is granted in the one case is conferred in the other. And the uniform practical exposition of the constitution, as to the regulation of foreign commerce, is equally applicable to that among the several states. Suppose, instead of directing the legislation of this government constantly, as heretofore, to the object of foreign commerce, to the utter neglect of the interior commerce among the several states, the fact had been reversed, and now, for the first time, we were about to legislate for our foreign trade: Should we not, in that case, hear all the constitutional objections made to the erection of buoys, beacons, lighthouses, the surveys of coasts, and the other numerous facilities accorded to the foreign trade, which we now hear to the making of roads and canals? Two years ago, a sea wall, in other words, a marine canal, was authorized by an act of Congress, in New Hampshire;[12] and I doubt not that many of those voted for it who have now constitutional scruples on this bill. Yes, any thing, every thing, may be done for foreign commerce; any thing, every thing, on the margin of the ocean. But nothing for domestic trade; nothing for the great interior of the country! Yet, the equity and the beneficence of the constitution equally comprehends both. The gentleman does, indeed, maintain that there is a difference as to the character of the facilities in the two cases. But I put it to his own candor whether the only difference is not that which springs from the nature of the two elements on which the two species of commerce are conducted—the difference between land and water. The principle is the same whether you promote commerce by opening for it an artificial channel where now there is none, or by increasing the ease or safety with which it may be conducted through a natural channel which the bounty of Providence has bestowed. In the one case, your object is to facilitate arrival and departure from the ocean to the land. In the other, it is to accomplish the same object from the land to the ocean. Physical obstacles may be greater in the one case than in the other, but the moral or constitutional power equally includes both. The gentleman from Virginia had, to be sure, contended that the power to make these commercial facilities was to be found in another clause of the constitution—that which enables Congress to obtain cessions of territory for specific objects, and grants to it an exclusive jurisdiction. These cessions may be obtained for the "erection of forts, magazines, arsenals, dockyards, or other needful buildings." It is apparent that it relates altogether to military or naval affairs, and not to the regulation of commerce. How was the marine canal covered by this clause? Is it to be considered as a "needful building?" The object of this power is perfectly obvious. The Convention saw that, in military or naval posts, such as are indicated, it was indispensably necessary, for their proper government, to vest in Congress the power of exclusive legislation. If we claimed over objects of internal improvement an exclusive jurisdiction, the gentleman might urge, with much force, the clause in question. But the claim of concurrent jurisdiction only is asserted. The gentleman professes himself unable to comprehend how concurrent jurisdiction can be exercised by two different governments at the same time over the same persons and things. But, is not this the fact with respect to the state and federal governments? Does not every person, and every thing, within our limits, sustain a two-fold relation to the state and to the federal authority? The power of taxation as exerted by both governments, that over the militia, besides many others, is concurrent. No doubt embarrassing cases may be conceived and stated by gentlemen of acute and ingenious minds. One was put to me yesterday. Two canals are desired, one by the federal, and the other by a state government; and there is not a supply of water but for the feeder of one canal—which is to take it? The constitution, which ordains the supremacy of the laws of the United States, answers the question. The good of the whole is paramount to the good of a part. The same difficulty might possibly arise in the exercise of the incontestible power of taxation. We know that the imposition of taxes has its limits. There is a maximum which cannot be transcended. Suppose the citizen to be taxed by the General Government to the utmost extent of his ability, or a thing as much as it can possibly bear, and the state imposes a tax at the same time, which authority is to take it? Extreme cases of this sort may serve to amuse and to puzzle; but they will hardly ever arise in practice. And we may safely confide in the moderation, good sense, and mutual good dispositions, of the two governments to guard against the imagined conflicts.

It is said by the President, that the power to regulate commerce merely authorizes the laying of imposts and duties. But Congress has no power to lay imposts and duties on the trade among the several States. The grant must mean, therefore, something else. What is it? The power to regulate commerce among the several States, if it has any meaning, implies authority to foster it, to promote it, to bestow on it facilities similar to those which have been conceded to our foreign trade. It cannot mean only an empty authority to adopt regulations without the capacity to give practical effect to them. All the powers of this Government should be interpreted in reference to its first, its best, its greatest object, the Union of these States. And is not that Union best invigorated by an intimate, social, and commercial connexion between all the parts of the confederacy? Can that be accomplished, that is, can the federative objects of this Government be attained, but by the application of federative resources?

Of all the powers bestowed on this Government, Mr. Clay thought none were more clearly vested, than that to regulate the distribution of the intelligence, private and official, of the country; to regulate the distribution of its commerce; and to regulate the distribution of the physical force of the Union. In the execution of the high and solemn trust which these beneficial powers imply, we must look to the great ends which the framers of our admirable constitution had in view. We must reject, as wholly incompatible with their enlightened and beneficent intentions, that construction of these powers which would resuscitate all the debility and inefficiency of the ancient confederacy. In the vicissitudes of human affairs, who can foresee all the possible cases, in which it may be necessary to apply the public force, within or without the Union? This Government is charged with the use of it, to repel invasions, to suppress insurrections, to enforce the laws of the Union; in short, for all the unknown and undefinable purposes of war, foreign or intestine, wherever and however it may rage. During its existence, may not Government, for its effectual prosecution, order a road to be made, or a canal to be cut, to relieve, for example, an exposed point of the Union? If, when the emergency comes, there is a power to provide for it, that power must exist in the constitution, and not in the emergency. A wise, precautionary, and parental policy, anticipating danger, will beforehand provide for the hour of need. Roads and canals are in the nature of fortifications, since, if not the deposites of military resources, they enable you to bring into rapid action, the military resources of the country, wherever they may be. They are better than any fortifications, because they serve the double purposes of peace and of war. They dispense, in a great degree, with fortifications, since they have all the effect of that concentration, at which fortifications aim. I appeal from the precepts of the President to the practice of the President. While he denies to Congress the power in question, he does not scruple, upon his sole authority, as numerous instances in the statute book will testify, to order, at pleasure, the opening of roads by the military, and then come here to ask us to pay for them.[13] Nay, more, sir, a subordinate but highly respectable officer of the Executive Government, I believe would not hesitate to provide a boat or cause a bridge to be erected over an inconsiderable stream, to ensure the regular transportation of the mail. And it happens to be within my personal knowledge, that the head of the Post Office Department,[14] as a prompt and vigilant officer should do, had recently despatched an agent to ascertain the causes of the late frequent vexatious failures of the great northern mail, and to inquire if a provision of a boat or bridge over certain small streams in Maryland, which have produced them, would not prevent their recurrence.

I was much surprised at one argument of the honorable gentleman. He told the House, that the Constitution had carefully guarded against inequality, among the several states, in the public burthens, by certain restrictions upon the power of taxation; that the effect of the adoption of a system of internal improvements would be to draw the resources from one part of the Union, and to expend them in the improvement of another, and that the spirit, at least, of the constitutional equality would be thus violated. From the nature of things, the constitution could not specify the theatre of the expenditure of the public treasure. That expenditure, guided by and looking to the public good, must be made, necessarily, where it will most subserve the interests of the whole Union. The argument is, that the locale of the collection of the public contributions, and the locale of their disbursement, should be the same. Now, Sir, let us carry this argument out; and no man is more capable than the ingenious gentleman from Virginia, of tracing an argument to its utmost consequences. The locale of the collection of the public revenue is the pocket of the citizen; and, to abstain from the violation of the principle of equality adverted to by the gentleman, we should restore back to each man's pocket precisely what was taken from it. If the principle contended for be true, we are habitually violating it. We raise about twenty millions of dollars, a very large revenue, considering the actual distresses of the country. And, Sir, notwithstanding all the puffing, flourishing statements of its prosperity, emanating from printers who are fed upon the pap of the public Treasury, the whole country is in a condition of very great distress. Where is this vast revenue expended? Boston, New York, the great capitals of the North, are the theatres of its disbursement. There the interest upon the public debt is paid. There the expenditure in the building, equipment, and repair, of the national vessels takes place. There all of the great expenditures of the government necessarily concentrate. This is no cause of just complaint. It is inevitable, resulting from the accumulation of capital, the state of the arts, and other circumstances belonging to our great cities. But, Sir, if there be a section of this Union having more right than any other to complain of this transfer of the circulating medium from one quarter of the Union to another, the West, the poor West {Here Mr. Barbour explained. He had meant that the Constitution limited Congress as to the proportions of revenue to be drawn from the several states; but the principle of this provision would be vacated by internal improvements of immense expense, and yet of a local character. Our public ships, to be sure, are built at the seaports, but they do not remain there. Their home is the mountain wave; but internal improvements are essentially local; they touch the soil of the states, and their benefits, at least the largest part of them, are confined to the states where they exist.} The explanation of the gentleman has not materially varied the argument. He says that the home of our ships is the mountain wave. Sir, if the ships go to sea, the money with which they were built, or refitted, remains on shore, and the cities where the equipment takes place derive the benefit of the expenditure. It requires no stretch of the imagination to conceive the profitable industry—the axes, the hammers, the saws—the mechanic arts which are put in motion by this expenditure. And all these and other collateral advantages are enjoyed by the seaports. The navy is built for the interest of the whole. Internal improvements, of that general, federative character, for which we contend, would also be for the interest of the whole. And, I should think their abiding with us, and not going abroad on the vast deep, was rather cause of recommendation than objection.

But, Mr. Chairman, if there be any part of this Union more likely than all others to be benefitted by the adoption of the gentleman's principle, regulating the public expenditure, it is the West. There is a perpetual drain from that embarrassed and highly distressed portion of our country, of its circulating medium to the East. There, but few and inconsiderable expenditures of the public money take place. There we have none of those public works, no magnificent edifices, forts, armories, arsenals, dockyards, &c. which more or less are to be found in every Atlantic state. In at least seven states beyond the Alleghany, not one solitary public work of this Government is to be found. If, by one of those awful and terrible dispensations of Providence, which sometimes occur, this Government should be unhappily annihilated, every where on the seaboard traces of its former existence would be found; whilst we should not have, in the West, a single monument remaining on which to pour out our affections and our regrets. Yet, sir, we do not complain. No portion of your population is more loyal to the Union, than the hardy freemen of the West. Nothing can weaken or eradicate their ardent desire for its lasting preservation. None are more prompt to vindicate the interests and rights of the nation from all foreign aggression. Need I remind you of the glorious scenes in which they participated, during the late war—a war in which they had no peculiar or direct interest, waged for no commerce, no seamen of theirs. But it was enough for them that it was a war demanded by the character and the honor of the nation. They did not stop to calculate its cost of blood, or of treasure. They flew to arms; they rushed down the valley of the Mississippi, with all the impetuosity of that noble river. They sought the enemy. They found him at the beach. They fought; they bled; they covered themselves and their country with immortal glory. They enthusiastically shared in all the transports occasioned by our victories, whether won on the ocean or on the land. They felt, with the keenest distress, whatever disaster befel [*sic*] us. No, sir, I repeat it, neglect, injury itself, cannot alienate the affections of the West from this Government. They cling to it, as to their best, their greatest, their last hope. You may impoverish them, reduce them to ruin, by the mistakes of your policy, and you cannot drive them from you. They do not complain of the expenditure of the public money, where the public exigencies require its disbursement. But, I put it to your candor, if you ought not, by a generous and national policy, to mitigate, if not prevent, the evils resulting from the perpetual transfer of the circulating medium of the West to the East. One million and a half of dollars annually, is transferred for the public lands alone; and, almost every dollar goes, like him who goes to death—to a bourne from which no traveller returns. In ten years it will amount to fifteen millions; in twenty to—but I will not pursue the appalling results of arithmetic. Gentlemen who believe that these vast sums are supplied by emigrants from the East, labor under great error. There was a time when the tide of emigration from the East bore along with it the means to effect the purchase of the public domain. But that tide has, in a great measure, now stopt. And as population advances farther and farther west, it will entirely cease. The greatest migrating states in the Union, at this time, are Kentucky first, Ohio next, and Tennessee. The emigrants from those states carry with them, to the states and territories lying beyond them, the circulating medium, which, being invested in the purchase of the public land, is transmitted to the points where the wants of government require it. If this debilitating and exhausting process were inevitable, it must be borne with manly fortitude. But we think that a fit exertion of the powers of this government would mitigate the evil. We believe that the government incontestibly possesses the constitutional power to execute such internal improvements as are called for by the good of the whole. And we appeal to your equity, to your parental regard, to your enlightened policy, to perform the high and beneficial trust thus sacredly reposed. I am sensible of the delicacy of the topic to which I have reluctantly adverted, in consequence of the observations of the honorable gentleman from Virginia. And I hope there will be no misconception of my motives in dwelling upon it. A wise and considerate government should anticipate and prevent rather than wait for the operation of causes of discontent.

Let me ask, Mr. Chairman, what has this government done on the great subject of Internal Improvements, after so many years of its existence, and with such an inviting field before it? You have made the Cumberland road only. Gentlemen appear to have considered that a western road. They ought to recollect that not one stone has yet been broken, not one spade of earth has been yet removed in any Western State. The road begins in Maryland and it terminates at Wheeling. It passes through the states of Maryland, Pennsylvania, and Virginia. All the direct benefit of the expenditure of the public money on that road, has accrued to those three states. Not one cent in any Western State. And yet we have had to beg, entreat, supplicate you, session after session, to grant the necessary appropriations to complete the road. I have myself toiled until my powers have been exhausted and prostrated to prevail on you to make the grant. We were actuated to make these exertions for the sake of the collateral benefit only to the West; that we might have a way by which we should be able to continue and maintain an affectionate intercourse with our friends and brethren —that we might have a way to reach the Capitol of our country, and to bring our councils, humble as they may be, to consult and mingle with yours in the advancement of the national prosperity. Yes, Sir, the Cumberland road has only reached the margin of a Western State; and, from some indications which have been given during this session, I should apprehend it would there pause for ever, if my confidence in you were not unbounded; if I had not before witnessed that appeals were never unsuccessful to your justice, to your magnanimity, to your fraternal affection.

But, Sir, the bill on your table is no Western bill. It is emphatically a national bill, comprehending all, looking to the interests of the whole. The people of the West never thought of, never desired, never asked, for a system exclusively for their benefit. The system contemplated by this bill looks to great national objects and proposes the ultimate application to their accomplishment of the only means by which they can be effected, the means of the nation— means which, if they be withheld from such objects, the Union, I do most solemnly believe, of these now happy and promising states, may, at some distant (I trust a far, far, distant) day, be endangered and shaken at its centre.[15]

Washington *Daily National Intelligencer,* January 27, 1824. Published also, under erroneous date, in Lexington *Kentucky Reporter,* February 23, 1824; *Annals of Cong.,* 18 Cong., 1 Sess., XLI, 1022-41; Chambers, *Speeches of the Hon. Henry Clay,* 130-48; [Swain], *Life and Speeches of Henry Clay,* I, 162-84. On dating the speech see *Niles' Weekly Register,* XXV (January 17, 1824), 319.

Debate on the bill for surveys for roads and canals (see above, Remarks, January 12, 1824) had been resumed in Committee of the Whole of the House of Representatives on January 13, when Philip P. Barbour had supported his motions, held over from the preceding day, and had been answered by George Holcombe, of New Jersey. The Committee had then risen at Clay's request, which entitled him to the floor when the House again sat in Committee of the Whole on the bill.

[1] See above, II, 311n; Clay to Johnson, April 12, 1822, note.

[2] On January 22, 1823, President Monroe had sent to the House a report stemming from legislation of April 14, 1820 (3 *U. S. Stat.*, 563; above, II, 793). The document, submitted by Brigadier General Simon Bernard (a French engineer serving in the United States Army, 1816-1831, at this rank) and Major Joseph G. Totten (of Connecticut, brevetted a lieutenant colonel for gallantry in the War of 1812), was not so encouraging as Clay stated, the writers commenting that an experiment at dike construction to deepen the channel was justifiable because of the "very great importance of the object in view" but that they were "not sanguine in their belief of its efficiency in all cases requiring remedy." *House Docs.*, 17 Cong., 2 Sess., no. 35, p. 17.

Tabled for the remainder of that Session, the report was taken up in February, 1824, in connection with a bill "to improve the navigation of the Ohio and Mississippi rivers." See below, Remarks, March 12, 1824; Remarks, May 7, 1824.

[3] Built in 1819, this vessel had struck a snag and sunk about a hundred miles above Natchez, during the night of February 8, 1823, with great loss in lives and property.

[4] Pennsylvania and Virginia, principally because of the rejection of Philadelphia and Richmond as terminals.

[5] See above, I, 845. Two canals through New Jersey were in contemplation at this time—the Delaware and Raritan, which had been surveyed in 1816 and again in 1823, and the Morris Canal between the Delaware River and New York Harbor over a route surveyed prior to incorporation of the Morris Canal and Banking Company in 1824. Construction on the latter was begun in this year and completed by 1832; work on the Delaware and Raritan, not begun until 1831, was completed in 1834. The Chesapeake and Delaware Canal project, long under contemplation, had been recently revived: construction on the canal was begun in 1824; it was partially in use by 1828 and completed by 1830. A Chesapeake and Ohio Canal, via the Potomac River, had received particular attention in November, 1823, when, following revocation of the charter of the earlier Potowmack Company and issuance of a new charter to a successor in February of that year, a convention, called by the Maryland legislature, had been held in Washington to discuss feasibility of the undertaking. Construction on this system was begun in 1828, but it was built only as far as Cumberland, Maryland, and not completed to that point until 1850.

[6] "Message from the President of the United States, with His Objections to the Bill for the Preservation and Repair of the Cumberland Road; Also a Paper, containing His Views on the Subject of Internal Improvements," *House Docs.*, 17 Cong., 1 Sess., no. 127, p. 25.

[7] *Ibid.*, 27. [8] *Ibid.*, 37-40. [9] See above, Speech, February 7, 1822, note.

[10] *Annals of Cong.*, 17 Cong., 1 Sess., XXXIX, 1803. See above, Clay to Johnson, April 12, 1822.

[11] *Annals of Cong.*, 17 Cong., 1 Sess., XXXIX, 1804.

[12] 3 *U. S. Stat.*, 699 (May 7, 1822).

[13] See above, II, 491n, 629n. [14] John McLean.

[15] When Clay finished speaking, a majority of the Committee voted against striking out the enacting clause of the bill, and the blank for appropriation was filled with the sum of thirty thousand dollars. The Committee then rose and reported, a motion to engross the bill was approved, and the following day was designated for third reading.

From Robert Scott

Dr. Sir Lexington 16th. Jany. 1824

My last respects were of 5th. inst. enclosing your a/c with Colo. Morrison's estate down to 1st. inst.— Since then, had [*sic*] the pleasure of receiving your favor of 29th. Ulto.[1] and enclosures therein referred to— Mr. Turner[2] charges liberally—quite too much I think Indeed I do not know of any thing he did of consequence in the claim against Smith, except in the adjustment of the partnership Accts[3]—for which he charges 250$. Why he should charge a 1000$ in the other case[4] I am quite at a loss to know— Enclosed is the evidence of the U S B Stock—6 Shares—[5] Since my last have paid Mrs. Clay 165$ Coms., collected of Wilkins &c for rent of S. Cooper for Jonathans hire— I have issued Warrt. of Distress vs Colo. Whaley— Mr Todd says it is necessary that you should answer Shreve's Bill— If I am not mistaken you informed me otherwise— As you are a judge of this matter, I enclose a copy of the Bill and Shreves letter, which was the inducement to receive the Note of Shreve & Co. from Poague— When you have the papers before you, you will know what is best for you to do in the matter— The Jessamine Co. Ct. begins on 3rd. Monday in April—[6]

On the Bank Stock, I presume there is some dividend due— J. Henderson & Sons, Natchez[7] inform me they have sold between 2 & 300 Coils of the rope but do not say at what price nor time of credit given—

Mrs. Morrison & family are well— As were yours a day or two since— very respectfully Your obt. Servt. ROBT. SCOTT

The Honble H. Clay Congress.

ALS. KyLxT. [1] Not found.

[2] Fielding Turner, prominent New Orleans lawyer.

[3] See above, Morrison to Clay, February 18, 1821. John K. Smith, listed as "Insolvent," owed the estate $30,932.61, as estimated in August, 1826. Fayette County, Will Book F, 233; Conjectural Estimate of the Condition of Col. Morrison's Estate . . . August, 1826 (KyLxT).

[4] Not found.

[5] Cf. above, Scott to Clay, December 4, 1823; Clay to Gratz and Brother, February 1, 1824.

[6] On June 14, 1823, Clay, as executor of James Morrison, had taken an assignment (not found) of a note for $1,581.79, given to Alexander Dougherty, of Mason County, Kentucky (brother of Thomas), by William Shreve and his sons, Leven L. and Thomas T., as partners in ownership of an iron works in Greenup County of that State. Dougherty had transferred the note to Robert Poague, who, owing a comparable sum to the Morrison estate, had made the assignment to Clay. The understanding between the Shreves and Dougherty had been that the note was to be redeemed in currency, provided that the obligee was not to lose more than twenty per cent by depreciation of the paper. Clay had brought suit and won a judgment in Jessamine Circuit Court to enforce payment of the whole sum in specie. The Shreves' bill was a petition in equity for an injunction against Clay's claim to $354.04, representing interest charges and a discount of twenty per cent for specie payment, said to have been already provided for in the assignment from Dougherty to Poague. Scott's copies of letters from William Shreve to Scott, June 13, 1823, and from Levi L. Todd to Scott, January 1, 1824, and of the Shreves' bill of complaint, including a letter from Dougherty to Leven L. Shreve, September 12, 1823, stating the terms of the transaction are filed in KyLxT. At the April Term of Jessamine Circuit Court the injunction was denied. Jessamine Circuit Court, File 183.

[7] John Henderson, a Scotchman, had long engaged in business in Natchez, Mississippi, where he had also been Recorder of Adams County, County Treasurer, and Receiver for the Government Land Office in the Mississippi Territory, west of Pearl River. His firm became John Henderson and Sons in 1821.

From Baptis Irvine

Sir, January 18th, 1824.

To economize in paper and space, as well as bulk, I have crowded the preceding copy into a nutshell[1]— Should the *President* condescend to glance at it, (if you can conveniently show it to him,) he will perceive more clearly perhaps the nature of the damage done to me by the kidnappers here, and the deception practised on the U. S. gov't. as well as on that of Holland.

I wave all remark about Mr. Parker.[2]— Suffice it to say, once for all, that Cantzlaar (who in the short term of 3 years has accumulated a fortune by the prostitution of his office,) *with the testimony before him,* dispatches a messenger to La Torre,[3] and informs him, that he had arrested *an expedition!* He well knew the fiction he was relating; as no man in his senses would put in here, *eight days or more out of his course,* on his way to Porto-Rico. Remember, that the fiscal himself[4] admits there was none. The object was *to enhance the price of the offered service.*— He could easily pledge the servile court to anything whatever; knowing, as he did, that the *same men* were every one bribed in the case of *Ellis* vs. *Van der Moehlen,*[5] which has made a great noise even here, and that a nod from him is irresistible—especially as S——e— & co.[6] have already prepared them for any purpose. In truth, their excessive pliancy put the governor in perplexity, who (stunned perhaps by my letters on their *unlawful* outrages) shrunk from executing their sentence, sent for the drunken judge, and requested an appeal, "as a particular accommodation to *himself.*" These are his very words. Still, he would screen them, and make common cause against any one likely to expose their turpitude. They are his puppets & his breastwork.

A person[7] well versed in the language and usages here has collected a sketch of some leading briberies & *harasseries,* in the different offices, from the governor's downwards, through four of them —and means to publish it in *the United States.* I have read it,— and would have been surprised, if my own experience had not damped all wonder.— To others it will be a rare curiosity; and prove the identity of despotism on a grand scale or a small one, in a spacious empire, or a worthless colony.

I concluded by telling you that, as I cannot relish to be bartered or sold by a Dutch kidnapper at a fixed pries [*sic*], as I have been;— I still rely *on the President* to avenge my wrongs.

Supposing that *he* may believe I had unlawful designs, relatively to my obligations as a citizen; that would be a question *in* the United States, not elsewhere— Will he suffer *an Algiers* to exist in shape of a *petty* Dutch colony, whose coinage of illicit sea-papers has robbed so many honest Americans of vessels & cargoes? I cannot think it. Did Parker never inform on, or protest against the odious practice?

The ship from Holland, with the Minister's decisio[n] expected a month ago, not yet arrived.—Should she soon come, I will go over to La Guayra[8] probably, until I hear from the United States. May that be soon!

Letters to-day from Colombia represent this country very tranquil at the rumor of a Spanish expedition. Preparation would do no harm— Much talk of war between England & France. All this *you* know better than Your humble servant B. IRV[INE]

Hon. H. Clay.

ALS. DNA, RG59, Misc. Letters.

1 An enclosure, copy of a letter dated January 12, 1824, from Irvine to William Prince, identified by Irvine as "Govt. Secy. Caracas," but soon thereafter "master and commandant of the Brig Romp of Boston" in the Caribbean trade. Irvine, who in the autumn of 1822 had been associated as Government Secretary, pro tempore, of a revolutionary movement led by H. LaFayette Villaume Ducoudray-Holstein against the Spanish Royalist refugee base on the island of Puerto Rico, had been captured with other members of the expedition when, en route, they had put into the Dutch port of Curaçao. A native of Germany and a former general under Napoleon, Ducoudray-Holstein was at this time serving under Bolívar. Sentenced by the local tribunal of Curaçao to thirty years of labor in the salt mines, Irvine in this letter protests against the actions of the Dutch governor, Cantzlaar, who had refused to notice Irvine's previous memorial of December 20, 1823, which had sought redress for his imprisonment or permission to address the Baron Antoine Reinhard Falck, Dutch Minister of Public Instruction, National Industry, and the Colonies (1818-1827). ALS copy. DNA, RG59, Misc. Letters.

2 Cortland L. Parker, of New Jersey, United States Consul at Curaçao since 1819.

3 Miguel de la Torre, Military Governor of Puerto Rico, formerly in command of the Spanish forces of Tierra Firme.

4 Not identified. 5 Case not found. 6 Not identified.

7 Not identified; no publication has been found. 8 Venezuela.

To Nicholas Biddle

Sir

Washington 20h. Jan. 1824

I am extremely sorry to have to inform you that there has been another failure of the Federal Court at Columbus in Ohio, owing to the non-attendance of both the Judges. This makes three successive failures of the January term of that Court. I had given such instructions and made such arrangements that, if there had been a Court, the business of the Bank would have proceeded without detriment from my absence.[1] As it is, we must look forward to the September term, with better hopes. At the May term and that in November, both of which I shall, I trust, be able to attend in Kentucky I think we may reasonably anticipate upon the despatch of the mass of the business of the Bank in that State. In the mean time it is very important to get the Supreme Court, at its approaching term, to adjudicate upon all the principles of our Execution laws, in the several cases which I have brought up for that purpose.[2] The doctrines which the Court may settle must necessarily apply both to Kentucky and Ohio. I transmitted to Mr. Sergeant and to

Mr. Cheves, the same decision of our Court of Appeals, of which I had the honor to send you a Copy.[3]

With great respect I am Your obedt. Servant H. CLAY

Nicholas Biddle Esqr.

P. S. I duly received your letter of the 14h. inst.[4] respecting the business of Col. Johnson,[5] and will attend to its contents. H C.

ALS. PHi-Etting Collection.

1 See above, Clay to Este, December 15, 1823.

2 See above, Clay to Hammond, July 14, 1822, note; Clay to Biddle, December 27, 1822, note.

3 John Sergeant; Langdon Cheves. Letters transmitting the decision, probably in the case of Blair and Others *vs.* Williams, have not been found.

4 Not found.

5 Richard M. Johnson.

Resolution on European Intervention in America

[January 20, 1824]

Resolved by the Senate and House of Representatives of the United States of America in Congress assembled, that the people of these States could not see, without serious inquietude, any forcible interposition by the Allied powers of Europe, in behalf of Spain, to reduce to their former subjection those parts of the Continent of America which have proclaimed and established for themselves, respectively, Independent Governments, and which have been solemnly recognized by the U. States.

AD. DNA, HR 18A-B3. Published in *House Reports,* 18 Cong., 1 Sess., H. Res. no. 5; Washington *Daily National Intelligencer,* January 21, 1824; Lexington *Kentucky Reporter,* February 9, 1824; *Annals of Cong.,* 18 Cong., 1 Sess., XLI, 1104. Immediately after the House had resolved itself into Committee of the Whole on the state of the Union, Clay offered his resolution, "which he desired to lay on the table for consideration."

Remarks on Foreign Policy Resolutions

[January 20, 1824]

Mr. CLAY then rose, and said he hoped the Committee would not rise. He trusted that gentlemen were now prepared to act on the resolutions, with respect to Greece; and as to that which he had himself submitted, and which the gentleman from Virginia had, he must say, gratuitously, and without just reason, alluded to in his observations, it was by no means his wish that it should be now considered. He had distinctly stated, at the time he offered it, that he wished merely to lay it on the table that it might be reflected on. At a proper time he should call it up for discussion. He would, however, incidentally remark, since it had been made the subject of animadversion, what he hoped incontrovertibly to prove, that that resolution, or something like it, must be adopted, or we might prepare to surrender our liberty. If the gentleman wished time to consider it, he should be accommodated: he might take days, or weeks, if he pleased, for more mature reflection: but if the liberty of the country was worth preserving we must rouse ourselves; we must take decided ground, or we are gone, at least in prospect. He trusted that the committee would now proceed; he pledged himself to show to it that this tocsin of war which had been sounded with so much effect from one side of the house to the other, was, when examined, a mere creature of the imagination. He hoped that the resolution of the gentleman from Massachusetts would be adopted. The measure for which it prepared was in strict accordance with the policy of this country, and with the practice of all our Presidents, from the days of our immortal Washington to this hour. He was disposed to accord to the gentleman from Virginia every reasonable accommodation; but, asked Mr. C. has it come to this? Have we yet to *make up* our minds on the question of the Greek cause? Has there, then, been no pillow reflections on such a subject? Is it now that we are for the first time to "sleep upon it?" He trusted[1] not. He did hope that, ere this time, every gentleman had made up his mind on such a question. The proposition is before us. It asks us to speak a cheering word to the Greeks. Gentlemen had only to say yes or no. That monosyllable was all that was asked of them. Let them say, distinctly, whether they would give so much encouragement as this to a nation of oppressed and struggling patriots in arms, or whether they would shut themselves up in a cold, shivering, contracted, but mistaken policy, which must in the end react upon ourselves. If, in a proposition so simple, so plain, so harmless, so free from all real danger as this, we were to shut our hearts from the influence of every generous, every manly feeling, let gentlemen say so at once. But he could tell the gentleman from Virginia, that he who follows the dictates of a heart warmed with humanity, and with the love of freedom, has a better guide than that cold, unfeeling, pence-calculating policy, which shrinks before it is menaced, and will never do a noble deed, for fear of some remote, possible consequences, of conceivable danger.

[Randolph begged Clay's pardon. He had not meant to interfere with his resolution. He "presumed (judging from the source from which the observations just uttered had proceeded) that they were held to be perfectly in order; but the gentleman from Kentucky would pardon him, if the lofty promises that gentleman had given, with respect to what he would show and prove when his resolution came to be considered, left his mind somewhat in doubt as to their realization. He recollected that, in the case lately before the House, on the motion of his honorable colleague, promises equally large had been given by the gentleman from Kentucky, which in his judgment, had failed of their fulfilment."[2] He had made up his mind regarding Greece and South America, but this was no reason why the resolutions should not be printed. "As to consulting, in legislation, the heart rather than the head, he had indeed, learned from much higher authority than that of the gentleman from Kentucky, that our passions may sometimes instruct our reason; but the question was, whether the present was one of those cases?"]

Mr. CLAY, in answer, said, that he had presented his resolution in no invidious spirit; he had simply read it, and asked to lay it on the table; and any thing that had since fallen from him respecting it, had been drawn forth entirely by the allusions to it in which the gentleman from Virginia had, unnecessarily he must think, indulged himself. As to the realization of promises, it was possible, in the instance referred to, he might, in the judgment of the gentleman, have failed: but that gentleman was one with whom, in any effort he might make, he should not calculate on much success. Complete, however, as his failure might have been, he would venture to assure that gentleman, that it had not been greater than *his* would be in attempting to prove the danger he had attributed to the resolution now before the committee. Observations of this kind, he said, were painful--they were extorted from him with reluctance. He hoped the discussion would be conducted calmly, fairly, and with good feelings. So far as his own resolution was concerned, he could assure that gentleman, and every other, that he should ever be ready to afford the amplest time for deliberation and discussion.[3]

Washington *Daily National Intelligencer,* January 21, 1824. Published also in Lexington *Kentucky Reporter,* February 16, 1824; *Annals of Cong.,* 18 Cong., 1 Sess., XLI, 1113-15. After Clay had offered his resolution (above, this date) the Committee of the Whole had resumed consideration of a resolution, submitted by Daniel Webster, December 8, 1823, recommending "That provision . . . be made by law for defraying the expenses incident to the appointment of an agent or commissioner to GREECE, whenever the President shall deem it expedient to make such appointment." U. S. H. of Reps., *Journal,* 18 Cong., 1 Sess., 35. The resolution had been defended by Webster on January 19. Now, on January 20, Joel R. Poinsett had argued against it and offered a substitute, which merely expressed deep interest in "the heroic struggle of the Greeks," "sympathy for their sufferings," and "ardent wishes for their success." (A second resolution, similar to that proposed by Clay, had been offered, then withdrawn, by Poinsett.)

John Randolph had thereupon moved that the Committee rise and that both Webster's and Clay's resolutions be printed. Referring to "this quixotism" in regard to Greece and Latin America, Randolph "saw as much danger, and more, in the resolution proposed by the gentleman from Kentucky, as in that of the gentleman from Massachusetts. The war that may follow on the one, is a distant war—it lies on the other side of the ocean. The war that may be induced by the other, is a war at hand—it is on the same continent. He was equally opposed to the amendment, as well as to that which had since been offered to the original resolutions. Let us look a little further at all of them. Let us sleep upon them, before we pass resolutions, which I will not say are mere hooks to hang speeches on, and thereby commit the nation to a war, the issue of which it is not given to human sagacity to calculate." *Annals of Cong.,* 18 Cong., 1 Sess., XLI, 1112-13.

Following Randolph's remarks, Alfred Cuthbert expressed a hope that the Committee would rise in order that the resolutions, which "threw open for discussion the entire field of our foreign relations," might "be printed, and submitted to the most deliberate reflection."

1 Printed in *Intelligencer* as "wusted"; corrected to "trusted" in *Annals of Congress.*

2 See above, Speech, January 14, 1824; below, Speech, January 30, 1824.

3 After further discussion and a speech by Henry W. Dwight in support of Webster's resolution, the Committee rose and obtained leave to sit again.

From Baptis Irvine

Sir, Curaçao, 20th January 1824

I hope you will do me the farther favor of laying the two articles within, marked (II) (III)[1] before the *President;* and I hope too, that he will consider them.

Although vile money was the spring of all movements against me here, the conspirators ventured on the desperate game entirely on the calculation, that *misrepresentation* from P——r[2] and others would effectually prevent the United States from interfering.— First, in hope of its being only a formality;—next in prospect of *going to Holland,* as promised from week to week;—and chiefly, because I was inexpressibly ashamed of a momentary dupery &c., I deferred writing to America. But hearing, that the most scandalous fabrications have been circulated there, I think it a duty to present an occasion of inquiry and interposition,—not without confidence that the *President* will think it *his* duty to move in the matter. — Is it only the pirates of Cuba & Porto-Rico that need chastisement?[3] Look into Curaçao, and you will find baser wretches.

I am, Sir, most respectfully Your servt. B. I——.

Hon H. Clay.

I take the liberty of requesting, that when the enclosed shall have been perused by THE CHIEF, you would have them pubished.[4] I submit it to your descretion [*sic*].—Though the conspirators have tried to gild our prison, given us comfortable *debtors'* apartments, increased *per diem,* as to those whom the chief conspirator ridiculously terms in his instructions to F—l[5] *"prisoners of distinction!"* yet their crimes & insults are unpardonable.—

ALI. DNA, RG59, Misc. Letters. Endorsed, apparently by a clerk in the State Deportment: "with Mr. Speaker Clay's Letter to the President of 12 June 1824." Cf. above, Irvine to Clay, January 18, 1824.

1 Enclosure "II" is a copy of a letter dated January 20, 1824, from Irvine to A. R. Falck, asking that complaints against Cantzlaar be laid before the King. Enclosure "III" is a copy of the letter of January 12, 1824, from Irvine to William Prince.

2 Cortland L. Parker.

3 See above, Warfield to Clay, December 10, 1822.

4 No publication has been found.

5 Not identified, possibly "Fiscal."

From Thomas Diehl and Others

Henry Clay Esqr. Philad. Jany. 21. 1824

Sir

In consequence of your Letter[1] from Lexington informing us, you expected the voucher of your haveing paid the Amot. due the Estate of Mr. Jacoby.[2] was at Washington with your papers, we addressed you a Letter their [*sic*] dated 27th. Ultimo.[3] to which we have not as yet Recd. an answer, we expect on the Recpt. of this, you will give the buisness [*sic*] prompt attention, and either forward coppy of the Voucher of the Money haveing been paid. or remit the Amot, the amot. due as appears from papers in our possession including Interest to 14 April 1823 is $730..27 the necessaty of bringing the Estate to a close compells us to urge your prompt attention, Your obat Servt THOMAS DIEHL

FRANCIS JACOBY

WM. J BAKER

ALS by Diehl, signed also by Francis Jacoby and William J. Baker. Fayette Circuit Court, File 665 (1828). Directed to Washington, "favoured by J. Sergant [*sic*] Esqr." Endorsed by Clay on cover: "Jacoby's business (Remitted a check for $250 to the within drawn by the Washn. Office on the B. U. S. dated 15 May 1824)." Check not found. Diehl was Leonard Jacoby's son-in-law; Francis Jacoby, probably a son of Leonard, and Baker have not been further identified.

1 Not found. 2 Leonard Jacoby. 3 Not found.

From Thomas Fletcher

Dear Sir Owingsville Ky. Jany. 21st. 1824

Since my return from Frankfort[1] I have seen those concerned in the Suit Littlepage against Fowler and others, in which the Heirs of Col Hart are also interested against the claim of Littlepage. they Claiming under Mosbey Those concerned are anxious for you to defend the Suit now in the Supreme Court, they will give you $200– in Currency, that being the sum you proposed to take; On this Subject please write me & say will the Cause be tried at the ensuing Term or not.[2]–

I hope you are geting on well with your Presidential Election. The Stubenville & Cincinnati Resolutions not with Standing, from the best information we have been able to Obtain from Ohio the Clinton Ticket will not Succeed against you I presume Genl. Jackson does not consider it a compliment on the part of the People of Ohio to nominate him as Vice President,[3] I met Col W. P Anderson in Frankfort a few days before I left there. he States that Genl. Jackson will not Get over one half of the votes of Tennessee, partly Owing to his success over Col Williams[4] for the Senate– Williams & his friends will exert themselves against Jackson however in this Col. A may be mistaken

how does Mr. Barbour feel towards you after the prodigious beeting you Gave him[5]

when at leasure please Give me a line Yours most Sincerely

TH: FLETCHER

P.S. No local news here worth your attention. TF

ALS. DLC-TJC (DNA, M212, R12). Addressed to Clay at Washington.

[1] The legislature, which Fletcher had attended as Representative from Bath County, had adjourned January 8.

[2] Letter not found. At the June Term, 1822, the Federal Circuit Court for the District of Kentucky had ruled in favor of the defendants, John Fowler and others, against the claim of John Carter Littlepage, of Hanover County, Virginia, to a prior entry on a location of 20,000 acres at the mouth of Fox's Creek, on the north bank of the main fork of the Licking River, about 35 miles above the Upper Blue Lick. The heirs of Colonel Thomas Hart were involved as claimants under the patent to Littleberry Mosby for property conveyed to Joel Havens by Clay as Hart's executor (see above, II, 891). The case was tried, on appeal, in the United States Supreme Court at the February Term, 1826, and the decision of the lower court affirmed. U. S. Circuit Court, Seventh Circut, District of Kentucky, Complete Records, P, 404-41; 24 *U.S.* (11 Wheaton) 215-25.

[3] See above, Clay to Stuart, December 19, 1823, note.

[4] John Williams.

[5] See above, Acceptance, December 1, 1823, note.

From Sidney Montgomery

Sir) Baltimore 21st Jany. 1824.

I have received a letter from Mr. Robt. Scott of date 1st Nov. 1823, stating, that you as one of the executors of Col. Morrisons estate requested him to inform me, that You were willing to pay me the same sum for My Annuity, you paid to My sister Mary,[1] that is $350, upon my giving you Notice of My Agreeing to it, & giving a receipt in full for the Annuity, & that you would arrange for paying me when you came to washington.

I Now give you Notice that I accede to your proposal Made through Mr. Scott, & upon sending Me the Amount of $350, I will execute A receipt which you will please to prepare & send with the Money, in full of my Annuity. your obt. Servt.

SIDNEY MONTGOMERY

LS. DLC-TJC (DNA, M212, R12). Addressed to Clay at Washington. Endorsed by Clay: "Answd. & inclosed a Check for $350 on the Off. of Dt. & Dt. Washn City the 16 Feb. 1824." Answer not found. Sidney Montgomery was a sister of Mrs. James Morrison.

[1] Mary Montgomery. James Morrison had willed to each of the sisters forty dollars per annum for life. Fayette County, Will Book F, 65, 67.

To Francis T. Brooke

My dear Sir Washn. 22d. Jan. 1824

I duly recd. your obliging letter of the 18h. instant.[1] I am glad to hear of the probability of the recovery of Col. Taylor's health.[2] With respect to his opinions on the subject to which you refer, whatever they may be,[3] they cannot diminish that habitual veneration for him which I have ever cherished.

On the point of a Caucus, in a spirit of perfect desparation [*sic*], a continued effort is making to get one up. It will be defeated, you may rely, either by being voted down, in a general attendance of the republican members, or by a resolution of a large majority of them not to attend. If they make one, it will be a faction, a Cabal. My friends say that, on the score of mere expediency, they have no objection to a Caucus which shall be composed of the Republican members generally; that they have no fears of the result of such a Caucus; but that they have no idea of consenting to make part of a Caucus in which they should act the part of mere figuranti, which would be the case, if the friends of other Candidates, who it is well known will not attend should be absent.

The election, in all human probability, will come to the H. of R. In that case, if Mr. Crawford, Mr. Adams and I should be the three highest, as is most probable, my friends do not entertain a doubt of my election. They even confidently believe that, on the very first ballot, I should receive the vote of at least twelve states, among which would be those of Pennsa. and Ohio. Information from the latter leaves no earthly doubt of its support of me, and that from Indiana is equally conclusive.

With great regard I am faithf ly Yr. friend H. CLAY

The Honble F. Brooke.

ALS. KyU. Published in part in Colton (ed.), *Private Correspondence of Henry Clay*, 86.

1 Not found.

2 The death of John Taylor of Caroline had been reported in the Washington *Daily National Intelligencer* on January 13, 1824. The following day there had been a retraction of the report and the next day a comment that his physicians had "*some* hopes of his recovery." On January 23, it was noted that his condition had so improved "as to allow, not only sanguine hopes of his recovery, but of his being able before long to undertake the journey to the seat of government." He died, however, on August 21 of that year.

3 Cf. above, Brooke to Clay, August 14, 1823.

Speech on Mission to Greece

[January 23, 1824]

Mr. CLAY then rose, and commenced his speech by distinctly stating the original resolution, as moved by Mr. Webster, and the amendment proposed by Mr. Poinsett. The resolution proposed providing the means to defray the expense of a mission, whenever the President, who knows, or ought to know, the dispositions of all the European powers, Turkish or Christian, shall deem it proper to send one: The amendment goes to withhold any appropriation, and to make a public declaration of our sympathy with the Greeks, and our good wishes for their cause. And how, sir, (asked Mr. C.) has this simple, modest, unpretending, this harmless proposition been treated? It has been argued, as if it proposed aid to the Greeks; as if it proposed the recognition of their government; as an act of unjustifiable interference; as a measure of war. And those who thus argue the question, while they themselves give unbounded range to their imagination, in conceiving and setting in array the monstrous consequences which are to grow out of so simple a proposal, impute to us who are its advocates, Quixotism, Quixotism. While they are taking the most extravagant and limited[1] range, and arguing any thing and every thing but the question before the House, they accuse us of enthusiasm, of giving the reins to feeling, of being carried away by our imagination. No, sir, the proposition on your table is no proposition for aid, nor for recognition, nor for interference, nor for war.

I know that at least some of the objections to the original proposal are occasioned by the source from which it has proceeded. There are individuals in this House, who look at the mover of this resolution, as if its value or importance was to be measured by inquiring who brought it forward. Sir, I have long had the pleasure of knowing the honorable gentleman who originated this resolution—I have sometimes had the pleasure of acting with him; and I would suggest to those to whom I have alluded, that, if they seek to be regarded as the sentinels of freedom, they must disregard the source from which any measure favorable to its interest may happen to have proceeded, and must take it upon its own intrinsic merits. If a gentleman who happens to belong to a different party, in political sentiment, shall bring forward a proposition fraught with liberal principles and noble sentiments, is it to be rejected for his sake? if this is the case, we cease to be republicans, and those who act on principles the reverse of ours, will be the men who truly deserve that name; and, sir, if all republicans must oppose this doctrine and all federalists advocate it, I for one, should cease to be a republican, and would become a federalist.

Mr. Chairman, is it not extraordinary that, for, now, these two years, the President of the United States should have been allowed, not only without censure, but with universal applause, to express all the feelings which either the resolution or the amendment on your table go to sanction or to declare?[2] So far is this from having met the disapprobation of the American people, that, from Maine to Georgia, and from the Atlantic to the Gulf of Mexico, the sentiment of approbation has blazed with the rapidity of electricity! That it is felt with the deepest intensity, that it is expressed in almost every possible form, and that it increases with every new day and passing hour. And, Sir, are we alone to be insulated from the common moral atmosphere of the whole land? Shall we shut ourselves up in apathy, and separate ourselves from our country? from our constituents? from our Chief Magistrate?

The measure, Sir, has been unwarrantably magnified. Gentlemen speak of the watchful jealousy of the Turks, and seem to think that the lightest [*sic*] movements in this body will be matter of speculation at Constantinople. He could assure the gentlemen that the European powers attached no such vast importance to our acts and deliberations as some seemed to suppose. The Turk will in all probability never hear of the gentlemen's names who either advocate or oppose the resolution. The resolution is certainly not without its value, but that value is wholly a moral value; it throws our little tribute into the vast stream of public opinion, which, sooner or later, must regulate the physical action upon the great interests of the civilized world. But, sir, rely upon it the Turk is not about to declare war because this unoffending proposition has been offered by my honorable friend from Massachusetts, of whom, however eminent in our own country, the Sublime Porte has never yet heard. The Allied Powers are not going to be thrown into a state of alarm by a resolution appropriating two or three thousand dollars to send an agent to Greece.

The question has been argued as if the Greeks were likely to be exposed to increased sufferings in consequence of such a measure; as if the Turkish cimetar [*sic*] would be sharpened by its influence, and dyed deeper and yet deeper in Christian blood. Sir, if such is to be the effect of the declaration of our sympathy, it must have happened already. That expression is very fully and distinctly given, in the message of the President to both Houses of Congress, not only this year, but last. And I would again remind the gentleman, that it is the President's Message, and not any record of our debates, that goes the rounds of the European Cabinets. This document is translated into their several languages, and is read by their Ministers of State, and possibly by some of the Sovereigns themselves: possibly by the Divan; but our resolutions are all for domestic use—for home consumption; they never will meet either royal or imperial eyes. In that Message, the President, after a most eloquent and touching representation of the feelings excited by the Greek insurrection, tells you, that the dominion of the Turk over that people is gone forever, and that the most sanguine hope is entertained that they will succeed in establishing their independence. Well, Sir, if this is the fact, if their independence is almost achieved, if the allied powers themselves, possibly before we shall again meet in this Hall, may acknowledge that independence, is it not fit to make provision that our President may be among the foremost in that acknowledgment—or, at least, not among the last?

But, Sir, so far from this resolution being likely, if passed, to produce injury to the Greeks, it is likely to have a directly opposite effect. Sir, the Turk with all his power, and in all the elevation of his despotic throne, is at last but man; he is made as we are, of flesh, of muscle, of bones, and sinews; he can feel; and, Sir, he has felt the uncalculating valor of American freemen[3] in some of his dominions; and when he is made to understand, that not only the Executive of this government, but that this nation; that our entire political fabric, base, column and entablature, rulers and people, with heart, soul, mind, and strength, are all on the side of the nation he is crushing, he will be more likely to restrain, than to increase his atrocities upon suffering and bleeding Greece.

The gentleman from New Hampshire has made, on this subject, a very ingenious, sensible, and ironical speech, an admirable *debut* for a young member, and such as I hope we shall often have repeated on this floor. But, Sir, permit me to advise my young friend to remember that declaration, "sufficient unto the day is the evil thereof," and when the resolution which I have had the honor of laying on the table shall come to be discussed, I hope he will not think it sufficient to say, as he has now done, that the measure, or the argument in its support, is "a very extraordinary one," but that he will then let us hear an argumentative speech to prove that it is our duty to lay prostrate every fortress of human hope, and to see with complacency the last outwork of liberty taken.[4] This, however, is foreign to the question now before the House.

It has been said, that the proposed measure will be a departure from our uniform policy with respect to foreign nations;—that it will provoke the ire of the Holy Alliance;—and will, in effect, be a repetition of their own offence, by an unwarrantable interference with the domestic concerns of other powers. No, sir; not even if it proposed, which it does not, an immediate recognition of Grecian independence. What has been the uniform policy and practice of this Government, from the days of Washington to this moment? In the case of France, President Washington, and his successors, received Genet, Fuchet [*sic*],[5] and all who followed them, whether sent from king, convention, anarchy, or emperor. Sir, the rule we have followed has ever been this: to look at the state of the fact, and to recognize that government, be it what it might, which was in actual possession of soverign power. When one of these governments was overthrown, and a new one established on its ruins, without embarrassing ourselves with any principles involved in the contest, we have ever acknowledged the new and actual Government as soon as it had positive existence. Our simple inquiry has been, which is the Government *de facto*? An example has recently been furnished in relation to the Government of Spain. When the foreign ministers were driven or retired from Madrid, and refused to accompany Ferdinand to Cadiz, our Minister sought at that port, to present himself to the constitutional Ferdinand—why? This Government held Ferdinand to be the actual king.[6] Did this produce any declaration of war? Were any diplomatic notes ever received complaining of this proceeding? Nothing like it, sir. The lines are so plainly marked in which we are to go, that there is no mistaking them. We are to engage in no interference with their disputes, no contests for either party, no entangling alliances, but to maintain our diplomatic intercourse with existing Sovereignties. It has been admitted by all, that there is impending over this country a threatening storm, which is likely to call into action all our vigor, courage, and resources.[7] Is it a wise way of preparing for this awful event, to talk to this nation of its incompetency to resist European aggression, to lower its spirit, to weaken its moral force, and do what we can to prepare it for base submission and easy conquest? If, Sir, there be any reality in this menacing danger, I would rather adjure the nation to remember that it contains a million of freemen capable of bearing arms, and ready to exhaust their last drop of blood and their last cent, in defending their country, its institutions, and its liberty. Sir, are these to be conquered by all Europe united? But I am quite sure that that danger, so far at least as this resolution is concerned, is perfectly ideal and imaginary. But, if it were otherwise, any danger is best guarded against by invigorating our minds to meet it—by teaching our heads to think, our hearts to conceive, and our arms to execute the high and noble deeds which belong to the character and glory of our country. Sir, the experience of the world may instruct us that conquests are achieved when they are boldly and firmly determined on: and that men become slaves as soon as they have ceased to resolve to live freemen. If we wish to cover ourselves with the best of all armor against perils, let us not discourage our people, let us stimulate their ardor, let us sustain their resolution, let us show them that we feel as they feel, and that we are prepared to live or die like freemen. Surely, sir, we need no long or learned lectures about the influence of property or of rank;[8] let us rather remember that we can bring into the field a million of bayonets; let us remember that we are placed over a nation capable of doing and of suffering all things for its liberty. I can never forget what was once said to me by a most illustrious female, the first of the age, if not of her sex,[9] on this subject. "Mr. Clay, (said that enlightened lady,) a nation never yet was conquered." No, sir—no united nation can be, that has the spirit to resolve not to be conquered; such a nation is ever invincible. And, sir, has it come to this? Are we so humbled, so low, so despicable, that we dare not express our sympathy for suffering Greece, lest, peradventure, we might offend some one or more of their imperial and royal majesties? If gentlemen are afraid to act rashly on such a subject, suppose, Mr. Chairman, that we draw an humble petition addressed to their Majesties, asking them that of their condescension they would allow us to express something on the subject. How, sir, shall it begin? "We, the representatives of the free people of the United States of America, humbly approach the thrones of your Imperial and Royal Majesties, and supplicate that of your Imperial and Royal clemency"—I will not go through the disgusting recital; my lips have not yet learnt the sycophantic language of a degraded slave. Are we so low, so base, so despicable, that we may not express our horror, articulate our detestation, of the most brutal and atrocious war that ever stained earth, or shocked high heaven, with the ferocious deeds of a brutal soldiery, set on the clergy and followers of a fanatical and inimical religion, and rioting in excesses of blood and butchery, at the mere details of which, the breast sickens?

If the great mass of Christendom can look coolly and calmly on, while all this is perpetrated on a Christian people in their own vicinity, in their very presence, let us, at least shew, that, in this distant extremity, there is still some sensibility and sympathy for Christian wrongs and sufferings, that there are still feelings which can kindle into indignation, at the oppression of a people endeared to us by every ancient recollection, and every modern tie.

Sir, the House has been attempted to be alarmed by the dangers to our commerce, and a miserable invoice of figs and opium have [*sic*] been presented to us to repress our sensibilities, and to eradicate our humanity.[10] Ah, Sir, "What shall it profit a man if he gain the whole world and lose his own soul?" or what shall it profit a nation to save the whole of a wretched commerce, and lose its liberties?

As to the question of American interests, hitherto, it has not been necessary to depart from the rule of our foreign relations laid down in regard to Europe. Whether it shall become us to do so or not, will be discussed when we take up another resolution[11] that lies upon your table. But we may not only pass this resolution; we may go further; we may recognize the government in the Morea,[12] and yet it will not be any cause of war, nor will it be war, nor even aid. Besides, Sir, what is Greece to the Allies? A part of their own dominions? By no means. Suppose the people in one of the Philippine Isles, or in any other spot still more insulated [*sic*] and remote, in Asia or Africa, were to resist their former rulers, and set up and establish a new government; are we not to recognize *them* for fear of the Holy Alliance? If they are going to interfere on the principle of example, here is the spot where they must strike. *This* government, you, Mr. Chairman, and the body over which you preside, are the living reproach to allied despotism. If they attack us at all, they will do it *here*. They will assail us in our own happy land. They will attack us because you, Sir, sit beneath that canopy, and we sit freely debating and deliberating upon the great interests of freemen. They will strike because we pass one of those bills on your table. The passing of the least of them by our authority is as galling to despotic powers as will be the passage of this so-much-dreaded resolution.

Pass the resolution, and what, sir, do you do? You exercise an act of indisputable sovereignty for which you are responsible to none of them. You do the same act as when you pass a bill—no more. If the Allies object, let them forbid us to take a vote in this House—let them disperse us—let them strip us of every attribute of sovereignty.

Do gentlemen attempt to maintain that, on the principles of the laws of nations, these powers have *cause* of war? Sir, if there is any principle settled for ages, any which is founded in the very nature of things, it is, that every sovereign power has the right to judge as to the fact of the existence of other sovereign powers. I admit there may be a state of inchoate, inactive sovereignty, in which a new government is struggling into being, and may not be said yet perfectly to exist; but the premature recognition of such a new Government can give offence justly to no other than its ancient sovereign. The right to recognize comprehends the right to be informed; and the means of information must depend upon the sound discretion of the party seeking it. You may send out a commission of inquiry, and charge it with a provident attention to your own interests and your own people. If you adopt it, no act necessarily follows. You merely grant the means by which the Executive may act when he thinks proper. What does he tell you in his message? that Greece is struggling for freedom—that all sympathise with her, and that no power has declared against her. You pass this resolution, and what does it say to the President? "You have sent us grateful intelligence: we feel for Greece, and we grant you money, that, when you think it proper, when the interests of this nation shall not be jeopardized, you may depute a Commissioner, a public functionary, to Greece." This is all it says; and the whole responsibility is left with the Executive, where the Constitution puts it. But, sir, it is not first and chiefly for Greece, that I wish to see this measure adopted. It will give them but little aid, and that aid purely of a moral kind. It is, indeed, soothing and solacing in distress, to hear the accents of a friendly voice, (we know this as a people.) But, sir, it is principally and mainly for America herself, for the credit and character of our common country, that I hope to see this resolution pass: it is for our own unsullied name that I feel.

What appearance on the page of history would a record like this make, Mr. Chairman, "In the month of January, in the year of our Lord and Saviour, 1824, while all European Christendom beheld with cold and unfeeling apathy, the unexampled wrongs and inexpressible misery of the Christians in Greece, a proposition was made in the Congress of the United States, almost the sole, the last, the greatest depository of human hope and of human freedom, the Representatives of a nation capable of bringing into the field a million of bayonets, while the freemen of that nation were spontaneously expressing its deep-toned feeling, its fervent prayer for Grecian success, while the whole continent was raising, by one simultaneous emotion, solemnly and anxiously supplicating and invoking the aid of heaven to spare Greece and to invigorate her arms, while temples and senate houses were all resounding with one burst of generous feeling—(gentlemen may call it enthusiastic declamation if they please; would to God we could hear such declamation, and the utterance of such feeling from them)—in the year of our Lord and Saviour, that Saviour alike of Christian Greece and of us—a proposition was offered, in the American Congress, to send a Messenger to Greece, to inquire into her state and condition, with an expression of our good wishes and our sympathies—and it was rejected." Go home, if you dare; go home, if you can, to your constituents, and tell them that you voted it down—meet, if you *dare,* the appalling countenances of those who send you here, (he meant no defiance,) and tell them that you shrank from the declaration of your own sentiments—that you cannot tell how, but that some unknown dread, some indescribable apprehension, some indefinable danger, affrighted you—that the spectres of cimetars and crowns, and crescents, gleamed before you, and alarmed you; and that you suppressed all the noble feelings prompted by religion, by liberty, by national independence, and by humanity. He could not bring himself to believe, Mr. C. said, that such would be the feeling of a majority of this House. But, for himself, though every friend of the measure should desert it, and he be left to stand alone, with the gentleman from Massachusetts, he would give to the resolution the poor sanction of his unqualified approbation.

[John Randolph moved that the Committee rise but suspended his motion at the request of Cuthbert, who desired from Clay an explanation of some parts of his speech: ". . . as he understood them, they seemed to contain reflections and insinuations, respecting those who opposed the resolution, which were of an unpleasant kind; if its opponents had in them the spirit of freemen, they were not to be terrified from their posts by menaces. He could not believe the gentleman meant all his words seemed to convey—if he did, he would say that he, for one, defied the insinuations, and scorned the denunciation."]

Mr. CLAY explained. He had no intention to disturb the gentleman; he should take back nothing of what he had said; but he could assure the gentleman, that he had no personal allusion to him, or to any other gentleman on that floor: far from it—his feelings on the subject were strong, and he might have expressed them strongly. The advocates of the motion had been called Don Quixotes; and he had meant to repel imputations of that kind.

[Cuthbert "requested to be more clearly informed whether the Speaker had intended to support the original resolution or the amendment: for such was his zeal, that it was not always easy to understand his precise intention. At one time, he tells us with that sneer he so well knows how to employ (for the honorable gentleman commands the whole armory of the orator) that the European monarchs do not read our resolutions: at another, he says, they are jealous of our government." He further asked if Clay wished to "abandon this continent for a war in Europe" and if he were not aware "that the Emperor of Russia, without one hostile word being publicly uttered, has only to withdraw his troops from certain points they now occupy, to bring down immediate ruin on the Greek cause?"]

Mr. CLAY said, in reply, that, it appeared he had been very unfortunate in the speech he had delivered, since the gentleman felt obliged to make the present inquiry; but he must have been more unfortunate than ever he had been before, if the gentleman was, indeed, ignorant that it was the original motion he meant to support. He was, indeed, in favor of both, and he should like to see them incorporated together.

Washington *Daily National Intelligencer*, January 24, 1824. Published also in Lexington *Kentucky Reporter*, February 9, 1824; and, dated erroneously, in *Annals of Cong.*, 18 Cong., 1 Sess., XLI, 1170-78; Chambers, *Speeches of the Hon. Henry Clay*, 149-56; [Swain], *Life and Speeches of Henry Clay*, I, 185-93; Mallory, *Life and Speeches of the Hon. Henry Clay*, I, 488-95; Colton, *Life, Correspondence, and Speeches of Henry Clay*, V, 246-53. Clay had not participated in the continuing debate on the Greek question since his remarks on January 20. He now followed Alfred Cuthbert, who obtained the floor when the House again resolved itself into Committee of the Whole.

1 The word printed as "unlimited" in *Annals of Congress* and as "boundless" in Chambers, Swain, Mallory, and Colton.

2 In both his annual messages to Congress, December 3, 1822, and December 2, 1823, Monroe had expressed "A strong hope" that the Greeks would succeed in their struggle for independence.

3 The word printed as "freedom" in *Annals of Congress*.

4 Ichabod Bartlett, who had taken his seat as Representative from New Hampshire on the preceding December 12, had on January 22 spoken at some length against the resolution concerning Greece. Our ground of complaint against the Holy Alliance, he had pointed out, is "that they claim to interfere with the governments of other Powers." That being true, "What right have we to interfere with the internal concerns of the Government of Turkey?" Developing further this aspect of the question and noting that the Greeks had been subjects of the Ottoman Sovereign for four hundred years, he had commented: "Suppose that a certain part of the population of the United States should attempt to take the government, by force, into their own hands— and they have not been four hundred years under their masters— should the sovereign of Hayti send 'an agent or commissioner' to encourage them— and we cannot deny he has a right to feel for them as much sympathy as we do for the Greeks—should we take it kindly? Would we not expound the law to him, and, if necessary to convince him of his error, resort to the *ultima ratio regum*? But, if we pass this, and another extraordinary resolution on your table, do we not at once furnish an authority against ourselves? Is not our principle abandoned?" *Annals of Cong.*, 18 Cong., 1 Sess., XLI, 1151, 1152. See above, Resolution, January 20, 1824.

5 Edmond Genêt; Joseph Fauchet, who had succeeded Genêt as French Minister to the United States.

6 Hugh Nelson's instructions, dated April 28, 1823, after the French attack on Spain (see above, Lafayette to Clay, November 5, 1822), noted that his credentials had been addressed "to Ferdinand the King of Spain under the Constitution." Secretary Adams had stipulated: "So long as the Constitutional Government may continue to be administered in his name, your official intercourse will be with his Ministers. . . ." DNA, M77, R4.

7 Cf. above, Scott to Clay, December 15, 1823. The prevalent popular belief in the "grave danger which menaced the United States" as a consequence of President Monroe's message of December 2 and the "self-confident nationalism" which "took for granted . . . the ability of the country to repel any threat which might be offered" are discussed in Dexter Perkins, *The Monroe Doctrine, 1823-1826* (*Harvard Historical Studies*, XXIX; Cambridge, 1932), 144-49. See also Adams, *Memoirs*, VI, 226.

8 In the debate of January 21, Silas Wood had explained that "Property is the basis of power in society. . . . The hereditary descent of property and established ranks, with exclusive privileges, lie at the foundation of the European Governments. . . ." So long as "the feudal principles of rank and property remain," the power of the great mass of the people "would be unavailing to withstand their influence." The Greeks, like the revolutionists of Cromwellian England and of France and South America, lacked "the elementary principles of freedom." "The adoption of the resolution, under these circumstances, would be premature. . . ." *Annals of Cong.*, 18 Cong., 1 Sess., XLI, 1135-37.

9 Probably Madame de Staël.

10 Both Bartlett and Christopher Rankin, during the debate on the previous day, had warned that the Turks might retaliate for passage of the resolution by attacks upon American commerce in the Mediterranean. *Annals of Cong.*, 18 Cong., 1 Sess., XLI, 1154, 1159.

11 See above, this document, note 4.

12 Following the meeting of a national assembly at Epidaurus, a constitutional government had been proclaimed for Greece on January 13, 1822.

Reply to Attack by Ichabod Bartlett

[January 24, 1824]

Mr. CLAY rejoined. The gentleman from N. Hampshire, he believed, was a new member of this House. If he had ever been here before, he was ignorant of it. He had never, till now, heard of his name, in the House or out of it. In his speech on the resolution of the gentleman from Massachusetts, this gentleman had gone out of his way, to attack a resolution laid on the table by the Speaker, and which was not then under consideration. He had replied to him, he thought—he certainly intended it—with great respect, with great decorum;[1] it was his habit so to treat every member of this House, and particularly a new member, on his trial, for the first time, before this House and this country. He chose to travel out of his track, said Mr. C. to assail my resolution; but I must say, he did not more mistake the dimensions of that resolution, than he has done his own. And now, after lying on his pillow for twenty-four hours, he comes here with a conned reply. What I now say, I say not for him, but out of respect to this House. If that gentleman had felt himself aggrieved, and had, at the time, requested an explanation, it would, with all readiness, have been furnished; but he has chosen to go on, and to seek it in the manner we have just witnessed, and now let him get it where he can. On this floor he shall never get it from me. The honorable gentleman has further permitted himself to introduce a topic the most unfit that can be brought before this committee: he has alluded to a relation in which I stand to this country, (which has not been of my seeking,) and he has ventured to insinuate that the ground I have taken in the present discussion has been influenced by motives derived from, or connected with, that relation.—{Here the Chairman interposed, and reminded the gentleman now speaking, that the gentleman last up had expressly disclaimed the imputation of such motives, and had said that it would be unjust.} Mr. Clay resumed—I know he disclaimed them, and yet he made them, sir—I know the import of words. If a man says a thing is black, and then tells me he meant by that to say that it was white, I know how to understand him; but if he did mean to cast the insinuation upon me, I cast it back with scorn and contempt upon his own shoulders, and there it rests.[2]

Washington *Daily National Intelligencer,* January 26, 1824. Published also in Lexington *Kentucky Reporter,* February 9, 1824; *Annals of Cong.,* 18 Cong., 1 Sess., XLI, 1201-1202. As the debate of this day on the resolution relating to Greece (above, Speech, January 23, 1824) drew to a close, Ichabod Bartlett "proceeded to say, that however young he might be, either personally, or as a member of that House, he felt it incumbent on him to rise, and to repel the charge of personality which had been cast by the honorable Speaker upon the opponents of the resolution of the gentleman from Massachusetts; were that charge, as stated, indeed applicable, the parties involved in it, would be more worthy of the cells of a criminal penitentiary, than of a seat on this floor. The charge had been made very broadly—and if the loud voice, the menacing look, and sneering gesture, which accompanied it, were intended to apply to him personally, he must send it back as unjust, ungenerous, untrue." He then referred admiringly to Daniel Webster's defense of the resolution, which through ability in argument and "corruscations of wit" had been "an intellectual treat." Turning again to Clay, Bartlett "did not *advise,* but he must say to the honorable Speaker, that it was unwise to throw out the insinuations which had escaped him as to the motives of the opposition; they were as little merited as would be the insinuations of one who should say to that Hon. gentleman, 'You, sir, have a great personal and political object in view—you perceive that, on this question, the whole country is in a tempest—you feel it to be necessary for you to "buy golden opinions from all sorts of men"—and you have aimed to "ride on the whirlwind and direct the storm."' Insinuations of this kind, would be, as to that gentleman, unjust as they would be disgraceful; to he who should make them, but not more so than those which had been thrown out against the opponents of the resolution. He had been 'seriously advised' by the Hon. Speaker, he ought, doubtless, to receive the advice with all due deference; yet, however criminal it might be, he felt inclined to say to him, 'I thank you for your advice—more, forasmuch as it was altogether gratuitous and uncalled for; but, however inexperienced I may be, or however young, when I feel any need of lessons on the subject of political integrity, I feel myself of age to select my instructor.'"

In the same vein, he concluded by saying that "Somewhat too, of *terror* had been resorted to. Gentlemen were asked if they *dare* go home to their constituents after voting against the resolution. Whether to vote against the resolution, or against the opinion of that honorable gentleman were the more daring, he would not attempt to determine; where he should go when he left this House, he might not be able to say, but if not to his constituents, he certainly should not go to the Grand Seignior, for he should make a bad slave either at Constantinople or in this House. However obscure he might be, he had no constituents so humble as not to know that he dare do all his duty."

1 See above, pp. 606, 612n.

2 Clay apparently did not participate further in the debate on the Greek question, which was resumed on Monday, January 26, and was ended on the same day when the Committee rose without having voted on Webster's resolution, Poinsett's amendment, or a last-minute amendment proposed by John C. Wright.

From Peter B. Porter

Dear Sir, Albany, Sunday Evg, Jany 25. 1824

I came here yesterday, where I found the political elements in great commotion on the presidential question. When, or in what precise shape, they may eventually subside, it is impossible, at present, to say— My decided opinion, however, is, that the Electoral votes of this State will ultimately be given in favour of H. Clay.

The published proceedings of our Members either in their legislative or individual characters, on the subjects of *Caucusses* & of giving the choice of Electors to the people, will furnish no clue by which you can determine the relative strength of the several candidates. It is not improbable that the Assembly many of whom are committed will pass a Bill giving the choice of the electors to the people, but it is pretty well understood that the bill will not receive the sanction of the Senate.[1] It is perhaps more important to you than to any other candidate, that the appointment of the electors should be retained by the Legislature—for (so far as the observations I have made for the short time I have been here, enable me to judge) I feel much confidence in saying that you will have a decided majority of our Legislature with you. On the other hand, if the election goes to the people, the votes will be much scattered, and it is not improbable that Clinton may get a plurality of the votes.

The Republicans of this State are *Caucus Men,* & the strongest & most frequent objection which the friends of Mr Crawford make to you is, that you & your friends are opposed to a Congressional caucus. A letter from known [*sic*] & respectable member to me, stating (if such are the facts, & such I have understood them to be) that you are willing to submit your pretensions to a caucus composed of the Members of Congress generally—or to a *general* (not however going so far as to require an *universal*) meeting of the Republican Members. But that you are not disposed to advise a caucus composed of all of Mr Crawfords friends, & a part only of yours, many of whom are restrained from attending either by personal scruples, or legislative restrictions—or something of this sort would be usefull.— Mr Crawfords friends here rest all their hopes on a Congressional Caucus. And if a caucus is held at Washington I trust that care will be taken, to have it either a very *general* one—*or as limited in point of numbers as possible,* so as to render it harmless.

Be very circumspect in your letters to this place, particularly to Doct. Stuart,[2] who, altho a zealous & devoted friend, is not distinguished for great discretion, nor for political influence. Genl. McClure[3] is equally your friend but lacks a little in the virtue of prudence. It will be generally better for your friends to write to them. Please write me. Yours with great respect & regard.

P. B. PORTER

ALS. DLC-HC (DNA, M212, R1).
1 Cf. above, Woods to Clay, August 27, 1823, note.
2 Josephus B. Stuart. 3 George McClure.

From [John E.] Hall

Mr. Clay Honoured Sir, Deliberation-Seat 27 Jany *1824*

Allow me to ask you; are the members of Congress still to *sleep* upon the subject of *slavery*? Have they yet to *make up their minds,* whether the *black population* of this Country should be set free? Have they had no *pillow-reflections* respecting the manumitting of *them,* poor wretched creatures! and despatching *them* to the *Morea* under the *flag* of the United States to fight for the Greeks, in *their* glorious struggle with the Turks for *religious* and civil liberty? Surely, in such a Country as this, where the *feeling* of *sympathy* and of *freedom* runs so high there can be no hesitation in putting an end to all kinds of slavery and to all kinds of *religious oppression*— Are the coloured people, then, to be held in slavery by Christians, like *you,* who are ready and willing to act the *noble* and *praise worthy part* of *Don Quixottes* for the liberation of a degraded and enslaved world? Can our respected friend Mr. Randolph be really in earnest when he denominates the rash interference of *the States* with foreign matters, *Quixotism?* Quixotism!— Yes it is Quixotism— And how honourable to be Quixotes in such a cause!—! Yes! Yes! We shall, Mr Clay, put down *Holy* and Impure Alliances and cause the cap of freedom to dance either *madly* or wisely on every head. Talk no more of *ploughing* and *sowing* of *canals* and internal *improvements;* for we *shall* neither *eat, drink* nor SLEEP upon the *subject* of *Grecian Independence* until, by our *potent* and *eloquent* speeches, *Mr. Clay,* we cause the *Turks* and the other *alliances* to come into our terms and fix the politics of the whole earth according to our wise and infallible contrivances—*Sleep* before this is accomplished! No! This would be below OUR Spirit, Mr Clay, and altogether unworthy of the *hot* and *Quixotic* state of our *invincible* blood! Hold to your position, my Dear Sir, and, *then, sleeping* or *waking*—whether you *dream,* that you are in Greece, or in the *President's Chair,* in America, you will always find a faithful and staunch frend [*sic*] in— QUIXOTTE-HALL

ALS. NHi-John W. Taylor Papers. Addressed: "The Honourable Mr. Taylor Member of Congress Washington D. C." Postmarked at Philadelphia, January 27. This political diatribe, probably by John E. Hall, may not have reached Clay. Cf. above, Remarks, January 20, 1824.

From Ichabod Bartlett

Sir Washington 29. January 1824.

The remarks, which I made in the House of Representatives on Saturday last, were delivered under an impression, that your previous observations had left an existing imputation upon me of improper motives for my official conduct. Considering myself authorized to view the explanation, which you had previously made, as extending to myself, and being since satisfied, by information from those, who were seated nearer to you, that such an explanation was made, as, had it been known to me at the time, would have prevented my remarks, I now frankly state my regret, that expressions which were intended to repel, what I then deemed an unjust imputation, should have been made, when no such imputation attached to me—

However desirous I may be to disclaim the influence of improper motives, I am not less desirous to correct any misapprehension, or remove any misunderstanding, that may have produced unpleasant feelings in the mind of a gentleman towards whom I have ever entertained sentiments of high respect.— I have the honor to be Sir Your obedient Servant ICHABOD BARTLETT.

To the Honorable Henry Clay.—

ALS. DLC-HC (DNA, M212, R1). This letter and that which follows resulted from negotiations described in an unsigned, undated (*ca.* January 30, 1824) memorandum of eleven manuscript pages, drawn up by an unidentified friend of Clay and endorsed by the latter on verso: "Papers respecting personal affair with Mr. Bartlett." According to this account, Clay reported that on the morning of January 26 he had been approached by the senior Senator from New Hampshire, John F. Parrott, "in reference to the controversy which took place betwen him (Mr C) and Mr. Bartlett, . . . in the Ho of Rep: on Saturday the 24th—" Parrott, declaring that he acted voluntarily, though with the approval of Bartlett, desired "to have such explanations between Mr. C & Mr. B as would put them on a footing of amity." In reply Clay had stated "that he was on all occasions amicably disposed, but held that on this he was so situated that he had no explanations to offer on his part unless they were made proper by previous explanations on the part of Mr B.— That, however, he had no objections to name a friend who should converse with Mr. Parrott.—" That evening Parrott had called on Clay's friend, who had agreed that an "amicable accommodation" was possible; "That, however, Mr. Clays situation appeared to me to be such that he could make no advances tho' I had no doubt of his willingness to meet any on the part of Mr. B, Which should be Consistent with his honor—that his [fe]elings were strong but his nature generous—" He had further maintained that Bartlett had been entirely in the wrong, perhaps "acting under bad advice—" (of which Parrott immediately disclaimed any part); that in his first speech Bartlett had been the assailant; that no "well Constituted mind, at all experienced in Parliamentary proceedings, who was not governed by hostile feelings and not heated by debate would Consider" Clay's remarks exceptionable; that Clay's reply to Alfred Cuthbert "ought to have Satisfied the most jealous mind & Still more so Mr B. to whom he had alluded in the most Complimentary manner in the Speech itself"; that Bartlett had slept on it and seen the explanation in print "and after all had made a most violent & disorderly attack on the Speaker"; that the attack was "the more exceptionable" from having been "made on one who from his relations to the House was forbidden the full use of the means of repelling it which an other member would have enjoyed"; and that the first step "must be a removal of the aspersion which Mr B's remarks had Cast upon Mr. Clay"

Parrott had replied that if Bartlett, who held "no hostile feelings to Mr. Clay," had understood himself included in Clay's explanation to Cuthbert, "he would not have opened his lips." To this Clay's friend had commented "that I was Certain Mr. Clay had no feelings towards Mr B. which would prevent a reconciliation, if the aspersion apparently Cast upon him were properly removed, that I was also Sure he wished nothing from Mr. B. that would be humiliating to him & that I hoped & believed the declarations of Mr B which he, Mr P., had just mentioned if put in a proper shape & Coupled with the usual apt expressions of Courteous regret would Call from Mr. C a reply that would heal the feelings of Mr B.—"

On Wednesday, January 28, the mediators again had met and agreed that Bartlett should address a note directly to Clay; that Parrott should place it in the hands of Clay's friend "under the promise . . . that no use should be made of it & that it should be returned to him, without retaining any Copy of it, unless it was finally accepted"; and that, if it were found to be satisfactory, Clay's reply would be put in Parrott's hands under the same promise. During the conversation Parrott "took pains to have it understood that any act of Mr. B. Should be Considered as entirely *Voluntary* & not the result of any *threat*." Parrott further "was in the act of stating that while Mr. B. desired an amicable adjustment of the misunderstanding, he was of a Character that would not shrink from any different result," when Clay's friend "stopped him & told him I could not hear a word on that subject—that it did not belong to the nature of our Confereces [*sic*] & I could not listen to it—he was about to explain by referring to the impressions of New England on such subjects, but I again stopped him & said I could not hear a Word on the subject."

On the following morning Clay's agent received from Parrot a note, in Parrott's hand but drafted with Bartlett's approval, and promised to submit it to Clay for his consideration. That night a reply, framed by Clay, was handed to Parrott. Upon agreeing that the notes were satisfactory, the negotiators agreed to meet the next day and exchange them "in form." Consequently, on January 30, the "Notes were exchanged as agreed upon in the precise terms of the papers originally submitted—"

It was next agreed "that some respectable member of the House should be selected to Announce to it, the Arrangement between the parties—" Louis McLane, Chairman of the Ways and Means Committee, was first asked to perform this task; but, when he manifested some hesitation and embarrassment, the intermediaries requested James Hamilton, Jr., "to make the annunciation." AD. DLC-HC (DNA, M212, R1).

Accordingly, on January 30, at the end of debate in Committee of the Whole on the bill for surveys for roads and canals (see below, Speech of that date) but before the presiding officer had left his chair, "Mr. HAMILTON rose in his place, and stated that he wished, though in a very informal way, to make a communication, to which, from its nature, he was sure every gentleman would listen with interest The House had all witnessed, with regret, the very unpleasant altercation which during a late debate, had taken place between two honorable members of this House He was now the bearer of the agreeable intelligence that, through the spontaneous interposition of friends, the state of feeling which arose on that occasion had been successfully removed, and had been exchanged in a manner highly honorable to both parties, for a happier one; the gentlemen had been restored to each other in relations of mutual amity and personal respect, and every painful recollection removed—he congratulated the House on so happy an issue of an affair which all who witnessed it could not but deeply deplore." *Annals of Cong.*, 18 Cong., 1 Sess., XLI, 1317.

To Ichabod Bartlett

29 Jan. 1824

Mr. Clay hastens to acknowledge the receipt of the note of Mr. Bartlett of the — day[1] which he has perused with very great satisfaction. The frank and manly spirit which dictated it leaves Mr. C. at entire liberty to declare, as he does in the most unreserved manner, that no observation whatever of his in the debate on the Greecian resolution which took place prior to saturday last was intended to question the motives or to cast the slightest imputation of any sort on Mr. B. On the contrary Mr. C. participated largely in the general gratification felt by the House in listening to a speech which indicated a considerable acquisition of talent; and any remarks which he made respecting Mr. B. or his speech were intended for encouragement and to stimulate to fresh exertions rather than to to [*sic*] reproach or assail him. The general observation of Mr C. on the objection which he had heard that some had made to the source of the proposition, under consideration, was not even designed to comprehend Mr. B. but to refer to others who had not shared in the debate. And as to them it was far from his intention to wound their feelings. His sole wish by it was to rally his republican friends to the support of a resolution which seemed to him to afford some small aid to the liberal cause which they have ever espoused.

Mr. C. seizes the occasion to express the hope that the painful incident which has given rise to this correspondence may be improved to promote the public service and an amicable personal relation

AN draft. DLC-HC (DNA, M212, R1).
1 See above, this date.

From Baptis Irvine

Sir, January 29. 1824

To encourage you to glance over these notes & expostulations, I promise to trouble you no farther. Mr P. . . . e[1] is no honester than the rest of the band. I *use* him solely as a medium. All began with *Parker* & the notorious Von Spengler.[2] Cantzlaar &c. followed.

The ship expected at *New Year,* with a decision, or [*sic*] suppression of farther farces, not yet arrived—perhaps gone to the bottom.

[. . . .][3]

Seeing that *Parker* is a man who STICKS AT NOTHING, it is probable that he has poisoned the ear of Mr—[4] or of the *President,* by false representations of D—y's[5] project. This may be one source of

Cantzlaar's insolence.— If the President be once undeceived, as he must be on enquiry, I trust to his prompt and energetic interference.[6] Ought he not *make an example of this gang of legalized freebooters before all the West-Indies*?—

I hope *you* will coincide with your obedt servt. B. IRVINE

Hon H. Clay

ALS. DNA, RG59, Misc. Letters. Probably received with Irvine's letter, above, January 20, 1824.

1 William Prince. 2 Cortland Parker; Von Spengler not identified.

3 Extracts copied from a letter written by Irvine to Prince, January 25, 1824, again protesting the illegality of his imprisonment, are here omitted by the editors.

4 Probably John Q. Adams. 5 H. La Fayette Villaume Ducoudray-Holstein.

6 The Administration, forced to extend assurances to the British, disclaiming any part in the venture, viewed it as a violation of American neutrality law. After nearly a year and a half of imprisonment Irvine and Ducoudray-Holstein were released upon orders of the King of the Netherlands and ordered from Dutch territory. *Niles' Weekly Register,* XXVI (April 10, 1824), 96; Adams, *Memoirs,* VI, 104, 430-31.

Speech on Surveys for Roads and Canals

[January 30, 1824]

Mr. CLAY rose in reply to Mr. RANDOLPH. It had certainly, he said, been far from his intention again to trouble the committee on the present subject. He felt restrained, not only by a consideration of the time that had already been spent upon it, but also by the state of his own health; but allusions so frequent, and of such a marked character, had been made to him, (especially by the honorable gentleman who had just taken his seat,) that he trusted it would not be deemed a trespass on the committee if he should briefly notice some of them.

The gentleman from Virginia, (Mr. Archer,) [1] for the general character of whose discussion he felt the highest respect, and whose intelligent mind never led him to say what was not, at least, worthy of serious consideration, had observed, in the course of his speech, (which I regret that I heard only in part,) that he was quite sure I would concede that, in ascertaining what were lawful means to be taken for carrying into effect either of the granted powers in the constitution, a congruity would be required in such means with the power to be executed. To this I then nodded assent; and I now repeat the expression of my concurrence. But I submit it to the committee to say, whether there is any discrepancy between roads and canals as a means, and the transportation of troops and munitions of war as an end; between good roads as a means, and the transportation of the mail as an end; between roads and canals as a means, and the regulating and facilitating of internal commerce as an end.

Another gentleman from Virginia, (Mr. Stevenson,) whose speech

I had the pleasure of hearing throughout, alluded to a speech of mine, delivered on a former occasion, and which contained, as he contended, sentiments in opposition to those expressed by me in the present debate.[2] Although I think it somewhat unfair to travel out of the proceedings of this House in search of arguments advanced on a different occasion and in another body, yet, whatever others may say, I, for one, have never felt the slightest difficulty in owning any and every part of the course I have pursued, and in avowing the motives by which I have been actuated. It is true that I was opposed to the renewal of the charter of the old Bank of the United States. My opposition to it arose from various motives, involving not merely the constitutional question, but the expediency of the measure. I admit that I did not, at that time, believe that Congress could, constitutionally, grant the incorporation. But, on another occasion, after much experience had, in a state of war and in the most perilous times, of the urgent necessity of such an institution, I did, on farther consideration, change my opinion,[3] and, in having done so, I stand in company with some of the best, the wisest, and the purest men of our country, and especially with that man who most deserves the gratitude of this country for the establishment of this government, I mean the late chief magistrate of the United States, and with one not less honest, though less distinguished, the present Governor of Virginia.[4] The conviction was forced upon us by necessity and the lights of experience. But, while I acknowledge this, I must, at the same time, be permitted to say, that I think the gentleman who urged this has utterly failed of establishing the slightest contradiction between the principles I then held and those on which I advocate the present bill. His failure is most signal.—He first assumes it for granted that, if Congress does not possess the power of incorporation, it has no power to make internal improvements; and then he urges my objections against the former power to disprove the existence of the latter. But I am sure that, to do away this assumption, I may appeal not only to his own candor, (for I never admitted what he assumes,) but to the example of his own state, which has, at this moment, a Board for Internal Improvements, sanctioned and aided by the state Legislature, and yet not incorporated; and to the example of this government, which made the Cumberland road without granting any act of incorporation to effect it. So that, even granting him the full benefit of the opinion I formerly held and expressed in the Senate, and which he now quotes against me, it does not advance him one step in his argument.

A member on my right (Mr. Randolph) has done me honor to notice an argument I brought forward some eight or ten days ago, and although he set out with declaring that he should treat it with more respect than I had treated that of the chief magistrate,[5] I think, I may appeal to the committee to decide whether he has redeemed the pledge. Sir I am growing old. I have had some little measure of experience in public life, and the result of that experience has brought me to this conclusion, that, when business of whatever nature, is to be transacted in a deliberative assembly, or in private life, courtesy, forbearance, and moderation, are best calculated to bring it to a successful conclusion. Sir, my age admonishes me to abstain from involving myself in personal difficulties; would to God that I could say I am also restrained by higher motives. I certainly never sought any collision with the gentleman from Virginia. My situation, at this time, is peculiar, if it be nothing else, and might, I should think, dissuade at least a generous heart from any wish to draw me into circumstances of personal altercation. I have experienced this magnanimity from some quarters of the House.[6] But I regret that, from others, it appears to have received no such consideration. The gentleman from Virginia was pleased to say that, in one point at least, he coincided with me—in an humble estimate of my grammatical and philological acquirements.[7] I know my deficiencies. I was born to no proud patrimonial estate; from my father I inherited only infancy, ignorance, and indigence. I feel my defects; but, so far as my situation in early life is concerned, I may, without presumption, say they are more my misfortune than my fault. But, however I may regret my want of ability to furnish to the gentleman a better specimen of powers of verbal criticism, I will venture to say, it is not greater than the disappointment of this committee, as to the strength of his argument. Sir, I am no preceptor: when I desire perfect accuracy of definition, or correctness of pronunciation, I may go to the highest authority in this House—probably in this country—the gentleman himself: but, in the meantime, I am very sure that my commentary on the word in question, has not yet been fairly met and refuted. The hon. gentleman from Virginia has asked, whether, in the preamble of the Constitution, the people of the United States are made to say that they adopt that instrument "in order to *construct* justice," or to *make* justice. I answer, sir, in one sense, yes. In all that relates to that part of the penal code which assigns punishment to acts not immoral in themselves, but only criminal because prohibited by law, whatever is malum prohibitum, and not malum in se, the law *creates* the crime: the crime, as such, had no existence till the law defined and prohibited it. Here criminal justice is *created,* and a crime is *constructed,* and *made* by force of law.

The gentleman from Virginia says that the settled sense of the Constitution for these thirty years past, may be gathered from the practice under it. But if his construction be true, no post road has yet been *established;* for, according to him, every one of them may be abrogated at pleasure by the States. The gentleman has gone for illustration to the small but respectable State of Delaware —and has said something about her "getting her back up," and "resisting the passage of the United States troops."[8] Sir, is the Legislature of the State of Delaware, or of any other State, large or small, to resist and defeat the laws of Congress made by delegates from every part of the Union? I know that the interest of the States is, in general, a guarantee against any resistance on their part, to the exercise of a power so beneficial as that of transmitting the mail; but we have seen cases of contest between a State and the General Government, in which their attachment to the confederacy, has not always been sufficient to restrain them, and we have seen them in peace and in war. A late instance occurred between the States of New York and Connecticut.[9] When men's passions get up, there is no telling before hand into what measures they may be precipitated.

But, has the gentleman met my argument on the difference between the Constitution and the old Confederation? That the government acts under the one by its own intrinsic energy, while by the other, it was dependent for every act upon the power of the State Legislatures? Has he shewn that this principle of difference does not apply to Post Roads, as well as to any other branch of the powers of the government? It is possible, I admit, that cases may be produced, in which the sense which the gentleman attributes to the word "establish" may hold[10]—but, in the Constitution, as well as in the President's Message, it is used in the sense for which I contended.

It has been said that one leading motive which led to the adoption of the Federal government, was the necessity of some general regulation for foreign commerce. I grant this; but I ask, are we to refer to the various motives which prevailed on the People to adopt the Constitution, or to the Constitution itself, for the principles of its interpretation? I will draw an illustration of this part of my subject from the records of that profession, of which the gentleman from Virginia has spoken, in no very respectful terms,[11] but which has produced in all countries some of the ablest, wisest, and best men that have ever adorned our species. I advert to a case which is no doubt familiar to the gentleman's historical recollection—the famous Coventry act,[12] which was passed in consequence of an affray that took place in the public streets of London, between some knights and other persons of distinction, and which prohibited, under severe penalties, the "drawing of blood in the streets"—no doubt ever did or could exist as to what was intended to be prohibited by this act; and yet, if its interpretation had been limited by the motive of its enactment or the preamble, it would have been restrained to the particular case which led to its passage. We must look into the instrument, to its words, and not out of it, for its true meaning. Resort may indeed be had to the preamble—but even the preamble is not suffered to control the interpretation. It is only used to assist in finding the meaning of equivocal and doubtful phrases. So in the present case—I know that commerce and revenue were leading considerations in the formation and adoption of the Constitution; but we are to look at the words of the grant, and though I would not say that we are wholly to reject all consideration of the motives, yet they are but of small avail in interpreting plain words in the instrument itself. Now, the self same words being applied in the Constitution to the powers of Congress over internal, that are applied to its powers over external, commerce, I contend that all powers given for the one are given for the other: the words are the same—the objects are the same. It is true, indeed, that, in the origin of the government, it might not be necessary to insist on this interpretation, because there was then no pecuniary means to exercise the power, or at least, in a very partial extent: the same may be said of the power to establish post roads. The country was just out of a distressing war, followed by a distressing peace. The public revenue was in such a state, that it was doubted if it would be competent to pay the civil list—it is not wonderful that, at such a time, the government did not use all the powers which it possessed.

Gentlemen have misstated, or misunderstood, what I said in relation to the exercise of powers confided to the government. I never said that simply not to exercise these powers was treachery:[13] but that when the public good required their exercise—and especially when none but Congress could exercise them, when Congress must exercise them, or they would not be exercised at all, then, not to use the power was treachery; and I still hold and repeat the sentiment. Although commerce and revenue were at first very leading motives to the Federal Constitution, are we to limit the Constitution by this rule? Let us remember that then the country had scarcely any interior—there were few settlements, and but few settlers, beyond the Alleghany [*sic*] Mountain. The whole interior has grown up since the Constitution was adopted—and tho' this gives no power, yet it may and ought to call forth every dormant power conveyed by that instrument, the exertion of which may tend to the public prosperity. It presents a new case—new relations—new interests; and certainly it is the duty of Congress to look to the whole—to remember we have an internal as well as an external commerce; and to seek to enable this country to say, what has been so often proudly said in England—"England is England's best customer." I hope that it will yet be said, America is America's best customer. Sir, a new world has come into being since the Constitution was adopted. Are the narrow limited necessities of the old thirteen States, of indeed parts only of the old thirteen states, as they existed at the formation of the present Constitution, forever to remain a rule of its interpretation? Are we to forget the wants of our country? Are we to neglect and to refuse the redemption of that vast wilderness which once stretched unbroken beyond the Allegany [*sic*]? I trust not, sir. I hope for better and nobler things. The gentleman intimates that the General Government may have powers in time of war which it does not possess in time of peace;[14] but I ask, has it any powers but what it holds by grant of the Constitution, expressed or fairly implied? And if not, does it not possess the same powers at all times? True it is, that in peace many of these powers are not called forth into action and exercise—but they exist nevertheless, or the Constitution is a nullity. Sir, is war a source of power? Is necessity a source of power? Surely not. The government holds its powers not by peace, or war, but by the Constitution. I ask whether, while peace yet continues, the government has no powers which are preparatory, but which have a direct relation to war? May it not cast cannon? May it not provide muskets, to put into the hands of a hardy and gallant yeomanry? May it not make forts?—and if it may do all these, do I advance a single step, when I ask, may it not make roads also? Yes, sir. I do say that roads are in place of forts, and in a great measure dispense with the necessity of building them: roads collect the moveable force of the country, and condense it on whatever point may be attacked or threatened by an enemy. What was told us when, the other day, we voted for a road in Arkansas?[15] That the great body of population in that territory was separated by a wilderness, from that in other states, impracticable [*sic*] and impassable; and we voted for that road as a measure of defence—and it is a measure of defence—far more effectual than fortifications would have been.

Another gentleman from Virginia (Mr. Archer) employed a species of argument, the propriety of which I again submit to his candor. He takes up all the various constitutional sources, whence the friends of the bill draw the power, and examines them separately and in detail. And, contending that no one of them would induce Congress to pass the bill, dismisses the whole in succession. Now, sir, is not this treating the subject upon grounds of expediency and not of power? He asks if you would make these internal improvements for the purpose merely of transporting the mail? Or for that of facilitating the distribution of the public force? Or for that of promoting internal commerce among the several states? And, emphatically pronouncing the negative, in reference to each of those several objects, the gentleman seemed to think that the committee ought to come to the same conclusion to which he brought himself, that this power does not exist. Is it fair, thus to pass in review the various objects, and to pronounce, that, since no one of them, considered by itself, would lead to the adoption of the proposed policy, the bill ought not to pass? The motive for the exercise of power is one, and a totally different thing, from the power itself. It might be conceded, that no one of the objects suggested, considered apart, would present a sufficient motive to enact the bill; and yet, that the aggregate effect of the whole of them united, would present an adequate motive. In truth, almost the whole argument against the bill is virtually an argument on expediency, rather than power. The gentlemen argue from extreme cases; but, if their argument amounts to any thing, it is good against the exercise of any power whatever, and applies as much to any and every other power of the government, even to those literally and expressly granted, as it does to the incidental power now in dispute. The power of taxation is a power expressly granted; and taxation may be carried so far as to take away the last dollar from every man in the community. But, is this good argument against the existence of the power? So gentlemen ask us if we are going to make 80,000 miles of post roads? No, sir; but this does not operate as a reason why we may not such as are called for by the wants and the safety of the country.

The gentleman from Virginia has reminded me of the many obligations conferred by this Government upon the West—and, among them, has spoken of the grants of land for education.[16] I ask the gentleman, Were not these paid for? Have not these school lots raised the value of the whole body of U. States' land, by which they were surrounded? Sir, the Western States have never yet received any thing from this Government, for which they have not given an equivalent. They have paid a *quid* for every *quo*. Was the West allowed to buy its land of the Indians? or, did not the whole avails go into your own exchequer? You yourselves desired it. And, as to the Indian wars, were they not necessary for the safety of the whole Union? {Here Mr. Randolph interposed, and denied having adverted to the Indian wars.} If he did not, said Mr. C. then I must say he has made out a wretched list of benefits. Sir, I regret the introduction of such a topic. It is one on which I should never have dwelt, unless forced into its discussion. But I will say, in leaving it, that the sale of your land to the people of the West, has brought more money into your treasury than has been acquired in the sale of the public domain of all the powers of Europe together, who own American colonies. I know it may be said, that there is no compulsion, and that the whole of this revenue is from voluntary purchase. True, Sir, But, is this parental Government to look, in the spirit of Shylock, only at the bond? If its policy, by whatever circumstances, has practically operated to drain one portion of the country of its money, ought not the Government, like a wise and considerate parent, to counteract this enfeebling process, by the adoption of a broad and beneficent national policy, especially when that may be done, not only without doing injury to any other part, but so as to advance the prosperity of all? With this appeal to the equitable feelings and the sound discretion of the committee, Mr. C. said he should close what he had now to say; and, as it had been with reluctance that he rose, he now sat down with equal pleasure.[17]

Washington *Daily National Intelligencer,* February 24, 1824, where the speech is mistakenly dated January 31. Published also in Lexington *Kentucky Reporter,* March 22, 1824, also dated erroneously; and in *Annals of Cong.,* 18 Cong., 1 Sess., XLI, 1311-17. The bill providing for surveys for roads and canals (see above, Speech, January 14, 1824) had been given its third reading on January 15. Debate on the measure had then resumed but had ended with the adoption of a motion, offered by John Randolph "(it is supposed with a view to allow the Speaker to take part in the debate)," to recommit the measure to a Committee of the Whole. *Annals of Cong.,* 18 Cong., 1 Sess., XLI, 1053-63. Taken up in Committee of the Whole on January 27, the bill was again the subject of prolonged consideration. John Randolph had begun the debate of January 30 by attacking the arguments advanced by Clay two weeks previously.

1 William S. Archer had spoken on January 28.

2 Speaking on January 29, Andrew Stevenson had quoted portions of Clay's speech in the United States Senate, February 15, 1811, opposing a bill to recharter the Bank of the United States (above, I, 531, 532).

3 See above, II, 199-205.

4 James Madison, in his message to Congress on December 15, 1815, had recommended consideration of the need for a national bank, and he had subsequently signed the measure establishing the second Bank of the United States. Among the members of the House Committee which had been appointed to consider this portion of Madison's message and had reported the bill to create the bank was James Pleasants, now Governor of Virginia (1822-1825).

5 Randolph had said, near the beginning of his speech on this day, "that, in my notice of the argument of that member [Clay], I shall show at least as much deference to it as *he* showed to the Message of the President of the United States of America, on returning a bill of a nature analogous to that now before us—I say at least *as much*—I should regret if not *more.*" *Annals of Cong.,* 18 Cong., 1 Sess., XLI, 1296. For the remarks to which Randolph refers, see above, pp. 576-77, 593n.

6 See above, Bartlett to Clay, January 29, 1824.

7 In his attack on Clay, Randolph had said "He was happy to be able to agree with that gentleman in at least one particular, to wit: in the estimate the gentleman had formed of his own powers as a grammarian, philologer, and critic—particularly, as those powers had been displayed in the dissertation with which he had favored the Committee, on the interpretation of the word *establish.*" *Annals of Cong.,* 18 Cong., 1 Sess., XLI, 1297.

8 Randolph had said: "But, we are asked, what if little Delaware should erect her back, or New Jersey, and should undertake to stop the transportation of the United States mail? It would be something like the attempt virtually made by another State

during the late war, or an attempt to stop the transit of the United States troops through the territory of a State." *Ibid.*, 1300.

9 Probably a reference to the conflict over the New York law prohibiting navigation of her waters by steam vessels without a license from that State, which had granted the privilege as a monopoly to Robert R. Livingston and Robert Fulton. In 1822 Connecticut had enacted retaliatory legislation providing that no one might enter her waters with a steam vessel under New York license. New Jersey and Ohio had also enacted laws directed against the New York action. *Niles' Weekly Register*, XXII (June 8, 1822), 226. The issue culminated in the case of Thomas Gibbons *vs.* Aaron Ogden before the United States Supreme Court at the February Term, 1824, wherein the Court, under an opinion delivered by Chief Justice John Marshall on March 2, held the New York laws in collision with the acts of Congress regulating the coasting trade, which having been made under the authority of the Constitution held supremacy. 22 *U. S.* (9 Wheaton) 1-240.

10 Stevenson had taken "issue with the Speaker, as to the meaning of this word 'establish.' If we go to philological authority, or common usage, it is much oftener used to signify 'confirm,' 'adopt,' 'designate,' than to create, construct, or build. Establish is to render certain, fixed." *Annals of Cong.*, 18 Cong., 1 Sess., XLI, 1269. Caustic in his reference to Clay's definition, Randolph had called "establish" "one of the plainest words in the English language." *Ibid.*, 1297.

11 Randolph had said he had learned "that *words*—the counters of wise men, the money of fools—that it is by the dextrous cutting and shuffling of this pack that is derived one-half of the chicanery, and more than one-half of the profits, of the most lucrative profession in the world. . . ." *Ibid.*, 1298.

12 In December, 1670, following a reference in Parliamentary debate to Charles II's interest in actresses, the speaker, Sir John Coventry, had been assaulted on the street and his nose slit to the bone. Parliament had thereupon enacted a law (22 & 23 *Car. II*, c. 1) providing that anyone who "of Malice fore-thought, and by lying in wait, shall unlawfully cut off or disable any limb or Member of any Subject of his Majesty, with Intention in so doing to maim or disfigure," the perpetrator of the act, together with his counsellors and abettors "are hereby declared to be Felons and shall suffer Death as in Cases of Felony without Benefit of Clergy." The first six sections of the statute, including the preamble, had dealt specifically with the assault upon Sir John.

13 This was Randolph's interpretation of Clay's argument.

14 Under the power to make war, said Randolph, "what may we not do? Quarter troops upon you; burn your house, sir, or mine; burn your own ships and your navy yards, that the enemy may not have the pleasure of doing it. But would any man contend that, in time of peace, all the incidents to the war-making power take effect?" *Annals of Cong.*, 18 Cong., 1 Sess., XLI, 1300.

15 A bill "to authorize the surveying and making a road from a point opposite to Memphis, in the State of Tennessee, to Little Rock, in the territory of Arkansas" had passed the House on January 7 and became law on January 31. 4 *U. S. Stat.*, 5.

16 Randolph had asked "What have we *not* done for the West? Do gentlemen want monuments? Unless the art of printing should be lost, posterity will find them in your statute books, and in the journals of this House. They may find them in Indian treaties for the extinguishment of title to lands—in grants of land, the effects of which begin now to be felt in Ohio, Kentucky, and Tennessee, as they have long been severely felt in Maryland, Carolina, and Virginia; they will find them in laws granting every facility for the nominal payment—and, he might also say, for the spunging, of the debts due this Government, by purchasers of the public lands—in the grants, which cannot be found in the older States, for the establishment of schools, and for other great objects of public concernment, for which nothing has been given to the States of the East." *Annals of Cong.*, 18 Cong., 1 Sess., XLI, 1298-99.

17 The committee now "rose and reported, and obtained leave to sit again."

From Robert Scott

Dr. Sir, Lexington, 30th. Jany. 1824

My last was of 22nd inst.[1] accompanying a statement of Colo. Troups A/C with the late Colo. Morrison[2]— Since then, have recd. your favor of 17th. Currt.[3] and also a patent for 2 half quarter sections land in the Dist. of St. Louis Missouri[4]—Your confidential communication will be preserved from all except my self and attended to altho I doubt whether the object referred to can be effected— However I will keep a look out—and see what may be done —In the packet of papers which I put up and which you took with you, were the certificates I beleive, and other papers in relation to the titles of two tracts of land near St. Louis, the patents for which have not yet been obtained— If you can have time it would be desirable to obtain them whilst you are in Washington—

James Wilson has enjoined part of the 450$ due by him, and I now enclose a copy of his Bill, as it is desirable to endeavor to dissolve his Injunction at the April Court— From it you will see Mr Bibb is also made a deft and as he is now in Washington please procure his answer.—[5]

Colo. A Butler, whose note for 3000$ payable in the U S. B Bank at Orleans on 1st. inst. has suffered it to come back protested— Do you wish any suits to be brought prior to your return?[6] I [*sic*] you do, have the goodness to refer to the balance list and point them out— I have not seen, or heard from Mr. Carneal since you left us, altho I wrote to him at Frankfort on the subject of his debt, he did not reply[7]— My brother arranged with Mr. Cox for amt in his hands[8]— Specie at Louisville is 190 to 192$ in Coms.[9]—here 198 to 200$. Aunt Morrison and family are well—

very respectfully Yr. Obt. Servt. ROBT. SCOTT

The Honble H. Clay

ALS. DLC-TJC (DNA, M212, R12).

1 Not found.

2 No record found.

3 Not found.

4 See above, Receipt, November 15, 1823, note; Scott to Clay, December 4, 1823.

5 The bond, due November 16, 1822, was still in suit in Pendleton Circuit Court, in August, 1826. Conjectural Estimate of the Condition of Col. Morrison's Estate . . . August, 1826 (KyLxT). George M. Bibb was in attendance at the sitting of the United States Supreme Court.

6 Anthony Butler's note, due January 1, 1824, was placed in suit in the Federal Circuit Court, Mississippi District, and remained under contest in August, 1826. *Ibid.*

7 Thomas D. Carneal owed two notes to the Morrison estate: the first, for $2778, due September 16, 1818; the second, for $555.50, due September 23, 1821. Fayette County, Will Book F, 234.

8 Cf. above, Receipt, December 30, 1823.

9 Bank of Commonwealth notes.

To Peter B. Porter

My dear Sir Washn. 31 Jan. 1824

I perceive by your letter of the 25h. inst. that you have arrived at Albany. The interest which you take in the approaching election of a President induces me to say to you, in regard to a Caucus here, that there will be none, and that you must discredit all assertions to the contrary. My friends are perfectly willing fairly to submit my pretensions, whatever they may be, to a caucus composed of the great body of the republican party in Congress, or indeed to a Caucus composed of all the members of Congress, without reference to party. They believe that any practical decision to which a Caucus, composed in either of those modes, would come *must* be favorable to me. But they are unwilling to submit them to a Caucus which should be made up of a section of the republican party—to a caucus which would exhibit the appearance of a Cabal, a faction—to a caucus, which would be constituted of *all* the friends of one Candidate, and a few only of those of the other Candidates, who would play the part of mere figuranti, of mere cyphers. Now without going into a minute detail it is sufficient to observe, that no *general* Caucus can be assembled. Some will not, and many are instructed not to go into Caucus. If there were a *general* caucus, however the results might appear on the first ballotings, my friends believe that on the final vote a majority would be concentrated on me. Thus we perceive that a partial Caucus would probably exhibit one result, and a general caucus another and a different result. In this condition of things whatever deference my friends entertain for the opinions of those highly respectable States which favor the convention of a Caucus, they cannot consent to lend themselves to a purpose which might defeat the wishes of the great body of the Republican party of this Country. They are still less inclined to do this because they believe that an election by the H. of Representatives (however unwilling they may be to devolves [*sic*] on that body the choice) will correspond with what would be the final opinion of a general caucus.

Such, my dear General, is the state of things here— I know that other and different representations will be made to you. But I have rarely been deceived in my opinions on public affairs. I have never deceived you and rest assured that I do not in this instance.

We entertain high hopes of the passage of the Tariff. The South as usual is against it, but we trust that the coincidence of opinion which happily exists between the West and the middle states will ensure the passage of that salutary measure.

I am ever with great respect Your's faithfully H. CLAY

Genl. P. B. Porter.

ALS. NBuHi.

To Peter B. Porter

My dear Sir (Private & confidential) Washn. 31 Jan. 1824

I am truly rejoiced that you have reached Albany. My interests there wanted your presence, your powers of direction and your combination. They have suffered for the want of your [*sic*] But your arrival is in time to set every thing right. Be assured that the

Crawford interest is in the greatest confusion and despondency here. To preserve appearances, and probably to acquire strength at Albany, his partizans continue to assert that there will be a Caucus here; but they do not themselves believe it. It has been I understand *ascertained* that there are 181 members against a Caucus, 68 for one, and the residue doubtful. The truth is that statements are made up here for Albany, and, in return, there for this place. *There cannot be any Caucus here.*

The election will come into the House. If, as is probable, Crawford Adams and I should be the three highest, I believe, on the first ballot, I should get the vote of twelve states, without including New York, New Jersey, or any New England State. The only point of danger which I run is from Jackson's interference. But of Ohio, Kentucky, Indiana, Illinois, Missouri, and Louisiana I continue to be absolutely certain. The state of Mississippi is some what doubtful. The delegation from this State here is united for me— In Maryland I am positively certain of at least two and if there be a general ticket probably of the whole number of votes: for my strength lies in the most populous parts of that State. If I get into the House I consider my election secure; if Jackson should even get it [*sic*] into it, leaving me out, *he* cannot be elected. A decision by N. York in my favor would put the election beyond all doubt. The view which I have presented will render it important to me to get *some* if not all of the votes of that State. That same view (the collision between Jackson and me, and the utter impossibility of his election) may determine some of those States favorable to him, at this time, ultimately to drop him and take me up; for all the States to the West which prefer him first, prefer me next.

You will be told that a coalition is forming between Adams' friends and Crawfords. Don't credit it. They are now making the effort with Adams' friends which was first made with mine—that is coaxing them to come over to the Secretary of the Treasury. Finding themselves sternly repulsed by my friends, they have flattered themselves that they will find more pliancy else where. And, if they should not, they hope to gain something by propagating the opinion that the Department of State will be content with remaining in statu quo, or with the Vice Presidency, and yielding the higher office to him of the Treasury. In short, every nerve is strained, to secure their object— But I believe it will be all unavailing.

I thank you for your hints about my correspondents at Albany.[1] The want of some such medium of communication as yourself threw me upon them; but I think I have not written any thing which can commit me— Let me hear frequency from you— Will Rochester[2] be at Albany? I am faithfully Your friend H. CLAY

Genl. P. B. Porter.

ALS. NBuHi.
1 See above, Porter to Clay, January 25, 1824. 2 William B. Rochester.

To Simon Gratz and Brother

Gent. Washn. 1 Feb. 1823

Holding as Exor of Col. Morrison[1] six shares in the Bank of the U. S. I inclose a Certificate of them, accompanied by a Certified Copy of his will and a power of Atto. authorizing you to make sale of them. I will thank you to effect a sale accordingly and remit me the proceeds in a check or post note of the said Bank. Be pleased to return the Copy of the will, and I will thank you also to ascertain and let me know the amount of dividends standing in my testators name. I am Yr. ob. Servt. H. CLAY

Mess. Simon Gratz & Brother.

ALS. PHi. 1 James Morrison.

Remarks on Need for Two Additional Indian Agents

[February 2, 1824]

Cited in Washington *Daily National Intelligencer,* February 3, 1824; *Annals of Cong.,* 18 Cong., 1 Sess., XLI, 1320-21. On motion of John Cocke, Chairman of the Committee on Indian Affairs, the House had gone into Committee of the Whole to consider a bill authorizing the President to appoint two additional Indian Agents, to be stationed west of the Mississippi River. Although Cocke had "assured the House" that the bill "would not detain them ten minutes, . . . a desultory debate arose, which continued till past three o'clock." Clay was among those who advocated the bill. Reported only in general terms, "The grounds insisted on in its favor were the disorderly state of the Indians on the Arkansas River and its vicinity, produced in part by the removal of the remnants of other tribes into that Territory and its neighborhood, in consequence of an exchange of their lands elsewhere for lands there. Some of these were from tribes who inherited an ancient grudge against each other, and almost the whole of them were more or less dissatisfied with the arrangement which had placed them there.— They were now in a very lawless state, and committed great depredations on the property of the settlers; and recent intelligence had been received of actual hostilities and bloodshed. Two agents were as few as could be assigned for this region, and it was hoped that their presence and influence with the ordinary means employed in such agencies, would have an operation to restrain these excesses."

The bill was recommitted. Amended to provide for only one additional agent, it finally passed the House on April 7 and became law May 18. 4 *U. S. Stat.,* 25.

To Peter B. Porter

Dear Sir Washn. 4h. Feb. 1824

I have your favor of the 27h. Ulto.[1] The Lieut Govr. of your state,[2] I have just learnt, has *written* to a friend of Mr. Crawford here that there is a *majority* at Albany for me of those who are there in favor of a Congressional Caucus; but that he thinks, if there be a nomination here, the nomination will be supported in N. York.

You may rely that we shall have no Caucus unless a minority short of eighty should resolve to hold one and I do not believe they will. I have been informed that an attempt has been made to obtain authentic information of the number opposed to a Caucus of the present Congress and that it has been found to be not less than 180. Some of the public prints have labored to prove that my friends have been most active in defeating a Caucus. It is not so. They have constantly said secure a general attendance and we will go; but we will not go to a Cabal, to a factious assemblage; we will not consent to be made mere cyphers. They are willing to make common cause and to sink or swim with the great body of the Republicans. They know that there are no better republicans than those whom they represent. But they will not be cajoled.

If the Legislature of N. York were to nominate me, the election would be fixed by two thirds of the Union, without coming into the House; and then N. York would have accomplished two great objects 1st. She would have, in effect, determined the election; and 2dly. *She* would have prevented its coming into the House. And powerful as she undoubtedly is such a result can only *certainly* happen by a declaration for me—

I will write you again shortly.

Be pleased to shew this letter to Genl. McClure[3] and, with my best respects, tell him that I recd. his favor of the 28h. Ulto. for which I sincerely thank him. Your's faithf ly H. CLAY

Genl. P. B. Porter.

ALS. NBuHi. [1] Not found. [2] Erastus Root.
[3] George McClure. His letter has not been found.

Remarks on Surveys for Roads and Canals

[February 4, 1824]

{Here Mr. CLAY explained. He said he never contended that, if a majority of the States withheld their co-operation, the General Government might not be dissolved; but, his principle was, when the General Government is once organized, and [*sic*] moves by its own inherent energy, and acts independently of State power.}

[Rives stated that, not having heard Clay's speech, he had only read a newspaper report, which had given the principle (to which he had referred) in a manner that required qualification. "But, even as now qualified, by the explanations of the Speaker, he was not prepared to give his assent to it."

[Rives continued his argument and, some moments later, challenged Clay's contention "that in one sense, we do create justice—

we create, he says, the criminal justice of the country, because we create the crimes, which are prohibited and punished by our laws. But in what sense do we create a crime? We do not create the fact which constitutes the crime, we only create the legal character which is imposed upon that fact."]

{Here Mr. CLAY explained. He said there was a distinction between acts which are *mala in se,* and those which are *mala prohibita.* As to the latter, they are wrong, only because the Legislature has made them so, and in relation to them, therefore, the law creates the crime.}[1]

Annals of Cong., 18 Cong., 1 Sess., XLI, 1346, 1349. The debate on the bill for surveys of roads and canals had been resumed in Committee of the Whole on February 3. Clay had remained silent until the next day when William C. Rives, of Virginia, in the course of a speech, accused him of having "deduced, as a general principle, that the Government of the Union, as now organized, is wholly independent of the States for the execution of any of its powers." Rives declared that he, himself, had "always supposed directly the contrary: that the General Government is dependent upon the States for the execution of all its powers, for it cannot exist, without the concurrence of the States."

1 Rives retorted that "this view of the subject was not affected by the explanation of the honorable gentleman." After Rives finished speaking, others followed until four o'clock, when the Committee rose and the House adjourned. Seven days later the bill was passed by the House and on April 24 by the Senate. The President approved it April 30. 4 *U. S. Stat.,* 22-23.

From Robert Scott

Dr. Sir, Lexington, 8th. Feby. 1824

The last of your favors recd. is that of 17th. Ulto.[1] the receipt of which I acknowledged on 30th.

Enclosed herewith is your Account with the Estate for the month of Jany. 1824—[2]

9th. I have just returned from C Farm[3]— Your Stock there look quite as well as is usual for stock to look at this season of the year— Mr. Hawkins[4] has some time since finished breaking up your ground, so that he will be in complete readiness for the spring crop when the period arrives— Mrs. Clay and family are well— Mr. Erwin & Lady[5] sets [*sic*] out in a day or two for N Orleans— Mrs. Morrison & family are well and she thanks you for your attention to her request to get her a *Cook*[6]— We have nothing new—

Very respectfully Yr. Obt. Servt. ROBT. SCOTT

The Honble H. Clay

ALS. DLC-TJC (DNA, M212, R12). 1 Not found.

2 Private account not found. For the executor's accounts, see below, *ca.* June 8, 1824.

3 The "Carlisle Farm." 4 Francis Hawkins. 5 Mr. and Mrs. James Erwin.

6 Cf. above, Scott to Clay, January 5, 1824. Scott ran an advertisement until the following July for "A GOOD PLAIN COOK, A WOMAN between 30 and 40, without children, of good character and good constitution." Lexington *Kentucky Reporter,* January 19-July 26, 1824. Clay may have lent her a cook during the interim.

From Erastus Root

Dr Sir, Albany 9 Feb. '24

I had the honor of receivg. your inclosure of a newspaper containing your *"internal improvement"* speech[1] which I have read with that pleasure which I always feel when either reading or hearing the effusions of my friend's fine genius.— Your zeal upon that subject fastens your friends in the western part of this state— But permit me to say, that your friends in our legislature are Crawford's friends & generally, his are yours— C. & C. are considered the democratic candidates & A. & Calh.[2] if not entirely, partially the reverse.— You know I am for Crawford— I was in 1816— I wish a *caucus* to decide the question between you & whichever might be successful could assure himself of the votes of this state— Your friends at Washn. declining to *caucus*[3] does not *add* to your strength here— Very respectfully &c ERASTUS ROOT

ALS. DLC-HC (DNA, M212, R1). Addressed to Clay at Washington.

1 See above, January 14, 1824.

2 Adams and Calhoun.

3 The New York *American* at the end of January had carried a report relative to a general caucus by the members of Congress, stating that Clay's friends in Washington had met and "positively decided that they would *not* attend one, unless for the purpose of defeating its object, by voting against any recommendation. . . ." Reprinted in Washington *Daily National Intelligencer,* February 2, 1824.

To Peter B. Porter

My dear Sir Washn. 10 Feb. 1824

You will have seen the Caucus and Anti Caucus Notifications published in the Intellr.[1] Those who are urging a Caucus are perfectly desperate and despondent. I think it far from being certain that if they should even assemble, any thing will be done. If they do meet their number will not exceed seventy and probably will be short of it. What will be thought of a Caucus of such a minority? And many of that very slender number *mis*representing their respective states and district [*sic*]? Was ever any thing more silly, not to say wicked, if they should attempt a nomination? There are some moderate men among them, and if they should actually get together, I should not be surprized if they disperse without doing any thing.

Our information is that the same distraction reigns at Richmond that is perceived at Albany and here among the Crawford party. Is it possible that N. York which, by one decisive course of action, can terminate all contention, will continue to wait for what she cannot possibly obtain, under actual circumstances, a fair expression of the opinion of the Republican party here?

Be pleased to make my respects to Genl. McClure and tell him that I am greatly obliged by his kind communications which I regularly receive;[2] and ask him to excuse me for not acknowledging them at present, as I am much engaged in both the Supreme Court and the H. of R. We took up the Tariff to day.

Your's faithfully H. CLAY

ALS. NBuHi. Endorsed in Porter's hand: "H. Clay 10. Feby 1824."

1 On February 7 the Washington *Daily National Intelligencer* had carried an announcement by a committee of 24 members of Congress, representing the supporters of Clay, Adams, Calhoun, and Jackson, that 181 of the 261 members "deem it inexpedient, under existing circumstances, to meet in Caucus, for the purpose of nominating Candidates for President and Vice President . . . and they have good reasons to believe, that a portion of the remainder will be found unwilling to attend such a meeting." The same issue of the journal had carried a call for a caucus to meet on February 14, signed by eleven Crawford supporters.

2 No letter from George McClure, after that above, July 23, 1823, has been found.

Remarks on Tariff Bill, Duty on Spirits

[February 11, 1824]

Mr. CLAY said, he was far from wishing to prevent a fair and deliberate discussion of the bill; but some regard must be had to time. Numerous petitions had been presented on the general subject of a revision of the tariff, the reading of which had been dispensed with, and they still lay on the table of this House. Would it not be respectful to these numerous petitioners, (and they amounted to thousands,) to have some further disposition given to these documents? They should either be taken up and read, or referred to a committee, to have their contents presented in a condensed form, to the Committee of the Whole. The voice of almost the whole country had come up to the House, setting forth a picture of distress, invoking the interposition of Congress—that voice ought at least to be heard.

[Cambreleng, commenting that much time would be required to read the petitions, the number of which he estimated to be over a hundred, suggested that they be referred to the Committee on Manufactures. He withdrew his motion for the Committee to rise, and the reading of the bill was completed. Samuel A. Foot then moved to strike out the provision of the bill "containing a duty on imported spirits; the enacting of which clause would not increase but rather impair the revenue, and would, besides, operate as a bounty on intemperance."]

Mr. CLAY expressed a hope that the motion would not prevail.

[Foot "was not to be driven from his opposition to the measure by a mere suggestion or wish of any gentleman" and stated his belief that the clause would injure the West India trade. After an exchange between Foot and David Trimble, George McDuffie declared that the duty already being imposed on foreign spirits had reduced the revenue from that source by two million dollars and the bill under consideration would reduce it further. He maintained also, in relation to the manufacture of whisky, that it was the least worthy of all manufactures to be encouraged.]

Mr. CLAY differed entirely from the gentleman from South Carolina; but he was very unwilling to go into discussion of the general principles of the bill on one of its mere incidental details. A better course would be for some gentleman to move to strike out the enacting clause, and then to let the committee take up the measure on general grounds. It had been said that the clause in question would diminish the revenue. This might possibly be the fact; but must it, therefore, necessarily diminish the wealth of the country? Suppose we had imported ten millions of gallons of foreign spirits. It is true, we derived the amount of the revenue upon it, which, so far, was a gain; but, so far as we thereby encouraged foreign agriculture, we paid an equivalent for what we gained. But, if, instead of having been manufactured abroad, and paid for abroad, the same quantity had been made at home, and paid for at home, which would have been the greatest gain to the country? Wealth at home was to preferred to that which was brought into the country from abroad. And were this duty, instead of being diminished, to be increased yet more than is now proposed; were the tax on it to be increased, so as to go to an absolute prohibition, I, for one, said Mr. C. am prepared, for myself, and, I may say, for my constituents, to meet a tax on our home products. I am not to be frightened by that ominous word "excise—excise," if the wealth of the country is substantially to be promoted. I agree that the western country is interested in the manufacture of spirits; but I ask, by importing spirits, are you not encouraging the foreign manufacturer? We may experience the same vicissitude in seasons and in crops that other countries have experienced—we may experience times of scarcity, and even of famine. Whatever encourages the extensive growing of grain, provides you with a resource against such a calamity. But this article affects not only the grain-growing, but the fruit-growing, the cane-growing, and the malt-making districts of our country—they are all interested in the exclusion of foreign spirits. Look at the example of England; she excludes the brandies of France and the gin of Holland; and so do France and Holland exclude England and each other. The duty has a double operation; it not only encourages home manufactures, but home agriculture likewise—while the admission of foreign spirits not only goes to encourage the foreign manufacturer, but the foreign agriculturist also.

But, I will not anticipate the discussion of the general question—when that comes up, I think I shall be able clearly to show that the national wealth is the only substratum on which to raise taxation.

[Gideon Tomlinson, of Connecticut, one of the speakers who

followed, accused Clay of favoring agriculture over commerce and stated that under the proposed duty the West India trade, languishing even under the existing rate, would be destroyed. He was interested in Clay's reference to an excise and was "prepared to go with him" in an excise on domestic spirits equal to the duty of those imported. James Hamilton, Jr., referred, as had others, to the moral issue involved and professed to see a danger of "a loathsome *still* on every side of the picture." "The honorable Speaker," said he, "no doubt, prefers whiskey to brandy, and we seem in a fair way to have, in abundance, the pure western stuff, fresh from the still." Concluding on a serious note, Hamilton said the subject had "been so ably argued on both sides of the Atlantic, and . . . was . . . so fully understood and settled, he had really been surprised to find a provision of this kind introduced into the bill."]

Mr. CLAY rejoined. He had been much amused with the witticisms of the honorable gentleman from South Carolina—but he was restrained from entering into any thing like a general discussion of the question, by a fear that this was not *a favorable time of the day* for such discussion.

Yet he could not refrain from noticing the argument of his honorable friend from Connecticut. If he had rightly apprehended that argument, it was in substance this: The produce of Connecticut is sent to the West Indies, and spirits constitute the return cargo. If you impose a higher duty on spirits, the produce of Connecticut can no longer be sent to the West Indies. But this same argument is urged with equal reason against the whole Tariff. If it taxes an article raised in the Middle States, then the gentlemen from the Middle States urge this argument. If you tax an article that is the produce of the South, then gentlemen from the South urge it. Each different section of the country holds the same language. The honorable gentleman is quite ready to concur in an excise on the Western whiskey, because that will not affect Connecticut—but if any duty is proposed that touches Connecticut, then our commerce is gone at once! The glory of the nation is annihilated; the country is going to speedy ruin!

The argument is fallacious. Its fallacy consists in this: it assumes that those persons in the West Indies, who want the produce of Connecticut, will not take it unless the Connecticut trader will take rum in exchange, (which he will not do if the duty is raised;) but this is not the fact: I say that, if they want the produce of Connecticut, as they do, and will, and must continue to want it, and the Connecticut trader refuses rum, they will give him something better. They only give rum now because he will take it, and it is the worst thing they have to part with. As he did not intend to pursue the discussion now, Mr. Clay said he should conclude with expressing a hope that all deliberations and discussion, of the committee would be marked with a spirit of moderation, amenity, and mutual forbearance.

[Alfred Cuthbert said "the course the discussion was taking, was, in itself, a proof that the committee ought now to rise and report. The honorable Speaker, it appeared, was averse to this skirmishing mode of warfare–and why? It deranges his legions–it breaks the order and system of his array, and thereby impairs his strength." He hoped the Committee would rise, though he preferred that the motion to that effect should "come from the other side."]

Mr. CLAY then said he would with great pleasure oblige the honorable gentleman from Georgia. The only reason why he had before objected to rising was the early hour.

Mr. CLAY then made the motion, and the committee rose and reported, and had leave to sit again.

Washington *Daily National Intelligencer,* February 12, 1824. Published also in Lexington *Kentucky Reporter,* March 1, 1824; *Annals of Cong.,* 18 Cong., 1 Sess., XLI, 1481, 1482-83, 1485-86. Discussion of a bill for the revision of the tariff had begun in Committee of the Whole on the preceding day, with little progress. When the House again in Committee of the Whole had returned to the subject, John Tod, Chairman of the Committee on Manufactures, had explained the measure, after which opponents of revision (first, John Randolph, and, after his motion had been rejected, Churchill C. Cambreleng) had attempted to prevail on the Committee to rise.

Remarks on Tariff Bill, Duty on Spirits

[February 12, 1824]

Mr. CLAY, (Speaker,) explained. If an equivalent was given by the *exclusion* of the foreign article, so as to give to our manufacturers the whole supply of the market, he would consent to a tax on the domestic article equal to that now derived from the same foreign article.[1]

Washington *Daily National Intelligencer,* February 13, 1824. Published also in *Annals of Cong.,* 18 Cong., 1 Sess., XLI, 1498. During continued debate in Committee of the Whole on the tariff, George McDuffie stated that he had understood Clay to have said "that he was perfectly willing that an excise should be established to supply any deficiency which might be produced by this bill," and "he asked that gentleman if he would consent to introduce into this bill a provision for such an excise?"

[1] McDuffie retorted that "he could not conceive what the manufacturer could gain by such an arrangement." Clay did not reply.

From E. I. Du Pont

The Honorable Henry Clay Wilmington february 13th 1824.
Speaker of the House of Representatives.
Sir

To an early and decided friend of american manufacturers, to a warm, active and powerful advocate of all measures calculated to

Support the dignity and encrease the prospertiy of the Nation, I must take the liberty to submit some remarks on the part of the tariff connected with the woolen interest and claim your indulgence.

You will perhaps remember that when the tariff of 1816 was before Congress, I observed to you[1] that the duty on Salt petre could not protect the working of your caves in time of peace, and would only be a tax on the industry of the country. fortunately Gunpowder being at the same time protected by *a Specific duty* could bear without inconvenience the tax on the raw material.

But this will not be the case with fine cloths, which are only protected by a Small addition on the present insufficient rate of *ad valorem duty,* to [*sic*] easily evaded; and the result will be that Cloth and wool will both be prostrated if the reported tariff pass Congress in its present Shape.

I beg Sir that you will excuse the liberty I have taken and I have the honor to be with great respect your most obedt. Servt.

E. I. DU PONT

ALS. PKsL.

1 No communication of this nature has been found.

To ———

Dr Sir Washn. 15h. Feb. 1824

I duly recd. your letter of the 13h. inst.[1] with its inclosure. I wish you were a member of Congress; you would then practically feel all the difficulties of our actual situation. Do you ever expect to see a tariff adopted which will satisfy every body? Do you ever expect to find perfection in any thing which is human? I have seen three different tariffs attempted at three different periods. And each of them was pronounced, by some, to be the most bungling essay at a scheme of national policy that ever was presented. You must recollect that in the H. of R. there are 213 persons to satisfy & 1000 interests to conciliate. And you complain of a miserable affair of quills and rifles & muskets! We must aim at great results. Perfection in matters of detail, if ever attainable, must be left to the future. You would limit the tariff to cottons woolens & iron ware. And what then becomes of the West in its hemp & hempen manufactures? A tariff is an affair of mutual concession; and without the observance of that principle none will ever be adopted.

I am inclined to think it might be improved as to fine Cloths. But what are they at last? Who wears them? Coarse woolens are those which enter into the consumption of the great body of the Country; and we have difficulties almost insuperable about them. With respect to your correspondent Mr. Wolcott,[2] he is a sour grumbling unmannerly fellow. And I will thank you to tell him that Congress is not legislating only for the Wolcott Woolen Manufacturing Company[3] but for a great nation & a great national interest. Yr. friend

H. CLAY

ALS. ICHi. [1] Not found. [2] Probably J. Wolcott, of Southbridge, Massachusetts. [3] Established a decade earlier, the firm had factories at Southbridge and Woodstock, Massachusetts, manufacturing broadcloths and cassimeres. Wolcott was not at this time among the officers of the company.

To E. I. Du Pont

Dr Sir Washington 15h Feb. 1824

I have duly received your letter of the 13h. instant with the observations inclosed with which you have favored me on the pending Tariff. I recollect, with high satisfaction, the advantage I derived in 1816 from your judicious views communicated to me in respect to the important interest of American Manufactures. And I shall give to these new ones a consideration corresponding with my high opinion of the intelligent source whence they have emanated. We have great difficulties to encounter—to reconcile jarring interests, and especially to accommodate the protection proposed for the Manufacturing industry of the Country to the National Agriculture, the first and greatest of all our interests. Whatever may be the final result, I am sure we shall find in you a liberal and considerate judge of our perplexing labors.

With great respect I am faithfy Your's H. CLAY

Mr. Dupont.

ALS. PKsL.

To Peter B. Porter

My dear Sir Washington 15th. Feb. 1824

The contemplated meeting of Mr. Crawford's partizans took place last night. The whole week, indeed I may say the Session, had been employed by them in the endeavor to collect together as many as possible. Persuasions, threats, coaxing, entreaties were unsparingly used. These conjoint means brought together sixty six persons! This small assemblage nevertheless has undertaken to recommend their favorite as President and Albert Gallatin as V. President. Deduct from the total number, those members who come from States which have expressly declared themselves against Mr. Crawford, and it will reduce the sixty four (including two *proxies*) who concurred in his nomination to about forty four.[1] Deduct the Senators, and it will leave just about the vote that was given for Mr. Barbour as Speaker, at the commencement of the Session.[2] Mr. Crawford never could have been elected President; but if he ever stood any chance the *mere fact* of such a nomination, with its train of necessary consequences, must inevitably destroy all his prospects.

From Richmond my friends assure me that Mr. Crawfords interest is rapidly on the decline; and that mine is fast rising. They assure me that *nearly* one moiety of the Legislature there is for me at this time. The Phœnix, a paper established some months ago and conducted with much ability at Richmond[3] has just taken a bold & decisive stand for me in an editorial article written with very great talent. It is as certain that if New York would declare for me Virginia would follow as that you and I exist. And is it not better that your great State should take the lead, instead of being lead [*sic*], in this interesting subject?

The effect of the stand taken here by Mr. Crawfords friends partizans and presses will be to alienate all the friends of the other Candidates. Now, as the question cannot be kept out of the H. of R. by him even if N. York declare for him, how is he to be elected by that house more than three fourths of which are thus estranged from him?

Be pleased to present my respects to my friend Genl. McClure[4] and shew him this letter. With great regard. I am faithfully Your friend H. CLAY

Genl. P. B. Porter.

P.S. I wish you or Genl. McClure would address a letter to E S. Duncan Esqr. at Richmond, a respectable member of the Senate of Virginia,[5] and a decided friend of mine, giving a true and faithful account of my prospects at Albany. Information is wanted there of what exists with you. H.C.

[Enclosure][6] (Strictly Confidential)

The affair of the Vice Presidency becomes one of much interest, as time elapses. My friends are desirous of running some one from your State. Mr. Thompson, yourself and Mr. Young[7] have been thought of. Your unfortunate deafness forms an objection to you, and besides there is another place in which I think you can render more service to the public. Will you turn this matter over in your mind, and advise us? And I pray you to throw this note into the fire. What I have said in respect to yourself is more than I have ever said in relation to any other person whatever. I trust I need not apologize to you for saying it. *You* can never misconceive the *purity* of *my* motives.

Genl. P. B. Porter

ALS. NBuHi.

1 See above, Clay to Porter, February 10, 1824, note. At the meeting 64 votes were cast for Crawford, including two by proxy; two for Adams; and one each for Jackson and for Nathaniel Macon—a total of 68. Gallatin received 57 votes for the vice-presidential nomination. Washington *Daily National Intelligencer,* February 16, 1824.

2 See above, Acceptance, December 1, 1823, note.

3 Established in November, 1823, by Samuel Crawford and Company, the paper apparently expired in 1824.

4 George McClure.

5 On January 5, 1824, Edwin S. Duncan had been nominated as Attorney for the Western District of Virginia. This appointment was confirmed on March 4, and he was reappointed in January, 1828. During the session of the Virginia General Assembly for 1830-1831 he was elected a judge of the General Court and held that post until his resignation in 1848.

6 AN. NBuHi. On the placement of this document, see below, Clay to Porter, March 3, 1824.

7 Smith Thompson; Samuel Young.

Remarks on Tariff Bill, Duty on Cotton Bagging

[February 16, 1824]

Mr. CLAY then rose, and said that it had not been his intention to engage in any discussion on the details of the bill; but this was one in which his own district was so specially interested, and its provisions had now been attacked from so unexpected a quarter, that he should hold himself culpable if he refused to answer. He would, therefore, say to the gentleman from Pennsylvania that, if this article would not bear the duty proposed to be laid upon it, there was not an article in the bill that would.

The great articles which it was proposed to protect, were cotton, wool, hemp, and iron—but if the country could manufacture any article whatever, that article certainly was cotton bagging. Having a personal acquaintance with the mode of its manufacture, he begged to state a few of the facts respecting it to the House. The buildings in which it was conducted were of the slightest and cheapest kind, much resembling rope walks; the hands employed in spinning were, for the most part, small negro boys, and a few negro girls. The weavers are all either negroes or common laborers; and such is the facility with which the manufacture can be extended, that, if the bill shall pass, I am willing to pledge myself, said Mr. Clay, in any form, that, within 12 months, 20 millions of yards can be produced, and almost without a special[1] effort. I am well acquainted with the article, and it is one which, of all others, I should select to illustrate the propriety of the principles of the present bill. Who are our competitors in the manufacture? The weavers of Inverness and Dundee, two small towns in Scotland—before the war they had the entire monopoly of this article. During the war, a portion of our domestic labor was directed to this article, and, as might be expected, the manufacture being in its infancy, the prices first demanded were very high—after the close of the war, the factories still continued—but, in a languishing condition, till by the joint competition of the American and the Scotch manufactures they were completely prostrated. No sooner was this effected, than immediately the price was raised upon the cotton grower; and the extra price then paid would be more than equal to ten years protection of our own fabric. What is it, on the general principles of political economy, that secure [*sic*] an abundant supply of any article made, and its good quality? It is competition. And the real question now before Congress is, whether these men of Inverness and Dundee shall continue to have the monopoly, or whether there shall be an American competition to counteract them? The gentlemen ask, what is to hinder the competition at present? why cannot we now make the article? I reply to them—that it is only for want of a certain and a steady market, guarded against the sudden influx of goods sent into it from abroad for the very purpose of prostrating our manufactures. The Scotch merchant reasons in this way—if I can, by selling my goods for one year at half or a quarter of their value, or by throwing them away altogether, secure a monopoly of those goods for ten or for twenty years, I shall, on the whole, be a gainer. But, if it is asked, how a sudden influx at a low price can so soon destroy the American manufacturer? the answer is not difficult. It is to be found not only in his comparatively small capital, but in the character of our people, which has in it a mixture of impatience with its activity. They soon become disgusted and discouraged with a business that is not immediately productive; and, in this particular manufacture, the persons employed are so easily turned to some other branch of industry, that, unless a steady market is secured, the establishments can have no permanency or success. But, from my knowledge of this manufacture, I now assert, allowing the present average price to be 30 cents, that, if the proposed encouragement is given, in less than 12 months the American will be furnished at a lower rate than the Scotch article.

Something was said about the nature of the American hemp. It is true, that a large portion of that now raised is dew-rotted—but, in the State of New York, and other parts of the Union, as well as in Kentucky and Ohio, much is also water-rotted. And there is not a doubt, that, if protection be given, enough could be obtained for all uses, both maritime and manufacturing. The quantity required was not so very great—a yard of bagging weighs only a pound and an half. So that, allowing four millions of yards to be made, only six millions of lbs weight of hemp is needed. But there is another improvement lately discovered in the preparation of it, by which the necessity of both dew-rotting and water-rotting is completely done away with—and that is, by suffering it to remain one year in stack; a process takes place which renders the hemp, at least in texture and appearance, equal to any of the Russian. Besides all which, late improvements have been introduced into the dressing, which supersede either rotting or stacking.[2]

Mr. Clay then went into a calculation to shew that the estimate of the rate per cent. stated by some of the gentlemen in opposition, was incorrect.

But what, sir, is the principle on which the gentleman from Pennsylvania means to go? He will protect our manufactures as soon as we are able, without protection, to go on with the manufacture. Sir, protection comes first in the order of nature: it is while a thing is in feeble infancy that it needs protection. If the gentleman is going to wait till the American manufactures, operated against by the legislation of the universe—opposed by foreign governments—resisted by foreign capital—combined against by foreign companies, and towns, and cities in every part of Europe—shall, unaided, attain to strength and vigor before he will protect them, he will never have the opportunity, or, if he have, his protection will be as thankless as it will then be unnecessary. Sir, it not only can happen, but it has happened—Dundee and Inverness have driven America off the field. They prostrated us in 1816 and 17, and they had the undisputed monopoly of our whole market till 1822,[3] and they knew how to use it too.

But this may happen, even where there is no hostile design against our establishments. The market failing him in Europe, the European manufacturer finds an accumulation of goods upon his hands; and this is the market in which he has the best chance to dispose of them; he pours them into our auction rooms, and the effect is just as baneful as if it were done out of the most determined hostility. Gentlemen seem to wish this state of things to continue—they would leave the monopoly where it is—leave us dependent on a little Scotch town. We, sir, wish to destroy that dependence by setting up an American competition.

Mr. C. here referred to a letter[4] from a person of competent information at Lexington, which stated, on the revival of manufactures, in 1822, a million of yards of bagging had been made there, and had reduced the Scotch price from 30 to 20 cents.[5]

Washington *Daily National Intelligencer,* February 17, 1824. Published also in Lexington *Kentucky Gazette,* March 13, 1824; *Annals of Cong.*, 18 Cong., 1 Sess., XLI, 1547-50. Debate on the tariff bill for the past two legislative days had centered largely around an amendment, offered on February 13 by William L. Brent, to strike "out the clause which proposes to lay a duty of six cents per square yard on all cotton bagging imported." *Annals of Cong.*, 18 Cong., 1 Sess., XLI, 1515. Clay had taken no part in the discussion until James Buchanan, who "approved the duty on hemp [of which cotton bagging was made], and was willing to make that on bagging equal to it," had stated that "He thought the proposed duty out of proportion, and much greater than needful." Buchanan deplored "implied threats of resistance" but warned against "going too far" in the imposition of duties.

[1] Word printed as "social" in *Intelligencer;* corrected from *Annals of Congress* version.

[2] None of the "improvements" mentioned proved satisfactory in practice.

[3] Apparently the revival was attributable merely to general improvement in business at this time. No relief under tariff legislation was afforded until 1824.

[4] Not found.

[5] Shortly after Clay had finished, the Committee rose for the day and the House adjourned.

To Richard Bache

My dear Sir (Confidential) Washington 17h. Feb. 1824

I recd. your letter of the 14h. inst.[1] without the packet to which it refers.

In regard to the P. question, the states which may be *certainly* relied on for me are Ohio, Kentucky, Indiana, Illinois, Missouri and Louisiana. There is not a doubt here about one of them. The States which may be certainly relied upon for Mr. Crawford are Virginia, North Carolina and Georgia. Tho' with respect to Virginia, my friends at Richmond entertain great confidence of giving the support of the antient dominion and I understand are about forming an electoral ticket for me.[2] The States which may certainly be relied on for Genl. Jackson are Tennessee and Alabama, the latter with less certainty than the former. Mr. Adams will receive the votes of Maine, Massachusetts, Connecticut Rhode Island New Hampshire and Vermont. Mr. Calhoun may certainly count upon South Carolina.

Such is the condition of the various interests in point of certainty. That view of the subject leaves New York, Pennsylvania, New Jersey, Delaware, Maryland and Mississippi as uncertain.

All our information represents my interest as best at Albany. Genl. Jackson will get Pennsa. I presume. How New Jersey and Delaware will go I cannot say. Maryland will give a divided vote, and I think the largest number to me. Mississippi is for Jackson or me.

If the election comes to the H. of R. (as it will do unless N. York should make a decisive nomination of me) my election I think certain, if I should be one of the three highest.

If Jackson, Adams and Crawford should be the three highest, Adams or Crawford will be elected.

Pennsylvania will go for Jackson, and that cannot now be prevented. I told you long ago that the friends of Mr. Calhoun were making a vain and fruitless effort there for him.[3] They would not believe me. I told you that the same effort directed to my support would have secured me the vote of your State. Can you now doubt it?

The ridiculous farce of last Saturday night[4] destroys Mr. Crawford effectually, unless in the contingency within indicated. His friends evidently believe the battle lost. There is general dissatisfaction with Gales and Seaton;[5] to such a degree that I have no doubt if an election were now to take place they would lose the place of public printers.

Mr. Calhoun's friends are in great despondency. They are preparing to admit openly the utter hopelessness of his prospects. Genl.

Rogers[6] told me to day, that all was over, and that Jackson would be nominated at Harrisburg.

Give my best respects to Mrs. Bache and to Mrs. Campbell.[7] and believe me Faithfully Your friend H. CLAY

P.S. Be pleased to shew this letter to Mr. Norvell[8] H. C.

R. Bache Esqr.

ALS. Bristol, Rhode Island, Historical Society.

1 Not found. 2 See below, Clay to Brooke, March 16, 1824.

3 See above, Clay to Woods, May 22, 1823. During the intervening period a succession of popular meetings endorsing Jackson's candidacy had been held in Pennsylvania. The final collapse of Calhoun's cause was signalized at a meeting in Philadelphia, February 18, when George M. Dallas, formerly a leading supporter of Calhoun, presented a resolution recommending Jackson's election and urging that the local delegates to the Harrisburg Convention (see below, Clay to Brooke, March 6, 1824) support his candidacy. The resolutions were adopted unanimously. Washington *Daily National Intelligencer,* February 24, 1824. Calhoun later wrote that Dallas had informed him a week before the Philadelphia meeting "that he thought the cause was lost in Pena. and that we should have to yield there, at the Harrisburg convention." Calhoun to V. Maxcy, February 27, 1824, in John Spencer Bassett, *The Life of Andrew Jackson* (2 vols., Garden City, New York, 1911), I, 334.

4 See above, Clay to Porter, February 15, 1824.

5 Who had been supporting Crawford's candidacy and the procedure of nomination by caucus of the members of Congress. See also below, Clay to Porter, April 26, 1824, note.

6 Thomas J. Rogers.

7 Maria Charlotte Dallas Campbell, Mrs. Bache's sister and the wife of Alexander Campbell, of Philadelphia, formerly of Norfolk, Virginia.

8 John Norvell.

To Nicholas Biddle

Sir H. of R. 17h. Feb. 1824

We argued the other day the cause of the Bank with the State of Ohio, and I entertain strong hopes of success. But the Court has since directed an argument of the question whether the Bank has a right to institute suits in the Federal Courts.[1] I think I can get along very well with that question in the particular cause; because it is undoubtedly one *arising under the Constitution and Laws of the U. States.* In regard to the general right of the Bank to sue in those Courts, in all cases, that is a question, which I argued for the Bank in Kentucky, and which was there decided in its favor.[2] Still it is one about which I have never ceased to entertain the most serious apprehensions. Its importance you will readily perceive. Decided against the Bank it sweeps the dockets of Kentucky and Ohio, and calls in question all that has been decided for the Bank in that State. I understand from Mr. Sergeant that the question of general jurisdiction is adjourned from Georgia. And I shall endeavor to have an arrangement made to effect an argument of both cases at once.[3]

I have thought it my duty to make this communication to you; and to assure you that, although I do not wish to excite unneces-

sary alarm, I think it proper at the same time to warn you against the indulgence of too much confidence. There is certainly a division among the Judges. I am Sir Your Most obedient H. CLAY
Nicholas Biddle Esqr

ALS. PHi-Etting Collection. Endorsed: "recd. Feby. 19. 1824."

1 Argument on the latter question was heard on March 11, and on March 19 Chief Justice John Marshall handed down the Supreme Court ruling in the case of Osborn and Others *vs.* The President, Directors, and Company of the Bank of the United States. The Court here reiterated its stand in the case of McCulloch *vs.* The State of Maryland and Others (see above, II, 674n) and held (1) that the act chartering the Bank was in accordance with the Constitution; (2) that under this legislation the Federal circuit courts were given jurisdiction of suits by and against the Bank; (3) that while in general a decree would not be rendered against an agent where the principal was not made a party to the suit, nevertheless, when the principal (as a sovereign State) was not subject to the jurisdiction of the courts, the rule might be overridden; (4) that an injunction, rather than a simple trespass, was justified to forestall "the avowed purpose of expelling the Bank from the State." The Court thereupon affirmed the decree of the Circuit Court for the District of Ohio (see above, Clay to Cheves, September 8, 1821) so far as it affected the $98,000 unlawfully removed from the Bank and in the possession of Samuel Sullivan when the injunction of September, 1820, had been awarded; also affirmed the decree directing payment of the remaining $2,000 held by Ralph Osborn and John L. Harper; but reversed the ruling which had allowed the Bank interest on the coin, part of the $98,000, which Sullivan had been restrained from using. Justice William Johnson dissented on the basic issue of the Court's jurisdiction of Bank disputes. 22 *U.S.* (9 Wheaton) 738-903.

2 The general question of the jurisdiction of the Federal courts in Bank suits had been argued in the Roberts case, above, II, 720-21, 723n.

3 Both arguments were made on the same day, March 11, and by the same attorneys, Clay, Daniel Webster, and John Sergeant for the Bank of the United States and John L. Harper, Ethan Allen Brown, and John C. Wright for Osborn and Others and for the Planters' Bank of Georgia. For the Court on March 20, Chief Justice Marshall accepted the argument and ruling in the Osborn case as determinate of the jurisdiction in the Georgia dispute. A complicating circumstance in the latter contest, however, was the fact that the State of Georgia was one of the incorporators of the Planters' Bank. Was it then unconstitutional that the suit, against a State, should have originated in circuit court? The Supreme Court here ruled that the State as a partner in any trading company assumes the character of a private citizen in such concern. The jurisdiction of the lower court had also been challenged under the eleventh article of the Judiciary Act, which restricted the circuit courts from acting in suits involving recovery on notes under assignment when such contests would not have been allowed in those Federal courts without such assignment. In this case the note on which the Bank of the United States sought to collect had been made out to a citizen of Georgia and assigned to the Bank, which included citizens of Georgia among its stockholders. Again the issue returned to the section of the act chartering the Bank of the United States, which empowered it to sue and to be sued in the Federal circuit courts; and again the Supreme Court upheld the terms of the charter. Justice Johnson repeated his dissent on the jurisdictional question. 22 *U. S.* (9 Wheaton) 904-14.

Remarks on Tariff Bill, Duty on Cotton Bagging

[February 17, 1824]

Mr. CLAY rose and said, he would answer the gentleman with pleasure. In the first place, his honorable friend had entirely mistaken his argument. What I said, was, that it was desirable there should be a competition, not between American and American, but between the American manufacturer and the Scotch manufacturer. He is equally mistaken in his fact. He said, I believe, in a former speech, that there was but one factory of cotton bagging in all Kentucky. {Here Mr. BRENT explained: that he had said, that in 1822, there was but one, according to the report of the Census of Manufactures, and that in a languishing condition.} Yes, continued Mr. CLAY, in a most languishing condition, and why? For want of the protection of a parental government. But now there are, I believe, ten, certainly not less than eight, in a single village, in Kentucky. The gentleman is equally mistaken as to the number of hands employed. It is calculated that one able-bodied man can make 1000 yards of hempen bagging in one year. The largest of the establishments I refer to, has about one hundred hands, and it made 100,000 yards of bagging, and 40,000 yards of baling rope in a year. Here is the datum on which the honorable gentleman can make calculations for himself.

But compare the arguments of the two last gentlemen. One tells us that 500 hands will make enough of the article to supply the whole of the United States; the other tells us that the whole United States cannot make enough to supply the Southern States.[1] When these gentlemen shall reconcile these two statements, we shall have something more satisfactory to go upon. But, being up, I claim permission to make some reply to arguments adduced by others. The gentleman from South Carolina,[2] who never speaks without illuminating his subject, began, by saying, that the present is purely a sectional question between two portions of the Union, and Congress is called to act as umpire between them. Yet the gentleman professes to be in favor of some degree of protection being extended to some branches of manufacture. But if he applies this species of argument to other of the articles enumerated in the bill, it will destroy them each in succession. There is not an article in it that does not principally affect some limited district of the Union. One important article is iron: but that affects only Pennsylvania, and New Jersey, (and, I think I heard a faint sound like asking protection for it, from a part of *Virginia.*[3]) One of the honorable gentlemen presented a petition from Virginia, (last year also,[4]) and, when this article comes up, he will tell us that this is a question between the United States and Pennsylvania, and we must be umpires; so with cotton; and so with every other article in this beneficent bill. We shall have the Union versus Kentucky—the Union versus Pennsylvania—and so on, till every item is destroyed by umpirage.

But my idea is, that the happiness of a nation is the happiness of the several parts that compose it; that the protection of the several parts of a nation, is the protection of the nation.

I did not say that this manufacture required *no* capital or skill—but only *comparatively* none. I know it must have buildings to shelter the hands employed, looms to weave, and implements to spin. But these are all nothing in comparison to what is required in other branches of manufactures. Where slaves are used, the capital is chiefly in slaves and hemp.

The gentleman from Louisiana asks, why this manufacture cannot subsist of itself? I'll tell the gentleman. It is because doubly protected and bountied industry can put down industry that has neither bounty nor protection. Britain proects her manufacturer; nay, she is not content with protecting—she superadds to all a bounty to encourage him, and purposely to enable him to prostrate the foreign manufacture [*sic*], even in his own market. This is the reason. The honorable gentleman from South Carolina has laid down a proposition to which I assent, but with some qualifications. He says no Government can guard trade against fluctuation. This is true in general; but Government can guard it against all such fluctuations as are the result of legislation in other countries; against such overwhelming fluctuations as are purposely occasioned by the acts of other Governments with a hostile design. We do not ask, we never thought of asking, protection against our own citizens. It is against the foreign manufacturer, protected, encouraged, aided, bountied, by a foreign Government. A steady market is equally desirable to the maker and the consumer of the article. With this, the manufacturer can make some sort of calculation to guide him; but not if he is to guard against the acts of the whole universe of hostile governments. It is only within the circle of our own glorious republic that he asks or seeks to have his market made secure; and to this extent his request can be granted him. Cotton growers have had to pay fifty and sixty cents a yard for bagging. Now, from a Charleston price current, it appears the price is 20 and 22. Are not such appalling fluctuations as this, produced by the cupidity of foreign monopolists, to be deprecated alike by planter and manufacturer?

Mr. Clay said the question before Congress was whether the country shall submit to a Scotch monopoly, or shall raise up an American competition? Surely the cotton growers would be the better for having two instead of one to supply them. He would put a case. Supposing one American manufacturer, or one village or town, had, till now, enjoyed the undisturbed monopoly of this article, (sometimes raising it on the planter to 60 cents a yard,) and it was now proposed to admit some other town into the trade for competition; would not Southern gentlemen listen to the proposal? Would they not hail it with joy? and will they be indifferent to it because the new competitor is in America and the old in Dundee? Or, can it be that gentlemen will be indifferent because the competitor resides in the West?

But, surely, Louisiana was the last that should complain. Cotton bagging goes from Kentucky to that state almost free of all expense for transportation. While Louisiana pays one cent or a cent and a half, Augusta pays four or five cents for transportation, besides the expense of two commission establishments, one in New Orleans and the other at Savannah. Yet, the gentleman from Louisiana continues his attacks upon the bill with a perseverance which plainly shows that, when his constituents chose him, they knew whom they were sending.

I have heard one most extraordinary species of argument used in reply to those urged from the bounty on sugar.[5] It is that the *quo animo* with which a duty was laid, is to be considered, rather than its actual operation in practice. Sir, what have we to do with the motives of the laws? We have only to inquire what is the law, and how does it operate?

We have been told that Egypt, that South America, that the West Indies, and Asia, are all beginning to cultivate this plant,[6] (a plant that seems designed by Providence to furnish the clothing of the whole human race.) And so, too, are Virginia and even Illinois —for nature herself is violated by the necessities of suffering industry.

As to the gentleman from Virginia; he is answered by the gentleman from Louisiana. He seems to have complained that certain statements were not laid before the House by the gentleman who introduced this bill:[7] but it was equally the duty of every gentleman to search for information, and to lay it before the House for general advantage. The gentleman from Virginia has done this. But, after all his calculations, the fact will turn out to be, that there are about four millions of yards of bagging consumed annually in the United States. Is it not important to put in motion all the active industry necessary to manufacture this amount, and to provide the materials for its fabrication? It seems to have come to this, that the Southern district of the Union is to separate itself from all the rest, and unite itself with Inverness and Dundee! that the prosperity or distress of Inverness and Dundee are to be the prosperity or distress of the Southern states of this Union. Sir, is it not better that the manufacturers, with whom our brethren are to be so closely united, should reside in the Union, than out of it?

Mr. Clay then went into an argument illustrative of the general nature of trade, which always moves in a circle, and shewed that the trade between the Western and Southern States, was mutually advantageous, it formed (especially as soon to be promoted by internal improvements) part of the great *home system* which would build up the strength and prosperity of the Union.

He next replied to the gentleman from Va. (Mr. Mercer,) who still persists to say that the duty will be, in effect, 10 cents on the running yard. I ask him, said Mr. C. whether the three cents allowed by England as a bounty, and met by a countervailing duty on our part, is not honestly to be deducted—for, what does it avail for protection that we lay 3 cents if England meet this by a bounty to the same amount—our protection is so far neutralized—it is, therefore, only what is laid over and above this bounty, that can operate as any protection at all—this on the square yard is by this bill made 6 cents, but the running yard being 6 inches wider, it will be exactly 7 cents on that yard.[8]

Washington *Daily National Intelligencer,* February 18, 1824. Published also in Lexington *Kentucky Reporter,* March 8, 1824; *Annals of Cong.,* 18 Cong., 1 Sess., XLI, 1559-63. The House, in Committee of the Whole, had returned to the motion offered by William L. Brent, on February 13, to strike from the tariff bill the provision for a duty on cotton bagging. After several other speakers had been heard, Brent directed a question specifically to Clay: "That gentleman says we ought to lay this duty, to excite a competition in the United States; but the committee will immediately perceive that four or five hundred hands are sufficient to make all the bagging that can be consumed in the whole cotton country—and I wish to ask the hon. Speaker, whether it is fair, that the Southern States should be taxed 400,000 dollars, to support five hundred Western men?"

1 The second statement here cited may have been made by Charles F. Mercer, whose remarks in the debate of this date were not fully reported.

2 George McDuffie, who had opened the day's debate.

3 Mercer, who had opposed the duty on cotton bagging, had, nevertheless, commented, relative to the bill, that he "intended to vote in the integrity of his heart for such parts of it as he believed to be favorable to the interests of the country." *Annals of Cong.,* 18 Cong., 1 Sess., XLI, 1559. On January 26 of this year, Representative William McCoy of Virginia had "presented a memorial of sundry inhabitants of the state of Virginia," asking that the duty on imported iron and iron castings be raised. On February 2 and 9 Jared Williams, also of Virginia, had presented similar petitions from his constituents. U. S. H. of Reps., *Journal,* 18 Cong., 1 Sess., 174, 194, 212.

4 None has been found in 1823.

5 The report of Clay's remarks in this and the next following paragraph is garbled. Proponents of the tariff argued that it would benefit agricultural interests, as well as manufacturing. Cotton and sugar growers, it was asserted, had received such support in the form of import duties since the founding of the Nation. John Tod had specifically cited the cost of cotton growing in South America and some parts of the West Indies as lower than in the United States and had maintained that the import duties were, in fact, protection for the Southern planters at the expense of consumers largely resident in other sections of the Union. Opponents of the measure retorted that these duties had been levied for revenue purposes and that Southern producers would gladly forego such benefits to escape the proposed tariff on bagging. *Annals of Cong.,* 18 Cong., 1 Sess., XLI, 1516-22 *passim,* 1526, 1552-53.

6 Cotton.

7 Mercer had complained that neither the statements of the Chairman of the Committee on Manufactures nor the papers "prepared for the use of the House" had provided "the information which ought to be the only foundation of the debate . . . that is, the real value of the article proposed to be taxed, the amount of the tax, and the effect of the tax, as a prohibitory duty; and, if it should have that effect, the competency of the manufactories of the country to supply the demand for the article thus proposed to be prohibited." *Annals of Cong.,* 18 Cong., 1 Sess., XLI, 1557.

8 Mercer replied to Clay, and several other members spoke briefly before the Committee rose and the House adjourned.

From James Slaughter

Henry Clay Esqr. Bards Town Feby. 18th. 1824

Sir

Although I have not the pleasure of an Acquaintance with you I take the liberty of addressing you upon a subject of great importance to myself, There is a suit now pending in the Supreme Court of the Nation in the Name of Mays Heirs vs me.[1] Removed from the District Federal Court at Frankfort, which suit was decided in favour of myself at Frankfort last May, I am told that it cannot come to trial this term, but as it is a suit of very considerable importance. I wish you to bestow some Attention on it, be pleased to examine the Docket & if you find that it will come to trial this term, if you will be so good as to Defend for me I will pay you a handsome fee on your return to Kentucky, it is necessary for me to call your particular attention to the Defence set up by me as it is entirely on paper, your own Superior Knowledge will Govern you, I have no Attorney there but should my Adversaries Attorney Mr. Wickliffe[2] urge a trial I confidently trust that you will appear and Defend for me, this suit is for a tract of land worth from five to six thousand and [*sic*] Dollars—& prosecuted in the Name of May's Heirs by a Hord [*sic*] of Speculators—I will thank you to write to me immediately the probable prospect of its being call [*sic*] or tried this term[3] I am Sir with great esteem & high Respect.

Yr Hble Servt. JAMES SLAUGHTER

P S I have had peaceable & adverse possession of this land for thirty years & 5 or 6 Months

ALS. DLC-TJC (DNA, M212, R12). Slaughter, a resident of Nelson County, had been many years earlier a member of the Kentucky House of Representatives.

1 The suit, involving in its final form the question of possession of 200 acres of land in Nelson County, had been instituted several years earlier by John L. May and others, heirs of John May, against Slaughter as tenant. A jury on May 27, 1823, had found that Slaughter held the superior right to the tract, but both parties in the dispute had filed exceptions to specific points of the decision. U. S. Circuit Court, Seventh Circuit, District of Kentucky, Order Book H, 461; I, 178, 182-92, 229-30; Complete Records, U, 40-66. The United States Supreme Court appears to have taken no action on this case.

2 Charles A. Wickliffe, identified below, 728n.

3 No letter found.

To Simon Gratz and Brother

Gent. Washington 19h. Feb. 1824

I duly received your obliging letter of the 17h. instant[1] transmitting a Check for $754 19/10 [*sic*] being the nett amount of the proceeds of the sale of six shares in the B. of the U. States and of dividends thereon, and also dividends on public stock, all being in the name of the late Col. James Morrison.[2] I thank you for your prompt and kind attention to this affair. I also received the two notes of John Coleman[3] for $150 each, given to the deceased, under date the 1 Septr. 1813, one payable five and the other seven years after date. I regret that the amount of them could not be collected. Is it worth while to sue the maker? Be pleased to inform me when you shall have occasion to write again to Mess Simon Gratz and Brother.

Yr ob. Servant
H. CLAY

ALS. PHi. [1] Not found.
[2] Cf. above, Nourse to Clay, January 12, 1824; Simon Gratz and Brother to Clay, January 16, 1824; Scott to Clay, January 16, 1824; Clay to Simon Gratz and Brother, February 1, 1824.
[3] A Philadelphian who had come to Lexington in 1813 and for several years had operated the Lexington Brewery before returning to the East.

To Peter B. Porter

Dr Sir Washn. 19h. Feb. 24

The inclosed letter is from one of the most eminent members of the Bar at Richmond.[1] I transmit it to you to be used according to your discretion in exhibiting the true state of things in Virginia. The meeting spoken of among my friends is a meeting of the members of the Legislature to designate persons to form an Electoral ticket to support me.[2] And the Mr. Duncan[3] mentd. is a gentleman of the Senate and one of its most prominent members.

Mr. Calhoun will be dropt in a few days. The course of events in Pennsa. has rendered that inevitable.[4] It is rumored that he means to lend his support to Genl. Jackson! We are waitng [*sic*] anxiously to hear from Albany. Yr's faithfully H. CLAY

Genl. P. B. Porter.

ALS. NBuHi. [1] Letter not found; correspondent not identified.
[2] Cf. below, Clay to Brooke, March 16, 1824. [3] Edwin S. Duncan.
[4] See above, Clay to Bache, February 17, 1824.

From John Chew

Dear Sir, Fredericksburg Feb. 21st. 1824.

Your esteemed favr. of the 16th. lays before me.[1] The failure of Mr. R Dunbar,[2] and the doubt as to the liability of Mr. Botts[3] estate for improper indulgence, induced me to enquire whether Genl. Taylor[4] would accept a draft from Dunbars receiver, at short sight, which might secure the debt, and as the General, probably has funds in hand, I advise you *at all events* to write him on the subject.

Majr. Croughan & Col: Morrison[5] were agents for Mrs: H. Kemp, of Richmond, to investigate & sell her title to 3000. acres Military lands in Kentucky—one tract of 1000 acres lies in Mc.Clarin County,[6] for which she has an application, but does not wish to close a bargain, without Knowing what steps have been taken by her agents. Can you from memory, state, any thing relative to them? and whether the lands situated within the Indian boundary,[7] have been surveyed and patented, whether any taxes have been charged on those lands, and what is the *probable* value of the tract in Mc.Clarin?

The anxiety of several persons to purchase, induces Mrs: K— to hope that the land is becoming valuable.

I have the honor to be, very respectfully Dr. Sir, Your mo: obt. Servt JNO. CHEW.

ALS. DLC-TJC (DNA, M212, R12). Addressed to Clay at Washington. Chew, of Spotsylvania County, Virginia, had been Clerk of the Circuit Court there, 1787-1806.

1 Not found.

2 Possibly Robert Dunbar, a Scottish merchant resident in Falmouth, Virginia.

3 Cf. above, I, 413. The Botts referred to in both instances was more probably Benjamin Botts, Richmond, Virginia, lawyer, who had died in the theater fire of December 26, 1811 (above, I, 602n).

4 James Taylor. 5 Probably William Croghan, Sr.; James Morrison.

6 No such county exists in Kentucky. 7 West of the Tennessee River.

To [Charles Hammond]

Dr Sir Washn. 22 Feb. 24

I thank you most cordially for your obliging letter of the 9h. inst.[1] You are right in your conjecture that my multifarious vocations are very oppressive. Still I should have been glad to hear from you more frequently. Indirectly, through Wright[2] and others, I have had that satisfaction, and have learnt the very zealous and efficient support that you have been, at Columbus and at Cincinnati, rendering to my interests. The question, on which you have been thus kindly exerting yourself, begins, by the developement of successive events, to be seen in a more distinct light. The Caucus of the 14h. is believed to have terminated Mr. Crawfords prospects.[3] His friends have not formally given him up, but it is evident that they feel conscious that his election cannot be secured. Mr. Calhoun is no longer regarded as a Candidate, and is spoken of by all his friends here as withdrawn. This result has been produced by the unequivocal indications recently given in Pennsa. of a determination to support Genl Jackson & not Mr. C.[4] The circle of competition is thus much circumscribed. And I do not now entertain a doubt that Mr. Adams, Genl. Jackson or myself will be elected. If I am brought into the H. of R. as one of the three highest, I consider my election safe. My opponents will direct their great aim to exclude me; but they cannot effect it, if my Western friends do not desert me. It is well known here that my strength is greatest at Albany. We are awaiting anxiously to know what course Mr. Crawfords friends there will take when they shall know the results of the Caucus here. In Maryland I am certain of the two upper districts with a good prospect of obtaining others. In Virginia they are about to form a ticket to run for me in opposition to the Crawford ticket, if that should be insisted on.[5] In New Jersey my prospects are good.

My affair with Mr. Bartlett[6] gave me great pain. His attack was premidated [*sic*], stimulated and unjustified. What I said was to repel it in a manner to secure me tranquillity for the future. It has had that effect. I was clearly in the right and he clearly in the wrong. Such was almost the unanimous opinion here. It has been accommodated by an *apology* from *him*.

I have great fears about the extension at this Session of the Cumberland road.[7] New York (would you believe it?) is opposed. That is the joint effect of her having completed, by her own separate resources, her great Canal,[8] and of the Crawford influence on her delegation. But don't sell your farm. The road will be extended at no distant day.

I hope you will execute your purpose of writing on the Slave subject if necessary.[9] With great regard I am faithfully Your's

H. CLAY

P.S. We have argued the Bank Cause. You will lose it, which will not excite your surprize. But the Ct. has directed an argument of the question of the jurisdiction of the Fed. Courts, about which in this *particular* case you know there can be no difficulty.[10] H.C.

ALS. InU. 1 Not found. 2 John C. Wright.
3 See above, Clay to Porter, February 15, 1824.
4 See above, Clay to Bache, February 17, 1824.
5 See below, Clay to Brooke, March 16, 1824. 6 Ichabod Bartlett.
7 Two bills for the extension of the road from Wheeling, Virginia, westward were introduced during this Session of Congress, but neither was adopted.
8 See above, Porter to Clay, January 29, 1823, note. 9 No publication found.
10 See above, Clay to Biddle, February 17, 1824.

To Francis T. Brooke

My dear Sir (Confidential) Washn. 23 Feb. 1824

It is some time since I had the pleasure of hearing from you. In the interval several events of importance have occurred. The miserable attempt at a Caucus you will have seen accounts of.[1] Mr. Crawford never could have been elected; but I venture to predict that the mere *fact* of seeking by means of a Caucus so got up & so constituted will destroy whatever prospects he ever had. Mr. Calhoun is withdrawn: This has been produced by events in Pennsa. evincing, beyond all doubt, the determination of that State to support Genl. Jackson.[2] The circle of competition is thus much circumscribed. And you may rely upon it that you will have, as your next President, Adams, Jackson or myself. You will have in Virginia to choose between those three evils. It is madness; it is perfect infatuation to think, at this time, of any body else. Our intelligence from N. York continues to be favorable to the hopes of my friends. Still we shall have nothing absolutely decisive from that quarter until time has elapsed to enable us to hear what the consequences there will be of the Caucus. The present moment is one of great importance to me in Virginia. Now is the time to make a demonstration for me there, if ever. My friends accordingly I understand contemplate the formation of an electoral ticket for me at Richmond and think of putting you at the head of it, if you consent.[3] Such a ticket, announced at this time, whatever may be its ultimate fate in Virginia, will have the very best effects out of Virginia.

As soon as I hear from N. York I will communicate to you. In the mean time I should be glad to hear from you. Mr. Crawfords friends will make an effort, as long as they adhere to him, to exclude me from the H. of R. in the hope that my Western friends will take him if they cannot get me. They utterly deceive themselves. If they accomplish that object, and bring him into the House—with Adams and Jackson, to my exclusion, he *cannot* be elected. As I have told you before, the N. Western States will go for Mr Adams, if they cannot get me. They will vote for no man residing in a Slave state but me, and they vote for me because of other & chiefly local considerations outweighing the Slave objection. On that you may depend. Mr. Adams then will have the six New England States & three N. Western States, with the chance (and the best chance) for N. York (if I am out of the way) New Jersey, Maryland, to say nothing of Alabama, Mississippi, Louisiana.

I am faithfully Your friend H. CLAY

The Honble F. Brooke.

ALS. KyU. Published in Colton (ed.), *Private Correspondence of Henry Clay,* 86-87.

1 See above, Clay to Porter, February 15, 1824.

2 See above, Clay to Bache, February 17, 1824. Calhoun had not formally withdrawn. Writing to Virgil Maxcy on February 27, he commented: "Our friends have come to the conclusion that we ought to hold to our position, and wait events." Quoted in Bassett, *Life of Andrew Jackson,* I, 334.

3 See above, Clay to Porter, February 19, 1824; below, Clay to Brooke, March 16, 1824.

From C[onstant] F[reeman]

23d February 1824

Constant Freeman, of Massachusetts, a retired Army officer, a veteran of the Revolution and the War of 1812, who was Fourth Auditor in the Treasury Department from 1817 to his death February 27, 1824, informs Clay, as executor of the estate of James Morrison, "late Navy Agent at Lexington," that there is on the books of the Fourth Auditor a balance of $892.26 against Morrison, as reported on settlement February 28, 1820. Copy. DNA, RG217, Records of the Fourth Auditor, General Correspondence: Letters Sent, vol. 20, p. 102. This sum was listed as an advance to Morrison for disbursements as Navy Agent. *House Docs.,* 17 Cong., 2 Sess., no. 102, p. 28.

Remarks on Tariff Bill

[February 24, 1824]

Mr. CLAY was glad that gentlemen would, with whatever views, now vote on the general question; but he saw no cause for so much excitement against the course of the honorable gentleman from New York. It was, to be sure, unusual; it was not one to which he should have advised him. But it had only been adopted to bring up for discussion the general principle of the bill as separated from its details. But, though the course, in its form, was unusual, it was not so very unusual to see gentlemen make a speech on one side of a question, and afterwards vote on the other. He had seen frequent instances of this in his public life. He trusted gentlemen would not vote in favor of striking out. As to the bill going to tear up commerce, and God knows what—all that belonged to the discussion of its merits. And if the honorable gentleman from Virginia thought that such was its tendency, he should shew it by argument rather than by violent expressions. He hoped to hear that gentleman (to whom he always listened with interest) in answer to the arguments in favor of the bill.

[Several members joined in discussion of the propriety of considering the general principles of the bill. Stevenson took occasion to observe "in reply to the Speaker . . . that, while complaining of excitement in others, he seemed to have shown quite as much himself." George McDuffie, who saw the bill as "a mass of particulars" to which no general principles applied, suggested that the motion be withdrawn. Martindale refused to comply, and Clay rose again.]

Mr. CLAY observed, that some experience in legislative bodies had taught him that more stress was often laid upon the modes and forms of doing public business than was at all necessary. If a discussion of the general principle was desired, it might be brought up on any one of the items of the bill. It would necessarily come up in a variety of forms. It was, however, the established parliamentary usage that a motion to strike out the enacting words (formally the first section) of a bill should precede the motions to alter its several features. This was the course lately pursued on the bill for internal improvements. Mr. C. again defended the gentleman from New York.[1]

Washington *Daily National Intelligencer,* February 25, 1824. Published also in *Annals of Cong.,* 18 Cong., 1 Sess., XLI, 1656-57, 1658. On February 23 Henry C. Martindale had charged that the strategy of opponents of the tariff bill was to attack each of its separate items with the same arguments repeated again and again. In order to save time, to prevent defeat, and to test "the general principles of the bill," he had therefore moved to strike out the enacting clause. He had then begun a speech in opposition to his own motion, had given way at four o'clock for adjournment, and had concluded on the following day. Andrew Stevenson had then argued against discussing the general principles of the bill. "He thought the course pursued by the gentleman from New York, was without a parallel. After the House had, for two weeks, been engaged in a discussion which touched the vital interests of the country—after the two sides of the House, in relation to that discussion, had agreed, first to go into the several items of the bill; then to take up its general principles; and, if a decided majority should appear to be in its favor, then to agree to make its provisions as little exceptionable as possible—for that gentleman to get up and occupy the Committee for two days, with a speech against his own motion, and on the general principles of the bill—this was offering an indignity to the House, and was a course which this House ought to spurn." He urged a unanimous vote, without discussion, against the motion. Stevenson's fellow Virginian, John Floyd, had disagreed. Ordinarily he would have opposed a motion of this kind, but he would support it in this instance because "this bill was of such an enormous character . . .; it ought rather to have been entitled a bill to tear up commerce and destroy agriculture, than to amend the duties on imported articles." Clay's remarks followed.

1 Soon afterward the motion to strike out the first section of the bill was defeated, and the Committee resumed consideration of the motion earlier introduced by William L. Brent (see above, Remarks, February 16, 1824, note).

From E—— P——

[*ca.* February 24, 1824]

Describing himself as "a stranger whose head is bleached with the frosts of fifty-six winters; whose humble and unassuming and obscure situation in life, has rendered him a stranger in the political world," the writer addresses himself to Crawford, Adams, Clay, and Calhoun, appealing to them to withdraw from the presidential race in favor of Andrew Jackson, "the only surviving hero of the Revolution, whom we can elevate to the Presidential Chair," "the second . . . Washington." The document was inserted in the newspaper at the request of "A Representative in Congress." Washington *Daily National Intelligencer,* February 25, 1824.

Remarks on Tariff Bill, Duty on Cotton Bagging

[February 25, 1824]

Mr. CLAY was happy to hear such a declaration from the honorable member from Louisiana, and he was now about to put those declarations to the test. I, said Mr. C. am a hemp grower (that is, at such times as the situation of the country and the regulations of government render it possible, without loss.) The gentleman seems to believe that it is impossible, in this country, to make the article good. Sir, as nature delivers it to our hands, it is of as fine a quality as any in the world; it has no natural, inherent defect of any kind whatever. The only difficulty attends the treatment of it after it is cut down or pulled up, (for both modes are pursued.) It is then either dew-rotted, or water-rotted. When it is to be dew-rotted, it is stacked till the month of December or January, and then spread under the snow till February—this is called dew-rotting. In the other process, the hemp is immersed in ponds or running streams, where some process goes on, by which the glutinous part of the vegetable is dissolved, and when dry, it is submitted to an operation called breaking. When thus prepared, the hemp of this country is, in all respects, equal to the Russian, and commands as high a price.

The gentleman from Massachusetts, on my right, (Mr. Lathrop,) [1] tells me that he always water rots his hemp. I have known in Kentucky entire crops to be water rotted; and it may be done wherever hemp is raised, if we were only favored with the protection of Government to secure to us our own market.

The gentleman from Louisiana says that we have already a bounty of $80 a ton, and yet the manufacturer won't take the hemp we raise. Does not the gentleman know that this observation applies only to the dew-rotted? And besides, what is the bounty without any certainty of the market? A cargo of three or four hundred tons imported, will destroy the market for a whole crop. If the gentleman doubts this, will he guaranty the market? The farmers of Kentucky have given this matter a sufficient trial—pressed by suffering at home, and lured by the flattering promises of hope, they have again and again ventured, and again and again they have been broken down by foreigners—by the serfs and boors of Russia. If adequate protection was given, the water-rotted hemp would speedily supersede the dew-rotted article, and all the hemp of the country would become good. But, even the dew-rotted hemp will answer every purpose for cotton bagging, provided the bales are not exposed to the wet. But the gentleman asks, with an air of triumph which I was sorry to witness, Why don't you do it? If you can make good bagging, why is bagging of your make always 10 cents a yard below the imported? And he quotes from a price current, to shew that ours is put down at half price. But what is the date of that paper? 1822.[2] The very year in which the manufacture was languishing and almost destroyed, and in the latter part of which it began to revive. Yet he reiterates upon us the question, Why don't you at once make it both cheap and good? Sir, we want to breathe. We are, in this respect, just born. Our factories are but 18 months in being; and already they have reduced the Scotch price. The gentleman objects to the recent paper quoted by my honorable friend over the way, (Mr. Sharpe,) [3] because the planters, he says, are all supplied, nothing is doing in the market, and the price is nominal merely. But, sir, I am in possession of another paper, only 2 or 3 days later than that quoted, and a different price is given, which shews that there is, at this time, some activity in the market. The majority of the planters may be supplied—but there are, also, provident men, who reserve their purchases till the market is lowest. When I left my home,[4] which was at the time when the purchases are usually made, I saw letters from highly respectable men, which stated that the bagging of Kentucky, (from one particular factory at Lexington,)[5] was then bringing a price equal to the Scotch article. Sir, we only ask you to let our manufactures exist *under hope*, and in 18 months, my word for it, you will have bagging as good as the Scotch, in equal abundance, and at a less price.

Before I sit down, I must add a word or two in reply to a gentleman from New York, (Mr. Hogeboom,)[6] who told us that the manufacturers of Dundee lived in a cold climate, bought their fuel, and brought their hemp from Dantzic, though they had nothing to give for it in exchange. Why, sir, though I do not in the least doubt that honorable member had fully convinced his own mind that this was so, did he know so little about trade, as not to be aware that it was not the manufacturer, but the merchant who imports the material of British manufactures? And does he suppose that nothing goes from Britain up the Baltic, for the hemp and iron that come down the Baltic? I repeat what I before mentioned, that the Scotch manufacturer may afford to make a sacrifice for a time—that he may enjoy the monopoly in the end. But if that gentleman is really convinced that there must be a monopoly of this article somewhere, would he not rather give it to the American than to the Scotch manufacturer? I put it to his patriotism.

The gentleman from Louisiana says, that this manufacture is in no need of protection, because we have been obliged to take our hands from it, and employ them in other occupations. Sir, we have done so, it is true—lamentably true. We have tried the raising of tobacco—we have tried horses—we have tried hogs—we have tried hemp: the industry of the country roams from object to object, trying every thing, and alike in vain. We want protection—we ask this government for protection—not against our brethren—not against other states, but against strangers.[7]

Washington *Daily National Intelligencer,* March 1, 1824. Published also in *Annals of Cong.,* 18 Cong., 1 Sess., XLI, 1672-74. Again the House, in Committee of the Whole, was debating William L. Brent's motion to strike from the tariff bill the proposed duty on cotton bagging (see above, Remarks, February 16, 1824). Clay rose to reply to Edward Livingston, who had repeatedly criticized the quality of Kentucky hemp and had said: "When the American manufacturer will consent to take our hemp at all, then a protecting duty may, with more propriety, be asked for."

1 Samuel Lathrop.

2 Livingston had "quoted a price current of 1822, to prove that when the price of the imported bagging was 45 to 50 cents, that of the home made was only 25; there was always a difference of at least 10 cents a yard." *Annals of Cong.,* 18 Cong., 1 Sess., XLI, 1666.

3 Peter Sharpe had "quoted a Louisiana price current of last month, to show that while the foreign article is bringing from 24 to 26 cents, the home-made brings from 18 to 19—a very different proportion from that quoted by the gentleman from Louisiana." *Ibid.,* 1667.

4 In mid-November, 1823.

5 Not identified.

6 James L. Hogeboom had spoken on the preceding day.

7 After a brief exchange of comment by other members, the Committee rose. On the following day a vote was taken and Brent's amendment was defeated. An amendment was then adopted to change the proposed duty on cotton bagging from six to four and one half cents a square yard. On April 12, after prolonged efforts by John

Tod, this proposal was amended so as to provide a supplementary clause setting the rate at five and a half cents after June 30, 1825—the action being carried "by the Speaker's casting vote." *Annals of Cong.*, 18 Cong., 1 Sess., XLII, 2294. 2315.

From Asher Robbins

Honble. Henry Clay. Newport. R. I. Feby. 25th, 1824
Dear Sir

Among all our public men, you have long been the object of my preferrence for the Presidency of the United States; I have been led to this preferrence by an attentive observation of your political course; and the wisdom which it appears to me to have displayed.

Of all our public men, I think you best understand the great interests of this great Country; are the most devoted to them; and the best able to promote them: nothing therefore would give me more satisfaction than to see you, our Executive Cheif [*sic*]; and nothing more pleasure than to be instrumental in making you so.

This letter is intended merely, as a pledge of my cordial cooperation with your friends for the attainment of this object; in every way in which I can be usefull to them: And to say that I should be happy to receive any of their communications; particularly on the Subject of your prospects of support; as we have no information here that can be depended on: the partizans of the Several candidates, aiming to throw, all but their own, out of the combat, state the account of the support to be expected by each, according to their wishes, rather than according to the fact.—

With Sentiments of high esteem and devoted attachment I am. D.Sir Your obed. Servt. ASHER ROBBINS—

ALS. DLC-HC (DNA, M212, R1). Robbins, born in Connecticut and graduated from Yale College in 1782, had taught in Rhode Island College, had studied law, and had begun practice in Providence. Having moved to Newport in 1795, he had been United States District Attorney, and was now (1818-1825) a member of the State Assembly. He later served as United States Senator from Rhode Island (1825-1839), was again briefly a member of the State Assembly, and was postmaster at Newport from 1841 to his death four years later.

To Francis T. Brooke

My dear Sir (Confidential) Washn. 26 Feb. 1824

During your sojourn at home I did not write you any letter except one,[1] which I addressed you some days ago at Fredericksburg, with a direction to the Post Master at that place to forward it to you at Richmond, if you had gone thither. I hope it has safely come to hand. I am glad that you have returned to the metropolis. Inclosed I transmit you two letters which I have recd. to day from N. York[2] which you may return or destroy after perusing their contents. Other letters to other persons here from Albany corroborate their statements, and represent 1st. that Mr. Crawford cannot possibly obtain the vote of N. York; 2dly that great dissatisfaction prevails at Albany with such a Caucus as was held here, and especially with the person nominated as Vice President;[3] and 3dly that there is no contest in New York but between Mr. Adams and me. Pennsylvania is gone inevitably to Jackson. Will you still persevere in the hopeless support of Mr. Crawford in Virginia? That is what we are left to suppose by the proceedings of Saturday night last.[4] Well; be it so. You will find that he will not even come into the H. of R. You will find that he has no other aid to get there, but that which Virginia, No. Carolina & Georgia can give him, and they cannot carry him into the House. One thing is certain, that Mr. Crawford cannot be elected, whoever may be. If he Adams and Jackson go into the House, Adams will be elected. If he Adams and I go into the House, he will still not be elected.

Be pleased to make my respects to Mr. Call[5] and to say to him that I recd. his favor of the 24h. and that I will write to him when I shall receive that which is promised in it. I yet think that the formation of a respectable Electoral ticket in Virginia for me wd. have the best effect, but I do not wish to place my friends there in an uncomfortable position. Faithfully Yr friend H CLAY

The Honble F Brooke.

ALS. KyU. Published in part in Colton (ed.), *Private Correspondence of Henry Clay,* 88.

1 See above, Clay to Brooke, February 23, 1824.

2 Not found.

3 See above, Clay to Porter, February 15, 1824, note.

4 A caucus of members of the Virginia legislature on February 21 had nominated Crawford by a vote of 139 to 7 for Adams, 6 each for Nathaniel Macon and Jackson, and 5 for Clay.

5 Daniel Call. Correspondence not found.

Defense of Appointments to Committee on Agriculture

[February 27, 1824]

Mr. CLAY rose, not to enter into the discussion, but to reply to the observations of the gentleman from Va. respecting the Committee on Agriculture. He said, that when he had placed at the head of that Committee, a gentleman from New York, the largest agriculturist in the Union, (Gen. Van Rensselaer,) a gentleman from Pennsylvania who had ploughed hundreds of acres where the gentleman from Virginia had ploughed one; when he had put on it other gentlemen who were either themselves agriculturists, or the decided friends of agriculture—above all, when the gentleman from

Virginia, himself a host, was added to the Committee[1]—and, he might add, when the presiding officer of this House was one who had formerly ploughed hundreds of acres with his own hands, he did think the interests of agriculture were pretty well taken care of here. In the commencement of a session, the occupations of all the members could not be known at once—the presiding officer had to exercise a faculty which he had heard was peculiarly possessed in some parts of the United States, he had to *guess* a little in the appointment of Committees—but he felt some doubt whether the gentleman from Virginia would have found it easy to make a better selection. That gentleman seemed to think there existed some general conspiracy against the interests of agriculture—if all who had petitioned for the Tariff were to be considered as conspirators, the conspiracy was extensive indeed—(here Mr. Clay enumerated 17 states.) The whole State of New York *en masse* was in the plot, so was all Pennsylvania *en masse*—nay, there were conspirators even in Virginia—the mischief seemed to extend throughout the Union—and, considering its extent, and the character of those concerned in it, the interests of agriculture must be in serious danger.

[Baylies declared that the interests of agriculture and manufacturing "were inseparably connected, especially in the Eastern States." Garnett again expressed the belief that, though the members of the Committee on Agriculture "were upright and sincere, . . . their principles were, in their tendency, hostile to agriculture." Garnett concluded his remarks by saying: "As to the compliments of the Hon. Speaker, the agricultural interest would have been much more indebted to him, if he had taken a few more members of the Committee from South of the Potomac."]

Mr. Clay again explained, as to the structure of the Committee. The members were all either farmers, or persons decidedly attached to the farming interest. It was not always possible to observe latitudes, especially where the number of a committee consisted but of 7. Not one Western man had been put on it. The Committee on Manufactures, too, consisted almost entirely of farmers. Surely the gentleman from Virginia ought rather to suspect the soundness of his own views, than to set himself up as a standard, and arraign all who differed from him in sentiment. For himself, Mr. C. believed that the interests of agriculture would be prostrated, not if the bill did, but if it did not pass.[2]

Washington *Daily National Intelligencer,* March 1, 1824. Published also in *Annals of Cong.,* 18 Cong., 1 Sess., XLI, 1690, 1691. During debate in Committee of the Whole on a motion, offered the preceding day by Philip P. Barbour to strike from the tariff bill the clause laying an import duty of twenty five cents a bushel on wheat, Robert S. Garnett had been critical of the Committee on Agriculture: "A majority of the committee were in favor of the protecting duty system, no doubt honestly, conscientiously. But, whilst the manufacturers were provided with a committee, to prepare, organize, and concentrate the means of attack, the agriculturists had no committee to prepare, organize, and concentrate the means of defence. He owed it to justice to say, that he had the best reason to believe, that the competition [*sic*] of the committee was purely the result of accident or inadvertence—and inadvertence to the concerns of agriculture, no one had a right to impute, as a fault, to another, for all were equally culpable. But, if it were any advantage at all to have a committee, it was one which the agriculturists were deprived of. It was now time for the agriculturists to change their conduct, if they did not wish to be driven to choose between the alternatives of ruin and resistance." *Annals of Cong.*, 18 Cong., 1 Sess., XLI, 1686.

Clay took the floor after John W. Taylor had replied briefly to Garnett.

1 Members of the committee were Stephen Van Rensselaer; Francis Baylies, of Massachusetts; Garnett; Robert Harris, of Pennsylvania; Robert S. Rose; Lemuel Whitman, of Connecticut; and Thomas Patterson, of Pennsylvania.

2 Debate on Barbour's motion continued.

Remarks on Tariff Bill, Duty on Wheat

[February 27, 1824]

Mr. CLAY regretted, exceedingly, the course the debate had taken. It was certainly altogether unnecessary. The great merits of Virginia and Pennsylvania were known to all, and need not be repeated on this floor. Why should gentlemen indulge in such a course of reflection? It had no connexion with the subject before the House, and he hoped it was now over.

[When debate was resumed, Daniel Webster argued against the proposed duty on wheat. In regard to Canadian wheat, he observed, "the true question is, whether the expenses of going round by Montreal and Quebec will so raise its price in the foreign market that the gain upon the wheat we sell there will more than compensate us for the loss of the ad valorem duty, the transit toll, and the commercial commission and charges for the shipment?"]

Mr. CLAY said he was greatly surprized at the argument of the gentleman from Massachusetts. It was certainly not correct that, if the Canada wheat did not come down our canal, it would get as cheaply to the foreign market by the way of the St. Lawrence.

{Mr. W. explained. He had not been so absurd as to say this.}

Mr. CLAY. Then the gentleman surrenders the argument; for it gets to the West Indies, in that route, burdened with additional costs of transportation; it is no longer able to compete with ours, and the market is secured to our own agriculturist. The Canada flour is certainly eaten somewhere, either in the United States or in a foreign market; if in the United States, then so much of our own is displaced, and, to its whole amount, it is an injury to the American wheat grower; if in a foreign market, then, if that market was great enough to consume both all the Canada wheat and all ours, the gentleman's argument might hold. But such is not the fact. Ours and the Canada must compete for the same consumer. Why, then, bring the Canada wheat to that consumer any cheaper, by the use of our canal? Wherever the Canada wheat goes, go where it may, it takes the place of so much American wheat, whether at home or abroad. Besides, if you cut off their flour from the use of our canal, you keep it at home for all that portion of the year that the St. Lawrence is closed with ice, while our canal is open. The British warehousing system did not apply to this case. Gentlemen did not seem to be aware of the advantage of the home consumption. The city of New York alone did not consume less than 800,000 barrels of flour annually. If Canada flour comes to New York for consumption, so much American is excluded. No matter, says the gentleman from Massachusetts, because so much more American goes abroad. Very true: if there was a market ready abroad to receive it—but this is not the case; and therefore it is a dead loss to the American farmer. Such was the fertility of the Canadian peninsula, between Lakes Erie and Ontario, and so cheap were the lands sold by the British government, that the settler there could afford to undersell the farmer of the United States, whose land costs him ten times as much.[1]

Washington *Daily National Intelligencer,* March 1, 1824. Published also in *Annals of Cong.,* 18 Cong., 1 Sess., XLII, 1699, 1700-1701. On February 26, when Barbour had first offered his motion (see above, this date) in Committee of the Whole, Clay had risen to a point of order—"is it in order to move to strike out this line untill we arrive at it in due progress from line 105—" Upon the Chairman's affirmative ruling, the debate had been opened. Minutes in Committee of the Whole . . . from 18 Cong., 1 Sess., to 26 Cong., 1 Sess. (DNA, 18A-C21.1).

During the discussion Samuel D. Ingham, of Pennsylvania, had been critical of Virginia, saying, "could she look beyond her own boundary for any thing else than political power, she might have discovered that her neighbors have some interest in such a duty, if she has none." Barbour challenged the statement and the resulting verbal exchange was halted by the Chairman of the Committee of the Whole, who called Ingham to order. Clay then rose.

1 After a rejoinder by Webster, the Barbour amendment was defeated and the Committee rose.

From Robert Scott

Dr. Sir, Lexington 28th. Feby. 1824

Your favors of 12 & 13th. inst.[1] have been recd. The former enclosed your answer to Shreves Bill[2]— Enclosed is the Clerks certificate of your qualification as Executor of Colo. Morrison s estate—[3]

The Gentleman who contemplated renting your house declined it, having rented another— However I do not think you will lose any thing by it, as if you rented to one person, I do not think it would bring more than 300$ curry or perhaps 350$ including the iron store and cellar—as it is, it will bring you something more— In a few days I can rent all the end occupied by Mr. Hawes[4] &c. and will do so—

Latterly our weather has been pretty cold and very unfavorable

for out work– Your domestic affairs are all I beleive [*sic*] doing well– Aunt Morrison & family are well– Wishing your health may continue good and that you may succeed in your efforts for the encouragement of Internal Improvements &c. I am Dr Sir Most respectfully Yr Obt. Servt. ROBT. SCOTT
The Honble H. Clay

ALS. DLC-TJC (DNA, M212, R12). [1] Not found.
[2] See above, Scott to Clay, January 16, 1824.
[3] Not found. See above, Warfield to Clay, June 1, 1823, note.
[4] Richard Hawes, Jr. See above, Agreement, November 1, 1819; below, Rental Agreement, March 26, 1824.

To Francis T. Brooke

My Dear Sir, Washington Feby. 29, 1824–

I received your favor of the 27th instant.[1] The secondary declaration of your Caucus would have been of considerable service to me; for I have no doubt it will be alleged & perhaps believed out of Virginia, that both Gen. Jackson & Mr. Adams are preferred there to me.[2] The expectation which has been excited in other States, that a demonstration would be made in my favor at Richmond will be dissappointed [*sic*], if nothing be done. Whether it be advisable to adopt any measure, my friends are the most competent Judges. Your willingness to be placed at the head of the electoral ticket for me, is a new & valuable proof of the fidelity & zeal of your friendship. I should regret, however, that you should be placed, by your regard for me, in any position which might affect your social or political relations to those with whom you have so long moved. I assure you that it is my decided conviction that Mr. Crawford has not the remotest chance of being elected. I do not believe that he will come into the house of Representatives, for I think his total vote will will [*sic*] be limited to the three States of Virginia, N. Carolina & Georgia, if he gets them. Penna. is gone absolutely, & without any manner of doubt, to Jackson. New York will not support Mr. Crawford, whoever else they may support, & however her electors may be appointed. All our information from Albany continues to assure us, that the only contest in New York, is between Mr. Adams & me; that great disatisfaction [*sic*] has been produced there by the selection of Mr. Gallatin; & that Mr. Crawford's friends are in the utmost despair.

As to the tariff, I have expressed no new opinion. They [*sic*] have been formed & declared for these 12 years past. Mr. Crawford, at the last session of Congress, as well as at this, recommended the encouragement of domestic manufactures, & recommended the specific duty of 6 cents per yard on Cotton bagging, which we have been so long debating in the house of Representatives.[3] At the North his friends every where proclaim him as friendly to the tariff. The same is asserted here in reference to all the candidates. The difference between them & me is, that I have ever been placed in situations in which I could not conceal my sentiments.

When will your legislature rise?—Will it be before you are enabled at Richmond to hear of the result of the Convention at Harrisburg?[4]— I am faithfully Your friend H. CLAY

The Honble F. Brooke

Copy. DLC-HC (DNA, M212, R1).

1 Not found. 2 See above, Clay to Brooke, February 26, 1824, note.

3 Crawford had recommended "a judicious revision of the tariff" as "advantageous to the revenue, salutary to commerce, and beneficial to the manufactures of the country"; but he particularly deplored the differing rates at which articles "composed of wool, cotton, flax, and hemp" were assessed. "It is, therefore, respectfully submitted, that all articles composed of wool, cotton, flax, hemp, or silk, or of which any one of these materials is a component part, be subject to a duty of twenty-five per cent. ad valorem." "Letter from the Secretary of the Treasury, Transmitting His Annual Report on the State of the Finances, December 27, 1822," *Sen. Docs.*, 17 Cong., 2 Sess., no. 8, p. 12; "Report from the Secretary of the Treasury, on the State of the Finances, January 2, 1824," *Sen Docs.*, 18 Cong., 1 Sess., no. 16, p. 12.

4 See below, Clay to Brooke, March 6, 1824. The Virginia legislature remained in session until March 10.

To [Peter B. Porter]

Dr Sir Washn. 3d. March 1824.

I recd. your letter[1] acknowledging the receipt of two of mine of the day & of the 13h. Feb.[2] But I wrote you one, after the Caucus here, of which you have made no acknowledgment. It sought to obtain information from you in respect to the opinions of my N. York friends in regard to the V. Presidency; and contained a note marked "Strictly Confidential."[3] Have you received them?

There is at this moment an eddy in politics here. We are all waiting to hear which way the current will break out at Albany. If N. York should not be in favor of Mr. Crawford, I do not believe that *he* will come into the House. If it should decide for him still I think that he cannot possibly be elected.

Inclosed I send you a letter from Richmond[4] written by one of the most distinguished members of the Senate of Virginia.

Yr faithful friend H. CLAY

ALS. NBuHi. Endorsed, in Porter's hand: "H. Clay 3. March 1824."

1 Not found. 2 Not found.

3 See above, Clay to Porter, February 15, 1824. 4 Not found.

From Robert Scott

Dr. Sir, Lexington, 4th. Mar: 1824

This serves to hand you, your A/Cs. with Colo. Morrison's Estate for the month of February Ulto.[1] The Boswells have not yet paid the interest, but promise it in 3 or 4 days.[2]

On yesterday Mr Hawkins[3] recd. a Stud Horse from John Mason of Montgomery[4] which the latter says you made a bargain with him for during the season— Mr. H. was not apprised of this, but will retain the horse and do the best he can with him— He says the horse is rough and will not be in complete order to put to mares under a month or near it—

From the Cash A/C you will observe I have paid J. M. Morrison 250$ of his legacy[5]— This includes 100$ he recd. of Mr Cox[6] in Oct. last and debts he had contracted at Louisville to something more than 100$— The balce. of the 250$ I gave him in money to keep him from beggary— I have endeavored to get him to give me a deed of Trust for his benefit and to go on his land, but have failed[7] If I had discretionary power, I beleive [*sic*] I would buy out his legacy on the best terms I could and give what might be saved to the use of his child[8] or other relations, as he will squander the whole of it without doubt—except his land which he has made over to his wife and child—Mr. Hawes[9] and others inform me that he has the power to sell his legacy, and I fear he will do it—Hence my anxiety to obtain his deed of Trust to prevent it—

We are all well Respectfully ROBT. SCOTT

On the 27 Ulto. Judge Bledsoe[10] fell from his horse and broke his leg—His case is considered to be a doubtful one—

ALS. DLC-TJC (DNA, M212, R12).

1 Private account not found. For the executor's accounts, see below, *ca.* June 8, 1824.

2 Joseph and George Boswell had borrowed from James Morrison a sum of money, on which the interest was $1,200 per year.

3 Francis Hawkins. 4 Montgomery County, Kentucky.

5 Under the terms of James Morrison's will, James M. Morrison was to receive $2,000 in cash and $4,000 worth of land.

6 Probably Nathaniel Cox.

7 Such an indenture, dated February 24, was recorded upon acknowledgment of signature by Morrison and Scott in Fayette County Court on March 11, 1824. Fayette County, Deed Book X, 295-97.

8 Henry Morrison. 9 Richard Hawes, Jr.

10 Jesse Bledsoe, who survived the accident.

To Francis T. Brooke

My dear Sir Washington 6h. Mar. 24

I have received the three last letters which you have done me the favor to write to me.[1] On the subject to which they relate there appears to be an eddy at this moment. We shall soon see which way the currents will break out. Information from every quarter assures us that the Caucus here[2] has impaired instead of advancing Mr. Crawfords prospects. The Convention at Harrisburg no doubt the day before yesterday recommended Genl. Jackson; and they probably forebore to make any recommendation of a Vice Presidt. or if they did make any I think it was Mr. Calhoun.[3] At Albany they are probably looking to Harrisburg and waiting for events. It is now believed that the Senate of N. York will reject the Electoral bill, the Commee. of that body having made a report against it.[4] But rest assured that all inferences derived from that fact in favor of Mr. Crawford are utterly fallacious. He cannot obtain the vote of that State.

I concur with you in thinking that my friends at Richmond & in Virginia ought to avoid, if possible, all misunderstanding with those of Mr. Crawford; and a temperate and conciliatory character would, therefore, be best to be given to any appeal made to the people, in my behalf.

I have just heard that Dewit [*sic*] Clinton has arrived, here. I pray you not to think it necessary to answer every letter which I may address to you. I should be glad to hear from occasionally [*sic*] & when perfectly convenient. Yr faithful friend H. CLAY

The Honble F. Brooke.

[Marginal addendum]

P.S. The Pennsa. delegation are the most mortified men in the world. They lament the course which is taking in that State for Genl. Jackson; and now regret that the unavailing effort which has been made there for Calhoun had not been directed to my support. They own that it would have been successful, if it had been so directed.

ALS. KyU. Published without the marginal note in Colton (ed.), *Private Correspondence of Henry Clay,* 88-89.

1 Not found. 2 See above, Clay to Porter, February 15, 1824.

3 At the Pennsylvania convention, held at Harrisburg on March 4, Jackson had been nominated for the Presidency with only one dissenting vote; Calhoun had been chosen as the vice-presidential candidate by a vote of 87 to 10 each for Clay and Albert Gallatin, 8 each for William Findlay and John Tod, and one for Daniel Montgomery, Jr. (of Danville, Pennsylvania, member of the State House of Representatives, 1800, and of Congress, 1807-1809, and an active proponent of canal development).

4 See above, Woods to Clay, August 27, 1823, note; below, Clay to Brooke, March 16, 1824.

From George Wallace

Sir Braddocks Field 6h. March 1824

It was not until lately, that I understood you were the Executor of the late Colo. Morrison[1]— It is therefore necessary for me to inform you that I am in possession of several title papers to land belonging to him—they are now held subject to your order; or should you pass thro' Pittsb on your way home, & will apprise me of the time you will be there I will make it my business to see you— I hold a claim (as the Executor of the late Henry Reed) for money recd. by the Col., and which was retain'd by him (by consent) in consequence of the claimants being minors, & residing in Ireland;[2] they are now pressing a settlement of the estate, which will make it necessary for me to ask payment as soon as you will tell me it is proper to apply— I should also be glad to see you on another account, which Mr. Baldwin[3] can explain, if he is yet at Washington—it relates to a claim of the Colo. against the estate of late Geo McDowall [*sic*]—also another against the estate of Joseph Scott, in the hands of Parker Campbell Esqr of Washtn. Pa. for collection[4]— Respectfully Yr. Obdt. St. GEO. WALLACE

The Hnble Henry Clay

ALS. DLC-TJC (DNA, M212, R12). Wallace owned and lived on a tract known as Braddock's Field, the scene of General Edward Braddock's defeat in 1755, located some eight miles southeast of Pittsburgh.

1 James Morrison.

2 Reed, a Louisville, Kentucky, merchant, who had died in 1793 or 1794, had bequeathed one fourth of his estate to his brother, James, in Ireland, or to James' children.

3 Henry Baldwin. 4 On both these claims, see below, Wallace to Clay, May 17, 1824.

Remarks on Tariff Bill, Reciprocal Clause

[March 8, 1824]

Cited in Washington *Daily National Intelligencer*, March 9, 1824; *Annals of Cong.*, 18 Cong., 1 Sess., XLII, 1758-61. The House, in Committee of the Whole, had renewed debate on a resolution offered by John Forsyth on Saturday, March 6, to strike from the tariff bill its third section, which provided that after June 30 of this year there should be added to import duties on certain goods "the full amount of such bounty or premium, or allowance in nature thereof, as" might be given in the country or place from which the goods should be exported or in which they should be produced or manufactured.

Those who favored the resolution argued that the operation of this section would violate the most favored nation clause of the treaty of 1815 with Great Britain (above, II, 57-58). Since "England grants to her exporters a bounty on certain articles on which other countries grant none," the effect of this provision would "be to charge such English goods with a higher duty than articles of the same kind brought from elsewhere; and it will therefore break the treaty, and compromit the faith and honor of the nation." *Annals of Cong.*, 18 Cong., 1 Sess., XLII, 1759.

Opponents of the resolution, Clay, Andrew Stewart of Pennsylvania, and John Tod (their remarks not reported individually), replied that the object of the tariff bill, to protect domestic industry, "could never be attained, and the whole bill must be rendered nugatory, if a bounty granted by a foreign nation on the exportation of its commodities might not be met by an equivalent duty here. It was well known, that England grants bounties for the express purpose of forcing her goods into foreign markets; and if the objection to this section of the bill is held valid, she will still be enabled to do so with respect to this country.

"But it is not valid. In that article of the treaty which this section of the bill is said to violate, two objects were intended. The first was to secure a perfect reciprocity between the two nations, with respect to their navigation. Preferences had previously been given, both by France and England, which threatened altogether to deprive America of the carrying trade—which course of things led to the adoption of what has been called the American policy on this subject—a policy which has proved completely triumphant, and has brought both England and France to terms. But this section of the bill leaves this reciprocity untouched—for no difference is made in our duties, whether merchandise is imported in British or in American bottoms.

"The second object aimed at, in the article of the treaty alluded to, was to secure to British goods an entrance into our country on as good terms as those of any other nation; nor does this section make any discrimination to their prejudice; its provisions are general, no more directed against the goods of one country than another. It adds the amount of all foreign bounties to the duty on those goods on which the bounty is granted; and if, in consequence of this general measure of self-defence, British goods have more duty to pay than French, it is not the result of *our* legislation, but of *her own,* and when two parties make a contract, no act of one of them is, of itself, to constitute a violation of the contract by the other party."

After further discussion, amendments offered by Stewart and Tod were defeated. Forsyth's motion then carried by a vote of 114 to 66.

From John Harvie

Henry Clay Esqr Washington City Bk of Ky March 8th. 1824

My Dear Sir, The majority of the persons whose notes were transfered to you under the ill judged agreement of Mr. Mils [*sic*] with you have been making application for the annullment of that agreement and the reinstatement of the notes upon accommodation or at all events for permission, which they contend is their priviledge under the 8th. section of the act concerning the Bk of Ky passed 8th. Feby. 1815,[1] to discharge them with notes of said Bk.[2] Your atto[3] has addressed, either at their instance, or with the view of propitiating the application a letter to the Directors intimating his opinion of your willingness in the event of a disposition on the part of the Directors to comply with their request by reassuming the debt to you, to grant an indulgence thereupon of 6 . 12 . 18 & 24 months whether with or without interest he omits to state. It is with the view of determining this latter point that I now address you. To be candid I do not well know what other course the Directors can well take than to leave the transaction to its natural channel The notes have been transfered. they are now your property before the parties can avail themselves, if indeed they can at all, of the privilege of making paymt. in the notes of the Bk the tender must be made in open court.[4] Should it be ascertained that under the law such tender is valid and available it will then be full time enough, either, for yourself, or the Bk to receive the notes, and grant an acquittance But it is possible they may challenge the assignment upon other grounds. It is understood here that they have high professional authority for questioning the legallity of such transfers It is affirmed with much confidence that it is a species of dealing not within the chartered powers of the corporation to embark in and therefore upon its face void and of no virtue This I do not believe nor does the counsel of the Bk whose attention has been particularly called to the subject. It is however well worthy of your consideration. should it have any force or weight a motive might be engendered on your part as well as ours by a little concession to have this matter amicably adjusted. I know that you are playing upon the safest side of the ground Miles in his unremitting zeal to get rid of your claim which bye the bye I was just as anxious to see extinguished as he was entered without authority into our agreement with you totally variant from the resolution which had been adopted by the Directors by which all these embarrassing points and questions were devolved upon the Bk and to be guarranteed against, instead of being according to the resolution and intentions of that body devolved and thrown upon yourself. When he returned from Lexn. and presented me with the agreement I was both surprized and dissatisfied and pointed out to him the discrepancy between it and the resolution. conformably to the latter the assignments were to be made "without recourse" agreeably to the first the Bk was to guarantee against every thing save the insolvency of the parties. But as I was satisfied you had formed the contract under the belief of the sufficiency of his authority to make it and had left the state under the firm conviction of a faithful execution on the part of the Bk I conceived that good faith enjoined its ratification and therefor voted for carrying it into effect. Had you remained in the state it would never have been confirmed. It is in this way we have been left to encounter these questions, which in the adoption of the resolution it was never designed that we should have been exposed to. Indeed in the discussion that occurred upon the subject it was expressly asserted that these were questions and matters unnecessary for the Directors to enquire into, in as much as they would be consequences that the assignee in taking assignments without recourse would assume upon himself. Altho in the event that there are any good pleas in bar of your recovery *we* shall be the principal and substantial sufferers yet I would put it to you how far your own interests may be concerned in promoting in that contingency by reasonable yielding an amicable settlement of the transaction I do not apprehend much danger of any such result but I am no lawyer and I conceive it my duty to present it to you as an eminent lawyer well able to decide upon it, for consideration. Respectfully J.HARVIE Prest

Copy. Bank of Kentucky, Frankfort, Letter Book G (1822-1825), 192 [*i.e.* 292]-293. See above, Agreement, November 10, 1823; Assignment, November 18, 1823; Clay to Paynes, November 20, 1823, note; Clay to Biddle, December 6, 1823; Clay to Harper, December 22, 1823.

1 "*And be it further enacted,* That the notes of the mother bank, and each of the branches now established, or which may hereafter be established, shall be current in each other, and be received on account, or for any debt due to the bank of Kentucky or either of its branches."

2 On February 24 and again on March 2, 1824, the board of directors of the Bank had postponed consideration of the "proposition of Thomas Wallace & others to place their notes to Henry Clay upon the same footing of other debtors to the Bank. . . ." Bank of Kentucky, Frankfort, Record Book D, 211, 213.

3 Either James Harper or Richard Hawes, Jr. The letter has not been found.

4 This was the distinction in the differing decisions under the litigation, discussed above, Clay to Harper, December 22, 1823, note.

Remarks on General Appropriation Bill

[March 12, 1824]

Mr. CLAY (Speaker) expressed his hope that his colleague would withdraw his amendment. He admitted that the course was not unusual; that, in an appropriation bill at a former session, at *his* instance, a similar provision had been introduced for a nearly similar purpose.[1] But he hoped that, if the amendment was withdrawn, the House would feel disposed to indulge a spirit of liberality towards the bill which had been reported upon this subject, and would permit his colleague to call it up at a period as early as possible.[2]

Annals of Cong., 18 Cong., 1 Sess., XLII, 1773. During discussion in Committee of the Whole "on the bill making appropriations for the support of Government for the year 1824," Robert P. Henry had moved to amend the measure by adding an appropriation of $75,000 for removing obstructions to navigation of the Ohio and Mississippi rivers. He had already (on February 28) reported a bill for the same purpose; but now, fearing his measure would not be reached before the end of the Session, he "thought proper to introduce the proposition in the present shape." Louis McLane stated a hope that Henry would withdraw his amendment, for he "had no doubt" that the bill would be called up before adjournment.

1 See above, II, 793.

2 Henry withdrew the amendment. See above, Speech, January 14, 1824, note; below, Remarks, May 7, 1824.

To Francis T. Brooke

My dear Sir Washington 16h. Mar. 1824.

I recd. your obliging favor of the 14h. instant.[1] The ticket formed by my friends at Richmond appears to me, upon the whole, to be extremely judicious;[2] and its good effect elsewhere I think I am not deceived in. The Senate of N. York has by a vote of 17 to 14 postponed the Electoral bill.[3] The first and most certain effect of that vote is to prevent Mr. Clinton[4] from being a Candidate. And I have no doubt that that was a principal object with the majority. If there had been a popular election of Electors he wd. probably have come out, and very likely wd. have obtained the vote of that State. I am thus relieved from all collision with him in Ohio, where he wd. have given me trouble, 'tho' I have no doubt that I should have beaten him. Genl. Porter[5] thinks that I am more interested than any other Candidate in the Legislature of N. York retaining the choice of electors. He believes that the vote of the State will be given to me. Mr. Crawfords friends, on the contrary, will claim the postponement of the bill as evidencing a purpose to support him. They are deceived. Even if he should get the vote of that State, he would lose it in the House, there being a decided majority of the N. York delegation against him.

You may rely upon it that Ohio, Kentucky, Indiana Illinois,

Missouri and Louisiana will support me, and that I shall get two if not four votes in Maryland. I stand well in Delaware and New Jersey. If I were withdrawn it is my opinion that the entire West would go to Jackson. His election can only be prevented, by my continuing to be supported.

The course of Mr. Randolph's[6] friends about Richmond surprizes me. My conscience acquits me entirely of all blame towards that gentleman, throughout all our acquaintance. He has ever been the assailant. I have ever been on the defensive. The H. of R. has always taken part with me and against him in every collision that I ever had with him. I am faithf y Your friend H. CLAY
The Honble F. Brooke.

ALS. KyU. Published in part in Colton (ed.), *Private Correspondence of Henry Clay*, 89.
[1] Not found.
[2] A meeting of members of the Virginia legislature favoring Clay for the Presidency had been held at Richmond on March 8. Hector Davis, of the House of Delegates, and Edwin S. Duncan had been authorized to draw up an "Address to the People of Virginia" on the merits of Clay's candidacy and to prepare a list of Clay electors. Brooke's name headed their roster, published in Washington *Daily National Intelligencer*, March 15, 1824.
[3] See above, Woods to Clay, August 27, 1823, note.
[4] DeWitt Clinton. [5] Peter B. Porter. [6] John Randolph.

To Amos Kendall

WASHINGTON, 18th March 1824.

Dear Sir: I thank you for your favor of the 3d inst.;[1] of the kind and friendly suggestions contained in which, I will make the best use in my power. The attack upon you by Cowan was most unjustifiable, and terminated as all such appeals to violence should do.[2]

New-York continues to be a contested State. My decided opinion is, that it will give its support to Mr. Adams or to me, or perhaps divide it between us. In that case, Mr. Crawford cannot come into the House. My friends are confident in the belief, that if I enter the H. as one of the three highest, no matter with what associates, I shall be elected. If, contrary to all probability, Mr. Crawford should obtain the vote of New-York, the contest for an entry into the H. will probably be between Jackson and me. In Maryland, Delaware and New-Jersey, I have reason to count upon some support. Without entering into further particulars, my opinion is, that my friends have every motive for vigorous, animated and persevering exertion. I am faithfully your friend, H. CLAY.
AMOS KENDALL, Esq.

Frankfort *Argus of Western America*, July 9, 1828. Published also in Washington *United States Telegraph-Extra*, I (July 26, 1828), 318-19.
[1] Not found.

2 On March 1, 1824, James Cowan had assaulted Kendall "with a Hickory cudgel" for publishing a series of articles entitled "Wictorian Dinner, an 'Expose' of the Minority 'System' of Kentucky; or the Curtain Drawn from the Holy Alliance of America," by one signing himself "Patrick Henry," which attacked the Bank of the United States, the United States Supreme Court, the Kentucky Court of Appeals, and their Kentucky supporters for overriding the will of the majority as expressed in relief legislation (see above, Clay to Dougherty, December 7, 1821, note; Scott to Clay, December 30, 1823, note).

Kendall reported: "No great harm was done, and one party received just about as much injury as the other." Both parties having been summoned into court, Cowan was fined $20, or ten days' imprisonment. *Argus of Western America,* March 3, 1824. The "Patrick Henry" series was continued through nine numbers and then announced for publication by Kendall in pamphlet form the following June.

To Nicholas Biddle

Dr Sir Washn. 19h. Mar. 1824

I have the satisfaction to inform you that the Supreme Court has this moment decided the general question of Jurisdiction in cases in which the Bank is a party in favor of the institution; and that it has also decided the case with the State of Ohio in favor of the Bank on all the points occurring in it except that of interest on the Coin part of the funds of the Bank which had been seized.[1] Interest is refused because the defendants were restrained, by the injunction, from using the funds. The necessity of that restraint is however very apparent from the opinion, because if the funds had been disbursed by the State, in the current service, the amount never could have been recovered from *the State.* I congratulate you upon these auspicious results.

The argument is now going on in the Court upon the Kentucky relief laws.[2]

I have the honor to be with great respect Your ob. Servant

Nicholas Biddle Esqr. &c. &c. &c. H. CLAY

ALS. PHi-Etting Collection. Endorsed: "recd March 22. 1824."

1 See above, Clay to Biddle, February 17, 1824.

2 See above, Clay to Hammond, July 14, 1822; Clay to Biddle, December 27, 1822, note.

Remarks on Tariff Bill, Duty on Wines

[March 20, 1824]

Mr. CLAY opposed the amendment, as being injurious to the revenue, and the navigating interest, without being beneficial to any branch of American industry.[1]

Washington *Daily National Intelligencer,* March 22, 1824. Published also in *Annals of Cong.,* 18 Cong., 1 Sess., XLII, 1871. In Committee of the Whole on the tariff bill Samuel A. Foot had proposed raising the duty on wines from 15 to 25 cents per gallon.

1 After Clay and others had spoken Foot "withdrew his motion, to give time for farther inquiry."

Remarks on Tariff Bill, Duty on Hemp

[March 23, 1824]

Cited in Washington *Daily National Intelligencer,* March 24, 1824; *Annals of Cong.,* 18 Cong., 1 Sess., XLII, 1888. In Committee of the Whole on the tariff bill, Clay, with James Buchanan and John Tod, opposed an amendment, offered by Churchill C. Cambreleng on March 20, lowering the duty on hemp from two to one and one half cents per pound. Clay's remarks were not recorded. At the conclusion of the debate, "abounding with fact and argument, and occasionally enlivened with attack and retort in which humor was chastened by decorum," the amendment was defeated.

To Josephus B. Stuart

Dr Sir Washn. 24 Mar. 1824

I recd. your favor of the 20h. inst. and your several previous communications all came safely to hand.[1] I should written [*sic*] you sooner but that I had nothing in particular to communicate. Albany is now the great point of attention. Mr. Crawfords friends here assert with the greatest confidence that he has a majority of your Legislature. As to the idle report which you state them to have put in circulation that my friends had with drawn me, it is too ridiculous to merit a serious contradiction.[2] There is not a doubt that out of your state there is a greater *certain* support of me than of him. Nobody doubts here that I shall receive the votes of Ohio, Kentucky, Indiana, Illinois, Missouri, & Louisiana and a part of Maryland. Where, out of N. York, will he receive an equal support? New Jersey is believed also to incline towards me; and many of my friends in Virginia are sanguine of my success there. All agree that if I enter the House I shall be elected. And is not the difficulty of entering it as great in the cases of the other gentlemen as in mine? With great regard I am faithfly Yrs H. CLAY

Dr. Stuart.

ALS. NcD. [1] None of these letters has been found.

[2] The rumor was apparently widespread. On April 13, 1824, the Washington *Daily National Intelligencer* reprinted a denial of it, taken from the Cincinnati *Advertiser,* which noted that the story had been previously published in the Louisville *Advertiser* and copied into the Washington *National Republican,* coupled with the statement that Clay "would probably accept the appointment of Attorney General."

Remarks on Tariff Bill, Duty on Sail Duck

[March 24, 1824]

Mr. CLAY supported Mr. Tod's motion. The article now made was of an excellent quality. The American Navy had adopted the use of it. It was a manufacture for which this country was well adapted; and it diminished a trade the most disadvantageous of any in which we are engaged.

[Benjamin W. Crowninshield (now serving the first of four successive terms as Congressman from Massachusetts) discussed the manufacture and importation of sail duck and "gave a detailed account of the factory at Salem, in its first abortive attempt at using the American flax, and its late successful manufacture of sail cloth from flax imported from Ireland." The duck from Irish flax was "of the very first quality, but furnished at a price which the Navy alone would pay. The factory was kept in being by Navy contracts alone—not a bolt of its duck had ever been used in a merchant ship, notwithstanding it was situated in the most commercial district in all the Union." Crowninshield continued with "a course of general argument against the bill." He was answered, first, by George Kremer, of Pennsylvania.]

Mr. CLAY spoke in reply to the gentleman from Massachusetts, (Mr. CROWNINSHIELD,) so far as he had not been answered by the speech of the honorable gentleman from Pennsylvania. The gentleman had said that the Navy distributed its contracts at high prices with a view to become popular with the nation.[1] He wished that government would pursue, throughout, the policy of encouraging our own ingenuity, industry, and enterprise. There could be no more certain or more honorable path to popularity. But he thought the gentleman's argument went to confute himself. He said that, but for the patronage of the navy, the factory at Salem must die. What did this show? That nothing was wanting to the manufacturer but governmental protection—the very thing for which the friends of the bill contended. Mr. C. insisted that the effects of the American efforts had greatly lowered the price of this article. It had been furnished to the navy since the peace, at $22, but could now be supplied at $17, while the best Russian was at from 16 to $20. The report of the Secretary of the Treasury recommended an ad valorem duty of 25 per cent,[2] the very rate at which this amendment would place it.[3]

Washington *Daily National Intelligencer*, March 25, 1824. Published also in Lexington *Kentucky Reporter*, April 26, 1824; *Annals of Cong.*, 18 Cong., 1 Sess., XLII, 1895, 1896-97. In Committee of the Whole on the tariff bill, John Tod had moved to strike out specific rates proposed on designated types of sail duck. In reply to a question, he had explained "that the ad valorem duty laid on duck in the other part of the bill, was 25 per cent.; that proposed in this, amounted to about 20 per cent. so that striking out would raise the duty 5 per cent."

1 The report of Crowninshield's speech does not mention such a statement.

2 See above, Clay to Brooke, February 29, 1824, note.

3 Among the speakers who followed, "Mr. Crowninshield replied to Mr. Clay, in relation to the quantity of cloth in a bolt of American duck." The part of Clay's remarks here referred to was not recorded.

When the question was put, Tod's amendment carried.

Motion and Remarks on Tariff Bill, Duty on Molasses

[March 24, 1824]

Mr. CLAY moved to increase the existing duty on the article of

Molasses. He believed there was no fairer object of taxation in the proposed tariff. His great wish was to promote American agriculture; and, with this view, to encourage the production of the raw material of any subject of manufacture to which our own country was adapted, rather than the importation of the rival foreign article. Molasses was to be considered—1st, As an article of subsistence. As such, the existing duty bore no proportion to that on brown sugar. It was capable of being applied, and was in fact applied, to almost all the purposes of brown sugar. This latter article was subject to a duty of three cents per pound. A gallon of molasses, containing not less than eight pounds, paid a duty only of five cents; that is, a little more than half a cent a pound. 2ndly, As a substance capable of conversion into spirituous liquors. The least duty imposed on them was thirty-eight cents per gallon. If the policy of the country be well founded, in imposing this high duty on spirits manufactured *abroad,* it equally dictates that a high duty should be imposed on an article produced *abroad,* susceptible of easy conversion into spirits, and which comes into competition with articles raised at home, capable of similar conversion. 3rdly, As a raw material of manufacture. On this point, it appeared to Mr. C., that we ought to discourage, even for the purpose of manufacture, any raw material, raised abroad, of which articles, capable of a similar fabrication, can be certainly produced in abundance at home. No one will doubt that the grain of our country produces a spirit equal, at least, to that which is distilled from molasses; nor our ability to produce it in the greatest abundance. He did not mean to take up the moral consideration of the question. He intended to ask the attention of the committee to the matter practically. A certain amount of spirituous liquors will be consumed, whatever we may think or wish upon it as moralists or philanthropists. Assuming that practical principle, we are to consider whether it is not better for our country to derive the whole profit, both as to the production of the raw material and the distillation of it, rather than divide it with foreigners. Every gallon of spirits, distilled from foreign molasses, and consumed within the country, takes the place of a gallon of spirits distilled from domestic produce. The foreigner enjoys the benefit of the value of the raw material, and we that of its manufacture only. This latter advantage we should still possess, if we substituted a native raw material to that which is furnished us from abroad; and, consequently, the mere interest of manufacturing would not suffer by the exclusion of the foreign material. There would, at most, be only a change in the theatre of distillation.

The increase in the import of molasses was very great, so great as to threaten the supplanting of the native materials of distillation. From 1790 to 1800, inclusive of both years, the total quantity of molasses imported was 53,323,607 gallons; that is, an average of 4,847,600 gallons for each of these eleven years. From 1801 to 1811, inclusive of both those years, the total quantity imported was 78,224,651 gallons; that is, upon an average, 7,111,320 for each of the latter term of eleven years.—The population of the United States increases in a ratio of about four per cent. per annum. And the increased importation of molasses, during the latter term of eleven years, beyond that of the previous term of eleven years, was about what it ought to have been, supposing the increase of consumption to be according to the progressive augmentation of our population. Applying the same principle, the quantity of molasses imported in 1822 ought to have been 9,375,040, instead of which the actual quantity was 11,990,569 gallons for that year, and for the last year it rose to 13,019,328 gallons! The principle which Mr. C. thought ought to govern our manufacturing policy was to encourage—1st, the manufacture of our own raw materials; 2ndly, the manufacture of foreign raw materials which do not come into competition with any that are native; and 3rdly, but least of all, those which compete with our own produce. Of all parts of our country, the grain growing now suffers the most. Whatever, therefore, would tend to reanimate that, without material detriment to others, ought to meet with a favorable consideration. According to an estimate of a former Secretary of the Treasury, in 1810, of the 6,834,878 gallons of molasses, then imported, five millions were supposed to be distilled, and the residue, 1,834,878, were consumed for other domestic purposes.[1] Applying that rule—of the 13,019,328, imported last year, 2,786,413 gallons were consumed in domestic purposes other than that of distillation, and 10,232,915 gallons in distillation. Supposing (which is a low estimate) a gallon of molasses to produce only a gallon of spirits, there was distilled 10,232,915 gallons of spirits. To produce this quantity from grain, would require about five millions of bushels. And the total export of the breadstuffs of the last year did not equal five millions of bushels of grain. Thus, by excluding the foreign raw material of molasses as an object of distillation, we should create an additional market at home, for a quantity of grain equal to about the whole export, in the form of breadstuffs, of that article last year. Suppose it were attempted to import grain from abroad, for the purpose of distillation, would not every one cry out against it? And where is the difference between such an operation as that would be, and the importation of molasses convertible into a worse spirit than that which is distilled from grain?

Fourthly, and lastly, molasses ought to be considered as a source of revenue. The effect of the additional duty, which he meant to propose, would be merely to lessen the importation, and thereby give greater scope for the consumption of our native produce. To what amount it would lessen it could only be matter of conjecture.— If one half, and the duty which the committee might fix should be twelve and a half cents per gallon, there would be an augmentation of revenue in the ratio of twenty-five per cent. upon the present amount. Taxed at that rate, the duty would still be greatly below the standard which is furnished by that on brown sugar, or on that of spirits.

So far as it may be considered as an article of mere subsistence, Mr. Clay felt no disposition to increase the duty, low as it would be, if his proposition were adopted, in comparison to brown sugar. If there could be a discrimination made between that portion of the material which was distilled and that which was consumed in other domestic uses, he would, with pleasure, adopt the discrimination. He knew of none that was practicable. He finally proposed to insert in the bill a duty of 12½ cents per gallon on molasses, but subsequently reduced the proposed amount of duty to 10 cents.

[Though not informed in advance that this motion was to have been made, Gideon Tomlinson "still felt it his duty to state his views," which were contrary to those expressed by Clay. During his argument Tomlinson stated that a duty of twelve and one half cents would be 125 per cent on the first cost of molasses in the West Indies and would exclude this commodity altogether. Considering the price of Kentucky whisky in New Orleans, "He could not believe, that the manufacturer of whiskey needed this duty as an encouragement."

Timothy Fuller accounted for the different results obtained by Clay and Tomlinson, in examining certain statistics, "from the fact, that large quantities of the imported molasses were refined and converted into loaf sugar, for exportation; and that a part of the rum distilled from molasses is also exported. Both these amounts must be deducted from the apparent amount consumed."]

Mr. CLAY rejoined. Admitting that part of the molasses is converted into sugar, (though this was the first time in his life he had heard of such a thing; he always supposed that molasses was a residuum which could not be grained.) Still, he asked, if there was any just proportion between the duty on sugar and that on molasses? If the molasses was to be considered as sugar, the case was still worse than if it was to be considered as spirits. Touch it but with the wand of the manufacturer, and straight it would bring, as sugar, a protecting duty of 3 cents a lb.; but, as molasses, it paid only

5 cents a gallon. He repelled the idea, that this was a duty for the West. He knew not that it would benefit that section of country more than others. Nor did he care where the benefit fell; it would fall somewhere. Wherever grain was grown throughout the Union, its effects would operate—nor are grain growers alone—the fruit raising districts, (including that of the gentleman from Connecticut,) would all be aided by it. Peach brandy and apple brandy would both be benefitted by excluding West India molasses, and diminishing the rum made from it. He aimed not at the eaters, but at the drinkers, of New England; and if the gentleman could devise a plan by which they could be separated, so that the duty would bear upon the latter only, he would immediately vote with him in its favor. As to its taxing the food of the poor, he asked, whether it was equal to the duty on brown sugar, or bohea, both of which were food of the poor?

Mr. C. here quoted a statement from a work by Mr. Picton,[2] (on whom he passed a merited encomium, and who is a citizen of the same State with Mr. T.) to corroborate the position he had taken in respect to the proportion of molasses distilled, to that used for food; and closed, by reducing his motion to a duty of 10 cents per gallon.[3]

Washington *Daily National Intelligencer,* March 26, 1824. Published also in *Annals of Cong.,* 18 Cong., 1 Sess., XLII, 1898-1900, 1903-1904. Immediately after the adoption of Tod's amendment (above, this date), Clay again took the floor.

1 No such "estimate" has been found. Albert Gallatin had reported to the United States Senate in 1811 that 7,651,682 gallons of molasses had been imported during the preceding year. Clay appears to have garbled certain statements found in Timothy Pitkin, *A Statistical View of the Commerce of the United States of America: Its Connection with Agriculture and Manufactures: and an Account of the Public Debt, Revenues, and Expenditures of the United States . . .* (Hartford, 1816). According to this work (p. 102), about five million gallons of spirits manufactured in the country in 1810 had been distilled from molasses, and "The average quantity of spirits imported and consumed from 1801 to 1812 inclusive [had been] 6,834,878" gallons.

2 *I.e.,* Pitkin, who had not sought re-election to Congress in 1818 but had been returned to the State legislature, 1819-1830.

3 During his rejoinder Clay was interrupted several times by Jonas Sibley, of Massachusetts, but refused to yield the floor. When the question was taken, Clay's motion carried.

Rental Agreement with Thomas Curry

[March 26, 1824]

An Agreement between Robert Scott for and on behalf of H. Clay and Thomas Curry.

The said Scott for and on behalf of said Clay, hereby leases to the said Curry, the two lower rooms lately occupied by Richard Hawes Jur. in the Brick House on Short and Market Streets in the Town of Lexington and the Kitchen thereto appertaining, from this day inclusive until the last day of February 1825 inclusive—

In consideration whereof the said Curry, hereby agrees and obliges himself to pay to the said Clay, the sum of One hundred and twenty one dollars & 10c. in Kentucky Currency payable quarterly—and to surrender the said premises on the said last day of Feby. 1825, in as good order as he receives them, natural decay and inevitable accidents excepted—

The right of distress for any of the rent in arrear is reserved to the said Clay— And also the right of the occupants of the rooms in the 2nd. or 3rd. Story to use the back privy.

Witness the hands and Seals of the parties this 26th. day of March 1824.

ROBT. SCOTT for
H CLAY } Seal
THO CURRY

[Endorsement][1]

Memorandum of deficiencies in the above premises— viz
3 panes Glass broken out of 2 front room windows—
1 Do out & 1 fractured back room windows—
5 do out & 1 sash out of the Kitchen lower windows—
2 do do up stairs Kitchen windows—
No Lock & key to Kitchen door—One of the floors of the privy torn up
Booth [*sic*] doors of Smoke House without keys.
No Key to Lock from back room to the passage in big house
The rest of the premises in good order except that the painting-plastering is very black & dirty— THO CURRY

[Endorsement on verso][2]

23 April 1823 Mr. Curry took possession of the room up Stairs— RS.

ADS by Scott, signed also by Curry. DLC-TJC (DNA, M212, R16). Curry, in August, 1823, had assumed editorship of the Lexington *Western Monitor*.

1 ES, in Scott's hand. 2 AEI.

Notes for Speech on Tariff

[*ca.* March 30, 1824]

See 4th. Vol. of Hallam[1] page 224 for the Woolen Manufacture of Flanders, "which first animated the Northern division" of Europe—

page 226— Wool, "the great staple of England, upon which more than any other, in its raw or manufactured state, our wealth has been founded."

Prohibitions began in 1261—

page 228 —A more prosperous æra began with Edward III; the father of English Commerce—

Invited the manufacturers from Flanders—

☞ See note—

See 4h. Vol. of Las Casas[2] for Bonaparte's policy in regard to Manufactures.

Examination of the alleged tax on the Consumer–

It is incidental – It is voluntary –

He may fabricate –

The Cotton grower and the English Manufacturer unite– The Cotton grower tells him that if he will buy his Cotton he shall have the market for the sale of his fabrics not of the Cotton growing Country but of all the U S.

Examine the assertion that every one should be left to the unfettered use of his own labor capital & skill– There is no such thing. The world is but one vast theatre of Coml. restriction; each nation striving to secure to itself the greatest advantages of all others: And the question in this state of things is whether we shall submit to their monopolies to their exclusive policy to their Legislation or to our own.

It is a calumny that our laws have diminished commerce & navigation.

AD. DLC-TJC (DNA, M212, R10).

1 Henry Hallam, *View of the State of Europe during the Middle Ages . . .* (4 vols.; Philadelphia, 1821). This work had been published in England in 1818.

2 Emmanuel, Comte de Las Cases, *Memorial de Sainte Hélène, Journal of the Private Life and Conversations of the Emperor Napoleon at Saint Helena* (6 vols.; Philadelphia, 1823).

Speech on Tariff

[March 30-31, 1824]

The gentleman from Virginia (Mr. BARBOUR) has embraced the occasion produced by the proposition of the gentleman from Tennessee, to strike out the minimum price, in the bill, on cotton fabrics, to express his sentiments at large on the policy of the pending measure; and it is scarcely necessary for me to say, that he has evinced his usual good temper, ability, and decorum. The parts of the bill are so intermingled and interwoven together, that there can be no doubt of the fitness of this occasion to exhibit its merits or its defects. It is my intention, with the permission of the committee, to avail myself also of this opportunity, to present to its consideration those general views, as they appear to me, of the true policy of this country, which imperiously demand the passage of this bill. I am deeply sensible, Mr. Chairman, of the high responsibility of my present situation. But that responsibility inspires me with no other apprehension than that I shall be unable to fulfil my duty; with no other solicitude than that I may, at least, in some small degree, contribute to recal [*sic*] my country from the pursuit of a fatal policy, which appears to me inevitably to lead to its impoverishment and ruin. I do feel most awfully this responsibility; and, if it were allowable for us, at the present day, to imitate ancient examples, I would invoke the aid of the MOST HIGH. I would anxiously and fervently implore His divine assistance; that He would be graciously pleased to shower on my country His richest blessings; and that He would sustain, on this interesting occasion, the humble individual who stands before Him, and lend him the power, moral and physical, to perform the solemn duties which now belong to his public station.

Two classes of politicians divide the people of the United States. According to the system of one, the produce of foreign industry should be subjected to no other impost than such as may be necessary to provide a public revenue; and the produce of American industry should be left to sustain itself, if it can, with no other than that incidental protection, in its competition, at home as well as abroad, with rival foreign articles. According to the system of the other class, whilst they agree that the imposts should be mainly, and may, under any modification, be safely relied on as a fit and convenient source of public revenue, they would so adjust and arrange the duties on foreign fabrics as to afford a gradual but adequate protection to American industry, and lessen our dependance on foreign nations, by securing a certain, and, ultimately, a cheaper and better supply of our own wants from our own abundant resources. Both classes are equally sincere in their respective opinions, equally honest, equally patriotic, and desirous of advancing the prosperity of the country. In the discussion and consideration of these opposite opinions, for the purpose of ascertaining which has the support of truth and reason, we should, therefore, exercise every indulgence, and the greatest spirit of mutual moderation and forbearance. And, in our deliberations on this great question, we should look fearlessly and truly at the actual condition of the country, retrace the causes which have brought us into it, and snatch, if possible, a view of the future. We should, above all, consult experience—the experience of other nations as well as our own, as our truest and most unerring guide.

In casting our eyes around us, the most prominent circumstance which fixes our attention, and challenges our deepest regret, is, the general distress which pervades the whole country. It is forced upon us by numerous facts of the most incontestable character. It is indicated by the diminished exports of native produce; by the depressed and reduced state of our foreign navigation; by our diminished commerce; by successive unthreshed crops of grain, perishing in our barns and barn-yards for the want of a market; by the alarming diminution of the circulating medium; by the numerous bankruptcies, not limited to the trading classes, but extending to all orders of society; by an universal complaint of the want of employment, and a consequent reduction of the wages of labor; by the ravenous pursuit after public situations, not for the sake of their honors, and the performance of their public duties, but as a means of private subsistence; by the reluctant resort to the perilous use of paper money; by the intervention of legislation in the delicate relation between debtor and creditor; and, above all, by the low and depressed state of the value of almost every description of the whole mass of the property of the nation, which has, on an average, sunk not less than about fifty per cent. within a few years. This distress pervades every part of the Union, every class of society; all feel it, though it may be felt, at different places, in different degrees. It is like the atmosphere which surrounds us—all must inhale it, and none can escape it. In some places, it has burst upon our people without a single mitigating circumstance to temper its severity. In others, more fortunate, slight alleviations have been experienced, in the expenditure of the public revenue, and in other favoring causes. A few years ago, the planting interest consoled itself with its happy exemption; but it has now reached this interest also, which experiences, though with less severity, the general suffering. It is most painful to me to attempt to sketch or to dwell on the gloom of this picture. But I have exaggerated nothing. Perfect fidelity to the original would have authorized me to have thrown on deeper and darker hues. And it is the duty of the statesman, no less than that of the physician, to survey, with a penetrating, steady, and undismayed eye, the actual condition of the subject on which he would operate; to probe to the bottom the diseases of the body politic, if he would apply efficacious remedies. We have not, thank God, suffered, in any great degree for food. But distress, resulting from the absence of a supply of the mere physical wants of our nature, is not the only, nor, perhaps, the keenest distress, to which we may be exposed. Moral and pecuniary suffering is, if possible, more poignant. It plunges its victim into hopeless despair. It poisons, it paralyzes, the spring and source of all useful exertion. Its unsparing action is collateral as well as direct. It falls with inexorable force, at the same time, upon the wretched family of embarrassment and insolvency, and upon its head. They are a faithful mirror, reflecting back upon him, at once, his own frightful image, and that, no less appaling [*sic*], of the dearest objects of his affection. What is the CAUSE of this wide-spreading distress, of this deep depression, which we behold stamped on the public countenance?—We are the same people. We have the same country. We cannot arraign the bounty of Providence—The showers still fall in the same grateful abundance. The sun still casts his genial and vivifying influence upon the land; and the land, fertile and diversified in its soils as ever, yields to the industrious cultivator, in boundless profusion, its accustomed fruits, its richest treasures. Our vigor is unimpaired. Our industry has not relaxed. If ever the accusation of wasteful extravagance could be made against our people, it cannot now be justly preferred. They, on the contrary, for the few last years at least, have been practising the most rigid economy. The causes, then, of our present affliction, whatever they may be, are human causes, and human causes not chargeable upon the people, in their private and individual relations.

What, again I would ask, is the CAUSE of the unhappy condition of our country, which I have faintly depicted? It is to be found in the fact that, during almost the whole existence of this government, we have shaped our industry, our navigation, and our commerce, in reference to an extraordinary war in Europe, and to foreign markets, which no longer exist; in the fact that we have depended too much upon foreign sources of supply, and excited too little the native; in the fact that, whilst we have cultivated, with assiduous care, our foreign resources, we have suffered those at home to wither, in a state of neglect and abandonment. The consequence of the termination of the war of Europe, has been the resumption of European commerce, European navigation, and the extension of European agriculture and European industry, in all its branches. Europe, therefore, has no longer occasion to any thing like the same extent as that which she had during her wars, for American commerce, American navigation, the produce of American industry. Europe in commotion, and convulsed throughout all her members, is to America no longer the same Europe as she is now, tranquil, and watching with the most vigilant attention all her own peculiar interests, without regard to the operation of her policy upon us. The effect of this altered state of Europe upon us, has been to circumscribe the employment of our marine, and greatly to reduce the value of the produce of our territorial labor. The further effect of this twofold reduction has been to decrease the value of all property, whether on the land or on the ocean, and which I suppose to be about fifty per cent. And the still further effect has been to diminish the amount of our circulating medium, in a proportion not less by its transmission abroad, or its withdrawal by the banking institutions, from a necessity which they could not control. The quantity of money, in whatever form it may be, which a nation wants, is in proportion to the total mass of its wealth, and to the activity of that wealth. A nation that has but little wealth, has but a limited want of money. In stating the fact, therefore, that the total wealth of the country has diminished, within a few years, in a ratio of about fifty per cent. we shall at once fully comprehend the inevitable reduction which must have ensued, in the total quantity of the circulating medium of the country. A nation is most prosperous when there is a gradual and untempting addition to the aggregate of its circulating medium. It is in a condition the most adverse, when there is a rapid diminution in the quantity of the circulating medium, and a consequent depression in the value of property. In the former case, the wealth of individuals insensibly increases, and income keeps ahead of expenditure. But, in the latter instance, debts have been contracted, engagements made, and habits of expense established, in reference to the existing state of wealth and of its representative. When these come to be greatly reduced, individuals find their debts still existing, their engagements unexecuted, and their habits inveterate. They see themselves in the possession of the same property, on which, in good faith, they had bound themselves. But that property, without their fault, possesses no longer the same value; and hence, discontent, impoverishment, and ruin arise. Let us suppose, Mr. Chairman, that Europe was again the theatre of such a general war as recently raged throughout all her dominions—such a state of the war as existed in her greatest exertions and in our greatest prosperity; instantly there would arise a greedy demand for the surplus produce of our industry, for our commerce, for our navigation. The languor which now prevails in our cities, and in our sea-ports, would give way to an animated activity. Our roads and rivers would be crowded with the produce of the interior. Every where we should witness excited industry. The precious metals would re-flow from abroad upon us. Banks, which have maintained their credit, would revive their business, and new banks would be established, to take the place of those which have sunk beneath the general pressure: for, it is a mistake to suppose that they have produced our present adversity; they have somewhat aggravated it, but they were the effect and the evidence of our prosperity. Prices would again get up; the former value of property would be restored; and those embarrassed persons who have not been already overwhelmed by the times, would suddenly find, in the augmented value of their property, and the renewal of their business, ample means to extricate themselves from all their difficulties. The greatest want of civilized society is a market for the sale and exchange of the surplus of the produce of the labor of its members. This market may exist at home or abroad, or both, but it must exist somewhere, if society prospers; and wherever it does exist, it should be competent to the absorption of the entire surplus of production. It is most desirable that there should be both a home and a foreign market. But, with respect to their relative superiority, I cannot entertain a doubt. The home market is first in order, and paramount in importance. The object of the bill under consideration, is to create this home market, and to lay the foundations of a genuine American policy. It is opposed; and it is incumbent upon the partisans of the foreign policy (terms which I shall use without any invidious intent) to demonstrate that the foreign market is an adequate vent for the surplus produce of our labor. But is it so? 1. Foreign nations cannot, if they would, take our surplus produce. If the source of supply, no matter of what, increases in a greater ratio than the demand for that supply, a glut of the market is inevitable, even if we suppose both to remain perfectly unobstructed. The duplication of our population takes place in terms of about twenty-five years. The term will be more and more extended as our numbers multiply. But it will be a sufficient approximation to assume this ratio for the present. We increase, therefore, in population, at the rate of about four per cent. per annum. Supposing the increase of our production to be in the same ratio, we should, every succeeding year, have, of surplus produce, four per cent. more than that of the preceding year, without taking into the account the differences of seasons which neutralize each other. If, therefore, we are to rely upon the foreign market exclusively, foreign consumption ought to be shown to be increasing in the same ratio of four per cent. per annum, if it be an adequate vent for our surplus produce. But, as I have supposed the measure of our increasing production to be furnished by that of our increasing population: so the measure of their power of consumption must be determined by that of the increase of their population. Now, the total foreign population, who consume our surplus produce, upon an average, do not double their aggregate number in a shorter term than that of about 100 years. Our powers of production increase then in a ratio four times greater than their powers of consumption. And hence their utter inability to receive from us our surplus produce.

But, 2dly, If they could, they will not. The policy of all Europe is adverse to the reception of our agricultural produce, so far as it comes into collision with its own; and, under that limitation, we are absolutely forbid to enter their ports, except under circumstances which deprive them of all value as a steady market. The policy of all Europe rejects those great staples of our country, which consist of objects of human subsistence. The policy of all Europe refuses to receive from us any thing but those raw materials of smaller value, essential to their manufactures, to which they can give a higher value, with the exception of tobacco and rice, which they cannot produce. Even Great Britain, to which we are its best customer, and from which we receive nearly one half in value of our whole imports, will not take from us articles of subsistence produced in our country cheaper than can be produced in Great Britain. In adopting this exclusive policy, the states of Europe do not inquire what is best for us, but what suits themselves, respectively; they do not take jurisdiction of the question of our interests, but limit the object of their legislation to that of the conservation of their own peculiar interests, leaving us free to prosecute ours as we please. They do not guide themselves by that romantic philanthropy, which we see displayed here, and which invokes us to continue to purchase the produce of foreign industry, without regard to the state or prosperity of our own, that foreigners may be pleased to purchase the few remaining articles of ours which their restrictive policy has not yet absolutely excluded from their consumption. What sort of a figure would a member of the British Parliament have made; what sort of a reception would his opposition have obtained, if he had remonstrated against the passage of the Corn Law,[1] by which British consumption is limited to the bread-stuffs of British production, to the entire exclusion of American, and stated that America could not, and would not buy British manufactures, if Britain did not buy American flour?

Both the inability and the policy of foreign powers, then, forbid us to rely upon the foreign market as being an adequate vent for the surplus produce of American labor. Now, let us see if this general reasoning is not fortified and confirmed by the actual experience of this country. If the foreign market may be safely relied upon, as furnishing an adequate demand for our surplus produce, then the official documents will show a progressive increase, from year to year, in the exports of our native produce, in a proportion equal to that which I have suggested. If, on the contrary, we shall find from them, that, for a long term of past years, some of our most valuable staples have retrograded, some remained stationary, and others advanced but little, if any, in amount, with the exception of cotton, the deductions of reason and the lessons of experience will alike command us to withdraw our confidence in the competency of the foreign market. The total amount of all our exports of domestic produce for the year, beginning in 1795, and ending on the 30th September, 1796, was $40,764,097. Estimating the increase according to the ratio of the increase of our population, that is, at four per cent. per annum, the amount of the exports of the same produce in the year ending on the 30th Sept. last, ought to have been $85,420,861. It was in fact only $47,155,408. Taking the average of five years, from 1803 to 1807, inclusive, the amount of native produce exported was $43,202,751 for each of those years. Estimating what it ought to have been, during the last year, applying the principle suggested to that amount, there should have been exported $77,766,751 instead of $47,155,408. If these comparative amounts of the aggregate actual exports, and what they ought to have been, be discouraging, we shall find, on descending into particulars, still less cause of satisfaction. The export of tobacco in 1791 was 112,428 hogsheads. That was the year of the largest exportation of that article; but it is the only instance of which I have selected the maximum of exportation. The amount of what we ought to have exported last year, estimated according to the scale of increase which I have used, is 266,332 hogsheads. The actual export was 99,009 hogsheads. We exported in 1803 the quantity of 1,311,853 barrels of flour; and ought to have exported last year 2,361,333 barrels. We, in fact, exported only 756,702 barrels. Of that quantity we sent to S. America 150,000 barrels, according to a statement furnished me by the diligence of a friend near me (Mr. Poinsett) to whose valuable mass of accurate information, in regard to that interesting quarter of the world, I have had occasion frequently to apply.[2] But that demand is temporary, growing out of the existing state of war. Whenever peace is restored to it, and I now hope that the day is not distant when its independence will be generally acknowledged, there cannot be a doubt that it will supply its own consumption. In all parts of it, the soil, either from climate or from elevation, is well adapted to the culture of wheat; and no where can better wheat be produced than in some portions of Mexico and Chili. Still the market of South America is one which, on other accounts, deserves the greatest consideration. And I congratulate you, the committee, and the country, on the recent adoption of a more auspicious policy towards it.[3]

We exported, in 1803, Indian corn to the amount of 2,074,608 bushels. The quantity should have been, in 1823, 3,734,288 bushels. The actual quantity exported was 749,034 bushels, or about one fifth of what it should have been, and a little more than one third of what it was more than twenty years ago. We ought not then to be surprised at the extreme depression of the price of that article, of which I have heard my honorable friend (Mr. Bassett)[4] complain, nor of the distress of the corn growing districts adjacent to the Chesapeake Bay. We exported 77,934 barrels of beef in 1803, and last year but 61,418, instead of 140,274 barrels. In the same year, (1803,) we exported 96,602 barrels of pork, and last year

55,529, instead of 173,882 barrels. Rice has not advanced, by any means, in the proportion which it ought to have done. All the small articles, such as cheese, butter, candles, &c. too minute to detail, but important in their aggregate, have also materially diminished. Cotton alone has advanced. But whilst the quantity of it is augmented, its actual value is considerably diminished. The total quantity last year exceeded that of the preceding year by near thirty millions of pounds. And yet the total value of the year of smaller exportation, exceeded that of the last year by upwards of three and a half millions of dollars. If this article, the capacity of our country to produce which was scarcely known in 1790, were subtracted from the mass of our exports, the value of the residue would only be a little upwards of $27,000,000, during the last year. The distribution of the articles of our exports throughout the United States, cannot fail to fix the attention of the Committee. Of the $47,155,408, to which they amounted last year, three articles alone, (cotton, rice, and tobacco,) composed together $28,549,177. Now these articles are chiefly produced to the South. And if we estimate that portion of our population who are actually engaged in their culture, it would probably not exceed two millions. Thus, then, less than one-fifth of the whole population of the United States produced upwards of one half, nearly two thirds of the entire value of the exports of the last year.

Is this foreign market, so incompetent at present, and which, limited as its demands are, operates so unequally upon the productive labor of our country, likely to improve in future? If I am correct in the views which I have presented to the committee, it must become worse and worse. What can improve it? Europe will not abandon her own agriculture to foster ours. We may even anticipate that she will more and more enter into competition with us in the supply of the West India market. That of South America, for articles of subsistence, will probably soon vanish. The *value* of our exports, for the future, may remain at about what it was last year. But, if we do not create some new market; if we persevere in the existing pursuits of agriculture, the inevitable consequence must be, to augment greatly the quantity of our produce, and to lessen its value in the foreign market. Can there be a doubt on this point? Take the article of cotton, for example, which is almost the only article that now remunerates labor and capital. A certain description of labor is powerfully attracted towards the cotton growing country. The cultivation will be greatly extended, the aggregate amount, annually produced, will be vastly augmented. The price will fall. The more unfavorable soils will then be gradually abandoned. And I have no doubt that, in a few years, it will cease to be profitably produced, any where North of the 34th degree of latitude. But, in the mean time, large numbers of the cotton growers will suffer the greatest distress. And whilst this distress is brought upon our own country, foreign industry will be stimulated by the very cause which occasions our distress. For, by surcharging the markets abroad, the price of the raw material being reduced, the manufacturer will be able to supply cotton fabrics cheaper, and the consumption in his own country, and in foreign nations, other than ours, (where the *value* of the import must be limited to the value of the export, which I have supposed to remain the same,) being proportionally extended, there will be consequently an increased demand for the produce of *his* industry.

Our agricultural is our greatest interest. It ought ever to be predominant. All others should bend to it. And, in considering what is for its advantage, we should contemplate it in all its varieties, of planting, farming, and grazing. Can we do nothing to invigorate it? nothing to correct the errors of the past, and to brighten the still more unpromising prospects which lie before us? We have seen, I think, the causes of the distresses of the country. We have seen, that an exclusive dependence upon the foreign market must lead to still severer distress, to impoverishment, to ruin. We must then change somewhat our course. We must give a new direction to some portion of our industry. We must speedily adopt a genuine American policy. Still cherishing a foreign market, let us create also a home market, to give further scope to the consumption of the produce of American industry. Let us counteract the policy of foreigners, and withdraw the support which we now give to their industry, and stimulate that of our own country. It should be a prominent object with wise legislators, to multiply the vocations and extend the business of society, as far as it can be done, by the protection of our interests at home, against the injurious effects of foreign legislation. Suppose we were a nation of fishermen, or of skippers, to the exclusion of every other occupation, and the Legislature had the power to introduce the pursuits of agriculture and manufactures, would not our happiness be promoted by an exertion of its authority? All the existing employments of society, the learned professions, commerce, agriculture, are now overflowing. We stand in each other's way. Hence, the want of employment. Hence, the eager pursuit after public stations, which I have before glanced at. I have been again and again shocked, during this session, by instances of solicitation for places, before the vacancies existed. The pulse of incumbents, who happen to be taken ill, is not marked with more anxiety by the attending physicians, than by those who desire to succeed them, though with very opposite feelings. Our old friend, the faithful sentinel, who has stood so long at our door,[5] and the gallantry of whose patriotism deserves to be noticed, because it was displayed when that virtue was most rare and most wanted, on a memorable occasion, in this unfortunate city, became indisposed some weeks ago. The first intelligence which I had of his dangerous illness, was by an application for his unvacated place. I hastened to assure myself of the extent of his danger, and was happy to find that the eagerness of succession, outstripped the progress of disease. By creating a new and extensive business, then, we should not only give employment to those who want it, and augment the sum of national wealth by all that this new business would create, but we should meliorate the condition of those who are now engaged in existing employments. In Europe, particularly in Great Britain, their large standing armies, large navies, large even on their peace arrangement, their established church, afford to their population employments which, in that respect, the happier constitution of our government, does not tolerate, but in a very limited degree. The peace establishments of our army and our navy are extremely small, and I hope ever will be. We have no established church, and I trust never shall have. In proportion as the enterprise of our citizens, in public employments, is circumscribed, should we excite and invigorate it in private pursuits.

The creation of a home market is not only necessary to procure for our agriculture a just reward of its labors, but it is indispensable to obtain a supply of our necessary wants. If we cannot sell, we cannot buy. That portion of our population (and we have seen that it is not less than four-fifths,) which makes comparatively nothing that foreigners will buy, has nothing to make purchases with from foreigners. It is in vain that we are told of the amount of our exports, supplied by the planting interest. They may enable the planting interest to supply all its wants: but they bring no ability to the interests not planting, unless, which cannot be pretended, the planting interest was an adequate vent for the surplus produce of the labor of all other interests. It is in vain to tantalize us with the greater cheapness of foreign fabrics. There must be an ability to purchase, if an article be obtained, whatever may be the price, high or low, at which it was sold. And a cheap article is as much beyond the grasp of him who has no means to buy, as a high one. Even if it were true that the American manufacturer would supply consumption at dearer rates, it is better to have his fabrics than the unattainable foreign fabrics; for it is better to be ill supplied than not supplied at all. A coarse coat, which will communicate warmth and cover nakedness, is better than no coat.—The superiority of the home market results, 1st. from its steadiness and comparative certainty at all times; 2d, from the creation of reciprocal interests; 3d, from its greater security; and, lastly from an ultimate and not distant augmentation of consumption, and, consequently, of comfort, from increased quantity and reduced prices. But this home market, highly desirable as it is, can only be created and cherished by the PROTECTION of our own legislation against the inevitable prostration of our industry, which must ensue from the action of FOREIGN policy and legislation. The effect and the value of this domestic care of our own interests will be obvious, from a few facts and considerations. Let us suppose that half a million of persons are now employed abroad, in fabricating for our consumption those articles of which, by the operation of this bill, a supply is intended to be provided within ourselves. That half a million of persons are, in effect, subsisted by us; but their actual means of subsistence are drawn from foreign agriculture. If we could transport them to this country, and incorporate them in the mass of our own population, there would instantly arise a demand for an amount of provisions equal to that which would be requisite for their subsistence throughout the whole year. That demand, in the article of flour alone, would not be less than the quantity of about 900,000 barrels, besides a proportionate quantity of beef and pork, and other articles of subsistence. But nine hundred thousand barrels of flour exceeded the entire quantity exported last year, by nearly one hundred and fifty thousand barrels. What activity would not this give? What cheerfulness would it not communicate to our now dispirited farming interest! But if, instead of these five hundred thousand artisans emigrating from abroad, we give, by this bill, employment to an equal number of our own citizens now engaged in unprofitable agriculture, or idle, from the want of business, the beneficial effect upon the productions of our farming labor would be nearly doubled. The quantity would be diminished by a subtraction of the produce from the labor of all those who should be diverted from its pursuits to manufacturing industry, and the value of the residue would be enhanced, both by that diminution and the creation of the home market to the extent supposed. And the honorable gentleman from Virginia may repress any apprehensions which he entertains, that the plough will be abandoned, and our fields remain unsown. For, under all the modifications of social industry, if you will secure to it a just reward, the greater attractions of agriculture will give to it that proud superiority which it has always maintained. If we suppose no actual abandonment of farming, but, what is most likely, a gradual and imperceptible employment of population in the business of manufacturing, instead of being compelled to resort to agriculture, the salutary effect would be nearly the same. Is any part of our common country likely to be injured by a transfer of the theatre of fabrication for our own consumption from Europe to America? All that those parts, if any there be, which will not, or cannot, engage in manufactures, should require, is, that their consumption should be well supplied; and if the objects of that consumption are produced in other parts of the Union that can manufacture, far from having, on that account, any just cause of complaint, their patriotism will and ought to inculcate a cheerful acquiescence in what essentially contributes, *and* is indispensably *necessary,* to the prosperity of the common family.

The great desideratum in political economy is the same as in private pursuits; that is, What is the best application of the aggregate industry of a nation, that can be made honestly to produce the largest sum of national wealth? Labor is the source of all wealth; but it is not natural labor only. And the fundamental error of the gentleman from Virginia, and of the school to which he belongs, in adducing,[6] from our sparse population, our unfitness for the introduction of the arts, consists in their not sufficiently weighing the importance of the power of machinery. In former times, when but little comparative use was made of machinery, manual labor and the price of wages were circumstances of the greatest consideration. But it is far otherwise in these later times. Such are the improvements and the perfections in machinery, that, in analyzing the compound value of many fabrics, the element of natural labor is so inconsiderable as almost to escape detection. This truth is demonstrated by many facts. Formerly, Asia, in consequence of the density of her population, and the consequent lowness of wages, laid Europe under tribute for many of her fabrics. Now Europe reacts upon Asia, and Great Britain in particular, throws back upon her countless millions of people the rich treasures produced by artificial labor, to a vast amount, infinitely cheaper than they can be manufactured by the natural exertions of that portion of the globe. But Britain is herself the most striking illustration of the immense power of machinery. Upon what other principle can you account for the enormous wealth which she has accumulated, and which she annually produces? A statistical writer of that country, several years ago, estimated the total amount of the artificial or machine labor of the nation, to be equal to that of one hundred millions of able-bodied laborers.[7] Subsequent estimates of her artificial labor, at the present day, carry it to the enormous height of two hundred millions. But the population of the three kingdoms is 21,500,000. Supposing that, to furnish able-bodied labor to the amount of 4,000,000, the natural labor will be but two per cent. of the artificial labor: In the production of wealth she operates, therefore, by a power (including the whole population,) of 221,500,000; or, in other words, by a power eleven times greater than the total of her natural power. If we suppose the machine labor of the United States to be equal to that of 10,000,000 of able-bodied men, the United States will operate, in the creation of wealth, by a power (including all their population,) of 20,000,000. In the creation of wealth, therefore, the power of Great Britain, compared to that of the United States, is as eleven to one. That these views are not imaginary, will be, I think, evinced, by contrasting the wealth, the revenue, the power, of the two countries. Upon what other hypothesis can we explain those almost incredible exertions which Britain made during the late wars of Europe? Look at her immense subsidies! Behold her, standing unaided and alone, breasting the storm of Napoleon's colossal power, when all continental Europe owned and yielded to its irresistible sway; and, finally, contemplate her vigorous prosecution of the war, with and without allies, to its splendid termination, on the ever-memorable field of Waterloo!

The British works which the gentleman from Virginia has quoted, pourtray a state of the most wonderful prosperity, in regard to wealth and resources, that ever was before contemplated. Let us look a little into the semi-official pamphlet, written with great force, clearness, and ability, and the valuable work of Lowe, to both of which that gentleman has referred.[8] The revenue of the United Kingdom amounted, during the latter years of the war, to seventy millions of pounds sterling; and one year it rose to the astonishing height of ninety millions sterling, equal to four hundred millions of dollars. This was actual revenue, made up of real contributions from the purses of the people. After the close of the war, ministers slowly and reluctantly reduced the military and naval establishments, and accommodated them to a state of peace. The pride of power, every where the same, always unwillingly surrenders any of those circumstances which display its pomp and exhibit its greatness. Cotemporaneous with this reduction, Britain was enabled to lighten some of the heaviest burthens of taxation, and particularly that most onerous of all, the *income tax*. In this lowered state, the revenue of peace, gradually rising from the momentary depression incident to a transition from war, attained, in 1822, the vast amount of fifty-five millions sterling, upwards of two hundred and forty millions of dollars, and more than eleven times that of the United States for the same year; thus indicating the difference, which I have suggested, in the respective productive powers of the two countries. The excise alone (collected under twenty-five different heads) amounted to twenty-eight millions, more than one-half of the total revenue of the kingdom. This great revenue allows Great Britain to constitute an efficient sinking fund of five millions sterling, being an excess of actual income beyond expenditure, and amounting to more than the entire revenue of the United States.

If we look at the commerce of England, we shall perceive that its prosperous condition no less denotes the immensity of her riches. The average of three years' exports, ending in 1789, was between thirteen and fourteen millions. The average for the same term, ending in 1822, was forty millions sterling. The average of the imports for three years, ending in 1789, was seventeen millions. The average for the same term, ending in 1822, was thirty-six millions, showing a favorable balance of four millions. Thus, in a period not longer than that which has elapsed since the establishment of our constitution, have the exports of that kingdom been tripled; and this has mainly been the effect of the power of machinery. The total amount of the commerce of Great Britain is greater since the peace, by one-fourth, than it was during the war. The average of her tonnage, during the most flourishing period of the war, was two million four hundred thousand tons. Its average, during the three years, 1819, 1820, and 1821, was 2,600,000; exhibiting an increase of 200,000 tons. If we glance at some of the more prominent articles of her manufactures, we shall be assisted in comprehending the true nature of the sources of her riches. The amount of cotton fabrics exported, in the most prosperous year of the war, was eighteen million sterling. In the year 1820, it was 16,600,000; in 1821, 20,150,000; in 1822, 21,639,000 pounds sterling; presenting the astonishing increase in two years of upwards of five millions. The total amount of imports in Great Britain from all foreign parts, of the article of cotton wool is five millions sterling. After supplying most abundantly the consumption of cotton fabrics within the country (and a people better fed, and clad, and housed, are not to be found under the sun than the British nation) by means of her industry, she gives to this cotton wool a new value, which enables her to sell to foreign nations to the amount of 21,639,000*l.*, making a clear profit of upwards of 16,500,000 pounds sterling! In 1821, the value of the export of woollen manufactures was 4,300,000*l.* In 1822, it was 5,500,000. The success of her restrictive policy is strikingly illustrated in the article of silk. In the manufacture of that article she labors under great disadvantages, besides that of not producing the raw material. She has subdued them all, and the increase of the manufacture has been most rapid. Although she is still unable to maintain, in foreign countries, a successful competition with the silks of France, of India, and of Italy, and, therefore, exports but little, she gives to the two millions of the raw material which she imports, in various forms, a value of ten millions, which chiefly enter into British consumption. Let us suppose that she was dependent upon foreign nations for these ten millions, what an injurious effect would it not have upon her commercial relations with them! The average of the exports of British manufactures during the peace exceeds the average of the most productive years of the war. The amount of her wealth annually produced is three hundred and fifty million sterling, bearing a large proportion to all of her pre-existing wealth. The agricultural portion of it is said by the gentleman from Virginia to be greater than that created by any other branch of her industry. But that flows mainly from a policy similar to that proposed by this bill. One-third only of her population is engaged in agriculture; the other two-thirds furnishing a market for the produce of that third. Withdraw this market, and what becomes of her agriculture? The power and the wealth of Great Britain cannot be more strikingly illustrated than by a comparison of her population and revenue with those of other countries and with our own. {Here Mr. Clay exhibited the following table, made out from authentic materials:}

	Population.	Taxes and public burthens.	Taxes per capita.
Russia in Europe	37,000,000	*l*18,000,000	*l*0 9 9
France, including Corsica,	30,700,000	37,000,000	1 4 0
Great Britain, exclusive of Ireland, (the taxes computed according to value of money on the European continent,)	14,500,000	40,000,000	2 15 0
Great Britain and Ireland, collectively,	21,500,000	44,000,000	2 0 0
England alone,	11,600,000	36,000,000	3 2 0
Spain	11,000,000	6,000,000	0 11 0
Ireland	7,000,000	4,000,000	0 11 0
The United States of America,	10,000,000	4,500,000	0 9 0

From this exhibit, we must remark, that the wealth of Great Britain (and, consequently, her power) is greater than that of any of the other nations with which it is compared. The amount of the contributions which she draws from the pockets of her subjects is not referred to for imitation, but as indicative of their wealth. The burthen of taxation is always relative to the ability of the subjects of it. A poor nation can pay but little. And the heavier taxes of British subjects, for example, in consequence of their greater wealth, may be easier borne than the much lighter taxes of Spanish subjects, in consequence of their extreme poverty. The object of wise governments should be, by sound legislation so to protect the industry of their own citizens against the policy of foreign powers as to give to it the most expansive force in the production of wealth. Great Britain has ever acted, and still acts, on this policy. She has pushed her protection of British interest further than any other nation has fostered its industry. The result is, greater wealth among her subjects, and, consequently, greater ability to pay their public burthens. If their taxation is estimated by their *natural* labor alone, nominally it is greater than the taxation of the subjects of any other power. But if, on a scale of their natural and artificial labor compounded, it is less than the taxation of any other people. Estimating it on that scale, and assuming the aggregate of the natural and artificial labor of the United Kingdom to be what I have already stated, 221,500,000, the actual taxes paid by a British subject are only about three and seven-pence sterling. Estimating our own taxes on a similar scale,—that is, supposing both descriptions of labor to be equal to that of 20,000,000 of able bodied persons,—the amount of tax paid by each soul in the United States is 4*s.* 6*d.* sterling.

The committee will observe, from that table, that the measure of the wealth of a nation is indicated by the measure of its protection of its industry; and that the measure of the poverty of a nation is marked by that of the degree in which it neglects and abandons the care of its own industry, leaving it exposed to the action of foreign powers. Great Britain protects most her industry, and the wealth of Great Britain is consequently the greatest. France is next in the degree of protection, and France is next in the order of wealth. Spain most neglects the duty of protecting the industry of her subjects, and Spain is one of the poorest of European nations. Unfortunate Ireland! disinherited, or rendered, in her industry, subservient to England, is exactly in the same state of poverty with Spain, measured by the rule of taxation. And the United States are still poorer than either.

The views of British prosperity which I have endeavored to present, show that her protecting policy is adapted alike to a state of war and of peace. Self-poised, resting upon her own internal resources, possessing a home market carefully cherished and guarded, she is ever prepared for any emergency. We have seen her coming out of a war of incalculable exertion, and of great duration, with her power unbroken, her means undiminished. We have seen that almost every revolving year of peace has brought along with it an increase of her manufactures, of her commerce, and, consequently, of her navigation. We have seen that, constructing her prosperity upon the solid foundation of her own protecting policy, it is unaffected by the vicissitudes of other states. What is our own condition? Depending upon the state of foreign powers—confiding exclusively in a foreign, to the culpable neglect of a domestic policy, our interests are affected by all their movements. Their wars, their misfortunes, are the only source of our prosperity. In their peace, and our peace, we behold our condition the reverse of that of Great Britain, and all our interests stationary or declining. Peace brings to us none of the blessings of peace. Our system is anomalous; alike unfitted to general tranquillity, and to a state of war or peace on the part of our own country. It can succeed only in the rare occurrence of a general state of war throughout Europe. I am no eulogist of England. I am far from recommending her systems of taxation. I have adverted to them only as manifesting her extraordinary ability. The political and foreign interests of that nation may have been, as I believe them to have been, often badly managed. Had she abstained from the wars into which she has been plunged by her ambition, or the mistaken policy of her ministers, the prosperity of England would, unquestionably, have been much greater. But it may happen that the public liberty, and the foreign relations of a nation, have been badly provided for, and yet that its political economy has been wisely managed. The alacrity or sullenness with which a people pay taxes depends upon their wealth or poverty. If the system of their rulers leads to their impoverishment, they can contribute but little to the necessities of the state; if to their wealth, they cheerfully and promptly pay the burthens imposed on them. Enormous as British taxation appears to be in comparison with that of other nations, but really lighter as it, in fact, is, when we consider its great wealth, and its powers of production, that vast amount is collected with the most astonishing regularity. {Here Mr. Clay read certain passages from Holt,[9] showing that, in 1822, there was not a solitary prosecution arising out of the collection of the assessed taxes, which are there considered among the most burthensome, and that the prosecutions for violations of the excise laws, in all its numerous branches, were sensibly and progressively decreasing.}

Having called the attention of the committee to the present adverse state of our country, and endeavored to point out the causes which have led to it; having shewn that similar causes, wherever they exist in other countries, lead to the same adversity in their condition; and having shewn that, wherever we find opposite causes prevailing, a high and animating state of national prosperity exists, the committee will agree with me in thinking that it is the solemn duty of government to apply a remedy to the evils which afflict our country, if it can apply one. Is there no remedy within the reach of the government? Are we doomed to behold our industry languish and decay yet more and more? But there is a remedy, and that remedy consists in modifying our foreign policy, and in adopting a genuine AMERICAN SYSTEM. We must naturalize the arts in our country, and we must naturalize them by the only means which the wisdom of nations has yet discovered to be effectual—by adequate protection against the otherwise overwhelming influence of foreigners. This is only to be accomplished by the establishment of a tariff, to the consideration of which I am now brought.

And what is this tariff? It seems to have been regarded as a sort of monster, huge and deformed; a wild beast, endowed with tremendous powers of destruction, about to be let loose among our people, if not to devour them, at least to consume their substance. But let us calm our passions, and deliberately survey this alarming, this terrific being. The sole object of the tariff is to tax the produce of foreign industry, with the view of promoting American industry. The tax is exclusively levelled at foreign industry. That is the avowed and the direct purpose of the tariff. If it subjects any part of American industry to burthens, that is an effect not intended, but is altogether incidental, and perfectly voluntary.

It has been treated as an imposition of burthens upon one part of the community by design for the benefit of another; as if, in fact, money were taken from the pockets of one portion of the people and put into the pockets of another. But, is that a fair representation of it? No man pays the duty assessed on the foreign article by compulsion, but voluntarily; and this voluntary duty, if paid, goes into the common exchequer, for the common benefit of all. Consumption has four objects of choice. 1. It may abstain from the use of the foreign article, and thus avoid the payment of the tax. 2. It may employ the rival American fabric. 3. It may engage in the business of manufacturing, which this bill is designed to foster. 4. Or it may supply itself from the household manufactures. But, it is said by the honorable gentleman from Virginia, that the South, owing to the character of a certain portion of its population, cannot engage in the business of manufacturing.[10] Now, I do not agree in that opinion to the extent in which it is asserted. The circumstance alluded to may disqualify the South from engaging in every branch of manufacture as largely as other quarters of the Union, but to some branches of it that part of our population is well adapted. It indisputably affords great facility in the household or domestic line.

But, if the gentleman's premises were true, could his conclusion be admitted? According to him, a certain part of our population, happily much the smallest, is peculiarly situated. The circumstance of its degradation unfits it for the manufacturing arts. The well being of the other, and the larger part of our population, requires the introduction of those arts. What is to be done in this conflict? The gentleman would have us abstain from adopting a policy called for by the interests of the greater and freer part of our population. But is that reasonable? Can it be expected that the interests of the greater part should be made to bend to the condition of the servile part of our population? That, in effect, would be to make us the slaves of slaves. I went, with great pleasure, along with my Southern friends, and I am ready again to unite with them in protesting against the exercise of any legislative power, on the part of Congress, over that delicate subject, because it was my solemn conviction, that Congress was interdicted, or at least not authorized, by the constitution, to exercise any such legislative power.[11] And I am sure, that the patriotism of the South may be exclusively relied upon to reject a policy which should be dictated by considerations altogether connected with that degraded class, to the prejudice of the residue of our population. But, does not a perseverance in the foreign policy, as it now exists, in fact, make all parts of the Union, not planting, tributary to the planting parts? What is the argument? It is, that we must continue freely to receive the produce of foreign industry, without regard to the protection of American industry, that a market may be retained for the sale abroad of the produce of the planting portion of the country; and that, if we lessen the consumption, in all parts of America, those which are not planting, as well as the planting sections of foreign manufactures, we diminish to that extent the foreign market for the planting produce. The existing state of things, indeed, presents a sort of tacit compact between the cotton grower and the British manufacturer, the stipulations of which are, on the part of the cotton grower, that the whole of the United States, the other portions as well as the cotton growing, shall remain open and unrestricted in the consumption of British manufactures; and, on the part of the British manufacturer, that, in consideration thereof, he will continue to purchase the cotton of the South.

Thus, then, we perceive, that the proposed measure, instead of sacrificing the South to the other parts of the Union, seeks only to preserve them from being absolutely sacrificed under the operation of the tacit compact which I have described. Supposing the South to be actually incompetent, or disinclined to embark at all in the business of manufacturing, is not its interest, nevertheless, likely to be promoted by creating a new and an American source of supply for its consumption? Now foreign powers, and Great Britain principally, have the monopoly of the supply of Southern consumption. If this bill should pass, an American competitor in the supply of the South would be raised up, and ultimately, I cannot doubt, that it would be supplied cheaper and better. I have before had occasion to state, and will now again mention, the beneficial effects of American competition with Europe, in furnishing a supply of the article of cotton bagging.[12] After the late war, the influx of the Scottish manufacture prostrated the American establishments. The consequence was, that the Scotch possessed the monopoly of the supply; and the price of it rose, and attained, the year before the last, a height which amounted to more than an equivalent for ten years protection to the American manufacture. This circumstance tempted American industry again to engage in the business, and several valuable manufactories have been established in Kentucky. They have reduced the price of the fabric very considerably; but, without the protection of government, they may be again prostrated—and then the Scottish manufacturer, engrossing the supply of our consumption, the price will probably again rise. It has been tauntingly asked, if Kentucky cannot maintain herself in a competition with the two Scottish towns of Inverness and Dundee?[13] But is that a fair statement of the case? Those two towns are cherished and sustained by the whole protecting policy of the British empire, whilst Kentucky cannot, and the general government will not, extend a like protection to the few Kentucky villages in which the article is made.

If the cotton growing consumption could be constitutionally exempted from the operation of this bill, it might be fair to exempt it upon the condition that foreign manufactures, the proceeds of the sale of cotton abroad, should not enter at all into the consumption of the other parts of the United States. But such an arrangement as that, if it could be made, would probably be objected to by the cotton growing country itself.

2. The second objection to the proposed bill is, that it will diminish the amount of our exports. It can have no effect upon our exports, except those which are sent to Europe. Except tobacco and rice, we send there nothing but the raw materials. The argument is, that Europe will not buy of us, if we do not buy of her.

The first objection to it is, that it calls upon us to look to the question, and take care of European ability in legislating for American interests. Now, if, in legislating for their interests, they would consider and provide for our ability, the principle of reciprocity would enjoin us so to regulate our intercourse with them, as to leave their ability unimpaired. But I have shewn that, in the adoption of their own policy, their inquiry is strictly limited to a consideration of their peculiar interests, without any regard to that of ours. The next remark I would make is, that the bill only operates upon *certain* articles of European industry, which, it is supposed, our interest requires us to manufacture within ourselves; and, although its effect will be to diminish the amount of our imports of *those* articles, it leaves them free to supply us with any other produce of their industry. And, since the circle of human comforts, refinements, and luxuries, is of great extent, Europe will still find herself able to purchase from us what she has hitherto done, and to discharge the debt in some of those objects. If there be any diminution in our exports to Europe, it will probably be in the article of cotton to Great Britain. I have stated that Britain buys cotton wool to the amount of about five millions sterling, and sells to foreign states to the amount of upwards of twenty-one millions and a half. Of this sum, we take a little upwards of a million and a half. The residue, of about twenty millions, she must sell to other foreign powers than the United States. Now their market will continue open to her, as much after the passage of this bill, as before. She will, therefore, require from us the raw material to supply their consumption. But, it is said, she may refuse to purchase it of us, and seek a supply elsewhere. There can be but little doubt that she now resorts to us, because we can supply her cheaper and better than any other country. And it would be unreasonable to suppose that she would cease, from any pique towards us, to pursue her own interest. Suppose she was to decline purchasing from us: The consequence would be, that she would lose the market for the twenty millions sterling which she now sells other foreign powers, or enter it under a disadvantageous competition with us, or with other nations, who should obtain their supplies of the raw material from us. If there should be any diminution, therefore, in the exportation of cotton, it would only be in the proportion of about one and a half to twenty, that is, a little upwards of five per cent.; the loss of a market for which, abroad, would be fully compensated by the market for the article created at home. Lastly, I would observe, that the new application of our industry, producing new objects of exportation, and they possessing much greater value than in the raw state, we should be in the end amply indemnified, by their exportation. Already the item in our foreign exports of manufactures is considerable; and we know that our cotton fabricks have been recently exported, in a large amount, to South America, where they maintain a successful competition with those of any other country.

3. The third objection to the tariff is, that it will diminish our navigation. This great interest deserves every encouragement, consistent with the paramount interest of agriculture. In the order of nature, it is secondary to both agriculture and manufactures. Its business is the transportation of the productions of those two superior branches of industry. It cannot, therefore, be expected, that they shall be moulded or sacrificed to suit its purposes; but, on the contrary, navigation must accommodate itself to the actual state of agriculture and manufactures. If, as I believe, we have nearly reached the maximum in value of our exports of raw produce to Europe, the effect, hereafter, will be, as it respects that branch of our trade, if we persevere in the foreign system, to retain our navigation at the point it has now reached. By reducing, indeed, as will probably take place, the price of our raw materials, a further quantity of them could be exported, and, of course, additional employment might, in that way, be given to our tonnage; but that would be at the expense of the agricultural interest. If I am right in supposing that no effect will be produced by this measure upon any other branch of our export trade, but that to Europe; that, with regard to that, there will be no sensible diminution of our exports; and that the new direction given to a portion of our industry will produce other objects of exportation, the probability is, that our foreign tonnage will be even increased under the operation of this bill. But, if I am mistaken in these views, and it should experience any reduction, the increase of our coasting tonnage, resulting from the greater activity of domestic exchanges, will more than compensate the injury. Although our navigation partakes in the general distress of the country, it is less depressed than any other of our great interests. The foreign tonnage has been gradually, though slowly, increasing, since 1818. And our coasting tonnage, since 1816, has increased upwards of one hundred thousand tons.

4. It is next contended that the effect of the measure will be to diminish our foreign commerce. The objection assumes, what I have endeavored to controvert, that there will be a reduction in the value of our exports. Commerce is an exchange of commodities. Whatever will tend to augment the wealth of a nation must increase its capacity to make these exchanges. By new productions, or creating new values in the fabricated forms which shall be given

to old objects of our industry, we shall give to commerce a fresh spring, a new aliment. The foreign commerce of the country, from causes, some of which I have endeavored to point out, has been extended as far as it can be. And I think there can be but little doubt that the balance of trade is, and, for some time past has been, against us. I was surprised to hear the learned gentleman from Massachusetts, (Mr. Webster,) rejecting, as a detected and exploded fallacy, the idea of a balance of trade.[14] I have not time nor inclination now to discuss that topic. But I will observe, that all nations act upon the supposition of the reality of its existence, and seek to avoid a trade, the balance of which is unfavorable, and to foster that which presents a favorable balance. However the account be made up, whatever may be the items of a trade, commodities, fishing industry, marine labor, the carrying trade, all of which, I admit, should be comprehended, there can be no doubt, I think, that the totality of the exchanges of all descriptions made by one nation with another, or against the totality of the exchanges of all other nations together, may be such as to present the state of an unfavorable balance with the one or with all. It is true that, in the long run, the measures of these exchanges, that is, the totality in value of what is given and of what is received, must be equal to each other. But great distress may be felt long before the counterpoise can be effected. In the mean time there will be an export of the precious metals, to the deep injury of internal trade, an unfavorable state of exchange, an export of public securities, a resort to credit, debt, mortgages. Most of, if not all, these circumstances, are believed now to be indicated by our country, in its foreign commercial relations. What have we received, for example, for the public stocks sent to England? Goods. But those stocks are our bond, which must be paid. Although the solidity of the credit of the English public securities is not surpassed by that of our own, strong as it justly is, when have we seen English stocks sold in our market, and regularly quoted in the prices current, as American stocks are in England? An unfavorable balance with one nation, *may* be made up by a favorable balance with other nations; but the fact of the existence of that unfavorable balance is strong presumptive evidence against the trade. Commerce will regulate itself! Yes, and the extravagance of a spendthrift heir, who squanders the rich patrimony which has descended to him, will regulate itself ultimately. But it will be a regulation which will exhibit him in the end safely confined within the walls of a jail. Commerce will regulate itself! But is it not the duty of wise governments to watch its course, and, beforehand, to provide against even distant evils; by prudent legislation stimulating the industry of their own people, and checking the policy of foreign powers as it operates on them? The supply, then, of the subjects of foreign commerce, no less than the supply of consumption at home, requires of us to give a portion of our labor such a direction as will enable us to produce them. That is the object of the measure under consideration, and I cannot doubt that, if adopted, it will accomplish its object.

5. The fifth objection to the tariff, is, that it will diminish the public revenue, disable us from paying the public debt, and finally compel a resort to a system of excise and internal taxation. This objection is founded upon the supposition that the reduction in the importation of the subjects, on which the increased duties are to operate, will be such as to produce the alleged effect. All this is matter of mere conjecture, and can only be determined by experiment. I have very little doubt, with my colleague, (Mr. Trimble,) that the revenue will be increased considerably, for some years at least, under the operation of this bill.[15] The diminution in the quantity imported will be compensated by the augmentation of the duty. In reference to the article of molasses, for example, if the import of it should be reduced fifty per cent. the amount of duty collected would be the same as it now is. But it will not, in all probability, be reduced by any thing like that proportion. And then there are some other articles which will continue to be introduced in as large quantities as ever, notwithstanding the increase of duty—the object in reference to them being revenue, and not the encouragement of domestic manufactures. Another cause will render the revenue of this year, in particular, much more productive than it otherwise would have been; and that is, that large quantities of goods have been introduced into the country, in anticipation of the adoption of this measure. The eagle does not dart a keener gaze upon his intended prey, than that with which the British manufacturer and merchant watches the foreign market, and the course even of our elections as well as our legislation. The passage of this bill has been expected; and all our information is, that the importations, during this spring, have been immense. But, further, the measure of our importations is that of our exportations. If I am right in supposing that, in future, the amount of these, in the old or new forms of the produce of our labor, will not be diminished, but probably increased, then the amount of our importations, and, consequently, of our revenue, will not be reduced, but may be extended. If these ideas be correct, there will be no inability on the part of the government to extinguish the public debt. The payment of that debt, and the consequent liberation of the public resources from the charge of it, is extremely desir-

able. No one is more anxious than I am to see that important object accomplished. But I entirely concur with the gentleman from Virginia, (Mr. Barbour,) in thinking that no material sacrifice of any of the great interests of the nation ought to be made to effectuate it.[16] Such is the elastic and accumulating nature of our public resources, from the silent augmentation of our population, that, if, in any given state of the public revenue, we throw ourselves upon a couch and go to sleep, we may, after a short time, awake with an ability abundantly increased to redeem any reasonable amount of public debt with which we may happen to be burthened. The public debt of the United States, though nominally larger now than it was in the year 1791, bears really no sort of discouraging comparison to its amount, at that time, whatever standard we may choose to adopt to institute the comparison. It was, in 1791, about seventy-five millions of dollars. It is now about ninety. Then we had a population of about four millions. Now we have upwards of ten millions. Then we had a revenue short of five millions of dollars. Now our revenue exceeds twenty. If we select population as the standard, our present population is one hundred and fifty per cent, greater than it was in 1791; if revenue, that is four times more now than at the former period; whilst the public debt has increased only in a ratio of twenty per cent. A public debt of three hundred millions of dollars, at the present day, considering our actual ability, compounded both of the increase of population and of revenue, would not be more onerous now than the debt of seventy-five millions of dollars was, at the epoch of 1791, in reference to the same circumstances. If I am right in supposing that, under the operation of the proposed measure, there will not be any diminution, but a probable increase of the public revenue, there will be no difficulty in defraying the current expenses of government, and paying the principal, as well as the interest of the public debt, as it becomes due. Let us, for a moment, however, indulge the improbable supposition of the opponents of the tariff, that there will be a reduction of the revenue to the extent of the most extravagant calculation which has been made, that is to say, to the extent of five millions. That sum deducted, we shall still have remaining a revenue of about fifteen millions. The Treasury estimates of the current service of the years 1822, 1823, and 1824, exceeds, each year, nine millions. The lapse of revolutionary pensions, and judicious retrenchments which might be made, without detriment to any of the essential establishments of the country, would probably reduce them below nine millions. Let us assume that sum, to which add above five millions and a half for the interest of the public debt, and the wants of government would require a revenue of fourteen and a half millions, leaving a surplus of revenue of half a million beyond the public expenditure. Thus, by a postponement of the payment of the principal of the public debt, in which the public creditors would gladly acquiesce, and confiding, for the means of redeeming it, in the necessary increase of our revenue from the natural augmentation of our population and consumption, we may safely adopt the proposed measure, even if it should be attended (which is confidently denied) with the supposed diminution of revenue. We shall not then have occasion to vary the existing system of taxation; we shall be under no necessity to resort either to direct taxes, or to an excise. But, suppose the alternative were really forced upon us of continuing the foreign system, with its inevitable impoverishment of the country, but with the advantage of the present mode of collecting the taxes, or of adopting the American system, with its increase of the national wealth, but with the disadvantage of an excise, could any one hesitate between them? Customs and an excise agree in the essential particulars, that they are both taxes upon consumption, and both are voluntary. They differ only in the mode of collection. The office for the collection of one, is located on the frontier, and that for the other within the interior. I believe it was Mr. Jefferson, who, in reply to the boast of a citizen of New York, of the amount of the public revenue paid by that city, asked who would pay it if the collector's office were removed to Paulus' Hook, on the New Jersey shore?[17] National wealth is the source of all taxation. And, my word for it, the people are too intelligent to be deceived by mere names, and not to give a decided preference to that system which is based upon their wealth and prosperity, rather than to that which is founded upon their impoverishment and ruin.

6. But, according to the opponents of the domestic policy, the proposed system will force capital and labor into new and reluctant employments; we are not prepared, in consequence of the high price of wages, for the successful establishment of manufactures, and we must fail in the experiment. We have seen that the existing occupations of our society, those of agriculture, commerce, navigation, and the learned professions, are overflowing with competitors, and that the want of employment is severely felt. Now what does this bill propose? To open a new and extensive field of business, in which all that choose may enter. There is no compulsion upon any one to engage in it. An option only is given to industry, to continue in the present unprofitable pursuits, or to embark in a new and promising one. The effect will be to lessen the competition in the old branches of business and to multiply our resources for increasing our comforts and augmenting the national

wealth. The alleged fact of the high price of wages is not admitted. The truth is, that no class of society suffers more, in the present stagnation of business, than the laboring class. That is a necessary effect of the depression of agriculture, the principal business of the community. The wages of able-bodied men vary from five to eight dollars per month; and such has been the want of employment, in some parts of the Union, that instances have not been unfrequent, of men working merely for the means of present subsistence. If the wages for labor here and in England are compared, they will be found not to be essentially different. I agree with the honorable gentleman from Virginia, that high wages are a proof of national prosperity;[18] we differ only in the means by which that desirable end shall be attained.—But, if the fact were true, that the wages of labor are high, I deny the correctness of the argument founded upon it. The argument assumes, that natural labor is the principal element in the business of manufacture. That was the ancient theory. But the valuable inventions and vast improvements in machinery, which have been made within a few years past, have produced a new era in the arts. The effect of this change in the powers of production may be estimated from what I have already stated, in relation to England, and to the triumphs of European artificial labor over the natural labor of Asia. In considering the fitness of a nation for the establishment of manufactures, we must no longer limit our views to the state of its population, and the price of wages. All circumstances must be regarded, of which that is, perhaps, the least important. Capital, ingenuity in the construction, and adroitness in the use of machinery, and the possession of the raw materials, are those which deserve the greatest consideration. All these circumstances, (except that of capital, of which there is no deficiency,) exist in our country in an eminent degree, and more than counterbalance the disadvantage, if it really existed, of the lower wages of labor in Great Britain. The dependence upon foreign nations for the raw material of any great manufacture, has been ever considered as a discouraging fact. The state of our population is peculiarly favorable to the most extensive introduction of machinery. We have no prejudices to combat, no persons to drive out of employment. The pamphlet to which we have had occasion so often to refer, in enumerating the causes which have brought in England their manufactures to such a state of perfection, and which now enable them, in the opinion of the writer, to defy all competition, does not specify, as one of them, low wages. It assigns three—1st, capital; 2dly, extent and costliness of machinery; and, 3dly, steady and persevering industry. Notwithstanding the concurrence of so many favorable causes, in our country, for the introduction of the arts, we are earnestly dissuaded from making the experiment, and our ultimate failure is confidently predicted. Why should we fail? Nations, like men, fail in nothing which they boldly attempt, when sustained by virtuous purpose and firm resolution. I am not willing to admit this depreciation of American skill and enterprise. I am not willing to strike before an effort is made. All our past history exhorts us to proceed, and inspires us with animating hopes of success. Past predictions of our incapacity have failed, and present predictions will not be realized. At the commencement of this government, we were told that the attempt would be idle to construct a marine adequate to the commerce of the country, or even to the business of its coasting trade. The founders of our government did not listen to these discouraging counsels; and behold the fruits of their just comprehension of our resources! Our restrictive policy was denounced, and it was foretold that it would utterly disappoint all our expectations. But our restrictive policy has been eminently successful; and the share which our navigation now enjoys in the trade with France, and with the British West India Islands, attests its victory. What were not the disheartening predictions of the opponents of the late war? Defeat, discomfiture, and disgrace, were to be the certain, but not the worst, effect of it. Here, again, did prophecy prove false; and the energies of our country, and the valor, and the patriotism of our people, carried us gloriously through the war. We are now, and ever will be, essentially, an agricultural people. Without a material change in the fixed habits of the country, the friends of this measure desire to draw to it, as a powerful auxiliary to its industry, the manufacturing arts. The difference between a nation with, and without the arts, may be conceived, by the difference between a keel-boat and a steam-boat, combatting the rapid torrent of the Mississippi. How slow does the former ascend, hugging the sinuosities of the shore, pushed on by her hardy and exposed crew, now throwing themselves in vigorous concert on their oars, and then seizing the pendant boughs of over-hanging trees: she seems hardly to move; and her scanty cargo is scarcely worth the transportation! With what ease is she not passed by the steam-boat, laden with the riches of all quarters of the world, with a crowd of gay, cheerful, and protected passengers, now dashing into the midst of the current, or gliding through the eddies near the shore! Nature herself seems to survey, with astonishment, the passing wonder, and, in silent submission, reluctantly to own the magnificent triumphs, in her own vast dominion, of Fulton's immortal genius!

7. But it is said, that, wherever there is a concurrence of favorable circumstances, manufactures will arise of themselves, without

protection; and that we should not disturb the natural progress of industry, but leave things to themselves. If all nations would modify their policy on this axiom, perhaps it would be better for the common good of the whole. Even then, in consequence of natural advantages, and a greater advance in civilization and in the arts, some nations would enjoy a state of much higher prosperity than others. But there is no universal legislation. The globe is divided into different communities, each seeking to appropriate to itself all the advantages it can, without reference to the prosperity of others. Whether this is right or not, it has always been, and ever will be, the case. Perhaps the care of the interests of one people, is sufficient for all the wisdom of one Legislature; and that it is among nations as among individuals, that the happiness of the whole is best secured by each attending to its own peculiar interests. The proposition to be maintained by our adversaries, is, that manufactures, without protection, will, in due time, spring up in our country, and sustain themselves, in a competition with foreign fabrics, however advanced the arts, and whatever the degree of protection may be in foreign countries. Now I contend that this proposition is refuted by all experience, ancient and modern, and in every country. If I am asked, why unprotected industry should not succeed in a struggle with protected industry, I answer, the FACT has ever been so, and that is sufficient; I reply, that UNIFORM EXPERIENCE evinces that it cannot succeed in such an unequal contest, and that is sufficient. If we speculate on the causes of this universal truth, we may differ about them. Still the indisputable fact remains. And we should be as unwise in not availing ourselves of the guide which it furnishes, as a man would be who should refuse to bask in the rays of the sun, because he could not agree with Judge Woodward as to the nature of the substance of that planet, to which we are indebted for heat and light.[19] If I were to attempt to particularize the causes which prevent the success of the manufacturing arts, without protection, I should say, that they are—1st, the obduracy of fixed habits. No nation, no individual, will easily change an established course of business, even if it be unprofitable; and least of all is an agricultural people prone to innovation. With what reluctance do they not adopt improvements in the instruments of husbandry, or in modes of cultivation! If the farmer makes a good crop, and sells it badly, or makes a short crop, buoyed up by hope, he perseveres, and trusts that a favorable change of the market, or of the seasons, will enable him, in the succeeding year, to repair the misfortunes of the past. 2dly, The uncertainty, fluctuation, and unsteadiness, of the home market, when liable to an unrestricted influx of fabrics from all foreign nations; and, 3dly, The superior advance of skill, and amount of capital, which foreign nations have obtained, by the protection of their own industry. From the latter, or from other causes, the unprotected manufactures of a country are exposed to the danger of being crushed in their infancy, either by the design or from the necessities of foreign manufacturers. Gentlemen are incredulous as to the attempts of foreign merchants and manufacturers to accomplish the destruction of ours. Why should they not make such attempts? If the Scottish manufacturer, by surcharging our market, in one year, with the article of cotton bagging, for example, should so reduce the price as to discourage and put down the home manufacture, he would secure to himself the monopoly of the supply. And now having the exclusive possession of the market, perhaps for a long term of years, he might be more than indemnified for his first loss, in the subsequent rise in the price of the article. What have we not seen under our own eyes? The competition for the transportation of the mail, between this place and Baltimore, so excited, that to obtain it, an individual offered, at great loss, to carry it a whole year for one dollar! His calculation, no doubt, was, that, by driving his competitor off the road, and securing to himself the carriage of the mail, he would be afterwards able to repair his original loss by new contracts with the department. But the necessities of foreign manufacturers, without imputing to them any sinister design, may oblige them to throw into our markets the fabrics which have accumulated on their hands, in consequence of obstruction in the ordinary vents, or from over-calculation; and the forced sales, at losing prices, may prostrate our establishments. From this view of the subject, it follows that, if we would place the industry of our country upon a solid and unshakable foundation, we must adopt the protecting policy, which has every where succeeded, and reject that which would abandon it, which has every where failed.

8. But if the policy of protection be wise, the gentleman from Virginia, (Mr. Barbour,) has made some ingenious calculations to prove that the measure of protection, already extended, has been sufficiently great. With some few exceptions, the existing duties, of which he has made an estimate, were laid with the object of revenue, and without reference to that of encouragement to our domestic industry; and, although it is admitted that the incidental effect of duties, so laid, is to promote our manufactures yet, if it falls short of competent protection, the duties might as well not have been imposed with reference to that purpose. A moderate addition may accomplish this desirable end; and the proposed tariff is believed to have this character.

9. The prohibitory policy, it is confidently asserted, is condemned

by the wisdom of Europe, and by her most enlightened statesmen. Is this the fact? We call upon gentlemen to show, in what instance a nation, that has enjoyed its benefits, has surrendered it. {Here Mr. Barbour rose, Mr. Clay giving way, and said, that England had departed from it in the China trade, in allowing us to trade with her East India possessions, and in tolerating our navigation to her West India colonies.} With respect to the trade to China, the whole amount of what England has done is to modify the monopoly of the East India Company in behalf of one and a small part of her subjects, to increase the commerce of another, and the greater portion of them. The abolition of the restriction, therefore, operates altogether among the subjects of England, and does not touch at all the interests of foreign powers. The toleration of our commerce to British India is for the sake of the specie, with which we mainly carry on that commerce, and which, having performed its circuit, returns to Great Britain in exchange for British manufactures.[20] The relaxation from the colonial policy, in the instance of our trade and navigation with the West Indies, is a most unfortunate example for the honorable gentleman; for, it is an illustrious proof of the success of our restrictive policy, when resolutely adhered to. Great Britain had prescribed the terms on which we were to be graciously allowed to carry on that trade. The effect of her regulations was, to exclude our navigation altogether, and a complete monopoly, on the part of the British navigation, was secured. We forbade it, unless our vessels should be allowed a perfect reciprocity. Great Britain stood out a long time; but finally yielded, and our navigation now fairly shares with hers in the trade.[21] Have gentlemen no other to exhibit than these trifling relaxations from the prohibitory policy, which do not amount to a drop in the bucket, to prove its abandonment by Great Britain? Let them show us that her laws are repealed which prohibit the introduction of our flour and provisions; of French silks, laces, porcelain, manufactures of bronze, mirrors, woollens; and of the manufactures of all other nations; and then we may be ready to allow, Great Britain has really abolished her prohibitory policy. We find there, on the contrary, that system of policy in full and rigorous operation, and a most curiously interwoven system it is, as she enforces it. She begins by protecting all parts of her immense dominions against foreign nations. She then protects the parent country against the colonies; and, finally, one part of the parent country against another. The sagacity of Scotch industry has carried the process of distillation to a perfection which would place the art in England on a footing of disadvantageous competition, and English distillation has been protected accordingly.—But suppose it were even true that Great Britain had abolished all restrictions upon trade, and allowed the freest introduction of the produce of foreign labor, would that prove it unwise for us to adopt the protecting system? The object of protection is the establishment and perfection of the arts. In England, it has accomplished its purpose, fulfilled its end. If she has not carried every branch of manufacture to the same high state of perfection that any other nation has, she has succeeded in so many that she may safely challenge the most unshackled competition in exchanges. It is upon this very ground that many of her writers recommend an abandonment of the prohibitory system. It is to give greater scope to British industry and enterprise. It is upon the same selfish principle. The object of the most perfect freedom of trade, with such a nation as Britain, and of the most rigorous system of prohibition, with a nation whose arts are in their infancy, may both be precisely the same. In both cases, it is to give greater expansion to native industry. They only differ in the theatres of their operation. The abolition of the restrictive system, by Britain, if by it she could prevail upon other nations to imitate her example, would have the effect of extending the consumption of British produce in other countries, where, her writers boldly affirm, it could maintain a fearless competition with the produce of native labor. The adoption of the restrictive system, on the part of the United States, by excluding the produce of foreign labor, would extend the consumption of American produce, unable, in the infancy and unprotected state of the arts, to sustain a competition with foreign fabrics. Let our arts breathe under the shade of protection; let them be perfected as they are in England, and we shall then be ready, as England now is said to be, to put aside protection, and to enter upon the freest exchanges. To what other cause, than to their whole prohibitory policy, can you ascribe British prosperity? It will not do to assign it to that of her antiquity; for France is no less ancient, though much less rich and powerful, in proportion to the population and natural advantages of France.—Hallam, a sensible and highly approved writer on the Middle Ages, assigns the revival of the prosperity of the North of Europe to the success of the woollen manufactories of Flanders, and the commerce of which their fabrics became the subject; and the commencement of that of England, to the establishment of similar manufactures there, under the Edwards, and to the prohibitions which began about the same time. As to the poor rates, the theme of so much reproach, without England, and of so much regret within it, among her speculative writers, the system was a strong proof, no less of her unbounded wealth, than of her pauperism. What other nation can dispense, in the form of regulated charity, the enormous sum, I believe, of ten or twelve millions sterling! {Mr. Barbour stated, it was reduced to six; to which Mr. Clay replied, that he entertained no doubt but that the benign operation of British protection of home industry had greatly reduced it, within the last few years, by the full employment of her subjects, of which her flourishing trade bore evidence.} The number of British paupers was the result of pressing the principle of population to its utmost limits, by her protecting policy, in the creation of wealth, and in placing the rest of the world under tribute to her industry.—Doubtless the condition of England would be better without paupers, if, in other respects, it remained the same. But, in her actual circumstances, the poor system has the salutary effect of an equalizing corrective of the tendency to the concentration of riches, produced by the genius of her political institutions, and by her prohibitory system.

But, is it true that England is convinced of the impolicy of the prohibitory system, and desirous to abandon it? What proof have we to that effect? We are asked to reject the evidence, deducible from the settled and steady practice of England, and to take lessons in a school of philosophical writers, whose visionary theories are no where adopted; or, if adopted, bring with them inevitable distress, impoverishment, and ruin. Let us hear the testimony of an illustrious personage, entitled to the greatest attention, because he speaks after a full experiment of the unrestrictive system, made in his own empire. I hope I shall give no offence in quoting from a publication issued from "the mint of Philadelphia;" from a work of Mr. Carey,[22] of whom I seize, with great pleasure, the occasion to say, that he merits the public gratitude, for the disinterested diligence with which he has collected a large mass of highly useful facts, and for the clear and convincing reasoning with which he generally illustrates them. The Emperor of Russia, in March, 1822, after about two years' trial of the free system, says, through Count Nesselrode:

"To produce happy effects, the principles of commercial freedom must be generally adopted. *The State which adopts, whilst others reject them, must condemn its own industry and commerce to pay a ruinous tribute to those of other nations.*"

"From a circulation exempt from restraint, and the facility afforded by reciprocal exchanges, almost all the governments at first resolved to seek the means of repairing the evil which Europe had been doomed to suffer; *but experience and more correct calculations, because they were made from certain data, and upon the results, already known, of the peace that had just taken place, forced them soon to adhere to the prohibitory system.*

"England preserved hers. Austria remained faithful to the rule she had laid down, to guard herself against the rivalship of foreign industry. France, with the same views, adopted the most rigorous measures of precaution. And Prussia published a new tariff in October last, which proves that she found it impossible not to follow the example of the rest of Europe."

"In proportion as the prohibitory system is extended and rendered perfect in other countries, *that state which pursues a contrary system, makes, from day to day, sacrifices more extensive and more considerable. * * * It offers a continual encouragement to the manufactures of other countries; and its own manufactures perish in the struggle which they are, as yet, unable to maintain.*

"It is with the most lively feelings of regret we acknowledge it is our own proper experience which enables us to trace this picture. *The evils which it details have been realized in Russia and Poland, since the conclusion of the act of the* 7-19 *December,* 1818. AGRICULTURE WITHOUT A MARKET, INDUSTRY WITHOUT PROTECTION, LANGUISH AND DECLINE. SPECIE IS EXPORTED, AND THE MOST SOLID COMMERCIAL HOUSES ARE SHAKEN. The public prosperity would soon feel the wound inflicted on private fortunes, if new regulations did not promptly change the actual state of affairs."

"Events have proved that our Agriculture and our Commerce, as well as our Manufacturing Industry, are not only paralyzed, but brought to the brink of ruin."

The example of Spain has been properly referred to,[23] as affording a striking proof of the calamities which attend a state that abandons the care of its own internal industry. Her prosperity was greatest, when the arts, brought there by the Moors, flourished most in that kingdom.—Then she received from England her wool, and returned it in the manufactured state; and then England was least prosperous. The two nations have reversed conditions. Spain, after the discovery of America, yielding to an inordinate passion for the gold of the Indies, sought in their mines that wealth which might have been better created at home. Can the remarkable difference in the state of the prosperity of the two countries, be otherwise explained, than by the opposite systems which they pursued? England, by a sedulous attention to her home industry, supplied the means of an advantageous commerce with her colonies. Spain, by an utter neglect of her domestic resources, confided altogether in those which she derived from her colonies, and presents an instance of the greatest adversity. Her colonies were infinitely more valuable than those of England; and if she had adopted a similar policy, is it unreasonable to suppose that, in wealth and power, she would have surpassed that of England? I think the honorable gentleman from Virginia does great injustice to the Catholic religion, in specifying that as one of the leading causes of the decline of Spain. It is a religion entitled to great respect; and there is nothing in its character incompatible with the highest degree of national prosperity. Is not France, the most polished, in many other respects the most distinguished state of Christendom, Catholic? Is not Flanders, the most populous part of Europe, also Catholic? Are the Catholic parts of Switzerland and of Germany less prosperous than those which are Protestant?

10. The next objection of the honorable gentleman from Virginia, which I shall briefly notice, is, that the manufacturing system is adverse to the genius of our government, in its tendency to the accumulation of large capitals in a few hands; in the corruption of the public morals, which is alleged to be incident to it; and in the consequent danger to the public liberty. The first part of the objection would apply to every lucrative business—to commerce, to planting, and to the learned professions. Would the gentleman introduce the system of Lycurgus?[24] If his principle be correct, it should be extended to any and every vocation which had a similar tendency. The enormous fortunes in our country—the nabobs of the land—have been chiefly made by the profitable pursuit of that foreign commerce, in more propitious times, which the honorable gentleman would so carefully cherish. Immense estates have also been made in the South. The dependents are, perhaps, not more numerous upon that wealth which is accumulated in manufactures, than they are upon that which is acquired by commerce and by agriculture. We may safely confide in the laws of distributions, and in the absence of the rule of primogeniture, for the dissipation, perhaps too rapid, of large fortunes. What has become of those which were held two or three generations back in Virginia? Many of the descendants of the ancient aristocracy, as it was called, of that state, are now in the most indigent condition. The best security against the demoralization of society, is the constant and profitable employment of its members. The greatest danger to public liberty is from idleness and vice. If manufactures form cities, so does commerce. And the disorders and violence which proceed from the contagion of the passions, are as frequent in one description of those communities as in the other. There is no doubt but that the yeomanry of a country is the safest depository of public liberty. In all time to come, and under any probable direction of the labor of our population, the agricultural class must be much the most numerous and powerful, and will ever retain, as it ought to retain, a preponderating influence in our councils. The extent and the fertility of our lands constitute an adequate security against

an excess in manufactures; and also against oppression on the part of capitalists towards the laboring portions of the community.

11. The last objection, with a notice of which I shall trouble the committee, is, that the constitution does not authorize the passage of the bill. The gentleman from Virginia does not assert, indeed, that it is inconsistent with the express provisions of that instrument, but he thinks it incompatible with the spirit of the constitution. If we attempt to provide for the internal improvement of the country, the constitution, according to some gentlemen, stands in our way. If we attempt to protect American industry against foreign policy and the rivalry of foreign industry, the constitution presents an insuperable obstacle. This constitution must be a most singular instrument! It seems to be made for any other people than our own. Its action is altogether foreign. Congress has power to lay duties and imposts, under no other limitation whatever than that of their being uniform throughout the United States. But, they can only be imposed, according to the honorable gentleman, for the sole purpose of revenue. This is a restriction which we do not find in the constitution. No doubt revenue was a principal object with the framers of the constitution, in investing Congress with the power; but, in executing it, may not the duties and imposts be so laid, as to secure domestic interests? Or, is Congress denied all discretion as to the amount or the distribution of the duties and imposts?

The gentleman from Virginia has, however, entirely mistaken the clause of the constitution on which we rely. It is that which gives to Congress the power to regulate commerce with foreign nations. The grant is plenary, without any limitation whatever, and includes the whole power of regulation, of which the subject to be regulated is susceptible. It is as full and complete a grant of the power, as that is to declare war. What is a regulation of commerce? It implies the admission or exclusion of the objects of it, and the terms. Under this power, some articles, by the existing laws, are admitted freely; others are subjected to duties so high as to amount to their prohibition; and various rates of duties are applied to others. Under this power, laws of total non-intercourse with some nations, and embargoes, producing an entire cessation of commerce with all foreign countries, have been, from time to time, passed.—These laws, I have no doubt, met with the entire approbation of the gentleman from Virginia. {Mr. Barbour said that he was not in Congress.} Wherever the gentleman was, whether on his farm, or in the pursuit of that profession of which he is an ornament, I have no doubt that he gave his zealous support to the laws referred to.

The principle of the system under consideration has the sanction of some of the best and wisest men, in all ages—in foreign countries, as well as in our own; of the Edwards, of Henry the Great, of Elizabeth, of the Colberts, abroad; of our Franklin, Jefferson, Madison, Hamilton, at home. But it comes recommended to us by a higher authority than any of these, illustrious as they unquestionably are —by the master spirit of the age—that extraordinary man, who has thrown the Alexanders and the Caesars infinitely farther behind him than they stood in advance of the most eminent of their predecessors—that singular man who, whether he was seated on his imperial throne, deciding the fate of nations, and allotting kingdoms to the members of his family, with the same composure, if not with the same affection, as that with which a Virginia father divides his plantations among his children, or on the miserable rock of St. Helena, to which he was condemned by the cruelty and the injustice of his unworthy victors, is equally an object of the most intense admiration. He appears to have comprehended, with the rapidity of intuition, the true interests of a state, and to have been able, by the turn of a single expression, to develop the secret springs of the policy of cabinets. We find that Las Casas[25] reports him to have said:

"He opposed the principles of economists, which, he said, were correct in theory, though erroneous in their application. The political constitution of different states, continued he, must render these principles defective; local circumstances continually call for deviations from their uniformity. Duties, he said, which were so severely condemned by political economists, should not, it is true, be an object to the Treasury: they should be the guarantee and protection of a nation, and should correspond with the nature and the objects of its trade. Holland, which is destitute of productions and manufactures, and which has a trade only of transit and commission, should be free of all fetters and barriers. France, on the contrary, which is rich in every sort of production and manufactures, should incessantly guard against the importations of a rival, who might still continue superior to her, and also against the cupidity, egotism, and indifference of mere brokers.

"I have not fallen into the error of modern systematizers," said the Emperor, "who imagine that all the wisdom of nations is centered in themselves. Experience is the true wisdom of nations. And what does all the reasoning of economists amount to? They incessantly extol the prosperity of England, and hold her up as our model; but the custom-house system is more burthensome and arbitrary in England than in any other country. They also condemn prohibitions; yet it was England set the example of prohibitions; and they are, in fact, necessary, with regard to certain objects. Duties cannot adequately supply the place of prohibitions: there will always be found means to defeat the object of the legislator. In France we are still very far behind on these delicate points, which are still unperceived or ill understood by the mass of society. Yet, what advancement have we not made? What correctness of ideas has been introduced by my gradual classification of agriculture, industry and trade; objects so distinct in themselves, and which present so great and positive a graduation!

"1st. *Agriculture;* the soul, the first basis of the empire.

"2d. *Industry;* the comfort and happiness of the population.

"3d. *Foreign trade;* the superabundance, the proper application of the surplus of agriculture and industry.

"Agriculture was continually improving during the whole course of the revolution. Foreigners thought it ruined in France. In 1814, however, the English were compelled to admit that we had little or nothing to learn from them.

"Industry or manufactures, and internal trade, made immense progress during my reign. The application of chemistry to the manufactures, caused them to advance with giant strides. I gave an impulse, the effects of which extended throughout Europe.

"Foreign trade, which, in its results, is infinitely inferior to agriculture, was an object of subordinate importance in my mind. Foreign trade is made for agriculture and home industry, and not the two latter for the former. The interests of these three fundamental cases are diverging and frequently conflicting. I always promoted them in their natural gradation; but I could not, and ought not, to have ranked them all on an equality. Time will unfold what I have done, the national resources which I created, and the emancipation from the English, which I brought about. We have now the secret of the commercial treaty of 1783. France still exclaims against its author; but the English demanded it on pain of resuming the war. They wished to do the same after the Treaty of Amiens; but I was then all powerful; I was a hundred cubits high. I replied, that if they were in possession of the heights of Montmartre, I would still refuse to sign the treaty. These words were echoed through Europe.

"The English will now impose some such treaty on France, at least if popular clamor, and the opposition of the mass of the nation, do not force them to draw back. This thraldom would be an additional disgrace in the eyes of that nation, which is now beginning to acquire a just perception of her own interests.

"When I came to the head of the government, the American ships, which were permitted to enter our ports on the score of their neutrality, brought us raw materials, and had the impudence to sail from France without freight, for the purpose of taking in cargoes of English goods in London. They moreover had the insolence to make their payments, when they had any to make, by giving bills on persons in London. Hence the vast profits reaped by the English manufacturers and brokers, entirely to our prejudice. I made a law that no American should import goods to any amount, without immediately exporting their exact equivalent. A loud outcry was raised against this: it was said that I had ruined trade. But what was the consequence? Notwithstanding the closing of my ports, and in spite of the English, who ruled the seas, the Americans returned and submitted to my regulations. What might I not have done under more favorable circumstances?

"Thus I naturalized in France the manufacture of cotton, which includes:—

"1st. *Spun-cotton.*—We did not prevoiusly spin it ourselves; the English supplied us with it as a sort of favor.

"2d. *The web.*—We did not yet make it; it came to us from abroad.

"3rd. *The printing.*—This was the only part of the manufacture that we performed ourselves. I wished to naturalize the two first branches; and I proposed to the Council of State, that their importation should be prohibited. This excited great alarm. I sent for Oberkamp,[26] and I conversed with him a long time. I learned from him, that this prohibition would doubtless produce a shock, but that, after a year or two of perseverance, it would prove a triumph, whence we should derive immense advantages. Then I issued my decree in spite of all; this was a true piece of statesmanship.

"I at first confined myself merely to prohibiting the web; then I extended the prohibition to spun cotton; and we now possess within ourselves the three branches of the cotton manufacture, to the great benefit of our population, and the injury and regret of the English—which proves that in civil government, as well as in war, decision of character is often indispensable to success."

I would trouble the committee with only one other quotation, which I shall make from Lowe, and from hearing which the committee must share with me in the mortification which I felt on perusing it. That author says: "It is now above 40 years since the United States of America were definitively separated from us, and since their situation has afforded a proof that the benefit of mercantile intercourse may be retained, in all its extent, without the care of governing, or the expense of defending, these once regretted provinces." Is there not too much truth in this observation? By adhering to the foreign policy, which I have been discussing, do we not remain essentially British, in every thing but the form of our government? Are not our interests, our industry, our commerce, so modified as to swell British pride, and to increase British power?

Mr. Chairman, our confederacy comprehends within its vast limits great diversity of interests—agricultural, planting, farming, commercial, navigating, fishing, manufacturing. No one of these interests is felt in the same degree, and cherished with the same solicitude, throughout all parts of the Union. Some of them are peculiar to particular sections of our common country. But all these great interests are confided to the protection of one government—to the fate of one ship; and a most gallant ship it is, with a noble crew. If we prosper, and are happy, protection must be extended to all: it is due to all. It is the great principle on which obedience is demanded from all. If our essential interests cannot find protection from our own government against the policy of foreign powers, where are they to get it? We did not unite for sacrifice, but for preservation. The inquiry should be, in reference to the great interests of every section of the Union, (I speak not of minute subdivisions,) What would be done for those interests if that section stood alone and separated from the residue of the Republic? If the promotion of those interests would not injuriously affect any other section, then every thing should be done for them, which would be done if it formed a distinct government. If they come into absolute collision with the interests of another section, a reconciliation, if possible, should be attempted, by mutual concession, so as to avoid a sacrifice of the prosperity of either to that of the other. In such a case, all should not be done for one, which would be done if it were separated and independent, but something; and, in devising the measure, the good of each part and of the whole should be carefully consulted. This is the only mode by which we can preserve, in full vigor, the harmony of the whole Union. The South entertains one opinion, and imagines that a modification of the existing policy of the country, for the protection of American industry, involves the ruin of the South. The North, the East, the West, hold the opposite opinion, and feel and contemplate, in a longer adherence to the foreign policy, as it now exists, their utter destruction. Is it true, that the interests of these great sections of our country are irreconcilable with each other? Are we reduced to the sad and afflicting dilemma of determining which shall fall a victim to the prosperity of the other? Happily, I think, there is no such distressing alternative. If the North, the West, and the East formed an independent state, unassociated with the South, can there be a doubt that the restrictive system would be carried to the point of prohibition of every foreign fabric of which they produce the raw material, and which they could manufacture? Such would be their policy, if they stood alone; but they are, fortunately, connected with the South, which believes its interest to require a free admission of foreign manufactures. Here, then, is a case for mutual concession, for fair compromise. The bill under consideration presents this compromise. It is a medium between the absolute exclusion and the unrestricted admission of the produce of foreign industry. It sacrifices the interest of neither section to that of the other; neither, it is true, gets all that it wants, nor is subject to all that it fears. But, it has been said, that the South obtains nothing in this compromise. Does it lose any thing? is the first question. I have endeavored to prove that it does not, by showing that a mere transfer is effected in the source of the supply of its consumption from Europe to America; and that the loss, whatever it may be, of the sale of its great staple in Europe, is compensated by the new market created in America. But does the South really gain nothing in this compromise? The consumption of the other sections, though somewhat restricted, is still left open by this bill, to foreign fabrics purchased by Southern staples. So far its operation is beneficial to the South, and prejudicial to the industry of the other sections, and that is the point of mutual concession. The South will also gain by the extended consumption of its great staple, produced by an increased capacity to consume it in consequence of the establishment of the home market. But the South cannot exert its industry and enterprise in the business of manufactures! Why not? The difficulties, if not exaggerated, are artificial, and may, therefore, be surmounted. But can the other sections embark in the planting occupations of the South? The obstructions which forbid them are natural, created by the immutable laws of God, and therefore unconquerable.

Other and animating considerations invite us to adopt the policy of this system. Its importance, in connexion with the general defence in time of war, cannot fail to be duly estimated. Need I recal [*sic*] to our painful recollection the sufferings, for the want of an adequate supply of absolute necessaries, to which the defenders of their country's rights and our entire population were subjected during the late war? Or to remind the committee of the great advantage of a steady and unfailing source of supply, unaffected alike in war and in peace? Its importance, in reference to the stability of our Union, that paramount and greatest of all our interests, cannot fail warmly to recommend it, or at least to conciliate the forbearance of every patriot bosom. Now our people present the spectacle of a vast assemblage of jealous rivals, all eagerly rushing to the sea-board, jostling each other in their way, to hurry off to glutted foreign markets the perishable produce of their labor. The tendency of that policy, in conformity to which this bill is prepared, is to transform these competitors into friends and mutual customers; and, by the reciprocal exchanges of their respective productions, to place the confederacy upon the most solid of all foundations, the basis of common interest. And is not government called upon, by every stimulating motive, to adapt[27] its policy to the actual condition and extended growth of our great republic? At the commencement of our Constitution, almost the whole population of the United States was confined between the Alleghany mountains and the Atlantic ocean. Since that epoch, the western part of New York, of Pennsylvania, of Virginia, all the western states and territories, have been principally peopled. Prior to that period we had scarcely any interior. An interior has sprung up, as it were, by enchantment, and along with it new interests and new relations, requiring the parental protection of government. Our policy should be modified accordingly, so as to comprehend all, and sacrifice none. And are we not encouraged by the success of past experience, in respect to the only article which has been adequately protected? Already have the predictions of the friends of the American system, in even a shorter time than their most sanguine hopes could have anticipated, been completely realized in regard to that article; and the consumption is now better and cheaper supplied with coarse cottons, than it was under the prevalence of the foreign system.

Even if the benefits of the policy were limited to certain sections of our country, would it not be satisfactory to behold American industry, wherever situated, active, animated, and thrifty, rather than persevere in a course which renders us subservient to foreign industry? But these benefits are twofold, direct, and collateral, and in the one shape or the other, they will diffuse themselves throughout the Union. All parts of the Union will participate, more or less, in both. As to the direct benefit, it is probable that the North and the East will enjoy the largest share. But the West and the South will also participate in them. Philadelphia, Baltimore, and Richmond, will divide with the Northern capitals the business of manufacturing. The latter city unites more advantages for its successful prosecution than any other place I know, Zanesville, in Ohio, only excepted. And where the direct benefit does not accrue, that will be enjoyed of supplying the raw material and provisions for the consumption of artisans. Is it not most desirable to put at rest and prevent the annual recurrence of this unpleasant subject, so well fitted by the various interests to which it appeals, to excite irritation and to produce discontent? Can that be effected by its rejection? Behold the mass of petitions which lie on our table, earnestly and anxiously entreating the protecting interposition of Congress against the ruinous policy which we are pursuing. Will these petitioners, comprehending all orders of society, entire states and communities, public companies and private individuals, spontaneously assembling, cease in their humble prayers by your lending a deaf ear? Can you expect that these petitioners, and others, in countless numbers, that will, if you delay the passage of this bill, supplicate your mercy, should contemplate their substance gradually withdrawn to foreign countries, their ruin slow, but certain, and as inevitable as death itself, without one expiring effort? You think the measure injurious to you; we believe our preservation depends upon its adoption. Our convictions, mutually honest, are equally strong. What is to be done? I invoke that saving spirit of mutual concession under which our blessed Constitution was formed, and under which alone it can be happily administered. I appeal to the South—to the high-minded, generous, and patriotic South—with which I have so often co-operated, in attempting to sustain the honor and to vindicate the rights of our country. Should it not offer, upon the altar of the public good, some sacrifice of its peculiar opinions? Of what does it complain? A possible temporary enhancement in the objects of consumption. Of what do we complain? A total incapacity, produced by the foreign policy, to purchase, at any price, necessary foreign objects of consumption. In such an alternative, inconvenient only to it, ruinous to us, can we expect too much from Southern magnanimity? The just and confident expectation of the passage of this bill has flooded the country with recent importations of foreign fabrics. If it should not pass, they will complete the work of destruction of our domestic industry. If it should pass, they will prevent any considerable rise in the price of foreign commodities, until our own industry shall be able to supply competent substitutes.

To the friends of the tariff I would also anxiously appeal. Every arrangement of its provisions does not suit each of you; you desire some further alterations; you would make it perfect. You want what you will never get. Nothing human is perfect. And I have seen, with great surprise, a piece signed by a member of Congress, published in the National Intelligencer, stating that this bill must be rejected, and a judicious tariff brought in as its substitute.[28] A *judicious* tariff! No member of Congress could have signed that piece: or, if he did, the public ought not to be deceived. If this bill do not pass, unquestionably no other can pass at this session, or probably during this Congress. And who will go home and say that he rejected all the benefits of this bill, because molasses has been subjected to the enormous additional duty of five cents per gallon? I call, therefore, upon the friends of the American policy, to yield somewhat of their own peculiar wishes, and not to reject the practicable in the idle pursuit after the unattainable. Let us imitate the illustrious example of the framers of the Constitution, and, always remembering that whatever springs from man partakes of his imperfections, depend upon experience to suggest, in future, the necessary amendments.

We have had great difficulties to encounter. 1. The splendid talents which are arrayed in this House against us. 2. We are opposed by the rich and powerful in the land. 3. The Executive government, if any, affords us but a cold and equivocal support. 4. The importing and navigating interests, I verily believe from misconception, are adverse to us. 5. The British factors and the British influence are inimical to our success. 6. Long established habits and prejudices oppose us. 7. The reviewers and literary speculators, foreign and domestic. And, lastly, the leading presses of the country, including the influence of that which is established in this city, and sustained by the public purse.

From some of these, or other causes, the bill may be postponed, thwarted, defeated. But the cause is the cause of the country, and it must and will prevail. It is founded in the interests and affections of the people. It is as native as the granite deeply embosomed in our mountains. And, in conclusion, I would pray GOD, in His infinite mercy, to avert from our country the evils which are impending over it, and, by enlightening our councils, to conduct us into that path which leads to riches, to greatness, to glory.[29]

Washington *Daily National Intelligencer,* April 19, 20, 1824. Published also in Lexington *Kentucky Reporter,* May 10, 17, 24, 1824; Lexington *Kentucky Gazette,* June 3, 10, 17, 24, 1824; *Annals of Cong.,* 18 Cong., 1 Sess., XLII, 1962-2001; [Swain], *Life and Speeches of Henry Clay,* I, 219-66; Mallory, *Life and Speeches of the Hon. Henry Clay,* I, 496-538; Colton, *Life, Correspondence, and Speeches of Henry Clay,* V, 225-94; and, widely, as a separate imprint. Cf. above, Notes, this date.

On March 26, in Committee of the Whole, Jacob C. Isacks, of Tennessee, had moved to strike from the tariff bill the provision that all imported cotton cloth, "excepting nankeens imported directly from China, . . . be taken and deemed to have cost thirty-five cents per square yard, and . . . be charged with duty accordingly." Philip P. Barbour, believing that this motion afforded an opportunity "to present his views of the general principles involved," had spoken at length in opposition to the tariff bill. *Annals of Cong.,* 18 Cong., 1 Sess., XLII, 1915-45.

During the next few days the attention of the House had been directed mainly to the general appropriation bill. Debate on the tariff was not resumed until March 30, when Clay spoke from about eleven o'clock in the morning until three-thirty that afternoon. He then "gave way to a motion for the Committee to rise" and concluded his speech on the following day.

1 See above, II, 846n.

2 See above, Clay to Poinsett, *ca.* January 5, 1824.

3 The Monroe Doctrine. See above, Scott to Clay, December 15, 1823, note.

4 Burwell Bassett.

5 Benjamin Burch, Maryland veteran of the Revolutionary War, had been Assistant Doorkeeper of the United States House of Representatives from 1809 to 1821 and was Doorkeeper from the latter date to 1831. During the War of 1812 he had been captain of a volunteer artillery unit which had participated in the defense of the Washington area in 1814.

6 Word substituted from version in *Annals of Congress;* printed as "reducing" in *National Intelligencer.*

[7] Reference not found.

[8] In his speech Barbour had cited "the Ministerial exposé of the British resources, published in 1823," and Lowe's description and explanation "of the national embarrassment of England since the peace of 1814." *Annals of Cong.*, 18 Cong., 1 Sess., XLII, 1935, 1937-38. He was referring to Frederick John Robinson, 1st Earl of Ripon, Viscount Goderich, *Speech of the . . . Chancellor of the Exchequer, Delivered in the Committee of Ways and Means, on Friday, 21st of February, 1823, on the Financial Situation of the Country . . .*, and to Joseph Lowe, *The Present State of England in Regard to Agriculture, Trade, and Finance . . .* (London, 1822).

[9] Francis Ludlow Holt, English legal writer and dramatist, admitted to the bar in 1809, a member of the King's Council and bencher of the Inner Temple in 1831.

[10] Barbour had asked "what hope is there, in the career of competition [in regard to manufacturing], between two sections of the country, in one of which there is a combination of the three great advantages of large capital, dense population, and free labor; and in the other of which there is a combination of the three great disadvantages of a deficient capital, sparse population, and slave labor?" *Annals of Cong.*, 18 Cong., 1 Sess., XLII, 1920.

[11] See above, II, 670n, 742, 777n.

[12] See above, pp. 642-43, 644, 649.

[13] Speaking on February 26, George McDuffie had commented: "They [the western States] cry out for protection against the little towns of Inverness and Dundee, as if some army was invading them, because the poor Scotch weaver can work for sixpence a day. It was vain to compete, while the labor in Kentucky was four times as high as in Scotland. The Speaker cries out, Save us from the overwhelming influence of—what? Little Dundee." Charles A. Wickliffe had at that time "resisted with warmth the implied charge of indolence, which he understood as cast upon the Kentucky population." *Annals of Cong.*, 18 Cong., 1 Sess., XLII, 1677, 1678.

Wickliffe, a brother of Robert Wickliffe, was a lawyer of Bardstown, Kentucky. He had served as general's aide in the War of 1812; had been a member of the Kentucky legislature, 1812, 1813, 1822, 1823; represented his district in Congress, 1823-1833, and again from 1861-1863; acted as Governor of Kentucky, 1839-1840, filling the office upon the death of the incumbent; and held Federal appointment as Postmaster General, 1841-1845.

[14] In debate on March 19 Daniel Webster had "remarked with severity on the doctrine that a balance resulting from a comparison of the amount of imports and exports to any particular country, shows whether we gain or lose by trade with that country—which he denominated jargon and nonsense. We export nothing to the South Seas, and bring back great amounts from there; so the balance of trade is against us. Is it therefore a losing trade?" Later on the same day he had added that "The value of trade was not altered by its being circuitous—provided it was profitable in the end, the more circuitous and multifarious in its intermediate stages the better for the interests of navigation." *Ibid.*, 1867, 1869.

[15] On February 12 David Trimble had risen, "not to enter into a discussion of the merits and principles of the bill, but merely to state facts. It had been said, repeatedly, in the course of the debate, that, to impose an additional duty, would have an effect to diminish the revenue. On this subject he had a statement to lay before the House, which would show that the operation of the duty would be very different from what gentlemen seemed to think." The figures he had then presented had indicated continuation of the same revenue from imported spirits after, as before, enactment of the tariff of 1816.

When it was later proposed that an inquiry be made as to the effect the proposed tariff was likely to produce upon the public revenue and whether it would "diminish the revenue to a greater extent than the expenditures of Government will admit of," Trimble had protested again, on February 20: "He must correct an error into which gentlemen had fallen. They seemed to represent it as a thing conceded by the friends of the bill, that it was to diminish the revenue. . . . The friends of the bill made no such concession. On the contrary, if he could not demonstrate that it would increase the revenue from three to five millions of dollars, in three years, and beat down completely all arguments to the contrary, he should think he had taken leave of his senses." *Ibid.*, XLI, 1494, 1614.

[16] On March 26 Barbour had commented that he would not support the bill "even if it were . . . designed to raise revenue, and if such would be its effect." Though he considered a public debt an evil, he advised against haste in paying it. *Ibid.*, XLII, 1917-18.

[17] Reference not found.

[18] In his discussion Barbour, referring to the nature of wages, had said, "every pursuit to be continued must yield about the average rate of profit in the country after paying all expenses; now wages are a part of those expenses; when, therefore, it is

said that manufactures cannot pay the rate of wages that other pursuits do, it shows that those others are more beneficial; besides, high wages, if the business yet goes on, is the best sign of the prosperity of the country; they are paid the laboring class of the community, who are always a majority; it shows, therefore, that the class is in a comfortable condition." *Ibid.*, 1939.

19 Augustus Brevoort Woodward, born in New York, graduated from Columbia College in 1793, and established as a lawyer in Georgetown, D. C., in 1797, had been appointed one of the first three judges of Michigan Territory in 1805. Serving until expiration of his term in February, 1824, he had not been reappointed by President Monroe, who had been given false information regarding Woodward's character and habits. Monroe soon revised his opinion and in August, 1824, appointed Woodward to the Federal Court in Florida, where he served until his death in 1827. Woodward had been influential in the founding of the University of Michigan in 1817; and, though somewhat of an eccentric, had undertaken to stimulate "scientific conjecture." In 1801 he had published a brochure, entitled *Considerations on the Substance of the Sun,* wherein he had put forward the hypothesis *"that the substance of the Sun is electron,"* defined as "an elementary substance, not compounded of any other substances presented to our observation upon this earth. . . ."

20 Cf. above, II, 123. The phrase "China trade" is apparently used broadly in reference to that with the East Indies, for the monopoly of the East India Company in the Canton trade was not broken until the act of 3 & 4 William IV, c. 85 (August 28, 1833).

21 See above, II, 564-66. A second countervailing measure had been enacted by Congress in May, 1820 (3 *U. S. Stat.*, 602-604), under which legislation the ports of the United States after the following September 30 were to be closed against British vessels coming from any of Britain's American colonies, and no wares were to be imported into the United States from those colonies unless they were wholly the growth or manufacture of the colony from which they were directly imported. On July 24, 1822, the British had responded by permitting the importation of certain enumerated articles into specified ports of their American colonies. But Clay's statement failed to cover the subsequent events. The United States Congress under act of March 1, 1823 (3 *U. S. Stat.*, 740-42) had opened the ports of this country to British vessels which sailed directly from enumerated British colonial ports, including the West Indies, and had permitted importation of articles grown, produced, or manufactured in the British colonies to which the specified ports belonged, provided they could be exported from the colonial ports on equal terms in vessels of either state and provided that American ships and goods were admitted to those ports without payment of any higher duties or charges than were levied on British vessels or "upon the like goods, wares, and merchandise" entering those ports "from elsewhere." The latter qualification, which had thus sought to place American ships on equal terms with the British in the colonies, had again proved unacceptable to the British Ministry, which had issued on July 17, 1823, an order in council fixing discriminatory duties upon American vessels entering ports of British colonies in America and the West Indies. Negotiations to resolve this impasse had been opened at the end of January, 1824, but remained deadlocked. F. Lee Benns, *The American Struggle for the British West India Carrying-Trade, 1815-1830* (Indiana University *Studies*, X, no. 56; March, 1923), 67-103 *passim.*

22 Mathew Carey, born in Ireland and embarked there upon a journalistic career, had emigrated to the United States as a young man, in 1784, to escape governmental opposition. After a brief period of editing several successive journals at Philadelphia, he had set up a profitable business as bookseller and publisher. In 1802 he had been elected a director of the Bank of Pennsylvania. He had urged renewal of the charter of the first Bank of the United States, and he was an ardent advocate of universal education, internal improvements, and a protective tariff. A voluminous pamphleteer in support of his interests, he had grouped many of his tariff writings into the *Essays on Political Economy . . .*, published at Philadelphia in 1822. The same year he had also published *Facts and Observations, Illustrative of the Past and Present Situation and Future Prospects of the United States: Embracing a View of the Causes of the Late Bankruptcies in Boston, To Which Is Annexed, a Sketch of the Restrictive Systems of the Principal Nations of Christendom . . .*, where the quoted passages may be found (2d. edn.; Philadelphia, 1822, pp. 38-39).

23 By Barbour, on March 26.

24 Traditionally, framer of the Spartan laws and institutions, with their severe discipline and subordination of the individual to the state.

25 Las Cases, *Memorial de Sainte Hélène,* IV, 196-200.

26 Guillaume-Philippe Oberkampf, native of Germany but a naturalized Frenchman, who around 1759 had established the manufacture of printed calicoes in France.

27 Word corrected from *Annals of Congress* version; printed as "adopt" in *National Intelligencer*.

28 The Washington *Daily National Intelligencer*, March 30, 1824, had carried a letter addressed to the editors and signed, "A MEMBER OF CONGRESS," in which the writer had protested against the urgency of passing the current tariff bill. He noted that there were members of Congress who would oppose it but who did believe in a " 'judicious' revision of the tariff," "a new regulation of duties, favorable to domestic manufactures, but more discriminating, more moderate, and less *dangerous* to the existing interests of the government and of individuals, than that which is now under consideration."

29 During the following several days other speakers also discussed the principles of the tariff.

From Charles Hammond

[*ca.* April, 1824]

How is it that no one speaks freely of this man?[1] Is he not acting the part of a most contemptible seeker after popularity? Instead of being a frank, open, fearless, honest man, is he not the victim of strong passions and prejudices, violent when irresponsible, cautious when differently situated, ambitious, vain and hasty, a fit instrument for others to work upon, subject to be governed by flatterers, and still inclined to hate every man of talents who has firmness to look through him, and speak of him as he deserves? I think he is strongly endowed with these traits of character, and that if classed as a mere animal, he would be a kind of monkey-tiger. I do not know but that it would be well for such a monster to be placed in the Presidential chair for the next term. King Snake succeeding King Log, and the citizen frogs made to scamper. I am almost sure that if I had been this winter at Washington, I should have contrived to quarrel with him. I dislike him for cause, I hate him peremptorily, and I could wish that his supporters for the presidency, one and all were snugly by themselves in some Island of Barrataria,[2] and he be their King, provided, that they constituted the entire population. They would make a glorious terrestrial pandemonium, and as fast as they cut each other's [*sic*] throats the world would be rid of very troublesome politicians, and, in general, right worthless citizens.

William H. Smith, *Charles Hammond and His Relations to Henry Clay and John Quincy Adams; or, Constitutional Limitations and the Contest for Freedom of Speech and Press, an Address Delivered before the Chicago Historical Society, May 20, 1884* ([Chicago], 1885), 35-36. An extract.

1 Andrew Jackson.

2 Barataria, base of the Louisiana smuggling band led by Jean Lafitte.

Receipt from John H. Morton

Transylvania University, April 1st. 1824.

John H. Morton, as Treasurer of Transylvania University, acknowledges receipt from Clay of $20, "for Tuition in CP." DS, partially printed. DLC-TJC (DNA, M212, R16). Payment was probably for Henry Clay, Jr. Cf. above, Receipt, January 5, 1824.

Account with Thomas Smith

[April 1, 1824]

[Henry Clay, as executor of the estate of Thomas Hart, Sr., owes a balance of $246.46 on account of $323.54, against which he is credited with repairs on a dwelling house on Poplar Row, Lexington.]

[Endorsement][1]

Received of H. Clay 2d. July 1825 the above balance of $246:46/100 in full THO. SMITH

D. DLC-TJC (DNA, M212, R16). 1 ES, in Clay's hand.

To Peter B. Porter

My dear Sir Washn. 3d. Apl. 1824.

From a letter which I had the pleasure yesterday to receive from Mrs. Porter, I find that you have returned to Albany, which I am extremely glad to hear. There is quite a stagnation in respect to the Pl.[1] question. One thing I find here, that, in proportion as the prospects of Mr. Crawford recede, his friends come nearer and nearer to me. They begin now to apprehend that he stands no chance of being elected even if he enter the H. no matter with whom. And on that hypothesis some of them are desirous to secure, at all events, my entry into the H. knowing that I will be elected, no matter who my other two associates may be. In Virginia I understand that this idea begins to be felt & distinctly acted on by even Mr. *Crawfords friends,* that is to give me if necessary such a portion of votes there, even if his ticket prevail, as shall accomplish the above object.

I am extremely desirous to know what are the views and wishes in your State in regard to the V. Presidency, prior to the adjournment of your Legislature. On that subject I have written to you several times, without having had the good fortune to obtain a reply.

Yr's faithfully H CLAY

Genl. P. B. Porter—

P. S. I have almost prostrated myself on the Tariff—I fear it will keep us here until June. H C.

ALS. NBuHi. 1 Presidential.

From Peter B. Porter

Dear Sir, Albany April 5th. 1824

You will hear various & contradictory rumors from this place on the subject of the Presidential election— such as, that Col. Young & his friends have been bought over, in consideration of his nomination for Governor,[1] to the support of Mr Crawford &c &c &c. I write to correct these reports & to give you some just idea of the state of things here.

Col. Young has been, during the winter, the open advocate of your election, & decidedly in favour of giving the choice of Electors to the People.[2] He left this, for home, about two weeks since, & returned the day only before the last caucus. It was during his absence that the popular current began to set in his favour to such a degree as to ensure almost a certainty of his nomination. I have spent an hour with him, alone, today. He tells me that on the day of his return, he was privately waited on by a certain member of the Legislature who is in the confidence, and a principal agent of the Crawford party, who proffored [*sic*] him the support of Mr Crawford's friends, if they could be satisfied on two points. First, that he (Col. Y.) would support the Washington nomination[3] and Second, that he would approbate the rejection of the Electoral Bill. These corrupt propositions, for such they were, met a prompt & unqualified rejection—and the negociator was moreover informed by Col. Y. that he did not consider the Washington Caucus (composed as it was of a decided minority of Congress, against the express wishes of a majority) as entitled to any respect; that his preferences were, as they always had been, for you; and that his opinions in regard to the electoral law had undergone no change. These are sentiments which he will continue openly and unhesitatingly to express on all proper occasions.

This simple statement, on the truth of which you may implicitly rely, will at once remove from your mind all fears, if you should have entertained any, that your friends had been bought over.

I consider the prospects of Mr. Crawford in this state as entirely annihilated by the nomination of Col. Young, although his friends still affect to have confidence in his success, and that the contest hereafter will be between you & Mr. Adams. Genl Jackson is out of the question. If we could have assurances of some little accession of strength from abroad—If, for instance, either Pennsylvania, Virginia, or even New Jersey, would give some unequivocal manifestations in your favour, there is scarcely a doubt but you would get the whole of the votes of this State. I confess that nothing in the course of this canvas [*sic*] has surprised me more than that Pennsylvania should have selected Jackson in preference to yourself.[4] Is it the *Cumberland Road*, that has induced them to abandon the course in which, I could have almost sworn their political interests as well as personal predilections would have led them?[5] If no change takes place abroad before November it is probable that our Legislature will give a divided vote.[6] No nomination will be made during the present session, and if any allusion is made to the subject in the Gubernatorial address from the Legislature, it will be merely to say that the members are uncommitted, and that, in their appointment of Electors, they will be governed by what they shall believe to be the sentiments of their constituents.

I hardly know what to say on the subject of the vice presidency.[7] If my feelings were to be consulted we should not seek another vice president from this State. Judge Thompson would perhaps be the most popular candidate but I doubt whether he would stand. Mr. Sanford[8] would be a good one in case his friends & Mr Crawfords friends should unite with us. Could anything be gained by taking old Mr. *Macon*.[9] If so, I think he would pass here.

I beg you to understand that this letter is not written for *effect* at Washington. There are undoubtedly many others from this place, which will answer that purpose quite as well, & perhaps better. I must request you to consider this as strictly confidential, most especially as regards the friends of Mr Crawford from this State and their allies. Among other reasons for asking this— These people feel already extremely sore toward me, & I would not irritate their wounds, because I have great hopes that they may yet be induced to unite amicably in our views. Have you & Van Buren broken off all intercourse? If not, I hope that, if he should evince a disposition to make advances, you will encourage them.

My business requires me to leave this for home in the course of a day or two. I hope however that you will still continue to write me at Black Rock. I shall leave directions for letters addressed to me at this place to follow me.

With sincere respect & regard—your Obt. Sert. P. B. PORTER
Honble. Henry Clay.

ALS. DLC-HC (DNA, M212, R1).
1 On April 3, Samuel Young had been nominated by a legislative caucus.
2 See above, Woods to Clay, August 27, 1823; Clay to Brooke, March 16, 1824.
3 See above, Clay to Porter, February 15, 1824.
4 See above, Clay to Brooke, March 4, 1824.
5 Cf. above, pp. 575, 593n. 6 See below, Clay to Brooke, November 26, 1824, note.
7 Cf. above, Clay to Porter, February 15, 1824.
8 Nathan Sanford, Chancellor of New York (1823-1826), had been United States Attorney for the District of New York (1803-1816), a member of the State legislature for several years, and United States Senator (1815-1821). He was again elected to the United States Senate in 1826 and served until 1831, when he retired to the practice of law.
9 Nathaniel Macon.

Motion to Amend Tariff Bill, Duty on Copper; General Remarks

[April 6, 1824]

On all manufactured copper in sheets and bottoms of every description, three cents per pound.[1]

Washington *Daily National Intelligencer,* April 7, 1824. Published also in *Annals of Cong.,* 18 Cong., 1 Sess., XLII, 2210; and in Lexington *Kentucky Reporter,* April 19, 1824, where the word "bottoms" is misprinted as "buttons." In Committee of the Whole, Clay proposed to amend the tariff bill by inserting this clause.

1 The motion was defeated.

Toward the close of consideration of the tariff bill in Committee of the Whole, on this date, Clay again "rose to speak in explanation on one or two points which had been touched upon in debate" (his remarks not further reported). When he concluded his comment, the Committee rose, Clay resumed the Speaker's chair, "and the report was made from the Committee of the Whole." *Annals of Cong.,* 18 Cong., 1 Sess., XLII, 2212.

To Francis T. Brooke

My dear Sir (Confidential) H. of R. 8h. Apl. 1824

Our information is very encouraging from Albany.[1] A caucus of the Legislature has nominated Mr. Young, who is an open and avowed friend of mine, for the office of Governor; and there is no doubt of his election. A principal ground of the opposition to Yates,[2] the former Governor, was his support of Mr. Crawford. There will probably be no expression of the opinion of that legislature, on the subject of the presidency, but my friends are animated & sanguine. All this you may rely upon. Every assurance from that quarter which I receive is that it is not possible for Mr. Crawford to obtain the vote of New York.

I have just seen our friend Taliaferro[3] and beg leave to reciprocate the friendly messages which he bore from you. Your faithful friend

H. CLAY

The Honble F. Brooke.

ALS. NcD. 1 Cf. above, Porter to Clay, April 5, 1824. 2 Joseph C. Yates.

3 John Taliaferro, who had this day again taken a seat in Congress, as the result of an interim election in Virginia.

From Robert Scott

Dr. Sir, Lexington, 12th Apl. 1824

Herewith is your A/Cs. with Colo. Morrison's Estate for the month of March Ulto.[1]— Since the closing date of the Accts. I have paid Mrs. Dodge 1004$50 in Coms. Notes in full of the balance due her[2]— And have advanced Mr. Hawes 1500$. in Coms. Notes to be retained by him on Acct. of his wife's legacy,[3] should you fully approve it, if not he is to return it immediately on application. therefore inform me if you please, in your first letter, whether you assent or dissent from the arrangement, in order that I may reclaim the 1500$ in case you should disapprove of it—I was induced to make this arrangement with Mr. H. from the fact of the currency becoming worse and the opinion of our friends that it will continue to depreciate—and not being able as you proposed to invest it in C Bagging at a price which I think would not even promise any thing like a reasonable compensation for trouble and risk—I have enquired of most of our manufacturers and the prices asked has been 18 @ 20c. specie or its equivelant [*sic*] in Coms. Notes, which prices you know would not justify a purchase on speculation—Mr. Hawes has received the 1500$. @ 2 for 1— It was then and yet is, at 105$ on specie— On advising with our friend Mr Gratz[4] he recommended the advce. being made to Mr Hawes on the terms stated—

Mr. Hawkins[5] has planted some corn—altho' our weather has been, and stil [*sic*] is very unfavorable to out door's business— The Hemp breaking machine[6] has not yet been put into complete operation, but will be put in motion this week I understand—I have seen a hand of hemp which was broke in it—the hemp looks well and it is beleived [*sic*] the machine will answer the intended purpose—

We are all well— Most respectfully Yr. Obt. Servt. Robt. Scott

P. S. I have a letter from J Stricker Jnr. relative to his father s[7] Ky land—the deed for which you have amongst the packet of papers I sent in with you— I mean a deed from the Register to Colo Morrison as assee. of my self—having purchased the land at the Registers Sale— The intention was in the purchase, to secure repayment I beleive and strenthen [*sic*] the title of Gl. Stricker— I have said nothing of this to Mr Stricker—leaving the thing with your self— Perhaps if you can get as much time it would be well to inform Mr Stricker he is of Baltimore—

The Honble H. Clay

ALS. DLC-TJC (DNA, M212, R12).

1 Private account not found. For the executor's accounts, see below, *ca.* June 8, 1824.

2 This balance, paid in notes of the Bank of the Commonwealth, was due Dorcas Dodge "for Hemp furnished and spinning Bale Rope &c for acct. the Est & in completion of a Contract made with Col Morrison before his death." Fayette County, Will Book F, 380.

3 Richard Hawes, Jr., and Hetty Morrison Nicholas, youngest daughter of George Nicholas, had been married in November, 1818. Morrison, who had been guardian of Hetty Nicholas, had bequeathed to her $8,000 in cash and land to the value of $10,000.

4 Benjamin Gratz. 5 Francis Hawkins.

6 Cf. above, Toast, June 6, 1822. In the spring of 1824 another hemp breaker, one marketed by Abraham K. Smedes of Lexington under the patent issued to William Cumberland of New York, July 9, 1822, had been placed on exhibition at "Ashland." Beginning May 10, the Lexington *Kentucky Reporter* advertised that the machine was "in successful and daily operation," cleaning hemp in the unrotted state and producing "a handsome and valuable article, either for Bagging or Cordage of every description."

7 General John Stricker, born in Fredericktown, Maryland, had fought throughout the American Revolution and had been in command of the Baltimore militia when they stopped the British landing at North Point, in Chesapeake Bay, in September, 1814. Engaged in commercial pursuits in Baltimore since shortly after the Revolution, he had held the post of Naval Agent for that port for nearly a decade from the turn of the century. Though in ill health during the early twenties, he was still active as the president of a Baltimore bank when he died in June, 1825.

To Joshua Gist

Dr Sir Washn. 14 Apl 1824

I received your letter[1] communicating your wish to have a son of Mordecai Gist, late from Kentucky, now residing in Ohio, placed in the public academy at West Point. The persons designated as Cadets for that institution were all appointed on the 4h. March last and are usually appointed on that day annually so that at present I know of no vacancy. in the quota of any State. That situation is now much sought after & there exists great competition for it

Under other circumstances it would have given me much satisfaction to have been able to contribute towards the attainment of your wishes. With great respect I am Yr. ob. Servt H. CLAY

Joshua Gist Esq.

ALS. NcD. [1] Not found.

To Joseph Anderson

Sir Washington 15th. April 1824

At the request of Mr. Jackson, British Commissioner &c &c &c[1] I have great pleasure in stating that in 1815 on passing over from Paris to London, in my public character as one of the Commissioners to treat with G. Britain, I found an order at Dover, issued by the proper authority at London, directing my baggage to pass free from duties and from inspection, and it was accordingly allowed so to pass. I am with great respect Your ob. Servant.

Jos. Anderson Esqr. H. CLAY

ALS. DLC-TJC (DNA, M212, R10). Endorsed: "Let Mr. Jackson's goods be admitted free from duty—J[ames] M[onroe]."

[1] George Jackson, British diplomat, brother of Francis James Jackson, had been appointed commissioner, under the terms of a convention concluded by the United States and Great Britain at St. Petersburg in 1822, to settle American claims, arising under Article 1 of the Treaty of Ghent, relating to indemnification for slaves carried away by British forces during and immediately after the War of 1812. Cf. above, I, 1002, 1011.

To William B. Giles

My dear Sir Washington 19h. April 1824

Always recollecting, with pleasure, our acquaintance in public life, I have ever felt an unaffected interest in whatever concerns you, and particularly in respect to your health, which I had learnt was not good. I am, therefore, really happy in being authorized to infer, from certain ingenious and learned essays with which you have enlightened the public, through the respectable medium of the Enquirer,[1] that the state of your health, if not entirely reestablished, is much improved; and that the unfortunate disputes and prosecutions in which, according to public rumor, you have been so long engaged with your Miller or Overseer,[2] allow you sufficient leisure once more to dedicate, to the public service, those fine talents which I have so often had occasion to admire. I hope that you will be able to command, from those unprofitable occupations, sufficient time to peruse a Speech (of which I have the honor to transmit you a copy herewith) which I felt it to be my duty to deliver in the H. of Representatives.[3] It is sent to you for the sole purpose of exhibiting my real opinions, on the interesting subject of which it treats, and under the conviction that it will be considered by you with, at least, the same candor and liberality with which you have, in the essays above mentioned, discussed the public acts and public conduct of those who had the honor to concur and to co-operate with you, in important measures adopted, in a most eventful crisis of our common country.[4] Wishing you sincerely an entire restoration of your health and much happiness I am Faithfully Yr. ob. Servant H. CLAY

William B. Giles Esqr.

ALS. DLC-TJC (DNA, M212, R10). Giles had resigned from the United States Senate in 1815, his ill health being a major consideration in this move.

1 On April 9, Giles, who had remained apart from politics since 1817, had published in the Richmond *Enquirer* the first in a series of sharp attacks on Clay, James Monroe, and John Quincy Adams for their views inimical to states rights. In this first letter he had described Clay's Congressional stands as "electioneering schemes" and had charged that such motives had determined his position on South American recognition, the Greek cause, internal improvements, and the tariff.

2 No reference found.

3 See above, Speech, March 30-31, 1823.

4 Giles had been a War Hawk and had ardently supported the embargo laws of Jefferson's Administration.

To Edward Everett

Dr Sir Washington 22d. Apl. 24

I owe you very many apologies for not earlier acknowledging the receipt of your obliging letter of the 21st. Feb.[1] which I read with great pleasure. The truth is, that the pressure of my numerous engagements, at a time too when my health is not in the best state, leaves me no command whatever of my time. I have been therefore compelled to suffer my correspondence to languish much more than I could have wished.

I rejoice to find such men as yourself and Mr. Webster[2] cherishing correct opinions, as I think, on the great subject of Internal Improvements. It would certainly be a very narrow and selfish principle to oppose them, upon the ground that New England would not participate in their benefit, to the same extent, as some other sections. And yet it is only the liberal & enlightened that can, in the first instance, withstand the influence of that principle. What would New England think of an opposition to the Fishing interest, which is peculiar to her, or to the Navigating interest, of which she enjoys most, on the ground that other sections did not participate at all, or but in a limited degree, in those interests? The fact is that each section, if it would think correctly, must perceive that it enjoys an equivalent, for the attention of the General Govt. to the peculiar wants of other sections, in the care which is taken of its own particular concerns.

Your idea of interpreting the Constitution is ingenious, and I think may be advantageously used in interpreting the actual grants of the Constitution. But the principle would be, perhaps, rather broad, and would create considerable alarm to assert that the Union, per se, was a source of power, without regard to the specific delegations of authority contained in the Constitution. For what is the Union? It is precisely what the Constitution makes it, neither more nor less; and then we must look to that instrument for its terms, powers, &c which wd. carry us back to the original question.

Did you ever read Mr. Madisons draught of the answer of the Virginia Legislature to the Massachusetts & other resolutions on the subject of the Alien & Sedition laws, published about the year 1799?[3] It is one of the ablest, if not the very ablest, exposition [*sic*] of the Constitution that I have ever seen.

I have sent you one of my Tariff speeches.[4] I know not whether you do or do not concur in the opinions of the North American Review, in respect to the prohibitory policy.[5] If you do, I entreat you to reconsider the subject; and particularly to give just weight to the consideration of the different state of the arts in England & in this Country.

We want in Transylvania a Professor of Mathematics to teach the higher branches. We can give a Salary of $1200 (Specie) I should be glad to get a person of established character, of good habits, and one free from objection & from peculiarity on the score of religion. Will you do me the favor to consult with your President[6] and tell me if you both can recommend such a person as I have described? I do not wish any engagement actually made at present; but I desire to know a suitable person, with whom I may correspond when necessary. We derive our ability to establish this Professorship from the benefaction of the late Col. Morrison, whose name it will bear.[7] The fund which he has provided is amply sufficient to insure the most punctual payment of the Salary.

With great respect I am Your's faithfully H. CLAY

Edward Everett Esq.

ALS. MHi. [1] Not found.

[2] In his argument before the Supreme Court in the case of Gibbons *vs.* Ogden, at the February term, 1824, Daniel Webster had maintained that when a road constituted "a matter of great commercial concern . . . there is no doubt of the power of Congress to make it." Similarly in speaking on the tariff bill on April 2, he had cited the progress of internal improvements as an evidence of national prosperity, "which the present generation is usefully vesting for the benefit of the next." While no speech by him was reported in the debates on the bill for survey of roads and canals (above, Remarks, January 12, 1824; Speeches, January 14, 30, 1824; Remarks, February 4, 1824), he had voted for passage of the measure. *Annals of Cong.*, 18 Cong., 1 Sess., XLII, 1467-69, 2030; Daniel Webster, *Works* (5th edn., 6 vols.; Boston, 1853), VI, 14-15.

[3] See above, II, 448, 464n. [4] See above, March 30-31, 1824.

[5] Since 1820 Everett had been editor of the *North American Review,* launched in 1815 under the auspices of the Anthology Club of Boston and highly reputed among scholarly readers. The journal had repeatedly reflected editorial hostility to the "restrictive policy" embodied in a protective tariff, and Clay's speech failed to change this viewpoint. Cf. *North American Review,* XVII (July, 1823), 214-28; (October, 1823), 424-36; XVIII (April, 1824), 413-14; XIX (July, 1824), 223-53.

[6] John Thornton Kirkland, graduated from Harvard College in 1789, for a brief period a tutor in logic and metaphysics at that institution, and from 1794 to 1810 pastor of the New South Church of Boston, had thereupon returned to Harvard as president and remained in that post until his resignation because of ill health in 1828.

[7] See above, Report, October 5, 1823, note.

From David Harris

The honble Henry Clay Baltimore 24 April 1824

Dr. Sir,

I have recd. your favor of the 21st. Curt. & am much obliged by your prompt attention to my letter of the 19th.—[1] It would appear from Col. Morrison's will, as regards the bequest to my Son, Jas. Morrison Harris,[2] that he had an expectation that the debt due him by the late firm of Harris & Donaldson would be paid, at least some part of it. I have now to inform you, Sir, that Col. Morrison, on his way to Washington through Baltimore, a few months previous to his death, was fully apprised that the aforesaid debt was lost!—

You may, probably, recollect that when I was with you at Col. Morrison's death-bed-side I requested you to inform me whether or not he had made any provision in his Will to relieve me from said claim—You told me he had not. I then would have spoken to him on the subject but the day after you left Washington, he sank so fast I could not think of agitating his last moments by any concerns of mine—

Some years since, Harris & Donaldson assigned sundry debts due them to Col. Morrison, part of which, only, were recovered. At that time, H. & Donaldson were confident that they would be able to pay off his claim in full.

Soon after this, the firm of H. & Donaldson was dissolved & the whole settlement of the concern rested with Jos. Donaldson (my late partner) he had sanguine hopes that there was still enough to pay all— he was mistaken. And very heavy losses made our house insolvent. Col. Morrison's friendly, &, certainly, disinterested conduct towards us entitled him to a preference, this was not given him, & I lament to say that I had no control of the business when the thing might have been done. I was stretched on a bed (supposed to be my death bed) & totally incapacitated for business.— My late partner, Jos. Donaldson, has, I have been told, taken the benefit of the Insolvent laws, &, I assure you that I have not a cent in my power—and what is worse, I am almost constantly confined to the house by sickness—

These things are all Known to Mrs. Morrison & she promised to intercede so far as to use her influence to prevent any means that the Executors might think it thier [*sic*] duty to use against me. I do hope & trust, Sir, that you will cherish the like disposition towards a Man that, I assure you has sacrificed his private interests, has lost his health, his time & his money in the late War. For this I refer you to Genl. Smith[3] of this place. I beg, Mr. Clay, that you will excuse me for taking up so much of your time, but I must still further intrude, by requesting another communication from you, in which you will be so good as to state whether or not Mr. Wilson[4] will take charge of Esther's property in Ohio[5] & to afford me his address. You will find the Will enclosed, & be assured, that I am, with great respect, your obliged servant

DAV HARRIS

ALS. DLC-TJC (DNA, M212, R12). 1 Neither letter found.

2 Nephew of Mrs. James Morrison, the brother of Esther Morrison Harris, and the son of Sarah Montgomery Harris. Under Morrison's will he had been bequeathed $1000 of the debt due Morrison by "the late firm" of Harris and Donaldson and also land to the value of $1000. Fayette County, Will Book F, 63. The debt of Harris and Donaldson was carried in the accounts of the estate as $4,251.39, listed as "Bad." Conjectural Estimate of the Condition of Col. Morrison's Estate . . . August, 1826 (KyLxT).

3 Samuel Smith. 4 Probably Thomas Wilson.

5 See above, Scott to Clay, November 23, 1823.

From James Madison

Dr. Sir Montr.[1] Apl. [24] 1824.

I have recd. the copy of your Speech on "American Industry"[2] for which I pray you to accept my thanks. I find in it a full measure of the ability & Eloquence so often witnessed on preceding occasions. But whilst doing this justice to the task you have performed, which I do with pleasure as well as sincerity, candor obliges me to add that I cannot concur in the extent to which the pending Bill carries the Tariff, nor in some of the reasonings by which it is advocated.

The Bill, I think loses sight too much of the general principle which leaves to the judgment of individuals the choice of profitable employments for their labour & capital; and the arguments in favor of it drawn from the aptitudes of our situation for manufacturing Establishments, tend to shew that these would take place without a legislative interference. The law would not say to the Cotton planter you overstock the Market, and ought to plant Tobacco; nor to the Planter of tobo., you would do better by substituting Wheat. It presumes that profit being the object of each, as the profit of each is the wealth of the whole, each will make whatever change the State of the Markets & prices may require. We see, in fact, changes of this sort frequently produced in agricultural pursuits, by individual sagacity watching over individual interest. And why not trust to the same guidance in favor of manufacturing industry, whenever it promises more profit than any of the Agricultural branches,—or more than mercantile pursuits, from which we see Capital readily transferred to manufacturing establishments likely to yield a greater income.

With views of the subject such as this, I am a friend to the *general* principle of "free industry" as the basis of a sound system of political Economy. On the other hand I am not less a friend to the legal patronage of domestic ma- [*sic*] manufactures, as far as they come within particular reasons for exceptions to the general rule, not derogating from its generality. If the friends of the Tariff, some of them at least, maintain opinions subversive of the rule, there are, among its opponents, views taken of the subject which exclude the fair exceptions to it.

For examples of these exceptions, I take 1. the case of articles necessary for national defence. 2 articles of a use too indispensable to be subjected to foreign contingences. 3. Cases where there may be sufficient certainty, that a *temporary* encouragement will introduce a particular manufacture, which once introduced will flourish without that encouragement. That there are such cases is proved by the Cotton manufacture, introduced by the impulse of the war & the patronage of the law, without wch. it might not for a considerable time have effectually sprung up. It must not be forgotten however that the great success in this case was owing to the advantage in the raw material, and to the extraordinary degree in which manual labour is abridged by mechanical agency. 4. A very important exception results from the frequency of wars among the manufacturing nations, the effect of a state of war on the price of their manufactures, and the improbability that domestic substitutes will be provided by establishments which could not outlast occasions of such uncertain duration. I have not noticed any particular reference to this consideration, in the printed discussions,—the greater cheapness of imported fabrics being assumed from their cost in time of peace. Yet it is clear that if a yard of imported cloth which costs 6 dollars in peace, costs 8 in war, & the two periods should be as for the two last Centuries taken together, nearly equal, a tax of nearly one dollar a yard, in time of peace could be afforded by the Consumer, in order to avoid the tax imposed by the event of war.

Without looking for other exceptions to the principle restraining Legislative interference with the industrious pursuits of individuals, those specified give sufficient scope for a moderate tariff that would at once answer the purpose of revenue, and foster domestic manufactures.

With respect to the operation of the projected Tariff, I am led to believe that it will disappoint the calculations both of its friends and of its adversaries. The latter will probably find that the increase of duty on articles which will be but partially manufactured at home, with the annual increment of consumers, will balance at least, the loss to the Treasury from the diminution of tariffed imports: Whilst the sanguine hopes of the former will be not less frustrated by the increase of smuggling, particularly thro' our East- & North- frontiers, and by the attraction of the labouring classes to the vacant territory. This is the great obstacle to the spontaneous establishment of Manufactories, and will be overcome with most difficulty wherever land is cheapest, and the ownership of it most attainable.

The Tariff, I apprehend, will disappoint those also, who expect it to put an end to an unfavorable balance of trade. Our imports, as is justly observed, will not be short of our exports. They will probably exceed them. We are accustomed to buy not only as much as we can pay for, but as much more as can be obtained on credit. Until we change our habits therefore, or manufacture the articles of luxury, as well as the useful articles, we shall be apt to be in arrears, in our foreign dealing, and have the exchange bearing agst. us. As long as our exports consist chiefly of food & raw materials, we shall have the advantage in a contest of privations with a nation supplying us with superfluities. But in the ordinary freedom of intercourse the advantage will be on the other side; the wants on that being limited by the nature of them, and on ours as boundless as fancy & fashion.

Excuse a letter which I fear is much too long, & be assured of my great esteem & sincere regard J. M

P. S. Mrs. Madison desires me to offer the proper return for the kind wishes expressed in your note introducing Mr. Ten Eyck,[3]

who with his companion made the time very agreeable which they passed with us.

ALI copy. DLC-James Madison Papers (DNA, M212, R22). Published in Colton (ed.), *Private Correspondence of Henry Clay,* 89-92; James Madison, *Letters and Other Writings* (Published by order of Congress, 4 vols.; Philadelphia, 1865), III, 430-33; Gaillard Hunt (ed.), *The Writings of James Madison . . .* (9 vols.; New York, 1900-1910), IX, 183-87. The date and the postscript are taken from Colton, who doubtless used the document that Clay received.

1 "Montpelier," Madison's home, in Orange County, Virginia.

2 See above, March 30-31, 1824.

3 Probably Egbert Ten Eyck; his companion, not identified.

To Peter B. Porter

My dear Sir (Confidential.) Washn. 26h. Apl. 1824

I recd. the three last letters which you did me the favor to write to me from Albany, just before your departure for Black rock;[1] and as I did not expect that a letter from me would find you at the former place, I defered writing until I supposed you should have arrived at home.

Your observation as to the course of Pennsa. is very just. There were several causes combined (of which the Cumberland road is the principal one) to detach that State from my support. Still I always had and yet have a strong interest in it. The delegation here, almost to a man, are united on me; and if both Jackson and I should be brought into the H. several of them are disposed, even on the first balot [*sic*], to decide for me; and there is no doubt that a majority of them will, after giving a formal vote in conformity to the anticipated decision of their State. They are much mortified; and several of them (such as Todd, Stewart[2] &c) say that they believe the State may yet be withdrawn from Jackson, and induced to support me &c. and that they will, on their return, make efforts to that effect. However I confess to you freely that I do not entertain that opinion.

One of the views of my interest which deserves to be much urged is that there is not a doubt of my election if I am one of the three highest that enter the H. of R., no matter who my two associates may be. I believe myself that I should obtain the votes of 15 or 16 states against any one of the Candidates. The great point of exertion therefore for my friends is to endeavor to secure my entry into the H. What are the prospects of this result? The six States which I have before named to you remain firm and unshaken. From Ohio we learn that the ticket, which is composed of some of the most eminent men in that State, and which was agreed upon at the late Session of its legislature, is now published;[3] that no doubt is entertained of its success; that my interest is every day becoming stronger and stronger; and that those who were inclined towards Clinton are giving him up and waiting on me. This is evident from the zeal which is now manifested in my behalf by several papers at Steubenville and other points which were lately for Mr. Clinton.

Our information is not less satisfactory from Indiana, Illinois and Missouri. And I yesterday recd. a letter from Govr. Robertson[4] assuring me that I may continue to count upon the vote of Louisiana with entire confidence, notwithstanding the Tariff. The upper districts in Maryland are generally conceded to me. What other Candidate can now certainly count upon a greater strength in his support than that which I have stated to be in mine?

Any one of these contingencies must exclude Mr. Crawford from the House, that is either if N. York should give her vote to Mr. Adams or to me or divide it between us. On the other hand if N. York decide for Mr. Crawford it is far from certain that Mr. Adams can enter the House.

You see nothing now in the papers respecting the health of Mr. Crawford. The truth is it is extremely precarious; he is greatly reduced, almost blind in one eye, and the other also affected. Those who know best his condition think it extremely doubtful if he will live through the Summer.

Congress will probably adjourn about the 17h. of next month.[5] An address of N. Edwards implicating the official conduct of the Secy of the Treasury[6] is likely to protract the Session to that period if not beyond it. The Tariff is before the Senate, and its fate there is doubtful.[7] The bill respecting Internal improvements is passed. So that one of the two great measures which I have been so anxious about now only waits the President's signature.[8]

I sent one of my Tariff speeches[9] to both Mrs. Porter and yourself. Be pleased to present her my best respects. Your's faithfully

H. CLAY

Genl. P. B. Porter.

P.S My friends in Congress are considering the subject of the Vice Presidency. Their present inclination is towards Mr. Sanford.[10] H.C.

ALS. NBu.

1 See above, Porter to Clay, April 5, 1824. The other two letters have not been found.

2 John Tod; Andrew Stewart.

3 The list of electors was reportedly chosen at a meeting of Clay supporters at Columbus, January 9, 1824. Stevens, *Early Jackson Party in Ohio,* 78, 107. For composition of the ticket, see Lexington *Kentucky Reporter,* April 12, 1824; Washington *Daily National Intelligencer,* April 23, 1824; *Niles' Weekly Register,* XXVI (May 22, 1824), 195.

4 Thomas B. Robertson. Letter not found.

5 Cf. below, Simkins to Clay, May 27, 1824, note.

6 Charges against William H. Crawford's conduct of the Treasury Department (see above, Shaw to Clay, April 4, 1822) had been continued in 1823 through a series of letters, signed "A. B.," published in the Washington *Republican,* ostensibly protesting against the suppression by the public printers, Gales and Seaton, of "parts

of those documents implicating Mr. Crawford the most strongly." Investigation by two committees of the House of Representatives had vindicated the printers but had failed to affix responsibility for the deletions. On March 22, 1824, Crawford, in further compliance with a House resolution of May 8, 1822, had submitted a lengthy report relating to the charges against his department and in his letter of transmittal had refuted testimony given by Ninian Edwards before one of the House committees, on February 13, 1823. Meanwhile, Edwards on March 5, 1824, had resigned as United States Senator from Illinois to accept appointment as Minister to Mexico.

Stung by results of the investigation during the last Session of Congress, by Crawford's recent report, and by "all the canting about an 'A. B. plot,'" Edwards on April 6, 1824, on his way to assume the duties of his office, had sent back from Wheeling, Virginia, a communication containing specific and detailed charges against Crawford and admitting his own authorship of the "A. B." letters. Clay, as Speaker, had submitted this communication to the House on April 19; and, after discussion, the matter had been referred to a committee "empowered to send for persons and papers." President Monroe, even before receiving a request from the House, had directed that Edwards be stopped "and instructed not to proceed in his mission, but to await such call as might be made on him, either by the house or its committee."

The committee made a preliminary report on May 25 and, since Edwards had not yet reached Washington, recommended that the investigation continue beyond the end of the Session. Edwards appeared June 7 and was examined. On June 21 the committee ended its sittings and drew up a report exonerating Crawford. *Annals of Cong.*, 17 Cong., 2 Sess., XL, 652-56, 735-39, 829-55, 860-85, 1126-34, 1324-36; 18 Cong., 1 Sess., XLII, 2431-55, 2459-60, 2471-79, 2713-57, 2766-2916; *House Docs.*, 18 Cong., 1 Sess., nos. 139-41, 145; *House Repts.*, 18 Cong., 1 Sess., nos. 128, 133; Adams, *Memoirs*, VI, 296-310 *passim*, 339-40, 355, 361-76 *passim*, 384-95 *passim*.

7 See below, Remarks, May 15, 1824, note.

8 See above, Remarks, February 4, 1824, note.

9 See above, March 30-31, 1824.

10 Nathan Sanford.

To Mathew Carey

Dear Sir Washn. 2d. May 1824

I duly recd. your obliging letter of the 30h. Ulto.[1] My allusion to your retirement was produced by an expression in one of your letters in which you spoke of a "valedictory." I am extremely rejoiced to find that I mistook your intention. For every new number of Hamilton[2] (I have had the pleasure of receiving as far as No. 6) proves what an irreparable loss we should sustain, if you were to withdraw from that cause which is so much identified with you.)

The hope & belief, at this time here, are that the Senate will return the bill with the duty on Iron restored, and with no other material modification than a reduction in the duty on Hemp (not altogether stricken out) and a rejection of the prospective increase of that on Cotton bagging. In this State we shall endeavor to accept & pass the bill.[3] Yr's respectfully H. Clay

Mathew Carey Esqr.

P. S. You have read Websters Speech,[4] which Mr. Walsh so much extols.[5] You must have remarked that it is a Speech on both sides, and that the whole effort of the orator was to make the bill a little more a New England measure than was consistent, in our opinion, with what was due to all parts of the Union. H. C.

ALS. MH.

1 Not found.

[2] For several years Carey had been writing under the pseudonym "Hamilton" in support of a protective tariff. The series to which Clay refers, having been rejected by the editors of the Washington *National Intelligencer* from space considerations (see "Hamilton" to Gales and Seaton, in *Daily National Intelligencer,* October 5, 1824), had been published in pamphlet form, running to ten numbers between March 31 and May 17, 1824. A nearly complete file is located at MWA.

[3] See above, Remarks, February 25, 1824, note; Remarks, March 23, 1824, note; below, Remarks, May 15, 1824, note.

[4] Daniel Webster's speech on the tariff, delivered April 1 and 2, may be found in Washington *Daily National Intelligencer,* April 30, 1824, and Supp.; *Annals of Cong.,* 18 Cong., 1 Sess., XLII, 2025, 2026-68; Fletcher Webster (ed.), *The Writings and Speeches of Daniel Webster . . .* (National edn., 18 vols.; Boston, 1903), V, 94-149.

[5] Robert Walsh, in the Philadelphia *National Gazette and Literary Register.*

Remarks on Supreme Court Quorum

[May 3, 1824]

Robert P. Letcher, on February 9, had presented to the House the remonstrance of the Kentucky General Assembly against the decision of the Supreme Court in the case of Green *vs.* Biddle (see above, Clay to Brooke, March 9, 1823, notes). In Committee of the Whole on May 3 he had offered resolutions proposing that in cases before the Supreme Court involving "the validity of any part of the Constitution of a State, or of any act passed by the Legislature of a State, . . . — Justices shall concur in pronouncing such part of the said constitution or act to be invalid," and that the justices be required "to give their opinions, with their respective reasons therefor, separately and distinctly," if their judgment be against the validity of such constitutional provision or legislative act. John Forsyth had then offered an amendment, as a substitute for Letcher's first resolution, proposing that a quorum of the Supreme Court be such "that a majority of the quorum shall be a majority of the whole court, including the Chief Justice." Clay and others spoke "at considerable length on the question." His remarks were not recorded (cf. below, Remarks, May 14, 1822). Cited in Washington *Daily National Intelligencer,* May 4, 1824; *Annals of Cong.,* 18 Cong., 1 Sess., XLII, 2527.

To Samuel L. Southard

My dear Sir 4h. May 24

Will you be good enough to inform me if it be practicable to have two young gentlemen from N. York, at this time, appointed Mid Shipmen? Or do you still refrain from making any appointments? With great respect I am faithfy Yours H. CLAY

ALS. DNA, RG45, Misc. Letters Received, 1824, vol. 3, p. 101. Addressed: "The Honble Mr. Southard Present." Endorsed: "No appts. will be immediately made—Th F." Thomas Fillebrown, Jr., was a clerk in the Navy Department.

Remarks on Bill Concerning the Post Office Department

[May 6, 1824]

Mr. CLAY now rose, and observed that a bill of such great extent, containing more than forty sections, and involving some new principles of criminal law, could not, at this late period of the session, receive that mature attention which it required. There was scarcely a possibility that it could pass both Houses at the present session, and it would only consume time peculiarly precious. He therefore moved, that the committee rise, with an understanding that leave be refused to sit again.[1]

Washington *Daily National Intelligencer,* May 7, 1824. Published also in *Annals of Cong.,* 18 Cong., 1 Sess., XLII, 2552. A bill "reducing into one, the several acts for establishing and regulating the Post Office Department" had been introduced by Francis Johnson, Chairman of the Committee on the Post Office and Post Roads, on February 9 and had been discussed in Committee of the Whole on May 4 and 5. Clay's action came shortly after further consideration of the measure had begun in Committee of the Whole, May 6.

1 Johnson "opposed this motion, on account of the importance of the bill, &c." Clay then "replied, in a few words" (his remarks not recorded), and his motion carried. The Committee rose and was refused leave to sit again. In the House the bill was tabled.

Remarks and Motions on Awards under Treaty with Spain

[May 6, 1824]

Mr. CLAY maintained that, by the treaty, we are not bound to pay interest on the capital of five millions, and thought it was premature to pay it at this time. The mode selected to discharge the debt was the most onerous of those pointed out in the treaty,[1] and though something had been said of getting the money at four per cent. he doubted if such would turn out to be the fact. If it could be had at that rate, why was not such rate put down in the bill? He went into a discussion of the stipulations of the treaty, and compared the three optional modes of paying the money agreed on. He differed from Mr. BARBOUR in the opinion that the interest must be paid, whether the lands are sold or not. He thought both principal and interest were payable out of the sales of the lands in Florida. He would prefer issuing a stock, both the principal and interest of which should be payable out of the fund created by the sales of the Florida lands. The saving proposed by the bill, between five and six per cent was deceptive. The stock, when thrown into the market, would not bring more than 75 per cent. and yet must be paid at par. He opposed the bill, and gave warning that, if its passage were pressed, he should offer amendments, the effect of which should be to make the stock payable only out of the sales of the lands.

[McLane said "He had spoken on authority, when he had said the money could be got at four and a half per cent. Such an Offer had actually been made—and *five* had been inserted in the bill as a measure of precaution, to cover fluctuations in the money market." He also "insisted that the difference between the interest of 4½ and 6 per cent. would be an actual saving to the Government." After further debate, during which Clay continued his opposition to the bill (his remarks not recorded), the Kentuckian moved that the Committee "rise & report prog."[2] This proposal failing to win support, an amendment was adopted "reducing the rate of interest at which the five millions may be borrowed, from *five* per cent. to *four and a half* per cent." At this point Clay again took the floor.]

Mr. CLAY moved so to amend the bill as to make it read—

"The Secretary of the Treasury be, and he hereby is, authorized, with the approbation of the President of the United States, to cause to be issued certificates of stock of the United States to any amount not exceeding the sum of five millions of dollars, and bearing an interest of six per centum per annum, from the — day of June, 1824, which stock, so created, shall be redeemable out of the proceeds of the sale of the lands ceded to the United States by the aforesaid treaty."[3]

Washington *Daily National Intelligencer,* May 7, 1824. Published also in *Annals of Cong.,* 18 Cong., 1 Sess., XLII, 2553-54. A bill to provide for issuance of stock, not to exceed five million dollars in face value, to cover awards by the Commissioners under the treaty with Spain of February 22, 1819 (see above, II, 678n), had been introduced in the House on January 8, 1824, by Louis McLane, from the Committee of Ways and Means, and had now been brought up for discussion in Committee of the Whole. McLane, urging passage of the measure, "objected to the creation of a 6 per cent. stock, payable out of the public lands [in Florida], and maintained that it would be a saving of nearly one million of dollars at once to pay the money at the Treasury, borrowing a like amount at a rate not exceeding five (possibly four) per cent. per annum." Philip P. Barbour expressed a belief "that the payment of the capital of the five millions might be postponed till the public lands were sold; but, that, in the interim, the interest must be paid on the amount awarded." Clay was the next participant in the debate.

1 According to the treaty, payment of the claims, to the maximum of five million dollars, "shall be made by the United-States, either immediately at their Treasury or by the creation of Stock bearing an interest of Six per Cent per annum, payable from the proceeds of sales of public lands within the Territories hereby ceded to the United-States, or in such other manner as the Congress of the United-States may prescribe by Law." Miller (ed.), *Treaties,* III, 14 (Art. 11).

2 This action reported from Minutes in Committee of the Whole . . . from 18 Cong., 1 Sess. to 26 Cong., 1 Sess. (DNA, 18A-C21.1).

3 McLane opposed the amendment, which Clay defended (his remarks not recorded), and it was rejected by a vote of 89 to 62. On the following day the bill, with certain amendments, was passed and sent to the Senate. It became law on May 24. 4 *U. S. Stat.,* 33.

From Daniel Brent

Department of State 6th. May, 1824.

Daniel Brent presents his compliments to Mr. Clay, and has the honour to inform him, in answer to his note of yesterday to the Secretary,[1] that copies of all the answers to [*sic*] the Spanish Government to Mr. Nelson's[2] demands for papers interesting to Citizens of the United States under the 11th. ar: of the Florida treaty,[3] including Mr. Meade's, are nearly prepared, and will be sent to the Board of Commissioners tomorrow.[4]

Copy. DNA, RG59, Domestic Letters, M40, R18, p. 364.
1 John Quincy Adams. Letter, not found. 2 Hugh Nelson.
3 See above, II, 678n; Remarks and Motions, May 6, 1824, note.
4 Cf. above, Clay to Meade, March 12, 1821; Meade to Clay, February 8, 15, 1823.

From S[amuel] L. S[outhard]

Hon. Henry Clay, In Congress. Navy Dep'mt. 6. May, 1824.

Sir,

In reply to your note of the 4th. instant, I have the honor to inform you that it is not contemplated to make any additional appointments of Midshipmen immediately. I am, respectfully, &c.

S. L. S.

Copy. DNA, RG45, Letters to Members of Congress, vol. 1820-26, p. 142.

Remarks on Improvement of the Ohio and Mississippi Rivers

[May 7, 1824]

Mr. CLAY suggested the following modification, viz. to strike out the clause which describes the mode of improving the river by dams sluices, &c. and inserting the following: "so as to ensure, at the driest season, a uniform depth of three feet of water over each of said bars; and, for this purpose, the President is authorized to employ any of the Engineers in the public service which he may deem proper."

["The amendment, thus modified, was agreed to, *nem. con.*"; another amendment was added; and blanks in the bill were filled.]

Mr. CLAY moved to rise and report the bill, and accompanied the motion with a series of observations on the circumstances of the case for which the bill provides.[1]

Washington *Daily National Intelligencer,* May 8, 1824. Published also in *Annals of Cong.,* 18 Cong., 1 Sess., XLII, 2558. On motion of Robert P. Henry the House had gone into Committee of the Whole on two measures, one of which was his bill "for improving the Ohio and Mississippi rivers" (see above, Remarks, March 12, 1824, note). To begin the discussion, Henry had moved that the following be substituted for the first two sections of the bill: "That the President of the United States is hereby authorized to take prompt and effectual measures for improving the navigation of the waters of the Ohio river, by causing channels to be cut through all the bars which cross the current of said river, from Brownsville, in Pennsylvania, to the Mississippi, upon which said bars there shall not be, at the lowest stage, at least three feet of water; or by causing dykes or sluices, and wing walls, to be constructed upon said bars, or by such other mode as, in each particular case, may be deemed most advisable." Objections to the proposal were voiced, and Henry defended it.

1 The Committee rose and reported the bill. As finally approved, on May 24, after considerable alteration, the measure appropriated $75,000 for improvement of

navigation over five, enumerated, sand bars, if an initial experiment upon two of the bars should prove successful, and "for the removal of all trees which may be fixed in the bed of said river . . . , commonly called 'planters, sawyers, or snags.'" 4 *U. S. Stat.*, 32-33.

To James Taylor

My dear Sir Washn. 9h. May 1824

I owe you a thousand apologies for not writing to you. The truth is that I have been overwhelmed with business and engagements, and with all I have not been in the best health. I have regretted that I could not get out in time for the present Court at Frankfort, on account of your suit;[1] but if I should not reach there before it is tried I have no doubt that the Court will continue it, if you desire it. The next term is to commence on the second monday in October, which will admit of my attendance.

I transmit you a letter[2] from Col. Mercer.

I am faithfully Your friend H. CLAY

Genl. James Taylor.

ALS. OCHP-Whelpley Autographs. Directed to Frankfort and endorsed on cover: "To be forwarded to N. Port, if Genl. Taylor should have left Frankfort."

1 See above, Mercer to Clay, April 1, 1823. 2 Not found.

Remarks on Beaumarchais Claim

[May 10, 1824]

A special committee, appointed December 24, 1823, had made, on February 16, 1824, a detailed report on the claim of the heirs of Caron de Beaumarchais (see above, Lafayette to Clay, November 5, 1822, note). Consideration of the report in Committee of the Whole on Friday, April 30, had ended when the Committee had risen, "on motion of Mr. CLAY, with an understanding that this subject shall be taken up on Monday next." The matter was not discussed further until May 10, when the report was again taken up in Committee of the Whole. Joining the debate at this time, "Mr. CLAY, in a short speech, expressed a very decided opinion in favor of the claim" (his remarks not further reported). Cited in Washington *Daily National Intelligencer*, May 11, 1824; *Annals of Cong.*, 18 Cong., 1 Sess., XLII, 2594.

To Nicholas Biddle

Sir Washington 11h. May 1824

I received your letter of the 6h. instant[1] communicating an enquiry of Mr. Jones, Agent of the Bank at Cincinnati, and a question of difficulty in respect to executions suggested by Mr. Wilson.[2]

Mr. Jones's enquiry relates to costs in cases in which the Bank, suing in the Federal Courts, shall recover an amount less than the sum of five hundred dollars. By the 20h. section of the act establishing the Judiciary of the U. S. it is provided "that where in a Circuit Court a plaintiff in an action originally brought there, or a petitioner in equity other than the United States, recovers less than the sum or value of $500, or a libellant, upon his own appeal, less than the sum or value of $300, he shall not be allowed, but, at the discretion of the Court, may be adjudged to pay costs."[3] The Circuit Court of Kentucky, composed of Judges Todd and Trimble,[4] have decided that, notwithstanding the unlimited right conferred on the Bank to sue in the Fed. Courts, in cases where the amount of the Judgment is less than $500, it has no right to recover Costs.[5] It has, however, in no such instance been compelled to pay Costs. The decision of the Supreme Court lately rendered, on the appeal of Ralph Osborne against the Bank, does not, as Mr. Jones seems to suppose settle the question.[6] That decision merely affirms the general right of the Bank to sue in the Federal Courts, without settling the conditions on which this right is to be exercised in the particular case of a Judgment for a less sum than $500. Altho' the costs in each particular action are trivial yet the aggregate amount in all causes where the Judgment is under $500 are worth attending to. I do not consider the question as a clear one for or against the Bank, but being inclined to think it was with us it was and yet is my intention to endeavor to prevail upon the Court in Kentucky or Ohio to divide pro forma, so as to adjourn the question to the Supreme Court, that being the only mode of getting it there. I should be glad to receive your instruction on this point, and I beg leave to suggest the propriety of your consulting on it your Counsel at Philada.

In regard to the case suggested by Mr. Wilson, a diversity of opinion exists among the profession in Ohio (and I know of no judicial opinion on the question in that State) whether in the case of a levy upon a part of the property of the debtor, on a prior judgment, which turns out to be insufficient to satisfy the execution, on a final sale of it, and a subsequent levy upon the residue of the debtor's property, in virtue of junior executions, the latter levy would not hold to the prejudice of the elder judgment? I think, under the laws of Ohio, as they existed, prior to the late Session of the Legislature of that State, the levy under the younger executions would be valid; but then I think also that the officer would be liable to the plaintiff in the senior judgment for having made an *insufficient* levy under the execution which issued upon it. But at the late Session of the Ohio Legislature a new alteration has been made in its execution laws.[7] What that is I do not at present know. But as I shall go to Columbus in the month of July to attend the Circuit Court of the U. S. there, I will examine at that time into this matter particularly and write you the result; & I will also cause an enquiry to be made into the sufficiency of the levies heretofore made on executions[8]

I have the honor to be with great respect Your obedient Servant.

H. CLAY

N. Biddle Esqr. &c &c &c

ALS. PHi-Etting Collection. Endorsed: "recd May 14. 1824."

1 Not found.

2 George W. Jones; Thomas Wilson.

3 1 *U.S. Stat.*, 83.

4 Thomas Todd; Robert Trimble.

5 Case not found.

6 See above, Clay to Biddle, February 17, 1824.

7 See above, Clay to Biddle, May 22, 1824.

8 Cf. below, Clay to Biddle, August 7, 1824.

From Simon Gratz and Brother

Dear Sir Philada. May 11. 1824

The last mail brought us a check on the F & M Bank[1] for Eight hundred eighty two Dollars & 16/100 from Mr Robt Scott subject to your order as Exr. of J Morrison Decd. which is placed to your credit— we do not think it probable that any thing will ever be recd. for John Coleman [*sic*] notes, forwarded you some time ago,[2] he some years since took the benefit of the insolvent Laws and is not now in a situation to pay— Very Respectfully Your Obt Serts

Hone Henry Clay Washington City SIMON GRATZ & BRO.

ALS. DLC-TJC (DNA, M212, R12).

1 Farmers and Mechanics' Bank of Philadelphia.

2 See above, Clay to Gratz and Brother, February 19, 1824.

Amendment to Bill for Extinguishing Indian Title

[May 12, 1824]

During consideration of a bill "to extinguish the Quapau title to lands in the Territory of Arkansas," Henry W. Conway, surveyor, townsite developer, and delegate to Congress from the Territory, had offered an amendment proposing to appropriate $5,000 "to enable the President of the United States to make a treaty with the Quapau Indians." At Clay's suggestion "the sum was increased to $7,500." The bill, thus amended, became law May 26, 1824 (4 *U. S. Stat.*, 41). Cited in Washington *Daily National Intelligencer,* May 13, 1824; *Annals of Cong.*, 18 Cong., 1 Sess., XLII, 2605.

Rental Agreement with Philbert Ratel

[May 12, 1824]

I have rented of H. Clay, his Brick House & Lot on Market Street, lately occupied by Colo. Whaley[1] and the Small frame building on Said lot, for the term of three months, commencing with this day, for which I am, and hereby obligate myself to pay him thirty two dollars and fifty Cents in Ky. Currency, and deliver up said premises on the expiration of said three months, in as good repair as they now are, or in which they may be rendered by repairs, natural decay and unavoidable accidents only excepted— The rent commencing this day— Given under my hand this 12th. day of May 1824

P. Ratel

[Endorsement on separate sheet][2]

By forty eight dollars for four Scholars at dancing Scholl [*sic*] one quarter	48—
By Seven dollars for glazing[3]—	7
By four —— for small house during the time that the old woman[4] Kept it—	4
By Cash	6
Rent to 12 Nov. 1824—	$65.[5]

DS, in Robert Scott's hand. DLC-TJC (DNA, M212, R16). Ratel was a dancing and music instructor in Lexington..

1 Benjamin Whaley. 2 AE, by Clay.

3 An endorsement by Robert Scott (AES) at the bottom of this sheet states that "a charge for putting in Glass of 7$ is to be allowed Mr. Rattel [*sic*] out of the rent and he is to leave the windows full glazed when he gives up the house."

4 Not identified.

5 Additional endorsements in Scott's hand (the first two, AES; the remainder, AE) indicate that payments of $32.50 in notes of the Bank of the Commonwealth were made February 16, May 23, August 18, and December 7, 1825; February 18, May 19, September 9, and December 23, 1826; February 26, May 17, and December 12, 1827. Payments of $25 in specie were made December 12, 1827; March 4, July 2, September 4, and November 21, 1828. On May 13, 1829, the sum of $50 was paid for two quarters' rent, and regular payments of $25 each followed on October 1 and December 7. The last payment, $50 for the two quarters ending May 12, 1830, was made in November of that year by John Brand, administrator of the estate of Ratel, who had died.

Remarks on Extending Land Suit Privileges

[May 13, 1824]

The House in Committee of the Whole was considering a bill "enabling the claimants to lands within the limits of the state of Missouri, to institute proceedings to try the validity of their claims," when Henry W. Conway offered an amendment to extend the provisions to the Territory of Arkansas. Clay spoke in favor of the amendment (his remarks not further reported). Washington *Daily National Intelligencer,* May 14, 1824. Thus amended, the measure was adopted and became law on May 26. 4 *U. S. Stat.,* 52-56.

Remarks on Resolutions Concerning the Supreme Court

[May 14, 1824]

Mr. CLAY spoke in opposition to the amendment, and in defence of the resolution as offered by Mr. LETCHER. He objected to that part of the amendment which prescribes that a majority of the judges, "competent" to decide, shall be required—there being no umpire to decide upon their competency, and if two declined, a majority will be only three judges. He thought that when four judges should be found on one side, and three on the other, the united decisions of the State Legislature and State Judiciary, together with the three Supreme Court judges, would outweigh the judgment of the remaining four. He insisted on the equity and policy of requiring five judges to concur when the whole authority of one or of many states was to be set aside. He adduced the case of the bankrupt laws, passed by a majority of all the states, as an illustration of the position. He thought that no danger could arise from such an arrangement to the interest of the General Government. It would sooth [*sic*] the States whose laws were set aside, and conciliate the confidence of all parties concerned.

[Philip P. Barbour countered one objection to Letcher's proposal, that it would permit a minority to "control a majority, by refusing to concur in their decision," by stating that "This . . . was no more, but much less, than happened every day in the case of an ordinary jury, where one man's refusal controlled the decision of eleven men." Webster replied that the two cases were different, "since, in the one, a minority did virtually give a decision, (because the court must decide, one way or the other,) whereas, in the other, the refusal prevented a verdict, and no decision was given on either side."

[Webster continued by discussing "the general principles on which the Supreme Court was erected, by the constitution, as a safeguard to the General Government against the State Governments, when disposed to violate the constitution. He maintained that no greater number should be required when a state was a party, than when an individual, claiming under a state law, was a party—because the authority of the state was involved in its laws. He stated the improbability that all the seven judges should, in each case, attend; and, if one judge should be involved in the question, five only would be left. If this resolution passed, not even four out of these five, could decide. He referred to the late case of the steamboat monopoly.[1] In that case one judge was absent, and if it had happened, as it might, that another was indisposed, or interested in the question, so as to leave a court of five judges only, four out of five would not have been competent to pronounce a decision, if the provision of Mr. Letcher's resolution had been law. It was a fair presumption, that state judges would lean toward the authority of their own state. A mere majority of those judges could decide against the United States; but now, more than a majority was to be required to decide against a state. This was unequal. The very case of the bankrupt laws, quoted by gentlemen, furnished a strong instance. He protested against a greater number being required to decide a cause one way than the other."

[Webster concluded with "a eulogy on the Supreme Court as a tribunal," and quoted from a lecture, cited as the "introductory lecture," in which James Kent had delivered "a very decided testimony to the distinguished character of the Supreme Court."[2]]

Mr. CLAY replied—and while he subscribed to a very high opinion of the Supreme Court, he could not acknowledge that the moment a man was appointed a member of that Court, he became exalted above his whole species in intellect and virtue. He spoke of their power practically to *make* the Constitution, by giving, authoritatively, their interpretation of it. He warned the country of the consolidating influence of this power, and maintained the necessity of guarding the State tribunals. The Supreme Court was virtually an umpire between the General Government and the States—its appointment was by one of these two parties, and its bias might be expected to be towards that party on which every member of the tribunal was dependent.

On the subject of the attendance of Judges, he had attended sixteen or seventeen terms, and had never witnessed more than two, at the most three, where a full Court was not present. In the Steamboat case, he asked whether, had four Supreme Court Judges decided against three, the opinion of the Supreme Court of New York; of Judge Kent, (than whom there was not more, at the utmost, than one greater jurist on the bench of the Supreme Court,) and of the Court of Errors of that State, added to the opinion of three Judges of the Supreme Court, ought not to outweigh the opinions of four Supreme Court Judges?

In reference to the argument respecting a jury, he observed, that the want of a verdict, when all did not agree, was not owing to the mere declaration of law, but to the reason of the case, on which the law was founded. He viewed the amendment of the gentleman from Mass. as worse than nothing in the case, and he concluded by expressing an earnest hope that it would not be adopted.[3]

Washington *Daily National Intelligencer,* May 15, 1824. Published also in *Annals of Cong.,* 18 Cong., 1 Sess., 2618-19, 2620. In Committee of the Whole, on the resolutions offered earlier by Robert P. Letcher (see above, Remarks, May 3, 1824), Daniel Webster had moved to amend the first resolution by inserting a proposal that in suits before the United States Supreme Court involving "the validity of any treaty or statute of the United States, or . . . the validity of any statute of a state, or the constitution thereof, or of any authority exercised under any state, on the ground of repugnancy to the constitution, treaties, or laws, of the United States," judgment should not be "rendered until a majority of all the justices of said court, legally competent to sit in the cause, shall concur in the opinion . . .," provided that the court not "be prevented from rendering judgment in any such suit, when it should be of opinion that the final adjudication of the merits thereof did not require the decision of such continuance on legal question as aforesaid."

The Chair had ruled this amendment out of order, because the one previously offered by John Forsyth was still pending. Forsyth thereupon had withdrawn his amendment in order to permit discussion of Webster's.

1 Gibbons *vs.* Ogden (see above, Speech, January 30, 1824, note). The following passage, explaining the relevance of this case to Webster's argument, is here reprinted from the corrected version in *Annals of Cong.,* 18 Cong., 1 Sess., XLII, 2619-20.

2 Specific reference not found, but Judge Kent paid tribute to the role and the caliber of the Court at several points in his Columbia College lectures, published as his *Commentaries on American Law* (5th edn., 4 vols.; New York, 1844), I, 439-45, 448-50.

3 The debate was thereafter briefly continued, whereupon "the Committee rose and had leave to sit again"; but the Session of Congress terminated without further action.

Remarks on Tariff Bill

[May 15, 1824]

During consideration, in Committee of the Whole, of the tariff bill as amended by the Senate, a question had arisen on a Senate proposal to strike out the following clause: "On cotton bagging, four and a half cents per square yard, until the 30th day of June, 1825; and, afterwards, a duty of five and a half cents per square yard." Cf. above, Remarks, February 25, 1824, note. Clay "requested a division of the question." The question being put on deleting the first half of the statement, it was negatived; the second section was then abandoned "without opposition." Washington *Daily National Intelligencer,* May 17, 1824; *Annals of Cong.,* 18 Cong., 1 Sess., XLII, 2624.

On the question of striking out the fourth section of the bill, concerning drawbacks, Clay and others "advocated striking out the whole section, not on its principle, but as objecting to a disagreement with the Senate on a matter of this kind—and, also, apprehending frauds on the revenue" (their remarks not further reported). When put to a vote, the proposal to strike out the section was defeated. Washington *Daily National Intelligencer,* May 17, 1824; *Annals of Cong.,* 18 Cong., 1 Sess., XLII, 2625.

Soon afterward the Committee rose and reported the bill to the House, which agreed to the amendments thus reported, with one exception. On May 17, on the question of agreeing to a Senate amendment to reduce the rate of duty on woolens valued at less than 33⅓ cents a square yard, the vote was 94 to 93 in the affirmative, but "The Speaker voted in the negative, by which an equal division was produced and the question was thereby decided in the negative." U. S. H. of Reps., *Journal,* 18 Cong., 1 Sess., 533.

Two days later the report of a conference committee on the measure passed both houses, and the bill was finally approved May 22. The most important provisions called for duties on sail duck and burlap at 15 per cent ad valorem; cotton bagging, 3¾ cents a square yard; hemp, 35 dollars a ton; wool, 20 per cent ad valorem for one year, 25 per cent during the following year, and thereafter, 30 per cent, excepting wool valued at not more than 10 cents a pound, which was to be charged no more than 15 per cent ad valorem; woolen manufactures, 30 per cent ad valorem for one year and thereafter 33⅓ per cent, excepting worsteds, blankets, and goods other than flannels valued at not more than 33⅓ cents a square yard, which were to be charged at 25 per cent ad valorem; iron in bars or bolts, unmanufactured by rolling, 90 cents per 112 pounds; iron castings, one cent a pound; lead in pigs, two cents a pound; copper vessels, 35 per cent ad valorem; wheat, 25 cents a bushel; and flour, 50 cents a hundredweight. Cotton and silk manufactures coming from beyond the Cape of Good Hope were to be charged 25 per cent ad valorem, provided that all cotton cloths, except nankeens imported directly from China, were to be valued at a minimum of 30 cents a square yard. Minimum valuations of 60 cents a pound on unbleached cotton twist, yarn, or thread and 75 cents a pound on the bleached product were also set. 4 *U. S. Stat.,* 25-30.

From George Wallace

Sir Braddocks Field 17h. May 1824

A few days after the receipt of your letter,[1] requesting me to send you the title papers to three tracts of land in this neighbourhood belonging to Col Morrison, your order to Mrs. Carruthurs (one of the legatees of the Col.)[2] was presented to me by James, Scott[3] (the brother of Robt) the deeds &c. were accordingly deliver'd to him–

At an early period Col. M purchased a claim on a certain Geo. McDowall (now dead) – Many years after suit was brought and Judgt. obtain'd in our Court of Comn. Pleas– McD own'd a valuable tract of land in this neighbourhood, which was purchased by my father & Genl. Wilkins[4] from Euphronia Grant of Scotland, the sole heir of McD.– Mr. Baldwin[5] was the Colns. Atty, and is of opinion that the Judgt. is a lien on the land, on the ground that my father had a Knowledge of the existance of the claim previous to his purchase (the Judgt. I think was obtain'd after) – James Ross Esqr.[6] is of a different opinion, from the circumstance of suit not being brought after the expiration of 14 years– I am interested in two ways in this claim, first as Exor. & an heir of my father, also the Coln. (Several years ago) gave me an equal interest with himself in the amt. that should be recover'd–

The Coln. also had a claim against the estate of his relative Joseph Scott[7] (the father of Robt.) for money expended in patenting land; he gave the papers to Wm Wilkins with a fee & directions to bring suit–nothing was done–W became a Judge, & I was directed to employ another Attorney,– I accordingly directed Parker Campbell Esqr. to call on Wilkins for the papers, and conform to the instructions given by the Coln.–the business seems now to be suspended, and appears of so little consequence, that I think Robt. Scott ought to settle it and obtain your directions to me to have the papers withdrawn from the hands of Mr. Campbell,–I think it very doubtful, whether any thing could be obtain'd from Jos Scotts estate–

With regard to the claim (I mention'd in my last letter) [8] that I have against the estate of Mr. Morrison,–it will probably become necessary for me to go to Lexington after you return home. of this you will be able to advise me, on receiving a full explanation from Mr. Scott– With much respect Yr. Obet St. GEO WALLACE

The Hnble. Henry Clay

ALS. DLC-TJC (DNA, M212, R12). 1 Not found.

2 Order not found. Mrs. Carruthurs has not been identified. This name does not appear in James Morrison's will, and it has not been found in the accounts of the estate.

3 Probably of Warren, Ohio.

4 George Wallace; John Wilkins, Jr. George Wallace, the father, had established the family home at Braddock's Field. Though not a lawyer, he had been a judge in Allegheny County, Pennsylvania, from 1788 to 1814.

5 Henry Baldwin.

6 A Pittsburgh lawyer, born in York County, Pennsylvania, member of the United States Senate, 1794-1803.

7 A veteran of the Revolution and for some years thereafter a resident of Allegheny County, Pennsylvania, where he had held several judicial posts.

8 Above, March 6, 1824.

To Francis T. Brooke

My Dear Sir Washn. 19h. May 24

I duly recd. your favor of the 16h. inst.[1] I did not become acquainted with Col. Gooch[2] whilst he was here. An incident that occurred may serve to explain the charge to which you refer. It is the duty of the Speaker to admit Stenographers. Mr. Stevenson[3] said to me "Col Gooch is here, and probably wd. like to take down the debates &c. for the Enquirer[4] during his say [*sic*], but I am not authorized to apply for his admission." I replied if Col. Gooch wants a seat within the Hall bona fide for that purpose he shall be admitted; but that I could not consent to his admission, merely to give him a comfortable place, without reference to the duties of a Stenographer. Mr. Stevenson said he should advise him not to apply & he did not make an application. I afterwards understood that he complained, but I was also told that, after an explanation with Mr. Stevenson, he left here entirely satisfied with my conduct.

I inclose you the extract of a letter[5] which has been sent me from N. York respecting a contemplated call of the Legislature. I have very little doubt that such a measure has been determined on, and will take place, unless the Governor changes his intention.[6] If my efforts on the Tariff have affected me in Virginia they have benefited me in other quarters; and my friends have increased confidence of my success in New York, & New Jersey, and are not even without hopes as to Pennsylvania whose predilection for Genl. Jackson has greatly abated. In the Western States opposition is rapidly declining and will finally disappear. I transmit you a pamphlet from Cincinnati which I have recd. this morning. I know not who the Author is but I conjecture it is Mr. Hammond.[7]

I am faithfully Your friend H. CLAY

The Honble F. Brooke.

ALS. KyU. Published in Colton (ed.), *Private Correspondence of Henry Clay,* 92.

1 Not found.
2 Claiborne W. Gooch.
3 Andrew Stevenson.
4 The Richmond, Virginia, *Enquirer*.
5 Not found.
6 See above, Woods to Clay, August 27, 1823. note.
7 Charles Hammond; the pamphlet, not found. William Henry Smith noted that during the 1824 campaign Hammond "in a pamphlet formulated the platform for the Adams-Clay party. It was *Protection to American Industry, and Internal Improvements.*" Smith, *Charles Hammond and His Relations to Henry Clay and John Quincy Adams,* 35.

From Peter Hagner

Sir, Treasury Department 3rd Auditors Office May 20th. 1824

I have the honor to state in reply to your personal application that the Account of the late Colo. James Morrison for boats sold by him for Account of the United States cannot be settled without the evidences of the debts contracted by the Purchasers who have failed to pay the Amount of the purchase money being forwarded to this office— With great respect Your Obt. Servt.

The Hon. Henry Clay H, R, PETER HAGNER Aud

ALS. DLC-TJC (DNA, M212, R12). Records of this transaction, not found.

To Nicholas Biddle

Dr Sir Washington 21st. May 1824

I received this day your letter of yesterday[1] respecting the case of the mortgage of Mess. Carneal and Johnson.[2]

The lien which has been created in behalf of the Bank by the execution of the mortgage can not be impaired or affected, in the smallest degree, by any indulgence which the Bank may extend to the mortgagors. short of twenty years. The most that other creditors of the mortgagors can do is to compel the Bank, if they please, by suit to proceed to the foreclosure of the mortgage so as to allow the surplus, after satisfying the debt due to the Bank, to be applied to the satisfaction of their debts. This is not likely or usual.

With respect to the mode of giving the contemplated indulgence, it may be effected in either of three ways. 1st. The suit now pending may be dismissed, in which case, if it should become necessary to renew it, what has been gained in the prosecution of the existing suit would be lost. 2dly. The present suit may be continued upon the docket, during the time of the proposed indulgence, which would subject the parties to costs amounting to about four or five dollars per annum. 3dly. A decree may be entered to foreclose the equity of redemption and for a sale of the mortgaged premises, to be made after the forbearance intended has expired. One of the two last modes is undoubtedly best, and the third is preferable.

I have received your two letters[3] respecting the execution laws of Ohio, and the laws themselves, which you had the goodness to forward, 'though the last act did not come to hand until the day before yesterday. I am now considering that subject and I will have the honor of writing to you on it in a day or two.[4]

With great respect I am Your ob. Servant H. CLAY

N. Biddle Esqr. &c. &c. &c.

ALS. PHi-Etting Collection. Endorsed: "recd. 24th. Reffd to Comm. on the Offices —May 25, 1824."

1 Not found.

2 No mortgage, and no suit involving one, between these parties and the officers of the Bank of the United States has been found. Thomas D. Carneal, at this time removed to Campbell County, Kentucky, had, however, assumed obligations amounting to $40,000 in return for mortgages on property of Richard M. and James Johnson. Scott County, Deed Book E, 79-80, 110-12.

3 Not found.

4 See below, Clay to Biddle, May 22, 1824.

To Nicholas Biddle

Dr Sir Washington 22d. May 1824

I duly received your two letters of the 15h. and 17h. instant with the three acts of the Legislature of Ohio, to which they refer and which accompanied them. I have attentively examined these several acts and now have the honor to submit to you such observations as appear to me proper to the occasion.

The two acts regulating Judgments and executions passed in 1822 and 1824 are most interesting to the Bank. It is much to be regretted that the Supreme Court did not decide, at its late term, the questions presented to it on the Kentucky execution laws,[1] as the principles which it may settle must form a safe guide in ascertaining how far similar laws in Ohio are applicable to the execution of the Judgments of the Federal Courts. Until that decision is pronounced, it is safest for the proceedings of the Bank to be conducted upon the supposition of the validity of the Laws of Ohio.

The act of 1824 is a revisal and contains a repeal of the previous act of 1822.[2] The principal variance between the two acts relates to personal estate which, by the latter act, until the 4 July 1822, could not be sold unless it brought one half of its appraised value. This restriction no longer exists, and all such estate may now be sold for whatever it will command. The provision of both acts is, that real estate shall be bound from the first day of the term at which 'Judgment is pronounced, in all cases where it lies within the County *where* the Judgment is entered. Both require the execution to be *levied* on lands lying without the County where the Judgt. is rendered, in order to subject them to it; and that unless the execution be sued out, within one year, and actually levied, the lien acquired by the Judgment shall not operate to the prejudice of any other Judgment creditor. Both acts also require that the real estate shall not be sold for less than two thirds of the amount of its appraised value, and declare that, if it shall appear that two thirds of the appraised value of the real estate levied upon is sufficient to satisfy the execution with all costs, the Judgment shall not operate as a lien on the residue of the debtor's estate, to the prejudice of any other bona fide judgment creditor. Both acts also provide that where real estate has been twice offered for sale, and will not produce its appraised value, the plaintiff may set aside the appraisement by application to the Court.

As to the Judgment debtor himself, it will be seen, that the lien which the creditor acquires by his Judgment is unaffected and remains in full force, whether execution be sued out or not within the year, or whether the real estate taken in execution be appraised or not in such manner that two thirds of its appraised value will satisfy the execution. It is only in behalf of other Judgment creditors, that the prior judgment loses its lien altogether as to them by a neglect to sue out execution within the year, and loses it as to the residue of the real estate of the debtor, after so much of it has been taken as that two thirds of the appraised value there of will be sufficient to pay the execution. Supposing the execution to be issued in the proper time, and two thirds of the real estate, at its appraised value, *not* to be sufficient to discharge the execution, then the lien of the Judgment continues in full vigor as to the residue of the debtor's Estate both in regard to other Judgment creditors and the debtor himself. I should imagine that the cases must be few, if any, where two thirds of the appraised value of Estate levied on will be equivalent to the amount of the execution. Examples unfortunately are much more frequent where the Estate seized and valued does not cover but a small part of the amount of the execution. In all such the Bank will preserve its lien on the residue of the debtor's Estate. In the smaller number of instances if any in which two thirds of the appraised value of the Estate are sufficient to pay the debt, the Bank can sustain ultimately no loss, unless the valuation has been erroneous; and the extent of its loss, in any event, can only be the difference between the amount at which the Estate has been valued and that at which it shall be finally sold.

With this view of the laws and their effects I can only repeat here in writing advice part of which I have repeatedly given to the Agents of the Bank in Ohio verbally.

1st. That in all cases of Judgments, execution shall be forthwith sued out.

2dly. That the execution be actually levied; and this precaution is the more necessary, because of the provision in the law of Ohio that the lien of the Judgment does not operate exterior to the County where the Judgment was rendered. This provision probably does not apply to the Federal Court, in consequence of its jurisdiction being co extensive with the limits of the State; but until it shall be decided by the Supreme Court that it does not apply, we had better proceed as if it did.

3. That the officer be always enjoined (as indeed it is his duty) to take care and levy enough to satisfy the execution.

4. That, where two experiments to sell, under the execution, and according to the appraised value of the Estate, have been unsuccessfully made, if the Agents of the Bank have reason to believe that the appraisement is enormous, application to the Court be made to vacate the appraisement.

And 5thly. that where the real estate of a debtor is seized, and he is manifestly insolvent, and consequently no prospect existing of any thing more being obtained, with a view to the close of the transaction, that the Agents of the Bank buy in such real estate.

I have also examined the third act which you transmitted, "to regulate Judicial proceedings where Banks and Bankers are parties, and to prohibit issuing bank bills of certain descriptions."[3] It is most probable that it was the intention of the Legislature of Ohio that this act should be applicable only to the local banks and bankers of that State. The only provisions of it, which may affect your institution upon which I will make any observations, are to be found in the ninth and 23d sections. The ninth section, after allowing a joint action to be prosecuted against the maker and indorser of a note &c. contains this proviso: "That in all suits or actions prosecuted by a Bank or banker or persons claiming as their assignee or under them in any way for their benefit, the Sheriff upon any execution in his hands in favor of such bank or banker their or his assignee as aforesaid shall receive the note or notes of such bank or banker from the defendant in discharge of the judgment" &c According to one construction of this proviso it might matterially [*sic*] affect the Bank in those cases in which it has received transfers from the Cincinnati Banks of the notes of their debtors, as they would have the right to discharge those notes or the Judgments upon them by paying the notes of such Banks, altho' any of them should happen now to be insolvent. I am inclined to think that the true construction of the act will not admit this to be done, except in cases where notwithstanding the assignment made by the Bank, the debt transfered still belongs to it. At all events, I think the offset cannot be made, if the Bank of the U.S should not avail itself of the priviledge of suing in the State Courts in the mode authorized by the ninth section. And this consideration furnishes a new motive for adhering to the resolution, to which the Bank has heretofore come, of appealing exclusively to the Federal tribunals. Indeed according to the 23d. section of the act it is provided "that no action shall be brought upon any note bill bond or other security given and made payable to any such bank, unless such bank shall be incorporated and authorized by the laws of *this* State." &c. &c If the expressions "the laws of this State" be interpreted to exclude the laws of the U. States, the Bank has no alternative, in the cases specied [*sic*] in the 23 section, but to resort to the Federal tribunals. and this I respectfully submit it is for the interest of the Bank generally to do. Mr. Jones[4] has, I believe, heretofore taken the precaution where notes have been transfered to the B. of the U.S. by the Cincinnati banks, to give immediate notice to the makers, of such transfer; if he has omitted it, no time should be lost in giving such notice.

I shall leave this place probably on Saturday the 29h. inst. and of course there will be time for me to receive any further commands with which you may honor me.

I am, with great respect, Your obedient Servant H. CLAY

N. Biddle Esqr. &c. &c. &c.

P.S. Anxious that this letter should reach you without further delay I send it without copying. Will you have the goodness to direct one of your Clerks to return me a Copy? I send the acts by the next mail H.C.

ALS. PHi-Etting Collection. Endorsed: "recd May 25th. 1824. & read to the Board." Cf. above, Clay to Biddle, May 21, 1824.

1 See above, Clay to Hammond, July 14, 1822, note; Clay to Biddle, December 27, 1822, note.

2 Ohio Gen. Assy., *Acts of a General Nature,* XXII (1823-1824), 108-119 (February, 4, 1824).

3 *Ibid.,* 358-66 (January 23, 1824).

4 George W. Jones.

Remarks Relative to Arkansas Boundary

[May 25, 1824]

Mr. CLAY advocated the passage of the bill—represented the hardships of the circumstances of the settlers—considered the new territories as younger daughters in the common federative family, and, as such, entitled to an indulgent policy—denied that the size of the territory must necessarily govern the size of the future state to be formed out of it, and even if it did, he urged the policy of making Arkansas a strong frontier state. The bill only asks the Indians to consent to remove the line farther west, and does not violate any treaty. It had received the deliberate consideration of the Senate, and he hoped it would pass this House.

[Rankin rejoined that "If this extension of the limits be allowed, the whole must be received as a state, or a small section of its western part must remain (probably forever) a territory, or else the Indians must be driven still farther west."]

Mr. CLAY responded. If Louisiana was not as large as the gentleman could wish, it was an argument rather for than against this bill. He (Mr. C.) had opposed the treaty by which Texas was ceded and Louisiana consequently reduced in extent. If Louisiana was comparatively weak, the greater need that the adjoining frontier state should be a strong one.[1]

Washington *Daily National Intelligencer,* May 26, 1824. Published also in *Annals of Cong.,* 18 Cong., 1 Sess., XLII, 2758. In Committee of the Whole on a Senate bill "to fix the western boundary line of the territory of Arkansas," Christopher Rankin had "opposed the extention [*sic*] of the present boundary of that territory, as violating the provision of Indian treaties, as giving an improper size to the future state into which this territory will soon be formed. He denied the right of the settlers to the lands they occupied, and contended that that territory ought to afford a resting place to the Indians from the eastern side of the Mississippi, &c." Others had contributed to the debate before Clay arose.

1 Following some further debate, the Committee rose and reported to the House, where the bill was defeated by a small margin. On the next day the vote was reconsidered and the bill passed. 4 *U. S. Stat.*, 40-41 (May 26, 1824).

To [James Monroe]

To the President of the United States [*ca.* May 26, 1824]

The undersigned beg leave respectfully to recommend to your attention William W. Blair of St. Augustine as a person well qualified to perform the duties of Judge in the middle Judicial District of Florida.[1]

Previous to leaving his native state Mr Blair had filled a judicial station, in which his talents, integrity, and firmness of character, acquired for him the respect and confidence of the whole community. His reputation for genious and legal attainments, is perhaps equal to that of any man of his age in our Country. His appointment to the office now solicited, we feel well assured would not only be acceptable to the People of Florida. (many of whom have expressed their solicitude on the subject) but would contribute greatly to the happiness and prosperity of the Territory.

R. K. CALL — P. THOMPSON
J. T. JOHNSON — SAM HOUSTON
T. P. MOORE — D. WHITE JR
D. P. COOK — BOB P LETCHER
H. CLAY — DAVID TRIMBLE
ROBT. P. HENRY — C A WICKLIFFE[2]

ALS by Call, signed also by Clay and others. DNA, RG59, Applications and Recommendations for Office.

1 The act establishing this office was approved May 26. Blair was nominated for the post on May 27, and the nomination was confirmed on the same day. 4 *U. S. Stat.*, 45-47; U. S. Sen., *Executive Journal*, III, 390-91. He held the post only three months before he died of a longstanding "pulmonary complaint." Lexington *Kentucky Reporter*, September 6, 1824.

2 All members of Congress. Of those not previously identified, Richard K. Call was delegate from the Territory of Florida; Thomas P. Moore, Philip Thompson, and David White, Jr., were from Kentucky; and Houston was from Tennessee.

Remarks on Resolution on European Intervention in America

[May 26, 1824]

While the House remained in committee of the whole, on the state of the Union, Mr. CLAY rose and said, that he would ask a single moment's attention of the committee whilst he said only one word in respect to a resolution which he had had the honor to present some time ago.[1] The resolution, to which he referred, was that which proposed an expression of the feelings of Congress in regard to an attack supposed to be meditated by Allied Europe upon the independence of Spanish America. He had offered that resolution, in consequence of information disclosed in the President's message, at the opening of the present session of Congress;[2] and most certainly, if the design imputed to the allies had really been entertained, every consideration connected with the interest, the safety, and even the independence of this country, called for the most deliberate attention to his proposition. But such a purpose, abominable as it would have been, ought not to be attributed upon any other than the strongest evidence. Events and circumstances, subsequent to the communication of the message, evinced, that, if such a purpose were ever seriously entertained, it had been relinquished. For his part, whilst he was disposed to keep a vigilant eye on every movement of the Allies, as to America, and to be ready to give his feeble co-operation to every measure calculated to repel their aggressions, if any such should be attempted, on the Independence of any part of America, he was, on the other hand, unwilling to give them any just cause of offence against us. But, to pass the resolution, after all that has occurred—in the absence of any sufficient evidence of their cherishing inimical designs on this Continent—might be construed by them as unfriendly, if not offensive. Under the full conviction, therefore, that they did not entertain any purpose so diabolical as that would be of attempting to reduce Spanish America to its ancient subjection, or of compelling it to adopt the monarchical form of government, he should continue to abstain from pressing upon the attention of the House, his resolution; and should allow it to sleep where it now reposes, on the table.

Washington *Daily National Intelligencer,* May 27, 1824. Published also in *Annals of Cong.,* 18 Cong., 1 Sess., XLII, 2763-64. Clay's remarks were offered immediately after a discussion in Committee of the Whole on another matter.

1 See above, Resolution, January 20, 1824.

2 See above, Scott to Clay, December 15, 1823.

Check to William Gunton

27 May 1824

Pay to William Gunton or order Seventeen dollars and eighteen Cents H. CLAY

Cashr. of the off. of Dt. & Dt. Washn.

$17.18/100

ADS. DLC-TJC (DNA, M212, R16). Gunton has not been identified.

Receipt from John Rowlett

[May 27, 1824]

Received Washington D.C. 5th. Mo. (May) 27th. 1824 of Henry Clay Speaker of the House of Representatives of the United States Thirty eight Dollars in full for one copy "Tanner's American Atlas"[1] bound in blue Morocco, gilt & the Maps of No. & So. America folded on Tape —pr. Subscription.— JOHN ROWLETT
Dolrs. 38.

ADS. DLC-TJC (DNA, M212, R16). Rowlett has not been identified.

1 Henry S. Tanner, born in New York, had learned the art of engraving from his brother, Benjamin, with whom he had launched a map publishing business at Philadelphia in 1811. Outstanding among his many works is *A New American Atlas; Containing Maps of the Several States of the North American Union, Projected and Drawn on a Uniform Scale from Documents found in the Public Offices of the United States . . . and Other Original and Authentic Information* (5 parts; Philadelphia, 1818-1823).

From Eldred Simkins

Dear Sir, Edgefield Courthouse So.Ca. 27. May 1824.

From the great lapse of time which has intervened since I had the honor of addressing you on the subject of your claim against the Estate of the late Mrs. Willison [*sic*] for costs which you were so very liberal as to pay for her, I presume you have nearly or quite abandoned the hope of ever getting the amount[1]— The truth is the estate was much involved, but both young Mr. Willison and his uncle Mr. Stark[2] have continued to say that the debt would be paid. The former wishes to wait the result of a suit in the fedl. Court involving the principal part of Willison's Estate— He is sanguine that he will succeed, in wh. Event the Estate will be quite ample to discharge all debts.[3] I write that you should see that I have neither abated vigilance or abandoned hope as it relates to your interest; and rely upon it that as soon as I can avail myself of any thing advantageous to your interest in this matter you shall be apprized of it. Hoping that you have arrived safely in the bosom of your family and friends after your late very laborious session of Congress[4] & wishing you health & happiness I am dear Sir Very respectfully & truly your friend ELDRED SIMKINS
Hon. Henry Clay Esqr.

ALS. DLC-TJC (DNA, M212, R10). 1 See above, II, 871-73, 883-84.

2 Thomas Willisson; Robert Stark.

3 The suit, Thomas Willisson *vs.* Anderson Watkins, involving 600 acres on the Savannah River, was decided in Willisson's favor in 1830 on appeal to the United States Supreme Court from the ruling of the Circuit Court for the District of South Carolina. 28 *U.S.* (3 Peters) 43-56.

4 Congress adjourned the day this letter was written.

To Francis T. Brooke

My dear Sir (Confidential) Washn. 28h. May 1824

The state of Mr. Crawfords health is such as to scarcely leave a hope.of his recovery. It is said that he has sustained a paralytic stroke. His friends begin to own that his death is now but too probable, and that in any event he can no longer be held up for the Presidency.

I conjecture that a visit which Mr. Van Buren & Govr. Dickinson [*sic*] of New Jersey are about to make to Virginia[1] is connected with this circumstance, and that they are about to take measures for a fresh campaign. I thought, prior to my departure on tomorrow, I would put you in possession of these matters.

Be pleased to make my best respects to Mr. Call[2] & believe me ever Faithfully Your friend H. CLAY

The Honble F. Brooke.

ALS. KyU. Published in Colton (ed.), *Private Correspondence of Henry Clay*, 93.

1 After the adjournment of Congress, Martin Van Buren and Senator Mahlon Dickerson visited Thomas Jefferson at "Monticello." Dickerson, an old friend of Jefferson, had been Governor of New Jersey from 1815 to 1817 and was United States Senator from 1817 to 1833. He later served as Secretary of the Navy under Presidents Jackson and Van Buren and was appointed United States District Judge for New Jersey in 1840.

2 Daniel Call.

To George Graham

29 May 24

Mr. Clay's Compliments to Mr. Graham and he sends him the note of Mr. Abbott,[1] the amt. of which Mr. G. promised to receive, information of the receipt of which, if paid, Mr. C. will thank Mr. G. for—

[Endorsements on cover][2]

Mr. Abbots Note. Received $200 the 6 or 7h. Septr. 1825. H.C.

Recd. $100 on the 23d. Decr. 1825.

Recd. $100—the 9h. March 1827.

AN. DLC-TJC (DNA, M212, R12).

1 John Abbott. Cf. above, Graham to Clay, July 15, 1823.

2 The first, AEI; the remainder, AE.

Receipt from John Davis

[May 29, 1824]

Received of H. Clay the sum of Twelve hundred & seventy three dollars and 74 Cents in full of all accounts including and up to the 29h. May 1824. JOHN DAVIS

DS, in Clay's hand. DLC-TJC (DNA, M212, R16).

From William B. Rochester

Hon. H, Clay Bath Steuben Co. N. Y. 29th. May 1824.
Dear Sir

About a fortnight ago I took the liberty of addressing to *you* a hastily written letter[1] which, doubtless You recd, previously to Your departure from Washington. Within a few days the political horizon of this State (always mutable) is beginning to assume a new aspect. —It has been confidently asserted for several weeks, by individuals near the person of the Govr, that he intends to convene the Legislature by proclamation on a day (perhaps in the latter part of Sepr,) sufficiently early to enable them to pass a law giving the choice of Electors to the people[2]— To this rumour I had not myself given credence, untill Yesterday; but last evening I received the information in Such manner, as leaves no doubt upon my mind, but that Such is his present determination.— Suffice it to Say that this intelligence comes to me thro' the most credible channel direct from his Excellency.—

Judge Thompson[3] (late Secy. of the Navy to whose opinions, whether in relation to law or politics, the Govr. has uniformly paid great deference, and who it is Said has himself transferred his preference from Mr. Calhoun to Mr, Adams) has contributed by his advice and persuasions mainly to bring our Execution [*sic*] to this conclusion— Yet judging from the past vacillating course of the latter upon the subject in question, he may yet abandon this recent determination, for surely, a moments reflection ought to satisfy him, that however he may be lauded *pendente lite,* by those to whom such a course may seem to point to the attainment of particular objects, Yet when the feverish impatience of the day shall have passed off with its exciting causes the estimation in which his views will be ultimately held can not be favourable to his character for wisdom or purity of intention—but perhaps the Govr. has become a little desperate, and thinking that he has nothing to lose on the score of respect yielded to his Stability and firmness of purpose, has adopted the hazardous adage that "reason would lose what rashness may obtain"—& possibly a Spice of revenge enters into his composition, for I learn that he has conceived a most deep-rooted hatred for Mr, V, Buren and his immediate adherents, usually denounced by the Federal journals as "the Albany junto."[4]—

Some of our friends think that the promise indirectly held out that he shall succeed Rufus King in the Senate of the U.S.[5] is a tub [*sic*] which his irritated feelings will not allow him to play with and are uncharitable enough, to surmise that his object is to obtain a nomination from the proposed minority Convention in opposition to Colo. Young[6]—this I can-not beleive [*sic*], tho' I apprehend he is not in such a frame of mind as will enable him to part with power as gracefully as Ceasar [*sic*] declined the crown—and upon the whole I am apt to think that he will be exceedingly puzzled to assign a good reason for the course proposed i.e. one which will be consistent with his views on the same subject, submitted in his last Anniversary Message.[7]—

But to the purpose of this letter. Assuming as a fact that the Governor means to carry the project above indicated, into effect, What will be the probable decision of the Legislature upon a reconsideration of their proceedings? And should they refer the choice of Electors to the People, what will be its probable bearing upon the Presidential question? In my last a supposition was indulged that Mr. Crawford can in no event get the vote of this State, provided *Your* friends do not falter— More recent information confirms this impression, as well as the one which I believe I also expressed, that under the existing State of things, the prospect of Mr. Adams was the best—

Without trespassing upon Your patience with a detail of my crude notions as to what will be the probable result of a Second attempt by the Legislature (in the event of their being convened by proclamation) to alter the mode of choosing Electors, I submit it as my humble opinion, that it will most probably depend upon the course which *your* friends in the Senate Shall deem it expedient to mark for their guidance—Among these I am warranted in enumerating Messrs Redfield and Bowman[8] (both from this district) who voted for the postponement of the question, and who, on account of the closeness of that vote, have it in their power alone by changing their ground, to give a totally different direction to the entire question. But should the choice of Electors be given directly to the people, then Mr Crawford (unpromising as is his chance now) will be more completely hors de combat—and unless the choice be made by Districts, the hopes of your friends will be greatly diminished if not utterly annihilated—the hopes of Mr. Adams will not be advanced and unless Mr. Clinton (who I think might carry this State before the people) be brought forward, a most determined effort will be made by the last last named gentleman and his friends (a band which includes nine tenths of all the Federalists in the State, always excepting the coterie of Rufus King) to get Electors favourable to Genl, Jackson.—

After all if the People shall be allowed to choose the Electors, much very much must obviously depend upon the manner in which their voice is to be ascertained—and going upon the assumption that Mr. Clinton is already so far committed to Genl. J that he cannot, with any decency, set up for himself, I venture to predict that if it shall be 1st. by Districts—there will be a tri partite division of the vote of the State among A., J. & yourself—a plurality probably for the first named, for which he will be indebted to the Northern and Eastern prepossessions of very many of our Citizens—

2ndly. if by general ticket requiring a majority of all the votes given, I am firmly persuaded (Mr Clinton out of the question) that the People will fail of making a choice—

And 3rdly. if a plurality of votes is to govern candour requires me to express my belief that it cannot be counted on for *you;* and my reasons for this opinion I predicate upon the following facts—namely: the apparently mad determination of many of our leading and more influential Republicans to sink or swim with Crawford—The fast hold which the location of Mr Adams gives him upon the attachment of a vast many [*sic*], and lastly the cause of Genl, Jackson being (wit[h] few exceptions) undoubtedly espoused by what is designated among us the *Clintonian* party—a party-coloured party—just such an one as Mr Monroe (partly under the advice and direction of Genl, J) [9] seems to have contemplated organizing throughout the Union and in our State comprehending besides, all the croakers and disappointed office Seekers, of which description the corps in New York is far from being inconsiderable either on the score of numbers or persevereance [*sic*].—

I feel in common with many more of your N.Y. friends, the pressing necessity of looking well and immediately to all the emergencies of the occasion and of doing promptly all that prudence and patriotism require; to that end I have set apart a month at least (as I shall have abundance of leisure—between the 15th. July and 1st. Sept,) to spend at the Springs of Saratoga (the County in which Col Young resides) the great Summer resort of invalids, fashionables, politicians, et id omne genus, where any man (even a Judge) may appear with impunity. I shall there make it a point to see Col. Young and many others of *your* friends and Shall doubtless meet with Mr Van Buren &c and perhaps with the Govr,. I shall also visit Albany and most probably N.Y. before my return. I shall take occasion from thence to give you at large my further views and hopes and fears touching the premises, unless indeed *you* shall previously signify a disinclination to be thus intruded upon by the jejune speculations of an humble but I can assure you an ardent friend.

I congratulate *you* on the passage of the tariff-bill—meager as it appears—I perceive that even Gales confesses that it will have a tendency to increase the annual revenue to from 1 to 4 millions—but with our great debt staring him in the face he has the characteristic impudence to add that there is no need of addition to our treasury![10]

Be kind enough to present me cordially to my old friend Doct. Pindell:[11] tell him that my venble. Father at the advanced age of more than seventy years still retains a great share of his mental and bodily activity, so much so, that I believe he is on the eve of taking upon himself the Presidency of a Bank, lately authorized to be established in his flourishing *City of Rochester,* at the falls of the Genesee river.[12]—

Before concluding this long letter permit me to add one more surmise— In the event of the choice of Electors in this State being given to the people, May not Mr Clinton suffer *his name* to be brought forward, with the ulterior veiw [*sic*] of transferring the vote of the Electors, (after they shall be chosen) to Genl, Jn. making it on his part a merit of declining that which will be found unavailable in advancing his own immediate views to the Chief Magistracy? The General no doubt would feel obliged by such a Manœuvre. The Story has become quite current that Mr. Clinton is to be *Prime Minister* to President Jackson. But I will trouble you no longer.— Yours faithfully. W B. Rochester

P.S. the draught of the above letter was written in so illegible a hand, that I had to resort to the aid of a very indifferent copyist— my youngest brother—Henry[13]—who resides with me— I mention this that Mr. C. may not suppose that I have made an improper exhibition of the privilege which he has accorded me, of writing to him freely & frankly— W B R.

LS, the postscript in Rochester's hand. DLC-HC (DNA, M212, R1). Addressed to Clay in Washington, marked for forwarding to Lexington, and postmarked at Washington on June 14.

1 Not found.

2 See above, Woods to Clay, August 27, 1823, note.

3 Smith Thompson.

4 Otherwise known as the Albany "Regency."

5 King's term expired March 3, 1825.

6 Following the nomination of Samuel Young by legislative caucus as a candidate for Governor of New York (see above, Clay to Brooke, April 8, 1824), a group of legislators who opposed this nomination and favored popular choice of electors (the People's Party) had held a caucus on April 7. One of the recommendations of this body was that a convention friendly to an electoral law be held at Utica, September 21, for the purpose of nominating candidates for Governor and Lieutenant Governor. Cf. below, Storrs to Clay, September 23, 1824.

7 In his message at the opening of the legislative session of 1824, Governor Yates had called for amendment of the Federal Constitution to fix the mode of choosing electors. Since such a procedure could not have been accomplished before the current presidential election, his message had been commonly interpreted as "an executive recommendation to the legislature to retain, in their own hands, the power of appointing the electors." Hammond, *History of Political Parties in the State of New York,* II, 141-42.

8 Heman J. Redfield, of Batavia, Genesee County, and John Bowman, of Clarkson, Monroe County, at this time represented the Eighth District in the New York Senate; but they were staunch adherents to Van Buren and supported Crawford, not Clay. Weed, *Autobiography,* 108, 109.

9 Rumors that Jackson in 1816 and 1817 had recommended bipartisan Cabinet appointments to Monroe had set off controversy early in 1824 and had eventuated in publication of the relevant correspondence. See Washington *Daily National Intelligencer,* May 8, 12, 1824.

10 See editorial of Joseph Gales, Jr., in Washington *Daily National Intelligencer*, May 20, 1824.

11 Richard Pindell.

12 Later in the year Nathaniel Rochester became the first president of the Bank of Rochester, chartered during the New York legislative session of 1824 after extended political maneuvering.

13 Henry E. Rochester.

From Sir James Mackintosh

My Dear Sir London 3 June 1824

This Note will be presented to you by Mr Stanley a Grandson of the Earl of Derby; a young Gentleman who has [a]lready shewn in Parliament Talent, equally brilliant & solid & whom I can hardly be mistaken in considering as destined to perform a great Part in the public affairs of this Country.[1] He is accompanied by three other Gentlemen one of whom Mr Wortley I know & highly value & the other two I know to be most respectable.[2] I know that you will consider this first Visit of such a body of English Travellers to the United States as an Event which ought to interest & gratify the Friends of both Countries. I hope that I may venture to ask your good Offices in guiding the Enquiry & aiding the Observation of Mr Stanley & in procuring Access for Him & his Friends to those Individuals & Societies which may afford them sufficient specimens of the great English Common wealth in which you perform so distinguished a Part.

The enlightened Curiosity of Mr Stanley will direct his Comprehensive Understanding to your Laws & Government & manners; to the State of Industry Wealth & Knowledge & to the Effect of all these on the Nature & Happiness of the People. There is no one more able than yourself to aid him in so difficult a Study.

I intended to have taken the same Liberty with Mr. Adams & Mr Crawford. But I am so very much hurried (besides being indisposed) at this Moment that I am reduced to the Necessity of requesting that you would introduce Mr Stanley to them as holding the first Place among those who are the Hope of this Country After this sincere Testimony to his extraordinary Merit it is perhaps presumptuous in me to add that I should consider their Attention to Hi[m] as a most pleasing mark that the[y] have not forgotten the Degree in which I have had the Pleasure of enjoying their Society.

I am My Dear Sir with great Esteem Your faithful Ser[t]

J MACKINTOSH

ALS. DLC-TJC (DNA, M212, R10). Published in Colton (ed.), *Private Correspondence of Henry Clay*, 93-94.

1 Edward George Geoffrey Smith Stanley, grandson of Edward Stanley, twelfth Earl of Derby, in 1851 became himself the fourteenth bearer of that title. His long career in politics, during which he changed from Whig to Conservative, had

begun in 1822, when he entered the House of Commons. In addition to holding numerous lesser offices, he was three times Prime Minister. He became a member of the House of Lords in 1844.

2 John Stuart-Wortley in 1823 had entered the House of Commons, where he sat until his succession to the peerage in 1845 as the second Baron Wharncliffe. The other two travelers were John Evelyn Denison and Henry Labouchere. Denison had been elected to the House of Commons in 1823, was several times re-elected, and from 1857 to 1872 served as Speaker. In February, 1872, he was created Viscount Ossington and entered the House of Lords. Labouchere, member of a prominent mercantile family, was first elected to the House of Commons in 1826. He was successively a lord of admiralty, Master of the Mint, Vice President and President of the Board of Trade, and, from 1855 to 1858, Secretary of State for the Colonies. In 1859 he became Baron Taunton of Taunton and the following year took his seat in the House of Lords.

The four companions on this visit to America had been students together at Christ Church, Oxford.

Bill of Sale from Ruth Carter

[June 4, 1824]

I do hereby declare and make known that as administratrix of William Carter[1] deceased and in my own right I have authorized Ralph St. John[2] to sell a negro boy named Jerry, now a little upwards of twenty years of age, who is bound to serve until he becomes twenty eight years of age. And my said Attorney having accordingly sold him to Henry Clay for the price of One hundred and twenty five dollars, I do hereby ratify and confirm the said sale. Witness my hand & seal this 4th. day of June 1824.

Signed Sealed & Delivered in presence of — RUTH CARTER {L.S.}

Isaac Tucker Thomas Tucker[3]

[Endorsement on verso][4]

Jerry (A Pennsa. negro)

Sold Jerry to Mr. James Erwin & made a bill of Sale for him 4 July 1825.[5] Mr. Erwin agreeing to pay to Jerry on his arrival at full age the sum of thirty five dollars. H. CLAY

DS, in Clay's hand. DLC-TJC (DNA, M212, R16). Accompanied by certification, dated June 4, 1824, by the justices of the peace of Washington County, Pennsylvania, that Ruth Carter, of Amwell Township, in that county, was the owner of the Negro, Jerry, aged twenty years and three months, a servant until the age of twenty-eight years, and that she was moving him to Wheeling, Virginia (now West Virginia), with his consent, as evidenced under private examination.

1 Probably the coroner of Washington County, 1814-1817. 2 Not identified.
3 Neither of the witnesses has been identified. 4 AES. 5 Not found.

Order to Forsythe, Dobbin and Company

5 June 1824

Clay, as executor of the estate of James Morrison, directs the Cashier of the Washington Branch of the Bank of the United States to pay Forsythe, Dobbin and Company the sum of one hundred dollars. ADS. DLC-TJC (DNA, M212, R16). The payee was a Wheeling, Virginia firm.

From William Ingalls

Boston June 5. 1824

The Honorable Henry Clay, Esqr., Speaker of the House of Representatives in Congress.

Sir,

Enclosed are the names[1] of a few names [*sic*] Gentlemen, who are warmly interested & engaged in the promotion of your election to the Presidential Chair. Those belonging to this district are active, enterprising & influential men. We have just commenced organizing your friends, & making arrangements to carry into effect such measures as may tend to advance the cause, in which we are engaged. In one district there is already a majority in your favour. Our object in addressing you, is to ascertain whether you intend to continue a candidate, & in what manner we can best co-operate with your friends in different parts of the Union.

I am, with respect, Your obedt. servant WILLIAM INGALLS

ALS. PHi. Ingalls, a native of Newburyport, Massachusetts, had received the M. D. degree from Harvard in 1801 and had settled in Boston. In 1811 he had been appointed professor of anatomy and surgery at Brown University, a position he retained until 1823, although in the later years of this period his lectures were delivered in Boston.

[1] Not found.

Account of Sales of the Estate of James Morrison

[June 8, 1824]

As only acting executor of the estate of James Morrison, Clay signs an account of sales at auction of part of Morrison's estate, held at "Carlisle Farm," October 21 and 28, 1823, and, in addition, a few sales in Lexington. Produced in open court at the August Term, the account was approved and ordered to record. Fayette County, Will Book F, 366-69.

Executor's Specie Account with Morrison Estate

[*ca.* June 8, 1824]

As only acting executor of the estate of James Morrison, Clay files a cash account, covering the period from June 9, 1823, through June 8, 1824. A commission of five per cent on receipts of $36,878.59 is allowed the executor. Examined and certified, August 6, 1824, by commissioners appointed by the court; approved by the Fayette County Court at its August Term and ordered to record. Fayette County, Will Book F, 370-73.

Executor's Note Account with Morrison Estate

[*ca.* June 8, 1824]

As only acting executor of the estate of James Morrison, Clay files an account of the settlement in notes of the Bank of the Commonwealth from June 9, 1823, through

June 8, 1824. A commission of five per cent on receipts of $16,274.89 is allowed the executor. Examined and certified by commissioners appointed by the court; approved by the Fayette County Court at its August Term and ordered to record. Fayette County, Will Book F, 374-81.

To James Monroe

Sir Ashland 12th. June 1824

I comply with the request of Mr. B. Irvine in laying the inclosed papers before you.[1] I transmit them just as I have received them. My acquaintance with Mr. Irvine is probably not more extensive than that which you may happen to have had. He has been the Editor of one or more news papers in the U. S. & afterwards an agent in the employment of Government in South America. It was after he filled this latter situation that I personally knew him. Of his participation in the plans on Porto Rico, and of the causes of his imprisonment I know nothing except what is to be collected from the news papers and from the inclosed documents. Doubtless you have full information on those matters, and I shall be glad if it be such as to admit of the effectual interposition of the American Government to obtain the liberation of Mr. Irvine.

I have the honor to be with the highest respect

Your obedient Servant H. CLAY

The President.

ALS. DNA, RG59, Misc. Letters. Endorsed: ". . . Registered in Dept of State 10th July."

[1] See above, Irvine to Clay, January 18, 20, 29, 1824.

To John Rodgers

Sir Ashland 14 June 1824

I have had forwarded to Mess. Forsyth, Dobbin & Co. of Wheeling 2060 lb. of Hemp which has been broken out on my farm in the new method, that is without having been previously either water or dew retted.[1] I directed it to be carefully put up, and understand that has been done accordingly. Mess. F. Dobbin & Co. are directed to forward this Hemp to the Commrs of the Navy Board, agreeably to what passed between us.

In making the experiments which you contemplate wd. it not be well to have some made with the hemp in its present state, and some after it has been boiled &c?

I have the honor to be with great respect Your ob. Servant

H. CLAY

John Rogers Esq. &c &c &c.

ALS. DNA, RG45, Navy Comrs., Misc. Letters Received, 1825-1831, vol. 10.
[1] See above, Scott to Clay, April 12, 1824, note.

To Josephus B. Stuart

Dr Sir (Confidential) Ashland 14h. June 1824

Your favor of the 29h. Ulto.[1] addressed to me at Washington reached me here. Public sentiment, on this side of the mountains, in respect to the P. question remains, according to all the information which I have received, faithful to its attachment. It is more and more approximating towards unannimity [*sic*] in the three N. Western States, and in Kentucky, Missouri and Louisiana there never has existed a doubt.

We are anxiously waiting to see the course your Executive will pursue in respect to the call of your Legislature.[2] I presume, from all that I have heard, that his proclamation is already published. I observe what you say in respect to assurances from Mr. Clinton of his being uncommitted. I understood last fall that he had avowed publicly favorable opinions of me. Subsequently I learnt that he had espoused the fortunes of Genl. Jackson. Doubtless he has been misrepresented in both instances. The public, at a distance from New York, has been much at a loss to comprehend the causes of his exclusion from the Board of Canal Commissioners,[3] and how it happens that your State denies to itself the use of the fine talents of one of its most distinguished Citizens, in any station.

The designation of a person suitable for the office of Vice President neither can or ought to control the choice of the State, of which he may happen to be a Citizen, in regard to the Presidency. In considering the pretensions of Chancellor Sandford,[4] I take it for granted that his merits and qualifications have been principally, if not exclusively regarded. What may finally be the disposition of the Western States towards him cannot be certainly known at present. All that can be safely affirmed is that he seems to be well spoken of in several places.

I should like that you would make the acquaintance of the honble J. S. Johnston, a Senator of the U. S. from Louisiana, who will pass the summer in New York. He is a gentleman of honor, of intelligence and of discretion, and a particular friend of Your's faithfy

H. CLAY

Dr. J. B. Stuart

ALS. NHi. [1] Not found. [2] See above, Rochester to Clay, May 29, 1824.
[3] The New York legislature, on the last day of the Session, April 12, 1824, had removed DeWitt Clinton from the office of Canal Commissioner, a post he had held for many years. No reason had been given for this action, which stemmed from the partisan rancor of the "Regency" supporters. It precipitated a strong public reaction in Clinton's favor.
[4] Nathan Sanford.

To Josiah S. Johnston

Dr Sir (Confidential) Ashland 15h. June 1824

I transmit you the inclosed just as I have received it.[1] The person who writes it (and whose acquaintance I would like you to make, if convenient) became known to me at Columbus in Ohio in Jan. 23. He travelled with Judge Burnett & myself from that place to Wheeling, and interested us both by the variety & extent of his information, particularly in regard to personal characters now on the stage.[2] He subsequently manifested a good deal of zeal in my behalf, and has frequently written me letters, to which I have some times replied respectfully but cautiously. If the communication from Mr. Clinton is to be considered in the nature of an overture, there can be but one answer given. I can make no promises of office, of any sort, to any one, upon any condition whatever. Whatever support shall be given to me, if any, must be spontaneous and unbought. I cannot but believe that Mr. Clinton's friend must have allowed his zeal to carry him further than was authorized.

We have nothing new in this quarter. All that we believed in respect to its favorable dispositions towards me is well founded.

Be pleased to make my best respects to Mrs. Johnston.[3]

I am faithfly Your friend H. CLAY

The Honble Mr. Johnston.

ALS. PHi. Published in Colton (ed.), *Private Correspondence of Henry Clay*, 94. Endorsement by Johnston on wrapper: "Mr. Clay—1824 Clinton wanted a foreign Embassy."

1 Probably the letter (not found) from Josephus B. Stuart to Clay, May 29, 1824. Cf. above, Clay to Stuart, June 14, 1824.

2 See above, Clay to Hammond, October 29, 1823.

3 In 1814 Johnston had married Eliza Sibley, of Nachitoches, Louisiana.

Rental Agreement with John C. Buckner

[June 16, 1824]

[Henry Clay leases to John C. Buckner, "the said Buckner acting in his own right and as Agent of the Penitentiary," two rooms in the house at the corner of Market and Short streets, "one of them fronting Short Street and the other immediately back and adjoining," for one year. Clay is to be at no expense for repairs; Buckner is privileged to move to the front room any shelving from the cellar. Buckner agrees to pay the sum of $200 rent per year, in quarterly installments, and to return the rooms in good order.]

[Endorsements][1]

Recd. the quarters rent due the 16 Sept 1824. H CLAY

Recd. the quarters rent due the 16. Decr. 1824—this 4 Jany 1825.

for H Clay—R SCOTT

17 March 1825 recd. Fifty dollars Coms. Notes—One quarters rent due 16 inst. for H. Clay R. SCOTT

Sale of Penitentiary articles 3 Monday 20 June 1825 Key not given up til some days afterward

Dead & Insolvent

ADS. DLC-TJC (DNA, M212, R16).

[1] The first three, AES; the fourth, E, in Scott's hand; and the last, E, in strange hand. Buckner died in Lexington in early July, 1825.

Rental Agreement with John Deverin

[June 16, 1824]

[Henry Clay leases to John Deverin "the room, in the House now in the possession of the said Deverin, which room was formerly occupied by the Athenæum, for the term of three years commencing on the first day of this present month." Deverin agrees to pay $70 per annum, in quarterly installments, and to return the room in good order.]

[Endorsement][1]

This lease is to be credited by 16 days rent in the first quarter.

H. CLAY.

ADS by Clay, signed also by Deverin. DLC-TJC (DNA, M212, R16). Cf. above, Rental Agreement, July 5, 1823.

[1] AES.

Toasts and Speech at Public Dinner

[June 17, 1824]

14. HENRY CLAY—Our friend and guest; Agriculture, Domestic Manufactures, Internal Improvements, and Struggling Liberty claim him as their foremost champion.

{This sentiment was received by the company with a general burst of enthusiastic applause. After silence was restored Mr. Clay rose, (we do not pretend to give all that he said, nor in his precise language) and with deep feeling expressed the thanks, he said, of a heart over-flowing with gratitude for the cordial reception and hearty welcome which his constituents had again and again given him, upon his return from the national councils, and especially for this new proof of their esteem. In all the vicissitudes of his public life, their confidence, affection and approbation had been to him a source of the greatest consolation and encouragement. These sentiments had not been measured out to him in a cold and sparing spirit, but with a generous, unreserved, lavish dispensation. He was happy to find that they approved of the most prominent measures of the last session of Congress, which in his opinion had entitled itself to a distinguished place in the American annals. If in respect to the Tariff,[1] the degree of protection which has been extended to objects of American industry, against rival articles produced abroad, is not as great in every instance as might have been desired, we must not forget how difficult is the task of reconciling what are the conflicting interests (erroneously supposed, as he verily believed, to be conflicting) in the different quarters of the union; that its moderation will tend to lessen if not to reconcile opposition; and that it affords a new and animating pledge of the fostering care of our own government. But we ought always to remember, that the business of government is defence and protection;—that it does not produce nor create—that it must be left to individual exertion and enterprize to repair the losses in private fortunes, and to make those accumulations which form the subject of commercial exchanges with foreign powers; and hence, that we should second the beneficent intentions of Congress by steady and persevering industry, and by calculating and unflinching economy. The kindred measure which was adopted, in respect to the internal improvement of the country,[2] was also one of the highest importance. As far as the decision of Congress can settle such a question, the constitutional power had been maintained; and hereafter it was to be hoped the only point would be, one of discrimination between objects which were national, and therefore entitled in their execution to the application of national resources; and those which belonged more peculiarly to the different states. In connection with this great interest, in which all parts of the union were concerned, a bill was passed which demanded grateful acknowledgments from the people of the valley of the Mississippi. It was not in the amount of the appropriation for the improvement of the navigation of the Mississippi and Ohio rivers,[3] though it was far from being contemptible, that he saw occasion for particular satisfaction, but it was the principle which that appropriation recognizes and proclaims; and that is, that those rivers will be regarded as our SEAS—as our Atlantic ocean and Mexican gulph, and as such are considered as entitled to special care and attention; and he entertained no doubt but that adequate appropriations will be from time to time made, to effect every practicable improvement of which their navigation may be deemed fairly susceptible. He felt much gratification in referring to the liberal support which this important bill experienced in its passage through the House of Representatives, from the North and East, to that of the latter in particular, because he knew that prejudices had sometimes unhappily existed between it and the Western section. Nor was the measure without the concurrence of some highly respectable Southern members; and he knew that other prominent and influential members from Virginia and the South were only restrained by their constitutional opinions, from giving to it their approbation. From the success of the measures to which he had thus adverted, Mr. Clay said, there was one cheering conclusion,—that however for the moment great interests may seem to be neglected— however those of a particular section may appear to be forgotten or put aside, the day would at length arrive, when they would obtain from Congress a just and parental attention; and this view of the subject would, he trusted, tend to give fresh strength and attachment to that union, which at last is the best and safest guarantee of all our rights and interests. Mr. Clay sat down with the expression of his best wishes for the prosperity of each of the gentlemen assembled.}

. . . .

Henry Clay—May his nomination to the Presidency be the signal for rallying around the palladium of Internal Improvements and American Industry.

Lexington *Kentucky Reporter,* June 21, 1824. Published also in Washington *Daily National Intelligencer,* July 22, 1824. The dinner, given Clay "by his Constituents, as a testimonial of their personal regard for him, and approbation of his public conduct," was held at "Mrs. Keen's Inn" (Sanford Keen had died in October, 1823, and his wife, the former Martha Threshly, continued to operate the inn). Officers for the occasion were John Bradford, president, and Edmund Bullock, Richard Higgins, and William W. Worsley, vice presidents.

1 See above, Remarks, May 15, 1824, note.

2 See above, Remarks, February 4, 1824, note.

3 See above, Remarks, May 7, 1824, note.

Account with Lexington Post Office

[*ca.* June 17, 1824]

The account, headed "Henry Clay Esqr to Jos Ficklin Dr," is similar to those above, July 3, *ca.* October 10, 1823, except that no newspapers are mentioned. Entries include letter postage from October 9, 1823, to June 17, 1824; box rent for two quarters, to July, 1824 (60¢); and a credit of $1.25 for overcharge on a letter. The total sum due is $14.71. Fifteen of the separate charges for postage, an amount stated at $5.18½ (should be $5.43½), are for "Mr. Claiborne." Ficklin notes that the account has been paid in full. ADS. DLC-TJC (DNA, M212, R15).

William Charles Cole Claiborne, son of William C. C. Claiborne (who had died in 1817), resided in the Clay household while a student at Transylvania University, from which he was graduated in 1826. He returned to Louisiana, where he was later a member of the legislature and of the constitutional convention of 1845.

To James Erwin

Dr Sir Ashland 19h. June 1824

You have been in such a movable position that I have not written to you, being unaware where a letter would find you; and I now address you at Nashville under some uncertainty if my letter will reach its destination. I returned to this place on the 9h. inst. and found my family in good health. My own is better than it was when I left home or at the corresponding period of the last year; but it is nevertheless not good, and I experience occasionally some of the symptoms of my old complaint which I fear will increase as the summer advances. I shall leave home about the 4h. of next month for the Federal Court in Ohio, and must necessarily be absent during the greater part of it: We are extremely anxious that you and Anne[1] should join us at Ashland, and I hope you will not delay giving us the gratification of seeing you one day longer than is indispensible. We feel this wish the stronger since it seems that we are not to have the happiness of seeing Mr. and Mrs Duralde[2] this summer. In the absence of so many of those who are most dear to us Ashland will appear dreary. We shall be delighted to see here any of your relations who may feel disposed to retire to a more temperate climate than that in which they reside, and to pass the summer with us. Your father,[3] whose acquaintance I had the satisfaction to make at Washn., would not allow me to expect the pleasure of seeing him here this summer; but possibly some circumstances may have arisen to change his inclination in that respect, and I beg you therefore to assure him how much he would gratify us by a visit. Mrs. Clay and I have returned to day from an excursion to Woodford to see my mother[4] and relations whom we left well.

I can add very little to the stock of information which is derivable from the public prints in respect to the Presidential Election. The state of Mr. Crawfords health is such that I entertain no doubt that he will be withdrawn sooner or later; of that I think you may be quite certain. If the support, or the major part of it, which he seems likely to obtain, if he should continue, shall be transfered to me, I shall be elected; if to Mr. Adams, he will be elected. I do not think that there is any prospect whatever of Genl. Jackson's election. Whether Virginia and the other States prefer ing Mr. Crawford will assign their votes to Mr. Adams or to me, I believe to be uncertain. I can not yet persuade myself that Virginia will give to that gentleman a preference over me, but perhaps I am too much influenced by my own interests. If I were to say whose prospects appear to me to be best at this moment, I should designate Mr. Adams. The result is yet however involved in almost as much uncertainty as has, at any time, heretofore, attended it; and circumstances which may here after arise, such as the time when Mr Crawford shall be withdrawn, the passage of an Electoral law in New York[5] &c. may give a new face to the contest. If I am carried into the H. of R. with any thing like a pretty respectable vote I believe I shall be elected. Ohio, Indiana, Illinois, Missouri Louisiana, and Kentucky, according to all my information remain firm in their determination to support me. I think I shall receive several votes in Maryland, and my friends are sanguine in respect to both New York and New Jersey. I do not enterain [*sic*] a single doubt myself that the vote of N. York will be given to Mr. Adams or to me. There does not exist the smallest probability of Genl. Jackson obtaining it. I pray you to consider as confidential whatever I write on this delicate subject.

Give my love and that of her Mama to our dear Anne; and I repeat again that I hope we shall see you both as soon as it is possible.

Your's affectionately H. CLAY

James Erwin Esqr.

ALS. THi. [1] Mrs. Erwin. [2] Martin Duralde (Jr.).
[3] Andrew Erwin. [4] Mrs. Henry Watkins.
[5] See above, Woods to Clay, August 27, 1823, note; below, Clay to Hammond, June 21, 1824.

To Charles Hammond

Dear Sir (Confidential) Ashland 21st. June 1824

I had intended to write you from Washn. but defered [*sic*] it until my return. We will talk over the matter of the decision of the S. Court in the case of Osborn and the Bank when I have the pleasure to see you. I shall not put the parties to any inconvenience, in respect to the bal. of the decree, if it be supposed that the Legislature, at its ensuing Session, will make provision for it.[1]

The bad state of Mr. Crawfords heath [*sic*], should he even survive the summer, (of which *I know* his most intimate friends entertained serious doubts) you may rely on it, will lead to his ultimate withdrawal. When may be uncertain, but that it will happen, sooner or later, I have no doubt. I hope I shall obtain credit with you when I assure you that it gives me no pleasure to speculate on such an event. My interest even would appear to me to recommend that, if he be withdrawn at all, it should not be hastily done. It is of consequence to me that there should be time for the anti tariff fever, now raging in the South, to abate. Should he be withdrawn, I shall be elected if the vote of Va. be given me. Mr. Adams will be elected if he obtains it, unless that of N. York (which I should then hardly expect) should be bestowed on me. If the withdrawal of Mr. Crawford should take place, I can hardly believe that Virginia will support Mr. Adams. The great mass of the friends of the Secy of the Treasury have constantly assured mine that I am the next person of their choice. I do not think that there is any contingency likely to happen which will lead to the election of Genl. Jackson.

We have just heard of the call of the Legislature of N. York.[2] That measure must in all probability deprive Mr. Crawford of all prospect of obtaining the vote of that State, if, contrary to expectation, he should continue a Candidate. If the Law proposed should pass the only contest in that State will be between Mr. Adams and me, unless Mr. Clinton should be brought out, which I consider as possible.

I have thought you might like to receive these impressions of mine. In any view of the subject which presents itself to me, I think vigorous perseverance the true policy of my friends. There is much to hope; there is nothing discouraging.

I shall be at Columbus at the approaching term of the Fed. Court. The arrangement between Tod[3] & myself is that we shall go together; and we shall probably pass by Cincinnati. I pray you however not to mention this, as we shall both desire a quiet and undisturbed journey. With great regard I am faithfully Your's

Charles Hammond Esqr. H. CLAY

ALS. InU.

1 See above, Clay to Biddle, February 17, 1824, note. Later in the year the Ohio legislature appropriated a sum "not exceeding three thousand dollars" to cover the judgment in this case. Ohio Gen. Assy., *Acts of a General Nature, 1824-1825*, p. 9 (December 16, 1824).

2 The call for a special session of the New York legislature, beginning August 2, had been issued by Governor Joseph C. Yates on June 2. See above, Woods to Clay, August 27, 1823, note.

3 Thomas Todd.

To Josiah S. Johnston

Dear Sir Ashland 21 June 1824

I recd. your obliging favor of the 7h. inst.[1] from Philada. with the proclamation of the Govr. of N. York[2] inclosed. I was of course prepared to expect that measure, the only effect of which will be, should the Legislature pass the proposed law, to place the vote of that State to some Candidate other than Mr. Crawford.

We have nothing new to the West, where I find every thing to be as I had expected. You will see Candidates announced for Electors in this State for Mr. Adams, Genl. Jackson &c. This is the result of the absence of all sort of concert, by means of Caucus's or other nominating assemblages in Kentucky. Every body who chooses puts himself forward as a Candidate. The State is divided into three districts, according to which it has given its Electoral vote for many years past.[3] No change was made, in consequence of one of its own Citizens being brought forward, because it was known that no change was necessary to ensure him the entire vote of the State. Nor is there a County, parish, or respectable neighbourhood in the whole State in which he wd. not obtain the majority over all competition. In Ohio, Indiana and Illinois, as well as in Missouri, the result I believe to be equally certain. I shall go to Columbus to attend the Fed. Court which begins there on the second monday in July. Should you write to me at any time after the receipt of this letter and before the 20h. of July be pleased to address me at that place. I am anxious to see the indications which will shortly be given to the South of the dispositions of Mr Crawfords friends, should he be withdrawn, of which I do not doubt, sooner or later. My interest, I think, will be benefited by his being continued to be held up for some time to come. The Tariff fever will have then somewhat abated. My respectful compliments to Mrs. Johnston.

I am faithfully Your's H. CLAY

The Honble J. S. Johnston.

[Postscript in margin] Shall I continue to address you at New York? H C.

ALS. PHi. Published in Colton (ed.), *Private Correspondence of Henry Clay,* 95.
1 Not found. 2 See above, Clay to Hammond, this date.
3 Under the Kentucky law the State's total number of electors was allotted equally among the districts and the choice made from among residents of the respective districts. Littell (comp.), *Statute Law of Kentucky,* IV, 410-12.

To Walter Dun

Dr Sir Ashland 22d. June 1824

At the term of the Federal Court, which is just closed, the injunction obtained by H. Banks against you as exor of Mr. Graham &c.[1] was dissolved; but at the very close of the Court he filed an amended bill, with several letters from you and obtained an order for a new injunction. I shall direct a Copy of this Amended bill & the exhibits to be made out, and if I do not transmit them to you before, I will carry them with me over to the Federal Court at Columbus in next month when I expect I shall have the pleasure to see you

Montjoy continued his injunction until the next term.[2]

With great regard I am faithfy Yr's H. CLAY

Walter Dun Esqr.

ALS. Ross County Historical Society, Chillicothe, Ohio. Endorsed: "recd. Augt 16. 1824 on my return from Va."
1 See above, Clay to Dun, July 2, 1823.
2 See above, Clay to Dun, April 23, 1822; November 3, 1823.

To Thomas Diehl

Sir Ashland 24 June 1824

Inclosed I send you an a/c. with Mr. Leonard Jacoby bal. due me $81:30—You will see accompanying it a fee bill of the Clk of the Fed. Court; and a Certificate of the Clk of the Fayette Circuit Court of my having paid the fees in the suits agt. Jordan & Keizer.[1] These persons were unfortunately all insolvent, and therefore nothing was made out of them. I have no doubt that I paid other fee bills, particularly that of the Marshall on which I cannot now lay my hands. The truth is I supposed (and yet believe) that I long since closed this matter with Mr. Jacoby. I am Your ob. Servant

H. CLAY

Tho. Deihl [*sic*] Esqr For the assignees of Leonard Jacoby

P. S. On the subject of interest I neither feel bound in law or conscience to pay it in such a stale transaction. It will be seen moreover that I was in advance for Mr. Jacoby several years before I recd. any money on his a/c. I am willing however that the whole affair may be considered now closed, without demanding the bal. of $81.30. H. CLAY

ALS. WHi.

1 Enclosures not found. Cf. above, I, 294. In Fayette Circuit Court, at its January Term, 1807, Leonard Jacoby, endorsee of Christopher Keiser, had won a judgment against John Jordan, Jr., to recover the sum of $912.66, with interest from October 18, 1806, until paid, and costs. Fayette Circuit Court, Order Book D, 69. No suit against Keiser has been found, and no action in the Federal court.

To Josiah S. Johnston

Dr Sir Ashland 25 June 1824

I transmit you the inclosed just as I have recd. them. I have merely acknowledged the receipt of the letter & said that *you* will probably communicate the information desired. I cannot imagine that any effort for me in that State wd. be availing; but what my interest wants & most stands in need of is *demonstration*. In that view a display in that City might have a good collateral effect.

I red. the circular. Always Faithfly Yrs H CLAY

The Honble J. S. Johnston.

ALS. PHi. The documents mentioned in this letter have not been found.

Mortgage Deed from John Tilford

[June 25, 1824]

[Indenture by which John Tilford, "for and in consideration of the debt herein after mentioned, and for the further consideration of the sum of five shillings" paid by Clay to Tilford, conveys to Clay the house and lot on Main Street, Lexington, "at present occupied by the said Tilford as a store and dwelling house, fronting on the said Main Street twenty eight feet more or less and extending back at right angles to Water Street, bounded by Dr. Elisha Warfield on the North West, and by the house and lot lately owned by George Trotter used now by Elijah [W.] Craig on the South East." Whereas

Tiford is indebted to Clay in the sum of $1191.66 "lawful money of the U. States,"[1] for which he has given Clay three promissory notes in the amount of $397.22 each, bearing interest from this date, "the first payable one year, the second two years and the third three years after date," if Tilford shall pay these notes as they come due, with interest, "this deed is to be void otherwise to remain in full force and virtue."

Signed by Tilford and on the same day recorded in the office of James C. Rodes, Clerk of the Fayette County Court.]

DS, in Clay's hand. DLC-TJC (DNA, M212, R10).

[1] See above, Agreement, November 10, 1823; Clay to Harper, December 22, 1823.

To Simon Gratz and Brother

Gent. Lexington 26 June 1824

I have this day drawn upon you in favor of Robert Scott at Sixty days after sight for $6759 and at one hundred and twenty days after sight for $6759. These bills I have negotiated with the office of discount[1] here; and you will perceive that I have consulted your convenience, agreeably to your letter[2] addressed to me at the City of Washington. They will leave, according to our account, a small balance yet remaining due to the Estate in your hands, which we cannot ascertain until the payment of the bills and we shall be favored with your statement. This is exclusive of the affair of Geo. G. Taylor & Co.[3] and the controversy which grew out of it, respecting which I will thank you for any information in your power to communicate.

I am with great respect Your ob. Servant H. CLAY

acting Exor of James Morrison deced

Mess Simon Gratz & Brother. Philadelphia

ALS. PHi. Endorsed: "Red 12 July Ansd." Answer not found.

[1] Lexington branch, Bank of the United States. [2] Not found.

[3] Of Philadelphia, against whom the Morrison estate on March 26, 1826, won a judgment for $4213.10. Fayette County, Will Book G, 364.

From Isaac Chauncey

Sir 26th. June 1824

The Commissioners of the Navy have had the honour of receiving your letter of the 14″ inst. When the yarns therein referred to[1] shall arrive, the experiment will be made.

I have the honor to be. &c &c I. CHAUNCEY

To the Honorable Henry Clay Ashland near Lexington Kentucky

Copy. DNA, RG45, Navy Comrs., Misc. Letters Sent, vol. 3, p. 285. Chauncey was a member of the Board of Navy Commissioners, 1821-1824, 1832-1840.

[1] The hemp had not yet been spun into yarn.

From Josiah S. Johnston

Dear Sir. Philadelphia June 27h. 1824

I have just returned from N. York where I spent ten days. That state is in great doubt & Confusion—& Certainly no Conjecture can be formed of the vote of it for President. There are three parties—One for Crawford—one for Adams & one for yourself— Neither has a majority— What measures will be adopted—What Combinations formed—or Arrangements made—is beyond Calculation— A Committe [*sic*] of Correspondence was organized in the City to write to all your friends throughout the state— They are now on the guard—& will be alert— Their organization was too long neglected —& the other parties have gain'd ground by our supineness— It is now understood that they will be all present at the meeting of the Legislature[1]— They have the power now to Controul the Election Law & Can either retain it or repeal it by a new one— They will be governed by Circumstances—& with a view to your interest— Neither party under the present Law are strong enough to Carry a General ticket without the Concurrence of your friends— If therefore the parties form a ticket, dividing the state equally with you—It will be Concurred in In this event you Can not fail to be returned to be returnd [*sic*] to the House & the fourth person[2] must be sought for among the other Candidates

Public opinion is so divided—the population so numerous—the partizans so active—that as a stranger I can form no Idea of the result— I trust to the numbers Zeal—& influence of your friends to do all that Can be done— They are now fully apprized of your strength—& the importance of their adherence— The Evening Post[3] & the Statesman both offerd to come out freely & openly in your Cause—your friends hesitated—dreading the unfavorable influence of their politicks— I left it altogether to Mr. Tillotson the District atto[4] who I found the most intelligent & able friend there— My own opinion was that the effect would be favorable— Some hopes were entertaind of the *Patriot* & the *Advocate*—[5]

I have not yet heard from Genl Porter—[6]

There was a meeting some days ago in Jersey—in which three Counties were to meet to nominate you— We have not receivd the result—[7]

Great exertions are making every where but most of the Nominations are merely expressions of Minorities— The doubt with regard to the fourth Candidate is as great as to the Presidency & depends upon as many Contingencies— It is of the first importance that the Western States remain firm & United They have every motive to adhere—& little to hope by seperation— They will be lost by division— You will see that the strength of the parties is nearly equal— The loss of one of the states may throw either of them in the rear—& it will be extraordinary if there are not greater changes— If the West feel any pride or interest in the Event, Let them adhere with Confidence—I am told we may depend on three Districts in Maryland.

I found many friends here—who have written to their friends in the Country—There is great division. But the *nomination*[8] will probably Carry— Crawfords friends had a meeting here which only served to show their weakness—& was very unadvised—[9] North Carolina is ballancing—& it is very doubtful if they will not go over to the Genl.—[10] It is now of the first importance, to Let your friends in Kentucky place this question fairly before the people of the western states—& to send to your friends here & in *Albany*—the papers expressive of their determination to adhere.

If they remain firm—all is safe——

With great regard Yr. obt sert J. S. JOHNSTON

ALS. InU. Addressed to Clay at Lexington.

1 Cf. above, Clay to Hammond, June 21, 1824.

2 Cf. above, Clay to Porter, January 31, 1824.

3 Founded as a Federalist organ in 1801 and edited by William Coleman until his death in 1829.

4 Robert Tillotson, of New York, who had been appointed the Federal Attorney in January, 1820, and reappointed at the expiration of his commission in 1824.

5 The New York *National Advocate*.

6 Peter B. Porter.

7 A meeting at Paterson, New Jersey, on June 19, of residents of Bergen, Morris, and Essex counties had "decidedly recommended" Clay for the Presidency and appointed a committee of correspondence to further this end. Lexington *Kentucky Reporter,* July 19, 1824.

8 See above, Clay to Brooke, March 6, 1824.

9 The meeting had been held at the county courthouse on June 16, when an address to the public had been issued and delegates appointed to meet with Crawford supporters from the rest of the State in formation of an electoral ticket.

10 Andrew Jackson.

Receipt from Robert Scott

[June 28, 1824]

[Robert Scott, guardian for Mary Ann Holmes, acknowledges receipt from Henry Clay, as executor of the state of James Morrison, of the sum of $1,000, "in full of a legacy of that sum bequeathed by the Will of the deceased to Mary Ann Holmes,[1] which said sum was loaned for her use to Richd. Hawes by the said Clay on the 31 day of Octr. 1823." Received in addition, $40, the interest on the loan to date, "the said Hawes having repaid the said principal sum and paid the said interest."]

ADS. DLC-TJC (DNA, M212, R16).

1 Besides the monetary legacy, Morrison had bequeathed land to the value of $3,000 to his grand niece, the daughter of Daniel Holmes, deceased. Scott had been urged "to pay particular attention to the child who is an orphan that has lost both her father and mother." Fayette County, Will Book F, 65.

From James Gambier

IVER GROVE, June 29, 1824.

MY DEAR SIR,—I had great pleasure in receiving your very friendly letter by the hand of the worthy Bishop Chase,[1] and in hearing of your well being from him. I have found him, as you truly describe him, a learned, pious, and highly estimable clergyman; he passed a few days with me here, on his first arrival in this country, and I have had much agreeable communication with him since that time; he gains the esteem and affection of all persons with whom he has become acquainted, he is highly respected, and has been received with great kindness wherever he has gone, and I am happy to say he has been very successful in the important object of his visit in this country. I very much regret that he is under the necessity of returning so soon to his diocese; but he leaves an excellent Christian savour among the good and pious of our land. I hope we shall add more to the collection that has been made for the good and laudable work in which he is so piously and zealously engaged.

It is a cause of great satisfaction to me that so much success has attended the good Bishop's visit to this country, for I greatly rejoice on every occasion that in any way promotes mutual friendship and good will between the people of our two countries.

I feel very sensibly the kind and friendly expressions in your letter, toward me, and happy in every opportunity of assuring you of my high esteem and sincere regard.

Colton (ed.), *Private Correspondence of Henry Clay,* 95-96.
[1] See above, Clay to Gambier, August 20, 1823.

From Daniel Call

Dear Sir, Richmond June 30th. 1824

Your letter, of the 5th. Instant,[1] came to hand several days ago, and would have been attended to sooner, but some political phenomena were beginning to appear, which I thought it would be well enough to watch the progress of a little before I wrote—

The tarif [*sic*] had produced such excitement in this State, that, upon the first news of Mr Crawfords ill health, his friends were mostly inclined to favour M[r] Adams; but the letter of the latter to some person in Ohio relative to internal Improve[ments][2] either is, or is affected to be, the cause of a total revulsion of opinion among many of them: The Richmond party as it is called, although they have not expressly committed themselves, have yet dropt hints upon several occasions which indicate a dereliction of Mr Adams, and a disposition towards you, if Mr Crawford should, from *any* cause, not continue a candidate; and I hear from several parts of the country, that the sentiment is diffusing itself— Indeed, until the late accounts of Mr Crawfords probable recovery of his health, your friends were making arrangements for a new edition of your ticket, with a supplemental address, and a substitution of several more popular electors, than some of those originally named[3]— But the convalescence of that gentleman has suspended operations; for so long as he is considered as a candidate, it will be in vain to expect that the votes of this State will be given to any other person— If however he should relapse, or New York should abandon him, I have not the least doubt that the suffrages of Virginia will finally centre on you— In the mean time, I stil[l prac]tise myself, and recommend it to others, to bend before the storm, and carefully to avoid giving any offence to the friends of Mr Crawford— This conduct, I am persuaded, has had the happiest effects hitherto, and will gradually smooth the way to success, if either of the above mentioned occurrences should take place— There is a very current opinion here, that General Jackson will get North Carolina; and if so it will lessen the Chanc[e] of Mr Crawfords election; but as it will not be absolutely decisive, I do not beleive [*sic*] that that circumstance alone will make the Virginians give him up— Besides [w]hat is said in the Washington Republican of the 26th. Instant,[4] it is rumoured this morning that there were unfavourable accounts relative to the health of Mr Crawford, brought by a gentleman from Washington last evening— But there is so much uncertainty in all intelligence of that kind, that I never [*credit*] it. Great efforts are making by the friends of Mr Adams, whose election is supported wi[th] great vivacity by the Whig;[5] but, notwithstanding all that, I think Virginia will not consent to go to New England for a President. The Enquirer[6] of yesterday accused him of being a friend to the Tarif; and an ultra federalist in his exposition of the constitution: Two or three hits more of that kind from the same party would ruin his cause in the old dominion— I am apprehensive that I shall find it necessary to go to the Western country this summer; and, if so, I will endeavour to see you, although I shall probably be in a hurry when I pass through the upper parts of Kentucky—Should any thing material occur before I go, I will communicate it; for as the Election approaches every thing relative to it is important to the candidates— With best respects to Mrs Clay and the family, I am dear Sir your very sincere friend and well wisher DAN CALL

ALS. DLC-HC (DNA, M212, R1). Addressed to Clay at Lexington. MS. torn and faded.

1 Not found.

2 In the letter, addressed to a resident of Washington County, Adams claimed that his resolution of February 23, 1807, in the United States Senate, represented "the *first* resolution . . . that ever was presented to the Congress, contemplating a *general system* of Internal Improvement." He stated his belief that the Congress had the

power to appropriate money and to authorize works for such improvements, "subject always to the territorial rights of the several States in or through which the improvement is to be made, to be secured by the consent of their legislatures, and the proprietary rights of individuals to be purchased or indemnified." He expressed "heartfelt satisfaction" that the opposition was "gradually yielding to the paramount influence of the *general welfare*." Washington *Daily National Intelligencer*, July 15, 1824, reprinted from the Hagerstown, Maryland, *Torch Light*.

3 Cf. above, Clay to Brooke, March 16, 1824.

4 The item noted that for the past nine months Crawford had been "incapable of attending to the duties of his Department" and that there was not "the least probability" that he would "be able to discharge its duties for months to come, notwithstanding the flattering accounts of his rapid recovery." The writer then commented upon the illegality of conducting the business of the Treasury Department over a facsimile signature. Reprinted in Lexington *Kentucky Reporter*, July 12, 1824.

5 The Richmond, Virginia, *Constitutional Whig* had been established in January, 1824, as a semiweekly journal and continued publication, under various titles, until 1888. Its founder, John Hampden Pleasants, son of James Pleasants, had been graduated from William and Mary College in 1817, had studied law, and had begun practice in Lynchburg, Virginia. Turning from the law, he had edited the Lynchburg *Virginian* for a short time in 1823 before settling in Richmond.

6 Richmond *Enquirer*.

Receipt from Thomas S. Page

State of Kentucky Auditors Office Frankfort 1st July 1824

Received of Henry Clay & John Rowan by Porter Clay the treasurers receipt for two thousand two hundred and fifty six dollars dated the 29th of January last, and the Treasurers receipt of this date for five hundred dollars making in all two thousand seven hundred & fifty six dollars in specie, the same being in part of the money, directed by the Legislature at their November Session 1823 to be refunded by them as Counsel to Virginia, and to the Supreme Court of the United States[1]

Given under my hand as Clk. for Porter Clay Auditor of Public Accounts the date above— THOS. S. PAGE

ADS. DLC-HC (DNA, M212, R1). Page, born in New York and reared in Virginia, as a young man had removed to Frankfort and was himself State Auditor for two decades (1839-1859).

1 See above, Legislative Act, December 18, 1823. The Treasurer's receipts have not been found.

To Edward Everett

Dr Sir Lexington 3 July 1824

I recd. your obliging letter of the 14h. Ulto.[1] and thank you for the trouble which you have had the goodness to take in designating a person supposed by you and President Kirkland to be the most eligible Candidate, that you can name, for the vacant professorship in Transylvania. I shall lay what you have stated, in relation to Mr. Hayward,[2] the gentleman proposed, before the Board of Trustees which I have no doubt will give it a consideration corresponding with the very high respect which the Board entertains for both yourself and President Kirkland. The appointment of the professor to the existing vacancy is an affair of great importance to the interests of our University, and one therefore on which the Board will take full time for thorough deliberation. It will probably not be made until towards or during the autumn, if it should not be longer delayed.

In respect to the question, on which some observations have passed between us, regarding the interpretation of the Constitution, you are certainly right, I think, in stating that the Union is not the Nation. The Constitution is however the instrument according to which the Nation has agreed it shall be governed; and we must look therefore to its provisions for the powers of government. The nation may alter that constitution, in the mode which itself has prescribed; but until altered it is the grant and the limit of the government. The *government* can not go out of the Constitution, and appeal to our existence as a Nation for a source of power. If the Union were dissolved, the Nation would continue undoubtedly to exist, but it would exist in the form of its unassociated elements —in the shape of the 24 Sovereign states which compose it, unless out of its fragments other combinations should be formed. If there be powers, relating to the whole, which the parts cannot exercise, because of that relation; and which the whole cannot exercise because they are not to be found in the constitution, we must conclude that they lie dormant only to be called forth by a regular amendment of the Constitutional instrument. Such powers its framers believed might exist & hence the provision in regard to amendments to supply defects as well as to curtail excesses.

You need not fear that I shall ever consider speculative suggestions made by you as formed opinions.

With high respect I am faithfully Yrs H. CLAY

E. Everett Esqr.

ALS. MHi. Cf. above, Clay to Everett, April 22, 1824.

1 Not found.

2 Probably James Hayward, who, having been graduated from Harvard College in 1819, had remained there as tutor of mathematics. He did not come to Transylvania but, instead, in 1826 became a professor at Harvard. Three years later he left academic life to devote himself to the profession of civil engineering.

From Thomas S. Hinde

Hon H Clay. Newport Ky July 7th 1824

Dear Sir/

I am preparing to go on to Columbus, having recently returned from Chillicothe—

Charles Vattier Offers $5000 in notes well secured for the lot Sold

Lytle—& pay 250$ towards the *Costs* Lytle bought 70 *odd feet*— Vattier agrees to suffer a decree to be entered against himself & Co. Defts— I think he ought to give $7000. As you are interested, I wish an expression of your mind on the Subject early in the day if you please— The contract with Lytle has been *rescinded,* he being unable to pay anything— I am in possession of Lytle's part, I wish your advice on the subject Yr friend TH: S. HINDE

ALS. DLC-TJC (DNA, M212, R12). Addressed to Clay at "Hotel Cincinnatti [*sic*]." See above, Bond, January 6, 1821.

From Francis T. Brooke

My Dear Sir July 12h 1824

I Should reproach myself for not writing you Sooner, if my Silence had in the Smallest degree prejudiced your interest, The precarious State of Mr Crawfords health gave some ground for the expectation that ere this, he would have been left out of veiw [*sic*] to the Presidency, when your friends would exert all their zeal and activity in your behalf— before I left Richmond I ascertained as certainly as possible in Such case, that in that event a majority of his committee would prefer you to either of the other candidates—if I may use that expression in relation to an office so important,— on the receipt of your Short Letter,[1] I intimated the information it contained to Mr Chapman Johnston, and others and was happy to find that though reluctantly they would embrace the alternative of Supporting you in preference to anyone else after Mr Crawford, your Speeches on the Tariff had made a Strong impression against you, and on that acct the Editors of the Enquirer[2] were casting about for some other Successor to Mr Crawford, and I have no doubt that the opinions of Johnston Nicholas & Leigh[3] who I heard declare their opinions on the alternative, indeed I pressed them with an explicit declaration that they would not Support Adams or Jackson—has influenced the gentlemen to again change their ground and if Mr. Cs health declines I am pretty Sure they must Support you— I received a letter from Mr Colston recanting his preference for Mr Crawfd and availing myself of it I as you will perceive by the papers prompted him to get up a meeting in his County in your behalf[4]— before I left Richmd I prepared Some preliminary remarks on the Claims of Jackson & Adams to a Set of resolutions to be brought on in Goochland,[5] and but for the supposed recovery of Mr Crawford they would have appeared before this in that county you are really Stronger than any of them, but your friends think, that it will be useless to aggrevate the dissentions in the

State— and untill it is understood that Mr Crawford is out of the question either from bad health or his loosing N.Y— they are disinclined to further disturb its harmony— whatever you may think of appearances in Virga. I think it impossible that either Mr Adams or Genl Jackson can get its vote, I may be mistaken but I am confident that in the absence of Mr Crawfords pretensions—you will be preferred to either of them— I have received a Letter from Messrs Fitzhugh Mason &c of Fairfax[6] asking a cooperation, against the caucus candidate but I have declined it, for reasons which I have well considered, Mr Crawford will be preferred in Virga to any body— and it is most favourable to your interest to let the gentlemen fret & vex his friends, as much as possible in the event, that he is dropt, you will more certainly get their vote, I am now Setting out to the Sulphur Springs[7] for my Sons[8] health and Somewhat for my own, I shall have an opportunity to See and hear more of the actual feelings of Virginia on the Subject of the Presidential election than at home and on my return will be at the Convention (if one can be gotten up) at Charlottesville,[9] where much may be done in the event that Mr Crawford is then out of the question, which I think is highly probable if not certain— by that time N Y will have declared herself &c— I have written you in haste and fear you will not easily read my Scrawl— but you must take the will for the deed and beleive me Sincerely your friend FRANCIS BROOKE

ALS. DLC-HC (DNA, M212, R1). Addressed to Clay at Lexington.

1 See above, May 28, 1824.

2 Thomas Ritchie and Claiborne W. Gooch, of the Richmond *Enquirer*.

3 Chapman Johnson; Philip N. Nicholas; Benjamin W. Leigh.

4 Edward Colston, of Berkeley County, Virginia (now West Virginia), a member of the State House of Delegates. A graduate of Princeton, Colston had become a lawyer, had served in the War of 1812, had been a member of the Fifteenth Congress (1817-1819), and was long active in State and local politics.

The Berkeley County meeting had been held at the courthouse in Martinsburg on June 14, when resolutions had been adopted calling for cooperation with Clay's Virginia friends to elevate him to the Presidency and appointment of committees to prepare an address to the public and to correspond in his support. Lexington *Kentucky Reporter,* July 5, 1824.

5 No record of a Goochland County meeting has been found.

6 William Henry Fitzhugh of "Ravensworth," Fairfax County, Virginia, was proprietor of extensive land holdings and a director of the Fairfax Turnpike Road, later a vice president of the American Colonization Society, a member for one term of the Virginia legislature, and a delegate to the State constitutional convention of 1829. He died in 1830, at the age of forty.

The reference here is probably to James Murray Mason, rather than to his father, General John Mason, both of Analosten Island. The younger man had been admitted to the bar in 1820 and served in the Virginia House of Delegates from 1826 to 1832, the United States House of Representatives, 1837-1839, and the United States Senate, 1847-1861.

7 Probably the White Sulphur Springs, Greenbrier County, Virginia (now West Virginia). This famous resort had been developed by James Calwell (Caldwell), formerly a Baltimore merchant, who had acquired an interest in the property in 1795 and had become sole proprietor by 1816.

8 Probably the youngest son, Francis E., who lived until 1874.

9 No convention was held.

From William B. Astor

Dear Sir, New York 13th. July 1824.

I have had the honor to receive your letter of the 28th ulto enclosing a check for $6000 & one for $1500 together Seven Thousand five Hundred Dollars on the U S. Bank[1] to be placed to the credit of your bond held by my father[2]— At Foot you have statement of the interest that will be due on your bond the 24 August next

I am with great regard Your most obedient Servant

To, The Honorable Henry Clay Lexington Kenty. Wm. B Astor

Interest on Bond for $20,000 to 1st Augst 1 yr.		$1400
Less interest on $5000 frm 8 Decr.		
7 mo. 24 Dys	227.50	
" " 7500 " 16 July 16	23.33	250.83
due 1st Augst 1824		$1149.17

ALS. DLC-TJC (DNA, M212, R12).

1 The letters and checks have not been found. 2 See above, II, 686, 687n.

To Joseph Anderson

Dr Sir Columbus 14h. July 1824

I have been induced to recommend to your indulgence the case of Mr. Robert McCllaran [*sic*][1], a debtor of the U.S. against whom Judgment has been recovered in this State, believing that it is your disposition to extend it as far as you can consistently with the duties you owe to Government. Mr. McClaran [*sic*] is not very particularly known to me, but from what I do know and have heard of him, I think him entitled to all the lenity which can be shewn compatible with the public safety and security. He has experienced already some evidence of that disposition in the terms which have been heretofore extended to him, with which he has been able to comply only in part. What he would now solicit is a forbearance of two years for the entire balance which he owes instead of enforcing payment of the several instalments which he has heretofore stipulated to pay; and this he asks upon giving the most abundant additional *security* that may be required. His means, he tells me, are ample, provided he could convert them without ruinous sacrifices, into cash. But the impracticability of doing that at present is a fact which I am persuaded you will readily believe. Can Government be injured by the indulgence requested? Is it not better that it should wait the time proposed, upon the condition suggested, rather than ruin an industrious and meritorious Citizen?

If you can conceive it, as I hope you may, to be proper to accord to him this indulgence, the Atto. or Marshall for this district might be instructed to take the additional security, to be such as he should deem sufficient, and a suspension of the execution accordingly ordered. Be pleased to inform Mr. McClaran at Wooster in Wayne County in Ohio of your determination on this subject.

I have the honor to be Your obedient Servant H. CLAY.

Jos. Anderson Esq. Comptroller &c &c. &c

ALS. DNA, RG206, Misc. Letters Received. Handwritten postmark: "Wooster O July 19." Endorsed on cover: "Respectfully refered [*sic*] to the Agent of the Treasury J A–"; endorsed at bottom of letter: "Wrote to the Attorney of ohio [*sic*] the 6 Augt 1824. S[tephen]. P[leasanton]."

1 Robert McClarren had been a member of the Ohio House of Representatives during the Session of 1823-1824.

From Thomas Diehl

Henry Clay Esqr. Sir Philad. July. 15. 1824

The assignees of Leonard Jacoby have Recd. your favour of 24 Ultimo. we do not acquies [*sic*] in the Statement or acct. you render relative to the bals.[1] due from you. collected of Banks & owins.[2] you say you do not feell [*sic*] bound in Law or conceince [*sic*] to allow Interest, it is a universal practice among mercantile men to allow Interest on Running accts, & I am inclined to think in this case it should be more strictly adheared to, as mercantile men reciprocate [*sic*] advantages, but when a man acts as an agent for which he receives a compensation, I cannot conceive be [*sic*] he is at least in conceince bound if not in Law to allow Interest for money in his hands perticulary [*sic*] such a length of time, however I have Stated the acct. inclosed upon liberal prnicipals saying nothing about the Interest due from Bank & owing [*sic*], which is certainly due the Estate of Mr. Jacoby, but commenced the acct. 30 augt. 1808 being the date you Settle [*sic*] with B & owins. and allowing you Interest on your charges which leaves a bals. due the Estate of Mr. Jacoby of $78.17– this mode I think cannot but be satisfactory to you, *on reflection,* by your remitting us the the [*sic*] Said bals. we will then close the transaction. we wish to hear from you early whilst the buisness [*sic*] is fresh on our minds

Your obat [*sic*] Servt THOMAS DIEHL
for the Assignees of Leonard Jacoby

[Enclosure][3]

Dr. Henry Clay Esqr in acct. with Leonard Jacoby.

1808		
Augst. 30th.	To this Sum Recd. of Banks & Owins this date	$291.22
	To interest on the able [*sic*] to 21 May 1824–	274.56.
		$565.78

1824	Cr.		
July. 15.	By. Amot. of your bill of charges.	$122.50	
	By Interest on the above from 30 Augt. 1808 to 21. May 1824	115.11	
	By Cash Recd. p Letter dated 21 May. 1824	250.—[4]	
			$487.61
	Bals due	Dollars	78.17

Philad. July 15. 1824

THS. DIEHL for the Assignees of Leonard Jacoby

ALS. Fayette Circuit Court, File 665 (1828).

1 Balance. 2 Owings.

3 ADS. Fayette Circuit Court, File 665 (1828).

4 Letter not found. See above, Diehl and Others to Clay, January 21, 1824, note. On November 12, 1824, Clay filed suit against Leonard Jacoby's assignees and Andrew F. Price in an effort to recover this sum, which, he declared, he had paid without recollecting that he had already fully accounted to Price, agent for the assignees. The defendants answered that the sum had not been paid by mistake, that it had been applied to Clay's account with them, and that a balance was yet due. The Fayette Circuit Court decreed, on September 20, 1826, that Price, the only one of the defendants resident in Fayette County, pay Clay so much of the property of Jacoby's assignees as he might have to the amount of $250 with interest from May 21, 1824, until paid. Fayette Circuit Court, Order Book no. 5, p. 29; File 638 (1826).

In a second suit, begun December 4, 1826, Clay charged that the proceeds from the sale of four tons of iron castings, upon which execution of the former judgment had been levied, had not satisfied the obligation. He contended further that the answer, exhibits, and commissioner's report in the earlier suit indicated that he should have had a larger sum than that awarded. Price answered, March 3, 1827, and on February 6, 1828, the case was dismissed on motion of Clay's attorney. Fayette Circuit Court, File 665 (1828).

Speech at Chillicothe Banquet

[July 17, 1824]

Upon Clay's arrival in Chillicothe, Ohio, returning from the sitting of the Federal Court at Columbus, a public dinner was held for him, "attended by between fifty and sixty gentlemen." A number of toasts were drunk, "among which was one in honour of Mr. CLAY; for which he returned thanks in an appropriate address . . . [not further reported]." Lexington *Kentucky Reporter,* August 2, 1824.

From William B. Astor

Dear Sir, New York. 17th July 1824

I have had the honor to receive your letter of the 3d inst[1] covering a check for $500 Five Hundred Dollars on account of the interest which will become due on your bond to my father the 1st Augst next— I am with great regard your most obedient Servant

WM. B ASTOR

To, The Honorable Henry Clay Lexington Kenty.

ALS. DLC-TJC (DNA, M212, R12). See above, Astor to Clay, July 13, 1824.
1 Not found.

From S[amuel] L. S[outhard]

Sir, Navy Dep'mt. 20. July, 1824.

In order to discharge a public duty, I wish to procure the most extensive and accurate information respecting the cultivation and manufacture of Hemp in the United States. I shall be thankful for any information you can furnish or procure for me, at an early day, respecting the places where, and the extent to which it may be cultivated; the manner of raising, and preparing it for market—its quality, compared with foreign Hemp, and every thing relating to its manufacture; with any suggestions as to the manner in which its cultivation, curing, or manufacture, may be improved.

I am, respectfully, &c. S. L. S.

Copy. DNA, RG45, General Letter Book, vol. 14, p. 431. Copies of this letter were sent to David Barton; James De Wolf; James Lloyd; Thomas H. Benton; John F. Parrott; Winslow Lewis, of Boston, Massachusetts, ship captain, lighthouse designer, contractor, and manufacturer of rope and duck; Walter Heron (Herron), a wealthy ropemaker of Norfolk, Virginia; Tucker and Carter, of New York; John Travers and John Elliott, both of Paterson, New Jersey; and the Commissioners of the Navy.

To Josiah S. Johnston

Dear Sir Columbus (Ohio) 21st. July 1824

Your favor under date at Philadelphia on the 27h. June has followed me from Lexington to this place. I thank you for it. The picture which it pourtrays of the condition of things in N. York, compared with other means of ascertaining its correctness, I should suppose faithful. It certainly offers every motive to animated and persevering exertion. I concur with you in thinking that the appearance in my favor of the two papers you have mentd. as being willing so to come out, would be advantageous. On their part it is perfectly voluntary. They are unbought. No imputation of that kind could be possibly made. None can be made against me either of Clintonian or Federal taint. Or if such imputations were made they would not be credited by the unbiased and impartial which must compose a large portion of the American population.

Before I came to this State, popular meetings in various Counties had been held. Some have occurred since I entered it. The evidence derivable from their expression of preference among the P. Candidates, places beyond all sort of doubt the final result here. These meetings have been held in some of the most populous Counties in the State. And my friends speak in a tone of the most perfect confidence. A meeting was called here of casual attendants on the

Fed. Court, but many of whom were among the most respectable Citizens of this State. About 300 assembled on a short public notice. I transmit you their proceedings.[1] On the same night, in the same house those of Mr. Adams assembled. They amounted in number, I understand, only to 14, 'though the address of my friends, from abundant caution, states it not to have exceeded 20. They too published an address, which you will see, and from which you will remark they rest principally upon "hope." Mortified at the paucity of their numbers, they have since got up another meeting (last night) the persons principally composing which were actually brought down in carriages and waggons from Worthington, a neighbouring settlement composed chiefly of N. England emigrants. Bets have been offered that the electoral ticket pledged for me will be chosen by more than 10.000 over all the Candidates.[2]

There is not a County in K. in which I shall not obtain a decided majority; and measures are in progress to prevent any possible loss of a vote from the multitude of Electoral Candidates in my favor.

The effort at New Orleans for Genl. Jackson, by means of a public meeting, you will have heard was defeated by another meeting much more numerously & respectably attended, which was afterwards convened.[3] Indiana, Illinois and Missouri continue firm and unshaken.

I have just heard of the result of the New Jersey meeting, though I have seen no account which shews how far it may be relied on as a fair expression of the sentiment of the three Counties.[4]

Was ever any thing more singular than the incident which occurred at the City of Washington on the celebration of our anniversary? The indiscretion in excluding Mr. Edwards was not greater than that of the voluntary exclusion to which it gave rise.[5]

I shall leave this place tomorrow for Lexington—

With great regard I am faithfly Yrs H. Clay

The Honble J. S. Johnston

ALS. PHi. Published in part in Colton (ed.), *Private Correspondnece of Henry Clay*, 97.

1 At this meeting, held at the United States Circuit Courthouse on July 15, the ticket of electors already published (see above, Clay to Porter, April 26, 1824), with one change, was approved. Nathan Sanford was nominated for Vice President; a general committee, composed of one person in each county of the State, was established; and a committee was appointed to prepare and publish an address and a record of the proceedings of the meeting. Lexington *Kentucky Reporter*, July 26, August 2, 9, 1824.

2 Cf. below, Clay to Brooke, November 26, 1824.

3 The first meeting was reported, without record of date, in Washington *Daily National Intelligencer*, June 28, 1824; *Niles' Weekly Register*, XXVI (July 17, 1824), 333. Further reference to the second meeting has not been found.

4 See above, Johnston to Clay, June 27, 1824.

5 The committee of arrangements for a public dinner at Washington on July 4 had been prevailed on by friends of William H. Crawford to exclude Ninian Edwards from the affair (cf. above, Clay to Porter, April 26, 1824, note). Unwilling to be placed in the position of tacitly approving this exclusion, Secretaries Adams and Calhoun and Postmaster General McLean had published a joint letter announcing the withdrawal

of their subscriptions to the dinner. Adams, *Memoirs,* VI, 396-99; *Niles' Weekly Register,* XXVI (July 10, 1824), 299.

From R. D. Richardson

Dear Sir, New Orleans, July 21st. 1824.

Allow me to introduce to your acquaintance, and civilities, Mr. Ira Ingram, formerly of Nashville.[1] Mr. Ingram is my particular friend, and my confidential agent. I have intrusted to him, the arrangement and liquidation of all my pecuniary affairs, in the western States, and I shall feel particularly obliged, by any assistance you may render him, in any transaction in my behalf, in which he may be engaged. The two hundred dollars referred to in a letter[2] transmitted some days by mail, if not forwarded by the medium of the post office, previous to the receipt of this, you will greatly oblige me by paying over to Mr. Ingram— This sum having been advanced by me to your son Theodore.

You will find Mr. Ingram a gentleman of intelligence and urbainty [*sic*]; and any questions which friendship or curiosity may prompt you to make, in regard to me, he will able [*sic*] to answer.

Truly and Sincerely I am dear Sir, Your friend, & obt. srt.

Hon: H. Clay. Lexington Ky R. D. RICHARDSON

[Endorsement on verso][3]

Recd. a check[4] on the off. of Dt. & Dt. of Lexn. for the within sum of Two hundred dollars. 12 Aug. 1824.

IRA INGRAM Agent for R. D. Richardson.

ALS. DLC-TJC (DNA, M212, R12). Richardson, formerly a resident of Ohio, was (1823-1826) editor of the New Orleans *Louisiana Gazette.*

1 In January, 1826, Ingram, originally from Vermont, settled on the San Bernard River in Texas, where he became a merchant and planter and figured prominently in the revolt against Mexico. He was later Speaker of the House in the first Congress of the Republic of Texas.

2 Not found. 3 ES, in Clay's hand. 4 Not found.

From Jabez D. Hammond

Dear Sir, Albany (N. Y.) July 28″ 1824

I had last evening a conversation with Genl. Mc.Clure,[1] a Member of the Legislature of this State, in which he informed me that he had ascertained to *a certainty* that your Friends in the Legislature tho' not numerous were yet sufficiently so, to prevent the choice of Electors either for Mr. Crawford or Mr. Adams— They have he says to a man determined to *continue* to give their votes for 36 Electors who will vote for you. The result then will be that either the votes of this State will be given to you or the electoral vote of New York will be lost— The only way in which this result can be avoided is by some of the Friends of Mr. Adams joining the Friends of Mr.

Crawford or by a desertion of Mr. C's friends to Mr. A– But the Adams men say they prefer you to Mr. Crawford and the Crawford men that *they* prefer you to Mr. Adams– With these feelings towards each other it is hardly possible for them to coalesce– Genl. Jackson can scarcely be said to have a party in our Legislature

Much ill nature will be illicited [*sic*] at the meeting of the Legislature next Week—but no inteligent [*sic*] man seriously anticipates the passage of an Electoral Law[2]—

If the *real* state of things in New York is not known to your friends at the west it strikes me it ought to be– The only apology I can offer for troubling *you* with this letter is that I am not acquainted with any person in your State with whom I can with safety & propriety communicate on this subject—

Should the State of New York give no vote at all or should its 36 Votes be given for you I consider your election as almost certain; an event to me most desireable, not only on account of the high respect I entertain for your talents and character, but because I religiously believe that the Northern & Western States immediately, and the whole Nation eventually must depend for prosperity on the perseverance of the government in the *"Domestic policy"* you have so ably sustained and that you are the *only* Candidate for the Presidency who is committed to that policy–

With highest respect I am Your Obedt. Servt.

The honle. H. Clay– JABEZ D. HAMMOND

ALS. DLC-HC (DNA, M212, R1). 1 George McClure.

2 See above, Woods to Clay, August 27, 1823, note: Clay to Charles Hammond, June 21, 1824.

To Benjamin W. Leigh

My dear Sir Ashland 31st. July 1824

My absence from home, attending the Fed. Court at Columbus, has delayed my acknowledgment of the receipt of your obliging letter under date the 4h. inst.[1] communicating the very satisfactory result of the action for Euphraim.[2] I am sure that my brothers will share with me in feeling the great obligation under which you have placed us by your prompt constant and successful attention to this matter. On my arrival at Washn. next autumn I will defray any cost incident to the prosecution of the suit, of which reimbursement may not be effected from the defts, together with an extra fee of fifty dollars for your kind attention to our interests.

In respect to the possession, I would be glad, if you should happen to see Mr. Tinsley[3] of Hanover, that you would request him to take it for us and to rent out the property for this year; or Col. Burfoot of Manchester,[4] who I am sure will take this trouble for us. I suppose the persons in possession will wish to rent the property for the present year, and a line from you stating that Mr. Tinsley or Col. B. (as the one or the other may be good enough to assume the agency) is authorized to lease it will supercede [*sic*] the necessity of a formal power of attorney.

Your advice not to prosecute for the mesne profits shall be pursued, with the reservation only that the defts shall abstain from giving us further trouble in litigation.

The regard which you have felt and manifested towards our State induces me to say one word on its present condition. The affair of the occupying claimant laws[5] does not continue to create much excitement. The public hopes appear to rest on the forfeiting law passed at the last Session of our Legislature[6] and on the prospect, however uncertain, of a future change in the opinion of the Supreme Court,[7] or the adoption of some equitable rule of compensation for improvements. But there is, at this moment, the eve of our general elections, very great agitation in relation to certain decisions of our local Courts, which have grown out of the "Relief system,"[8] terms with which you are familiar. In regard to that system, public sentiment was fast correcting itself, and the vessel of state would have soon been righted. These decisions constitute a new, 'though collateral, cause of division, which produces as much zeal, heat and intolerance as the parent cause ever did. The question now is, with the different parties, between the Judiciary and the Legislature, whether the acts of the latter supposed to be incompatible with the Constitution shall be declared null by the former or not. The issue on that point is to be tried the three first days of next week, and what the verdict will be is very doubtful.[9]

On the general proposition, that it belongs to the Judiciary to declare the invalidity, in the particular causes before it, of those acts of the Legislative authority which are seriously believed to be repugnant to the Constitution, I never could doubt. I am however rather inclined to think that the Courts have some times pushed the principle too far and that, creating themselves into a sort of tribunal to remedy *all* the public evils, at least *all* the evils of bad legislation, they have not allowed to operate other probably more efficacious correctives. If the basis of all our free institutions be sound (of which I cannot doubt) that is, that man is competent to self government, there can be no doubt that, in the end, most of the pernicous [*sic*] acts of legislation would be rectified by the operations of public sentiment. When so corrected there is always tranquillity & general acquiescence— But if, during the existence of the excitement, the Courts interpose, the consequence is that the public disorders are prolonged instead of being healed. Such is our experience. I do not condemn our Courts. I have great confidence in them; and I do not entertain a doubt but that they have discharged what they deemed a conscientious duty. I believe nevertheless that we should have gotten back to our former wholesome state of laws much sooner if they had not been compelled to give the decisions which they have pronounced.

I pray you to make my best respects to Mrs. Leigh and to Mrs. Wickham[10] and to believe that I remain Cordially & faithfully
Your friend & obedient Servant H. CLAY

B. W. Leigh Esqr.

ALS. ViU. 1 Not found.
2 Cf. above, Clay to Leigh, December 22, 1823. 3 Garland Tinsley.
4 Lawson Burfoot, later for many years Treasurer of Virginia. Manchester, across the James River from Richmond, was consolidated with the latter city in 1910.
5 See above, Leigh to Clay, February 12, 1823; Clay to Brooke, March 9, 1823; Clay to Leigh, December 22, 1823.
6 The act, approved January 7, 1824, to become effective July 1 of that year, provided that no person should sell or purchase land of which another person held possession adverse to the title so sold and that an attempt to recover "such pretended right or title to land . . . of which adverse possession is held under conflicting title as aforesaid," should result in forfeiture of such "right, title, interest or claim" to the Commonwealth for "the benefit of the person in possession. . . ." Among additional provisions of the measure was a requirement that "every proprietor or claimant of any tract of land within this Commonwealth" carry out before August 1, 1825, certain specified practices of cultivation and improvement or lose the land by forfeiture; a section repealing the act of December 20, 1820, concerning occupying claimants, and restoring to full force the act of January 31, 1812, which had been repealed by the 1820 statute; and a proviso that the occupants of a claim should "not be permitted to plead or rely upon the said forfeiture to the commonwealth" in land suits if the "adversary claimant whose rights, interests or claims" were forfeited for want of cultivation and improvement should, before commencing legal action, file with the court "a written engagement, under hand and seal, to the occupant or occupants," agreeing to abide by Kentucky's occupying claimant laws, including consent "that the occupant shall have a lien upon the land for payment" of the value of improvements. Ky. Gen. Assy., *Acts, 1823-1824*, pp. 443-50.
7 In 1831 the United States Supreme Court, in the case of John Hawkins and William May *vs.* Joshua Barney's Lessee, appealed from the Circuit Court of Kentucky, upheld the validity of Kentucky's limitation act, "the seven years law." Justice William Johnson, who wrote the decision of the Court in this instance, declared it "impossible to take any reasonable exception to the course of legislation pursued by Kentucky on this subject." 30 *U.S.* (5 Peters) 456-68.
8 See above, Clay to Dougherty, December 7, 1821, note; Scott to Clay, December 30, 1823, note.
9 The general election, held August 2-4, inclusive, resulted in victory for the Relief Party, although a commentator noted that "it is not believed that there will be a *Judge-breaking* majority (two-thirds) in either House" of the legislature. Joseph Desha was elected Governor. Lexington *Kentucky Reporter*, August 16, 1824.
10 Mrs. John Wickham.

From William B. Astor

Dear Sir, New York 5 August 1824

Your letter of the 24th ulto[1] I have had the pleasure to receive with a check on the United States Bank for $500 Five Hundred Dollars to be credited against the interest due on your bond to my father on the 1st inst— Receipt of the two former remittances for

$7500. & $500. together Eight Thousand Dollars I acknowledged in my letters of the 13th & 17th July which were directed to Lexington— I am with great regard Your most obedient Servt.

WM. B ASTOR.

To, The Honorable Hy Clay Lexington, Kentucky.

ALS. DLC-TJC (DNA, M212, R12). [1] Not found.

From Asher Robbins

Honble. Henry Clay. Newport. R Island Augst. 5th. 1824.

Dear Sir— The prospect here now is that your & Mr Crawford's friends, will unite. in a joint Ticket, dividing the votes equally between you; in that event there is every probability of success; but without that union, Mr. Adams I think will get a plurality.—

You have many friends here, and they are increasing; our manufacturers feel the debt of gratitude due to their great patron. This Union is the plan I have advised from the beginning, & the friends of Mr Crawford are now fast falling in with it.— I have taken the present opportunity to give you the above information, tho' the special occasion of my writing now is one personal to myself. The Office of District Judge for this District is now become vacant by the recent death of Judge Howell;[1] and my freinds [*sic*] here have been pleased to recommend me for that office; will you do me the favor to befriend the application?[2]

I am Dear Sir very, respectfully Yr freind & hble Servt

ASHER ROBBINS

ALS. DLC-HC (DNA, M212, R1).

[1] David Howell, delegate from Rhode Island to the Continental Congress (1782-1785), professor of law in Brown University since 1790, and judge of the United States District Court for Rhode Island since 1812, had died July 21, 1824.

[2] See below, Clay to Monroe, August 30, 1824.

To Nicholas Biddle

Dr Sir Lexington 7h. August 1824

I returned a few days ago from Columbus. During the term most of the actions brought by the Bank were tried and judgments obtained. The two cases against Genl. Lytle, one founded upon the judgment of the Court of Common pleas of Hamilton,[1] and the other to foreclose his equity of redemption in the property mortgaged by him near and adjoining Louisville, were both continued by the Court.[2] The grounds of this continuance were, that he had a negotiation pending with the Bank for a compromise; that Mr. Jones[3] had agreed with him that no step should be taken in the cause in Hamilton until August, from which he infered that none would be taken in the suit founded on the Judgment of Hamilton in the Federal Court; and that, under all the circumstances, connected with the change in the time of holding the Circuit Court,[4] he would be surprized, if ruled into trial. The Court continued the causes with some hesitation. I need not suggest the utility of bringing the alleged negotiation, if there be one really yet pending, to a close time enough to prevent the use of the same pretext to postpone them again. We lost two causes, one against E. Stone, in consequence of the irregularity of the notice given to him, and the other against Mack and Bates, partners of Spence,[5] who were held not to be chargeable with a transaction of their partner, who negotiated a bill with the Bank in the name of the firm for the purpose of paying his individual debt, with the knowledge of the officers of the Bank. I took exceptions to the opinion of the Court, and I directed copies of them to be transmitted to you. I was not sufficiently persuaded that the Court erred, to prosecute writs of error, and was at the same time unwilling to close all opportunity of revising its decision, if the Board shall wish to obtain the judgment of the Supreme Court on the points involved. I should have regretted the failure of the Bank to recover in these cases more, if the defendants had been certainly able, or if there were any other causes depending upon the same principles. But it was not believed that the amount of the demands could be coerced from the defendants, if judgments had been rendered against them, nor are there any suits resting on the same principles. If the Board desire the causes to be taken up to the Supreme Court, directions can be accordingly given to that effect.[6]

I again pressed upon Mr. Jones, as well as the Solicitor of the Chillicothe Office,[7] the necessity of preserving unimpaired the liens acquired by the Bank in the recovery of Judgments, and, to this end, the issuing of executions. I was assured that it had been, and would continue to be, particularly attended to in every case in which it was or might be necessary.

We feel in this State the want very much of the decision of the Supreme Court on our execution laws.[8] We must however hobble on as well as we can until the next term, when I suppose it will be certainly pronounced.

I am with great respect Your obedient Servant H. CLAY

Nicholas Biddle Esqr &c. &c. &c

ALS. PHi-Etting Collection.

1 See above, Clay to Biddle, June 11, 1823.

2 Cf. above, I, 348-49, 829; II, 127, 416; De Wolf, Jr., to Clay, January 1, 1821, note.

3 George W. Jones.

4 Under an act approved April 22, 1824, the meetings of the Circuit Court of the

United States for the District of Ohio had been shifted from the previous dates, the first Monday in January and September, annually, to the second Monday of the following July, with subsequent sittings called for the first Monday in January and June, annually, 3 *U. S. Stat.*, 544 (March 4, 1820); 4 *U. S. Stat.*, 18-19.

5 See above, Clay to Este, December 15, 1823. Spence has not been identified.

6 The cases were apparently not appealed. 7 Possibly William Key Bond.

8 See above, Clay to Hammond, July 14, 1822, note; Clay to Biddle, December 27, 1822, note.

From William Ingalls

Honle Henry Clay, Speaker of the House of Representatives in Congress. Boston August 8, 1824.

Sir,

Perhaps it may not be unacceptable to receive the following copy of a letter, addressed to the Honl. J. S. Johnson of the above date.[1]

I am, with sentiments of esteem, your obedient servant

WILLIAM INGALLS.

ALS. DLC-HC (DNA, M212, R1).

1 Ingalls had written to Johnston that the friends of Crawford in Boston proposed to nominate Clay rather than Albert Gallatin for the Vice Presidency so that, in case of Crawford's death, "we should then have a gentleman every way qualified to perform the duties of a President, & one that would be acceptable to the great majority of the people." Ingalls had expressed himself as "decidedly opposed to taking a different ground from that announced in the circular" and had requested delay until he could communicate with Clay's friends. He asked Johnston's opinion on the matter.

The circular to which he referred had been released in Washington, under date of May 25, as an announcement by "The friends of Mr. CLAY" that "they now determine to *adhere* to him steadily to the end." Recognizing that the election would pass to the House of Representatives, they continued: "If, contrary to all probability, Mr. CLAY should not be returned to the House, his friends having done their duty, will be able, by concentration, to control the event—they will hold in their hands the balance—they will determine between the opposing and conflicting interests, and secure to the country a republican administration." Washington *Daily National Intelligencer*, June 16, 1824.

Agreement with James Minter

[August 9, 1824]

[Henry Clay and James Minter agree to the following exchange of property: Clay is to convey to Minter the Tammany Mills, now in Minter's possession, "with all the houses improvements and ground appurtenant thereto," and a pair of millstones in the millhouse, the conveyance to be made upon "receipt of a clear and unincumbered title to the Land hereafter mentioned."

["In consideration of the above," Minter is to convey to Clay a farm of 220 acres, "lying on the Winchester road, now in the possession of Nathl. Petit,[1] lately the property of Thomas Wallace, and adjoining the farm of Robert Wickliffe Esqr., which was conveyed to the said Minter by Thomas Wallace." Clay is to obtain possession of the farm by January 1, 1826 (or by March 1, 1826, if Petit's lease extends to that date). Minter promises to remove a mortgage of $2,000 on the farm, held by the Bank of the United States, and another mortgage of the same amount, held by the Bank of the Commonwealth and payable in paper of that bank. Clay engages to remove a mortgage (of unspecified amount) on the Tammany Mills, held by the Bank of the Commonwealth. Both parties "agree to execute reciprocally clear titles to the above property . . . on or before the first day of January. 1826." Clay agrees to pay Minter $958 by October 1, 1825, "as the difference in the estimated value of the said Mills and farm," which sum he is not to pay, however, "until the removal of the said incumbrances from the said farm."

[Minter's lease of the Tammany Mills[2] is hereby cancelled, and he is released from the payment of any rent now due. Clay "is to convey the same extent of ground that was conveyed to him by William Allen[3] as belonging to the said mills." Clay further "agrees that he will not purchase any claim upon the said Minter as an offset against his the said Clays note aforesaid." Witnessed by Andrew McCalla.]

ADS, signed also by Minter and McCalla. DLC-TJC (DNA, M212, R16).

1 Petit (Petitt, Pettit, Pettitt) later resided about six miles from Lexington near the Tate's Creek Road.

2 Above, June 20, 1822. 3 See above, Property Deed, *ca.* May 4, 1821.

From Josiah S. Johnston

Dear Sir. Saratoga Augt. 9h. 1824

In passing through N. York, from which place I had been absent a month, I found your several favors[1]—to which I shall give due attention—

I made my arrangements to be in Albany last week The prompt declaration of the Senate with regard to the Call of the Legislature left no hope—that any new measure would be adopted— I attended the debate in the House of Representatives—where a similar sentiment was manifested, although with Less Unanimnity [*sic*][2]— I requested Mr. Rochester[3] to write you fully on the subject He is fully informed & entirely to be relied on—

The impression will now go abroad that Mr. Crawford will get this state—Which is perhaps Correct but I doubt Whether he has a majority of the State. It is my opinion that either Crawford or Adams require the Concurrence of your friends to Carry a ticket—

What use they may make of this advantage Cannot at this time be Calculated— It may result in a Compromise very favorable to you— If you Can obtain a respectable portion of this state with either it will put you on the foreground— all your friends will assemble at Albany at the Meeting of the Legislature in November & will doubtless profit by their position[4]— The Western States & your friends, have every motive to stand firm— No one Can foresee the events that may happen to give a new turn to the public mind.

There are now large *minorities* in every state— Unexpected Combinations & Compromises may be made—Candidates may die or become incapable— Some of these states may Secede—Various occurrences may intervene to render it important, that the West should act steadily & Consistently—

I understand a great change has taken place in Virginia (or Richmond) among the *Regulators* there, in Relation to Mr. Adams[5]— His Conduct—with the Editors of the Intelligencer & with regard to Edwards & his writing in his own favor in the National Journal[6]—have alienated their affections—& they have now openend [*sic*] their batteries upon him—

It was doubtless true at the close of the Session as we Conjectured—That anticipating the Issue of Mr. Crawfords illness, they had determind [*sic*] to sustain Adams & five or six men by that means would have at once Contrould the event of the Election— The friends of Crawford & Adams Consider the Contest now lies between them & their hostility will be principally directed against each other—

Mr. Crawford Continues in feeble health—& incapable of engaging in the Duties of the Executive—& I lament the necessity of *taking* him with all his infirmities—or Adams with all his passions & prejudices— Crawford had no doubt a slight paralitic stroke—he speaks with difficulty, & can scarcely pronounce many words—his tongue was much affected—his eys [*sic*] are still weak—& he is incapable of reading or writing—& I have no doubt he Uses a fac simile His walk is feeble & hobling [*sic*]— I see no indications of restoration— I see no reason to hope he Can ever recover his faculties— The members of Congress will know the truth of this before they vote & if any unfavorable turn should take place, It may throw him out of the Contest— I hope in that [*sic*] the friends of Crawford may have gone too far to rally upon Adams— You see how numerous are the Contingencies upon which the event rests— Your experience in Political life will enable you to Look Calmly upon it—

I have read the Letter of Dr. S. which you inclose me your answer is very proper[7]— He is a Political *Broker*— The proposition is a Corrupt one—& if answerd can only be answerd indignantly— If Mr. C.[8] authorized such a proposition—he has lost all integrity as well as all sense of decency— He merits all the Contempt of his enemies— I do not believe he knows any thing of it He wants public employment, & his fear of sinking into naught would no doubt induce him to go far to obtain it— His friends are Zealous & perhaps not very scrupulous & they might make such a proposition—It is an X Y & Z business[9]—

If they mean to put themselves up to sale, they will go to the highest bidder— The Doctor Calld on me on my first visit— He is an active, busy, & knowing politician & his political morality is well Calculated for the meridian of Albany & N.York—of which he has only furnished you a Common instance— you Can not escape such propositions

your Correspondence should be limited to men of high character & well known friends—& very guarded—to others you Can say that the Delicacy of your situation, pending the present Canvass, deprives you the pleasure of writing them freely upon subjects Connected with that question— In such a Contest individuals are nothing—you Can only act upon Masses— After all much will be found to depend upon Geographical Considerations—or other great Causes over which an Individual has no Controul— Mr. Adams can not write himself into that office & every time he acts personally on the Election it will hurt— The public greatly approves a dignified & retired Course— It remains to be seen whether management intrigue or Corruption Can eventually succeed—

I go from this place tomorrow to Albany & thence to N. York— from which place I shall write you again. I have just recd. yours from Columbus[10]— with great regard yr. obt Servt

J. S. JOHNSTON

ALS. InU. Addressed to Clay at Lexington.

1 See above, Clay to Johnston, June 15, 21, 25, 1824.

2 See above, Woods to Clay, August 27, 1823, note; Clay to Hammond, June 21, 1824. The Senate had promptly adopted a resolution declaring the call of the legislature unconstitutional; the House, by a vote of 66 to 53, concluded that it was "an indiscreet exercise of the Executive prerogative." Washington *Daily National Intelligencer,* August 9, 11, 1824, reprinting reports from Albany *Argus.*

3 Probably William B. Rochester. No letter to Clay from him around this date has been found.

4 See below, Clay to Stuart, December 6, 1824, note.

5 Cf. above, Call to Clay, June 30, 1824.

6 On July 1, 1824, Joseph Gales, Jr., and William W. Seaton, the editors of the Washington *Daily National Intelligencer,* had stated that the Secretary of State, who had ignored their efforts to obtain the list of awards of the Florida Claims Commission, had directed that the report be published in the Washington *National Journal* (*National Government Journal*), established by Peter Force in November, 1823, as an organ devoted to Adams' candidacy. On July 3, Adams, after consultation with the President and John C. Calhoun, had issued a reply, in which he charged that the editors of the *Intelligencer* had maligned both himself and the Administration in failing to publish supporting documents relative to the recently ratified convention for the suppression of slave trade, during the time it was under attack in the Senate. Adams protested against "the general course of the Editors of that paper, for some time past, towards the present administration. . . ." In issues of July 8, 12, 17, and 22, the editors of the *Intelligencer* had explained that their failures had been attributable to lack of space, not to ill will; that they felt that their columns should be opened to both sides of the controversial convention; that they had, in fact, supported it; and that they had long been friendly to the Republican administrations. Adams had reiterated his charges in the *Journal* of July 10, 14, and 21.

Peter Force, a native of New Jersey, who had learned the printing trade in New York City, had removed to Washington in 1815, where for some years prior to the founding of the *Journal* he had held the Government printing contract. He had held several posts in the city administration of Washington and from 1836 to 1840 served as mayor. He is best known as a collector and editor of historical and statistical data.

For the incident involving Ninian Edwards, see above, Clay to Johnston, July 21, 1824, note.

[7] See above, Clay to Stuart, June 14, 1824; Clay to Johnston, June 15, 1824.

[8] DeWitt Clinton.

[9] Prior to the quasi-war with France in 1797-1798, French emissaries, popularly identified as "X," "Y," and "Z," had requested a large loan as a condition for negotiation, a proposal which the Americans had viewed as an attempt to obtain a bribe.

[10] Above, July 21, 1824.

From John Harvie

Bank of Ky. Aug. 10th 1824

Henry Clay Esqr. Lexington Dear Sir

Our Board just now terminated its sitting. Your letter was before it and the determination was formed to accept the overture therein contained.[1] You can therefore receive of Mr Wallace the amount of the claim transferred to you in the notes of this Bank and they will be redeemed by a payment of two thirds Specie and one third notes of the Bank of the Commonwealth of Kentucky

respectfully J HARVIE Prest

Copy. Bank of Kentucky, Frankfort, Letter Book G (June 19, 1822-June 10, 1825), 374. See above, Agreement, November 10, 1823; Assignment, November 18, 1823; Clay to Harper, December 22, 1823, note; Harvie to Clay, March 8, 1824, note.

[1] The letter, not found. The action of the board is recorded in Bank of Kentucky, Record Book D, 258.

Receipt from R. D. Richardson

[August 12, 1824]

Attached to Richardson to Clay, July 21, 1824.

To [John C. Calhoun]

Sir Ashland 15h. Aug. 1824

Mr. John Bruce intending to apply for a contract to clear out a section of the Ohio river, under the act of Congress passed, at the last session,[1] I take great pleasure in expressing my belief that entire confidence may be placed in his faithful execution of any contract that he may make with Government for that purpose I have the honor to be Your obedient Servt. H. CLAY

The Honble The Secy. of War.

ALS. CU-Wakefield Collection of Autographs.

[1] See above, Remarks, May 7, 1824, note.

To Walter Dun

Dr Sir 15h. Aug. 24

Mr. Mountjoy has this day notified me of his intention to take depositions in the suit with Mr. Taylor,[1] at the office of Saml. Treat Esq.[2] in Maysville on the 24h. inst. or the 25th. if prevented on the 24h.. As I cannot attend, I have thought it best to advise you of the fact, and to recommend that you should afford every facility to the taking of depositions, as being most likely to ensure a speedy trial.

I am Yr's faithfully H. CLAY

ALS. Ross County Historical Society, Chillicothe, Ohio. Addressed to Dun at Chillicothe. Endorsed: ". . . recd. Augt. 18th. 1824 & ansd." Answer not found.

1 Thomas Mountjoy, Jr.; James Taylor, Jr. See above, Clay to Dun, April 23, 1822, note.

2 Not further identified.

To Nicholas Biddle

Dr Sir Ashland 16 August 1824

I received your letter of the 27th. Ulto[1] with the resolutions of the Board inclosed, respecting the debt of Col. Todd.[2] He has returned, but I have not yet seen him. The intentions of the Board, as indicated in those resolutions and your letter, so far as their execution depends upon me, shall have particular attention. I have always supposed Mr. Sneed to be competent to pay the debt for which he is responsible, 'though I do not believe that he has the command of much active capital. The other indorsers of Col. Todd I believe are in a very different situation.

As to the amount of damages accruing on protested bills, which was included in the debts of Col. Johnson[3] and his connexions, it is true that Mr. Harper[4] and I thought it might be well enough, upon the final completion of the arrangement which was entered into respecting those debts,[5] to obtain a release of all claim on the part of the debtors on account of those damages. The situation of the question, in regard to them, was this: By an act of the Legislature of this State ten per Cent. damages were allowed on the return, in certain cases, of bills of exchange protested: According to a long settled practice in this State, on the part both of individuals and corporations, this percentage was charged on all protested bills, payable out of this State and within the United States, without regard to the place of residence of the parties to the bill: It was of course charged on the bills drawn by Col. Johnson and his connexions, which were dishonored, and constituted an item of some fifteen or twenty thousand dollars in the above debts: By a recent decision of our appellate Court it would seem that the Bank had no right to make the charge of damages, under the particular circumstances of those bills. That decision stands alone, is, I think, by no means satisfactory, and it is not very certain that the same Court, upon a review of it, would not change it. The Federal Court has not yet passed upon any similar case, and of course we do not know whether it would conform to it or not.[6]

Assuming the correctness of the decision of the Kentucky Court (the safer ground to take) I never thought the Bank in any danger of having to repay those damages. The debts of Col. Johnson &c. were compounded of principal interest damages costs &c. This mass of debt, so constituted, it was proposed by Col Johnson to extinguish, without his questioning any part of it, by the transfer of real estate, which was taken at the most extravagant prices. It would now be too late, I think, to object to the item of damages in that compounded mass of debt, or to set up a claim to have it refunded by the Bank. A court would consider that the composition agreed upon was the result of all the circumstances of the debt, of which the disputable character of the damages was a material one. It would be monstrous to decree the Bank to refund those damages in specie, after receiving such payment as has been made it in land. The most that a Court could possibly think of doing would be to set aside the arrangement which has been made, to purge the debt of the item of damages, and to leave the debtors subject only to the residue, payable in money. But the parties themselves would not be willing to accept redress upon such conditions. I think it will be at any time a sufficient answer to the claim, on account of the damages, for the Bank to say, if it should ever be made, that it is willing to set aside the whole arrangement, to give up the damages, and to receive *in money* the balance only, after deducting the damages.

Such have always been my views of the case, and I believe I communicated them to Mr. Harper. Still I concurred with him in thinking that, as a precautionary measure, it was well enough to obtain some evidence from Col. Johnson & his associates, in the form of a release, or in some other form, that they had no claim on the Bank founded on those damages. I attach however no importance to it, and still less after what subsequently occurred between Col. Johnson and myself. One of his brothers and a Mr. Offutt,[7] against whom Judgments had been obtained by the Bank, filed bills in chancery, claiming credits against those judgments for the amount of damages which they alleged they had erroneously paid to the Bank on protested bills. Upon enquiring at the office I found that they had paid no damages except such as were finally merged in the *arranged* debts of Col. Johnson. I stated this to him, and that there could be no foundation for any claim to damages included in those arranged debts. He readily admitted it, and his brother and Mr. Offutt afterwards abandoned the claim, respecting which I did not doubt that I should have defeated them, if they had persevered in it. Thus it appears that both sides coincide in the view that no right can be set up to have the amount of damages, comprehended in the arranged debts, refunded. I think therefore that it is of very little consequence to obtain any release on account of them; but if it be wished, I will endeavor to procure it.

I have the honor to be, with great respect, Your obedient Servant

H. CLAY

Nicholas Biddle Esqr. &c &c &c

ALS. PHi-Etting Collection. Endorsed: "recd Sept 3d. 1824. . . . Reffd to Comm. on Offices Sep. 3, 1824."

1 Not found.

2 Charles S. Todd, whose mission to Colombia had ended earlier in the year. See above, Todd to Clay, May 8, 1823, note.

3 Richard M. Johnson. 4 James Harper.

5 See above, Clay to Cheves, June 11, 1821, note.

6 See above, Clay to Cheves, October 26, 1821, and notes.

7 In the suit, The President, Directors, and Company of the Bank of the United States *vs.* John T. Johnson and Hugh Offutt (above, Clay to Biddle, June 11, 1823, note), the defendants had protested that the officers of the Bank had refused to grant the loan on a promissory note, which would have yielded interest at the rate of six per cent, but instead had handled the arrangement under the form of an out-of-state bill of exchange, though all the parties to the transaction had been at the time in Kentucky. Such a bill had carried a six per cent interest deduction on the amount paid by the Bank; but when the bill had not been paid at maturity, it had then been also subjected to a charge of ten per cent as damages. A second bill of exchange, drawn as a renewal of the loan, had included these charges for damages and protest; and, when it, too, had not been paid at maturity, ten per cent of the total on the second bill had also been charged. The defense had rested upon the illegality of such charges as evidenced by court decision (in the Hopkins case, above, Clay to Cheves, October 26, 1821). In an interlocutory decree at the May Term, 1823, the Federal Circuit Court had upheld the Bank's statement of the amount due. U. S. Circuit Court, Seventh Circuit, District of Kentucky, Complete Records, W, 182-86.

From William B. Astor

Dear Sir, New York 16th August 1824

I have the honor to acknowledge receipt of your letter of the 31st ulto enclosing a check for $149 17/100 One Hundred & forty nine 17/100 dollars[1]— If you wish it I will receive for my father a lien on the Estate[2] mentioned in your letter in lieu of your bond[3]—

I have the honor to be with great regard Your obedient Servant

WM. B ASTOR

To, The Honorable Henry Clay Lexington Kentucky—

ALS. DLC-TJC (DNA, M212, R12).

1 Letter and check not found. Cf. above, Astor to Clay, July 13, 17, August 5, 1824.

2 "Ashland." 3 See above, II, 686.

Receipted Bill from Richard Pindell and Others

[August 16, 1824]

1823		Henry Clay Esqr.	
Jany.	1st.	To Bal: due Ridgely Pindell & Satterwhite[1]	
		For Medical Services &c—to this date	$ 475.12½
		By Check[2] on CommonWealths Bank	200 —
			$ 275.12½

1824

Jany. 1st.	For Amt of acct due Pindell & Satterwhite[3] from 1st. Jany. 1823 to this date	303.25
		$ 578.37½

Recd. Augst. 16th. 1824 Three hundred Dols on the above Balance R. PINDELL

ADS. DLC-TJC (DNA, M212, R15).

1 Frederick Ridgely; Thomas P. Satterwhite. The latter, born in Virginia in 1795, became a highly esteemed physician and surgeon in Lexington.

2 Not found.

3 Cf. below, Account, *ca.* November 10, 1824. Ridgely died November 21, 1824.

From Josiah S. Johnston

Dear Sir. New York Augt. 19h. 1824

I Recd. the inclosed from Mr. Ingalls,[1] which I think it proper to send you, with my Veiws [*sic*] on the subject. I wrote him some days ago, the real state of things here & the probability of dividing the Vote of this State— Their hope of doing some thing in Jersey— Which would Certainly bring you into the House—& stated that a Similar arrangement might possibly be affected [*sic*] in Massachusetts.

I have now written him in Reply to this— That the first object is to secure your return to the House. That there is a reasonable expectation of affecting that object without relying on the arrangements & Contingent events above alluded to. That there is every motive to Continued & Strenuous exertion & that the Single Vote in that State may be all important.

I put it—this Candid Statement—

Mr. Clay has 6 States & 46 Votes—

Genl. Jackson 4 —— & 47 Votes[2]— You depend on two Districts in Maryland which make you 48—one more than the Genl. & equal to Crawford— Mr. Adams will have the Votes of S. Carolina— Delaware & Jersey & the remainder of Maryland— Then if N. York is thrown into the Scale of Mr. Crawford you will be returned the third— If N. York is divided you will be Second & Crawford third— There is no expectation that Genl. Jackson Can now receive any Vote except the 4 States. Upon this view alone your Chances are equal to his—& it requires only Constancy & good faith in your friends to obtain the *first* object which we have to Accomplish

I have told him he will See from this statement how important it is to obtain the Vote even of one District in that state & Urge upon him the necessity to securing it—

If Mr. Adams has a majority, he will receiv[*sic*] the Vote of this State & Mr. Calhoun the Vote as Vice Prest. & the efforts of the friends of Mr. Crawford will be Unavailing & the proposition to run you as Vice P. is nugatory: But if the two parties are Strongest & Can by Union defeat Mr. Adams, It is of the greatest moment to Mr. Crawford, in the peculiar state of things that now exists to secure half of that State—& Weaken his adversary— It is so essential—that they will not hesitate to divide this State equally—or at Least to give you a just proportion— I Urge it therefore in this not to accept of any proposition but a just Division— They Cannot give you the Vote as Vice P. Unless they Can Command the Vote of the State, & it would be extreme folly to give up your expectations for Such a Compromise & Unreasonable on their part to ask it— It would be in fact with drawing from the Contest— I entertain no doubt they would Consent to With draw Mr. Gallatin & to nominate you as Vice President— You might probably be elected— & I think would be— But I doubt whether it would elect Mr. Crawford— Your States Seem much more inclined to the other Candidates & the interest of three of Jacksons States will be for Adams—If left to the people —— My Opinion has been for Some time that they had this in Contemplation & that this movement in Massachusetts is the begining [*sic*]— They would be very Willing to accomplish their purpose in this State by the Same means— Without any instructions or advice on the means of Consultation— I shall Continue to hold up your Claims to the highest place without listning [*sic*] to any schemes of this Kind— I regret to be placed in a Situation, where I may do you great injury & defeat the hopes of the other party. But I shall not Change while the Contest stands as it is— Unless more Correct information should enable you to give a new direction to this business— I should be glad to see you Vice P. for the reasons assigned in this Letter— If there was no reasonable hope of your Success— I think at this time there is no motive to dispair [*sic*] of being returned to the House.—although the Issue is so doubtful & depends upon so many events that it ought not to excite any expectations—

I have given Mr. Warfield[3] a Similar View of your Chances & Urge him to the necessity of making an effort in Maryland—& by all means to Secure two Districts— He is now apprized of the extreme importance of that object—

A Meeting is advertized in Philadelphia of your friends[4]— I have heretofore opposed this— I was Sure it would result as Crawfords meeting did[5]—But it may have a good affect & produce Similar meetings in different parts of the State—& give Countenance to your friends else where—particularly in Jersey and Delaware—In speaking of an Union in Jersey a friend of Crawford said, it is better to wait untill a Contest is Created there by the friends of Jackson against Adams—& then the arrangement will be practicable—

In speaking the other day with Mr. Goram[6] of Boston— He said Mr. Adams would probably receive the Vote of N. England & the day after have as little popularity there as any Man in it— He said he thought it advisable & Suggested to your friends the propriety of Coming out as a Candidate for the Vice Presidency—he said the N. England states had the best feelings towards you & would Support you. He said he then thought it very doubtful, whether you could be elected President—& he said many of your friends to the North, doubted whether in justice the Western States were intitled [*sic*] to the Presidency yet— But in this way you would make sure of it in good time—& besides the possibility of the Death of the Next President—made it more important to secure that place in judicious hands There is little feeling in N. England for Adams— The Ultra Federalists hate him—the moderates feel indifference—The Republicans are not Cordial— He is supported merely on Sectional grounds— But strange—the Ultras will join the Radicals[7]—the extremes meet—

Genl. La Fayette has been received with distinguished honors & departed this morning for Boston—his whole journey will be a procession—What a Glorious reward![8]

I shall leave here in a few days for Philadelphia Where I think it important to be— I hope Carey[9] will Come out—& possibly We may be joind [*sic*] by the friends of Adams & Crawford—I shall press Carey warmly— With great regard yr Obt. Sert.

J. S. JOHNSTON

ALS. DLC-TJC (DNA, M212, R12). Addressed to Clay at Lexington. Brief extract published in Colton (ed.), *Private Correspondence of Henry Clay*, 98.

1 William Ingalls. Enclosure not found, but cf. above, Ingalls to Clay, August 8, 1824, and note.

2 Clay's supporters were counting on the votes of Ohio, Indiana, Illinois, Kentucky, Missouri, and Louisiana; they reckoned Pennsylvania, Tennessee, Alabama, and Mississippi as Jackson strongholds.

3 Henry R. Warfield.

4 See below, Johnston to Clay, September 11, 1824.

5 See below, Johnston to Clay, June 27, 1824.

6 Benjamin Gorham.

7 See above, Creighton to Clay, May 2, 1822, note.

8 In response to an invitation extended by Congressional resolution (4 *U. S. Stat.*, 78 [February 4, 1824]), Lafayette made an extended visit to the United States in 1824-1825. With his son, George Washington Lafayette, his secretary, and his valet, he had landed at New York, August 15.

9 Mathew Carey.

From William Ingalls

To the Honle. Henry Clay, &c. [*ca.* August 20, 1824]

Sir,

The following is the copy of a letter, addressed to the Honl J. S. Johnson, dated August 20th. 1824—

Sir, I received yours of the 15. Inst. yesterday, & was so much impressed with the importance of a press favorable to Mr. Clay, that I called on Mr. Buckingham, Editor of the Gallaxy,[1] to ascertain his views with regard to the presidential question. He is disposed to support the claims of Mr. Clay, & had already prepared an article, which will be found in his paper to day, & intends to prepare another for next Friday.[2] He will receive essays from the friends of Mr. Clay, appears desirous to engage in any measures, that may tend to promote his elevation to the presidential chair. I have directed to days Gallaxy to be sent to you, & to the gentlemen to whom I am referred in your letter. It is presumed by competent judges, that the Gallaxy is read by ten thousand people, & of course it is a valuable vehicle for the diffusion of political sentiments. From the extensive circulation of this paper, & the talents of the editor, it would be judicious in the friends of Mr. Clay to make it their official organ of communication, & to give it as much currency in every part of the United States as possible. No one has felt the want of a paper devoted exclusively to the interests of Mr. Clay more than myself.

We are diligently here organizing an opposition to Mr. Adams. Mr. Clay has many influential adherents in Rhode Iland [*sic*].

With great respect, your obedient servt, William Ingalls.

ALS. DLC-HC (DNA, M212, R1).

1 Joseph T. Buckingham, a native of Connecticut, had settled in Boston, where in 1817 he had founded the weekly paper, *The New England Galaxy and Masonic Magazine,* with which he was connected until 1828. Early in 1824 he had established a daily newspaper, the *Boston Courier,* which became highly successful but which, as yet, had a small number of subscribers. Buckingham continued as editor of the *Courier* until 1848. He was at various times a member of the Massachusetts Senate and House of Representatives and was the author of several books.

2 The first article somewhat backhandedly argued that Clay's talents were more dangerous to New England commercial interests when he was Speaker of the House of Representatives than they would be were he President. The second piece did not appear until September 3. Further comment, deploring Clay's oratorical efforts in behalf of the tariff but applauding his dignity and public service, was published in succeeding issues.

From Josiah S. Johnston

Dear Sir. Philadelphia Augt. 25h. 1824

I hand you inclosed a Letter recd. from Boston.[1] It is presumed that the majority of Mr. Adams is not decisive in that state & that an arrangement may be made. The Galaxy will have the effect to present your views fairly before the people

The other Candidates have availd [*sic*] themselves of all the presses —& all the aid of Caucus'—Conventions & party names.—& While yours stood still, trusting every thing to the Judgement of the people a Concurrent effort of all parties was made to withdraw your name from the Contest.— It is difficult even now to Communicate the truth even to a small portion of the Cities—impossible to diffuse Correct information among the people. The Galaxy is extensively read & will present fairly your claims to that portion of the Country— I Know nothing of its political character.— I have impressed strongly upon Mr. Ingalls—Mr. Shaw[2] & others the necessity of securing a portion of that State— I communicate the same to Maryland—

It is very doubtful if the friends of Mr. Adams are the strongest in the New England States. & it is probable an effort may be made in each of them against him a Combined attack upon his ranks will be very formidable. The example of one state might dissolve the charm—

It is now said with Confidence that Delaware is fixed for Mr. Crawford. I expect it is true.— Maryland will be much divided— I have seen Mr. Elliot from Georgia[3]— He is of opinion that South Carolina will vote for Genl. Jackson— all this only serves to show the great doubt, that rests upon this subject every where—& how little any one knows of the result—

The Contest between Crawford & adams grows warmer & warmer— It is too violent, to remain long friends— They begin to speak very plain & open of Mr. Adams They strongly Condemn his Conduct in the Edwards business[4] & Consider him secretly at the bottom of it— They disapprove of his attempt to Controul or to punish the Intelligencer—& they Consider the National journal as speaking his sentiments—perhaps his words[5]— I think in no event Can there be a Coalition— I wish that state of things to exist— The quarrel is Coming to a Crisis—

Mr. Crawfords health is said to be better But he is Liable to relapse—to a renewal of the attack— his life is Certainly very precarious— I want a Declaration from his friends with regard to the Course they will persue [*sic*]— I will bind them up to this—as a sine qua non—

I had a Conversation with Mr. Elliot to day— he speaks with Warmth of Mr. Adams Course & says that sentiment prevails to the South— Mr. Crawfords friends generally entertain the same opinion— Both parties will Commit themselves into a fierce hostility.—Mr. Elliot said you was always his second choice, he wished the Republicans to have nominated you as vice President with Mr. Crawford— that if any accident Occurrd [*sic*] you would be President— I explaind [*sic*] to him as I did to V.Buren[6] how it would have fail'd— He said he wished now to have you run as vice President, as it was, with his friends—so that point Could be secured—I said I presumed Mr. Gallatin[7] would withdraw for that object He said he would— He agreed with me in the improper Course they had persued in depreciating your claims—that you ought to have been held up & brought into the House—Because they see clearly that if Crawford Comes into the House with the other two—They will Ultimately Coalese [*sic*] against him. You see this Idea of vice President has been suggested to me several times from different quarters which proves the subject much discussed & much at heart— But I tell them expressly that there is not a possibility of either of the 6 states[8] going to Mr. Crawford in the Electoral vote if you was withdrawn— But if you & Mr. Crawford are in the House together, with Mr. Adams, then in the Last resort—the Coalition would be against Adams & that this is the only hope— I do not know if I present this subject Correctly But I think they feel the truth of the remarks & I will Cause them to alter the tone of the prints—

It is entirely in the power of the friends of Mr. Crawford to Elect you to the House—& to Carry you if they Cannot Carry him.— I shall Communicate to you frequently what Occurs—mainly that you may know every thing that is thought & said here—They my letters are free & unreserved & altogether private— when you Come to Washington seal them up & give them to me—as I am obliged to write of men & things—intrigues & combinations & things not to be *letterd* [*sic*]— I think it probable they will determine to run you as vice President on Crawfords ticket—so that you may be *put up* against Calhoun, against whom there is some desire to act— But as at present advised I shall insist on your being Continued as a Candidate for the Presidency & shall impress on them the necessity of giving you such support as will bring you into the House— If Genl. Jackson is not returned I calculate you Can Command the vote of Pennsylvania—Alabama & Tennessee in the House—

I have a Letter from Mr. Brown[9]—his health is better & Mrs. Brown has her Usual good health Paris is improving very much & becoming as dear[10] as London— With great regard yr. Obt Sert

address me to Philadelphia J. S. JOHNSTON

ALS. InU. Addressed to Clay at Lexington.

1 See above, Ingalls to Clay, *ca.* August 20, 1824. 2 Henry Shaw.

3 John Elliott, lawyer, resident of Sunbury, Liberty County, Georgia, United States Senator (1819-1825).

4 See above, Clay to Porter, April 26, 1824.

5 Cf. above, Johnston to Clay, August 9, 1824.

6 Martin Van Buren. 7 Albert Gallatin.

8 See above, Johnston to Clay, August 19, 1824.

9 James Brown. 10 Word not clear.

To James Monroe

Sir Ashland 30h. Aug. 1824

Having been informed that the office of district Atto. is vacant in Rhode Island, and been requested to express my opinion to you of Mr. Asher Robbins, an applicant for it, I have the honor to state that I have known him for many years; that I became acquainted first with him at the Bar of the Supreme Court; and that I have always understood and considered him as an Attorney & Coun-

seller of great eminence, holding firmly his station among the most distinguished of the Bar of his State. I will only add that I shall be glad if circumstances shall admit of your conferring on him the appointment.[1] I have the honor to be Your obedient Servant
The President. H. CLAY

ALS. DNA, RG59, Applications and Recommendations for office (MR1). See above, Robbins to Clay, August 5, 1824.
[1] Robbins was not appointed.

From Josiah S. Johnston

Dear Sir. Philadelphia Augt. 30th. 1824

I have the pleasure to hand you a printed letter of Genl. McClure— which speaks for itself.[1] with the speech of Mr. Wheaton[2]— It confirms the belief that what I have said to you about that state—is true— This declaration will have a good effect— But it would have been more judicious to have omitted the Name of Mr. Crawford— It is generally understood that in the Legislature Adams has 61— Crawford 59 Clay 34. Jackson 6. This is perhaps nearly Correct It is clear that neither party will have a Commanding majority, without your friends—that they are perfectly aware of the power in their hands—& that they *will use it*— all the friends will be at Albany at the meeting. & their force will be Concentrated— The Coalition will be made with Adams.[3] McClures declaration is explicit & founded upon a perfect understanding of the parties—& moreover the Confidence of Van Buren induced him to believe that your friends would Come into his views & he expected to Carry measures by force—not by Conciliation— I have a Letter of Genl. McClures which is much stronger—which I retain to shew to some friends—& will then send you[4]— Van Buren & Forsythe have gone on a visit to Dickinson[5] There is an Alarm in the Camp— My fear is that they mean to have the Credit of Controuling the event— that if they find they Cannot Carry Crawford—they will Unite upon one whom they Can Certainly Carry— If defeated in N. York they may throw their might upon Adams to exclude you— But I think their influence will be Cautiously Used against you as long as they have hope—because they are aware that he Can have no expectation of an Election in the House, except by the aid of your States—

The Conflict between Adams & Crawford grows fiercer—see the National Journal. Enquirer—Intelligencer. Argus[6] &c—

This is one advantage at least you enjoy by having no press— you certainly provoke no hostility—. Your friends still approve of not engaging any of the Federal-Clintonian Presses in N. York[7]— One of them has gone over to Crawford & you perceive by the papers, what a Serious charge it is made & how much pains is taken to shew that Adams has three times as many papers of that discription [*sic*][8]— I wish you to have McClures Letter published— I shall have it published here— The friends of Adams & Jackson will be desirous of publishing it. In a few days, I will send you McClures Letter—

with great regard J. S. JOHNSTON

ALS. InU. Addressed to Clay at Lexington.

1 George McClure to the Editors of the New York *Statesman,* written from Bath, Steuben County, New York, August 18, 1824, correcting reports of the meeting of the New York legislature (see above, Johnston to Clay, August 9, 1824; below, Clay to Johnston, August 31, 1824), denying that he had joined the "Albany Regency," criticizing Crawford, and praising Clay. He had "no hesitation in saying that, if the choice of electors were given to the people, Mr. Clay would get the votes of this state, and, as it is, I can assure you that I consider his chances of success equal at least to any other candidate." *Niles' Weekly Register,* XXVII (September 11, 1824), 23-24; Lexington *Kentucky Reporter,* September 20, 1824.

2 Henry Wheaton, who sat in the New York legislature for one term, 1823-1824. The reference is probably to his speech of August 3 before the House of Assembly, when he "supported his motion at considerable length, and with great ability," urging that a joint committee of the House and Senate be appointed to draft a bill providing for popular choice of presidential electors. *Niles' Weekly Register,* XXVI (August 14, 1824), 396.

3 See below, Clay to Porter, September 2, 1824; Stuart to Clay, September 6, 1824.

4 Cf. below, Stuart to Clay, September 6, 1824.

5 Martin Van Buren; John Forsyth; Mahlon Dickerson.

6 Washington *National Journal;* Richmond *Enquirer;* Washington *National Intelligencer;* Albany *Argus.*

7 See above, Johnston to Clay, June 27, 1824.

8 When William Coleman in August, 1824, had announced the support of Crawford by the New York *Evening Post,* the New York *American* had emphasized the link between the "leading ultra Federalists, and the radical democrats." Cited in Shaw Livermore, Jr., *The Twilight of Federalism, the Disintegration of the Federalist Party, 1815-1830* (Princeton, 1962), 147-48. Cf. also *Niles' Weekly Register,* XXVII (October 16, 1824), 100; Washington *Daily National Intelligencer,* October 21, 1824.

To Josiah S. Johnston

Dear Sir Ashland 31 August 1824

Your obliging favor of the 9h. inst. dated at Saratoga, and those subsequently at New York[1] have all safely arrived. They reached Lexington during my absence, on a short excursion to one of our watering places,[2] from which I am but just returned.

I concur with you in thinking that, considering all the combinations that may arise and the contingencies that may happen, my friends ought to persevere in their support of me. That I believe is the course which they have determined on generally. And I think the six States heretofore supposed to be disposed to support me may still be relied on. You have heard, no doubt, from Louisiana. Your Governor elect[3] passed through Lexington and I presume you will have seen him. The information derived from him and other sources assures us of the unaltered state of Louisiana, altho' in the City of New Orleans the Jackson ticket prevailed in the greater part.[4] Those opposed to me in that State admit a plurality of the Legislature to be for me; whilst my friends confidently claim the majority. What is most to be apprehended is, that my friends in the West, or at least in some of the more doubtful States, may become discouraged by the little prospect of my being supported to any extent in the East, and especially by the statements in the N. Intellr[5] and other papers, according to which it would seem that I have not a friend in the New York Legislature. Would it not be well to have these statements corrected or contradicted in some prominent Eastern papers? One consideration may however detain even the timid portion of my friends, that is the difficulty of knowing to whom to go. Another has also much effect, and that is that the adjournment of the Legislature of New York without passing an Electoral law,[6] if it operates against me, or rather in favor of Mr. Crawford, is more prejudicial to Mr. Adams. Now he is really the only person that I seriously feel in those states which are inclined to support me, and hence, on the part of any of my friends, I should think there would be no disposition to exchange one bad cause for another no better.

The anticipated coalition in New York I should suppose was very probable, unless it should be prevented by the apprehension of imputations of corruption, bargaining &c. Perhaps there may be nerve enough to encounter all the odium of these imputations, considering the *quarter* from which they must emanate. If there be a majority of the legislature who prefer either of two candidates to a third,[7] there is much reason in an equal division of its vote between those two. The effect of such a division would doubtless be to exclude the third from the H. of R. and it would lead to the election of one or other of them most certainly. In the actual state of the circumstances of the election, New York would have two strings to her bow by dividing her suffrage and more certainly secure influence in the new administration than by risking her whole vote upon one of the Candidates, since if she were so to concentrate it she could not be sure of effecting his election.

What about the Vice President? Is New York desirous of ele[c]ting Mr. Sandford?[8] Has he any and what interest there? In Ohio there is a strong disposition to elect a Vice P. from New York, and Mr. Sandford has been favorably brought forward there.[9] Here also his name has been advantageously announced to the public,[10] and there would not be the slightest difficulty in his obtaining the votes of both States, and probably of the other States inclined to give me their suffrages. Be pleased to write me fully on this subject.

I have such information from Virginia as does not leave a doubt that she will support me, if Mr Crawford should be withdrawn.[11] The incidents at Washn. on the 4h. of July[12] and since have confirmed, if they have not contributed to produce this disposition.

The Legislature in this State that nominated me,[13] at the same time appointed a Comee. of correspondence, comprizing some of our most eminent Citizens. I understand that this Comee will, in the course of a few days, address a Circular to my friends in other States advising perseverance &c &c[14]—

I shall direct the Reporter[15] & some other papers to be forwarded to you.

Be pleased to present my respects to Mrs Johnston and believe me Faithfully & Cordially Yr friend H. CLAY

The Honble J. S. Johnston.

P.S. I was glad to learn from Mr. H. Johnson that he was friendly to you. He does not think that you are in any danger of a re-election.[16] On that subject I have written very particularly to Duralde,[17] and I shall communicate my wishes to others. H.C.

ALS. PHi. Published in part in Colton (ed.), *Private Correspondence of Henry Clay,* 98-99.

1 Of letters from New York, only that above, August 19, has been found.

2 Probably either the Olympian Springs or Greenville Springs.

3 Henry Johnson, who was Governor of Louisiana from 1824 to 1828.

4 Cf. above, Clay to Johnston, July 21, 1824. Bernard Marigny, identified with a ticket of Jackson supporters, had polled nearly twice as many votes as Johnson in New Orleans during the State elections, held July 6-8. A division of the French vote between two candidates contributed to Johnson's over-all victory; at the same time, the American vote in the city had been curtailed by the absence of a large proportion of that segment of the population during a serious outbreak of yellow fever. Washington *Daily National Intelligencer,* August 5, 1824.

5 See, e.g., *ibid.,* August 10, 11, 12, 1824.

6 See above, Woods to Clay, August 27, 1823, note.

7 Cf. above, Johnston to Clay, August 30, 1824.

8 Nathan Sanford.

9 See above, Clay to Johnston, July 21, 1824, note.

10 The address of delegates supporting Clay in Kentucky's Third Electoral District, meeting at Paris on August 9, had recommended consideration of Sanford for the Vice Presidency.

11 See above, Brooke to Clay, July 12, 1824.

12 See above, Clay to Johnston, July 21, 1824; Johnston to Clay, August 9, 1824.

13 See above, Clay to Porter, October 22, 1822, note.

14 The circular, issued over the names of William T. Barry, George Robertson, John Rowan, Benjamin W. Patton (Hopkinsville lawyer), and John J. Crittenden, acknowledged that reference of the presidential election to the United States House of Representatives "appears unavoidable," argued that no single candidate could defeat Clay in that body, and urged that the friends of the other candidates, considering him as their "second choice," give him the support to bring him into the House. Noting the revival of rumors of Clay's withdrawal as a candidate following his reelection to Congress earlier in August (cf. above, Clay to Stuart, March 24, 1824, note), the circular denied that Clay had "placed himself in a situation dissimilar to that occupied by the other candidates" and termed "all reports that Mr. Clay has withdrawn from the contest or that he has been abandoned by his friends as hopeless . . . utterly idle and unfounded." Frankfort *Argus of Western America,* September 22, 1824.

15 Lexington *Kentucky Reporter.*

16 See above, John Clay to Henry Clay, December 13, 1822, note.

17 Martin Duralde (Jr.). Letter not found.

To Asher Robbins

Dr Sir Ashland 31 Aug. 1824

My absence from home at one of our watering places[1] has delayed my acknowledging the receipt of your letter[2] in regard to the vacant office of Atto. for the district of Rhode Island. The same cause I fear will prevent a letter which I have addressed to Mr Monroe in your favor[3] from reaching him in time. I shall be extremely happy if it have any favorable effect.

If R. Island could be detached from the interest of Mr. Adams, even by the division of its vote between Mr Crawford & me, it would be more than I ever anticipated. I have supposed the Secretary of State to be invulnerable in New England. My friends in the West are very animated, and are sufficiently sanguine. Information which has been communicated to me from New York, of probabilities there, is quite encouraging.

With great regard I am faithfly Yrs H. CLAY

ALS. CtY-Col. John Mason Brown and Maj. Gen. Preston Brown Papers. Addressed to Robbins at "New Port. Rhode Island."

1 See above, Clay to Johnston, August 31, 1824.

2 Not found. 3 Above, August 30, 1824.

From Josiah S. Johnston

Dear Sir Philadelphia 1 Sept. 1824

I now hand you the letter of Genl. Mc.Clure, which I promised you in my last, when I handed you the printed Letter[1]—

I purposely avoided seeing Genl. McClure at Albany, satisfied it was better for Rochester[2] to Communicate with him, than Me.— & that the objects & views of your friends are better accomplished by a Corresponding Committee— Besides I was told your friends were as firm & stanch as was necessary—& from the tone & tenor of this letter I have no doubt— I will now write to all of them & let them understand distincly [*sic*], the views taken of the state of your interests in N. York—

If our expectations are realized, you will be returned triumphantly to the House—

The fate of Crawford rests upon N. York. The Contest in N. Carolina is animated & doubtful in its Issue— But I yet Consider it fair to Count it for him—Jackson disputes S. Carolina with Mr. Adams—& Adams who now seems the strongest—may by an accident loose [*sic*] some of the N. England States—& be last on the List—so doubtful is the Issue every where

with great regard J S. JOHNSTON

ALS. DLC-HC (DNA, M212, R1). Published in part in Colton (ed.), *Private Correspondence of Henry Clay*, 99-100. Addressed to Clay at Lexington.

1 See above, Johnston to Clay, August 30, 1824. The manuscript letter, from McClure to J. B. Stuart, dated August 14, 1824 (ALS. DLC-HC [DNA, M212, R1]), covers much the same ground discussed in the letter to the New York *Statesman*. McClure comments, "You already perceive how our extraordinary session terminated, not by any means so disastrous as the Statesman has declared; that paper has made verry [*sic*]

erroneous strictures on my conduct. . . . I am the last man in the Union that will desert Mr. Clay, at all events I never can be brought to support Crawford." He admits that he voted "against the Governor. . . . Still I was of opinion (notwithstanding I considered this call of the Executive indiscreet) that we had a right to Legislate, but to press the matter beyond reasonable bounds after the Senate had positively declared they would not act would have been a fruitless inquiry—

"As it respects the prospects of Mr. Clay I candidly beleive [*sic*] they are verry flattering he is certainly gaining strength every day in the Legislature, we hold the ballance of power in our hands and will use it to the best advantage— Our policy will be to shut Crawford out of the house— The friends of Clay must rally to a man and rendezvous at Albany in Novr.—there will be the field of action when something can be done to effect. You must urge upon your acquaintances the necessity of being there— I have conversed with a number of Adams' men members of the Legislature who have lately come out for Clay; depend upon it he is gaining every day."

2 William B. Rochester.

To Peter B. Porter

Dr. General. Lexn. 2d. Septr. 1824

Since the adjournment of your Legislature, I have recd. several communications informing me of the disposition of Mr. Adams friends in the Legislature of New York to form a coalition with mine and to divide the electoral vote of the State between us. I have said, in reply, that the rule which I have prescribed to myself utterly forbids any interposition by me in respect to such an arrangement.[1] I doubt whether it be practicable. If it were effected, Mr. Crawford would undoubtedly be excluded from the H. of R.. And you may rely upon it that he cannot be elected in that House against any of the Candidates, except perhaps Genl. Jackson. If your State shd. prefer either of two Candidates to a third, I do not know that it might not be for its interest to divide its vote beween those two, as it could thereby certainly secure the election of one of them.

My friends are unalterably determined to persevere in support of me to the last; and anticipate with great confidence the vote in my favor of the six Western States, including Louisiana, which have been generally counted for me.[2] My information from Virginia leaves me without a doubt that that State will support me, if Mr. Crawford be withdrawn.[3] I have also recd. encouraging intelligence from Rhode Island, New Jersey and a part of Maryland.[4]

Give my respects to Mrs. Porter and believe me ever

Faithfully Yr friend H. CLAY

Genl. P. B. Porter.

ALS. NBuHi.

1 See above, Johnston to Clay, August 30, 1824; Clay to Johnston, August 31, 1824; below, Stuart to Clay, September 6, 1824. No other letters on this subject have been found.

2 See above, Johnston to Clay, August 19, 1824.

3 See above, Clay to Brooke, July 12, 1824.

4 See above, Robbins to Clay, August 5, 1824; cf. above, Johnston to Clay, June 27, 1824, note; Johnston to Clay, August 19, 25, 1824.

To Josiah S. Johnston

Dr Sir Ashland 3d. Septr. 1824

I duly received your obliging favor of the 19h. Ulto. under date at New York, transmitting a letter from Mr. Ingalls, from whom I had previously received a duplicate. I did not however answer his letter. I entirely approve of what you have said to him in reply. Eight months ago I supposed there would have been no difficulty in my election as V. President, if my friends had thought it advisable to press me for that office. It would now be extremely difficult, if not impracticable, to effect that object, if it were desirable. My friends in the West do not attach any very great, perhaps not sufficient, importance to the office; and it would be, I apprehend, nearly impossible now to induce them to divert their support of me from the first to the second office. And if they could be prevailed on to do it, the Electoral colleges would hardly be induced, by any possible exertion, to unite their undivided suffrages on any other Candidate for the Presidency. There could therefore be no support secured for me in the Atlantic States for the V. P., if it depended upon concert among my Western friends in regard to the office of President. And consequently, if I received any, it must be spontaneous and without reference to the direction which my interest would take as to the Presidency.

If my Eastern friends think proper to bring me forward for the office of V.P. I wish it distinctly understood that it is their own movement, unprompted by me. If an idea were taken up that the office was sought by me, after all that has occurred, it could not fail to be injurious to me. It would be said to display a most inordinate desire for office, which I certainly am not conscious of feeling. It could not look well, in any aspect, if it were supposed that I was instrumental in the attempt to elect me. It is certainly a high and dignified office—such as no American Citizen could readily decline.

With respect to the movement in Massachusetts to which Mr. Ingalls refers, whilst I concur with you entirely in the state of public feeling in New England towards Mr Adams, I do not believe that there is the smallest prospect of diverting the vote of Massachusetts from him. There may be some probability of such a diversion in other states of that section, but none whatever I apprehend in Massachusetts. Depend upon it that local pride, if not attachment, will secure to each of the Candidates the support of his own state, doubtless with more opposition in some instances than in others. It would be therefore an act of extreme indiscretion, justified by no motive whatever, for me or for any of my friends out of Massachusetts to say to Mr Ingalls and to those who are co-operating with him—to say in other words to the American public—that I am willing to give up all pretensions to the office of President and to be contented with that of V.P. By the bye, it has been said here that a feeling is prevailing in some of the Atlantic Cities to make the Marquis LaFayette V. President. Such a disposition of the office would be highly creditable to the national gratitude, if it could be made without any constitutional impediment.

I do not anticipate much from the Philada. meeting. It is a little remarkable that my support of the Tariff has excited against me in the South, a degree of opposition, which is by no means counter-balanced by any espousal of my cause in Pennsa. and other quarters, where the Tariff was so much desired. Is this owing to the greater activity which the losing party most always displays than the gaining?

I expect every day that the Comee. of Correspondence, appointed by the Legislature of this State, will prepare their general Circular, as suggested in my last.[1] A Copy of it shall be forwarded to you. Do you correspond with Genl. Peter B. Porter?[2] His residence is Black Rock.

I cannot close without expressing to you my thanks for the zeal and interest which you manifest in my favor; nor without adding that you have fulfilled entirely all my expectations as to the discretion which you would manifest. I remain faithfly Your's

The Honble J. S. Johnston. H. CLAY

ALS. PHi. Published in Colton (ed.), *Private Correspondence of Henry Clay*, 100-102.

1 See above, Clay to Johnston, August 31, 1824.

2 Cf. above, Johnston to Clay, June 27, 1824.

From William L. Brent

My dear Sir Washington City 3rd. Septr—1824

When Mr. McClure's letter[1] appeared here I waited upon all the editors of the Newspapers and urged them to publish it— The Journal hesitated, but agreed to do it, The Gazette promised to reflect upon it[2] and what astonished me our friend Gales[3] refused— I told him that if he would not do it of his own accord, to state *that it was at my request* and if he wished any responsibility he might give my name in his paper. He has this day published it, with remarks of rather an unkind and unfriendly feeling[4]—. We ought to have had a paper here, our friends have been remiss, we have been too silent—. There is not one paper here in which we can reply so as to give that letter the weight it is entitled to—. If our friends would act decisively and with warmth, I still have hopes that we will bring you into the House—I can discover that both the friends of Crawford and Adams fear you—. Genl. Jackson has no chance, it is almost admitted by his friends here—Rely upon it that the plan is to use Jackson to keep you out— It is an intrigue—. In the electoral College he will be abandoned and I fear things will be so managed by Mr. Adams & Calhoun as to throw his (Jacksons) votes into Adams' scale.— Is it possible, that Pensylvania [*sic*] is so blind as to not see these things? Jackson out of the question you ought to get the votes of that State—your friends ought now to make the exertion— This is the crisis—.

Robertson[5] writes to me that he is much yr. friend, but he fears Louisiana will vote for Jackson. Your conduct upon the Tariff question has impaired you—but was not Jackson as much a Tariff man as you were— His conduct was more covert, but he went the lengths[6]— These things ought to be known in Louisa. I have written to Duralde[7] and told him how to meet this thing— Can you not get some of your friends to state Jacksons conduct upon the Tariff Question— Do write to your friends in Louisa. and urge them— If Jackson should get the electoral vote of Louisiana, he will never get the vote in our House—Livingston[8] is his only friend.

What can I do here— I wish you would write to me and say how I can be usefull. —Give me the news of S Ca.—

I have been reelected after a warm contest, by a large and flattering majority over my opponent— Yr. friend WM L BRENT

P. S— It would be well to have your services to Louisa. enumerated. —I have stated some of them to Duralde, such as yr. proposition to *protect molasses,*[9] your *oppositio*[n to the][10] *increase* of duty upon our [. . .]e, and your conduct at [. . .] *in saving for the state,* the duty upon sugar— These things occurred under my observation no doubt there are other services rendered. Your friends are too inert in every direction— yrs W L BT

ALS. DLC-HC (DNA, M212, R1). Addressed to Clay at Lexington.

1 See above, Johnston to Clay, August 30, 1824.

2 Washington *National Journal; City of Washington Gazette.*

3 Joseph Gales, Jr.

4 See Washington *Daily National Intelligencer,* September 3, 1824, which attributed McClure's letter to "the same sanguine temper and ardent zeal that dictated the letters written from Albany to this city during the last winter, which so completely deceived the friends of Mr. CLAY, by exaggerations of his strength in New York." Cf. above, Porter to Clay, January 25, April 5, 1824; Clay to Stuart, December 19, 1823.

5 Thomas B. Robertson.

6 Jackson had taken his stand in support of American manufactures as early as his "Grass Hat" letter of May 17, 1823, written in thanks for a gift to Mrs. Jackson from two young girls of Philadelphia. Marquis James, *Andrew Jackson, Portrait of a President* (New York, 1937), 54-55. During Senate consideration of the tariff in April and May, 1824, Jackson appears to have taken no part in debate but had voted consistently against drastic revision of the House bill. He had reasserted his position in a widely publicized letter to Dr. L. H. Colman, of Virginia, dated April 26, 1824, wherein he presented arguments supporting a "judicious," "a careful Tariff," affording protection for the development of home markets and national defense. Bassett, *Life of Andrew Jackson,* I, 344-48.

7 Martin Duralde (Jr.). 8 Edward Livingston.

9 See above, Remarks . . . on Molasses, March 24, 1824.

10 MS. torn—two words missing at indicated passages.

From Josiah S. Johnston

Dear Sir. Philadelphia Sept. 4h. 1824.

I attended a meeting of your friends To wit Mr. Carey & son.—Mr. Hemphill—Mr. Tilman Mr. Wharton—Dr. Chapman—Dr. Godman—Mr. Ed. Ingersol[1] &C. to Consult about the meeting of your friends— It was called without their knowledge— They determined to postpone the meeting until this day week— Mr. Carey Consents to be Chairman—a Committe [*sic*] of Correspondence will be Organized & delegates appointed[2]— I have no doubt the Meeting will be Numerous & respectable— This state might have been secured at a proper time & this state would have secured you— your affairs have been trusted to providence— I send you two Letters from Boston[3]— I hope you have recd. Genl. McClures[4]—.

The friends of Crawford are still very anxious to make you Vice President— Mr. Elliot[5] often speaks of it— It is much a subject of Correspondence among them— They Count Confidently upon most of your Votes in that event— They say Gallatin would not be in the way— with great regard yr. Obt Sevt J. S. JOHNSTON.

ALS. DLC-TJC (DNA, M212, R12). Published in Colton (ed.), *Private Correspondence of Henry Clay*, 102-103. Addressed to Clay at Lexington.

1 Mathew Carey; his eldest son, Henry C. Carey, who continued the family publishing business until 1835, when he devoted himself exclusively to writing on political economy, expounding strongly nationalist and protectionist views; Joseph Hemphill; Benjamin Tilghman, lawyer; Thomas I. Wharton; Dr. Nathaniel Chapman, graduated from the Medical School of the University of Pennsylvania in 1801, a professor at that institution from 1810 to 1850, founder of the Medical Institute of Philadelphia in 1817, and president at various periods of the Philadelphia Medical Society, the American Medical Association, and the American Philosophical Society; John D. Godman; Edward Ingersoll, poet and political writer, author of *Digest of the Laws of the United States* (Philadelphia, 1821), and a brother of Charles Jared Ingersoll.

2 See below, Johnston to Clay, September 11, 1824.

3 Not found.

4 See above, Johnston to Clay, August 30, September 1, 1824.

5 Jonathan Elliot.

From Henry Vethake

Mess. H. Clay & B. Gratz Carlisle, September 4th. 1824.

Gentlemen,

Your communication of the 16th ult.[1] was received on my arrival on the 31st. from an excursion to the eastward. A reply would have been sent without delay, but sickness has for a day or two prevented me from writing.

Private considerations relating to my mother's family,[2] residing in New Jersey, at present forbid me to think of removing farther to the West than my present situation. I am fully aware of the eligibility in many respects of a residence in the literary capital of West, and especially of the excellent state of society with you, which has frequently been represented to me by visiters [*sic*] in the most favourable terms, and most enthusiastically so by my brother resident at Chillicothe,[3] who has written to me in anticipation of your present offer to urge my acceptance of it. On account of the above obstacle however, independent of other difficulties at present in the way, I must decline your kind offer.

requesting you, gentlemen, to present to the Board of Trustees my acknowledgements of the honour intended, and assuring you that I shall always feel a peculiar interest in the prosperity of your university and town, I have the honor to be, Gentlemen,

Your obt. servt. HENRY VETHAKE

Mess H. Clay and B Gratz.

ALS. KyLxT. Vethake had held positions as a professor of mathematics and natural philosophy at Columbia, Queen's College (now Rutgers University), the College of New Jersey, and Dickinson College, in which last post he had remained since 1821. In 1829 he returned to the College of New Jersey and later removed to the University of the City of New York, to Washington College, Lexington, Virginia, to the University of Pennsylvania, and finally to the Polytechnic College of Philadelphia. He published *Principles of Political Economy* in 1838 (revised edition, 1844) and edited the *Encyclopedia Americana, Supplementary Volume* (1848) and various other works.

1 Not found. 2 Not identified. 3 Not identified.

To Board of Navy Commissioners

Gent. Ashland 6h. Septr. 1824

The Ton of Hemp, got out by the new Breaker from unretted hemp, which I engaged to deliver for the use of the Navy Department, by way of an experiment,[1] has been sent from Wheeling to Mess. Macdonald & Ridgely merchants Baltimore. Supposing that you might possibly prefer to have the contemplated experiment on the article made either at Balto. or Philadelphia rather than Washington, I inclose herein a letter,[2] addressed to those gentlemen, requesting them to deliver the ton of hemp to your order at either of those three places which you may be pleased to designate; and I have to request that you will instruct them accordingly.

I have the honor to be Your obedient Servant H. CLAY

The Honble The Commissioners Of the Navy Board.

P.S. Be pleased to transmit the inclosed with your instructions to Mess. Mc. D. & R. as soon as practicable. H C.

ALS. DNA, RG45, Navy Commissioners' Misc. Letters Received, 1825-1831, vol. 10.
1 See above, Clay to Rodgers, June 14, 1824. 2 Not found.

From Josephus B. Stuart

My dear Sir. New York: 6th. Septr. 1824.

Your favor of the 14th. of June[1] came duly to hand, & would have been acknowledged ere this, but the unsettled state of our Political

Market induced me to delay from time to time untill something decisive should take place. Two days since I forwarded you M. M. Noah's pamphlet, & to day the Evening Post containing Judge Van Ness s statement, with a short reply & a prospectus.[2]— This blew up in the Crawford ranks, in this City— if followed up by Noah, will ruin Mr. Crawford in this state: & it will do so in time to have its effect on other states prior to the Election. Several canvasses of our Legislature were made during the August session, & the following may be confidently relied on as the strongest against yourself—For Adams 61. Crawford 59. Clay 34. & Jackson 6. As it requires 81 to elect—neither party can carry their ticket without the aide [*sic*] of the 34 Clay Men— Van Buren endeavored to impress the public with the belief that the Clay men would vote for Crawford; this produced a letter from Genl. McClure to the editors of the Statesman which together with a private letter from Mc.Clure to me I sent J. S. Johnston at Philada. to be forwarded to you.[3]—Since which I have letters from Genl. Porter & Mr. Hammond also Mr. Leake[4] in which they spoke with considerable confidence of carrying the whole vote of the state for you; but as this can be done only by a total abandonment of Mr. Crawford a [*sic*] transfer of his votes to you, I have never had much faith in such a result.— On the other hand a number of Adams men in the Legislature—with some of the leaders out— (including the editors of the American[5]) oferred [*sic*] a negociation with Mr. Tillotson[6] for the purpose of making a joint ticket of 18 Adams & 18 Clay men.— We have closed with this proposal which I think will be carried into effect in good faith, This is all I have anticipated & with this I shall be satisfied.— Forsyth & Van Buren made an excursion 10 days since to New Jersey[7]—where they met with such a reception as induced them to beat a speedy retreat.— I am authorized to say that Messs. Dickerson & Penington[8] of N. J. have abandoned Mr. Crawford. The state is divided between Adams. Jackson & yourself—but in what proportions I have not be [*sic*] able to ascertain with any certainty. Mr. Crawford stands no possible chance east of this State. I yesterday saw some intercepted correspondence from a Crawford Missionary to the east,—he describes Crawfords case as hopeless.—

With great regard I am truly Yours. J. B, STUART

H. Clay Esqr.

ALS. DLC-HC (DNA, M212, R1). 1 Not found.

2 Early in September, 1824, Noah had published a pamphlet describing the financial difficulties of his editorship of the New York *National Advocate*, complaining of the controls asserted by the proprietors, and attributing the differences which had arisen between them to "the unhappy divisions now existing in the republican party." Noah believed that his opponents anticipated Crawford's withdrawal from the presidential campaign and wished to hold the journal available "to make terms" upon a personal basis "with any of the other candidates"; while Noah, himself, was thought to have leaned toward Clinton. In conclusion the editor announced his plans to establish a second journal under the same name, "to be published under the protection

of the republican general committee, and to take the rank which the National Advocate now holds, to support the same principles, and the same men."

On August 31 William P. Van Ness, the current proprietor of the journal, had explained that, when Noah sought in the preceding May to liquidate his indebtedness, the previous owner had objected to the *"manner"* in which Noah was conducting the paper and had feared that the editor might support "our political adversaries, particularly as it regarded the pending question of the electoral law." This situation having since been resolved, Van Ness had concluded by offering to convey the journal to Noah or his friends upon the latter's "refunding the amount of the advances which have been made." On September 2 Noah had, nevertheless, announced his withdrawal from editorship of the journal, and on the following day Van Ness had published a detailed statement of the financial transactions involved and had released the earlier correspondence.

The incident was settled when, on September 6, Van Ness surrendered title to the journal to the Republican General Committee of New York and that organization, on September 16, adopted a formal resolution "That it be recommended, that Mr. NOAH resume his former station as Editor of the NATIONAL ADVOCATE, and use his best efforts as heretofore, in supporting the honor and interests of the country and the accredited usages of the Republican party." *Niles' Weekly Register*, XXVII (September 11, 18, 1824), 24-28, 36; Washington *Daily National Intelligencer*, September 23, 1824.

3 See above, Johnston to Clay, August 30, September 1, 1824.

4 Peter B. Porter; Jabez D. Hammond; Isaac Q. Leake.

5 New York *American*. 6 Robert Tillotson.

7 See above, Johnston to Clay, August 30, 1824.

8 Mahlon Dickerson; probably William Sandford Pennington, a veteran of the Revolution, member of the State Assembly, 1797-1799, licensed as an attorney in 1802, reporter and justice of the State Supreme Court, 1806-1813, Governor, 1813 and 1814, and Federal judge for the district of New Jersey from 1813 till his death in 1826.

To Josiah S. Johnston

Dear Sir Ashland 10h. Septr 1824

I received this day your obliging letter of the 25h. Ulto. with that of Mr. Ingalls inclosed, for both of which I thank you. I am perfectly sensible of the very great disadvantage under which I have labored, in respect to the Presidency, for the want of a support by the presses in the large Cities. It has been unavoidable but by a resort to means which my principles forbade. Although I believe the number of my personal friends is not exceeded by that of either of the other Candidates, there is a large, indeed the larger, mass of the Community who do not stand in the relation of friendship to any of the candidates. On that mass the Secretaries are able to throw out, from their respective departments, a more intense & vivifying heat than I am capable of ejecting. The Cities are focal points for the collection and subsequent distribution of this heat. The evil is great but I have seen no conscientious course but that of patiently bearing it.

I do not believe that any thing can be effected in New England against Mr. Adams. Impressions may be made abroad of the extent of opposition to him there but that is all, except possibly in Rhode Island. Still the support of me by the Galaxy, if it should be rendered, will not be without its value. I think my friends in New York were mistaken in not allowing the two papers there, inclined to espouse my cause, to pursue the bent of their inclination. One of them I remark is since become favorable to Mr. Crawford.[1]

In respect to the Vice Presidency, I wrote you some days ago.[2] When my name was first brought forward seriously, I resolved neither to offer nor to accept any arrangement in regard to myself or to office for others. I have adhered to that resolution hitherto, and shall continue to abide by it to the last. I considered that I was and ought to be in the hands of the public to be disposed of as it pleased. Most undoubtedly the office of V. President is one of high respectability and great dignity, preferable in my opinion to any place in the Cabinet. If the acceptance of it were offered to me (I mean by the public having the right to tender it) I could not decline it; but I cannot seek it, much less make any sacrifices of honor or duty to obtain it. Nor, if I were capable of lending myself to an arrangement with the friends of Mr. Crawford to secure it, do I think it would be attainable certainly. If Mr. Gallatin were dropt, and Mr. Calhoun and myself only were run, Mr. Calhoun would be elected, if Mr. Adams's friends vote for him, unless mine were to drop me for the first office and give me their suffrages for the Vice Presidency. But my Western friends could not now, if it were desirable, be induced to withdraw me for the first and hold me up for the second office; and if they could, I do not think it certain that Mr. Crawford would obtain the *electoral* vote of any one of the states believed to be favorable to me. They would divide between Genl. Jackson and Mr. Adams, principally for the latter. What the representatives of those states may do in the House, if, notwithstanding their vote for me, I should not enter it, is another question. In that contingency they would stand uncommitted, as between the other Candidates, and would be left free to make their selection according to their sense of the public interest. Besides, public sentiment in Ohio and Kentucky has taken a strong direction towards Mr. Sanford of N. York for the Vice Presidency. He has been recently, in one of the three electoral districts, into which this State is divided, recommended by a convention of delegates assembled to fix on an Electoral ticket for me to the consideration of the people as a fit person for Vice President. He had been before recommended in the same way by another of those districts.[3] You are aware that he was recommended in a similar way by an imposing assemblage at Columbus in Ohio in the month of July.[4] If Mr. Sandford [*sic*] should be voted for as Vice President by all the electors who may support me as President, and I should be supported by all those (including New York) who are claimed to be favorable to Mr. Crawford, Mr. Calhoun obtaining the residue, he would enter the Senate so advantageously as that his election there would be certain. There is but one contingency on which I could probably be elected, and that requires the extremely improbable conjunction of all Mr. Crawfords friends with a portion of those of Mr. Adams. Doubtless if I should be run for that office by the friends of either of those gentleman [*sic*], that circumstance would have, I presume, a favorable consideration with my friends in determining the direction of their vote in the House of R. if I should be excluded from it. To what extent it would operate you are as competent to judge as I am. As my friends, upon the supposition of their acting in concert, will have great weight, and therefore will be anxiously courted, in the H. of R. should I not be carried there, it is not unlikely that if Mr. Crawfords friends were known to contemplate dropping Mr. Gallatin and taking me up, that Mr. Adams's friends would also run me, to prevent any advantage being obtained of them by that circumstance.

The determination of my friends, as far as I know it in in [*sic*] the West, is to persevere to the last in their support of me. I understand that the circular, mentioned in my last, announcing that determination, will be published in a few days by the Kentucky Comee. of Correspondence.[5]

I recd. by the last mail letters from Genl McClure and Judge Rochester.[6] The former is sanguine, and the latter not without hopes, that I shall obtain the whole or a part at least of the vote of N. York. They speak of considerable popular movements, in various Counties, which are expected in my favor. You can judge of these matters better than I. There can be no doubt I think that the breach between Mr. Adams' friends and those of Mr. Crawford has become too wide for them to get together, unless the death of the latter should unfortunately happen. In that event I doubt if the animosity could survive so as to prevent Mr. Adams from deriving any support from that quarter. The reserve too which you describe as having been manifested by Mr. V. Buren shews that he means to hold himself free to act as he pleases, if Mr. Crawford should be out of the way.

My information from Virginia continues to assure me of the support of that State, if the Secretary of the Treasury should be dropt.[7] There is one danger which if possible ought to be guarded against. That is, that they may not know at Richmond of Mr. Crawfords loss of the vote at Albany (should that happen) and continuing to support him to the last I may be sent into the House with such disparity of numbers compared to Mr. Adams, (if he should get the N. York vote) as to place him decidedly on the vantage ground. If the vote of Virginia were given to me that, in addition to what there is every probability of my obtaining, would place me on such high ground as to render my election almost certain. Tennessee remains firm in its attachment to me in the second instance; and as between Genl. Jackson Mr. Adams and me I think I should get ultimately the vote of that State Pennsylvania, Alabama, Mississippi, and possibly South Carolina and Maryland.

I shall not violate your confidence in the letters which you have obligingly writ me or those with which you may continue to favor me. I need not say that mine are addressed to you in like confidence, nor how much I am obliged by the zeal and discretion which you have displayed. I am faithfly Your friend H. CLAY

The Honble J. S. Johnston.

ALS. PHi. Brief extract published in Colton (ed.), *Private Correspondence of Henry Clay*, 103.

1 See above, Johnston to Clay, June 27, 1824; August 30, 1824.

2 See above, Clay to Johnston, September 3, 1824.

3 See above, Clay to Johnston, August 31, 1824. Delegates to the meeting for selection of Clay electors in the Second Electoral District, at Harrodsburg on September 6, had also recommended nomination of Sanford.

4 See above, Clay to Johnston, July 21, 1824, note.

5 See above, Clay to Johnston, August 31, 1824.

6 George McClure; William B. Rochester. Letters not found.

7 See above, Brooke to Clay, July 12, 1824; unsigned letter to editor, Lexington *Kentucky Reporter*, August 16, 1824.

Receipt from Robert Scott

[September 10, 1824]

Lexington 10th. Septr. 1824 recd. of H. Clay only acting Executor of J. Morrison decd. the Sum of Sixteen hundred and eighty five dollars & Seventy five Cents (Amt of Gratz & Bruce's two Notes) on Acct. of a legacy of Fifteen thousand dollars in money bequeathed to me by the deceased.[1] ROBT. SCOTT

$1685,,75

ADS, "Duplicate." DLC-TJC (DNA, M212, R16).

1 See above, Receipt, October 31, 1823.

To John C. Calhoun

Sir Lexington 11 Septr. 1824

Being informed by Mr. Cleon Hawkins[1] that he intends to make application to your Department for some contract, for the supply of the Army, I have the honor to state that, from the very high character which Mr. Hawkins sustains, I have no doubt that he will execute, with fidelity, any contract into which he may enter.

I have the honor to be Your ob. Servant H. CLAY

The Honble The Secretary of War. &c &c &c

ALS. Owned by Thomas D. Clark, Lexington, Kentucky.

1 A Georgetown, Kentucky, merchant.

From Josiah S. Johnston

Dear Sir. Philadelphia Saturday 11" Sept. [1824]

It has rain'd all day, & we had the most gloomy prospect & forebodings of the meeting[1]— But it had excited much interest & would have resulted in a powerful meeting if the weather had permitted— & notwithstanding the weather & th [*sic*] unpropitious appearances, a very respectable meeting has been held—highly respectable in point of Character, property, Talent & principle Mr. Cary [*sic*] was Chairman—Mr. Richards Secy[2]—

An address was deliverd [*sic*]—& resolutions passed all which will be printed & distributed in every direction The address is appropriate—manly—& popular[3]

I will send it in a few days— The following Gentlemen appointed a Committe [*sic*] of Correspondence Langdon Cheves. R. W. Meade. M. Carey. Jas Harper Cadwallader Evans. Wm. Young. Mark Richards B. McCredy J. T. Wharton. J. D. Godman. J. G Longstreth— Turner Camac Edwd. Ingersol. T. B Freeman Wm. Rawle Jr. They are also to form the Electoral Ticket[4]—

They are in very high spirits—& will push their example & influence throughout this state & else where— I hope your other friends in different places will be induced to Come out— you are very strong in this state—& nothing but early exertions was necessary to have given you the Vote— I hope yet to See a Strong expression— The Vote of this state is still liable to Change— The meeting & th Committee will be a good demonstration— It is equally supported by all parties—

I send you the inclosed Letter[5] to shew you that the Spirits are at work in the North—

If Adams is broken in N. England—he is gone— Your friends seem to be firm in N. York.—

There is a great disposition in Mr. Crawfords friends to run you as Vice President in his Ticket— To this I can make no reply— I cannot change your position—or make any promise—you are nominated by six states—who can do with you as they please—you are in the hands of the people & must yield with a good grace, to whatever is done you *are neutral—neither seeking nor declining*—

Many plausible pretexts are urged—the first is the necessity of defeating Adams— The necessity of securing th the [*sic*] 2nd. Place in your hands in the event of Mr. Crawfords death— To defeat Calhoun— To place you in the foreground hereafter— But above *all to insure Mr. Crawfords Election*— They seem quite Confident that with your Concurrence It could be Carried, by the Electoral vote— I do not think your States would Come into the measure— It is too lat [*sic*]—your claims to the first place cannot be withdrawn— They will in all probability run you as Vice President without any Understanding— They say if you or your friends Consent. Gallatin will not be in th way

The Presidential election is involved in the deepest doubt, uncertainty & perplexity—you see the Chances & Can estimate probabilities—

Suppress your feelings—your hopes & ambition distrust all the Sanguine Calculations of your friends— Wait Calmly & patiently th Issue—

You have receid. the most honorable testimony of public favor— If you are not elected it is th misfortune of your position. If you was a Citisen of N. York—Pennsylvania or of N. England you would be.—

They were quite mistaken in Supposing Genl. Jackson would yield to Mr. Adams he will not give an Inch— He is now pressing closely on him in South Carolina & Jersey— This must be a delicate business for the War & Navy Departments— They do not know which foot to tread on—

Crawford be assured has recd. a mortal blow—from which he can never rise— He may live along as Genl. Brown[6] does— They are Cases of partial Death—The functions of Nature either from excessive action or diminished force of life—refuse to act The muscular power is enfeebled—beyond renovation—

I respect his misfortunes.—But his is a living death— They say he is Convalescing— It is true— But the power of life cannot be restored— He must be always feeble—frail—infirm—liable to relapse & sudden Death— all that we Conjectured about his state—& the views of his friends—*was true*— But they say—Their eyes are now opened"

If I warn you against encouraging any hopes, that may aggrivate disappointment—you may soon read me a Lesson on the same Subject—& teach me to look with a Phylosophic indifference upon the Versitility of my Constituents— But your Lecture will be entirely useless— I have the benifit of Some experience, which you have never had— I can be turnd out without an emotion—& be beaten with a good grace— They delight to *put me* up *& take me* down,[7] without much reason—& according to the natural order of things—it is my time to go out— yrs. truly. J. S. JOHNSTON

ALS. InU. 1 See above, Johnston to Clay, September 4, 1824.

2 Mathew Carey; Mark Richards, Philadelphia merchant and manufacturer.

3 See *Niles' Weekly Register*, XXVII (September 25, 1824), 61-63.

4 Harper, a native of Ireland, educated in the public schools of Philadelphia, was a manufacturer of brick, a wholesale grocer, and later a Whig member of Congress, 1833-1837. Cadwalader Evans, formerly representative from Montgomery County in the Pennsylvania General Assembly (1790-1800), had removed to Philadelphia in 1812, where he became a merchant, active in the promotion of internal improvements. Young and Freeman were Philadelphia publishers and booksellers, the latter also operating an auction house. Turner Camac, owner of large estates in Ireland, had settled in Philadelphia around the turn of the century and embarked in mercantile affairs—he was one of the managers in construction of the Union Canal in 1824. Rawle

was a lawyer, one of the founders of the Historical Society of Pennsylvania and long active in that organization. Bernard McCready and J. G. Longstreth (Langstreth, Langstroth), not further identified. Thomas I., not J. T., Wharton served on the Committee. See *Niles' Weekly Register,* XXII (September 25, 1824), 62.

5 Not found.

6 Jacob J. Brown had "been severely attacked by the palsy" in 1821 and had been incapacitated for almost a year. *Niles' Weekly Register,* XXI (November 3, 1821), 159; XXIII (October 5, 1822), 80.

7 Johnston had been an unsuccessful candidate for re-election to Congress in 1822.

To Robert P. Henry

My dear Sir (Confidential) Ashland 14th. Sept. 1824

I have received your favor of the 4h. inst. by your brother,[1] whose acquaintance I shall be extremely happy to make and which I shall take an early opportunity of cultivating. I pray you to give my best respects to your venerable father, one of my earliest and steadiest friends, and express to him how much I lament his present infirmities.[2]

I wish I could satisfy the curiosity which your kindness towards me prompts you to feel, in regard to the Presidential election; but really the issue of it continues involved in as much uncertainty as ever. It is not true that my friends in the New York Legislature have abandoned me; on the contrary I am assured that they remain firm and determined to support me throughout; that neither Crawford nor Adams has a majority in the Legislature; that my friends hold the balance in their hands; and that overtures have been made to them by those of Mr. Adams to divide the electoral vote of the State between us.[3] I have recently received letters from Genl. McClure, who you know is a member of the Legislature, and from Judge Rochester.[4] The former is very sanguine and the latter entertains strong hopes that I shall obtain the whole or a part of the vote of that State. From Virginia I am assured, and I do not doubt, that the vote of that State will be given to me, if Mr. Crawford should be withdrawn, or should lose the vote of N. York, which would be tantamount to his withdrawal.[5] In Rhode Island strong hopes are entertained that a joint ticket for Mr. Crawford and me, which it is proposed to run, will prevail.[6] I have heard nothing decisive from New Jersey, since the meeting in June of the three Eastern Counties, in which I was nominated.[7] Mr. Kinsey[8] informed me that on that occasion one thousand persons at least attended. And the Secretary of the Navy,[9] prior to my departure from Washington, told me that if those three Counties should support me, I might confidently count upon the vote of New Jersey. Maryland is greatly divided, but I still think that I shall receive some votes in that State.

I do not think that the cause of Genl. Jackson has, upon the whole advanced, since the adjournment of Congress. In Pennsa.

he has certainly lost ground, if he should obtain the vote of that State. The claim which his friends set up to Louisiana is without foundation. I have every reason to believe that I shall receive its vote; but it would be given to Mr. Adams in preference to the General. South Carolina is inclined to support him; but South Carolina is prudent and will not cast away its vote.

I think my friends have no occasion to despair, although it must be admitted that the issue of the Election continues very doubtful. Many circumstances may arise; many combinations of interest in other States may take place. And it appears to me that the best course for us to pursue is to persevere with hope and confidence, and leave the result to events. I am faithfully Your friend

R. P. Henry Esqr. H. CLAY

ALS. Owned by Dr. George A. Robertson, Louisville, Kentucky.

1 Probably Gustavus Adolphus Henry, a student at Transylvania University, from which he was graduated in 1825. Born in Scott County, Kentucky, in 1804, he had moved with his parents to Christian County in 1818. He studied law, was admitted to the bar, and began practice in Hopkinsville. From 1831 to 1833 he was a member of the Kentucky House of Representatives. He then removed to Clarksville, Tennessee, attained success as a lawyer and orator, was active in politics as a Whig, and served in the Tennessee legislature, 1851-1852. Unsuccessful as a candidate for Governor in 1853, he was later elected a Senator in the Confederate Congress.

The letter to which Clay refers has not been found.

2 William Henry died November 23 of this year.

3 See above, Stuart to Clay, September 6, 1824.

4 George McClure; William B. Rochester. Cf. above, Clay to Johnston, September 10, 1824.

5 See above, Brooke to Clay, July 12, 1824; Clay to Johnston, September 10, 1824.

6 See above, Robbins to Clay, August 5, 1824.

7 See above, Johnston to Clay, June 27, 1824.

8 Probably Charles Kinsey, New Jersey paper manufacturer, several times a member of the State legislature, United States Congressman, 1817-1819, 1820-1821. He was later judge of the court of common pleas and of the orphans' court in Bergen County. No letter from Kinsey has been found.

9 Samuel L. Southard.

From Thomas S. Hinde

Dear Sir/ Newport Septr 15 1824.

In haste, I dropped you a few lines by W W Southgat[e] a few days ago.[1] Vatteir's [*sic*] propositions were mere *smoke;*[2] I procured a list of his notes & the persons are scattered from Maine I beleive [*sic*] to Georgia! Some at *Boston,* Some at *N. Orleans* and many in the other world! The property he held in Security for these debts is Some lots in a little village on the Ohio in the State of Indiana; Sold in 1818 in the *age* of folly & *landed mania,* now of no value.

Under an impression that I will not take his offer, he has obtained a reconveyance from *Lytle quit* claim as *usual.* Lytle having relinquished previously his right of possession to me, & my tenants holding under me have been *notified* that next month he will Sue them for *rent monthly*: this no doubt will be a *magistrate* proceeding,

Knowing, or being advised by Council that if he Commences with an Ejectment that I will take it up to the Circuit Court. Is there not Some remedy? You recollect that the decree was drawn up that I should remain in peaceble [*sic*] & quiet possession—. Should Vatteir proceed in any way; could we not get an order from the Circuit Judge to stay any proceeding Contrary to the decree— I should like to be advised & proceed immediately if Such a step be found practicable—. I shall anxiously wait an answer. Yours Sincerely

TH: S. HINDE

P S—In case any step be necessary papers may be directed to Timothy Kirby Esqr of of [*sic*] Cincinnatti [*sic*]—

In case of Hinde vs Humphrey,[3] at Frankfort, may require a little Attention— Yr friend TH. S, H

Could not a writ be issued agt Vatteir &c for back rents

ALS. DLC-TJC (DNA, M212, R12). Addressed to Clay at Lexington, "Fav of Mr Benj. Fowler—" (of Kenton County, Kentucky). Endorsed by Clay: "Answered & gave advice 24 Septr. 1824." Answer not found.

1 Letter not found. William W. Southgate, of Newport, Kentucky, had received the LL.B. degree from Transylvania University earlier in the year and was married in Lexington in December. He represented Campbell County in the State legislature, 1827-1828, 1832-1833, and 1836-1837, and afterward moved to Covington, Kentucky.

2 See above, Hinde to Clay, July 7, 1824.

3 Not found; Humphrey, not identified.

From Josiah S. Johnston

Dear Sir. Philadelphia Sept. 16h. 1824

Since I wrote you last—The Aurora[1] has adopted your Cause— Having no press—It was impossible to present your claims or your Chances before the people—or to Counteract the United efforts of all parties to withdraw you from the Contest. This paper has now espoused your Cause. It has explained itself in a neat & plain article. & will hereafter be devoted to your Interest This paper is in the hands of your friends & attention will be paid to it. —It will be Widely distributed— He publishes a daily paper + Three Times & twice a Week—so that it Circulates widely— I shall send them to your friends in N. York. Boston Rhode Island & the West. I send you an acct. of the meeting in Western part of N. York[2]—which will be followed— you will see the statement of Genl. McClure Corroborated by 13 members in answer to Mr. Wheaton.[3] all the evidence Concurs to demonstrate that you will get half of that state.

I send you the address of the meeting in this City favorable to yr. Election[4]— I shall also send you Circulars to yr. friends in different states— This—must be republished throughout the W. & South.

Mr. Crawfords friends are very sanguine & never doubt, where there is a hope—They speak with Confidence of N. Carolina—New York & part of N. England— But allowing him North Carolina his fate rests upon N.York— If he does not get N.Y. you will be a head of him—

If Adams looses [*sic*] half of N. England, he is gone—

I trust there is as much reason to expect Confidence & Constancy in your friends to the West as in any other part— I rely they will be faithful

The affair must terminate against all Chances & Calculations if you are not returnd— But so it may be— all things are uncertain—

I do not receive the Reporter[5]— with great regard

J. S. JOHNSTON

ALS. InU. Addressed to Clay at Lexington.

1 Formal announcement of the Philadelphia *Aurora's* support of Clay was issued on September 18. The journal in 1823 had been sold by John Sanderson to one of his former pupils, Richard Penn Smith, who had studied law and had been admitted to the bar in 1820. After about five years Smith gave up the editorship of the *Aurora* and returned to the practice of law. He was also a writer of essays, novels, short stories, plays, and a biography.

2 A meeting had been held on September 4 in Bath, Steuben County, at which resolutions had been adopted endorsing the candidacy of Clay and Nathan Sanford, urging the State legislators to designate presidential electors in conformity with this sentiment, and specifically requesting the appointment of Peter B. Porter as one of the State's electors. Lexington *Kentucky Reporter,* October 4, 1824.

3 See above, Johnston to Clay, August 30, 1824. On August 4, Henry Wheaton had addressed a letter to thirteen members of the New York legislature, known opponents of Crawford's candidacy, asking whether there was a majority of that governing body for or against his election. James Burt, for many years State Senator from Orange County, and the other twelve correspondents, agreed that Crawford did not hold the support of the majority. Washington *Daily National Intelligencer,* September 15, 1824.

4 See above, Johnston to Clay, September 11, 1824.

5 Lexington *Kentucky Reporter.*

To John J. Crittenden

My dear Sir Ashland 17 Sept. 1824

Although I know how utterly unavailing are the condolences of friends, however sincere, and that nothing but time can assuage the grief which is excited by a loss so irreparable and afflicting as that which you have recently sustained, I cannot deny to myself the melancholy satisfaction of expressing to you my deepest sympathy for your heavy bereavement. In the lamented death of Mrs. Crittenden[1] I do not merely recognize the loss of the wife of a friend, but that of a friend herself. I knew her I believe, before you did; and altho' her residence in another and distant part of the State prevented my seeing her for many years, I never ceased to feel the respect and esteem for her which was inspired by our early acquaintance.

Altho' thus early deprived of a mother's care and a mothers tenderness, it must be some consolation to you to know that your children will find their mother's place supplied, as far as that is possible, in the affections and attentions of Mrs. Wilkinson and Mrs. Price.[2]

One would be almost inclined sometimes to think that our State had lost, in these last years, divine favor. The afflictions, by death, have been numerous and distressing in the extreme. Frankfort, in particular, appears to have suffered more than its due proportion. My family is not wholly exempt from disease. Theodore, just returned from New Orleans, is down with a threatening fever; and I have myself had a slight attack.

With best wishes I remain faithfully Your friend H. CLAY

John J. Crittenden Esqr.

ALS. NcD. [1] On September 14.

[2] Mrs. Lyddall Wilkinson; Mrs. Andrew F. Price—sisters of Mrs. Crittenden. The former, born Elizabeth Taylor Lee, had married Dr. Lyddall Wilkinson, of Frankfort, about 1812.

From C[harles] H[ay]

Hon. Henry Clay, Lexington, Ky. Navy Dep'mt. 18. Sept. 1824.

Sir,

I have received your letter of the 6th. inst. in behalf of Mr. Hart.[1]

His name shall be registered on the list of applicants, and will receive due consideration when an increase of Midshipmen is required for the service. I am, respectfully, &c.

For the Sec. Navy, C.H.

Copy. DNA, RG45, General Letter Book, vol. 14, p. 455. Charles, son of George Hay, was Chief Clerk of the Navy Department.

[1] Letter not found. John S. Hart, son of Thomas Hart, Jr., was appointed a midshipman in the Navy on January 1, 1825.

To Josiah S. Johnston

My dear Sir Ashland 19h. Septr. 1824

I recd. to day your favor, under date the 4h. with its inclosures, as I did your former letters with theirs, including Genl. McClures letter.[1] I thank you for them. I have directed twenty copies of the Circular, prepared by the K. Comee. of Correspondence[2] (which I have not seen) to be forwarded to you for distribution. Copies have been also ordered to most of our friends in Philada. and N. York. Altho' I have not perused it, I presume from the pen from which it will issue that it is well composed. An address from the same quarter has been written to Virginia, intended for that region, but so guarded as to do mischief no where, if it be published,[3] which is to be anticipated. These papers will, I think, contribute to arouse and animate my friends. The remark which you make is but too true that there has not been sufficient united exertion among them. Every thing is yet going well in the West. It is amusing to see the mistakes or mis statements made about it to the Eastward. For example: Strother was said to be elected in Missouri & was claimed by the Franklin gazette for Genl. Jackson. No says the Nat. Journal, altho' he is elected, we *know* he is for Adams. Now it turns out that Scott is elected and that Strother declared himself for me.[4]

Faithfully Your friend H. CLAY

The honble J. S. Johnston.

ALS. PHi. Published in Colton (ed.), *Private Correspondence of Henry Clay,* 100.
1 See above, Johnston to Clay, August 25, 30, September 1, 1824.
2 See above, Clay to Johnston, August 31, 1824. 3 Not found.
4 In August John Scott had won re-election to Congress over George F. Strother and a third candidate.

From Josiah S. Johnston

Dear Sir. Philadelphia Sept. 19h. 1824

I have sent you the address of the Philaa. meeting[1]—Which is a strong statement of your Case. I hope your friends will Cause it to be extensively Circulated to the West—as We have to the North I send you ten papers of the twice a week paper (Aurora) for which I have subscribed for 6 months at 2$ each—$20—which you may send to me for the printer— I send also ten to Trimble & to F. Johnston—[2] The rest I distribute to friends in all directions. This paper will Contain all the pieces in the daily paper— There is no talent in the Editorial department— But this will be partially supplied— I recommend great respect delicacy, & moderation with regard to the Candidates.

The War between them is Carried in a way to excite the most angry passions & the most violent conflict—a man goaded to madness & wriathing [*sic*] under the Lash is not in the best temper of mind, to place himself at the head of a great nation—besides it will place you on much higher grounds before the Country & the world —& even in the opinions of those Gentlemen.—

With great regard yrs truly. J. S. JOHNSTON

I have Recd. ys of the 3rd. Inst.

ALS. InU. Addressed to Clay at Lexington.
1 See above, Johnston to Clay, September 11, 1824.
2 David Trimble; Francis Johnson.

To John Bradford

20 Sepr 1824

We request you to call a meeting of the Board of Trustees this evening at 3 O Clocok [*sic*]. H CLAY
John. Bradford Esqr. Chairman JAMES TROTTER
E. I. WINTER

ANS, signed also by Trotter and Winter. KyLxT. Endorsed by Bradford: "Mr. [William] Macbean will please notify the trustees agreeably to the above request." Cf. below, Resolutions, September 24, 1824.

From John Rodgers

Sir 20h. September 1824

The Commissioners of the Navy have had the honor of receiving your letter of the 6h. ins. On the 15h. ins they received from Messrs. Macdonald and Ridgely, a bill of lading of the hemp shipped by them to this Navy Yard—and they immediately gave direction to the Commandant of the Yard, to receive the hemp, and report its state and condition.

When it shall be received here, the Commissioners will have the honour of again writing to you upon the subject.

I have the honor to be &c JNO. RODGERS

Honorable Henry Clay Ashland Lexington Ky.

Copy. DNA, RG45, Navy Commissioners' Misc. Letters Sent, vol. 3, p. 311.

Receipt from Daniel Bradford

[September 21, 1824]

Recd. Sept. 21, 1824, from Bro. Henry Clay, Ten Dollars and fifty Cents, in full of his dues to Lexington Lodge No 1.[1]

DAN BRADFORD, Secretary.

ADS. DLC-TJC (DNA, M212, R16).

[1] Free and Accepted Masons.

Executor's Account with Nicholas Estate

[*ca.* September 22, 1824]

As the only acting executor of the estate of James Morrison, Clay files the settlement account of the estate of George Nicholas, for whom Morrison had served as executor, covering the period from July 9, 1810, through September 22, 1824. Examined and certified, October 12, 1824, by commissioners appointed by the court; approved by the Fayette County Court at its November Term, 1824, and ordered to record. Fayette County, Will Book G, 25-31.

From Josiah S. Johnston

Dear Sir Phila Sept. 22nd. 1824

The Aurora is sent you, from which you will see the manner it will be Conducted— Let your friends send them to Indianna [*sic*] Illinois &c— I send ten to Johnson & 10 Trimble 10 to Duralde[1]— & I send some to Ohio— The Committee[2] have been active— They distribute about 100 papers over the Union— It will have a good effect. It will Keep alive your Cause which sank every where under the want of direction & management.— I had myself no Idea untill the adjournment of Congress of the total want of Interest or Zeal or arrangement among your friends With a little activity & money a sufficient number of presses would have been engaged—

Your being out of view has had the effect to raise a war among the Candidates in which you may possibly profit by your neutrality.

Mr. Duponts[3] tells me that it is not impossible you may get Delaware— He says you had many friends there—but you was thought to be almost withdrawn[4] & they went over to the other Candidates— at present They are nearly equally divided between the other three Candidates—neither having a majority—& they are all pledged against the *opposing Candidates*

He therefore thinks it more probable they will at length Unite on you—

This is Conjectural & probable—

The Committee will encourage this—

I learn that the Patriot can be had in New York for some money & will be enlarged— I go therefore to morrow morning to accomplish this object— It is in vain to strive against the United influence of the press without one— I will set one a-going before I return—

A pamphlet is Coming out there by Mr. Lockwood,[5] I Know nothing of the Talent displayd in the work— I wish I could have seen it before the publication— you will have it in a few days.—

I wait the Letter of yr. Committee[6] which I expect will be able—

The War is fiercer among the Beligerents [*sic*]. heavy disclosures are making agt. Mr. Adams, in the affair with Mr. Ker[7] It is very Characteristic of the Man The prevailing opinion is that Adams will loose [*sic*] S. Carolina & Jersey although very lately he was thought to be strongest

If Crawford should unexpectly [*sic*] get N. York—Adams will be Confined to the N. England States—They are in great agitation & Confusion & it is not possible to Say what be [*sic*] the result There is then a reasonable expectation of going to the House to his *exclusion* Jackson is beating him in S. Carolina & Jersey at present—

I write this scrawl in haste yrs. J. S JOHNS[TON]

There is to be a meeting in Jersey in a few days to form a new ticket[8]

ALS. InU. Addressed to Clay at Lexington.

1 Martin Duralde (Jr.). Cf. above, Johnston to Clay, September 19, 1824.

2 The Committee of Correspondence established at the Philadelphia meeting of Clay supporters. See above, Johnston to Clay, September 11, 1824.

3 Probably Eleuthère I. du Pont.

4 See above, Clay to Stuart, March 24, 1824, note; Clay to Johnston, August 31, 1824, note.

5 Ralph Ingersoll Lockwood, young New York lawyer and political writer, later the author of at least two novels, published *An Address to the Republicans and People of New York, Pennsylvania and Virginia, upon the State of Presidential Parties, By a*

Citizen of New York, To Which Are Added, Questions and Answers on the Presidential Elections (New York and Philadelphia, 1824).

6 See above, Clay to Johnston, August 31, September 19, 1824.

7 Alexander Kerr, Cashier of the Bank of the Metropolis, Washington, D. C., who held a protested note of Mrs. Mary G. Moulton, also of Washington, for $187.50, which John Quincy Adams had endorsed as security. In a diary entry of March 20, 1824, Adams had explained that the note had been given to aid the woman and her small children when her furniture had been seized under a distress warrant obtained by Kerr for unpaid rent. Adams maintained that Kerr had taken advantage of a deception by which the note had been written to cover nine months' rent, when the order of distraint had been issued for only $125.00, the sum due for six months. Though Adams had paid the note in full early in April, Kerr had refused to surrender it because the further amount of $1.75 in protest charges remained unpaid.

Adams' friend Edward Wyer had reported to him on April 15 that the matter had been discussed at the tavern dinner table. During the succeeding months Adams several times noted the repetition of slander upon his public and private character. Finally, on October 27, 1824, Peter Force, in the Washington *National Journal,* publicly accused Kerr of forgery, by altering documents so as to change the terms and conditions of the note. In his accompanying statement, the editor commented: "We have permitted him [Kerr], for months past, to exercise his ingenuity and to obey the dictates of his malignant heart, in devising slanderous accusations against Mr. Adams in silence; we had hoped that a consciousness of his own moral obliquity, and the invulnerable nature of the character which he assailed would have taught him to desist; but he has been blind to the consequences of calling down upon him the eye of the public. . . ."

When Kerr subsequently brought suit for libel, Force offered as his defence that he had undertaken "to justify the said Mr. Adams against the slander of the plaintiff [Kerr], by showing that no credit was due to the statements of the plaintiff in support of such slanders. . . ." Justice William Cranch in November, 1826, ruled: "The point of the slander seems to me, in every instance to be avoided. The slander is not in the words themselves, but in the ideas which those words excite in the minds of those who hear them, and the inferences which the world draws from them. These inferences are not met by the allegations of the plea." He did find grounds for trial of the forgery charge, but a jury which heard the evidence in January, 1828, was unable to reach agreement. The case was continued until December of that year, when it was compromised by the defendant's confession of judgment with one cent as damages. John Quincy Adams, Diary (Microfilms of The Adams Papers, owned by the Adams Manuscript Trust and deposited in the Massachusetts Historical Society, Part I, Reel 38; Boston, 1954), entries of March 20, April 1, 14, 15, July 27, 31, August 27, 1824; Kerr *vs.* Force, 14 *Fed. Cas.* 386-404.

8 At a convention of Republican delegates, meeting at the State House in Trenton, October 19, friends of Adams sought to adjourn without forming a ticket of presidential electors. After defeating this proposal by a vote of 45 to 15, the body selected a ticket and adopted an address to the public favoring Jackson as President and Calhoun as Vice President. Washington *Daily National Intelligencer,* October 25, 1824.

From Henry R. Storrs

Dear Sir Whitestown [*sic*] Sepr 23rd 1824

The Convention which was directed against the nomination of Colo. Young as Govr. met at Utica on Tuesday and last evening nominated Mr. Clinton for Gov. and Mr Tallmadge for Lt. Govr.[1] It has been a mere *Clintonian* party movement. The object of Mr. C's party in the measure has been to turn the present excitement in the State against Mr Van Buren and Mr. Crawfords party to the advantage of Mr. Clinton and his friends only. His friends (i.e. the [larges]t portion of them) came there predetermined and doubtless preinstructed. Instead of sacrificing all personal predilection to the great object of overthrowing the influence of Mr. Vn Buren and

Mr. Crawford in the State (an object perfectly attainable). I have no doubt that the remote if not the immediate effect of their proceedings will be to strengthen V. B. & Cd. If Mr. Clinton should succeed he cannot stand longer than two years and by that time Mr. V B. will be no doubt at the head of a united republican party opposed to him—and if Mr. Crawford fails now it is about two years hence when Mr. V. B. will need all his strength at home. Indeed I scarcely hesitate to say that Mr. V. B. would on the whole prefer Mr. Clintons election at this time to Colo. Young. Whether Mr. Crawford succeeds or not it is morally certain that the party of Mr. Vn. Buren must be prostrated. Should Colo. Y. be elected Mr. V. B. knows that he (Colo. Y) has too much sagacity not to discover the true *"signs of the times."* The only pernicious result of the whole affair which I fear is that this nomination against Colo. Young *may* drive him into union with V. B.: in the choice of Presidential Electors.—for it is *certain* that your friends in the Legislature, if not false, can control that choice. It is in their power, if they are firm and fearless to compel Mr. Crawfords friends to divide the Electoral tickett [*sic*]. If they do not *sell* you or themselves it will be done. whatever may be the result of the election for Govr., it is the true interest of Colo. Y. and his friends to divide the Electors.

Mr. V. B. I say, would probably prefer Mr. Clintons election. He has two objects to effect.—the first to obtain Mr. C's[2] election and to acquire for that end the Presidential electors of this State—secondly, if defeated either in that object or in acquiring the control of the next legislature, then being prostrated his next object must and will be to redeem his lost power and standing. By means of this nomination of Mr. Clinton he will exert all his power to draw Colo. Y. and his friends towards him when the Legislature meet to choose Electors If Clinton should succeed (and the result will probably be known before the choice of Electors) it is impossible to foresee its effect on the course of Colo. Y.'s friends. If Colo. Young should be defeated then Mr. V B. has two years to reorganize against Mr. Clinton and in the mean time Colo. Young has been put out of the way of V. B. and thrown into the same common fate. The result of that misfortune would be to unite them hereafter. and I have no doubt whatever that even if Mr. Clinton is elected that he can stand but two years. The present excitement will subside or be supplanted by new combinations of feeling—the Governor has little or no patronage under the present Constitution and Mr Clint[on] is too far removed in private life from the *present generation* of political men to maintain himself in the place.

I regret extremely the movements of the Convention for I cannot doubt that Colo. Y. and his friends are truly possessed of right and honorable views and feelings both towards the State and towards *Mr. V. B.* He could never have been brought to an alliance with Mr. V. B. and he has enough of sagacity to have known that when elected he would have triumphantly sustained [*sic*] by the great body of the republican party and also the People of this State against Mr. V. B. and his adherents. That course he would have taken. But Clinton and his *personal* party are destined to distract the State only. I hope that even now Colo Young may succeed, for if Mr. C.[3] is unsuccessfull, Colo. Y. may yet have his way open, clear and honorable. It is chiefly the *intermediate* consequences which I apprehend at this *peculiar* time. If he is *firm* and *sincere* he cannot fail to see that let the result of the Govrs. election terminate as it may, he will stand on elevated and honorable ground.

I have lately heard a suggestion that the friends of Mr. Adams, with the view of excluding you from the H. of Reps. may perhaps give to Mr. Crawford the entire tickett of Electors if they find that they cannot carry their own. I have no doubt they would do so, if they cannot elect their own, unless they should be deterred by the fear of actually electing Mr Crawford by that very course. They would take any step short of actually electing Mr Crawford, which should exclude you from the House.

I am sick of writing to you, or to any one not of this State on these subjects.—for one can scarcely write any thing relating to our State which can honor our political character abroad. The profligacy of the times the thirst for public office and emolument and the unwearied and artfull efforts to corrupt and purchase others have truly sunk our State in public estimation. If there is any virtue or honor or pride of character or firmness left in the State which can operate on our legislature I do not by any means dispair of an honorable result at their meeting in November. The feeling of this State against Mr. V. B. and Mr. Crawford is [ove]rwhelming. I do not believe that on a ballott by the People either of them could obtain a quarter of the votes. But such ha[s] been the influence of the V. B. party that many of *your* friends appear to "cow" under it. I have found many of them timid and some treacherous.—ready for the attainment of some paltry *promise* merely to sacrifice any opinion or principle.

I have no doubt that the next *legislature* will be decidedly [opp]osed to Mr Crawford & Mr. V. B's party. Nothing *can* prevent it but this ridiculous nomination of Mr. Clinton and I do not think that even that can prevent it. Whatever hostility there is to Mr. Clinton in that part of the republican party which has broken off from Mr. V. B. they will still in their County nominations for the

Assembly support their own man. Their only hope of escape from actual insignificance must now be by their power in the popular branch of the State legislature. If Colo. Young and his friends do not abandon the ground which they have once taken in the Presidential election[4] our Electoral vote will and must be divided. If my honorable efforts to induce them to remain firm can succeed the result need not be feared

I expect to be at Albany attending the Sup. Ct. when the legislature meet and if any thing of interest to you [occu]rs it will give me pleasure to communicate it to you. I am, Dr. Sir. Yours truly
Hon. Mr. Clay HENRY R STORRS

ALS. DLC-HC (DNA, M212, R1). Postmark, handwritten: "Whitesboro N. Y. Septr 24th." Margins ragged.

1 See above, Rochester to Clay, May 29, 1824, note. The nominees were DeWitt Clinton and James Tallmadge, Jr.

2 Crawford's. 3 Clinton. 4 See above, Porter to Clay, April 5, 1824.

Resolutions on Morrison Professorship

[September 24, 1824]

Resolved that it is expedient to make a temporary appointment for one year of a Morrison professor of Natural Philosophy and Mathematics with a salary of one thousand dollars, lawful money of the U. S. to commence with the commencement of the ensuing Session on the last wednesday of September 1824

Resolved that the arrears of interest on the legacy of $20.000 bequeathed by the late Col. James Morrison to the University which shall be due on the last wednesday of September 1824, together with two hundred dollars, the residue of the legal interest which will accrue on the said legacy during the year beginning with the commencement of the next session, after deducting the one thousand dollars allowed for that year to the temporary appointment of a Morrison Professor, this day made, be appropriated to the purchase of Philosophical Apparatus and instruments for the use of the Morrison Chair.

Resolved that the Chairman notify Thos J Mathews of his temporary appointment to the Morrison Chair,[1] and assure him that if, at the end of the year for which he is appointed, it be agreeable to both parties, his appointment shall be then rendered permanent, and a Salary of Twelve hundred dollars shall thereafter be allowed him in like Money—

AD. KyLxT. Endorsed on verso: "Resolution 24th. Sept. 1824." See above, Report, October 5, 1823, note.

1 Thomas Johnson Matthews held this post for eight years and was acting president of the University for a short time before leaving the institution in 1832. At the time of his death, in 1852, he was a professor at Miami University, Oxford, Ohio.

Account with Samuel Redd

Henry Clay To Saml Redd Dr Lexington Sept 24th. 1824.

	Mending Both pole Braces for your light Carriage with new Leather	$ 1 –
Oct 7h.	2 new Swingletree Braces for your carige [*sic*]	3 –
Nov 6th	Puting a new Iron plate on the Sway bar of your family carriage	2 50
	A large piece of Leather over the footboard & Boot of of [*sic*] the Drivers Seat	2 –
	Taking the Tyre off one of the front wheels cuting a piece out of the fellow, cuting welding & puting on tyre	1 75
	11 new Tyre nails	0 50
	Repaing [*sic*] the cushion for Coachman seat puting one [*sic*] a new Bottom new Tufting & stufing Do	1 25
	Triming the pole with new Leather Repaing the Harness	3 50
	Piecing Two of the Traces with new Leather	2 25
	Piecing two of the hame tugs with new Leather & puting four new Rivits in the hame clips	2 –
	Three large new Leather pipes on the hame tugs	1 –
	One new Housing Strap	0 25
	A new Strap for the Belly band	0 25
	Mending one crupper & puting on two new loops	0 25
	Mending the Britchband	0 25
	Mending two howsing [*sic*] Tugs with new Leather	0 50
	A new plated Buckle & leather Strap on collar	0 50
Novr 9th	Repaing Chariottee after it was Tund [*sic*] over—	
	Plating one of the pillars with Iron & puting in new Rivits & screws in the other & puting a board under the Seat rale in front	2 –
	Piecing one skein with new Iron one new Staple & a large shoulder washer on front axle	1 25
	Mending the curtains in Several places	1 –
	2 new plated Dees for the harness & mending the Bridles & howsing tugs	0 75
	Piecing the perch Bolt with new Iron	0 50
		$ 28 25
	Speie [*sic*] at one half	
		$ 14 12½

AD. DLC-TJC (DNA, M212, R16). Endorsed in margin: "Commonwealth Paper," *i.e.*, notes of the Bank of the Commonwealth.

From Josiah S. Johnston

Dear Sir. Phila Sept 26h. 1824

I have made a running visit to New York. Secured the Patriot & returned this morning.[1] It will at least have the effect to dissemminate [*sic*] the truth—I shall send the paper to you & other friends to Circulate especially in Illinois Indianna [*sic*] & Missouri—

This is the first money spent for papers or presses & this is only for so much room in his[2] daily paper— He is to enlarge his paper & publish whatever is requested— Mr. Lockwood will attend to it principally—he has some talent & Zeal— I send you the address— *"by a Citizen of N. York,"* which is well written—& contains very excellent views— It may perhaps be advisable to republish it in Lexington in the same form & to distribute it through the adjoining states—& to give it a wide Circulation in the papers—It is from the pen of Mr. Lockwood.[3] These views might be greatly extended —Indeed there are subjects enough to furnish a pamphlet of the same size—which I have suggested to him, but if he pays proper attention to the Patriot, he may not have time—except by seperate [*sic*] articles in that paper

Yours of the 10 Inst. is at hand—your views of the Contest Correspond entirely with my own

But I have not time to say more with great regard

J. S. JOHNSTON

ALS. InU. Addressed to Clay at Lexington.

1 Cf. above, Johnston to Clay, September 22, 1824.

2 Charles K. Gardner's.

3 See above, Johnston to Clay, September 22, 1824.

From Josiah S. Johnston

Dear Sir. Philaa. Sept. 26h. 1824

I have read With pleasure & with attention your favor of the 10th. Sept. We agree in every particular, with regard to the vice Presidency. You Can not Change your position & your friends are not disposed— You must abide the Issue. I have uniformly given the same reply. It was a Strange Idea of Crawfords friends to Count on the Western States, by your Withdrawal— I have often explaind [*sic*] that to them— They now see & feel the truth— The object of Crawfords friends *now* will be to put down Adams & if possible to prevent his being returnd— under the Idea that his being with drawn, the N. England states will vote for him They now perceive that the Chance of the N. England votes is greater than of your Six

States[1]— They Will therefore in every Case run Jackson against Adams especially in Maryland & Jersey— If Mr. Adams therefore does not get New York—he will probably not be returnd—

The friends of Adams are every where decided against Crawford & they will exert their influence to exclude him— If they prevent his getting the Votes of N. York—I think he Can not Come in—

The friends of Adams and Jackson both affirm with great Confidence that Jackson will Certainly receive N. Carolina & they say that in that event your Cause will be as successfully Maintain'd by giving Mr. Adams New York as by taking half of the state With Mr. Crawford—

We shall Keep Virginia advised of the progress of things at Albany & if possible they shall know the state of the vote before they vote— This is a Very important point—& will be duly impressed upon your friends

If it is Unfavorable to Mr. Crawford—It will inevitably result in your Election— The friends of Crawford & Adams Can never Unite— This is the advantage of our Neutrality— We Will Keep fair with all of them—

If Mr. Adams is withdrawn from the Contest, by being beaten by Jackson out of the middle states & by Crawford out of N. York—which now seems to me the object of that party—I think you Will in all probability get the N. England Votes

The friends of Adams will Unite with you rather than Crawford— & your own friends are Strong there— The friends of Crawford will put every engine in motion— When I find them Crawfords[2] fixd in their purpose with regard to adams, & there is a Strong expectation of getting the Vote of N. York—I will suggest the policy of giving you half of the Votes of that state to render the defeat of Adams Certain so that he may have the N. England States open to him in the House. If Crawford excludes you he will be beaten by Jackson & Adams— His only hope must be to exclude Adams & depend upon his Chance in N England—

It Must be Suggested to both Adams & Crawfords friends—that they more effectually exclude the other, by giving you half of N. York than by taking the Whole Vote of that State.

I do Count therefore with much Confidence upon half of this State— & that you will be returned to the House— If Mr. C looses [*sic*] N. York, you Will be returnd very high on the List by the accession of Virginia— We shall republish the address here[3]—which is well receivd— The Convention at Utica have Nominated Clinton[4] But this I apprehend will not interfere with the Presidential Election—

Little has been said about a Vice President & I do not think it will materially aid you I have been surprised that Crawfords friends, who are hostile to Calhoun, do not seize on him Sandford[5] to defeat his hopes— This may yet be done—

I have as yet recd. no Letter from Genl. Porter[6]— But I understand he is doing all that Can be done— I will Keep him advised— I entertain strong hopes of Delaware— You Must excuse My hasty Letters—

We receive Genl. La Fayette tomorrow— The Concourse of people here is very great— The preparations, are very expensive & Very grand—

I Presume he is will be [*sic*] receivd by both houses in the Center building— With great regard J. S. JOHNSTON—

There is no Idea of making him Vice President.

ALS. DLC-TJC (DNA, M212, R12). Published in part in Colton (ed.), *Private Correspondence of Henry Clay,* 103.

1 See above, Johnston to Clay, August 19, 1824.

2 This word interlined.

3 Probably the *Address to the Republicans and People of New York. . . .* See above, Johnston to Clay, September 22, 26, 1824.

4 See above, Storrs to Clay, September 23, 1824.

5 Nathan Sanford.

6 Peter B. Porter. On this and subsequent topics discussed in this letter, cf. above, Clay to Johnston, September 3, 1824.

From Macdonald and Ridgely

H Clay Esqr. Baltimore September 28th. 1824

Dear Sir:

We received a letter dated 31st. augt. from F Dobbin & Co[1] of Wheeling in answer to our inquiries as to the disposal of the last parcel of your Hemp, in which they directed us to forward it to the Commissioners of the Navy Board at Washington which we immediately did, & since then have received under cover from Jno Rogers Prest. of said Board your letter of 6th. inst. requesting us to send the same Hemp to whereever the said Commissioners should order it; the recit [*sic*] of our letter to the Board, inclosing bill of Lading for the Hemp was acknowledged by them & we presume ere this they have informed you of its arrival at Washington.[2] The person who bought the first parcel of your Hemp was very desirous of getting the last also

Your obt. Sevts MACDONALD & RIDGELY

Your A/C is charged for

Carriage 2240 lbs. Hemp fr: Wheeling @ 1½	33 60
Postage [. . .]:[3] Rect.	19
Drayage to Packets	50
and has credit for	$34 29
Nt. Pro. Hemp P A/S. rendd.	126.91
Leaving subject to your order a Bal. of	$92.62

ALS. DLC-TJC (DNA, M212, R12).
1 Forsythe, Dobbin, and Company.
2 See above, Rodgers to Clay, September 20, 1824.
3 Word illegible.

To Josiah S. Johnston

My dear Sir Ashland 2d. Oct. 1824

I duly received your favors of the 16h. and 19h. Ulto. with the Philada. address. I also received one or two preceding letters from you which I did not before acknowledge the receipt of.[1] I am infinitely obliged to you for the activity which you have given to my friends and my interest to the Eastward. If I should not succeed it will be because the same exertion had not been made in the same quarter a year ago. It appears to me however that the prospect of success is yet sufficient to animate the highest zeal of my friends. I do not think that we shall be deceived in any calculation of support in the West which we have made. In both Ohio and Indiana I think you will find, from the result, that my friends will outnumber those of Genl. Jackson and Mr. Adams together. The General has the best interest in Mr. Gazlay's[2] district including Cincinnati; but I shall beat him in every other Congressional district in the State, and he will in the general vote of Ohio be behind Mr. Adams.

The K. Comee. of Correspondence has issued its general Circular, which is published in all the prints. I transmit you inclosed a Copy of that which was sent to Virginia and intended for that region exclusively.[3] If I get the whole or half the vote of N. York, I have much reason to believe that Virginia, seeing that Mr. Crawford is lost, will give me her suffrage. If the insulting tone of the Nat. Journal should be continued towards that State, I shall not doubt that she will bestow her vote on me.

Mr. Holley,[4] just returned from an Eastern trip, saw Mr. Crawford about a fortnight ago at Frederick town, on his return from the Springs.[5] He says that his gait, articulation, and general appearance indicated most clearly the paralysis under which he has labored; and that he appeared to be much more infirm than Mr. Jefferson, at the age of 82, whom he also saw.

I thank you for your kind admonition about the uncertainty of the pending election, and the utility of repressing a too great anxiety. I hope you will not, as you seem to anticipate, have any occasion for philosophical exertion on the account of your own election. I have written to Durald [*sic*][6] who will do whatever is in his power to secure it. I will write discreetly also to some other friends. The Govr. elect,[7] if he is to be confided in, assured me when here of his determination to support you.

Brent[8] has tendered to me his services. He may be useful in writing to the members of the Louisiana Legislature, particularly in stating to them, what was most certainly the fact, that I prevented, at the last Session, the reduction in the H. of R. of the duty on brown sugar.[9]

The access which you have secured to the Pennsa. & Eastern public through the Aurora will enable my friends to obtain correct information of the state of my interests in other quarters. I inclose a check[10] for the subscription which you have made to that paper for me.

I think it would be useful for you to correspond with Genl. Saml. Ringgold & Col. Otho Williams at Hagerstown[11] and Michal [*sic*] Sprigg at Cumberland in Maryland. Nothing is wanting to secure me the two upper districts but to keep up the spirits of my friends.

I have some thought of passing through Virginia and visiting Mr. Jefferson, Mr. Madison and Govr. Barbour.[12]

The Reporter has been regularly sent to you.

You do not acknowledge the receipt of any of my letters of which I have written three or four.

I am faithfully Your friend H. CLAY

J. S. Johnston Esq.

ALS. PHi. Published in part in Colton (ed.), *Private Correspondence of Henry Clay,* 104.

1 See above, Johnston to Clay, September 11, 1824.

2 James W. Gazlay, Cincinnati lawyer and United States Congressman, 1823-1824, who had shifted his support from Clinton to Jackson in early January, 1824. Stevens, *Early Jackson Party in Ohio,* 84, 89.

3 See above, Clay to Johnston, September 19, 1824.

4 Horace Holley.

5 Crawford had left Washington on August 9, passing by way of Fredericktown, Maryland, to the Berkeley Springs in Virginia (now West Virginia). He returned to the city on September 12.

6 Martin Duralde (Jr.). 7 Henry Johnson. 8 William L. Brent.

9 Clay's action in relation to the various proposals for reducing the duty on brown sugar was not reported.

10 Not found.

11 Samuel Ringgold, large landholder in western Maryland, had served as a judge in Washington County and as a member of the State legislature and the United States House of Representatives (the latter in 1810-1815, 1817-1821). He was a militia officer and a veteran of the War of 1812.

Otho Holland Williams, also a militia officer and at one time a Washington County judge, was Clerk of the Washington County Court from 1800 to 1845.

12 James Barbour.

Resolution on Lafayette Visit

[October 2, 1824]

Resolved, That a Committee be appointed in behalf of the citizens of Fayette and Lexington, to invite Gen. La Fayette to visit this place;—that the Committee be instructed to assure him of the entire participation of the citizens of this county and town in the general sensibility excited throughout the U. States on the occasion of his arrival among us; of the grateful recollection which they cherish of his signal, and eminent, and disinterested services, rendered to the cause of American Independence; of their warm admiration of his uniform and zealous devotion to Liberty; of their deep solicitude for his welfare and happiness;—and of their desire to testify these feelings to him personally if it should comport with his convenience and inclination to visit Kentucky.

Lexington *Kentucky Reporter,* October 4, 1824. The resolution, offered by Clay at a public meeting, was adopted unanimously. Lafayette visited Lexington May 16-17, 1825, while Clay was in Washington.

From Josiah S. Johnston

Dear Sir. Phil. Octr 3rd. [1824]

I have this morning recd. your Circular[1] which is Well Composed— Contains just views—& will be multiplied here & distributed widely—

We have had 500 additional Copies of the address by a Citizen of N. York[2] published here & sent abroat [*sic*].— Some delay I presume with regard to paper has Occurd with the Patriot[3]— It is of the first importance to bring that paper out strongly—especially to publish all these papers—

The Committee of Correspondence here[4] receive very flattering intelligence from their Correspondents— In truth your friends are very numerous & influential every where— But parties—Caucus'—presses a few managing men—& the want of Concert & Confidence have kept them in the back ground—

With great regard yr. obt. Svt J. S. JOHNSTON

ALS. InU. Addressed to Clay at Lexington. Encloses the following extract, in Johnston's hand, of a letter addressed to R. W. Meade from Rochester, New York:

"Mr. Clays standing with the Republicans in this section of the state, has never been better than at this time. The paper which I conduct in this village has a Circulation probably as extensive as any other in the western part of this state—I took an early & decided stand for Mr. Clay (he having been a favorite with me for years) & other republican papers have subsequently done the same. If the people had the Choice of Electors, we Could in my opinion Carry a Clay Ticket with ease Crawford has no supporters—Jackson not more than one in a hundred & Adams none but Federalists—

"Whatever may be said to the Contrary you may rely on it that the Legislature is about equally divided between Clay Crawford & Adams—

"The Crawford presses are endeavouring to make the public believe that there is no chance for Mr. Clay to succeed & therefore his friends ought to support Crawford although it is impossible to tell how the votes of the state may finally go, yet I think Mr. Clay Cannot fail to get some of them—

"Hugh McGee of Allegany will in 2 weeks publish a paper 'the decided advocate of Mr. Clay & of Republican Men & Measures' D. Sibley—"

Derrick Sibley, publisher of the Rochester *Republican,* was later a member of the New York legislature. McGee's paper has not been identified.

[1] Of the Kentucky Committee of Correspondence. See above, Clay to Johnston, August 31, 1824.

[2] See above, Johnston to Clay, September 22, 26, 1824.

[3] New York *Patriot.* [4] See above, Johnston to Clay, September 11, 1824.

From William B. Astor

Dear Sir, New York 4 October 1824

I have had the honor to receive your letter of the 19th ulto covering a check for $3300.[1] say Three thousand three hundred Dollars to be applied to the payment of your bond to my father[2]—Agreeably to your request I shall in the course of a few days send the Bond to the President or cashier of the Office of Disct & Depit. Lexington to be delivered to you on your executing a bond for the balance with Mr. Wickliffe[3]— I should not ask for Mr Wickliffe's name did the bond belong to me; but acting for my father who is absent you will be pleased to excuse my doing so—

I am with great regard Your most obedient Servant

WM. B. ASTOR

To, The Honorable Henry Clay Lexington Kentucky.

ALS. DLC-TJC (DNA, M212, R12).

1 Letter and check not found. 2 See above, II, 686.

3 Robert Wickliffe. Apparently no further bond was executed. Cf. below, Endorsement, November 1, 1824; Mortgage, November 15, 1824.

From Henry Shaw

My Dear Sir Lanesborough Oct. 4. 1824

It is a long time since I have heard from you, or since I have written you, but the interim has been employed by you in securing new and additional Laurels, and making new claims upon the publick confidence and fixing yourself still deeper in the affections of the People—while, in a humble way I have been busily engaged in producing a state of things in Mass: not unfriendly I hope, for securing to you, sooner or later, a glorious reward for all your publick labours— you will forbear the smile, I know will rise, at vanity [*sic*] of the above paragraph, in consideration of the affectionate regard I bear you— and I have simiular [*sic*] follies your good natur [*sic*] will be called on to pardon, not in me alone, but in all that wide circle of enthusiastik friends, the frankness and generosity of your natur has created— if we address you with familiarity if we approach you with too much freedom, blame your own kindliness of natur for it— And let the issue of the present contest result as it may, a lasting consolation is afforded in the reflection, that no imprudent or dishonorable step has been taken, by either our Candidate or his supportes [*sic*]— I shall have to speak much of myself in what follows, it does not arise from any other cause, than a desire, in so doing to give you frankly the state of the case with us— I took a seat in the Legislature last spring, not however believing that we could carry Mass: off from Q,[1] but under the hope that something might arise, that could be used to advantage.— I was not disappointed— The Electoral Law afforded this occasion[2]— the Q. Party took the side of a Genl. Ticket— a most unpopular step for them.— The friends of Crawford, who by the bye are few in number United with us, and we came to the Understanding, that in opposition to Q. we could unite, & in the resulting Electoral Vote, if we had any, it should be equally divided, as few on that vote could be controulld by us— in truth Crd. has not a supporter in Mass: that does not really prefer our Candidate, but they were early committed—and could not so easily abandon— after the passage of the Law we took the resolution of getting up an Opposition Ticket without reference to Candidates, but merely to resist the Law— We began the device in Berkshire District by calling a District Convention— we placed Old Eustis & Brooks[3] at the head, the thing has taken beyond even our hopes— every District has concurred, & we shall shortly give to the Publik [*sic*] our list— in the mean time Eustis has been prevailed upon by the Q Junto to withdraw his Nam [*sic*]. If Brooks does not follow suit, we shall on with another & in my opinion give them a hard run— The best consequences will flow from E.s withdrawl [*sic*].— he declines a[nd] it is said, he claims he will not have his Name on the same Ticket with Brooks— this reason will rouse all the Federal Party, who so easily ballance the State, and Brooks is decidedly the most Popular Name in the Commonwealth— what will be the result, we cannot with much certainty predict— we never expected so favourable a state of things as now actually exists— our movement was intended for our friends abroad— it may turn out quite a different thing— Q. has no personal popularity in the State, and is deservedly *hated* by all the leading Federalists—Our Ticket is a mixed one—and it may be pretty confidently stated that the chances are equal, that Mass: will give a divided Vote— Our People are full of fire and zeal— the Jenniers[4] and Wool Growrs [*sic*] are rallying, and the Tariff is the word And altho Our Delegation are nearly unans:, the People are a Majy. in favor of that Measure— we have circulated your Speech[5] by 1000s into every quarter of the State— we do not mean to give up the contest if Q prevails— we shall fight on —your friends are increasing day by [*sic*], and form now the efficient strength of the State— had we got District Electors Berkshire would have given you her vote by more than 1000 Majy, & I would have had the pleasure of being her Organ— N York is, as usual, a Pandemonium—but your friends there hold the ballance if they are faithfull— [. . .][6] it N.Y. is corrupt to the core— V.B.[7] has more than [. . .] halted, & would now if possible change his Candida[. . .] of Sanford[8] was well done— he is delighted with [. . .] the other day— the thing has taken well,— [. . .] is I fear too late— the People there Trust [. . . .]

[Y]ou know more about prospects there than I [. . . .] Johnson[9] wrote me the other day, that there was [. . .] and after all you must not depend upon any thing [*from*] us— we shall do any thing in our Power— the result may be better than we hope—it may be worse— but at all events—may I advise you—hold yourself, as you have done, above all compromising Arrangements we support you for President, & for nothing else— if we fail, let the champion make his own Cabinet—but let us stand clear— you are better off by maintaining an independency on all of them—a day sooner or later at the head is of less importance, to us, or our friend, than that he keep clear of combinations in which he can not controul, but in which he may be ruined— we go for the whole, or nothing— a Seat in Congress will be more honorable & popular too with the People, than a Seat in the Cabinet— may I hear from you one day—

your sincere friend: H. SHAW

ALS. DLC-HC (DNA, M212, R1). MS. faded and torn. Addressed to Clay at Lexington.

1 John Quincy Adams.

2 The law providing for a general electoral ticket in Massachusetts had passed the Senate by only one vote, with 18 yeas to 17 nays. Washington *Daily National Intelligencer,* June 16, 1824.

3 William Eustis; John Brooks. The latter, a veteran of the Revolutionary War, had practiced medicine, had been a member of the State legislature, and as a Federalist had been elected seven times as Governor of Massachusetts (1816-1822).

4 Word not clear.

5 See above, March 30-31, 1824.

6 Two or three words illegible in each of the indicated passages.

7 Van Buren.

8 Nathan Sanford.

9 Josiah S. Johnston.

From Peter B. Porter

Dear Sir, Black Rock Oct. 6th. 1824.

Your favour of the 2nd. of Sept.[1] reached me some time ago. I have, within a few days past, received letters from many of your best and most influential friends in different parts of the State, all of whom are very sanguine in the belief that a respectable proportion, at least of the votes of this State, may be secured to you. But it must be recollected that our Legislature is so divided between three candidates that neither can command a majority; and that the game is therefore completely in the power of *any* two of the parties, so that neither can count with certainty even on a participation in the stake. The relations, however, between your friends & those of each of the other candidates are certainly more amicable than those which exist between the other two parties, so that, in this point of view, our chance of being one of the parties in the compromise, is the best.

Since the last meeting of the Legislature, repeated intimations have been thrown out to me, by the friends of Mr Adams, of a disposition to divide the votes between him and you in proportion to the number of your respective supporters in the two houses, which they estimate as nearly two to one in his favour.[2] Such a proposition however I have invariably discountenanced. I have reason to beleive [*sic*] that, at the November session your relative strength will prove to be greater than has generally been allowed. I received, two days ago, a letter from one of our Senators, whose vote on the Presidential question has generally been put down as "uncertain." He expresses his full determination to support you, & his belief that your friends, by a firm & united course may secure at least one half of the votes. He tells me too, that the two members of Assembly from his County, who have also been counted "uncertain," have declared for you. That part of the delegation from the city of New York, amounting probably to five or six, who have favoured Genl. Jackson, will I think in the first instance come out decidedly for you. The utter hopelessness of Genl. J's cause in this state—the intimacy between him & Clinton whom most of them detest—their hatred of Crawford & his friends—and their aversion to Mr Adams on the ground of his former federalism—will all conspire to produce this result. If a compromise is effected by your friends it will probably, from present appearances, be with those of Mr Adams; and the effect in such case I think would be to exclude Mr Crawford from the house of Reps., and place you in it. This may perhaps be the most desirable state of things, as Mr Crawfords friends, he being hors du combat, will more probably unite on you than either of the other candidates.

I shall leave home in the course of next week for Montreal, where a meeting of our Boundary Commission[3] is appointed to be held on the 25th. Inst, and return by way of Albany. If the business of the commission does not, and I presume it will not, occupy more than four or five days, I shall reach Albany before the meeting of the Legislature. Your friends will generally attend.

I sent you by mail, two days ago, a News paper, containing a letter from me to the chairman of a republican meeting in Steuben County on the subject of the presidency.[4] It may possibly have some Little effect in this State.

I remain, Dr Sir, very respectfully & truly yours. P. B. PORTER

Hon. H. Clay.

If you should see any of the members of Mrs. Breckenridges[5] family, please say to them that their friends here are all well.

ALS. DLC-HC (DNA, M212, R1). 1 Not found.

2 Cf. above, Johnston to Clay, August 30, 1824; Clay to Johnston, August 31, 1824; Clay to Porter, September 2, 1824; Stuart to Clay, September 6, 1824; Clay to Henry, September 14, 1824.

[3] See above, II, 162n.
[4] In the letter, dated September 16, Porter declined candidacy as a presidential elector (see above, Johnston to Clay, September 16, 1824, note) but avowed his great admiration for Clay and for his advocacy of a protective tariff. Lexington *Kentucky Reporter*, October 25, 1824.
[5] Mrs. John Breckinridge, Porter's mother-in-law.

Account with Bennet P. Sanders

Henry Clay Esqr. [October 8, 1824]
1824 To B. P. Sanders Dr.
Oct. 8th
Pulv. Rhei ℥j Sem. Anisi ʒ.ss Cort. Aurantii[1] Self 37½
[Endorsements on verso][2]
I do certify the within to be Correct. LEM,L SANDERS[3]
received the within in full J, MURPHY JR.[4] Colr.

D. DLC-TJC (DNA, M212, R16). Sanders was a Lexington physician.
[1] Powdered rhubarb; anise seed; orange peel.
[2] Both AES. [3] Physician and druggist.
[4] Lexington shoemaker, possibly John Murphy, Jr.

Agreement with William S. Dallam

9h. Oct. 1824.

I do hereby agree with H. Clay that any indulgence or accommodation which he may give to Daniel Bryan respecting his note for upwards of six thousand dollars, with Romaine [*sic*] as security, assigned by me to said Clay,[1] either in extending the time of payment or taking other securities, shall not impair the ultimate rights of the said Clay to come back to me, if he fails finally to receive the said debt or any part thereof. WILL S DALLAM

DS, in Clay's hand. DLC-TJC (DNA, M212, R16).
[1] See above, Agreement, October 18, 1822.

From Josiah S. Johnston

Dear Sir. Phila Oct 9h. 1824

During the next Week a meeting of your friends will take place in the City of New York—Which will be numerous & respectable—& will have the best effect in that State— We have recd. here numerous answers to the Letters of the Corresponding Committee[1]—Which are very flattering— We have furnished these Letters with all the great names we have among your friends to be Used at the meeting in N.York—

Mr. Mallory[2] (whom you have seen & who knows you well) came here from N. York—to whom was exhibited all the information we have— He orderd 1000 Copies of the Kentucky address[3]—Which he has taken with him to day to N. York— He is very Zealous, sanguine, & active—& has a very extensive acquaintance in N. York & N England & the Western States— I requested him to write you, which he promised The Committee have distributed 1000 Copies of the Pamphlet from N. York—with the Interogations [*sic*][4]

I go to N. York the day after tomorrow

I wish to be there during the week—& besides the Patriot has for some reason disappointed me[5]— The next is an important Week & much must be done— I have suggested to Elliot[6]—that if Crawfords friends do not secure you half of N. York—His Election is inevitably lost—

They must exclude Adams to stand any Chance in the House—Crawford has but 3 States—to which we may add Delaware in the House. He might obtain the N. England States, which would give him 10 States.

If they exclude you—what expectation Can he have of succeeding to your States— Especially as your 6 States[7] added to his will not Carry the Election

If you are excluded The attachment of the Western States—the desire to decide at once the Election will induce the W. States to go to Genl. Jackson. Who having T, M, A, P., S C,[8] & Jersey—will have twelve States— Maryland or Delaware will decide the question—

or If Crawford has but 4 States—the rest will be divided between Jackson & Adams—in which case he will struggle in vain—

They Will I think make an effort to exclude Adams—

The friends of Crawford are deceived by their friends in the W. States—who represent that he will Certainly get their votes if you are with drawn— They still say they wish you as Vice President, but I do not Know what they will do—

With great regard J. S. JOHNSTON

I have sent all the Papers—Pamphlets addresses to Duralde[9]—

ALS. InU.
1 See above, Johnston to Clay, September 11, 22, 1824.
2 Daniel Mallory.
3 See above, Clay to Johnston, August 31, 1824.
4 See above, Johnston to Clay, September 22, 1824.
5 Cf. above, Johnston to Clay, September 22, 26, October 3, 1824.
6 Jonathan Elliot.
7 See above, Johnston to Clay, August 19, 1824.
8 Tennessee, Mississippi, Alabama, Pennsylvania, South Carolina.
9 Martin Duralde (Jr.).

From Ralph Lockwood

Hon. H. Clay New York, Oct. 9, 1824.

Dear Sir,

I took the liberty to address to you, a few days since a Copy of a *pamphlet,* which I had procured to be published here.[1]– Though written in great haste, and intended rather to effect a partial change in the current of popular opinion here, than to circulate beyond the State, I learn from Mr. Johnston at Phila. that he has had a new and large Edition published there and he flatters me that it may produce some benefit. *My* primary object here was to counteract the idea, which was getting to be alarmingly familiar to the republicans in the Legislature–& out of it, that no mode could be hit upon to avoid an election by the House but for this state to vote for Mr. Crawford, in the *hope* that Penna. would be induced to change her vote, *after our electors were appointed* and that your friends in the *west* would then naturally fall into this compromise.– I believe I may flatter myself that my hasty production may have had some effect, in that way, in counteracting the current of the hour which was begining [*sic*] to set in that direction.

I have returned from *Albany,* within the last three days;–and had full and frequent conversations with Mr. *Van Buren* upon the subject of the present state of of [*sic*] parties, while there. He *openly* calculates upon the support of yourself, with all your friends, when the question shall come to the house; and as evidently, plays his game, in relation to the votes of this state, so as to ensure, if possible, *your own* exclusion. At least, I can make nothing else of his Language. He even goes so far, as to presume that the very weight of *his* name and influence will be sufficient to carry the entire vote of New York to Mr. Crawford. He *is* mistaken in his conceit, as I am abundantly well informed.–

At the same time, to do him justice, I have no doubt, that if he was less sanguine of final success in the house, he would, upon a *fair prospect* of standing as well *personally,* under your own administration, as under that of Mr. *Crawford,* be very glad to quiet the parties in this State and as he certainly thinks, consolidate his own influence, *in it,* by giving up Mr. Crawford. He is alarmed at the aspect of things, as he in fact acknowledged to me. And, I think, I succeeded in convincing him that his interests, in reference to this State, require that course. But I have no idea that he will abandon Mr. Crawford, without a pretty distinct intimation to him, of the *actual* position he might expect *personally* to occupy.– This I have no direct authority from him for saying– But I have no doubt that it would tend very much to smooth the way, in case, our state elections should drive him, (which is next to certain) from his present position.–

Mr. *Young,*[2] if he does succeed, and I most sincerly [*sic*] hope & trust he will, will succeed rather *in spite* of the support of Mr. V. Buren than by aid of it. Under such circumstances he will owe his election almost entirely, to the exertions of your friends in the

Western Districts. He and his friends will therefore pursue their own course, without, any obligations to the Crawford party. The influence of Mr. *Sanford's*[3] name is now felt & dreaded— We shall not *yield,* to either party, as I am assured in the Legislature; and the rest you are probably as fully able to judge of already, as you would be by any detail I could go into.

Mr. *Sanford* informs me that Judge Rochester had written to you upon this subject,[4] and the Judge certainly understands the State of parties as well as any man in the State. However, though the Judge may *then* have supposed that Mr. *Crawford* would get the votes of this State, this opinion was given with reference to the *then* state of things. He is a little too much (*habitually*) afraid of the influence of certain gentlemen at Albany. But for my own part, after taking a full view of the ground and of the measures which will undoubtedly be resorted to give [*sic*] the vote to Crawford, I can see nothing to warrant the opinion *at this time.*— The judge thinks only of *numbers,* in estimating the present posture of parties in our Legislature. But for my own part, I attach more importance to *position* than to numbers.— I therefore, see no reason to coincide with the Judge's apprehensions at present.—

With the highest respect, I have the honor to be D Sir, Your obt. and faithful Servt. RALPH LOCKWOOD

ALS. DLC-HC (DNA, M212, R1).
1 See above, Johnston to Clay, September 22, 1824.
2 Samuel Young. See above, Storrs to Clay, September 23, 1824.
3 Nathan Sanford. 4 Cf. above, Clay to Johnston, September 10, 1824.

Property Deed to Mann Satterwhite's Heirs

[October 11, 1824]

[In consideration of the payment of $3,480 to James Morrison and Joseph H. Hawkins, or one of them, as agents of Wilson Cary Nicholas, under the terms of an agreement of March 11, 1811, between Mann Satterwhite, on the one hand, and Morrison and Hawkins, on the other, Henry Clay, "sole acting Executor of James Morrison who was trustee for the heirs of George Nicholas," conveys to Satterwhite's heirs a tract of 174 acres (excepting 14 acres sold by Satterwhite to Asa Wilgus) in Fayette County, Kentucky.]

Fayette County Court, Deed Book Y, 273-75. Recorded November 1, 1824.

Receipt from John C. Richardson

[October 11, 1824]

Recd. Lexington Oct. the 11. 1824. of Henry Clay Esqr. Eight

Dollars fifty cents being the full amt. of Debt. & cost. of an Execution, which issued from the Clerks office of the Scott circuit in favour of Parkes & Mc.Clay vs Said Clay & Watkins[1]—

J. C. RICHARDSON D S For Js Wood[2] Shff

ADS. DLC-TJC (DNA, M212, R16). Endorsed by Clay on verso: "Receipts relating to business with Isham Talbot Esqr." Cf. above, I, 577.

1 John Watkins. Case not found; plaintiffs not identified.

2 James Wood, formerly a justice of the peace and militia officer in Fayette County.

From Philander Chase

My Dr. Sir; Worthington 14. Ocr.—24

I have delayed, I fear, far beyond the proper period, forwarding to you the inclosed letter from Lord Gambier.[1]— My apology is the very sincere wish I have all a[lon]g entertained of a personal interview, on the Subject, of which I presumed, the letter treated, namely his Lord Ship's great regard for you, and the essential service, of which your letter to him, proved to me.

I wished also to see you, (perhaps at the U S. Court) [2] that I might assign the reasons and obtain your pardon, for using your name as the Umpire, in a certain deed of donation of my estate to the Contemplated Theological Seminary,[3] for the education of young men for the Christian ministry. As it is, I can only send you a *copy* of that inStrument;[4] and to it beg your *favourable* attention.

The meeting of our Convention[5] takes place, in Chillicothe, on the 3d. of Novr. next. Nothing of the kind could give me more pleasure, than to see you there, if business, or the great importance to posterity of our plan, should so incline you. Your very sincere friend, Charles Hammond, who has been of such essential service in the great work of founding this Seminary will be there and, as I trust, assist us with his most valuable advice. Pray communicate with him on the subject any thing which, you think, will do us good.

I take the liberty of sending you a letter—addressed to Lord Kenyon, on the subject of my errand to Engd. Presuming you have seen what has *preceed*[*ed*] this, no apology is deemed necessary

With most grateful sentiments, I am very Dr. Sir your faithful & sincere friend, PHILANR. CHASE.

ALS. DLC-HC (DNA, M212, R1). Published in Colton (ed.), *Private Correspondence of Henry Clay*, 96-97. Addressed: "The Honourable Henry Clay Kentucky."

1 Above, June 29, 1824. 2 At Columbus, Ohio. 3 Kenyon College.

4 On November 27, 1823, Bishop Chase had proposed to execute a deed to Lord Gambier for donation of "his farm and all things thereunto pertaining" to the proposed school whenever adequate funds had been pledged to establish the institution, the money not to be "transferred to America until his Lordship shall have been satisfied, through the Hon. Henry Clay, who is frequently in Ohio, that all the above

conditions are in good faith fulfilled. . . ." Such a deed had been executed shortly thereafter. Chase, *Reminiscences*, I, 254-55.

5 Of the Protestant Episcopal Diocese of Ohio.

From Nathan Sanford

My Dear Sir Albany 14th. October 1824.

I thank you for your letter of the twenty sixth of September,[1] which I have this day received.

No man can predict with certainty, to whom the votes of this state will be given, at the approaching election. The legislature have determined to retain the choice of electors in their own hands; and there is no majority of free opinions in the legislature, in favor of any one of the candidates for the Presidency. The refusal of the legislature to give the choice of electors to the people,[2] has produced great irritation; the state elections are approaching; and the members of the legislature will convene in November, in a state of excitement, arising from these various causes. An obstinate struggle will probably, then take place; and the result of it may be, to give all the votes of the state to Mr. Crawford, or all to Mr. Adams, or all to yourself. But an event which I think more probable than any other, may be, that the votes will be given partly to yourself, and partly to another. In what proportions they will be divided, if this should be the event, is utterly uncertain.

It is singular but still true, that the question who will receive the votes of this state, is now more doubtful, than it would have been, had the choice of electors been given to the people. The course which a few members of the legislature may take, may decide every thing; and the state elections which will be closed a few days before the electors will be chosen, may have much influence upon the conduct of some members. A result which may be so much the effect of accident or something else, will not at all indicate the real strength of any of the candidates, in the estimation of the people of this state.

I thus give you all that can be said with truth as I believe, upon this subject, in its present situation. Others pretend and proclaim that they know more; but they speak either without knowledge, or with too much assurance.

Your numerous friends in this state, are as well disposed to serve you, as any friends can be. Judge Rochester and Mr. Lockwood[3] I believe, sometimes write to you; and these gentlemen in my opinion, deserve all your confidence.

With great respect and esteem I am Yours truly and faithfully

NATHAN SANFORD—

The Honorable Henry Clay.

ALS. DLC-HC (DNA, M212, R1). [1] Not found.
[2] See above, Woods to Clay, August 27, 1823, note.
[3] William B. Rochester; Ralph Lockwood.

From Francis Brooke

My Dear Sir Richmd Octo 15h, 1828 [*i.e.*, 1824]

I came here a few days ago and have devoted some portion of my time to find out what the C committee mean to do,[1] there is a growing opinion here that Mr Cs health is so bad that he must be given up— this I had from Leigh,[2] and there is a project on foot to name you as vice President in the place of Galatin [*sic*]—with a veiw [*sic*] to an ulterior vote for you as President in the event that Mr C on account of imbecility is relinquished by the electors when they meet here, the Editor of the A paper[3] calls this treason— in the mean time I fear that there being no strong indications in Virginia in your favour, your friends in the west will go over to J,[4] and Virginia loose [*sic*] even her Second choice, this ought to be avoided if possible— Your friends here have forbourn to manifest their Strenth [*sic*], because they are under the impression that it would be useless untill Mr C is out of the way— by adopting this course they have conciliated the friends of Mr C— You will See that Ritchie again repeats in his last paper that Virga can not vote for A or J— it is my own opinion, though no one has done more to bring about Such an event than Mr Ritchie,— I believe after Colol Gouchs [*sic*] return from Washington last Spring finding you had lost ground here by the Tariff &c he had determined to take up A, but upon casting about he found that Johnson Leigh &c &c were opposed to it,[5] this you may have remarked if you have been attentive to the tone of his paper— it would be more than a letter could contain to detail to you all the facts I know on that Subject— I am preparing to Set out for York to meet Genl La Fayette[6] in the morning and hasten to conclude this Letter and to assure you of my high respect & Sincere Esteem

Francis Brooke

ALS. InU. Addressed to Clay at Lexington.

[1] The Central Corresponding Committee for Crawford's candidacy announced from Richmond, on September 18, that Albert Gallatin had withdrawn as vice-presidential nominee and that the Crawford electors would vote "for such person as Vice-President, as may be best entitled to public confidence, and calculated to unite the votes of the people of the United States." Washington *Daily National Intelligencer*, October 22, 1824, reprinted from the Richmond *Enquirer*.

[2] Benjamin W. Leigh.

[3] John H. Pleasants. Cf. above, Call to Clay, June 30, 1824.

[4] Jackson. [5] See above, Brooke to Clay, July 12, 1824.

[6] On October 17 Lafayette and his entourage left Alexandria, District of Columbia (now Virginia), on board a steamboat which took them to Mount Vernon, thence, on the eighteenth, to Yorktown, Virginia, where they remained for two days before continuing the tour through that State. The party returned to Washington November 23.

Receipted Account with Lexington Post Office

[*ca.* October 17, 1824]

The account, in continuation of those above, July 3, October 10, 1823, June 17, 1824, covers the period from July 1 through October 17, 1824 (the first entry: "July 1 to Ballance from 17 June to 1 July $1—"). Included in the total sum of $47.26 are box rent to January 1 (six months), sixty cents; postage to November 1 for the Washington *National Intelligencer, City of Washington Gazette,* Boston *New England Galaxy,* "Cincinnati paper" (probably *Liberty Hall and Cincinnati Gazette),* Cincinnati *Literary Gazette* (a short-lived weekly, published from January to December, 1824, by John P. Foote, Cincinnati editor and banker), Frankfort *Argus of Western America,* Frankfort *Commentator,* "New Orleans paper" (not identified), "Huntsville paper" (*Alabama Republican,* established in 1816 by Thomas B. Grantland and edited in 1824 by Henry Adams), and *Nashville Whig* (established in 1812, now edited by John P. Erwin, Nashville merchant and bank director, postmaster, 1826-1828, mayor in 1834, long a member of the board of aldermen, brother of James and son of Andrew Erwin); and letter postage through October 30 (three entries under this heading are for William C. C. Claiborne). The document includes the following statement: "Note News Papers are charged to the first of November when they become free untill the 4th of April next Joseph Ficklin"; it closes as follows: "Recd payment in full J Ficklin PM." ADS. DLC-TJC (DNA, M212, R16).

From Lafayette

On Board the Steam Boat Near York town October 18h 1824

My dear friend

Your kind Congratulations and Affectionate letter[1] Are New testimonies of those Sentiments which I am proud and Happy to Have obtained from You and which are Most Cordialy [*sic*] Reciprocated; I am Now on My Way to the Anniversary Meeting at York town, and shall from there proceed to Norfolk, Richmond, Monti-Celo, Montpellier, and Again to Washington[2] Where I intend to await the Meeting of Congress. it is My fond determination to Visit the Southern and Western States, and I Anticipate the pleasure to find Myself under your friendly Roof at Ashland. But it Cannot Now Be Before I Have Met You at Washington Where Every Motive of propriety, respect, and Gratitude demand My Early visit to the Members of Both Houses Whose Unanimous invitation[3] Has Called me to the Most Honorable and Gratifying Enjoyments in Which the Human Heart Can delight. I am Happy to think the time is Not far removed When I shall Have the pleasure to present You in person the Expression of My High Regard and Most Sincere affection. My son[4] desires His Best Aknowledgments [*sic*] and Respects to You. Most truly Your grateful friend

LAFAYETTE.

ALS. DLC-HC (DNA, M212, R1). Published in Lexington *Kentucky Reporter,* November 15, 1824; Colton (ed.), *Private Correspondence of Henry Clay,* 155. Addressed to Clay at "Ashland Near Lexington"; postmarked at Norfolk, Virginia, October 21.

[1] Not found. [2] See above, Brooke to Clay, October 15, 1824, note.

[3] See above, Johnston to Clay, August 19, 1824, note.

[4] George Washington Lafayette.

Receipt from Robert Scott

[October 18, 1824]

Lexington, 18th. October 1824, recd. of H. Clay Acting Executor of J. Morrison decd. the sum of Four hundred dollars on Acct. of a legacy of Fifteen thousand dollars in money bequeathed to me by the decd.[1] said 400$. being the price of negroes George Q & Louisa purchased of sd. Executor Robt. Scott

ADS. DLC-TJC (DNA, M212, R16). [1] See above, Receipt, October 31, 1823.

From Josiah S. Johnston

Dear Sir 20th. Octr. [1824]

The Revolution of public opinion in this state is Rapidly going on—a very great majority west of Utica are favorable & decided There will a [*sic*] numerous meeting here tomorrow[1]— Since the notification in this City—meetings are called in several places to nominate Delegates to meet at Albany to form the Ticket for Electors— The Delegation from all parts will be full— a meeting has already taken place at Pou keepsie[2]— There is a great stir in Politicks & I hope for a Revival— The friends of Crawford still assuming a bold tone of Confidence—are I apprehend secretly dispairing both of the Electoral & Legislative vote— N. Carolina is doubtful & much depends on it— In the discomfiture of this party, It is impossible to say when & how they will go— It is believed that Van Buren Cannot lead them about. & that they will divide— It is of immense importance in Delaware, Maryland & Virginia, that the doubtful state of N Carolina & N. York should be known—

I understand a great majority of the members of Congress of this state are favorable to you & a larger number of the New Congress

There will be a meeting of your friends at Albany at the opening of the Session— I write to Genl. Porter now at Montreal[3] to be there pressing on him the importance of his pressence [*sic*]

The Change here is Rapid—if it is not entire It will be because the time is too short— But much will be done—every thing will be done There has been a meeting at Wors ter [*sic*] in Massachusetts[4]— Your friends are again in motion in Jersey—

With great regard J. S. Johnston

The fals hoods invented & Circulated—of your withdrawing—or being abandoned in the West—or Combination with Crawford—or accepting the Vice Presidency &c have no effect here[5]— They are thought to be Con*temptible* & the men who lend their names to them des*picable* Your friends adhere firmly now & will to the end—

ALS. InU. Addressed to Clay at Lexington. Postmarked: "NEW-YORK OCT 20."
[1] A meeting of the "republican general committee of nomination" was to be held

at Tammany Hall on October 21, to select candidates to be "reported to a general meeting of the republican electors of the city and county of New York." *Niles' Weekly Register,* XXVII (September 18, 1824), 35.

[2] No account of this meeting has been found.

[3] Cf. above, Porter to Clay, October 6, 1824.

[4] Meetings of friends of Clay and of Jackson, at Boston and other points in Massachusetts, resolved to support an unpledged ticket in opposition to the electors pledged to Adams.

[5] Cf. above, Clay to Johnston, August 31, 1824, note.

To Charles Hammond

My dear Sir (Confidential) Frankfort 25h. Oct. 1824

Dr. Drake[1] handed me this morning, as I was leaving Lexington, your obliging letter of the 20th. instant.[2] You treated the proposition from the friends of Mr. Crawford, in regard to the Vice Presidency, transmitted to you through the medium of the post office, with much discretion & propriety. The same proposition has been communicated to other friends in various quarters, and I find that, without any concert between them, they have agreed substantially in the same answer.[3] It was impossible to accede to it, and it was impracticable, if it had been accepted. As for me, before I could listen to it, I must entirely change my nature and character, and violate all the principles which I have made my guide during the agitation of the Presidential question. According to these principles, I have felt it my duty to abstain from every species of compromitment; to reject every overture looking to arrangements or compromises; and to preserve my perfect freedom of action whether I am elected or not. Standing in the position in which I have been placed, it has appeared to me that I ought to avoid, as I have avoided, either giving or receiving promises from or to persons or parties. There is a great difference in the condition of the individual whose name is held up for office, and that of the public. Candidates (I do not like the expression, but I cannot employ a better) ought to be neutral and neither seek nor agree to compromises. They are personally too much interested. They ought to be (as in name and fact I have endeavored honestly to be) Clay in the potter's hands. And that potter is the public. Doubtless the public itself or even respectable portions of it, upon public principles, may make what compromises or arrangements it pleases, in regard to those who are nominated for public offices. Appointment to them is the proper affair and for the benefit of the public. Nor is there, in that case, danger from the illusions of personal interest or personal ambition.

No, my dear Sir, of one thing you and the rest of my friends may be perfectly assured, that if I am elected, I shall enter upon the office without one solitary promise or pledge to any man to redeem; and if I am not elected, I will at least preserve unsullied that public integrity and those principles which my friends have supposed me to possess.

What course my friends may take, what it may be proper for me to pursue, in the event of my not entering the H. of R. I have not yet determined. I have indeed purposely postponed the consideration of that question, partly from a hope that it may not be necessary to decide it, and partly from the embarrassments incident to it.

There are strong objections to each of the three gentlemen from among whom we may have to make a selection.

How can we get over, in regard to Mr. Crawford,

1 The Caucus nomination of him by *a minority*.

2 The state of his health.

3. The principles of administration which there is reason to fear will be adopted by him from his position and his Southern support?

To each of the other gentlemen there are strong if not decisive objections. Let me hear from you on these matters when I reach the City. What I am very desirous of is that our friends should act together and especially your state and Kentucky. I would make great sacrafices to that object.

The N. York pamphlet[4] 'though it bears marks of hasty composition was extremely well written. It has had a most extensive circulation. Its real author I presume you know is Mr. Ralph Lockwood of New York. I believe we shall not be disappointed in results in the States west of us. It is possible I may lose one vote in Illinois. In Missouri, some of my friends have published under their own names a spirited and animating short address, similar to that which you & others issued at Cincinnati.[5] After all, my entry into the House depends upon N. York. If that State divides its vote with either Mr. Adams or Mr. Crawford and myself I shall be returned. Or if it gives its vote wholly to Mr. Adams I do not absolutely despair of Virginia. By the bye, Mr. Adams' prospect of being one of the three highest is I think much less favorable now than it was some months back—

I regret the issue of some of the Ohio elections, particularly that in McArthurs and Ross s districts.[6] As to Gazley[7], he is not without some talents, but he had no utility in the H. I am rejoiced at the success of Wright, Sloane & Beecher and Whittlesey.[8] I take it for granted that in the other districts there have been no changes, except in your old one, where there has been an improvement.[9]

Be pleased to mention me respectfully to your good Bishop. I am delighted that my letter to Lord Gambier proved of some benefit to him.[10] There is no more pious or better man in England than his Lordship, whose letter I have not yet received.[11]

I am cordially & faithfly Yr friend H. CLAY

C. Hammond Esqr.

ALS. InU. [1] Daniel Drake. [2] Not found.

[3] Cf. above, Ingalls to Clay, August 8, 1824, note; Johnston to Clay, August 19, 25, September 11, 1824; Brooke to Clay, October 15, 1824.

[4] See above, Johnston to Clay, September 22, 1824.

[5] In an announcement dated October 7, Hammond and Jacob Burnet had denied reports that a coalition existed between the Clay and Crawford supporters, under which the presidential electors pledged to Clay would yield. William H. Harrison, campaigning as a Clay elector, had published a similar statement about the same time. At St. Louis on the same date, eighteen Missouri supporters likewise signed an address repudiating rumors of Clay's withdrawal. Lexington *Kentucky Reporter*, October 25, 1824.

[6] Duncan McArthur, who had not been a candidate for re-election to Congress, was succeeded by John Thomson, a physician of New Lisbon, Ohio, who had served in the State legislature, 1814-1820, and who sat in the United States House of Representatives from 1825 to 1827 and from 1829 to 1837. Thomas R. Ross had been defeated by John Woods, of Butler County, who served two terms in Congress, became editor of the Hamilton (Ohio) *Intelligencer* in 1829, and was later State Auditor, 1845-1851, and a railroad president.

[7] James W. Gazlay had been defeated by James Findlay.

[8] John C. Wright; John Sloane; Philemon Beecher, of Lancaster, lawyer, militia officer, member of State House of Representatives, 1803, 1805-1807, United States Congressman, 1817-1821, 1823-1829; Elisha Whittlesey.

[9] David Jennings had defeated the incumbent, John Patterson. Both were residents of St. Clairsville; both had held local offices and served in the State legislature. Jennings was a lawyer; Patterson, half brother of Thomas Patterson, was a merchant.

[10] Above, August 20, 1823. The letter had been instrumental in winning a hearing for the project of Bishop Philander Chase in England. See Chase, *Reminiscences*, I, 265.

[11] Above, June 29, 1824. Cf. above, Chase to Clay, October 14, 1824.

Bill of Sale from Daniel Bryan

[October 28, 1824]

Know all men by these presents that I. Daniel Bryan. have bargained and sold and by these presents do bargain and sell unto Henry Clay the negro slaves Humphrey, Peter and John, which said slaves were mortgaged by me to William Roman & Samuel Bryan, and the said mortgage has been assigned or agreed to be assigned to the said Clay[1]— And for and in consideration of the sum of Eleven hundred and fifty dollars, to be credited to me against the debt to secure payment of which the said mortgage was executed, I do hereby release to the said Clay all equity of redemption which I have in the said slaves or either of them. Hereby warranting and defending the title and the soundness of the said slaves to the said Clay his heirs and assigns.

Witness my hand & seal this twenty eight [*sic*] day of Octr 1824

Teste John Womack DAN'L. BRYAN {L.S.}

Robt. Scott

DS, in Clay's hand. DLC-TJC (DNA, M212, R16).
1 Cf. above, Agreement, October 18, 1822.

From James Smith, Jr.

Esteemed Friend, 28h. October 1824

(Tomorrow is the day of Election[1]—and I hope to see you in the presidents chair)

In your favour of 27h. May last[2] you say you have in hand about 50$ which I may either draw on you for, or that you will bring the same with you at the next session— As I have not drawn, I conclude of course I shall receive the same when you arrive at Washington.— permit me to say, and to request that, (as you will probably receive this before you set out) you will endeavour to ascertain what other sums are coming to me and altho' you may not have recived [*sic*] the same, yet, if they, or any part is so secured as that you are confident, you will receive the same— You will accomodate [*sic*] me by handing me at the same time with the 50$ as much more as you think I ought to have & am justly entitled to—

These matters have been a long time depending & it has given me pain to trouble you so frequently— I do want them settled— and I shall be much obliged by your handing me on your arrival at Washington any sum that you think I ought to have in addition to the 50$—so that I may send you a receipt in full— I am much in want of money—and hope you will do the needful & oblige

Yr Friend JAS SMITH JR

P S. I think there must me [*sic*] several hundred Dollars still coming from the different items— please to look into it.— If you can send me 250 Dollars I shall be willing to send you a receipt, in full for services rendered with many thanks— and as you say Woodson Wrens circumstances are good—you will probably recive this sum from him— Nothing will ever be got for the drft on Gray & Taylor—which he ought to make good—

please to do the best you can for me—

ALS. DLC-TJC (DNA, M212, R12). Addressed to Clay at Lexington.
1 Of presidential electors, in Pennsylvania. 2 Not found.

Property Deed to John Montgomery

[*ca.* November 1, 1824]

[For a stated[1] sum, paid and acknowledged, of which Henry Clay's share is one hundred and seventy five dollars, he and Isham Talbot sell to John Montgomery the 27 acres on which Montgomery now resides, part of a survey of 1500 acres patented in the name of Henry Watkins. Title guaranteed only against claimants under Clay and Talbot. Signatures witnessed by Joseph Lindsay and G. Y. Saltonstall;[2] deed recorded in Scott County Court, November 1, 1824.]

Scott County Court, Deed Book F, 323-24. Recorded copy partially destroyed.
1 Amount missing.
2 Gordon Y. Saltonstall, of Scott, later of Christian County, Kentucky.

Memorandum on Bond to John J. Astor

1 Nov. 1824

After having made sundry payments on the within bond, I paid a check this day for four thousand and odd dollars, obtained from the Off of Discount and Deposit of the B. of the U. S. in Lexington, which was remitted by Mr. Harper,[1] the Cashier to J. J. Astor.

H. CLAY

AES. On verso of Bond, April 10, 1819 (see above, II, 686, 687n).
1 James Harper.

To Nicholas Biddle

Sir

Lexington 1st. Nov. 1824

The off. at Lexington has made a contingent arrangement with D Weisiger of his debt due to the Bank of the U.S., depending upon the final ratification or rejection of the Board at Philada. Having advised that arrangement under the firm belief that it was for the interest of the Bank I wish now to assign my reasons for this opinion.

Mr. Weisigers principal means consist of a farm of 600 Acres of land near Frankfort, a large Tavern establishment in that town, which he now occupies, and some 20 or 30 slaves. His debt to the Lexington office, including interest &c, amounts to upwards of $13.000;[1] and to that at Louisville to about $2000,[2] besides $3000 or there abouts which he contests, but which I think we shall finally make him responsible for. The total amount to both offices may be assumed at upwards of $18.000. You will probably possess from those offices, respectively, a more precise statement in detail of this mass of debt.

The arrangement which has been made contemplates the reception of the farm at $7000 in absolute payment, and a mortgage upon the Tavern Establishment for the residue of his debt,[3] with the exception of the $2000 to the Louisville office which is secured by a lien upon the slaves and Tavern furniture, in common with other debts, which lien is I have no doubt adequate to the debts charged upon it. If he fail to pay the interest upon that residue annually during the term of five years, for which the credit is extended, the Bank is to be at liberty to proceed to enforce payment of both principal & interest. The debts which he owes other than those to the Bank of the U. S. amount to between five and seven thousand dollars in the currency of this State and $3000 in Specie, besides a responsibility which he is under as surety of a late Marshall of this district to the U.S., hereafter mentioned, which he contests.

Mr. Weisiger about a year ago executed to his son and to Robert Alexander a conveyance of his Tavern Establishment, furniture and slaves,[4] to secure payment of certain debts therein specified and as a provision afterwards for his wife and children. His pretext for making this conveyance is his responsibility to the U.S. as surety for a late Marshall. The U.S. claim of him & other sureties about $20.000 upon the Marshall's bond. He says that it is an old office bond of long standing, and that he does not believe the debt a just one. From my own knowledge of the late Marshall and his habits (Col. Jo. Crockett) I do not believe that he justly owes the Government the sum claimed of him.[5] Still I do not think Mr. Weisiger stands justified in making the conveyance which he has executed; because nothing can justify an incumbrance of one's property to evade the process of Law.

That conveyance I entertain no doubt we could set aside by a Suit in Chancery; but we should probably be a year or two at law to accomplish that object.

The considerations which appear to me to recommend the ratification of the arrangement which has been made are these:

1st. That the whole of Mr. Weisigers debt to the Bank can be only extinguished by the means which he possesses. If all compromise be rejected, we must look forward to the time, sooner or later, when they would be put under the hammer, and then the Bank would probably have to purchase, to save itself from loss.

2. We must, in the mean time, bring and prosecute what might prove to be a tedious suit in chancery. We might indeed sell the property on a fifa[6] and hazard actions of trespass; but that is a course of too much peril, and therefore I have always advised (except in a few extraordinary cases) when the alternative is presented of a Suit in Chy or a Sheriffs Sale upon executions issued on Judgments at law to adopt the first branch of the alternative.

3. The farm which it is proposed that the Bank shall take at $7000, I believe to be worth that sum. I have made very particular enquiries about it, the result of which is that it is the best farm within three or four miles of Frankfort; that it consits [*sic*] of 600 acres of land, of which one half is first rate and the residue good farming land; that there is a good brick house two stories high

on it, with four rooms on each, in excellent order; that it has all necessary out houses, orchards, garden & well fenced, and well watered. The title is indisputable. The Judge of the U. States District Court and the Marshall[7] are both desirous of owning it, but at this time, for some particular reasons, cannot purchase it; but they both think it cheap at the price at which it is offered. The residue of the debt to the Bank will be well secured.

4. We get also secured the debt of $3000 contested by Mr. Weisiger, for which the Bank has now no security. This debt he disputes on the ground that, being an indorser, the Bank has not pursued the proper course to charge him.

5. The whole of the debt which Mr. W. owes at both offices arises from his *indorsements*. Now, although this consideration does not lessen his just responsibility, it ought not to be overlooked in estimating the future, if all arrangement be rejected. I have feared that finding the B. of the U. S. unaccommodating he might propose some incumbrance of his property to the U. S. or some other disposition of it to disable the Bank from recovering.

& 6. By making this arrangement, the weight upon him being lessened, he will continue, with redoubled vigor and good heart, to exert himself in his Tavern to meet the residue of his debt. In justice to him I must say that I know no person who is making greater personal exertions to disentangle himself. His character has heretofore stood high both for integrity and industry. His present embarrassments are brought upon him by the injudicious speculations of a Son in law.[8]

In determining upon the proposed arrangement there are but two questions:

1st. The taking of the farm. The title is good; and I do not think ultimately that there will be any loss. I would myself purchase the property if I could command the means to pay for it, at the price at which it is offered.

2. The time which is given for the residue of the debt. Although I am well acquainted with the neighbourhood in which the farm is situated, my opinion is formed principally from information. I intend, if I can command the time when at Frankfort this week to ride & see it; in which case I may write you the result of my personal view of it.

With great respect I am Yr. ob Servt. H. CLAY

P.S. I understand from Mr. Weisiger that he has insured for several years past to the amt. of $10000 on the Tavern; and that he means to renew the policy when the present one expires. H C.

Nicholas Biddle Esqr. &c. &c. &c.

ALS. PHi-Etting Collection. Endorsed: "recd Novr. 17. 1824 Nov. 19. Reffd to Comm on Offices."

1 This debt represented a total of four or more replevy bonds signed in settlement of executions issued against Weisiger by the Federal Circuit Court for Kentucky during 1822.

2 The note was for $1,900, executed on February 19, 1823, by Weisiger and William Hunter, with Robert Alexander and Daniel Weisiger, Jr., as sureties, to the Louisville office of the Bank of the United States. It was secured by a mortgage on Weisiger's slaves, blacksmith shop, carriage house, and stables. Franklin County, Deed Book K, 334-37.

3 The farm, about 600 acres on the Kentucky River, had been conveyed outright to the Bank under indenture of October 22, 1824. *Ibid.*, L, 319-20. The mortgage deed, covering the tavern and other Frankfort property and including the valuation of $7,000 credited for the farm, was dated December 25, 1824. *Ibid.*, 354-56.

4 Indenture dated May 21, 1823, between Daniel Weisiger, of the first part, and Joseph Weisiger, of Mercer County, and Robert Alexander, of the second part. *Ibid.*, K, 334-37. The latter parties accordingly also entered into the conveyance under the mortgage deed cited above, note. 3. Alexander had married Daniel Weisiger's daughter, Eliza R., in 1814.

5 Claims by the United States against Joseph Crockett had amounted to $614.26 in 1812, had risen to a total of $94,673.06 by 1820, and had been reduced to slightly less than $10,000 by 1823. Litigation against him and his sureties continued for several years. *House Docs.*, 17 Cong., 1 Sess., no. 116, p. 5; 17 Cong., 2 Sess., no. 100, p. 4; 18 Cong., 1 Sess., no. 148, p. 6.

6 Writ of *fieri facias*.

7 Robert Trimble and Chapman Coleman. The latter, born in Orange County, Virginia, had been brought to Woodford County, Kentucky, at an early age, whence after service in the War of 1812, he had removed to Louisville and engaged in banking and mercantile activities. He had been appointed marshal in January, 1823, and was reappointed in January, 1827.

8 George Adams, probably the representative of Franklin County in the Kentucky General Assembly, 1810, 1811, 1814, who had married Anna M. Weisiger in 1811. Weisiger had been named in two executions, amounting to over $7,000, issued against Adams by the Federal Circuit Court in 1822, on debts due to the Bank of the United States.

Receipt from T. H. Clarke

[November 1, 1824]

T. H. Clarke, Collector, by Henry Allen, in a document similar to the Receipt, above, September 15, 1823, acknowledges payment from Henry Clay "by the hand of Col. T. H. Blake eight dollars and twenty and an half cents" for taxes for the year 1824, "together with the commission thereon and cost of advertising," on two tracts of land in Vigo County, Indiana. State and road taxes are the same as in the earlier document; the county tax is now 80 cents on each tract; advertising charges are 12½ cents for each tract; and a charge of two per cent commsision on the tax amounts to 15½ cents. ADS, by Henry Allen. DLC-TJC (DNA, M212, R16).

Receipt from John Wirt

[November 1, 1824]

Recd. Lexington Novr. 1st. 1824 of H. Clay esqr. Seventy Dollars & Sixty five cents his town tax for the present year

JOHN WIRT Colr. T.L.

ADS. DLC-TJC (DNA, M212, R16).

Receipt from John Wirt

[November 1, 1824]

John Wirt acknowledges receipt of nine dollars, Lexington town tax for 1824, paid by Clay as executor of the estate of Thomas Hart, Sr. DS. DLC-TJC (DNA, M212, R16).

From William Lytle

Cincinnati 3 Nov. 1824.

Hon. Henry Clay acting Exr. of James Morrison decd.
Dear Sir:

Mr. Scotts[1] letter of 25 Sept I have. On reexamining the taxes paid by me for Col. Morrison I find some errors both ways so as to leave that account about even and no balance due to me as I supposed.

The $346 which I paid to Fielding[2] for the Col. will be satisfied with the ⅔ of the 100 & 125 acre tracts of land—for which I wish a deed & transfer— one is patented & the other not & both of which I was authorised by Col. Morrison to sell.

The conveyance for my share of the 1000 acres I shall want whenever it is in the power of the Exr. to convey or when titles are obtained from O Hara & Bowsman.[3]

The taxes on said land can be paid at Columbus any time (I think) before Jany without penalty for this year.

Respectfully Yours &c. WM. LYTLE

LS. DLC-TJC (DNA, M212, R12). 1 Robert Scott.
2 Robert Fielding, not further identified.
3 Lytle had served as land locator for Morrison, James O'Hara, and Nicholas Bausman (Bowsman), the latter two having been pioneer settlers of Pittsburgh. O'Hara, quartermaster general of the Army during the Indian campaigns of the mid-nineties, had in 1797 erected the first glass-making works in Pittsburgh. Bausman was a farmer.

From John Harvie

Bank of Kentucky Frankfort Kentucky Nov. 4th. [1824]
Henry Clay Esqr. City of Washington Dear Sir

I have just this moment risen from addressing the President of the Bank of the United States on the subject of aiding in rebuilding our State House.[1] But as the Northen [*sic*] people have few sympathies for us especially since the era of the relief system,[2] I deem it necessary to endeavour to entice in advocation of the application some advocate better calculated from eminence and standing to give it consequence influence and effect. To your good offices then I resort—from the united consideration of your sympathies with our townsmen upon their calamity zeal in behalf of every thing appertaining to the state, and capacity to promote and propitiate our objects. Your personal knowledge of the various considerations which ought to be presented to the notice of the Bank of the United States and which is [*sic*] calculated to be operative upon the deliberations upon the subject is so full and ample as to render my dilating into details totally superfluous. The value of the larger portion of the property of that Bank in this town depends from its construction and nature essentially upon the continuation of the seat of Government at Frankfort—as indeed in a preeminent degree does the value of all property in the place. Although Frankfort has decided resourses and advantages, yet they are of that character as can only be active in an advanced stage of society with a dense population redundant Capital, and at a future period.— At present they are of no avail.— Her building materials are of the finest cast and first order abounding to excess. Marble firm and flexible, easily worked and fashioned in all forms and moulds, susceptible of high polish adapted for frames and facings for all manner and kinds of openings. Lime strong and adhesive, either for the purposes of cement or stucco sand of all qualities from the finest to the coarsest. and Clay of the best texture for bricks. Timber in the neighboring woods of all the various pecies [*sic*] of the country and of the loftiest and most stately growth.

A River, occasionally the most magnificent when elevated from forty to fifty feet above the ordinary level, flowing thro' the core of the most plenteous beautifull and fine country on the globe containing in its Banks enexhausteble stores of coal salt Marble &c. &c. and which in future times must render its surface the seat of an extensive and fruitfull commerce, Altho' owing to the peculiar constitution of our climate, is during the droughts of summer and fall incapable of being navigated for any usefull purposes but which when the progress of wealth shall have furnished a sufficient redundancy of Capital to be employed in the improvement of the navigation of our streams may be rendered at an inconsiderable expense navigable and traversable at all seasons of the year. These are matters which appear to me well worthy of the consideration of the Bank of the United States. But there is another consideration not less calculated in my estimation to have an influence upon that corporation. It is the opportunity which is furnished of conciliating the country and of lulling to rest those angry feelings which have heretofore prevailed in relation to that corporation. Should it comport with your Views to facilitate this application I shall be happy in the circumstance. Your friends are all elated with the prospect of Virginia going in your favour.[3]

Respectfully J. HARVIE Prest.

Copy. Bank of Kentucky, Frankfort, Letter Book G (June 19, 1822-June 10, 1825), 441.

1 The structure had burned in the morning of this day. Harvie's action, as president of the Bank of Kentucky, in soliciting this support for rebuilding of the capitol was repudiated by the Kentucky House of Representatives, which on January 12, 1825, adopted a resolution stating that "this house does *not* and will *not* approve such appropriations. . . ." Ky. H. of Reps., *Journal, 1824-1825*, pp. 602-603.

2 See above, Clay to Dougherty, December 7, 1821, note.

3 Rumors had been current in Frankfort that Crawford was about to be withdrawn as a candidate for the Presidency and that Virginia and New York would consequently support Clay. See Frankfort *Argus of Western America*, November 17, 1824.

Agreement with George J. Brown and Others

[November 6, 1824]

An agreement between George J. Brown, Francis P. Hord & Thomas E. West Commissioners of the Farmers Bank of Jessamine and Henry Clay.

The said Commissioners hereby agree to sell to the said Clay the frame house and lot situated in Lexington on Short street fronting the public square, adjoining the lot of Tibbatts[1] on the one side and that of the B. of the U. States, occupied by B. Gratz, on the other, formerly the property of Andrew McCalla; and the said Commissioners agree to assign to the said Clay the mortgage which they hold on the said lot from the said McCalla, and to convey the title which they have acquired to the same, under a Sheriff's sale; but they are not to be personally liable for the goodness of the title hereby transfered.

The said Clay is to receive the rents accruing from the tenants in possession on the said house and lot from the first instant.

In consideration whereof it is agreed that the suit in Chancery depending in the Circuit Court of Jessamine whereon the said Clay is Complt and the said Commissioners defendants[2] shall be dismissed agreed, each party paying his own Costs, and the notes of the said Nicholasville Bank, for the recovery of the amount of which the said suit was commenced, shall be surrendered to the said Commissioners.

And as a further consideration for the said house and lot the said Clay agrees to pay to the said Commissioners in notes of the Commonwealths Bank the sum of five hundred dollars six months hence at which time the said Commissioners agree to execute the assignment of the mortgage as afd. and to convey the title derived from the Sheriff's sale as above stipulated.[3] Witness the seals of the parties this 6th. day of Novr. 1824. H. CLAY {L.S.}
Signed Sealed &c in presence of GEO J BROWN {L.S.}
THO. E. WEST {L.S.}
{L.S.}

ADS. signed also by Brown and West. DLC-TJC (DNA, M212, R16).
1 Thomas Tibbatts.
2 Jessamine Circuit Court, File 185. See above, Receipt, July 16, 1822; Memorandum, December 26, 1822.
3 See below, Property Deed, June 22, 1825.

To Nicholas Biddle

Sir Lexington 8h. Nov. 1824

Since my last the Capitol at Frankfort has been burnt.[1] This event will give rise to an attempt to remove the Seat of Government from that place. Its establishment there has been the occasion of much dissatisfaction always, although a Constitutional majority (two thirds of the Legislature) has never heretofore been obtained to fix it any where else. Such a majority will not I think be procured at the present time. Nevertheless I do not think it at all improbable that the Legislature will refuse to make an appropriation to rebuild the Capitol,[2] strange as it may appear. In that case the proprietors in the town, prompted by the motive of self interest, will endeavor to rebuild it, and may solicit the aid of the Bank, as one of the largest proprietors. I mention this probable application that you may be prepared to consider and decide on it.

The event alluded to deserves to be estimated in considering Mr. D. Weisigers proposition.[3] If, on the one hand, it may diminish somewhat the value of the farm which he tenders, on the other, it diminishes still more the value of his Tavern Establishment, and consequently his ultimate ability to pay the debt which he owes to the Bank. My opinion is that it should not have any tendency to dissuade the Bank from ratifying the contingent arrangement which has been made here, but rather the contrary.

I have rode over the farm since I wrote you last.

It does not equal my expectation in all respects. The soil is as good and the timber and water better than I expected; but the land does not lay in as good a form as I hoped to find it. The dwelling house answered my expectations; the out houses did not. Nevertheless I do not believe that the Bank will sustain a material if any loss in the acquisition of that property; and I am still of the decided opinion that the arrangement ought to be sanctioned.

I transmit you inclosed a letter from Col. Todd.[4] He has been long and seriously indisposed, as has been his father Judge Todd.[5] I think the time which he solicits to complete the arrangement with the Bank had better be granted.

I have the honor to be with great respect Your ob. Servt.

Nicholas Biddle Esqr. &c. &c. &c. H. CLAY

ALS. PHi-Etting Collection. Endorsed: "recd Novr. 22. 1824."

1 See above, Harvie to Clay, November 4, 1824.

2 On January 6, 1825, a bill providing for removal of the seat of government was defeated on the question of engrossment, 34 ayes to 53 nays. Ky. H. of Reps., *Journal, 1824-1825,* p. 545. The Kentucky legislature met in local church buildings until the session of 1829-1830. Authorization for construction of a new capitol was not enacted until January 12, 1827, when an appropriation of $15,000 was allotted. Subsequently two additional grants of $20,000, each, were made, together with authorization for use of any materials which could be supplied by the State penitentiary. Ky. Gen. Assy., *Acts, 1826-1827,* pp. 32-34; *1827-1828,* pp. 175-76 (February 12, 1828); *1828-1829,* pp. 116-17 (January 29, 1829). The total cost of the new building was $85,000. Bayless E. Hardin, "The Capitols of Kentucky," Kentucky State Historical Society, *Register, XLIII* (1945), 181, 183.

3 See above, Clay to Biddle, November 1, 1824.

4 Charles S. Todd. The letter has not been found. On his debt to the Bank of the United States, see above, Todd to Clay, May 8, 1823, note; Clay to Biddle, August 16, 1824.

5 Thomas Todd.

Assignment from William S. Dallam

[November 8, 1824]

For value recd. I assign the within to Henry Clay

WILL S. DALLAM

ES. Fayette Circuit Court, File 605 (1825). On verso of a note for $6,000, from Thomas January to Dallam, dated January 2, 1815, and payable on or before January 1, 1825. On January 11, 1825, Clay filed suit for its collection, but an endorsement on the sheriff's writ reported failure of execution because of January's death, which occurred on January 26.

Agreement with William S. Dallam

[November 8, 1824]

I do hereby agree that H. Clay need not prosecute actions at law on the notes of Thos. January which I have assigned to him:[1] 8h. Nov. 1824 but to pursue the bill in equity on the mortgage[2]

WILL S. DALLAM

DS, in Clay's hand. DLC-TJC (DNA, M212, R16).

1 See above, Assignment, this date; below, Account, *ca.* December 7, 1824; and cf. above, Agreement, October 18, 1822.

2 Cf. above, Receipt, *ca.* October, 1823, note.

Receipt from William H. Prentiss

[November 8, 1824]

Recd. 8h. Nov. 1824 of H. Clay Fifty dollars in Specie under the order of my father on a/c. of monies collected by the said Clay for the trust of the Purviances. WM. H. PRENTISS

DS, in Clay's hand. DLC-TJC (DNA, M212, R16). Prentiss has not been identified.

Property Deed to Robert Scott

[November 9, 1824]

[As executor of James Morrison, Henry Clay, with Esther Morrison, Robert Wickliffe, Farmer Dewees, and Richard Hawes, Jr., nominated but not qualified as executrix and executors of the deceased, conveys to Robert Scott, in partial fulfillment of the grant of $30,000 worth of property bequeathed to him by Morrison,[1] two tracts adjacent to Louisville—viz, a lot known as "the point of Beargrass" and an undivided moiety of 35 acres purchased by Morrison and Thomas D. Carneal from William Lytle—together valued at $6,400 in the list of property appraisals accompanying Morrison's will. Signed and acknowledged by all the named executors; recorded in Fayette County Court on January 21, 1825, and in Jefferson County Court on March 19, 1825.]

Jefferson County Court, Deed Book X, 92-94.
1 See above, Receipt, October 31, 1823, note.

Memorandum from Richard H. Chinn

Nov 9. 1824.

In the case of Dallam vs. January Mr. Clay has handed to me two notes of Thomas January dated 2. Jany 1815 due 1st. Jany. 1825— The one for Six thousand dollars & the other for $360—to be used in the above Suit in Chany. in Fayette Court

R. H. CHINN

ADS. DLC-TJC (DNA, M212, R16). See above, Agreement, November 8, 1824.

Account with Richard Pindell and Others

1819.		Henry Clay Esqr [*ca.* November 10, 1824]	
Feby.	28th.	To Ridgely & Pindell Dr.	
		For Amt of Medical Acct from 15th. July 1817 to this date	$88. 00
1823		To Ridgely Pindell & Satterwhite	
Jany.	1st.	For Amt of Medical Acct Obstetric Fees & Surgical Cases from 1st. March 1819 to this date	$506. 12½
1824		To Pindell & Satterwhite	
Augst.	20th.	from 1st. Jany. 1823 to this date	$423. 25
Nov.	9th.	To Amt. of Acct Sons Since	113. 50
			$1123„87½

1822		Cr	
Nov	22d	By Vials & Med returned	$2.00
		" Yr Check for	100. —
1823		" Do Do	200. —
		" Sugar of Mr. Smith[1]	43:16
		" By Bushels Corn Meal @	9
1824		" By one Acre of Timothy	10
Augst	16th.	" By Cash R Pindell	300.00
		By a fee agst F Ridgely[2] Mc.Durmits Case	100.00

1824

Nov.	10th.	By Cash pd this day day [*sic*] T. P. Satterwhite	200.00

By Hay omitted furnished by J. Watkins . . 7:50[3]

There is an Acct. agst. you on Ridgely & Dudleys[4] Books

1552 lb	Pork	R Pindell	69.84
1070	do.	Satterwhite	48.15
			$1089.65

	1123.87½
	1089.65
	34.22½
Since	27 50.
	61.72½

[Endorsement on verso][5]

Up to 10h Novr. 1824

Memo. Some credits to be given as within—Pork furnished this fall to be charged.

D. DLC-TJC (DNA, M212, R16). Cf. above, Receipted Bill, August 16, 1824.

1 Probably Thomas Smith. 2 Case not found; the next line not clearly legible.

3 This entry is in Clay's hand. 4 Dr. Benjamin W. Dudley. 5 AE, by Clay.

To John J. Crittenden

My dear Sir Ashland Wednesday Evening 10 Nov 24

Inclosed I transmit you a paper to be used in the suit of Gernon agt. Vimont. It consists of a Certificate of deposit (the plea of lender making that necessary) of $500 and the written admission of Mr. Gratz (to whom the note sued upon has been indorsed for collection) that the tender was made. It was made as soon as the maker of the note knew where to make it.[1] There is a deposition filed to which I would request your attention. Be pleased to attend to this cause for me, about which I feel solicitude. Its justice is with my client and so I think the Court has substantially decided.

With respect to my business generally in the Federal Court I must ask your friendly attention. My wish is that it may be continued over, which I presume will be generally acquiesced in.

I believe the Ohio election has resulted agreeably to your friendly wishes, 'though it remains involved in some uncertainty.[2]

I have received a letter from La Fayette which I have allowed to be published, and which therefore you will see.[3]

The information from Richmond runs in the same current with increased force.[4]

With my best wishes I remain Faithfully & cordially Your friend

H. CLAY

J. J. Crittenden Esq

ALS. DLC-John J. Crittenden Papers (DNA, M212, R20).

1 Richard Gernon, at this time a resident of France, was suing Lewis Vimont, of Millersburg, Kentucky, for collection of a note payable "in bank notes current in the State of Kentucky at the time the said note became due towit on the 15th. day of November 1821." When Vimont had tendered payment to Gernon's agent, Benjamin Gratz, in notes of the Bank of Commonwealth, this currency had been rejected. The case, instituted in November, 1823, was finally discontinued, on motion of the plaintiff, May 31, 1826. U. S. Circuit Court, Seventh Circuit, District of Kentucky, Order Book, I, 339; K, 188, 222; L, 247.

2 The voting for presidential electors had been held in Ohio on October 29. Although early reports had placed Clay in the lead, final results were not known for about two weeks, when Clay's plurality over Jackson had been reduced to 766 votes. Lexington *Kentucky Reporter,* November 1, 8, 15, 22, 1824.

3 See above, October 18, 1824. 4 See above, Harvie to Clay, November 4, 1824.

To Robert Scott

11 Nov. 1824

Mr. R. Scott will be pleased to make for H. Clay the following Collections.

From R. C Buckner[1] on the 16 Decr. next	*pd.*	$50.
From P. Ratel on the 10 Feb. next	*pd.*	32:50
From R. Breckenridge[2] for nine months rent		*63.87½ pd*
From Tho. Curry now due		60:55
Do. on 1 Feb. next		60:55
From Winn and Ayres[3] on 25 Decr. next	*pd.*	150:
From J. Plasted [*sic*][4] for four months rent	*pd.*	26:66
From Mr. Deverin[5] due the 1st. Decr. next *123„87½ pd. 7 Decr. 24*		125: –
From Wilkins McIlvaine & Co. due 1st. Octr 1824	*pd.*	62:50
do. do. due 1 Jan. 1825	*Jany 1825*	62:50
From Mr. Richardson for exon agt. Whaley[6]	*pd.*	141„23½

H. Clay

Memo.

The ro[of] of the house on [*sic*] which Mr. Ratel lives is wanting some shingles to stop a leak. Will you mention to Mr. Kennedy[7] to have them put on. H C.

ANS. DLC-TJC (DNA, M212, R16). Italics, supplied by editors, delineate subsequent annotations by Scott.

1 John C. Buckner.

2 Robert J. Breckinridge, who in April, 1824, had announced the location of his law office, "on Short street fronting the corner of Cheap Side," in Lexington. Lexington *Kentucky Reporter,* April 19, 1824. No rental agreement with him has been found. Clay's record of the amount due for this entry, "75:," crossed out in the account.

3 The firm has not been identified, but cf. above, Scott to Clay, December 30, 1823.

4 Probably joined with W. Williams in the partnership of Williams and Plaisted, who earlier in the year had advertised their "English and Classical Academy" in Lexington. Williams continued as proprietor of a school in the town for many years. No rental agreement with either partner has been found.

5 John Deverin.

6 Probably John C. Richardson; Benjamin Whaley. Cf. above, Scott to Clay, January 5, 16, 1824.
7 Matthew Kennedy.

Mortgage Deed to Bank of the United States

[November 15, 1824]

This indenture made this 15th. day of November 1824 Between H. Clay and The President Directors and Company of the Bank of the U. States Witnesseth that for and in consideration of the sum of one dollar to the said Clay in hand paid the receipt whereof from the said Company is hereby acknowledged he hath granted bargained and sold and by these presents doth grant bargain and sell to the said Company a certain tract of land lying and being near Lexington, containing four hundred acres, and bounded by the Boones & Taits creek roads, the lands of the Estate of Col. James Morrison, Cornelius Coyle, John McNair and Geo. Trotter, being the same known by the name of Ashland, on which the said Clay at present resides, with the appurtenances To have and to hold the said tract of land, with the appurtenances, to the said President Directors and Company of the Bank of the U. States and their successors in fee simple: Upon this condition nevertheless that if the said Clay shall well and truly pay to the said Company a note[1] given by him on the first day of this month, at their office of discount and deposit in Lexington, payable Sixty days after date, for the sum of three thousand dollars and any note or notes that may be given for the renewal thereof or any part thereof, then this deed to be void otherwise to remain in full force. And the said Clay doth hereby covenant and agree to and with the said Company that he will warrant and defend the right and title to the land hereby conveyed against all and every person whatsoever.

In testimony whereof the said Clay hath hereunto set his hand and seal the day and year above written. H. CLAY {L.S.}

Signed Sealed & Delivered
In presence of

[Endorsement on verso][2]

I do hereby certify as Cashier of the Office of the Bank of the United States at Lexington that a debt due to the said Bank from H Clay to secure payment of which a mortgage was executed by him on the 15 day of November 1824. has been fully paid & satisfied and the said mortgage discharged

Witness my hand this 8 Decr 1830 J HARPR [*sic*], Cashr

ADS. Elsie Jackson Kelly Collection, Henry Clay Memorial Foundation, Lexington, Kentucky.
1 Not found. 2 AES, by James Harper.

From William B. Astor

Dear Sir, New York 15th. November 1824

I have received your letter of the 1st inst[1] also one from Mr Harper of the same date covering a check on the U S. Bank for $4315.21/100 Forty three hundred & fifteen 21/100 Dollars—

I remain with great regard Your most obedient Servant

WM. B ASTOR

To, The Honorable Henry Clay Lexington (Kenty)

ALS. DLC-TJC (DNA, M212, R12). Postmarked at Lexington, November 30, and forwarded to Washington. Cf. above, Endorsement, November 1, 1824.

1 Not found.

To Francis T. Brooke

Hardins[1] near Charlottesville 26 Nov. 24

My dear Sir (Confidential)

I felt, in your prompt public contradiction of the letter of Mr. Dayton stating that my name had been withdrawn as a Candidate for the Presidency, a new proof of your friendship, which I have ever so highly valued, and at the same time a self reproach for my not having written to you, since the adjournment of Congress.[2] The truth is that, in the first letter which I received from you, after I reached home, you stated your intention to visit the watering places and I did not well know where to address you; and the last which you did me the favor to write was received but a few days before I sat [*sic*] out on this journey.[3] I concluded therefore to defer the pleasure of writing you until I passed the mountains.

Your prediction has been well nigh being verified as to Genl. Jackson's taking the Western vote from me. My friends have prevailed over him in Ohio by only about 7 or 8 hundred votes.[4] This result has been owing to the conjoint causes of their discouragement, as to the prospect of my being carried into the H. of R., fabrications of tales of my withdrawal and imputations of sinister designs, on the part of my friends, to promote the election of Mr. Crawford.[5] But for these adverse causes my friends believe that they would have prevailed over the General by 15 or 20 thousand votes.

I have received no conclusive information as to the result of the election in Indiana and Illinois, the two of the six Western States counted for me, which were believed to be most doubtful. That which has reached me is favorable and such as to induce me to think the issue there has been auspicious. Missouri never was doubted, nor do I think Louisiana uncertain.[6]

Events on this side of the mountains have surprized me, particularly in N. York & N. Carolina,[7] in the former State especially. I know not the secret springs which have produced such a strange result as has occurred in N. York. I have moved none of them. I know nothing but what we see in the public prints. From these it is evident that, if the friends of Mr. Crawford and myself had all amicably cooperated the vote of that State might have been secured to the one or the other or been divided between us. I am uninformed of what prevented that concert.

It is now evident that Genl. Jackson, and Mr. Adams must each enter the H. with not less than eighty votes, and there is every probability that I shall be the third. What will Mr. Crawfords friends, what will Virginia do? If they adhere to him, I shall enter the H. so crippled that my election can scarcely be anticipated. If they concentrate on me (and we should not be disappointed as to the Western vote yet remaining to be heard from) I shall be placed highest on the list of the three, and I think there would be but little doubt as to the final result. Even if we should be disappointed as to the votes of Indiana, Illinois and Louisiana, if all Mr. Crawfords friends unite on me, there is much probability of success. I should not despair with the vote of Virginia alone added to that which I shall receive in the West. Thus your State has it yet in her power to secure her second choice, if, as my Virginia friends believe, I am the object of it.

I propose visiting Mr. Jefferson tomorrow, and afterwards Mr. Madison. I shall remain a day or two with each of them and expect to reach Fredericksburg, on my way to the City of Washington, on the 2d. or 3d. of December.

I remain faithfully & Cordially Your friend H. CLAY

The Honble Francis Brooke.

ALS. KyU. Published in part in Colton (ed.), *Private Correspondence of Henry Clay*, 106-107.

1 The Albemarle Hotel, owned and operated from 1805 to around 1827 by Benjamin Hardin, was located about one mile west of present day Ivy Depot, in Albemarle County, Virginia.

2 A few weeks earlier the Philadelphia *Columbian Observer*, strongly pro-Jackson, had printed a letter addressed to its editor, Stephen Simpson, by J. Ogden Dayton. Writing from Salem, New Jersey, October 9, 1824, Dayton had said, in part: "I have just received a letter from col. Samuel Swartout [*sic*] of Hoboken in this state, containing some important information from the west. A gentleman of great respectability by the name of *Thompson,* has just arrived in New York, from Fredericksburg in Virginia, who, just before his departure, saw and read a letter addressed by Mr. *Clay* to Judge *Brooke* of that place, in which he says, that he had given up all expectation of getting into the house of representatives as a candidate for the presidency, and that consequently general Jackson will obtain the electoral votes of *all the western states,* and if he should not succeed by the suffrage of the electors he will receive the support of all those states in the house. This is intelligence that may be relied on."

On October 23, 1824, Brooke had written to R. W. Meade the following letter, which was released to the Richmond *Enquirer*: "I this moment, on my return from York, received your letter of the 16th inst. and promptly reply to it, that I have received no letter of any description from Mr. Clay since he left Washington in June last. If the Mr. Thompson, alluded to in the publication signed J. Ogden Dayton, at Salem, the 9th inst. is from Culpeper Courthouse, he is a gentleman of high respectability [probably William Mills Thompson, merchant and lawyer], and I am assured never made the communications stated in the publication covered by your letter to me. I have no recollection of, and am very sure I had no conversation with him in relation to Mr. Clay on the presidential election. I would not have intimated to him, from any source, Mr. Clay's intention to withdraw from the canvass for the presidency, because I then had and now have every assurance to the contrary." *Niles' Weekly Register,* XXVII (October 23, November 6, 1824), 113, 149.

3 See above, Brooke to Clay, July 12, October 15, 1824.

4 See above, Clay to Crittenden, November 10, 1824, note.

5 Cf. above, Clay to Hammond, October 25, 1824.

6 Clay was defeated in both Indiana and Illinois—in the former, all five votes going for Jackson and, in the latter, two votes for Jackson and one for Adams. Clay did receive the three votes of Missouri. On the outcome of the election in Louisiana, see below, Clay to Porter, December 26, 1824.

7 On the New York vote, see below, Clay to Brooke, December 5, 1824. The maneuvering which had produced a fusion of the Clay and Adams forces in the selection of electors by the New York Assembly and the breakdown of the arrangement on joint ballot of the two houses, which deprived Clay of four votes that could have brought him into the election by the House of Representatives, is discussed in Hammond, *History of Political Parties in the State of New York,* II, 176-78.

In North Carolina the "People's ticket," in some instances identified with Adams but in a majority of cases composed of Jackson supporters, had decisively defeated the Crawford forces. The vote in the electoral college was given to Jackson without division. *Niles' Weekly Register,* XXVII (November 20, 27, December 18, 1824), 187n, 196, 241.

From Robert Scott

Dr. Sir Lexington, 1st. Decr. 1824

Herewith enclosed, please receive your A/C with the Estate of Colo. Morrison from 7 to 30th. Novr. inclusive[1]— By it you will perceive I have paid Mr Hawes the balance of Mrs. Hawes's legacy.— Having heard you say that you beleived [*sic*] Coms. Notes would get better, I have replaced the 1500$. loaned Mr Hawes on 6th. April last[2] by giving the 750$ Specie charge—

I have paid Mrs. Clay 200$ Coms. Notes— Please say how much you wish her to have monthly until your return and I will pay it to her whether I collect it for you or not— On 26 ulto. I forwarded to Maysville 2240 lb due-rotted and 521 lb unrotted Hemp being all on hand—with instructions to forwarded [*sic*] thence to Forsythe, Dobyn [*sic*] & Co. Wheeling to be held subject to your order— I saw Mrs. Clay this morning and her and family are well—as are all your domestic affairs—I regret I cannot say as much for your political prospects—tho' your friends here stil [*sic*] hope the best—but are much vexed and mortified at the vote of some of the western States[3]—

There is a debt of something upwards of 200$. due Genl. Lytle, payable in lands[4]— Would it not be well to let Genl. Harrison settle that debt, as the collection from him I apprehend will not be made in any reasonable time and suppose he would pay dollar for dollar of that paid for him, which was in Comths. Notes,[5] for that due Gl. Lytle?—

Since you set out, our weather has been, and yet is, extremely mild for the season— So much so that your people have made but one killing as yet of your hogs and that was a day or two after you left us—

Aunt Morrison[6] and family are well—

Respectfully Yr. obt. Servt. ROBT. SCOTT

The Honble H Clay.

ALS. KyLxT.
[1] Private account not found. For the executor's accounts, see below, June 13, 1825.
[2] See above, Scott to Clay, April 12, 1824.
[3] See above, Clay to Brooke, November 26, 1824, note.
[4] Cf. above, Lytle to Clay, November 3, 1824.
[5] A year and a half later William Henry Harrison was carried on the estate accounts as owing $275, due August 25, 1825. Conjectural Estimate of the Condition of Col. Morrison's Estate . . . , August, 1826. KyLxT.
[6] Mrs. James Morrison.

To David Chambers

Dear Sir Washn. 3d. Dec. 1824

I thank you for the kind congratulations, contained in your letter of the 18h. Ulto.,[1] on the occasion of my friends having prevailed in Ohio. Whatever may be the result of the pending election, I shall ever have occasion to be highly gratified with the honorable proofs of zeal, confidence and friendship which have been exhibited in your State. I am not surprized at the closeness of the competition, when I consider all attending circumstances.

The issue of the N. York vote is yet matter of contest and uncertainty here.[2] Tomorrows mail or that of next day will decide. My friends here yet believe that I shall receive about one half of the 11 uncertain votes.

Virginia voted for Mr. Crawford, and for Mr. Macon as Vice President.[3] I remain faithfy Yr friend H. CLAY

Genl. Chambers.

ALS. DLC-HC (DNA, M212, R1). Chambers, editor of the Zanesville *Ohio Republican,* had moved from Pennsylvania to Ohio in 1810 and joined a journalistic partnership which acquired the contract as State printer. After serving in the War of 1812, he had held a succession of posts as recorder and mayor of Zanesville, member of the State House of Representatives (1814), clerk of the State Senate (1817), clerk of the Muskingum County Court of Common Pleas (1817-1821), and member of Congress (1821-1823). He was later returned to the State legislature, as member of both the House (1836-1838, 1841, 1842) and Senate (1843 and 1844).
[1]Not found. [2] See below, Clay to Brooke, December 5, 1824.
[3] The votes had been unanimous; but prior to taking action, the Virginia electors had expressed their regret at the withdrawal of Albert Gallatin as candidate for the Vice Presidency. *Niles' Weekly Register,* XXVII (December 11, 1824), 225.

To Francis T. Brooke

My dear Sir Washn. 5h. Decr. 1824

Your favor of the 29h. Oct. addressed to me at Lexn. not finding me there has returned and been duly received by me here. Events subsequent to its date render it unnecessary for me to say any thing in regard to Mr. Ritchies communication about the Vice Presidency. I have also recd. your obliging letter of the 1st. inst.[1] I had before learnt the issue of the Electoral vote of Virginia.[2] I was prepared to expect it by all that I had previously observed. Two weeks ago a course might have been taken, which would probably have prevented that result of the Presidential election now most likely to happen; and that was to have prevailed upon Mr. Crawford to withdraw which might have been done, I should suppose, without mortification to his friends, by placing it on the ground of the continued precarious state of his health. As it is, I shall yield a cheerful acquiescence in the public decision. I should indeed have been highly gratified if my native state had thought me worthy of even a second place in her confidence and affection. The obligations and respect which I owe her forbid my uttering one word of complaint, on account of her having thought otherwise.

Mr. Calhoun deserves all that you say of him He is a most captivating man.

With great esteem I remain faithfly Yr friend— H. CLAY

The N. York vote is just received

Adams 26 Clay— 4
Crawford 5 Jackson 1.

ALS. KyU. Published in Colton (ed.), *Private Correspondence of Henry Clay*, 107. Addressed to Brooke at Richmond, Virginia.

1 Neither letter has been found. On the announcement in the Richmond *Enquirer* concerning the Vice Presidency, see above, Brooke to Clay, October 15, 1824, note.

2 See above, Clay to Chambers, December 3, 1824.

To Josephus B. Stuart

Dear Sir Washington 6h. Decr. 1824

I recd. your obliging favor of the 1st. instant.[1] and thank you for its contents. If events at Albany have not realized the hopes and expectations of my friends, I have every reason to be highly thankful for their zeal, firmness and fidelity. The difficulties of their position were great, and I cannot doubt that the course which they pursued, under all circumstances, appeared to them best, even if another course might have produced a more auspicious result.

The event in other States is pretty generally known, with the exception of Louisiana. The same causes—the fabrication of tales of my being withdrawn—the discouragement of my friends &c &c which nearly lost Ohio and have occasioned the loss of Indiana, may reach Louisiana and deprive me of the vote of that State.

In that issue of its election, I shall be excluded from the House. I am prepared for any result, and can only say that I shall ever retain a friendly & thankful recollection of the exertions of yourself and other friends. With great esteem I am faithfly Yrs H. CLAY
Dr. J. B. Stuart.

ALS. NcD. See above, Clay to Brooke, November 26, 1824, notes.
[1] Not found.

Account with William S. Dallam

[*ca.* December 7, 1824]

The account lists four notes from D. & S. Bryan, dated November 7, 1816, maturing February 20, annually, in 1820 to 1823, with accruing interest charges, and five notes from Thomas January, dated January 2, 1815, maturing January 1, annually, 1819 to 1823, with interest charges—amounting to $3,733.04, as payments on a farm valued at $10,300—leaving a debt of $6,566.96 due Clay on January 2, 1823, with interest to January 2, 1824, bringing the total to $6,960.96. Credit entries, a note of D. & S. Bryan, dated November 7, 1816, maturing February 20, 1824, and one of Thomas January, dated January 2, 1815, maturing January 1, 1824, reduce the amount due Clay on January 2, 1824, to $6,203.70, which, with interest charges, totals $6,549.70 on December 7, 1824. Dallam then transfers to Clay a note of D. Bryan and W. Roman for $6,621.40, due on that date, leaving a balance of $71.30 owed by Clay to Dallam. Further transfer by Dallam of two notes of Thomas January, one for $360, the other for $6,000, both due January 1, 1825, and of another note of D. & S. Bryan, for $231.76, due February 20, 1825, bring the total of Clay's debt to Dallam to $6,663.06. AD by Dallam. DLC-TJC (DNA, M212, R16). Cf. above, Agreement, October 18, 1822; Assignment, October 18, 1822; Agreement, November 8, 1824; Memorandum, November 9, 1824.

To Peter B. Porter

My dear Sir Washn. 7 Decr. 1824

I recd. at this place your two favors of the 16h. and 17h. Novr. dated at Albany and Schenectady.[1] The event at Albany has not realized the well founded expectations of yourself and other faithful friends. Had the vote there been given to me, as you had every reason to anticipate, my entry into the H. of R. would have been secured, without taking into the account the contingency of the vote of Louisiana. The result of that vote is yet unknown to us. But the causes which were nigh losing to us the vote of Ohio, and occasioned the loss of those of Illinois and Indiana—the discouragement of my friends—the power of the Atlantic press—the influence of Governmental patronage—the fabrication of tales of my being withdrawn, propagated so late as to accomplish their object before they could be contradicted—will probably transfer the vote of Louisiana from me. Thankful to my friends and especially to yourself, for their zeal firmness and fidelity, I shall bear with great fortitude the result. I only wish that I could have been spared such a painful duty as that will be of deciding between the persons who are presented to the choice of the H. of R.

Be pleased to present my best respects to Mrs. Porter and to Mrs. Breckenridge, if she is yet with you[2]—

I remain cordially Your friend H. CLAY

Genl. Porter.

ALS. NBuHi. See above, Clay to Brooke, November 26, 1824, notes.
[1] Letters not found. [2] Cf. above, Porter to Clay, October 6, 1824.

Mortgage Deed from William Weatherhead

[December 8, 1824]

[Henry Clay, acting executor of James Morrison, having obtained, at the February Term, 1824, of Fayette Circuit Court, a decree for $1,500 in specie, with interest at six percent per annum from June 1, 1823, founded on a mortgage executed to Morrison in his lifetime by William Weatherhead,[1] the latter now, to better secure payment of the obligation, conveys to Clay two additional slaves upon the condition that if the sum of $1,500 with interest be paid by September 1, 1825, this indenture shall be void.]

Fayette County Court, Deed book Y, 320-21. Acknowledged and recorded December 8, 1824. Weatherhead (Weathered) was a Lexington auctioneer.
[1] Fayette County Court, Deed Book V, 300-301; Fayette Circuit Court, Order Book no. 1, p. 439.

Address to Lafayette

[December 10, 1824]

GENERAL: The House of Representatives of the United States, impelled alike by its own feelings and by those of the whole American People, could not have assigned to me a more gratifying duty than that of being its organ to present to you cordial congratulations upon the occasion of your recent arrival in the United States, in compliance with the wishes of Congress,[1] and to assure you of the very high satisfaction which your presence affords on this early theatre of your glory and renown. Although but few of the members who compose this body shared with you in the War of our Revolution, all have a knowledge, from impartial history, or from faithful tradition, of the perils, the sufferings, and the sacrifices, which you voluntarily encountered, and the signal services, in America and in Europe, which you performed for an infant, a distant, and an alien people; and all feel and own the very great extent of the obligations under which you have placed our country. But the relations in which you have ever stood to the United States, interesting and important as they have been, do not constitute the only motive of the respect and admiration which this House entertains for you. Your consistency of character, your uniform devotion to regulated liberty, in all the vicissitudes of a long and arduous life, also commands its highest admiration. During all the recent convulsions of Europe, amidst, as after the dispersion of, every political storm, the people of the United States have ever beheld you true to your old principles, firm and erect, cheering and animating, with your well-known voice, the votaries of Liberty, its faithful and fearless champion, ready to shed the last drop of that blood which, here, you so freely and nobly spilt in the same holy cause.

The vain wish has been sometimes indulged, that Providence would allow the Patriot, after death, to return to his country, and to contemplate the intermediate changes which had taken place—to view the forests felled, the cities built, the mountains levelled, the canals cut, the highways constructed, the progress of the arts, the advancement of learning, and the increase of population. General, your present visit to the United States is the realization of the consoling object of that wish. You are in the midst of posterity! Every where you must have been struck with the great changes, physical and moral, which have occurred since you left us. Even this very city, bearing a venerated name, alike endeared to you and to us, has since emerged from the forest which then covered its site. In one respect, you behold us unaltered, and that is in the sentiment of continued devotion to liberty, and of ardent affection and profound gratitude to your departed friend, the father of his country, and to your illustrious associates, in the field and in the Cabinet, for the multiplied blessings which surround us, and for the very privilege of addressing you, which I now exercise. This sentiment, now fondly cherished by more than ten millions of people, will be transmitted, with unabated vigor, down the tide of time, through the countless millions who are destined to inhabit this Continent, to their latest posterity.[2]

Register of Debates, 18 Cong., 2 Sess., 3-4. Published also in Washington *Daily National Intelligencer,* December 11, 1824; Lexington *Kentucky Reporter,* December 27, 1824; Mallory, *Life and Speeches of the Hon. Henry Clay,* I, 540-41; Colton, *Life, Correspondence, and Speeches of Henry Clay,* V, 297-98. On December 6, at the beginning of the Session, immediately after Clay had taken the Speaker's Chair and the roll had been called, the House of Representatives had begun considering the matter of a proper reception for Lafayette. After having agreed with the Senate that each body should receive him separately, the House on December 8 had resolved that he "be invited by a committee to attend the House on Friday next, at one o'clock; that he be introduced by the committee, and received by the members standing, uncovered, and addressed by the Speaker, in behalf of the House. . . ."

At the appointed time Lafayette, escorted by the committee, appeared and was introduced. "Mr. SPEAKER then rose, and, in behalf of the House, addressed the Nation's Guest, in the following eloquent strain, adorned by those graces of oratory for which he is distinguished."

1 See above, Johnston to Clay, August 19, 1824, note.

2 After Lafayette had replied to this address, the House adjourned. "The SPEAKER then descended from the Chair, and most affectionately saluted the General. His example was followed by the members of the House, individually, and some time was spent in this agreeable manner before the General retired."

To James Erwin

My dear Sir Washington 13h. Decr. 1824

I received, at the moment of my leaving home, your letter under date at Cahawba the 22d Oct.[1] I thank you for your attention to my business with Mr. Grundy,[2] and hope that the means which you have adopted will bring it to a close. I am convinced that there is a considerable sum yet remaining in his hands.

The public prints will inform you of all events relating to the P. Election. Had my Western and Louisiana friends been able to realize our expectations a different result would have taken place from that which is now likely to happen in the Election. Mr. Crawfords friends now feel their error and are full of professions to me and express great regrets that a different direction had not been given to their exertions. This resembles the eulogiums which are pronounced upon a man after his death. I cannot tell you who will be elected, most probably it will be either Genl. Jackson or Mr. Adams. And what an alternative that is!

My health is pretty much as it was when we parted. I think another year will relieve me from my old complaint. I am anxious to hear often from you and my dear Anne, and hope that you will keep me regularly advised of all that concerns you

You will hear with satisfaction that I have paid off and taken up my bond to Astor.[3]

I will thank you to continue to pay some attention to the business of Col. Morrisons Estate with Trudeau[4] &c.

Give my love to my dear Anne, and believe me

Affectionately Yr's H. CLAY

J. Erwin Esq

ALS. THi. 1 Not found.
2 Felix Grundy. See below, Power of Attorney, June 6, 1825.
3 See above, Astor to Clay, October 4, 1824; Endorsement, November 1, 1824.
4 Charles Leveaux Trudeau.

To William D. Ford

Dr Sir Washington 13h. Decr. 1824

Your obliging letter of the 23d Oct[1] addressed to me at Lexington followed me to this place, and has just been received by me here Events, in relation to the subject of it, have followed each other so rapidly and have placed such a different face on the P. Election from that which it bore, at the date of it, that it is not necessary for me to answer its several topics further than to express to you my grateful thanks for your kind and friendly consideration of me. Now that the friends of Mr. Crawford see their error they are full of professions to me, and express the greatest regret that they had not given a different direction to their exertions. We have not yet heard from Louisiana, but I apprehend the vote of that State has been given to Genl. Jackson; and with respect to the result here I feel very indifferent about the vote.

We have the prospect of but little public business this Session which is likely to excite much interest in Congress. The Election which has devolved on the H. of R. will engross the chief attention of the members.

With great regard I remain faithfy & Cordially Yr. ob Servt

Wm. D. Ford Esq H. CLAY

ALS. Owned by Malcolm Stearns, Jr., Haddam, Connecticut. Ford, an attorney at law of Watertown, Jefferson County, New York, had been a member of the State Assembly and of the United States House of Representatives (1819-1821). He later held several local offices before moving to Sacket's Harbor, about 1830.

[1] Not found.

Order for Payment to William Ryland

13 Decr. 1824.

Pay to William Ryland for the use of Edward Lacy[1] or order the sum of one hundred and eighty two dollars and twenty five Cents.

Cashr. of the Off. of Dt. & Dt Lexn. H CLAY

ADS. DLC-TJC (DNA, M212, R16). Ryland had been Chaplain of the United States Senate, 1820-1822.

[1] Possibly the former Kentucky militia officer, who had removed to Jefferson County, Alabama, in 1816.

To Benjamin W. Leigh

My dear Sir Washington 14h. Decr. 1824

In your letter by Mr. Wickham,[1] for the pleasure of an acquaintance with whom I am much indebted to you, a wish was expressed to know the state of Kentucky politics. I am sorry to be obliged to tell you that I derive very little satisfaction from the contemplation of them. The party, in opposition to the Judges of the Court of Appeals, prevailed at the elections in August, so as to secure a majority in both branches of the General Assembly. That majority does not, however, it is believed, amount to two thirds, the requisite number to effect a removal of the Judges by address. Nevertheless I perceive that they are attempting to accomplish their object in that mode. Should they fail, as I think probable, what is to be feared is that the ouster of the Judges will be sought by a repeal of the Law organizing the Court. Already bills I observe, having I presume that for their object, are authorized to be introduced in each branch of the Legislature. I do hope that, as the effect of such a procedure would be to violate the Constitutional security intended for the Judiciary, the good sense of the Legislature will reject it.[2] But I can speak with no certainty as to the issue.

You will find inclosed a check for $50.[3]

I remain, with high regard, Faithfully Your friend H. CLAY

B. W. Leigh Esq.

ALS. ViU. [1] John Wickham. Letter not found.

[2] See above, Clay to Leigh, July 31, 1824; below, Kendall to Clay, December 22, 1824.

[3] For prosecution of Clay's suit relating to "Euphraim." See above, Clay to Leigh, July 31, 1824.

From John B. Morris

To the Honble Henry Clay Balt Decr 16th 1824

Sir

Some time during the last spring letters of administration on the estate of Gen W. H Winder[1]—were granted me— For the f[. . .][2] execution of the duties incident to that trust, it became necessary for me to examine the proceedings of the Commissioners acting under the Florida Treaty[3] to ascertain the particular cases that had been entrusted to Gen Winders proffessional [*sic*] care—& on which his estate necessarily had the right to charge for his services rendered in the successful prosecution of those claims & which had been brought to issue previous to his death—One of the many cases which appeared to have attained a favourable result through Gen. Ws. attention was that of Alexander Saunders owner of the schr "Narcissa" on which there was a nett award for $2„346„67„[4] In July last I address[ed] a letter to "Alex Saunders Lexington Kentucky" & in a few weeks received a reply from B S Saunders[5] bearing date August 9th. in these words "your letter of the 24 July to Alex Saunders Esq has, been, received by his widow[6] who requests me to say to you that the management of the business named in that letter is now in the hands of the Honble Henry Clay, to whom you are refered for an adjustment—Mr Clay will be at Washington City in the fall where you can see him"—

This referance will plead my apology for intruding the subject upon your attention— That the claim may be presented in a distinct shape I have stated an account against the estate of Mr Saunders, a copy of which is herewith subjoined[7]—by which you will perceive that a commission of 5 per cent is the charge in the present case— That being the standard uniformly controuling the measure of compensation in cases such as the one in question—particularly when the subject had been wholly entrusted to the care of an individual—a fact that prevails in the present case— May hoped [*sic*] to be excused when I respectfully sollcit [*sic*] an attention to this subject as early as convenient– I am persuaded that if an apology is necessary for making this request–That a sufficient one would be found in your estimation, when it is observed That it is my duty as well earnest [*sic*] desire to draw the estate entrusted to my care, to a conclusion as early as possible– That it may be distributed to those who are entitled to it & that we may vest in the family of Gen Winder [*the*] modicum that will accrue to them in the shape of commission [. . . adm]inistration[8] which is wholly to be [*assigned*] to their benefit– Although I h[ad the] honor of a personal introduction to you [I] cannot prevail on myself to suppose that it would have made such an impression as to insure a place in your remembrance–& as I forward no credentials to warrant my recognition as the representative of Gen Winders estate–I beg leave to refer you to my friends Messers McKim & Little[9] to sustain in the absence of other proofs that which surely it would be prudent & proper to know–

With Sentiments of great respect I am your very obt. Servant

JOHN B MORRIS–

ALS. DLC-TJC (DNA, M212, R12). Morris, a Baltimore banker, had studied law under the direction of William H. Winder and, during the War of 1812, had served on Winder's military staff. He was president of the Mechanics' Bank of Baltimore for over thirty years, a trustee of the Bank of Maryland, a member of the first board of directors of the Baltimore and Ohio Railroad, and a State Senator, 1832-1835.

1 Winder had died May 24, 1824.

2 MS. torn; part of word missing.

3 See above, II, 678n.

4 Saunders had estimated his loss at $4,783.25, for the vessel and her cargo of flour and corn, when she was seized in the port of Trinidad, Cuba, in June, 1802. DNA, RG76, Spain, Treaty, February 22, 1819, Article 11, vol. IV, no. 248-1331: Sloop *Narcissa.* At that time a resident of New York, Saunders had subsequently moved to Lexington, Kentucky.

5 Not identified, unless misread by Morris for Bennet P. Sanders.

6 Catharine Halstead Saunders, who operated a millinery store on Main Street, Lexington. Her husband's will had been probated in Fayette County Court in June, 1823.

7 The account, also dated December 16, 1824, charges Alexander Saunders five per cent commission on $2,346.67, amounting to $117.33, due to Winder's estate.

8 About two words missing.

9 Isaac McKim; Peter Little. The former, a Baltimore merchant, industrialist, and shipowner, had been a Maryland State Senator, 1821-1823, and was a member of Congress from 1823 to 1825 and from 1833 until his death in 1838. He was one of the organizers and a director of the Baltimore and Ohio Railroad Company.

To [Rufus Easton]

Dear Sir Washington 18h. Decr. 1824

I received your friendly letter of the 20h. Nov.[1] I am greatly honored and obliged by the favorable opinion of me which is entertained in Missouri, and shall ever feel thankful for the recent expression of it. If the other States, which had been supposed to prefer me for the high office in question had not disappointed the hopes of my friends, I should have been one of the three returned to the H. of R. As events have happened I am excluded, but I cheerfully submit[, as][2] is my duty, to the public decision. It is impossible at present to predict the choice which the H. of R. may finally make. Whatever it may be I hope it will tend to promote the happiness of our Country.

Our present Session will not I think be marked by much activity.

With great respect I am Yr. ob. Servant [. . . .]

AL. MoSHi. Bottom quarter of page missing. Recipient identified by endorsement in strange hand on verso. Easton, a St. Louis lawyer, had been born in Connecticut, had lived briefly in Indiana, and from 1804 to 1815 had been postmaster of St. Louis. He had been Delegate to Congress from the Territory of Missouri, 1814-1816, and had served as Attorney General of the State since 1821.

1 Not found. 2 MS. torn.

To John Q. Adams

19h. Decr. 1824

Mr. Clay has the honor to accept the invitation[1] of Mr— and Mrs. Adams to dinner on thursday next[2]—

AN. KyU. Addressed: "The Honble J. Q. Adams." 1 Not found.

2 For the names of Adams' dinner guests on December 23, see Adams, *Memoirs*, VI, 453.

Request for Permission to Vote

[December 22, 1824]

When the yeas and nays had been called and recorded, the SPEAKER rose, and observing that, having been precluded, by the place he held, from the expression of his sentiments in relation to either the principle or the form of the bill, he requested of the House that he might be permitted so far to give expression to his feelings, in relation to both, as to record his vote with those of the other members; and, leave having been promptly given, the Clerk called the Speaker's name, and his vote was recorded in the affirmative.

Register of Debates, 18 Cong., 2 Sess., 55-56. Published also in Washington *Daily National Intelligencer,* December 23, 1824; Lexington *Kentucky Reporter,* January 10, 1825. Cf. above, II, 311, n.7; Hinds, *Precedents of the House of Representatives,* V, 514. The House had just approved a bill authorizing monetary and land grants to Lafayette (see below, Clay to Brooke, this date).

To Francis T. Brooke

My dear Sir Washn. 22d. Decr. 1824

I recd. your letter by your son, and had great pleasure in furnishing him with a letter of introduction to Commodore Rogers.[1]

I have also recd. that of the 21st. inst.[2] and I will examine the claim to which it refers with all the prepossessions which arise from your opinion and my high regard to[*sic*] you.

The result in Louisiana did not surprize or afflict me. There was much misfortune attending it nevertheless. On the final vote, the coalition between Adams and Jackson was only able to secure 30 to my 28 votes. Two of my friends in the Legislature were overset in a gig the day before and thereby prevented from attending; two others who were expected did not arrive, and three were seduced. Such is the faithful account which Mr. Bouligny, the newly elected Senator,[3] and letters which I have received, communicate. We must not despair of the Republic. Our institutions, if they have the value which we believe them to possess, and are worth preserving, will sustain themselves, and we shall yet do well.

A bill passed the H. of R. to day (166 to 26) giving to La Fayette $200.000. and a Township of land.[4]

I remain Yrs. affectionately H. CLAY

The Honble Mr. Brooke—

ALS. KyU. Published in part in Colton (ed.), *Private Correspondence of Henry Clay,* 107-108.

1 John Rodgers, who on December 15 had resigned from the Board of Navy Commissioners so that he might return to sea duty, as commanding officer of the *North Carolina,* which sailed early in March for the Mediterranean. John Francis Brooke received a commission as Surgeon's Mate in the United States Navy, May 16, 1825, and was promoted to Surgeon on November 4, 1834. The two letters here mentioned have not been found.

2 Not found.

3 Dominique Bouligny, New Orleans lawyer, had been elected to the United States Senate to fill the vacancy caused by the resignation of Henry Johnson. He served until March 3, 1829.

4 The Senate, which had been considering a slightly different measure, adopted the House bill on December 23, and the President signed it five days later. 6 *U. S. Stat.,* 320.

To Benjamin W. Leigh

My dear Sir Washington 22 Decr. 1824

If, as intimated in your letter of the 20h. inst.[1] you have any matter of business here in which I can aid you, I pray you freely to command my services.

I will thank you to desire Col. Burfoot[2] to continue his friendly attentions to Ephraim [*sic*], and to rent out the property another year as he may think right. In respect to the property of one of the defendants, which has been seized for the costs,[3] you will oblige me to act for me as you would for yourself, under similar circumstances. Whatever you may do, shall receive my approbation and indemnity.

I share with you in all your feelings excited by the present posture of our public affairs. You have as much if not more at stake, as a member of the crew and part-owner of the Cargo, in the Ship of state, as I have; but then you are a looker-on, whilst I am compelled to be an actor in the public concerns here. And an actor in such a scene! An alternative made up of Andrew Jackson and John Quincy Adams! For to that we shall undoubtedly have to come, notwithstanding the infatuated hopes which are even yet cherished in regard to another. It is the issue as to one of them. (I may now speak freely to you) of the question which has agitated the Country for the last two years, that I dreaded, & distinctly foresaw but had not the power to prevent. Mr. Crawfords friends have been fairly dealt with by mine—they were given long since, again and again, to understand that the interest disposed to support me would not take him up. They were incredulous. I have no reproaches, I thank God not one, to make of myself. My duty was that of passive submission. Except to answer letters which have been, without solicitation, addressed to me, I have taken no concern in the past events. And I have not written nor spoken a syllable, to the publication of which to the whole world, with its attending circumstances, I would object.

You say that "you expect to find me at the board of general officers." I would not cross Pennsylvania Avenue to be in any office under any Administration which lies before us. To my friends I have no doubt, from all quarters, every sort of profession will be made. Since my exclusion from the H. of R. I enjoy the rare felicity, whilst alive, which is experienced by the dead, if they then have a consciousness of what passes here—that of hearing every kind of eulogium and panegyric pronounced upon me. To those, who favor me with any portion of their regard, I can only say that the duty which I have to perform shall be fulfilled with an anxious and solemn determination to promote the public good, if I can discern it, and without the slightest reference to personal considerations. If, my dear Sir, you can assist me in this purpose—if you can cast the slightest light upon the dark and difficult path which I have to pursue, you will confer lasting obligations upon

Your faithful & Cordial friend H. CLAY

B. W. Leigh Esqr.

P.S. I write for your own observation only. H C.

ALS, photostat. NN. [1] Not found. [2] Lawson Burfoot.
[3] See above, Clay to Leigh, December 22, 1823; July 31, 1824.

From Amos Kendall

Dear Sir, Frankfort Dec 22d. 1824.

I have just been conversing with Mr. Crittenden[1] and in consequence of what passed between us now address you. A resolution has been some days prepared to be presented to the Legislature requesting the Representatives of this state in Congress to vote for Jackson.[2] It would probably be better to leave you to take that course voluntarily, but I do not think it possible for your friends here to prevent the offering or the passage of this resolution. I have, therefore, with the advice of Mr. Crittenden concluded to advise you of it, that, if any advantage can be gained by a voluntary movement on the part of the Kentucky representation in favor of Jackson, their course may be indicated before the arrival of this resolution.

On Monday the address for the removal of the Judges was lost in the House of Reps. by a vote of 61 to 39 and in the Senate by 23 to 12.[3] A bill to repeal all laws organizing the Court, and providing for the appointment of four new Judges, has passed the Senate by 22 to 16, and has been under Discussion in the House two days, in which there has been much warmth. Candles are now lighted and the debate will continue till a late houre [*sic*]. There are believed to be 57 in favor of the bill. It will probably pass tomorrow.[4] Your friend AMOS KENDALL.

ALS. DLC-HC (DNA, M212, R1). Addressed to Clay at Washington.

1 John J. Crittenden.

2 Resolutions to this effect passed both houses; they were approved January 11, 1825. Ky. Gen. Assy., *Acts, 1824-1825,* p. 279.

3 Ky. H. of Reps., *Journal, 1824-1825,* pp. 398-438; Ky. Sen., *Journal, 1824-1825,* pp. 288-90.

4 Senate action on the bill had occurred December 9. Ky. Sen., *Journal, 1824-1825,* pp. 240-41. Debate had begun in the House on December 21 and ended at a late hour on December 23, with a vote of 54 to 43 in favor of the measure. Ky. H. of Reps., *Journal, 1824-1825,* pp. 440-54. The act, approved December 24, was to take effect immediately. Ky. Gen. Assy., *Acts, 1824-1825,* pp. 44-56. Cf. above, Scott to Clay, November 23, December 30, 1823, notes.

This legislation initiated the old court-new court controversy, during which, for a period of two years, two State courts of appeal, with separate judges and officers, claimed jurisdiction. The antirelief forces won control of the State House of Representatives in the election of 1825 and of both the House and Senate in 1826, after which the legislature, on December 30, 1826, enacted a bill repealing the law to reorganize the court and declaring the justices of the old court "the rightful and constitutional Judges of said Court." Ky. Gen. Assy., *Acts, 1826-1827,* pp. 13-14. Efforts to compromise the issue through new judicial appointments were complicated as the relief forces regained control of the Senate in 1827 and 1828. The subject remained a source of political agitation until the spring of 1829, when, the entire composition of the court having been changed, it ruled the acts of the judges and clerk of the so-called "new court" "totally null and void." Hildreth's Heirs *vs.* M'Intire's Devisee, 24 *Ky. Reports* (1 J. J. Marshall) 206-209.

From John B. Morris

D Sir Balt. Decr 22. 1824

I have to acknowledge the receipt of yours of the 20h[1] expressing a readiness to pay the estate of Gen Winder $117„33. it being the commission of 5 per cent on the nett amount on claim of Alex Saunders—in the case of the Schooner "Narcissa"—

It is uncertain whether I shall have occasion to visit Washington this winter & as it is desirable to expedite the settelment [*sic*] of Gen Winders estate—I herewith close the account with a receipt on the *back* of the Voucher which shews that letters of administration have been granted to me— A check[2] for the amt. payable to order on either of the Banks of Baltimore or Washington City as may be most convenient to you will be a mode of remittance equally acceptable to your Very obliged & obt Servant

To the Honble Henry Clay Washington City JOHN B MORRIS

[Enclosure][3]

Balt Dec 22. 1824 Recd from the estate of Alex Saunders (thro the hands of the Honble Henry Clay) the sum of one hundred & seventeen dollars & thirty three cents in full for the commission as above stated— JOHN B MORRIS admr of Wm H Winder

$117 33/100

ALS. DLC-TJC (DNA, M212, R12). Cf. above, Morris to Clay, December 16, 1824.

1 Not found. 2 Not found.

3 AES, on a copy of the account of Saunders' debt to Winder's estate, written on verso of the voucher mentioned above. DLC-TJC (DNA, M212, R16).

Check to James Smith, Jr.

23 Decr. 1824

Pay to Jas. Smith Jr. of Philadelphia or order the Sum of Fifty dollars. H. CLAY

Cashr. of the Off. of Dt. & Dt. Washington

ADS. DLC-TJC (DNA, M212, R16). Cf. above, Smith to Clay, October 28, 1824.

To Board of Navy Commissioners

Gent. Washington 24 Decr. 1824

I have a Ton of hemp[1] on its way from my farm near Lexington to Baltimore, which has been prepared in a new method. The usual practice of dew retting hemp is to spread it down the fall or winter after it is pulled or cut from the field. Mine has been kept in stack one year, and then spread down to be dew retted. During that period it undergoes some sweat, fermentation, or other natural process, which has a most material effect upon the appearance of the article. When delivered from the brake it looks as light in color, and as lively as Russia Hemp. Such is the mode in which the ton above mentioned has been prepared, and such is its appearance. What effect it has upon the quality of the hemp, in other respects, I know not; but I should suppose it worth an experiment to ascertain. The ordinary dew retted hemp is dark & ill looking.

If the Board would like to have the ton to have an experiment made upon it, I will deliver it to their order at such price as may

be deemed reasonable— I should prefer delivering it at Baltimore.
I am Gent Yr. ob Servant H. CLAY
The Navy Commissioners.

ALS. DNA, RG45, Navy Commissioners' Misc. Letters Received, 1825-1831, vol. 10.
[1] See above, Scott to Clay, December 1, 1824.

To Hubbard Taylor

Dear Sir Washn. 25h. Decr. 1824

I recd your favor of the 8h. inst.[1] I am happy to be able to tell you that Majr. William Taylor, who has just left here, obtained his pension.[2]

The unexpected results of the Electoral votes in New York, Indiana, and Louisiana are such as to exclude me from the House. We have to make a choice from among Genl. Jackson, Mr. Adams and Mr. Crawford, and I can not now venture to conjecture the issue. As for myself, my friends need entertain no fears about my bearing with grace and fortitude our defeat. I think you ought at home to leave us free to make the best selection we can. It is impossible that you should there possess a knowledge of all the circumstances now existing and which may arise before the first wednesday in February that must assist in making up our judgments.

I am glad to learn that you are making in your private affairs provision for any contingency that may happen. I feel and cordially sympathize with you on the evils of any sort of pecuniary embarrassment. I am Sincerely Your friend H. CLAY
Hubbard Taylor Esq

P. S. Will you be good enough to write me where Edward Bradley, in the neighborhood of the Cross plains, has moved to? He is gone to Missouri I believe, but I do not know the part.[3]

ALS. TxU-Humanities Research Center. [1] Not found.
[2] His pension, originally granted May 1, 1818, and terminated May 1, 1820, had been restored on November 23, 1824.
[3] By 1826 he had settled in Jackson County, Missouri, on the trail to Santa Fe.

To Peter B. Porter

My dear Sir Washn. 26 Decr. 1824

I recd your letter of the 4h. inst.[1] respecting a son of Mr. Holley[2] for whom a situation is desired at West Point. Success in the object mainly depends on your delegation, but I have told the Patroon[3] that I will co-operate with him, with much pleasure, towards its attainment.

You have heard of our disappointment in Louisiana. Thirty one members out of 58 met and agreed upon a ticket for me. Two other friends were expected to arrive before the election. After the meeting, two of my friends went to the Country and having got overturned from a gig were unable to attend. The two that were expected did not arrive. Three deserted, in consequence of false rumors; and with all these disadvantages the coalition between Jackson's friends & Adams' was only able to carry their joint ticket by 30 to 28.

I laugh off, and bear with unaffected fortitude, our defeat. We have no reproaches to make ourselves, and it is a source of high satisfaction that my character has not suffered but been elevated by the whole Canvass.

The final issue between the Candidates returned is doubtful. All that can be safely said is that it is probable the contest will be limited to the two highest.

With the Compliments of the Season to yourself and Mrs. Porter I remain Faithfully Yr friend H. CLAY

Genl. Peter B. Porter.

ALS. NBuHi. [1] Not found.

[2] Probably Myron Holley, born in Connecticut, educated at Williams College, and admitted to the bar in 1802. He had shortly thereafter moved to Canandaigua, New York, where he had given up practice of law and had become county clerk (1810-1814), State Assemblyman (1816), and member and treasurer of the board of commissioners of the Erie Canal (1816-1824). Retiring from the last post to Lyons, New York, and around 1836 removing to Rochester, he subsequently became active in support of the anti-Masonic and antislavery movements. He was one of the organizers of the Liberty Party in 1840 and edited the Rochester *Freeman* as a party organ. He was a brother of Horace Holley. Myron had six sons, none of whom was admitted to West Point.

[3] Stephen Van Rensselaer.

From William Bainbridge

Sir 27th december 1824

The Commissioners of the Navy have received your letter of the 24th ins

They have instructed the Navy Agent at Baltimore James Beatty Esqr.[1] to receive the ton of hemp referred to, and to allow for it the price of best Russia hemp—and they have given directions to ship it to Norfolk, where it is to be made up into running rigging and delivered to one of our public ships {probably the Constellation} with a view to test its strength and durability.[2]

You will be pleased to direct your Agent to deliver the hemp to Mr. Beatty.

I have the honor to be &c WM. BAINBRIDGE Prest.

Honorable Henry Clay.

Copy. DNA, RG45, Navy Commissioners' Misc. Letters Sent, vol. 3, p. 349. On December 23, 1824, Bainbridge had been appointed to the Board of Navy Commissioners in place of John Rodgers, resigned (see above, Clay to Brooke, December 22, 1824, note). Because of his seniority in age Bainbridge became the presiding officer of the Board.

[1] Beatty was also a Baltimore merchant and powder manufacturer.

[2] It was probably this hemp of which John Rodgers wrote to Samuel L. Southard, December 17, 1827: "Cordage made of American hemp, stacked one year, and then dew-rotted, was fitted on one side of the Frigate Constellation. . . . The other side of the ship . . . was fitted with cordage of Russia hemp; and, after being thus worn for nearly a year, it was found, on examination, that the Russia rope, in every instance, after being much worn, looked better, and wore more equally and evenly than the American; that the yarns of the former were rather stronger, and the number of broken yarns not so great as in the American." After nearly two years of the experiment, the commander of the *Constellation* said: "I have given a fair trial to the Kentucky hemp for rigging. If there is any preference, I would give it in favor of the Russia." *House Docs.,* 20 Cong., 1 Sess., no. 68, p. 5.

To Board of Navy Commissioners

Gent. Washington 28h. Decr. 1824

I have received your note of the 27h. int. stating that you had given orders to Mr Beatty to receive the ton of hemp described in mine of the 24h.. I have accordingly directed, upon its arrival at Balto., Mess. Macdonald & Ridgely to deliver it to Mr. Beatty.

I have the honor to be, with great respect Your obedient Servant

The Honble The Commissioners of the Navy Board. H. CLAY

ALS. DNA, RG45, Navy Commissioners' Misc. Letters Received, 1825-1831, vol. 10.

To George McClure

[December 28, 1824]

I have no hesitation in saying, that I have long since decided in favor of Mr. Adams, in case the contest should be between him and General Jackson. What I would ask, should be the distinguishing characteristic of an American statesman? Should it not be a devotion to civil liberty? Is it then compatible with that principle, to elect a man, whose sole recommendation rests on military pretensions? I, therefore, say to you unequivocally, that I can not, consistently with my own principles, support a military man.

Colton, *Life and Times of Henry Clay,* I, 387n. This extract was included in a letter from McClure to Robert S. Rose, September 1, 1827, with the following explanation: "After the electors of president and vice-president were chosen in 1824, it was ascertained, that the election would come before the house of representatives, and that Mr. Clay would not be among the number returned. Not knowing his sentiments in relation to the candidates, I addressed a letter to him, stating, that in all probability, the contest would be confined to Mr. Adams and General Jackson; and in that case, wished to know which of them he would prefer? Mr. Clay answered me promptly, by letter, bearing date December 28, 1824, of which the following . . . is an extract." *Ibid.,* 387n-88n.

To Jonathan Russell

My dear Sir Washn. 29h. Decr. 1824

I recd. your letter of the 21st. inst.[1] and I have great pleasure in transmitting to you inclosed a Certificate for your son George, who I hope will realize all his expectations in Chile. I have no acquaintance with any of the Natives of that part of So. America, to whom I could address letters of recommendation in his behalf.

With the Compliments of the Season I remain Faithfully Yr's
Jonathan Russell Esq. H. CLAY

ALS. DLC-Shaler Family Papers. 1 Not found.

Receipt from Jonathan Elliot

[December 30, 1824]

1824 Dec. 30. Recd. from the Hon Henry Clay ten dollars in full for Subscription to the Wash Gazette to March 3d. 1825
$10 00 JON ELLIOT

ADS. DLC-TJC (DNA, M212, R16).

To [William S. Dallam]

Dr Sir Washn 31 Decr. 1824

Inclosed I transmit to you a letter[1] which I have received from Mr. Ridgely[2] respecting the business as to which you desired me to make an inquiry.

With the Compliments of the Season, I am Respectfully Yr's
H. CLAY

ALS. NcD. Addressee identified in strange hand. Endorsed in same hand: "Act. in Md. due to Dallam $4000—deposd. in U. S. B. as security given to Clay by [James] Harper to collect."
1 Not found. 2 Possibly Nicholas G. Ridgely.

To William Goldsborough

Dr Sir [*ca.* December 31, 1824]

I recd. your letter of the 6h. inst.[1] and I will take pleasure in suggesting the defect which you mention in the Judiciary of the U.S. to the Commee. charged with that subject. From the station which I hold in the House I am disabled myself from originating any measure to cure the defect.

In cases such as yours, the Federal Courts where I have practised have had no difficulty in maintaining jurisdiction, upon a sugges-

tion that one or more of the parties resided out of their jurisdiction, provided the parties actually sued were those against whom a decree could be rendered. Upon making such a suggestion the Courts have conceived that they might depart from the rule of equity which requires all who are concerned in interest to be brought before the Court. I am Yr. ob. Servt. H. CLAY
Wm. Goldsborough Esqr.

ALS. NcD. Goldsborough was probably of Frederick, Maryland. 1 Not found.

INDEX

INDEX

ABOUT THE PAPERS OF HENRY CLAY

THE EDITORS: James F. Hopkins is professor of history in the University of Kentucky, where he received the M.A. degree in 1938. He received the B.A. degree from the University of Mississippi in 1929 and the Ph.D. degree from Duke University in 1949. He is the author of A HISTORY OF THE HEMP INDUSTRY IN KENTUCKY and THE UNIVERSITY OF KENTUCKY—ORIGINS AND EARLY YEARS.

Mary W. M. Hargreaves received the A.B. degree from Bucknell University (1935), the M.A. degree from Harvard University and Radcliffe College (1936) and the Ph.D. degree from Harvard University and Radcliffe College in 1951. Mrs. Hargreaves is the author of DRY FARMING IN THE NORTHERN GREAT PLAINS.

FORMAT: The text is set in Linotype Baskerville, a revival of the classic typeface cut about 1760 by John Baskerville of England, the greatest printer and typefounder of his time. The pattern for the cutting by the Mergenthaler Linotype Company is a complete font cast from Baskerville's own matrices and exhumed at Paris, France, in 1929. The paper is "1854," a text stock made to order for these volumes by the S. D. Warren Company, founded in 1854 at Boston, Massachusetts. The binding fabric is Bradford Buckram, manufactured in a gray blue color designed for this set by the Columbia Mills of Syracuse, New York.

The book was composed and printed in the University of Kentucky printing plant. It was bound by the C. J. Krehbiel Company, Cincinnati, Ohio.

AF606022